Business Law Guide to Belgium

Business Law Guide to Belgium

Van Bael & Bellis

KLUWER LAW INTERNATIONAL
THE HAGUE / LONDON / NEW YORK

Published by:
Kluwer Law International
P.O. Box 85889, 2508 CN The Hague, The Netherlands
sales@kluwerlaw.com
http://www.kluwerlaw.com

Sold and Distributed in North, Central and South America by:
Aspen Publishers, Inc.
7201 McKinney Circle
Frederick, MD 21704
USA

Sold and Distributed in all other countries by:
Turpin Distribution Services Limited
Blackhorse Road
Letchworth
Herts SG6 1HN
United Kingdom

Van Bael & Bellis
Avenue Louise/Louizalaan 165
1050 Brussels
Belgium
Tel: +32-(0)2/647.73.50
Fax: +32-(0)2/640.64.99
E-mail: info@vanbaelbellis.com

www.vanbaelbellis.com

Geneva office:
15, bd. Des Philosophes
CH-1205 Geneva
Switzerland
Tel: +41-(0)22/320.90.20
Fax: +41-(0)22/320.94.20
E-mail: vbb@vanbaelbellis.ch

A CIP Catalogue record for this book is available from the Library of Congress

Printed on acid-free paper.

ISBN 90-411-2133-1
© 2003 Kluwer Law International

PUBLISHER'S NOTE

FOREWORD AND ACKNOWLEDGEMENTS

This book offers a comprehensive overview of Belgian business law. The book was conceived as an update of its predecessor which was published in 1993. Over time, however, the book began a life of its own. It therefore ended up being far more than a second edition of the initial manuscript. Certain chapters have been entirely re-written, while subject-matters that were not covered in the first edition (*e.g.*, e-commerce and data protection) have been added. The book provides evidence of the pace of change and development of Belgian business law.

As was the case for the first edition, this book is the result of a team effort by partners and associates of Van Bael & Bellis. Contributors to the book are, in alphabetical order, Jane Arkell, Philippe De Baere, Steven De Schrijver, Pascal Faes, Martin Favart, Tinne Gilles, Joost Haans, Jennifer Huybrechts, Peter L'Ecluse, Monika Kuschewsky, Catherine Longeval, Capucine Rosenfeld, Inge Mannaerts, Hajar Mouatassim, Yves Melin, Charlotte Nassogne, Vincent Roobaert, Guy Rulkin, Jochen Schraeyen, Benoit Servais, Kris Somers, Filip Van den Bulcke, Hans Vandendael, Kris Van Hove and Markus Wellinger. The native English-speaking lawyers of Van Bael & Bellis helped proof-read the book. Steven De Schrijver and Pascal Faes acted as editors. Sophie Bertrand and Gwenda De Pril provided secretarial support.

In this book, the law is stated as of 31 December 2002.

Van Bael & Bellis

Brussels

March 2003

CONTENTS

1. BELGIUM: AN INTRODUCTION

I. INTRODUCTION

1. Belgium is a constitutional and parliamentary monarchy. It became independent in 1830 and has been a unitary state for 140 years. Its political structure has however changed dramatically in the last 3 to 4 decades. Firstly, Belgium has witnessed the transfer of a substantial amount of its sovereignty to the European Union. There is hardly any aspect of Belgian law which has been left untouched by EC legislation, either directly, through directly applicable EC Regulations or, indirectly, through the mandatory incorporation into Belgian law of rules contained in EC Directives. Taxation, labour law, company law, competition law, banking and financial law, customs law, investment incentives, intellectual property and many other areas of the law have undergone major changes as a result of Belgium's membership in the European Union. This process of change is expected to continue as Belgium further integrates into the European Union.

2. Secondly, through 4 sets of institutional reforms (in 1970, 1980, 1988-1989 and 1993), Belgium has undergone a metamorphosis from a unitary state to a federal state. Pursuant to Article 1 of the Constitution (*grondwet/constitution*), "*Belgium is a federal state made up of communities and regions*" (the multiple amendments brought to the 1831 initial text of the Constitution resulted on 17 February 1994 in a new co-ordinated version of the Constitution). The decision-making power in Belgium is no longer exclusively held by the national authorities but shared among several national and regional authorities, which exercise their respective competences independently from one another in different fields.

3. Recently, important institutional reforms aimed at transferring new competences to the communities and the regions have been adopted. These new revisions, in effect as from 1 January 2002, have brought about further drastic changes to the Belgian political landscape.

II. BASIC PRINCIPLES OF BELGIAN FEDERALISM

A. Introduction

4. Belgium has a hybrid and fairly complex state structure. The Belgian State is headed by a monarch and comprises a federal government and a 2-chamber federal parliament (the House of Representatives and the Senate). The constitutional reforms have created 3 communities (*gemeenschappen/communautés*): the Flemish Community, the French Community and the German-speaking Community; and 3 regions (*gewesten/régions*): the Flemish Region, the Brussels-Capital Region and the Walloon Region (the communities and the regions are hereinafter together referred to as the "federate entities"). The country is further divided into 10 provinces: 5 within the Flemish Region (*Antwerpen, Limburg, Oost-Vlaanderen Vlaams-Brabant and West-Vlaanderen*) and 5 within the Walloon Region (*Brabant Wallon, Hainaut, Liège, Luxembourg and Namur*), and 589 municipalities (*gemeenten/communes*). The constitutional reforms have also consolidated the division of the Belgian territory into 4 linguistic regions (*taalgebieden/régions linguistiques*).

5. Belgium is a democratic state. All power emanates from the nation (Art. 33 of the Constitution). Voting is compulsory at all levels for citizens over 18, and Belgium applies the principle of proportional representation.

B. Linguistic regions

6. There are 4 linguistic regions: the single-language Dutch, French and German linguistic regions, and the bilingual (Dutch and French) region of Brussels-Capital. Each municipality belongs to a specific linguistic region and the borders of these regions may only be changed by law. Such a law can only be passed if certain special quorum and majority voting requirements are met (Art. 4 of the Constitution). In this chapter, laws whose adoption require a special quorum and voting majority will be referred to as "Special Laws" *(bijzondere wetten/lois spéciales)*. Such quorum and voting majority requirements are intended to prevent one community or region from being able to pass legislation that conflicts with the interests of the other communities or regions.

7. The linguistic regions are a mere division of the territory and do not have their own political organisation. The purpose of these linguistic regions is, first, to indicate which national language is the official language applicable in that region and,

second, to define the geographical regions in which the communities have legislative and executive authority (*See*, para. 9).

8. The Dutch linguistic region basically covers the northern half of the country and comprises the provinces of *Antwerpen, Limburg, Oost-Vlaanderen, Vlaams Brabant* and *West-Vlaanderen*. The French linguistic region, which covers the southern half of the country, comprises the provinces of *Brabant Wallon, Hainaut, Liège* (with the exception of the municipalities which together constitute the German linguistic region), *Luxembourg* and *Namur*. The German linguistic region covers 9 municipalities located in the province of *Liège*, close to the border with Germany (*i.e., Amel, Büllingen, Burg-Reuland, Bütgenbach, Eupen, Kelmis, Lontzen, Raeren* and *Sankt-Vith*). Finally, the bilingual region of Brussels-Capital comprises the municipality of Brussels and 18 other surrounding municipalities (*See*, Arts. 3 through 6 of the Law of 18 July 1966 co-ordinating the Legal Provisions governing the Use of Languages in Administrative Matters).

C. Communities

9. There are 3 communities in Belgium: the Flemish Community, the French Community and the German-speaking Community (Art. 2 of the Constitution). The decrees issued by the communities have force of law in the following language regions:
    (i) *Flemish Community:* the Dutch linguistic region and, to some extent (*See*, para. 40), the bilingual region of Brussels-Capital;
   (ii) *French Community:* the French linguistic region and, to some extent (*See*, para. 40), the bilingual region of Brussels-Capital;
  (iii) *German-speaking Community:* the German linguistic region (*See*, Arts. 127 through 130 of the Constitution).

D. Regions

10. Article 3 of the Constitution defines 3 regions: the Flemish Region, the Walloon Region and the Brussels-Capital Region. The Flemish Region comprises the provinces of *Antwerpen, Limburg, Oost-Vlaanderen, Vlaams Brabant* and *West-Vlaanderen*. The Walloon Region includes the provinces of *Brabant Wallon, Hainaut, Liège, Luxembourg* and *Namur*. The Brussels-Capital Region coincides with the territory of the administrative district of Brussels, that is, the 19 Brussels bilingual municipalities (*See*, Art. 5 of the Constitution, Art. 2 of the Special Law of 8 August 1980 on Institutional Reforms – *Bijzondere wet tot hervorming der instellingen/Loi spéciale de réformes institutionnelles* (as amended) and Art. 2 of

the Special Law of 12 January 1989 relating to the Brussels Institutions – *Bijzondere wet met betrekking tot de Brusselse instellingen/Loi spéciale relative aux institutions bruxelloises* (as amended)).

E. Division of powers between the Federal State and the federate entities

11. The federal structure of the Belgian State is based on the principle that the powers of the communities and the regions are attributed powers. In other words, the communities and the regions have no other powers than those specifically attributed to them by the Constitution or by law. It follows that the residual powers – those powers that are not attributed to any body in particular – are vested in the federal authorities. It should however be noted that this process will be inverted eventually. Following the constitutional revision of 1993, Article 35 of the Constitution indeed provides that the residual competence will be based on the federate entities but only when a definite and detailed list of all the areas of federal competence is introduced into the Constitution. This list has not yet been drawn up and requires a new constitutional revision and the adoption of a Special Law determining the conditions and modalities of the exercise of the residual competences by the communities and the regions.

    The communities and the regions nevertheless hold certain implied powers. This principle is recognised in Article 10 of the Special Law of 8 August 1980 on Institutional Reforms (as amended), which provides that decrees issued by the communities and the regions may contain provisions relating to matters for which they are not competent, provided this is necessary for the exercise of their authority in matters for which they are competent.

12. Another important principle is that the powers of the federal authorities, the communities, and the regions are mutually exclusive. Any given matter is therefore subject to only one legislative and executive authority to the exclusion of all other authorities. The Special Law of 8 August 1980 on Institutional Reforms (as amended), however, recognises in limited circumstances the existence of parallel competences, that is, situations where more than one authority may exercise its competences. For example, in the field of scientific research, the communities and the regions may each intervene insofar as the research relates to matters for which they are responsible. On the other hand, the Federal State is competent for scientific research linked to matters for which the Federal State is competent.

13. Finally, a crucial aspect of the Belgian federal system is that there is no hierarchy between national or federal law on the one hand and community or regional law (decrees or ordinances) on the other hand. Therefore, the Constitution and Special

Laws provide for various co-operation and conflict resolution mechanisms (*See*, paras. 69 *et seq.*). Moreover, the concept of federal loyalty, incorporated into the Constitution (*See*, Art. 143, para. 1 of the Constitution), plays an essential role in the Belgian federal model.

III. THE FEDERAL AUTHORITIES

A. Organisation

§1. The federal legislature

14. Pursuant to Article 36 of the Constitution, legislative power is exercised collectively by the King, the House of Representatives and the Senate. The House of Representatives and the Senate constitute the Federal Parliament (Art. 72 of the Constitution).

15. The House of Representatives currently consists of 150 deputies directly elected by universal suffrage, while the Senate consists of the following 4 categories of senators:
    (i) 40 directly-elected senators (25 from the Dutch-speaking electoral college and 15 from the French-speaking electoral college);
    (ii) 21 senators appointed by and within the legislative assemblies of the 3 communities (10 from the Flemish Community, 10 from the French Community and 1 from the German-speaking Community);
    (iii) 10 co-opted senators, 6 of whom are appointed by the above elected Dutch-speaking senators and 4 by the above elected French-speaking senators; and
    (iv) the royal Princes (currently 3), who are automatically appointed as senators at the age of 18 after having taking the oath. They have a right to vote as of the age of 21 and are not taken into account for the determination of the quorum of attendance.

16. All members of Parliament (except the royal Princes and the senator from the German-speaking Community) belong to either the Dutch- or French-speaking linguistic group. Parliamentary elections take place every 4 years, unless an early election is called (Arts. 65 and 70 of the Constitution).

17. The federal legislature has 5 main powers: (i) the adoption of federal laws, (ii) the approval of international treaties, (iii) the control of the federal executive, (iv) the reform of the Constitution and (v) the conduct of parliamentary enquiries (*i.e.*, the analysis of societal problems followed by the right to propose solutions). Since the

federal reform of 1993, the 2 chambers no longer have the same federal legislative powers. Three systems of power-sharing exist:

(i) *Optional double-chamber system*: as a general rule, the House of Representatives has the most influence on law enactments. The Senate, as a reflection assembly, plays a secondary role. For a bill to become law, a majority vote in the House of Representatives alone may suffice, but the Senate examines bills submitted to the House of Representatives and may propose amendments. The House of Representatives always has the final word.

(ii) *Double-chamber system:* the 2 assemblies act on an equal footing in some fields of parliamentary activity, such as the revision of the Constitution, the legislation relating to the Belgian state structure, the approval of international treaties, *etc.* (Art. 77 of the Constitution).

(iii) *Single-chamber system*: the House of Representatives is the only decision-making body for laws relating to the civil and criminal liability of Ministers, for the state budget and finances, for establishing army quotas and for granting naturalisation (Art. 74 of the Constitution). Only the House of Representatives has the power of political control over the Federal Government. The Senate is exclusively competent to solve conflicts of interest between the federal and federate bodies.

18. Both deputies and senators can submit private members' bills (Art. 75 of the Constitution).

19. Finally, it should be noted that there is currently a proposal to reform the composition and the powers of both the House of Representatives and the Senate. The reform, if adopted, would be effective as of 2007. The Senate would become a genuine federate entities' assembly with 35 Flemish-speaking members and 35 French-speaking members (including one representative of the German-speaking Community), appointed by the respective legislative assemblies of the 3 communities, and would be granted specific powers. Simultaneously, the number of deputies at the House of Representatives would increase to 200.

20. The King (and the Ministers of the Federal Government) also share the legislative power. The King through the Federal Government has (i) a right of initiative (the Federal Government may submit government bills to the Federal Parliament), (ii) a right of amendment (the Federal Government may propose amendments to both its own bills and the laws proposed by the Federal Parliament), and (iii) a right of sanction (a law adopted by the Federal Parliament enters into force only after having been sanctioned by the King).

§2. The federal executive

21. The powers of the federal executive are vested in the King (Art. 37 of the Constitution). Pursuant to Articles 88 and 106 of the Constitution, however, all acts by the King must be countersigned by one or more Ministers who bear political responsibility for these acts *vis-à-vis* the Parliament. The King thus appoints Federal Ministers who, in practice, exercise the federal executive powers. The number of Federal Ministers is limited to a maximum of 15. With the possible exception of the Prime Minister, the Belgian Council of Ministers includes as many French-speaking members as Dutch-speaking members. Finally, the Federal Government also comprises the Federal Secretaries of State, who are deputies to a Minister. Both the Ministers and the Secretaries of State are appointed and dismissed by the King (Arts. 96 and 104 of the Constitution.).

22. The role of the federal executive is to execute the laws passed by the federal legislature by means of Royal Decrees (*koninklijke besluiten/arrêtés royaux*) or Ministerial Decrees (*ministeriële besluiten/arrêtés ministériels*). The Constitution also attributes some specific powers to the Federal Government, such as: (i) the exclusive power to regulate the internal organisation of the Federal Government, including the attributions of the Ministers; (ii) the appointment of judges; (iii) the appointment of officials of the federal administration and the foreign service (including, the power to regulate the status of these officials); (iv) the management of international relations and the conclusion of international treaties (without prejudice to the powers of the communities and the regions in international matters that concern them); (v) the command of the army and the conferring of military ranks; (vi) the determination of the state of war and the cessation of hostilities; (vii) the execution of courts' judgements; (viii) the right to grant pardons or to reduce sentences pronounced by judges; (ix) the minting of money as determined by law; and (x) the bestowal of titles of nobility (Arts. 105 through 114 and 167 of the Constitution). The executive's powers furthermore include the powers to convene the Federal Parliament for extraordinary sessions, to adjourn Federal Parliamentary sessions, and to dissolve the Federal Parliament (Arts. 44 through 46 of the Constitution).

§3. The judiciary

23. The judiciary is the only function not to have been modified following the reform of the State. The judicial power remains entirely federal; there is no equivalent power within the federate entities. Only the Youth Protection Office (*Dienst Jeugdbescherming/Office de Protection de la Jeunesse*) was transferred to the communities and regions in 1989. The constitutional revisions have, however, had some

consequences on the judiciary in that a Court of Arbitration (*Arbitragehof/Cour d'arbitrage*) has been created (*See*, paras. 73 *et seq.*) and the powers of the Council of State (*Raad van State/Conseil d'Etat*) have been amended.

24. The organisation and the powers of the judiciary are described in Chapter 21.

B. The Competences of the federal authorities

25. The powers of the Federal State can be subdivided into 3 categories:
    (i) competences which are specifically attributed to the federal authorities as, for example, pursuant to Title VI of the Constitution as regards the army and police force;
    (ii) competences which are exceptions to competences specifically attributed to the communities and the regions: these exceptions are provided for in the Constitution or in the institutional laws and are to be interpreted restrictively; and
    (iii) residual competences, *i.e.*, competences which are not attributed to a federate entity in particular and are for that reason vested in the federal authorities.

26. Broadly speaking, the Federal State has retained authority over all matters that fall within the sphere of the national interest: finance, defence, justice, foreign policy (without prejudice to the powers of the communities and the regions in these matters), social security, important parts of public health and domestic affairs, *etc.*

27. The Federal State thus retains control over a large part of Belgian society, including the judicial branch, the army, the federal police, social security and the major laws relating to social welfare (unemployment, pension, family allowances, health insurance, *etc.*), the public debt, monetary policy, wage and price policy, the protection of savings, nuclear power, state-owned companies (such as the Belgian Railways and the post office), federal culture and scientific institutions (such as the Museum of Modern & Ancient Art and the Royal Library), the use of languages in the German linguistic region and the bilingual region of Brussels-Capital, and over anything that does not fall within the express powers of the communities or the regions (residual powers), at least currently.

IV. THE COMMUNITIES

A. Organisation of the Communities

28. The 3 communities – Flemish, French and German-speaking – each have an executive and a legislative branch. They are, however, structured differently:

Flanders has merged its community and regional institutions. In contrast, the French Community and the Walloon Region each have their own institutions, while the French Community may transfer the exercise of its competences to the Walloon Region and to the French Community Commission in Brussels (Art. 138 of the Constitution). Finally, the Walloon Region may transfer the exercise of some competences to the German Community.

29. Furthermore, the communities enjoy constitutional autonomy. This means that they are able, subject to a special majority requirement, to organise the election, composition, and operation of their own parliament – also called Councils – and their own Government. The German-speaking Community does not enjoy such autonomy.

§1. *The Flemish Community*

30. The institutions of the Flemish Community are the Flemish Parliament *(Vlaamse Raad/Parlement flamand)* and the Flemish Government *(Vlaamse Regering/ Gouvernement flamand).*

31. The Flemish Parliament consists of 118 directly elected members from the Flemish Region plus 6 elected members from the Dutch-linguistic group of the Council of the Brussels-Capital Region. As a result of the most recent constitutional reforms of July 2001, as of the next elections (namely in spring 2003), those 6 members will be directly elected inhabitants of Brussels and will no longer be part of the Council of the Brussels-Capital Region. The members of the Flemish Government are designated by the Flemish Council. Their number may not exceed 11, including the President. At least one Flemish minister must have his/her domicile in the Brussels-Capital Region.

32. As noted above, the Flemish Parliament and the Flemish Government are in charge of both community and regional matters. The main function of the Flemish Parliament is to issue decrees *(decreten/décrets)* concerning the regional and community matters for which it is competent. The members of both the Flemish Parliament and the Flemish Government may take legislative initiatives. Decrees passed by the Flemish Parliament must be ratified and promulgated by the Flemish Government. These decrees have the same legal force as the laws passed by the federal legislature.

§2. *The French Community*

33. The institutions of the French Community are the Council of the French Community *(Franse Gemeenschapsraad/Conseil de la Communauté française)* and the

Government of the French Community *(Franse Gemeenschapsregering/Gouvernement de la Communauté française)*.

34. The Council of the French Community consists of 75 directly elected members of the Walloon Region Council plus 19 members elected from and by the French-linguistic group of the Brussels-Capital Region Council. The Government of the French Community consists of a maximum of 8 ministers elected by the Council (including the President of the Government of the French Community). As in the Flemish Government, at least one minister must have his/her domicile within the Brussels-Capital Region.

35. The principles governing the functions of the French Community institutions are, *mutatis mutandis*, the same as those governing the Flemish institutions except that the institutions of the French Community are only competent for community matters. Separate institutions exist for regional matters *(See,* paras. 51 *et seq.).*

§3. *The German-speaking Community*

36. The statute of the German-speaking Community is set forth in detail in the Law of 31 December 1983 reforming the Institutions of the German-speaking Community *(Wet tot hervorming der instellingen voor de Duitstalige Gemeenschap/Loi de réformes institutionnelles pour la Communauté germanophone)* (as amended). The institutions of the German-speaking Community are the Council of the German-speaking Community *(Rat der deutschsprachigen Gemeinschaft/Duitstalige Gemeenschapsraad/Conseil de la communauté germanophone)* and the Government of the German-speaking Community *(Executive der deutschsprachigen Gemeinschaft/Duitstalige Gemeenschapsregering/Gouvernement de la communauté germanophone).*

37. 25 directly elected members sit on the Council of the German-speaking Community. The executive power is vested in the Government of the German-speaking Community, which consists of one President and two ministers appointed by the Council.

38. The structure and functions of the German-speaking Community's institutions are similar to those of the 2 other communities except that the German-speaking Community does not enjoy constitutional autonomy. It should also be noted that the Constitution provides that the German-speaking Community may exercise some Walloon regional responsibilities in the German-linguistic region by decree or otherwise. This transfer of competence is subject to an agreement concluded between the Council of the Walloon Region and the Council of the German Community and ratified by a vote in each council (Art. 139 of the Constitution).

Currently, the German-speaking Community exercises the Walloon Region competences in relation to monuments and places of interest and to employment policy in the German-linguistic region.

§4. Community institutions for Brussels

39. The 19 Brussels bilingual municipalities do not constitute a separate community as there are only 3 communities in Belgium. The community competences exercised within those 19 Brussels municipalities are subject to a complex allocation which will be described briefly below.

40. With respect to Brussels, the decrees of the Flemish and the French Communities relating to cultural matters (including education) and the so-called "matters attached to the person" *(persoonsgebonden aangelegenheden/matières personnalisables)* (health policy and assistance to people) only have force of law with respect to institutions established in the bilingual region of Brussels-Capital. These institutions must be considered as belonging to the Flemish or the French Community, on account of their activities (for cultural matters) or of their organisation (for personalised matters). Thus, the decrees of the Flemish Community apply to the Dutch-speaking schools of Brussels and those of the French Community apply to the French-speaking schools of Brussels. However, the decrees issued by both the Flemish and the French Communities do not have force of law with respect to (1) people domiciled in the 19 bilingual municipalities of Brussels and (2) institutions that do not belong to either the Flemish or the French Community, *i.e.*, bilingual institutions. 3 other institutions have therefore been created in order to exercise these other community competences within the 19 bilingual municipalities of Brussels: the Flemish Community Commission (*Vlaamse Gemeenschapscommissie/Commission communautaire flamande*), the French Community Commission (*Franse Gemeenschapscommissie/Commission communautaire française*) and the Joint Community Commission (*Gemeenschappelijke Gemeenschapscommissie/Commission communautaire commune*). Each Commission has an assembly and a college.

41. The Joint Community Commission exercises the community competences with respect to the Brussels inhabitants and the bilingual institutions and, as such, has powers similar to those of the Flemish and the French Communities. Thus the Joint Community Commission enacts ordinances that have the same legal force as laws and decrees. These ordinances are enforced by the college of the Joint Community Commission. The power of the Joint Community Commission is, however, limited to "matters attached to the persons", with the exception of education and cultural matters. It is indeed the Federal State that is responsible for cultural and

11

education matters when the institutions located in the bilingual region of Brussels-Capital may not be considered as belonging exclusively to the Flemish or the French Community.

42. On the other hand, unlike the Flemish and the French Communities, neither the Flemish nor the French Community Commissions may issue ordinances. They act as decisional authorities for the monolingual institutions of Brussels, and, as such, may create and manage institutions, or grant subsidies. The Flemish and the French Community Commissions adopt regulations which have less legal force than laws, decrees and ordinances, and are subject to the control of their respective Community. As far as the bilingual institutions of Brussels are concerned, this decisional power is exercised by the Joint Community Commission under the control of both the Flemish and the French Communities.

43. Finally, when the French Community Commission exercises the competences transferred by the French Community pursuant to Article 138 of the Constitution, it is not subject to the supervision of the French Community and issues decrees which have the same legal value as the decrees and ordinances adopted by the federate entities.

B. Competences of the Communities

44. The powers of the 3 communities cover 4 broad areas: (i) cultural matters, (ii) education, (iii) the so-called "matters attached to the person" and (iv) the use of language. The communities also have the power to engage in international relations (as of 2004, the communities will also have power over certain aspects of the development cooperation insofar as these aspects are related to the communities' other areas of competence) and conduct scientific research in these 4 areas.

§1. Cultural matters

45. Cultural matters include, among other things, the protection and promotion of the language, the arts, museums, cultural and scientific institutions, libraries, radio and television, youth policy, tourism and leisure, sports and physical education, and vocational training.

§2. Education

46. Subject to 3 exceptions, the communities are fully responsible for their respective educational systems. These 3 exceptions are (i) the determination of the start and the end of the compulsory schooling period, (ii) minimum requirements regarding the issuing of diplomas, and (iii) teachers' pensions. These 3 matters fall within the competence of the federal legislature.

§3. Matters attached to the person

47. This concept refers to 2 broad areas in which the communities have competences: public health policy and welfare for individuals (*e.g.*, family policy, protection of youth, and, with some exceptions, social welfare).

§4. Use of languages

48. The use of languages in administrative matters, in public schools and schools sub-sidised or recognised by public authorities, in social relations between employers and employees, and in business documents the use of which is prescribed by law, are all covered by the competences of the communities. Since some of these rules may have an important impact on foreign businesses operating in Belgium, they will be discussed in more detail in a separate section (*See,* paras. 84 *et seq.*).

V. THE REGIONS

A. Organisation of the Regions

49. Like the communities, each region has a legislative and an executive branch (*See,* however, para. 28 above about the asymmetric character of Belgian federalism). Both the Flemish and the Walloon Regions enjoy constitutional autonomy, but not the Brussels-Capital Region. Such constitutional autonomy may however be granted to the Brussels-Capital Region at the time of the next institutional reform, which should take place after the 2003 elections.

§1. The Flemish Region

50. As mentioned earlier, the Flemish region, unlike the Walloon Region and the Brus-sels-Capital Region which each have specific institutions responsible for regional matters, is headed by the same institutions as the Flemish Community, that is, the Flemish Parliament and the Flemish Government (*See,* paras. 30 *et seq.*). When the Flemish Parliament votes on regional matters, the 6 members of the Flemish Parliament who were elected in Brussels may not participate in the vote. Any de-cree passed by the Flemish Parliament must specifically indicate whether it covers a community or a regional matter.

§2. *The Walloon Region*

51. The institutions of the Walloon Region are the Council of the Walloon Region *(Waalse Gewestraad/Conseil de la Région wallonne)* and the Executive of the Walloon Region *(Waalse Gewest Executieve/Exécutif de la Région wallonne).*

52. The Council of the Walloon Region – also called the Walloon Parliament – consists of 75 directly elected members. The executive of the Walloon Region consists of a maximum of 9 members. Members of the executive of the Walloon Region are appointed by the Council of the Walloon Region.

53. The Council of the Walloon Region operates in substantially the same way as the Council of the French Community. Its decrees have the same legal force as federal law in all matters for which it is competent. Legislative initiative rests both with individual members of the Council and with the executive. Decrees must be passed by the Council and ratified and promulgated by the executive. As mentioned above, the Walloon Region may exercise the community competences transferred by the French Community, but not within the German-speaking Community.

§3. *The Brussels-Capital Region*

54. The institutions of the Brussels-Capital Region are: the Council of the Brussels-Capital Region *(Raad van het Brussels Hoofdstedelijk Gewest/Conseil de la Région de Bruxelles-Capitale),* and the Executive of the Brussels-Capital Region *(Executieve van het Brusselse Hoofdstedelijke Gewest/Exécutif de la Région de Bruxelles-Capitale).*

55. The Council of the Brussels-Capital Region (*i.e.*, the Brussels-Capital parliament) consists of 75 directly elected members belonging either to the Dutch or to the French linguistic group depending on the election list from which they are chosen. However, as of the next elections, the Council of the Brussels-Capital Region will consist of 89 members and the linguistic repartition will be fixed: 72 members will be French-speaking members and 17 members will be Dutch-speaking. A member of the Council of Brussels-Capital Region may not simultaneously be a member of the Flemish Parliament. The Executive currently consists of 5 Ministers: a president, 2 Dutch-speaking members and 2 French-speaking members. The Brussels-Capital Government is assisted by 3 regional Secretaries of State who, unlike the Federal Secretaries of State, are not members of the Government. The Ministers and the regional Secretaries of State are chosen by the Council. As of the next elections in 2003, they will not be eligible for election as members of the Flemish Government at the same time.

56. The Council issues ordinances *(ordonnanties/ordonnances)* which are ratified and promulgated by the Executive. The ordinances have the same legal force as laws passed by the Federal Parliament or decrees issued by the Flemish Council and the Councils of the French Community and the Walloon Region.

B. Competences of the Regions

57. Each of the 3 regions have power over the same areas. These areas are for the most part listed in the Special Law of 8 August 1980 on Institutional Reforms (as amended). Like the communities, the regions also have the power to conduct international relations (like the communities, the regions should, as of 2004, have power over certain aspects of the development cooperation insofar as those aspects are related to areas of competences allocated to the Regions) and scientific researches in their areas of competences. These areas are:
    (i) regional development and town planning;
    (ii) environment and water policy;
    (iii) rural development and nature conservation;
    (iv) housing policy;
    (v) agriculture policy;
    (vi) energy policy;
    (vii) employment policy;
    (viii) public works and transport;
    (ix) economic policy; and
    (x) supervision of the provinces and municipalities and their financing.

58. Since January 2002, the regions' competences have been further extended to include:
    (i) foreign trade (the Federal State however retains authority over 2 matters: (a) the power to grant guarantees against risks linked to export, import and investment, and (b) the multilateral commercial policy (*e.g.*, within the WTO, FAO, OECD));
    (ii) agriculture and maritime fishing (with some exceptions aimed at ensuring the protection of the food chain);
    (iii) organisation and operation of the municipalities (with some limitations with respect to the Brussels-Capital Region).

59. In the area of economic policy, the powers of the regions, although very extensive, are subject to important restrictions. The Federal State remains in charge of matters such as monetary policy, pricing policy, competition law and trade practices, corporate law, intellectual property, *etc*. Moreover, in the exercise of their

economic powers, the regions must respect the principles of free movement of persons, goods, services and capital, the freedom of commerce and industry and the general regulatory framework designed to maintain the economic and monetary union.

60. Finally, it should be noted that, by virtue of Article 138 of the Constitution, the French-speaking Community handed over to the Brussels-Capital and the Walloon Regions a range of powers relating to tourism, social advancement, vocational training, school transport, sport infrastructure and, to a certain extent, health policy and social aid and assistance.

VI. COMMUNITY AND REGIONAL FINANCES

61. The community and regional finances are for the most part governed by the Special Law of 16 January 1989 concerning the Financing of the Communities and the Regions (as amended) (*Bijzondere wet betreffende de financiering van de Gemeenschappen en de Gewesten/Loi spéciale relative au financement des Communautés et des Régions*). There are no restrictions on how the regions and the communities decide to spend their budgets. In this respect, the regions and the communities have full discretionary powers. The finances of the communities and the regions are made up of fiscal resources (own and shared taxes), non-fiscal resources and loans. Moreover, the regions benefit from a solidarity intervention provided by the federal authorities.

A. Fiscal resources

§1. Own taxes

62. Article 170, paragraph 2 of the Constitution and its implementing law of 23 January 1989 provides that the communities and the regions have independent fiscal powers over matters which are not already subjected to taxes by the federal authorities or over which the federal authorities have not prohibited such taxes.

63. As far as the communities are concerned, the implementation of such autonomous power is, in practice, quite cumbersome in the Brussels territory as this region is bilingual. The implementation requires an agreement between the French and the Flemish Communities whereby the fiscal power is exercised jointly. This was the case for the radio and television tax, the sole community tax which has recently been taken away from the communities and has been replaced by a compensation.

64. The regions may levy 3 types of taxes:
    (i) *12 regional taxes*: taxes on gambling and lotteries, taxes on automatic amuse-
        ment machines, taxes on the first opening of pubs, inheritance taxes, taxes on
        real property, registration duties on the transfer of real estate, registration du-
        ties on mortgages and partition of real estate; registration duties on donations
        of movable property or real estate, the radio and television tax, road taxes and
        the Eurovignette (*i.e.*, a tax on heavy goods vehicles);
    (ii) *additional taxes*: the regions may raise, or grant reductions on, personal in-
        come taxes. To avoid discrepancies between regions, the decision to raise such
        additional taxes is subject to a preliminary consultation between the regions;
    (iii) *general taxes*: the general fiscal power is quite limited as the regions may not
        levy taxes in matters which are not subject to federal taxes. Water and non-
        nuclear waste are expressly recognised as regional competences in respect of
        which they can levy taxes.

§2. Shared taxes

65. The community and regional finances also comprise shared taxes. These are taxes
    collected by the Federal State and transferred to the communities and the regions.
    The communities and the regions are thus entitled to a portion of the proceeds
    from personal income taxes. The communities also benefit from a portion of the
    value added taxes (VAT) for education expenses.

B. Non-fiscal resources

66. The non-fiscal resources of the communities and the regions come from the sale
    of goods and services related to community and regional competences (such as
    entrance fees, sale of properties, *etc.*), as well as donations and legacies.

C. Loans

67. Both the communities and the regions may have recourse to loans. The public
    issue of loans in Belgium requires co-ordination between the Federal State, the
    communities and the regions, and the approval of the Minister of Finances of
    the Federal Government is necessary. The communities and the regions may also
    issue private loans, as well as short-term bonds after having informed the Minister
    of Finance of the Federal Government. It should be noted that such loans are in
    principle not guaranteed by the Federal State.

D. Solidarity contribution

68. The regions, but not the communities, may benefit from a so-called solidarity intervention provided by the federal authority. This system is based on a comparison between the average personal income taxes *per capita* at the federal level with the same average at the regional level. The region or regions whose average is below the national average benefit from a solidarity intervention borne by the federal authorities.

VII. CO-OPERATION AND CONFLICT RESOLUTION

A. Introduction

69. As mentioned above, the communities, the regions and the Federal State must observe federal loyalty, *i.e.*, in exercising their competences, they must refrain from acting against the federal structure and against the interests of the other entities. The constitutional reforms have provided for various mechanisms of co-operation and consultation between the Federal State and the federate entities (*See,* para. 70). 2 types of conflicts may nevertheless arise: (i) conflicts of interests, which are of a political nature and are thus dealt with by a political entity (the Consultation Committee – *See*, para. 71) and (ii) conflicts of competences, which are of a legal nature and are therefore brought before a tribunal (the Court of Arbitration or the Council of State – *See*, paras. 72 *et seq.*).

B. Mechanisms of co-operation

70. Various forms of co-operation exist in the Belgian federal system:
    (i) The role of the Consultation Committee is not limited to the resolution of conflicts: any matter may be the subject of a consultation within the Consultation Committee between the federal authority, the communities and the regions.
    (ii) In some matters, the adoption of a decision by a federate or federal entity requires the opinion or the approval of the other entity. Prior consultation is sometimes compulsory.
    (iii) The communities, the regions and the Federal State may also conclude co-operation agreements. Such agreements are either authorised or imposed by law. For instance, co-operation agreements may be concluded in order to jointly create and manage services or to jointly exercise competences.

C. Conflicts of interests: the Consultation Committee

71. The Consultation Committee consists of the Prime Minister and 5 members of the Federal Government, the President and one member of the Flemish Government, the President of the French Community Government, the President of the Government of the Walloon Region and the President and one member of the Executive of the Brussels-Capital Region. The President of the Government of the German-speaking Community takes part in the meeting but may only vote when the decision concerns the German-speaking Community. The main task of the Consultation Committee is to find solutions to any conflict of interest which may arise between the federal authorities, the regional authorities and the community authorities.

D. Conflict of competences

§1. Conflict prevention: the Council of State

72. The Council of State *(Raad van State/Conseil d'Etat)* has an important role to play in the prevention of conflicts of competence. The legislative section of the Council of State may be consulted by the president of any of the legislative assemblies on any draft bill. The Council of State must be consulted on any draft bill, decree, or ordinance proposed by a Minister of the Federal Government or by a member of a community or regional government. If the Council of State finds that the draft bill which it is called upon to examine exceeds the competence of the entity which has submitted the request for revision of the bill, the matter will be referred to the Consultation Committee. The Consultation Committee must render a unanimous opinion on the issue within 40 days. If the Committee confirms the opinion of the Council of State, it will request that the relevant government or executive amend the bill to avoid a conflict of competence.

§2. Conflict resolution: the Court of Arbitration

73. Conflicts of competence relating to existing legislation, as opposed to draft bills, are handled by the judiciary. The Court of Arbitration and the Council of State have, under certain circumstances, the power to annul legislation and regulations which are in breach of legal or constitutional principles. The other courts do not have the power to annul legislative or regulatory acts, but must refuse to apply regulations which violate the law (Art. 159 of the Constitution).

74. The Court of Arbitration has the power to annul, wholly or partly, federal laws and regional or community decrees or ordinances of the Brussels-Capital Region in the following cases:

(i) violation of a constitutional or implementing legal provision on the division of competences between the regions, the communities and the federal authorities; and

(ii) violation of Articles 10 (principle of equality of treatment), 11 (principle of non-discrimination) and 24 (freedom of and the equality in the educational system) of the Constitution.

75. Applications for annulment may be filed by (i) the Federal Government or a regional or community government, by (ii) the presidents of the legislative assemblies, as well as by (iii) any interested natural person or legal entity. In principle, applications for annulment must be filed within 6 months of the date of publication of the law, decree or ordinance.

76. The Court of Arbitration is the only court which has the power, within the above limits, to review the constitutionality of laws or regional and community decrees and ordinances of the Brussels-Capital Region. These regional and community decrees are legal instruments with the same authority as laws. The ordinary courts and tribunals have no such powers, apart from a limited power of control over ordinances of the Brussels-Capital Region (Art. 9 of the Law of 12 January 1989).

77. The second main function of the Court of Arbitration is to rule on references for preliminary rulings from other courts regarding the following issues:

(i) violation by a law, decree or ordinance of a constitutional or implementing provision on the division of competences between the regions, the communities and the federal authorities;

(ii) conflicts between decrees or ordinances emanating from different authorities insofar as these conflicts concern the scope of application of the respective decrees or ordinances;

(iii) violation by a law, decree or ordinance of Articles 10, 11 and 24 of the Constitution.

78. Any court before which one of the above issues is raised must suspend proceedings and refer the matter to the Court of Arbitration. This principle is subject to only limited exceptions. The Court of Arbitration settles the matter in a judgment which is binding upon the court before which the issue was raised, as well as upon any other court before which the same case will be heard.

§3. Conflict resolution: the Council of State

79. The Council of State also enjoys the power to annul certain legal instruments. While the Court of Arbitration has competence to rule on the constitutional validity of laws, decrees and ordinances, the Council of State has the power to annul

administrative regulations and individual administrative decisions. The administrative section of the Council of State (as opposed to the legislative section which
provides advisory opinions on draft legislation) is in charge of these matters. The
grounds for annulment are violation of substantial formal requirements, lack of
competence and misuse of power *(machtsafwending/détournement de pouvoir)*.
Any party showing the existence of a direct interest may introduce an application
for annulment. This must be done within a period of 60 days following the notification or the publication of the administrative act or regulation.

VIII. PROVINCES AND COMMUNES

80. Besides the federal authority, the communities and the regions, Belgium also comprises 10 provinces and 589 communes. The main difference between the Federal
State, the communities and the regions on the one hand and the provinces and the
communes on the other hand is that the provinces and the communes may enact
regulations, but not laws.

81. The institutions of the provinces are the provincial council *(provinvieraad/conseil
provincial)*, the permanent deputation *(bestendige deputatie/députation permanente)*
and the provincial governor *(provinciegouverneur/gouverneur de province)*. The
members of the provincial council are directly elected every 6 years. Their number
varies between 47 and 84 depending of the number of inhabitants. The permanent
deputation consists of 6 members and a provincial governor who acts as a president but without the power to vote. The 6 members are elected by and within the
provincial council, while the provincial governor is appointed by the King.

82. The institutions of the communes are the municipal council *(gemeenschapsraad/
conseil communal)*, the college of the mayor and deputies *(college van burgemeester
en schepenen/ collège des bourgmestre et échevins)* and the mayor *(burgemeester/
bourgmestre)*. The members of the council are elected every 6 years by the inhabitants of the commune (including EU citizens). Their number depends on the number
of inhabitants and varies between 7 and 55. The deputies are in principle elected
by and within the municipal council. The deputies present their candidate for the
mayor position to the King, who ultimately appoints the mayor.

83. The provinces and the communes exercise power over:
    (i) all matters that are of provincial or municipal interest, unless the Federal State,
    the communities or the regions decide to regulate the matter themselves;

(ii) missions assigned by a superior authority: the federal authority, the communities or the regions may entrust the provinces and communes with the implementation of their politics.

IX. USE OF LANGUAGES

A. The official languages of Belgium

84. There are 3 official languages in Belgium: Dutch, French and German. In certain situations, it may be required by law or decree to use one particular language. As this may have a significant impact on the way in which foreign companies may operate in Belgium, the main principles governing the matter are set forth below.

85. Article 30 of the Constitution contains the general principle that the use of languages in Belgium is optional. Exceptions to this principle may only be made by law and must relate to the acts of public authorities and to judicial matters. Article 129, paragraph 3, of the Constitution further provides that the communities are competent to regulate the use of language in administrative matters; in schools created, subsidised, or recognised by the public authorities; in social relations between employers and their personnel; and with respect to documents the use of which is prescribed by law or regulation.

86. Both the federal authorities and the Communities have used their powers to regulate the use of languages. The federal authorities have passed laws relating to the use of languages in administrative matters (Law of 2 August 1965 co-ordinated by Royal Decree of 18 July 1966 on the Use of Languages in Administrative Matters – *Wetten op het gebruik van de talen in bestuurszaken/Lois sur l'emploi des langues en matière administrative*) and in judicial matters (Law of 15 June 1935 on the Use of Languages in Judicial Matters – *Wet op het gebruik der talen in gerechtszaken/ Loi concernant l'emploi des langues en matière judiciaire*). The principal area in which the communities have used their legislative powers, and which is of interest to foreign companies conducting business in Belgium, is that of employment relations. For the Flemish Community, the relevant legislative instrument is the Decree of 19 July 1973 regulating the Use of Languages in Social Relations between Employers and Employees as well as for the Documents of Companies which are Prescribed by Law (*Decreet tot regeling van het gebruik van de talen voor de sociale betrekkingen tussen de werkgevers en de werknemers, alsmede van de voor de wet en de verordeningen voorgeschreven akten en bescheiden van de ondernemingen*) which, due to its date of publication, is often referred to as the

"September Decree". For the French Community, the relevant texts are the Decree of 12 July 1978 on the Protection of the French Language (*Décret sur la défense de la langue française*) and the Decree of 30 June 1982 on the Protection of the Freedom of the Use of Languages and the Use of the French Language in Social Relations between Employers and their Personnel as well as the Documents of the Companies which are Prescribed by Law (*Décret relatif à la protection de la liberté de l'emploi des langues et de l'usage de la langue française en matière de relations sociales entre les employeurs et leur personnel ainsi que d'actes et documents des entreprises imposés par la loi et les règlements*).

B. Social relations

87. The language to be used in the official correspondence between employers and their employees is either Dutch, French or German, depending on the location of the place of business *(exploitatiezetel/siège d'exploitation)*. If the place of business is located in the Dutch language region (with the exception of certain municipalities which benefit from an exceptional language status – the so-called *faciliteitengemeenten/communes à facilités)*, the language to be used is Dutch (Arts. 1 and 2 of the Decree of 19 July 1973). If the place of business is located in the French linguistic region (with the exception of certain municipalities), the language to be used is French (Arts. 1 and 2 of the Decree of 30 June 1982). If the place of business is located in the German linguistic region, the language to be used is German (Art. 52 of the Royal Decree of 18 July 1966). The bilingual region of Brussels also remains subject to the federal Law of 2 August 1965 co-ordinated by Royal Decree of 18 July 1966 on the Use of Languages in Administrative Matters. Employers which have their place of business in the Brussels-Capital Region must use Dutch or French in the employment relationship with employees depending on whether the employees are Dutch or French-speaking (Art. 52 of the Royal Decree of 18 July 1966).

C. Documents prescribed by law

88. Documents the use of which is prescribed by law must be drafted in the language of the area of the place of business. This category of documents is extremely wide. It covers, for example, all accounting documents insofar as the accountancy laws prescribe their use (*See*, Chapter 4), invoices, bills of lading, bills of exchange and most corporate documents.

D. Sanctions

89. The sanctions to be applied for violations of the rules governing the use of language depend on the applicable legal instrument. If the situation is governed by the federal Law of 2 August 1965 co-ordinated by Royal Decree of 18 July 1966, the only sanction is an obligation to replace the document with a document drafted in the appropriate language. The decrees issued by both the Flemish and the French Community have stricter sanctions. Documents which contravene the language requirements contained in these decrees are null and void. The nullity sanction covers not only the document itself, but also the legal act which it embodies. The Flemish decree specifies in Article 10 that the nullity sanction does not prejudice the rights of the employee, nor the vested rights of third parties. The Flemish decree also provides that violations may lead to the imposition of administrative fines and criminal sanctions.

2. COMPANY LAW

I. INTRODUCTION

A. Sources of law

90. On 7 May 1999, the Belgian Parliament adopted a new Company Code (*Wetboek van Vennootschappen/Codes des Sociétés* – the "Company Code"), which regroups and restructures the main provisions of Belgian company Law. The Company Code was completed by a Royal Decree of 30 January 2001 that further details some of the principles contained therein.

91. For several years, authors and practitioners had been complaining that the provisions governing Belgian Company law were fragmented in several laws and regulations. This fragmentation was mainly due to the fact that, in the last decade, several amendments had been made (mainly in 1991 and 1995) to the main code, without serious reflection on the structure and transparency of the legislation.

92. The main objective of the legislator in introducing the new Company Code was therefore not to introduce considerable changes to the legal provisions relating to commercial companies, but to adopt a code that regroups all these provisions in a consistent and structured outline. Therefore, some provisions on accounting and annual accounts, as well as provisions on transparency, which were previous set out in separate laws and regulations, were also included in the Company Code.

93. The Company Code came into force on the 6 February 2001.

B. Definition of a company under Belgian law

94. Article 1 of the Company Code gives the following definition of a company under Belgian law:

> "*A company is incorporated by an agreement, whereby 2 or more parties agree to put something in common with the intention to carry out one or more precisely defined activities and with a view to providing the shareholders with a direct or indirect benefit.*

In cases as determined by this Code, it can be incorporated by a legal act of a single person who designates some assets to the use for one or more precisely defined activities.

In cases as determined by this Code, the deed of incorporation can determine that the company was not incorporated with a view to providing the shareholders with a direct or indirect benefit."

C. Forms of corporate organisation

95. There are several forms of companies (with legal personality) in Belgium (Art. 2, para. 2 of the Company Code):
    - The public limited liability company (*naamloze vennootschap/société anonyme*) (*NV/SA*);
    - The closely held limited liability company (*besloten vennootschap met beperkte aansprakelijkheid/société privée à responsabilité limitée*) (*BVBA/SPRL*);
    - The co-operative company with limited liability (*coöperatieve vennootschap met beperkte aansprakelijkheid/société coopérative à responsabilité limitée*) (*CVBA/SCRL*);
    - The co-operative company with unlimited liability (*coöperatieve vennootschap met onbeperkte aansprakelijkheid/société coopérative à responsabilité illimitée*) (*CVOA/SCRI*);
    - The general partnership (*vennootschap onder firma/société en nom collectif*) (*VOF/SNC*);
    - The limited partnership (*gewone commanditaire vennootschap/société en commandite simple*) (*Comm. V/SCS*);
    - The limited partnership with shares (*commanditaire vennootschap op aandelen/société en commandite par actions*) (*Comm. VA/SCA*);
    - The Economic Interest Grouping (*economisch samenwerkingsverband/groupement d'intérêt économique*) (*ESV/GIE*).

96. The first and second form, *i.e.*, the public limited liability company and the closely held limited liability company, are the most common forms of business enterprises. All the aforementioned companies do however have a distinct legal personality.

97. The Company Code also lists 3 types of business enterprises which do not have legal personality: a partnership (*maatschap/société de droit commun*), a temporary commercial company (*tijdelijke handelsvennootschap/société momentanée*), and a company in participation (*stille handelsvennootschap/société interne*) (Art. 2, para. 1 of the Company Code). These will however not be discussed here.

98. A foreign company wishing to do business in Belgium can also opt not to establish a subsidiary but, instead, form a Belgian branch of the foreign company.

D. Use of languages when setting up a business in Belgium

99. The Law on the Use of Languages in Administrative Matters as co-ordinated by Royal Decree of 18 July 1966 (*Wetten op het gebruik van de talen in bestuurszaken/ Lois sur l'emploi des langues en matière administrative*) stipulates that all official corporate documents must be drawn up in the language of the region in which the company has its registered office or a centre of operations.

100. If a subsidiary of a branch is established in the Dutch-speaking region, all official corporate documents must be exclusively in Dutch. If a subsidiary or branch is constituted in the French-speaking region, all official corporate documents must be in French. For subsidiaries or branches established in Brussels, the documents can be either in Dutch, in French or in both languages. However, companies are free to add an English translation to these documents.

101. The Decree of 19 July 1973 provides a sanction of nullity for documents established in violation of this legislation in the Dutch-speaking region. The Decrees of 12 July 1978 and 30 June 1982 provide the same sanction for documents established in violation of the legislation in the French-speaking region. As to the region Brussels-Capital, the Royal Decree of 18 July 1966 also provides for the sanction of nullity for any violations.

102. The legislation regarding the use of languages is mandatory and it is, therefore, impossible for foreign companies wishing to set up a subsidiary or branch in Belgium to derogate from its application.

II. REQUIREMENTS FOR THE ESTABLISHMENT OF A BRANCH OFFICE (*BIJKANTOOR/SUCCURSALE*)

A. Definition of a branch office

103. The Company Code does not contain a definition of a "branch office". Inspiration should therefore be sought in the case-law of the European Court of Justice, where this concept is further defined.

104. 2 characteristics are of vital importance:
    (i) the economic dependence of the branch;
    (ii) the durability and the relationship with the economic activity of the head office.

105. In its *Somafer/Ferngas*-judgment of 22 November 1978 (ECJ, 22 November 1978, Case 33/78, *Somafer S.A. v. Soar-Ferngas AG*, [1978] E.C.R. 2183), the European Court of Justice defined the concept of a branch as follows:

> *"The concept of branch, agency or other establishment implies a place of business which has the appearance of permanency, such as the extension of a parent body, has a management and is materially equipped to negotiate business with third parties so that the latter, although knowing that there will if necessary be a legal link with the parent body, the head office of which is abroad, do not have to deal directly with such parent body but may transact business at the place of business constituting the extension."*

106. From this case law, it can be concluded that a branch is considered to be a permanent, economically dependent establishment of the head office.

107. Under Belgian law, this concept has not been properly defined as yet. The Supreme Court did however state in several judgements that a foreign company has a centre of activities in Belgium when it regularly carries out activities in Belgium which fall within its commercial purpose and when it is represented by a representative who may bind it with respect to third parties (Cass. 24 March 1930, *Pas.*, 1930, I, 170; Cass. 18 December 1941, *Pas.*, 1941, I, 467).

108. A branch is therefore dependent on another company for whose account and under whose name it operates. It can have its own management, but is not in itself an independent legal entity.

109. Once the office of a foreign company in Belgium is considered to be a branch of that foreign company, it becomes subject to a distinct set of rules, which govern its corporate organisation.

B. Requirements for the formation of a branch

110. In order to form a Belgian branch of a foreign company (hereinafter the "head office"), the head office should file certain information with the registry of the commercial court prior to the opening of the branch.

111. A distinction is made depending on whether or not the head office is incorporated under the laws of an EC Member State. Where the head office is incorporated under the laws of a member state of the European Union, the following information should be filed (Art. 81 of the Company Code):
     (i) the deed of incorporation and the current articles of association of the head office;

  (ii) the name and legal form of the head office;

 (iii) the trade registry with which the head office is registered and the trade registry number of the head office;

 (iv) an extract of the entry of the head office with the trade registry;

  (v) the address and activities of the branch as well as its name (where this differs from the name of the head office);

 (vi) the appointment and the identity of the persons authorised to represent the company; and

(vii) the annual accounts and the consolidated annual accounts of the last financial year.

112. Where the head office is not incorporated under the laws of an EC Member State, the following information should be filed (Art. 82 of the Company Code):

  (i) the address of the branch;

 (ii) the activities of the branch;

 (iii) the law of incorporation of the head office;

 (iv) the trade registry with which the head office is registered and the trade registry number of the head office;

  (v) an extract of the entry of the head office with this trade registry;

 (vi) the deed of incorporation and the current articles of association of the head office;

(vii) the legal form, the registered office and activities of the head office;

(viii) the name of the head office and the branch (if it would differ from the name of the head office);

 (ix) the appointment and identity of the persons authorised to represent the company;

  (x) the extent of the powers of representation of these persons as well as the fact whether they are entitled to act alone; and

 (xi) the annual accounts as well as the consolidated annual accounts of the last financial year.

113. It is however important to note that these documents are to be submitted to a notary public of the country of incorporation of the head office for certification.

114. In addition, the certified copies are to be submitted to the competent authorities to provide the certified copies with an apostil, *i.e.*, a statement indicating that the signature on the document is authentic. It is only after affixation of an apostil to the certified copies by those authorities that they can be filed with the registry of the commercial court having jurisdiction over the branch. At the time of filing, a specific registration form must be filled out.

115. Furthermore, no document can be filed without being accompanied by a translation from a certified translator.

116. The use of the apostil in the above procedure is however only possible if the head
office is located in a country that adhered to the "Apostil Treaty", that is, the Hague
Treaty for the Abolishment of the Requirement of Legalisation of Foreign Official
Documents of 5 October 1961. If the Hague Treaty does not apply, although it
currently counts 57 states, the full chain of signature legalisations will have to
be followed. In practice, the internal procedure of the relevant country should be
followed, after which the documents are to be presented to the Belgian Consulate
in that country and, thereafter, to the Belgian Ministry of Justice. There is an
exception to this where a specific bilateral agreement exists between Belgium and
the country where the head office is located.

117. Finally, the board resolution stating the decision of the head office to establish a
branch and operating its representatives and the articles of incorporation and association should be published in the *Annexes to the Belgian Official Journal* (*Bijlagen
tot het Belgisch Staatsblad/Annexes au Moniteurs belge*). The forms submitted for
that purpose should be signed by the legal representative of the branch.

C. The publicity formalities to be complied with by the branch after it has started to operate

118. Once a branch has been set up, a particular body of rules will apply to both the
foreign company and its branch office.

119. Obligations imposed by Belgian law on foreign companies operating through a
Belgian branch (Arts. 59, 81, 82 and 107 of the Company Code) include:
    (i) filing and publishing in Belgium any modification to the documents as listed
    above (Arts. 81, para. 1 and 83 of the Company Code) within 30 days after
    the events;
    (ii) publishing of the bankruptcy, liquidation or related procedures in which the
    head office is involved;
    (iii) depositing every year the annual accounts of the head office. (Art. 83 of the
    Company Code); and
    (iv) publishing the closure of the branch.

120. The Belgian branch office will be required to use a specific letterhead for all external correspondence and/or invoicing. It must contain the following information
(Art. 86 of the Company Code):
    (i) the name of the head office;

(ii) the legal form of the head office;

(iii) the registered office of the head office;

(iv) the trade registry with which the head office is registered and its number;

(v) the commercial court competent for the place where the branch is situated; and

(vi) if applicable, the fact that the head office is in liquidation.

III. REQUIREMENTS FOR THE ESTABLISHMENT OF A SUBSIDIARY (*DOCHTERVENNOOTSCHAP/FILIALE*)

A. General characteristics of a subsidiary (*dochtervennootschap/filiale*)

121. Foreign companies may choose to establish a subsidiary in the form of a Belgian company having a legal personality distinct from the parent company.

122. Several reasons may support the establishment of a subsidiary:
    (i) the subsidiary is, as a rule, a means to limiting the potential liability of the business partners to the capital to which they have subscribed;
    (ii) the subsidiary is a framework for organised collaboration between active share-holders and passive investors;
    (iii) the subsidiary may offer tax advantages;
    (iv) the subsidiary may be a useful tool to settle inheritance questions *e.g.*, since any assets as contributed to the company can be transferred easily by trans-ferring the bearer shares of the company.

123. As was mentioned before (*See*, para. 96), the principal types of Belgian companies are all either limited liability companies or partnerships. A specific type of company, the public limited liability company (*naamloze vennootschap/société anonyme*) (*NV/SA*) is most often used by foreign investors who wish to establish a Belgian subsidiary.

124. The main characteristics of the NV/SA are that it is a company with separate legal personality in which the shareholders' potential liability is normally limited to their subscription. An NV/SA must have at least 2 shareholders who may be either Belgian or foreign individuals or companies. There is a minimum capital require-ment of € 61,500 (Art. 439 of the Company Code). The shares are eligible for quotation on a stock exchange.

125. The legal provisions governing the NV/SA are contained in Articles 437 through 653 of the Company Code.

126. In the following sections, the legal provisions relating to the incorporation and operation of an NV/SA in Belgium will be discussed in more detail.

B. The rules governing the incorporation of an NV/SA

§1. Requirements for the incorporation of an NV/SA

127. As is the case for most domestic corporations, the co-operation of a Belgian notary public is required for the incorporation of an NV/SA. Indeed, the articles of association of an NV/SA must be enacted in the form of a deed drawn up by a notary public. The deed must, in accordance with the Royal Decree of 18 July 1966 on the Use of Languages in Administrative Matters (*Wetten op het gebruik van de talen in bestuurszaken/Lois sur l'emploi des langues en matière administrative*) (*See*, para. 86), be drawn up and executed in Dutch, French or German, depending on the region where the registered office is located. If the registered office is located in Brussels, the language of the deed can be in either French or Dutch.

128. The basic substantial requirements for the formation of an NV/SA are:
    (i) There must be a minimum of 2 shareholders who may be individuals or companies, Belgian or foreign. After the formation of the NV/SA, the number of shareholders may not drop below 2 for any period longer than 12 months. The Company Code provides that, if there are fewer than 2 shareholders at the end of such a 1-year period, the remaining shareholder will be held jointly liable with the company for all the company's obligations which have been entered into by the company after the concentration of the shares in the hands of one shareholder until the entry of a new shareholder, the transformation of the NV/SA into a closely held limited liability company, or the winding up of the NV/SA (Art. 646 of the Company Code);
    (ii) There must be a minimum stated capital of € 61,500, which must be fully subscribed. Violations of this requirement are penalised by the founders being considered by law as the subscribers with the ensuing liability (Art. 456 of the Company Code);
    (iii) At least 25 per cent of each share and the minimum capital must be fully paid up (Art. 448 of the Company Code);
    (iv) There must be a draft budget (Art. 440 of the Company Code) (*financieel plan/plan financier*), which provides a forecast covering the company's first 2 years of activity. The budget should demonstrate a balanced relationship between the amount of the corporate capital and the intended activities of the company. If the NV/SA is declared bankrupt within the first 3 years of its creation, the founding shareholders may incur personal liability if the court

considers that the capital was manifestly insufficient to carry out the planned activities for at least 2 years. The draft budget must be submitted to and kept by the notary. The notary will file the draft budget with the court or with the office of the public prosecutor in the circumstances determined by law (Art. 456 of the Company Code).

129. The incorporation of an NV/SA before a Belgian notary public does not require the physical presence of the founding shareholders. The shareholders may be represented by special proxyholders. If this is the case, special proxies should be drafted, which should list the main features of the draft articles of association of the company in accordance with the last paragraph of Article 453 of the Company Code.

§2. Payment of capital: contributions in cash or in kind

130. Contributions to the capital may be made either in cash or in kind.
    (i) With regard to contributions in cash, Article 449 of the Company Code stipulates that the cash should be transferred into a blocked bank account which must be opened for this purpose with a Belgian bank in the name of the company in formation prior to the day of enactment of the articles of association. The delivery of a bank certificate in this respect by the bank will be a condition for the notary public to pass the deed.
    (ii) With regard to contributions in kind, the founding shareholders must prepare a special report in which they state their assessment of the value of the assets concerned and the reasons for the contribution in kind. In addition, the founding shareholders must appoint a statutory auditor who will prepare a report concerning, among other things, the description and valuation of the assets as made by the founding shareholders (Art. 444 of the Company Code). Both reports must be completed prior to the incorporation of the company and must be deposited with the registry of the competent commercial court within 2 weeks of the date of incorporation. Moreover, the statutory auditor's name and the conclusions of the report must be mentioned in the excerpt of the deed of incorporation which is deposited with the trade registry and published in the *Belgian Official Journal (Belgisch Staatsblad/Moniteur belge)*.

§3. Minimum provisions to be included in the articles of association

131. The articles of association of an NV/SA must, amongst other information, contain information regarding the following matters (Art. 453 of the Company Code):
    (i) *the corporate name*: this name should be different from the names of any other company (Art. 65 of the Company Code);

(ii) *the corporate purpose*: the purpose of the company should be defined with care because it defines the permitted scope of activity of the company (in addition, a change of corporate purpose is subject to stringent requirements) (Art. 69, para. 11 of the Company Code);

(iii) the registered office of the company (Art. 69, para. 2 of the Company Code);

(iv) the duration of the company, unless it is unlimited (Art. 69, para. 3 of the Company Code);

(v) the stated capital of the NV/SA and the amount of the capital which has been subscribed to (Art. 69, para. 5 of the Company Code);

(vi) if applicable, the amount of the authorised capital, that is, the amount by which the board of directors is allowed to increase the stated capital (*See*, paras. 152 *et seq.*);

(vii) the number and method of designation of members of the board of directors (in principle, minimum 3 physical persons or companies, which are not subject to any Belgian residence requirement), the person(s) in charge of the daily management of the company (physical persons, who are not subject to any Belgian residence required), and the statutory auditors (Art. 453, para. 2 of the Company Code);

(viii) the number and the nominal value of the shares of the company (Art. 453, para. 3 of the Company Code);

(ix) any restriction on the transfer of the shares (Art. 453, para. 3 of the Company Code);

(x) the number of the non-capital shares (*winstbewijzen/parts bénéficiaires*) and their attached rights (Art. 453, para. 4 of the Company Code);

(xi) any restrictions on the transfer of non-capital shares (Art. 453, para. 4 of the Company Code);

(xii) the nature of the shares (that is, bearer or registered (Art. 453, para. 5 of the Company Code) shares (*See*, para. 170);

(xiii) a description of any contributions in kind (Art. 453, para. 6 of the Company Code);

(xiv) the cause and the extent of the special benefits granted to the founding shareholders (Art. 453, para. 7 of the Company Code);

(xv) the total cost of incorporation (Art. 453, para. 8 of the Company Code);

(xvi) the bank which holds the special blocked account (Art. 453, para. 9 of the Company Code);

(xvii) any transfers of real estate contributed to the company during the preceding 5 years (Art. 453, para. 10 of the Company Code);

(xviii) any mortgages or charges that encumber the goods contributed to the company (Art. 453, para. 11 of the Company Code);

(xix) the conditions under which any contributed option rights can be exercised.

132. The provisions of Article 69, paragraphs 1, 2, 3, 5, 11 and Article 453, paragraph 2 of the Company Code must be mentioned explicitly in any proxies to represent shareholders at the incorporation meeting.

133. If the above information is not included in the notarial deed, the founding shareholders may be held civilly and criminally liable. Moreover, if the deed drawn up by a notary public does not contain specific clauses relating to matters such as the corporate purpose clause or the stated capital, any party whose interests are directly prejudiced may request the competent commercial court to declare the NV/SA null and void.

§4. Formalities to be completed after the formation of the company

1. Registration

134. Within 15 days of the formation of the company before the notary public, an excerpt of the deed of incorporation must be deposited with the registry of the commercial court (*dienst akten van vennootschappen/service actes de sociétés*) in whose jurisdiction the registered office of the company is located (Arts. 67 and 68 of the Company Code). Subsequently, an application can be made for an entry in the trade registry (*handelsregister/registre de commerce*) of the commercial court (where a separate file is kept of all the companies).

135. The excerpt should also be published in the *Annexes to the Belgian Official Journal* (*Bijlagen tot Belgisch Staatsblad/Annexes Moniteur belge*) within 15 days of the above-mentioned filing (Art. 73 of the Company Code). In the absence of such a publication, the NV/SA shall not be entitled to be represented in court as a separate legal entity and it will only be possible to rely on the content of the incorporation deed as against third parties where the NV/SA proves that the third parties had knowledge of it (Art. 76 of the Company Code).

2. Corporate books

136. The rules pertaining to the corporate books are discussed in paragraphs 290 *et seq.*

3. Registration tax

137. A 0.5 per cent registration tax is payable on the amount of the corporate capital contributed.

4. Government approvals

138. No specific government approvals are needed for the formation of an NV/SA. However, in certain regulated industries, the company may have to apply for specific government approvals or licenses prior to starting its operations.

5. Certificate of establishment

139. In order to be able to register some small and medium-sized companies with the trade registry, an application needs to be made to obtain a so-called certificate of establishment (*vestigingsgetuigschrift/attestation d'établissement*) at the Chamber of Crafts and Trades. The certificates of establishment then needs to be deposited at the trade registry, as part of the registration with that registry.

140. In view of Article 2, 1°, 3 of the Law of 10 February 1998, this obligation however only applies to small or medium-sized companies (the so-called "SMEs") that do not meet one of the following thresholds:
    (i) the number of employees exceeds 50 persons;
    (ii) the turnover exceeds € 7,000,000; and
    (iii) the balance sheet exceeds € 5,000,000.

141. In order to make such application for a certificate of establishment, certain documents are required:
    (i) a copy of the deed of incorporation of the company, mentioning the founding parties and the appointment of the directors;
    (ii) proof of the deposition by the notary public of the deed with the Companies' Registry or an excerpt from the publication in the *Belgian Official Journal*; and
    (iii) proof for each company that one of the directors possesses a basic knowledge of corporate management.

142. Basic knowledge of corporate management may be proven either by means of certain documents or, alternatively, by means of sufficiently corroborated professional experience.

143. Basic knowledge of corporate management may be proven by the following documents:
    (i) certificate of higher general or technical secondary education, of secondary art education or of professional secondary education obtained in "trade", "accounting", "sales" or "office";
    (ii) any college or university degree;
    (iii) certificate of the first year of training for "head of undertaking";
    (iv) certificate of a recognised accelerated course in "corporate management";

(v) degree or certificate of training in "social promotion";

(vi) certificate by the central exam commissions of the Ministry of Education; and

(vii) documents which are equivalent to any of the above by force of international commitments.

144. Proof of professional experience may take one of the following forms:

i. Experience as an independent head of undertaking or as a person, not bound by an employment contract, who is responsible for general affairs management of a company

The experience must have occurred within the last 15 years and have lasted 3 years where it constituted the main activity of the director or 5 years where it constituted a secondary activity. The following documents must be provided:

(i) the registration with the trade registry of a business activity in personal name; or a contract of subsidiary management; or the proof of the appointment by a company (*i.e.*, the excerpt from the publication in the *Belgian Official Journal*); and

(ii) and the social security certificate, mentioning the period of enlistment and the nature of the profession.

ii. Experience as an "independent assistant" for 5 years out of the last 15 years

The following documents must be provided:

(i) certificate by the employer, indicating the period of employment; and

(ii) and the social security certificate, mentioning the period of enlistment and the nature of the profession.

iii. Experience as white-collar worker with a leading function for 5 years out of the last 15 years

The following documents must be provided:

(i) the employment contract in so far as this concerns the leading function; or a certificate by the employer, indicating function and period; and

(ii) and any corporate document confirming said leading function.

145. In view of the fact that the obtaining of a certificate of establishment can be a cumbersome and lengthy procedure, an important exception was however included. No application for a certificate of establishment needs to be made if one of the shareholders, holding at least 25 per cent of the shares, meets one of the above-mentioned thresholds and makes a written statement on honour in this respect.

C. Rules governing the operation of an NV/SA

§1. The rules pertaining to the capital of an NV/SA

1. The stated capital

146. The stated capital is the capital which is determined in the incorporation deed and whose main purpose is to constitute a guarantee for the creditors of the company. For an NV/SA the stated capital must amount to at least € 61,500.

2. Capital increases

147. The rules relating to capital increases are contained in Articles 581 through 611 of the Company Code.

148. A decision to increase the capital of the company will usually be taken by a general shareholders' meeting. Such a decision entails the modification of the company's articles of association in the form of a notarial deed. If agreed by the shareholders, a capital increase can only take place if at least one-half of the stated capital is present or represented at the general shareholders' meeting, and provided a special majority of at least two-thirds of the votes present or represented supports the decision to increase the capital.

149. The deed containing the decision to increase the capital must be filed with the registry of the commercial court and an excerpt of the deed must be published in the *Belgian Official Journal (Belgisch Staatsblad/ Moniteur belge)* (Arts. 73 and 588 of the Company Code). The entry of the company with the trade registry must be amended accordingly.

150. If a capital increase is achieved through a contribution in kind, the statutory auditor must prepare a special report containing a description of the contribution in kind and the method of valuation. The board of directors must also prepare a report containing a description of the importance for the company of the capital increase and the contribution in kind. The 2 reports are filed with the registry of the commercial court (Art. 602 of the Company Code).

151. If the capital increase is achieved through contributions in cash, Article 600 of the Company Code requires that the cash be transferred into a blocked bank account, opened for this purpose with a Belgian bank in the name of the company, prior to the enactment of the deed by the notary public (Art. 589 of the Company Code). The delivery of a bank certificate in this respect by the bank will be a condition for the notary public to pass the deed. After the enactment of the notarial deed, the notary public will issue a certificate to release the money on the blocked bank account.

3. Powers of the board of directors to proceed with capital increases

152. The articles of association may empower the board of directors to increase the stated capital once or several times up to a predetermined amount over a specific period of time, not exceeding 5 years. The amount by which the board is accordingly allowed to increase the stated capital constitutes the authorised capital (Arts. 603 through 607 of the Company Code).

153. The Company Code (Art. 604 of the Company Code) provides that the board should establish a detailed and precise report when it requests the general shareholders' meeting to grant or renew the board's right to increase the capital in the framework of the authorised capital. The report must contain a description of the circumstances under which the board will make use of its right to increase the capital and of the purposes for which this may be done. If the board fails to establish a report or to follow the guidelines contained in its report, it can be held responsible by the company or by third parties.

154. The report should be mentioned in the agenda of the general shareholders' meeting and a copy of the report should be forwarded to the holders of registered shares. In addition, each shareholder has the right to obtain a copy of the report free of charge at least 15 days prior to the general meeting. The Company Code limits the power of the board of directors to obtain a capital increase through contributions in kind. Article 606, paragraph 1 of the Company Code prohibits the board from increasing the capital if such an increase is achieved primarily through a contribution in kind by a shareholder who holds shares of the company which represents at least 10 per cent of the voting rights.

4. The rules pertaining to the application and abolition of the preferential right

155. A preferential right is a right given to existing shareholders to participate with preference over other parties in a capital increase achieved by contributions in cash by providing funds in proportion to the shares they hold (Art. 592 of the Company Code).

156. This preferential right can be exercised during a term that is agreed upon by the general shareholders' meeting, or by the board of directors if the capital increase is effected in the framework of the authorised capital. The term should be at least 15 days from the day the subscription time is opened (Art. 593, para. 1 of the Company Code). The existence of the right to exercise the preferential right must be notified in advance to the existing shareholders (Art. 593, para. 2 of the Company Code). The preferential right can be traded during the subscription time in the

same manner as the share to which it is attached (Art. 593, para. 4 of the Company Code).

157. Shareholders of shares without voting rights will in principle have a preferential right when new shares are issued, regardless of whether the latter are with or without voting rights. However, if the capital increase is effected by the issue of 2 classes of shares, one with voting rights and the other without, each class of shares must be presented first to shareholders who already own that class of shares.

158. The preferential right cannot be abolished or limited in the articles of association (Art. 595 of the Company Code). However, the general shareholders' meeting, which is convened to decide on a capital increase, can limit or abolish the preferential right in the interest of the company (Art. 596 of the Company Code). In that case, the invitation to that general shareholders' meeting has to make specific mention of this intention.

159. If the preferential right is limited or abolished, the general shareholders' meeting or the board of directors can nevertheless determine that priority should be given to the existing shareholders for the allocation of the new shares. In this case, the subscription time for the new shares should be 10 days. (Arts. 67 and 599 of the Company Code).

160. If the preferential right is limited or abolished in favour of one or more persons (other than employees of the company or of the company's subsidiaries), the identity of the beneficiaries of such limitation or abolition must be mentioned in both of the special reports which have to be prepared in this respect by the board and the statutory auditor and in the invitation to the meeting. The Company Code also contains specific provisions designed to avoid that the offer price would be lower than the value of the shares.

5. The rules pertaining to a decrease of the capital of a company

161. A decision to decrease the capital of a company requires a modification of the articles of association and can only be taken by the general shareholders' meeting convening before a notary public (Art. 612 of the Company Code). The shareholders must be treated equally if they find themselves in similar circumstances. The invitation to the meeting must contain the reasons for the decrease in the capital and the method that will be followed to achieve that end.

6. The rules applicable in case of substantial losses

162. Article 633 of the Company Code provides for a mandatory procedure in case the company sustains substantial losses. The board of directors must convene an

extraordinary shareholders' meeting in the event that the net assets of the company have reached a level that is inferior to one-half of the stated capital. The term "net assets" is defined in Article 617, paragraph 2 of the Company Code as being "*the difference between the total value of the assets, as determined in the official balance sheet, on the one hand, and the sum of all the debts and provisions for potential future liabilities on the other hand.*"

163. The extraordinary shareholders' meeting must be convened within 2 months from the date when the directors had actual knowledge of the substantial losses or should have been aware of them. The shareholders must then decide either to dissolve the company or to accept the measures aimed at restructuring the company's financial situation, which the board of directors may propose in a special report (Art. 633, para. 1 of the Company Code). A capital increase may constitute one of those measures. The decision to dissolve the company is taken in accordance with the rules that govern a modification of the corporate articles of association. If the loss amounts to more than three-quarters of the company's stated capital, the decision to dissolve the company can be taken by one-quarter of the votes represented at the meeting (Art. 633, para. 4 of the Company Code).

164. The penalty where the board does not convene such a general shareholders' meeting in due time, promotes for the board of directors being liable towards third parties for the losses which the third parties have sustained as a result of the fact that the meeting was not held. There is a legal presumption, until proof of the contrary, that any damages sustained by third parties result from the fact that the general shareholders' meeting of was not convened in due time.

165. Article 634 of the Company Code provides that if the net assets have sunk below the amount of the minimum stated capital (that is below € 61,500 in case of an NV/SA), any interested party may request the court to dissolve the company. The court can allow the company a period of grace to allow the directors to regularise its situation.

§2. The rules pertaining to the shares of an NV/SA

  1. Capital shares (aandelen/actions) and non-capital shares (winstbewijzen/parts bénéficiaire)

166. Capital shares are those shares belonging to shareholders who contributed to the stated capital in cash or in kind. Those shares can be shares with or without nominal value, registered or bearer shares and shares with or without voting rights.

167. Non-capital shares do not represent the stated capital but entitle their owner to any dividends that the general shareholders' meeting may decide to grant. The articles

of association may provide that owners of non-capital shares also have the right to vote in the general shareholders' meeting (possibly limited to specific types of decisions). However, owners of non-capital shares are not entitled to more than one vote per share and the total number of votes attached to non-capital shares cannot be more than one-half of the votes attached to the capital shares, and cannot account for more than two-thirds of the actual votes of the owners of capital shares at a general shareholders' meeting (Art. 542 of the Company Code).

2. Shares with or without nominal value

168. The capital of an NV/SA can be divided into shares with or without an indication of their nominal value (Art. 460 of the Company Code). The advantage of issuing shares without nominal value is that they do not have to be adjusted in the case of a capital increase or decrease. However, a major disadvantage of issuing shares without nominal value is that, in the case of a capital increase, shares can be issued for a lower price than the price for which the original shares were subscribed. The existing shareholders would thus be disadvantaged with respect to the new share-holders, the latter having equal voting rights even though they have paid less for their shares.

169. Article 582 of the Company Code attempts to prevent that such situation occurs by offering protection to the existing shareholders. This Article provides that only the general shareholders' meeting can decide whether shares without nominal value can be issued below the par value of the existing shares. The board of directors as well as the auditor must prepare an extensive report on the issuance price of the shares and on the financial consequences of the operation for the shareholders.

3. Registered shares or bearer shares

170. Registered shares are shares which are recorded in a special register – the share-holders' register – in the name of the shareholder who is exclusively entitled to exercise the rights attached to those shares (Art. 463, para. 1 of the Company Code). The shareholders register must be kept at the registered office of the com-pany and contains the following information (Art. 463, para. 1 of the Company Code):
   (i) the name and address of each shareholder and the number of the shares he owns;
   (ii) the payments made for those shares; and
   (iii) the transfers with the dates of the transfer or of the conversion of the regis-tered shares into bearer shares (if permitted by the articles of association).

171. According to Article 465 of the Company Code, the ownership, and thus also the transfer, of registered shares is proven by the inscription of the shares into the shareholders' register. The shareholders may ask for certificates to prove that their shares have been recorded in the shareholders' register.

172. According to Article 477 of the Company Code, shares remain registered and cannot be converted into bearer shares until they are fully paid up.

173. A bearer share does not mention the identity of the owner. Article 466 of the Company Code states that bearer shares must contain at least the following information:
    (i) the signature or name stamp of at least 2 directors;
    (ii) the date of incorporation of the company and of the publication of that incorporation;
    (iii) the number and type of shares, the nominal value of the shares and the number of votes attached to those shares;
    (iv) a brief description of the contributions;
    (v) special benefits granted to the founding shareholders;
    (vi) the duration of the company; and
    (vii) the date and time of the annual shareholders' meeting.

174. The transfer of bearer shares is effected by the mere transfer of the title (Art. 45 of the Company Code).

175. According to Article 462 of the Company Code, owners of bearer shares can, at all times and at their own cost, request that their shares be converted into registered shares.

4. Shares with or without voting rights

176. The Law of 18 July 1991 introduced the concept of shares without voting rights (Art. 476 of the Company Code) and thus now permits a company to find financial resources without this having an impact on the distribution of the company's voting rights.

177. The following requirements should be satisfied for the issue of non-voting shares (Art. 480 of the Company Code):
    (i) the non-voting shares should not represent more than one-third of the capital;
    (ii) in cases where the legal conditions for a distribution of profits are met, non-voting shares should give the right to a preferential dividend which can be carried forward, unless the articles of association provides otherwise. The amount of this dividend is determined when the shares are issued. The non-

voting shares should also entitle the holders thereof to receive a part of the profits for an amount equivalent to or lower than that accruing to voting shares;

(iii) non-voting shares should have a preferential right to a refund of their contribution to the capital and to the balance of the proceeds remaining after liquidation of the company, for an amount not lower than that accruing to voting shares.

178. Notwithstanding any provision to the contrary in the articles of association, non-voting shares will acquire voting rights under the following circumstances:

   (i) if one of the above-mentioned conditions is no longer fulfilled;

  (ii) if the general shareholders' meeting must decide on either of the following subjects:

    (a) the liquidation, merger or division of the company;

    (b) the modification of the company's purpose;

    (c) the conversion of the company;

    (d) the reduction of the capital of the company;

    (e) the limitation or abolition of the preferential right; or

    (f) the delegation to the board of directors of the power to increase the capital with limitation or abolition of the preferential right;

 (iii) if, pursuant to Article 558 of the Company Code, the general shareholders' meeting modifies the articles of association; and

 (iv) if the preferential dividends have not been made available or been paid for 3 consecutive financial years and until they are paid up in full.

179. The issue of shares without voting rights can take place on the occasion of the incorporation of the company, a capital increase, or the conversion of existing shares with voting rights. Such a conversion is governed by special rules.

180. The Company Code contains specific rules governing the acquisition by the company of its own non-voting shares.

5. Limits on the transferability of shares

181. An approval clause is a clause in the articles of association, in an authentic deed relating to the issue of convertible bonds or subscription rights, or in a shareholders' agreement which requires any transfer of shares to be approved by the board of directors or another decision-making body of the company. A pre-emption clause is a clause whereby a shareholder who wishes to sell his shares undertakes to offer these to the shareholders before selling them to a third party.

182. In principle, the articles of association, the deeds regarding the issue of convertible bonds or warrants and any other agreements can limit the transferability of shares, warrants or any other instrument which entitle the owner to shares. Such limitations should however be limited in time and should always be in the interest of the company. However, if such limitations result from a pre-emption clause or an approval clause, its application may not have the effect that the intransferability would last longer than 6 months after a request for approval was made or after an initiation to exercise the right.

183. Special rules exist with respect to approval clauses and pre-emptive rights in case of a public take-over bid.

6. Subscription by an NV/SA to its own shares

184. The company is not allowed to subscribe for its own shares, either directly, or through a subsidiary or person acting in their own name but for account of the company or its subsidiary. Several exceptions and technical consequences of these rules are however included in the Company Code. They will not be discussed in detail.

7. Acquisition by an NV/SA of its own shares

185. The acquisition by a company of its own shares, either directly or by a person acting in his own name but for the account of the company, must meet the following conditions:
    (i) the acquisition must be approved by the general shareholders' meeting;
    (ii) the nominal value (or the fraction value) of the acquired shares by the company, a directly controlled subsidiary or any person acting for account of the company or such directly controlled subsidiary may not exceed 10 per cent of the stated capital;
    (iii) only funds that could be made subject to profit sharing can be used to acquire own shares;
    (iv) only fully paid up shares can be acquired by the company; and
    (v) the company must treat all shareholders equally.

8. Acquisition of shares by employees

186. Art 609 of the Company Code governs the issue of shares for the benefit of employees. On the basis of this provision, a company may issue voting shares that are fully or partially reserved for the employees of that company or that company's subsidiaries.

187. Article 609 of the Company Code subjects the creation of such shares to a number of strict conditions:
    (i) the issuing company should have proceeded to at least 2 dividend distributions during the preceding 3 financial years;
    (ii) the issue should be discussed in the works council;
    (iii) successive capital increases designed to create stock for employees should not exceed 20 per cent of the company's stated capital during a period of 5 years;
    (iv) the issued shares should be registered shares; and
    (v) the shares cannot be transferred during a period of 5 years from the date of subscription.

188. Further requirements relating to personnel seniority, the term given to employees for exercising their subscription rights, the term allowed for full payment of the shares and the subscription price of the shares have to be determined by the corporate body that has decided on the capital increase, *i.e.*, the general shareholders' meeting or the board of directors (in the framework of the authorised capital (*See*, paras. 152 *et seq.*).

189. Article 620 of the Company Code contains further detailed rules that govern the acquisition by a company of its own shares (*See*, para. 185). However, the decision by the general shareholders' meeting, which is normally required for an acquisition of this type will not be necessary if it is intended that the shares will be offered to the company personnel (Art. 620, para. 1 of the Company Code). According to Article 622, paragraph 2 of the Company Code, the shares must be offered to the employees within a period of 12 months from the date they were acquired by the company.

190. Finally, Article 629 of the Company Code now allows companies to finance or guarantee operations which are effected in view of the acquisition of company shares by or for the personnel of the company. This is an exception to a general prohibition imposed on limited liability companies to finance or guarantee the financial obligations resulting from the acquisition of its own shares by third parties (Art. 629 of the Company Code). The exception not only benefits company employees but also related companies in which at least one-half of the voting rights are controlled by company personnel, provided the related companies acquire stock that carries at least one half of the voting rights in the company. The modification is regarded as an important step towards simplifying management buy-outs in Belgium.

9. Cross participation (Arts. 631 and 632 of the Company Code)

191. A cross participation can be defined as a situation whereby 2 companies hold equity stakes in each others' capital.

192. The Company Code (Arts. 631 and 632 of the Company Code) distinguishes cross participations between unrelated companies from cross-participations between parent companies and their subsidiaries.

i. Between parent companies and their subsidiaries

193. Under the Company Code, subsidiaries (whether individually or jointly) are not allowed to hold an equity stake in their parent company, if such a holding entitles them to represent more than 10 per cent of the voting rights (Art. 631 of the Company Code). The voting rights of shares which are held by a subsidiary in the parent company are suspended.

194. Article 6 of the Company Code contains a definition of what is meant by the notions "parent company" and "subsidiary" in this context. A "parent company" is defined as a company which has a power of control over another company, and a "subsidiary" is defined as a company over which another company exercises a power of control. "Power of control" means, amongst others, the power in law or in fact to exercise a decisive influence on the appointment of the majority of the directors or managers or on the orientation of the management of the company.

195. The Company Code establishes a special notification procedure:
   (a) the subsidiary must inform the parent company of the nature and number of the voting shares which it holds in the parent company (Art. 631, para. 2 of the Company Code);
   (b) the notification must take place within 2 days off the date on which the company is informed of the participation by the new parent company in its stated capital, or from the date of later acquisitions or sales which take place (Art. 631, para. 2 of the Company Code); and
   (c) the shares of the subsidiary which have been obtained in violation of the above rules, should be sold within one year from the date the situation arose.

ii. Between unrelated companies

196. Cross-participations between 2 unrelated companies, of which at least one is an NV/SA having its registered office in Belgium, are not permitted if each of these holdings represents more than 10 per cent of the voting rights in the other company (Art. 632, para. 1 of the Company Code).

197. If a company acquires shares representing more than 10 per cent of the voting rights in another company, the Company Code provides for a specific notification procedure:
   (a) the first company (Art. 632, para. 2 of the Company Code) must immediately notify the other company by registered letter mentioning the number of shares

it owns and the number of voting rights attached to those shares. Any subsequent change in the participation must be notified in the same manner. This notification is not required if a disclosure has already resulted from the application of the Law of 2 March 1989 governing the Publication of major shareholdings in Companies listed on a Stock Exchange and Regulation of Public Take-Over Bids (*Wet op de openbaarmaking van belangrijke deelnemingen in ter beurze genoteerde vennootschappen en tot reglementering van de openbare overnameaanbiedingen/Loi relative à la publicité des participations importantes dans les sociétés notées en bourse et réglementant le offres publiques d'acquisition* – the "Transparency Law");

(b) the company which receives the said notice is no longer entitled to acquire shares in the first company which have more than 10 per cent of the voting rights attached to them (Art. 632, para. 3 of the Company Code);

(c) shares which were obtained in violation of the above rules must be sold within one year of the date that the illegal situation arose, unless the parties can agree to comply with these rules in another manner. The voting rights attached to shares which were obtained in disregard of the rules and which therefore must be sold, are suspended (Art 632, para. 4 of the Company Code).

§3. The rules pertaining to the management of an NV/SA

198. According to Article 517 of the Company Code, the NV/SA is managed by legal or natural persons or legal entities acting in the name and on behalf of the company, who may or may not be remunerated.

1. The board of directors

199. The directors of an NV/SA are subject to the following rules.

i. The appointment of directors

200. The NV/SA is managed by a board of directors which must be composed of at least 3 members (Art. 518, para. 1 of the Company Code). A company which only has 2 shareholders, can however opt for a board of directors composed of only 2 members. The directors are appointed by the general shareholders' meeting. Their appointment is for a fixed term which may not exceed 6 years but which may be renewed, unless the articles of association provides otherwise (Art. 520 of the Company Code). The general shareholders' meeting can, at any time, decide to dismiss the directors. If a director is dismissed or if he resigns, and as a result the number of directors falls below the minimum number that is foreseen by the Company Code as in the articles of association of the company, the remaining directors have the right to co-opt a temporary director, unless the articles of association provide otherwise, until the next general shareholders' meeting.

201. If a legal entity is appointed as member of the board of directors or member of the management committee, it will designate a single natural person to execute such mandate in the name and for the account of the legal entity. Such natural person will additionally be civilly and criminally liable as if he were executing such mandate in his own name and for his own account. The Company Code does not impose any other requirements (*e.g.*, nationality, qualifications) for the appointment of directors.

202. The appointment of the directors must be published in the *Belgian Official Journal* (*Belgisch Staatsblad/Moniteur belge*) and must be filed with the registry of the commercial court (Art. 74 of the Company Code).

   ii. The powers of the board of directors

203. Article 522 of the Company Code states that the board of directors is competent to take all measures which are necessary or useful to accomplish the corporate purpose of the company, unless the law expressly reserved the power to take specific measures for the general shareholders' meeting.

204. As a result, the general shareholders' meeting only has the powers which are expressly granted to it by law. All residual powers are within the competence of the board of directors. However, the powers of the board can be limited in the articles of association of the company. Yet, in principle, any such limitations on the powers of the board cannot be relied upon as against third parties, even if they were published (Art. 522, para. 2 of the Company Code). Accordingly, these limitations are only operative within the company.

205. The board of directors represents the company in court proceedings as a plaintiff or a defendant (Art. 522 of the Company Code).

206. In principle, the board must act collectively as a group in which decision are taken by a majority. But, in accordance with Article 522, paragraph 2 of the Company Code, the articles of association can give one or more directors the power to represent the company and this mandate can be relied upon as against third parties, provided it is published in the *Belgian Official Journal* in accordance with the provisions of Article 76 of the Company Code.

207. The board of directors can also appoint proxyholders for the performance of specific assignments.

208. In exceptional cases, if required by the interest of the company and by extreme urgency, the board of directors can decide by means of unanimous written consent of the directors, if this is provided for by the articles of association. This procedure

can however not be applied for the approval of the annual accounts, the use of the authorised capital or any other case that is excluded by the articles of association.

209. Article 226 of the Company Code provides that the company is bound *vis-à-vis* third parties, by all the actions taken by the board of directors, even if these actions are outside the corporate purpose, unless the company proves that the third party knew that the action was outside the corporate purpose or that the third party could not have been unaware of this fact.

iii. The conflicting interest of a director (Art. 523 of the Company Code)

210. A conflict of interest arises when the direct or indirect patrimonial interest of a director conflicts with a decision to be taken by the board of directors.

211. According to Article 523 of the Company Code, a director who has such a conflict of interest should inform the board of this conflict before the board takes the relevant decision. His declaration as well as any grounds for justification are to be included in the minutes of the board of directors. In case the company has appointed one or more auditors, the director concerned should also inform those auditors of his conflict of interest. In view of publishing such conflicts in their annual report, the board of directors must describe the nature of the decision and its patrimonial consequences in their minutes.

212. In companies which made an appeal to the public for funds, the consequences of a conflict of interest are more severe. In such companies, a director is not allowed to participate in the deliberations proceeding the relevant decision and is to refrain from casting a vote. The rules however do not apply if the relevant decision(s) of the board of directors relate to dealings between companies where one owns 95 per cent of the voting rights of the other or between companies where 95 per cent of the voting rights of each of these companies are controlled by a third party.

213. If the information procedure described above is not followed, the company can request the annulment of the relevant board decision if the counter party was aware or should have been aware of this violation.

iv. Conflicting interest of the board of directors regarding intra-group dealings

214. By means of the Law of 2 August 2002, an important amendment of the Company Code was adopted concerning the provisions on intra-group transfers relating to Belgian listed companies and conflicts of interest relating thereto, since the existing provisions were considered insufficient to achieve an appropriate balance between such listed company and its controlling shareholders and other affiliates.

215. The scope of application of Article 524 of the Company Code is extended in order to cover any dealings with other entities of the same group, not merely the parent company. In an attempt not to impede the efficiency of the decision-making process, the procedure outlined below does however not apply to:
(a) Dealings at arm's length;
(b) Dealings representing less than 1 per cent of the net assets of the company (as based on the consolidated annual accounts).

216. All agenda items relating to intra-group dealings need to be presented to a committee of 3 independent directors, assisted by one or more independent experts. This committee defines the transaction, assesses the financial impact and advises on the potential unlawful or detrimental nature of the transaction at hand. After receipt of the written non-binding advice of said committee, the board of directors deliberates and decides whether or not to follow the advice. The minutes of the board of directors should reflect whether the above procedure was followed and why, if relevant, the advice of the committee of independent directors was not followed. The auditor will draft a separate report on the reliability of the numbers and information contained in the advice and the minutes of the board of directors, which will be attached to the minutes.

217. Dealings of a non-listed Belgian subsidiary of the Belgian listed parent company with other entities of the group will, in addition, require the approval of the parent company, with application of the above procedure.

218. Independent directors should at the very least comply with the following criteria:
(a) they should not have exercised any mandate within the company or any of its affiliates in the 2-year period prior to their appointment;
(b) they should not have a spouse, concubine or relative (to the second degree) exercising a mandate within the company or any of its affiliates, nor having a financial interest in the company or any of its affiliates;
(c) they should not hold any security in the company that represents more than 10 per cent of the capital. Even if they hold less than 10 per cent of the capital in their own name, the combined shareholding of their own securities and securities held by companies they control should not exceed 10 per cent. They should not be tied by any agreements or unilateral commitments with respect to such securities; and
(d) they should not be in contact with any company that would compromise their independence.

219. Non-compliance with the new Article 524 of the Company Code may render the dealings null and void.

220. The new provisions will come into force as from the financial year beginning 31 December 2003.

    v. Director's liability

  (a) Liability against third parties. The NV/SA is a so-called "full" legal entity. Therefore shareholders are not considered to be personally liable towards third parties for the debts of the company. Similarly, directors are not considered to be liable for the obligations entered into by the company, *i.e.*, which were entered into by the directors on behalf of the company in the context and in the framework of the representative powers of the directors (Art. 61 of the Company Code).

221. A director may commit a tort, for example if he commits a so-called *culpa in contrahendo, i.e.*, a pre-contractual fault, during and as a result of a contract negotiation. A director will always be held personally liable for torts that he committed, within or outside his capacity as a director. If, however, the director was acting within his powers as a director, *i.e.*, in such a way that he validly represented the company, this tort will be directly attributed to the company as well. Indeed, under general civil law, the legal entity is personally responsible for committed tortuous acts by its organs. The person who suffered damage may therefore take action against both the company and the director(s) committing the tort.

222. On the contrary, torts committed by the directors in the execution of a contract to which the company is a party will not lead to their liability. Either the director would have acted as the representative body of the company: in that case the contractual error can only be attributed to him personally if at the same time this error would be considered to be negligence. Under Belgian law, however, it is very unlikely that a default under an agreement also constitutes a tort given the legal doctrine honoured in Belgium by the Supreme Court regarding co-existence of contractual and tort liability. Or, the director was acting as an agent of the company and not as the representative body of the company. Here the chanced of him being personally liable are also virtually non-existent because the possibility of a third party turning against an agent executing an agreement does not exist under Belgian law (personal immunity of the executing agent).

223. Directors in an NV/SA may also be held personally and severally liable for damage suffered by third parties as a result of infringements of the Company Code or of the articles of incorporation by the said directors (Art. 62 of the Company Code).

    There are other cases in which directors in an NV/SA could be held jointly and severally liable to interested parties. More specifically, the law imposes the same kind of liability upon the directors for the subscription and effective payment of the capital amount in case of a capital increase as is imposed on the incorporations of the company at the time of incorporation (Art. 610 of the Company Code). The directors will be considered to be the subscribers for the full amount of any of the company's capital not validly subscribed. In addition, they are liable to interested parties for the effective payment of one-quarter of the shares and of payment in full of those shares which have been issued wholly or in part for a contribution in kind.

224. Finally, if, on bankruptcy of a company, its liabilities exceed its assets, the directors, or former directors, may be held personally liable for all part of the liabilities of the company, up to the amount of the shortfall, provided it has been established that such director committed a manifestly serious mistake that contributed to the bankruptcy of the company. It is up to the courts to decide whether or not such directors will be held liable jointly and severally, and the part of the existing liabilities they will have to bear. There is no need to establish a causal relationship between the serious mistake and the bankruptcy; it suffices that the error contributed to the involuntary liquidation. It must also be noted that not only the "official" directors can be held liable under this Article, but also all other persons who had *de facto* authority to manage and administer the business of the company (Art. 530 of the Company Code).

(b) *Liability against the company.* Directors in all companies with a "full" legal personality cannot be regarded as the agents of the shareholders, or as an agent of the company (unless of course he is charged with a special mandate).

225. Nevertheless, their liability *vis-à-vis* the company is judged as if the directors were agents of the company. This applies equally to the managing director. As the director is contractually liable *vis-à-vis* the company, it is obvious that the authority to decide whether or not to start proceedings against the directors (the so-called "*actio mandate*") rests with the general shareholders' meeting. If the general shareholders' meeting decides to institute a claim against the directors on behalf of the company, it may appoint one or more agents to implement such decision and to institute a suit (Art. 561 of the Company Code). In order to prevent the majority of shareholders from neglecting to commence proceedings against the board of directors, although there are valid reasons to do so, the law provides the possibility for the minority shareholders to institute an action for the account of the company (Art. 562 of the Company Code). Such minority action can only be instituted by one or more shareholders who (i) oppose the discharge from liability to be given to the directors, (ii) hold securities representing not less than 1 per cent of the existing voting rights within the company, or (iii) represent such part of the capital having a value of not less than € 1,250,000. Holders of non-voting shares can institute an action only for those cases in which they are entitled to vote (Art. 481 of the Company Code).

226. The minority action is instituted on behalf of the company. All damages to be paid by the director(s) will be paid to the company, and not to the individual plaintiff. Individual shareholders can only institute an action against the director if a tort has been committed by the directors inflicting damage directly upon the shareholder personally.

227. The directors are responsible in accordance with civil law for any shortcomings in their management and administration. This refers to the normal liability of a professional *vis-à-vis* his client – here, the company. For example, the directors could be held liable if the company suffers damage resulting from the erroneous non-execution of an agreement by the company.

228. The directors shall also be jointly and severally liable *vis-à-vis* the company or *vis-à-vis* third parties for any loss resulting from an infringement of the provisions of the Company Code or the articles of association. Each director may, however, avoid liability for an infringement in which he had no part and was not able to prevent it (for example, by not being present at a board of management meeting where he could have been present). In addition, to avoid liability, he must have brought the issue to the attention of the first general shareholders' meeting held after he became aware of it.

2. The daily management of the company

229. In accordance with Article 522 of the Company Code, the daily management of the company can be entrusted to one or more persons, whether or not they are directors, empowered to act alone or jointly. Any appointments and dismissals of daily managers must be published in the *Belgian Official Journal* (*Belgisch Staatsblad/Moniteur belge*) in accordance with Article 73 of the Company Code.

230. The authority of persons entrusted with the daily management of the company to bind the company as against third parties cannot be made subject to any limitations insofar as any matters normally falling under the scope of the notion of "daily management" are concerned.

231. The law does not define which areas of competence are covered by the notion of daily management. Case law defines the term "daily management" as "*any actions which are necessary in the normal course of business or which can be taken without a formal decision of the board of directors because of their minor importance or their urgency*" (Cass., 17 September 1968, *Pas.*, 1969, I, 61).

232. Examples of powers which fall under the scope of the notion of daily management are the hiring and firing of personnel, all actions which are necessary for the preservation of the company's real estate or business, the organisation of the compa-

ny's accounting system and the signing of minor contracts in the ordinary course of business.

233. If any doubt arises as to whether the person in charge of the daily management could have taken any given decision, a practical solution would be for the board of directors to ratify that decision.

234. The powers of the person in charge of the daily management can be revoked at any time (Art. 2004 of the Civil Code).

235. The person in charge of the daily management may receive a remuneration, the amount of which is generally determined by the board of directors.

3. Management committee

236. Although several, mostly large, public limited liability companies already had a management committee, the Company Code only recently introduced the management committee as a legal concept. The Company Code was amended by means of the Law of 2 August 2002 to offer public limited liability companies the possibility (since they are under no obligation to do so) to organise such committee within the legal framework of the Company Code (Art. 524*bis* of the Company Code).

i. Organisation

237. The organisation and functioning of such management committees will be organised by the board of directors or the articles of association, including provisions governing the appointment and the dismissal of members of the management committee.

238. Article 524*bis* of the Company Code provides for a minimum of 2 members, but does set a maximum duration of their mandate.

239. The Company Code does not impose any other requirements (*e.g.*, nationality, qualifications) for the appointment of the members of the management committee.

240. The appointment of such members must be published in the *Belgian Official Journal* (*Belgisch Staatsblad/Moniteur belge*) and must be filed with the registry of the competent commercial court.

241. Under the new rules, the management committee will therefore report to the board of directors and the board of directors will report on the management committee to the general shareholders' meeting.

ii. Powers

242. Within the new framework, all powers of the board of directors can be delegated to the management committee, with exception of (i) the strategic management, (ii) the control on the management committee, and (iii) the powers that are legally reserved to the board of directors.

243. If established, such management committee will automatically possess the full powers of representation regarding all matters of interest of the company (with however the same 3 exceptions as listed hereabove), even if the board of directors or the articles of association opt not to delegate all of such powers to the management committee.

244. Possible limitations to the powers transferred to the management committee therefore merely constitute internal limitations that are not enforceable *vis-à-vis* third parties.

245. In principle, the management committee must act as a collective group in which the majority decides. But, the articles of association can give one or more members the power to represent the company and this mandate can be relied upon as against third parties, provided it is published in the *Belgian Official Journal* in accordance with the provisions of Article 76 of the Company Code.

246. The board of directors can also appoint proxyholders for the performance of specific assignments.

247. Article 226 of the Company Code provides that the company is bound *vis-à-vis* third parties, by all the actions taken by the management committee, even if these actions are outside the corporate purpose, unless the company proves that the third party knew that the action was outside the corporate purpose or that the third party could not have been unaware of this fact

iii. The conflicting interest of a member of the management committee (Art. 524*ter* of the Company Code)

248. The same provisions apply as to the members of the board of directors. (*See*, paras. 210 *et seq.*)

iv. Liability

249. The members of the management committee will, to the same extent as directors, be liable for the improper execution of their task.

4. The general shareholders' meeting

250. The general shareholders' meeting is subject to the following rules:

   i. Powers of the general shareholders' meeting

251. Article 522 of the Company Code states that the board of directors is competent to take all measures which are necessary or useful to accomplish the corporate purpose of the company, unless the law expressly reserved the power to take specific measures for the general shareholders' meeting. As a result, the general shareholders' meeting only has the powers that are expressly granted to it by law.

252. Pursuant to Article 531 of the Company Code the general shareholders' meeting has nevertheless extensive powers to take or ratify decisions which are in the interest of the company.

253. The general shareholders' meeting is accordingly empowered to take 2 different types of action:
   (a) actions which relate to the proper functioning of the company: *e.g.*, the appointment and dismissal of directors, the approval of the annual accounts and the allocation of the results (profit or loss);
   (b) actions which relate to the corporate structure of the company : *e.g.*, the modification of the articles of association, the liquidation and the transformation of the company.

There are 2 different kinds of general shareholders' meetings:
   (a) the ordinary or annual shareholders' meeting *(jaarlijkse vergadering der aandeelhouders/assemblée annuelle des actionnaires)* which takes place at the same time every year on the date determined in the articles of association in order to approve the annual accounts, to allocate profits or losses and to appoint directors and statutory auditors (Arts. 532 and 535 of the Company Code);
   (b) the extraordinary shareholders' meeting *(buitengewone vergadering der aandeelhouders/assemblée extraordinaire des actionnaires)* which is called whenever the articles of association need to be modified or when a decision must be taken on whether to liquidate or transform the company. An extraordinary general shareholders' meeting takes place whenever a request to this effect is made by shareholders representing at least one-fifth of the capital (Art. 532 of the Company Code).

ii. Written declaration

254. Since the most recent amendment to the Company Code (by means of the Law of 2 August 2002), a shareholders' meeting can be held by means a written resolution of the shareholders (without any further formalities), upon condition that the decisions are taken unanimously and do not concern any decisions that need to be incorporated in a notarial deed.

iii. The general shareholders' meeting notice and quorum

255. The notice for the general shareholders' meeting must contain the agenda of that meeting (Art. 533 of the Company Code) and must be published in the *Belgian Official Journal (Belgisch Staatsblad/Moniteur belge)* at least 8 days before the meeting is held and in both a national and local newspaper, with a minimum interval of 8 days between these 2 publications. The second publication must take place at least 8 days before the date of the general shareholders' meeting (Art. 533 of the Company Code). For listed companies, all intervals of 8 days are extended to 15 days.

256. However, if all the shares are registered, it is sufficient to send the notice by registered post to all shareholders (Art. 533, para. 3 of the Company Code).

257. Unless the articles of association prescribe otherwise, the general shareholders' meeting decides by a majority of the votes cast. The general meeting can only modify the articles of association if such modification is proposed in the agenda, and if at least one-half of the stated capital is represented at the meeting. The modification can only be accepted if at least three-quarters of the shareholders present or represented vote in favour of such a modification.

258. In accordance with Article 543 of the Company Code, preferential shares without voting rights and shares whose voting rights have been suspended will not be taken into account in order to determine whether the requirements regarding presence and majority are satisfied.

iv. Vote at the general shareholders' meeting

259. Prior to the recent amendment (Law of 2 August 2002) of the Company Law, shareholders of listed companies were only granted the right to participate in and to vote on the general shareholders' meeting if (i) they were registered in the companies shareholders' register, (ii) they had deposited their bearer shares or (iii) they had filed a certificate from an acknowledged account holder or clearing house, stating that the dematerialised shares would be unavailable until the date of the general shareholders' meeting. In order however to stimulate active participation

of institutional investors in the general shareholders' meeting and the decision-making process within listed companies in general, the articles of association of listed companies now can provide for a reference date (between 15 and 5 days before a general shareholders' meeting) upon which the ownership of shares is established, without the need to deposit shares or filing of a certificate. As a result of this, such shareholder can participate in and vote on the general shareholders' meeting, without any impediments to simultaneous trading in such listed shares.

260. As a general principle, all shares of equal value are entitled to one vote (*see*, however, above concerning shares without voting rights). Alternatively, each share is entitled to a number of votes in proportion to the capital it represents.

261. The corporate articles of association determine the voting rights, if any, attached to non-capital shares (Art. 542 of the Company Code). Article 542 of the Company Code contains important restrictions regarding the total level of voting power that can be given to non-capital shares.

262. Voting by proxy is allowed by Article 547 of the Company Code. The articles of association cannot deny the right of a shareholder to be represented by a proxy, but it can regulate the use made of this right. The articles of association may, for example, provide that a shareholder can only appoint another shareholder as its proxy, or that, prior to the meeting, the proxies must be deposited at the registered office of the company.

263. The articles of association may also allow the vote by proxy through the use of a standard form which must contain the information specified in the articles of association (Art. 550 of the Company Code). The shareholder must have the possibility to indicate, without leaving any doubt, in which manner he wants to cast a vote.

v. The general shareholders' meeting – access

264. The directors and statutory auditors must, in principle, be present at the general shareholders' meeting even if they are not shareholders and do not have voting rights (Arts. 540 and 554, para. 1 of the Company Code). Although third parties have no right to be present at the general shareholders' meeting, the shareholders can explicitly allow third parties to attend the general shareholders' meeting. Legal commentators generally agree that a shareholder may be accompanied by legal counsel.

vi. Minutes of the general shareholders' meeting – presence list

265. The Company Code requires the preparation of a presence list and of minutes of the proceedings (Art. 539 of the Company Code).

266. The minutes of the meeting must be signed by the president of the meeting, its secretary and its vote-collectors, if any, whose function it is to organise the voting proceedings. All shareholders who specifically request to sign the minutes may do so (Art. 546 of the Company Code).

vii. Shareholders' agreements that govern the use of shareholders' voting rights

267. The Company Code specifically allows for shareholders' agreements to govern the use of shareholders' voting rights (Art. 551 of the Company Code). Such agreements have to be limited in time and in the interest of the company.

268. Article 551, paragraph 1 of the Company Code specifically lists 3 categories of shareholders' agreements which are null and void:
   (a) shareholders' agreements that violate the provisions of the Company Code, or that are contrary to the company's interests;
   (b) agreements in which a shareholder agrees to vote in accordance with the directives as given by the company, one of its subsidiaries or its decision-making bodies; and
   (c) agreements in which a shareholder agrees to accept the proposals of the decision-making bodies of these companies.

269. Votes resulting from such void shareholders' agreements are of course also void. The decisions taken will also be void unless the void votes have had no influence on the validity of the voting process. An action for the annulment of a decision must be brought within 6 months of the date of the vote.

viii. The annual general shareholders' meeting: purpose, procedure and filing of annual accounts

270. Each year the directors must prepare the annual accounts (Art. 92 of the Company Code) (*jaarrekening/comptes annuels*) which are composed of a balance sheet (*balans/bilan*), a profit and loss statement (*resultatenrekening/compte des résultats*) and notes on the accounts (*toelichting/annexe*). The directors are also required to prepare an annual report (*jaarverslag/rapport annuel*) in which they must account for their management of the company (Art. 95 of the Company Code). This report must contain a comment on the balance sheet as well as information regarding important events which occurred after the closing of the fiscal year and on developments which are likely to have an impact on the company's business. The report must also contain details regarding the activities of the company in relation to research and development, regarding any capital increases and regarding the acquisition by the company of its own shares.

271. The directors are required to transmit this information at least one month before the date of the annual general shareholders' meeting to the statutory auditor who will then, in turn, provide comments in a special report.

272. 15 days before the annual general shareholders' meeting, the shareholders have access to the annual accounts and the discussed reports at the registered office of the company (Art. 553 of the Company Code).

273. Moreover, a shareholder is entitled to a free copy of these documents (Art. 535, para. 3 of the Company Code).

274. The annual general shareholders' meeting takes place at the venue, date and time determined in the articles of association (Art. 552 of the Company Code). The shareholders are required to meet within 6 months of the closing of the fiscal year. The board of directors is entitled to postpone the annual meeting once for 3 weeks (Art. 534 of the Company Code). After the approval of the annual accounts, the shareholders must decide on the discharge (*kwijting/décharge*) to be given to the directors and the statutory auditor (Art. 554 of the Company Code).

275. The annual accounts must be deposited (together with the annual report prepared by the directors and that of the statutory auditor), within 30 days of their approval (Art. 98 of the Company Code), at the local office of the National Bank (*Nationale Bank van België/Banque nationale de Belgique*).

276. According to Article 102 of the Company Code, the filing of the annual accounts of a company is deemed to be accepted on the day the accounts are received by the National Bank. However, the National Bank can inform the company within 8 business days that the filing cannot be accepted as long as any of the requirements for such filing have not been complied with. Within 15 business days of acceptance of the filing of the accounts, the National Bank draws up a summary of the accounts and publishes the summary in the *Annexes to the Belgian Official Journal* (*Belgisch Staatsblad/Moniteur belge*). The same text is sent by the National Bank to the registry of the commercial court that keeps the company file. Third parties may also examine the annual accounts of the company at the registry.

5. The control of the company's financial condition

277. The control of the financial condition of the company is subject to the following rules.

i. The appointment and task of the statutory auditor

278. In accordance with Article 142 of the Company Code, the NV/SA is, in principle, required to appoint one or more statutory auditors (*bedrijfsrevisoren/réviseurs*

d'entreprises) if more than one of the thresholds mentioned in Article 15 of the Company Code is exceeded or if the company has more than 100 employees (*See*, para. 553).

279. The statutory auditor must monitor the financial situation of the company, and must review the annual accounts and the transactions contained therein to ensure their conformity with the Company Code and the articles of association of the company (Art. 142 of the Company Code).

280. The statutory auditor is appointed by the general shareholders' meeting for a renewable period of 3 years and can, in principle, not be dismissed during that period, unless there are serious reasons to do so. The statutory auditor receives a fixed remuneration that is also determined by the general shareholders' meeting in the beginning of its mandate.

281. The Company Code emphasises the importance of the independence of auditors. By means of the Law of 2 August 2002, the Belgian legislator even increased the level of independence of the auditors by amending the Article 133 of the Company Code with respect to the provision of additional services and employment with the audit client. Auditors will no longer be able to take up a mandate as director, manager or any other function, within a period of 2 years after the termination of their mandate as auditor of a specific company or affiliate thereof.

282. An auditor, nor any of its employees, affiliates of partners with whom he has a professional relationship may not perform any services additional to the ones required by law, in so far as the total amount of such services would exceed the agreed fixed remuneration. Services provided to audit the financial and economic data of companies, as recently acquired by the company or any of its subsidiaries will, however, not be taken into account. This obligation is however limited to services provided to listed companies and companies belonging to a group of companies required to draft consolidated accounts. The rules on additional services however do not apply if:
    (a) such was approved by an audit committee, as established within the company by the articles of association;
    (b) the new "Advice and Control Commission" (providing advice on the compatibility of specific services with the auditor's independence) granted a positive advice;
    (c) a committee of mutually independent auditors was set up within the company.

283. An auditor will, in any case not be considered as independent if, during his mandate or within a period 2 years prior to his mandate, the auditor, one of his employees or

affiliates of a partner with whom he has a professional relationship, performed services (that are not required by law) to the company for which such auditor audits the annual accounts, its Belgian affiliates or a foreign subsidiary. At a later stage, the list of such services will be specified by Royal Decree.

ii. The liability of the statutory auditor

284. In accordance with Article 140 of the Company Code, the statutory auditor can be held liable:
    (a) for the improper execution of his task as statutory auditor;
    (b) for damages suffered by the company or by third parties as a result of a violation by the statutory auditor of the Company Code or of the company's articles of association.

285. Moreover, in accordance with Article 1382 of the Civil Code, statutory auditors can be held liable for tort. Finally, in some specific instances, the statutory auditor can also be exposed to criminal sanctions (Arts. 196, para. 1 and 347, 387, 434, 648 of the Company Code).

iii. The control of the company if no statutory auditor is appointed

286. In companies where the appointment of a statutory auditor is not mandatory, every shareholder has, notwithstanding any provisions in the articles of association to the contrary, individually, the powers of investigation and control which would normally belong to the statutory auditor (*See also*, Art. 166 of the Company Code). These powers imply that the shareholder is entitled to examine, at any time, the corporate books, the minutes of meetings and every other document belonging to the company at the registered office of the company. For this purpose, a shareholder may be represented by an accountant.

287. A majority of legal commentators are of the opinion that a shareholder who exercises the powers of a statutory auditor does not have the same liability against third parties as an auditor would have, since a shareholder, unlike a statutory auditor, is deemed to exercise those powers in his own interest and not in the interest of third parties.

iv. Expert examination of books and records of the company

288. Shareholders that own at least 1 per cent of the shares or a number of shares representing at least € 1,250,000 of the stated capital, may request the commercial court to have the books and records of the company as well as the decisions of the decision-making bodies examined by an independent expert (Art. 168 of the Company Code).

289. The request is brought before the commercial court. The procedure is initiated by writ of summons. The court hears the parties in chambers but it gives its judgement in public. The judgement defines the problem areas which should be examined by the expert.

D. Accounting, auditing and corporate documents

290. The rules regarding accounting, auditing and the attendant documents are described in Chapter 4.

291. The Company Code contains a few provisions that explicitly address legal obligations in relation to corporate documents. Article 463, paragraph 1 of the Company Code requires the establishment of a register of registered shares (*See*, para. 170). This register should be kept at the registered office of the company in order to avoid rendering the shareholders' right of access to the register devoid of substance. The establishment of a register is mandatory even if all shares of the company are bearer shares. Article 462 of the Company Code indeed entitles owners of bearer shares to have their shares converted into registered shares at all times.

292. Companies are required to prepare and keep minutes of board of directors' and general shareholders' meetings and to keep both sets of minutes in corporate books at the company's registered office.

E. Conflict resolution, dissolution, liquidation and bankruptcy of an NV/SA

§1. Conflict resolution

293. Before the conflict resolution provisions were added to the Company Code, shareholders in conflict were forced to resort to a dissolution of the company by a court decision, if the co-operation between the shareholders became impossible. Perfectly viable companies were thus dissolved. In order to safeguard the interests of the company and the shareholders, it became possible for a shareholder to request the exclusion of another shareholder (Art. 636 of the Company Code) or the take over of his shares by another shareholder (Art. 642 of the Company Code).

294. One or more shareholders may file an action for a forced transfer if he holds:
    (i) shares whose nominal value or par value represents 30 per cent of the capital of the company;
    (ii) 20 per cent of the voting rights for the total number of existing securities if the company has issued securities that do not represent the capital; or

(iii) securities representing 30 per cent of the voting rights related to the total number of existing securities.

295. Any shareholder may file an action for a forced take-over.

1. Justification

296. The Company Code requires a plaintiff to have "well-founded" reasons for a forced transfer or take-over.

297. These include circumstances under which (i) the defendant can no longer reasonably be accepted as a shareholder or (ii) the plaintiff can no longer reasonably be obliged to indulge the defendant as a shareholder. While the interests of the company are the main criteria in applying Article 636 of the Company Code, Article 642 of the Company Code protects mainly shareholders' interests.

298. The commercial courts are very reluctant to allow a forced transfer or a forced takeover. They will avoid a forced transfer if (i) there are other ways to resolve the problem; (ii) the plaintiff caused the conflict; (iii) the defendant has not committed a breach; or (iv) a particular breach was insufficient to constitute a "well-founded" reason. The commercial courts will also avoid a forced take-over if (i) the plaintiff contributed to the well-founded reasons; or (ii) the plaintiff has not proven well-founded reasons.

2. Consequences

299. If a plaintiff succeeds in an action for a forced transfer, a court will order the defendant to transfer its shares to the plaintiff at a price determined by the court. In a successful forced take-over, the court will order the defendant to purchase the plaintiff's shares for a price determined by the court. This price is binding on all parties, even the plaintiff. A plaintiff may not unilaterally waive this order if it disagrees with the selling or purchase price.

300. The Company Code only provides that the court determines the purchase price. However, it does not indicate how a court must determine the price. The court may determine the price itself, or ask for an expert's non-binding opinion (for example, an accountant or auditor).

301. The moment the value of the shares is determined is crucial. In most cases, this is the moment the procedure was started or the date on which the expert determines the price. However, the parties sometimes object to this valuation by claiming that the value of the shares had decreased between the defendants' breach and the court's decision (for example, by abuse of majority).

3. Procedure

302. The legal action must be filed with the President of the commercial court in the district where the Company's corporate seat is located. This composition of the Court is the same as in summary proceedings. The company must also be a party to the proceedings.

303. During the "forced-transfer" procedure, the defendant is not allowed to transfer or encumber its shares.

§2. Dissolution (ontbinding/dissolution) of an NV/SA

304. An NV/SA can be dissolved in 3 different ways:
     (i) by force of law;
     (ii) on a voluntary basis; or
     (iii) by a court decision.

1. The dissolution of an NV/SA by force of law

305. An NV/SA can be dissolved simply because the duration for which it was constituted has expired.

306. In accordance with Article 645 of the Company Code, an NV/SA is considered to be constituted for an indefinite duration, unless its articles of association expressly provide that the NV/SA is constituted for a definite period. If the NV/SA is constituted for a definite period, the general shareholders' meeting can extend this duration before its expiration in accordance with the rules that govern a modification of the articles of association (Art. 645 of the Company Code).

307. The NV/SA will also be dissolved if the corporate purpose has been realised, or if it becomes impossible to realise the corporate purpose. Although rarely applied, this provision illustrates the importance of describing the corporate purpose as broadly as possible in the company's articles of association.

2. The dissolution of an NV/SA on a voluntary basis

308. The general shareholders' meeting can, at any time, decide to dissolve the company in accordance with the rules that govern a modification of the company's articles of association (that is, at least one-half of the stated capital must be represented, and at least three-quarters of the shareholders voting must cast an affirmative vote).

309. If the company has lost half of its capital, Article 633 of the Company Code requires that the directors convene a general shareholders' meeting which must decide as to whether to continue the corporate activities or to dissolve the com-

pany (*See*, paras. 162 *et seq.*). The meeting must take place within 2 months after such loss was discovered or should have been discovered. The decision to dissolve the company must be taken in accordance with the rules that govern a modification of the corporate articles of association (Arts. 645 and 646 of the Company Code).

310. If the loss amounts to more than three-quarters of the company's capital, the decision to dissolve the company can be taken by one-quarter of the votes represented at the meeting.

3. The dissolution of an NV/SA by a court decision

311. Articles 45 and 645 of the Company Code determine that the dissolution of an NV/SA can be requested from the court for "legitimate reasons". The law does not define such "legitimate reasons". However, the case law indicates that these reasons must be so serious that they threaten the future of the company by hindering its activities or by preventing the company from realising its corporate purpose.

312. Article 634 of the Company Code contains an illustration of such a reason. It states that, when a company's net assets are smaller than the minimum amount referred to in Article 439 of the Company Code, any interested party can request the dissolution of the company before the court. An individual shareholder can be an interested party in the context of Article 634 of the Company Code. However, the court can decide to grant the company a period within which to cure its financial situation.

§3. Liquidation (vereffening/liquidation) of an NV/SA

1. Definition

313. An orderly liquidation of a company requires compliance with a specific procedure in order to allow for the distribution of the remaining assets between the shareholders upon the complete payment of all the company's creditors. For the duration of the liquidation procedure, the company will maintain its distinct legal personality (Art. 183, para. 1 of the Company Code).

314. During the liquidation procedure, all the documents that emanate from the company must mention its state of affairs (Art. 183 of the Company Code).

315. Following the dissolution of the company, the company will be deemed to continue to exist for liquidation purposes only (Art. 183 of the Company Code).

2. The appointment and resignation or discharge of liquidators

316. The general shareholders' meeting determines the procedure to be followed for the liquidation of the company and appoints the liquidators (Art. 184 of the Company

Code). If no liquidators have been appointed, the directors will be considered to be the liquidators (Art. 185 of the Company Code).

317. The appointment of the liquidators must be filed with the registry of the commercial court and must be published in the *Annexes to the Belgian Official Journal* (*Bijlagen tot Belgisch Staatsblad/Annexes aux Moniteur belge*) in accordance with Articles 74, paragraph 2 and 73 of the Company Code.

318. The shareholders may discharge the liquidators at any time by a simple majority of the votes cast (Art. 194, para. 2 of the Company Code).

3. *Powers of the liquidators*

319. The liquidators form a collective body, deliberating in accordance with the rules contained in Article 63 of the Company Code. The shareholders may however explicitly stipulate that a liquidator will have the authority to act alone.

320. The shareholders enjoy absolute freedom in conferring powers on the liquidators, notably those contained in Articles 186 and 187 of the Company Code. For certain important decisions, the liquidators will need the prior approval of the shareholders. Article 187 of the Company Code provides in particular that the shareholders may authorise the liquidators to contribute the assets of the company to another company. The liquidators may request payment of the amounts that the shareholders previously agreed to contribute if these are needed to pay the debts of the company and the costs resulting from the liquidation (Art. 188 of the Company Code).

4. *Liabilities of the liquidators*

321. Liquidators are responsible both *vis-à-vis* the company and *vis-à-vis* third parties for a proper execution of their tasks and any shortcomings in their administration of the liquidation (Art. 192 of the Company Code). Liquidators are typically exposed to claims by third parties, as disgruntled creditors may question the manner in which the company's debts have been settled.

322. The statute of limitations for all actions brought against the liquidators in relation to the execution of their task is 5 years from the date of the contested act or omission or from the date that the act or omission was discovered in cases where facts have been intentionally concealed (Art. 198 of the Company Code).

5. *Effect of the liquidation of a company*

323. The liquidators are obliged by law to pay all creditors in a proportional manner and without taking account whether or not the claims of these creditors are imme-

diately enforceable. However, the liquidators are required to safeguard the rights of creditors holding preferential claims (Art. 190, para. 1 of the Company Code).

324. If the assets of the company in liquidation clearly exceed its liabilities or if the long-term debts of the company are sufficiently secured, the liquidators may pay first, at their own risk, the creditors who hold claims that are immediately enforceable. In such situation, every creditor maintains the right to bring legal proceedings to enforce his rights (Art. 190, para. 1 of the Company Code).

6. Description of the liquidation procedure

325. The liquidation procedure normally comprises the following 3 steps:
    (i) the realisation of the company's assets;
    (ii) the payment of its debts; and
    (iii) the division of the remaining monies among the shareholders.

326. The shareholders can freely determine, in the company's articles of association or in a separate decision, how the assets of the company must be realised by the liquidators. They can modify the rules contained in Articles 186 and 187 of the Company Code regarding the powers of the liquidators. The only restraint on the shareholders' freedom is contained in Article 188 of the Company Code, which holds that the liquidators are empowered to request payment of the sums the shareholders agreed to contribute if these are needed to pay the debts of the company and the costs of liquidation.

327. Article 190, paragraph 1 of the Company Code determines in which order the debts must be paid:
    (i) the creditors holding certain preferential rights must be paid first; and
    (ii) then, all the other creditors must be paid in a proportional manner.

328. The creditors need not file a declaration of their claim with the court (as is the case in bankruptcy proceedings). The liquidators must identify the creditors of the company from the company's books. The liquidators are required to keep necessary provisions aside in case of contested claims. The Supreme Court held on 16 June 1988 that costs incurred by the liquidators in performing their tasks must be reimbursed before the other debts of the company are paid. (Cass., 16 June 1988, *T.R.V.*, 1988, 352)

329. Each year the liquidators must present the shareholders with a report outlining the progress made in respect of the liquidation and the reasons why the liquidation could not be completed (Art. 193 of the Company Code). At least one month before the general shareholders' meeting, the shareholders must meet again. The liquidators must then report to the shareholders on how the assets of the company

were used and submit their calculations together with the required supporting documents (Art. 194 of the Company Code). These reports are controlled by the auditor (Art. 194 of the Company Code). If there is no auditor, the shareholders have an individual "investigation right" for which they can be assisted by an accounting expert or by a statutory auditor (*bedrijfsrevisor/réviseurs d'entreprise*). (Art. 155 of the Company Code) The closure of the liquidation will be published in accordance with Articles 67 and 73 of the Company Code, namely it will be filed with the registry of the competent commercial court and it will be published in the *Annexes to the Belgian Official Journal* (*Bijlagen tot Belgisch Staatsblad/Annexes au Moniteur belge*) within 15 days. The publication will contain:

(i) the place (to be determined by the shareholders) where the books and documents of the company will be kept for a period of at least 5 years (Art. 195, para. 1 of the Company Code); and

(ii) the measures taken to safeguard funds or values that are destined for creditors or shareholders (Art. 195, para. 1 of the Company Code).

330. The company ceases to exist on the date of publication. On the same date, a 5-year period starts running within which any action against the liquidators must be commenced (Art. 198, para. 1 of the Company Code).

§4. The rules pertaining to the bankruptcy (faillissement/faillite) of an NV/SA

331. The rules pertaining to bankruptcy are discussed in Chapter 20.

IV. OTHER CORPORATE FORMS

A. The closely held limited liability company (*besloten vennootschap met beperkte aansprakelijkheid/société privée à responsabilité limitée*) (BVBA/SPRL)

332. The closely held limited liability company is governed by Articles 210 through 349 of the Company Code and defined as:

> "*A company incorporated by one or more parties who only commit their own contribution and in which the rights of the shareholders can only be transferred under specific conditions.*"

333. This definition clearly demonstrates the closely held character of a BVBA/SPRL. However, many of the rules that were discussed for the NV/SA also apply to the BVBA/SPRL. The specific provisions, which only apply to the BVBA/SPRL are discussed briefly in this section.

§1. The constitution of a BVBA/SPRL

334. A BVBA/SPRL can be constituted if the following conditions are satisfied:
   (i) the stated capital must be fully subscribed (Art. 216 of the Company Code);
   (ii) a minimum capital of € 18,550 must be contributed;
   (iii) at least one third of the minimum capital of the capital must be paid up on the day of incorporation;
   (iv) each share that represents a contribution in cash must be paid up to at least one-fifth (Art. 223 of the Company Code); and
   (v) the shares representing contributions in kind must be fully paid up (Art. 223 of the Company Code).

335. It is prohibited by law to raise funds for a BVBA/SPRL through a public rights issue (Art. 346 of the Company Code, which contains criminal sanctions for people violating the prohibition). A prohibition on subscribing to its own shares, either directly, or indirectly through a subsidiary or a person acting for account of these companies, is also imposed on the BVBA/SPRL (Arts. 217, 304 and 314, para. 3 of the Company Code).

336. A BVBA/SPRL must be constituted by a notarial deed (Art. 66 of the Company Code). Excerpts of the deed must be published within 15 days of the incorporation in the *Belgian Official Journal* (Belgisch Staatsblad/Moniteur belge) and must be registered with the registry of the competent commercial court (Arts. 67, 68, 72, 73 of the Company Code).

337. The rules contained in Article 444 of the Company Code regarding reporting requirements for contributions in kind made in an NV/SA also apply to the BVBA/SPRL (Art. 219 of the Company Code). The same goes for the rules that govern the financial plan to be drawn up by the founding shareholders (Arts. 440, 219 and 224, para. 5 of the Company Code).

338. The following information must be contained in the notarial deed by which the BVBA/SPRL is constituted (Art. 226 of the Company Code):
   (i) the corporate form and the name (Art. 69, para. 1 of the Company Code);
   (ii) the purpose of the company (Art. 69, para. 11 of the Company Code);
   (iii) the registered office of the company;
   (iv) a precise indication of the shareholders of the company (Art. 69, para. 4 of the Company Code);
   (v) the duration of the company, unless this is unlimited (Art. 69, para. 3 of the Company Code); and
   (vi) the amount of the capital that was subscribed to and an indication of the part of the capital that was paid up (Art. 69, para. 5 of the Company Code);

339. The shareholders may be represented at the incorporation meeting by special proxyholders. For this purpose, special proxies containing the main features of the draft articles of association must be drawn up (Art. 226 of the Company Code).

340. A BVBA/SPRL can be incorporated by one natural person (Art. 212 of the Company Code). In principle, the same rules will apply as for the incorporation of a BVBA/SPRL with more than one shareholder. A major difference is that a natural person can only incorporate a single "one-person BVBA/SPRL" (Art. 212 of the Company Code). If this person sets up a second "one-person BVBA/SPRL" or if he acquires the shares of such a BVBA/SPRL, he will be held jointly and severally liable with the company for the obligations assumed by the second BVBA/SPRL (Art. 212, para. 2 of the Company Code). If the "one-person BVBA/SPRL" is incorporated by a company, the company will be held jointly and severally liable for all the obligations assumed by the BVBA/SPRL, until such time as the company is no longer the only shareholder of the BVBA/SPRL (Art. 123, para. 8 of the Company Code).

341. A major difference from the rules that apply to an NV/SA is the fact that every party which participates in the incorporation of a BVBA/SPRL will be considered to be a founding shareholder, notwithstanding any provision to the contrary. In other words, it is not possible to participate in the incorporation of a BVBA/SPRL as a mere subscriber to the capital (Art. 225 of the Company Code).

§2. *The capital of a BVBA/SPRL*

342. According to Article 302 of the Company Code, each capital increase must be decided by the general shareholders' meeting in accordance with the rules that apply to a modification of the company's articles of association (which are contained in Art. 136 of the Company Code and which are identical to those applicable to an NV/SA). As a result, the notion of authorised capital does not exist in the context of a BVBA/SPRL. The formal requirements that govern the incorporation of a BVBA/SPRL also apply to a capital increase (Arts. 119 and 120 of the Company Code, as discussed above).

343. The closely held nature of the BVBA/SPRL entails the existence of a preferential right for the existing shareholders to subscribe to a capital increase. Article 309 of the Company Code states that if the company intends to receive contributions in cash, the new shares must be presented first to the existing shareholders in accordance with the amount of the capital which is represented by their shares. In contrast to the position applying to the NV/SA, the preferential right contained in Article 309 of the Company Code cannot be limited or abolished either in the

company's articles of association or by a decision of the general shareholders' meeting.

344. If some or all of the existing shareholders do not fully exercise their preferential right, only the other shareholders, the spouse of a shareholder, his ascendants or descendants, or other persons indicated in the articles of association will be entitled to participate in the capital increase (Arts. 249, para. 2 of the Company Code). Third parties can only participate in the capital increase if they obtain the consent of at least one-half of the shareholders whose shares represent at least three-quarters of the capital (Arts. 310 and 294, para. 1 of the Company Code).

345. The rules for a capital decrease are contained in Article 316 of the Company Code. They generally resemble the rules that govern a capital decrease in the NV/SA (*See*, para. 161).

§3. *The shares of a BVBA/SPRL*

346. The stated capital is divided into equal shares. The shares are all registered in order to preserve the closely held character of the company. Each share entitles the holder to an equal part in the profits of the company. A BVBA/SPRL can only issue capital shares. Non-capital shares are not allowed (Art. 232 of the Company Code).

347. A shareholders' register must be kept in the registered office of the company (Art. 233 of the Company Code). Each shareholder and any interested third party is entitled to consult the shareholders' register (Art. 233 of the Company Code).

348. If a shareholder intends to transfer his shares in a BVBA/SPRL to a third party, he is required to obtain the prior approval of at least one-half of the shareholders whose shares represent three-quarters of the capital (Art. 249, para. 1 of the Company Code). The company's articles of association may provide even stricter rules by, for example, subjecting the transfer of shares to unanimous shareholders' approval. An exception to this approval requirement exists, subject to a provision to the contrary in the company's articles of association, for transfers of shares to specific categories of parties namely:
  (i) other shareholders;
  (ii) the spouse of the transferor;
  (iii) the ascendants or descendants of the transferor; and
  (iv) other persons mentioned in the articles of association

349. If the shareholders refuse the required approval, all interested parties can bring summary proceedings before the President of the commercial court (Art. 251 of the Company Code). The company's articles of association may, however, bar the

possibility of such an action. The rules regarding approval obviously do not apply to the "one-person BVBA/SPRL".

§4. The management and control of a BVBA/SPRL

350. A BVBA/SPRL is managed by one or more paid or unpaid persons (*zaakvoerders/ gérants*). The relationship between these persons and the company is one of principal and agent as covered by Articles 1984 to 2010 of the Civil Code and who may, but need not, be shareholders. A company can however not become the manager of a BVBA/SPRL

351. The general shareholders' meeting appoints the manager(s). The status of the manager is determined by the procedure of appointment:
    (i) a manager appointed in the articles of association of the company can only be dismissed by a unanimous decision of the shareholders or for serious cause, unless the articles of association determine differently.
    (ii) a manager who is appointed by a majority decision of the general shareholders' meeting can be dismissed at any time by a new majority decision of the general shareholders' meeting, unless the company's articles of association determine differently.

352. The appointment of the manager(s) must be published in the *Belgian Official Journal (Belgisch Staatsblad/Moniteur belge)*.

353. According to Article 257 of the Company Code, each manager has the power to take all actions necessary or useful to accomplishing the corporate purpose of the company, unless such action falls within the scope of the powers expressly reserved by law for the general shareholders' meeting.

354. The powers of the managers can be limited in the articles of association but such limitation is not enforceable against third parties, even if such limitation is published in the *Belgian Official Journal*. By contrast, the company's articles of association may give one or more managers the power to represent the company individually or collectively, and this power is enforceable against third parties provided that it was published in the *Belgian Official Journal (Belgisch Staatsblad/ Moniteur belge)*.

355. In cases where there is a conflict of interest between one or more managers and that of the company, the rules that govern such a situation in the NV/SA will apply (Art. 259 of the Company Code – *See*, paras. 210 *et seq.*). Article 260 of the Company Code contains a special procedure if the company has only one manager. Article 261 of the Company Code describes the required course of action for one-person BVBA/SPRLs which are managed by the sole shareholder.

356. The same applies for the rules regarding the liability of the managers. (The rules for the NV/SA are analogous to the rules contained in 262 through 265 of the Company Code for the BVBA/SPRL)

357. The control of the BVBA/SPRL is regulated in the same manner as in the NV/SA.

358. The rules that govern the general shareholders' meeting in the NV/SA generally apply to the BVBA/SPRL.

B. The co-operative company with limited liability (*coöperatieve vennootschap met beperkte aansprakelijkheid/société coopérative à responsabilité limitée*) (CVBA/SCRL)

359. Article 350 of the Company Code defines the CVBA/SCRL in relevant part as follows:

> "*A company which is constituted by a variable number of shareholders who make variable contributions [...]. In the co-operative company with limited liability, the shareholders' responsibility for the company's debts is limited to their contribution.*"

§1. The constitution of a CVBA/SCRL

360. The CVBA/SCRL can only be constituted by a notarial deed. It must have at least 3 shareholders (Art. 351 of the Company Code). The deed is required to contain the following information (Art. 355 of the Company Code):
   (i) the form, the name and the registered office of the company;
   (ii) the corporate purpose;
   (iii) the precise information regarding shareholders; and
   (iv) information regarding the contributions made and the invariable part of the stated capital.

361. The following rules should be taken into account for the establishment of a CVBA/SCRL:
   (i) the invariable part of the stated capital may not be less than € 18,550, and at least one third of the minimum stated capital must be paid up at the date of the incorporation;
   (ii) each share which represents contributions in cash or in kind must be paid up to at least one-quarter; and
   (iii) contributions in kind are only valid if they can be assessed in accordance with economic criteria.

362. The notarial deed must expressly mention that the above requirements have been complied with. A number of the rules applicable to the NV/SA are also valid for the CVBA/SCRL. These include (i) the requirement to establish a financial plan (Art. 341 of the Company Code), (ii) the reporting requirement for contributions in kind (Arts. 394 and 395 of the Company Code) and (iii) the potential liability of the founding shareholders (Art. 405 of the Company Code).

§2. The capital of a CVBA/SCRL

363. The capital of a CVBA/SCRL consists of an invariable and a variable part (Art. 144 of the Company Code).

§3. The shares in a CVBA/SCRL

364. The shares in a CVBA/SCRL are transferable to other shareholders in the manner determined in the articles of association (Art. 362 of the Company Code). The shares can only be transferred to third parties that were explicitly named in the articles of association or that belong to a specific category of potential transferees mentioned in the articles of association (Art. 364 of the Company Code).

365. A shareholders' register must be kept in the registered office of the CVBA/SCRL (Art. 356 of the Company Code).

366. The CVBA/SCRL is precluded from subscribing to its own shares (Art. 354 of the Company Code).

§4. The management and control of a CVBA/SCRL

367. According to Article 378 of the Company Code, the CVBA/SCRL is managed by one or more managers, which may, but need not, be shareholders.

368. The control is essentially governed by the same rules as apply to the NV/SA.

§5. The dissolution and liquidation of a CVBA/SCRL

369. The duration of the CVBA/SCRL is mentioned in the company's articles of association. If the articles of association do not regulate this matter, the CVBA/SCRL will be deemed to exist for an indefinite period (Art. 386 of the Company Code). The dissolution and the liquidation of the CVBA/SCRL are governed by rules similar to those applying to the NV/SA.

C. The co-operative company with unlimited liability (*coöperatieve vennootschap met onbeperkte aansprakelijkheid/société coopérative à responsabilité illimitée*) (CVOA/SCRI)

370. Article 352 of the Company Code defines the CVOA/SCRI in relevant part as follows:

> "*A company which is constituted by a variable number of shareholders who make variable contributions. [...] In the co-operative company with unlimited liability, the shareholders are jointly and severally liable for the debts of the company.*"

371. In addition to the potentially unlimited liability of the shareholders, the following factors differentiate a CVOA/SCRI from a CVBA/SCRL:
   (i) no notarial deed is required for its establishment (although there must be a written document);
   (ii) there is no minimum requirement for the invariable part of the stated capital;
   (iii) there is no requirement to pay up the shares;
   (iv) the managers of a CVOA/SCRI are obliged by law (Art. 373 of the Company Code) to file a list of all shareholders with the registry of the commercial court every 6 months.

D. The general partnership (*vennootschap onder firma/société en nom collectif*) (VOF/SNC)

372. The VOF/SNC is a partnership which is formed by 2 or more partners, which jointly conduct commercial or non-commercial activities under a common name (Art. 201 of the Company Code). That name may contain the names of the partners.

373. The most important characteristic of the VOF/SNC is that the liability of the partners for the debts of the partnership is unlimited, joint and several, even if only one of the partners assumed the debt in the name of the partnership (Art. 204 of the Company Code). However, Article 203 of the Company Code provides that the partners of a VOF/SNC cannot be held personally liable for obligations of the partnership as long as the partnership itself has not been held liable.

374. Unlike partners in, for instance, the NV/SA, BVBA/SPRL and CVBA/SCRL, partners in a VOF/SNC are allowed to contribute their labour to the company/partnership. This makes the VOF/SNC a suitable corporate form for persons who exercise an independent profession, such as attorneys. The VOF/SNC must be created by a written document (Art. 4*quater* of the Company Code). An excerpt of this docu-

ment must be published in the *Belgian Official Journal* (*Belgisch Staatsblad/ Moniteur belge*) (Art. 7a of the Company Code).

375. There are no minimum capital requirements in the VOF/SNC.

376. Because of the nature of the VOF/SNC, the shares can generally not be transferred unless all the partners agree.

377. One or more managers can be appointed in the VOF/SNC.

378. The VOF/SNC is not obliged to publish its annual accounts.

379. The VOF/SNC can be dissolved on a voluntary basis provided all the partners agree. The VOF/SNC can also be dissolved by a court decision based on legal reasons (Art. 45 of the Company Code).

E. The limited partnership (*gewone commanditaire vennootschap/société en commandite simple*)

380. The limited partnership is a company which is formed by one or more partners which are jointly and severally liable and which are referred to as "managing partners" (*beherende vennoten/associés commandités*), and one or more partners which merely invest in the partnership and which are referred to as "limited partners" (*stille vennoten/associés commanditaires*) (Art. 202 of the Company Code).

381. The name of the limited partnership can contain only the name(s) of one or more of the managing partners (Art. 65 of the Company Code).

382. The limited partnership must be incorporated by a written document and an excerpt of this must be published in the *Belgian Official Journal* (*Belgisch Staatsblad/ Moniteur belge*).

383. There are no minimum capital requirements.

384. Because of the nature of the limited partnership, the shares can generally not be transferred unless all the partners agree.

385. As a rule, one or more of the managing partners will take care of the management of the partnership. The law explicitly prohibits limited partners from becoming involved with the management of the partnership (Art. 207 of the Company Code).

F. The limited company with shares (*commanditaire vennootschap op aandelen/société en commandite par actions*)

386. The limited company with shares is a company with 2 types of shareholders with a distinct legal status: (i) shareholders of the first category are jointly and severally liable with the company for the company's obligations; and (ii) shareholders of the second category only commit their contribution to the company.

387. The name of the company can only contain the name of one or more of the shareholders who are jointly and severally liable with the company (Art. 65 of the Company Code).

388. Most of the rules applicable to the NV/SA also apply to the limited company with shares (Art. 657 of the Company Code).

389. A limited company with shares can only be constituted by notarial deed. The deed must be filed with the registry of the competent commercial court and an excerpt must be published in the *Belgian Official Journal (Belgisch Staatsblad/Moniteur belge)*.

390. The shares of the company can, in principle, be transferred freely. The company can raise funds through a public rights issue.

391. The names of the managers, who must be chosen from the category of jointly and severally liable shareholders, must be mentioned in the company's articles of association (Art. 658 of the Company Code). The shareholders with limited liability are precluded from interfering with the external management of the company unless they act as a proxy-holder for the company (Art. 656 of the Company Code).

392. A statutory auditor must be appointed if the relevant criteria of size are satisfied (*See*, para. 553).

393. Unless the company's articles of association determine otherwise, the limited company with shares ceases to exist when the managing shareholder dies (Art. 660 of the Company Code).

G. Economic interest grouping

§1. Definition

394. EC Council Regulation No. 2137/85 of 25 July 1985 on the European Economic Interest Grouping (EEIG) ("Regulation No. 2137/85") (O.J. [1985] L 199/1), was implemented in Belgium by the Law of 12 July 1989. At the same time, it was also decided to make it possible to create a national Economic Interest Grouping (EIG)

(*Economisch Samenwerkingsverband (ESV)/Groupement d'intérêt économique (GIE)*) which is similar to the EEIG without, however, having its multinational requirement (at least 2 members must have their central administration or principal activities in different EC Member States).

395. The EIG was recently incorporated in the new Company Code. Unless otherwise specified, all following references pertain to provisions of the Law of 17 July 1989.

396. Article 839 of the Company Code defines the EIG as a grouping established by 2 or more parties the sole aim of which is to facilitate or develop the economic activities of its members or to improve or increase the profits derived from these activities. The activities of the grouping must be related to the activities of its members and must not be more than ancillary to these activities. This means that an EIG may not replace the activities of its members.

397. The EIG could be used as a vehicle for co-operation in a number of areas including lobbying, co-operation between law firms, joint purchasing of raw materials, advertising, provision of ancillary services in the context of franchise networks and research and development. The purpose of an EIG may not be to pursue profits (Art. 840 of the Company Code). However, this does not mean that an EIG cannot make profits in the course of its activities.

398. An EIG is constituted for either a limited or an unlimited duration. The EIG has a distinct legal personality as from the moment of the formation contract.

§2. *Members*

399. An EIG must include at least 2 legal entities or 2 natural persons or a legal entity and a natural person (Art. 839 of the Company Code). Special governmental authorisation is needed for public credit institutions to become members of an EIG and an EIG may itself not be a member of another EIG, or of an EEIG.

400. The members of an EIG are jointly and severally liable for the obligations of the EIG (Art. 843 of the Company Code).

401. The contract for the formation of the EIG can provide that the members are required to make a contribution in cash or in kind or to contribute their labour to the EIG (Art. 842 of the Company Code). For each non-cash contribution a statutory auditor must evaluate the contribution and draw up a report. Article 840 of the Company Code prohibits an EIG from being financed through the issue of bonds.

§3. Procedure to form an EIG

1. Contract

402. A contract for the formation of an EIG must include at least the following information (Art. 845 of the Company Code):
  (i) the name of the grouping;
  (ii) the aims for which the grouping is formed;
  (iii) the names, business names, legal form, corporate purpose, permanent address or registered office and the number and place of registration, if any, of each member of the EIG;
  (iv) the duration of the EIG, except when this is indefinite;
  (v) the official address of the EIG;
  (vi) the procedure to be followed for the appointment and dismissal of the managers;
  (vii) the kind and value of the contributions, if any, as well as the name or business name of the members making such contributions;
  (viii) the place and date of the assembly of the members; and
  (ix) the way in which the management and control of the EIG is organised.

403. The members are free to conclude a private written contract or to establish the EIG by means of a notarial deed.

2. Registration and publication

404. An EIG must be registered with the registry of the commercial court of the place where the EIG has its official address. The registration formality applies to the contract for the formation of the EIG as well as to a number of other documents and particulars including:
  (i) any amendments to the contract of formation, including any change in the composition of the EIG;
  (ii) the judicial decisions establishing or declaring the nullity of the EIG;
  (iii) the notice of appointment and termination of the manager(s) and of the way in which he or they may act;
  (iv) any decision by members or any judicial decision to wind up the EIG;
  (v) the notice of the appointment and termination of the liquidators of the EIG;
  (viii) the notice of the conclusion of the EIG's liquidation;
  (ix) any clauses exempting a new member from the payment of debts and other liabilities which originated prior to his admission.

405. The particulars which must be included in the contract for the formation of the EIG and any amendments thereto, the number, date, and place of registration, and

the documents and particulars which must be registered, must all be published in the *Belgian Official Journal* (*Belgisch Staatsblad/Moniteur belge*).

§4. *Operation and control of an EIG*

406. The bodies of an EIG are the members, acting collectively, and the manager(s). The contract of formation may provide for other bodies and determine their powers. Under specific circumstances, it will be necessary to call upon the services of a statutory auditor.

1. *Collectively acting members*

407. The members, acting collectively, may take any decision to achieve the aims of the EIG. Each member shall have one vote unless the contract for the formation of the EIG provides otherwise (Art. 854 of the Company Code).

408. Article 854 of the Company Code lists a number of matters which require a unanimous decision of the members, such as, for instance, the decisions to admit new members, to alter the aims of the EIG and to alter the number of votes allocated to each member.

409. The contract for the formation of the EIG may prescribe the conditions for a quorum and for a majority in order to decide on matters for which the law does not impose a unanimity requirement. If the contract does not prescribe a specific voting procedure regarding these matters, decisions on these matters must also be taken unanimously.

410. The members convene at least once a year on the date and at the place provided for in the contract for formation of the EIG. The assembly of members will also convene upon request of the manager or of a member of the EIG. The agenda of the meeting must be sent to the members by registered mail at least 15 days before the assembly (Art. 861 of the Company Code).

411. On the occasion of the annual assembly, the manager will present the annual accounts to the assembly of members for their approval.

2. *Manager(s)*

412. An EIG must be managed by one or more natural persons appointed in the contract for the formation of the EIG or by decision of the members (Art. 854 of the Company Code). The managers may, but need not, be members of the EIG. Notwithstanding any contractual provision to the contrary, each member can request the removal of a manager for justified reasons.

413. The contract for the formation of the EIG shall lay down the powers of the managers.

414. The managers are required to prepare the annual accounts of the EIG and to submit them to the assembly for its approval within 6 months following the end of the financial year. The approved accounts must be published 30 days following their approval (Art. 866 of the Company Code).

3. Statutory auditor

415. The appointment of a statutory auditor to monitor the EIG's financial affairs is only compulsory if one of the members of the EIG is itself subject to statutory auditor's control. The EIG can also, on its own initiative, decide to appoint a statutory auditor. His tasks and responsibilities are identical to those laid down in the pertinent provisions of the Company Code (*See*, Chapter 4).

416. A report of a statutory auditor will be required for each contribution by a member which is not in cash.

4. Relations with third parties

417. Only the manager, or where there are 2 or more managers then each of these, shall represent a grouping in respect of dealings with third parties. The contract for the formation of the EIG may provide that the EIG shall be validly bound only by 2 or more managers, acting jointly. Such a clause may be relied on by third parties if it has been published in the *Belgian Official Journal* (*Belgisch Staatsblad/Moniteur belge*).

418. All documents, letters, invoices, announcements, orders and other written materials used by an EIG must indicate:
   (i) the name of the EIG;
  (ii) the indication "*economisch samenwerkingsverband*" or "*groupement d'intérêt économique*" (economic interest grouping in Dutch or French depending on the language of registration). The abbreviation "*ESV*" (Dutch) or "*GIE*" (French) may also be used;
 (iii) the location of the registered office of the EIG; and
 (iv) the words "*register van de economische samenwerkingsverbanden*" or the letters "*RESV*" (Dutch). In French, these words read "*registre des groupements d'intérêt économique*" and the abbreviation, "*RGIE*". These indications must be followed by the name of the place where the commercial court with which the EIG is registered is located, and by the registration number.

§5. Profits

419. The profits resulting from the EIG's activities are profits belonging to the members and must be allocated among them in the proportions laid down in the contract for the formation of the EIG or, in the absence of any such provision, in equal shares.

420. As far as the taxation aspects of EIGs and EEIGs are concerned (*See*, paras. 841 *et seq.*).

§6. EEIG

421. As mentioned above (*See*, para. 394), the EIG has a European counterpart, the EEIG, which allows individuals and enterprises in the European Community to co-operate through a legal entity which is governed by a uniform set of rules, laid down in EC Council Regulation No. 2137/85 as implemented in Belgium by the Law of 12 July 1989. Except for the multinational requirement, which implies that at least 2 members must have their central administration or principal activities in different EC Member States, the EEIG is very similar to the EIG.

3. MERGERS & ACQUISITIONS

I. INTRODUCTION

422. One of the most important features of the Belgian M&A market consists in the fact that, unlike in neighbouring countries, most medium-sized companies are still family-owned. The strong entrepreneurial spirit, which still exists in these companies, implies that numerous smaller M&A transactions are carried out in Belgium, many of which address inheritance concerns. This creates interesting opportunities for new investors. The family nature of these businesses as well as the succession related concerns, however, also creates specific legal problems.

423. In Belgium, the provisions governing mergers, acquisitions, joint ventures, divisions and transformations are contained in: (i) the Company Code (the "Company Code"), (ii) the Royal Decree No. 185 of 9 July 1935 on the Control on Banks and the Issue Requirements for Securities (*Koninklijk Besluit nr. 185 op de bankcontrole en het uitgifteregime voor titels en effecten/Arrêté Royal no. 185 sur le contrôle des banques et le regime des emissions des titres et valeurs* – "Royal Decree No. 185"), (iii) the Law of 2 March 1989 on the Publication of Major Shareholdings in Companies Listed on a Stock Exchange and the Regulations of Public Takeover Bids (*Wet op de openbaarmaking van belangrijke deelnemingen in ter beurze genoteerde vennootschappen en tot reglementering van de openbare overname-aanbiedingen/Loi relative à la publicité des participations importantes dans les sociétés cotées en bourse et réglementant les offers publiques d'acquisition* – the "Law of 2 March 1989"); and (iv) the Royal Decree of 8 November 1989 on Public Takeover Bids and Change of Control (as amended by the Royal Decree of 21 April 1999) (*Koninklijk Besluit op de openbare overnameaanbiedingen en de wijzigingen in de controle op vennootschappen/Arrêté Royal relative aux offers publiques d'acquisition et aux modifications du contrôle des sociétés* – the "Royal Decree of 8 November 1989"). These provisions are completed by specific legislation related to the labour, tax and environmental aspects of such transactions, which will not, however, be discussed in this chapter.

II. MERGERS UNDER BELGIAN LAW

424. The Company Code (*Wetboek van vennootschappen/Code des Sociétés*) covers both mergers by acquisition and mergers by incorporation of a new company. Since most mergers involve companies that have taken the form of a public limited liability company (*naamloze vennootschap/société anonyme- N.V./S.A.*), this chapter does not deal with specific rules for mergers involving other types of companies.

A. Merger by acquisition

§1. Definition

425. A merger by acquisition is the *"legal act by which one or more companies transfer all their assets and liabilities, including rights and obligations, to another company, following a winding up, without liquidation, in exchange for the acquiring company issuing shares to the shareholders of the acquired company, increased, as the case may be, by additional cash not more than one tenth of the nominal value or the par value of the issued shares"* (Art. 671 of the Company Code).

426. In order to be enforceable against third parties, the transfer of certain assets (*i.e.*, real estate, *etc.*) requires compliance with certain formalities and conditions.

427. A merger in accordance with Article 671 of the Company Code differs from a contribution of a universality of assets and liabilities in that the merger, contrary to a contribution of a universality of assets and liabilities, results by law in the dissolution of the acquired company and allows a limited cash payment.

§2. Procedure

1. Merger proposal

428. The boards of directors of the merging companies must draw up the merger proposal. The merger proposal, included in a notarial deed or in a private instrument, sets out the basic conditions of the merger and should at least contain the information required by Article 693 of the Company Code, including, for example, the names and addresses of the merging companies, the exchange rate and special benefits as granted to the management of the merging companies. Each company involved in the merger must submit the merger proposal to the clerk's office of the competent Commercial Court at least 6 weeks prior to the extraordinary general shareholders' meeting that will decide on the merger.

2. Merger reports

429. A detailed written report is prepared by the board of directors of each company, setting out the current status of the stated capital of the merging companies as well as the legal and economic justification for the merger (Art. 694 of the Company Code). For each company, the statutory auditor, a certified auditor or a registered accountant (Art. 695 of the Company Code) prepares a written report on the merger proposal, specifically focussing on the share exchange rate.

3. Preparation of the extraordinary general shareholders' meeting (Art. 697 of the Company Code)

430. The board of directors of each company must draw up a notice to convene an extraordinary general shareholders' meeting, which will decide on the merger, and must send this notice to the general shareholders of their respective companies. The agenda for the extraordinary general shareholders' meeting must refer to the merger proposal and the merger reports, and must mention that shareholders are entitled to obtain a free copy of the merger proposal. A copy of the agenda must be sent to the registered shareholders at least one month before the extraordinary general shareholders' meeting. Each shareholder may inspect the documents mentioned under Article 697 paragraph 2 of the Company Code at the latest one month prior to the date of the extraordinary general shareholders' meeting. Each shareholder may obtain a free copy of all or part of of these documents.

4. Extraordinary general shareholders' meeting (Arts. 699 and 700 of the Company Code)

431. In order to be valid, the extraordinary general shareholders' meeting of each company deciding on the merger must be held before a notary public and its minutes must be recorded in a notarial deed. After examining the deed, the notary must confirm that the company complied with the law. Subject to more stringent provisions in the articles of association of the companies concerned and the special provisions contained in the Company Code, the merger must be approved by the extraordinary general shareholders' meeting in accordance with the following rules on attendance and majority requirements:
    (i) The shareholders present must represent at least half of the stated capital of the company. If this condition is not satisfied, a new extraordinary general shareholder's meeting must be convened, which may then in principle validly vote even though the meeting does not satisfy the quorum requirement; and
    (ii) A merger proposal must receive 75 per cent of the votes of the general shareholders' meeting in order to be adopted.

432. Any changes, if required, to the articles of association of the acquiring company, including amendments to the corporate purpose, will have to be adopted immediately after the resolution to merge is adopted and in accordance with the rules on quorum and majority as required by the Belgian Company Code. Until this takes place, the resolution to merge shall remain without effect (Art. 701 of the Company Code).

5. Publication (Art. 702 of the Company Code)

433. The deeds establishing the merger, and the resolutions adopted by the acquiring company and the acquired company, must be submitted to the clerk's office of the competent commercial court and must be published in the *Belgian Official Journal* (*Belgisch Staatsblad/Moniteur belge*) in the form of an extract. The same requirement applies to any amendments made to the articles of association of the acquiring company. The acquiring company may itself perform the formalities of publication on behalf of the acquired company.

434. The extracts from the resolutions on the merger adopted by the acquiring company and the acquired company must be published simultaneously in the *Belgian Official Journal* within 15 days of the submission of the instrument establishing the merger resolution at the latest general shareholders' meetings.

6. Simplified procedure

435. Article 676 of the Company Code provides a simplified procedure for transactions "ranked as a merger". A transaction will be ranked as a "merger" if: (i) all the assets and liabilities of one or more companies are transferred to the acquiring company; and (ii) the shares and other voting securities of the acquired company were already entirely held by the acquiring company, or by a person who held these shares and securities in his own name but for account of the acquiring company. In case of a transaction ranked as a merger, the merger proposal may be drawn up in a more simplified form and no merger report is required.

B. Merger by incorporation of a new company

§1. Definition

436. A merger by incorporation of a new company is "*a legal act, transferring all assets and liabilities of several companies (including all rights and obligations), to a new company formed by them, following a winding up, without liquidation, in exchange for the new company issuing shares to the shareholders of the dissolving companies, increased, as the case may be, by additional cash of not more than one*

tenth of the nominal value or the par value of the issued shares. " (Art. 672 of the Company Code).

§2. *Procedure*

437. With some exceptions, the procedure for a merger by acquisition also applies to a merger by incorporation of a new company (Arts. 705 of the Company Code *et seq.*). If the conditions are fulfilled, the simplified merger procedure can also be applied.

III. ACQUISITIONS UNDER BELGIAN LAW

A. Methods of Acquisition

438. Under Belgian law, an acquisition may take the form of: (i) a purchase of shares in exchange for a cash amount or shares (a "share deal"); (ii) a purchase of assets in exchange for a cash amount or shares (an "asset deal"); or (iii) a capital increase in cash.

B. Share deal

§1. *Formalities*

439. According to Article 1583 of the Civil Code, an acquisition is valid once the parties agree on the price and the shares to be transferred. The transfer of bearer shares will be enforceable against third parties, including the seller, as from the physical delivery of the shares, while the transfer of registered shares must be effected by a registration of the transfer in the shareholder register of that company, dated and signed by the seller and the buyer or their representatives (Art. 504 of the Company Code).

§2. *Quasi-contribution (Arts. 445 through 447 of the Company Code)*

440. In the event that assets are acquired by a company from a founder, director or shareholder within 2 years following its incorporation and at a price that is equivalent to at least 10 per cent of the value of the subscribed capital of the company, a special report must be dawn up by: (i) the board of directors; and (ii) the statutory auditor or, if there is no statutory auditor, a certified accountant appointed by the

board of directors. The general shareholders' meeting must approve the acquisition in advance. However, the foregoing does not apply to:
- (i) an acquisition made in the normal course of business, on the terms and with the guarantees that are typical in such transactions;
- (ii) a stock exchange acquisition; or
- (iii) an acquisition following a judicial sale.

§3. Contractual restrictions

441. Certain restrictions on transfers of shares can be created in the articles of association of the company or in a shareholders' agreement. Such restrictions may result from the application of an approval clause or a pre-emptive rights clause. However, the use of such clauses may not extend the non-transferability of the shares for more than six months from the date of the request for approval or the exercise of the pre-emptive right (Art. 510 of the Company Code).

442. Other contractual restrictions, such as tag-along rights (*i.e.*, a shareholder may not sell its shares without giving the other shareholders the right to participate in the sale), and stand-still provisions (*i.e.*, a contractual restriction to the negotiability of the shares) must always be in the interest of the company. Additionally, stand-still provisions should be limited in time.

§4. Legal restrictions

443. Belgian law restricts the transfer of shares in the following situations:
- (i) Certain cross shareholdings are restricted or prohibited (Arts. 631 and 632 of the Company Code);
- (ii) The acquisition of own shares or profit certificates by a company or a directly held subsidiary (Art. 620 of the Company Code);
- (iii) The transfer of shares that are not fully subscribed is only enforceable towards third parties after publication by mention of the deposit of the list of shareholders who did not fully subscribe their shares (Art. 506 of the Company Code);
- (iv) Profit-sharing certificates or similar securities may only be transferred 10 days after the deposit of the second annual accounts following their issue, or by a public deed or a private instrument served on the company within one month after the transfer (Art. 508 of the Company Code);
- (v) Shares subscribed by employees of the company or a subsidiary may not be transferred for 5 years following the subscription (Art. 609 of the Company Code); and

(vi) During the time of a takeover bid, shares that are subscribed following an issue of subscription rights exclusively destined for certain persons may not be transferred for 12 months following the subscription (Art. 500 of the Company Code).

C. Asset Deal

§1. Introduction

444. The applicable procedure in a purchase of assets may be different depending on whether the assets are considered as:
    (i) a branch of activity (*bedrijfstak/branche d'activité*) being "*a unit which conducts a business activity autonomously from a technical and operational perspective and which is capable of functioning by itself*" (Art. 680 of the Company Code) or a universality of goods (*algemeenheid van goederen/universalité des biens*), or
    (ii) a mere collection of assets.

445. If the purchase concerns a branch of activity or a universality of goods, the Company Code (Art. 760 of the Company Code *et seq.*) may apply, in addition to Belgian civil law. Only Belgian civil law will apply in case of a transfer of a mere collection of assets.

§2. Civil law

446. Belgian civil law requires that each and every part of the operational activities is transferred between the parties, but additionally requires such transfers to be made enforceable against third parties. A complete list of assets, rights and obligations must be made by the parties and treated in the acquisition agreement. To make the different transfers enforceable against third parties, compliance with different sets of formalities may be required depending on the assets and liabilities involved.

447. If an asset or a branch of activity is acquired by the company from a founder, director or shareholder in the 2 years following its incorporation at a price that is equivalent to at least 10 per cent of the value of the subscribed capital, additional formalities will apply in accordance with Articles 445 through 447 of the Company Code.

§3. The Company Code

1. Principle

448. In order to avoid the formalities of the Belgian civil law procedure, Article 760 *et seq.* of the Company Code, introduced the concepts of "a contribution of a universality of goods" or "a contribution of a branch of activity". Both forms of contribution are made in exchange for shares in the transferee company.

2. Procedure

449. The procedure set out in Article 760 *et seq.* of the Company Code, is similar to the procedure for mergers. The procedure includes the following stages: (i) the drawing up of the transfer terms, (ii) the filing by each party of these terms with the clerk of the commercial court, (iii) a report of the competent corporate body, (iv) the notarial deed of transfer, (v) the filing of the notarial deed with the clerk of the commercial court and (vi) the publication of an extract of the notarial deed in the *Annexes to the Belgian Official Journal* (*Belgisch Staatsblad/Moniteur belge*). However, unlike in the case of mergers, the report of the competent corporate body is not subject to the scrutiny of the statutory auditor.

450. The procedure is mandatory for the contribution of a universality of goods and optional for the contribution of a branch of activity. If the procedure is applied, all assets and liabilities are then transferred without any further formalities once the procedure has been completed and the transfer is enforceable against third parties from the date of publication. However, in the case of a contribution of a branch of activity, related assets and liablities are not automatically transferred, unless the contribution is explicitly made subject to the procedure of Article 760 *et seq.* of the Company Code in express terms (Arts. 763 and 764 of the Company Code). It is therefore important to state explicitly in the transfer proposals and the transfer agreement that the transaction is subject to the procedure.

451. Notwithstanding the above procedure, some specific formalities related, *inter alia*, to the transfer of permits, pending legal proceedings and specific provisions in contracts, such as change of control provisions, would still need to be complied with.

452. The procedure only applies to a transfer between 2 Belgian companies, and, in case of a branch of activity, to a transfer by a physical person to a Belgian company. According to some legal authors, a foreign company may transfer a branch of activity under the Company Code if its constitutive elements are situated in Belgium and if the transfer agreement is governed by Belgian law.

§4. Advantages and disadvantages of Company Code procedure and civil law procedure

453. If the parties invoke the Company Code procedure, the operational activities and related assets and liabilities will transfer by law. Otherwise, civil law requires that each and every part of the operational activities be transferred and that a list of all the assets transferred be drawn up and incorporated in the agreement. If an item is not mentioned on the list, this will imply that it will not be transferred.

454. The Company Code procedure lasts up to 8 weeks as a result of the various (cumbersome) formalities that have to be complied with.

D. Capital increase in cash

455. Subscribing to a capital increase in cash may also be a way to acquire control over a company.

456. The general shareholders' meeting of a company or its board of directors (within the authorised capital) may decide to increase the capital of the company through a cash contribution. To enable the subscription by a third party, existing shareholders' preferential rights must be restricted or excluded by the general shareholders' meeting or, if permitted by the articles of association of the company, by the board of directors in favour of one or more designated persons. Restriction or exclusion of preferential rights must be done under a special procedure set out in Articles 595 through 599 of the Company Code. The company must obtain a detailed report from the board of directors dealing particularly with the issue price of the new shares and the financial consequences of the transaction for the existing shareholders. An additional report of the statutory auditor, a certified auditor or a registered accountant is required certifying that the financial and accounting information in the board of directors' report is correct and that, if the preferential rights are to be limited or restricted by the general shareholders' meeting, the information provided in the board's report is sufficient to permit the general shareholders' meeting to take a decision. In case of restriction or exclusion of the shareholders' preferential rights in favour of one or more designated persons, the identity of the persons must be mentioned in the reports of the board of directors, of the statutory auditor, and in the notice to convene the general shareholders' meeting. The shareholders may also waive their preferential rights at the time of the capital increase.

E. Acquisition processes

457. An acquisition may be effected through: (i) a negotiated process, whether or not in the form of a controlled auction; (ii) a public takeover bid; or (iii) a forced transfer of shares effected under the procedures of either forced transfer, forced takeover of shares (*See*, paras. 293 *et seq.*) or a squeeze-out procedure (Art. 513 of the Company Code).

F. Negotiated acquisition

458. In Belgium, negotiated acquisitions are not regulated by any specific provisions. The main regulations which could be applicable to a negotiated acquisition can be found in the Civil Code and relate to the theory of contract, the contractual responsibility, *etc.*

459. However, some further specific provisions which could affect negotiated acquisitions can be found in the Belgian Company Code and other regulatory texts.

§1. Principles under Belgian civil law.

1. Rights and obligations of the parties during the negotiation

i. Pre-contractual liability

460. Under Article 1382 of the Civil Code, a person who causes injury to the interests of another person must compensate that other person. By extension, each party must consider the interests of the other during the negotiation. This principle, called the "principle of good faith", includes, *inter alia*, the obligation on each party:
    (a) to provide correct information on the terms of the agreement;
    (b) to inform the other party about any new elements that may arise during negotiations; and
    (c) not to break off negotiations in a sudden manner and without any well-founded reasons if the other party reasonably believed that negotiations would presumably succeed.

461. In order to establish that the principle of good faith has been breached, the non-breaching party must show that it has suffered damage for which it should receive compensation, for example, costs incurred and time lost, and a causal connection between the termination and the damage.

ii. Obligation to inform

462. Belgian law does not provide for an obligation for the seller to disclose information, unless required by law, agreement, or by virtue of the seller's profession.

Non-compliance with such an obligation may lead to extra-contractual liability or possibly nullity of a signed agreement in case of fraud. Such obligation does not, however, discharge a purchaser from his obligation to investigate, the extent of which depends on his profession and level of expertise.

2. *Seller's obligations after the closing of the transaction*

i. Obligation to deliver and guarantee the property sold (Art. 1603 of the Civil Code)

463. The seller must deliver the object sold and may not disturb the purchaser's possession by his own acts. If a third party has rights over the object sold that reduce the rights of the purchaser, the seller must indemnify the purchaser for the third party's claims.

ii. Guarantee against hidden defects

464. According to Article 1641 of the Civil Code, the seller must indemnify the purchaser against hidden defects that prevent or limit the purchaser's use of the goods in such a way that the purchaser would not have bought the goods or would have paid less for them, if he had had knowledge of those defects. Unless otherwise agreed, the seller must also indemnify the purchaser for the hidden defects of which he was not aware. The guarantee is in principle limited to the rights attached to the shares and the existence of the company at the time of the closing (*i.e.*, the object of the purchase), to the exclusion of the company itself (*e.g.*, the assets and liabilities of the company, the value of the shares, *etc.*) (*Liège* Court of Appeal, 1 April 1992, *R.P.S.*, 1993, 102).

iii. Non-competition obligation

465. The foregoing implies that, in an asset deal, the seller may not do anything that would cause a depreciation of the goods sold. Thus, the seller should not do anything which could affect the value of the goods as sold, including engaging in competitive activities. In contrast, in a purchase of shares, the purchaser has no protection against competitive acts unless a non-competition clause is included in the acquisition agreement. The purchaser may, however, institute proceedings for pre-contractual breaches or for unfair commercial practices under the Law of 14 July 1991 on Trade Practices and Information to and Protection of the Consumer (*Wet betreffende de handelspraktijken en de voorlichting en bescherming van de consument/Loi sur les pratiques du commerce et sur l'information et la protection du consommateur*).

§2. Different steps in the acquisition process

1. *The letter of intent (also known as memorandum of understanding or the heads of agreement)*

466. A letter of intent is a preliminary agreement that is intended to set forth the basic terms of a future final agreement. Generally speaking, a letter of intent is not binding, except for certain clauses related to exclusivity, confidentiality, the applicable law, certain costs, *etc.* However, according to Belgian law principles, if the parties agree on the price and the object of the sale in the letter of intent, the letter may be considered to be binding (Art. 1583 of the Civil Code).

467. Moreover, courts will also look at other elements such as the intention of the parties or their behaviour. Therefore, care must be taken in regard to the binding effect of a letter of intent. One might indicate the object in a vague manner or give a price range rather than an amount in order to deprive a letter of intent from having a binding effect.

2. *Due diligence*

468. The due diligence investigation has an essential role in the acquisition process. It allows the purchaser to evaluate and identify the risks linked to the acquisition, and to assess the value and the interest of the target. The decision whether or not to proceed with the acquisition is mainly based on the results of the investigation. Due diligence investigations focus mainly on an examination of issues related to corporate matters, real estate portfolios, equipment, shareholdings, financing arrangements, insurance, employment matters, tax matters, litigation and claims, licences, environmental risks, intellectual property and commercial matters. The material that has to be examined as part of due diligence is either put at the purchaser's disposal by the seller itself (*i.e.*, by allowing access to a data room and giving the opportunity to ask information and questions to management), or directly sought by the purchaser (*e.g.*, the articles of association at the companies' registry of the district in which the company is situated, the annual accounts at the National Bank). The letter of intent usually contains the timing, procedure and scope of the due diligence.

3. *The acquisition agreement*

i. Validity

469. In principle, an acquisition is legally enforceable as soon as a clear offer and acceptance have occurred. However, the following conditions must also be satisfied:
   (a) The parties must have the capacity to contract; and

(b) The parties' consent must not have been vitiated through error, fraud, misrepresentation, duress or detriment.

470. A sale of real estate can also be null and void if the sale price was less than seven-twelfths of the fair market value.

ii. Main provisions

471. An acquisition agreement usually includes the following provisions:
(a) *Representations and warranties*: Specific contractual representations and warranties are disclosures reflecting the situation of the company at the time of the closing. They are intended to increase the protection of the purchaser.
(b) *Indemnification*: Procedure, contents and types of indemnification will depend largely on the parties' negotiating position and on the due diligence results.
(c) *Means of recourse*: This provision specifies the compensation the seller will pay the purchaser in case of a breach.
(d) *Non-competition obligation:* A seller usually agrees not to compete with the company or the business sold. The Decree of 17 March 1791 (*décret d'Allarde*) however provides that any person may engage in trade and commerce and may practice a profession. The Decree is mandatory on grounds of public policy, which means that any provision breaching it is void. Non-competition clauses are therefore not prohibited, but must be limited in duration, in geographical scope and in the scope of activities. The aim of a non-competition clause must be to ensure that the purchaser effectively obtains the benefit of the goodwill of the business that he has acquired.

4. The closing

472. The closing is the moment that the purchase price and the ownership of the company are transferred. Closing can either consist of a 1-step transaction which is accomplished with the signing of the acquisition agreement, or a 2-step transaction in which the closing is effective upon the attainment of certain conditions or after having procured certain consents, permits, licences, *etc.*

§3. Controlled auctions

473. Under Belgian law, negotiated acquisitions may take the form of a controlled auction. A controlled auction is a procedure by which the seller offers assets or shares to several potential purchasers.

474. Generally speaking, a controlled auction consists of 3 phases:
(i) *The preparatory phase*: identification of the potential purchasers, the drawing up of an offering memorandum, and the setting up of an internal due diligence;

(ii) *The bidding phase*: contacts with the selected potential purchasers, submissions of non-binding offers by those potential purchasers, reduction of the selection of potential purchasers, access to information (*i.e.*, the data room) for the candidates, drafting a standard acquisition agreement, submission of binding offers by the candidates;

(iii) *Decision phase*: selection of the candidate, final negotiations and conclusion of the acquisition agreement.

G. Public Takeover bids

475. In Belgium, the first laws passed addressing takeover bids were the Law of 2 March 1989, and the Royal Decree of 8 November 1989. Due to the entry into force of the Thirteenth EC Directive on Company Law concerning Takeover Bids (O.J. [2003] C 045/E), Belgium will need to amend its legislation in the next few months, thereby mainly focussing on: (i) defensive measures; (ii) compulsory take-over bids; (iii) rights of minority shareholders; and (iv) the scope of application of the legal provisions.

476. It should be noted that although takeover bids mainly involve companies quoted on a stock exchange, the scope of application of the laws concerning takeover bids is not limited to such companies.

477. Only voting securities and securities conferring a right to subscribe to, convert into or acquire voting securities are relevant in case of a takeover bid under Belgian law (Art. 1, para. 3 of the Royal Decree of 8 November 1989).

478. The Royal Decree of 8 November 1989 regulates share purchase takeover bids and share exchange takeover bids.

§1. Launching of a public takeover bid

1. Procedure

479. According to Article 3 of the Royal Decree of 8 November 1989, the bidder must ensure that: (i) the information it gives to the market is correct; (ii) it treats all shareholders equally and safeguards their interests; and (iii) it respects the transparency and proper functioning of the market.

480. All securities issued by the target company must be covered by the bid. However, the bid may be conditional on the acquisition of a minimum number of securities.

i. Consideration

481. With regard to a share purchase, funds comprising the total consideration for

acquiring all the securities issued must be blocked in an account at a financial institution registered in Belgium. Alternatively, the bidder may also obtain an irrevocable and unconditional letter of credit from a financial institution registered in Belgium.

482. In the case of a share exchange, the bidder must either hold the securities he proposes to offer, or at least have the means to obtain those securities.

ii. Notification of the bid (Arts. 4 and 5 of the Royal Decree of 8 November 1989)

483. The intention to launch a public takeover bid must be notified to the Banking and Finance Commission (*Commissie voor Bank- en Financiewezen/Commission Bancaire et Financière*) at least one month before the launch, together with:
    (a) a draft prospectus;
    (b) the resolution of the bidder's board of directors to launch the bid;
    (c) drafts of the press releases required by law; and
    (d) details of the intended announcement of the bid and the availability of the prospectus.

484. A public announcement of the notification must be made by the Banking and Finance Commission no later than one business day after receiving the notification (Art. 6 of the Royal Decree of 8 November 1989), after which the target and the authorities of the market where the securities are listed are informed of the announcement.

iii. Information to the Banking and Finance Commission

485. All contacts between the bidder and the target occuring after reception of the notification described above must be notified to the Banking and Finance Commision (Art. 9 of the Royal Decree of 8 November 1989).

iv. Dealings (Art. 11 of the Royal Decree of 8 November 1989)

486. During the offer period, all dealings in the target's issued securities must be disclosed to the Banking and Finance Commission. In case of a share exchange, dealings in the bidder's issued securities must be notified as well. The obligation applies to the bidder, the target, or any person who holds, directly or indirectly, at the time of the public announcement of the bid, at least one per cent of the issued securities of the bidder or of the target. Securities quoted on a regulated market and admitted on the official listing may only be traded on that market during the time of the bid (Art. 10 of the Royal Decree of 8 November 1989). Under Article 11, paragraph 4 of the Royal Decree of 8 November 1989, brokers dealing in securities of the target company must disclose to the Banking and Finance Commission the identity of the person for whom they are acting.

v. Revision or withdrawal of a bid (Arts. 12 and 13 of the Royal Decree of 8 November 1989)

487. In principle, the bid may not be revised once notified unless:
    (a) it is revised in favour of the holders of securities;
    (b) the Banking and Finance Commission requires an amendment;
    (c) the bid is extended or reopened;
    (d) the Banking and Finance Commission grants an exemption under Article 15, paragraph 3 of the Royal Decree of 8 November 1989;
    (e) there is a counter bid or a higher bid; or
    (f) the target company's board of directors or shareholders' meeting take, within the limits of their powers, any action intended to modify the terms of the offer.

488. The bid may not be withdrawn after its public announcement unless:
    (a) the Banking and Finance Commission refuses to approve the bid;
    (b) the target company's board of directors or shareholders' meeting take, within the limits of their powers, any actions intended to modify the terms of the offer;
    (c) the bid cannot proceed for reasons beyond the bidder's control;
    (d) the administrative approvals required to acquire the securities have not been obtained; or
    (e) the conditions of the bid have not been satisfied for reasons beyond the bidder's control.

vi. Limitations of rights and obligations of the target company's board of directors (Art. 8 of the Royal Decree of 8 November 1989)

489. The rights of the target's board of directors are limited during the bid period. Between the reception of the notification of the bid and the end of the bid, the target's board of directors may not:
    (a) increase the target company's capital by a contribution in cash or in kind while limiting or suspending the shareholders' preferential subscription right; nor
    (b) take decisions or enter into transactions that may modify the target's assets and liabilities; nor
    (c) issue securities or grant rights to subscribe or acquire securities unless those securities are first offered to existing shareholders in proportion to their share in the capital.

490. However, the board of directors may still:
    (a) conclude transactions, provided they were at a sufficiently advanced stage before the receipt of the communication of the notification;

    (b) satisfy the obligations validly undertaken before the receipt of the communi-
cation of the notification;

    (c) increase the company's capital upon approval of the shareholders' meeting,
according to a 50 per cent attendance and 75 per cent majority, dated not
more than three years before the communication of the notification, provided:
(1°) the shares issued at the capital increase are fully paid up when issued;
(2°) the issue price for the newly issued shares is not lower than the offer price;
and (3°) the newly issued shares do not represent more than 10 per cent of the
total shares representing the issued capital before the capital increase; and

    (d) acquire own shares and own profit shares of the company under Article 620
of the Company Code.

The board of directors must inform the bidder and the Banking and Finance Commission of any of the above decisions and make the decision public.

491. Within 5 days following the receipt of the draft prospectus, the board of directors
must give its position on the bid and its opinion on the prospectus. Furthermore,
the directors must indicate their opinion in their capacity of securities holders and
as representatives of other securities holders (including whether they would accept
the bid). In the event that there is no unanimity, the directors must identify those
among them who dissent from the majority view. Finally, the board of directors
must also present the view of the works council. The position of the board of
directors will be publicly announced in the prospectus or another document. The
board of directors' position does not bind securities holders.

2. The prospectus

i. Content

492. The prospectus must indicate the conditions of the offer and the necessary information for the making of a decision on the bid. The information to be indicated in
the prospectus concerns the Banking and Finance Commission approval of the
prospectus, the person responsible for the prospectus, the bidder, the target and the
offer. That information is indicated in the scheme for drafting a prospectus, annexed to the Royal Decree of 8 November 1989.

ii. Approval procedure

493. The prospectus may not be published until approved by the Banking and Finance
Commission (Art. 17 of the Royal Decree of 8 November 1989). The Banking and
Finance Commission has one month from the date of completion of the file sub-
mitted to decide to approve the prospectus.

494. In the case of a negative opinion, the bidder has 15 days to appeal the decision to the Minister of Finance, who will have 2 months to issue a decision. The Minister of Finance's decision may be appealed to the Council of State (*Raad van State/ Conseil d'Etat*). Once approved, the prospectus is made public by the Banking and Finance Commission in the form of a brochure. Following the publication, any new elements arising that may influence the decision of the securities' holders must be dealt with in a supplement to the prospectus. It must be approved and announced in the same form.

3. Offer period (Art. 26 of the Royal Decree of 8 November 1989)

495. The offer period must last between 10 and 20 working days from the date of the public announcement. The offer period must be extended for a 15-day period from the date of the general shareholders' meeting if the general shareholders' meeting of the target:
   (i) decides to increase the target company's capital by a contribution in cash or in kind while limiting or suspending the shareholders preferential subscription right;
   (ii) takes decisions or enters into transactions which may modify the target's assets and liabilities;
   (iii) issues securities or grants rights to subscribe; or
   (iv) acquires securities unless those securities are first offered to existing shareholders in proportion to their share in the capital.

4. Results of the bid

496. The results of the bid are publicly announced within 5 working days following the end of the bidding period (Art. 27 of the Royal Decree of 8 November 1989). Even if the law does not provide for the way in which the results are announced, it is generally accepted that it must be announced in the same way as the prospectus.

497. In a share exchange take-over bid where the shares of the target company are quoted on a regulated Belgian market, the bidder must request, within one month after the closing of the offer, the listing of the securities offered on the same regulated Belgian market (Art. 31 of the Royal Decree of 8 November 1989).

5. Reopening of the bid (Art. 30 of the Royal Decree of 8 November 1989)

498. If the bidder has promised to increase the offer price before the end of the offer period, he must reopen the bid at a higher price and pay the difference to all shareholders who accepted the original offer. If he holds 90 per cent or more of the target company's securities or if he requests a withdrawal of the target company's securities from the market within 3 months from the end of the bid, the bidder

must reopen the bid under the same conditions (Art. 32 of the Royal Decree of 8 November 1989).

6. Squeeze-out

499. As part of a share purchase, a bidder who: (i) controlled the company, directly or indirectly, alone or together with others, before the initial public takeover bid, and; (ii) following the public takeover bid, owns 95 per cent or more of the securities of the company and at least 66 per cent of the securities which he did not yet own, may reopen the bid under the same conditions for 15 days after making the results of the bid public in order to launch a purchase offer in the meaning of Article 513 of the Company Code. This possibility must have been explicitly mentioned in the prospectus. The securities that are not offered after the closing of this reopened bid are considered transferred to the bidder by operation of law. However, this procedure is only possible if the target is a public company as defined in Article 438 of the Company Code.

7. Counter bid and higher bid (Arts. 33 to 37 of the Royal Decree of 8 November 1989)

500. During the offer period, another bidder can make a counter bid or the bidder can make a higher bid. The counter bid or higher bid must be made at least 2 days before the closing of the bid, counter bid or higher bid. The price of each counter bid or higher bid must be at least 5 per cent higher than the last bid, counter bid or higher bid. A counter bid and a higher bid are subject to the same rules and conditions as a normal public takeover bid. However, Article 35 of the Royal Decree of 8 November 1989 provides the following:
   (i) the Banking and Finance Commission must send the draft prospectus of the counter bidder to the bidder and, if the bidder's prospectus has not yet been approved by the Banking and Finance Commission, the bidder's draft prospectus must be sent to the counter bidder;
   (ii) the position of the company's board of directors on the counter bid must be sent to the bidder; and
   (iii) the target's Board of Directors will compare the bid and the counter bid.

501. The bidder, counter bidder and higher bidder must be treated equally with respect to the information disclosed by the target company. A higher bidder whose offer is already listed in a prospectus approved by the Banking and Finance Commission must amend the prospectus to include the higher offer.

§2. Defense against takeover bids

502. The usual instruments to protect against takeover bids are the following:
  (i) pre-emption and refusal clauses;
  (ii) authorised capital;
  (iii) limitation of the voting rights;
  (iv) issuance of non voting shares;
  (v) selling of "crown jewels" (restricted by the Art. 8, para. 1, 3° of the Royal Decree of 8 November 1989 and Art. 557 of the Company Code);
  (vi) use of "white knight" protection;
  (vii) issuance of preference shares; and
  (viii) involvement of a trustee company issuing depository receipts representing the beneficial interest in the shares, while the trustee retains the voting rights.

H. Change of Control

§1. General

503. A physical person or a legal entity who intends to purchase a given percentage of securities in a Belgian publicly held company must notify the Banking and Finance Commission at least 5 working days before the purchase where this will lead to a change of control in the company (Art. 38 of the Royal Decree of 8 November 1989).

504. A Belgian publicly held company is: (i) a company whose securities are listed on Belgian regulated markets or whose securities are regularly traded at the periodic auctions of a stock exchange; or (ii) a Belgian company whose securities are publicly distributed. The notification is not required if the acquisition is a public takeover bid and the acquisition follows a subscription of securities issued following a capital increase decided by the general shareholders' meeting or the exercise of a right of conversion or a warrant.

§2. Procedure

505. The notification to the Banking and Finance Commission must evidence that:
  (i) complete information is given to the shareholders,
  (ii) shareholders are treated equally,
  (iii) shareholders' interests are safeguarded, and
  (iv) transparency and proper functioning of the financial market is ensured (Art. 39 of the Royal Decree of 8 November 1989).

506. Subsequently, the Banking and Finance Commission makes comments on the notification and may, if necessary, suspend the transaction or apply for an injunction
from the President of the Commercial Court.

1. Mandatory takeover bid (Art. 41 of the Royal Decree of 8 November 1989)

507. When the control of a company is acquired at a price higher than the market price,
the new controller must propose to the remaining shareholders to buy their securities at the same price as the securities previously acquired if only one transaction
occurred. If several transactions occurred, the price will be the higher price offered
during the last 12 months before the acquisition of control of the company.

508. This proposition takes the form either of a public takeover bid or of a stock price
maintenance (*i.e.*, an undertaking to buy all securities presented on the stock exchange market at the same price). The public takeover bid or the stock price maintenance must be announced within 3 days following the acquisition of the control,
and must start at the latest within 30 days. The stock price maintenance must last at
least 15 days.

2. Squeeze-out (Art. 41, para. 3 of the Royal Decree of 8 November 1989)

509. As part of a share purchase, a physical person or legal entity owning 95 per cent or
more of the securities of a public company following an acquisition of control may
convert a mandatory takeover bid into a purchase offer under Article 513 of the
Company Code. The securities not offered after the closure of the offer are considered transferred to the bidder by operation of law.

I. Squeeze-out

510. Article 513 of the Company Code (as well as the relevant Royal Decree implementing this provision) sets out the procedure for a squeeze-out or purchase offer.
An important distinction must be made between public companies and non-public
companies. In case of a non-public company, a shareholder is entitled to retain
ownership to the shares, if he expressly indicates such in a written manner.

§1. Public companies

511. A physical person or legal entity may acquire through a purchase offer all voting
securities of a Belgian public limited liability company if it holds alone, or in
concert with another person, 95 per cent of the voting securities of that company,
upon the following conditions:

    (i) The offeror must make a public offer for: (a) all voting securities, which may
or may not represent capital, not yet owned by the offeror, affiliated persons

or persons acting in concert with the offeror; and (b) all securities that give a right to subscribe to, acquire or convert those securities.

(ii) The offeror must alone (directly or indirectly) or in mutual concert own 95 per cent of the voting securities (including the voting securities of affiliated persons or persons acting in concert with the offeror).

(iii) The price must be a sum of money available in a bank account or under an unconditional and irrevocable bank credit.

(iv) The terms of the offer must be in line with the above-mentioned Royal Decree and must (in particular regarding the price) safeguard the minority shareholders' interests.

(v) The offeror is not allowed to acquire securities under conditions other than those of the offer (except if it extends those conditions to everybody).

(vi) A credit institution or a stock company should intervene and pay the price.

512. Before launching a purchase offer, an offeror must give the Banking and Finance Commission: (i) a notice of one month in advance; (ii) a draft prospectus; (iii) a report of an independent expert; and (iv) the board of director's opinion on the prospectus.

513. The prospectus must clearly indicate that:

(i) any increase of the price will apply to all securities' holders who accepted the bid before the increase; and

(ii) any acceptance before the prospectus is made public is not binding on the securities' holders.

514. The Banking and Finance Commission must make the notice public not later than one day after receiving the notice. This publication must also indicate where the public can obtain, without any charges, the expert report. On the same day, the management committee of the stock exchange, the competent market authorities and the target company will be informed.

515. Upon publication of the notice, neither the offeror, the company nor persons acting in mutual concert may make documents public or make declarations or communications which might influence the public.

516. After the issuance to the public of the notice to the Banking and Finance Commission, the minority shareholders have 15 days to provide comments to the Banking and Finance Commission (especially regarding the price of the securities). The Banking and Finance Commission may then decide to send such comments to the offeror, the target company, the stock market authorities, the securities holders and the public.

517. The offeror then has 15 days to react to those remarks and to modify its offer in a way more favourable to the securities holders. At the end of this period, the Banking and Finance Commission decides whether to approve the prospectus.

518. Once the contents of the prospectus have been approved, any new element arising that may influence the decision of the holders of securities must be dealt with in the supplement to the prospectus. The supplement must be approved by the Banking & Finance Commission and publicly announced in the same way as the prospectus.

519. The offering must last at least 10 days and at most 20 days, starting from the date of publication of the prospectus. The results of the purchase offer procedure must be published within the 5 days following the closing of the offering.

§2. Non-public companies

520. A physical person or legal entity may acquire through a purchase offer all voting securities of a Belgian non-public limited liability company if it holds alone or with another person 95 per cent of the voting securities of that company, whereby, in principle, the same conditions of a purchase offer for the securities of a public company will apply.

521. Unlike a purchase offer for securities of a public company, however, the Banking and Finance Commission does not intervene nor does an independent expert.

522. The offeror must draft a detailed written report mentioning all necessary information so the owners of the securities can make a comprehensive judgement about the transaction. This report must include information about the offeror, the transaction and the company. A report by an accountant or a certified auditor and the opinion of the board of directors of the target must be attached to the offeror's report. The accountant or certified auditor must certify that the valuation methods are adapted to the specific characteristics of the company. Moreover, they must indicate whether the price offered safeguards the interests of the holders of the securities. The board of director's opinion must include the same information as for a purchase offer on securities of a public company.

523. The minority shareholders have 30 days to make comments to the offeror, especially regarding the valuation and the price, from the second publication of the offer or from sending the registered letter. The offeror has 15 days to maintain its offer or to modify it in a way more favourable to the holders of the securities. In both cases, the offeror must make its decision public. If all securities are registered, this is done in a single publication in a nationally distributed and in a re-

gional paper. This publication must include the starting date and the closing date of the offering and any modifications to the first offer.

524. The offering must last at least 10 days and no more than 20 days, starting from the second notification.

525. The ownership of the securities transfers by law to the offeror upon payment of the price, unless the owner explicitly objects in writing.

IV. DIVISIONS, DEMERGERS AND SPLIT-UPS

A. Forms of a division

526. The Company Code covers the division by acquisition, the division by incorporation of new companies and the division through a mix of both acquisition and incorporation. The focus of the discussion below will be on transactions involving companies havind adopted the form of an NV/SA.

B. Definition

§1. Division by acquisition

527. A division by acquisition is the legal act by which one company, following its winding up without liquidation, transfers all of its assets and liabilities to several other companies, in exchange for the issue of shares to the shareholders of the dissolving company and, if necessary, for the payment of an additional cash amount, the value of which is not more than one tenth of the nominal value or the par value of the issued shares (Art. 673 of the Company Code).

§2. Division by incorporation of new companies

528. A division by incorporation of new companies is the legal act by which a company, following its winding up without liquidation, transfers, all of its assets and liabilities to several new companies formed specifically for this purpose, in exchange for the issue of shares by the newly formed company to the shareholders of the dissolving company, increased, if necessary, by an additional cash amount, the value of which may not be more than one tenth of the nominal value or the par value of the issued shares (Art. 674 of the Company Code).

§3. Mixed division

529. A mixed division is the legal act by which, following its winding up without liquidation, a company transfers to one or more existing companies and to one or more
new companies formed by it, all its assets and liabilities, in exchange for the issue
of shares to the shareholders of the dissolving company.

C. Procedure (Arts. 728 through Art 758 of the Company Code)

530. The procedure for division of a company under Belgian law is very similar to the
procedure applicable to mergers of companies. The main difference occurs when
the proposal does not allow for the determination of the allocation of a given asset.
In this case, the element of assets or its exchange value shall be shared proportionally among the beneficiary companies.

4. ACCOUNTING

I. INTRODUCTION

531. This chapter contains a discussion of the rules that govern the establishment and maintenance of the accounting system of commercial businesses, as well as the preparation of the inventory and financial statements of such businesses. In addition, this chapter provides an overview of current disclosure requirements and briefly explains the role of certified accountants and statutory auditors in the commercial businesses' compliance with the accounting and auditing rules.

II. APPLICABLE LAW

A. Principal legislation

532. The principal legislation relating to accounting and auditing is the Law of 17 July 1975 on Accounting (as amended) (*Wet op de boekhouding van de ondernemingen/ Loi relative a la comptabilité des entreprises* – the "Law on Accounting"). The Law on Accounting sets out the basic rules with respect to accounting requirements and principles of valuation.

533. The Law on Accounting is complemented by a number of Royal Decrees that regulate in detail various aspects of the accounting system and financial reporting. A first Royal Decree of 12 September 1983, as amended (the "First 1983 Decree"), regulates mainly the simplified system of accounting which applies to small unincorporated businesses and partnerships and sets forth the requirements regarding the preparation and retention of books. A second Royal Decree of 12 September 1983 (the "Second 1983 Decree") lays down the content and presentation of a minimum standard chart of accounts.

534. Reporting and disclosure requirements of commercial businesses are regulated by a number of provisions contained in the Company Code of 7 May 1999 (*Wetboek van Vennootschappen/Code des Sociétés* – the Company Code – *See*, Chapter 2), which is complemented by the Royal Decree of 30 January 2001 (the "2001 Decree").

535. Guidelines on the interpretation of the rules regarding accounting and auditing in Belgium are laid down in several opinions and recommendations issued from time to time by the Commission for Accounting Standards *(Commissie voor Boekhoud-kundige Normen/Commission des Normes Comptables* – the "CAS"). The CAS was created both to assist the Government and the Parliament with matters of accounting law and to issue opinions and recommendations that would contribute to the development of principles of proper accounting *(See,* Art. 13 of the Law on Accounting). While not legally binding, the opinions and recommendations of the CAS are of high authoritative value. They are published at regular intervals.

536. Banks and credit institutions, insurance companies and, to a certain extent, holding companies are subject to particular sets of accounting, auditing and reporting rules that are designed for their specific activities. These specific rules will not be discussed in this chapter.

B. Scope of the Law on Accounting and its implementing Royal Decrees

537. The Law on Accounting applies to all businesses listed in its Article 1. These include:
   (i) individual traders;
   (ii) commercial companies listed in the Company Code, civil companies which have adopted the form of a commercial company, European economic interest groupings and other economic interest groupings;
   (iii) public institutions with a statutory mission of a commercial, financial or industrial nature;
   (iv) specific categories of entities not listed under the above second and third indents which engage in commercial, financial or industrial activities and to which the Law on Accounting has been made applicable by Royal Decree.

538. Very small unincorporated businesses with a turnover not exceeding € 500,000 are exempt from a large number of requirements which would normally result from the application of the Law on Accounting and its implementing Decrees.

539. Branches of foreign companies also fall under the scope of the Law on Accounting. Article 1 of the Law on Accounting specifies that books, accounting records and supporting documentation of such branches must be kept in Belgium. Belgian branches of foreign companies which do not have their own revenues from the supply of goods or services are, however, no longer subject to the rules imposed by the Second 1983 Decree pertaining to the minimum standard chart of accounts.

Table 1: Overview of the application of the rules governing accounting and financial reporting requirements (1)

Obligations in respect of	I *Businesses which, irrespective of their legal form, do not satisfy more than one of the following criteria:* • *personnel: 50* • *turnover: € 6,250,000* • *balance sheet total: € 3,125,000 unless the total number of employees of such businesses exceeds 100 (2)*	II *Businesses other than those identified in I*
1. Accounting	Are required to maintain a complete accounting system in accordance with Arts. 3 and 4 of the Law on Accounting.	
2. Chart of accounts	Are required to maintain a chart of accounts in accordance with the minimum standard chart of accounts provided by the Second 1983 Decree. (3)	
3. Inventory of assets	Are required to establish an annual inventory in accordance with the rules of valuation. (3)	
4. Annual accounts	Are required to establish annual accounts in accordance with the rules of valuation and presentation. (3) Annual accounts may be in abridged form.	Annual accounts must be drawn up following the complete presentation.

112

5. Publication	a) Businesses operating under the form of: (i) a public limited company (*naamloze vennootschap/société anonyme*); (ii) a closely held limited company (*besloten vennootschap met beperkte aansprakelijkheid/société privée à responsabilité limitée*); (iii) a co-operative company with limited liability (*coöperatieve vennootschap met beperkte aansprakelijkheid/société coopérative à responsabilité limitée*); (iv) a limited company with shares (*commanditaire vennootschap op aandelen/société en commandite par actions*); (v) an economic interest grouping (*economisch samenwerkingsverband/groupement d'intérêt économique*) are required by Article 98 of the Company Code to publish their annual accounts by filing them with the National Bank of Belgium (*Nationale Bank van België/Banque Nationale de Belgique*); b) Businesses operating under the form of: – a general partnership (*vennootschap onder firma/société en nom collectif*); – a limited partnership (*gewone commanditaire vennootschap/société en commandite simple*); – a co-operative company with unlimited liability (*coöperatieve vennootschap met onbeperkte aansprakelijkheid/société cooperative à responsabilité illimitée*) are not required to publish their annual accounts.	are required to publish their annual accounts in accordance with Article 98 of the Company Code. (4)

Notes to Table 1

1. This overview does not take account of the less stringent rules that apply to mall unincorporated businesses or partnerships whose turnover does not exceed € 500,000.
2. Article 15 of the Company Code.
3. Not applicable to branches of foreign companies established in Belgium which do not have revenues from the supply of goods or services to third parties or to the foreign company of which they form part.
4. Not applicable to partnerships or co-operatives with unlimited liability composed of natural persons.

540. Non-profit associations *(verenigingen zonder winstoogmerk/associations sans but lucratif)* do not normally come within the scope of the Law on Accounting, unless a given association is considered to be a commercial business in accordance with the pertinent rules of the Commercial Code. The statutory context of these associations is, however, under revision, and it is likely that the accounting requirements for such associations will be increased.

541. An overview of the application of the rules of the Law on Accounting and its implementing Decrees is given in Table 1. Table 1 also contains references to the relevant provisions of the Company Code and demonstrates that certain businesses (small unincorporated businesses, branches of foreign companies, small and medium-sized companies) may benefit from less stringent rules as regards accounting, reporting and disclosure requirements.

C. Accounting records

542. The Law on Accounting sets out the general legal requirements as regards the keeping of accounting records. First and foremost, the Law on Accounting requires each business to maintain an accounting system that is best suited to its nature and size (Art. 2 of the Law on Accounting). In addition, the accounting system should encompass the totality of a business's operations, assets, rights, liabilities, debts and commitments (Art. 3 of the Law on Accounting).

543. The accounting system must include a system of books and accounts and must be maintained in conformity with generally accepted rules of double-entry bookkeeping (Art. 4 of the Law on Accounting). All transactions must be recorded chronologically, on a timely basis and in a true and complete manner. This should be done in either a central journal or an auxiliary journal that may be subdivided into individual journals. The entries must be made consistently in the relevant ledger accounts (Art. 4). If auxiliary or individual journals are used, the entries must be consolidated in the central journal at least on a monthly basis (Art. 4 of the Law on Accounting).

544. The accounts used must be specified in a chart of accounts that must be adapted according to the activities of the business (Art. 4 of the Law on Accounting). The minimum standard chart of accounts is provided by the Second 1983 Decree.

545. Each entry must be justified by a reference to a dated supporting document. The supporting documents (either original documents or photocopies) must be kept for a period of 10 years. However, documents not required for evidentiary purposes against third parties do not have to be kept longer than 3 years (Art. 6 of the Law on Accounting).

546. The Law on Accounting contains a number of requirements regarding the way in which books should be used (Arts. 7 and 8 of the Law on Accounting). The books must be numbered and form an uninterrupted series for each category. The books must be identified by category and must state their place in the series. They must mention the name of the business. The books have to be kept in a manner that ensures physical continuity as well as regularity and irreversibility of the entries. They must be kept in chronological order and may not contain blanks or omissions. When corrections are made, the original entry must remain legible. Books must be kept for a period of 10 years starting on 1 January of the year following the year in which the books were closed.

D. Inventory

547. According to Article 9 of the Law on Accounting, every business is required, at least once a year, to make the necessary inspections, verifications and assessments in order to establish a complete inventory of its assets and liabilities. The inventory must be prepared in accordance with the presentation of the chart of accounts of the business.

548. The ledger accounts must be reconciled with the data provided by the inventory, summarised and laid down in the annual accounts. The annual accounts (*jaarrekening/comptes annuels*) are composed of a balance sheet (*balans/bilan*), a profit and loss statement (*resultatenrekening/compte des résultats*) and explanatory notes to the accounts (*toelichting/annexe*) (Art. 92 of the Company Code). The annual accounts must give a "true and fair view" of the assets and liabilities, the financial position and the results of the business.

549. Article 28 of the 2001 Decree provides that every business must determine its own valuation rules in accordance with the legal requirements and the particular nature of the business. The valuation rules pertain to a variety of matters including depreciation, devaluations and revaluations, as well as provisions for liability and charges. These rules must be determined by the body responsible for the management of the business and must be stated in the book in which the annual accounts and the inventory documents are recorded. Moreover, the rules must be summarised in the notes to the accounts. The valuation rules are in principle based on the assumption that the business will be carried on as a going concern.

550. Article 30 of the 2001 Decree requires that, as a general rule, the valuation rules should be applied consistently from one financial year to another. Pursuant to Article 31 of the 2001 Decree, each asset and liability must be subject to individual valuation. Valuations, depreciation, devaluations and provisions for liabilities and

charges must satisfy the criteria of prudence, sincerity and good faith (Art. 32 of the 2001 Decree).

III. FINANCIAL STATEMENTS

A. Content

551. Within 30 days following the approval of the annual accounts, the annual accounts must be deposited with the National Bank of Belgium (*Nationale Bank van België/ Banque Nationale de Belgique*). The annual accounts comprise a balance sheet, a profit and loss statement and notes to the accounts. The 2001 Decree specifies the mandatory presentation and headings of the annual accounts. An English version of the mandatory presentation of the balance sheet and the profit and loss statement is given in Table 2. There are 2 optional formats for the profit and loss statement. Only the format in so-called "vertical form" is contained in the table.

Table 2: Presentation of the balance sheet and of the profit and loss statement

1. PRESENTATION OF THE BALANCE SHEET

Assets

Fixed Assets

I. Formation expenses

II. Intangible assets

III. Tangible assets

    A. Land and buildings

    B. Plant, machinery and equipment

    D. Furniture and vehicles

    E. Assets under construction and advance payments

IV. Financial assets

    A. Affiliated enterprises

        1. Investments

        2. Amounts receivable

B. Other enterprises linked by participating interests
1. Investments
2. Amounts receivable
C. Other financial assets
1. Shares
2. Amounts receivable and cash guarantees

Current Assets

V. Amounts receivable after one year
A. Trade debtors
B. Other amounts receivable
VI. Stocks and contracts in progress
A. Stocks
1. Raw materials and consumables
2. Work in progress
3. Finished goods
4. Goods purchased for resale
5. Immovable property acquired
6. Advance payments
B. Contracts in progress
VII. Amounts receivable within one year
A. Trade debtors
B. Other investments and deposits
VIII. Investments
A. Own shares
B. Other amounts receivable
IX. Cash at bank and in hand
X. Deferred charges and accrued income
TOTAL ASSETS

Liabilities

Capital and Reserves

I. Capital

    A. Issued Capital

    B. Uncalled capital

II. Share premium account

III. Revaluation surplus

IV. Reserves

    A. Legal reserve

    B. Reserves not available for distribution

        1. In respect of own shares held

        2. Other

    C. Untaxed reserves

    D. Reserves available for distribution

V. Accumulated profits (losses)

VI. Investment grants

Provisions for Liabilities and Charges

VII. Provisions and deferred taxes

    A. Provisions for liabilities and charges

        1. Pensions and similar obligations

        2. Taxation

        3. Major repairs and maintenance

        4. Other liabilities and charges

    B. Deferred taxes

Creditors

VIII. Amounts payable after one year

    A. Financial debts

        1. Subordinated loans

        2. Unsubordinated debentures

        3. Leasing and similar obligations

        4. Credit institutions

5. Other loans
B. Trade debts
   1. Suppliers
   2. Bills of exchange payable
C. Advances received on contracts in progress
D. Other amounts payable

IX. Amounts payable within one year
A. Current portion of amounts payable after one year
B. Financial debts
   1. Credit institutions
   2. Other loans
C. Trade debts
   1. Suppliers
   2. Bills of exchange payable
D. Advances received on contracts in progress
E. Taxes, remuneration and social security
   1. Taxes
   2. Remuneration and social security
F. Other amounts payable

X. Accrued charges and deferred income

TOTAL LIABILITIES

2. PRESENTATION OF THE PROFIT AND LOSS STATEMENT
(presentation in vertical form)

I. Operating income
A. Turnover
B. Increase (+) or decrease (–) in stocks of finished goods and work and contracts in progress
C. Fixed assets – own construction
D. Other operating income

II. Operating charges
A. Raw materials, consumables and goods for resale

    1. Purchase

    2. Increase (–) or decrease (+) in stocks

  B. Services and other goods

  C. Remuneration, social security costs and pensions

  D. Depreciation, and amounts written off formation expenses and intangible and tangible fixed assets

  E. Increase (+) or decrease (–) in amounts written off stocks, contracts in progress and trade debtors

  F. Increase (+) or decrease (–) in provisions for liabilities and charges

  G. Other operating charges

III. Operating profit (+)

Operating loss (–)

IV. Financial income

  A. Income from financial fixed assets

  B. Income from current assets

  C. Other financial income

V. Financial charges

  A. Interest and other debt charges

  B. Increase (+) or decrease (–) in amounts written off current assets other than those mentioned under II E

  C. Other financial charges

VI. Profit on ordinary activities before taxes (+)

Loss on ordinary activities before taxes (–)

VII. Extraordinary income

  A. Adjustments to the depreciation of and to other amounts written off intangible and tangible fixed assets

  B. Adjustments to amounts written off financial fixed assets

  C. Adjustments to provisions for extraordinary liabilities and charges

  D. Gain on disposal of fixed assets

  E. Other extraordinary income

VIII. Extraordinary charges

  A. Extraordinary depreciation of and extraordinary amounts written off formation expenses, intangible and tangible fixed assets

B. Amounts written off financial fixed assets

C. Provisions for extraordinary liabilities and charges

D. Loss on disposal of fixed assets

E. Other extraordinary charges

IX. Profit for the year before taxes

Loss for the year before taxes

IX *bis*. A. Transfer to deferred taxes

B. Transfer from deferred taxes

X. Income taxes

A. Income taxes

B. Adjustment of income taxes and write-back of tax provisions

XI. Profit for the year

Loss for the year

XII. Transfer to untaxed reserves

Transfer from untaxed reserves

XIII. Profit for the year available for appropriation

Loss for the year available for appropriation

Appropriation Account

A. Profit to be appropriated. Loss to be appropriated

1. Profit for the year available for appropriation

Loss for the year available for appropriation

2. Profit brought forward. Loss brought forward

B. Transfers from capital and reserves

1. From capital and share premium account

2. From reserves

C. Appropriations to capital and reserves

1. To capital and share premium account

2. To the legal reserve

3. To other reserves

D. Result to be carried forward

1. Profit to be carried forward

2. Loss to be carried forward

E. Shareholders' contribution in respect of losses

F. Distribution of profit

    1. Dividends

    2. Directors' entitlements

    3. Other allocations

B. Consolidated accounts

552. The Company Code and the 2001 Decree contain a system of consolidated accounting. Pursuant to Article 110 of the Company Code, each parent company is required to establish consolidated annual accounts and a consolidated annual report if it controls, solely or jointly, one or more Belgian or foreign subsidiaries. The term "control" is defined in Article 5 of the Company Code in such a manner that control can be exercised independently or jointly. Moreover, Article 5 makes a distinction between instances where control will be deemed to exist automatically (Art. 5, para. 2 of the Company Code), and instances where the existence of control must be established by reference to concrete circumstances (Art. 5, para. 3 of the Company Code). The 2001 Decree lists a number of exemptions from the obligation to consolidate in Articles 107 through 111. Articles 113 through 132 of the 2001 Decree discuss in detail the structure of the consolidated accounts and the rules of valuation that apply to them. Articles 133 *et seq.* of the 2001 Decree state the various consolidation methods available. The 2001 Decree also contains specific rules that govern the consolidated annual report, the audit of the consolidated accounts and their publication.

C. Control of the annual accounts

553. Article 141 of the Company Code requires public limited liability companies (*naamloze vennootschappen/sociétés anonymes*), closely held limited liability companies (*besloten vennootschappen met beperkte aansprakelijkheid/sociétés privées à responsabilité limitée*), co-operative companies with limited liability (*coöperatieve vennootschappen met beperkte aansprakelijkheid/sociétés cooperatives à responsabilité limitée*) and limited partnerships with shares (*commanditaire vennootschappen op aandelen/sociétés en commandite par actions*) to appoint one or more statutory auditors (*bedrijfsrevisoren/reviseurs d'entreprises*) if they exceed more than one of the thresholds mentioned in Article 15 of the Company Code or

employ more than 100 employees. It is the task of a statutory auditor to monitor the financial position of the company, its annual accounts as well as the regularity of the operations which are reflected in the annual accounts. In addition, general partnerships (*vennootschappen onder firma/sociétés en nom collectif*), limited partnerships (*gewone commanditaire vennootschappen/ sociétés en commandite simple*), and co-operative companies with unlimited liability (*coöperatieve vennootschappen met onbeperkte aansprakelijkheid/sociétés cooperatives à responsabilité illimitée*) must also appoint an auditor if they exceed more than one of the thresholds mentioned in Article 15 of the Company Code or employ more than 100 employees. However, general partnerships, limited partnerships and co-operative companies with unlimited liability are not required to appoint an auditor if all the shareholders are natural persons.

554. Economic interest groupings (*economische samenwerkingsverbanden/ groupements d'intérêt économique*) and European economic interest groupings (*Europese economische samenwerkingsverbanden/groupements européens d'intérêt économique*) are under an obligation to appoint a statutory auditor if one of their members is subjected to the statutory regime of financial control.

555. Statutory auditors are appointed by the general shareholders' meeting and, if applicable, by the works council for a renewable period of 3 years. Audit fees are based on a fixed fee that is negotiated between the company and the auditor prior to his appointment. The audit fee has to be approved by the general shareholders' meeting.

556. The Company Code emphasises the importance of the independence of auditors. By means of the Law of 2 August 2002, the Belgian legislator even increased the level of independence of the auditors by amending Article 133 of the Company Code with respect to the provision of additional services and employment with the audit client.

557. Auditors will no longer be able to take up a mandate as director, manager or any other function within a period of 2 years after the termination of their mandate as auditor of a specific company or affiliate thereof.

558. Neither an auditor, nor any of its employees, affiliates of partners with whom the auditor has a professional relationship, may perform any "services" additional to the ones required by law for as far as the total amount of such services would exceed the agreed fixed remuneration. Services provided to audit the financial and economic data of companies recently acquired by the company or any of its subsidiaries will, however, not be taken into account. This obligation is, however,

limited to "services" provided to listed companies and companies belonging to a group of companies required to draft consolidated accounts.

559. The rules on "additional services", however, do not apply if:
   (i) the additional services were approved by an audit committee, as established within the company by the articles of association;
   (ii) the new "Advice and Control Commission" (providing advice on the compatibility of specific services with the auditor's independence) granted a positive advice; or
   (iii) a committee of mutually independent auditors was set up within the company.

560. An auditor can in any case not consider himself independent if, during his mandate or within a period 2 years prior to his mandate, the auditor, one of his employees, affiliates of a partner with whom he has a professional relationship, performed "services" (that are not required by law) to the company for which such auditor audits the annual accounts, its Belgian affiliates or a foreign subsidiary thereof. At a later stage, the list of such "services" will be specified by Royal Decree.

D. Reporting requirements

561. A number of businesses are required to publish their annual accounts. This requirement may either be the consequence of the legal form in which the business in question operates (for example, a public limited liability company), or stem from the size of the business (for example, a large co-operative company with unlimited liability). These rules are summarised in Table 1 above.

562. The annual accounts must be deposited with the National Bank of Belgium within 30 days following their approval. At the same time, a number of additional documents must be deposited (Art. 100 of the Company Code), namely:
   (i) a document containing the name (forename and surname), profession and place of residence of each of the directors and statutory auditors;
   (ii) the allocation of the financial result;
   (iii) a document describing the status of the corporate capital (See, Art. 479 of the Company Code);
   (iv) a document containing the dates on which amendments to the company's articles of association were published;
   (v) the report of the statutory auditor; and
   (vi) the annual report prepared by the company directors pursuant to Article 95 of the Company Code.

IV. AUDITING AND ACCOUNTING PROFESSIONS

A. Auditing profession

563. Statutory auditors play an important role in the financial control of Belgian enterprises. For many businesses, their appointment is mandatory. Statutory auditors are all members of the Institute of Statutory Auditors (*Instituut der bedrijfsrevisoren/ Institut des réviseurs d'entreprises* – the "Institute"). The Institute was established by the Law of 22 July 1953. Its functions are the organisation of the auditing profession, the training of candidate-auditors, the adoption of technical, ethical and disciplinary regulations and the monitoring of its members' compliance with these regulations.

B. Accounting profession

564. The Law of 21 February 1985 (Arts. 69 *et seq.*) governs the status and role of certified accountants (*accountants/experts-comptables*). While the accounting and auditing rules confer a less visible role as regards the financial control of businesses on accountants than on statutory auditors, there is, nonetheless, an elaborate set of rules which regulates the accounting profession and entrusts accountants with specific statutory tasks. The Institute of Accountants (*Instituut der accountants/Institut des experts-comptables*) must supervise the training of new accountants, organise the profession and act as a disciplinary and ethical body.

5. TAXATION

565. Foreigners doing business in Belgium will inevitably have to face certain aspects of the Belgian tax system. As a corporate entity or as an individual, they may be subject to income tax. If they supply goods or services to Belgians or in Belgium, questions of value added tax will arise. Foreigners will also encounter a variety of other taxation questions. Attention will therefore be given to the most important registration taxes which are due on business or personal transactions and, briefly, inheritance tax. Customs and excise duties are dealt with in Chapter 6. Belgium also has a wide variety of very specific taxes, for example, taxes or duties on insurance contracts, on the use of a car, on gambling machines and on the issuing of official documents. These taxes and duties are not discussed in this book.

I. INTRODUCTION

A. Main tax categories

§1. National taxes

566. Belgium's tax system can be divided into 4 main categories of taxes levied at the national level:
  (i) income taxes (*inkomstenbelastingen/impôts sur les revenus*);
  (ii) value added tax (*belasting op de toegevoegde waarde/taxe sur la valeur ajoutée*);
  (iii) registration taxes (*registratierechten/droits d'enregistrement*); and
  (iv) customs duties and excise duties (*douane- en accijnsrechten/droits de douanes et d'accises*).

567. These taxes are governed by a series of separate tax codes, each specifically regulating a particular tax:
  (i) the Income Tax Code (*Wetboek van de inkomstenbelastingen/Code des impôts sur les revenus* – the "ITC"), as further implemented by the Royal Decree implementing the Income Tax Code (*Koninklijk Besluit tot uitvoering van het WIB/Arrêté Royal d'exécution du CIR* – the "RD-ITC");

- the Value Added Tax Code (*Wetboek van de belasting over de toegevoegde waarde/Code de la taxe sur la valeur ajoutée*);
- the Registration and Mortgage Tax Code (*Wetboek der registratie, hypotheek en griffierechten/Code des droits d'enregistrement, d'hypothèque et de greffe*); and
- the Code on Customs and Excise Duties (*Wetboek van douane- en accijnsrechten/Code des droits de douanes et d'accises*).

§2. Local taxes

568. Communities (*gemeenschappen/communautés*), regions (*gewesten/régions*), provinces (*provincies/provinces*) and municipalities (*gemeenten/communes*) are financed or co-financed through allocations by the national government. However, the regions, provinces and municipalities also have limited taxation powers and may impose local levies. These typically take the form of surcharges on income tax, or specific levies, such as a tax on personnel employed, on the use of energy, sewers, roads, motorcycles and so on. More recently, local taxes have also been levied to protect the quality of the environment. Starting in 1997, the inheritance tax originally levied as a national or federal tax has been transformed into a regional tax.

§3. International tax treaties

569. Belgium maintains an extensive network of double taxation treaties with all Western European countries, except Iceland, and with many other major countries. Most of these treaties are based upon the OECD Model Convention. A notable exception is the tax treaty concluded with France.

B. Amount of taxes received

570. Total fiscal receipts in Belgium for 2001 amounted to € 73.14 billion. Total fiscal receipts for 2002 are estimated at € 74.5 billion, representing an approximate 2 per cent increase as compared to 2001. Major sources of fiscal receipts are income taxes (more than 50 per cent) and VAT, registration and inheritance taxes (almost 30 per cent).

571. OECD statistics indicate that, in 1998, governments of the OECD Member States collected almost US$ 8 trillion in taxes. The countries with the highest tax/GDP ratio – over 45 per cent of GDP – are Sweden, Denmark, Finland, Belgium, France and Luxembourg. It should be noted that these statistics take into account all fiscal and parafiscal levies imposed by the EC Member States, whether at national or local level. While the tax level in Belgium, as measured as a percentage of GDP,

has fallen somewhat since 1985, Belgium still ranks as the fourth heaviest tax burden country among the OECD Member States.

572. In 1999, the Belgian Government announced its firm intention to proceed with a reduction of the income tax burden so as to bring it in line with that of Belgium's neighbouring countries. The first tangible effects are expected for assessment year 2002 (income year 2001) and substantially result from a reform of the individual income tax that will be implemented gradually over assessment years 2002 through 2005. In parallel, effective as of assessment year 2004, the Belgian Government has reduced the standard corporate income tax rate from 39 per cent to 33 per cent.

II. INDIVIDUAL INCOME TAX

A. Scope of taxation

573. Resident individuals are subject to individual income tax on their global world-wide income. However, some exemptions, deductions and credits are made with regard to non-Belgian source income in the ITC or in international tax treaties to which Belgium is a party, in order to avoid or limit double taxation.

574. An individual is considered to be a resident of Belgium for income tax purposes if his domicile, or normal residence, is in Belgium or if his seat of wealth (*zetel van fortuin/siège de la fortune*) is located in Belgium. The domicile, or customary residence, is defined as the place where an individual maintains a residence under circumstances indicating that this residence is to be retained permanently. The seat of wealth criterion implies that an individual who has no customary residence in Belgium, but whose centre of wealth, where actual management decisions are made, is located in Belgium, will also be considered to be a resident taxpayer. Individuals who are registered in the National Register of Individuals (*Rijksregister van de natuurlijke personen/Registre national des personnes physiques*) are deemed to be residents of Belgium, unless they provide evidence to the contrary. Effective as of 1994, an irrefutable presumption applies pursuant to which married taxpayers (who are not treated as single taxpayers) are deemed to have their fiscal domicile where their household is established.

575. Foreign diplomats and career consular agents assigned to Belgium, as well as, under certain conditions, officials, agents or representatives of foreign countries and officials of international organisations, are not subject to Belgian individual income tax.

B. Sources of taxable income

576. Resident individuals are subject to Belgian individual income tax on income derived from the following sources:
    (i) real property;
    (ii) personal property;
    (iii) business and professional activities and employment; and
    (iv) miscellaneous sources.

577. Although the tax on each source of taxable income is computed on a different basis, with separate rules applying to withholding tax and tax credits, total taxable income equals the total income from all 4 sources. A few types of income, such as certain capital gains, income from occasional services and certain other miscellaneous income, are not included in the total amount of taxable income and are, in general, taxed separately at flat rather than progressive rates. Each of the different income categories is briefly discussed below.

C. Income from real property

§1. Taxable income

578. The determination of the taxable income derived by resident taxpayers from real property is dependent upon the use of such property and the location thereof, *i.e.*, whether in Belgium or abroad. The following 4 categories may be distinguished:
    (i) privately used property;
    (ii) real property used for professional purposes;
    (iii) rented real property located in Belgium; and
    (iv) real property located outside Belgium

1. Privately used property

579. The amount of taxable income from real property located in Belgium that is not used for professional activities is equal to the presumed or deemed annual net rental income of the property. This presumed income, the so-called cadastral income (*kadastraal inkomen/revenu cadastral*), is determined by an official appraisal that should be revised every 10 years. However, the last revision took place in 1975. Because of the long periods of time between revisions, assessed net rental income usually reflects only a fraction of actual rental income. Pending a general revision, the cadastral income is adjusted annually on the basis of the retail price index in order to reduce the difference between the actual rental and cadastral income.

580. Taxable income from second residences that are not rented is equal to the cadastral income plus 40 per cent.

2. *Real property used for professional purposes*

581. If the owner uses part of his property for professional or business activities, the corresponding fraction of the cadastral income will be included in the taxable income as income from the business or professional activity, not as income from real property.

3. *Rented real property located in Belgium*

582. When the real property is rented to an individual who uses the property for private habitation purposes, the taxable income is the cadastral income increased by 40 per cent. The tax base is different when the property is rented to a lessee who uses it for professional or business purposes. Irrespective of whether such lessee is an individual, a company, a public entity or an entity without legal personality, the tax base will be equal to the amount of the actual net rent received (but not less than the cadastral income). For this purpose and subject to certain corrections, the net rent corresponds to 90 per cent (for land) or to 60 per cent (for buildings) of the gross rent received, the deductions representing maintenance and repair costs.

4. *Real property located outside Belgium*

583. A resident's income from real property located outside Belgium is calculated on the basis of the presumed rental value if the property is not rented, and on the basis of the actual net rent and rental charges received if it is rented. No distinction is made between property that is used for residential purposes and property that is used for business or professional purposes. The tax base corresponds either to the rental value or to the rent and rental charges received after deduction of the foreign taxes directly related to the property and an additional 40 per cent (for buildings) or an additional 10 per cent (for land) for maintenance and repair expenses. Many tax treaties provide that income from Belgian-owned real property located abroad is taxable only in the foreign country and not in Belgium. In this case, the income will still be included in the taxpayer's taxable income, but only to determine the tax rate applicable to the total income, from which foreign real property income will have been deducted. In the absence of a tax treaty, Belgium grants unilateral tax relief by reducing the amount of Belgian income tax on foreign real property income by 50 per cent.

§2. Exemptions and deductions

584. The cadastral income of real property used, on a non-profit basis, for religious, educational or medical purposes is exempted from tax.

585. When real property cannot be completely used because of damage, destruction or any other reason, the cadastral income is reduced in accordance with the duration and importance of the reduction in the productivity of the property. The taxpayer must provide evidence that the non-productivity of the real property is of an involuntary nature.

586. Interest paid on debts incurred for the sole purpose of acquiring or maintaining real property is deductible from the real property income. The loan does not need to be secured by a mortgage in order for the interest to be deductible. The interest will be deducted from the total income from all real property even if the loan was entered into for the acquisition of only part of the property. If the amount of interest exceeds the income from the real property, the excess is not deductible from any other source of income, nor can it be carried over to previous or subsequent tax years.

587. If an individual taxpayer occupies a house that he owns, the cadastral income of the house is exempted up to € 3,000 plus an additional € 250 for the spouse and each dependent person living together with the taxpayer on 1 January of the tax year (the so-called "housing deduction"). These amounts are adjusted annually on the basis of the retail price index. For assessment year 2003 (income year 2002), the maximum exemption amounts to € 3,950 plus an additional € 330 for the spouse and each other person dependent on the taxpayer. If the house is also used for professional purposes, the exemption is reduced proportionally.

588. An additional interest deduction is granted to individual taxpayers for interest paid on mortgage loans concluded to acquire or construct a new house located in Belgium. The additional interest deduction, which is a deduction from global income rather than a deduction from real property income, only applies for the first building acquired or constructed by the taxpayer.

§3. Real property withholding tax

589. Individuals are subject to an advance levy on real property located in Belgium, *i.e.*, real property withholding tax (*onroerende voorheffing/précompte immobilier*). The real property withholding tax is calculated as a percentage of the cadastral income of the real property concerned. The basic rate of the withholding tax is 1.25 per cent of the cadastral income in the Walloon Region; 1.25 per cent of the cadastral

income in the Brussels Region; and 2.5 per cent in the Flemish Region. Reduced percentages apply to social housing. However, due to the surcharge which provincial and local authorities are entitled to levy on the basis of the real property withholding tax, the total burden generally amounts to between 30 per cent to 50 per cent of the cadastral income, depending on the municipality where the property is located.

590. Real property withholding tax is payable by the person who owns the building on 1 January of the taxable period, even if the property changes ownership between 1 January and the actual date on which the tax must be paid (which is usually in the course of the second half of the year). Therefore, agreements concerning the sale of real property usually contain an obligation undertaken by the purchaser to reimburse the seller that part of the withholding tax corresponding to the portion of the year after the date of the sale. While enforceable among the parties, the tax authorities continue to be entitled to claim the withholding tax from the selling party only.

591. Exemptions from, or reductions in, real property withholding tax are available for certain types of real property (*e.g.*, real property used for charitable purposes or real property falling within the public domain) or certain categories of taxpayers (*e.g.*, disabled persons).

592. The real property withholding tax pertaining to the taxpayer's principal private dwelling is creditable against his final individual income tax liability. In all other cases, the real property withholding tax constitutes a final tax. The tax credit is limited to 12.5 per cent of the cadastral income of the real property. The tax credit may only be applied when the cadastral income is included in the taxpayer's global taxable income. The latter requirement is important, as in many cases the housing deduction will lead to a situation where no real property income is effectively included in the taxpayer's global taxable income. This is even more important when the taxpayer has deductible interest available. In such cases, the housing deduction will only be applied if it is to the benefit of the taxpayer.

D. Income from capital and personal property

§1. Taxable income

593. Income from capital and personal property consists of several types of either Belgian or foreign origin income, the principle features of which are that it is derived from an investment and is not obtained through the performance of a business

activity. If the latter condition is not met, the income will be considered to be business income.

594. Income from capital and personal property include the following categories of income:
   (i) dividends;
  (ii) interest;
 (iii) royalties; and
 (iv) life annuities.

1. Dividends

595. Dividends include any benefits obtained from shares and profit parts, in any form, issued by a company. The shares concerned may be registered shares, bearer shares, ordinary shares or preference shares. Dividends also include total or partial reimbursements of a company's capital, where such reimbursements are not made pursuant to a decision to reduce that company's capital, that complies with applicable corporate law requirements. Dividends also include liquidation surpluses and gains resulting from redemption of a company's capital.

596. Interest on advances granted to their companies by directors of stock corporations, partners of private companies, their spouses and their children, are taxable as dividends if and to the extent that (i) such interest exceeds the market interest rate as defined in the statute, or (ii) the total amount of the interest-bearing cash advances exceeds the company's capital at the end of the taxable period plus the taxed reserves at the beginning of the taxable period.

2. Interest

597. Interest income includes, *inter alia*, interest, late interest (other than interest allowed by judgement or otherwise for late payment of a debt), premiums and any other revenues derived from (i) securities (whether or not carrying a right to fixed interest), (ii) loans not represented by securities, (iii) debt claims and (iv) cash deposits.

3. Royalties

598. Royalty income includes income from the lease of personal property as well as income derived from industrial and intellectual property rights and concession agreements.

4. *Life annuities*

599. Life annuities paid by a business or a legal entity are taxed at a rate of 3 per cent of the capital.

§2. *Exemptions*

600. The ITC provides for a number of tax exemptions for certain types of personal property income. The main exemptions relate to (i) income from preferred shares issued by the national railroad company; (ii) income from shares paid or attributed on the occasion of the total or partial reimbursement of the capital or on the occasion of a redemption of shares by non-resident companies or by qualifying Belgian investment companies; (iii) the total or partial reimbursement of a company's paid-in capital where such reimbursement is made in compliance with corporate law requirements; and (iv) the first € 1,250 per year and per household of interest derived from qualifying savings deposits.

601. Effective as of 1 January 2002, but with a grace period for liquidations that have been completed prior to 25 March 2002, distributions resulting from the total or partial reimbursement of a company's paid-in capital or resulting from a share redemption, are subject to a 10 per cent withholding tax.

§3. *Tax base*

602. In general, taxable income derived from capital and personal property consists of the total gross amount irrespective of recovery and maintenance costs as well as withholding tax, all of which may reduce the amount received but not the taxable income. For royalties and rentals, the taxable amount equals the gross amount less the expenditures or charges paid to acquire or preserve the income. If the taxpayer is not able to provide evidence of these expenditures or charges, he will be allowed to make a lump-sum deduction.

§4. *Personal property withholding tax*

603. When income from capital or personal property is distributed, the institution or person making the distribution must give notice to the tax authorities within 15 days of the payment and retain an amount equal to the withholding tax. The standard rate of the withholding tax is, in principle, 25 per cent for dividends and 15 per cent for personal property income other than dividends. Personal property withholding tax on interest from bonds and securities issued before 1 March 1990 is 25 per cent. Dividends paid on so-called "tax advantage" (*fiscaal voordeel/avantage fiscal*) shares (*AFV* shares) benefit from a reduced withholding tax of 20 per cent,

while certain categories of dividends on shares issued as of 1 January 1994, are eligible for a reduced rate of 15 per cent.

604. Income on which withholding tax has already been paid remains part of a taxpayer's taxable income, although the withholding tax paid may be credited in the calculation of final tax liability. Since 1984, taxpayers who have paid withholding tax, are no longer obliged to declare in their annual tax return the income on which the withholding tax has been retained. Taxpayers can choose between the 2 systems, unless it would appear that taxation at the progressive rates of the individual income tax applicable to the beneficiary's global taxable income were to be to his advantage. In principle, the latter will only be the case if the taxpayer's global taxable income is lower than the minimum taxable income.

E. Professional income

§1. Taxable income

605. Professional income includes all income resulting directly or indirectly from professional activities of any kind. It includes profits (*winsten/profits*), gains (*baten/bénéfices*), profits and gains resulting from a former professional activity, remuneration and salaries (*bezoldigingen/rémunérations*) and pensions, annuities and similar payments.

1. Profits

606. Profits include any income derived from industrial, commercial and agricultural enterprises carried on by individual taxpayers. The terms "industrial, commercial and agricultural operations" must be broadly interpreted and include, for example, trade activities, handicraft activities and the provision of services. Activities performed under private works agreements are also considered to fall into this category, although the distinction between such agreements and employment contracts is sometimes difficult to make. Transactions in real estate are considered to be business activities if performed by a real estate company or if the real estate concerned is used for professional activities. Moreover, transactions entered into by independent insurance agents or agents of financial institutions working under an agency contract are also considered to be business activities.

607. Article 24 of the ITC establishes 4 categories of taxable income derived from industrial, commercial or agricultural businesses.

608. The first category relates to income *sensu stricto*, *i.e.*, income directly or indirectly resulting from industrial, commercial or agricultural activities. Article 25 of the

ITC contains a non-exhaustive list of such income. It includes the salary which an entrepreneur takes for his personal labour and the benefits in kind which he obtains in the context of his activities, such as, for example, the use of a company car and related expenses paid by the company. Claims which are certain and the amounts of which are fixed are also considered to be income *sensu stricto*, as well as subsidies or premiums granted by governmental administrations or agencies, unless it is specifically provided that such premiums are tax-free. All abnormal payments made by a Belgian taxpayer to enterprises abroad which are linked directly or indirectly to the taxpayer or to any person or enterprise having a common interest therewith will be added to the income of the Belgian taxpayer. In addition, all abnormal payments made by a Belgian taxpayer to foreign persons or enterprises, which, in their home country, are subject to a considerably more advantageous tax regime, will also be included in the taxable income of the Belgian taxpayer. The amount of any abnormal payment made by a Belgian taxpayer to an individual or legal entity shall likewise be included in the taxable income, unless such payments are taken into account for the calculation of the taxes due by the beneficiary in Belgium.

609. The second category contains capital gains resulting from increases in the value of assets or decreases in the value of liabilities. All surplus value on assets used in the course of professional activities (including raw materials, products and merchandise) becomes taxable at the time that it is realised or expressed in the bookkeeping or the annual accounts of the taxpayer.

610. The third category relates to reserves that are present in the enterprise without having been realised or expressed in the accounts of the taxpayer (so-called "latent" reserves). In principle, such reserves are not taxable. An exception relates to non-expressed or non-realised gains on financial fixed assets and portfolio securities.

611. The fourth category relates to so-called "latent" or "hidden" reserves, *i.e.*, reserves resulting from a conscious and intentional under-valuation of assets or over-valuation of liabilities. Such reserves are treated as profits of the taxable period in which they are discovered, regardless of whether or not the normal assessment period has expired.

2. *Gains*

612. Gains include any income resulting from a liberal profession (*e.g.*, doctors, lawyers, dentists, architects and artists), a function or position (*e.g.*, bailiffs, notaries public) or any other profit-seeking activity. Income from these activities includes (i) any and all receipts, regardless of how they are named, obtained by said individuals, whether in cash or in kind; (ii) any capital gains realised on assets used for

the exercise of the professional activity; and (iii) any payments in lieu obtained to compensate for a decrease in activity, a decrease in gains or a temporary loss of gains.

3. Profits and gains resulting from a former professional activity

613. Capital gains realised or established on the occasion or by reason of the complete and definitive cessation of an enterprise, a liberal profession, a function or position, or any other profit-seeking activity, where such income is derived from gains on assets used for the professional activity, constitute profits and gains derived from a former professional activity. So-called forced capital gains realised or established as a direct consequence of the cessation of a business also fall into this category. For example, if a businessman ceases all activities due to the destruction of his factory by fire, the proceeds from the fire insurance policy are taxable as professional income. Other types of income falling into this category concern profits or gains acquired by the taxpayer before the cessation of the professional activity but effectively obtained after such cessation, and any compensation in lieu obtained after the cessation of the professional activity which compensates for a decrease in activity, a decrease in profits or gains, or a temporary loss of profits or gains.

4. Remuneration and salaries

614. Remuneration includes salaries of employees and remuneration of directors and active partners, regardless of the identity of the debtor, the qualification of the income or the manner in which such income is determined or attributed.

i. Salaries

615. The term "employee" refers to all employed persons working under an employment contract and those with similar arrangements, such as civil servants and trainees. In general, all compensation for an employee's activities paid by or on behalf of the employer constitutes income subject to personal income tax, regardless of the debtor, the qualification of the income or the means of payment used. Employees' remuneration can be divided into 2 main categories, *i.e.*, (a) income from professional activities and (b) income upon termination of employment relationships or replacement income.

(a) Income from professional activities

616. *General.* Income from professional activities includes all salaries, commissions, bonuses, tips and other similar payments obtained by an employee in the context of a professional activity. It also includes reimbursement by the employer of ex-

penses which are normally borne by the employee, such as housing or heating allowances. Compensation paid to an employee for expenses paid on behalf of the employer are not regarded as part of an employee's income. For example, travel expenses for sales representatives or allowances to buy special clothing required by safety regulations are not regarded as taxable income.

617. *Benefits in kind.* Income from professional activities also includes all benefits in kind provided for the employee's activities, which are also available to the employee for his private use, such as the personal use of a company car, free petrol and discounts on the purchase price of goods purchased from the employer. The value of such benefits must be established according to their real value to the recipient. The real value is normally the amount saved by the beneficiary by the benefits granted. Lump-sum valuations have been established for specific benefits, such as the use of a company car, interest-free loans and the services of a domestic servant or driver. Detailed rules on the calculation methods for these benefits are contained in the RD-ITC.

618. *Stock options.* Special rules for the valuation of the benefit in kind granted under stock option plans have been developed by the Law of 26 March 1999. The rules for determining the taxable benefit in kind distinguish between whether or not the stock options are listed or traded on a stock exchange. If the options are listed, the taxable benefit is determined on the basis of the closing price of the option on the day preceding the day of the offer. If the options are not listed, the taxable benefit is valued on a lump-sum basis corresponding to a percentage (in principle, 15 per cent) of the value of the underlying shares on the day of the offer. However, if the options are granted for a period exceeding 5 years (to be counted as of the date of the offer), this percentage is increased by one per cent for each year or fraction of a year that exceeds the 5-year period. If the exercise price of the option is lower than the value of the shares at the time of the offer, the difference must be added to the taxable benefit. The basic percentage of 15 per cent is reduced to 7.5 per cent if the following cumulative conditions are met: (i) the exercise price of the option must be determined at the time the offer is made; (ii) the option may not be exercised before the end of the third calendar year nor after the end of the tenth year following the calendar year in which the offer has been made; (iii) the option may not be transferred, except for reason of death; (iv) the option may not be covered by a hedge; and (v) the option must relate to shares of the company that is the employer of the beneficiary or to shares of another company that has a direct or indirect stake in that company. The option is deemed to be granted on the sixtieth day following the date on which the offer to participate in the stock option plan was made by the grantor to the beneficiary, even if the option is subject to condi-

tions precedent or subsequent. These rules are applicable to stock options granted as from 1 January 1999 onwards.

(b) Income upon termination of employment relationships and replacement income

619. Income resulting from the existence of a prior or suspended employment relationship includes the following types of income:
   (i) benefits granted as a result of the termination of employment (including compensation for the dismissal of employees, both in individual cases and when a business ceases trading). Indemnities falling within this category are taxed at the average rate of the total taxable income of the last year during which the taxpayer carried out a normal professional activity;
   (ii) compensation for temporary loss of income (especially including benefits which are granted on the basis of social security legislation in cases of illness, accident, unemployment or early retirement schemes, as well as other compensation paid by third parties who were liable for the loss of income); and
   (iii) remuneration which the employer pays to the employee after the employment terminates (or, after his death, to his widow and/or children).

ii. Directors of companies

620. In general, all income received by a person acting in the capacity of a director, receiver or other person who performs activities similar to those of a director in a Belgian or foreign stock company or in any similar legal entity is taxable income in this category (Art. 32 of the ITC). This is the case whether or not such income is received pursuant to an employment agreement.

iii. Remuneration of active partners in private limited liability companies and partnerships

621. The remuneration of active partners in private limited liability companies or in partnerships constitutes business income (Art. 33 of the ITC). Active partners are defined as those who are both shareholders of and actively involved in the management of the following types of companies: the general partnership (*vennootschap onder firma/société en nom collectif*), the limited partnership (*gewone commanditaire vennootschap/société en commandite simple*), the co-operative company (*coöperatieve vennootschap/société cooperative*) and the private limited liability company (*besloten vennootschap met beperkte aansprakelijkheid/société de personnes à responsabilité limitée*).

622. The taxable income of active partners in private limited liability companies or partnerships consists of all revenue received by such partners in payment for their professional activities in these companies. Revenue that does not represent remu-

neration for services rendered is excluded. In particular, the following types of income are excluded:

(i) income from invested capital and from interest on advances, which is taxable as personal property income;

(ii) revenue obtained from the total or partial liquidation of a company; and

(iii) refunds by the company to a partner of costs normally borne by the company and paid by a partner on behalf of the company.

5. Pensions and annuities

623. In general, all income which partially or totally compensates for a permanent loss of professional income is taxable as professional income. Permanent loss of income may result from a variety of causes such as retirement or physical disability, and the compensation may take a number of different forms (*e.g.*, interest or capital paid on the basis of a life insurance contract, social security payments and individual or collective private pension schemes). No distinction is made between employees or self-employed persons. The taxable person is the actual person who suffers the definitive loss of income, his assignees or his beneficiaries. Compensation for temporary loss of income or profits is dealt with above.

624. Proceeds from voluntary pension schemes (the so-called "pension savings"), whether collective or individual, and from individual life insurance contracts (so-called insurance savings), are taxable as professional income only if part or all of the contributions to such pension schemes or insurance contracts have been previously deducted from taxable income. Under specific conditions, a reduced tax rate of 16.5 or 10 per cent applies to life insurance contracts or pensions settled in a single capital payment rather than in recurring interest. Such capital payments are taxed separately in the year they are paid out. It should be noted, however, that annuities paid out of capital formed by contributions, which did not benefit from any tax exemption, may nevertheless be taxable as personal income if the annuities cover both capital and income from capital (mixed annuities). The part of the annuity which represents income (a fixed 3 per cent of the capital) is taxable as income from personal property.

§2. Calculation of net taxable income

625. The rules relating to the calculation of an individual taxpayer's net taxable business income can be summarised as follows. The gross business income will first be reduced by the amount of social security contributions due. Secondly, business expenses (actual or estimated) and losses are deducted. Finally, certain other items may be deducted or exempted.

1. Social security contributions

626. Social security contributions which have been withheld from the income of employees or which have been paid directly by the self-employed taxpayer, are deductible.

2. Business expenses

627. The taxpayer may deduct the business expenses he has made or sustained during the tax period in order to acquire or conserve taxable income, and which he can prove both as to their amount and their reality. Some of these expenses may only be partially deducted. Expenses that cannot be easily justified may be determined by mutual agreement between the tax administration and the taxpayer. If no expenses at all can be justified, the taxpayer will usually opt for a lump-sum deduction (*See*, para. 630).

628. Deductible business expenses include, *inter alia*, the following types of expenses:
    – commuting expenses from home to work and *vice versa*, fixed at € 0.15 per kilometre;
    – expenses relating to the rent or use of real estate for professional purposes;
    – interest on loans;
    – insurance premiums, commissions and advertising costs;
    – salaries and other remuneration paid to employees;
    – depreciation of goods used in the exercise of one's profession;
    – some taxes which are not related to the taxable income (for example, part of the real property withholding tax and car tax).

629. Non-deductible expenses include:
    – personal expenses which are necessary to exercise one's profession; and
    – fines;
    – income tax;
    – 25 per cent of the expenses relating to the use of a car for professional purposes (fuel excepted); and
    – 50 per cent of restaurant bills and entertainment expenses incurred within a professional context.

630. If the taxpayer does not itemise his business expenses, a lump-sum deduction for business expenses is available. Moreover, the lump-sum deduction will also apply if the taxpayer's itemised deductions are lower than the lump-sum deduction. The lump-sum deduction cannot be combined with itemised deductions. The lump-sum deduction is limited to a maximum amount of € 2,500 (assuming a gross taxable income of € 12,400 or more). Company directors and similar persons may

deduct a lump sum of 5 per cent of their gross income, up to a maximum of € 2,500. The maximum threshold is adjusted annually and, for assessment year 2003, the applicable maximum threshold is € 2,950.

3. Other deductions or exemptions

631. Certain other deductions or exemptions are available. These include (i) employment incentives, (ii) deduction of losses suffered during the taxable period (even if related to another professional activity) or brought forward losses and, subject to strict conditions, (iii) life insurance premiums as well as (iv) interest charged on mortgages and (v) part of the redemption of capital on a mortgage loan.

§3. Tax treatment of business income earned by spouses

632. The business income of spouses is taxed separately. Other items of income (from real property, from personal property and miscellaneous sources of income) are aggregated and any tax payable is due by the spouse with the highest business income.

633. If only one spouse has a business income, 30 per cent of his or her gross income, up to a maximum of € 6,700, is attributed to the other spouse and taxed separately. In case the other spouse has business income not exceeding 30 per cent of the business income earned by both spouses, part of the business income of the first spouse is attributed to the other spouse (up to 30 per cent of the total business income of the 2 spouses with a maximum of € 6,700). For assessment year 2003 (income year 2002), the applicable maximum is € 7,900.

§4. Payroll taxes and advance payments

634. Income tax on professional income is paid either by way of withholding tax or by way of advance payment.

1. Payroll taxes

635. Payroll withholding tax applies to all forms of employment income (including pensions and annuities) and to the income of directors, other corporate officers and active partners in private limited liability companies or partnerships, and must be retained by the employer, the company or the institution distributing the income.

636. Withholding tax is computed on a progressive scale on the basis of gross business income, net of social security contributions, and takes into account the lump-sum business expenses deduction and exemptions for dependants. The updated amount of the payroll withholding tax on monthly salaries and periodic remuneration, as well as detailed instructions on how to calculate the relevant income figures, are

published annually. In general, the retained amounts must be paid to the tax administration within 15 days following the month in which the income was paid or awarded. Before 1 March of the year following the year the income was earned, the employer, company or institution which retained and paid the withholding tax must deliver an individual salary slip to each person to whom income was paid and on which withholding tax was retained. A copy of this salary slip indicating the net amounts paid and the taxes retained must also be sent to the tax administration.

2. Advance payments

637. Advance payment of income tax applies to income from agricultural, industrial or commercial activities, as well as to income from self-employed activities. If no advance payment is made, the taxpayer concerned will have to pay an increased amount. This is because employees and other persons, part of whose income is retained as withholding tax, actually pay the income tax at the same time as they receive their income. Those who are self-employed or who are engaged in business activities normally pay their taxes the year after the year in which the income was earned. The system of advance payments ensures that both categories of taxpayers are treated in the same way. Directors of companies and active partners in private limited liability companies and partnerships must make advance payments if insufficient withholding tax has been retained by the company or partnership. Anyone under the age of 35 establishing himself for the first time in a self-employed profession is not obliged to make advance payments in respect of income earned in the first 3 years. In addition, there is no penalty if the shortfall in the advance payments is less than € 25 (for assessment year 2003: € 30) or 1 per cent of the total tax due.

638. Taxpayers owing advance payments must estimate their income for the whole year and pay 25 per cent of the tax due each quarter. The payments must be made before 10 April, 10 July, 10 October and 20 December. Failure to make such payments up to an amount equal to 106 per cent of the income tax due will result in a penalty. There are alternative payment schedules allowing the taxpayer to avoid a tax increase. If no advance payments are made at all, a tax increase will be applied, the amount of which is a function of the base interest rate of the European Central Bank on 1 January of the year preceding the year after which the assessment year is named. However, as far as individuals are concerned, only 90 per cent of the tax increase so calculated will have to be paid.

639. Taxpayers who do not have to make advance payments because their income is subject to withholding tax may nonetheless make such payments on a voluntary basis if they foresee that the retained withholding tax will be insufficient to pay the

amount of tax finally due. In those circumstances, tax relief is granted. This relief is also granted to taxpayers who are obliged to make advance payments for the quarterly payments made in excess of the 25 per cent due to avoid a tax increase. Those who pay, for example, the full amount of the estimated taxes due during the first quarter (before 10 April) receive the largest tax relief. It is common practice to finance such a payment through a bank loan. The interest due to the bank is tax deductible and the amount of the net cost of the loan is, therefore, in general, less than the relief which the taxpayer receives from a substantial advance payment during the first quarter of the year.

F. Miscellaneous income

640. Income that does not fall within the above-mentioned categories of taxable income is considered to be miscellaneous income if it falls within one of the categories listed in Article 90 of the ITC. The most important categories of miscellaneous income are:

(i) the net income from speculations or from occasional services, outside the exercise of a professional activity. Losses may be carried forward for a period of 5 years and can be offset against income of the same category only. This income may not be included in the total amount of income subject to personal income tax, but is taxed separately at a flat rate of 33 per cent;

(ii) regular support or alimony payments made to the taxpayer in accordance with the provisions of the Civil Code, by individuals who are not members of the taxpayer's household, for example, by a divorced spouse. This category is included in the taxpayer's total taxable income, up to a maximum 80 per cent of the amount received;

(iii) the net capital gains upon the sale of undeveloped land in Belgium, made by individuals who are not real estate agents, are taxable when the land is sold within eight years of its acquisition. The gains are not included in the taxpayer's total taxable income, but are taxed separately at 33 per cent if the property is sold within 5 years following its acquisition and at 16.5 per cent if it is sold after the fifth year following its acquisition. The net capital gain consists of the net sales price after deduction of all costs relating to the acquisition less the purchase price and purchase expenses. The purchase price is adjusted by 5 per cent for each year the property has been held to take account of inflation; and

(iv) capital gains realised on the transfer of privately owned shares are, as a general rule, not taxable. However, net capital gains realised by an individual shareholder on the transfer of shares will be taxable if the shareholder and his family have, at any time during the 5 years preceding the transfer, directly or indirectly, held more than 25 per cent of the shares in a company which has its registered office or principal place of business in Belgium and if the shares are transferred to a company or association which does not have its registered office or principal place of business in Belgium. The tax is not applicable to a transfer or exchange of shares in the context of a liquidation, merger or division of the company. The amount of the capital gain consists of the difference between the net sales price and the acquisition price of the shares. Taxable capital gains are taxed separately at a rate of 16.5 per cent.

G. Deductions from the global taxable income

641. An individual's global taxable income is computed by combining all his net income from all sources, *i.e.*, income from real property, from capital and personal property, business income, and those items of miscellaneous income that are not taxed separately at reduced rates.

642. The following deductions may be made from the global taxable income so calculated:
    (i) 80 per cent of regular support and alimony payments made by the taxpayer to individuals who are not members of the taxpayer's household pursuant to the provisions of the Civil Code;
    (ii) contributions to recognised charitable, cultural and scientific organisations;
    (iii) compensation paid to domestic staff and expenses relating to day-nursery for children below the age of 3; and
    (iv) interest paid on a mortgage loan entered into with a view to acquiring or constructing a new dwelling or renovating a house or apartment which is at least 15 years old. The property must be located in Belgium and must be the only one owned by the taxpayer. This additional interest deduction will only be available if the interest to be paid exceeds the real property income.

H. Computation of tax

643. Apart from those categories of personal income which are taxed separately at a flat rate, all individual income, after deduction of the specific expenses and exemptions for each category, is added. The sum of all such individual income, less the deductions mentioned above, provides the basis for the final calculation of the income tax due, which is levied on a sliding scale of total taxable income. This tax is levied at a progressive rate on total individual taxable income. The individual income of married couples is taxed jointly, except for the business income of each spouse, which is taxed separately on a sliding scale.

644. The income tax due on the basis of this sliding scale is increased by a variable local surcharge of up to 9 per cent levied on the full amount of tax due by the municipal authorities of the taxpayer's place of residence. In the Brussels area, an additional 1 per cent of the tax due is levied by the conurbation (*agglomeratie/ agglomération*).

645. For single taxpayers without dependent persons, the first € 4,095 (assessment year 2003: € 5,480) is exempt from tax, while married taxpayers do not pay tax on the first € 3,250 (assessment year 2003: € 4,350) of their respective taxable income. The tax-exempt portion is increased for descendants and children who are dependent on the taxpayer, as follows:
   – for one child   € 870 (assessment year 2003: € 1,160)
   – for 2 children   € 2,240 (assessment year 2003: € 3,000)
   – for 3 children   € 5,020 (assessment year 2003: € 6,720)
   – for 4 children   € 8,120 (assessment year 2003: € 10,860)
   – for more than 4 children   € 8,120 (assessment year 2003: € 10,860) plus
                            € 3,100 (assessment year 2003: € 4,150) for each child after the fourth child

646. The tax-exempt portion is further increased for certain other persons who are dependent on the taxpayer or for persons meeting certain conditions. An additional allowance is made for each child less than 3 years old on 1 January of the assessment year provided the taxpayer does not claim the deduction for day-nursery costs.

I. Tax rates

647. Individual income tax rates are as follows:
   – 25 per cent on the income bracket from € 0.01 to € 5,705 (assessment year 2003: € 6,730);
   – 30 per cent on the income bracket from € 5,705 to € 7,565 (assessment year 2003: € 8,920);
   – 40 per cent on the income bracket from € 7,565 to € 10,785 (assessment year 2003: € 12,720);
   – 45 per cent on the income bracket from € 10,785 to € 24,800 (assessment year 2003: € 29,260);
   – 50 per cent on the income bracket from € 24,800 to € 37,185 (assessment year 2003: € 43,870);
   – 52 per cent on the income bracket exceeding € 37,185 (assessment year 2003: € 43,780).

648. These rates do not take into account the 3 per cent crisis surcharge (which will be abolished gradually between 2001 and 2005) or the variable local surcharges.

649. The income tax liability calculated by applying the above-mentioned tax rates is adjusted by taking into account the tax-exempt portion (*See*, para. 645). The tax liability is further reduced by a number of tax reductions granted for, or in connection with, (i) long-term saving (*e.g.*, premiums of qualifying pension schemes), (ii) construction saving, (iii) replacement income, (iv) bridge pensions and (v) advance tax payments. The ultimate outcome is the final income tax liability to which the crisis surcharge and the local surcharges will be added.

J. Filing of tax return and payment

650. Individual income tax returns must be filed annually on the standard form supplied by the tax administration before the filing date indicated on the form. If a taxpayer does not receive a form, he should request one before 1 June of the assessment year. The assessment year for the individual income tax is the calendar year following the year in which taxable income was earned.

651. The taxpayer is not required to calculate the exact amount of income tax due. This calculation is made by the tax administration that also calculates all credits, reduction and penalties. The taxpayer will then receive an assessment notice in which a detailed calculation of the tax liability is given. Payment (if any) must be made within 2 months from the receipt of the assessment notice by the taxpayer. Interest is charged on late payments.

652. In principle, the statute of limitations for reviewing the tax return is 3 years from the beginning of the assessment year. This period may be extended to 5 years in case of fraud.

III. CORPORATE INCOME TAX

A. Companies subject to corporate income tax

653. In general, all entities which are, for fiscal purposes, resident in Belgium, and which have legal personality and which are engaged in profit-making activities, are subject to corporate income tax on their worldwide income.

§1. Fiscal residence

654. Companies or associations having their registered office, principal place of business, or place of management in Belgium are considered to be tax resident in Belgium. Non-resident companies and associations with a branch or permanent establishment in Belgium are subject to non-resident income tax.

§2. Legal personality

655. The following entities are considered to have legal personality under Belgian law:
    (i) commercial companies (partnerships, public limited liability companies, private limited liability companies and cooperative companies);
    (ii) civil companies which have adopted the form of a commercial company;
    (iii) non-profit associations and other associations which have acquired legal personality pursuant to specific Acts (mutual insurance associations, mutual assistance associations, professional associations, international associations with philanthropic, religious, scientific, artistic or educational objectives and institutions for public welfare); and
    (iv) certain public institutions which have been specifically granted legal personality.

656. If a company or association has been established in accordance with foreign company law, that law will determine whether or not the company or association concerned has legal personality.

§3. Profit-making activities

657. All industrial, commercial and agricultural businesses are deemed to engage in profit-making activities. These activities are the same as those considered that generate business income pursuant to the provisions for individual income tax. Activities subject to individual income tax if performed by a private person are subject to corporate income tax if performed by companies or associations with legal personality. In addition, all other activities normally producing profits are subject to corporate income tax, irrespective of the legal entity's corporate purpose.

§4. Excluded legal entities

658. Certain legal entities are specifically exempted from corporate income tax. The exception mostly concerns non-profit associations and associations and institutions exercising specific tasks in the public interest (public transport, ports, and water purification companies, for example). These entities are subject to the tax on legal entities. Other entities, while having legal personality for corporate law pur-

poses, are deemed to lack legal personality for tax purposes. Examples of such entities are European economic interest groupings and Belgian economic interest groupings. These entities are treated as transparent vehicles for income tax purposes, meaning that their income is taxed not at the level of the entity, but at the level of their members.

B. Tax base

§1. General

659. In general, the calculation of the tax base for corporate income tax purposes is similar to the individual income tax. The sections of the ITC governing corporate income tax (Title III, Articles 179 through 219) frequently refer to the provisions on individual income tax. For example, Article 183 of the ITC expressly refers to the 4 categories of taxable income for individuals:
   (i) income from real property;
   (ii) income from personal property;
   (iii) business income; and
   (iv) miscellaneous income.

660. Article 183 of the ITC further provides that, subject to certain exceptions, the taxable profit of a company is determined according to the individual income tax provisions applying to industrial, commercial and agricultural activities conducted by non-incorporated entities (Art. 24 of the ITC). This means that all aggregated income is, in principle, treated as business income, regardless of its nature or origin.

§2. Amount of profit for each type of income

1. Real property

661. In general, the taxable income of companies earned from real property consists of the difference between the income and the expenses related to the real property. If the company owns the building it uses for its premises, the amount of rent saved will be included in taxable income. If the company leases the property to another company, the rent actually collected will be regarded as income. In both of these situations, actual expenses related to depreciation and maintenance of the real property are deductible from the taxable income. The company must be able to provide evidence of all expenses deducted.

2. *Personal property*

662. The rules for the calculation of company income derived from personal property are generally the same as those applicable to individuals. However, in order to determine the taxable income of corporations derived from personal property, the actual costs may be deducted from the calculated income but, contrary to the rules on individual income tax, no lump-sum deductions may be made. Moreover, unlike individuals, companies are taxed on all interest received from savings deposits. As far as dividend income is concerned, 95 per cent of all dividends received are tax exempt if the conditions for the "dividends-received" deduction are satisfied.

3. *Business income*

663. The amount of taxable business income is determined according to the rules applicable to industrial, commercial and agricultural occupations, as contained in Article 24 of the ITC.

4. *Miscellaneous income*

664. Taxable income of this type is also calculated according to the rules on individual income tax. Actual expenses incurred are deductible, however not by way of a lump-sum deduction.

§3. Accounting and tax rules

665. In principle, tax payable is calculated on the basis of normal accounting rules, unless there are any specific exceptions. In order to avoid confusion, it has been attempted to make tax and accounting provisions consistent. However, in some cases, differences continue to exist. For example, contrary to the accounting rules, the amount of income tax paid does not constitute a deductible expense under the corporate income tax rules. Also, the value of certain assets for tax purposes may be different from that for accounting purposes.

C. Calculation of taxable income

§1. General

666. The basic rule is that a company's taxable income consists of any increase in its total net value as shown by the difference in the balance sheet between the beginning and the end of the financial year, without taking into account capital increases carried through during that financial year. Although company income is not classified according to its sources, net taxable income is divided into 3 main categories of income: (i) retained earnings, (ii) certain non-deductible expenses and (iii) distrib-

uted profits or dividends. However, since the accounting rules imposed by tax law do not always coincide with the principles observed in the preparation of the annual financial statements or which are generally accepted for commercial purposes, several adjustments must be made when calculating net taxable income. The calculation of the net taxable income is accomplished through the following 6 steps:

- (i) determination of fiscal profits or losses;
- (ii) ventilation of the fiscal profits or losses according to their source (Belgian or foreign source);
- (iii) deduction of income which is exempt under tax treaties and certain other deductions;
- (iv) deduction of participation exemption;
- (v) deduction of previous losses; and
- (vi) investment deduction.

667. Each of these steps will be discussed in further detail in the following sections.

§2. First step: calculation of fiscal profits or losses

668. As mentioned above, taxable income includes retained earnings, non-deductible expenses and distributed profits (dividends).

1. Retained earnings, capital gains and subsidies

669. As a general rule, all retained earnings and provisions for reserves are included in the company's taxable income. This includes statutory and other reserves, depreciation allowances exceeding the levels permitted by depreciation rules, premiums and subsidies paid by the Belgian State, hidden reserves resulting from undervalued assets or overvalued liabilities and capital gains that are not exempt from corporate income tax. The amount of retained earnings is determined on the basis of the annual balance sheet and the financial statements as compared to the retained earnings of the former fiscal year.

i. Depreciation

670. For tax purposes, annual depreciation allowances are permitted only to the extent that they reflect the real depreciation in the asset's value during the fiscal year, although up to assessment year 2004 a full year of depreciation was allowed for the year during which an asset was acquired. For fixed assets that are acquired or created during a taxable period that is connected with assessment year 2004 or thereafter, depreciation of assets must be recorded *pro rata temporis* in the year of acquisition (except for formation expenses). If the accounting year is longer or shorter than one calendar year – for example during the first year of business – the annual depreciation allowance must be apportioned accordingly.

671. As far as straight-line depreciation is concerned, the annual depreciation allowance is calculated by dividing the original acquisition cost by the expected useful lifetime of the assets. The table below gives an overview of the most common depreciation rates. Any annual depreciation which exceeds the rates of depreciation shown in this table will in general give rise to an undervalued asset.

Depreciation rates for assets

Type of assets	Rate (in percentage)
Land	0 (unless the land actually depreciates as a result of the production process)
Buildings (manufacturing, commercial, office premises)	3-5
Equipment and furniture	10
Rolling stock	20
Small equipment	33
Equipment for scientific research	33

672. Whilst straight-line depreciation is the general method, the taxpayer may, under certain conditions, use the decreasing-balance depreciation method. Decreasing-balance depreciation is available at a fixed rate which cannot exceed twice the corresponding rate of depreciation allowed under the straight-line method. The decreasing-balance method may not be used for motor vehicles (with the exception of taxis), intangible fixed assets and fixed assets the use of which is transferred to third parties by the taxpayer who is allowed to depreciate them.

673. When the amount of the depreciation allowance as calculated on a decreasing-balance basis is equal to or less than the amount calculated using the straight-line method, the taxpayer may switch to the latter method until the assets are fully depreciated. If the taxpayer chooses the decreasing-balance method for assets acquired during a particular year, he must notify the tax administration and complete a special form. Having chosen this method, the taxpayer may not change his mind and must apply it to all assets in the same category acquired in subsequent years

unless the intention to discontinue the use of this method is notified to the administration. Special depreciation schemes are applied to establishment costs and intangible fixed assets.

ii. Capital gains

674. Capital gains realised on business assets are treated as ordinary company profits and are, therefore, normally taxed at the standard corporate income tax rate. However, capital gains realised on shares are fully exempt, provided the dividends paid on these shares, at the time of the realisation of the capital gain, can be deducted from the receiving company's taxable base profits under the participation exemption. For the capital gains to be exempt, reference is thus made to the conditions that allow a parent company receiving dividends to benefit from the 95 per cent participation exemption, it being understood, however, that the minimum participation and minimum holding period requirements must not be satisfied for the capital gains exemption. On the other hand, capital losses suffered on shares are in principle not deductible (unless incurred on the occasion of the liquidation of the company, in which case such losses are deductible up to the amount of the paid-up capital).

675. Capital gains realised on the occasion of the sale of tangible or intangible fixed assets held for more than 5 years in the company's business, and gains resulting from involuntary dispositions of tangible or intangible fixed assets, may be eligible for deferred taxation. Tax deferral will be available if the full sales price or insurance indemnity is reinvested in tangible or intangible fixed assets in Belgium within a period of 3 years, and if the reinvestment meets specific conditions. In that case, the capital gains will be taxed in proportion to, and over the same period as, the depreciation of the assets in which the proceeds from the sales were reinvested. Pending reinvestment in qualifying assets, the capital gains must be recorded in a blocked account, meaning that they may not be used for distribution purposes.

iii. Subsidies

676. In order to promote investment in specific sectors, public authorities may grant, under strict conditions, premiums or subsidies to companies. Such subsidies are granted either by way of capital or through the payment of part of the interest which a company must pay on a loan. Both types of subsidies are taxable. In the case of interest subsidies, the reduced financing charge for the company will inevitably increase its taxable income. In order to reduce the tax burden of capital subsidies, such subsidies are subject to taxation in proportion to the depreciation of the asset for the acquisition of which the subsidies have been granted.

2. *Non-deductible expenses*

677. Non-deductible expenses are expenses recorded in the financial statements of the company, but which are not deductible for tax purposes. As a general rule, expenses or charges incurred or borne by a company in order to acquire or preserve taxable business income are deductible, provided that the company can prove that the expenses or charges were effectively paid during the taxable period.

678. Expenses or charges that must be included in a company's taxable business income include:

(i) corporate income tax, including increases, fines, interest and advance payments. However, foreign corporate income tax subject to the rules laid down in tax treaties, as well as VAT which is not recoverable, and some insurance taxes are deductible;

(ii) excessive interest. Interest is only deductible to the extent that it does not exceed the rates which, for certain currencies, are laid down in a Royal Decree. No limits are imposed on the interest paid to or by Belgian financial institutions;

(iii) fines in general, tax penalties, criminal fines and transactional fines are not deductible;

(iv) abnormal advantages granted by Belgian companies to individuals or companies subject to Belgian taxation will be added to the taxable business income of the paying company, unless these advantages are included in the taxable income of the receiving party. Any abnormal advantages granted by a Belgian company to a foreign undertaking directly or indirectly connected to the Belgian company will be included in the Belgian company's taxable income. The same applies to advantages granted to a person or company established in a tax-haven country. An advantage is abnormal if it is received in a transaction that is not arm's length or if there is no counter obligation on the part of the receiving party. Examples of abnormal advantages are the sale of goods at cost price, the purchase of goods at excessive prices and interest-free loans;

(v) payment of interest or royalties to residents of tax-haven countries are not deductible unless the taxpayer proves that such payment does not exceed what is to be considered as normal; and

(vi) entertainment costs, restaurant expenses and business presents are, in general, only deductible up to 50 per cent. Expenses relating to the professional use of motor vehicles are deductible up to 75 per cent, except for petrol expenses which are deductible in full.

3. Distributed profits (dividends)

679. Dividends or other remuneration for invested capital paid by a company to its shareholders are included in the taxable income of the company. Normally, the dividend to be distributed is a gross amount on which the distributing company will withhold the withholding tax. If, however, the withholding tax is borne by the distributing company, the withholding tax paid by the company itself constitutes a non-deductible expense.

680. In the 1980s, the Belgian Government tried to attract investors and create employment in Belgium by granting tax incentives to companies which were willing to make important investments or to establish new plants in specific areas of high unemployment. The dividends paid by these companies were, under certain conditions, exempt from corporate income tax. These favourable tax rules are no longer applicable.

§3. Second step: Ventilation of profits and losses according to their source

1. General

681. If the sum of the retained earnings, non-deductible expenses and distributed profits results in a positive amount, the next step in calculating a company's taxable income is to determine the Belgian and foreign income of that company. In the event that the determination of the total income results in a loss, this can be set off against later profits.

682. If the calculation of total income results in a profit, it is divided up according to its origin. Income can be of Belgian origin, originate from a country with which Belgium has concluded a tax treaty or originate from a country with which Belgium has not concluded such a treaty. Foreign income can be generated from real estate, business income earned through a permanent establishment in that country, or income from capital when the shares, bonds or loans are managed by a foreign establishment of the Belgian company.

2. Methodology

683. Since Belgian income, income from a treaty country and income from a non-treaty country are subject to different tax rules, the taxable profit or loss of each foreign establishment must first be determined. Next, losses suffered in one or more establishments must be set off against profits made by other establishments. This calculation is made on the basis of the annual accounts and accounting documents of the Belgian company. However, adjustments may be made regarding the allocation of costs which are specifically borne by the foreign establishment rather than by the Belgian company, and the general overhead expenses of the Belgian company.

If the Belgian company has suffered losses in one or more of its establishments (Belgian or foreign), these losses may be set off against profits made by other establishments. In order to avoid that losses incurred by a foreign permanent establishment of a Belgian company are deducted twice, *i.e.*, first in Belgium and in a later fiscal year in the country where the establishment is located, because the loss can be carried forward, most double taxation treaties provide that Belgium may tax an equal amount of profits of other taxable periods attributable to that establishment.

684. Foreign income from treaty countries will, in general, be exempt from Belgian corporate income tax and thus is not included in the calculation of the Belgian company's taxable income. Foreign income from non-treaty countries that has been subject to taxation in the source country is reduced by 75 per cent. This means that foreign income from non-treaty countries is taxed at one-fourth of the corporate income tax rate. However, effective as of assessment year 2004, this tax reduction is no longer available.

§4. Third step: Deduction of income exempt under tax treaties and other tax-allowed deductions

685. Income exempt from tax in Belgium because of a tax treaty may be deducted from the total profit. Further deductions concern financial contributions to recognised charitable or cultural organisations, as well as some deductions for the employment of additional personnel or of scientific personnel.

§5. Fourth step: Participation exemption

686. The so-called "dividends-received" deduction, or participation exemption (*stelsel van definitief belaste inkomsten/régime des revenus définitivement taxés*) aims to avoid double taxation of income which has already been subject to corporate income tax at the level of the distributing company.

687. The participation exemption regime has been substantially modified by the implementation in Belgium of the EC Council Directive No. 90/435 of 23 July 1990 on the common System of Tax Applicable in the Case of Parent Companies and Subsidiaries of Different Member States (O.J. [1990] L 225/6 – the "Parent/Subsidiary Directive"). This was accomplished in 2 stages. Firstly, the Royal Decree of 14 October 1991 specified the conditions under which profits distributed by Belgian subsidiaries to their EC-parent companies are exempted from withholding tax. Secondly, the Law of 23 October 1991 deals with, among other issues, the taxation of dividends obtained by a Belgian company. It should be noted that, although the Parent/Subsidiary Directive only applies to the cross-border distribution of divi-

dends in the European Union, the Belgian legislature opted for a common system applicable to both foreign and Belgian dividends.

688. Under the participation exemption regime, 95 per cent of the dividends received is exempt. The remaining 5 per cent is regarded as management costs related to the holding. The recipient can deduct actual management costs as business expenses. All other costs relating to the shareholding, such as financing costs, remain deductible as well.

689. The dividends received are first included in the taxable income and it is only afterwards that they are deducted. It follows that a company that suffered a loss of 100 in the year in which it received dividends of 80 qualifying for the participation exemption will have a loss of 20. Because the result is negative, the dividends will effectively not be deductible and the loss to be carried forward will be 20 instead of 100. In other words, this system results in an indirect taxation of dividends through a reduction in the loss which can be carried forward to the next fiscal year. It is debatable whether this aspect of the participation exemption regime, as implemented by the Belgian tax legislature, is compatible with the Parent/Subsidiary Directive.

690. The following conditions must be met in order for dividends to be eligible for the participation exemption. First, the beneficiary of the dividends must have a shareholding of at least 10 per cent or with an investment value of at least € 1.2 million in the capital of the distributing company. Second, the distributing company must be subject to ordinary taxation. Third, the shares on which dividends are paid out must qualify as financial fixed assets within the meaning of accounting legislation and the participation must be held in full ownership during an uninterrupted period of 1 year (whereby the minimum holding period requirement must not necessarily have to be met at the time of the dividend distribution).

691. The taxation condition is deemed not fulfilled and, hence, the participation exemption is not available, in the following cases:
   (i) the distributing company is established in a country (other than an EC Member State) where the tax regime is considerably more advantageous than that in Belgium, which is deemed to be the case if the ordinary nominal tax rate or the effective tax burden in the foreign country is less than 15 per cent (tax haven exclusion);
   (ii) the distributing company is a financing, treasury or investment company subject to a tax regime derogating from common law;
   (iii) the distributing company is a company with offshore activities;

(iv) the distributing company is a company whose profits are realised through the intervention of one or more foreign establishments that are subject to a tax regime that is substantially more advantageous than the tax regime to which such profits would have been subject in Belgium (which is deemed to be the case if the cumulative tax that is actually levied on the profits of the establishment, *i.e.*, both at the level of that establishment and at the level of the head office, is less than 15 per cent; this exclusion does not apply if both the distributing company and the foreign establishment are located in an EC Member State); or

(v) the distributing company is a company, other than an investment company, re-distributing dividends which themselves would not be eligible for at least 90 per cent for the participation exemption.

692. The tax authorities published a list in the *Belgian Official Journal* (*Belgisch Staatsblad/Moniteur belge*) of 24 August 1991 creating 3 categories of countries or companies excluded from the participation exemption regime. List I A concerns countries where all companies are not subject to a tax similar to the Belgian corporate income tax (Andorra, Anguilla, Bahamas, Bahrain, Bermuda, Campione, Cayman Islands, Ciskei, Grenada, Nauru, Saint-Pierre-et-Miquélon, Sark, Tonga, Turks and Caicos Islands and Vanuatu). List I B refers to countries where certain types of companies are not subject to a tax similar to the Belgian corporate income tax. List II relates to countries where the common rules concerning taxes are markedly more advantageous than in Belgium (Alderney, the Netherlands Antilles, Aruba, Cook Islands, Djibouti, Guernsey, Herm, Hong Kong, Jersey, Liechtenstein, Macao, Isle of Man, San Marino, Svalbard and British Virgin Islands). List III lists the countries where all holding and financing companies, or certain types of those companies, are subject to a tax regime derogating from common law (the Netherlands Antilles, Jersey, Liechtenstein, Luxembourg and Uruguay). At the time of writing, a new but still provisional list of 57 countries has been drawn up by the tax authorities for the application of the tax haven exclusion. The final list will be introduced by Royal Decree.

693. Dividends that do not qualify for the participation exemption are taxable in full at the standard corporate income tax rate, without any tax credit being granted for the income tax paid in Belgium or abroad on the underlying income.

§6. Fifth step: Deduction of previous losses

694. If the above 4 steps result in a profit, the company may deduct from these profits losses made during previous business years. Previous losses are deductible without limitation in time or amount.

695. Specific anti-avoidance legislation was introduced in 1995 to counter trading in loss-making entities. Carry-forward losses are forfeited in case of a change of control or a change of ownership occurring during the tax year, unless such change of control or change of ownership can be justified by legitimate financial or economic needs. A ruling can be obtained from the tax authorities in this regard. The provision is not applicable in case of a change of control or a change of ownership involving companies belonging to the same consolidation perimeter.

§7. Sixth step: Investment deduction

696. The investment deduction (*investeringsaftrek/déduction pour investissement*) allows enterprises to deduct a certain percentage of the acquisition or investment value of qualifying assets from taxable profits. For large corporations, the investment deduction no longer has any practical meaning, since the deduction percentage has in the meantime, been reduced to zero (except for (i) patents, (ii) environment-friendly investments, (iii) energy saving investments and (iv) investments exclusively destined to the manufacturing process of certain forms of recycled packaging). At present, the investment deduction may be of importance only to small and medium-sized companies whose shares (and the voting power attached thereto) are owned, for more than 50 per cent, by individuals and which do not form part of a corporate group comprising a co-ordination centre. Investments made by such companies are eligible for an investment deduction at a basic rate of 3 per cent of the acquisition or investment value of qualifying assets. Higher percentages are available for (i) fixed assets used to promote research and development of new products and future technologies that do not affect the environment or that are aimed at limiting the negative impact on the environment, (ii) fixed assets that contribute to energy saving and (iii) patents.

697. The investment deduction must be made in the financial year in which the investments are made. Companies with less than 20 employees may, however, choose to spread the deduction over the period during which the assets concerned will be depreciated. The investment deduction can only be made after the deduction of previous losses. If the fiscal result in a particular assessment year is not sufficient to make the full investment deduction, the balance of the deduction not used during that assessment year may be carried forward to subsequent years.

698. A company wishing to benefit from the investment deduction must complete its tax return with a special request to that effect and provide an inventory identifying the relevant assets, the dates on which they were acquired, their value and their depreciation regimes. In the case of energy-saving investments or research and

development investments, the certificates referred to above must also be submitted to the tax authorities.

D. Corporate income tax rates

§1. Standard corporate income tax rate

699. The taxable income of a company will, in general, be subject to a standard corporate income tax rate of 39 per cent. Effective as of assessment year 2004, the standard corporate rate is 33 per cent.

§2. Reduced tax rates

700. Companies with taxable income below € 323,700 benefit from the following reduced tax rates:

Taxable income (in €)	Tax rate (in percentage)
0 – 25,000:	28
25,000 – 89,500:	36
89,500 – 323,750:	41

Effective as of assessment year 2004, the reduced tax rates are as follows:

Taxable income (in €)	Tax rate (in percentage)
0 – 25,000:	24.25
25,000 – 90,000:	31
90,000 – 322,500:	34.5

701. The reduced rates of tax do not apply if:
   (i) the company concerned is a financial company as statutorily defined;
   (ii) more than 50 per cent of the company is owned by one or more other companies;
   (iii) the company distributes dividends exceeding 13 per cent of the paid-up capital as it existed at the beginning of the taxable period;
   (iv) the company does not attribute to at least one director or active partner compensation equal to or exceeding the taxable income of that company if such payment is less than € 24,500; or

(v) the company forms part of a corporate group to which a co-ordination centre belongs.

§3. Crisis surcharge

702. A 3 per cent crisis surcharge is levied on the corporate income tax rates, bringing the aggregate standard corporate income tax rate to 40.17 per cent and the reduced corporate income tax rates to 28.84, 37.08 and 42.23 per cent, respectively.

§4. Tax credit

703. A tax credit of 7.5 per cent, with a maximum of € 19,850 of the positive difference between the paid-up capital at the end of the taxable period and the highest amount of the paid-up capital at the end of one of the 3 preceding taxable periods, may be offset against the corporate tax liability computed in accordance with the above-mentioned rules. Any excess credit can be carried over to subsequent assessment years.

§5. Special assessment on secret commissions

704. Companies which pay so-called secret commissions – payments where the beneficiary is not identified – are subject to a special tax levy of 300 per cent (increased by a 3 per cent crisis surcharge) on these commissions. Such commissions are not included in the taxable income which is subject to the basic corporate income tax rate. The secret commissions themselves are not deductible as a business expense, but the special tax paid is so deductible.

E. Payment of corporate income tax

705. Although corporate income tax is generally levied in the autumn of the year following the end of each tax year, tax on certain items is levied by way of withholding. In order to avoid substantial surcharges, companies must also make quarterly prepayments of their estimated tax liability.

§1. Withholding taxes

706. Withholding taxes are usually credited partially or completely against corporate income tax. In some cases, however, where no credit or only partial credit is given and no refund is available, withholding taxes may constitute an additional tax burden.

1. Real property withholding tax

707. While corporate income tax is levied upon actual real property income, real property withholding tax (*onroerende voorheffing/précompte immobilier*) is retained

on the deemed rental value (cadastral income) of the real property. Real property withholding tax paid by companies is deductible as a business expense.

2. *Personal property withholding tax*

708. Personal property withholding tax (*roerende voorheffing/précompte mobilier*) is a prepayment levied on personal property income (*i.e.*, (i) dividends, (ii) interest and (iii) royalties). Personal property withholding tax on dividends is, in principle, 25 per cent or 15 per cent. Special rules apply, however, to intercompany dividends. An exemption from personal property withholding tax on dividends applies, provided that both the distributing and the receiving companies are subject to Belgian corporate income tax and that the receiving company has maintained a shareholding of at least 25 per cent in the capital of the distributing company for an uninterrupted period of a minimum of 1 year. Pursuant to the implementation of the Parent/Subsidiary Directive into Belgian law, this exemption also applies to distributions made by Belgian subsidiaries to their parent companies established in the European Union, provided the above-mentioned minimum and permanency conditions are met. Both the Belgian subsidiary and the parent company must be subject to corporate income tax or to an equivalent foreign tax, without the possibility of an option or of being exempt. Moreover, they must be companies incorporated in one of the legal forms listed in the Annex to the Parent/Subsidiary Directive.

709. Personal property withholding tax is in principle fully creditable against the corporate income tax due and any excess prepayment is refundable. However, for income derived from securities other than dividends, personal property withholding tax may only be credited in proportion to the period during which the company had full ownership of the underlying securities. For interest on loans and receivables not represented by securities and for interest on cash deposits, the tax credit for personal property withholding tax is available only in proportion to the period during which the company was the creditor of the income. No tax credit is available if and to the extent that the attribution or payment of dividend income results in a write-down or a capital loss on the underlying shares.

3. *Foreign tax credit*

710. The foreign tax credit (*forfaitaire buitenlandse belasting/quotité forfaitaire de l'impôt étranger*) is a credit for foreign tax, *i.e.*, an amount deemed to correspond to foreign tax levied in the country where the income is sourced may be deducted from Belgian corporate income tax. The credit is available, subject to certain limitations, for (i) personal property income other than dividends and (ii) certain types of miscellaneous income derived by Belgian companies from foreign sources, provided that such income was subject to a foreign tax equivalent to Belgian

corporate income tax. The foreign tax credit is creditable against corporate income tax before the deduction of other refundable tax credits. Any excess foreign tax credit is not refundable.

§2. Advance payment of corporate income tax

711. Like individual entrepreneurs, company directors and members of the liberal professions, corporations must make prepayments during the year corresponding to their estimated tax liability for that year in order to avoid a substantial surcharge. The surcharge is calculated on the basis of the total corporate income tax less the withholding taxes which can be credited against the corporate income tax. In order to avoid this surcharge, prepayments equal to 25 per cent of the estimated income tax liability must be made each quarter. The dates before which such prepayments must be made are for the first quarter: on or before 10 April; for the second quarter: on or before 10 July; for the third quarter: on or before 10 October; for the fourth quarter: on or before 20 December. For companies which have an accounting year that differs from the calendar year, special rules determine the dates before which the prepayments must be made.

F. Reporting obligations

712. A yearly tax return must be filed with the competent authorities before the date mentioned on the form. The deadline for submission of the return may not be earlier than one month after the approval of the company's annual accounts and may not be later than 6 months following the date of closure of the annual accounts. If the company does not file its tax return, or files an incomplete or incorrect return, the corporate income tax due may be increased by a penalty, the amount of which depends on the seriousness of the infringement.

G. Special tax regimes

713. Belgium grants various tax incentives which aim to make the establishment or expansion of foreign multinational companies in Belgium more attractive, or to promote the development of particular regions with high unemployment or which are in need of innovative industrial activities. The major regimes relate to co-ordination centres, distribution centres and call centres.

714. These regimes have come under increased scrutiny as they have been labelled as amounting to "harmful" tax competition under the EC Code of Conduct. While a phasing-out period which expires in 2005, is set forth under the EC Code of Conduct in order to do away with tax measures deemed to result in "harmful" tax

competition, it is expected that Belgium will not give up these regimes unilaterally.

§1. Co-ordination centres

715. The Belgian legislation on co-ordination centres (*coördinatiecentrum/centre de co-ordination*) permits multinational groups to carry out a large variety of management activities and financial activities within Belgium under a special tax regime. The measures were originally enacted by Royal Decree No. 187 of 30 December 1982. Around 300 centres, which include the biggest international corporate groups, have been established to date.

1. Conditions for recognition

716. In order to be recognised as a co-ordination centre, the centre must be set up as a company incorporated under Belgian law or as a Belgian branch of a foreign company.

717. The co-ordination centre must form part of an international group of affiliated companies. In this respect, a company is deemed to be in a group with another company if one of the companies holds either at least 20 per cent of the capital or 20 per cent of the voting rights of the other company. The international group, of which the co-ordination centre forms a part, must have consolidated capital and reserves of at least € 24 million on a worldwide basis. The consolidated annual turnover of the group must reach at least € 240 million.

718. The group will be considered international if the following conditions are fulfilled:
   (i) the non-Belgian capital of the group must equal at least € 12 million or 20 per cent of the consolidated capital of the entire group, whichever is lower;
   (ii) the group must have owned subsidiaries in at least 4 different countries for an uninterrupted period of at least 2 years immediately preceding 1 January of the year in which the application for recognition as a co-ordination centre is made; and
   (iii) the group must have a turnover outside Belgium of at least € 120 million or 20 per cent of the total consolidated turnover of the group, whichever is lower.

2. Permissible activities for co-ordination centres

719. A co-ordination centre is only permitted to perform those activities which are listed in Royal Decree No. 187 and which are enumerated in the specific Royal Decree recognising the centre. The permitted activities can be divided into 2 categories. The first category covers general head office services and includes advertising and sales promotion, gathering and disseminating information, insurance and re-

insurance, scientific research, relations with national and international authorities, centralised accounting and administrative activities (including data processing), and certain preparatory and ancillary activities (such as the regional office functions of supervision and control, control of in-house legal services and tax management). The second category of activities relates to centralised financial transactions and the management of foreign exchange risks. These activities may include providing loans to group members, leasing, collecting debts, engaging in sale and lease-back transactions (subject to certain conditions) and re-invoicing group members for products or services which have been invoiced to the co-ordination centre by other members of the group.

720. A co-ordination centre's activities must be solely aimed at group members' benefit. The centre may not engage in manufacturing or other commercial activities. The remuneration received by the centre from the members of the group for the activities carried out must be no more than the centre would have received in an arm's length transaction. Banks, insurance companies and other financial or credit institutions cannot benefit from these provisions. Furthermore, co-ordination centres may not hold shares or any other interest in any company whatsoever.

721. Finally, to be eligible for the advantageous treatment granted to co-ordination centres, a centre must employ, by the end of the 2-year period following the commencement of its activities, at least 10 full-time employees. If employees of a Belgian member of the group are transferred to the centre, the Belgian member of the group must hire new personnel equal to the number of employees transferred in order for the transferred employees to be included as employees of the group.

3. Tax concessions for co-ordination centres

722. A recognised co-ordination centre benefits from concessions on corporate income tax, withholding tax, registration tax and real estate tax. The so-called deemed withholding tax (*fictieve roerende voorheffing/précompte mobilier fictif*), which was originally part of the package of incentives, was reduced to zero by the law of 23 October 1991. In 2002, a number of amendments to the existing tax treatment of co-ordination centres were introduced in an attempt to meet the proposals for useful measures made by the European Commission within the framework of the state aid rules contained in the EC Treaty.

i. Corporate income tax

723. The normal corporate tax rate is applied to a tax base for qualified co-ordination centres which is calculated as a percentage of the operating expenses borne by the co-ordination centre, except personnel costs and financial charges. This percent-

age is fixed for each co-ordination centre individually, generally according to the cost-plus basis that the centre charges for its services. This is generally about 8 per cent. However, the co-ordination centre's tax base may never be less than the sum of any non-deductible expenses and any abnormal or benevolent advantages granted to the centre (the so-called "alternative minimum tax base"). At the time of writing, this tax treatment was amended by law, but the entry into force of the new rules is still unclear as it will be determined by a Royal Decree yet to be adopted. Under the new rules, the cost-plus basis is redefined so as to encompass financial and personnel costs, and the applicable mark-up will need to be determined on a case by case basis in function of the specific characteristics of the transactions realised by the centre.

ii. Withholding tax

724. Co-ordination centres are exempt from paying withholding tax on payments of dividends, interest and royalties, unless the recipient thereof is an individual or a legal entity subject to the legal entities tax (resident or non-resident). The exemption of withholding tax extends to interest income from certain cash deposits made by the co-ordination centre with Belgian banks.

iii. Registration tax

725. An exemption from registration tax on capital and increases in capital is granted to recognised co-ordination centres.

iv. Real estate tax

726. Co-ordination centres are exempt from paying real estate tax on the buildings which they own and use for their activities in Belgium. At the time of writing, this exemption was established by law, but the exact entry into force of this abolition will be determined by a Royal Decree yet to be adopted.

4. *Related tax concessions for expatriate executives and researchers of foreign nationality*

727. Non-Belgian executives and researchers employed by a Belgian co-ordination centre who have, for Belgian tax purposes, non-resident status (primarily because they maintain the centre of their economic interest outside Belgium) are entitled to substantial concessions regarding personal income taxes. These concessions are principally tax-free allowances which may amount to a maximum of € 29,700. Income earned abroad by foreign executives during their Belgian assignment is not taxable in Belgium. The application of this favourable regime is dependent on

an explicit, individual authorisation by the tax administration, following a specific request by both the employer and the employee concerned.

5. Application for recognition as a co-ordination centre

728. The advantages provided by Royal Decree No. 187 are not automatically available. An application for recognition must be filed with the Ministry of Finance. The application consists of 3 parts. First, a general description of the group, its composition and its activities must be given. The co-ordination centre's proposed activities must be explained in the second part. This section is the most important because it must show that the co-ordination centre will carry out only activities permitted by the strict provisions of Royal Decree No. 187. The third part must provide certain statistics including, *inter alia*, the annual reports published by the group, in order to establish that the request complies with the conditions for recognition.

729. After approval of the written application by a working group of representatives from the Ministries of Finance, Economic Affairs, Employment and the Middle Classes, the services of the Ministry of Finance will draft a proposal for a Royal Decree. From the moment the Royal Decree is signed, the co-ordination centre will be entitled to benefit from the above-described advantages for a period of 10 years. Existing co-ordination centres may apply for a renewal of their status at the expiry of the 10-year period.

§2. Distribution centres

730. On 9 August 1989, the Ministry of Finance issued a circular letter (the "Circular Letter of 9 August 1989") on the taxation of distribution centres in order to promote the establishment of centralised purchase and transportation centres in Belgium.

1. Permitted activities

731. The special tax regime for distribution centres is based on a cost-plus system and is applicable only to Belgian companies and Belgian branches of foreign companies the activities of which consist solely of one or more of the following:
   (i) purchasing, on their own behalf or on behalf and account of companies in the group, raw materials and supplies intended for those companies;
   (ii) storing and packaging such raw materials and supplies;
   (iii) selling, including transportation and delivery, such raw materials and supplies exclusively to the companies of their group;
   (iv) storage and packaging for companies of the group of goods for resale and also of finished products owned by those companies; and

(v) transportation and delivery for resale of such goods and finished products on behalf of companies of the group. In this respect, it should be noted that distribution centres may not be involved in any way in sales transactions to companies outside their own group.

732. Distribution centres may not process the raw materials, supplies, goods for resale or finished products which they purchase, store, pack or sell on behalf of companies in the group. The packaging of the goods may not, therefore, give rise to any added value.

733. Companies are considered to belong to a group if they are affiliated companies, meaning that any company with at least 50 per cent common control or ownership constitutes a group member.

2. Taxable income

734. The taxable income of a distribution centre is generally the same as for other companies, *i.e.*, the sum of the retained earnings, disallowed expenses and dividends. However, according to the Circular Letter of 9 August 1989, distribution centres will not be considered to have granted abnormal advantages to related companies, provided that they have applied a profit margin of 5 per cent to their operating expenses. Raw materials and supplies may be resold to other companies of the group without any profit. For the purposes of the Circular Letter of 9 August 1989, operating expenses include all expenses except:
   (i) the purchase price of products resold by the distribution centre to group members during the taxable period;
   (ii) the price of services rendered to the distribution centre by third parties;
   (iii) non-deductible Belgian taxes and other non-deductible expenses; and
   (iv) reserves and certain provisions which must be considered as taxable reserves.

735. If the actual tax base is higher than the tax base computed on the lump sum basis (that is 5 per cent of the operating expenses), the former will be the tax base. In contrast, if the actual tax base is less than 5 per cent of the operating expenses, the balance will be considered to be an abnormal advantage and will be included in the taxable profit of the distribution centre if such advantage has been granted to a foreign group member. If the advantage was granted to a Belgian company, that company is disallowed from offsetting the abnormal advantages received against any carry-forward losses available to it.

736. In any case, the taxable profits of a distribution centre will not be lower than 5 per cent of the operating expenses as defined above. The 5 per cent safe harbour rule is only applicable if the activities of the distribution centre do not give rise to com-

mercial risks. In addition, the 5 per cent requirement must be maintained separately with regard to each company of the group.

737. The distribution centre's tax base, computed in accordance with the rules set out above, is taxable at the standard corporate income tax rate of 39 per cent (increased by the 3 per cent surcharge).

3. Application for recognition of a distribution centre

738. The tax regime provided for by the Circular Letter of 9 August 1989 is not automatically available. An application for recognition must be filed with the Ministry of Finance before establishing a distribution centre. The application must contain the address of the registered office of the company and provide the authorities with all the necessary information with regard to the activities which will be carried out.

§3. Call and Service Centres

739. On 26 July 1996, the Belgian tax authorities issued a circular letter (the "Circular Letter of 26 July 1996") designed to encourage multinational groups of companies to establish call and service centres in Belgium.

1. Eligibility conditions

740. A call or service centre may take the form of either a Belgian company or a branch of a foreign company and must be part of a group of companies. All companies with at least 50 per cent common control or ownership are regarded as group members for purposes of the Circular Letter of 26 July 1996.

2. Permissible activities

741. The activities of the centre must be confined to those described in the Circular Letter of 26 July 1996 and must be performed for the sole benefit of the group members. Call and service centres are authorised to carry out a variety of tasks which may be divided into 4 categories. First, a call or service centre may perform preparatory or auxiliary activities that form an essential part of the group activities (*e.g.*, managing a database within the context of a frequent-flyer program of a group of airline companies; logistical support for the continuing education of the group members' professional personnel). Second, a call or service centre may provide certain information services and thus act as an interface between group members and external customers or between group members themselves (*e.g.*, providing information about the availability and delivery terms of group member products). Third, the centre may contribute in a passive manner to group sales, thereby acting on behalf of the group members without assuming any entrepreneurial risk (*e.g.*,

collecting and confirming purchase orders without accepting such orders). Finally, a call or service centre may, in specific circumstances, be authorised to intervene in an active manner in sales activities, thereby acting in its own name but for the account of group members. The related entrepreneurial risk borne by the centre should be accurately described in the application request and should, in any event, be limited (*e.g.*, accepting purchase orders following terms and conditions previously determined and fixed by group members).

3. Tax treatment

742. Call and service centres remain fully subject to the standard corporate income tax rules and rates. However, call and service centres are deemed to carry out their activities in a market-conforming manner if they achieve a certain level of profitability. Applicable thresholds for determining a qualifying centre's minimum tax base are set forth in the Circular Letter of 26 July 1996. These thresholds serve as a transfer pricing safe haven. However, should the centre's actual profits exceed the minimum tax base determined on the basis of these thresholds, then the excess profits will be subject to corporate income tax.

743. The minimum tax base is defined by reference to a notional mark-up, to be calculated on the basis of a combined application of the cost-plus method and the resale-price method. For the first 3 categories of authorised activities listed above, the applicable mark-up must be determined on the basis of the cost-plus method. For preparatory and auxiliary activities, the centre must receive remuneration that may not be less than its operating expenses plus a 5 per cent mark-up. A 10 per cent mark-up applies to information services, while activities that contribute in a passive manner to group sales trigger a 15 per cent mark-up. For this purpose, operating expenses consist of all expenses incurred by the centre in rendering the services, excluding disallowed expenses, taxed reserves or the amount of turnover that is surrendered to group members. However, personnel costs and disbursements to third parties may be charged to group members without mark-up. In cases where the centre is actively involved in group sales, the minimum profit must be established on the basis of the resale-price method as a percentage of the sales realised through the intervention of the centre. The applicable resale minus, to be determined on a case by case basis, will depend on the outcome of a functional analysis. The resale minus may not exceed 5 per cent, but should be sufficient to cover the centre's operating expenses.

4. Application for recognition

744. The tax regime for call and service centres provided for by the Circular Letter is not automatically applicable. An application for approval must be filed with the

Central Tax Administration, either before the centre is established or during the financial period preceding the year in which the centre intends to take advantage of the regime. The application must contain detailed information on (i) the proposed activities, (ii) the identity of the group members that would benefit from the services rendered by the centre and (iii) the level of entrepreneurial risk assumed by the centre, if any. Once the approval is obtained, it will remain in force for renewable periods of 5 years. The approval may be withdrawn if the centre does not confine itself to the authorised services.

H. Corporate reorganisations

§1. Redemption of shares

745. If the purchase price paid by the company exceeds the par value of the paid-up capital corresponding to the redeemed shares (multiplied, where applicable, by a revaluation coefficient to take account of inflation), the resultant gain is treated as a dividend for tax purposes. The dividend distribution is deemed to be made at the time the company cancels the shares acquired or, when the shares are not cancelled, at the time that any write-downs are recorded or any capital losses are realised on the shares and, at the latest, upon liquidation of the company. Corporate income tax becomes due to the extent that the dividend distribution is charged to previously untaxed reserves. However, the gain is exempted from personal property withholding tax (although, at the time of writing, it has been announced that a 10 per cent levy will apply in certain cases in the future). Any gain realised by a Belgian corporate shareholder on the occasion of redemption of shares will benefit from the dividends received deduction.

§2. Liquidation of a company

746. Companies entering into liquidation remain subject to ordinary corporate income tax on their annual profits between the date of their dissolution and the date of closing of their liquidation. Such profits include any capital gains realised or established on the occasion of the distribution of the company's assets.

747. Liquidation distributions are treated as a repayment of capital up to the amount of the paid-up capital and, to that extent, such distributions are not subject to any taxation. Any amounts distributed in excess of the paid-up capital are treated as dividends. Hence corporate income tax is due to the extent that previously untaxed reserves are comprised in the distribution proceeds. Liquidation surpluses are subject to a 10 per cent withholding tax unless the beneficiary of such proceeds is a

Belgian company or an EC parent company qualifying under the Belgian implementation legislation of the Parent/Subsidiary Directive.

748. Liquidation gains realised by corporate shareholders subject to Belgian corporate income tax will generally qualify for the dividends received deduction. If the corporate shareholders suffer a capital loss on their shares, such a loss will be tax deductible, but only up to the amount of the paid-up capital represented by their shares.

§3. Mergers and divisions

1. General

749. By the Law of 29 June 1993, Belgium has implemented the Third and Sixth EEC Directives dealing with national mergers and divisions into Belgian company law. The Law of 6 August 1993 has transposed the new company law framework, including the defined concepts of "merger" and "division", into Belgian tax law.

750. In principle, mergers and divisions are subjected to the tax regime applicable to the liquidation of companies. It follows that corporate income tax should be applicable to all capital gains realised or established as a result of the merger or the division and that the liquidation distribution should be treated as a dividend.

751. However, a tax exemption regime is available for mergers, divisions and operations similar to a merger if the following 3 cumulative conditions are fulfilled:
  (i) the acquiring or receiving company must be a domestic company;
  (ii) the transaction must be realised in compliance with Belgian company law; and
  (iii) the transaction must meet legitimate financial or economic needs.

752. Once these conditions are met, the transaction automatically falls within the application of the tax exemption regime.

2. Tax treatment of the acquired or divided company

753. Under the tax exemption regime, the acquired or divided company is exempt from corporate income tax on the capital gains realized on the occasion of the merger or division, as well as on the unrealised capital gains on stocks and contracts in progress and on the capital gains that benefit from the tax deferral regime. The tax exemption may, however, not be total if the acquired or divided company has previously untaxed reserves and if the contribution of its assets and liabilities is not paid for solely by newly issued shares of the acquiring or receiving company(ies).

3. Tax treatment of the acquiring or receiving company(ies)

754. In the case of mergers and divisions carried out under the tax exemption regime, and provided that the contributions made to the acquiring or receiving company(ies) are paid solely by newly issued shares in the latter company(ies), depreciation allowances, investment deductions, capital gains and capital losses relating to the assets contributed, as well as the paid-up capital, must be determined in the hands of the acquiring or receiving company(ies) as if the transaction had not taken place. Moreover, the rules applicable to write-downs, provisions, overvaluations and under-valuations, subsidies, receivables and reserves which were part of the acquired or divided company remain applicable to the acquiring or receiving company(ies).

755. In the case of a tax-free merger, the losses incurred by the absorbed company prior to the merger continue to be deductible in the hands of the absorbing company, but only in the proportion that the fiscal net value of the former company (as determined prior to the transaction) bears to the total fiscal net value of both the absorbing and absorbed companies (as determined prior to the transaction). In the case of a tax-free division, the aforementioned rule applies to that part of the relevant losses which is determined as the proportion that the fiscal net value of the acquired assets bear to the total fiscal net value of the acquired company. Similar rules apply if the acquiring or receiving company(ies) has (or have) loss carry-forwards. As a result, it does not make any difference if the loss-making entity acquires the profit-making entity or vice versa. If both the acquiring or receiving company(ies) and the acquired or divided company have carry-forward losses, the calculation should be made at both levels.

4. Tax treatment of shareholders

756. If the merger or division is carried out under the tax exemption regime, Belgian resident individuals who held the shares in the acquired or divided company as a private investment are, in principle, not subject to tax on the capital gains realised on such shares, even if they had a significant shareholding in the acquired or divided company.

757. Capital gains realised or recorded by Belgian corporate shareholders on the occasion of a tax-free merger or division are treated as unrealised capital gains and, hence, are exempt from income tax, provided that such gains are included in a separate and non-disposable reserve account. Such gains will become taxable at the time the intangibility condition is no longer met and, at the latest, at the time of the liquidation of the corporate shareholder. The question whether a loss realised by the corporate shareholders at the time of the merger or division on their shares

in the acquired or divided company is tax deductible up to the amount of the paid-up capital of the acquired or divided company is debated.

5. Cross-border mergers or divisions

758. Under present legislation, a tax-free cross-border merger or division within the European Community is not yet possible. Belgium justifies this position on the ground that the company law framework currently in place does not permit cross-border mergers or divisions. It is questionable whether this justification is compatible with the requirement for EC Member States to bring into force their implementation measures of the EC Council Directive No. 90/434 of 23 July 1990 on the Common System of Taxation Applicable to Mergers, Divisions, Transfer of Assets and Exchanges of Shares Concerning Companies of Different Member States (O.J. [1990] L 225/1 – the "Tax Merger Directive") before 1 January 1992. Cross-border mergers and divisions within the European Community, whereby the acquired or divided company is a Belgian resident company, thus continue to necessitate both the dissolution and the liquidation of the Belgian company and, as a result, such transactions automatically trigger the application of the tax rules applicable to liquidations. The same holds true, *a fortiori*, for cross-border mergers or divisions involving Belgian companies, whereby the acquiring or receiving company(ies) are established outside the European Community.

§4. Contribution of a branch of activity or a universality of goods

1. General

759. In principle, a contribution in kind of assets used in the professional activity of the contributing party, whether an individual or a company, results in income taxation on any capital gains realised on that occasion. An exception to this rule applies if the contribution in kind concerns one or more branches of activity or a universality of goods. In such cases, subject to the conditions set out below, the capital gains realised by the contributing party are exempt from tax while the receiving company benefits from a regime of tax deferral.

760. A branch of activity refers to all the assets and liabilities of one or more divisions of an enterprise which each, from a technical point of view, constitutes an independent business unit. A universality of goods refers to all the assets and liabilities used by a taxpayer in the exercise of a professional activity.

2. Conditions for exemption

761. Capital gains realised by the contributing party on the occasion of a contribution of a branch of activity or a universality of goods to a company's capital are exempt

from tax if:

  (i) the contribution is made to a Belgian company or to a foreign company resident in an EC Member State;

  (ii) the contribution is made in exchange for the issue of shares representing the capital of the receiving company (a partial payment in cash is allowed if it does not exceed reasonable limits);

  (iii) the transaction meets legitimate financial or economic needs; and

  (iv) where the contribution is made by a company, the realised capital gains are booked in a separate blocked account on the liabilities side of the contributing company's balance sheet.

762. At the level of the receiving company, the neutrality or continuity principle will apply. This means that the receiving company must compute any new depreciation, write-downs, gains or losses in respect of the assets and liabilities transferred, as well as the investment deductions, according to the rules that would have applied to the contributing party if the contribution had not taken place.

3. Optional regime

763. The tax exemption regime is optional, so that the contributing party may waive this regime if a taxable transaction is more beneficial. This may be the case, for example, if the contributing party has losses available to neutralise the capital gains resulting from the contribution.

IV. LEGAL ENTITIES INCOME TAX

A. Taxable legal entities

764. The following 3 categories of taxpayers are subject to the Belgian legal entities income tax (*rechtspersonenbelasting/impôt des personnes morales*):

  (i) the state, the communities, the regions, provinces, agglomerations of municipalities, federations of municipalities, public welfare centres, intercommunal public welfare centres and public clerical institutions;

  (ii) legal entities which are expressly excluded from corporate income tax (*e.g.*, intermunicipal associations governed by the Law of 22 December 1986 on the Intermunicipal Associations (*Wet betreffend de intercommunales/Loi relative aux intercommunales*) and stock exchange companies); and

  (iii) legal entities which have their statutory seat, principal establishment or seat of management or administration in Belgium, provided that such persons do not carry on an enterprise or profit-making activities.

765. The third category includes, *inter alia*, non-profit associations (*verenigingen zonder winstoogmerk/associations sans but lucratif*) and any other legal entities without profit motive such as, for example, associations exclusively or primarily engaged in the protection and promotion of the professional or interprofessional interests of their members or associations which have as their exclusive or main purpose the organisation or support of education.

B. Taxable income

766. The income tax on legal entities is levied only on certain types of income. In addition, a distinction must be drawn between the 3 main categories of legal entity which are subject to the income tax on legal entities.

§1. All categories of taxpayers

767. The taxable income of the above-mentioned categories of taxpayers includes:
   (i) the deemed rental value (cadastral income) of real property located in Belgium, unless such income is exempt; and
   (ii) income from personal property and from certain miscellaneous sources.

§2. Third category of taxpayers

768. Taxpayers of the third category are also taxable on the following types of income:
   (i) income from real property located abroad, unless such income would have been exempt from the legal entities income tax had the property been located in Belgium;
   (ii) the net amount of rentals and rental charges relating to real property located in Belgium which exceeds the cadastral income of such property, unless the property is rented to an individual for private habitation purposes or is used by the tenant for agricultural or horticultural purposes;
   (iii) compensation obtained from the granting or the transfer of long-term rights on real property located in Belgium or abroad, subject to the above exceptions;
   (iv) capital gains realised on certain transfers of real property or real property rights; and
   (v) capital gains realised on the transfer of significant shareholdings.

§3. Second and third categories of taxpayers

769. Taxpayers of the second and third categories are also taxable on:
   (i) secret commissions (*i.e.*, payments to non-identified persons); and

(ii) employer contributions for additional insurance against old age and early death and for certain pensions and annuities, unless such contributions meet the conditions of deductible business expenses.

C. Tax rates

770. The tax owed by all 3 categories of legal entities on real property income or personal property income is equal to the equivalent real property and personal property withholding tax. Income, other than capital gains, which is taxable in the hands of taxpayers of the third category, is taxed at 20 per cent. Capital gains realised by taxpayers of the third category on real property are taxable at 33 percent or 16.5 per cent, depending on whether or not the land is sold within 5 year of its acquisition. Capital gains on significant shareholdings are taxable at 16.5 per cent. Extralegal pensions and payments which do not constitute tax deductible items are taxed at 39 per cent. A separate assessment is established in respect of secret commissions at 300 per cent. All these rates must be increased by the 3 per cent crisis surcharge (which will be abolished gradually over time).

V. NON-RESIDENT INCOME TAX

A. Taxable persons

771. Non-resident individuals, foreign companies and non-profit making legal entities are subject to Belgian non-resident income tax on income from Belgian sources. Non-residents are, for these purposes, persons who do not have their economic interests in Belgium or companies or associations not having their registered office, main establishment or a place of management in Belgium.

772. The tax treatment of non-residents is established in Articles 227 through 248 of the ITC. These rules may not apply, however, in cases where international double taxation treaties concluded by Belgium apply. Typically, these conventions are based on the OECD Model Convention and contain special rules determining the competence of a state to tax income from real property, business income obtained through a permanent establishment and foreign source interest, dividends and royalties.

§1. Non-resident individuals

773. Non-resident status for tax purposes is not necessarily precluded if the individual concerned lives or resides in Belgium on a semi-permanent basis. Individuals who

do not have their principal place of residence or the centre of their economic interests in Belgium qualify for this status. Foreign diplomatic agents and career consular agents assigned to Belgium fall within this category. Other members of foreign diplomatic and consular missions in Belgium and their family members living with them are included, provided they do not have Belgian nationality and their home countries grant reciprocal treatment. Officials, agents and representatives of foreign states, regional entities or public law institutions also fall within the scope of this category, provided that they do not have Belgian nationality and they do not provide their services on a commercial basis.

774. Non-residents are taxed on income gained in Belgium only. It follows that professional income gained outside Belgium will not be subject to Belgian income taxes. For such Belgian income, non-resident tax is levied according to the same rules and rates as for resident individuals. The municipal surcharge, however, is fixed at 6 per cent.

§2. Profit-seeking foreign entities

775. This category includes all companies, organisations and institutions which have legal personality or which are constituted in a legal form similar to a limited liability company or a partnership and which have their registered office, principal establishment or management seat outside Belgium.

§3. Non-profit making foreign legal entities

776. This category includes foreign countries, their regional and local entities and non-profit making companies, organisations and institutions with legal personality which have their registered office, principal establishment or management seat outside Belgium.

B. Taxable income

777. The taxable income of non-residents consists solely of income obtained in Belgium. Income acquired elsewhere is not subject to Belgian tax.

§1. Income from real property

778. Real property income is income from real property located in Belgium. The taxable amount of such income is determined on the basis of the same rules as those prevailing under the individual or legal entities tax. If the real property is used in the performance of a business activity, the income will qualify as business income.

§2. Income from personal property

779. Non-residents are subject to tax on income from their personal property obtained from:
    (i) a Belgian resident;
    (ii) a company or institution with its registered office or principal place of business in Belgium;
    (iii) the Belgian State, the regions, provinces or municipalities;
    (iv) the Belgian establishment of a non-resident; or
    (v) a non-resident, provided that the payment was made in Belgium.

780. The taxable income from personal property consists of dividends, interest and other income. Unless such income is obtained from personal property used in Belgium for professional purposes, in which case it will qualify as business income, personal property of non-residents will in principle be subject to withholding tax.

§3. Business income

781. The 4 main categories of business income which are subject to non-residents income tax are:
    (i) the profits resulting from industrial, commercial or agricultural activities,
    (ii) income from liberal professions;
    (iii) all types of remuneration of individuals; and
    (iv) pensions and annuities.

1. Income from industrial, commercial or agricultural activities

782. A distinction is made between income derived through a Belgian establishment and income obtained without the intervention of such a Belgian establishment. Taxpayers who have a Belgian establishment are taxable on all income earned, directly or indirectly, through that establishment irrespective of whether they do business with residents or non-residents and whether the Belgian establishment took the initiative to do business or only acted as an intermediary. The term "Belgian establishment" means a fixed establishment through which the professional activities of a foreign enterprise are wholly or partly carried out in Belgium. This includes a place of management, a branch, an office, a factory, a workshop, an agency, a mine, a construction site if it lasts for an uninterrupted period of more than 30 days, a warehouse or a stock of goods. Agents representing a non-resident in Belgium, who do not act as independent intermediaries, may qualify as a Belgian establishment. Finally, each partner in a partnership or member of an association without legal personality which has its registered office, principal establishment

or management seat in Belgium or which has a Belgian establishment, will itself be considered to have a Belgian establishment.

783. Non-residents who do not have a Belgian establishment may nevertheless be subject to tax in Belgium if they derive from Belgium:
   (i) income from the sale or lease of real property located in Belgium;
   (ii) income from transactions carried out in Belgium by foreign insurance companies which usually enter into contracts in Belgium. Reinsurance activities do not fall within this category. It should also be noted that the fact that goods which are located in Belgium or individuals who reside in Belgium are insured by foreign insurance companies does not result in the taxation of the foreign insurance company if it is not in the normal course of business of the latter to conclude policies in Belgium;
   (iii) income from performances in Belgium by artists or sportsmen, even if such income is paid to another individual or legal entity, such as an agency for artists;
   (iv) income earned by a non-resident company or association which is a director of a Belgian company or which carries out activities in a Belgium establishment; or
   (v) income earned by a partner in a Belgian partnership which has no legal personality.

   2. Income from activities by a self-employed person

784. Non-resident individuals are in principle taxable on all of the income earned from their self-employed activities, whether or not such income is obtained through a Belgian establishment. Most double taxation treaties provide that income from independent personal services or other activities of an independent character is only taxable in the country where the services are rendered if the non-resident has a fixed base in that country for the purpose of performing his activities.

   3. All types of remuneration, pensions and annuities

785. A non-resident is liable to income tax on any remuneration obtained as an employee or as an active partner in a company, as well as on pensions and annuities, provided that such remuneration is paid by a Belgian resident, a company with its registered office or principal place of business in Belgium, the Belgian State, the regions, provinces or municipalities or the Belgian establishment of a non-resident. This category of income also includes replacement income such as unemployment or sickness indemnities.

786. Remuneration paid to a non-resident by a non-resident which is not allocated to the results of a Belgian establishment will nevertheless be subject to the non-resident income tax if the beneficiary of such income resides in Belgium for more than 183 days a year.

4. Miscellaneous income

787. Non-residents are, in principle, taxed on all miscellaneous income (as defined in respect of resident individuals) which they obtain in Belgium.

C. Exemptions

788. Certain income items are not subject to Belgian non-resident income tax, mainly because they are not paid or obtained in Belgium. These include:

　(i) income from personal property or securities other than shares received from a Belgian resident or a company with its registered office or principal place of business in Belgium, provided that the income is not obtained in Belgium and is charged to an establishment outside Belgium. For example, interest on a loan paid by the permanent establishment in France of a Belgian company to a French bank will not be subject to Belgian non-resident income tax;

　(ii) income from non-Belgian securities which are deposited in Belgium under the conditions laid down by the Minister of Finance and which are not used for professional purposes in Belgium. The exemption from non-resident income tax implies also an exemption from withholding tax;

(iii) remuneration to employees, directors and active partners of companies, received from individuals or entities subject to Belgian personal income tax, corporate income tax or income tax on legal entities, provided that the remuneration is related to an activity performed outside Belgium and is paid through an establishment outside Belgium;

　(iv) income obtained in Belgium by a foreign company through the transactions of a representative who only takes orders from established clients and transfers them to such company. The representative may not solicit new customers; and

　(v) income obtained in Belgium by a foreign company which owns ships or airplanes which land in Belgium to load or unload goods or passengers.

D. Calculation of taxable income

789. Individuals, companies and legal entities are each subject to different rules for the calculation of their taxable income.

§1. Non-resident individuals

790. Non-exempted personal property income and miscellaneous income is always taxed separately by means of withholding taxes. Non-resident individuals who have no Belgian income other than such personal property income and miscellaneous income do not have to file a tax return. The only tax due is the withholding tax which is paid in Belgium by the party or intermediary who pays the income.

791. Non-resident individuals who receive Belgian business income or income from the rental of real property located in Belgium, or both, must file a tax return and will be taxed on this income.

792. Apart from the special tax regime which applies to expatriate executives (*See*, paras. 797 *et seq.*), non-resident individuals who maintain a residence in Belgium during an entire tax year are allowed to make the same deductions as resident taxpayers who are subject to individual income tax. Non-resident individuals who do not have such a residence may only deduct the following expenses and costs from their taxable income:
    (i) 80 per cent of allowances paid on the basis of a legal obligation of support to a Belgian resident;
    (ii) gifts to Belgian universities, cultural or welfare institutions; and
    (iii) payments made for the acquisition of long-term leases, building or planting rights or similar rights if these rights are established on real property in Belgium.

§2. Non-resident companies

793. Non-resident companies are subject to non-resident income tax on all income earned in Belgium through a Belgian establishment, as well as on certain items of income earned without the intervention of a Belgian establishment.

794. The net amount of the different types of taxable income is calculated in accordance with the corporate income tax rules. Business expenses are deductible only if they can be allocated to a Belgian establishment and are related to business income which is taxable in Belgium.

§3. Non-resident non-profit making legal entities

795. Non-profit making foreign legal entities are taxable on certain income from real property and also on certain payments received. The determination of the net taxable income of non-profit making foreign legal entities is generally identical to that of legal entities subject to the Belgian legal entities income tax.

E. Minimum taxable income

796. If the profits of a Belgian establishment cannot be determined, for example in the absence of evidential bookkeeping, its taxable profits are determined as a lump-sum minimum corresponding to 10 per cent of the turnover figure, or € 7,000 to € 24,000 per employee, depending upon the economic sector involved. However, the minimum taxable profit is € 9,500 in all cases. It is debatable whether the minimum tax base rules are compatible with the non-discrimination provisions contained in certain tax treaties concluded by Belgium or with the EC law principles of free movement.

F. Special tax regime for certain foreign executives

797. The relevant rules regarding foreign executives are primarily contained in an administrative circular of 8 August 1983 (hereinafter "the Circular Letter of 8 August 1983"). The special taxation regime was established to compensate for the higher level of taxation and cost of living which a foreign executive may face when coming to Belgium. Under this regime, part of the salary earned by the executive will be considered to be compensation for these higher costs, paid by the employer to induce the executive to work in Belgium. This compensation may be granted tax-free.

798. The result of the application of the special taxation regime is that an employer wishing to ensure the payment of a defined net salary to his employee, will have to sustain the burden of a lower gross salary than if he had to pay the net salary under the normal application of the Belgian tax laws. In other words, the special tax regime is regarded by the fiscal authorities as a benefit extended to the foreign employer wishing to conduct activities in Belgium.

§1. Conditions for the applicability of the special taxation regime

799. Both the employer and the employee must satisfy certain requirements for the special taxation regime to be applicable.

800. The employer must be part of an international group of companies. This condition will be deemed fulfilled if the employer is a Belgian branch or subsidiary of a foreign company. In addition, the activities of the employer must fit into one of the 3 categories set forth in the Circular Letter of 8 August 1983. These categories are:
   (i) a scientific centre or research laboratory;
   (ii) an office exclusively performing a controlling or co-ordinating function for an international group to which it belongs; or
   (iii) an enterprise creating goods or services.

801. The employee must satisfy the following conditions in order to benefit from the special taxation regime:
   (i) the employee must not have Belgian nationality;
   (ii) the employee must be an executive. According to the Circular Letter of 8 August 1983, an executive is a person performing a function which requires special knowledge and responsibility. An employee assigned to Belgium to set up a Belgian business unit will be considered to be an executive. In addition, other specific categories of personnel may benefit from the special tax regime as well. One such category is "specialised personnel". This is personnel which is very difficult or impossible to recruit in Belgium;
   (iii) the employee must have been transferred to Belgium from abroad, or must have been directly hired abroad by the Belgian entity; and
   (iv) the employee must be a non-resident for tax purposes. This is a very important requirement, and constitutes one of the reasons necessitating the provision of an extensive list of information to the tax authorities. Under Belgian tax law, a non-resident is a person whose tax domicile and place where his assets are administered are located outside of Belgium. To meet this condition, the employee will have to rely on a number of factual elements which should convince the authorities of the temporary nature of his stay in Belgium. The following elements may be considered: (a) spouse or children remaining abroad; (b) the availability of a dwelling abroad; (c) the attendance of children at a foreign school; (d) the possession of real estate or personal property abroad; (e) the subscription to life insurance abroad; (f) the continued participation in group insurance abroad; (g) the insertion of a "diplomatic clause" in a lease for a Belgian residence permitting early termination in the event of a move for professional reasons; (h) continued contributions to a foreign social security system; (i) an employment contract for a limited duration; (j) temporary employment in Belgium with a view to establishing or restructuring a company; and (k) the possibility that the employee might at any moment move his activities to another country because of contractual obligations or close links with a foreign company. This list is not exhaustive, nor is every component mandatory. Additional persuasive factors may be taken into consideration as well. In this context, it is important to mention that people who lived abroad prior to their employment in Belgium will be presumed to have non-resident status. This presumption can be rebutted only by an investigation demonstrating a change in the personal situation of the employee since his arrival in Belgium. As indicated, Belgian nationals will never be considered to be non-residents, even if assigned from or hired abroad.

§2. The request for the application of the special tax regime

802. The employer must file an application with the Deputy Director of the Service competent for the taxation of non-residents within the Ministry of Finance (*Dienst Buitenland/Service Étranger*). The application should include all necessary data regarding both the employer and the employee to enable the tax authorities to take a decision. In addition, the following information should be added:
    (i) an approximate calculation of the part of the salary of the employee that will benefit from the special tax regime; and
    (ii) the effective remuneration of the employee in question for the year prior to his employment in Belgium.

803. The application must be filed within 6 months following the month in which the employment in Belgium commenced.

§3. Tax savings

804. Under the special tax regime, income earned for work performed abroad is not taxable in Belgium ("travel exclusion").

805. As regards income earned for work performed in Belgium, a part of the income may be considered as compensation paid by the employer to help the employee face the higher tax burden and costs of living in Belgium. These "costs borne by the employer" are tax-exempt, provided they are reasonable. For certain types of expenses (for instance the costs of moving to Belgium and the costs of refurbishing a Belgian dwelling), the reasonableness will be determined on a case by case basis. Other types of expenses will be accepted only if they do not exceed certain limits. In this regard, 2 limits are applicable: € 11,150 for employees of an enterprise creating goods or services; and € 29,700 for employees exercising a co-ordinating function in a controlling or co-ordinating office. The expenses included in these amounts are the following:
    (i) allowances aimed at compensating for the additional cost of living and housing, which are based on a hypothetical basic salary in the home country. The basic salary is equal to the gross salary paid in Belgium, minus a foreign service premium (usually 10 per cent), multiplied by an index reflecting the difference between the wage scale in Belgium and in the home country. This index varies according to the country of origin of the applicant;
    (ii) an allowance aimed at compensating for the different levels of taxation. It is equal to the difference between Belgian taxes on the hypothetical basic salary (as calculated above), increased by the foreign service premium and decreased by Belgian social security contributions, remuneration for work performed

abroad and a fixed deduction for professional expenses, and taxes which would be due on the hypothetical salary in the home country less the foreign service premium, social security contributions and standard deductions provided for all residents of the home country;

(iii) costs of an annual trip to the country of origin; and

(iv) travelling costs caused by exceptional circumstances such as the death or illness of close relatives.

806. The employee must be able to demonstrate that all expenses were actually incurred and that all allowances were warranted. This suggests the importance of retaining documents for certain expenses (such as the invoice of the shipping company for moving expenses) or showing sensible calculations (for tax equalisation). Generally, only approximate calculations should be made at the time of the request for application of the special tax regime. Detailed calculations should be supplied at the time of submission of the tax return.

VI. INTERNATIONAL ASPECTS OF INCOME TAXATION

A. Bilateral double taxation conventions

§1. Purpose

807. Objectives of bilateral double taxation conventions are to avoid double taxation or to mitigate its consequences. Double taxation exists when 2 or more different national jurisdictions subject a taxpayer to taxation for the same taxable assets and during the same period.

§2. Double taxation treaties concluded by Belgium

808. Belgium maintains an extensive network of double taxation treaties. The vast majority of these treaties follow the OECD Model Tax Convention.

List of treaty countries	Date
Algeria	15 December 1991
Argentina	12 June 1996
Australia	13 October 1977 and 20 March 1984
Austria	29 December 1971
Azerbeidjan	17 December 1987
Bangladesh	18 October 1990

Belorussia	7 March 1995
Brazil	23 June 1972
Bulgaria	25 October 1988
Canada	29 May 1975
China	18 April 1985
Croatia	21 November 1980
Cyprus	14 May 1996
Czech Republic	16 December 1996
Denmark	16 October 1969
Egypt	3 January 1991
Finland	18 May 1976 and 13 March 1991
France	10 March 1964, 15 February 1971 and 8 February 1999
Georgia	17 December 1987
Germany	11 April 1967
Greece	24 May 1968
Hungary	19 July 1982
India	26 April 1993
Indonesia	16 September 1997
Ireland	24 June 1970
Israel	13 July 1972
Italy	29 April 1983
Ivory Coast	25 November 1977
Japan	28 March 1968 and 9 November 1988
Kazakhstan	16 April 1998
Korea (South)	29 August 1977 and 20 April 1994
Kuwait	10 March 1990
Luxembourg	17 September 1970
Macedonia	21 November 1980
Malaysia	24 October 1973 and 25 July 1979
Malta	28 June 1974
Mauritius	4 July 1995
Mexico	24 November 1992
Moldavia	17 December 1987

Morocco	4 May 1972 and 14 February 1983
Netherlands	19 October 1970 and 5 June 2001 (new treaty)
New Zealand	15 September 1981
Nigeria	20 November 1989
Norway	14 April 1988
Pakistan	17 March 1980
Philippines	2 October 1976
Poland	14 September 1976
Portugal	16 July 1969
Romania	4 March 1996
Russian Federation	16 June 1995
Senegal	29 September 1987
Singapore	8 February 1972
Slovakia	15 January 1997
Slovenia	22 June 1998
South Africa	1 February 1995
Spain	24 September 1970
Sri Lanka	3 February 1983
Sweden	5 February 1992
Switzerland	28 August 1978
Tajikistan	17 December 1987
Thailand	16 October 1978
Tunisia	22 February 1975
Turkey	2 June 1987
Ukraine	20 May 1996
United Kingdom and Northern Ireland	1 June 1987
United States of America	9 July 1970 and 31 December 1987
USSR	17 December 1987
Uzbekistan	14 November 1996
Venezuela	22 April 1993
Vietnam	28 February 1996
Yugoslavia	21 November 1980

809. Belgium has signed tax treaties with Cyprus, Gabon, Kuwait and Mongolia, but these treaties have not yet become effective. Belgium is honouring the USSR treaty with respect to the republics forming part of the Commonwealth of Independent States (CIS). It is honouring the Yugoslavia treaty with respect to the new republics comprising the former Yugoslavia, except for Macedonia, Montenegro and Serbia. Belgium and Portugal have signed an amendment to their tax treaty, but this amendment has not yet been ratified. A new treaty was signed with Spain, but has not yet been ratified.

§3. Belgian withholding tax rates under the tax treaties

810. Subject to exceptions, Belgian withholding taxes on dividends, interest and royalties under the relevant double taxation treaties are shown in the table below.

Residents of	Dividends (in percentage)	Interest (in percentage)	Royalties (in percentage)
Argentina	15	12(a)	15(e)(g)
Australia	15(i)	10	10
Austria	15(c)	15(a)	Nil
Bangladesh	15	15(a)	10(g)
Brazil	15	15(a)	15(e)
Bulgaria	10	10(a)	5
Canada	15	15(a)	10(f)
China	10	10(a)	10
Czech Republic	15	10(a)	5(e)
Denmark	15(c)	15(a)	Nil
Egypt	20(i)	15	15
Finland	15(c)(i)	10(a)	5(e)
France	15(c)(i)	15	Nil
Germany	15(c)	15(a)	Nil
Greece	15(c)	10	5
Hungary	10	15(a)	Nil
India	15	15	Nil
Indonesia	15	15	10
Ireland	15(c)	15(a)	Nil

Israel	15	15(a)	10(b)
Italy	15(c)	15(a)	5
Ivory Coast	15	15	10
Japan	15(i)	10	10
Korea (Rep.)	15	10	10
Luxembourg	15(c)(i)	15(a)	Nil
Malaysia	15	15(a)	10(e)
Malta	15	10(a)	10(e)
Mauritius	10(i)	10(a)	Nil
Mexico	15(i)	15	10
Morocco	15	15	10(f)
Netherlands	15(c)	10(a)	Nil
New Zealand	15	10	10
Nigeria	15(i)	12.5	12.5
Norway	15(i)	15(a)	Nil
Pakistan	15	15(a)	15(f)
Philippines	20(h)	15(a)	15
Poland	10	10(a)	10
Portugal	15(c)	15(a)	5
Romania	10	15(a)	10
Senegal	15	15	10
Singapore	15	15(a)	Nil
South Africa	15(i)	10(a)	Nil
Spain	15(c)	15(a)	5
Sri Lanka	15	10(a)	10
Sweden	15(c)	10(a)	Nil
Switzerland	15(i)	10(a)	Nil
Thailand	20(i)	25	15(f)
Tunisia	15	15(a)	15(e)
Turkey	20(i)	15(a)	10
Ukraine	15(i)	10(a)	10
United Kingdom	10(c)	15	0
United States	15(i)	15(a)	15

USSR	15	15(a)	Nil
Uzbekistan	15(i)	10	5
Venezuela	15(i)	10(a)	5
Vietnam	15(i)	10	15
Yugoslavia	15(i)	15	10
Non-treaty countries	25	15	15

Notes

(a) possible exemption (Ukraine: exemption or 2 per cent rate)

(b) a 5-per cent rate applies to royalties for the use of works of art, science or literature, other than motion pictures.

(c) Under the Parent/Subsidiary Directive, no withholding tax is imposed on dividends paid by a Belgian subsidiary to a parent company in another EC Member State, if the recipient owns at least 25 per cent of the capital of the paying company for an uninterrupted period of at least 1 year.

(d) A 10 per cent rate applies if the recipient owns more than 50 per cent of the capital of the Belgian company.

(e) A 0-per cent rate (Argentina and Tunisia: 5 per cent) applies to copyright royalties.

(f) A 0-per cent rate (Morocco and Thailand: 5 per cent) applies to copyright royalties other than for motion pictures.

(g) Subject to certain conditions, reduced to 10 per cent.

(h) A 15-per cent rate applies if the dividends are exempt from tax in the Philippines.

(i) Reduced rates apply if the recipients holds qualifying shareholdings, as follows:

	Reduced rate (in percentage)	Shareholding (in percentage)
Argentina	10	25
Egypt	15	25
Finland	10	10
France	10	10
Japan	5	25
Luxembourg	Nil	€ 6.20 million
Mauritius	5	10
Mexico	5	25

Nigeria	12.5	10
Norway	5	25
South Africa	5	25
Switzerland	10	25
Thailand	15	25
Turkey	15	10
Ukraine	5	20
United States	5	10
Uzbekistan	5	10
Venezuela	5	25
Vietnam	5	50
Vietnam	10	25 (but < 50)
Yugoslavia	10	25

B. European tax law

811. In 1990, with a view towards the achievement of a Single European Market, the EC Council of Ministers adopted 3 important measures in the field of direct company taxation that had been on the agenda for more than 20 years. The measures are:
    – EC Council Directive No. 90/435 of 23 July 1990 on the Common System of Taxation Applicable in the Case of Parent Companies and Subsidiaries of Different Member States (the so-called "Parent/Subsidiary Directive" – O.J. [1990] L 225/6);
    – EC Council Directive No. 90/434 of 23 July 1990 on the Common System of Taxation Applicable to Mergers, Divisions, Transfers of Assets and Exchanges of Shares Concerning Companies of Different Member States (the so-called "Tax Merger Directive" – O.J. [1990] L 225/1); and
    – Convention No. 90/436 of 23 July 1990 on the Elimination of Double Taxation in Connection with the Adjustment of Profits of Associated Enterprises (the so-called "Arbitration Convention" – O.J. [1990] L 225/10).

812. Another instrument which is also relevant in the tax area is EC Council Regulation No. 2137/85 of 25 July 1985 on the European Economic Interest Grouping (O.J. [1985] L 199/1 – the "EEIG Regulations").

§1. Parent/Subsidiary Directive

813. The Parent/Subsidiary Directive applies to intra-Community dividends, *i.e.*, to distributions of profits received by companies established in one EC Member State

which come from their subsidiaries of other EC Member States and to distributions of profits by companies of one EC Member State to companies of other EC Member States of which they are subsidiaries.

814. For purposes of the Parent/Subsidiary Directive, a parent company is defined as a company which has a minimum holding of 25 per cent in the capital of a company of another EC Member State. A subsidiary is a company the capital of which includes such a holding. EC Member States have the option of replacing, by way of bilateral agreement, the criterion of a holding in the capital by that of a holding of voting rights.

815. The Parent/Subsidiary Directive does not provide for a minimum holding period. However, EC Member States have the option of not applying the Directive to companies which do not maintain, for an uninterrupted period of at least 2 years, holdings qualifying them as parent companies or to companies in which a company of another EC Member State does not maintain such a holding for an uninterrupted period of at least 2 years. EC Member States are not allowed to require that the minimum holding requirement is satisfied at the time of the dividend distribution.

816. The Parent/Subsidiary Directive only concerns companies set up in one of the forms listed in the Annex thereto. For Belgium, these are the public limited liability company (*naamloze vennootschap/société anonyme*), the partnership limited by shares (*commanditaire vennootschap op aandelen/société en commandite par actions*), the private limited liability company (*besloten vennootschap met beperkte aansprakelijkheid/société privée à responsabilité limitée*) and those public law bodies that operate under private law. In addition, companies eligible under the Parent/Subsidiary Directive must be subject to tax without the possibility of an option or of being exempt (in Belgium: corporate income tax). A Proposal of 26 July 1993 aimed at extending the scope of application of the Parent/Subsidiary Directive to all companies subject to corporate income tax, regardless of their corporate form, is still pending.

817. Under the Parent/Subsidiary Directive, dividends received (excluding liquidation proceeds) by a qualifying parent company from a qualifying subsidiary will, in the EC Member State of the parent company, either be exempted or be eligible for a credit of that fraction of the corporate income tax paid by the subsidiary to which those profits relate. Each EC Member State retains the option of providing that any charges relating to the holding and any losses resulting from the distribution of the profits of the subsidiary may not be deducted from the taxable profits of the parent company. Where the management costs relating to the holding in such a case are fixed as a flat rate, the fixed amount may not exceed 5 per cent of the profits distributed by the subsidiary.

818. On the other hand, profits distributed by a qualifying subsidiary to its qualifying parent company are exempt from withholding tax, at least where the parent company holds a minimum of 25 per cent of the capital of the subsidiary. Said exemption overrides the provisions of applicable tax treaties between EC Member States.

819. The Parent/Subsidiary Directive does not preclude the application of domestic or agreement-based provisions required for the prevention of fraud or abuse.

820. The Parent/Subsidiary Directive has been implemented into Belgian law by the Law of 23 October 1991 and the Royal Decree of 14 October 1991. The Belgian requirements with respect to the minimum holding period have been amended by the Royal Decree of 6 July 1997 in order to do away with the condition that the minimum holding period had to be met at the time of the dividend distribution.

§2. Tax Merger Directive

821. The European Commission had 2 fundamental objectives in proposing to the EC Council of Ministers the common system of taxation applicable to mergers, divisions and contributions of assets. Since the main obstacle to merger-type reorganisations involving companies incorporated in different countries lies in the taxation costs of the operation, the European Commission had to develop a system whereby these transactions do not, by their very nature, give rise to tax liability. This step was deemed necessary so that companies wishing to extend their activities to other. EC Member States would no longer have to rely on the use of intermediate holding companies or on contractual co-operation with a foreign partner. On the other hand, the tax jurisdiction of the country of incorporation of the transferring or contributing company had to be safeguarded. Because the acquired company will normally become a permanent establishment of the company which has taken it over, the country of incorporation of such a company must be entitled to impose taxes on the transferred assets in the future.

822. EC Member States were required to comply with the provisions of the Tax Merger Directive before 1 January 1992, except for Portugal which was authorised to delay the application of the provisions concerning the transfer of assets and exchanges of shares until 1 January 1993. Belgium has not yet implemented the Tax Merger Directive in its entirety at the time of writing (*See*, para. 758).

823. The common system governing mergers also applies to divisions, transfers of assets and exchanges of shares in which companies from 2 or more EC Member States are involved. These transactions are defined in detail in the Tax Merger Directive. Central to the definitions is the concept that mergers and divisions are operations whereby the company or companies involved are dissolved without

going into liquidation. Under current Belgian company law, this is only possible for domestic mergers and divisions.

824. The provisions of the Tax Merger Directive apply to enterprises which are considered to be resident in an EC Member State for tax purposes and which, under the laws of said EC Member State, are subject to corporate income tax. These enterprises must take one of the forms listed in the Annex to the Tax Merger Directive. As far as Belgium is concerned, the qualifying companies are the public limited liability company (*naamloze vennootschap/société anonyme*), the partnership limited by shares (*commanditaire vennootschap op aandelen/société en commandite par actions*), the private limited liability company (*besloten vennootschap met beperkte aansprakelijkheid/société privée à responsabilité limitée*) and those public law bodies that operate under private law.

825. The Tax Merger Directive establishes a general (but provisional) tax exemption in respect of capital gains arising from the contribution of assets in a merger, division or transfer of assets. In order to safeguard the interests of the country in which the transferring company is incorporated, a general deferral of the payment of tax due is provided for with respect to capital gains until they are realised. Since the above transactions normally result in the transformation of the transferring company into a permanent establishment of the receiving company or in the assets becoming connected with a permanent establishment of the receiving company, the country in which the transferring company is incorporated will be allowed to tax the capital gains after the date of the actual realisation by the receiving company of the assets in question.

826. For this system of deferred taxation to be applicable, the receiving company must compute depreciation and any gains or losses in respect of the transferred assets and liabilities according to the rules that would have applied to the transferring company if the merger, division, or transfer of assets had not taken place.

827. The system of deferred taxation also applies to situations where 3 EC Member States are involved, for example, when the transferred assets include a permanent establishment of the transferring company which is situated in an EC Member State other than that of the transferring company or receiving company. The state in which the permanent establishment is located and the state of the receiving company will be subject to the provisions of the Merger Directive as if the state of the permanent establishment were the state of the transferring company. The state of the transferring company must renounce any right to tax the permanent establishment, except in those cases when the losses of the permanent establishment have previously been set off against the taxable profits of the transferring company

and have not yet been recovered as of the date of transfer. In this situation, the state of the transferring company may add an amount equal to such losses to the taxable profits of the company.

828. As an exception to this general rule, the EC Member State of the transferring company has the right to tax any profits or capital gains of a permanent establishment of the transferring company situated in another EC Member State resulting from a merger, division, or transfer of assets, provided it taxes world-wide profits and grants relief for the tax that would have been charged on those profits or capital gains in the EC Member State in which the permanent establishment is situated in the same way as if that tax had actually been levied by and paid to the EC Member State in which the permanent establishment is located.

829. The provisions and reserves of the transferring company, which have been accumulated under a partial or total tax exemption, may be carried over tax-free to the books of the permanent establishment of the receiving company which is located in the state of the transferring company. In this respect, the receiving company must also assume the associated obligations of the transferring company.

830. Losses which have not yet been set off against the profits of the transferring company may be assumed by the receiving company's permanent establishment located in the State of the transferring company. This rule only applies to EC Member States which allow a carrying-over of losses when both the receiving and the transferring companies are situated in its territory.

831. A receiving company holding at least 25 per cent of the capital of the transferring company will not be taxed on the gains made on the cancellation of the shares. The EC Member States may derogate from this provision and lower the required minimum holding.

832. The Tax Merger Directive also exempts from tax the exchange of shares of the receiving or acquiring company for shares of the transferring or acquired company if the value of the former for tax purposes is not higher than the value of the latter immediately before the merger, division or exchange.

833. EC Member States may refuse to apply or withdraw the benefit of the Tax Merger Directive where it appears that the merger, division, transfer of assets or exchange of shares has as its principal objective, or as one of its principal objectives, tax evasion or tax avoidance. The fact that the operation is not carried out for valid commercial reasons, such as the restructuring or rationalisation of the activities of the companies participating in the operation, may constitute a presumption that the operation has tax evasion or tax avoidance as its principal objective or as one of

its principal objectives. However, in order to be permissible under European law, domestic measures aimed at fighting tax evasion or tax avoidance must not be of a general scope and nature.

834. The Tax Merger Directive has been implemented in part into Belgian law by the Law of 23 October 1991 (exchange of shares) and the Law of 28 July 1992 (contribution of assets). The Law of 6 August 1993 further amended the tax regime for mergers and other reorganisations, but except for a contribution of a branch of activity or a universality of goods, the Belgian tax legislation is limited to domestic transactions. According to the European Court of Justice, however, provisions applicable to domestic transactions may be tested against the Tax Merger Directive if the national legislature, when implementing the Tax Merger Directive, attuned internal legislation to community law by deciding to grant the same treatment to purely internal situations and cross-border situations.

§3. Arbitration Convention

835. The Arbitration Convention provides for an arbitration procedure to resolve double taxation that may arise when tax authorities of different EC Member States reassess transfer prices between associated enterprises. Although the Arbitration Convention was originally proposed as a Directive in 1976, the EC Council of Ministers felt that the measure should be drafted in the form of a multinational convention. Belgium ratified the Arbitration Convention by the Law of 3 March 1993. Portugal was the last state to deposit the instrument of ratification on 28 October 1994. Thus, the Arbitration Convention entered into effect on 1 January 1995.

836. The key provision of the Arbitration Convention is Article 4, which provides that the profits made by one enterprise from dealings with an associated enterprise may be increased to the level they would have been had the enterprises been independent and dealing at arm's length. Such a provision is similar to Article 9(1) of the OECD Model Tax Convention. Further, the Arbitration Convention provides that the same principle applies to adjustments relating to permanent establishments. For the purposes of making adjustments to prices charged between an enterprise and its permanent establishment situated in another EC Member State, the latter is deemed to be an enterprise of the state in which it is located.

837. It is unclear whether European branches of non-EC enterprises (for example, US-based groups), are covered by the Arbitration Convention. Nevertheless, from a reading of Article 4 of the Arbitration Convention together with the Joint Declaration to the Arbitration Convention, it may reasonably be asserted that the Arbitration Convention excludes permanent establishments of non-EC enterprises situated

within the European Union. Thus, a transaction between a French company and the Brussels permanent establishment (for example, a co-ordination centre) of a US-based multinational would not be governed by the Arbitration Convention. This potential disadvantage for US corporations should, however, be seen in the light of applicable double taxation agreements. The US-German double taxation agreement, for example, provides for an arbitration procedure similar to the procedure set out under the Arbitration Convention.

838. The Arbitration Convention's main objective is to resolve issues of double taxation within a maximum of 3 years from the initiation of proceedings. In this context, if an enterprise is of the opinion that it is subject to adjustment in contravention of the principle set out in Article 4 of the Arbitration Convention, it may present its case to the tax authorities of the EC Member State concerned. If the parties do not reach an agreement, the following procedure can be initiated:

(i) a mutual agreement procedure in line with Article 25 of the OECD Model Tax Convention is provided by the Arbitration Convention; and

(ii) if the alleged double taxation has still not been eliminated within 2 years of the date on which the objection was first raised, the competent authorities of the EC Member States involved in the procedure are required to set up an advisory commission. Within 6 months following its constitution, the advisory commission has to deliver its opinion on the elimination of the double taxation in question. The competent authority involved then has an additional 6 months to take a decision.

839. Until this stage of the procedure, EC Member States involved are not compelled to reach agreement concerning the elimination of double taxation. Moreover they are allowed to deviate from the advisory commission's opinion. Only if EC Member States fail to reach an agreement before the last deadline will the opinion of the advisory commission become binding.

840. Finally, the Arbitration Convention provides for 2 types of exception. The first prevents EC Member States from reaching a settlement where such a settlement derogates from a court decision. The second exception entitles EC Member States to waive the procedure if legal or administrative proceedings have resulted in a final ruling imposing a serious penalty on an enterprise in respect of action taken to adjust the transfer of profits. Once the arbitration procedure has been initiated, however, the proceedings may only be stayed until the issue of such a final ruling by a joint decision of all tax authorities involved.

§4. European Economic Interest Groupings

841. EC Council Regulation No. 2137/85 of 25 July 1985 (O.J. [1985] L 199/1 – the "EEIG Regulation") introduced the European Economic Interest Grouping ("EEIG"). An EEIG is a legal vehicle for the cooperation of 2 or more enterprises situated in at least 2 different EC Member States in order to facilitate or develop the economic activities of its members and to improve or increase the results of those activities.

842. An EEIG thus exists to promote the interests of its members. Its purpose is not to make profits for itself. However, the EEIG is not prohibited from making profits. If profits accrue to its activities, they are deemed to be profits of the members and are to be apportioned among them in the proportion laid down in the contract for the formation of the EEIG or, in the absence of any such provision, in equal shares.

843. As regards the tax treatment of an EEIG, the EEIG Regulation merely spells out that the profits or losses from the activities of an EEIG are taxable in the hands of its members. This principle of tax transparency is not elaborated in the EEIG Regulation and must therefore be applied in accordance with national tax law of the EC Member States and the double taxation treaties concluded between them. With respect to the periodic attribution of profits to the members, the tax procedures and any tax obligations imposed, as well as the rules on the computation of annual profits, the tax law of the EC Member State under the law of which the EEIG has been constituted is applicable.

844. Belgium brought its legislation in line with the EEIG Regulation by the Law of 12 July 1989. Shortly thereafter, the Law of 17 July 1989 introduced legislation on the "Belgian" Economic Interest Grouping, enabling the constitution of economic interest groupings involving non-EC members. An EEIG constituted in Belgium (as well as a "Belgian" Economic Interest Grouping) is considered to be transparent for income tax purposes. Hence, the distributed profits, the reserved profits and the advances to the members are considered to be profits taxable in the hands of the members. Expenses are similarly considered to be expenses of the members, who may set them off against their taxable income.

VII. VALUE ADDED TAX

A. Definition and general principles

845. Value added tax (*Belasting over de toegevoegde waarde (BTW)/Taxe sur la valeur ajoutée (TVA)*) ("VAT") was introduced in Belgium as of 1 January 1971, replacing different categories of sales and cumulative turnover taxes. VAT was introduced to implement 2 EC Council Directives of 1967. Presently, VAT is charged in all EC Member States, although its application and rates may vary from EC Member State to EC Member State.

846. The rules on VAT are laid down in the VAT Code (*Wetboek van de belasting over de toegevoegde waarde/Code de la taxe sur la valeur ajoutée* – the "VATC"), introduced by the Law of 3 July 1969 as amended by the Laws of 27 December 1977 and 28 December 1992. Implementing legislation can be found in multiple Royal and Ministerial Decrees.

847. VAT is a general tax on consumption, but is levied on the occasion of each transfer on the basis of the price of the goods or services after deduction of the VAT directly bearing on the cost price of the various components constituting said price. Fundamentally, VAT is a tax levied at a flat rate and charged to the final consumer of goods and services within the country. The essence of VAT is that the tax has no cumulative effect regardless of the number of transactions taking place between the primary producer and the final consumer. It is paid to the tax authorities not by the final consumer, but by the intermediaries in the production and distribution process who, as taxpayers, are individually liable for their share of VAT due on the net value of their output. In this way, the total amount of VAT levied on the price of goods or services charged to the final consumer will be equal to the sum of partial payments made by the intermediaries to the tax authorities. It follows from these principles that intermediaries in the production and distribution process do not bear any tax, because they charge VAT on the value of their output to their customers and recover VAT paid on the value of their input, by retaining the amount of VAT paid to their suppliers from the amount of VAT received from their customers. Thus, the burden of the total amount of VAT rests completely with the final consumer, who can neither deduct the amount of VAT paid nor charge it to someone else, unless he uses the goods or services for professional purposes.

B. Taxable person

848. A VAT taxpayer is any person who independently carries out, in any place, any economic activity, whatever the purpose or results of that activity. Only supplies of

goods and services performed by a VAT taxpayer are subject to VAT. Only VAT taxpayers can exercise a right of deduction. Imports into Belgium are always subject to VAT, even if made by a non-taxable person. This is the sole instance in which transactions made by non-taxable persons are taxed, since the Government has not made use of the possibility to extend the application of VAT to non-taxable persons in order to avoid distortions of competition.

849. Individuals, companies or other legal entities solely engaged in activities that are specifically exempt from VAT are not deemed taxpayers for VAT purposes. This includes notaries, attorneys, medical professionals, hospitals, cultural and educational professions, insurance brokers and banks. Such entities are not obliged to charge VAT on goods delivered or services rendered by them. On the other hand, they may not deduct VAT paid on goods or services supplied to them. It should be noted, however, that several of these exempt categories (notaries and attorneys) are likely to become liable to charge and collect VAT in the near future.

850. Public entities such as the Federal State, the regions, the provinces and public institutions are exempt from paying VAT. However, if these entities perform commercial activities on a regular basis, they can be considered as entities obliged to charge VAT.

C. Taxable transactions

851. There are 4 categories of taxable transactions:
    (i) the supply of goods;
    (ii) the rendering of services;
    (iii) importation of goods; and
    (iv) the intra-Community acquisition of goods.

§1. Supply of goods

1. Definitions

852. A supply of goods refers to the transfer of the right to dispose of a good as an owner. Even if from a civil law point of view, no transfer of legal ownership occurs, there may be a supply where there is a transfer of a tangible good enabling the other party to effectively dispose of the good as if it were the owner thereof. Goods are tangible goods, whether movable or immovable. Electricity, gas, heat and cold are considered to be goods. Rights *in rem*, other than ownership rights, which give the holder thereof an authority to use real property as an owner are also considered to be tangible goods (*e.g.*, *usufruct*). Intangible goods such as shares, bonds or commercial paper are excluded from VAT.

853. The transfer of a universality of goods or a branch of activity, whether or not for consideration, by way of contribution to a company or otherwise, is not considered to be a supply if the transferee is a taxpayer who, had VAT been due as a result of the transfer, would have been able to deduct such VAT, either in whole or in part. This exception applies to, for example, a transfer of a business, even if the commercial receivables and liabilities are not comprised in the transfer. In contrast, the client base is an essential feature of such a transfer.

854. The sale of buildings that qualify as "new" for VAT purposes are subject to VAT. A building is "new" if it is sold within 2 years of its construction. In that case, no registration duties are levied (except on the fraction of the price related to the land).

855. A taxable supply is deemed to occur if a taxpayer applies goods forming part of his business assets for his private use or that of his staff. The same holds true if such goods are applied for the disposal free of charge, except if it concerns the giving of samples or the making of gifts of small value for the purposes of the person's taxable business.

856. A special rule applies to "commissionaires" (*commisionairs/commisionaires*), *i.e.*, persons acting in their own name but for the account of a principal. A purchase commissionaire is considered as purchaser and, towards its principal, as seller of the good that is purchased through its intervention. Conversely, a sales commisionaire is considered as seller and, towards its principal, as seller of the good that is sold through its intervention. Although there is only one sale, there is a double sale from a VAT point of view.

2. *Place and time of the supply of goods*

857. A supply of goods takes place in Belgium if:
    (i) the place where the good is put at the disposal of the acquirer or transferee is situated in Belgium;
    (ii) the dispatching or transportation of a good to the acquirer begins in Belgium;
    (iii) a good is installed or assembled in Belgium by or on behalf of the supplier; or
    (iv) a good is supplied on board of a ship, aircraft or train during the part of a transport of passengers effected in the Community that departed in Belgium.

858. Unless there is evidence to the contrary, goods are deemed to have been supplied in Belgium if one of the contracting parties has the seat of his economic activity or a permanent establishment in Belgium, or in the absence thereof, his domicile or a usual place of residence in Belgium.

859. The supply takes place at the time when a good is put at the disposal of the acquirer or transferee. If the good is dispatched or transported by or on behalf of the supplier, the supply takes place at the time when the good arrives with the acquirer or transferee. If the good is installed or assembled by or on behalf of the supplier, the supply occurs at the time when the installation or assembly is finished. A supply of a building is deemed to take place at the latest on 31 December of the year following the year of assessment. For goods such as electricity, gas or heat that are supplied on a continuous basis, supply is deemed to take place at the end of each period for which a statement of account or payment is made. If the goods are already at the disposal of the purchaser before the conclusion of the contract or if the seller keeps the goods in his possession after the conclusion of the contract, supply is considered to take place at the time the contract enters into effect.

3. Chargeable event

860. The chargeable event means the occurrence by virtue of which the legal conditions necessary for tax to become chargeable are fulfilled. In principle, this event coincides with the time at which the VAT becomes due. A derogation from this principle applies if the price or a portion thereof is invoiced or received prior to the time of supply. In that case, the chargeable event is deemed to occur at the time of invoicing or payment. Moreover, VAT becomes due at the time when the price must contractually be satisfied in whole or in part if this occurs before supply, invoicing or collection.

§2. Supply of services

1. Definition

861. A service is any transaction that does not constitute a supply of goods. Examples of services subject to VAT include (a non-exhaustive list is contained in the VATC):
    (i) the putting at the disposal of personnel;
    (ii) the fringe benefit related to private use of company cars;
    (iii) the transfer of a clientele or the attribution of rights on clientele;
    (iv) the undertaking not to exercise a professional activity;
    (v) the transfer or granting of rights on a sales or purchase monopoly;
    (vi) the transfer of patents, trade marks, copyrights, industrial drawings, industrial models or other similar rights or the granting of licenses concerning such rights;
    (vii) the putting at the disposal of space for the storage of goods;
    (viii) banking and financial transactions;
    (ix) transactions of radio and television broadcasting companies and telecom operators;

(x) the provision of parking facilities; and

(xi) the provision of hotel services.

862. Services that are rendered on the occasion of a transfer of a universality of goods or a branch of activity, by way of contribution or otherwise, are not considered to be services for VAT purposes. However, the use of goods forming part of the assets of a taxpayer's business, or the supplies of services carried out free of charge by the taxable person, for his own use or that of his staff, are considered to be supplies of services.

2. Place and time of the supply of services

863. In order to be taxable the service must be rendered in Belgium. The general principle is that a service is considered rendered in Belgium if the supplier has established his business, a permanent establishment, his domicile or a usual residence from where the service is rendered in Belgium. This principle has numerous exceptions:

(i) the place of supply of services connected with real property is the place where the property is located. A Royal Decree of 29 December 1992 (amending Royal Decree No. 5 of 27 December 1977) provides a list of such services, among which are warehousing, hotel services and management services for real property;

(ii) the place of supply of services consisting of material work or an assessment of goods other than goods immovable by nature is the place where the goods are located;

(iii) the place of supply of services in the case of transport services, both for goods and persons, is deemed to be in Belgium in proportion to the distances covered;

(iv) intra-Community transport of goods is deemed to be supplied in whole at the place of departure (subject to derogation); and

(v) the place of supply of services is the place where the service is physically carried out in the case of cultural, artistic, sporting, scientific, educational, entertainment or similar activities, including the activities of the organisers of such events and the supply of ancillary activities, ancillary transport activities such as loading, unloading and handling, and hotel and restaurant activities.

864. In the case of the leasing of means of transportation, the place of supply is the place where the means of transportation is used if leased by a lessor established in Belgium and to the extent that it is used outside the European Community. The same rule applies if the lessor is established outside the European Community. In all other cases the general principle applies.

865. For services rendered to a recipient who is established outside the European Community or to a recipient acting for professional purposes established within the European Community but outside the country of the supplier, the place of supply is the place where the recipient has established his business, a permanent establishment or his domicile or habitual abode. This rule applies to the following services:
   (i) transfer or assignment of copyrights, patents, licenses, trademarks or other similar rights;
   (ii) transfer or assignment of rights on clientele, a sale or purchase monopoly; the right to exercise a professional activity, the undertaking not to exercise a professional activity or a copyright, patent, license, trade mark or other similar right;
   (iii) advertising services;
   (iv) intellectual work carried out by legal counsel, engineers, consultants and accountants and data processing services, information services and similar services;
   (v) banking and financial transaction services, with the exception of the lease of safes;
   (vi) supply of personnel;
   (vii) services of agents who act in the name and on behalf of their principal when they supply the above-listed services;
   (viii) leasing of all movable tangible property, except means of transport; and
   (ix) telecommunication services.

866. As of 1 January 2000, telecommunication services are deemed to take place in Belgium if such services are used by a non-taxable recipient established in the European Community and are performed by service providers established outside the European Community.

867. As regards the timing of the supply of services, the taxable event occurs at the time when the service is completed. In case of a series of continuous services, the service will be deemed completed at the end of each period for which an invoice is issued or a payment is made.

§3. Importation of goods

1. Definition

868. Importation of goods means the entry into the fiscal territory of the European Community of a good from third countries (*i.e.*, countries that are not EC Member States) or third country territories. Importation of goods, by whomever, is subject to VAT if the importation takes place in Belgium.

2. *Place of importation*

869. Importation takes place in the EC Member State where the good is located at the time of the entry into the European Community. Unless evidence to the contrary, any person having acquired goods in a third country or having caused goods to be processed there for his own account will be deemed to have imported those goods into Belgium. Specific rulers relate to temporary importation or transit arrangements. The underlying principle is that where goods are imported into Belgium under arrangements for transit or temporary admission, the goods will become subject to VAT only when they cease to be covered by these arrangements and are declared to be used in Belgium.

§4. *Intra-Community acquisition of goods*

870. Intra-Community acquisition of goods is defined as the acquisition of the power to dispose, as an owner, of tangible movable goods dispatched or transported to the person acquiring the goods, by or on behalf of the vendor or the person acquiring the goods, to an EC Member State other than that from which the goods are dispatched or transported. VAT is due by the person who makes the intra-Community acquisition of goods in Belgium. However, the intra-Community acquisition of excise goods is always taxable in the EC Member State of arrival or destination. Certain intra-Community acquisitions of goods are not subject to VAT (*e.g.*, if the vendor is a small enterprise exempted from VAT in its EC Member State or if the regime for distance sales is applicable). Certain transaction are treated as supplies of goods effected for consideration followed by an intra-Community acquisition of goods for consideration (*e.g.*, the transfer by a taxable person of goods from his undertaking to another EC Member State). In principle, the place where an intra-Community acquisition of goods occurs is the place where the goods are located at the time of the arrival of the dispatch or transport to the person acquiring the goods. The intra-Community supply of goods by taxable persons to another EC Member State is exempt from VAT. Special rules apply to distance sales.

D. Taxable amount

871. The taxable amount consists of everything that is obtained directly in respect of the supply made or service rendered and the counter-value of which can be expressed in money. In case of self-supplies or internal supplies the purchase price or the cost price generally constitutes the taxable amount. The value for customs purposes is the taxable amount in respect of imported goods.

872. Price discounts, rebates, interest for late payment, costs for standard packaging materials if returned by the customer and reimbursed by the supplier, advances made by the supplier or service providers to cover expenses made on behalf of his contracting party and VAT itself do not form part of the taxable amount. Commissions paid by the supplier of goods and services to the agent are not included in the taxable base. Commission fees paid by the customer to the supplier's agent are added to the taxable base in order to calculate VAT due.

873. Where buildings and land are sold together for a single price and the sale of the building is subject to VAT rather than registration tax, the taxable amount for the sale of the building is determined by subtracting the fair market value of the land as of the date of the sale from the total amount of the purchase price. The taxable amount for the sale of a building may not be lower than the fair market value of the building at the time of the sale, or the costs of all construction work and materials supplied. The tax authorities may request an evaluation of the building by an expert in order to determine the taxable base.

E. Tax rates

874. The rate applicable to taxable transactions is the rate in force at the time of the taxable event. The standard rate is 21 per cent. A reduced rate of 6 per cent applies mainly to necessities and social and cultural services such as foodstuffs, water, books, animal feed, pharmaceuticals, works of art and services related thereto. A reduced rate of 12 per cent applies to, *inter alia*, phytopharmaceutical products, tires for tractors and agricultural equipment, fuel, pay television, supplies of new buildings and transfers of rights *in rem* related to such buildings, if the buildings are destined for social housing. The reduced rate of 1 per cent applicable to gold held as an investment has been abolished as of 1 January 2000, and replaced by a special exemption for the supply, the intra-Community acquisition and the import of gold held as an investment. A zero rate applies to newspapers and magazines.

F. Exemptions

875. There are 2 types of exemptions, *i.e.*, exemptions without and exemptions with a loss of the right of deduction. The second category of exemptions does not grant the right of deduction of the input VAT related to exempt transactions. Taxable persons effecting such transactions are taxable persons without the right of deduction, implying that VAT paid by such persons on goods supplied to them for professional use cannot be reclaimed from the tax authorities and cannot be credited against any VAT liability, since there is no such liability.

876. The main types of exempt transactions are the following:
    (i) exports and transactions assimilated to exports;
    (ii) international transportation and ancillary agency services related thereto;
    (iii) supplies and imports of certain goods and performance of services related thereto;
    (iv) air and sea passenger transportation and the transportation of goods which are considered to be in transit or for export, and all services connected therewith;
    (v) the storage of goods in bonded warehouses and the services connected therewith;
    (vi) services performed by the legal and medical professions, hospitals, retirement homes and non-profit sports establishments;
    (vii) services performed by teachers and teaching institutions, libraries, lecturers, non-profit museums, artists and athletes;
    (viii) publishing contracts;
    (ix) deposit of funds, credit and discount of notes, payment and collection services;
    (x) insurance, foreign exchange and securities brokerage; and
    (xi) placing by religious institutions of personnel at someone's disposal for medical or teaching purposes.

G. Right of deduction

877. The essence of VAT is the deduction of input VAT by non-consumers. A taxable person has the right to deduct from the tax for which he is liable, in respect of his supplies, the tax invoiced to him on goods or services supplied to him or (intra-Community) acquired or imported by him. Recovery of VAT takes place by charging the deductible VAT to the VAT that the taxable person has charged to his customers. Only the balance between input and output VAT must be paid to the treasury. In case of excess input VAT, the excess is refundable subject to certain conditions. The right of deduction is exercised by way of the periodical VAT return. Taxable persons not established in Belgium who do not dispose of a permanent establishment in Belgium or do not have a fiscal representative may exercise their right of deduction by way of refund. The right of deduction arises at the time when the deductible tax becomes chargeable.

878. In order to be able to exercise the right of deduction in respect of supplies of goods and services, the taxable person must possess an original invoice that is drawn up in conformity with the applicable rules. For imports, an import document mentioning the taxable person as the recipient and the payment of the tax is required.

879. Immediate deduction of input VAT on goods or services supplied to the taxable person or on imports or intra-Community acquisitions of goods made by him is available if and to the extent the taxable person uses such goods or services for:
  (i) taxable transactions;
  (ii) exempted exports, imports or international transport; or
  (iii) transactions abroad for which the right of deduction would arise if carried out in Belgium.

880. Limitations on the right of deduction apply with respect to the supply, import and intra-Community acquisition of motor vehicles for the transportation of persons and of the intra-Community supply of new transportation means. In certain cases the right to deduction is entirely excluded. If the taxable person engages in both transactions giving rise to the right of deduction and other non-taxable transactions, a *pro rata* right of deduction is available. The *pro rata* is calculated on the basis of the fraction with, as denominator, the total amount of all transactions giving rise to the right of deduction and, as nominator, the total amount of all transactions carried out by the taxable person in the calendar year. Upon request, or if the *pro rata* method creates inequitable results, the method of the so-called real use may be authorised, meaning that the right of deduction can be exercised in respect of purchases effectively connected with transactions giving rise to the right of deduction without using the *pro rata* method.

881. The right of deduction is subject to revision if it appears that the actual deduction is higher or lower than the deduction originally made or, for investment goods, within 5 years (movable property) or 15 years (buildings), commencing on 1 January of the year in which the deduction was originally made. For buildings used for business purposes in respect of which the right of deduction arose before 31 December 1995, the revision period is 10 years.

H. Administrative obligations

§1. VAT registration

882. Before engaging in activities that are subject to VAT, each individual or company must obtain a VAT registration number. This number must be included on all documents submitted by the taxpayer. When a taxpayer ceases or modifies his taxable activities, he must notify the tax administration within 15 days. The application for a registration number as well as the notification of cessation of taxable activities must be filed on forms supplied by the tax administration. It can take up to 6 weeks for a VAT registration number to be issued.

883. The registration and notification requirements also apply to non-resident individuals or companies engaging in taxable activities and which have a permanent establishment in Belgium. When a non-resident individual or company has no permanent establishment, there is no obligation to register for VAT purposes. However, before any taxable transaction is carried out in Belgium, a non-resident must appoint a local tax representative who has been approved by the Ministry of Finance and who will become responsible for all VAT matters. In some cases, such as the supply of intellectual services by non-residents, no tax representative need be appointed, but the Belgian customer will be jointly and severally liable for the payment of the VAT.

§2. Issuance of invoices

884. Taxpayers must issue an invoice for each supply of goods or services. Invoices must be issued at the latest on the fifth working day of the month following the month in which the VAT becomes chargeable. Issuance of invoices is not compulsory if the goods or services are supplied to individuals who destine such goods or services to their private use. However, invoices must in any event be issued for:
   (i) supplies of cars, aircrafts, buildings, building works and for instalment sales;
   (ii) distance sales, for supplies of goods which, by their nature, are obviously destined for economic use;
   (iii) maintenance and repair services for cars, ships or aircrafts the price of which, VAT included, exceeds € 62; and
   (iv) moving and storage services.

885. Invoices must include the following information:
   (i) the date of issue and the number of the invoice;
   (ii) the supplier's name, address, VAT number and trade register number (if any);
   (iii) the customer's name and address;
   (iv) the date of supply;
   (v) a description of the goods or services supplied;
   (vi) the price and other elements of the taxable base; and
   (vii) the applicable VAT rate and amount of tax due.

§3. Filing of VAT returns and payment of the tax

886. Taxpayers must file a VAT return at the latest on the twentieth of each month relating to the transactions of the prior month. The tax must be paid within the filing period of the VAT return. Taxpayers whose annual turnover does not exceed € 500,000 may file a return 3 times a year if they make, in the second and third

month of each quarter, an advance payment of one-third of the VAT that was due for the preceding quarter.

§4. Client listing

887. Before the end of the first quarter of each year (*i.e.*, on 30 March at the latest), each taxpayer must file a list of clients based on the clients' accounts and relating to goods and services delivered during the preceding calendar year. This list must contain the following information concerning each customer: (i) name, (ii) address, (iii) VAT registration number, (iv) total amount of sales (exclusive of VAT) and (v) the total amount of VAT charged during the preceding year.

§5. VAT accounting

888. Taxpayers must keep detailed records to permit the filing of periodic tax returns and review by the tax authorities. Taxpayers must retain all records, books, invoices, returns and other documents required by the VAT legislation for a period of 5 years beginning from the date such books or records were closed or such invoices or documents were issued. Taxpayers must keep a book of incoming invoices and a book of outgoing invoices. Both books must be kept in bound form, except if a prior authorisation from the tax administration is received to keep the books in loose-leaf form. In addition, taxpayers must keep a journal of receipts. Corrections or modifications to these records because of price rebates, cancellations of contracts, return of packaging materials or errors in invoices or tax returns, must be evidenced by credit notes issued in duplicate and kept by the taxpayer in a special register and by the customer in his book of incoming invoices. Clients' accounts recording the delivery of all goods and services must be kept for each customer who is a taxpayer in order to establish the annual client listing. The accounting requirements are simplified for taxpayers whose annual turnover, net of VAT, does not exceed € 500,000.

I. VAT developments in the European Community

§1. General

889. Progress in the area of harmonising or approximating VAT, which started with the first 2 VAT Directives in 1967 and culminated in the adoption of the Sixth VAT Directive in 1977, has proven to be a time-consuming and difficult process. A major reason for this is that tax measures are not amongst the subject matter included in the regime of qualified majority voting at the EC Council of Ministers.

The EC Member States' reluctance to accept constraints on their power to tax explains the existence of the unanimity rule for the adoption of tax measures.

890. Although harmonisation or coordination progress in the VAT area has been more overwhelming than in the direct tax area, the fact remains that the VAT rules applicable in the various EC Member States are still, to a large extent, country-specific. The great divergences between VAT rates within the European Community – from zero (on some items in Belgium, Ireland, Portugal and the United Kingdom) to 36 per cent in Greece and 38 per cent in Italy – are illustrative of this. In the 1980s the European Commission unsuccessfully proposed VAT rate ranges with upper limits. On 19 January 2001, the EC Council adopted Directive No. 2001/4/EC amending Directive No. 77/388 (O.J. [2001] L 022/1) as regards the length of time during which the minimum VAT standard rate, set at 15 per cent, is to be applied.

891. The 1987 proposal for an origin-based common VAT system was aimed at achieving a true Single Market in which intra-Community sales and purchases of goods would be treated in the same way as those taking place within the EC Member States. Since, by the time of the abolition of border controls on 1 January 1993, the origin based system had not been achieved, a transitional system involving taxation in the country of consumption, at the rates and under the conditions applicable in that country, was retained. In 1996, the European Commission proposed a program involving a stage by stage movement to the definitive origin system. In the last few years, however, it has become apparent that, because of the importance of VAT for tax revenues, most EC Member States are reluctant to agree to proposals designed to lead towards the definitive system. While movement to the definitive origin system remains a long-term objective of the European Commission, its present strategy – which was announced in June 2000 – concentrates on bringing about an overall improvement in the operation of the current VAT system that would directly benefit EC taxpayers. Said strategy focuses on simplification, modernisation and a more uniform application of present arrangements, as well as closer administrative co-operation.

§2. Electronic commerce

892. The first proposal made after the new strategy was announced in June 2000 concerns the modification of the rules applying VAT to certain services supplied by electronic means (Proposal 2000/C 337E/04 for a Council Directive amending Directive No. 77/388 as regards the Value Added Tax Arrangements Applicable to Certain Services Supplied by Electronic Means; the "Proposal" – O.J. [2000] C 337E/65). The Proposal has the principal objective of protecting EC competitiveness by eliminating a major disadvantage for EC service providers relative to their

non-EC competitors. Indeed, under the current VAT provisions, unless specifically provided, where a supplier of services is based outside the European Community, no VAT is payable on services supplied to customers within the European Community. Although the reverse charge mechanism is likely to ensure the correct taxation of most business-to-business transactions, the existing provisions do not comprehensively take account of the full range of services which can be delivered electronically today. In addition, the existing rules do not ensure that electronically delivered services can, in all cases, be exported free of charge and that a sufficient legal basis exists for charging VAT on services supplied to EC private consumers by foreign operators. What is being proposed to rectify this situation is the continued use of the reverse charge mechanism linked to the imposition of a registration obligation on operators supplying to EC non-taxable persons.

893. Under the Proposal, transactions between businesses will be taxed under the reverse charge procedures. For supplies to non-taxable persons in the Community, EC businesses will continue to charge VAT in the EC Member State where the supplier is established. For supplies to non-EC customers, however, electronic supplies will be exempt from VAT. Non-EC suppliers selling to customers in the Community will be required to apply taxes on the same basis as an EC operator when transacting business in the Community, meaning that they must charge and account for VAT on sales to final consumers in the European Community. To this end, a single registration of non-EC suppliers is envisaged and provision is made for a registration threshold to exclude very small non-Community operators or those making occasional supplies into the European Community. Obviously, in rendering non-EC operators to act as tax collectors of what is in essence a European tax, the Proposal has invited a lot of criticism as it is not clear on which legal basis this could be achieved.

§3. Fiscal representatives

894. On 17 October 2000, the EC Council adopted the proposal concerning the abolition of fiscal representatives (EC Council Directive No. 2000/65 amending Directive No. 77/388/EEC as regards the Determination of the Person Liable for Payment of Value Added Tax; hereinafter, "Directive No. 2000/65" – O.J. [2000] L 269). Currently, the person liable for VAT is the operator carrying out taxable transactions. Where the operator is not established in an EC Member State in which the transactions are carried out, present Community legislation enables the EC Member State involved either to require the appointment of a tax representative or to make the taxable customer liable to the tax instead of the supplier. Tax representation has proven to be a complex, cumbersome and costly system.

895. Under Directive No. 2000/65, the obligation incumbent on European traders to appoint a tax representative in EC Member States in which they are not established was abolished as of 1 January 2002. Directive No. 2000/65 provides that the appointment of a tax representative or agent will no longer be an obligation but an option for European traders carrying out taxable transactions in another EC Member State. EC Member States will retain the possibility of deciding that the recipient should be liable to VAT (reverse charge mechanism) in business relations between taxable persons.

896. Directive No. 2000/65 has been implemented into Belgian legislation by the Law of 7 March 2002 and 2 Royal Decrees of 2 April 2002.

§4. Future prospects

897. A Communication of 23 May 2001 set outs the European Commission's VAT legislative strategy for the next 5 years. The European Commission intends to carry on with the work on existing proposals (amongst which the proposal related to e-commerce) as well as to present new proposals focusing on the recasting of the Sixth VAT Directive, the place of supply of goods and on travel agents. Some of this work is already under way. Further action points are in the field of financial services and in the field of subsidies, activities of public authorities and services as well as co-ordination of customs and taxation policies. As for VAT rates, a review and rationalisation of the rules and derogatory regimes applying to the definition of reduced VAT rates should be considered in the medium term, but not before the end of 2002. Particular attention will be paid to the rates applying to virtual products compared with traditional products and the use of reduced VAT rates in Community policies (*e.g.*, protection of the environment; promotion of employment). As indicated, the movement to a definitive origin-based VAT system remains a long-term goal.

VIII. REGISTRATION TAX

A. Introduction

898. Registration taxes (*registratierechten/droits d'enregistrement*) are levied on certain transactions and on the presentation for registration of certain deeds, writs and other documents. In most cases, except for leases, the obligation to register the document does not rest with the parties to the agreement or transaction, but with the official issuing the document.

899. In addition to the compulsory registration of certain transactions, private documents can be registered with the authorities for the purpose of authenticating their dates.

900. The basic rules regarding registration are laid down in the Registration and Mortgage Tax Code (*Wetboek der registratie, hypotheek en griffierechten/Code des droits d'enregistrement, d'hypothèque et de greffe*), the "RMTC".

901. Only the most important registration taxes will be briefly discussed here: (i) the tax on the sale or exchange of real property, (ii) the tax on capital contributions, (iii) the tax on leases and (iv) the gift tax.

B. Sale or exchange of real property

902. The sale or exchange of real property located in Belgium is subject to a proportional registration tax, regardless of whether the sale is made by an individual or a company (Art. 44 of the RMTC). The applicable rate is, in principle, 10 per cent in the Flemish Region and 12.5 per cent in the Walloon Region and the Brussels-Capital Region. The tax is calculated based on the sales price plus charges or the fair market value of the property as estimated by the tax authorities, whichever is higher.

903. As mentioned above, the sale of new buildings is, under certain circumstances, subject to VAT at the rate of 21 per cent. When VAT is applicable, no registration tax will be due. In such cases, only the fair market value of the land will be subject to the registration tax.

C. Corporate transactions

904. Unless a specific exemption applies, Article 115 of the RMTC imposes a registration tax of 0.5 per cent on capital contributions and on transfers of assets to a Belgian company if such transfers are made in exchange for shares in the company. The tax is calculated on the basis of the value of the shares issued in exchange for the assets transferred (including any premium charged in excess of the stated value of the shares). The tax also applies to any incorporation of retained earnings or other reserves in the capital.

905. The transfer of assets to a company in exchange for consideration other than shares is not subject to registration tax (but may be subject to VAT), except for the transfer of real property. As described above, the transfer of real property is subject to a 10 or 12.5 per cent rate (depending upon in which Region the real property is situated) instead of a 0.5 per cent rate.

906. When assets, including real property, are transferred to a company partially in exchange for shares and partially in exchange for consideration other than shares, each category of consideration will be taxed at the appropriate rate on a *pro rata* basis. The tax authorities have the power to question the validity of any capital contribution in the form of real property and may, in some cases, determine that such transfer is a *de facto* sale.

907. Article 117 of the RMTC exempts mergers, divisions and acquisitions of so-called branches of activity (*universaliteit van goederen/universalité de biens*) from the registration tax if the transferring company has its registered seat or its principal place of management in an EC Member State and if the transaction is made for shares in the absorbing or newly established companies. In determining whether or not the assets are transferred for shares, the transfer of indebtedness is not taken into account and consideration in cash, of an amount not exceeding 10 per cent of the value of the shares, is allowed.

908. No registration tax is levied on the establishment of a branch office in Belgium, a change in company name, form or purpose, or the transfer of a company's registered seat or head office from one EC Member State to another.

D. Lease contracts

909. Written leases, including subleases and lease transfers, are subject to a registration tax of 0.2 per cent. The tax does not apply to oral agreements. The lease agreement must be submitted for registration within 4 months of its conclusion by the lessee. When the lease is for a fixed term, the tax is calculated on the basis of the total amount of rent payable under the lease contract, plus estimated charges. When the lease is for an indefinite term, the tax is calculated on the basis of the total amount of rent payable annually, plus estimated charges, multiplied by 10. Rent increases resulting from indexation clauses are not taken into account in determining the amount of tax due. There is no reimbursement of the registration tax when the lease is terminated before its expiration (Arts. 83 and 84 of the RMTC). As an exception to the above rules, lease contracts for private housing are only subject to a fixed registration tax of € 25.

E. Gift tax

910. A registration tax is also levied on gifts which are evidenced by a written document. Gifts of real property located in Belgium are always subject to this tax, even if no notarial deed exists.

911. The registration tax is levied on the gross amount of the gift, except when the gift is accompanied by an obligation to make a cash payment or the payment of a pension or annuity to a third party.

912. The registration tax on gifts is levied at a progressive rate determined by the value of the gift and by the degree of kinship between the donor and the beneficiary, as indicated in the table below.

Value of gift (in €)	Applicable percentage	Total tax on preceding brackets (in €)
Gifts between spouses or between parents and their children		
0.01 – 12,500	3	–
12,500 – 25,000	4	375
25,000 – 50,000	5	875
50,000 – 100,000	7	2,125
100,000 – 150,000	10	5,625
150,000 – 200,000	14	10,625
200,000 – 250,000	18	17,625
250,000 – 500,000	24	26,625
over 500,000	30	86,625
Gifts between brothers and sisters		
0.01 – 12,500	20	–
12,500 – 25,000	25	2,500
25,000 – 75,000	35	5,625
75,000 – 175,000	50	23,125
over 175,000	65	73,215
Gifts between uncles or aunts and nephews or nieces		
0.01 – 12,500	25	–
12,500 – 25,000	30	3,125
25,000 – 75,000	40	6,875
75,000 – 175,000	55	26,875
over 175,000	70	81,875

Gifts between unrelated persons

0.01 – 12,500	30	–
12,500 – 25,000	35	3,750
25,000 – 75,000	50	8,125
75,000 – 175,000	65	33,125
over 175,000	80	98,125

IX. INHERITANCE TAX

A. Application

913. Inheritance taxes (*successierechten/droits de succession*) are levied on a deceased's estate, regardless of whether it is transferred intestate or by testamentary disposition.

914. The inheritance tax applies only when the deceased was domiciled in Belgium at the time of his death, regardless of his nationality and regardless of the domicile or nationality of his heirs or legatees. An individual is deemed to have his domicile in Belgium if his residence or the place of management of his business and property is located there.

915. If the deceased was not domiciled in Belgium at the time of his death, Belgian inheritance taxes apply only to that part of the deceased's estate consisting of real property located in Belgium.

916. Belgium has concluded only 2 international treaties for the avoidance of double inheritance taxes: with Sweden (1956) and with France (1959). In the absence of a treaty, however, foreign inheritance taxes paid on the transfer of real estate located abroad may be credited against Belgian inheritance taxes with respect to such property (Art. 17 of the Inheritance Tax Code).

B. Tax base

917. The inheritance tax is levied on the net amount of the deceased's estate inherited by each heir or legatee. In general, assets must be reported in the tax return at their fair market value. If it is not possible to ascertain the fair market value of real property located abroad, such property will be valued at 30 times its estimated

gross rental income for buildings and at 20 times its estimated gross rental income for unimproved land.

918. In general, all of the deceased's outstanding liabilities at the time of his death, including medical expenses and funeral and church service expenses, are deductible for the purpose of determining the net tax base. No deductions are allowed if the deceased was not domiciled in Belgium at the time of his death. Expenses related to the filing of the tax return are never deductible.

919. In order to prevent inheritance tax avoidance schemes, the following items are included in the inheritance tax base (Arts. 5 through 14 of the Inheritance Tax Code):
   - any indebtedness contained solely in the deceased's testamentary disposition;
   - any life insurance proceeds, except from certain types of group insurance; and
   - any gifts made within 3 years of the deceased's death if no registration taxes were paid on such gifts.

920. The inheritance tax is levied at the different rates depending on whether the estate is located in the Flemish Region, the Walloon Region or the Brussels-Capital Region, as shown in the table below.

Value of the estate (in €)	Applicable percentage	Total tax on preceding bracket (in €)
(A) Flemish Region		
Between parents and their children, between spouses or between cohabitants		
0.01 – 50,000	3	–
50,000 – 250,000	9	1,500
over 250,000	27	19,500
Between brothers and sisters		
0.01 – 75,000	30	–
75,000 – 125,000	55	22,500
over 125,000	65	50,000
Between any other persons		
0.01 – 75,000	45	–
75,000 – 125,000	55	33,750
over 125,000	65	61,250

(B) Walloon Region

Inheritance tax is levied at the same rates as the registration tax applicable to gifts (*See* para. 912)

(C) Brussels-Capital Region

Inheritance gift is levied at the same rates as the registration tax applicable to gifts (*See* para. 912)

C. Tax returns and the payment of tax

921. A tax return must be filed within 5 months of the date of death if the death occurred in Belgium, within 6 months if the death occurred in another European country and within 7 months if the death occurred outside of Europe. The tax return must be filed by the heirs of the deceased or by the universal legatee. Each heir or legatee must pay the inheritance tax on his portion of the estate within 2 months following the expiry of the deadline for the filing of the tax return. In addition to cash payment, inheritance taxes may also be paid with certain bonds or works of art.

6. CUSTOMS AND EXCISE LAW

I. CUSTOMS LAW

A. Introduction

922. Foreign trade accounts for more than 60 per cent of Belgium's gross national product. Due to its central location and well-developed transport infrastructure, Belgium is also an important country of transit. All import, export and transit operations are subject to customs formalities in accordance with Belgian customs law.

B. Source of Belgian law

923. The main provisions of Belgian customs law are found in the Royal Decree of 18 July 1977, which constitutes the General Law on Customs and Excise ("CLCE" – *Algemene wet inzake Douane en Accijnzen/Loi générale sur les douanes et accises*), as confirmed by Article 1 of the Law of 6 July 1978, and as last amended by the Law of 30 June 2000. In addition, many provisions have been heavily influenced by the numerous international conventions to which Belgium is a signatory. Currently, matters which are essentially procedural in nature – such as customs inspections and verifications, the payment modalities of the customs debt, penalties and fines and dispute settlement – are governed by Belgian law. In contrast, more substantive matters such as the classification of goods, tariff rates, origin of products, customs valuation, preferential regimes and duty relief are almost exclusively governed by EC law.

C. Impact of customs unions and preferential trade arrangements

§1. Economic and customs unions of which Belgium is a member

1. Belgo-Luxembourg Economic Union (BLEU)

924. Since 1922 Belgium has belonged, along with the Grand Duchy of Luxembourg, to the Belgo-Luxembourg Economic Union, or "BLEU". The customs border between the 2 countries has been abolished and they are considered as one customs territory for the purposes of customs legislation, trade statistics and commercial relations with third countries. Belgian customs and excise law is also applied in

Luxembourg. Customs controls continue to be carried out at the internal borders of the BLEU, however, because of the remaining differences in excise duties and, in particular, the widely divergent VAT rates (*See*, Chapter 5, and in particular para. 890).

2. *Benelux Economic Union (Benelux)*

925. In 1960, the BLEU and the Netherlands created the Benelux Economic Union ("Benelux"). On the basis of the Agreement on the Unification of the Benelux Customs Territory, which came into effect in 1971, customs formalities have been abolished at the internal borders of the Benelux. Each member recognises the validity of each other's customs rules and formalities. Thus, goods imported from outside the Benelux that have been declared to customs in the Netherlands may subsequently be shipped to Belgium using the documents issued by Dutch customs. Documents issued by one of the members are valid in the whole customs territory of the Benelux. However, important parts of the customs legislation, for example, on certain forms of transit and on customs warehouses, have not yet been harmonised. Moreover, important differences in excise duties and VAT rates continue to exist. Accordingly, controls are still carried out at the Benelux internal borders. Since 1984, these remaining customs formalities have been simplified by the introduction of a single customs document, the "Benelux 50". This document may be used for most formalities concerning VAT, excises and statistical controls. Use of this document also makes it possible to deal with all formalities at the customs office at the border of the importing country.

3. *The European Community*

926. The most important impact on Belgian customs law has undoubtedly resulted from Belgium's membership of the European Community (the "EC"). The EC Treaty created a customs union among the EC Member States and has as its aim the establishment of an economic union. As of 1968, the 6 original EC Member States eliminated all customs duties and quantitative restrictions on the import and export of goods between them and all other measures having equivalent effect, and established a common customs tariff and a common commercial policy towards third countries. New EC Member States similarly eliminated such restrictions on the free movement of goods at the end of the transitional period specified in each Treaty of Accession. Also, since 1968, the EC institutions have gradually harmonised the customs legislation applicable in the different EC Member States. Initially, EC customs legislation concentrated on eliminating the most visible barriers to intra-EC trade and on ensuring a uniform application of the Common Customs Tariff towards third countries. Thus, matters such as the development of common

classification and valuations rules, as well as a common definition of the concept of origin, were given priority. Increasingly, however, efforts have been made to harmonise customs formalities in order to simplify and, eventually, abolish remaining customs formalities at borders within the European Community. For instance, in 1988, the Single Administrative Document (the "SAD") was introduced. This replaced a wide array of national customs documents and may now be used throughout the European Community for most import, export and transit operations. As this process of harmonisation progressed, the disparate nature of the customs legislation created the need to put an end to such a situation by bringing the different EC Regulations into a single structured legislative document, namely the Community Customs Code. The Community Customs Code, which was established by EC Council Regulation No. 2913/92 of 12 October 1992 (O.J. [1992] L 302), aims at codifying the provisions of customs law governing trade between the European Community and third countries.

927. On 2 July 1993, a code implementing the Community Customs Code was adopted by the European Commission (Commission Regulation No 2454/93, O.J. [1993] L 253). Both the Community Customs Code and its Implementing Code entered into force on 1 January 1994. However, in spite of the fact that the purpose of the Community Customs Code was to incorporate the customs legislation into a single instrument, 2 codes have been established (*i.e.*, the Community Customs Code and its Implementing Code) and subsequent legislation has amended most of the provisions of the Implementing Code. In other words, it is doubtful whether the codification process has made the reference to the existing customs legislation any easier: 2 codes and a number of amending acts still need to be consulted in order to be aware of the existing legislation concerning customs issues.

928. In addition, due to the remaining differences in customs formalities and, in particular, the existence of important differences in national excise duties and VAT rates, internal border controls continue to exist (*See*, Chapter 5, and in particular paras. 889 *et seq.*).

§2. Preferential trade arrangements

1. Types of arrangements: conventional or unilateral

929. The European Community has concluded association agreements or other preferential trade agreements, offering benefits more favourable than those resulting from a most-favoured-nation clause, with the following countries:
   – Turkey;

- the countries belonging to the European Economic Area (the "EEA") (Norway, Iceland, Liechtenstein);
- the Czech Republic, Hungary, Poland, Slovakia, Slovenia, Bulgaria, Romania, Estonia, Latvia, and Lithuania;
- the Faeroe Islands;
- Ceuta and Melilla;
- San Marino;
- Andorra;
- the FYROM;
- Israel;
- Malta;
- Cyprus;
- the Maghreb countries (Morocco, Tunisia and Algeria);
- the Machrak countries (Egypt, Jordan, Lebanon and Syria);
- certain Overseas Countries and Territories (overseas territories still closely linked to certain Member States);
- the African, Caribbean and Pacific (ACP) countries;
- Palestinian Authority;
- Mexico;
- South Africa;
- Azerbaijan; and
- Kazakhstan.

930. In addition, the European Community has unilaterally granted trade preferences to a large number of developing countries under its Generalised System of Preferences (the "GSP"), to the territories occupied by Israel and to Bolivia, Colombia, Ecuador, and Peru.

2. Scope of the arrangements

931. The preferential trade arrangements provide for unilateral (*e.g.*, the GSP) or reciprocal tariff concessions. Certain agreements, such as those with the Mediterranean countries, also extend tariff preferences to certain specified agricultural products. Except for the few agreements establishing a customs union, *e.g.*, with Turkey, (which extends tariff preferences to products in free circulation in the customs union, regardless of their origin), all arrangements limit the tariff preferences to products meeting the preferential origin rules set out in an annex to each agreement. Importers wishing to benefit from the preferences will accordingly have to submit evidence of the preferential origin upon importation.

D. The Belgian External Tariff

§1. Introduction

932. Since 1968, Belgium has applied the EC Common Customs Tariff (the "CCT"). The CCT consists of a product nomenclature, a tariff schedule listing the applicable tariff rate for each product in the nomenclature and a number of rules on the correct application of the nomenclature and tariff schedule, the so-called Preliminary Provisions. On the basis of the CCT, the Integrated Tariff of the European Communities (the "TARIC") was established. This lists, in addition to the customs duties applicable to imports from third countries under the CCT, the necessary information on specific duties and measures such as anti-dumping and countervailing duties, suspensions, autonomous and conventional tariff quotas, certain quantitative restrictions and tariff preferences.

§2. Nomenclature

933. The nomenclature used for the CCT (and TARIC) is the Combined Nomenclature (the "CN"), which has an eight digit code. The CN incorporates the nomenclature of the 1983 Convention on the Harmonised Commodity Description and Coding System (the "Harmonised System" or "HS") which was ratified by the European Community in 1987.

§3. Tariff schedule

1. Conventional and autonomous rates

934. For each product included in the nomenclature, the tariff schedule of the CCT lists the applicable duty rates. For each tariff heading and subheading, a conventional and an autonomous rate is listed. The conventional rates have been negotiated in the framework of the various rounds of GATT talks and are applicable to all goods originating in any of the countries which are signatories to GATT 1994 or any other countries which have concluded most-favoured-nation agreements with the European Community. In theory, the autonomous rates, which are normally higher, should apply to imports from other countries. However, the European Community has decided that the conventional rates should be applied to all imports from third countries unless the autonomous rate is lower. In such cases, the autonomous rate will be applied to all imports.

2. Types of duty

935. Most duties in the CCT are *ad valorem* – they are expressed as a percentage of the customs value of the product. In a number of cases, specific duties, taking the form

of a fixed amount of Euro per weight, volume or length unit, are applied. Finally, mixed duties also exist for a limited number of products. Mixed duties are normally expressed as an *ad valorem* duty with an additional monetary minimum or maximum.

§4. Preliminary Provisions

936. The Preliminary Provisions of the CCT contain the general rules for the interpretation of the CN as well as rules concerning duties. The rules for the interpretation of the CN are based on the General Rules for the Interpretation of the Harmonised System. These General Rules, including the headings and the section and chapter notes, are legally binding on the EC Member States. In addition, the Belgian External Tariff is preceded by a number of Benelux provisions, which have, however, only limited relevance. Additional tools for the interpretation of the CN include the Explanatory Notes to the Harmonised System, the Classification Opinions of the Harmonized System Committee of the World Customs Organisation (the "WCO") as well as those of the EC Committee on Tariff and Statistical Nomenclature.

§5. Annexes to the Tariff

937. The Belgian External Tariff is supplemented by a number of annexes. These annexes contain information on preferential duty regimes such as tariff suspensions and tariff quotas relating to imports from certain countries only (general tariff preferences are included in the tariff itself); variable duties and levies; anti-dumping duties; reference import prices; VAT; excise duties; export and import restrictions and other control measures; and import and export licences.

§6. Prospective classification rulings by the Belgian customs authorities

938. As described above, the classification of a product in the CN will determine which rate of duty and specific commercial policy measures are applicable upon importation or exportation of the product concerned. However, if, due to the complexity of the CN and TARIC, importers and exporters are uncertain as to the correct classification of the goods, they may request the customs authorities to inform them of the precise CN code to be used, prior to carrying out the envisaged import or export transaction, in the form of a so-called "binding tariff information". Similarly, binding origin information may be requested from the customs authorities. Pursuant to Article 12 of the Community Customs Code and Articles 5 through 14 of the Implementing Code, binding tariff information or binding origin information must be requested in writing from the central customs authorities and must relate to a commercial transaction that is actually planned. The application must contain all the data necessary to identify the applicant and the goods concerned and must be accompanied by samples of the product or, if this is impossible, by

full technical and commercial documentation. The decision taken by the customs administration as to the correct classification or origin of the goods must be notified to the applicant as soon as possible and, at the latest, within 3 months for the acceptance of the application in the case of tariffs or within 150 days in the case of origin. The information thus provided remains valid for a 6-year period from the date of issue in the case of tariffs and 3 years from the date of issue in the case of origin. Binding tariff or origin information can only be applied by its holder to identical goods cleared through customs after the date on which the information was officially notified to him.

E. Derogations from the External Tariff

§1. Tariff suspensions

1. Definition

939. Under Article 26 of the EC Treaty, the EC Council, acting on a qualified majority on the basis of a proposal from the European Commission, may temporarily suspend, partially or totally, the CCT applicable to imports of certain goods. EC Council Regulation No. 1255/96 ("Regulation No. 1255/96" – O.J. [1996] L 158/1) establishes the list of products for which duties are suspended (partially or totally). Such autonomous tariff suspensions are granted for an indefinite period of time. However, products can be added or removed from the list attached to Regulation No. 1255/96 through an EC Council Regulation.

2. Insufficient EC supply

940. Tariff suspensions are usually granted at the request of EC processors and manufacturers that face difficulties in obtaining an adequate supply of raw materials, semi-finished goods or components from European Community suppliers. Thus, no duty suspension may be granted where identical, equivalent or substitute products are manufactured in sufficient quantities within the European Community (Commission Communication Concerning Autonomous Tariff Suspensions and Quotas, O.J. [1998] C 128/2).

3. Application to the Ministry of Economic Affairs

941. In order to obtain a tariff suspension, the applicant must submit a request to the Belgian Ministry of Economic Affairs. The application must contain full technical information on the product, its classification in the CN, the value and quantity of estimated imports, the value and quantity of imports in the preceding year, details of the intended use of the imported product and particulars relating to the producer, importer and intended user. The applicant must also provide full details

about the EC companies approached with a view to the supply of equivalent, identical or substitute products, the results of these approaches and a full explanation of the unsuitability or inadequate supply of EC products for the purpose in question. Such approaches must be made before the products covered by the suspension request are ordered and, in the case of customised products, before initial contact is made with the third country producers concerned. Finally, the applicant must also submit a declaration that the products are not subject to purchasing or distribution restrictions.

4. Procedure at the national and the EC level

942. Upon receipt of the application, the Belgian authorities will verify the completeness and accuracy of the information provided and, in particular, examine whether any manufacturing companies located in Belgium would be able to supply the product concerned. If they are satisfied that local suppliers do not exist, the Belgian authorities will forward the application to the European Commission, which will inform the other EC Member States of the request through their representatives in the Economic Tariff Questions Group. Each EC Member State will then invite its national producers to comment on the request. If no objections are received, or the objections received appear to be unjustified after consulting the applicant, the European Commission will include the product in its proposal to the EC Council. The EC Council must adopt the proposal by qualified majority. Amendments to the proposal by the EC Council require unanimity.

§2. Tariff quotas

1. Definition

943. Tariff quotas allow the importation of products into the European Community at a reduced or zero tariff up to a certain limit expressed as a quantity or value. When this limit is reached, the normal rate is automatically reintroduced. Tariff quotas should thus be distinguished from autonomous tariff suspensions, under which the duty remains suspended during the entire period of the suspension regardless of the quantity imported. The current balances of tariff quotas are available on the Internet at the following address:

www.europa.eu.int/comm/taxation_customs/dds/en/home.htm

2. Types of tariff quotas

i. Autonomous tariff quotas

944. A quota may be unilaterally opened by the European Community on the basis of Article 26 of the EC Treaty in case EC production is unable to meet specific re-

quirements of the user industries in the European Community. The procedure to be followed is the same as for obtaining a tariff suspension. The regulations on opening tariff quotas are published throughout the year and usually take effect 7 days after publication.

ii. Conventional tariff quotas

945. In addition to autonomous tariff quotas, the European Community also imposes conventional tariff quotas on an annual basis. For instance, the European Community has undertaken, within the framework of GATT, to open annual tariff quotas for certain agricultural and industrial products such as plywood and newsprint. (*See*, EC Council Regulation No. 32/2000, O.J. [2000] L 5/1). Tariff quotas may also be opened in the context of preferential trade arrangements with developing countries. (*See, e.g.*, EC Council Regulation No. 747/2001, O.J. [2001] L 109/2).

3. Management of the quotas

946. The European Commission is responsible for the management of the various quotas. Tariff quotas are currently administrated on a first-come first-served basis, in accordance with the chronological order of dates of acceptance of declarations for import (*See*, Article 308a of the Implementing Code).

4. Formalities to be completed by importers

947. In order to benefit from a tariff quota, the importer must expressly request preferential tariff treatment, and the customs declaration may only cover the goods for which the preferential treatment is requested. Where the tariff quota does not apply to imports from all third countries, the importer will have to submit the relevant origin certificate. Moreover, the local customs office, after having obtained approval from the central customs authorities in charge of managing the quota at the national level, must give its prior authorisation. When an application to benefit from the preferential arrangements is approved and the entry for release into free circulation is accepted by the customs authorities, Belgium will, by notifying the European Commission, draw an amount corresponding to its requirements from the quota volume. Requests for drawings, indicating the dates on which the entries were accepted, must be sent to the European Commission immediately. The European Commission will then grant drawings in chronological order of the dates on which the customs authorities of the EC Member States accepted the entries for release for free circulation, provided the available balance so permits. If the quantities requested are greater than the available balance, the balance will be allocated among the applicants on a *pro rata* basis with respect to the quantities requested.

F. Substantive rules for the application of the External Tariff

§1. Customs valuation rules

1. Introduction

948. Most of the tariff rates in the Common Customs Tariff are *ad valorem* duties, *i.e.*, they are calculated as a percentage of the customs value of a product. The applicable rules for the determination of the customs value of imported goods are set out in Articles 28 through 36 of the Community Customs Code and in Articles 141 through 181 of the Implementing Code. In accordance with the WTO Code on customs valuation, the EC customs valuation rules are based on the principle that, for the determination of customs value, preference should be given to the transaction value of the imported goods, that is, the price actually paid or payable for the goods when sold for export to the customs territory of the European Community, provided that the conditions referred to in Article 29 of the Community Customs Code are satisfied.

949. In cases where the customs value cannot be established on the basis of the transaction value, alternative valuation methods are provided for in Articles 30 and 31 of the Community Customs Code.

2. Transaction value

i. Definition:

950. According to Article 29, paragraph 1 of the Community Customs Code, the transaction value is *"the price actually paid or payable for the goods when sold for export to the customs territory of the Community"*. The transaction value may be, but is not necessarily, equal to the invoice price. Indeed, the invoice price may not be the total price of the goods or, on the contrary, may include costs which are unrelated to the imported goods.

ii. Price actually paid or payable

951. Under Article 29, paragraph 3(a) of the Community Customs Code, the price actually paid or payable is the total payment made or to be made by the buyer to or for the benefit of the seller for the imported goods. This price includes all payments made or to be made as a condition of sale of the imported goods by the buyer to the seller or by the buyer to a third party to satisfy an obligation of the seller. Article 29, paragraph 3(a) of the Community Customs Code expressly mentions that the payment need not necessarily take the form of a transfer of money. Payment may be made by way of letters of credit or negotiable instruments and may be made directly or indirectly.

iii. Sale for export to the Community

952. In its Advisory Opinions, the Technical Committee on Customs Valuation of the WCO has consistently interpreted the concept of "sale" in a very wide sense. However, a transaction between entities which are not legally separate, such as a branch and its head office, does not constitute a sale within the meaning of the Community Customs Code. Also, the sale should be "for export to the Community". This does not mean that the buyer must be located in the European Community but rather that the goods sold by the seller to the buyer are intended for export to the European Community. According to Article 147 of the Implementing Code, the fact that the goods which are the subject of the sale are declared for free circulation in the European Community is to be regarded as an adequate indication that they were sold for export to the European Community. This principle also applies to successive sales. Thus, provided the goods have not been used or processed between the first sale and their release for free circulation in the European Community, the price of each of these sales can be used for customs valuation purposes provided that the sale on the basis of which the customs declaration is made took place for export to the customs territory of the European Community.

iv. Adjustments

953. Under Article 32 of the Community Customs Code, the price actually paid or payable should, where necessary, be adjusted upwards to take account of any indirect payments or to bring the price up to the level of a CIF price at the EC border. These adjustments, which are exhaustively listed in Article 32, are as follows:
   (i) commissions and brokerage except for buying commissions;
   (ii) cost of containers which are treated as being one with the goods in question;
   (iii) cost of packing, whether for labour or materials;
   (iv) certain goods and services supplied by the buyer free of charge or at a reduced cost;
   (v) royalties and licence fees of which the payment is related to the imported goods and is a condition of their sale;
   (vi) proceeds of subsequent resale, disposal or use accruing directly or indirectly to the seller; and
   (vii) costs of transportation, loading, handling and insurance up to the EC border.

954. The customs valuation rules also list a number of items which should not be included, provided they are distinguishable from the price of the imported goods either by means of a separate invoice or through a separate identification on the same invoice. These items are as follows:
   (i) transportation and ancillary expenses within the European Community;
   (ii) EC customs duties and other taxes paid upon importation;

   (iii) buying commissions;
   (iv) charges for construction, erection, assembly, maintenance or technical assist-
        ance undertaken after importation of imported goods such as industrial plants,
        machinery or equipment;
    (v) the value of engineering, development, artwork, designwork and plans and
        sketches necessary for the production of the imported goods, provided they
        have been undertaken in the European Community;
   (vi) the cost of research and preliminary design sketches;
  (vii) charges for the right to reproduce the imported goods in the European Com-
        munity;
 (viii) payments made by the buyer for the right to distribute or resell the imported
        goods, provided that such payments are not a condition of the sale for export;
        and
   (ix) interest charges under a financing arrangement entered into by the buyer and
        relating to the purchase of imported goods, provided that the financing ar-
        rangement has been made in writing and that the buyer can demonstrate that
        the goods are actually sold at the price actually paid or payable, and that the
        claimed interest rate does not exceed the level for such transactions in the
        country where the finance was provided.

3. Cases in which the transaction value must be rejected

955. In certain circumstances, no transaction value will exist or the transaction value
     will be considered unreliable and will be rejected by the customs authorities in
     favour of an alternative method of valuation. The latter will be the case in circum-
     stances where there are restrictions on the sale or use of the goods by the buyer
     which substantially affect the value of the goods and are not imposed by law or by
     the public authorities. Other examples are where the price for the goods is subject
     to conditions or consideration for which no value can be determined, or where a
     part of the proceeds of the subsequent resale accrues to the original seller and this
     part is not easily quantifiable.

956. That a sale is made between related parties, such as between 2 subsidiaries of the
     same company, is not in itself sufficient grounds for rejecting the transaction value.
     Where necessary, the customs authorities may request evidence that the relation-
     ship between the parties to the sale did not influence the price. Such evidence must
     be provided by meeting one of the tests listed in Article 29, paragraph 2(b) of the
     Community Customs Code.

4. Alternative valuation methods

957. Where a sale between related parties fails the arm's-length test or where the trans-

action value must be rejected due to any other of the above-mentioned reasons, one of the alternative methods of valuation provided by the Community Customs Code must be used. The alternative bases of valuation are as follows:

   (i) the transaction value of identical goods sold for export to the European Community and exported at or about the same time as the goods to be valued;

  (ii) the transaction value of similar goods sold for export to the European Community and exported at or about the same time as the goods to be valued;

 (iii) the resale price of the imported goods or identical or similar goods duly adjusted to bring the price to the EC border level (the so-called "deductive method"); or

 (iv) the computed value consisting of the cost of production increased by an amount for general expenses and profit, corresponding to the usual amount in the exporting country for sales to the European Community, and by the costs for transport, insurance, loading and handling up to the EC border.

958. It should be stressed that these methods must be applied in the order given above. The only exception is that, at the request of the importer, the computed value method may be applied before the deductive method.

§2. Rules of origin

1. Difference between non-preferential and preferential rules of origin

959. The non-preferential rules of origin applied by the Belgian customs authorities are those laid down in Articles 22 through 26 of the Community Customs Code and in Articles 35 through 65 of the Implementing Code. The non-preferential origin rules should be distinguished from the preferential origin rules applicable in the context of the various preferential arrangements applied by the European Community.

2. Non-preferential origin rules

i. Scope of application of the non-preferential origin rules

960. The non-preferential rules of origin are applicable in all cases where an exporter or importer does not intend to request preferential tariff treatment according to one of the preferential trade arrangements applied by the European Community. It should be noted that the origin of a product does not normally play a role in the application of the CCT. As explained above, the European Community applies the same duty rate to imports of products originating in all third countries. An exception is made regarding certain conventional tariff quotas not covered by any preferential trade arrangement, which are opened for imports from a certain country only, such as newsprint from Canada. Origin determinations are, however, essential for statistical purposes and, more importantly, for the application of specific commercial

233

policy measures such as anti-dumping or countervailing duties and quantitative import restrictions which apply to products from certain countries only.

ii. "Substantial transformation" rule

961. A product is deemed to originate in a certain country if it has been wholly obtained or produced in that country. As for products that involve production processes carried out in 2 or more countries, Article 24 of the Community Customs Code stipulates that they *"shall be deemed to originate in the country where they underwent their last substantial, economically justified processing or working in an undertaking equipped for that purpose and resulting in the manufacture of a new product or representing an important stage of manufacture"*. This "last substantial transformation" criterion has been interpreted by the European Court of Justice as requiring that the product obtained must have distinctive characteristics and features not to be found in any of its constituent parts.

962. In the *Brother* case (ECJ, 13 December 1989, *Brother International GmbH* v *Hauptzellamt Grießen*, Case C-26/88, [1989] ECR 4253), the European Court of Justice ruled that whether this criterion was met had to first be examined from a technical viewpoint. Where a technical analysis was inconclusive, the next issue to be addressed should be whether substantial value was added to the product. In practice, however, most customs authorities use the added value criterion, which is easier to apply. A product will be considered to have undergone a substantial transformation if the value added in the process amounts to more than 45 per cent of a product's *ex*-works price. In an effort at further clarification, the European Community has adopted a number of specific origin rules defining the meaning of "substantial transformation" for certain products. Such specific origin rules currently exist for most textile products, tape recorders, radio and television receivers, integrated circuits, photocopiers, eggs, spare parts, roller bearings, meat and offal, ceramic products and basic wines.

963. Finally, Article 25 of the Community Customs Code contains an anti-circumvention provision stating that even a substantial transformation within the meaning of Article 24 will not confer origin if it is ascertained that the sole object of the transformation being carried out in that country is to avoid the application of measures adopted by the European Community to goods from specific countries.

3. Preferential origin rules

i. Scope of application of the preferential origin rules

964. The preferential origin rules are different from the general origin rules outlined above. They apply within the context of the GSP and most preferential trade agree-

ments concluded by the European Community with third countries for the purpose of identifying the products which benefit from preferential duty treatment upon importation. The GSP origin rules are laid down in Articles 67 through 95 of the Implementing Code. As to the preferential origin rules applicable to trade agreements concluded by the European Community with third countries, they are generally contained in a protocol to each agreement. Although there are some differences between the various agreements, the same origin rules generally apply.

ii. "Sufficient processing" test

965. Products are deemed to originate in the country from which they have been wholly obtained or in which they have undergone "sufficient processing". "Sufficient processing" is generally deemed to occur when the product obtained is classified under a different tariff heading – the first 4 digits of the CN code are different from the first 4 digits of the CN code of any of the non-originating materials used in its manufacture. There are, however, a significant number of exceptions to this basic rule which are usually set out in annexes to the origin protocol of each preferential agreement. For some products, requirements besides the change in tariff headings must be met. For others, an alternative test must be met instead of the change in tariff heading. These alternative tests generally take the form of a specific processing test (certain processing operations must (or may not) be carried out or certain non-originating materials may not be used), a value added test (non-originating materials may only be used up to a certain percentage of the *ex*-works price of the product), or a combination of both tests. Finally, the protocols contain a list of certain minor processing operations which will never be sufficient to confer origin regardless of whether the other requirements have been fulfilled.

iii. "Direct transport" rule

966. In order to avoid the possibility of circumvention, the preferential origin rules require that a product which has acquired preferential origin in the exporting country must be shipped directly to the importing country. No other countries may be crossed except for geographical reasons, and the goods must remain under customs control in the transit country and must not undergo any operation other than normal handling or those necessary for their preservation.

iv. The territoriality principle

967. In accordance with the territoriality principle, the manufacture of a product to be imported into the European Community must be carried out without interruption in the exporting country with which the European Community has concluded a preferential agreement. The principle of territoriality is contained, for instance, in

the agreements that the European Community has concluded with the EEA countries, Switzerland, Poland, Hungary, the Czech Republic, Slovakia, Slovenia, Bulgaria, Romania, Estonia, Latvia, Lithuania and Turkey. Some derogations to the principle of territoriality exist in most of the agreements concluded by the European Community .

v. The "no-drawback" rule

968. The no-drawback rule prohibits the drawback of, or exemption from, customs duties of whatever kind applicable to non-originating materials used in the manufacture of products which acquired preferential origin in the European Community or in the partner country. This prohibition applies to any arrangement for refund, remission or non-payment, partial or complete, of customs duties applicable in the European Community or in the partner country to non-originating materials used in the manufacture, where such refund, remission or non-payment applies, expressly or in effect, when products obtained from the said materials are exported and not when they are retained for home use.

969. This rule is therefore aimed at inward processing arrangements, in which customs duties payable on third-country materials will be suspended or refunded when the final product manufactured with such materials is exported but not when the product is designed for domestic use. It should be noted that the no-drawback rule does not prevent the use, in the manufacture of a product to be exported to a partner country, of non-originating materials imported into the country of manufacture at a preferential duty rate applicable under another preferential arrangement (for example, under the GSP scheme or a preferential agreement with another third country) provided, of course, that such preferential duty is paid.

970. The application of the no-drawback rule entails that products will not benefit from preferential treatment when exported to a partner country unless the exporter can prove that he has not benefited from any drawback of, or exemption from, the customs duties payable on imports of non-originating materials.

vi. The "10 per cent-general tolerance" rule

971. In accordance with the "10 per cent-general tolerance" rule, non-originating materials which, according to the origin rule applicable to the product concerned, should not be used in the manufacture of the product, may nevertheless be used provided their total value does not exceed 10 per cent of the *ex*-works price of the product.

972. The 3 following points should be taken into account when applying this rule:
   (a) the "10 per cent-general tolerance" rule applies only in respect of non-originating materials which, in accordance with the origin rule concerned, may

not be used at all (as opposed to non-originating materials that can be used up to a given percentage);

(b) the percentage laid down in the origin rule for the maximum value of non-originating materials that can be used may not be exceeded by virtue of the "10 per cent-general tolerance" rule. This means that the "10 per cent-general tolerance" rule does not apply in respect of origin tests which already lay down a maximum percentage for the value of non-originating materials that can be used; and

(c) the "10 per cent-general tolerance" rule never applies where the origin rule provides that "the value of all the non-originating materials used may not exceed the value of the originating materials used" (the 50/50 test).

G. General customs procedures relating to the movement of goods

§1. Importation

1. Summary declaration

973. All goods entering the Belgian customs territory, even those exempted from import duties and taxes, must be presented immediately to a Belgian customs office at the border. When the goods enter by road or rail, they must be taken to the border office following a designated route and be presented during the normal opening hours of the office. At the time the goods are presented at the border office, or, at the latest, one working day later, the person who transported the goods into Belgium or who is responsible for their carriage after their introduction must lodge a summary declaration. This declaration may be made on the basis of commercial documents such as invoices, or on the basis of an official document such as a transit document. The document used must contain all the details necessary for the identification of the goods concerned. If, before the deadline for lodging a summary declaration has expired, the goods are released for free circulation or are placed under another customs procedure, no summary declaration needs to be lodged.

2. Temporary storage of goods

974. If the goods do not receive one of the forms of customs-approved treatment or use before the deadline and, thus, form the subject of a summary declaration, the goods will be placed in temporary storage under customs control.

3. Customs-approved treatment or use

975. Goods placed in temporary storage must be assigned customs-approved treatment or use within 45 days, if brought by sea, and within 20 days if brought by any other means of transport. The most common form of custom-approved treatment or use is release for free circulation or the placement of the goods under another customs procedure such as inward processing or the external transit procedure. Other forms of customs-approved treatment or use are the dispatch of the goods outside the European Community customs territory and the destruction of the goods under customs supervision.

i. Release for free circulation

976. Release for free circulation is the customs-approved treatment whereby goods coming from third countries become EC goods within the meaning of Articles 23 and 24 of the EC Treaty. According to Article 24 of the EC Treaty, *"products coming from a third country shall be considered to be in free circulation in a Member State if the import formalities have been complied with and any customs duties or charges having equivalent effect which are payable have been levied in that Member State, and if they have not benefited from a total or partial drawback of such duties or charges".*

ii. Release for home use

977. Release for free circulation must be distinguished from release for home use. Release for home use implies that, in addition to the compliance with the customs formalities and the payment of the import duties, the applicable national consumption taxes and excise duties have been paid. Since 1 January 1993, the release for free circulation in one EC Member State implies that the goods concerned have to be released for home use in that EC Member State.

4. Customs declarations

i. "Declarations"

978. Release for free circulation requires that a written declaration is lodged with the customs authorities. Article 61 of the Community Customs Code also provides that the customs declaration may be made by using a data processing technique where provided for by provisions laid down in the Implementing Code or where authorised, or by using a normal declaration or any other act where such a possibility exists in the Implementing Code. For release into free circulation of non-Community goods, the symbol IM (or EU in case of imports into an EFTA country) must be marked in the copies of the Single Administrative Document (the "SAD"). This declaration is frequently called the "IM declaration".

ii. "Declarant"

979. In order to make a customs declaration, it is in principle not necessary for the declarant to be the owner of the goods. It is enough that he is able to produce the goods concerned and all documents required for making the entry.

iii. Information to be contained in the written declaration

980. The information to be contained in the declaration is as follows:
    (a) the declarant's name and address and, if he is acting on behalf of a third party, the basic details of this arrangement;
    (b) where the declarant is not the consignee of the goods, the name and address of the consignee;
    (c) a reference to the summary declaration, if any;
    (d) in the absence of a summary declaration, a reference to the previous customs procedure under which the goods were entered, if any;
    (e) the number, kind, marks and serial numbers of the packages containing the goods or, in the absence of packing, the number of articles covered by the declaration;
    (f) identity and nationality of the active means of transport crossing the border;
    (g) mode of transport at the border;
    (h) mode of transport inland;
    (i) the location of the goods declared;
    (j) the CN code, description of the goods and the number of the item in question;
    (k) the net mass of the goods;
    (l) the customs value of the goods and, where necessary, the quantitative data used in the calculation if an *ad valorem* duty is applicable and, in the case of specific duties or mixed duties, the additional data necessary for their application;
    (m) the country of dispatch and the country of origin according to the general origin rules if no preferential duty treatment is requested, or otherwise the country of origin as determined according to the applicable preferential origin rules;
    (n) the procedure for which the goods are declared at destination;
    (o) statistical value and the calculation of taxes; and
    (p) any other information necessary for the release for free circulation of the goods concerned.

iv. Documents to be submitted with the entry

981. The documents which must accompany the entry are:
    (a) the invoice on the basis of which the customs value is declared;

(b) the declaration of particulars necessary for the assessment of the customs value (form D.V.1);

(c) the documents required for the application of any preferential tariff arrangements (a GSP Form A for goods originating in GSP beneficiary countries, a movement certificate EUR.1 for goods originating in countries that have concluded a preferential trade agreement with the Community); and

(d) all other documents required for the application of the provisions governing the release for free circulation of the goods declared.

982. The customs authorities may, for example, also require the production of documents relating to the previous customs procedure under which the goods were entered, the inward processing authorisation, and transport documents. They may also physically examine the goods before, or even after, their release for free circulation.

v. Date of the entry

983. The import duty rate and any commercial policy measures to which the goods may be subject will be those in force at the time the entry is accepted by the customs authorities. The date of acceptance of the entry and the release for free circulation of the goods will be indicated on the entry.

5. *Simplified import procedures*

984. In order to facilitate import formalities, Belgian customs authorities may authorise importers to use simplified import procedures, allowing importers to make incomplete declarations. The incomplete declaration form (the "bulletin") must contain information on (i) the declarant or the representative of the consignee, (ii) country of origin, (iii) consignment and description of the goods including nature, quantity and value of the goods, (iv) means of transport and (v) summary declaration. Missing documents have to be presented to customs no later than 1 month from the date of acceptance of the incomplete declaration. Also, upon a written request, the declarant may be authorised to make the declaration for release for free circulation in a simplified form. Such a simplified declaration may be in the form of an incomplete declaration or of an administrative or commercial document (*e.g.*, the invoice) accompanied by a request for free circulation. It must contain at least the particulars necessary for the identification of the goods. As to the importers that frequently import goods through the same customs office, they may be authorised to make a global declaration. The global declaration covers the release operations taking place over a one-month period (or another period). The conditions for obtaining such a declaration are that the consignee is established in Belgium, is au-

thorised to transmit data to the statistical office of the National Bank of Belgium, is authorised to postpone the payment of VAT and provides adequate security.

§2. *Exportation*

1. *Normal export procedure*

i. Obligation to lodge a declaration

985. As is the case for the importation of goods, all goods exported from Belgium must be presented to a customs office and leave the territory following a designated route. The exportation of goods is conditional upon the lodging of an export declaration with the appropriate customs office.

ii. Information to be contained in the export declaration

986. The export declaration is normally made using the Single Administrative Document ("SAD") and must include the following particulars:
     (a) the name and address of the declarant as well as a brief description of any agency arrangement if he acts for another party;
     (b) the name and address of the exporter, if different from the declarant;
     (c) the particulars necessary for the identification of the goods (including the number of items declared);
     (d) the location of the goods;
     (e) packages and description of goods and their net mass;
     (f) the classification of the goods under the CN;
     (g) the identity and nationality of the active means of transport crossing the border;
     (h) the country of destination;
     (i) mode of transport at the border;
     (j) mode of transport inland;
     (k) all other documents required for the application of the rules applicable to the export of the goods concerned; and
     (l) statistical value of the goods.

iii. Documents to be submitted with the export declaration

987. The export declaration must be accompanied by the following documents:
     (a) the transportation documents covering transport under customs control to the foreign destination. These may include a TIR ("Transport International Routier") carnet or the SAD as transport document;
     (b) transport documents relating to previous customs-approved treatment or use;
     (c) when a single item is presented in 2 or more packages, a packing list or equivalent document indicating the content of each package may be required;

(d) export licence, where applicable;

(e) origin certificates, where required; and

(f) the various certificates applicable in the context of the Common Agricultural Policy (the "CAP") for agricultural products.

2. Simplified export procedures

988. As is the case for customs formalities upon importation, the customs authorities may authorise the use of simplified procedures such as incomplete declarations, declaration prior to the presentation of the goods or simplified declarations including a global declaration.

§3. Transit

1. Types of EC transit procedures

989. EC transit procedures apply whenever goods move across an internal EC border. EC transit is based on the Community Customs Code. 2 different EC transit procedures apply depending on the customs status of the goods transported. The external EC transit procedure must be used for movements of non-EC goods for which customs duties and other charges at import are at stake, *i.e.*, goods not in free circulation in the European Community, and for EC goods, in cases and on conditions determined in accordance with the committee procedure, in order to prevent products covered by or benefiting from export measures from either evading or benefiting unjustifiably from such measures. This is, for example, the case when there are refunds payable under the common agricultural policy or drawback, remission or repayment of duty. The rules on internal Community transit apply to movements of Community goods, which, between their point of departure and point of destination in the European Community, have to pass through the territory of a third country without any change of their customs status. Internal Community transit is also applicable to the movement of EC goods to/from those parts of the customs territory of the European Community which fall outside the scope of directives on tax harmonisation, such as the Channel Islands and the Canary Islands. In those cases a "T2F-document" is used.

2. Transit operations excluded from the procedures

990. The EC transit procedures do not apply to the carriage of goods under cover of TIR carnets (TIR Convention), provided that the movement of the goods began or is to end outside the European Community. Similarly, the EC transit procedure does not apply to the movement under cover of an ATA (*Admission Temporaire/Temporary Admission*) carnet, the Rhine Manifest or the form 302 provided for in the Convention between the Parties to the North Atlantic Treaty regarding the Status

of their Forces, signed in London on 19 June 1951. Finally, the EC transit procedures do not apply to the movement of goods by post.

3. Benefits of the EC transit procedure

991. The advantages of the EC transit procedure are that goods may be moved across the internal borders of the European Community without having to undergo complete customs formalities at each border post. It also makes it possible not to clear non-EC goods through customs at the point of entry but to ship them instead to the customs office nearest to the place where they are intended to be used and to clear the goods for home use at that office.

4. Reform of the EC transit procedures

992. The EC transit procedures have undergone, and are currently undergoing, a reform. Special rules regarding the comprehensive guarantee for goods involving greater risk of fraud apply since 1 January 2001. Since 1 July 2001, a clear distinction between the regular or standard transit procedure and the use of simplifications is made. Further, it is envisaged to replace the current paper-based transit procedure, which turned out to be less than fraud-proof by the New Computerised Transit System (the "NCTS"). The paper-based system and the NCTS will, however, be used alongside each other until 2003.

5. External transit procedure

i. Declaration and other formalities

993. Non-EC goods must be placed under an external transit procedure by making a "T1-declaration" using the SAD, the official model for written declarations. The T1-declaration must be accompanied by the transport document during the transport. The office of departure shall accept and register the T1 declaration, prescribe the period within which the goods must be presented at the office of destination and take such measures for identification as it considers necessary by sealing their packaging or their means of transport. The goods must be transported from the office of departure to the office of destination by way of the offices of transit mentioned in the T1-document. The consignment, as well as copies 4 and 5 of the T1-document, must be produced at each office of transit. The carrier shall present a transit advice note made out on a form corresponding to the specimen in Annex 46 of the Implementing Code to each office of transit, where the note shall be kept. Each office of transit will retain a transit advice note. The office of transit shall not inspect the goods unless some irregularity is suspected which could result in abuse. It should be noted that under the simplified procedure, persons wishing to carry out Community transit operations without presenting the goods and the correspond-

ing transit declaration at the office of departure may, under certain circumstances, be granted the status of authorised consignor. Similarly, persons who wish to receive at their premises or at any other places goods entered for the Community transit procedure, without presenting them or copies 4 and 5 of the transit declaration to the office of destination, may be granted the status of authorised consignee provided that a number of conditions are fulfilled.

ii. Guarantee

994. To ensure that goods arrive at their announced destination under the external transit procedure, authorisation to use this procedure is conditional upon the provision of a guarantee. This guarantee may be an individual guarantee covering a single transit operation or a comprehensive guarantee covering a number of transit operations by a single declarant. The authorisation to use a comprehensive guarantee may be granted only to persons who are established in the EC Member State where the guarantee is furnished, to persons who have been regular users, either as principals or as consignors, of the Community transit system during the previous 6 months or to persons who are known by the customs authorities to have a good financial standing which is sufficient to fulfil their commitments, and who have not committed any serious or repeated infringement of customs or tax laws.

995. The individual guarantee must cover the full amount of the customs debt to be incurred, calculated on the basis of the highest rates applicable to the goods in the Member State of departure. The individual guarantee may take the form of a cash deposit lodged at the office of departure or it may be furnished by a guarantor in the form of individual vouchers for an amount of € 7,000 per voucher. The individual guarantee has to be drawn up in accordance with the specimen referred to in Annex 49 of the Implementing Code. Under the pre-reform system, the guarantor could also be allowed to furnish a single guarantee for a flat-rate amount of € 7,000. As a consequence of the reform, the use of the pre-reform flat-rate guarantee for the fixed amount of € 7,000 for a consignment of whatever value has been discontinued. A number of guarantee vouchers must be used in future to cover the whole amount of duties and other charges at stake. The validity of the vouchers is limited to a maximum of one year. As regards the comprehensive guarantee, it must be furnished by a guarantor and be the subject of a guarantee document conforming to the specimen of Annex 50 of the Implementing Code. Where a consignment has not been presented at the office of destination, a calculation is made of the amount of the customs debt which may be incurred for each transit operation. When the necessary data is not available, the amount is presumed to be € 7,000 unless other information known to the customs authorities leads to a different figure.

996. For certain modes of transport, *i.e.*, transit operations carried out by air, on the Rhine and the Rhine waterways, by pipeline or by the national railway companies of the European Community, it is not necessary to provide a guarantee. For rail transport, this only applies to cases where a simplified procedure is being used. The pre-reform guarantee waiver for journeys by sea has been withdrawn, except for the simplified procedure which applies to regular shipping services under the Community transit.

   iii. The end of a transport procedure and its discharge

997. Under the pre-reform transit procedure, a guarantor was released from his obligations as soon as the transit operation had been completed, that is, once copy 5 of the transit declaration had been returned to the office of departure by the office of destination duly certified as to the arrival of the goods. The Community Customs Code now distinguishes clearly between the "end" and the "discharge" of the transit procedure. The end of a transit operation is defined as the moment when the goods and accompanying documents are properly presented to the customs office of destination. Although the movement of the goods is considered to have ended at that moment, the procedure is not automatically discharged. This can only be done when the customs authorities of the country of departure, by comparing the information available at the office of departure with that sent back by the office of destination, are able to establish that the procedure has been properly concluded. The office of destination shall record on the copies of the T1-document the details of controls carried out and shall without delay send a copy to the office of departure. The person presenting a Community transit document to the office of destination together with the consignment to which that document relates may obtain a receipt on request.

998. If copy 5 of the transit declaration is not returned to the customs authorities of the Member State of departure within 2 months of the date of the acceptance of the declaration, those authorities shall inform the principal and ask him to furnish proof that the procedure has ended. The receipt which the person presenting a Community transit document to the office of destination together with the consignment may obtain on request may constitute such a proof. Where the customs authorities of the EC Member State of departure have not received proof within 4 months of the date of acceptance of the transit declaration that the procedure has ended, they shall initiate an enquiry procedure in order to obtain the information needed to discharge the procedure or to establish whether a customs debt has been incurred.

999. The guarantor shall be released from his obligations upon expiry of a period of 12 months from the date of the registration of the T1-declaration where he has not been advised by the customs authorities of the EC Member State of departure of the non-discharge of the external Community transit procedure. Where within the period of 12 months from the date of the registration of the T1-declaration the guarantor has been advised by the customs authorities of the non-discharge of the external Community transit procedure, he shall, in addition, be notified that he is or may be required to pay the amounts for which he is liable in respect of the Community transit operation in question. This notification shall reach the guarantor not later than 3 years after the date of registration of the T1-declaration. Where no such notification has been made before the expiry of that time limit, the guarantor shall likewise be released from his obligations.

6. Internal transit procedure

1000. The rules governing internal transit are *mutatis mutandis* the same as those applicable to the external transit procedure. A declaration for internal transit is made on the same forms as a declaration for external transit. However, the symbol T2 is used instead of the symbol T1. The internal transit procedure enables EC goods to move from one point to another within the customs territory of the European Community passing through the territory of a third country without any change in their customs status.

7. Regular transit procedure

1001. Following the reform of the EC transit procedures, a clear distinction between the regular or standard transit procedure and the use of simplifications is made since 1 July 2001. The regular transit procedure must be used by a trader who does not yet have a track record, qualifies for any simplification or who is an incidental user of the transit system. Under the regular transit procedure,

   (i) the goods are presented to customs for examination when the transit declaration is made;

   (ii) the goods and accompanying documents are presented to any offices of transit and at the office of destination;

   (iii) a guarantee valid only for one single transit operation for the full amount of the customs duties and other charges at stake (the "individual guarantee") is used;

   (iv) there is an obligation to seal the means of transport or the container for identification purposes;

   (v) there is an obligation to follow an economically justified route or sometimes (in the case of goods involving greater risks of fraud) even a binding itinerary;

(vi) a time limit is set within which the goods have to be presented at the office of destination, taking into consideration the route involved and the means of transport used; and

(vii) there is an obligation to state the harmonised system commodity code (the "HS code") when the goods concerned involve a greater risk of fraud, or, where the goods are declared for another customs procedure at the same time (*e.g.*, export), which itself requires the provision of the HS code.

8. Simplifications

1002 Since 1 July 2001, different derogations allow authorised traders to derogate from some of the requirements under the regular transit procedure. However, the use of these derogations is subject to: compliance with a set of general conditions and any conditions specific to the simplification involved; and issue of an authorisation to use a particular simplification.

i. Authorisation

1003. The authorisation is subject to withdrawal if the conditions are no longer met after it has been issued. The application for authorisation to use simplifications is to be made in writing and must include all the facts enabling the customs authorities to check that the conditions have been met. The application shall be lodged with the customs authorities of the EC Member State in which the applicant is established. The authorisation shall be issued or the application shall be rejected within 3 months at most from the date on which the application is lodged. The authorisation shall specify the conditions for use of the simplifications and lay down the operating and control methods. The authorisation is valid from the date of issue. It may be revoked or amended.

The authorisations are only granted to persons who are established in the European Community. This is subject to the *proviso* that authorisation to use a comprehensive guarantee may be granted only to persons established in an EC Member State where the guarantee is furnished, who regularly use the Community transit arrangements, whose customs authorities know that they can meet their obligations under the arrangements, or, in connection with the authorised consignee status, regularly receive goods that have been entered for the Community transit procedures, and who have not committed any serious or repeated offences against customs or tax legislation. The authorisations are only granted where the customs authorities are able to supervise the procedure and carry out controls, and the persons concerned keep records which enable the customs authorities to carry out effective controls.

ii. Scope of simplifications

1004. The simplifications include (a) the use of a comprehensive guarantee or a guarantee waiver; (b) the use of special loading lists; (c) the use of seals of a special type; (d) exemption from the requirement to use a binding itinerary for goods involving greater risk of fraud; (e) the status of authorised consignor and authorised consignee; (f) special simplifications for large containers and rail, sea, air or pipeline movements; and (g) other additional simplifications that may be granted on the basis of bi- or multilateral agreements between countries. The geographic scope of the application of the simplifications depends on the simplification in question. Whereas the authorisation to use the authorised consignee status applies solely in the EC Member State where the authorisation is granted, the authorisation to use seals of a special type, the exemption from the requirement to use a prescribed itinerary and the authorisation to use authorised consignor status shall apply only to Community transit operations beginning in the EC Member State where the authorisation was granted. All other authorisations apply in all EC Member States.

iii. Comprehensive guarantee and guarantee waiver

1005. The principal may use a comprehensive guarantee, or guarantee waiver, up to a reference amount which equals the amount of customs debt which may be incurred in respect of goods in the principal places under the Community transit procedure during a period of at least one week. The reference amount will be established by the office of guarantee in collaboration with the party concerned on the basis of the information on goods imported in the past and an estimate of the volume of the intended Community transit operations. The reference amount shall be reviewed annually and adjusted, if necessary. In certain cases, the amount to be covered by the comprehensive guarantee may be reduced to 50 per cent or 30 per cent of the reference amount. Since 1 January 2001, for certain goods involving a greater risk of fraud, specific minimum rates apply. The following goods are considered to involve greater risk of fraud: live animals of the bovine domestic species; meat of bovine animals, frozen, fresh or chilled; milk and cream, concentrated or containing added sugar or other sweeteners; butter and other fats and oils derived from milk; fresh bananas, excluding plantains; cane or beet sugar and chemically pure sucrose, solid; undenatured ethyl alcohol of an alcoholic strength by volume of 80 per cent or higher; spirits, liqueurs and other spirituous beverages; and cigarettes containing tobacco. A guarantee waiver may be granted where the principal demonstrates that he maintains certain standards of reliability, is in command of transport operations and has sufficient financial resources to meet his obligations. The criteria to be taken into account, including sufficient experience, high level of cooperation with the customs authorities, being in command of transport operations and sufficient financial resources to cover obligations, are further defined in Annex 46b of the Implementing Code. With respect to the goods involving greater risk of fraud, additional criteria must be met to be authorised to furnish a comprehensive guarantee. On the basis of the authorisation, the customs authorities shall issue the principal with one or more comprehensive guarantee certificates or guarantee waiver certificates corresponding to the specimen form in Annexes 51 and 51a of the Implementing Code. These certifications shall be valid for a period which does not exceed 2 years.

iv. Special loading lists

1006. The customs authorities may authorise principals to use loading lists which do not comply with all the requirements of Annexes 44a and 45 of the Implementing Code, provided the lists are produced by firms which use an integrated electronic or automatic data-processing system to keep their records; are designed and completed in such a way that they can be used without difficulty by the customs authorities; and, include, for each item, the information required under Annex 44a of the Implementing Code.

v. Use of seals of a special type

1007. Principals may be authorised to use special types of seals on means of transport or packages provided these seals have been approved. The principal shall affix the seals no later than when goods are released.

vi. Exemption regarding prescribed itinerary

1008. The customs authorities may grant an exemption from the requirement to follow a prescribed itinerary.

vii. Authorised consignor status

1009. Persons wishing to carry out Community transit operations without presenting the goods and the corresponding transit declaration at the office of departure may be granted the status of authorised consignor. This simplification shall be granted solely to persons authorised to use a comprehensive guarantee or granted a guarantee waiver. The authorisation shall specify, in particular, the office or offices of departure responsible for forthcoming Community operations; how and by when the authorised consignor is to inform the office of departure of forthcoming Community transit operations; the identification measures to be taken; and the excluded categories or movements of goods.

viii. Authorised consignee status

1010. Persons who wish to receive at their premises or at any other specified place, goods entered for the Community transit procedure without presenting them and copies No. 4 and 5 of the transit declaration at the office of destination, may be granted the status of authorised consignee. The principal is considered to have fulfilled his obligation to produce the goods intact at the customs office of destination by the prescribed time limit and with due observance of the measures adopted, and the Community transit procedure is deemed to have ended, when copies 4 and 5 of the transit declaration, together with the intact goods, have been delivered within the prescribed period to the authorised consignee at his premises or at the place specified in the authorisation, the identification measures having been duly observed. The authorisation shall specify, in particular, the office or offices of destination responsible; how and by when the authorised consignee is to inform the office of destination of the arrival of the goods; and the excluded categories or movements of goods. When the goods arrive at his premises or at the places specified in the authorisation, the authorised consignee shall immediately inform the office of destination and, without delay, send to the office of destination copies of Nos. 4 and 5 of the transit declaration, indicating the date of arrival and the condition of any seals affixed.

ix. Simplified procedures for goods carried by rail or in large containers, for transport by air, maritime transport or transport by pipeline

1011. Several simplifications have been introduced for the different kinds of transport.

9. New Computerised Transit System

1012. Under the reform, the current paper-based transit procedure is to be entirely replaced by a New Computerised Transit System (the "NCTS") by the end of 2003. As a general rule, the NCTS will be used for both external and internal Community transit and common transit in situations where they are currently carried out under the SAD made out as either "T1" or "T2". Therefore, the computerised system will not, at first, cover simplified procedures under which the goods are transported by rail, air, sea or by pipelines and where, essentially, the haulier's own documentation is used.

i. Entry into force

1013. The new rules are already in force for both Community and common transit. However, in order to give customs and trade the necessary time to adapt to the changes, during an intermediate period both the paper-based system and the NCTS are used alongside each other, depending on whether the office of departure is computerised or not. Up to now, only a limited number of offices in 7 pilot countries have started using the NCTS. When the change-over is complete, the paper-based system will be discontinued and the NCTS will be the only applicable system. The NCTS will be progressively extended to all customs offices in all countries by mid-2003.

ii. Advantages of the NCTS for trade and customs

1014. The European Commission expects that the NCTS will result in less time spent waiting at customs, because the declaration will have been sent electronically beforehand. Discharge of the transit procedure will be earlier because an electronic message is used instead of the return of the paper copy No. 5 by mail. At the same time, the high costs under the paper-based system will be reduced. For customs, the NCTS will also mean improved communication and coordination, which the European Commission expects to lead to the creation of a more coherent system.

iii. Which traders can use the NCTS?

1015. In principle, all traders can use the NCTS, provided they use the electronic data interchange (the "EDI") procedures. Each trader should obtain a trader identification number (the "TIN").

iv. Office of departure

1016. The transit declaration is presented at the office of departure, either in paper form (in which case the data is introduced in the system by the customs office) or in a computerised form. Electronic declarations can be made from terminals made available to traders at the customs office of departure or from a trader's own premises. The declaration must contain all the data required and comply with the system specifications. In case of an inconsistency in the data, the trader will be informed so that he can make the necessary corrections. Once the declaration is accepted, the system will provide the declaration with a unique registration number, the so-called movement reference number (the "MRN").

1017. Then, once any inspections have been carried out, either at the office of departure or at the authorised consignor's premises, and the guarantees are accepted, the goods will be released for transit. The system will print the transit accompanying document and, where appropriate, the list of items, either at the office of departure or at the authorised consignor's premises. The accompanying document and the list of items must travel with the goods and be presented at any office of transit and at the office of destination.

1018. When printing the transit accompanying document and the list of items, the office of departure will simultaneously send an anticipated arrival record to the declared office of destination. This message will mainly contain the information taken from the declaration, enabling the office of destination to control the consignment when it arrives.

1019. In case the movement has to pass an office of transit, the office of departure will also send an anticipated transit record, so that any office of transit has prior notification of the consignment concerned and can check the passage of movement.

v. Office of transit

1020. When the goods pass by an office of transit, the goods, the transit accompanying document and, where appropriate, the list of items have to be presented to customs. The anticipated transit record, already available in the system, will automatically be located when the MRN is entered and, subsequently, the movement may be approved for passage. A notification of crossing the frontier is sent to the office of departure.

1021. If the goods go via an office of transit other than the declared one, the message that had initially been sent to the declared office of transit is of no use. In this case the actual office of transit will send a message to the office of departure, requesting the anticipated transit record. Having checked the movement, it will send the notification of crossing the frontier to the office of departure.

vi. Office of destination

1022. Upon arrival, the goods must be presented at the office of destination, either directly or indirectly via the authorised consignee, together with the transit accompanying document and the list of items, if appropriate. The customs authorities will have had the possibility to decide beforehand what controls are necessary. When they enter the MRN into the system, it will automatically locate the corresponding anticipated arrival record, which will be used as a basis for any action or control, and send an arrival advice message to the office of departure.

1023. After the relevant controls have been carried out, the office of destination will notify the office of departure of the control results by using a control results message, stating which, if any, irregularities have been detected. The control results message is necessary to discharge the transit operation and to release the guarantees that were used for it.

1024. In case the goods are presented at an office of destination other than the declared one, the actual office of destination will request the office of departure to send the anticipated arrival record so that the new office of destination may obtain the necessary information on the consignment.

1025. The system will also automatically send a message to the declared office, notifying it where and when the goods have been presented, so that it can close the anticipated arrival record which would otherwise remain open.

vii. Authorised consignor and authorised consignee

1026. In addition to the requirements under the simplified procedure, under the NCTS the authorised consignor or authorised consignee will have to possess an adequate data-processing system for information interchange with their relevant customs offices. Under the NCTS, the consignor is authorised to:
   (a) create the transit declaration in their own computer system;
   (b) send the corresponding declaration message electronically to the office of departure without the goods having to be physically presented there; and
   (c) send and receive by electronic means subsequent messages, including requests for correction of the declaration, notification of its acceptance and notification of the release of the goods.

The authorised consignees are allowed to:
   (a) receive the goods and the accompanying document directly at their own premises;
   (b) send the arrival notification message to the relevant office of destination electronically; and
   (c) receive and send subsequent messages concerning permission to unload goods and the notification of the results of the unloading to customs electronically.

10. Common transit procedure with the EFTA countries

1027. Since 1 January 1988, the use of the Community transit procedures has been extended to the EFTA countries (Iceland, Norway and Switzerland – including Liechtenstein, as it forms a customs union with Switzerland) and the 4 Visegrad countries (Czech Republic, Hungary, Poland, Slovak Republic). It is based on the Common Transit Convention of 20 May 1987. This Common Transit Procedure applies to transit operations among EFTA countries and between EFTA countries and the EC. The "T1" or "T2" procedures are used depending on the duty position of the goods. The new rules set out above for the Community transit procedures also apply to the common transit.

H. Relief from import duties in cases of temporary importation or re-importation

§1. Temporary importation

1028. Goods temporarily imported for use in Belgium fall under a special customs procedure called temporary importation. Other forms of temporary importation are governed respectively by the rules on inward processing and the various transit procedures.

1. Conditions for obtaining relief from duty

1029. Pursuant to Articles 137 through 144 of the Community Customs Code, certain goods may be imported temporarily into the customs territory of the European Community with total or partial exemption from import duties, provided that prior authorisation has been obtained and that the goods are re-exported in an unaltered state before the expiry of the deadline determined in the authorisation. The exemption will be total or partial depending on the nature of the goods and their intended use.

2. Formalities

i. Application

1030. In order to benefit from the arrangements, the importer must submit a written application or an application by means of a data-processing technique to the customs authorities designated for the place where the goods are to be used. A specimen of the application is referred to in Annex 67 of the Implementing Code. For certain goods, the application may even be made by an oral customs declaration, subject to the presentation of a document containing certain additional information.

1031. An application for a single authorisation may be made in the event that it is expected that the goods will be used in several EC Member States. In that case, the application shall be submitted to the customs authorities designated for the place of first use. This customs authority shall then communicate the application and draft authorisation to the other customs authorities concerned. The other customs authorities concerned shall notify any objections within 30 days of the date of receipt of the draft authorisation. Where the objections are notified within that period and no agreement is reached, the application shall be rejected to the extent to which objections were raised. If no objections are received within the 30 days, the customs authorities may issue the authorisation. Authorisation for temporary importation shall be refused where it is impossible to ensure that the imported goods can be identified.

ii. Authorisation

1032. The customs authorities to which the application was presented will deliver the authorisation and determine the period within which re-exportation must take place or a new customs-approved treatment or use be assigned. The maximum period during which the goods may stay in Belgium under this arrangement is in principle 24 months, unless the applicant requests a shorter period. In exceptional cases, the customs authorities may extend the period determined in the authorisation.

iii. Entry for the arrangements

1033. Where personal effects, goods imported for sports purposes or means of transport are declared orally or by any other act for entry for the arrangements, customs authorities may require a written declaration when a high amount of import duties is at stake or a serious risk of non-compliance with the obligations of the arrangements exist. Particular rules apply if ATA (*Admission Temporaire/Temporary Admission*) / CPD (*Carnet de passage en Douane*) carnets are used.

iv. Guarantee

1034. In general, entry for the arrangements by written declaration shall be subject to the provision of security, except in the cases referred to in Annex 77 of the Implementing Code. These cases include, for example, packages imported empty, carrying indelible non-removable markings.

3. *Transfer of the goods to another EC Member State*

1035. It should be noted that it is possible to transfer goods temporarily imported into Belgium to other EC Member States. In such cases, a new authorisation must be requested using an information sheet INF6 (Art. 715 of the Implementing Code) conforming to the model in Annex 98.

4. *Goods qualifying for total relief*

1036. The types of goods benefiting from the total exemption of customs duties upon temporary importation and the relevant conditions are listed in Articles 555 through 578 of the Implementing Code. They include, *e.g.*, means of transport; personal effects and goods for sports purposes imported by travellers; disaster relief material; medical, surgical and laboratory equipment; sound, image or data carrying publicity material; certain types of professional and scientific equipment; packings, moulds *etc.*; goods for events or for sale; as well as spare parts thereof, accessories and equipment. Total relief may also be granted where other goods than those listed in Articles 556 through 577 and not complying with the conditions of these articles, are imported either occasionally and for a period not exceeding 3 months, or, in particular situations having no economic effect.

5. Goods qualifying for partial exemption

1037. All goods, except consumable products, may be imported under a partial exemption from import duties. This includes goods which are not covered by the temporary importation procedure qualifying for total relief or goods that are covered by those provisions, but do not fulfil all the conditions laid down therein for the grant of temporary importation with total relief. Under the partial relief system, 3 per cent of the total duties which would have been charged if the goods had been released for free circulation on the date they were placed under the arrangement is charged for every month or fraction of month they remain under the temporary importation procedure. However, the total amount of duties thus collected may not exceed the amount which would have been payable if the goods had been released for free circulation immediately.

6. Discharge of the arrangements

1038. Goods placed under the arrangements must remain in the same state. Repairs and maintenance, including overhaul and adjustments or measures to preserve the goods or to ensure their compliance with the technical requirements for their use under the arrangements, are admissible. Temporary importation agreements are discharged when the goods are re-exported outside the European Community or are placed under another customs-approved treatment or use. The consumption, destruction or distribution free of charge to the public of goods (except alcoholic beverages, tobacco goods or fuels) to be exhibited or used at a public event not purely organised for the commercial sale of the goods, or obtained at such events from goods placed under the arrangements, shall be considered as re-exportation, provided their quantity corresponds to the nature of the event, the number of visitors and the extent of the holder's participation therein. Goods which are placed under the arrangements in accordance with Article 576 of the Implementing Code (*i.e.*, goods for events or for sale) are also discharged by their entry for free circulation.

§2. Returned goods

1. Definition and scope

1039. Community goods which have been exported outside the EC Customs territory and which are subsequently re-imported into that territory may benefit from a relief from import duties upon their release for free circulation within the European Community pursuant to Articles 185 through 187 of the Community Customs Code and Articles 844 through 856 of the Implementing Code. The exemption will be complete in cases where the returned goods were in free circulation in the European Community at the time of their exportation. However, where the returned goods have been released for free circulation at reduced or zero import duty because of their use for a particular purpose, the relief of import duty will be granted if they are re-imported for the same purpose. If this purpose is no longer the same, the amount of import duties chargeable upon them will be reduced by the amount levied when they were first released for free circulation. Should the latter amount exceed that levied on the entry for free circulation of returned goods, no refund is granted. The returned goods will only be partially exempted from import duties if they are compensating products resulting from an inward processing authorisation. In this case, only goods originally imported under the inward processing operation but re-imported in an unaltered state will be treated as returned goods. Agricultural products for which an export refund or other financial benefit was granted under the Common Agricultural Policy (the "CAP") at the time of exportation will only qualify for relief upon re-importation in certain exceptional cases and provided additional conditions are fulfilled.

2. Conditions

1040. In order to benefit from the exemption, the goods must be returned within a maximum period of 3 years (which may be extended in order to take account of special circumstances) from the date of exportation. Moreover, the goods must be re-imported in the state in which they were exported. They must not have undergone any processing or treatment outside the European Community other than operations necessary for their preservation. Goods returned to the European Community after having undergone processing operations in third countries are thus excluded from the arrangements. However, they may obtain a partial relief under the EC outward processing arrangements.

3. Formalities

1041. The initial exporter may be aware at the time of exportation that the goods will subsequently be returned to the European Community in an unaltered state. In this case, the exporter should make a temporary export declaration, and an information sheet "INF3" will be delivered to the exporter. This information sheet must be delivered to the customs office of re-importation in order to facilitate the identification of the goods. In addition to the data normally provided on an export declaration, the declarant must indicate the reason for the temporary exportation and provide all details necessary for the identification of the goods at the time of re-importation. The customs authorities may also take additional measures to facilitate identification, such as samples or attaching identification marks. At the time of re-importation, an import declaration must be lodged along with a copy of the export declaration.

I. Relief from import duties upon permanent importation

§1. Introduction

1042. Total or partial exemption from import duties may be granted in cases of temporary importation or re-importation. In a limited number of cases, relief will also be granted upon permanent importation. The list of products, as well as the conditions which must be fulfilled in order to benefit from relief, are defined in EC Council Regulation No. 918/83 (O.J. [1983] L 105/1) setting up an EC system of reliefs. In addition, certain products may be imported permanently at a zero or reduced rate if they are intended for certain applications or uses. The conditions which need to be met in order to benefit from end-use relief are contained in Article 21 of the Community Customs Code and in Articles 291 through 300 of the Implementing Code.

§2. The EC system of reliefs

1043. The main products benefiting from the EC relief system are the following:
   (i) personal property of individuals who transfer their habitual residence from a third country to the European Community, that is, property intended for personal use, household effects and provisions for ordinary family requirements;
   (ii) capital goods and equipment imported by an undertaking ceasing its activities abroad and transferring its operations to the European Community, provided the transfer leads to a new activity being set up in the European Community similar to the previous activity and not to a merger with or an acquisition of an existing operation in the European Community. The goods transferred must have been used by the undertaking for at least 12 months before it ceased its activities abroad;
   (iii) goods contained in travellers' personal luggage;
   (iv) goods imported on the occasion of a marriage;
   (v) personal property acquired by inheritance;
   (vi) goods imported for trade promotion purposes:
   (vii) certain educational, scientific and cultural materials;
   (viii) scientific instruments and apparatus intended for public or approved private establishments principally engaged in education or research, to the extent that instruments or apparatus of equivalent scientific value are not being manufactured in the European Community;
   (ix) certain therapeutic substances of human origin; and
   (x) pharmaceutical products used at international sports events.

1044. Relief is granted, depending on the product concerned, by the head of the local customs office, the regional customs director or the central customs authorities.

Where the authorisation cannot be given immediately by the local customs office, a provisional authorisation may be given on condition that the importer provides adequate security.

§3. End-use relief

1. Definition

1045. For certain products listed in the CCT, preferential import duties apply upon definitive importation, provided the products are put to a specific end-use. These products are identified in the Belgian External Tariff by a footnote in the CN column containing the product description stating that *"Entry under this subheading is subject to the conditions laid down by the Minister of Finance"*.

2. Conditions

1046. In order to benefit from the regime, the importer must obtain, prior to importation, an authorisation from the Directorate-General of the Belgian customs administration. Applications must be made in writing using the model set out in Annex 67 of the Community Customs Code. The application must state the name and address of the applicant, the nature of the goods (CN code, description, quantity and value) as well as compensating and processed products, details of the planned activities and economic conditions. In particular circumstances, the customs authorities may allow the declaration for free circulation in writing or by means of a data-processing technique using the normal procedure to constitute an application for authorisation, provided that the application involves only one customs administration, the applicant wholly assigns the goods to the prescribed end-use, and the proper conduct of the operations is safeguarded. The importer, after having obtained the authorisation, must:
  (i) assign the goods to the prescribed end-use within the period and at the places referred to in the authorisation;
  (ii) not take actions incompatible with the intended purpose of the prescribed end-use;
  (iii) notify all factors which may affect the authorisation to the competent authority;
  (iv) provide security where necessary;
  (v) pay the amount of uncollected import duties if the goods are not put to the prescribed end-use within the period referred to in the authorisation;
  (vi) provide evidence of the assignment of the goods to the prescribed end-use and keep adequate records that will allow the customs authorities to carry out

any checks which they consider necessary to ensure that the goods are put to the prescribed end-use and to allow the inspection of the records; and

(vii) submit to any other control measures deemed necessary by the customs authorities.

1047. Goods released for free circulation benefiting from end-use relief may be transferred between different places designated in the same authorisation without any customs formalities. The transfer of goods between 2 authorisation holders established in different EC Member States has to be made by using the T5 control copy. However, this transfer may be made without using the T5 control copy if the customs authorities concerned consider that the proper conduct of operations is safeguarded.

J. Customs procedures with economic impact

1048. The customs procedures with economic impact include the following 5 arrangements designed to allow certain economic activities to be carried out without incurring customs duties: inward processing, outward processing, processing under customs control, customs warehousing and temporary importation. Each of the above-listed arrangements is explained hereunder, with the exception of temporary importation which is addressed at paragraphs 1028 *et seq*. The use of these arrangements is, amongst others, conditional upon the granting of a prior authorisation by the customs authorities and the keeping of a detailed bookkeeping for customs purposes. The entry into, and ending of, the arrangements is made by a customs declaration.

1049. Regulation No. 993/2001 simplifies and modernises the rules concerning customs procedures with economic impact. The conditions for being able to use the procedures have been liberalised, for example, regarding the way customs authorities determine whether economic conditions are met (*i.e.*, that the interests of EC producers are not harmed by the use of duty-free goods from abroad). For instance, for "non-sensitive" goods brought into the European Community for processing, the necessary authorisation may be granted without having to go through the former administrative procedure which was time-consuming both for customs authorities and for economic operators. In addition, simpler rules have been introduced for products that are re-imported after they have been processed outside the European Community. The movements of goods or products between different premises or operators have been facilitated by removing burdensome formalities. In response to a growing demand from operators, the provisions on single authorisations have been streamlined (*i.e.*, to allow the possibility for traders operating in more than one EC Member State to deal with a single customs administration for customs matters), and the possibility of granting retroactive authorisations has been considerably increased in order to meet cases of genuine need. For example, a need could occur when a trader imports raw material from a third country to process it in the European Community and sell it on the domestic market but, after processing, decides to export it instead. It is obvious that he wishes to get back the duty he has paid.

§1. Basic provisions common to all customs procedures with economic impact

1. Application for authorisation

1050. The use of any customs procedure with economic impact is conditional upon an authorisation being issued by the customs authorities. Application for authorisation must be made in writing using the model set out in Annex 67 of the Implementing Code. The customs authorities may permit renewal or modification of an authorisation, to be applied for by simple written request. In certain cases, the application for authorisation may be made by means of a customs declaration in writing or by means of a data-processing technique using the normal procedure. Where the customs authorities consider any of the information given in the application inadequate, they may require additional details. As to temporary importation, the application for authorisation may, under certain circumstances, be made by means of an oral customs declaration. Where the application is made by making a customs declaration, the customs authorities shall require that the application be accompanied by a document made out by the declarant containing at least the following information, unless such information is deemed unnecessary or can be entered on the form used for the written declaration:
  (i) name and address of the applicant, the declarant and the operator;
  (ii) nature of the processing or use of the goods;
  (iii) technical description of the goods and compensating or processed products and means of identifying them;
  (iv) codes of economic conditions;
  (v) estimated rate of yield or method by which that rate is to be determined;
  (vi) estimated period for discharge;
  (vii) proposed office of discharge;
  (viii) place of processing or use;
  (ix) proposed transfer formalities; and
  (x) in the case of oral customs declaration, the value and quantity of the goods.

2. Economic conditions

1051. In order to protect the interests of EC manufacturers, certain economic conditions must be met before authorisation will be given. Except where the economic conditions are deemed to be fulfilled, the authorisation shall not be granted without the examination of the economic conditions by the customs authorities (Art. 502 of the Implementing Code). The European Commission may be involved if the customs authorities concerned wish to consult the European Commission before or after issuing an authorisation; if another customs administration objects to an authorisation issued; or, on the initiative of the European Commission.

1052. In addition to the special conditions governing each of the arrangements in question, the authorisation shall only be granted to persons who offer every guarantee necessary for the proper conduct of the operations, and where the customs authorities can supervise and monitor the procedure without having to introduce administrative arrangements disproportionate to the economic needs involved.

3. Entry of goods under the arrangements

1053. With the exception of customs warehousing arrangements, the authorisation will stipulate a period of validity. Before the expiry of this period, the imported goods must be entered under the arrangements by means of an import declaration.

4. Discharge of the arrangement

1054. Where import or temporary export goods have been entered under 2 or more declarations for the arrangements by virtue of one authorisation, in the case of a suspensive arrangement, the assignment of goods or products to a new customs-approved treatment or use shall be considered to discharge the arrangements for the import goods in question entered under the earliest of the declarations; in case of inward processing (drawback system) or outward processing, the compensating products shall be considered to have been obtained respectively from the import or temporary export goods in question entered under the earliest of the declarations.

1055. Upon the expiry of the period for discharge, the bill of discharge or the claim for repayment or remission of import duties must be lodged.

§2. Inward processing

1. Definition

1056. Inward processing is a customs arrangement whereby goods, in particular raw materials or semi-manufactured goods, imported into the European Community for processing are exempted from import duties provided they are wholly or partly re-exported in the form of "compensating products". The inward processing arrangements are based on Articles 114 through 129 of the Community Customs Code and on Articles 536 through 550 of Commission Regulation No. 993/2001 of 4 May 2001 (O.J. [2001] L 141/1) amending the Implementing Code. There are 2 variants: one allows the duty to be suspended, while under the other it is paid and later repaid.

2. Authorisation

1057. The authorisation shall be issued at the request of the person who carries out processing operations or who arranges for them to be carried out. The authorisation shall be granted only to persons established in the European Community (persons established outside the European Community may be granted an authorisation in respect of imports of a non-commercial nature). Additionally, the authorisation shall only be granted where the import goods can be identified in the compensating products and where the inward processing procedure can help create the most favourable conditions for the export or re-export of compensating products, provided that essential interests of EC producers are not adversely affected (economic conditions).

1058. The application for an authorisation shall be submitted to the customs authorities designated for the place where the processing operation is to be carried out. The economic unviability of using EC sources must be established, taking into account the unavailability of EC-produced goods sharing the same quality and technical characteristics as the goods intended to be imported for the processing operations envisaged; differences in price between EC-produced goods and those intended to be imported; and contractual obligations. The economic conditions shall be deemed to be fulfilled except where the application concerns import goods mentioned in Annex 73 of the Implementing Code, namely agricultural products covered by Annex I to the EC Treaty as well as goods not covered by Annex I to the EC Treaty resulting from the processing of agricultural goods and fishery products. When goods mentioned in Annex 73 are concerned, the conditions shall nevertheless be deemed to be fulfilled provided that, for example,

i. The application concerns in particular
   (a) operations involving goods of a non-commercial nature;
   (b) a job processing contract;
   (c) the processing of compensating products already obtained by processing under a previous authorisation, the granting of which was subject to an examination of the economic conditions;

(d) usual forms of handling as defined for the warehousing arrangements in Annex 72 of the Implementing Code; and

(e) repair.

ii. The aggregate value of the import goods per applicant and per calendar year for each eight-digit CN Code does not exceed € 150,000.

1059. Additional conditions concerning the granting of the authorisation include that the applicant has the intention of re-exporting or exporting main compensating products. An authorisation may also be granted for the goods defined in accordance with the committee procedure which are not to be found in the compensating products, but which allow or facilitate the production of those products, even if they are entirely or partially used up in the process, with the exception of fuels and energy sources, lubricants, equipment and tools. The period of validity shall not exceed 3 years from the date the authorisation takes effect, except where there are duly justified good reasons. For certain goods, the period of validity shall not exceed 6 months. The authorisation shall specify the means and the methods of identifying the import goods in the compensating products and lay down the conditions for the proper conduct of operations using equivalent goods. The authorisation shall specify the period for discharge. For certain agricultural products, the period for discharge shall not exceed 2, 3, 4 or 6 months respectively.

3. *Systems for operating the arrangements*

1060. The inward processing arrangements offer 2 distinct systems:

(i) Under the suspension system, non-EC goods are imported without the payment of the applicable import duties, provided they are intended for re-export outside the customs territory of the European Community in the form of compensating products. This is the system most commonly used in Belgium;

(ii) Under the drawback system, non-EC goods are imported and released for free circulation – the applicable import duties must be paid. However, import duties levied on such goods are refunded or remitted if they are exported outside the customs territory of the European Community in the form of compensating products.

1061. An applicant must indicate for which system he wants to obtain the inward processing authorisation.

1062. In view of the procedural and legal differences between the 2 systems once the application has been lodged, the systems are explained separately in the following sections.

4. Suspension system

i. Conditions

1063. To use the suspension system, the applicant must actually intend, at the time he files the application, to export the main compensating products from the customs territory of the European Community. However, no obligation exists to actually export the compensating products resulting from the processing operation. It is enough that the applicant has a genuine intention to export at the time of the application. In case of doubt, the customs authorities may request the applicant to post an adequate security.

1064. In the authorisation, the customs authority will set a time limit for the processing operations to take place and by which the compensating products must be re-exported or assigned another customs-approved treatment or use. The customs authorities shall set either the rate of yield of the operation, *i.e.*, the quantity or percentage of compensating products obtained from the processing of a given quantity of import goods, or where appropriate, the method of determining such rate.

ii. Discharge of the arrangement

1065. The inward processing arrangement will normally be discharged by the definitive exportation of the compensating products. The declaration for definitive exportation must be lodged at the customs office indicated in the authorisation as being responsible for the supervision of the arrangement. Where another office is used, prior approval must be obtained. The compensating products must be presented at the office of exportation and the customs authorities may carry out all checks, including sampling, necessary to verify compliance with the conditions of the authorisation. The arrangement will also be discharged where the compensating products are placed under an equivalent customs regime, such as a second inward processing arrangement, the external Community transit procedure, the system of processing under customs control, the free zone procedure, the customs warehousing or temporary importation regime or where the goods are destroyed under customs supervision. As is the case for definitive exportation, the formalities for placing the goods under an equivalent customs regime must be completed at the customs office responsible for supervising the arrangements.

1066. The holder of the authorisation must submit a bill of discharge to the customs authorities within 30 days of the expiry of the period of discharge determined in the authorisation for the processing operations to take place. The bill of discharge must show that the inward processing authorisation for the suspension system was used in accordance with the conditions laid down in the authorisation.

iii. Release for free circulation

1067. If compensating goods or import goods are released into free circulation, the declarant must pay all import duties which would have been payable if the imported goods had been released for free circulation on the date they were first brought in under the inward processing arrangement. To avoid abuse of this possibility for deferring payment, the declarant must also pay compensatory interest on the deferred payment for the period involved. Interest shall be applied on a monthly basis, starting on the first day of the month following the month in which the import goods for which a customs debt is incurred were first entered for the arrangements. The period shall close on the last day of the month in which the customs debt is incurred. No compensatory interest shall be due, however, where:

(a) the period to be taken into account is less than one month;

(b) where the amount of compensatory interest applicable does not exceed € 20 per customs debt incurred;

(c) where a customs debt is incurred in order to allow the application of a preferential tariff treatment under an agreement between the European Community and a third country on imports into that country;

(d) where waste and scrap resulting from destruction is released for free circulation;

(e) where the secondary compensating products referred to in Annex 75 are released for free circulation, provided they are in proportion to exported quantities of main compensating products;

(f) where a customs debt is incurred as a result of an application for release for free circulation under Article 128, paragraph 4 of the Community Customs Code, as long as the import duties payable on the products in question have not yet actually been repaid or remitted;

(g) where the holder requests release for free circulation and submits proof that particular circumstances not arising from any negligence or deception on his part make it impossible or uneconomical to carry out the re-export operation under the conditions he had anticipated and duly substantiated when applying for the authorisation;

(h) where a customs debt is incurred and to the extent a security is provided by a cash deposit in relation to this debt; or

(i) where a customs debt is incurred in accordance with Article 201, paragraph 1(b) of the Community Customs Code or is due to the release for free circulation of goods which were entered for the temporary importation arrangements under Articles 556 through 561, 563, 565, 568, 573(b) and 576 of the Implementing Code.

1068. The authorisation shall specify whether compensating products or goods in the unaltered state may be released for free circulation without a customs declaration, without prejudice to prohibitive or restrictive measures. In this case, they shall be considered to have been released for free circulation, if they have not been assigned a customs-approved treatment or use on expiry of the period for discharge.

5. Drawback system

1069. In contrast to the suspension system, a number of imported goods are expressly excluded from the scope of the drawback system. Specifically, goods that are subject to quantitative import restrictions that might, within quotas, qualify for a preferential tariff measure or an autonomous suspensive measure or that are subject to an import charge under the CAP or under specific arrangements applicable to certain goods resulting from the processing of agricultural goods are excluded. The drawback system may also be used only if no export refund has been set for the compensating products at the time the declaration of release for free circulation of the import goods is accepted.

1070. As in the suspension system, the arrangement will be discharged if the compensating products are definitively exported outside the EC customs territory or are placed under an equivalent customs regime.

1071. In the event that the compensating products have been exported or have been entered under an equivalent regime, the holder of the authorisation must lodge a repayment or remission claim with the supervising office within 6 months, at the latest upon expiry of the period for discharge. In case the goods are released for free circulation, the declaration shall indicate that the drawback system is being used and shall provide particulars of the authorisation. Compensatory interest is due where release for free circulation is requested for compensating products or goods in the unaltered state placed under a customs procedure or in a free zone or free warehouse from the first day of the month following the month in which the import duties were repaid or remitted. The same exemptions as under the suspension system apply.

6. Special procedures: equivalent compensation and prior exportation

1072. The customs authority may, provided certain conditions are met, remove the requirement that the imported goods are re-exported as compensating products outside the customs territory of the European Community.

1073. Under the system of equivalent compensation, the customs authorities may authorise that the compensating products be obtained from equivalent EC goods instead of from the imported goods entered under the inward processing arrangement, provided these EC goods share the same 8-digit CN code, the same commercial quality and the same technical characteristics as the import goods. However, in specific cases, equivalent goods may be allowed to be at a more advanced stage of manufacture than the import goods.

1074. Under the system of prior exportation, the customs authorities may also allow the exportation of compensating products, obtained from equivalent goods, prior to the entry of the import goods for the arrangements using the suspension system. Where, in such a case, the compensating products would be liable to export duties if they were not being exported or re-exported under an inward processing operation, the holder of the authorisation shall provide a security to ensure payment of the duties should the import goods not be imported within the period described. Where the office of discharge is not the same as the office of entry, so-called triangular traffic, the information sheet INF5, for the communication to obtain duty relief for import goods, and the information sheet INF9, for the communication of information on compensating products to be assigned another customs approved treatment or use in triangular traffic, must be used.

§3. *Outward processing*

1. Definition

1075. Outward processing arrangements allow EC goods to be exported temporarily from the customs territory of the European Community in order to undergo processing operations. The products resulting from such operations (compensating products) are subsequently released for free circulation in the EC customs territory with total or partial relief from import duties.

1076. Under standard exchange arrangements, replacement products are allowed to be imported with partial or total exemption from import duties to replace compensating products. These standard exchange arrangements shall be allowed where the processing operation involves the repair of EC goods other than those subject to the CAP or to the specific arrangements applicable to certain goods resulting from the processing of agricultural products.

1077. The rules applicable to both arrangements are set out in Articles 145 through 160 of the Community Customs Code.

2. Conditions

1078. The use of the outward processing and standard exchange arrangements is subject to prior authorisation from the central customs administration. The application for an authorisation using the model in Annex 67 of the Implementing Code shall be submitted to the customs authorities designated for the place where the goods to be declared for temporary exportation are located.

1079. The application for authorisation may be made by means of a customs declaration in writing or by means of a data-processing technique using the normal procedure where the processing operations concern repairs, including the standard exchange system without prior importation, and, after outward processing, in the following cases:
  (i) for release for free circulation after outward processing using the standard exchange system with prior importation;
  (ii) for release for free circulation after outward processing using the standard exchange system without prior importation, where the existing authorisation does not cover such a system and the customs authorities permit its modification; and
  (iii) for release for free circulation after outward processing if the processing operation concerns goods of a non-commercial nature.

1080. Certain products are excluded from the scope of outward processing arrangements. This exclusion applies primarily to EC goods whose export gives rise to repayment or remission of import duties; or, which, prior to export, were released for free circulation with total relief from import duties by virtue of their end use, for as long as the conditions for granting such relief continue to apply; or, whose export gives rise to the granting of export refunds or of other financial advantages under the CAP.

1081. The authorisation may generally only be delivered to the person who arranges for the processing to be carried out and provided that he is established in the European Community. In addition, the customs authorities must be satisfied that it will be possible to establish that the compensating products have resulted from processing of the temporary export goods and that authorisation to use the outward processing procedure is not liable to seriously harm the essential interests of EC processors (economic conditions). In particular, the examination of the economic conditions shall establish whether carrying out processing outside the European Community is likely to cause serious disadvantages for EC processors, or whether carrying out processing in the European Community is economically unviable or is not feasible for technical reasons or due to contractual obligations. However, except where indications to the contrary exist, the essential interests of EC processors shall be deemed not to be seriously harmed. Where the arrangements are requested for repair, the temporary export goods must be capable of being repaired and the arrangements shall not be used to improve the technical performance of the goods.

1082. If the above conditions are met, the authorisation will be granted to the applicant specifying the period within which the compensating goods must be re-imported into the customs territory of the European Community and the period of discharge. In the authorisation or, at the latest, at the time the goods are entered under the arrangement, the customs authorities will also determine the quantity or percentage of compensating products obtained from processing a given quantity of exported goods, *i.e.*, the rate of yield of the operation or, where necessary, the method of determining that rate. Moreover, the authorisation shall specify the means and methods to establish that the compensating products have resulted from the processing of the temporary export goods or to verify that the conditions for using the standard exchange system are met. Such means and methods may include the use of the information document in Annex 104 of the Implementing Code and the examination of the records.

3. *Customs formalities upon exportation and re-importation*

1083. Exported goods must be presented and declared for exportation at the customs office indicated in the authorisation. The export declaration must contain the same information as a normal export declaration. In the case of prior importation, a copy of the authorisation must generally be joined to the declaration.

1084. The export goods must, after processing in a third country, be re-imported in the form of compensating products before the deadline set in the export declaration. Compensating products will be considered to have been re-imported when they are released for free circulation, entered under an inward processing arrangement or placed under a customs warehousing or external Community transit procedure.

1085. If the compensating products are released for free circulation, they will be entitled to total or partial relief from import duties only if they are declared by or on behalf of the holder of the authorisation or any other person established in the European Community, provided that the person has obtained the consent of the holder of the authorisation and the conditions of the authorisation are fulfilled. Thus, if the ownership of the export goods or the compensating goods has been transferred, the transferee may still benefit from the relief. In case one of the conditions or obligations relating to the outward processing is not fulfilled, total or partial relief will only be provided if it is established that the failures have no significant effect on the correct operation of the said procedures. The import formalities required to obtain relief upon re-importation will take the form of an entry for release for free circulation.

4. Calculation of the amount due

1086. The amount of import duties due will be calculated according to the so-called "differential taxation" method, that is, by deducting from the amount of the import duties applicable to the compensating products released for free circulation the amount of the import duties that would be due on the same date upon release for free circulation of the temporary export goods incorporated in the compensating products if they were imported in the customs territory of the European Community from the country in which they underwent the processing operation or last processing operation. The amount to be deducted shall be calculated on the basis of the quantity and nature of the goods in question on the date of acceptance of the declaration placing them under the outward processing procedure and on the basis of the other items of charge applicable to them on the date of acceptance of the declaration relating to the release for free circulation of the compensating products.

1087. In calculating the amount to be deducted, account should be taken of any reduced or zero-rated duty by virtue of their particular end-use, provided the exported goods underwent processing operations in the third country consistent with such end-use. Also, if the compensating products qualify for preferential trade arrangements, and similar arrangements exist for goods in the same tariff classification as the temporary export goods, the amount of the duty to be deducted should be calculated by applying the preferential rate. On the other hand, no account shall be taken of anti-dumping duties and countervailing duties.

5. Total relief from import duties

i. Repairs free of charge:

1088. Total relief from import duties will be granted to products that have been temporarily exported in order to be repaired where it is established to the satisfaction of the customs authorities that the repair was carried out free of charge, either because of a contractual or statutory obligation arising from a guarantee or because of the existence of a manufacturing defect and on condition that, at the time of their initial importation, account had not been taken of the defect. In case the repair is carried out in return for payment, partial relief from import duties will be granted.

ii. Exported goods returned in an unaltered state:

1089. Where, for any reason, the exported goods cannot undergo the intended operations and are consequently re-imported into the European Community in an unaltered state, they will be considered as returned goods for customs purposes and benefit from total relief.

6. Standard exchange arrangements

1090. If the processing operation involves the repair of EC goods other than those subject to the CAP or to the specific arrangements applicable to certain goods resulting from the processing of agricultural products, the customs authorities may permit the use of the standard exchange system. Under this system, the exported goods are not re-imported but are exchanged for replacement goods. The replacement goods must have the same tariff classification and have the same commercial quality and technical characteristics as the export goods would have had after having undergone the repair. Where the temporary export goods have been used before export, the replacement products must also have been used and may not be new products. Standard exchange shall be authorised only where it is possible to verify that the conditions laid down in Article 155 of the Community Customs Code are fulfilled.

1091. The customs authorities may also authorise importation of the replacement goods prior to the exportation of the export goods on condition that adequate security (in the amount of the import duties) is provided. In the case of prior importation, the export goods shall be temporarily exported within a period of 2 months from the date of acceptance by the customs authorities of the declaration relating to the release of the replacement products for free circulation.

7. Triangular traffic

1092. Where the office of discharge is not the same as the office of entry, e.g., if the compensating products are imported into an EC Member State different from the EC Member State from which the exported goods were temporarily exported, relief from import duties for compensating products may only be authorised on production of an information sheet INF2 delivered prior to the release of the compensating products into free circulation.

1093. This information sheet may be issued at the request of the person concerned or on the initiative of the customs authorities. It must contain precise information regarding the temporary export goods, the processing operations to be carried out and the compensating products to be re-imported in order to enable the customs authorities of the EC Member State of re-importation to assess whether the conditions laid down in the authorisation have been respected. The "INF2" must be endorsed by the customs office of exportation, which will return the original to the holder of the authorisation while keeping a copy. Upon presentation of the

endorsed original to the office of re-importation, and provided all other requirements are fulfilled, the compensating product will benefit from duty relief.

8. Special outward processing arrangements in the textile sector

1094. Pursuant to EC Council Regulation No. 3036/94 (O.J. [1994] L 322/1), special
rules apply to outward processing operations involving certain textiles and clothing products re-imported into the European Community after working or processing in other third countries. The main differences from the general outward
processing system are the requirement to obtain prior authorisation from the Central Office for Quotas and Licences (*Centrale Dienst voor Contingenten en Ver-
gunningen /Office des Contingents et Licences*) which forms part of the Ministry
of Economic Affairs, and the requirement that the exported goods are in free circulation in the European Community. Any person applying to benefit under the arrangement must either manufacture, in the European Community, products which
are similar to and at the same stage of manufacturing as the compensating products or perform in his own factory, within the European Community, the main
production processes on those products, *i.e.*, at least sewing and assembly, or knit-
ting in case of fully fashioned garments obtained from yarn.

§4. Processing under customs control

1095. Processing under customs control arrangements allow certain goods to be imported
into the European Community for processing which leads to products which are
subject to a lower duty rate than that applicable to the import goods (*e.g.*, PVC
materials subject to a duty rate of 8.3 per cent may be processed into film screens
with a duty rate of 2.7 per cent) without first having to pay import duties. The
import duty advantage obtained should contribute to creating or maintaining processing activities in the European Community. The arrangement shall also apply for
goods which have to undergo operations to ensure their compliance with technical
requirements for their release into free circulation.

1096. The application for an authorisation shall be submitted to the customs authorities
designated for the place where the processing operation is to be carried out.
Authorisation shall be granted at the request of the person who carries out the
processing or arranges for it to be carried out. Authorisation shall be granted only
to persons established in the European Community; where the import goods can
be identified in the processed products; where the goods cannot be economically
restored after processing to their description or state as it was when they were
placed under the procedure; where use of the procedure cannot result in circumvention of the effect of the rules concerning origin and quantitative restrictions

applicable to imported goods; and where the necessary conditions for the procedure to help create or maintain a processing activity in the European Community without adversely affecting the essential interests of EC producers of similar goods (economic conditions) are fulfilled. The examination of the economic conditions shall establish whether the use of non-EC sources enables processing activities to be created or maintained in the European Community. For the types of goods mentioned in Annex 76, Part A, of the Implementing Code, the economic conditions shall be deemed to be fulfilled. Annex 76, Part A, includes, for example, generally goods of any kind, provided the processing consists of reduction to waste and scrap or destruction, recovery of parts or components, or processing to correct the effects of damage to the goods. Annex 76, Part A, also includes specific products which are to be processed in a specific manner. For the types of goods and operations mentioned in Annex 76, Part B, and not covered by Part A, the examination of the economic conditions shall take place in the Committee. Annex 76, Part B, comprises any form of processing of all goods subject to an agricultural measure, a provisional or definitive anti-dumping duty, or a provisional or definitive countervailing duty.

1097. The authorisation shall specify the period for discharge. The period of validity shall not exceed 3 years from the date the authorisation takes effect, except where there are duly justified good reasons.

§5. *Customs warehousing*

1. Definition

1098. Customs warehousing is a customs regime whereby non-EC goods and, in certain cases, EC goods may be stored in places approved and supervised by the customs authorities without the collection of customs duties or the application of commercial policy measures. The regime is based on EC Council Regulation No. 2913/92 of 12 October 1992 (O.J. [1992] L 302/1), as last amended by EC Council Regulation No. 2700/2000 (O.J. [2000] L 311/17), as implemented by EC Commission Regulation No. 993/2001 of 4 May 2001 (O.J. [2001] L 141/1).

2. Types of warehouses

1099. The Implementing Code distinguishes between 6 different types of warehouses. The main distinction is between public and private warehouses. Further distinctions are made on the basis of whether the depositor or the warehousekeeper is responsible for the goods or on the nature, the customs value and the quantity of the goods and other special circumstances. Except for warehouses operated by the customs authorities themselves, the operation of all customs warehouses must be authorised by the customs authorities. An authorisation may be granted only if any intended usual forms of handling, inward processing or processing under customs control of the goods do not predominate over the storage of the goods. Authorisations shall, in principle, not be granted if the premises of the customs warehouses or the storage facilities are used for the purpose of retail sale.

3. Entry of goods for the arrangements

1100. The normal procedure for entry of goods for the arrangements requires that the goods must be presented at the customs office responsible for the control of the warehouse and that a declaration of entry is lodged. This declaration must be made in the form of an import declaration and, where applicable, reference must be made to any previous customs arrangements used. Under the simplified procedure, the customs authorities may authorise the declarant to make the entry on the basis of a commercial or administrative document, including computerised records, and exempt him from the obligation to present the goods. The control of the operations will be carried out on the basis of the entries in the stock ledger. The acceptance of the entry in the stock records by the control office has the same force in law as acceptance of the normal entry declaration. There is, in principle, no limit to the period during which the goods remain under the customs warehousing procedure.

4. Usual forms of handling

1101. Goods stored in customs warehouses may only undergo "usual forms of handling" as specified in Annex 72 of the Implementing Code. Such handling comprises, for example, ventilation, simple cleaning operations, repair of packaging, sampling, sorting, conservation, certain treatments, addition of goods or addition or replacement of accessory components as long as this addition or replacement is relatively limited or is intended to ensure compliance with technical standards and does not change the nature or improve the performances of the original goods, packaging and testing. Goods may be temporarily removed from the warehouse for a period not exceeding 3 months. Applications for permission to carry out usual forms of handling or to remove goods temporarily from the customs warehouse shall be made in writing on a case by case basis to the supervising office.

5. Discharge of the arrangement

1102. The arrangement will be discharged upon completion of the formalities for release into free circulation or entry for another customs procedure. The arrangement will also be discharged if the goods are exported or destroyed under customs supervision. If the goods are entered into free circulation, an import declaration using the SAD forms or the NCTS system must be made. However, the customs office may authorise the use of simplified procedures similar to those available for the entry for the customs warehousing arrangements.

K. The Customs debt

§1. Definition

1103. The customs debt is the obligation on a person to pay the import or export duties which apply to goods under the applicable provisions.

1104. The rules setting out on which occasions and at what time a customs debt is incurred are contained in Articles 201 through 216 of the Community Customs Code and in Articles 859 through 876a of the Implementing Code.

§2. Incurrence and extinction of a customs debt

1105. A customs debt on importation is incurred when goods subject to duties are released for free circulation or when goods are placed under the temporary importation procedure with partial relief of duties, or when goods liable to import duties are unlawfully introduced into the customs territory of the European Community. A customs debt is also incurred whenever an essential obligation or condition imposed in connection with the customs procedure under which the goods have been placed ceases to be fulfilled or when it is discovered that one of the conditions for granting the authorisation to use the arrangements was in fact not met. A customs debt on exportation is incurred whenever goods subject to export duties or levies are declared for export outside the EC customs territory or when the conditions for granting relief from export duties cease to be fulfilled.

1106. The customs debt is incurred at the time of acceptance of the import or export declaration or at the time the applicable condition ceases to be met. If no import or export declaration is made, the debt arises at the time the goods actually enter or leave the customs territory of the European Community.

1107. The amount of the customs debt is normally determined on the basis of the rules of assessment applicable to the goods at the time the customs debt is incurred.

1108. The customs debt is extinguished by payment of the import or export duties payable on the goods in question or by confiscation of the goods.

§3. Liability and form of payment

1109. The person in whose name the declaration or equivalent legal act was made is generally liable for the payment of the customs debt. The payment of the duties must be made immediately either in cash or by bank cheque. Payment may be deferred for one month as long as adequate security is provided.

L. Licences

§1. Introduction

1110. For the import, export or transit of certain goods, a licence delivered by the Central Office for Quotas and Licences is required. The authorisation to import, export or move these goods under a transit procedure must be obtained before the operation is carried out. The customs authorities will refuse acceptance of the import, export or transit declaration if no licence is produced at the time of the declaration. Accordingly, the refusal by the Belgian authorities to deliver the requested licence is equivalent to a prohibition to carry out the import, export or transit operation.

1111. Pursuant to the Law of 11 September 1962 on the Import, Export and Transit of Goods (*Wet betreffende de in-, uit- en doorvoer van goederen en de daaraan verbonden technologie/Loi relative à l'importation, à l'exportation et au transit des merchandises et de la technologie y afférente*), as implemented by the Royal Decree of 30 December 1993, licences may be imposed in order:
   (i) to safeguard the essential interests of an economic sector or the economy as a whole;
   (ii) to protect the interests of national security and public order;
   (iii) to implement treaties, agreements or decisions and recommendations of international or supranational organisations; and
   (iv) to contribute to the compliance with the general principles of law and society.

1112. Most of the licences imposed by Belgium are the result of decisions taken at the EC level. Indeed, on the basis of Article 133 of the EC Treaty, only the European Community has the power to adopt commercial policy measures involving third countries. Licences for the movement of strategic goods are imposed on the basis of the Law of 5 August 1991 concerning the Import, Export and Transit of Weapons, Ammunition and Other Materials Specifically Intended for Military Use and Related Technology (*Wet betreffende de in-, uit- en doorvoer van wapens, munitie en special voor militair gebruik dienstig materiel en daaraan verbonden technologie/Loi relative à l'importation, à l'exportation et au transit d'armes, munitions et de materiel devant server spécialement à un usage militaire et de la technologie y afférente*), as implemented by the Royal Decree of 8 March 1993.

1113. Licences for political or humanitarian reasons are sometimes imposed as a result of resolutions by the United Nations Security Council or to conform with common positions adopted by the EC Council of Ministers acting within the framework of European Political Co-operation; the Ministerial Decree of 8 August 1990 on Trade with Iraq (*Ministerieel besluit waarbij de in-, uit- en doorvoer van goederen aan vergunning onderworpen wordt/Arrêté ministériel soumettant à licence l'importation, l'exportation et le transit des marchandises*) and the Ministerial Decree of 23 October 1998 on Trade with the Federal Republic of Yugoslavia are examples of this.

1114. It should also be noted that the import, export and transit of certain types of waste requires prior notification pursuant to the Law of 9 July 1984 (*Wet betreffende de in-, uit- en doorvoer van afvalstoffen/Loi concernant l'importation, l'exportation et le transit de déchets*), as modified by the Decree of the Walloon Region (*Waalse Gewest/Région Wallonne*) dated 27 June 1996 and by the Decree of the Flemish Council (*Vlaamse Raad/Conseil flamand*) dated 20 April 1994.

1115. Finally, licences are also required for the import and export of agricultural products, in order to ensure the correct application of the CAP, pursuant to the Royal Decree of 26 July 1962 and the Royal Decree of 30 December 1993.

§2. Products concerned

1. Export and Transit Licences

1116. Exports of dual-use items and technology, listed in Annex I to EC Council Regulation No. 1334/2000 (O.J. [2000] L 159/1), are subject to the obtention of a licence to be delivered by the Central Office for Quotas and Licences. However, pursuant to the Ministerial Decree of 28 September 2000 concerning Exports of Dual-use Items and Technology (the "Ministerial Decree of 28 September 2000" – *Ministerieel besluit tot regeling van de uitvoer van producten en technologie voor tweeërlei gebruik/Arrêté ministériel réglementant l'exportation des biens et technologies à double usage*), no licence is required for products listed in Annex IV to Regulation No. 1334/2000 and exported to the Netherlands and Luxembourg. As to transit operations, the Ministerial Decree of 28 September 2000 provides that the transit of dual-use items is subject to the same requirements as those laid down in Regulation No. 1334/2000, unless:

(i) the dual-use items are consigned from or sent to the Netherlands and Luxembourg;

(ii) the dual-use items in transit are sent abroad without being unloaded or without any change in the means of transport; or

(iii) the dual-use items in transit are already covered by an export licence.

1117. Belgium currently requires that a licence be obtained for the export and transit of certain products destined to Myanmar (Ministerial Decree of 5 September 2000), to the Federal Republic of Yugoslavia (Ministerial Decree of 18 August 2000 and Ministerial Decree of 23 October 1998), to Angola (Ministerial Decree of 4 February 1999), to Rwanda (Ministerial Decree of 23 April 1997) and to Iraq (Ministerial Decree of 8 August 1990).

1118. Finally, it should be noted that exports from Belgium of products originating in the US or of products comprising more than 10 per cent of US parts or components listed in the US Export Administration Regulations may be subject to a licence from the Bureau of Export Administration (the "BXA") of the US Department of Commerce, depending on the destination of the products concerned. Similarly, exports of products having US origin or comprising at least 10 per cent of US parts or components are subject to a licence from the Office of Foreign Assets Control (the "OFAC") of the US Department of Treasury if they are intended to be exported to countries embargoed by the USA (such as, for instance, Lybia, Iran and Iraq).

2. Import Licences

1119. No import licence is necessary for imports of goods from the Netherlands or Luxembourg and in free circulation there. Moreover, import licences will usually not be required if the goods are already in free circulation in other EC Member States. The only exceptions concern the importation of wild animals and of certain weapons annexed to the Ministerial Decree of 15 September 1995 (*Ministerieel besluit waarbij de invoer van sommige goederen aan vergunning onderworpen wordt/ Arrêté ministériel soumettant à licence l'importation de certaines marchandises*). Other non-EC goods which require a licence upon importation are mainly those goods subject to quantitative import restrictions imposed on an EC-wide basis.

M. Dispute settlement procedures

§1. Infringement of tax provisions of customs law

1120. The Belgian customs administration has the authority to verify whether the applicable provisions of Belgian customs law have been complied with. In addition, the administration may prosecute any infringement of the tax provisions of Belgian customs law itself. Tax provisions are those which govern classification, valuation and origin of goods, that is, provisions aimed at ensuring that the correct amount of duty is collected. The provisions imposing the obligation to obtain a prior import, export or transit licence, although unrelated to the determination and collection of duties, are considered as equivalent to fiscal provisions. Any infringement of tax or equivalent provisions of Belgian customs law is considered as a "material" offence. Thus, it is not necessary to establish intent on the part of the perpetrator of the infringement; the mere fact that a tax provision has been violated is sufficient. The customs authorities command extensive investigative powers. For instance, they are entitled to search, at any time, all means of transport and to inspect any goods stored therein. They may carry out surprise on-the-spot checks on private and commercial premises during the daytime, provided they have been authorised by a judge; they may seize goods, means of transport and documents.

1121. The customs authorities may also carry out *a posteriori* investigations regarding customs declarations which were accepted previously but in which the authorities suspect the origin, customs value or classification of the goods has been incorrectly declared. The party responsible for the incorrect declaration may be prosecuted unless the wrong declaration was made more than 3 years before the discovery of its incorrect nature. Any person subject to such an investigation must disclose all relevant commercial documents and ledgers at the first request of the customs authorities.

1122. If an infringement is discovered, the investigating officials will draw up an official report on the basis of which the central administration will decide either to settle the dispute or to bring it before the criminal courts.

1123. In cases where the customs authorities decide to offer a settlement, the party responsible for the infringement must undertake to pay the amount of uncollected duties as well as a fine, which is usually less than the fines provided for under the terms of the General Law on Customs and Excise (the "GLCE"). In return, the administration agrees not to prosecute before the courts. In cases of minor importance, the customs authorities may accept a settlement in the form of a supplementary declaration whereby only the amount of uncollected duties is paid without any additional fine. The latter form of settlement may also be adopted where a person freely discloses the mistake on the declaration to the customs authorities and offers to pay the amount of duties due.

1124. Where the customs authorities do not offer a settlement, or the settlement offered is not accepted, the customs administration may submit the matter to the criminal court. In these circumstances, the normal rules governing court proceedings will apply.

1125. Pursuant to the GLCE, the infringement of tax provisions may be penalised by imprisonment, fines, confiscation, or a combination of all 3. For instance, a person importing goods without making the necessary customs declaration is liable to imprisonment for a period of 4 to 12 months. The fines provided for under the provisions of the GLCE range from 10 times the amount of the uncollected duties, in the case of an incorrect customs declaration, to twice the value of the goods, in cases involving the importation, exportation or transit of "prohibited" goods, that is, goods for which an import, export or transit licence is required. For repeat offenders, the amount of the fine will be doubled. It should be noted that the fine may not be reduced on the basis of the existence of mitigating circumstances. In addition to the fine, the court may order the confiscation of the goods which were incorrectly declared or imported without declaration as well as the means of transport and other equipment used to commit the customs infringement.

§2. Decisions against which an administrative appeal may be lodged

1126. Pursuant to the GLCE, as amended by Article 2 of the Law of 30 June 2000, any person has the right to lodge an administrative appeal against a decision taken by the customs authorities which concerns him directly and individually, provided that the following 3 conditions are fulfilled:
  (i) the decision must relate to the application of the legislation on customs and excise. This implies, for instance, that Article 2 of the Law of 30 June 2000 does not apply to decisions taken pursuant to the VAT legislation;
  (ii) the decision must not be taken on the basis of criminal law. In other words, no administrative appeal is allowed against a settlement of an infringement of customs law proposed by the customs authorities; and
  (iii) the decision must be taken by the Regional Director of customs and excise or by civil servants having a similar ranking (*See*, Ministerial Decree of 14 October 2000).

1127. The administrative appeal must be duly motivated and signed, and it should be lodged with the General Director of customs and excise by a registered letter within 3 months from the date on which the decision was sent to the person concerned or from the expiry of the 2-month period referred to in Article 211, paragraph 1, 2° of the GLCE. The appeal may contain a request to be heard. Also, pursuant to Article 244 of the Community Customs Code, the lodging of an appeal does not suspend the disputed decision. However, a duly motivated request for suspension of the disputed decision may be contained in the appeal. An acknowledgement of receipt is to be sent to the appellant upon reception of the appeal by the General Director. No time limit within which the General Director has to decide on the administrative appeal has been fixed in the GLCE. If the decision taken by the General Director on the administrative appeal is not favourable to the appellant, or if no decision is taken within 6 months from the reception of the appeal, the appellant may decide to lodge an action before the Court of First Instance (*Rechtbank van eerste aanleg/Tribunal de première instance*). It should be noted that until such an action is lodged, the General Director may decide on the administrative appeal even after the expiry of the 6-month period.

1128. Where a decision has been taken by the General Director, the action before the Court of First Instance must be lodged within 3 months from the sending of the General Director's decision by registered letter. An appeal against the judgement of the Court of First Instance may be lodged before the Court of Appeal (even if the amount involved is less than € 1,859.20) and, ultimately, the Supreme Court may be requested to review the judgement of the Court of Appeal.

II. EXCISE LAW

A. Definition

1129. Excise duties may be defined as indirect taxes which are levied on the consumption in Belgium of a limited number of products. A distinction must be made between ordinary excise duties and extraordinary excise duties. Most of the excise products are subject to both normal excise and extraordinary duty. Only non-alcoholic drinks, coffee and certain tobacco products are exempt from the extraordinary duty.

B. Taxable products

1130. The following products are subject to excise duties:
  (i) alcohol and alcoholic beverages (including beer, wine, sparkling wine and champagne) (Law of 7 January 1998);
  (ii) non alcoholic drinks (soft drinks, mineral water) (Law of 13 February 1995);
  (iii) tobacco products (Law of 3 April 1997);
  (iv) mineral oil (Law of 22 October 1997); and
  (v) coffee (Law of 13 February 1995).

C. Taxable event and date of payment

1131. Pursuant to the Law of 10 June 1997 (*Wet betreffende de algemene regeling voor accijnsproducten, het voorhanden hebben en het verkeer daarvan en de controles daarop/Loi relative au regime general, à la detention, à la circulation et aux contrôles des produits soumis à accise*), excise duties are due when the product is released for domestic use in Belgium. The production or processing in Belgium of the items referred to in paragraph 1130 may only be carried out in a fiscal warehouse (*entrepôt fiscal*). Also, the possession of the items listed in paragraph 1130 for which excise duties have not been paid may only take place in a fiscal warehouse. In general, the duties for all products must be paid when the declaration for release for home use are submitted to the excise authorities. Declarations for release for home use must be remitted to the customs authorities by the first working day following that on which the products were received. However, if the goods leave a fiscal warehouse or if they are received by a registered operator, the declaration for release for home use must be submitted until the Thursday of the week following the week during which the goods left the fiscal warehouse or were received by the registered operator.

D. Taxable base and amount of duty

1132. The taxable base and the amount of the excise duty are different for each excise product. Except for manufactured tobacco products, the taxable base is independent of the value of the product and is calculated based on weight or volume. Because the calculation of excise duties is extremely detailed and the tariffs change on a regular basis, this calculation is not dealt with in this book.

1133. At the EC level, the Council of Ministers adopted (on 25 February 1992) EC Council Directive No. 92/12 (O.J. [1992] L 76/7) on the general arrangement for products subject to excise duty and on the holding, movement and monitoring of such products. This directive applies to mineral oil, alcohol, alcoholic beverages and manufactured tobacco products and provides that these products will generally become subject to excise duties at the time of production in the European Community or upon importation from a country outside the European Community. The duty, however, becomes due when the products are released for consumption and products which are not released for consumption may circulate in the European Community under uniform excise duty suspension arrangements.

E. Exemptions

1134. No excise duties are levied on products which are exported, destroyed, stored in fiscal warehouses or used for industrial purposes.

§1. Exportation

1135. Non-alcoholic beverages and coffee exported to another EC Member State or to any third country are exempted from excise duties in Belgium.

§2. *Bonded warehouses*

1136. Bonded warehouses are considered not to form part of the customs territory. Duties are therefore not levied on products stored in these warehouses.

§3. *Industrial use*

1137. Certain excise products used for industrial purposes are exempted from excise duties. For example, alcohol used for scientific purposes and mineral oil used as a raw material in industry are exempted from excise duties.

F. Procedure

§1. *Excise documents*

1. *Request for authorisation (aanvraag/demande d'autorisation)*

1138. Anyone who owns an establishment where products subject to excise are manufactured or who possesses products subject to excise duties under a suspension regime must submit a request for authorisation to the excise office. This declaration must be made even if no products subject to excise are produced and the excise office must be notified of all changes in the situation.

2. *Declaration of production (werkaangifte/déclaration de travail)*

1139. Before commencing manufacture of a product subject to excise, the manufacturer must submit a declaration of production. This declaration must contain all the technical information concerning the manufacturing process in order to allow the excise authorities to calculate the duties and to carry out necessary investigations.

§2. *Powers of the excise authorities*

1140. The officials of the Administration of Customs and Excise (*Administratie der Douane en Accijnzen/Administration des Douanes et Accises*) have the right to inspect all vehicles used for the transportation of excise products and all excise establishments. In addition, such officials have the right to carry out inspections of other premises or private dwellings if they have received authorisation from the judicial authorities. The same officials are authorised to take samples and to verify the excise documents and accounting records of taxpayers.

§3. *Procedural rules*

1141. Reference is made to the procedural rules which are applicable to customs matters (*See*, paras. 1120 *et seq.*), which similarly govern excise duty procedure.

7. FINANCE

I. INTRODUCTION

1142. This chapter provides a general overview of the rules under Belgian law applicable to banking, credit and finance. First, the law relating to credit institutions will be addressed (*See*, Section II, paras. 1143 *et seq.*). Second, a general description will be provided of the legal regime governing certain forms of credit and finance, namely loan agreements, credit facility agreements, loan and credit facility agreements secured by a mortgage, and consumer credit agreements (*See*, Section III, paras. 1156 *et seq.*). Finally, a brief overview will be given of the law relating to the financial markets in Belgium (*See*, Section IV, paras. 1213 *et seq.*).

II. CREDIT INSTITUTIONS

A. General outline

1143. The statutory regime governing credit institutions is set out in the Law on Credit Institutions ("*Wet op het statuut van en het toezicht op de kredietinstellingen/Loi relative au statut et au contrôle des établissements du crédit*") of 22 March 1993, governing the legal context of and control on credit institutions (the "Law on Credit Institutions").

1144. Article 1 of the Law on Credit Institutions defines credit institutions as undertakings, Belgian or otherwise, whose business it is to receive deposits or other repayable funds from the public and to grant credit facilities for their own account.

1145. In general, only credit institutions incorporated in Belgium or in another EC Member State are entitled to receive deposits or other repayable funds from the public.

B. Establishment

1146. Prior to beginning their activities, credit institutions must submit an application for authorisation to the Banking and Finance Commission (*Commissie voor het Bank- en Financiewezen/Commission bancaire et financière*) (Art. 7 of the Law on Credit Institutions). The list of authorised credit institutions is published each year in the *Belgian Official Journal* (*Belgisch Staatsblad/Moniteur belge*) and is included in the Annual Report of the Banking and Finance Commission (Art. 13 of the Law on Credit Institutions).

1147. Credit institutions must normally be established as a commercial company (Art. 15 of the Law on Credit Institutions) and must have a minimum capital of € 6,200,000 (Art. 16 of the Law on Credit Institutions). In addition, an authorisation can only be granted if the Banking and Finance Commission considers the shareholders (with a shareholding of more than 5% in the capital of the credit institution) to be adequate (Art. 17 of the Law on Credit Institutions) and the managers to be experienced and reliable (Art. 18 of the Law on Credit Institutions). Finally, a credit institution is required to prove that it has a suitable organisation (Art. 20 of the Law on Credit Institutions) and that the main management is located in Belgium (Art. 21 of the Law on Credit Institutions).

1148. If a credit institution is (i) a subsidiary of a credit institution which has an authorisation in another EC Member State, (ii) a subsidiary of a company controlling another credit institution in another EC Member State or (iii) controlled by the same natural person(s) or legal entity(ies) as a credit institution which has an authorisation in another EC Member State, the Banking and Finance Commission will verify the authorisation with the national supervising authorities of these EC Member States.

C. Management

1149. Credit institutions are subject to special requirements relating to their management. These requirements mainly concern:
   (i) the qualifications required to be eligible for a managerial function (Arts. 18 and 19 of the Law on Credit Institutions);
   (ii) the incompatibility of a managerial function in a credit institution with some other functions (Art. 27 of the Law on Credit Institutions); and
   (iii) the dealings between a credit institution and its management (Art. 28 of the Law on Credit Institutions).

D. Operation

1150. Credit institutions must comply with a wide range of operational requirements. These requirements concern, among other things, the following matters:
   (i) minimum capital (Art. 16 of the Law on Credit Institutions);
   (ii) own funds (Arts. 23 and 43 of the Law on Credit Institutions);
   (iii) accounting (Arts. 44 and 45 of the Law on Credit Institutions);
   (iv) ownership of shares in other companies (Art. 32 of the Law on Credit Institutions);

(v) the use that is made of funds and deposits (Art. 33 of the Law on Credit Institutions);

(vi) opening branches in foreign countries (Arts. 34 through 37 of the Law on Credit Institutions);

(vii) performing banking activities in foreign countries without opening a branch (Arts. 38 through 40 of the Law on Credit Institutions);

(viii) performing banking activities by specialised subsidiaries in another EC Member State (Arts. 41 and 42 of the Law on Credit Institutions);

(ix) periodic information and accounting rules (Arts. 44 and 45 of the Law on Credit Institutions).

1151. It is important to note that mergers between banks (Arts. 30 and 31 of the Law on Credit Institutions) and, more generally, changes in the shareholdings of credit institutions are normally subject to prior approval by the Banking and Finance Commission (Arts. 24 and 25 of the Law on Credit Institutions).

E. Supervision

1152. The supervision of credit institutions is conducted in the first place by the bank auditors (*erkende revisoren/réviseurs agréés*). The Banking and Finance Commission approves the appointment of one or more bank auditors who will check the accounting documents of the credit institution, its compliance with the law and the regulations enacted pursuant to the law, its administrative and accounting organisation, its internal supervision, its solvency, liquidity and profitability (Arts. 53 and 55 of the Law on Credit Institutions).

1153. The bank auditors report to the Banking and Finance Commission and the management of the credit institution.

1154. In addition to the information obtained through the bank auditors, the Banking and Finance Commission supervises the credit institutions on the basis of reports they have to submit on a regular basis (Art. 44 of the Law on Credit Institutions). Furthermore, the Banking and Finance Commission is empowered to request additional information and may even conduct on-the-spot investigations (Art. 46 of the Law on Credit Institutions).

1155. If the Banking and Finance Commission finds that a credit institution does not operate in accordance with the law or the regulations enacted pursuant to the law, its management or financial condition is not satisfactory or its administrative and accounting organisation is not up to standard, it will impose a term within which the situation must be remedied. If the credit institution fails to cure the problem within the stated term, the Banking and Finance Commission is entitled to appoint a special auditor, suspend part or all of the activities of the credit institution or revoke its authorisation (Arts. 56 and 57 of the Law on Credit Institutions). The Banking and Finance Commission must provide reasons for its decision and the credit institution may lodge an appeal against the decision with the Minister of Finance (Art. 56 of the Law on Credit Institutions).

III. INTRODUCTION TO CREDIT AND FINANCE TRANSACTIONS

1156. Credit and finance transactions can take many forms. It is not the purpose of this chapter to provide a detailed and comprehensive overview or analysis of all the different types of such transactions. Instead, the discussion here will be limited to a general description of the legal regime governing loan agreements, credit facility agreements, loan and credit facility agreements secured by a mortgage and consumer credit agreements.

A. Loan agreements

§1. General outline

1157. A loan agreement can generally be defined as an agreement whereby one party (the borrower) borrows an amount of money from the other party (the lender), and the borrower undertakes to repay the amount borrowed to the lender, subject to certain terms and conditions. The legal regime generally applicable to loan agreements is contained in Article 1892 *et seq.* of the Civil Code.

§2. Interest

1158. The most common types of loan agreements are those requiring the borrower to pay interest. The obligation to pay interest is generally not presumed to be included in a loan agreement, and must be agreed, either expressly or tacitly, between the parties (Art. 1905 of the Civil Code). However, if the borrower pays interest to the lender where no interest rate is agreed upon or provided for in the loan agreement, such interest cannot be reclaimed or set off against the outstanding amount (Art. 1906 of the Civil Code).

1159. The parties to a loan agreement are free to determine the level of interest. Such interest may exceed the statutory interest rate (Art. 1907, para. 1 of the Civil Code). If the parties fail to specify the interest rate, the statutory interest rate applies, and no additional commission or compensation is due (Art. 1907, para. 4 of the Civil Code). The statutory interest rate amounts, at present, to 7 per cent per annum.

1160. Under certain circumstances, the court may, on the petition of the borrower, reduce the borrower's obligations to the mere reimbursement of the loan capital and
payment of the statutory interest rate. This will be the case if the following cumulative conditions are met:
   (i) the lender must have taken advantage of the needs, weaknesses, emotions or
   ignorance of the borrower; and
   (ii) the lender must have enacted a promise, for himself or a third party, of interest or other advantages clearly in excess of the normal interest and the covering of the risks of the loan (Art. 1907*ter* of the Civil Code).

1161. This reduction may also be claimed for past payments provided that the claim is
made within 3 years following the date of the payment being contested on the
basis of Art. 1907*ter* of the Civil Code.

1162. There are mandatory rules governing the conditions under which interest due on
loan capital can produce interest. Article 1154 of the Civil Code lists the following
cumulative requirements:
   (i) only interest due for at least one full year can produce interest; and
   (ii) a judicial summons or a special agreement must specifically provide that such
   interest shall produce interest.

§3. Reimbursement

1163. Loan agreements typically specify the date or dates on which reimbursement must
be made. If no date is provided, the court will decide when the reimbursement
becomes due (Art. 1900 of the Civil Code; *See also*: Cass., 20 April 1989, *R.W.*,
1989-90, 513). In doing so, the court will consider the factual circumstances of the
case, and, in particular, the time needed for the borrower to put the loan to its
expected use.

1164. The lender may object to an anticipatory reimbursement of the loan (Cass., 7 June
1900, *Pas.*, 1900, I, 289). However, if the lender accepts partial or total anticipatory reimbursement of a loan at interest, he may not claim, in addition to the loan
capital and the interest due, an indemnity for reinvestment exceeding 6 months of
interest calculated on the reimbursed amount at the rate fixed in the loan agreement (Art. 1907*bis* of the Civil code).

§4. Breach and termination

1165. One of the most controversial issues with regard to the legal regime governing
loans at interest is whether the lender may, in the absence of an express rescission
clause, claim rescission of the contract when the borrower fails to comply with his

contractual obligations. In other words, it is not clear whether, in loans at interest, a rescission clause is always presumed to be included in the agreement, albeit tacitly, in accordance with Article 1184 of the Civil Code. The majority view seems to be that Article 1184 of the Civil Code does not apply to loans at interest (Brussels Court of Appeal, 18 May 1962, *Pas.*, 1963, II, 138). Hence, if the parties would like to include the rescission remedy in their loan agreement, they are advised to provide for an express rescission clause. Thus, for instance, if the express rescission clause is intended to take effect without a prior notice of default, the clause must be carefully drafted so as to make this clear (Ghent Court of Appeal, 8 November 1978, *R.W.*, 1978-1979, 2828).

1166. The loan agreement may validly provide that the interest on the loan capital that must still be reimbursed shall be increased if the borrower delays his reimbursement. The increase in the interest rate may, in this case, not exceed 0.5 per cent per annum (Art. 1907, para. 3 of the Civil Code). In addition, the parties may include a liquidated damages clause in their loan agreement. This applies if the borrower fails to comply with his contractual obligations (Ghent Court of Appeal, 26 September 1980, *R.W.*, 1981-1982, 1026).

B. Credit facility agreements

§1. General outline

1167. Credit facility agreements can generally be defined as contracts whereby a credit institution makes certain funds (or guarantees) available for the beneficiary of the credit facility and the beneficiary may call upon such funds (or guarantees), generally within certain limits and subject to certain conditions. In return for this facility, the beneficiary pays a commission to the credit institution covering the period during which he has not called upon the funds (or guarantees), and he is obliged to repay the funds plus interest once he has availed himself of the facility. Legally speaking, credit facility agreements cannot be assimilated with loan agreements. Thus, the legal regime outlined in paragraphs 1157 *et seq.* concerning loan agreements does not apply. Since there are no similar provisions governing credit facility agreements, they are not subject to a general statutory legal regime. Specific statutory rules apply, however, to credit facilities extended to consumers.

§2. Interest

1168. The parties to the credit facility agreement are free to fix the interest rate level as they wish within the usual limits.

§3. Availability and reimbursement

1169. The credit institution is obliged to make the necessary funds available in accordance with the conditions contained in the credit facility agreement. Such conditions may include the grant of a security. If the beneficiary meets the contractual conditions, the credit institution must transfer the funds when and to the extent that the beneficiary so requests. Credit facility agreements typically include an upper limit. The fact that the credit institution did not object to funds being requested in excess of such limit does not automatically entail an increase of the contractually agreed maximum.

1170. As outlined above, the reimbursement obligation of the beneficiary of the credit facility may consist of the following items: (i) commissions relating to the period he has not called upon the funds, (ii) the funds themselves and (iii) the interest. In addition, credit institutions may stipulate reimbursement of certain costs. The beneficiary's reimbursement obligation is generally spelled out in detail in the credit facility agreement.

§4. Breach and termination

1171. If one of the parties fails to comply with his obligations under the credit facility agreement, the other party can rely on the remedies provided for in Article 1184 of the Civil Code.

1172. 3 categories of causes for termination of a credit facility agreement can be distinguished:
   (i) the first category is based on the *intuitu personae* character of credit facility agreements and includes such causes as the death of the beneficiary of the credit facility, in the case of a physical person, or the bankruptcy or dissolution and liquidation of the beneficiary, in the case of a legal entity. The credit facility agreement can, nevertheless, under certain circumstances exclude these causes or grounds for termination;
   (ii) the second category consists of the grounds or causes for termination expressly stipulated in the credit facility agreement. This category includes express rescission clauses relating to breaches of contract by one of the parties and contractually agreed time limits for the termination of the agreement;
   (iii) the third category consists of the hypothesis where no time limit is fixed and the credit facility agreement is of indefinite duration. In this case, the credit facility agreement may be terminated by either of the parties by giving notice in accordance with the provisions of the agreement or, if no notice requirements are included, by giving a reasonable notice period.

C. Loan and credit facility agreements secured by a mortgage

§1. General outline

1173. In addition to the legal regimes outlined above, some loan and credit facility agreements secured by a mortgage are subject to very specific legal rules. These rules are contained in the Law of 4 August 1992 on Loans and Credit Facilities secured by a Mortgage (*Wet op het hypothecair krediet/Loi relative au crédit hypothécaire* – the "Law of 4 August 1992").

§2. Scope of application

1174. In order to be subject to the requirements of the Law of 4 August 1992, loan and credit facility agreements must meet the following conditions:
    (i) the loan or credit facility agreement must be intended to finance the acquisition or preservation of real estate (mainly ownership and co-ownership) in Belgium or another country;
    (ii) granted to a natural person, acting exclusively with intentions not related to his commercial or professional activities;
    (iii) the debtor has, at the time of the signing of the agreement, his main residence in Belgium; and
    (iv) the creditor has his main residence in Belgium or outside Belgium on condition that the agreement was preceded in Belgium by a specific proposition or publicity and the debtor performed the essential acts for the conclusion of the agreement in Belgium.

1175. For the purposes of the Law of 4 August 1992, the following are considered to be loans or credit facilities secured by a mortgage:
    (i) the loan or credit facility secured by a mortgage, a privilege on real estate or by the pledge of a receivable secured in the same way;
    (ii) the receivable resulting from the substitution of one or more third persons in the rights of a creditor who has a privilege on real estate;
    (iii) the loan or credit facility which was granted with the right for the creditor to demand a mortgage, even if this right is included in a separate deed; and
    (iv) the loan or credit facility which is secured by a personal guarantee by a third person, to whom a mortgage is granted.

§3. Classification of agreements

1176. Article 5 of the Law of 4 August 1992 makes a distinction between 3 kinds of agreements for mortgage loans/credit facilities:

(i) with "redemption of capital", the debtor assumes the obligation to make payments (during the duration of the agreement), which immediately decrease the capital. This kind of agreement further varies as to the payments to be made: some agreements provide for equal payments, others for a varying amount;

(ii) with "reconstitution of capital", the debtor assumes the obligation to make payments (during the duration of the agreement), which do not immediately result in an equivalent release towards the creditor, although they are contractually intended for the repayment of capital: They only result in a decrease of capital at the time and upon the conditions as set out in the law or the agreement;

(iii) with "repayment of capital", the amount is to be decreased either at the end of the agreement or anticipated (in the latter form, there is no obligation of periodicity).

§4. Interest

1177. The interest is either fixed or variable.

1178. If one or more fixed interest rates were agreed upon, they prevail for the duration of the agreement.

1179. In case the debtor and creditor opted for a variable interest rate, there can only be one interest rate. The law no longer allows multiple variable interest rates per credit. The following rules apply to variable interest rates:

(i) the interest can increase as well as decrease;

(ii) the interest rate can only vary after a certain period, which can be no shorter than one year;

(iii) the variation has to be related to a referral index, based on several referral indexes in accordance with the duration of the periods of variation of the interest rate;

(iv) the original interest rate is the interest rate at which the interest is calculated which the debtor owes at the time of the first interest payment;

(v) the original value of the referral index is the referral index of the month which precedes the date of the offer;

(vi) after the periods as set out in the deed, the interest rate for the new period equals the original interest rate, increased with the difference between the value of the referral index in the calendar month preceding the date of the change and the original value of the index;

(vii) the deed caps the variation in the interest rate (in both directions), at a certain variation level from the original interest rate.

1180. The periods, terms and conditions of variations of interest rate as well as the original value of the referral index, have to be included in the notarial deed. Variations have to be communicated to the debtor at the latest on the date the interest will be calculated based on the new interest rate.

§5. Contents of the agreement

1181. Before the agreement is signed, the creditor has to communicate a written offer that contains all the modalities of the agreement and the duration of the offer. At the same time, the potential debtor has to be informed of the repayment schedule.

1182. The notarial deed containing the actual agreement cannot contain a clause allowing for the creditor to modify the conditions unilaterally. The capital itself has be put at the disposal of the debtor in the form of cash or electronically. The Law of 4 August 1992 forbids any agreements which are conditional upon the purchase of, exchange of or subscription to shares, bonds or related instruments.

1183. The debtor has the right to repay the capital in total at any time. Partial anticipatory repayments are allowed, unless the notarial deed provides otherwise.

§6. Breach and termination

1184. The rules governing breaches or termination of loan or credit facility agreements secured by a mortgage are generally the same as those applicable to ordinary loans or credit facility agreements. However, with regard to breaches of the requirements of the Law of 4 August 1992, specific sanctions are applicable. These sanctions include, *inter alia*, the nullity of the relevant clause or a reduction in the level of certain payment obligations to the statutory maximum. Given the complexity and variety of the sanctions contained in the Law of 4 August 1992, it is not appropriate to deal with this matter in any further detail in this chapter.

D. Consumer credit agreements

§1. General outline

1185. The rules governing consumer credit agreements are contained in the Law of 12 June 1991 on Consumer Credit Agreements (*Wet op het consumentenkrediet/Loi relative à la consummation* – the "Law of 12 June 1991").

1186. The Law of 12 June 1991 deals with the following matters: (i) publicity relating to consumer credit transactions, (ii) the formation and execution of consumer credit agreements, (iii) certain specific types of consumer credit agreements, (iv) intermediaries arranging for credit to be granted, (v) the treatment of personal data relating to consumer credit and enforcement procedures.

1187. A consumer credit agreement is defined as an agreement whereby a creditor provides or undertakes to provide credit to a consumer in the form of a suspension of payments, a loan, or any other similar arrangement (Art. 1, paragraph 4 of the Law of 12 June 1991).

1188. The Law of 12 June 1991 applies to credit agreements which have been concluded between, on the one hand, a consumer residing in Belgium and, on the other hand, a creditor having his principal place of business in Belgium. Credit agreements concluded by creditors having their principal place of business outside Belgium will only fall within the scope of the Law of 12 June 1991 if the agreement was preceded by a special offer or publicity in Belgium, or if the request for credit from the consumer was received in Belgium by the creditor or his representative (Art. 2 of the Law of 12 June 1991).

1189. The Law of 12 June 1991 does not apply in the following cases (Art. 3, para. 1 of the Law of 12 June 1991):
   (i) agreements for the provision, on a continuing basis, of a service or utility whereby the consumer has the right to pay for them, for their duration, by means of instalments;
   (ii) lease agreements which do not provide for a transfer of title;
   (iii) credit agreements, which are not credit facility agreements, under which the consumer is required to repay the credit within a period not exceeding 3 months;
   (iv) credit facility agreements repayable within a period not exceeding three months and relating to a maximum amount of € 1,250, unless a higher level is determined by Royal Decree;
   (v) credit agreements of an occasional nature and concluded without the objective of making profit;
   (vi) loans and credit facility agreements secured by a mortgage to which the Law of 4 August 1992 applies; and
   (vii) agreements of marriage counselling to which the Law of 9 March 1993 applies.

1190. The Law of 12 June 1991 is only partially applicable in the following cases (Art. 3, para. 2 of the Law of 12 June 1991):
   (i) credit agreements relating to an amount which is less than € 200;
   (ii) credit agreements established by an authentic deed relating to an amount exceeding € 20,000; and

(iii) credit agreements under which the consumer is required to repay the credit by a maximum number of three payments within a period not exceeding 9 months.

§2. Publicity

1191. The Law of 12 June 1991 contains a number of rules applicable to publicity in relation to credit agreements. In general, each form of publicity relating to a credit agreement must provide clear information regarding the advertiser, the type of credit to which the publicity relates, and the special conditions applicable to the type of credit involved (Art. 5 of the Law of 12 June 1991). The use of the promotional phrase "free credit" or similar phrases is prohibited (Art. 6 of the Law of 12 June 1991).

1192. Certain types of promotional activity relating to credit agreements are either prohibited or subject to specific conditions. These promotional activities include visits by the creditor to the residence of the consumer, promotion by mail or by telephone and visits to the consumer's place of work (Arts. 7 through 9 of the Law of 12 June 1991).

§3. Credit agreements

1. Conclusion of the credit agreement:

1193. Prior to the conclusion of the credit agreement, it is necessary for the creditor to obtain certain information from the consumer in order to determine the financial situation and the risks involved. The creditor is, however, restricted in the type of information that he may require the consumer to submit. This information should not relate to matters such as the race, health, political activities, religion and the like of the consumer (Art. 10 of the Law of 12 June 1991).

1194. If the creditor decides to make an offer for the provision of credit, the offer must, in general, remain valid at least for a period of 15 days. Detailed provisions set out the information that is required to be provided in the offer document (Art. 14 of the Law of 12 June 1991). The credit agreement is concluded by both parties involved signing the offer document. The acceptance of the offer by the consumer is subject to specific formal requirements (Art. 17 of the Law of 12 June 1991). No payments may be made between the creditor and the consumer until such time as the offer has been accepted (Art. 16 of the Law of 12 June 1991).

1195. Following the signature of the agreement, the consumer generally has 7 working days to renounce the agreement by registered letter in the following situations (Art. 18 of the Law of 12 June 1991):

   (i) if the credit agreement has been concluded on the first day of the period of validity of the offer indicated by the creditor; or

   (ii) if the agreement has been signed outside the business premises of the creditor or intermediary.

2. Execution of the credit agreement

1196. A number of provisions apply to the execution of credit agreements. It is provided that maximum annual percentages of the costs of credit will be established every 6 months by Royal Decree depending on the type, amount and duration of credit involved (Art. 21 of the Law of 12 June 1991). In addition, maximum repayment periods may be fixed by Royal Decree taking into account the amount and type of credit (Art. 22 of the Law of 12 June 1991).

1197. The consumer is entitled to make an early repayment of the credit at any time (Art. 23 of the Law of 12 June 1991). In this case, provided that the consumer informs the creditor by registered letter at least one month prior to the total repayment of the credit, the creditor is required to grant either a reduction of the total amount due or a similar compensation. The method for the calculation of this reduction or compensation will be determined by Royal Decree.

1198. Where the goods or services do not conform with the agreement between the consumer and the supplier of the goods or services, it is possible for the consumer, subject to a number of strict conditions, to invoke against the creditor the defences which the consumer can invoke against the supplier (Art. 24 of the Law of 12 June 1991).

1199. The Law of 12 June 1991 also mentions a number of clauses in credit agreements that are automatically considered void. These clauses include the following:

   (i) with a limited number of exceptions, clauses entitling the creditor to claim immediate repayment or express rescission clauses (Art. 29 of the Law of 12 June 1991);

   (ii) clauses entitling the creditor to modify the credit agreement unilaterally (Art. 30 of the Law of 12 June 1991); and

   (iii) obligations on the consumer to accept at the time of execution of the credit agreement another agreement with the creditor, the intermediary or a third party designated by one of them, unless the costs related thereto have been included in the total costs of the credit (Art. 31 of the Law of 12 June 1991).

§4. Specific types of credit agreements

1200. The Law of 12 June 1991 contains a number of special rules for particular types of credit agreements.

1. Sales agreements with deferred payment

1201. A sales agreement with deferred payment (*verkoop op afbetaling/vente à tempéra-ment*) is defined as a credit agreement for the acquisition of moveable property or the supply of services which is paid for by at least 3 instalments, not including the down payment (Art. 1, paragraph 9 of the Law of 12 June 1991).

1202. The Law of 12 June 1991 requires that certain supplementary information be provided in publicity made by the creditor. For instance, such publicity should include the price which would applicable in case of immediate payment, the total price to be paid under the credit agreement, the amount of the down payment and the number, amount and frequency of payments (Art. 40 of the Law of 12 June 1991). Similar requirements apply to offers made by the creditor relating to a sale with deferred payment (Art. 41 of the Law of 12 June 1991). In addition, specific rules apply to publicity for, or offers relating to, sales with deferred payments which provide for an annual cost percentage of zero per cent (Arts. 42 through 44 of the Law of 12 June 1991).

1203. Before the completion of a sales agreement with deferred payment, the seller must receive a down payment of at least 15 per cent of the purchase price applicable in the case of immediate payment. The sales agreement does not become binding until the down payment has been paid (Art. 45 of the Law of 12 June 1991).

2. Rent with deferred payment

1204. Under an agreement for rent with deferred payment (*financieringshuur/credit-bail*), the creditor agrees to allow the consumer the possession and use of moveable property against a fixed price which is paid periodically (Art. 1, paragraph 10 of the Law of 12 June 1991). The agreement must explicitly or implicitly include an offer for the purchase of the good involved and must be concluded for a fixed term. The Law of 12 June 1991 sets rules regarding publicity for or offers relating to agreements for rent with deferred payment (Arts. 48 through 54 of the Law of 12 June 1991). These rules are similar to those applicable to sales agreements with deferred payment.

3. Loan with deferred payment

1205. A loan with deferred payment (*lening op afbetaling/prêt à tempérament*) is a credit agreement whereby money or other means of payment are placed at the disposal of the consumer and the consumer undertakes to make periodic repayments (Art. 1, paragraph 11 of the Law of 12 June 1991). Publicity and offers in relation to such agreements must contain specific information (Articles 55 and 56 of the Law of 12 June 1991).

4. Credit facility

1206. Under a credit facility (*kredietopening/ouverture de credit*), the creditor puts money or other means of payment at the disposal of the consumer. The consumer can freely make use of the credit by making withdrawals, possibly by means of a payment card, while repayment can be made at the time of his choice (Art. 1, paragraph 12 of the Law of 12 June 1991). Apart from a number of obligations regarding the offer of and the publicity for credit facilities (Arts. 57 and 58 of the Law of 12 June 1991), the creditor must provide the consumer with monthly overviews of the amount of credit withdrawn, the payments made, as well as the interest and costs due (Art. 59 of the Law of 12 June 1991).

§5. Credit intermediaries

1207. Specific rules apply to the activities of intermediaries in the field of credit agreements (Arts. 62 through 67 of the Law of 12 June 1991). Credit intermediaries are natural persons or legal entities who contribute to the conclusion of performance of credit agreements within the context of their commercial or professional activities (Art. 1(3) of the Law of 12 June 1991). The credit intermediary must inform the consumer of his status and the nature and scope of its authority to act. In addition, credit intermediaries are not entitled to receive compensation from consumers. Intermediaries are only entitled to a commission for the credit agreements concluded through their intervention (Art. 65 of the Law of 12 June 1991). Credit intermediaries must, in principle, be registered with the Ministry of Economic Affairs prior to the commencement of their activities (Art. 77 of the Law of 12 June 1991).

§6. Protection of data

1208. Detailed rules apply to databases containing personal information regarding consumer credit. In this respect, it is provided that only data regarding the identity of the consumer, the amount and duration of the credit, the required frequency of the payment, the payment facilities granted, any delays in payment and the identity of the creditor may be included in such databases. The information is only allowed to be communicated to natural persons and legal entities active and recognised in the field of credit and finance, as well as to the supervisory body, the Banking and Finance Commission (*Commissie voor het Bank- en Financiewezen/Commission bancaire et financière*) (Art. 69, para. 4 of the Law of 12 June 1991, as amended). A maximum term for the storage of data may be determined by Royal Decree (Art. 69, para. 5 of the Law of 12 June 1991).

1209. The operator of the database is required to inform consumers as soon as they are registered for the first time in the database. Consumers must have free access to the information relating to them or their property in the database, and they may have any incorrect data corrected free of charge. Consumers can require the deletion of personal data that is incomplete or irrelevant for the purposes of the database (Art. 70 of the Law of 12 June 1991, as amended).

1210. The Law of 12 June 1991 provides for the creation of a central database for information regarding default payments in respect of credit agreements falling within its scope. The registration of default payments will be made by the National Bank (*Nationale Bank van België/Banque nationale de Belgique*). Access to the data will be provided to persons and entities recognized under the Law of 12 June 1991 and involved in the provision, conclusion or modification of credit agreements (Art. 71 of the Law of 12 June 1991).

§7. Enforcement

1211. In the event of violations of specific provisions of the Law of 12 June 1991, a variety of civil law sanctions can enter into play (Arts. 85 through 100 of the Law of 12 June 1991). If, for example, the creditor does not comply with the requirements applicable to offers made to the consumer (Arts. 14, 41, 49, 56 and 58 of the Law of 12 June 1991), the courts can decide to annul the credit agreement or to reduce the obligations of the consumer to the price which he would have to pay in the case of immediate, as opposed to deferred, payment (Art. 86 of the Law of 12 June 1991). The wide range of available sanctions makes detailed consideration of the Law of 12 June 1991 advisable in each individual case.

1212. In addition, criminal sanctions are provided for (Arts. 101 through 105 of the Law of 12 June 1991). These criminal sanctions concern, for instance, the registration and authorisation requirements included in the Law of 12 June 1991 for creditors and credit intermediaries (Art. 101 of the Law of 12 June 1991).

IV. FINANCIAL MARKETS

A. Introduction

1213. The following provides a brief overview of the laws applicable to the financial markets in Belgium. First, the rules relating to public offers of securities are addressed. (*See*, paras. 1214 *et seq.*) Secondly, the organisational and transactional aspects of trading in securities on the stock exchange are discussed. (*See*, paras. 1236 *et seq.*) Finally, the law applicable to the publication of significant participations in listed companies and the law concerning take-over bids are outlined. (*See*, paras. 1250 *et seq.*)

B. Public offers of securities

§1. General outline

1214. Public offers of securities are subject to specific regulations. The objective of these regulations is to ensure that potential purchasers of the securities are properly informed of the nature of the operation and the rights attached to the securities. In order to determine the scope of application of the regulations, the precise meaning of the concepts "public offer" and "securities" is essential.

1215. A Royal Decree of 7 July 1999 (the "Royal Decree of 7 July 1999") determines the conditions under which an offer of securities will be deemed to have a public character. Article 1 of the Royal Decree of 7 July 1999 provides that the public nature of an offer is presumed to exist when:
   (i) means of publicity of any kind aimed at more than 50 persons in Belgium are used in order to announce or recommend the offer. The relevant means of publicity are set out in Article 2 of the Royal Decree of 7 July 1999;
   (ii) one or more intermediaries are involved (the applicable concept of intermediary is set out in Article 2 of the Royal Decree of 7 July 1999);
   (iii) more than 50 people are solicited by the issuer or for his account.

1216. The list given in Article 1 of the Royal Decree of 7 July 1999 is however not exhaustive and the courts or the Banking and Finance Commission may consider other cases also to present a public character.

1217. Article 2 of the Royal Decree of 7 July 1999 is said not to apply:
   (i) if the operation requires payment of a minimum of € 250,000 per investor;
   (ii) if only institutional investors are involved;
   (iii) if the acquisition of the securities is a prerequisite to obtaining access to a particular profession or to exercise certain professional activities (Art. 3 of the Royal Decree of 7 July 1999).

1218. The concept of securities is defined in Article 26 of Royal Decree No. 185 of 9 July 1935 (the "Royal Decree No. 185"). Article 26 lists, *inter alia*, shares in companies and bonds.

§2. General notification and approval requirements

1219. Public offers of securities must be notified in advance to the Banking and Finance Commission (Art. 26 of Royal Decree No. 185) and the prospectus to be published when securities are offered to the public requires prior approval of the Banking and Finance Commission (Art. 29*ter* of Royal Decree No. 185). This requirement is important since any public offer of securities is, in principle, subject to the publication of a prospectus (Art. 29, para. 1 of Royal Decree No. 185).

1220. As part of the notification and approval procedure, the Banking and Finance Commission must be supplied with certain information. This information includes (i) a draft of the prospectus, (ii) a detailed overview of the liabilities of the company of which the securities are the object of the public offer, (iii) the motives behind the public offer, (iv) certain conditions relating to the offer, and (v) detailed information on existing participations in the company concerned (Art. 27 of Royal Decree No. 185). In addition, the Banking and Finance Commission is entitled to request, and, in practice, does request, all other information which it needs in order to scrutinise the prospectus.

1221. The prospectus must contain all the information that the public needs to make an informed assessment of the nature of the operation and the rights attached to the securities. It must also mention that the publication has been made following approval by the Banking and Finance Commission, but that such approval does not entail an appraisal of the transaction or the position of the offeror (Art. 29, para. 2 of Royal Decree No. 185).

1222. New significant facts which may have an influence on the assessment of the offer by the public and which occur as a result of the approval of the prospectus, but prior to the completion of the operation, must be published in an update of the prospectus. Failure to do so entitles the Banking and Finance Commission to suspend the operation until the new information has been made public (Art. 29, para. 2 of Royal Decree No. 185).

1223. Article 29*ter*, paragraph 1 of Royal Decree No. 185 provides that the approval decision must be communicated to the entities notifying their offer in accordance with Article 26 within a period of one month. If the Banking and Finance Commission is of the opinion that the offer would seem to be made under circumstances which may mislead the public as to the nature of the operation and the rights attached to the securities, it shall inform the notifying parties thereof. If the notifying parties do not duly take such communication into account, the Banking and Finance Commission may refuse to approve the offer. Such a refusal must be accompanied with reasons and sent by registered letter or by a letter requiring acknowledgement of receipt (Art. 29*ter*, para. 2 of Royal Decree No. 185).

1224. The notifying parties are entitled to lodge an appeal against a refusal decision of the Banking and Finance Commission.

§3. Financial markets in Belgium

1. General

1225. In accordance with the Law of 2 August 2002 on the Control on Financial Services and Products (*Wet betreffende het toezicht op de financiële sector en de financiële diensten/Loi relative à la surveillance du secteur financier et aux services financiers* – the "Law of 2 August 2002"), a financial market needs to comply with the following conditions in order to be considered a Belgian financial market:
    (i) the market guarantees the regular functioning of the market;
    (ii) the market establishes market rules in accordance with the Law of 2 August 2002 and supervises compliance there;
    (iii) the market guarantees compliance with transparency requirements in accordance with the Law of 2 August 2002 with respect to the traded securities;
    (iv) the market uses state of the art information technology in order to guarantee the efficient functioning of the market, to assess compliance with transparency requirements and to track market abuse;
    (v) the market uses clearing and settlement systems that provide sufficient guarantees to protect the interest of participants and investors and the proper functioning of the market;
    (vi) the market provides for sufficient structural measures in case of market deficiencies.

1226. A market is considered to be Belgian if the market authority has its registered office in Belgium, or, if it does not have a registered office, (in accordance with its national legislation) if it has its main office in Belgium.

1227. A financial market is required to draft market rules (Rule Book), which deals, amongst other subjects, with the following (after approval of the Banking and Finance commission):
    (i) conditions for acceptance, suspension and exclusion of members and other intermediaries;
    (ii) the obligations of their members and intermediaries;
    (iii) conditions and procedures for financial instruments to obtain listing or trading;
    (iv) the obligations of/on companies of which the financial instruments are listed or traded;
    (v) the functioning of the markets;
    (vi) the rules and procedures for reporting on and the publication of transactions;
    (vii) supervision on compliance with market rules.

2. Specific financial markets

1228. Currently, 2 important financial markets are considered to be Belgian financial markets:
   (i) Euronext Brussels
   (ii) Nasdaq Europe

i. Euronext

1229. Euronext is the common name for the official financial markets of Belgium, France and the Netherlands, which merged in the second half of the year 2000. As from June 2002, the Portuguese official market joined under the name "Euronext Lisboa".

1230. Euronext N.V., a public limited liability company incorporated under Dutch law, operates as a holding company for the 4 market companies. Its 4 subsidiaries continue to organize the existing financial markets, each for their own country. These financial markets are, however, connected by means of an integrated Euronext Trading Platform, as a result of which a virtual unified financial market is created. In addition, the market rules which apply to the financial markets are more and more harmonised.

1231. As a result of this merger, the 4 relevant financial markets changed their respective names to respectively Euronext Paris, Euronext Amsterdam, Euronext Brussels and Euronext Lisboa.

ii. Nasdaq Europe

1232. Nasdaq Europe is a subsidiary of "The Nasdaq Stock Market, Inc." and was set up as a pan-European market for financial instruments. Nasdaq Europe mainly focuses on young enterprises, attempting to attract European investors.

1233. As regards its legal structure, Nasdaq Europe was incorporated as a public limited liability company with the name "Nasdaq Europe N.V." and with registered office in Brussels, by consequence of which Nasdaq Europe is considered to be a Belgian financial market. The rules governing Nasdaq Europe concerning legal structure and organisation are incorporated in a Ministerial Decree of 21 May 2001, as amended by a Ministerial Decree of 9 July 2001.

§4. Admission to listing

1234. If a company wants its securities to be admitted to the official quotation of the stock exchange, it must, firstly, follow the procedure applicable to any public offer of securities. In other words, the company must submit to the Banking and Finance Commission, certain information, including a draft of the prospectus, and such prospectus must be approved by the Banking and Finance Commission.

1235. In addition, the company must make an application to the relevant market authority of the financial market. The conditions to be met and the procedure however differ for the different financial markets (and their different segments).

C. Trading in securities listed on a financial market

§1. Definition of qualified intermediaries

1236. The term "qualified intermediaries" usually comprises investment firms, investment advice companies and credit institutions, which offer or provide investment and ancillary services with regard to financial instruments (securities, units of undertakings for collective investments, *etc.*). It is worth mentioning that not only qualified intermediaries acting on behalf of a client in the trade in listed securities are made subject to specific statutory requirements, but also natural persons or legal entities which offer investment advice on a professional basis.

1237. The Law of 2 August 2002 limits the persons who are entitled to act in the course of their business as intermediaries in the trade in listed securities. On the other hand, the Law of 2 August 2002 allows financial intermediaries which are governed by the law of another EC Member State and authorised pursuant to the law of that EC Member State to trade in listed securities in Belgium by application of the "Home country control" principle, provided that the Banking and Finance Commission has been notified of its registration as a branch of an EC financial intermediary. Financial intermediaries governed by the law of countries that are not EC Member States and provide investment services in their home country may offer such services in Belgium, provided that they make themselves known to the Banking and Finance Commission in advance, which may refuse them the authorisation because the law of the EC Member State governing the financial intermediary does not offer reciprocal access under the same conditions.

1238. The setting up of an authorised financial intermediary in Belgium, that is a financial intermediary which is admitted to a special list drawn up by the Banking and Finance Commission, is made subject to various conditions regarding the minimum corporate capital, the shareholding structure, the identity of the managing directors, the internal organisation, etc. Furthermore, authorised financial intermediaries can neither hold shares in commercial companies, collect funds nor grant loans, unless under specific circumstances.

§2. The proper functioning of the market

1239. As mentioned, only authorised qualified intermediaries who are listed in Article 2 of the Law of 2 August 2002 are entitled to trade in listed securities. However, there are exceptions to this general rule for occasional transactions carried out between individuals, for assignments of securities representing more than 10 per cent of the voting rights of the concerned company or for assignments of securities between affiliated companies.

1240. In accordance with Article 11 of the Law of 2 August 2002, it could be imposed by means of a Royal Decree, that intermediaries must perform financial transactions in securities listed on a stock exchange via that stock exchange. However, this so-called principle of centralisation would only apply if:
- (i) the client instructing the transaction usually resides or is established in Belgium;
- (ii) the transactions do not fall under one of the exceptions as outlined under paragraph 1239;
- (iii) the securities traded are either listed on a Belgian financial market or negotiated on any regulated Belgian financial market; and
- (iv) the client has not expressly waived the duty to perform the transaction on such financial market.

1241. If these conditions would be met and if the intermediary would fail to perform the transaction on the appropriate financial market, the client would be entitled to refuse the transaction and request that the funds provided to the intermediary be returned to him.

1242. Finally, financial intermediaries co-operate with the Financial Intelligence Processing Unit in order to prevent the financial system to be used for money laundering purposes.

§3. Rules of conduct of financial intermediaries

1243. In performing financial transactions, financial intermediaries must comply with rules of conduct (Art. 26 of the Law of 2 August 2002), that can be summarised as follows. A financial intermediary should:
- (i) demonstrate loyalty, competence, care and effort in the interest of its clients and the integrity of the market;
- (ii) inquire as to the experience of the clients with respect to the financial products concerned, the goals, financial condition and limitations;
- (iii) inform their clients, in a clear and accessible manner, taking into account their experience, knowledge and goals;
- (iv) avoid any conflict of interest between themselves and their clients or among

their clients or, if this is unavoidable, make sure that their clients are treated in an equal and fair way;

(v) appropriately inform their clients on any received benefits with respect to the services rendered or to be rendered;

(vi) not propose or encourage any behaviour that entices their clients not to comply with their legal obligations;

(vii) not provide any investment advice if their service is limited to accepting and executing orders;

(viii) treat and execute the orders of their clients in their best interests and taking into account specific instructions;

(ix) in case of global orders for account of several beneficiaries, divide the financial instruments in accordance with equal criteria;

(x) to draft and keep documents relating to all the orders as received from clients;

(xi) not, in principle, compensate with respect to financial instruments as traded on a Belgian financial market;

(xii) issue a written or electronic confirmation of each transaction in financial instruments and to provide their clients with such confirmation;

(xiii) periodically inform their clients on their outstanding positions in derivatives.

1244. Presidential requirements specific to the offering of financial services via the Internet have been issued by the Banking and Finance Commission because of the risks attaching thereto (Circular of 5 May 2000 of the Banking and Finance Commission on Financial Services via the Internet: Presidential Requirements).

§4. Insider trading

1245. The rules governing insider trading are contained in Article 25 of the Law of 2 August 2002, defining the concept of inside information as information which has not been made public, of a precise nature relating to one or several issuers of transferable securities or other financial instruments which, if it were made public, would be likely to have a significant effect on the price of the transferable securities or other financial instruments in question.

1246. Any person who either by virtue of his membership of the administrative, management or supervisory bodies of the issuer, or by virtue of his holding in the capital of the issuer, or because he has access to such information by virtue of the exercise of his employment, profession or duties, possesses inside information and knows or should reasonably know that such information is inside information, is prohibited from acquiring or disposing of transferable securities or other financial instruments to which that information relates. The prohibition applies irrespective of whether that person acquires or disposes of such securities or other financial instruments for his own account or for the account of a third party, or whether he does so directly or indirectly.

1247. Moreover, any person subject to the prohibition laid down in Article 25 of the Law of 2 August 2002 who possesses inside information is prohibited from disclosing that inside information to any third party, unless such disclosure is mandatory or made in the normal course of the exercise of his employment, profession or duties and recommending or procuring a third party, on the basis of that inside information, to acquire or dispose of transferable securities or other financial instruments. Finally, the prohibition laid down also applies to any person, other than those referred to in the aforesaid provisions, who, with full knowledge of the fact, possesses inside information and knows, or reasonably should know, that such information is inside information and that the direct or indirect source of said information is a person referred to in Article 25 of the Law of 2 August 2002.

1248. Infringements of the provisions governing insider trading are subject to criminal sanctions.

1249. Current developments at a European level, might however entail some amendments to these rules in the coming years.

D. Publication of significant shareholdings in listed companies

1250. The rules governing the publication of significant participations in listed companies are contained in Articles 514 through 517 of the Company Code. The objective is to ensure that investors are adequately informed of major holdings and of any changes in those holdings in Belgian companies, the shares of which are officially listed on stock exchanges located or operating within the European Community.

1251. Where a natural person or legal entity acquires or disposes of a holding in a company incorporated under Belgian law, the shares of which are officially listed on a stock exchange or exchanges located or operating within one or more EC Member State, and where, following that acquisition or disposal, the proportion of voting rights held by that natural person or legal entity reaches, exceeds or falls below one of the thresholds of 5 per cent, 10 per cent, 15 per cent, 20 per cent (and so on up to 100 per cent), such natural person or legal entity shall notify the company concerned and the Banking and Finance Commission of the proportion of voting rights held following the acquisition or disposal. The notification must be made within 2 working days following the acquisition or disposal of said holding.

1252. The articles of association of a company may impose more severe obligations on natural persons or legal entities that acquire or dispose of a holding in a company incorporated under Belgian law. For instance, the articles of incorporation may provide for thresholds lower than those enumerated in Article 1, paragraph 1 of the Law of 2 March 1989. However, the threshold so stipulated may not be lower than 3 per cent. The articles of association may also impose an obligation of notification on companies incorporated under Belgian law which are not officially listed on a stock exchange located or operating in an EC Member State or which are not officially listed on any stock exchange.

1253. Where a natural person or legal entity holds 5 per cent or more of the voting rights of a company, and the shares of that company are listed for the first time on a stock exchange or exchanges located in an EC Member State, the shareholder shall notify the company and the Banking and Financial Commission of the voting rights held at that time. Also, where a natural person or legal entity acquires or disposes of the direct or indirect control over a company holding 5 per cent or more of the voting rights of a company incorporated under Belgian law, the shares of which are officially listed on a stock exchange or exchanges located or operating within the European Union, the latter company and the Banking and Finance Commission must be notified of the acquisition or disposal.

1254. For purposes of determining whether a natural person or legal entity is required to notify the authorities of their holding, the following shall be regarded as voting rights held by that person or entity:
   – voting rights held, acquired or disposed of by other persons or entities in their own name but on behalf of that person or entity;
   – voting rights held, acquired or disposed of by a natural person or legal entity affiliated with that person or entity;
   – voting rights held, acquired or disposed of by other persons or entities in their own name but on behalf of natural persons or legal entities affiliated with that person or entity;
   – voting rights held, acquired or disposed of by natural persons or legal entities acting jointly.

1255. In order to ensure compliance with these obligations, the legal provisions were amended by means of the Law of 2 August 2002. The Banking and Finance Commission was thereby granted the power to require filing of the transfer document itself entailing a notification. If such notification then appears to be late or partial, the voting rights attached to such shares will be suspended for a 1-year period.

8. EMPLOYMENT

I. INTRODUCTION

A. Definition of labour law

1256. "Labour law" generally refers to the rules and regulations governing individual and collective relationships between employers and employees. With regard to individual relationships, labour law governs employment agreements as well as a wide variety of other matters, such as working hours, annual vacation, minimum salary and working conditions. With regard to collective relationships, labour law contains rules governing collective bargaining procedures, the representation of employees and employers in various bodies, the organisation and composition of trade unions and the creation of binding obligations through collective bargaining agreements.

B. Definition of social security

1257. "Social security" refers to a system by which protection against various social risks is financed through mandatory contributions made by individuals and companies. Social security benefits may take the form of unemployment or retirement benefits, health insurance benefits, permanent or temporary disability benefits and family allowances.

1258. Whereas labour law relates exclusively to individual and/or collective relations between employers and employees, social security law regulates the relations between contributors (and the recipients of benefits) and the bodies entrusted with the administration and payment of benefits to those contributors. Social security beneficiaries need not necessarily be employed at the time they are claiming benefits (unemployed persons or retired persons, for example) or have ever been employed before (disabled or self-employed persons, for example).

II. LABOUR LAW

A. Introduction

1259. Belgian labour law applies only to parties to an employment contract. Employment contracts are usually defined as agreements whereby one party (the employee) agrees to work under the authority, direction and supervision of the other for a definite or indefinite period of time. The essential characteristic of an employment contract is the element of subordination. In the absence of that element, the parties are not subject to labour law.

1260. The rules and statutes which govern the relations between employers and employees can be classified into 3 main categories.

1261. The first set of rules covers the individual employment contracts between the employer and each of his employees. Although parties are generally free to determine the contents of their employment contracts, there are a number of mandatory rules. Most of these rules are contained in the Law of 3 July 1978 on Employment Contracts (*Wet van 3 juli 1978 betreffende de arbeidsovereenkomsten/Loi relative aux contrats de travail* – the "LEC").

1262. The second set of rules covers a wide spectrum of matters addressed in separate legislation, such as maximum working hours, legal holidays, minimum remuneration, working conditions, *etc.* These rules generally constitute a minimum level of protection granted to each employee and they are generally common to all employees. Collective bargaining agreements concluded at individual company level or at industry level may establish a higher level of protection.

1263. The third set of rules covers collective labour relations and governs the organisation of trade unions, the representation of employees and the mechanisms of collective bargaining.

B. The individual employment contract

§1. Introduction

1264. Whilst the parties are generally free to determine the content of their employment contracts, they are limited by mandatory provisions and requirements of public policy.

1265. The LEC applies to the vast majority of employment contracts and contains a large number of mandatory requirements covering the most important aspects usually addressed in employment contracts (*i.e.*, formality requirements, rights and obligations of the parties, duration, suspension and termination of the contract).

§2. Language legislation

1266. Belgian labour law also contains detailed legislation on which language must be used in the employer/employee relationship.

1267. The language to be used in social relations is either Dutch, French or German, depending on the place of business (*exploitatiezetel/siège d'exploitation*) at which the employee works.

1. Employers with a place of business in the Dutch language region

1268. If the place of business is located in the Dutch language region (with the exception of certain municipalities which benefit from an exceptional language status - the so-called "municipalities with facilities" (*faciliteitengemeenten/communes à facilités*), the language to be used is Dutch (Arts. 1 and 2 of the Decree of 19 July 1973). Infringement of this Decree is subject to criminal penalties. On a civil law-level, documents that are drafted in breach of this Decree are void *ex tunc*: they are deemed never to have existed. The annulment of the non-compliant documents can, however, not harm the employee's rights or the rights of third parties.

2. Employers with a place of business in the French language region

1269. If the place of business is located in the French language region (with the exception of certain municipalities), the language to be used is French (Arts. 1 and 2 of the Decree of 30 June 1982). Documents that are drafted in breach of this Decree are void *ex tunc*.

3. Employers with a place of business in the bilingual region of Brussels, the municipalities with facilities or the German language region

1270. The bilingual region of Brussels, the municipalities with facilities and the German language region remain subject to the national Laws on the Use of Languages in Administrative Matters co-ordinated by Royal Decree of 18 July 1966 (*Koninklijk Besluit houdende coördinatie van de wetten op het gebruik van de talen in de bestuurszaken/Arrêté royal portant coordination des lois sur l'emploi des langues en matière administrative* – the "Royal Decree of 18 July 1966"). Employers who have their place of business in the Brussels region must use Dutch or French in the relationship with their employees depending on whether the employees are Dutch or French-speaking (Art. 52 of the Royal Decree of 18 July 1966). Employers who have their place of business in the municipalities with facilities must use the language of the region where the place of business is located (for the municipalities of Spiere-Helkijn, Mesen, Ronse, Herstappe, Voeren, Bever, Drogenbos, Kraainem, Linkebeek, Sint-Genesius-Rode, Wemmel and Wezembeek-Oppem this will be Dutch, as they are located in the Dutch language region, and for the municipalities of Komen-Waasten, Moeskroen, Vloesberg, Edingen, Malmédy and Weismes this will be French as they are located in the French language region). Employers who have their place of business in the German language region must use German in the employment relationship with their employees (Art. 52 of the Royal Decree of 18 July 1966).

1271. The employers to whom the Royal Decree of 18 July 1966 applies may add translations to their communications with their employees if this is justified by the composition of the personnel. (Art. 52 of the Royal Decree of 18 July 1966).

1272. If the language requirements are not met, the employer must replace the non-compliant documents by compliant ones. The regularised document has effect as of the date of the replacement.

§3. Scope of application of the LEC

1273. The LEC has a wide scope. It covers most employment contracts and addresses a wide variety of issues relating, *inter alia*, to the formation, duration, content, suspension and termination of the employment contract. It covers employment contracts for 5 categories of employees: (i) blue-collar employees, (ii) white-collar employees, (iii) commercial representatives, (iv) home workers and (v) students.

1274. Blue-collar employees predominantly carry out manual labour, whereas white-collar employees are engaged in work which is more intellectual in nature.

1275. As a matter of principle, the nature of an employee's function is determined on the basis of the type of work performed and not on the basis of how the parties labelled the employment agreement. If the employee performs both manual and intellectual work, it must be established which element is decisive for the performance of the employment agreement.

1276. In any event, the parties to an employment agreement are free to grant the worker the benefits related to the status of white-collar employee (*i.e.*, a longer notice period, *See*, paras. 1360 *et seq.*), irrespective of the true nature of the work performed.

1277. A commercial representation agreement is defined as an agreement whereby a white-collar employee, the commercial representative, agrees, in return for the payment of a salary, to solicit and visit potential customers with a view to negotiating and/or concluding transactions under the authority, for the account and in the name of one or more employers. Commercial representation agreements are discussed in Chapter 10.

1278. The employment contracts of home workers and students fall outside the scope of this book.

1279. The essential characteristic of all employment contracts covered by the LEC is the performance of work by an employee under the authority, direction and supervision of an employer – the element of subordination. If that element is absent, the agreement is considered not to be an employment contract, and therefore falls outside the scope of the LEC. Although the parties are, in principle, free to characterise their agreement as they see fit, Belgian judges are not bound by the characterisation of the agreement by the parties. Judges will not only consider the wording used by the parties, but also their intentions and manner in which the agreement has been performed.

§4. Selection process

1. Equal treatment

1280. A number of provisions apply to the selection process. First, there are provisions relating to the equal treatment of men and women. Article 8 of the Law of 7 May 1999 on the Equal Treatment of Men and Women as Regards Working Conditions, Access to Employment and Promotion Opportunities, Access to Independent Professions and the Additional Regulations for Social Security (*Wet van 7 mei 1999 op de gelijke behandeling van mannen en vrouwen ten aanzien van de arbeidsvoorwaarden, de toegang tot het arbeidsproces en de promotiekansen, de toegang tot een zelfstandig beroep en de aanvullende regelingen voor sociale zekerheid/Loi sur l'égalité de traitement entre hommes et femmes en ce qui concerne les conditions de travail, l'accès à l'emploi et aux possibilités de promotion, l'accès à une profession indépendante et les régimes complémentaires de sécurité sociale* – the "Law of 7 May 1999") provides that equal treatment must be guaranteed in the provisions and practices regarding the conditions of access to employment and to independent professions and regarding the selection process, including the selection criteria. This applies irrespective of the sector or the activity concerned and irrespective of the level of the position concerned within the employer's hierarchy. In other words, it is prohibited to refer directly or indirectly to the gender of employees in employment offers, to determine directly or indirectly the access conditions or selection criteria on the basis of the employee's gender, *etc.* The conditions of access to a position or professional activity may only refer to the employee's or applicant's gender provided gender constitutes an essential aspect of the employment given its nature or the conditions of its performance. These cases can be determined by Royal Decree.

1281. Second, the Law of 30 July 1981 on the Punishment of Certain Acts Inspired by Racism or Xenophobia (*Wet van 30 juli 1981 tot bestraffing van bepaalde door racisme en xenophobia ingegeven daden/Loi tendant à réprimer certains actes inspirés par la racisme ou la xénophobie*) sanctions with imprisonment or fines all discriminatory behaviour engaged in during the selection process *vis-à-vis* a person on account of his/her race, colour, origin or nationality.

2. Offer of employment

1282. Article 24, paragraph 5 of the Decision of the Flemish Government of 21 December 1988 on the organisation of work placement (*arbeidsbemiddeling/recrutement et placement des travailleurs*) and professional education provides for an obligation to notify the employment office of a vacancy. This obligation applies to employers who employ at least 20 employees on average in the year prior to the vacancy and to any vacancy which the employer or a selection agency has announced in the press.

3. Work placement

1283. Until recently, work placement was a privilege of the government. The Decree of the Flemish Parliament of 13 April 1999 (the "Decree of 13 April 1999") now regulates work placement in return for payment in the Flemish Region. Operating an office for work placement in return for payment is only allowed under the conditions set forth by the Decree of 13 April 1999, and provided the office for work placement has obtained prior approval. Offices for work placement located in the Walloon Region and in the Brussels-Capital Region must comply with the provisions of the Ministerial Decree of 1 December 1975, as modified.

4. Outplacement

1284. Outplacement is regulated by Collective Bargaining Agreement No. 51, entered into at the level of the National Labour Council on 10 February 1992 ("CBA No. 51") and by Collective Bargaining Agreement No. 82 ("CBA No. 82").

1285. Outplacement is defined as a set of services and advice rendered in return for payment by a third party, *i.e.*, the outplacement office, at the request of the employer to an individual employee or group of employees in order to enable the employee(s) to find new employment or to develop a professional activity as a self-employed person.

1286. In the Flemish Region, the operating of a private outplacement office is subject to government approval. The Flemish Government has drawn up a code of conduct for outplacement offices (*See*, Annex to the Decree of the Flemish Government of 8 December 1993).

1287. Outplacement guidance may commence only upon the prior written consent of the employee. The costs involved with outplacement must be borne by the employer. Outplacement guidance may only be offered to the employee provided that the outplacement office undertakes to abide by a number of obligations, relating to, among other things, the duration of the assignment, confidentiality, *etc.* In addition, the outplacement office must also offer accident insurance covering the period of the assignment which guarantees the same protection as is guaranteed under the legislation on accidents at work.

1288. If the employer intends to offer outplacement services, he must consult the employees' representatives and inform them of his intentions.

1289. Since 15 September 2002, some employees are entitled to outplacement services if they are dismissed by their employer. This right is, more specifically, granted to employees who have reached the age of 45 at the moment of dismissal, and have at least 1 year's seniority. The termination of the employment agreement may, however, not be due to a serious cause or to early retirement (Art. 3 of CBA No. 82).

5. Application and selection

1290. Collective Bargaining Agreement No. 38 ("CBA No. 38") regulates the recruitment and selection of employees and lays down a code of conduct in this regard.

1291. More particularly, CBA No. 38 lays down the following principles:
    (i) the employer may not treat applicants in a discriminatory manner;
    (ii) the costs involved in the examination of applicants must be borne by the employer, if he ordered such an examination;
    (iii) if the applicant is subject to the control on unemployed persons, the employer must provide a record of the interview to the applicant upon his request, indicating the date and hour of the interview, as well as the reason why (s)he has not been hired;
    (iv) the employer must keep the documents relating to the application at the applicant's disposal for a reasonable period of time, if the applicant was not accepted;
    (v) the employer may only request a copy of diplomas, certificates, *etc.* when the selection procedure is completed;
    (vi) the employer must provide sufficient information to the applicant with regard to the employment on offer;
    (vii) the employer must respect the applicant's privacy throughout the selection procedure;
    (viii) the employer must treat any information regarding the applicant as confidential;
    (ix) the applicant must make his/her application in good faith and provide all necessary information regarding his education and professional experience, in so far as this information relates to the nature and the conditions for performance of the position concerned;
    (x) the applicant may not disclose any confidential information which he received during the selection procedure;
    (xi) the selection procedure must be completed within a reasonable period of time;
    (xii) if the selection procedure requires a practical test, this test may only last as long as is necessary to examine the applicant's competence; and

(xiii) the offering of fictitious employment for mere publicity purposes is prohibited.

§5. Formation of the employment contract

1292. In general, the LEC does not impose specific formalities as regards the formation of an employment contract. The agreement may be oral or even tacit. However, in order to avoid evidentiary problems if a conflict arises between the parties, it is preferable to have the agreement in writing.

1293. There are a few exceptions to the principle that employment contracts may be oral. The law provides that the following types of contracts must be in writing:
    (i) contracts for a fixed period or for a specific project;
    (ii) part-time employment contracts; and
    (iii) replacement contracts.

1294. When an employment contract is not in writing, it is always deemed to have been concluded for an indefinite duration.

1295. In addition, the following clauses must be in writing in order to bind the parties:
    (i) probationary period clauses (*See*, paras. 1298 *et seq.*);
    (ii) non-competition provisions (*See*, paras. 1306 *et seq.*); and
    (iii) notice period clauses for higher employees (*See*, para. 1373).

1296. Finally, it is reiterated that written employment contracts must comply with the provisions on the use of languages in labour relations (*See*, paras. 1266 *et seq.*).

§6. Duration of the employment contract

1297. The LEC identifies four different types of employment contract as far as their duration is concerned:
    (i) most employment contracts are concluded for an indefinite period of time. Either party may terminate such a contract at any time, but only in compliance with the mandatory provisions regarding termination set forth in the LEC;
    (ii) the employer usually enters into contracts for a fixed period or a specific project when he requires a temporary work force. The agreement must be in writing and entered into individually with each employee no later than the day on which the employment begins. Such agreements must clearly specify their duration or the project involved. If any doubt arises as to its term, the employment contract will be deemed to have been concluded for an indefinite period. In addition, Article 10 of the LEC stipulates that, where parties have concluded successive uninterrupted contracts for fixed periods or specific projects, they will be deemed to have concluded a contract for an indefinite

period unless the employer can provide evidence that such contracts were justified by the nature of the work or particular circumstances. This provision is intended to prevent employers from circumventing minimum notice requirements by concluding successive fixed-term employment contracts with their employees. Nevertheless successive contracts for a fixed term may be entered into provided the following conditions are met:

(a) no more than 4 successive contracts are entered into, each having a minimum duration of 3 months, without the total duration of these successive contracts exceeding 2 years; or

(b) the prior authorisation of the competent authority is obtained and the duration of the agreement may not be less than 6 months for each single contract and without the total duration of these successive contracts exceeding 3 years (Art. 10*bis* of the LEC).

If an agreement for a definite duration is continued after the contractual expiry date, it will be considered to have become an agreement for an indefinite duration (Art. 11 of the LEC LEC).

(i) the LEC entitles an employer to replace, under certain conditions, an employee whose contract has been suspended temporarily as a result of sickness, an accident at work, pregnancy, annual vacation, *etc.* However, no replacement contract is permitted if the suspension is due to a shortage of work for economic reasons, weather conditions, strike or lock-out. The replacement contract must be in writing and entered into individually for each employee concerned. It must contain the name of the replaced employee and the reason for the replacement. It is automatically terminated when the replaced employee returns to work. A replacement contract may normally not exceed 2 years. If it is not in writing, or if the period of 2 years is exceeded, it is deemed to have been concluded for an indefinite period.

(ii) a part-time contract must be in writing and mention the work timetable. If the work timetable is not mentioned in the contract, the employee may choose his work timetable from among the part-time work timetables established in the work rules *(arbeidsreglement/règlement de travail)* of the company or any equivalent document. Article 11*bis* of the LEC also provides that, in general, the work week of a part-time worker may not be less than one-third of the work week of a regular full-time worker. Where the contract provides for a shorter working week, the remuneration relating to the minimum period must nevertheless be paid.

§7. The probationary period clause

1298. It is common practice in Belgium to provide for a probationary period which entitles both the employer and the employee to terminate their agreement on short notice. The probationary period clause, which may be included in contracts of an indefinite duration, contracts for a fixed period or contracts for a specific project, must be established in writing before the employee starts performing the employment agreement. If a probationary period clause is added to an employment contract after the employment has begun, it will be deemed void.

1299. For blue-collar employees, the probationary period must be a minimum of 7 days and a maximum of 14 days. If the duration is not specified in the contract, in a collective bargaining agreement or in the work rules, the probationary period will automatically be 7 days.

1300. During the first 7 days of the probationary period, the employer may not terminate the contract except for serious cause (*See*, paras. 1387 *et seq*.). After the first 7 days and until the end of the probationary period, the employer may terminate the contract without any notice or the payment of any indemnity in lieu of notice.

1301. If the contract is suspended for any reason during the probationary period, the probationary period must be extended for a period equivalent to the period of suspension, with a maximum of 7 days. In this case, the employer may terminate the employment contract at any time, even during the period the contract is suspended, provided that the employee has already worked at least 7 days.

1302. For white-collar employees, including commercial representatives, the probationary period must be at least 1 month. The maximum probationary period is 6 months if the gross annual remuneration of the employee is € 31,073 or less and 12 months if the gross annual remuneration of the employee exceeds this amount (this figure is for 2003 and is adjusted annually on the basis of the index of the conventional salaries for white-collar employees). When the duration of the probationary period is not specified in the contract or in a collective bargaining agreement applicable to the employer or in the work rules, the minimum period applies.

1303. During the first month of the probationary period, the contract may be terminated by either party with 7 days' notice, but the termination of the employment agreement will only have effect at the earliest on the last day of the first month of employment. If the employer terminates the contract during the first month without notice, he must pay the employee's salary for the full first month, plus an indemnity equal to 7 days' salary, representing the 7 days' notice period. After the first month and until the end of the probationary period, the contract may be terminated on 7 days' notice or with immediate effect, provided an indemnity equal to 7 days' salary is paid.

1304. If the contract is suspended during the probationary period, the probationary period is extended to cover the duration of the suspension. If the contract is suspended for more than 7 uninterrupted days, the employer may terminate the contract without notice or indemnity in lieu of notice.

1305. Particular attention should be paid to the situation where an employer wishes to terminate an employment agreement during the last 7 days of the probationary period. In that case, the employer should terminate the agreement with immediate effect and pay an indemnity equal to 7 days' salary. Indeed, if the employer were to give notice, the period of notice would end after the expiry date of the probationary period and the contract could then only be terminated pursuant to the normal termination rules. As a result, the dismissed employee would be entitled to a normal indemnity, being at least 3 months' salary (*See*, 1371 and 1384).

§8. Non-competition clause

1306. Employment contracts may contain a non-competition clause whereby the employee is prevented, when he leaves his employer, from carrying out similar activities, either on his own behalf or by entering into an employment contract with a competitor.

1307. In order to be valid, the non-competition clause must comply with Article 65 of the LEC which imposes the following conditions:
  (i) it must be in writing;
 (ii) it must relate to similar activities;
(iii) the period during which it remains applicable may not exceed 12 months after the expiration or termination of the employment contract;
(iv) it must be geographically limited to the territory in which the employee can effectively enter into competition with the employer within the Belgian territory;
 (v) it must provide for the payment by the employer to the employee of a sum equal to at least half the gross remuneration of the employee corresponding to the duration of the non-competition obligation, except if the employer waives the non-competition clause within 15 days following the termination of the employment contract. The reference period for the calculation of compensation is the last month preceding the termination of the employment contract.

1308. The non-competition clause is null and void if the employee's gross annual remuneration is less than € 25,921. If it is between € 25,921 and € 51,842, the non-competition clause may only apply to specific areas of work fixed by collective bargaining agreements concluded within a joint committee (*paritair comité/ commission paritaire*) or within the company itself. When the gross annual remuneration exceeds € 51,842, the non-competition clause is valid except if otherwise stipulated by a collective bargaining agreement concluded within a joint committee or within the company.

1309. If the non-competition obligation is violated by the employee, the employer is entitled to receive from the employee an amount corresponding to twice the lump-sum compensation paid to the employee. However, depending on the period during which the clause was observed by the employee or the harm actually suffered by the employer, the judge may modify that amount.

1310. Non-competition clauses will have no effect if the contract is terminated during the probationary period or after the probationary period by the employer without serious breach on the part of the employee or by the employee for serious breach on the part of the employer.

1311. Non-competition clauses encompassing a territory larger than Belgium and/or extending beyond 12 months are valid, provided the company carries out its activities on an international scale, or has its own research and development centre. Furthermore, the employee must be entrusted with activities that enable him to directly or indirectly acquire information about practices whose disclosure might be harmful to the employer. In such cases, non-competition clauses remain applicable even if the employment contract is terminated during the probationary period or after the probationary period by the employer without serious cause (Art. 86 of the LEC).

1312. Irrespective of the existence of a non-competition clause, all employees are subject to Article 17 of the LEC which provides that, in the course of his employment, and after its termination, an employee must refrain from revealing any trade or business secret, or any secret of a personal or confidential nature that has come to his knowledge in the performance of his duties. Moreover, all employees must abstain from engaging in unfair competition. In case of violation of this obligation, the employer may sue for damages. Article 309 of the Criminal Code also provides for specific criminal sanctions in case employees reveal any technical secrets of their employer with fraudulent intent.

§9. *Duties and responsibilities of the parties*

1313. In addition to the general principle contained in Articles 1134, paragraph 3, and 1135 of the Civil Code which oblige contracting parties to perform any agreement in accordance with the principles of good faith and equity, Articles 17 and 20 of the LEC establish in general terms, the duties and responsibilities applicable to employees and employers.

1314. Employees must carry out their work with due care and at the agreed time and place and in accordance with the other conditions agreed between the parties. Employees may not divulge any secret or confidential information, nor engage or co-operate in any act of unfair competition.

1315. Article 18 of the LEC provides that an employee who has harmed his employer or any third party is liable for damages only where there is wilful misconduct or gross negligence. He is not liable for ordinary negligence unless it can be established that this negligence was not exceptional, but took place on a number of different occasions. Under certain conditions, the employer may deduct from the employee's remuneration certain amounts to cover damage caused by the employee (Art. 23, 3° of the Law of 12 April 1965 on the Protection of the Employees' Remuneration (*Wet betreffende de bescherming van het loon der werknemers/Loi concernant la protection de la rémunération des travailleurs* – the "Law of 12 April 1965").

1316. With regard to third parties, the employer remains liable for any harm caused by his employee in the course of their employment (Art. 1384, para. 3 of the Civil Code). The employer may only obtain indemnification from the employee under the conditions provided in Article 18 of the LEC.

1317. The main obligation of the employer is to employ the employee in accordance with the contractual conditions and ensure that the work can be carried out under satisfactory conditions. The payment of remuneration is subject to the protective rules of the Law of 12 April 1965 (*See*, paras. 1542 *et seq.*).

1318. The Law of 7 May 1999 relates to the equal treatment of men and women with respect to the access to employment, the possibility of promotion, access to independent professions and working condition. It also contains additional provisions regarding social security. Equal treatment is defined as the absence of any form of direct or indirect discrimination on the basis of gender. Sexual harassment at work is deemed to be a form of discrimination on the basis of gender. Equal treatment must be guaranteed in all provisions and practices relating to working conditions and conditions for dismissal (Arts. 11 and 12 of the Law of 7 May

1999). It is prohibited, *e.g.*, to refer to a person's gender as a condition for employment or to name an employee's gender as a reason for dismissal or to include factors in the employment conditions that are indirectly discriminatory. Discriminatory provisions within the meaning of the law are void. Article 19 of the Law of 7 May 1999 entitles parties to initiate legal proceedings seeking the application of this law. If the claimant adduces facts that might be deemed discriminatory, it is generally for the defendant to prove that he has not violated the principle of equal treatment. The Court can force employers to put an end to the discriminatory situation within a certain time-limit. Article 23 of the Law of 7 May 1999 grants special protection to employees who have filed a complaint or initiated legal proceedings on the basis of the law. If the employer terminates the employment contract or unilaterally changes its conditions within 12 months of the complaint or within 3 months of the date when the judgement was no longer appealable, he will have to prove that the dismissal or the unilateral modification of working conditions was unrelated to the complaint or to any court case initiated on the basis of the law.

1319. If the employer cannot justify the dismissal or unilateral modification of working conditions, he will have to reinstate the dismissed employee or respect his original working conditions. The employee must file a request to that effect within 30 days following the termination of his employment, the notification of the termination or the modification of the working conditions. If the employer refuses to reinstate the employee, the employee will be entitled to special compensation equal to 6 months' salary or the actual damage suffered, upon the employee's choice.

1320. On 12 December 2002, the Senate voted a new anti-discrimination bill (*Wetsontwerp tot bestrijding van discriminatie en tot wijziging van de wet van 15 februari 1993 tot oprichting van een Centrum voor gelijkheid van kansen en voor racismebestrijding/Projet de loi tendant à lutter contre la discrimination et modifiant la loi du 15 février 1993 créant un Centre pour l'égalité des chances et la lutte contre le racisme*). Acts of direct and indirect discrimination are prohibited. On a civil law level, all contractual clauses and agreements which fall foul of the law are void, as well as all clauses whereby a party to an agreement waives its rights thereunder. Discrimination is only allowed if it can be objectively and reasonably justified. As regards employment relations, Article 2, paragraph 5 of the law specifies in this respect that a person may be discriminated against on the basis of a certain characteristic if, in view of the nature of the professional activity or the context in which it is performed, this characteristic constitutes an essential or determined professional requirement provided the aim is legitimate and the requirement is proportionate in view of the aim. A person who feels discriminated against may request a cease-and-desist order with the Labour Court, file a complaint with the Social Inspection or follow the applicable internal company procedure, as a result of which he will be protected against dismissal: he may not be dismissed except for reasons that are unrelated to the complaint or the initiated legal proceedings or company procedure. Employers who do not observe this obligation or who modify the employee's working conditions must pay a compensation of six months' salary (which may be combined with a possible indemnity in lieu of notice). A dismissed employee may request his reintegration in the company or the re-modification of his working conditions.

§10. Suspension of the employment contract

1. General

1321. Article 26 of the LEC provides that the employment contract is suspended when either party is unable to perform its obligations under the employment contract as a result of *force majeure* not of a permanent character. If the *force majeure* has a permanent character, it is a cause for termination of the employment contract (Art. 32, 5° of the LEC, *See*, para. 1354).

1322. The LEC lays down a number of specific situations in which employees receive special protection during the suspension period. In such cases, the employer must unilaterally continue to perform his obligations under the employment contract even though the employee is unable to work due to, among others, illness or accident, pregnancy or annual vacation. These situations are further discussed below.

1323. The LEC also contains special provisions enabling the employer to unilaterally suspend the employment contract of blue-collar employees in particular circumstances.

1324. Not all grounds for suspension of the employment contract are regulated by the LEC. Employment contracts may, *e.g.*, also be suspended on the basis of the regulations on the "interruption of carreer" (*loopbaanonderbreking/interruption de la carrière professionnelle*), replaced by the system of "time-credit" (*tijdskrediet/système du crédit-temps*) as from 1 January 2002, or pursuant to the application of the *exceptio non adimpleti contractus* (contractual default).

1325. In addition, the parties may, at any time, mutually agree to temporarily suspend their respective obligations under the agreement. In such a case, the reciprocal obligations of the parties will resume once the suspension period has ended.

2. *Illness and accident*

1326. When the employment contract is interrupted because of illness or accident, the employment contract is legally suspended during the entire period the employee is unable to work (Art. 31 of the LEC).

1327. The employee must inform the employer immediately of his inability to work. The employee must provide the employer with a medical certificate if a collective bargaining agreement or the work rules require so or, in the absence thereof, at the request of the employer. Except in cases of *force majeure*, the medical certificate must be sent to the employer or handed in to the company within 2 days from the day of inability to work or from the receipt of the employer's request, unless a collective bargaining agreement or the work rules provide otherwise. If the medical certificate is submitted outside the time limit, the employee may no longer be entitled to the guaranteed salary relating to the days of inability to work preceding the day on which the medical certificate was submitted. Most employment contracts or work rules provide for a period of one or 2 days within which the medical certificate must be sent to the employer.

1328. The employer is entitled to have the employee's inability to work verified by a doctor paid by the employer.

1329. If the inability to work is work-related (*e.g.*, the inability is due to an accident at the work place), the employer must inform his insurance company of the accident or illness with a special form within 10 days of the event occurring. All employers must take out insurance with an approved company which covers accidents or illnesses related to work or occurring on the way to and from work. The employer must also inform the medical service responsible for his company as well as the competent technical inspection authorities as soon as possible.

1330. During the period of suspension of the employment contract, the employee is entitled in specific circumstances to a guaranteed remuneration payable by the employer.

1331. The rules regarding guaranteed remuneration are different for blue-collar and white-collar employees. For blue-collar employees, a further distinction must be made according to whether or not the illness or accident is work related:
   (i) *blue-collar employees:* if the illness or accident is not work related and the blue-collar employee has been employed for less than one month, no remuneration is due by the employer. If the employee concerned has a seniority of more than one month, the employer must pay the employee's full salary for the first 7 days of absence. From the eighth to the fourteenth day, the blue-

collar employee is entitled to 85.88% of his salary. From the fifteenth day to the thirtieth day, the blue-collar employee is entitled to 25.88% of his salary not exceeding € 2,619.65 and to 85.88% of that part of his salary exceeding that amount. If the illness or accident is work related, the blue-collar employee will be paid his full salary during the first 7 days. During the next period of 23 days, the employer must pay the blue-collar employee the difference between the amount paid by the insurance company and the net salary the employee would have received if he had been able to work.

(ii) *white-collar employees:* if a white-collar employee is employed for a definite duration of less than 3 months or to carry out specific work which will take less than 3 months or if he is still in his probationary period, and he has less than one month's seniority, no remuneration is due by the employer. If the same white-collar employee has at least one month's seniority, the employer must pay the employee's full salary for the first 7 days of absence. From the eighth to the fourteenth day, the white-collar employee is entitled to 86.93% of his salary. From the fifteenth day to the thirtieth day, the white-collar employee is entitled to 26.93% of his salary not exceeding € 2,619.65 and to 86.93% of that part of his salary exceeding that amount. Other white-collar employees are entitled to their full salary during the first 30 days of absence, to be paid by their employer. As far as work-related illnesses or accidents are concerned, the following distinction must be made: white-collar employees who are employed for a definite duration of less than 3 months or to carry out specific work which will take less than 3 months or who are still in their probationary period, are entitled to a remuneration which is identical to that of blue-collar employees. The other white-collar employees are entitled to their normal salary during the first 30 days, payable by the employer.

1332. If the employee gave notice, the suspension of the employment contract does not prevent the resulting notice period from elapsing (Arts. 38(1) and 62 of the LEC).

1333. If the employer has given notice to the employee prior to or during the suspension of the employment contract, however, such notice period will be suspended until the employee is able to return to work (Arts. 38(2) and 62 of the LEC).

3. Pregnancy

1334. Article 39 of the Labour Law of 16 March 1971 (*Arbeidswet/ Loi sur le travail*) provides that the employer must give a female employee, upon her request and upon presentation of a medical certificate, a rest period of a maximum of 7 weeks preceding the expected date of delivery. In no case is the employee allowed to work on or after the seventh day prior to the expected date of delivery. If delivery takes place at a later date, the rest period will be extended accordingly. The employment contract is also legally suspended during the 8 weeks following the delivery. If the employee has not taken full advantage of the non-compulsory pre-delivery 6 weeks' rest period, the unused part of this period may be added to the post-delivery rest period. In practice this means that the employment contract will be suspended for a total period of 15 weeks.

1335. Special protective rules also apply to mothers breastfeeding their babies and to employees carrying out dangerous work.

1336. During the period of suspension, the employer does not have to pay any salary. A special indemnity will be paid by the health insurance company during the employee's absence from work.

1337. Pursuant to Article 40 of the Law of 16 March 1971, the employer may not unilaterally terminate the employment contract from the moment he is notified of the pregnancy up to one month after the end of the post-delivery leave, unless he can prove that the termination is unrelated to the employee's physical condition resulting from pregnancy or giving birth. Failure to provide adequate proof will entitle the pregnant employee to a special indemnity equal to 6 months' salary in addition to the termination indemnity to which the employee would normally be entitled.

4. Annual vacation

1338. During the period the employee takes his vacation, the employment contract is suspended. Nevertheless, the employee continues to receive his full remuneration.

1339. The employer may give notice of termination of the employment contract during the vacation period. However, the notice period will only begin to run after the end of the vacation period. If the employer terminates the employment contract before the vacation period, the notice period is suspended during that period.

5. Unilateral suspension by the employer

1340. The employer may, under strict conditions, suspend the employment contracts of blue-collar employees if his establishment is temporarily closed as a result of bad weather conditions, technical problems or economic causes (Arts. 49, 50 and 51 of the LEC).

1341. The bad weather conditions must actually render work impossible. The technical problems must relate to the equipment of the undertaking while the economic causes must be responsible for a substantial reduction in workload.

1342. Specific procedures must be followed in each of the above cases. The employees will receive unemployment benefit for the duration of the suspension.

6. *Time-credit regime*

i. General

1343. A new system of so-called "time-credit" replaces the earlier regulation on "career interruption" as from 1 January 2002.

1344. Collective Bargaining Agreement No. 77 ("CBA No. 77") was entered into on 14 February 2001. In the meantime CBA No. 77 has been replaced by CBA No. 77*bis* of 19 December 2001, which clarifies certain of its provisions. On 10 July 2002, the social partners agreed on CBA No. 77*ter*, which contains certain transitional provisions that clarify the transition from the old system (of "career interruption") to the new system (of "time-credit"). CBA No. 77, as amended, introduces 3 new systems of career interruption:
- (a) full-time and part-time employees with at least one year's seniority will be entitled to time-credit;
- (b) full-time employees with at least 5 years' seniority can benefit from one-fifth career reduction in the form of one day per week or 2 half days per week;
- (c) full-time employees older than 50, having at least 20 years' seniority as an employee and at least 5 years' seniority with their employer are entitled to a reduction of their work performance.

1345. CBA No. 77 applies to employers and employees who fall within the scope of application of the Law of 5 December 1968 on Collective Bargaining Agreements and Joint Committees (*Wet betreffende de collectieve arbeidsovereenkomsten en de paritaire comités/Loi sur les conventions collectives de travail et les commissions paritaires*).

ii. Time-credit

1346. Under the system of time-credit, employees can suspend their work performance entirely or partially. The partial suspension of work performance is only possible for employees who are employed for at least 75 per cent. The employees can take up their time-credit only for periods of 3 months and only for a maximum period of one year throughout their professional career. A collective bargaining agreement at industry or company level can deviate from these limits. The employees receive a remuneration during the period of time-credit. There is no automatic right of time-credit for employees employed in undertakings with less than 11 employees. In these undertakings, time-credit can only be taken up upon the approval of the employer. If more than 5 per cent of the total number of employees take up time-credit simultaneously, a planning mechanism is worked out in order to guarantee the continuity of the organisation of labour within the company. The employer can postpone the taking-up of time-credit for serious internal or external reasons (*e.g.*, organisational needs, issues of continuity) for a maximum period of 6 months.

1347. Employees who have applied for time-credit can only be dismissed for serious cause or for a reason unrelated to their taking up of time-credit. If the employer disregards the protection against dismissal, he is liable to pay an indemnity equal to 6 months' remuneration to the employee.

iii. One-fifth career reduction

1348. Eligible employees must have at least 5 years' seniority, be full-time employed since at least 12 months and work at least 5 days a week. These employees can reduce their work performance by 20 per cent, *i.e.,* during 1 day per week or 2 half days per week, for a period of 6 months and for a maximum duration of 5 years throughout their professional career. The employees receive a remuneration during such period. There is no automatic right to one-fifth career reduction for employees employed in undertakings with less than 11 employees. In these undertakings, one-fifth career reduction can only be taken up upon the approval of the employer. If more than 5 per cent of the total number of employees reduce their work performance simultaneously, a planning mechanism is worked out in order to guarantee the continuity of the organisation of labour within the company. The employer can postpone the one-fifth career reduction for serious internal or external reasons for a maximum period of 6 months. The exercise of the right to reduce the work performance by one-fifth can also be withdrawn or modified provided the reasons and the duration are determined by the works council or, in the absence of a works council, by the employer and the trade union delegation, or in the absence of a trade union delegation by the work rules.

1349. Employees who have applied for the one-fifth career reduction can only be dismissed for serious cause or for a reason unrelated to their one-fifth career reduction. If the employer disregards the protection against dismissal, he is liable to pay an indemnity equal to 6 months' remuneration to the employee.

iv. Reduction of work performance for employees older than 50

1350. Eligible employees must be at least 50 years old, have at least five years' seniority in the undertaking where they apply for the career reduction and have at least 20 years' employment as an employee in general:

(a) full-time employees who work (at least) 5 days per week can reduce their work performance by 20 per cent, *i.e.*, during one day per week or 2 half days per week, for periods of 6 months for an unlimited number of times. Employees who have already benefited from a one-fifth career reduction under the system described above (*See*, para. 1348) must not necessarily be employed full-time and can, more specifically, switch immediately to the system applying to employees older than 50.

(b) employees who are employed for at least 75 per cent can start working half-time (*i.e.*, 50 per cent).

1351. The employees receive a remuneration during this period. There is no automatic right of work performance for employees employed in undertakings with less than 11 employees. In these undertakings, work performance can only be taken up upon the approval of the employer. If more than 5 per cent of the total number of employees reduce their work performance simultaneously, a planning mechanism is worked out in order to guarantee the continuity of the organisation of labour within the company. The employer can postpone the career reduction for serious internal or external reasons for a maximum period of 6 months. The exercising of the right to reduce the work performance can also be withdrawn or modified provided the reasons and the duration are determined by the works council or, failing a works council, by the employer and the trade union delegation, or failing a trade union delegation by the work rules.

1352. The employees who have applied for the work performance can only be dismissed for serious cause or for a reason unrelated to the career reduction. If the employer disregards the protection against dismissal, he is liable to pay an indemnity equal to 6 months' remuneration to the employee.

§11. Termination of the employment contract

1. Overview

1353. There are several ways to terminate an employment contract. The employment contract may come to an end by mutual agreement between the employer and the employee. The employment contract can be terminated by mutual consent at any time, *e.g.* during the notice period or when the contract is suspended, either with immediate effect or at a later date. Such a termination is not subject to any termination formalities. The employer may not exert pressure on the employee in order to have him agree to a termination of the employment agreement. Finally, a mutual termination of the employment agreement does not give rise to the payment of any indemnity. The employer is, however, free to pay compensation upon the termination of the employment agreement by mutual consent.

1354. The employment agreement may also come to an end at its expiration if the contract is for a fixed period or a specific task. It may also be automatically terminated if either party is unable to perform its obligations under the employment contract and the cause of such non-performance is permanent.

1355. In most cases, however, termination results from a unilateral decision taken by either party and usually takes one of the following forms: termination with notice (*See*, paras. 1360 *et seq.*); termination with payment of a severance indemnity in lieu of notice (*See*, paras. 1381 *et seq.*) and termination for serious cause (*See*, paras. 1387 *et seq.*). An employment agreement can also be deemed to be terminated due to the unilateral modification of one of its essential elements (*See*, paras. 1397 *et seq.*).

1356. There are particular rules protecting the employee in the event of termination of an employment contract for a fixed period or a specific project (*See*, paras. 1401 and 1402). In addition, certain categories of employees receive special protection in cases where their employment contract is terminated (*See*, paras. 1403 *et seq.*). Finally, the LEC contains special provisions protecting blue-collar employees against abusive dismissal (*See*, paras. 1435 *et seq.*).

1357. Belgian labour law also contains detailed rules governing the termination of employment contracts as a result of collective redundancy or plant closure. Although this legislation is not included in the LEC, it is convenient to discuss it in this section (*See*, paras. 1439 *et seq.*).

1358. The system of early pension will also be discussed briefly (*See*, paras. 1473 *et seq.*).

1359. Finally, an overview will be given of the social documents that must be handed over to the employee upon the termination of his employment agreement (*See*, paras. 1493 *et seq.*).

2. Termination with notice

i. General

1360. When an employer decides to dismiss an employee, he may either give him notice of termination, during which notice period the employee must continue to work, or terminate the employment contract immediately by paying a severance indemnity in lieu of notice (Arts. 37 and 39 of the LEC). It is also possible for the employer to terminate the employment contract during the notice period by paying a severance indemnity equal to the salary which the employee would have received for the remaining part of the notice period. An employee who resigns must also give notice to the employer or pay an indemnity in lieu of notice.

ii. Termination formalities (Art. 37 of the LEC)

1361. For individual dismissals, there is no need for an employer who wishes to terminate the employment contract of one of his employees to consult or obtain prior approval from the Works Council or any other regulating body or court (unless the employee has a protected status, *See*, paras. 1403 *et seq.*).

1362. Notice of termination may only be validly given in a written statement which specifies the starting date and the duration of the notice period. If the contract is terminated by the employer, the statement must be sent by registered mail or served by a bailiff. If the employee resigns, he may give notice by registered mail, by writ served by a bailiff or by simple letter handed to the employer. If notice is given by registered mail, the notification is deemed to be effective on the third working day following the day of mailing. For this purpose, Saturday is considered to be a working day.

1363. For blue-collar employees, the notice period commences on the first day of the week following the week in which notice was given. For white-collar employees, the notice period commences on the first calendar day of the subsequent month. If notice is given by registered letter at the end of a week or month, consideration should be given to the 3-working day rule explained above. If the notification does not become effective during the same week or month as it is given, the notice period will only start running one week or month later.

Example

If notice of termination is sent to a white-collar employee by registered mail on Monday 29 October, it will be deemed to be notified on Thursday 1 November. The notice period will commence on 1 December, that is, the first day of the month following the month in which the notification became effective. If the employer had sent the notice of termination by registered mail on Saturday 27 October, it would have become effective on Wednesday 31 October and the notice period would have started on 1 November.

1364. In general, notice periods given by the employer will be suspended during any period of suspension of the employment contract.

1365. The statement of notice must be drafted in Dutch if the place of business (*exploitatiezetel/siège d'exploitation*) where the employee works is located in the Dutch language region and in French if the place of business where the employee works is located in the French language region. If the employee is employed in the Brussels region, the notice must be in Dutch or French, depending on whether the employee is Dutch or French speaking (*See*, para. 1267).

iii. Duration of the notice period

1366. The LEC distinguishes between blue-collar employees and white-collar employees.

1367. As regards blue-collar employees, the LEC sets forth the following minimum notice periods. Blue-collar employees who are hired for an indefinite period of time may be dismissed with 28 calendar days' notice. If they have more than 20 years seniority, the notice period is 56 days. For workers with less than six months' seniority, a reduced notice period of not less than seven days may be agreed upon in the employment contract. Collective Bargaining Agreement No. 75 ("CBA No. 75") has recently considerably extended the notice periods to be observed by the employer.

1368. Under CBA No. 75, the following notice periods must be observed by the employer when he dismisses a blue-collar employee:

Seniority	Notice period
Between 6 months and 5 years	35 days
Between 5 and 10 years	42 days
Between 10 and 15 years	56 days
Between 15 and 20 years	84 days
More than 20 years	112 days

1369. Joint committees may deviate from the latter notice periods. If deviating collective bargaining agreements have not been entered into at the level of the sector or if there are no collective agreements in place that provide for additional employment stability or social security schemes, the provisions of CBA No. 75 will apply.

1370. With respect to white-collar employees, the LEC does not establish what constitutes adequate notice, except for employees whose total annual gross salary does not exceed € 25,921 (this figure is for 2003, and is adjusted annually to the index of the conventional salaries for white-collar employees by the Ministry of Employment and Labour).

1371. If a white-collar employee's annual gross salary is less than € 25,921, the employer must give at least 3 months' notice if the employee has been in the service of the company for less than 5 years and, upon commencement of any additional 5-year period, the notice period must be increased by 3 months. The parties may fix longer periods in the employment agreement. A number of collective bargaining agreements also provide for longer notice periods. When an employee wants to terminate his contract he need only give one-and-a-half months' notice if he has been employed less than 5 years and 3 months' notice if he has been employed for more than 5 years. A white-collar employee in this salary category may never be required to give more than 3 months' notice.

1372. If the annual gross salary of a white-collar employee exceeds € 25,921 but is lower than € 51,842, the duration of the notice period may not be fixed in advance in an employment contract. The notice period to be given by an employer in such cases must be agreed upon by the parties at the time of the termination of the contract or, failing such agreement, by the Labour Court. The notice period may not be less than the statutory minimum for white-collar employees whose annual gross salary is less than € 25,921. However, the Supreme Court has ruled that, once notice of termination has been given, the employee may waive the mandatory minimum notice period.

1373. If the annual gross salary of a white-collar employee exceeds € 51,842 at the moment of hiring, the duration of the notice period may be fixed in advance in the employment contract, concluded before the starting date of employment. The notice periods which can be agreed upon by the parties may not be less than the statutory minimum for white-collar employees whose annual gross salary is less than € 25,921. If no such notice period has been agreed upon by the parties, the rules explained in the previous paragraph apply.

1374. The employee may not be required to give more than 4.5 months' notice if his gross annual remuneration is between € 25,921 and € 51,842 and more than 6 months' notice if his salary exceeds € 51,842.

1375. When the employee has been given notice of termination by his employer and has found new employment, he may, at any time and notwithstanding any agreement to the contrary, terminate the existing contract by giving 1 month's counter-notice if his annual gross salary does not exceed € 25,921 and 2 months' counter-notice if his annual gross salary is between € 25,921 and € 51,842. If his annual gross salary exceeds € 51,842, the counter-notice period is to be agreed upon by the parties, but may not exceed 4 months.

1376. In the absence of an agreement between the parties on the notice period, the matter will be referred to the Labour Court which will award the employee an indemnity in lieu of notice if it considers that the employer gave insufficient notice.

1377. Labour Courts consider personal factors (such as seniority, age, the importance of the employee's position, his salary, his education and his professional experience) as well as social and economic factors (such as the employment market at the time of termination) to determine the length of the notice period.

1378. In practice, employers often calculate the notice period on the basis of certain statistical formulas developed by legal commentators which are designed to reflect the various factors relied upon by the courts to determine the duration of the notice period in particular cases. The most commonly used formula is the so-called "Claeys" formula. This formula is not, however, binding on judges. The "Claeys" formula is as follows:

Notice period in months =

(0.89 x seniority) + (0.08 x age) + (0.052 x indexed gross yearly remuneration) – 2

Both seniority and age are expressed in years and months. The remuneration is expressed in thousands of Euros and includes all fringe benefits, pension scheme contributions, bonuses and other benefits. Based on court decisions, the notice requirements to be observed considerably exceed the minima provided for in the LEC. Table 10.1 is an illustration of the notice periods granted recently by some Labour Courts.

1379. Finally, it should be noted that when the employee has reached the age of 65 the employer may terminate his employment with 3 months' notice if the employee has less than 5 years seniority and 6 months' notice in other cases. The employee, on the other hand, has the right to resign as of the age of 60 by giving 1.5 months' notice if he has less than 5 years' seniority and by giving 3 months' notice if he has a seniority of more than 5 years (Art. 83 LEC).

iv. Rights and obligations of the parties during the notice period

1380. During the notice period, the parties have, in principle, the same rights and obligations under the employment contract as before notice was given. However, during the notice period, employees whose gross annual salary does not exceed € 25,921 are entitled to take two half days or one full day off per week to find other employment. Employees earning more than € 25,921 are entitled to the same time off during the last 6 months of their notice period, but only to half a day per week during the preceding period (Art. 85 of the LEC).

Table 10.1: Notice periods

Seniority (yrs, mnths)	Age	Function	Indexed annual remuneration*	Notice (mnths)
0.10	42	Commercial representative	2,559,400	5
0.10	38	Executive	2,336,100	4
0.58	35	Assistant-Director	5,640,000	3
1.03	38	Commercial representative	1,254,100	4
1.04	29	Technician	729,400	4
1.06	33	Commercial representative	1,081,800	3
1.06	38	Manager	1,637,400	4
1.33	56	Commercial representative	964,514	4
2.00	48	Representative	756,100	6
2.05	29	Manager	1,083,400	5
2.09	37	Manager	1,487,800	8
3.00	42	Supervisory position	2,225,204	8
4.00	47	Secretary	822,500	8
4.03	43	Branch manager	4,300,200	10
5.03	36	Intern. sales manager	1,917,400	9
6.02	41	Commercial representative	908,600	9
6.06	24	Employee	786,900	6
7.06	38	Project manager	1,189,700	10
8.00	49	Commercial manager	2,153,000	14
9.03	32	Secretary	904,600	7
9.11	34	Representative	1,708,800	12
10.33	48	High-level position	6,445,305	14
12.05	51	Commercial representative	1,071,800	16
13.07	38	Manager	3,670,400	18
15.02	39	Assist. tech. manager	1,994,800	24
17.00	40	supervisory function	2,428,363	21
18.00	36	Manager	739,700	16
19.02	53	Chief of department	1,151,600	20
20.06	43	Medical representative	1,422,200	25

22.06	41	Analyst-programmer	1,297,100	15
25.01	47	Employee	720,700	29
27.00	54	Medical inspector	2,751,900	31
26.00	53.5	Senior adviser	4,783,675	28
29.04	48	Commercial manager	1,800,400	30
33.08	57	Adm. Manager	2,360,400	36
39.70	55	Administrative and IT	1,433,652	40
42.02	57	Employee	848,700	36

Amounts in BEF, as the reported case-law dates from before 1 January 2002 (40.3399 BEF = € 1).

3. Termination with payment of an indemnity in lieu of notice

1381. An indemnity in lieu of notice is due when the employer or employee terminates the employment contract without notice or with insufficient notice. At any time during the notice period, the terminating party may decide to pay an indemnity in lieu of notice.

i. Termination formalities

1382. There are no termination formalities to be complied with when a contracting party decides to terminate an employment contract with immediate effect. However, it is common practice to confirm such termination by registered letter. In addition, where a severance indemnity is offered, it is advisable to specify the amount of the indemnity or the duration of the notice period in lieu of which the indemnity is paid.

1383. The indemnity should be paid in one lump-sum at the time of termination. Article 39*bis* of the LEC permits, under certain conditions, payment of the indemnity in monthly instalments for companies which have been recognised as experiencing financial difficulties or exceptionally unfavourable economic circumstances.

ii. Amount of the indemnity

1384. The indemnity is equal to the salary which would have been due for the full duration or the remaining part of the notice period. The basis for calculation is the current salary at the time of termination. The salary includes all advantages to which the employee is entitled by virtue of his employment, for example, a "thirteenth month" bonus, use of a company car, group insurance premiums, and similar benefits, but not reimbursement of costs. According to the majority of case-law and legal commentators, stock options must not be taken into account for the calculation of the indemnity in lieu of notice. The reason is that stock options are not aimed at compensating the employee for his work, and therefore do not constitute salary. In any event, even under the assumption that stock options constitute a benefit within the meaning of Article 39 of the LEC, it is impossible to quantify such benefit (unless when the employee has exercised the option during a period of 12 months preceding the termination). For this reason also, they should not be taken into account for the purpose of calculating the total annual salary. The double vacation allowance will be deemed part of the salary of a white-collar employee if notice of termination is given by the employer. Certain Labour Courts of Appeal have excluded the double vacation allowance from the salary if notice of termination is given by the employee.

1385. The indemnity has a lump-sum character. With the exception of an indemnity for abusive dismissal, the indemnity in lieu of notice is presumed to cover all injury resulting from the termination of the employment relationship. The amount of the indemnity is calculated by the Labour Court without reference to the actual harm suffered by the employee. It is, therefore, of no relevance, for example, whether the employee has immediately found another job and has suffered little harm. Conversely, the Court would not award a higher indemnity if an employee's new job is not similar to the one which was lost or if the dismissed employee remains unemployed.

1386. Article 78 of the LEC allows the employer to dismiss a white-collar employee whose contract has been suspended for more than 6 months due to illness or accident by paying him an indemnity equal to the notice period to which the employee is normally entitled, less any remuneration paid to that employee since the beginning of his incapacity or, if notice has been given, since the date on which the notice took effect. This possibility only applies to contracts for an indefinite duration. Maternity leave may not be included in the calculation of the 6-month period.

4. *Termination for serious cause*

i. Termination formalities (Art 35 of the LEC)

1387. Either party may terminate an employment contract without notice and without paying an indemnity if there is serious cause (*dringende reden/faute grave*) for doing so.

1388. A contract may only be terminated for serious cause if the serious cause that justifies such termination has not been known to the terminating party for more than 3 working days. Moreover, for such a termination to be valid, the justification for terminating the contract without notice or before the expiry of its term must be notified to the other party within 3 working days following the termination of the contract. To be valid, such notification may be made either by registered mail, by writ served by a bailiff or by the hand delivery of a written document to the other party. However, in order to avoid problems of proof, it is advisable to use one of the first two methods.

1389. An employment contract can also be terminated for serious cause when the contract is suspended, during the notice period or during the probationary period.

   ii. Definition of serious cause

1390. Article 35 of the LEC provides little explanation of what is meant by "serious cause". It only states that it must be a fault that makes professional co-operation between the employer and the employee immediately and definitively impossible.

1391. The concept of serious cause is interpreted restrictively by the courts. The following events may constitute grounds for immediate dismissal of an employee for serious cause:
   - several unjustified absences from work;
   - serious insults directed to the employer;
   - violation of professional confidentiality;
   - theft in the context of the employment relationship, irrespective of the value of the stolen objects;
   - repeated drunkenness at work (although some courts consider this to be an illness which cannot justify a dismissal for serious cause);
   - violence against colleagues;
   - sexual harassment;
   - violation of an e-mail or internet policy;
   - smoking in a hazardous non-smoking area;
   - organisation of a wildcat strike;
   - refusal to perform a task within the scope of the employment contract; and
   - failure to return money or documents which belong to the employer.

1392. The following acts have been considered "serious faults" when committed by an employer:
   - non-payment or unilateral reduction of salary; and
   - physical violence against an employee.

1393. The above acts can be regarded as examples of justified serious cause, but in practice serious cause must always be interpreted in the light of the actual circumstances of each case.

1394. The party terminating the employment contract for serious cause must be able to provide the Labour Court, in case of litigation, with evidence of all the facts justifying the termination. As indicated earlier, the facts upon which the terminating party relies must also have been notified to the other party in writing within 3 working days following the termination.

1395. The courts have consistently held that the facts that are notified by the terminating party to the other party must be sufficiently precise and clearly identifiable. It is not sufficient to indicate that the employee "has been impolite" or "by his negligence caused serious harm to the employer" or "failed to respect discipline" without clearly mentioning the exact behaviour in question. The rationale behind this rule is that the party whose employment contract has been terminated for serious cause must be in a position to determine whether the invoked reason(s) may justify immediate termination without notice or indemnity or whether such question must be decided by the courts.

1396. In the event the serious cause invoked is rejected by the Labour Court, the party who terminated the employment contract must pay an indemnity in lieu of notice. For the calculation of such indemnity, reference is made to paragraphs 1384 *et seq.* above.

5. *Unilateral modification of a working condition*

1397. As a general rule, neither the employer nor the employee are allowed to modify working conditions unilaterally. Contractual clauses which entitle the employer to unilaterally modify contractual provisions are null and void (Art. of the 25 LEC).

1398. The courts have held that a unilateral modification of the working conditions will amount to an illegal termination under the following conditions:
  (i) the modification must either concern an essential element of the employment contract or a working condition expressly agreed upon. Traditionally the following constitute essential elements: place of work; duration and timetable of work; function and responsibilities and remuneration;
  (ii) the modification must be unilateral. A modification will become bilateral if the employee accepts the modification. Such acceptance may be express or result from the conduct of the employee. In this respect, the courts usually grant the employee a short period during which he may decide whether to accept such modification or not; and

(iii) the modification must be definitive.

1399. However, the courts have, within certain limits, also accepted that employment contracts may be modified unilaterally by the employer if the changes are justifiable for economic reasons.

1400. For instance, it has been ruled that an employee must accept a reorganisation, if his overall status is respected and the change is not "directed against the employee". Reductions in salary do not seem possible, but adjustments to the computation basis (commission schedules or targets, for example, or fluctuations in foreign currency) are sometimes allowed if the employee's overall earning potential is not affected and the possibility of modification is contractually foreseen. Changes of place of employment are accepted by the courts if the employee was hired in an international context (if the employee is an expatriate or on foreign assignment, for example).

6. Termination of an employment contract for a fixed period or for a specific project

1401. Article 40 of the LEC provides that where an employment contract has been concluded for a specific period or for a specific project, the party terminating the contract before its expiry date without a serious cause must pay to the other party an indemnity equal to the remuneration due until the expiry of the contract. However, such indemnity is limited to a maximum of twice the remuneration corresponding to the notice period which would have been required if the contract had been entered into for an indefinite period.

1402. Contracts concluded for a specific period, or for a specific project, can be terminated for serious cause or during the probationary period without giving rise to this indemnity.

7. Protected employees

1403. Some categories of employees receive special protection in case of dismissal. They cannot be dismissed under the general rules described above. Employers wishing to dismiss a protected employee will need specific grounds to do so and must follow special procedures.

1404. The main categories of protected employees are members and non-elected candidates of the Works Council and of the Committee for Prevention and Protection at Work (*See*, paras. 1405 *et seq.*), trade union delegates (*See*, paras. 1425 *et seq.*), and pregnant women (*See*, paras. 1431 *et seq.*). Other categories of protected employees will not be dealt with in this book.

i. Members of and candidates for the Works Council and the Committee for Prevention and Protection at Work

(a) General

1405. The Law of 19 March 1991 containing Special Dismissal Arrangements for Employee Representatives in the Works Councils and in the Committees for Prevention and Protection at Work and for Reserve Representatives (*Wet houdende bijzondere ontslagregeling voor de personeelsafgevaardigden in de ondernemingsraden en in de comités voor veiligheid, gezondheid en verfraaiing van de werkplaatsen alsmede voor de kandidaat-personeelsafgevaardigden/Loi portant un régime de licenciement particulier pour les délégués due personnel aux conseils d'entreprise et aux comités de sécurité, d'hygiène et d'embellissement des lieux de travail, ainsi que pour les candidats délégués du personnel* – the "Law of 19 March 1991") lays down very detailed and complex rules for the dismissal of elected representatives of the Works Council or the Committee for Prevention and Protection at Work, reserve representatives and unsuccessful candidates. Timing is of the utmost importance in this context. Failure to respect the compulsory time schedules set forth in the Law of 19 March 1991 will make it impossible to dismiss the employee concerned or result in the obligation to pay a very high severance indemnity. Even if the relevant timing requirements are met, the above employees can only be dismissed:
(1) for serious cause and with the prior written approval of the Labour Court; or
(2) for economic or technical reasons approved by the competent Joint Committee.

1406. The period during which the representatives and candidates benefit from the special protection runs from the thirtieth day before the announcement of the election until the time the representatives elected at the next elections assume office. Non-elected candidates are protected for the same period of time provided they are candidates for the first time. For candidates who are unsuccessful a second time, the protection applies during two years following the announcement of the results of the election. Finally, when the Works Council is discontinued because the required minimum number of employees is no longer met, the candidates elected at the last election continue to enjoy protection for a period of 6 months, starting on the first day of what would have been the next election period. Representatives or candidates who have reached the age of 65 do not benefit from protection unless it is the consistent practice of the company to continue to employ the category of workers to which they belong beyond the age of retirement.

1407. Representatives or unsuccessful candidates who are still in their probationary period also benefit from the special protection and can only be dismissed in conformity with the Law of 19 March 1991.

(b) Serious cause

1408. Articles 4 through 13 of the Law of 19 March 1991 establish very detailed and technical rules to be complied with by an employer who intends to dismiss a protected employee for serious cause.

1409. Within 3 working days following the discovery of the facts justifying the termination of the contract, the employer must notify his intention to terminate the contract to the employee concerned and to the trade union to which the employee belongs. This must be done by means of a registered letter which indicates all the facts justifying the termination of the contract for serious cause.

1410. Within the same time period, the employer must file a request with the President of the competent Labour Court. This request must be sent by registered mail and copies of the registered letters to the employee and his trade union must be attached to the request. If the above formalities are not respected, the procedure will have no effect.

1411. On the third working day following the day on which the employer sent the registered letters, a 5 working day negotiation period commences. The President of the Labour Court informs each of the parties individually about the procedure. The President sets a date on which the parties must appear before him and try to reconcile their differences. If no reconciliation is possible, the President will take note thereof in his decision. At the same time, the President takes a decision on the possible suspension of the contract of the employee representative during the subsequent procedure regarding the recognition of the serious cause. It should be noted that the employer does not need a decision from the President of the Labour Court on this issue where candidates are concerned: the employer may decide on his own initiative to suspend a contract with a non-elected candidate until the court has ruled on the serious cause issue.

1412. Article 9 of the Law of 19 March 1991 provides that the employer must pay the employee, during the period of suspension of the contract, a monthly amount equal to the difference between the unemployment benefits to which the employee is entitled and his normal monthly salary. The employee may not be required to reimburse the money received during the period of suspension, even if the Labour Court accepts that the contract may be terminated for serious cause. As a result, the employee concerned will receive a non-reimbursable guaranteed income during the legal proceedings, which are often lengthy.

1413. An employer who decides to proceed with the court case after the President of the Labour Court has established that no reconciliation is possible, must request the court to recognise the serious cause. This must be done by a writ of summons in accordance with the rules applicable to interim measures proceedings. The writ of summons must be served on the employee within 3 working days following the expiry of the negotiation period (for non-elected candidates) or within 3 working days following the decision by the President of the court regarding the suspension of the contract (for elected representatives).

1414. The court will then determine a time schedule, but must, in any case, hear the case within 45 days following the first court appearance of the parties. Parties may lodge an appeal against the judgment of the Labour Court within 10 days following the notification of the judgment.

1415. If the Labour Court or the Labour Court of Appeals does not recognise the serious cause, the employee will be entitled to continue performing his employment contract. If, on the other hand, the Labour Court or the Labour Court of Appeals does recognise the serious cause, the employer may terminate the agreement. The term during which this can be done takes effect on the third working day (1) following the expiry of the 10-day period during which the other party may lodge an appeal or (2) after the notification of the judgement by the Labour Court of Appeals.

(c) Economic or technical reasons

1416. The employment contracts of members of and candidates for the Works Council and the Committee for Prevention and Protection at Work can also be terminated for economic or technical reasons. The notion "economic or technical reasons" is interpreted narrowly.

1417. An employer cannot decide himself whether there are economic or technical reasons justifying the dismissal of one or more protected employees. Rather, the employer must request from the competent Joint Committee, or, if there is no such committee, the National Labour Council, a recognition of the economic or technical reasons (Art. 3(1) of the Law of 19 March 1991). Such request must be made by registered letter prior to the termination of the employment contract(s) concerned. The Joint Committee must rule on the existence of economic or technical reasons within 2 months following the request made by the employer. A decision by the Joint Committee can be appealed before the Labour Courts of Appeal.

1418. If the Joint Committee recognises that there are economic or technical reasons that justify the dismissal, the employer may proceed with the dismissal. If the decision is negative and the employer nevertheless terminates the employment agreement, the employee will be entitled to an additional indemnity (*See*, para. 1422).

1419. If the Joint Committee does not render its decision within this 2-month period, a dismissal for economic or technical reasons will only be possible in case of the closure of an undertaking or of a division thereof or in case of the dismissal of a specific category of personnel. As far as the procedures to be followed are concerned, a distinction must be made between the closure of an undertaking or of a division of an undertaking, on the one hand, and the dismissal of a specific category of personnel, on the other hand. In the first case of the closure of a whole or a division of an undertaking, the employer is not obliged to request the Labour Court to recognise the economic or technical reasons prior to the dismissal. In case of the dismissal of a specific category of personnel, the employer cannot terminate the employment contracts without having obtained prior recognition of the economic or technical reasons from the Labour Court. If the Labour Court has accepted the economic or technical reasons, the employer may notify the dismissal as from the third working day after the expiry of the appeal period or after the notification of the judgment of the Labour Court of Appeals. During the proceedings and until a final decision has been made, the employer must continue to employ the protected employee.

(d) Sanctions

1420. Articles 14 to 19 of the Law of 19 March 1991 set forth the sanctions related to an unjustified dismissal of a protected employee, *i.e.,* a dismissal carried out without observance of the afore-mentioned conditions and procedures.

1421. In case of an unjustified dismissal, the employee, or his trade union, may file a request by registered letter to be reinstated in the undertaking. This must be done within 30 days following the notification of the termination with notice, or following the date of termination without notice, or within 30 days following the presentation of the candidates if the termination precedes the announcement of the dismissed employee's candidacy. Only in the event of a dismissal prior to the announcement of the terminated employee's candidacy is the employee obliged to request reinstatement. In all other situations, the employee may directly claim a special indemnity.

1422. A dismissed employee who opts for the special indemnity and does not request to be reinstated will be entitled to an indemnity of 2, 3 or 4 years' salary, depending on whether the employee has been employed by the company for less than 10 years, more than 10 years but less than 20 years, or more than 20 years.

1423. In addition, the payment of the special indemnity does not prevent the employee from claiming damages for abusive dismissal or on any other grounds, if applicable.

However, the special indemnity cannot be cumulated with the normal indemnity in lieu of notice.

1424. If the employer refuses to reinstate the dismissed employee within 30 days after the request, the employee will be entitled to the special indemnity described above, plus an additional indemnity equal to his normal salary for the remaining part of the 4-year term following the date of dismissal. As a result, an employer who dismissed during the first year of his term a protected employee with 20 years' seniority for an unjustified reason, and who rejected the employee's request for reinstatement will have to pay an indemnity to the employee equal to 7 years' salary (4 years' special indemnity plus salary for the 3 remaining years of the employee's 4-year term).

ii. Trade union delegates

1425. Members of trade union delegations also benefit from special protection against dismissal. Article 18 of Collective Bargaining Agreement No. 5 of 24 May 1971 provides that trade union delegates may not be dismissed for reasons related to the exercise of their mandate.

1426. Unless the employer intends to dismiss a delegate for serious cause, he must previously inform the trade union delegation, as well as the trade union that has nominated the delegate, of his intention to dismiss the delegate. This notification must be sent by registered mail and will have effect on the third working day following the day on which it was sent.

1427. The trade union has 7 days to reject the validity of the proposed dismissal by registered letter. If the trade union fails to react within this 7-day period, it will be considered to have agreed with the dismissal. In case of a timely rejection by the trade union, any party may submit the case to the conciliation bureau of the competent Joint Committee. The employee cannot be dismissed during the procedure before the Joint Committee. The conciliation bureau has 30 days to reach a unanimous decision. Failing unanimous agreement, the case will be referred to the Labour Court.

1428. When a trade union delegate is dismissed for serious cause, the trade union must be informed immediately. A notification prior to the dismissal is not required, however.

1429. A special indemnity will be due to the dismissed trade union delegate when the employer has failed to observe the procedure of Article 18 of Collective Bargaining Agreement No. 5, or when the grounds for dismissal have been found to be invalid by a final decision of the conciliation bureau or the Labour Court, or when the purported serious cause has not been accepted by the Labour Court or when the contract has been terminated for serious cause committed by the employer.

1430. The indemnity amounts to the delegate's gross remuneration for 1 year. This indemnity can be cumulated with the indemnity in lieu of notice, but not with the special indemnity due in case of violation of the protection enjoyed by the personnel representatives in the Works Council or in the Committee for Prevention and Protection at Work.

iii. Pregnant women

1431. Article 40 of the Law of 16 March 1971 protects pregnant women against dismissal by their employer for reasons connected with their physical condition.

1432. The employer may not unilaterally terminate the employment contract as from the moment he has been informed of the employee's pregnancy until 1 month following the end of the post-delivery leave, unless he can prove that the termination is based on grounds which are not connected with the pregnancy or delivery. Legitimate grounds for termination can be economic or technical, but may also be related to the personal behaviour of the employee. It is not important how the employer has been informed about the pregnancy. The protection against dismissal also applies during the probationary period.

1433. If the employer terminates the employment contract of an employee who is protected by Article 40 of the Law of 16 March 1971 without observing these conditions, the employee concerned will be entitled to a special indemnity equal to 6 months' salary in addition to the severance indemnity. This special indemnity cannot be cumulated with an indemnity for abusive dismissal unless the latter indemnity is claimed on the grounds of a fault which is unrelated to the violation of Article 40 of the Law of 16 March 1971.

8. Abusive dismissal

1434. Both blue-collar and white-collar employees are entitled to a special indemnity in cases of abusive dismissal by the employer. A dismissal will be deemed to be abusive if the party who terminates the contract abuses its contractual rights in doing so, and therefore disregards its obligation of executing the contract in good faith.

1435. Blue-collar employees receive special protection under Article 63 of the LEC which provides that abusive dismissal will be found to exist if the reasons for termination of a contract of indefinite duration are unrelated to the skills or conduct of the employee or to the operating requirements of the employer's company or service.

1436. The employer bears the burden of proof. In case of an abusive dismissal, the blue-collar employee is entitled to a special indemnity equal to 6 months' remuneration in addition to his normal severance pay or notice period.

1437. The LEC does not provide for a specific indemnity in case of abusive dismissal of white-collar employees. Moreover, white-collar employees bear the burden of proof as to the abusive character of their dismissal. If, in a particular case, the Labour Court rules that the dismissal was abusive, it will determine an indemnity based on principles of equity.

1438. It must be noted that an employer who has dismissed an employee for serious cause, but who fails to persuade the Labour Court that such dismissal was justified, will not necessarily be condemned to pay an indemnity for abusive dismissal. The indemnity in lieu of notice is deemed to cover the injury resulting from the termination of the contract. A special indemnity for abusive dismissal will only be due if the termination has given rise to additional (material or moral) injury, *i.e.*, injury that is unrelated to the dismissal as such.

9. Collective redundancy

1439. The dismissal of several employees within a short period of time without the cessation of the employer's or the company's main activities or the activities of one of its divisions may result in additional liabilities for the employer. In the event of a collective redundancy, the employer must meet certain information and consultation obligations and pay a special indemnity. The notion of "collective redundancy" is not completely identical, however, in these 2 contexts.

i. Information and consultation obligations

1440. The procedures regarding disclosure of information to and consultation with personnel representatives in case of collective redundancy are laid down in Collective Bargaining Agreement No. 24 of 2 October 1975 ("CBA No. 24") and in the Royal Decree of 24 May 1976, implementing EC Council Directive No. 75/129 of 17 February 1975. This Directive has in the meantime been replaced by EC Council Directive No. 98/50 of 20 June 1998 (O.J. [1998] 201/88). Chapter VII of the Law of 13 February 1998 (the "Law on Collective Redundancy") contains supplementary provisions that are aimed at enhancing the effectiveness of the existing provisions.

(a) Definition of collective redundancy

1441. A collective redundancy is defined as any redundancy on economic or technical grounds affecting, over an uninterrupted period of 60 days:

(1) at least 10 employees in undertakings which employed more than 20 but less than 100 persons during the previous calendar year;

(2) at least 10% of the employees in undertakings where the average number of employees employed during the calendar year preceding the dismissal was at least 100 and not higher than 300; or

(3) at least 30 employees in undertakings where the average number of employees employed during the calendar year preceding the dismissal was at least 300 employees.

1442. The rules governing collective redundancy apply to undertakings which employed on average more than 20 employees during the previous calendar year.

1443. Employees whose employment contract is terminated because it had been entered into for a specific period or for a specific project and the period has expired or the task has been completed are not included in the calculation of the number of employees who are made redundant.

1444. Employees who are dismissed for cause (for example lack of skills or negligence) or serious cause are not taken into account either.

(b) Procedural requirements

1445. An employer who intends to proceed with a collective redundancy must first inform and consult the employees' representatives in the Works Council or the trade union delegation. In the absence of a formal employees' representation, the information must be transmitted directly to the personnel or its other informal representatives.

1446. In a first stage, the employees must be notified in writing of the employer's intention to proceed with a collective redundancy. The employer must give sufficient background information to the employees so as to allow them to enter into discussions during which they can formulate suggestions or objections. CBA No. 24 lists the information which must in any event be communicated to the representatives (reasons for the intended redundancy, number of employees to be made redundant, period during which this redundancy will take place, *etc.*). A copy of this notification must be sent to the director of the sub-regional employment office. The representatives must then be given the opportunity to formulate their opinions, suggestions, objections and questions, which the employer must address and answer, in order to guarantee the continuity of the dialogue. The employer must inform the employees about the consequences of the possible execution of his intentions.

1447. The consultation should aim at considering the possibilities of avoiding or reducing the extent of the collective redundancy as well as the mitigation of its consequences by accompanying social measures such as aid for the outplacement and retraining of the employees who are made redundant.

1448. The Works Council will determine the general criteria to be applied for the redundancy of employees (age, seniority, and so on) but only the employer will have the final word on whether a collective redundancy will take place.

1449. After the consultation procedure has ended, the employer must inform the director of the sub-regional employment office by registered mail about his intention to proceed with a collective redundancy so that the necessary measures can be taken in order to mitigate the consequences, which the collective redundancy entails for the situation on the labour market, in order to safeguard the continuity of the employment as much as possible. The Royal Decree of 24 May 1976 determines which information in particular must be included in this communication. In addition, the employer must provide a copy of this notification to the personnel representatives and to the employees whose employment agreement has already been terminated within the framework of the collective redundancy but before the threshold for collective redundancy was met (*i.e.*, if it appears only afterwards that, given the number of dismissals over an uninterrupted period of 60 days, a collective redundancy, within the meaning of the Law on Collective Redundancy is deemed to exist). The notification must also be affixed in the company. Notice of termination may not be given during a cooling-off period of 30 days from the mailing date of the notification to the sub-regional employment office. The director of the sub-regional employment office may, at the request of the employer, at his sole discretion reduce this period in case of a collective redundancy following a plant closure which is not the result of a court decision. The director may also extend the period for 30 days. The employer may lodge an appeal with the executive board of the sub-regional employment office against the decision to extend the cooling-off period. The executive board must decide on such an appeal within 30 days. After the cooling-off period, the employer may proceed with the redundancies.

1450. An employer who fails to comply with the above rules exposes himself to criminal sanctions (imprisonment of eight days to 1 month and/or fines).

ii. Supplementary indemnity

1451. In the event of a collective redundancy, the employer will have to pay a special indemnity to the employees concerned.

1452. The notion of collective redundancy in this context is slightly different from the one used in order to determine whether or not an employer must inform and consult personnel representatives and the sub-regional employment office. For the purpose of the indemnity, Article 2 of Collective Bargaining Agreement No. 10 of 8 May 1973 defines "collective redundancy" as any redundancy for economic or technical grounds affecting, over an uninterrupted period of 60 days, at least 10 per cent of the average number of employees employed during the previous calendar year. However, in an undertaking employing 20 to 59 employees, there will be a collective redundancy when at least six employees are dismissed in a 60-day period.

1453. If a collective redundancy is found to have taken place, all employees who were hired for an indefinite period of time, whose employment contract was terminated in the context of the collective redundancy, and who receive unemployment benefits, are entitled to a special indemnity. Unemployed employees who do not receive unemployment benefits for reasons independent of their will, employees who have found new employment but with a lower salary and employees who have taken up a professional training and receive a remuneration that is lower than their previous salary, are granted the same rights as employees who receive unemployment benefits.

1454. The special indemnity equals 50 per cent of the difference between the unemployment benefit or the net income earned in new employment/professional training and the so-called net "reference income". The net "reference income" is equal to the gross monthly salary, limited to a maximum ceiling which is revised periodically, less social security contributions and tax deductions. The maximum ceiling amounts to € 2,579.08 per month.

1455. The indemnity is due during a period of 4 months as from the termination of the employment agreement or upon the expiry of the period which is covered by an indemnity in lieu of notice. However, the indemnity is reduced by one month for each month of the notice period (or indemnity in lieu thereof) that exceeds 3 months. Thus, employees entitled to a notice period of seven months or more are not entitled to the supplementary indemnity.

1456. The indemnity cannot be combined with the indemnities for unjustified dismissal that are due to protected employees or trade union delegates or the plant closure indemnity.

10. Plant closure

i. Definition

1457. The Law of 28 June 1966 on the Indemnity to Be Paid to Employees who are Dismissed in the Context of a Plant Closure (*Wet betreffende de schadeloosstelling van de werknemers die ontslagen worden bij sluiting van ondernemingen/Loi relative à l'indemnisation des travailleurs licenciés en cas de fermeture d'entreprises* – the "Law of 28 June 1966") applies to undertakings which have employed at least 20 employees on average during the previous calendar year. A company division where, on average, at least 20 employees were employed during the previous calendar year will also be considered to fall within the scope of the Law of 28 June 1966. Non-profit organisations, professional organisations and interim offices are not covered by the Law.

1458. According to Article 2 of the Law of 28 June 1966, a plant closure will be deemed to have occurred when the 2 following conditions are met:
    (a) permanent cessation of the main activity of an undertaking or of one of its divisions; and
    (b) the number of employees of the undertaking or of the division concerned decreases below 25 per cent of the average number of employees during the previous calendar year.

1459. The plant closure will be deemed to have taken place on the first day of the month following the month in which the second condition set forth above is met.

   ii. Procedural requirements

1460. The Works Council or trade union delegation must be consulted before the decision to close the plant is taken, and, in any event, before the decision is publicly announced. The information must deal with the impact of the closure on employment prospects, the organisation of the work and employment policy in general.

1461. The employer who decides to close his plant or a division of it must inform his personnel of the fact by displaying a dated and signed notice in a visible place in the company. The decision must also be notified, preferably in writing, to the Works Council or the trade union delegation.

1462. Also, on the day of the notification of the personnel, a notification must be sent by registered letter to the Minister of Labour, the Minister of Economic Affairs, the director of the sub-regional employment office, the President of the competent Joint Committee and the Closure Fund *(Fonds tot vergoeding van de in geval van sluiting van onderneming ontslagen werknemers/Fonds d'indemnisation des travailleurs licenciés en cas de fermeture d'entreprise)*. The Closure Fund is financed by contributions made by all employers, the amount of which is determined in a Royal Decree.

1463. The above-mentioned notices must contain the following information (Art. 5 of the Royal Decree of 20 September 1967):
    (a) name and address of the undertaking;

(b) nature of the activity of the undertaking or division of it;

(c) the anticipated date of cessation of the main activity of the undertaking;

(d) a complete list of personnel employed on the date of notification, indicating for each employee: full name and address; date of birth; date of hiring; the statutory minimum notice period applicable; family situation; profession and professional capacities.

1464. Once the plant closure has taken place, the employer must, within 15 days, inform the Closure Fund by registered letter of the following (Art. 8 of the Royal Decree of 20 September 1967):

(a) the name and address of the undertaking;

(b) the nature of the activity of the undertaking or division of it;

(c) the competent Joint Committee;

(d) the number of employees in the undertaking, or division of it, during each of the 12 months preceding the closure;

(e) in alphabetical order, a list of the employees with at least 5 years' seniority whose employment contract of indefinite duration has been terminated during the 12 months preceding the plant closure or at the moment of the closure, listing for each employee: full name and address; date of hiring; by whom and how the employment agreement was terminated; the date on which the notice period took effect or on which the employment agreement was terminated; the amount of any closure premium paid and the date of payment; and the number of the employee's bank account.

1465. Finally, during a period of 12 months following the closure, the employer must inform the Closure Fund within 15 days of any dismissal of an employee bound by an employment agreement of indefinite duration and having at least 5 years' seniority. The notification must be made by registered letter and contain the same information as listed above. A limited number of Joint Committees have issued additional notification requirements. An employer who fails to comply with these requirements is exposed to criminal sanctions.

1466. When the plant closure is followed by a collective redundancy, both procedures for information and consultation of the personnel must be applied simultaneously.

iii. Closure premium

1467. The employer must pay a closure premium to all employees:

(a) having at least one year's seniority in the company;

(b) who are employed for an indefinite duration.

(c) who are not dismissed for serious cause;

(d) who are dismissed within a period beginning 12 months (for blue-collar employees) or 18 months (for white-collar employees) prior to the plant closure and ending 12 months after the date of closure.

1468. The employee is no longer entitled to the closure premium if he was transferred to another company while keeping his remuneration and seniority provided that his employment is not terminated by the new employer within a period of 6 months and he has not refused an offer of employment from another employer.

1469. The period of 12 months after the closure date is extended to 3 years for personnel who were involved in the winding up of the undertaking.

1470. Eligible employees are entitled to a plant closure premium of € 123.69 per full year of seniority up to a maximum of € 2,473.80 and € 123.69 per year that the employer is older than 45, up to a maximum of € 2,473.80 (the latter figure is for 2003 and is indexed yearly).

1471. The closure premium must be paid within 15 days after the closure date or the termination of the employment contract. If an employer fails to pay the premium within this time limit, the premium will be paid by the Closure Fund which will then have a claim against the employer for all amounts paid.

1472. The closure premium can be cumulated with an indemnity in lieu of notice, unemployment benefits and the special indemnities for protected employees.

11. Agreed early pension

1473. The system of agreed early pension (*conventioneel brugpensioen/prépension conventionnelle*) is an early retirement scheme for dismissed employees who meet certain requirements and which consists of a combination of unemployment benefits paid by the social security institutions and a supplementary allowance paid by the employer. The system of agreed early pension was introduced by Collective Bargaining Agreement No. 17 of 19 December 1974. Collective Bargaining Agreement No. 55 of 13 July 1993 has introduced the possibility of a half-time early retirement scheme which will, however, not be discussed in this book.

i. Conditions

1474. The Royal Decree of 7 December 1992 imposes a number of conditions which must be met in order for an employee to be entitled to an agreed early pension. These are discussed below.

(a) Age requirement

1475. Generally, in order to be entitled to an agreed early pension, the employee must be at least 58 years of age. This minimum age requirement must be met at the time when the employee effectively ceases his employment (for example, at the end of his notice period or at the time of termination of the contract).

1476. Collective bargaining agreements at industry or company level may deviate from this age requirement. However, in order for more favourable rules regarding unemployment benefits to apply, the age requirement must be determined at 58 years of age minimum.

1477. Some collective bargaining agreements can, under certain conditions, provide for a lower minimum age. Companies experiencing financial difficulties or which are in the process of restructuring may apply a minimum age requirement of 50 years of age.

(b) Seniority requirement

1478. The employee must have been an employee for at least 25 years. It is irrelevant whether such employment has been with the same employer. In order to determine whether the seniority requirement is met, account is also taken of the period of military service and certain periods of leave of absence during which the employee raised his children. There are a number of exceptions where a seniority of less than 25 years will suffice or where a seniority of more than 25 years is required.

(c) Nature of the dismissal

1479. An employee can only be entitled to an agreed early pension if he is dismissed for a reason other than serious cause. The employer must at least observe the statutory notice period provided for in the LEC or the notice period provided for in the applicable specific collective bargaining agreement, if any. The latter condition does not apply to undertakings experiencing financial difficulties or which are in the process of restructuring.

(d) Unemployment benefits

1480. The employee must be eligible for unemployment benefits. The payment by the employer of the early pension allowance is related to the right of the employee to unemployment benefits: the employer can request proof from the employee that he is entitled to such benefits.

(e) Additional early pension allowance

1481. The employee must be entitled to the additional early pension allowance, referred to in Collective Bargaining Agreement No. 17 or another collective bargaining agreement entered into at industry or company level.

ii. Payments and contributions under the early pension scheme

1482. The amount of the early pension allowance paid by the employer is equal to 50 per cent of the difference between the net reference income and the unemployment benefit payable.

1483. The net reference income is equal to the gross monthly salary, limited to a maximum ceiling which is revised periodically, less social security contributions and tax deductions. The maximum ceiling amounts to approximately € 2,900.10 per month.

1484. In addition, the employee is entitled to unemployment benefit, which is calculated on the basis of 60 per cent of his last salary before early pension. The unemployment benefit is limited to a maximum of approximately € 985.92.

1485. The employer must deduct from the early pension allowance a contribution of 3.5 per cent for the benefit of the pension sector. The early pension allowance is also subject to a solidarity contribution of 3 per cent.

1486. Depending on the family status of the employee and his last salary before early pension, the maximum supplementary allowance to which he will be entitled will amount to approximately € 400 per month.

1487. For each employee who receives an agreed early pension, the employer must pay a monthly contribution ranging from € 24.79 to € 111.55 to the unemployment authorities. In addition, a monthly contribution of € 24.79 is due to the pension authorities for each employee benefiting from an agreed early pension.

iii. Replacement requirement

1488. The employee must be replaced by one or 2 unemployed persons who are fully entitled to unemployment benefit. The number of hours to be performed by the substitutes must at least be equal to those performed on average by the employee who will benefit from the agreed early pension.

1489. In certain exceptional cases, the replacement requirement can be waived. In addition, the replacement requirement does not apply if the employee is older than 60 years (Art. 4, para. 7 of the Royal Decree of 7 December 1992).

1490. In order to comply with the replacement requirement the substitutes may not have been employed by the company concerned during the 6 months prior to the date on which they are engaged. There are a limited number of exceptions to this principle (Art. 4, para. 4 of the Royal Decree of 7 December 1992). Moreover, the company is obliged to keep the substitute(s) employed for a period of at least 36 months. However, within 30 days of his employment, the substitute can be replaced by another unemployed person (Art. 4, para. 6 of the Royal Decree of 7 December 1992).

1491. The employer must provide evidence of his compliance with the replacement requirement to the regional employment office *(gewestelijk werkloosheidsbureau/ bureau regional du chômage)*. Failure to comply with the replacement requirement may result in administrative fines and damages (Art. 6 of the Royal Decree of 7 December 1992), but will not result in the early pension being disallowed.

   iv. Derogations for companies experiencing financial difficulties or which are in the process of restructuring

1492. Certain conditions outlined above do not apply or are applied more leniently in the case of companies experiencing financial difficulties or which are are in the process of restructuring. In order to benefit from these derogations, the companies must meet the criteria set out in Article 9, paragraphs 1 and 1*bis* (companies with financial difficulties) or Article 9, paragraphs 2 and 3 (companies in the process of restructuring) of the Royal Decree of 7 December 1992. In addition, the companies must prove that they meet these criteria to the competent ministry and must receive formal recognition. The above derogations relate to the age and seniority requirements, the notice period to be granted to the employee and the replacement requirement.

   12. Social documents to be delivered upon termination

1493. Regardless of the reasons for the termination of an employment contract, the employer must deliver to the employee the following documents (Art. 21 of the LEC):
   (i) the certificate of employment *(getuigschrift van tewerkstelling/certificat de travail)* indicating the start and termination date of the employment agreement and the nature of the work. No additional information may be added save upon the employee's explicit request;
   (ii) the unemployment certificate *(werkloosheidsattest/certificat de chômage)* and information sheet (the so-called "C4"-form). This latter certificate provides all relevant information for the calculation of unemployment benefit. The employer must also indicate on this certificate the reason for termination of the contract. The termination of an employment contract does not need to be motivated in order to be valid, but the unemployment office requires this

information in order to determine whether the employee is entitled to un-employment benefit;

(iii) holiday certificate for white-collar employees *(vakantieattest/attestation de vacances),* which indicates the period during which the employee was em-ployed (or any equivalent periods), the gross amount of the holiday pay due and the percentage taken into account for the calculation of the holiday pay; this certificate allows a new employer to determine the rights of the employee with regard to future vacation;

(iv) statement of salary due *(afrekening van het nog verschuldigde loon/ décompte de paie pour les dernières prestations effectuées),* which allows the employee to verify whether he has received all amounts due (salary, premium, end-of-employment holiday pay, indemnity in lieu of notice, *etc.*) and to determine the amount of social security contributions and taxes which have been with-held;

(v) individual account for the current year *(individuele rekening voor het lopende jaar/compte individuel pour l'année en cours),* which contains all informa-tion concerning the salary paid from 1 January until the date of termination;

(vi) salary slip no. 281.10 *(loonfiche/fiche fiscale),* which must be joined to the employee's tax return; and

(vii) proof of payment of the contribution for health insurance *(bijdragebon voor ziekte en invaliditeitsverzekering/bon de cotisation pour l'assurance maladie-invalidité).*

1494. Many employers use the services of payroll agencies to prepare the above docu-ments.

§12. Interim Employment

1495. Interim employment is regulated by the Law of 24 July 1987 on Interim Employ-ment *(Wet betreffende de tijdelijke arbeid, de uitzendarbeid en het ter beschikking stellen van werknemers ten behoeve van gebruikers/Loi sur le travail temporaire, le travail intérimaire et la mise de travailleurs à la disposition d'utilisateurs* – the "Law of 24 July 1987"), Collective Bargaining Agreement No. 36 of 27 November 1981 ("CBA No. 36") and Collective Bargaining Agreement No. 58 of 7 July 1994 ("CBA No. 58").

1. The contract for interim employment

1496. An interim employment contract is a contract between the interim agency and the interim worker, whereby the latter undertakes to perform authorized temporary work for a third party ("the user") against the payment of a salary (Art. 7 of the

Law of 24 July 1987). Unless it is provided otherwise, the first 3 days of the interim employment contract are regarded as the probationary period, during which the contract may be terminated by either party, without notice or indemnity.

1497. A written agreement must be entered into for each interim employee at the latest at the moment when the worker starts to be employed by the interim agency. The Law of 24 July 1987 lists a number of data which must be included in the interim employment contract.

1498. The interim worker's salary may not be lower than the salary he would be entitled to if he were employed as a normal employee by the user under the same conditions.

2. The relation between the interim agency and the user

1499. The contract between the interim agency and the user must be in writing and executed within 7 days from the moment the interim worker starts to work for the user. The Law of 24 July 1987 lists a number of data which must be included in the contract between the interim agency and the user. Any provisions in this contract according to which the user must pay damages to the interim agency in case the interim worker becomes employed by the user are deemed to be void.

3. The relation between the interim worker and the user

1500. The contract for interim work between the interim worker and the user must be in writing and executed within 2 working days as from the moment the employee starts working. Whilst the interim agency is the employer of the interim worker, it is the user who must see to the application of provisions regarding the regulation of labour and the safety of the workplace.

4. Regulation of interim work

1501. Interim work is only allowed in order to:
     (i) provide for the replacement of a normal employee;
     (ii) deal with a temporary increase in work load; or
     (iii) see to the performance of exceptional work.

1502. As regards replacement of another employee and temporary increase in the work load, CBA No. 58 imposes strict conditions as to the application procedure and the duration of interim work. As regards the performance of exceptional work, regard must be had to the requirements laid down by CBA No. 36.

1503. The employment agreement between the interim agency and the interim worker will be terminated and the latter will be deemed to be bound by an employment agreement of indefinite duration with the user if:
  (i) the user employs the interim worker or continues the employment without observing the statutory limits/procedure; and
  (ii) the user employs an interim worker in the absence of an employment agreement and/or for the performance of other than authorised temporary work.

1504. Failure to comply with the provisions of the Law of 24 July 1987 may result in criminal sanctions (imprisonment and/or fines).

§13. Putting employees at the disposal of third parties

1. Principle

1505. With the exception of temporary or interim work, as described above, natural or legal persons are not authorized to put their employees at the disposal of users, whereby the latter exercise authority over those employees. However, the user will not be deemed to exercise authority over the worker in as far as he complies with the applicable obligations relating to the worker's well-being at the workplace and in as far as he regulates working hours and or instructs the worker in the performance of his work (Art. 31 of the Law of 24 July 1987).

1506. This prohibition is aimed at preventing the subcontracting of labour.

1507. The agreement whereby an employee is employed in order to be put at the disposal of a user is void from the moment when the employee starts working for the user. When a user has work performed by employees that are put at his disposal, the user and the employees are deemed to be bound by an employment agreement for indefinite duration from the moment when the employees start working for the user. However, the employees may terminate this agreement without notice or indemnity. They are entitled to do so until the day they would normally no longer be put at the user's disposal.

1508. The user and the person putting the employees at the user's disposal are jointly and severally liable for the payment of the social security contributions, salaries, remuneration and benefits to which the employee is entitled.

2. Exceptions

1509. Besides his usual activities, an employer may put his regular employees at the disposal of a user for a limited period of time provided he obtained the prior authorisation from the Social Inspection (Art. 32 of the Law of 24 July 1987). Prior authorisation is not required when an employee is exceptionally put at the disposal of a user within the framework of a collaboration between companies belonging to an economic and financial entity or with a view to the performance of specialised tasks requiring specific skills over a short period of time. In these circumstances, the Social Inspection must be informed 24 hours beforehand.

1510. Prior to putting an employee at the disposal of a user, the relevant conditions and the duration must be laid down in writing, signed by the employer, the user and the employee. The written consent of the employee is, however, not required if the sufficiency of tacit consent is generally accepted in the sector.

C. Regulation of labour

1511. The rules referred to in this section generally apply to all employees, and usually constitute a minimum level of protection which must be granted to each employee. These rules relate, in particular, to working time (*See*, paras. 1512 *et seq.*), legal holidays (*See*, paras. 1526 *et seq.*), paid and unpaid leave (*See*, paras. 1533 *et seq.*), remuneration (*See*, paras. 1537 *et seq.*), mandatory social documents (*See*, paras. 1566 *et seq.*) and work rules (*See*, paras. 1575 *et seq.*).

§1. Working time

1. Working hours

1512. Since 1 January 1999, standard working hours may not exceed 8 hours per day or 39 hours per week. However, it is permissible to provide for a 40-hour working week whereby the extra work hour per week is compensated by time off. As from 1 January 2003, the working week will be limited to 38 hours. Although it is common practice in Belgium to limit the working week to 5 working days, the Law of 16 March 1971 (*Arbeidswet/Loi sur le travail*) provides that work may be performed during 6 days per week (Art. 11 of the Law of 16 March 1971). In many sectors, collective bargaining agreements have limited the working week to 5 working days and to 37 or 38 hours per week.

2. Overtime

1513. The Law of 16 March 1971 lists a number of exceptions where the general prohibition on overtime does not apply (Arts. 22 to 27 of the Law of 16 March 1971). These exceptions generally relate to the type of work to be performed, such as shift work, urgent work, work which may not be interrupted and work in specific sectors. In these cases, the working time limits vary according to the type of work (*e.g.* 11 hours per day for shift work; 12 hours per day (or more, in which case overtime pay is due) for work which, given its nature, may not be interrupted).

1514. As regards work which gives rise to overtime as listed by the Law of 16 March 1971 (*e.g.* shift work (Art. 22, 1°), work on inventories (Art. 22, 3°), preparatory work (Art. 24, 1°) *etc.*), a work limit of 50 hours per week applies. For exceptional cases, however, even this limit may be exceeded (*e.g.* for urgent work to machinery). Also, for certain sectors or categories of undertakings the 50-hour limit may be exceeded upon a decision to this end by the government (Art. 27, para. 3 of the Law of 16 March 1971).

1515. In most cases where overtime is allowed, the employee must be granted time off. Moreover, overtime is only allowed provided that the normal work time limits are not exceeded on average during a specific reference period (of 3 months or a longer period of a maximum of 1 year). In addition, the Law of 16 March 1971 has determined an internal limit which applies during this reference period in order to prevent an employee from accumulating too much overtime over a short period of time.

1516. Not all work performed beyond the limits mentioned in paragraph 1512 will give rise to overtime pay. Overtime pay is only due for work performed as from the tenth hour per day or fourty-first hour per week. However, when a collective bargaining agreement has reduced working hours to less than 40 hours per week (in other words, when the reduction of working hours is not the result of the application of the Royal Decree of 11 December 1998), any work performed beyond this reduced number must be considered overtime work. In addition, work performed under the conditions that apply in case of flexible working hours (*See*, para. 1522), shift work, and work which may not be interrupted, among other things, is not regarded as overtime work (and therefore, no overtime pay will be due). However, an employee who has agreed to perform overtime work in breach of the law is entitled to overtime pay.

1517. Overtime pay normally amounts to one-and-a-half times regular pay, except for overtime pay for work performed on Sundays and on legal holidays which equals twice the employee's regular pay (Art. 29, para. 2, of the Law of 16 March 1971).

1518. The rules on overtime do not apply to, among others, persons entrusted with supervisory or high-level positions (directors, managers, assistant managers, heads of department, and so on) as well as sales representatives and home workers (Art. 3 of the Law of 16 March 1971).

   3. Night work

1519. The Law of 16 March 1971 defines night work as any work performed between 8:00 p.m. and 6:00 a.m. As a general rule, night work is prohibited, but the Law of

16 March 1971 provides for a large number of exceptions to this prohibition (Arts. 36 to 37 of the Law of 16 March 1971). Night work may only be performed in the exceptional circumstances listed by the Law of 16 March 1971. The company's work schedules must be adapted accordingly pursuant to a specific procedure (Art. 38 of the Law of 16 March 1971).

1520. Mention should also be made of Collective Bargaining Agreement No. 46 ("CBA No. 46"), relating to, among other things, night-shift work. As a general rule, the workers performing night work must be volunteers with an employment contract of indefinite duration. Certain categories of workers may apply for work not involving night work. CBA No. 46 also provides for specific financial compensation. Finally, Collective Bargaining Agreement No. 76 of 18 July 2000 states that certain categories of night workers are not allowed to work more than 8 hours in each period of 24 hours. Collective bargaining agreements providing for time off or overtime pay may deviate from this prohibition.

4. Sunday work

1521. Sunday work is prohibited (Art. 11 of the Law of 16 March 1971). However, the Law of 16 March 1971 provides for a number of exceptions to this prohibition, among other things, in cases where it is impossible to carry out the work on any other day of the week (Arts. 12 through 18 of the Law of 16 March 1971).

5. Flexible working time

1522. Article 20*bis* of the Law of 16 March 1971 provides employers with the possibility of organising working hours on a flexible basis. A collective bargaining agreement or, in the absence thereof, the work rules of the company may determine the maximum working hours on a yearly basis: the afore-mentioned maximum working hours per week will be observed on average on a yearly basis. If flexible working hours are introduced following a relevant collective bargaining agreement, the company's work rules will have to be adapted.

1523. If this option is pursued, the weekly average provided by the Law of 16 March 1971 or by the relevant collective bargaining agreement must be respected over a one-year period. In addition, no working week may be more than 5 hours more or less than the standard working week. For example, if the standard working week is 38 hours, the minimum working week would be 33 hours and the maximum working week would be 43 hours. The working day may not be more than 2 hours more or less than the normal working day and may in no event exceed 9 hours. If the requirements of Article 20*bis* are complied with, no overtime pay is due.

6. New working time provisions

1524. The Law of 17 March 1987 and Collective Bargaining Agreement No. 42 of 2 June 1987 have introduced new mechanisms, the purpose of which is to create additional jobs.

1525. The new working time provisions may deviate from the general rules on working hours, overtime, night work and Sunday work. They are introduced by a collective bargaining agreement at industry or company level, or, in the absence of a trade union delegation in the company, through a specific procedure by which the employees are individually informed about the employer's intentions in this regard and by which they are given the opportunity to formulate their remarks.

§2. Public holidays and paid vacation

1. Public holidays

1526. There are 10 public holidays in Belgium (Art. 1 of the Royal Decree of 18 April 1974): New Year's Day (1 January), Easter Monday, Labour Day (1 May), Ascension Day, Whit Monday, National Day (21 July), Assumption (15 August), All Saints Day (1 November), Armistice Day (11 November) and Christmas (25 December).

1527. When a public holiday falls on a Sunday or another day on which the employees would normally not work, employees are entitled to an additional day off (Art. 6 of the Law of 4 January 1974 regarding Public Holidays – *Wet betreffende de feestdagen/Loi relative aux jours fériés*). That day will be determined by the competent Joint Committee, by the Works Council, or by mutual agreement between the employer and the employees. If the replacement day has not been determined, the public holiday is replaced by the first working day following the public holiday. Employees are entitled to salary for public holidays or replacement days (Art. 14 of the Law of 4 January 1974).

2. Paid holiday

1528. Employees are entitled to 2 days of paid holiday per month worked during the previous calendar year in the case of a 6-day working week (Art. 60 of the Royal Decree of 30 March 1967). For a 5-day working week, employees are entitled to 20 days of paid holiday per year (Art. 68 of the Royal Decree of 30 March 1967). Collective bargaining agreements entered into in specific sectors or industries often contain more generous provisions.

1529. During the holiday period, all white-collar employees are entitled to a holiday allowance. They will receive:

(i) the normal remuneration for each holiday *(enkel vakantiegeld/simple pécule de vacances)*;

(ii) an extra holiday allowance corresponding to 92 per cent of the gross remuneration due for the month during which the employee takes his principal holiday *(dubbel vakantiegeld/double pécule de vacances)*.

1530. Because an employee earns his holiday for 2004 by working in 2003, his employer will have to pay him a holiday departure indemnity if the employee leaves his employment, for whatever reason, during the course of 2003. This indemnity, which amounts to 15.34% of the remuneration paid by the employer in 2003, is an anticipated payment of the 2004 holiday allowance and will therefore be deducted from the holiday allowance normally due by the new employer in 2004.

1531. In addition, if, at the time an employee leaves a job, he has not yet taken all his holiday days which he was allowed to take during that year, the employer must pay 15.34% of the remuneration received in the course of the previous year, reduced on a *pro rata* basis taking into account the holiday already taken.

1532. The system for blue-collar employees is different. The employer does not pay any salary for the holiday days, but the employee receives from the competent Holiday Fund a holiday allowance which amounts to 15.34% of the remuneration declared for social security purposes during the year preceding the year in which the holiday is taken. These Holiday Funds are financed by employers' contributions.

§3. *Paid and unpaid leave*

1. *Paid leave*

1533. In addition to the annual vacation, Article 30 of the LEC expressly authorises all employees to take paid leave, among other things, for certain family events. The Royal Decree of 28 August 1963 lists the situations where employees are entitled to take paid leave. For instance, employees are entitled to:

(i) 2 days for their wedding;

(ii) 3 days for the birth of a child;

(iii) 3 days for the death of a spouse or a child;

(iv) one day for the wedding of a child; and

(v) 3 days for the death of a parent.

1534. Individual collective bargaining agreements may provide for additional situations which entitle employees to paid leave.

1535. The Repair Law of 22 January 1985 containing Social Provisions *(Herstelwet houdende sociale bepalingen/Loi de redressement contenant des dispositions so-*

cials) entitles employees to take paid educational leave to attend recognised educational programmes. The organisation of the system of paid educational leave is conducted by the Works Council of the undertaking or by agreement between the employer and the employees or their representatives. Employees pursuing an education may be absent from work and maintain their normal remuneration for a maximum duration of 120 hours per year for a professional education, 80 hours per year for a general education and 120 hours per year in case the employee simultaneously follows a professional and a general education. There are a number of exceptions to these limits. The salary to which the employee is entitled under this law, is limited to € 1,920.00 per month (as per 1 January 2002). The employer may claim the reimbursement of the salary and the social security costs with regard to the educational leave from the Ministry of Employment.

2. Unpaid leave

1536. Collective Bargaining Agreement No. 45 of 19 December 1989 provides that employees are entitled to a maximum of 10 days per calendar year of unpaid leave of absence for unforeseeable reasons, such as the illness of a relative.

§4. Remuneration

1. Concept of remuneration

1537. In general, remuneration covers all benefits paid to an employee by the employer as compensation for the work performed in the context of an employment contract. However, the precise concept of remuneration may differ depending on the rules applied.

1538. Since the judgment of the Supreme Court of 9 September 1985 (*Cass.*, 9 September 1985, *R.W.*, 1985-86, 2692), it is generally accepted that end-of-year premiums or bonuses are part of an employee's remuneration, and must be paid to the employee on a pro rata basis if the employment contract is terminated before the normal date of payment of the premium. The employment contract itself or the relevant collective bargaining agreements may, however, provide exceptions to or modify this rule.

2. Determination of the level of remuneration

1539. In principle, the contracting parties are free to determine the level of remuneration. Typically, the remuneration will be a fixed amount, a variable commission fee or a combination of both. However, in most industrial sectors, collective bargaining agreements set minimum wages for each category of employee or function. In so far as minimum wages are determined by collective bargaining agreements, the parties to an employment agreement may not deviate from such provisions. For those sectors where no specific collective bargaining agreement exists, national Collective Bargaining Agreement No. 43 of 2 May 1988 imposes a guaranteed minimum monthly gross remuneration of approximately € 1,200. This amount is adjusted on a regular basis with reference to the index for consumer products. The guaranteed monthly remuneration for employees who are less than 21 years old is a percentage of the above amount, ranging from 70 per cent for 16 year olds to 94 per cent for 20 year olds.

1540. Since the early 1980s, the government has taken a number of measures by which the basic freedom to determine the level of remuneration has been limited to a certain extent. The Law of 26 July 1996 for the Promotion of the Employment and the Preventive Protection of the Ability to Compete (*Wet tot bevordering van de werkgelegenheid en tot preventieve vrijwaring van het concurrentievermogen/Loi relative à la promotion de l'emploi et à la sauvegarde préventive de la compétitivité*) constitutes the most recent development in this respect. It relates to the development of the employment in Belgium and ensures that the employment costs in Belgium and its 3 neighbouring countries are monitored. On the basis of this information, the social partners may take employment measures and determine the margin for the employment cost development. Failing agreement, the government will intervene. At present, 2 sets of measures as regards the determination of salaries are applicable as a result of government intervention. These measures have regard to, on the one hand, the manner in which salaries are adapted to the index for consumer products and, on the other hand, the margin for development of the employment cost.

1541. Collective Bargaining Agreement No. 25 of 15 October 1975 ("CBA No. 25") implements the principle that all men and women should receive equal pay for equal work. Article 5 of CBA no 25 gives employees the right to sue their employers to enforce the right for equal pay. Article 7 of CBA No. 25 grants special protection to employees who have filed a complaint against the employer for infringement of the equality principle. If the employer terminates the employment contract within a period of 12 months following the date on which the employee concerned filed a complaint against the employer, the employer will have to prove that the dismissal was unrelated to the fact that a complaint was filed. If the employer cannot justify the dismissal, he will have to reinstate the dismissed employee who must file a request to that effect within 30 days following the termination or the notification of the termination. If the dismissal cannot be justified and the employer refuses to reinstate the employee, the employee will be entitled to a special indemnity equal to 6 months' salary or an indemnity for the actual injury suffered, at the employee's choice.

3. Payment and protection of the remuneration

1542. The Law of 12 April 1965 on the Protection of Remuneration of Employees (*Wet betreffende de bescherming van het loon der werknemers/Loi concernant la protection de la rémunération des travailleurs* – the "Law of 12 April 1965") and its implementing legislation provide the employees with considerable protection with regard to their remuneration. The basic principle is that the employer may not in any manner whatsoever limit or restrict the employee's freedom to use his remuneration as he wishes (Art. 3 of the Law of 12 April 1965).

1543. For the purposes of this law, remuneration includes (Art. 2 of the Law of 12 April 1965):
    (i) any cash salary that an employee is entitled to receive from his employer by virtue of his employment;
    (ii) any tips or service charges that an employee is entitled to receive by virtue of his employment or by custom; and
    (iii) any fringe benefits capable of being quantified that an employee is entitled to receive from his employer by virtue of his employment.

1544. As of 1 January 2002, the remuneration must be paid in Euros if the employee is employed in Belgium. If the employee is employed abroad, his remuneration must, if he so requests, be paid wholly or partially in the currency of the country where he is employed (Art. 7 of Collective Bargaining Agreement No. 69 of 17 July 1998 and Article 4 of the Law of 12 April 1965).

1545. Article 6 of the Law of 12 April 1965 lays down the conditions under which part of the employee's remuneration may be paid in kind if this form of payment is customary or desirable. In any event, payment in kind should not normally exceed 20 per cent of the total remuneration, subject to exceptions if the employer provides the employee with housing.

1546. Blue-collar employees must be paid at least twice a month, at intervals not exceeding 16 days, and white-collar employees must be paid at least once a month (Art. 9 of the Law of 12 April 1965). Overtime must be paid at the same time as the normal remuneration due for that time period. Unless otherwise provided in collective bargaining agreements or work regulations, remuneration must be paid within 4 days following the period during which the work was performed. For every payment, the employer must give a statement of account to the employee. When an employment contract expires or is terminated, for whatever reason, any remuneration still due must be paid without delay and in any event by the first normal payment day following the end of the employment (Art. 11 of the Law of 12 April 1965).

1547. Remuneration automatically bears interest (currently at a rate of 7 per cent per year) from the date on which it may be claimed (Art. 10 of the Law of 12 April 1965). The interest is to be calculated on the net amount of remuneration to which the employee is entitled.

1548. Article 23 of the Law of 12 April 1965 specifies the nature and the maximum amount of the employee's remuneration which an employer may withhold. Only the following sums may be withheld: the employee's social security contributions, contributions towards group insurance or other contractual insurance plans, payroll tax, fines based on the applicable work rules, damages resulting from the employee's misconduct to the extent permitted by the LEC, cash advances received by the employee and the amount of the security provided as a guarantee for the performance of the employee's obligations. Unless the employer and the employee explicitly agree otherwise, the employer may not withhold any other amount without the prior authorisation of a court.

1549. The employer must withhold social security contributions and payroll tax. If the employer does not withhold social security contributions, he will himself be held liable for these payments without any possibility of claiming reimbursement from the employee. As far as the payroll tax is concerned, the situation is different. If not enough payroll tax has been withheld, the employer will be allowed to claim the difference from the employee. However, any fines or interest due because of the employer's failure to withhold the payroll tax must be paid by the employer.

1550. The total amounts withheld may not exceed 20 per cent of the remuneration due, after deduction of social security contributions, contractual insurance plan premiums and the payroll tax.

1551. Articles 1409 through 1412 of the Judicial Code and Articles 27 through 35 of the Law of 12 April 1965 specify in detail the conditions for attachment of remuneration by a creditor and for assignment of remuneration by an employee. The maximum amounts which can be attached or assigned are statutorily limited. No attachments or assignments are permitted if the employee concerned earns less than € 857 net per month. Between € 857 and € 1,111 net per month certain percentages qualify for attachment or assignment. Remuneration exceeding € 1,111 net per month can be attached or assigned in its entirety.

§1. *Prevention of violence, moral harassment and sexual harassment at work*

1552. Article 32*ter* of the Law of 4 August 1996 relating to the Well-being of the Employees in the Execution of their Work (*Wet betreffende het welzijn van de werknemers bij de uitvoering van hun werk/Loi relative au bien-être des travailleurs* *lors de l'exécution de leur travail*) protects employees against any form of violence, moral harassment or sexual harassment at work even if this emanates from outside the undertaking or is perpetrated by third parties who are present on the work premises (for example, customers, suppliers or service providers). This legal provision has been implemented by a Royal Decree of 11 July 2002.

1553. Article 32*ter*, 1° of the Law of 4 August 1996 defines "violence at work" as any incident where an employee is psychologically or physically disturbed, threatened or attacked while carrying out his/her work.

1554. "Moral harassment at work" is defined as any illegal and recurrent behaviour (in the form of speech, gestures or writing) inside or outside the undertaking which (i) is aimed at or results in affecting the personality, the dignity or the physical or mental integrity of an employee carrying out his/her work; (ii) is aimed at or results in putting the harassed employee's job at risk; or (iii) is aimed at or results in the creation of a threatening, hostile, offensive or humiliating environment (Art. 32*ter*, 2° of the Law of 4 August 1996).

1555. Finally, "sexual harassment at work" is any form of verbal, non-verbal or physical behaviour of a sexual nature which the perpetrator knows or ought to know is detrimental to the dignity of men and women at work.

1556. As of 1 July 2002, the employer's obligations to combat violence, moral harassment and sexual harassment at work are as follows:
  (i) all employers in the private and public sector (with the exception of employers of household personnel) must include in their annual action plan and in their global prevention plan a specific section dedicated to measures to combat violence and moral or sexual harassment at work after having carried out a risk assessment;
  (ii) all measures must be approved by the employee representatives in the Committee for Prevention and Protection at Work, or if this body is not established in the undertaking, by the trade union delegation (*See*, para. 1618), and included in the work rules;
  (iii) all employers must nominate a specialised prevention officer for each technical exploitation unit (*See*, para. 1597) by 31 December 2002, whose nomination must be approved by the employee representatives in the Committee for Prevention and Protection at Work, or if this body is not established in the undertaking, by the trade union delegation (*See*, para. 1618). If the employer and the Committee for Prevention and Protection at Work or the trade union delegation do not reach an agreement or if the undertaking has less than 50 employees, the prevention officer will be appointed by an external service for

prevention and protection at work. Optionally, and in addition to the special-ised prevention officer, employers may also appoint a confidant within the undertaking;

(iv) in undertakings or organisations where employees are in contact with the public, the employer must systematically take note of the declarations of em-ployees who find themselves a victim of violence, moral harassment or sexual harassment. These declarations are kept in a special register that is accessible only to the employer, the Social Inspection, the prevention officer and, if ap-plicable, the confidant. Declarations are kept in the special register for 5 years;

(v) when the employer is informed about violence, moral or sexual harassment, he must take effective remedies and provide for appropriate psychological assistance for the victim. In case of a failure to take effective remedies, the prevention officer is obliged to report to the Social Inspection.

1557. Any employee who is of the opinion that he/she is a victim of violence, moral harassment or sexual harassment may lodge an "internal" motivated complaint with the prevention officer or the confidential officer who will, at the victim's request, try to reconcile the parties. If such reconciliation fails or is impossible, the prevention officer or confidential officer will, at the victim's express request, offi-cially register the complaint, after which the employee is protected from dismissal. If the complaint is received by the confidential officer, he/she will transmit the complaint to the prevention officer. The prevention officer will immediately in-form the employer of the complaint and will transmit to the employer a copy of the declarations of the victim and the witnesses. The prevention officer will suggest specific measures to the employer. All of these steps must be documented.

1558. If an employee so wishes, he/she may also lodge his/her complaint directly with the Social Inspection or the Labour Courts.

1559. Trade unions are in principle always entitled to initiate legal proceedings on behalf of their members, except when the employee concerned has already initiated pro-ceedings, in which case the trade union will need the employee's approval. In specific cases, non-profit organisations may initiate proceedings after approval from the employee.

1560. If the labour court finds the employee's allegations to be well-founded, the of-fender and/or the employer may be ordered to pay damages and/or to cease the acts complained of.

1561. Any employee who has lodged a complaint or on whose behalf a complaint has been lodged (either internally, with the Social Inspection or before the Labour Court) as well as all intervening witnesses are protected from dismissal and from the unilateral modification of their working conditions by the employer from the moment the complaint is lodged.

1562. This protection entails that the employer may not unilaterally terminate the employment agreement of the protected employees nor modify their working conditions except for reasons that are unrelated to the complaint, the court action or the testimony. The burden of proof that the dismissal or the modification of the working conditions was unrelated to the complaint rests with the employer. The duration of the protection is not specified in the law.

1563. The protected employee or the trade union may request the employer who unilaterally dismisses a protected employee or who unilaterally modifies that employee's working conditions, to reinstate the protected employee or to restore the working conditions of the protected employee such as they existed before the facts that gave rise to the complaint. Such a request must be made within 30 days after notification of the dismissal or modification of the working conditions. The employer must respond to such a request within 30 days. If the employer accepts the reinstatement or restores the working conditions, he must pay the remuneration which the protected employee has lost due to the dismissal or the modification of the working conditions.

1564. If the employer refuses to reinstate the protected employee or refuses to restore the working conditions such as they existed before the facts that gave rise to the complaint, he will have to pay the protected employee an indemnity of 6 months' gross salary.

1565. Moreover, the indemnity of 6 months' gross salary will also be due (i) when the court finds that the violence, moral harassment or sexual harassment is proven; (ii) when the employee terminates the employment agreement because of the employer's behaviour with regard to the complaint; or (iii) when the employer has dismissed the employee for serious cause and the court does not uphold this serious cause and finds that the dismissal is related to the complaint.

§2. Mandatory social documents

1566. Royal Decree No. 5 of 23 October 1978 ("Royal Decree No. 5") requires employers to draw up and keep certain social documents. The obligation to draw up and keep these documents is subject to specific sanctions and monitoring measures. The content and format of the social documents, the time at which they have to be drawn up and possibly remitted to the employees, the place and period of their retention are established by Royal Decree.

1567. Royal Decree No. 5 mentions 2 main social documents which must mandatorily be drawn up by the employer: the personnel register (*personeelsregister/registre du personnel*) and the individual account (*individuele rekening/compte individuel*). In addition to these two main documents which must be kept by all employers, Royal Decree No. 5 also mentions the following documents which are mandatory only in certain industry sectors: the presence list (*aanwezigheidsregister/registre de présence*), and the individual card (*individuele fiche/fiche individuelle*). Finally, the employment contract for students, which is governed by Articles 123 and 124 of the LEC, and the employment contract for home workers, which is governed by Article 119 of the LEC, are also considered to be mandatory social documents within the meaning of Royal Decree No. 5.

1. Personnel register

1568. Each employer must draw up and keep a personnel register. The register must list all employees in chronological order based on the starting date of their employment. It contains detailed information on the employer and on each employee (Art. 5 of the Royal Decree of 8 August 1980). The personnel register must be comprised of one or more bound volumes with consecutively numbered pages. The register must be kept for a period of 5 years from the date of the last legally required entry.

1569. Employers who employ all their personnel at one location must keep the personnel register at that place. If the employer employs personnel at different locations, a separate special register must also be kept at each of these locations, except at the location where the central register is kept. The special registers contain less detailed information than the central register. Certain categories of employers are exempted from the obligation to keep a special personnel register.

2. Individual account

1570. Each employer must establish and maintain for every employee an individual account for each year. The purpose of the individual account is to provide a detailed overview of all payments made to the employee. Articles 14 through 17 of the Royal Decree of 8 August 1980 describe in considerable detail the information which must be provided in the individual account.

1571. The employer must provide each employee with a copy of the individual account before 1 March of the year following that to which the remuneration relates. When the employment contract is terminated, a copy of the individual account must be remitted to the employee within 2 months following the quarter during which the termination took place. All individual accounts must be retained by the employer for a period of 5 years.

3. Presence list

1572. Employers in certain industry sectors may be required by Royal Decree to maintain a presence list. This requirement applies, *e.g.*, to the diamond industry and the horticultural industry.

4. Individual card

1573. The use of an individual card is mandatory only in the construction industry, but this may be extended to other industry sectors by Royal Decree. The information to be mentioned on the card is listed in Articles 2 and 3 of the Royal Decree of 8 March 1990. Each individual card must be validated quarterly by using a sticker provided by the social security authorities. The purpose of the card and the validation procedure is to make sure that only personnel for which all social security contributions have been made is employed. The card must be handed over to each employee at the latest on the first day of work. The card must be returned to the employer when the employment contract terminates. Individual cards must be retained by the employer for a period of 5 years.

5. Employment contracts for students and for home workers

1574. Employment contracts for students are governed by Articles 120 through 130 of the LEC. Employment contracts for home workers are governed by Article 119 of the LEC. By including these agreements in the category of mandatory social documents, Royal Decree No. 5 makes the conclusion of these agreements subject to the special monitoring and sanction procedures applicable to other categories of mandatory social documents.

§3. Work rules

1575. The work rules (*arbeidsreglement/règlement de travail*) are governed by the Law of 8 April 1965 on Work Rules (*Wet tot instelling van de arbeidsreglementen/Loi instituant les règlements de travail* – the "Law of 8 April 1965"). They are binding upon both the employer and the employees. Individual derogations, within the limits of the law, are possible, but must be made in writing (Art. 4 of the Law of 8 April 1965). Different work rules may be established for different categories of employees or for different company divisions (Art. 5 of the Law of 8 April 1965).

1576. Articles 6 through 8 of the Law of 8 April 1965 list the information that must be contained in the work rules. The mandatory information relates to, among other things, (i) working hours and rest periods; (ii) the method of measuring and evaluating the employees' performance; (iii) the method, place and time of the salary payments; (iv) the duration of notice periods and the events justifying a dismissal for serious cause (without prejudice to the Labour Courts' discretion in this respect); (v) the rights and obligations of surveillance personnel; (vi) the disciplinary sanctions, the violation which they sanction and the amounts and allocation of penalties; (vii) the rights of recourse available to employees when sanctions are notified; (viii) the location where the person in charge of providing first aid in case of accidents can be reached; (ix) the location of the first-aid kit; (x) the dates of the annual vacation; (xi) the names of the members of the Works Council, of the Committee for Prevention and Protection at Work, and of the trade union delegation; (xii) the address of the social inspection services; (xiii) the applicable collective bargaining agreements; (xiv) the measures for the protection of the employees against sexual harassment at the work place (pursuant to the Royal Decree of 18 September 1992). This list of mandatory provisions may be extended by Royal Decree. In addition to this mandatory content, the work rules may contain other provisions agreed upon between the employer and the employees.

1577. For example, nowadays many employers include a policy on the use of e-mail and the Internet at the work place in the work rules. In this respect, it should be noted that the National Labour Council has adopted a Collective Bargaining Agreement No. 81 on the protection of the employees' privacy with regard to the control of electronic on-line communications ("CBA No. 81"). CBA No. 81 sets forth the conditions to be complied with when monitoring and identifying electronic on-line communications. It seeks to strike a balance between the rights of employers (right to monitor the performance of the employment agreement and the use of work equipment) and the rights of employees to privacy. In general, personal data may only be processed in a proportionate way for explicitly described and justified purposes. In addition, when installing a monitoring system the employer must observe certain information and consultation obligations towards the employees. Electronic on-line communications may only be identified (*i.e.*, attributed to a specific person) when there are indications of irregularities in the use of the system. In essence, the contents of the electronic communication may not be read by the employer, unless there exists an agreement to the contrary with the employee(s). If an employee is held liable for irregularities in the use of the e-mail or Internet facilities, he should be invited for a discussion prior to any decision on the matter by the employer.

1578. In companies which have a Works Council, the work rules are drawn up and amended by the Works Council. When the Works Council cannot come to an agreement, there is a mandatory conciliation procedure involving at a first stage an official from the Social Inspection and, subsequently, if the official's attempt at conciliation is unsuccessful, by the competent Joint Committee. If the Joint Committee does not succeed in reconciling the two parties, it may decide the issue itself. This requires a 75 per cent majority.

1579. Where there is no Works Council, the draft work rules are drawn up by the employer. The draft must be made known to the employees. To that effect they are posted in the work place and any employee may request a copy. During a period of 15 days, the employees must be given the opportunity to submit comments. These comments are made in writing in a special register provided by the employer. During the same period, the employees may also file their comments directly with the Social Inspection. Their names may not be revealed. After the 15-day period has expired, the employer sends the register to the Social Inspection. If no comments were made, the work rules, or the amendments to them, enter into force 15 days after the draft was posted in the work place. Where comments have been made, there is a conciliation and decision procedure similar to the one applicable when the Works Council cannot reach an agreement on the text of the work rules.

1580. The definitive version of the work rules must be available at all times for direct consultation by the employees. The place where a copy of the work rules is kept must be clearly posted. In addition, a copy of the work rules must be provided to each employee. Within 8 days of the entry into force of the work rules or any amendment thereto, a copy must be addressed to the Social Inspection. The provisions relating to the work rules are subject to specific sanctions and monitoring mechanisms.

D. Collective labour relations

§1. Institutional aspects

1. Representation of employees

1581. In Belgium, there exists both a "positive" and a "negative" freedom of association. Article 27 of the Constitution guarantees the freedom of association and Article 1 of the Law of 24 May 1921 on the Freedom of Association (*Wet tot waarborging der vrijheid van vereeniging/Loi guarantissant la liberté d'association*) specifically provides that nobody can be forced to become or not to become a member of an organisation. It is estimated that nearly 60 per cent of the active employee population in Belgium is affiliated with a trade union.

1582. The 3 largest employee organisations are, in descending order of size, *ACV/CSC* (Christian democratic tendency), *ABVV/FGTB* (socialist tendency), and *ACLVB/ CGSLI* (liberal tendency). *ABVV/FGTB* and *ACV/CSC* comprise various trade unions, each of which is active in a specific economic sector.

1583. Not all trade unions or employee organisations are recognised as so-called representative organisations. The status of representative organisation confers specific privileges, mainly the right to enter into collective bargaining agreements and the right to present candidates for the social elections. In order to be qualified as representative, an employee organisation must, cumulatively, be organised on an interprofessional and national scale, be represented in the National Labour Council and the Central Economic Council and must have at least 50,000 members. All professional organisations which are a member of or are affiliated with one of these interprofessional organisations are also considered representative employee organisations. Only the three main organisations mentioned above meet these criteria.

2. Representation of employers

1584. The main employer organisation in Belgium is *VBO/FEB*. It is organised on a national scale. Its members are various employer organisations that are each active in a specific industry or sector.

1585. On a regional basis, employers are organised as follows: Flemish region: *VEV*, Walloon region: *UWE*, and Brussels region: *VOB*.

1586. Representative employer organisations are:
 (i) interprofessional organisations which are organised on a national scale and which are represented in the National Labour Council and the Central Economic Council;
 (ii) professional organisations which belong to, or are affiliated with, such interprofessional organisations;
 (iii) professional employer organisations which have been recognised as representative for a specific industry sector; and
 (iv) national interprofessional and professional organisations which have been recognised pursuant to the Law of 6 March 1964 and which are representative of employers active as craftsmen, in small and medium-sized businesses or as independent workers exercising a liberal or intellectual profession.

3. Consultation bodies

i. National Labour Council (*Nationale Arbeidsraad/Conseil National du Travail*)

1587. The National Labour Council was constituted by Law of 29 May 1952 on the National Labour Council (*Wet tot inrichting van de Nationale Arbeidsraad/Loi organique du Conseil National du Travail* – the "Law of 29 May 1952"). It is a body governed by public law whose members are appointed by Royal Decree for a renewable period of 4 years. They are appointed from lists of candidates proposed by the representative employer and employee organisations. Employer and employee organisations are represented in equal numbers.

1588. The main functions of the National Labour Council are to advise the government or Parliament on social issues and to deliver an opinion when conflicts of competence arise between various Joint Committees (Art. 1 of the Law of 29 May 1952). Importantly, the Law of 5 December 1968 on Collective Labour Agreements and Joint Committees (*Wet betreffende de collectieve arbeidsovereenkomst en de paritaire comités/Loi sur les conventions collectives de travail et les commissions paritaires* – the "Law of 5 December 1968") provides that national collective bargaining agreements may be concluded within the National Labour Council. Approximately 88 such collective bargaining agreements are currently in force, many of them having been amended repeatedly. These collective bargaining agreements cover virtually all aspects of labour law.

ii. Joint Committees (*paritaire comités/commissions paritaires*)

1589. Joint Committees (and sub-committees) are governed by the Law of 5 December 1968. They are established by Royal Decree at the request of one or more representative employer or employee organisations or at the government's initiative. The Royal Decree whereby a committee is constituted defines the persons, the industry sectors, the businesses and the territory covered by the Joint Committee.

1590. Joint Committees are composed of an independent president and a vice-president, an equal number of delegates of the representative employer and employee organisations and at least two secretaries. All members of a Joint Committee are appointed for a 4-year term. The purpose of a Joint Committee is:
   (a) to assist in the conclusion of collective bargaining agreements between the representative organisations;
   (b) to prevent or to mediate in any dispute between employers and employees;
   (c) to advise the government, the National Labour Council and the Central Economic Council on all matters falling within its competence; and
   (d) to fulfill any other mission which the law attributes to it.

1591. Joint Committees are often attributed an important role in implementing legislation and collective bargaining agreements.

1592. At the request of a Joint Committee, the government may, by Royal Decree, create one or more joint sub-committees.

4. The Works Council (Ondernemingsraad/Conseil d'entreprise)

i. Applicable legislation

1593. The main provisions governing the Works Council are contained in the Law of 20 September 1948 on the Organisation of the Economy (*Wet houdende organisatie van het bedrijfsleven/Loi portant organisation de l'économie* – the "Law of 20 September 1948"), the Royal Decree of 25 May 1999 relating to the Works Council and to the Committee for Prevention and Protection at Work, Collective Bargaining Agreement No. 9 of 9 March 1972, the Royal Decree of 27 November 1973 containing rules on the economic and financial information to be provided to the Works Council, Collective Bargaining Agreement No. 39 of 13 December 1983 with regard to the introduction of new technologies and the Law of 19 March 1991 governing the Dismissal of Protected Employees.

ii. Establishment

1594. In principle, all businesses which normally employ on average at least 100 employees must have a Works Council (Art. 3, para. 1 of the Royal Decree of 25 May 1999). However, businesses which had established a Works Council, or were under an obligation to do so on the occasion of the previous social election, and which normally employ on average at least 50 persons must also establish a Works Council. In that case, the functions of the Works Council are exercised by the members of the Committee for Prevention and Protection at Work.

1595. The law provides detailed calculations to determine the average number of employees for purposes of establishing a Works Council (Art. 4, para. 1 of the Royal Decree of 25 May 1999).

1596. Businesses are covered by the rules governing the establishment of a Works Council even if they do not have a commercial or industrial purpose (Art. 3, para. 3 of the Royal Decree of 25 May 1999). However, only businesses in the private sector are covered.

1597. The word "business" does not necessarily refer to a legal entity. Rather, what is meant is a so-called "technical business unit" *(technische bedrijfseenheid/unité technique d'exploitation.)* The assessment of what constitutes a technical exploitation unit is based on economic and social criteria. In case of doubt, the social criteria prevail. A single legal entity may therefore comprise several technical exploitation units if these units are sufficiently economically and socially independent from one another. If these units meet the applicable employment threshold, a Works Council must be established in each such unit. By way of example, a company with headquarters in Brussels and a manufacturing plant in Liège may have to establish a Works Council at both locations. If a legal entity comprises several technical exploitation units which do not meet the employment thresholds, these units must either be joined together or joined with other units which meet the employment thresholds (Art. 5 of the Royal Decree of 25 May 1999).

1598. In addition, Article 14, paragraph 2, b) of the Law of 20 September 1948 creates a rebuttable presumption that several legal entities constitute together a technical exploitation unit if the following conditions are met:

(a) the legal entities form a part of the same economic group or the legal entities are managed by one and the same person or by persons who have mutual economic ties; or the legal entities have one and the same economic activity or have concerted economic activities; and

(b) there are elements that show a social cohesion between the legal entities.

1599. When the above-mentioned conditions are met, there exists a rebuttable presumption that the legal entities in question form a technical exploitation unit. The employer may rebut this presumption by demonstrating that the personnel management fails to show any social criteria. Lastly, the presumption applies without prejudice to the continuing existence of any Works Council which may already have been established within the separate legal entities.

1600. The employer must take the initiative to set up a Works Council. This obligation bears criminal sanctions. In principle every 4 years, nationwide social elections are held during which employee representatives are designated in each technical exploitation unit.

iii. Composition

1601. The Works Council is composed of, on the one hand, the employer and one or more employer representatives and, on the other hand, the representatives of the employees. The representatives of the employer may not exceed in number the representatives of the employees.

1602. The representatives of the employer are designated by the latter and must belong to the management personnel *(leidinggevend personeel/personnel de direction)*. This notion refers to 2 categories of employees. First, management personnel refers to employees who are charged with the daily management and who have the power to represent and bind the employer. Second, management personnel also covers employees who are directly subordinated to the first category of management employees, provided they are also charged with certain functions of daily management (Art. 1 (4) of Royal Decree of 25 May 1999). In this context, the notion of daily management does not have the same meaning as, for example, in company law. It is a specific term which refers to the decision-making power inherent in the function of the employer (*Cass.* 17 October 1983, *Pas.*, 1984, 1, 162). Prior to the social elections, the employer must indicate which of the employees are to be considered as management personnel. This determination may be challenged before the Labour Court by any interested employee or by the representative unions. Management personnel may not participate in the social election. They may not act as candidates for the function of employee representative, nor are they allowed to vote.

1603. The employee representatives, both effective and substitute representatives, are elected by the employees on the basis of lists introduced by the representative unions or, in the case of key employees *(kaderpersoneel/cadres),* by a minimum number of key employees or representative organisations of key personnel (Art. 31 of the Royal Decree of 25 May 1999).

1604. Under the current rules, the number of effective employee representatives varies between 4 and 22 as follows (Art. 20 of the Royal Decree of 25 May 1999):

Employees	Representatives
0-100	4
101-500	6
501-1000	8
1001-2000	10
2001-3000	12
3001-4000	14
4001-5000	16
5001-6000	18
6001-8000	20
8001 and above	22

1605. If key personnel is separately represented, these numbers are to be increased by one or 2 depending on whether there are less than 100 key employees or 100 or more than that number.

1606. The employer and the representative unions may agree unanimously to increase the numbers of employee representatives without, however, exceeding 25. The number of substitute delegates is equal to the number of effective delegates.

1607. Articles 21 through 26 of the Royal Decree of 25 May 1999 contain rules on the apportionment of the available seats among representatives of white-collar workers, blue-collar workers, key employees and young employees (below 25 years of age).

iv. Functions

1608. The main functions of the Works Council are described in Article 15 of the Law of 20 September 1948. Various other laws attribute further functions to the Works Council. Generally, it is to be noted that the Works Council has decision-making powers in only a limited number of matters. The main function of the Works Council is to act as a consultation body with advisory functions. To that effect, the employer must provide it with extensive financial and economic information. The main functions of the Works Council are:

   (a) to advise on all matters relating to the organisation of work, the working conditions and the productivity of the company;
   (b) to receive from the employer information regarding the company. The Royal Decree of 27 November 1973 and Collective Bargaining Agreement No. 9 define in considerable detail the information that must be disclosed to the Works Council. Information must be disclosed whenever a new Works Council is established, periodically (annually and quarterly) and occasionally, *i.e.,* whenever an important event occurs which may affect the affairs of the company. Articles 27 through 29 of the Royal Decree of 27 November 1973 provide for a procedure which enables the employer to obtain permission from the Ministry of Economic Affairs not to supply specific information when this is prejudicial to the company's interests;
   (c) to elect the company's statutory auditor (*See*, paras. 553 *et seq.*) from a list proposed by the board of directors;
   (d) to dismiss the company's statutory auditor (*See*, paras. 553 *et seq.*) during his mandate;
   (e) to establish or modify the work rules;
   (f) to receive information and to confer on the social impact of the introduction of new technologies;
   (g) to ensure that the industrial and social legislation for the protection of employees is rigorously applied;
   (h) to examine the general criteria used for hiring and dismissing personnel;
   (i) to establish the dates of the annual vacation;
   (j) to see to it that all legal provisions affecting the company from a social point of view or relating to the criteria of professional qualification are respected; and

(k) in certain cases, to carry out the tasks normally attributed to the Committee for Prevention and Protection at Work (Art. 85 of the Royal Decree of 25 May 1999).

v. Role of the statutory auditor (*bedrijfsrevisor/reviseur d'entreprise*)

1609. Any company which has established a Works Council must appoint a statutory auditor. The role of the statutory auditor is:
    (a) to report to the Works Council on the annual accounts and the management report filed by the company pursuant to Articles 143 through 144 of the Company Code of 7 May 1999;
    (b) to certify the accuracy and the completeness of the financial and economic information provided to the Works Council, in so far as this information is derived from the annual accounts or other accounting or verifiable records of the company;
    (c) to analyse and explain the economic and financial information supplied to the Works Council with respect to the financial structure and evolution in the financial state of the company; and
    (d) to inform the employer in case the statutory auditor is of the opinion that the economic and financial information supplied to the Works Council is inaccurate or incomplete. If the employer does not react within one month, the statutory auditor must inform the Works Council.

1610. These functions will be exercised by the company's statutory auditor in the case of Belgian companies established in the form of a public limited liability company, limited partnership with shares, a private limited liability company or a co-operative company (for a description of these corporate forms, *See* para. 95).

5. *The Committee for Prevention and Protection at Work (Comité voor Preventie en Bescherming op het Werk/ Comité pour la Prévention et la Protection au Travail)*

i. Applicable legislation

1611. The Committee for Prevention and Protection of Work is governed by the Law of 4 August 1996, the Royal Decree of 27 March 1998, and the General Labour Regulations ("*ARAB/RGPT*").

ii. Establishment and composition

1612. The rules governing the establishment and the composition of the Committee for Prevention and Protection at Work are substantially similar to those relating to the establishment and the composition of the Works Council. In principle, a Committee for Prevention and Protection at Work must be established by businesses which normally employ 50 persons on average (compared to 100 for the Works Council) (Art. 49 of the Law of 1996).

iii. Functions

1613. In general, the function of the Committee for Prevention and Protection at Work is to contribute to and to promote a healthy and safe working environment. For this purpose the Committee for Prevention and Protection at Work has a general advisory function in all matters related to health, safety and hygiene in the workplace.

1614. Typically, the Committee for Prevention and Protection at Work will be involved in:
    (a) the choice, the purchase, the maintenance and the use of protective clothing and equipment;
    (b) the ordering of new installations and machines;
    (c) ergonomic issues related to tools and machinery;
    (d) prevention of professional fatigue, stress and new health and safety risks;
    (e) determining the high-risk functions within the undertaking for which a specific medical examination is required;
    (f) drawing up the health and safety training program for the employees; and
    (g) the operation of the first aid services in the undertaking.

1615. The Committee for Prevention and Protection at Work will also be informed of:
    (a) the health and safety situation of the undertaking;
    (b) the yearly action plan of the employer, which cannot be put in practice before the Committee for Prevention and Protection at Work has given its advice;
    (c) the annual report of the work doctor;
    (d) the annual and monthly report of the prevention advisor;
    (e) the results of measurements ordered by the employer, the work doctor or the trade union delegation with respect to dangerous substances or damaging physical agents (for example noise, lack of ventilation, temperature and ionising rays); and
    (f) various environmental reports (annual environmental report and report of the environmental co-ordinator).

1616. The Committee for Prevention and Protection at Work must also:
    (a) help to identify health, safety and ergonomic risks and propose solutions;
    (b) inform the employees of health and safety issues and on the dates of the Committee for Prevention and Protection at Work meetings, their agenda, their resolutions, and their follow-up as well as on the annual action plan and annual report of the Internal Service for Prevention and Protection;

(c) have at its disposal a team which intervenes immediately when:
- there is an urgent reason to do so;
- there is (a threat of) a serious accident, a technical incident or an exposure to toxic substances; or
- one third of the employees so requests.

1617. The Committee for Prevention and Protection at Work also plays an important role in the prevention of violence, moral harassment and sexual harassment in the workplace.

6. Trade union delegation (vakbondsafvaardiging/délégation syndicale)

i. Applicable legislation

1618. Trade union delegations are governed by Collective Bargaining Agreement No. 5 of 24 May 1971 (as amended) ("CBA No. 5"). This collective bargaining agreement has been concluded at national level and is a framework agreement. The general principles contained in CBA No. 5 are further implemented by collective bargaining agreements entered into by the various Joint Committees and sub-committees or at company level.

ii. Establishment

1619. A trade union delegation must be established at the request of one or more trade unions which are a party to Collective Bargaining Agreement No. 5 (these unions are called the "representative unions"). This request must be addressed to the employer. The implementing collective bargaining agreements determine the minimum personnel required for the establishment of a trade union delegation, possibly the minimum number of demands that must be received from the employees to establish a trade union delegation, the number of trade union delegates, the procedures for designating or electing the trade union delegates and other similar provisions. These conditions may therefore vary from one industry sector to another.

iii. Functions

1620. The functions of the trade union delegation relate to, *inter alia*, labour relations within the company, negotiations leading to the conclusion of collective bargaining agreements at company level and the application in the company of the labour regulations, the applicable collective bargaining agreements and the individual employment agreements. Where there is a dispute of a collective nature, or a threat of such a dispute, the trade union delegation has the right to be received by the employer. For individual disputes, the trade union delegation may, if so requested, assist the individual employee concerned in his relations with the employer. In order to carry out its task, the trade union delegation must be informed in due course of (potential) modifications to the contractual or customary employment and remuneration conditions. However, the trade union delegation does not have access to information pertaining to individual employees. In an undertaking without a Works Council, the tasks of the latter may be carried out by the trade union delegation.

iv. Status of trade union representatives

1621. Trade union representatives benefit from special protection against dismissal. The protection regime which applies to them has been described at paragraphs 1425 *et seq.*

§2. Collective bargaining agreements

1. Applicable legislation

1622. Collective bargaining agreements are governed by the Law of 5 December 1968 (as amended).

2. Concept

1623. Collective bargaining agreements are defined as agreements entered into by one or more representative employee organisations and one or more representative employer organisations or employers which determine the individual and collective relations between employers and employees and which set forth the rights and obligations of the contracting parties (Art. 5 of the Law of 5 December 1968). Article 3 of the Law of 5 December 1968 defines which organisations are deemed to be representative for the purpose of entering into collective bargaining agreements.

3. Conclusion

1624. Collective bargaining agreements may be entered into at various levels. National collective bargaining agreements are concluded in the National Labour Council (*Nationale Arbeidsraad/Conseil National du Travail*). Industry-wide agreements are generally concluded in the competent Joint Committee or sub-committee. Collective bargaining agreements may also be entered into at company level.

1625. Collective bargaining agreements must be concluded in writing in French and in Dutch. However, where the scope of application of a collective bargaining agreement is limited to the Dutch, French or German-speaking linguistic region, the agreement must be drafted in, respectively, the Dutch, French or German language (Art. 13 of the Law of 5 December 1968).

1626. Collective bargaining agreements are entered into for a definite duration, an indefinite duration or for a definite duration with a renewal clause. Unless otherwise agreed, the latter two may be terminated in writing by any party (Art. 15 of the Law of 5 December 1968).

1627. All collective bargaining agreements must contain certain information relating to their signatories, the organisations on behalf of which the agreements are entered into, the Joint Committee, if any, in which the agreement is concluded, the persons bound by the agreement, the duration of the agreement, the dates of its conclusion and entry into effect. These items are listed in Article 16 of the Law of 5 December 1968.

1628. Collective bargaining agreements must be registered with the Ministry of Employment and Labour. They may only be accepted for registration if they meet the formal requirements imposed by law (Art. 18 of the Law of 5 December 1968).

4. Content

1629. Collective bargaining agreements contain 2 types of provisions: (i) normative provisions and (ii) obligatory provisions. Normative provisions determine the labour relations – individual or collective – between the employees and the employers covered by the agreement. Obligatory provisions relate to the contractual rights and obligations of the parties which have entered into the collective bargaining agreement, that is, the representative unions and the representative employer organisations or, as the case may be, the individual employers.

5. Binding force

1630. Collective bargaining agreements are binding upon:
   (i) the representative organisations which have entered into the agreements, the employers who are members of these organisations or who have entered into the agreements themselves;
   (ii) the representative organisations and the employers who have adhered to the agreement, as well as the employers who are members of such organisations;
   (iii) employers who join a representative organisation which is bound by an agreement; and
   (iv) all employees of an employer bound by a collective bargaining agreement (Art. 19 of the Law of 5 December 1968).

1631. For collective bargaining agreements entered into by the National Labour Council, by a Joint Committee or sub-committee, the provisions which deal with individual labour relations are also binding upon all other employers and all employees covered by the Joint Committee and by the terms of the agreement, unless their individual employment agreement contains written provisions which deviate from the collective bargaining agreement (Art. 26 of the Law of 5 December 1968).

1632. The normative provisions of a collective bargaining agreement which has been concluded by the National Labour Council, by a Joint Committee or sub-committee may be made generally binding by Royal Decree. This is done at the request of the joint body (National Labour Council, Joint Committee or sub-committee) in which the agreement was concluded or by a representative organisation which is a member of such body. If the request is granted, the collective bargaining agreement is published in the *Belgian Official Journal* (*Belgisch Staatsblad/Moniteur belge*) and becomes binding upon all employers and employees covered by the joint body in so far as the agreement contains provisions applicable to them (Arts. 28, 30 and 31 of the Law of 5 December 1968).

1633. Employers who violate the provisions of collective bargaining agreements which have been made generally binding by Royal Decree are liable to criminal sanctions (Art. 56.1° of the Law of 5 December 1968).

E. Transfer of undertakings, businesses or parts of businesses

§1. Introduction

1634. Belgium has implemented EC Council Directive 77/187/EEC of 14 February 1977 (O.J. [1977] L 61/26) and EC Council Directive 98/50/EC (O.J. [1998] L201/88) as codified in EC Council Directive 2001/23/EC of 12 March 2001 on the Approximation of the Laws of the Member States Relating to the Safeguarding of Employees' Rights in the Event of Transfers of Undertakings, Businesses or Parts of Undertakings or Businesses (O.J. [2001] L82/16).

1635. The implementing legislation consists of Collective Bargaining Agreement No. 32*bis* of 7 June 1985 (see Royal Decree of 25 July 1985) ("CBA No. 32*bis*"), as amended by Collective Bargaining Agreement No. 32*ter* of 2 December 1986 (see Royal Decree of 19 January 1987), Collective Bargaining Agreement No. 32*quater* of 19 December 1989 (see Royal Decree of 6 March 1990) and Collective Bargaining Agreement No. 32*quinquies* of 13 March 2002 (see Royal Decree of 14 March 2002). The provisions of CBA No. 32*bis* are mandatory.

1636. There is a transfer within the meaning of CBA No. 32*bis* where there is a transfer of an economic entity which retains its identity, meaning an organised grouping of resources which has the objective of pursuing an economic activity, whether or not that activity is central or ancillary (Art. 6, para. 2 of CBA No. 32*bis*).

1637. The scope of CBA No. 32*bis*, as amended, is not limited to the safeguarding of employees' rights in the case of the transfer of an undertaking, business or part thereof based on an agreement, but also concerns the safeguarding of certain rights of employees who are transferred in the context of a bankruptcy. Both aspects of CBA No. 32*bis* will be dealt with below. In addition, certain information and consultation obligations will also be addressed.

§2. *Transfer of an undertaking, business or part thereof by way of agreement (Chapter II of CBA No. 32bis)*

1. *Scope of application*

1638. Chapter II of CBA No. 32*bis* applies to the transfer "by way of agreement" of an undertaking, business or part thereof which includes transfers in a context of judicial composition (*gerechtelijk akkoord/concordat judiciaire*), except in the circumstances mentioned in Article 8*bis* of CBA No. 32*bis* (*See*, para. 1643).

1639. A number of conditions must nevertheless be met in order to bring the protective rules into play:
  (i) the rules apply only in cases where the transfer results in a change of employer; and
  (ii) the transfer may not result from the death of the employer. The employees' rights are in this case safeguarded by virtue of Article 33 of the LEC.

1640. The transfer of an undertaking, business or part thereof which triggers the application of Chapter II of CBA No. 32*bis* may take many forms. Examples of such transfers include changes in the legal status of the company, the incorporation of an unincorporated entity, mergers and acquisitions.

2. *Safeguarding of employees' rights*

1641. In the case of a transfer within the meaning of Chapter II of CBA No. 32*bis*, the rights and obligations of the transferring employer arising from a contract of employment existing on the date of the transfer are automatically transferred to the transferee (Art. 7 of CBA No. 32*bis*). The concept of transferee must be understood to include any natural or legal person who, by reason of the transfer, becomes the employer of the employees of the transferred business (Art. 2(4) of CBA No. 32*bis*). CBA No.32*bis* does not provide for the automatic transfer of old-age, invalidity or survivors' benefits under supplementary company or inter-company schemes (Art. 4 of CBA No. 32*bis*). However, if such benefits are included in a collective bargaining agreement concluded at company or industry level, they must be respected by the transferee (Art. 20 of the Law of 5 December 1968).

1642. After the date of the transfer, the transferring employer and the transferee are jointly and severally liable for the payment of debts existing at the time of the transfer and resulting from the employment contracts which pre-date the transfer (Art. 8 of CBA No. 32*bis*). This principle does not extend to the payment of debts relating to the supplementary schemes referred to above.

1643. Moreover, Article 8*bis* of CBA No. 32*bis* provides an exception to the principle of safeguarding employees' rights in case of a transfer in the context of judicial composition. In such a case, the transferor's debts arising from contracts of employment and payable before the transfer are not transferred to the transferee, provided that the payment of such debts is guaranteed by the Closure Fund (*Fonds tot vergoeding van de in geval van sluiting van ondernemingen ontslagen werknemers / Fonds d'indemnisation des travailleurs licenciés en cas de fermeture d'entreprise*). Moreover, in case of a transfer in the context of judicial composition, the transferee, transferor or person or persons exercising the transferor's functions, on the one hand, and the representatives of the employees on the other hand may agree to alter the employees' terms and conditions of employment to safeguard employment opportunities by ensuring the survival of the undertaking, business or part of the undertaking or business.

1644. The transfer of an undertaking, business or part thereof may not in itself constitute grounds for dismissal by the transferring employer or the transferee (Art. 9 of CBA No. 32*bis*). However, this does not preclude employees who are transferred being dismissed for serious cause or for economic, technical or organisational reasons. If an employment contract is terminated because the transfer involves a substantial change in working conditions to the detriment of the employee, the employer is to be regarded as having been responsible for the termination of the employment contract (Art. 10 of CBA No. 32*bis*).

§3. *Transfer of an undertaking, business or part thereof in the context of a bankruptcy*

1. *Scope of application*

1645. Chapter III of CBA No. 32*bis*, as amended, applies to employees who are transferred in the context of the transfer of an undertaking, business or part thereof following bankruptcy. The employees who benefit from the protective rules contained in Chapter III are the following:

   (i) employees who, on the date of the bankruptcy, were bound by an employment contract; and

   (ii) employees who were dismissed no earlier than one month prior to the date of the bankruptcy, provided that these employees are entitled to termination compensation and that such compensation has not been paid before the date of the bankruptcy.

1646. The employees in these 2 categories benefit from the protective rules only if they are transferred within a period of 6 months following the transfer of the undertaking, business or part thereof and the transfer of the undertaking, business or part of a business occurs within a period of 6 months following the date of the bankruptcy (Art. 11 of CBA No. 32*bis*).

2. Safeguarding of employees' rights

1647. As a general rule, the transferee may freely decide how many and which employees he wants to take over (Art. 12 of CBA No. 32*bis*). Employees who are transferred benefit from the following protection:

   (i) collective rights or benefits accepted by or binding on the previous employer are transferred to the transferee (Art. 13 of CBA No. 32*bis*). Changes to such collective rights can only be made if a specific procedure is followed (Art. 15 of CBA No. 32*bis*); and

   (ii) the seniority acquired under the previous employer, including any period between the transfer and the suspension of operations as a result of the bankruptcy shall be taken into account for the purpose of determining the notice period or the indemnity to be paid in case of termination of a new employment relationship by the transferee (Art. 14 of CBA No. 32*bis*), unless the employment contract is terminated by the transferee during the probationary period.

1648. It is important to note that Chapter III of CBA No. 32*bis* does not oblige the transferee to accept conditions included in individual employment contracts. The transferee is entitled to re-negotiate such conditions with the transferred employees.

§4. Special transitional indemnity for employees whose activity has been interrupted following a bankruptcy or a judicial composition and who are transferred to a new employer

1649. The Law of 12 April 1985 whereby the Closure Fund is Charged with the Payment of a Transitional Indemnity (*Wet waarbij het Fonds tot vergoeding van de in geval van sluiting der ondernemingen ontslagen werknemers belast wordt met de uitbetaling van een overbruggingsvergoeding/Loi chargeant le Fonds d'indemnisation des travailleurs licenciés en cas de fermeture d'entreprises du paiement d'une indemnité de transition* – the "Law of 12 April 1985") provides that employees whose professional activities have been interrupted due to bankruptcy or judicial composition are entitled to a transitional indemnity (*overbruggingsvergoeding/*

indemnité de transition) if they are eventually transferred to a new employer following bankruptcy or judicial composition.

1650. In order for such employees to benefit from the transitional indemnity, the following conditions must be met:

   (i) the transfer of the undertaking, business or part of a business must take place within 6 months following the bankruptcy or judicial composition (Art. 3 of the Law of 12 April 1985);

   (ii) the professional activity of the employee must be interrupted due to the bankruptcy or judicial composition (Art. 4 of the Law of 12 April 1985);

   (iii) the employee concerned must, on the date of the bankruptcy or judicial composition, have been bound by an employment contract, or the employee must have been dismissed no earlier than 1 month prior to the date of bankruptcy or judicial composition, provided that he is entitled to a termination indemnity which has not been paid by the date of bankruptcy or judicial composition (Art. 5 of the Law of 12 April 1985); and

   (iv) the employee must be hired by the transferee within a period of 6 months following the transfer of the undertaking, business or part thereof (Art. 5 of the Law of 12 April 1985).

1651. The transitional indemnity will be paid by the Closure Fund for the period between the date the employee's professional activity is interrupted and the date of employment by the new employer commences (Art. 4 of the Law of 12 April 1985). Subject to the usual social security and pay-roll deductions, the amount of the transitional indemnity is equal to the gross remuneration which the employee received before his professional activity was interrupted (Art. 8 of the Law of 12 April 1985) up to a maximum of € 2,331.19 per month.

1652. The transitional indemnity is not due to employees who have been hired by the new employer under a contract with a probationary clause and who have been dismissed during that probationary period (Art. 6 of the Law of 12 April 1985).

§5. Information and consultation

1653. If a company is involved in negotiations relating to a transfer within the meaning of CBA No. 32*bis*, it must inform the Works Council in good time and prior to the public announcement of any transfer. The information provided to the Works Council must relate to (i) the economic, financial and technical reasons for the transfer and (ii) to the transfer's economic, financial and social implications. In addition, the company must consult with the representatives of the employees in good time on envisaged measures in relation to the employees (Art. 11 of Collective Bargaining Agreement No. 9 of 9 March 1972, see, Royal Decree of 12 September 1972).

1654. Even when the company involved in negotiations relating to a transfer within the meaning of CBA No. 32*bis* does not have any employee representatives, the affected employees must be informed prior to the transfer of (i) the (envisaged) date of the transfer by way of agreement; (ii) in case of a bankruptcy, the (envisaged) date of the transfer of assets; (iii) the reasons for the transfer; (iv) the legal, economic and social consequences of the transfer for the employees; and (v) the envisaged measures *vis-à-vis* the employees (Art. 15*bis* of CBA No. 32*bis*).

F. Status of international employment contracts

§1. Introduction

1655. An international employment contract can be defined in this context as an agreement between an employer and an employee all the relevant elements of which are not Belgian. For instance, the employer or the employee may be of a different nationality or the employment agreement may have been concluded or is to be performed outside Belgium. With regard to such international employment contracts, specific choice of jurisdiction and choice of law rules apply.

§2. Choice of jurisdiction

1656. The Brussels Convention of 27 September 1968 as amended by the Treaty of San Sebastian of 26 May 1989 on jurisdiction and enforcement of judgments in civil and commercial matters (the "Brussels Convention") applies to international employment contracts as defined above. The relevant rules of the Brussels Convention are the following:

   (i) persons domiciled in a contracting state can, whatever their nationality, be sued in the courts of that state. Thus, Belgian courts will assume jurisdiction if an employer domiciled outside Belgium sues an employee who is domiciled in Belgium and vice versa (Art. 2 of the Brussels Convention);

   (ii) a person domiciled in a contracting state may be sued in another contracting state, in matters relating to a contract, in the courts of the place of performance of the obligation in question. In matters relating to individual contracts of employment, the place of performance is the place where the employee habitually carries out his work. According to recent case law, the place where an employee habitually carries out his work is the place where the employee has established the effective centre of his working activities. In order to identify that place, regard must be had to the amount of working time spent in the respective countries and the presence of an office from which the employee organises his professional activities and to which he returns after each trip abroad (ECJ, 9 January 1997, Case C-383/95, *Petrus Wilhelmus Rutten v. Cross Medical Ltd.*, ECR [1997] I-57). If the employee does not habitually carry out his work in any one country, the employer may also be sued in the courts of the place where the business which engaged the employee was or is now situated (Art. 5(1) of Brussels Convention).

1657. The validity of choice of forum clauses is governed by Article 17, final paragraph of the Brussels Convention, which provides that in matters relating to individual employment contracts an agreement conferring jurisdiction shall only have legal force if it is entered into after the dispute has arisen or if the employee invokes it to confer jurisdiction on courts other than those in the defendant's domicile or those specified in Article 5(1) of the Brussels Convention.

1658. As of 1 March 2002, the Brussels Convention has been replaced for all EC countries except Denmark by EC Council Regulation No. 44/2001 of 22 December 2000 on jurisdiction and the recognition and enforcement of judgements in civil and commercial matters (O.J. [2001] L 012/1) ("Regulation No. 44/2001"). In contrast with the Brussels Convention, Regulation No. 44/2001 contains a separate section on jurisdiction over individual contracts of employment (Section 5, Articles 18 through 21). The jurisdictional rules of Regulation No. 44/2001 with regard to individual employment contracts can be summarised as follows:

   (i) when the employer is not domiciled in an EC Member State, but has a branch, agency or other establishment in one of the EC Member States, the employer shall be deemed to be domiciled in that EC Member State in case of a dispute arising out of the operations of the branch, agency or establishment (Art. 18(2) of Regulation No. 44/2001);

  (ii) the employee may sue the employer in the Member State where the employer is domiciled (Art. 19(1) of Regulation No. 44/2001) or in the courts of the place where the employee habitually carries or carried out his work (Art. 19(2) a of Regulation No. 44/2001) or, if the employee does or did not habitually carry out his work in any one country, in the courts of the place where the business which engaged the employee is or was situated (Art. 19(2) b of Regulation No. 44/2001); and

(iii) the employer may only sue the employee in the EC Member State in which the employee is domiciled (Art. 20 of Regulation No. 44/2001).

1659. The provisions of Section 5 of Regulation No. 44/2001 may be departed from with a valid choice of forum clause (Art. 21 of Regulation No. 44/2001). Such clauses are valid if they are entered into after the dispute has arisen or when they allow the employee to bring proceedings in courts other than those which would result from the application of Section 5 of Regulation No. 44/2001.

§3. Choice of law

1660. The Law of 14 July 1987 contains specific choice of law rules applicable to individual employment contracts. Article 3 of the Law of 14 July 1987 provides for the general validity of choice of law clauses included in individual employment contracts having an international character, but at the same time Article 6 of the Law of 14 July 1987 also stipulates that such choice of law clauses may not deprive the employee of the protection afforded by the mandatory rules of the following laws:

   (i) the laws of the country in which the employee habitually carries out his work in performance of the contract, even if he is temporarily employed in another country;

   (ii) if the employee does not habitually carry out his work in any one country, the laws of the country where the business which engaged the employee is situated; unless

   (iii) it appears from the circumstances that the contract is more closely connected with another country, in which case the laws of that other country apply.

1661. There is a wide variety of protective rules of a mandatory nature under Belgian law which may limit the application of the law chosen by the parties. Based upon prior case law, the following mandatory rules can be referred to:

   (i) rules regarding the notice period to be respected in the case of termination and the power of the courts to fix the notice period in certain cases;

   (ii) rules regarding the calculation of salaries;

   (iii) rules regarding termination for serious cause;

   (iv) rules regarding the grounds for the suspension of an employment contract;

   (v) rules regarding minimum salaries, annual vacation and vacation allowance; and

   (vi) rules regarding post-term non-competition obligations.

G. Social Security Law

§1. Introduction

1662. This section gives a brief overview of the rules relating to social security contributions and benefits in Belgium.

1. General scope of application of Belgian social security laws

1663. There are 3 different schemes of social security in Belgium:
- (i) the general scheme which applies to blue-collar employees *(arbeiders/ ouvriers)* and white-collar employees *(bedienden/employés)*, that is, employees working in Belgium for a private employer;
- (ii) the scheme which applies to self-employed persons who carry out their activities in Belgium; and
- (iii) the scheme which applies to civil servants having life tenure in Belgian governmental institutions.

1664. In this section, the organisation of the general social security scheme for employees will be discussed under paragraph 2 (*See*, paras. 1674 *et seq.*) and the scheme for self-employed persons under paragraph 3 (*See*, paras. 1719 *et seq.*). Social security applicable to civil servants will not be discussed in this book. Extra-legal social security benefits such as additional sickness costs, insurance schemes or pension funds will not be dealt with either.

2. Territorial scope of application of Belgian social security laws

i. Principle

1665. The general scheme of social security is applicable to employees employed in Belgium. Self-employed persons will in general be subject to Belgian social security regulations if the activities of the self-employed persons are carried out in Belgium.

ii. EC Citizens who are active in several EC member states

1666. The social security regulations for EC citizens employed in an EC Member State are contained in EC Council Regulation No. 1408/71 of 14 June 1971 (O.J. [1971] L 149/2). In principle, the social security regulations of the country of employment will be applicable. However, if the EC citizen is employed in 2 or more EC Member States, the social security regulations of the country of residence will be applicable provided that the EC citizen also carries out activities in that EC Member State (Art. 14(2)(b) i of Regulation No. 1408/71). If the employee does not reside in any of the Member States where he is employed, the social security regulations of the EC Member State where the employer is located will apply (Art. 14(2)(b) ii of Regulation No. 1408/71). Moreover, if the EC citizen is only temporarily posted abroad, the social security regulations of the EC Member State where he carries out activities on a permanent basis will continue to apply (Art. 14(1)(a) of Regulation No. 1408/71). EC citizens who carry out self-employed activities in several EC Member States will be subject to the social security regulations of the country of residence if part of the activities are carried out in that country. If the self-employed EC citizen is not active in his country of residence, the social security legislation of the country where he carries out his main activity will be applicable (Art. 14*bis* (2) of Regulation No. 1408/71).

1667. When an EC citizen works as an employee in one EC Member State and as a self-employed person in another EC Member State, the social security regulations of the EC Member State where he is an employee will apply. However, Annex VII to Regulation No. 1408/71 provides for some exceptions to this rule. For example, a person who is self-employed in Belgium and an employee in another EC Member State will be subject to the social security legislation in each country separately.

iii. Countries with which Belgium has concluded a bilateral social security convention

1668. Belgium has entered into bilateral treaties on social security with the following non-EC countries: Algeria, Bosnia, Canada, Chile, Croatia, Israel, Macedonia, Morocco, Poland, San Marino, Slovenia, Switzerland, Tunisia, Turkey, the USA and Yugoslavia. Only the treaties with Canada, Chile, Switzerland, Turkey, and the United States deal with both employees and self-employed persons. The other treaties are only applicable to employees.

1669. The general principle in each of these treaties is that the employee or self-employed person is subject to the social security rules of the country where he carries out his activities.

1670. If employees from one of the above countries are assigned to work temporarily in Belgium, they will continue to be covered by the social security system of their country and no contributions will be due in Belgium. The maximum period during which an employee may be assigned to work in Belgium while remaining covered by the social security system of his own country is, in general, 12 months. Under the treaties with Canada and Chile this period is set at 24 months. The treaty between Belgium and the US provides for an exemption of up to 5 years. It should be noted that in order to benefit from an exemption, an application must be filed with the local authorities specified in the treaty.

1671. Each of the treaties also provides rules to determine the applicable legislation in cases where the employee or the self-employed person carries out activities in both countries.

3. *Risks and benefits of the Belgian social security systems*

1672. The social security contributions of employees serve to finance unemployment benefits, sickness and invalidity payments and old-age and survivors' pensions. In addition to these benefits, the social security payments of employers also finance educational leave, child benefits, and childcare. Finally, social security contributions of employers finance the payment of indemnities in case of labour accidents and occupational diseases.

1673. In addition, special legislation guarantees minimum allowances, in general, for all citizens living below subsistence level and, specifically, for handicapped persons.

§2. *The general scheme applicable to employees*

1674. The general scheme is, in principle, applicable to all employees working in Belgium. However, certain groups of employees are expressly excluded from the general scheme. This is, for example, the case for students working in the holiday season and certain seasonal workers.

1675. Special schemes also exist for certain groups of employees such as miners and seamen.

1676. Moreover, certain persons are expressly included in the general schemes in spite of the fact that they often do not have an employment contract. This is, for example, the case for performing artists, truck-drivers and taxi-drivers.

1. Contributions

1677. Social security for employees is, to a large extent, financed by contributions made by employees and by employers. These contributions are collected by the National Institute for Social Security (*Rijksdienst voor Sociale Zekerheid/Office National de Sécurité Sociale*) (*RSZ/ONSS*).

i. Registration as an employer with the RSZ/ONSS

1678. Every employer who employs one or more employees must notify the *RSZ/ONSS* by filling out a specific form (Art. 21 of the Law of 27 June 1969). The employer will then receive an *RSZ/ONSS* registration number.

ii. The quarterly statement to the RSZ/ONSS

1679. Every employer must file, on a quarterly basis, a form with the *RSZ/ONSS* which must contain the following information:
   (a) the identity of the employees;
   (b) the number of days they actually worked;
   (c) the number of vacation days or equivalent days;
   (d) the amount of vacation allowance which the white-collar employees earned;
   (e) the wages or salaries the employees earned; and
   (f) the amounts withheld from their remuneration for social security purposes.

iii. Payment of contributions to the RSZ/ONSS

1680. The employer must pay the amounts withheld from the wages or salaries of his employees and his own contribution into the account of the *RSZ/ONSS* within the statutory time limits (Art. 23, para. 2 of the Law of 27 June 1969).

1681. These time limits are determined as follows:
   (a) the contributions must be paid by the last day of the month following the end of a quarter, *i.e.*, on 30 April, 31 July, 31 October or 31 January.
   (b) companies who have declared more than € 6,197.34 in a certain quarter, must make a down payment for the next quarter by the fifth day of each month of at least 30 per cent of the contributions which were due for the previous quarter.

1682. If the contributions are not paid in due time, a 10 per cent penalty will be due. The *RSZ/ONSS* can also request interest for late payment at a rate of 7 per cent per year (Art. 54 of the Royal Decree of 28 November 1969). Finally, Article 35 of the Law of 27 June 1969 imposes criminal sanctions for employers who do not comply with the Law.

iv. Administration and payment through a payroll agency (*sociaal secretariaat/ secrétariat social*)

1683. In accordance with Article 27 of the Law of 27 June 1969, employers can request a recognised payroll agency (*sociaal secretariaat/secrétariat social*) to undertake the fulfilment of the employer's social security obligations.

1684. A list of the recognised payroll agencies is published every year in the Belgian Official Journal (*Belgisch Staatsblad/Moniteur belge*). These payroll agencies are private non-profit institutions. Their main purpose is to act in the name and on behalf of the employer towards the *RSZ/ONSS* and the tax administration.

1685. Typically the payroll agency carries out the following activities:
   (a) it handles the social security and/or tax administration of the employer;
   (b) it carries out specific tasks when employees are hired – initiation of claims for child benefits, organisation of medical examinations, application for a pension number and the like;
   (c) it calculates the net wages and salaries to be paid taking account of existing collective bargaining agreements, deals with payment orders with the various banks and provides employees with the required social security documents;
   (d) it calculates the precise amount of termination indemnities; and
   (e) it collects and passes on to the appropriate administration all social security contributions and payroll taxes.

v. Overview of social security contributions

1686. Social security contributions are calculated based on a percentage of the gross wage or salary before deduction of payroll taxes.

1687. Table 10.2 summarises the amounts due for the fourth quarter of 2002 by the employer and by the employee for the various social security categories.

Table 10.2: Social security contributions (in percentage)

	Blue-collar		White-collar	
	Employee	*Employer*	*Employee*	*Employer*
– Child benefit	–	7.0	–	7.0
– Sickness	3.55	3.8	3.55	3.8
– Invalidity	1.15	2.35	1.15	2.35
– Unemployment benefit	0.87	1.46	0.87	1.46
– Accident at work	–	0.3	–	0.3
– Occupational disease	–	1.1	–	1.1
– Pension	7.5	8.86	7.5	8.86
– Annual vacation	–	6.0	–	–
– Educational leave	–	0.04	–	0.04
– Wage moderation	–	7.48	–	7.48
– Child care	–	0.05	–	0.05
Subtotal	13.07	38.44	13.07	32.44
– Annual vacation with more than 10 persons employed	–	1.69	–	1.69
– Annual vacation additional	–	0.86	–	–

– Closing of plant(s) with 10 to 19 persons employed	–	0.21	–	0.21
– Closing of plant(s) with 20 or more persons employed	–	0.24	–	0.24
– Additional plant closure contribution	–	0.18	–	0.18
Total if 1 to 9 persons employed	13.07	39.69	13.07	32.83
Total if 10 to 19 persons employed	13.07	41.38	13.07	34.52
Total if 20 or more persons employed	13.07	41.41	13.07	34.55

2. Social security benefits

i. Child benefit

1688. The purpose of child benefit is to supplement the income of employees who have children to support. Child benefit for employees are governed by the Law of 19 December 1939, as amended (*Samengeordende wetten betreffende de kinderbijslag voor loonarbeiders/Lois coordonnées relatives aux allocations familiales pour travailleurs salaries* – the "Law of 19 December 1939").

1689. 2 kinds of child benefit exist:
  (a) a child birth allowance or adoption premium;
  (b) monthly allowances which vary according to the number and age of the children.

1690. These benefits are adjusted regularly to take account of the Retail Price Index.

1691. The administration of child benefits is undertaken by the *Rijksdienst voor Kinderbijslag voor Werknemers/Office National d'Allocations Familiales pour Travailleurs Salaries* (*RKW/ONAFTS*) and numerous private child benefit institutions (*kinderbijslagfondsen/ instituts d'allocations familiales*).

1692. Employers unable or unwilling to affiliate with one of the private institutions will automatically be enrolled with the *RKW/ONAFTS*.

1693. Beneficiaries of child benefit are listed in Articles 51 through 64 of the Law of 19 December 1939 and include:
   (a) employees employed in Belgium by an employer who is subject to the Belgian social security system;
   (b) unemployed persons receiving unemployment benefit;
   (c) employees who have suspended their professional activities; and
   (d) students.

1694. The Law of 19 December 1939 further requires that:
   (a) a family relationship exists between the beneficiary and the child;
   (b) the child is being raised in Belgium;
   (c) the child is younger than 18 years of age (or 21 years for handicapped children and 25 years of age for students).

1695. The recipient of the benefit is, in general, the person who is responsible for the child's education (Art. 64 of the Law of 19 December 1939). In practice, the child benefit will be paid to the mother.

   ii. Sickness and invalidity payments

1696. Sickness and invalidity payments reimburse some of the costs of medical care and provide a replacement income for employees struck by illness or invalidity.

1697. Sickness and invalidity payments are regulated by the Law of 14 July 1994, as amended (*Wet betreffende de verplichte verzekering voor geneeskundige verzorging en uitkeringen/Loi relative à l'assurance obligatoire soins de santé et indemnités –* the "Law of 14 July 1994")

1698. The administration of these payments is carried out by the *Rijksinstituut voor Ziekte- en Invaliditeitsverzekering/Institut National d'Assurance Maladie-Invalidité* (*RIZW/ INAMI*) and mutual healthfunds (*ziekenfondsen/mutualités*).

1699. Persons unable or unwilling to affiliate with one of the mutual health funds will be automatically enrolled with the *Hulpkas voor ziekte- en invaliditeitsverzekering/ Caisse auxiliaire d'assurance maladie-invalidité*.

1700. After a waiting period of maximum six months, the employee and his or her dependants become entitled to full or partial reimbursement of expenses for medical care (Art. 121, para. 2 of the Law of 14 July 1994). However, persons who can prove that they have been covered by a Belgian or foreign social security system in the six months preceding their affiliation will in most cases be immediately entitled to reimbursement. The medical care for which the expenses can be fully or partially reimbursed are listed in Articles 34 through 37*quater* of the Law of 14 July 1994 and include doctors' visits, dental care, drugs, hospitalisation and laboratory analysis. 2 separate systems of compensation exist in this respect:

(a) usually, the patient (that is, the employee or his dependants) will pay the costs directly to the person providing the care. He will receive a medical certificate which must be remitted to the sickness fund in order to obtain reimbursement. The beneficiary will rarely be completely reimbursed. He must pay a certain amount himself *(remgeld/ticket moderateur)*. The amounts of the reimbursements are fixed by Royal or Ministerial Decree and result from negotiations between sickness funds, representatives of the various medical professions and the government; and

(b) in other cases, the person who provided the care will be reimbursed by the sickness fund.

1701. Employees who are incapable of working as a result of sickness or of an accident can obtain allowances to substitute their wages or salaries. In certain cases there is a presumption that the worker or employee is incapable of working, for example, if he or she is hospitalised or taking maternity leave.

1702. During the first year the employee will normally receive at least 55 per cent of his regular salary. This allowance is referred to as the primary incapacity allowance *(primaire ongeschiktheidsuitkering/indemnité d'incapacité primaire)*. Articles 87 through 92 of the Law of 14 July 1994 govern the issue of this allowance.

1703. If the incapacity persists after the first one-year period, an invalidity allowance *(invaliditeitsuitkering/indemnité d'invalidité)* is granted which in general amounts to 60 per cent of the normal salary provided that the employee involved is head of the household. Otherwise, the allowance amounts to 40 per cent of the normal salary (Arts. 93 through 95 of the Law of 14 July 1994).

1704. Special legislation which covers incapacity to work due to accidents at work or occupational diseases will be discussed briefly under paragraph 1718 below.

1705. Allowances for women on maternity leave are also covered by sickness and invalidity insurance (Arts. 111 through 115 of the Law of 14 July 1994). The allowance usually amounts to 82 per cent of the employee's normal salary during the first 30 days and 75 per cent of the employee's normal salary (capped) from the thirty-first day to the fifteenth week.

iii. Unemployment benefits

1706. The Royal Decree of 25 November 1991 co-ordinated the administration of unemployment benefits at a national level and reorganised the competent national institution (*Rijksdienst voor Arbeidsvoorziening/Office National de l'Emploi*). This law now determines the conditions for granting the benefits as well as the procedure to be followed. However, work-placement is a responsibility of the regions. Thus, the Flemish region created an institution by Decree of 20 March 1984 (*Vlaamse Dienst voor Arbeidsbemiddeling (VDAB)*) which deals with the organisation of training and the assistance of unemployed in finding new employment. The Walloon region also created an institution (*Office Communautaire et regional de la formation professionnelle et de l'Emploi (FOREM)*) which has similar responsibilities for the Walloon region (Decree of the Walloon region of 16 December 1988). A Royal Decree of 16 November 1988 organised the *Brusselse Gewestelijke Dienst voor Arbeidsbemiddeling/Office Regional Bruxellois de l'Emploi (BGDA/ ORBEM)*, a similar institution for the Brussels region.

1707. Article 30 of the Royal Decree of 25 November 1991 provides that unemployment benefits can only be granted if the claimants have completed a minimum period of employment during a specific reference period as shown in Table 10.3.

1708. In principle, only the days for which social security contributions were withheld from the unemployed's salary are considered as working days for the purposes of calculating the minimum period of employment.

Table 10.3: Reference periods for unemployment benefit

Age of the claimant	*Minimum period of employment needed (in days)*	*Reference period*
Less than 36 years	312	18 months before claim is made
Between 36 and 50 years	468	27 months before claim is made
Older than 50	624	36 months before claim is made

1709. Moreover, unemployment benefits will only be granted if the following conditions are also fulfilled: the claimant must:
    (a) be under 65 years of age,
    (b) be physically fit to carry out normal employment,

(c) be willing to accept suitable work,

(d) have enrolled with an unemployment office,

(e) have lost his previous employment because of circumstances which were beyond his control, and

(f) be willing to submit to monitoring (Arts. 44 through 70 of the Royal Decree of 25 November 1991).

1710. The amount of the benefit is normally a percentage of the wage or salary which the unemployed person previously earned. However, maximum amounts are set by law. Usually, during the first 12 months of unemployment the benefit amounts to 55 or 60 per cent of the previous earnings. Depending on the family status of the unemployed, these percentages may be reduced after 12 months of unemployment.

iv. Old-age pensions and survivors' pensions

1711. The retirement age is fixed at 65 years for both men and women.

1712. The Royal Decree No. 50 of 24 October 1967 pertains to old-age and survivors' pensions and establishes a national institution for that purpose (*Rijksdienst voor Pensioenen/Office National des Pensions*).

1713. The Law of 20 July 1990 (*Wet tot instelling van een flexibele pensioenleeftijd voor werknemers en tot aanpassing van de werknemerspensioenen aan de evolutie van het algemeen welzijn/Loi instaurant un âge flexible de la retraite pour les travailleurs salaries et adaptant les pensions des travailleurs salaries à l'évolution du bien-être général* – the "Law of 20 July 1990") provides for flexibility concerning the age of retirement, that is, each worker or employee who is 60 years old can choose on which date he wants his retirement to commence.

1714. The claimant will only be entitled to an old-age pension on the first day of the month following the month of his application. He cannot, in any event, receive an old-age pension before the first day of the month following the month of his sixtieth birthday (Art. 2 of the Law of 20 July 1990).

1715. The old-age pension is a fraction of the gross wages or salaries earned by the claimant during his professional career. Generally, subject to certain statutory maxima, the pension amounts to 75 per cent or 60 per cent of the average wages earned during a full professional career (normally 45 years).

1716. A survivors' pension is a pension granted to the widower or widow of an employee who would have been entitled to an old-age pension. It usually amounts to 80 per cent of the old-age pension the deceased would have received.

v. Holiday allowances for employees

1717. Holiday allowances for white-collar employees are paid directly by their employer. For historic reasons, holiday allowances for blue-collar employees are part of the social security system, administered by the *RSZ/ONSS* and by the *Rijksdienst voor Jaarlijkse Vakantie/Office National des Vacances Annuelles.*

3. *Labour accidents and occupational diseases*

1718. These risks are governed by special legislation:
  (i) the Royal Decree of 3 June 1970 regulates allowances paid to persons suffering from occupational diseases. These allowances are paid from a special fund *(Fonds voor Beroepsziekten/Fonds des Maladies Professionnelles).*
  (ii) the Law of 10 April 1971 (*Wet betreffende de arbeidsongevallen/Loi sur les accidents du travail* – the "Law of 10 April 1971") regulates allowances paid to persons who are victims of labour accidents. In principle, all employers must subscribe to a labour accident policy with a recognised insurance company or insurance fund. This policy covers labour accidents and accidents occurring on the way from and to work. The insured risks are limited to those listed in the Law of 10 April 1971, that is, mainly reimbursement of medical expenses (under certain conditions) and compensation for the total or partial, temporary or permanent loss of salary. With respect to employers who have omitted to conclude a contract mandatory insurance coverage, a special fund *(Fonds voor Arbeidsongevallen/Fonds des accidents du Travail)* will pay out the indemnities. These indemnities will then be recovered from the employer. The allowances usually amount to a percentage of the wages or salaries earned during the year preceding the year in which the accident occurred or the disease was contracted. The percentage is based on the degree of the incapacity to work.

§3. *The residual scheme applicable to self-employed persons*

1719. Royal Decree No. 38 of 27 July 1967, as amended ("Royal Decree No 38"), governs the social security contributions and benefits of self-employed persons.

1720. Pursuant to Article 3, paragraph 1 of the Royal Decree, a self-employed person is any physical person who carries out professional activities in Belgium and who is not a civil servant nor bound by an employment contract. The Royal Decree contains provisions according to which persons are presumed to be self-employed persons, such as:

(i) persons who carry out professional activities in Belgium which result in an income which is taxable in accordance with Article 23, paragraph 1.1°, 23, paragraph 1.2° or 30.2° of the Income Tax Code of 1992;

(ii) directors in a Belgian company whether remunerated or not.

1721. The financing of the residual social security scheme for self-employed persons occurs mainly through contributions from the self-employed person.

1. Contributions

1722. Every self-employed person carrying out professional activities in Belgium must register with a special insurance fund of his choice (*Sociale Verzekeringskas voor Zelfstandigen/Caisse d'Assurances Sociales pour Travailleurs Independants*) within 90 days from the commencement of his professional activities. After the expiration of this period, self-employed persons who have not registered with such a fund will automatically be enrolled with the National Auxiliary Fund for the Social Security of Self-Employed Persons (*Nationale Hulpkas voor de Sociale Verzekeringen der Zelfstandigen/Caisse Nationale Auxiliaire d'Assurances Sociales pour Travailleurs Indépendants*) (Art. 9 of Royal Decree No. 38).

1723. Self-employed persons must pay social security contributions on a quarterly basis. The contributions are a percentage of the professional income. Contributions are collected by the *Rijksinstituut voor de Sociale Verzekering der Zelfstandigen/Institut National d'Assurances Sociales pour Travailleurs Indépendants* which obtains information regarding the income directly from the tax authorities (Art. 11 of Royal Decree No. 38).

1724. In practice, contributions amount to approximately 19.65 per cent of net annual income up to € 43,587.20. Contributions due on amounts between € 43,587.20 and € 64,238.84 will be approximately 14.16 per cent. No social security contributions are due on any income exceeding € 64,238.84. The social security contributions are increased with an administration fee which usually varies between 3 and 4.5 per cent of the contributions due. All social security contributions are fully tax deductible in the year of payment.

2. Benefits

1725. The social security system for self-employed persons includes limited sickness insurance and insurance for invalidity, old-age and survivors' pensions and child benefits.

1726. Self-employed persons, as opposed to employees, are only insured against major health risks such as hospitalisation. In order to be reimbursed for standard doctors' and dentists' fees, the self-employed person must take out a special "small risks" insurance policy with one of the mutual health funds *(ziekenfonds/mutualités)*.

§4. *Dispute settlement*

1727. Disputes between employees or self-employed persons and the social security administration services are handled by the Labour Court.

9. RESIDENCE AND WORK PERMITS

1728. This chapter describes the requirements faced by foreigners to take up residence or employment in Belgium.

I. RESIDENCE IN BELGIUM

1729. The rights of foreigners to gain access to, reside in and settle in Belgium are governed by the Law of 15 December 1980 on Access to the Territory, Residence, Settlement and Expulsion of Foreigners (*Wet van 15 december 1980 betreffende de toegang tot het grondgebied, het verblijf en de verwijdering van vreemdelingen/ Loi du 15 décembre 1980 sur l'accès au territoire, le séjour, l'établissement et l'éloignement des étrangers* – the "Law of 15 December 1980") and by the Royal Decree of 8 October 1981 on Access to the Territory, Residence, Settlement and Expulsion of Foreigners (the "Royal Decree of 8 October 1981"), as amended on numerous occasions. Apart from these general arrangements, Belgian regulations on foreigners include specific arrangements for a limited number of persons, such as diplomats or European Union nationals. Needless to say that these specific arrangements are in general less stringent.

A. General rules

1730. The Law of 15 December 1980 sets out the requirements applicable to foreigners in respect of entry and residence in Belgium. According to Article 1 of this law, a foreigner is a person who can not prove that he or she has the Belgian nationality.

§1. Conditions of entry

1731. Pursuant to Article 2 of the Law of 15 December 1980, a foreigner wishing to travel to Belgium must be in the possession of a valid travel document (in principle, a valid national passport) and a visa. During the last few years a lot of changes have been introduced to the Belgian rules on immigration through the signature of the Schengen Agreement on 14 June 1985 and through the Convention implementing the Schengen Agreement of 19 January 1990. At its entry into force, in March

1995, checkpoints and controls at the borders of the signatory states were abolished and a single external border, where immigration checks are carried out in accordance with a single set of rules, was created. Today common rules regarding visas, asylum rights and checks at the single external border have been adopted to allow the free movement of persons within the signatory states without disturbing law and order. One of these common rules concerns the compilation of a list of countries that are exempted from visa requirements. The first list dated from 1995, but was annulled since the European Parliament had not been consulted. The most recent list of exemptions can be found in Regulation No. 2414/2001 of 7 December 2001 amending EC Council Regulation No. 539/2001 (O.J. [2001] C 140/13) listing the third countries whose nationals must be in possession of visas when crossing the external borders of EC Member States and whose nationals are exempt from that requirements. Since this regulation allows the EC Member States to grant further exemptions in certain circumstances, Belgium compiled its own list that can be found in Annex 1 to the Royal Decree of 8 October 1981. More European countries have joined the Schengen Agreement over the past years. At present, there are 15 signatory states (Austria, Belgium, Denmark, Finland, France, Germany, Iceland, Italy, Greece, Luxembourg, Netherlands, Norway, Portugal, Spain and Sweden). Under the said Agreement, the Schengen States shall generally issue a visa valid for the entire Schengen territory: the so-called "uniform visa" or "Schengen visa".

1732. The Schengen visa entitles the holder to remain for an uninterrupted period of at most 90 days within the Schengen territory or to make within a 6 month period different visits over a 6-month period to the Schengen territory, starting from the date of first entry. There are 5 types of Schengen visa:

   (i) *Type A: Airport transit visa*: This is a type of visa that is established by the Joint Action 96/197/JAI of 4 March 1996 adopted by the EC Council on the basis of Article K.3 of the Treaty on European Union Airport Transit Arrangements. The Airport transit visa represents an exception to the principle of free transit allowing individuals to remain without a visa within the international transit area (*See,* Annex 9 to the Chicago Convention on International Civil Aviation and Article 8 of the Royal Decree of 8 October 1981). It is issued by the diplomatic or consular services of the EC Member States when it is ascertained that there is no security risk or risk of illegal immigration and it authorises transit solely through the international area of the airport. The countries concerned are: Afghanistan, Ethiopia, Eritrea, Ghana, Iraq, Iran, Nigeria, Somalia, Sri Lanka, Democratic Republic of the Congo. The Joint Action allows each individual EC Member State to extend this exception to other countries. Belgium has extended the above-mentioned exception to the following countries: Angola, Bangladesh, Guinea, Pakistan, Sudan, Syria (*See*, Annex 1 *bis* of the Royal Decree of 8 October 1981).

(ii) *Type B: Transit visa*: this document authorises transit through several countries starting from a third state and ending with a third state as the destination. The transit period is limited to 5 days.

(iii) *Type C: Short visit visa / Travel visa*: This is a type of visa that authorises non-nationals to enter the territory of the Schengen States for an uninterrupted maximum stay of 90 days (*i.e.*, 3 months) or for one or more visits over a period of 6 months, whereby the total period on the territory not exceed 90 days. Visas issued by Belgian diplomatic and consular authorities are valid for no more than 12 months. This means in concrete that the authorised visit(s) have to be made during this 12-month period.

(iv) *Type A, B, or C Collective visa*: This is a transit visa that authorises a visit of no more than 30 days. It is issued to foreigners travelling as a group on the condition that the group has already been in existence for a certain time and is socially and institutionally organized. Moreover, it must comprise at least 5 and no more than 50 persons and it must indicate the person liable for the eventual loss of the passport and for the departure of the entire group (*See*, Art. 4 of the Royal Decree of 8 October 1981).

(v) *Type D: national visa for a visit of up to 90 days*: This type will be discussed below (*See*, paras. 1737 *et seq.*).

1733. The person applying for a visa must fulfil the following conditions:

(i) The person must appear in person before the diplomatic or consular authorities.

(ii) The applicant must be in the possession of the following documents:

(a) A valid travel document to which a visa may be affixed. The validity of the travel document must be 3 months longer than that of the visa.

(b) Any original (or certified true copies of) documents substantiating the purpose and conditions of the planned visit (hotel, family address, *etc.*).

(c) Any documents proving that the foreigner has sufficient means of support to cover his journey (visit and return), as well as any medical expenses. If the applicant is unable to deliver this proof, Article 3*bis* of the Law of 15 December 1980 allows him/her to call upon a Belgian national or a foreigner residing or established legally and for a long period in Belgium, to act as a guarantor. In the case of such an undertaking of responsibility, it will be up to the guarantor to deliver the proof of sufficient means. The procedure to establish a valid undertaking of responsibility is laid down in Section 1*bis* of the Royal Decree of 8 October 1981.

1734. The aforementioned conditions will be applied even in the situation of an application for a business visa. Moreover, the Belgian diplomatic or consular authorities may require from the applicant to prove that, in the case of a self-employed applicant, he/she is listed in the trade registry (or in an equivalent document which is in use in the country of origin) or, in the case of a paid employee, he/she has in his/her possession a substantiating document drawn up by the employer on whose behalf the applicant wishes to visit Belgium. Evidence of sufficient means can be provided on the basis of one's own resources, the letter of invitation where it is mentioned that the inviting company will pay the accommodation expenses (transport, hotel, *etc.*) or by an undertaking of responsibility.

1735. Even when foreigners have obtained a visa (or where they did not because they are exempt from visa requirements), access to the Belgian territory can be denied in the following circumstances (Art. 3 of the Law of 15 December 1980):
   (i) where the foreigner is unable to hand over any document substantiating the purpose and the accommodation conditions of the visit;
   (ii) where the foreigner does not have sufficient means (and is unable to gain them lawfully), to cover the cost of the trip or the cost of the trip to a third country when he is on transit;
   (iii) where the foreigner has been declared unwanted in the Schengen States, either on the basis of the fact that his/her presence would constitute a danger to public order or national security, either on the basis of the fact that he/she was subjected to an expulsion order (which has not been suspended or quashed) based on an infringement of the national legislation on entry and residence.
   (iv) where the foreigner is considered to damage Belgian international relations (or those from a country party to an international agreement singed by Belgium and dealing with external borders);
   (v) where the foreigner, without having been convicted, poses a treat to society, public order or safety; and
   (vi) where the foreigner has been the subject of a Belgian deportation or expulsion order in the last 10 years. This exception does not apply if the order has been suspended or quashed.

1736. Pursuant to Article 5 of the Law of 15 December 1980, foreigners not staying in accommodation facilities such as a hotel, a camping site or a youth hostel must register with the municipal authorities in the district where the accommodation is located within 3 working days after entering Belgium. The municipal authorities will issue a declaration of arrival (*aankomstverklaring/déclaration d'arrivée*) which is normally valid for 3 months. However, Article 18 of the Royal Decree of 8 October 1981 has exempted 2 categories of persons, namely (i) foreigners that during their trip have been admitted to a hospital or a similar nursing home; (ii) foreigners that have been arrested and detained in a penitentiary. Foreigners who comply with the aforementioned requirements are in principle allowed to remain in Belgium for a maximum period of 3 months (Art. 6 of the Law of 15 December 1980 and Art. 20 of the Royal Decree of 8 October 1981).

§2. *Visits of more than three months*

1737. Foreigners intending to stay more than 3 months in Belgium need to apply for a type D Schengen visa, which allows the foreigner to stay up to 90 days. This type of visa counts as an authorisation to reside (*machtiging tot verblijf/authorisation de séjour*). In very exceptional circumstances, a foreigner can obtain this residence authorisation after his/her arrival in Belgium. In those circumstances, the authorisation will be delivered by the local municipal authorities (Art. 9 of Law of 15 December 1980).

The Belgian legislation only provides procedures for a limited number of applications (*i.e.*, employment purpose, studies, family reunification, cohabitation and marriage). This does not mean that residence for another purpose would not be accepted, but that the chances of obtaining a residence authorisation are more limited.

1738. In order to qualify for a residence authorisation, the applicant must provide a passport (valid for at least one year), a certificate of good conduct (issued 3 months earlier at the most and covering the last 5 years) and a medical certificate attesting good health. Where a foreigner is filing an application for employment purposes, he/she must also provide a work permit (*See*, paras. 1757 *et seq.*). The residence authorisation thus obtained remains valid for an undetermined period of time (in contrast to the residence permit, *See*, para. 1739), except when the authorization is limited in time due to the special circumstances related to the applicant or to his/her work (Art. 13 of the Law of 15 December 1980).

1739. A foreigner authorised or permitted to stay in Belgium for a period exceeding 3 months must, within 8 working days after his/her arrival in Belgium (or when the residence authorisation has been issued in Belgium, within 8 working days after the issuing of the said authorisation), request the local municipal authorities to formalise their stay by filing his/her name in the foreigners' register (*vreemdelingen-register/registre des étrangers*). He/she will then receive a residence permit (*verblijfsvergunning/titre de séjour*) which is normally valid for one year and renewable upon application (Art. 13 of Law of 15 December 1980).

§3. Residence in Belgium

1740. Provided that the foreigner complies with the conditions for entry into Belgium and has obtained an authorisation to reside in Belgium for an indefinite period of time and a residence permit (valid for one year), he/she is entitled to take up permanent residence in Belgium (Art. 14 of the Law of 15 December 1980). The request must be made to the local municipal authorities (Art. 16 of the Law of 15 December 1980). If these authorities decide to grant the request, they will issue a permanent residence permit (*vestigingsvergunning/titre d'établissement*) in the form of a special identity card which is valid for 5 years (Art. 31 of the Royal Decree of 8 October 1981). Moreover, the foreigner will have his/her name entered in the population register of the municipality in which he/she resides (Art. 17 of the Law of 15 December 1980).

1741. The special identity card can be renewed by an application to the local municipal authorities. Pursuant to Article 33 of the Royal Decree of 8 October 1981, this application has to be filed between the thirtieth and fifteenth day before the expiry date.

§4. Removal and expulsion

1742. A foreigner who has not (yet) obtained a permanent resident permit can be removed from the territory in the following situations:
  (i) where he/she has violated the principles of public policy or public security;
  (ii) where he/she has violated the conditions imposed on his/her visit to Belgium (Art. 20 of the Law of 15 December 1980).

1743. Only the Minister of Justice can issue a removal order (*terugwijzing/renvoi*). Moreover, Article 20 of the Law of 15 December 1980 states that when an international agreement determines that this measure can only be taken after the hearing of the foreigner in question, the removal can only be ordered after the recommendations of the Advisory Committee for Foreigners.

1744. A foreigner who has already obtained a permanent residence permit in Belgium can be the subject of an expulsion order (*uitzetting/expulsion*) issued by the King if that person has seriously violated principles of public policy or public security. In that case, the prior opinion of the Advisory Committee for Foreigners must be sought. If the expulsion measure is based on the political activity of the foreigner concerned, the measure must be discussed in the Council of Ministers (Art. 20 of the Law of 15 December 1980).

B. Nationals of the EC Member States

1745. Special rules (Tittle II, Chapter I of the Law of 15 December 1980) apply to nationals of the 14 other EC Member States who intend to exercise activities as employed or self-employed persons, provide services or exercise a continued right of residence in Belgium. These special rules will be set out below. The members of the family of an EC national gain equal rights to stay in Belgium (Art. 40, paras. 3 and 4 of the Law of 15 December 1980). The term "family members" covers:

   (i) the spouse of the EC national;
   (ii) the ascendants (and their spouses) of the EC national and his/her spouse provided they are supported by the EC national; and
   (iii) the descendants of the EC national and their spouses who are supported by the EC national or who are less than 21 years old.

§1. Conditions of entry

1746. EC nationals only need a national identity card or valid national passport to enter Belgium (Art. 41 of the Law of 15 December 1980) and to remain here for a maximum period of 3 months. Nonetheless, Article 43 of the Law of 15 December 1980 states that access to the Belgian territory can be denied. However, this is only possible in a limited number of cases (*See*, para. 1755).

1747. EC nationals intending to stay in Belgium for less than 3 months and not residing in accommodation facilities such as a hotel, a camping site, or a youth hostel, must register with the municipal authorities in the district where their accommodation is located within 8 working days after entering Belgium (Art. 41*bis* of the Law of 15 December 1980).

1748. Where an EC national travels to Belgium in order to work (this includes seasonal workers as well) for a period not exceeding 3 months, Article 47 of the Royal Decree of 8 October 1981 states that these persons need to submit to the municipal authorities: (i) a valid identity card (or passport); and (ii) a declaration of employment containing the duration or an employment contract certified by the competent authorities (*i.e.*, a document containing the signature of both the employee and the employer) or any documents necessary for the job-occupation. The municipal authorities will then issue a certificate. This document is for free but does not count as a residence permit.

1749. Article 48 of the Royal Decree of 8 October 1981 deals with the situation where an EC national travels to Belgium in order to provide services for a period not exceeding 3 months. In that case, the person concerned will have to be in the possession of a valid identity card or passport and has to prove that he/she will be providing services. Once proven, the person will obtain the necessary certificate for free. Again, this document will not count as a residence permit.

§2. Visits of more than 3 months

1750. The right of free movement of persons is a fundamental freedom granted by Title III of the EC Treaty. This right is primarily afforded to employees and self-employed persons.

1751. Article 42 of the Law of 15 December 1980 simply mentions that the right of EC nationals to reside in Belgium is subject to the conditions and deadlines stipulated by a Royal Decree in accordance to the EC regulations and directives. The Royal Decree of 8 October 1981 makes the distinction between 3 types of situations: (i) a residence of less than 3 months (*See*, paras. 1747 *et seq.*); (ii) a residence of more than 3 months but less than one year (Art. 46); and (iii) a residence of one year or more (Art. 45 of the Law of 15 December 1980).

1752. In the situation where an EC national travels to Belgium to occupy a professional activity (*i.e.*, an employed person, a self-employed person and a seasonal worker) for more than 3 months but less than one year, Article 46 of the Law of 15 December 1980 provides that he/she needs to be in the possession of: (i) a valid identity card or a valid passport; (ii) in case of an employed person: a declaration of engagement issued by the employer and stating the length of the engagement or an employment contract certified by the competent authorities; and (iii) in case of a self-employed person: the documents necessary for the occupation of a profession. The person concerned will be registered in the foreigners' register and he will obtain a registration certificate type B, *i.e.*, the certificate which is issued to EC nationals rather than type A, *i.e.*, the certificate which is issued to non EC nationals) which remains valid for the entire duration of the engagement.

Where a person travels to Belgium in order to provide services and this for a period of time exceeding 3 months, he/she will have to be in possession of a valid identity card or passport and has to prove that he/she will actually be providing services. Once proven, the local authorities will register the person concerned in the foreigners' register and he/she will obtain a registration certificate (Art. 48 of the Law of 15 December 1980).

1753. An EC national wishing to undertake a professional activity in Belgium for at least one year will have to submit a valid identity card or a valid passport and will have to get registered in the foreigners' register in the local municipality. He will then receive a registration certificate (type B) which remains valid for a period of 5 months (Art. 45). The procedure is, however, then still not completed at this stage. The EC national still needs to deliver the proof of his/her professional activity and this can be done through every relevant document. 3 possible scenarios must be distinguished:

(i) The EC national delivers the proof of his/her professional activity at the same time as his/her registration application or within the 4 months following the application. The municipal authority will transfer the documents to the Division and the Department of Federal Immigration. They will inform the Minister or his representative who will take a decision. The person concerned must address the municipal authorities within the period between one to 5 months following the application in order to obtain the notification of the decision that has been taken.

(ii) The EC national delivers the proof of his/her professional activity during the fifth month after the registration application: the municipal authority must renew the registration certificate for the period of one month. Moreover, they will transfer the documents to the Division and the Department of Federal Immigration that will inform the Minister or his representative who will take a decision. The person concerned must address the municipal authorities within the renewed period of one month in order to obtain notification of the decision that has been taken.

(iii) The EC national fails to deliver the necessary proof within the duration of validity of the registration certificate. In this case, the Minister or his representative will be obliged to refuse the residence application and to order the expulsion. This expulsion will be carried out even when the person concerned has not addressed the municipal authority in order to obtain notification thereof and this will occur within 30 days after the expiry of the residence certificate. However, this expulsion will not take place where the person concerned is nonetheless capable of proving either his/her professional activity or a realistic chance of finding a professional activity or the fact that he/she is about to start a self-employed activity.

1754. Where the person concerned is able to deliver the proof concerning his/her professional activities within the above mentioned time limits, the Minister or his representative have 2 options: (i) they may take a positive decision; or (ii) no decision at all. In the latter, the municipal authority must register the EC national in the population register (*bevolkingsregister/registre de la population*) and issue a residence card for EC nationals (Art. 49 of the Royal Decree of 8 October 1981). The issuing of this identity card must not be for free but the local municipalities are not allowed to impose a higher price than the one imposed for the creation of an identity card for nationals. However, they can also decide to postpone the residence application. This will be the case when there are serious reasons to believe that the applicant forms a threat to public order, public security or to the public health. This decision will mention the notification date of the final decision that can not be situated after the expiry of the registration certificate. This second decision can be a positive or a negative one. If the second decision contains a refusal of the residence application, it will have to be accompanied by an expulsion order that will be carried out within a minimum period of 15 days.

§3. *Deportation*

1755. If the foreigner does not comply with the conditions of entry, a deportation order can be issued by the Minister of Justice. For an EC national, such an order can only be granted for reasons involving public policy, public security or public health. Moreover, Article 43 of the Law of 15 December 1980 lays down that:

  (i) the reasons may not be invoked for economic purposes;

  (ii) the measure of public order or public security must be purely based on the personal attitude of the person concerned. The existence of a conviction for a criminal offence does not in itself constitute a sufficient ground for the adoption of such measures;

  (iii) the expiry of the documents authorising access and residence can not in itself justify the adoption of a removal order; and

  (iv) only the diseases and infirmities mentioned in Annex to the Law of 15 December 1980 may be invoked to refuse access or residence. After the issuing of such a permit, disease or infirmity can no longer be invoked to justify an expulsion or a renewal of a residence permit.

II. RULES APPLYING TO EMPLOYMENT OF FOREIGNERS

1756. As a general rule, any foreigner other than EC nationals intending to exercise professional activities in Belgium must obtain either a work permit (for employees) or a professional card (for self-employed persons). EC citizens are exempted from these obligations.

A. Work permit

1757. The acquisition by non-EC nationals of a Belgian work permit is governed by the Law of 30 April 1999 on the Employment of Foreign Workers (*Wet betreffende de tewerkstelling van buitenlandse werknemers/Loi relative à l'occupation des travailleurs étrangers* – the "Law of 30 April 1999") and by a Royal Decree of 9 June

1999 on the Employment of Foreign Workers (the "Royal Decree of 9 June 1999"). The exercise of professional activities by a foreigner in Belgium is in principle subjected to the system of permits that have to be applied for by the employee and the employer.

1758. Pursuant to Article 4 of the Law of 30 April 1999, an employer seeking to hire foreign employees must obtain the prior authorization by the competent authorities. In addition, Article 5 of the Law of 30 April 1999 provides that no foreign employee is entitled to work in Belgium without a work permit. In practice, the application for an authorisation for an employer to employ a foreign employee and the application by an employee to obtain a work permit are both made at the same time and on the same application form by the employer. It is possible to apply for a work permit through a proxyholder acting on behalf of the employer.

1759. However, pursuant to Article 2 of the Royal Decree, a large number of persons are exempt for the obligations laid down in Article 4 and 5 of the Law of 30 April 1999 (e.g. nationals of the European Economic Area, the spouse and the dependants of a Belgian national). As a consequence, these persons have unlimited access to the Belgian labour market. It should be underscored that some of the exempted categories are only exempt for a specified professional activity. They will not be exempt for other activities exercised on the side. At this moment, the Royal Decree contains 23 exempt categories of persons.

1760. There are 2 types of work permits: work permit A and work permit B:
    (i) *Work permit A*: This permit covers all kinds of salaried employment and has an indefinite validity (Art. 3 of the Royal Decree of 9 June 1999). Pursuant to Article 13 of the Royal Decree of 9 June 1999, only a limited number of applicants qualifies for this type of permit (*e.g.*, applicants having a work permit B and working in Belgium for more than 4 years, applicants residing legally in Belgium for an interrupted period of at least 5 year). Once the work permit of type A has been issued, Article 4 of the Royal Decree of 9 June 1999 states that it will no longer be necessary for the employer to obtain an employment authorisation. It is quite obvious that the application must be made by the entitled foreigner himself. He/she will have to fill in model forms specially created for this purpose and which can be found at the regional employment services (VDAB in Flanders, BGDA/ORBEM in Brussels and FOREM in Wallonia). It is important to mention that the applicant must address the regional employment service, which covers his/her place of residence (in contrast to the regional employment service covering the place of employment, such as is the case regarding the work permit B). Where the applicant is already residing legally in Belgium, he will have to fill in an extra

form (*i.e.*, an inquiry leaflet) which will be transferred to the migration service. In this case, the work permit will be directly issued to the worker by the municipal administration of his/her place of residence.

(ii) *Work permit B*: This type of work permit is only valid for employment by one employer and has a maximum validity of 12 months (Art. 3 of the Royal Decree of 9 June 1999). It is up to the employer to apply for an employment authorisation and whenever such an authorisation is issued, the employee concerned is automatically eligible for a work permit B (Art. 4 of the Royal Decree of 9 June 1999). The application must be filed with the regional employment services (VDAB in Flanders, BGDA/ORBEM in Brussels and FOREM in Wallonia) covering the worker's place of employment. The following documents must be joined together with the application form: (a) a medical certificate if the employee does not legally reside in the country where he will be working or if the employee resides less than 2 years in this country and if he is employed here for the first time (Arts. 14 and 15 of the Royal Decree of 9 June 1999); (b) an inquiry leaflet if the application is filed on behalf of a person residing already legally in Belgium; and (c) an employment agreement (Arts. 12 and 13 of the Royal Decree of 9 June 1999).

The file will then be transferred to the immigration service. An employment authorisation will only when the function which the applicant is going to fulfil cannot be exercised by a person already belonging to the Belgian and European (Economic Area) labor market (Art. 8 of the Royal Decree of 9 June 1999). This principle of the priority has nonetheless been attributed some important exceptions. Firstly, Article 38 of the Royal Decree of 9 June 1999, provides that the competent regional Minister of Employment may grant exceptions based on economic or social reasons. Secondly, Article 9 of the Royal Decree of 9 June 1999, provides a whole list of exceptions. The most important one in this context is the exception attributed to highly skilled staff (Art. 9, para. 6 of the Royal Decree of 9 June 1999) provided that the duration of their employment does not exceed 4 years and that their yearly salary is higher than € 25,921. A second category that is noteworthy contained in Article 9, para. 7 of the Royal Decree of 9 June 1999 since it deals with managerial staff provided for that their yearly salary is higher than € 51,842.

After the approval of the immigration service, the authorization will be accorded to the employer. If the foreign employee is already legally residing in Belgium, he will be entitled to collect his/her work permit at the municipal authorities of his/her place of residence. In the adverse situation, the employer will be entitled to collect the issued work permit at the municipal authorities of his/her place of residence or of the company's seat. It will be up to the employer to deliver this permit to his/her employee.

1761. The application for an employment and a work permit can be refused on the following grounds (Art. 34 of the Royal Decree of 9 June 1999):
  (i) the application contains incorrect or incomplete information or the conditions laid down in the law and the royal decree are not fulfilled;
  (ii) the employment is in conflict with public order, public security, Belgian legislation and (international) agreements on the employment of foreign employees;
  (iii) the existence of reasons relating to public order or public security purely based on the personal attitude of the employee concerned;
  (iv) the disrespect by the employer of legal employment obligations;
  (v) the employment is not in accordance with the provisions on pay and employment conditions applicable to the Belgian employees; and
  (vi) the application relates to an employment that does not procure any revenues capable of meeting the employee's needs or those of his/her family members.

1762. Where an application for a work permit (type A or B) is refused, the applicant (*i.e.*, the employee in case of a work permit type A or the employer in case of an authorisation/work permit B) will be informed by registered mail. He can thereupon, within one month following the receipt of the letter, lodge an appeal with the competent regional Minister of Employment.

1763. According to Article 31 of the Royal Decree of 9 June 1999, an employment authorisation and a type B work permit can be renewed provided that the employer submits a renewal application one month before the expiration of the validity of the running employment authorization and work permit. Only when the employee has attended special professional training (*i.e.*, training recognised by VDAB, ORBEM/BGDA, FOREM or the National Institute for Sickness and Invalidity Insurance (*Rijksinstituut voor ziekte- en invaliditeitsverzekering/l'Institut national d'assurance maladie invalidité – R.I.Z.I.V./I.N.A.M.I.*), he will not be bound to perform the same employment for which the first work permit was issued.

B. Professional Card

1764. The Law of 19 February 1965 on the Exercise of Self-Employed Professional Activities by Foreigners (*Wet betreffende de uitoefening van de zelfstandige beroepsactiviteiten der vreemdelingen/Loi relative à l'exercice, par les étrangers, des activités professionnelles indépendantes*) (and its various implementing decrees) regulates the exercise of self-employed professional activities by foreigners in

Belgium. Foreigners other than EC citizens, who wish to exercise self-employed professional activities in Belgium, must be in the possession of a professional card (*beroepskaart/carte professionelle*). If the applicant is not legally residing in Belgium, the application should be made at the Belgian Diplomatic or Consular services in the country of residence (Art. 1, para. 2 of the Royal Decree of 2 August 1985). Applicants already legally residing in Belgium should address the local municipal authorities (Art. 1 of the Royal Decree of 2 August 1985). The applicant must submit the following documents in order to obtain the professional card:

(i) a duly certified application form,

(ii) a medical certificate,

(iii) a certificate of good conduct issued by the authorities of the applicant's last country of residence, and

(iv) a copy of a passport.

In case of renewal, a document attesting that all social and fiscal obligations are fulfilled. A sum of € 87 must be paid when the application is filed before the municipal authorities and a sum of € 3 when the professional card is being isued (Arts. 3, para. 2 and 9, para. 1 of the Royal Decree of 2 August 1985).

1765. Once the application is approved, the professional card will be issued by the Ministry of Middle Classes (*Ministerie van Middenstand/Ministère des Classes Moyennes*). The card is personal and non-transferable. It defines precisely the nature of the activities the self-employed person will be authorised to exercise and the conditions under which such activities may be exercised (Art. 3, para. 1 of the Law of 19 February 1965). It stays valid for a maximum period of 5 years (Art. 3, para. 2 of the Law of 19 February 1965), but an application for renewal is possible. This application, however, has to be filed at least 3 months before the expiry date of the professional card that needs to be renewed (Art. 4 of the Royal Decree of 2 August 1985).

1766. Where a professional card is being issued for the first time, the applicant will receive a certified copy which is merely intended for the registration with the Trade Registry (Art. 11 of the Royal Decree of 2 August 1985).

10. DISTRIBUTION

I. INTRODUCTION

1767. Foreign suppliers who want to distribute their products on the Belgian market can choose from a wide variety of means. They can export their goods directly into Belgium (*See*, Chapter 6) or, in cases where local presence is necessary or advisable for commercial reasons, they can set up a branch or subsidiary (*See*, Chapter 2). Alternatively, foreign suppliers can make use of one or more commercial intermediaries, which is the subject of this chapter. Although Belgian law distinguishes between a wide variety of commercial intermediaries – some of whom are subject to specific legal rules – only the 4 most commonly used intermediaries will be discussed in this chapter, *i.e.*, distributors (*See*, Section II, paras. 1768 *et seq.*), commercial agents (*See*, Section III, paras. 1843 *et seq.*), commercial representatives (*See*, Section IV, paras. 1915 *et seq.*) and franchisees (*See*, Section V, paras. 1961 *et seq.*).

II. DISTRIBUTORS

A. Introduction

1768. Under Belgian law, distribution agreements (*verkoopconcessies/concessions de vente*) are usually defined as agreements whereby one party (*i.e.*, the supplier) agrees with another (*i.e.*, the distributor) to supply the latter with products or services for the purpose of resale. Such agreements can be entered into at different levels in the distribution chain: (i) between manufacturer and importer, (ii) between importer and wholesaler, or (iii) between wholesaler and retailer.

1769. One of the main characteristics of any distribution agreement is that the distributor sells the products or services in his own name and on his own account, unlike the commercial agent and the commercial representative. Hence, from a strictly legal point of view, the distributor does not act as an intermediary. A true (legal) intermediary acts on behalf of his principal in such a manner that the legal relationship is created directly between the principal and the customer. This is not the case with a distributor. He deals directly with his customer, and the resulting contractual relationships are established between the customer and the distributor. The latter bears the risks resulting from the individual resale agreements. However, from an economic point of view, distributors perform functions similar to those performed by true intermediaries, so it is appropriate to deal with them in this chapter.

1770. Distribution agreements establish a general framework within which future supplies of products or services will take place between the supplier and the distributor. It is common for such agreements not only to specify prices, quantities and other delivery conditions between the supplier and the distributor, but also to provide for warranty provisions, after-sales service, technical assistance, brand promotion, and so on. In other words, a distribution agreement is a framework agreement (*raamovereenkomst/contrat-cadre*) which is to be distinguished from the various individual sale and resale agreements implementing it. Each individual contract is governed by its own rules.

1771. With one important exception, Belgian law does not contain any specific rules governing distribution agreements. Therefore, the parties are free to determine between themselves the content of the distribution agreement. Questions not specifically addressed by the parties will be governed by the general rules of contract law as contained in the Belgian Civil Code. Nevertheless, the Law of 27 July 1961 on the Unilateral Termination of Certain Categories of Distribution Agreements (the "Law of 27 July 1961") (*Wet betreffende eenzijdige beëindiging van de voor onbepaalde tijd verleende concessies van alleenverkoop/Loi relative à la résiliation unilatérale des concessions de vente exclusive à durée indéterminée*) contains specific rules governing the unilateral termination of certain categories of distribution agreements. These rules are mandatory, and cannot be superseded even by the mutual consent of the parties. It is therefore appropriate to distinguish in this section between the general principles applicable to distribution agreements (*See*, paras. 1772 *et seq.*) and the specific provisions on termination contained in the Law of 27 July 1961 (*See*, paras. 1789 *et seq.*).

B. General principles applicable to distribution agreements

§1. Formation of the agreement

1772. In general, no specific formalities must be observed to form a valid distribution agreement. However, while the agreement may be oral or even tacit, the absence of a written document may create serious evidentiary problems if a conflict arises. In such cases, it may be difficult to prove the existence and the content of the agreement.

1773. While parties may characterise their contracts as they see fit, Belgian judges are not bound by this. They will consider the common intention of the parties rather than the literal meaning of the contract terms. If, for example, a contract bears the name 'agency agreement' but the so-called agent buys products from his principal in order to resell them in his own name and on his own account, the "agent" will be regarded as a distributor and the agreement will be deemed to be a distribution agreement subject to the rules governing such agreements.

1774. Finally, it is worth mentioning that the language used to draft a distribution agreement may be determined freely by the contracting parties.

§2. *Content of the agreement*

1. *Examples of typical clauses*

1775. Other than as discussed below, the parties to a contract may generally determine the content of their agreement as they wish. However, distribution agreements will typically contain some of the following:

(i) *grant clauses*, which define the respective roles of the parties and which grant the distributor the right to sell the supplier's products or services. This right may be non-exclusive, sole, or exclusive. Shared exclusivity and sole exclusivity are both possibilities. The distributor's right to sell the supplier's products or services may be subject to territorial restrictions, and is sometimes the counterpart of obligations to purchase the contract products or services exclusively from the supplier, or of an obligation not to sell competing products or services. If the agreement is not *de minimis*, these aspects must be reviewed carefully in the light of the applicable EC and Belgian competition rules.

(ii) *organisational clauses*, which set down the terms for ordering, invoicing, paying for and delivering the product, as well as transferring both the title and the risk. It is not uncommon to find provisions referring to the supplier's general conditions of sale for those aspects which are not expressly set out in the agreement.

(iii) *sales promotion clauses*, which may include minimum sales requirements, obligations regarding advertising, after-sales service, warranty provisions, the use of technically and commercially skilled staff, the appointment of sub-distributors, minimum stock provisions, obligations to sell the products or services under the trade mark of the supplier or using the latter's trade dress, *etc.*

(iv) *one or more clauses dealing with warranty provisions* in the relationship between supplier and distributor and, increasingly, with product liability issues (*See*, Chapter 18).

(v) *clauses governing the termination of the agreement*, including rules on early termination and the rights and obligations of the parties during the notice period (if any) and after termination, for example, with respect to existing sale orders, use of the supplier's trade marks and recovery of unsold stock.

(vi) *clauses concerning choice of law and choice of forum*, which are especially recommended in an international context.

2. *Implicit clauses*

1776. In addition to the provisions expressly provided for in the distribution agreement, Article 1134, para. 3, and Article 1135 of the Civil Code oblige contracting parties to perform the agreement in accordance with the principles of good faith and equity. These provisions have sometimes been interpreted in the case law to include supplementary obligations not expressly established in the agreement by the parties. For example, a supplier was held to have breached his contractual good faith obligations because he competed with his sole distributor at prices far below the prices he charged to his distributor (Antwerp Court of Appeal, 28 March 1984, *R.W.*, 1984-1985, 1713). However, the lower prices were charged by the supplier, not for the contract products, but for another brand of products which competed with the contract products. This practice was held to be part of an overall strategy by the supplier to evict his distributor from the market.

1777. A further important supplementary provision which is deemed to be part of any distribution agreement (unless the parties have expressly addressed the issue themselves) obliges the supplier to take back unsold stock on termination of the distribution agreement. This issue will be discussed in more detail in paragraph 1788.

3. *Restrictions regarding the content of the agreement*

1778. While parties are generally free to determine the content of their distribution agreement, this freedom is subject both to certain mandatory legal provisions and to the requirements of public policy. As indicated earlier, the Law of 27 July 1961 dealing with the termination of certain categories of distribution agreement contains several mandatory provisions, *i.e.*, provisions from which the parties may not derogate. (*See*, paras. 1789 *et seq.*) As far as public policy requirements are concerned, the basic principles are fairly straightforward. Under Belgian law, any contractual provision which violates principles of public policy will be deemed absolutely null and void (Arts. 6, 1131 and 1133 of the Civil Code). Any interested party (including the contract parties) may invoke the violation of public policy, and the judge must establish such violation *ex officio*, *i.e.*, at his own initiative. Contractual provisions which violate public policy are legally unenforceable ("*nemo auditur propriam turpitudinem allegans*"). In cases where the provision, which violates public policy, cannot be severed from the agreement as a whole or is determinant to the parties entering into the agreement, the nullity of this provision entails the nullity of the remaining contractual provisions. However, since the rules governing severability are not themselves considered mandatory legal provisions or public policy principles, parties may provide that the invalidity of one provision will not affect the validity of the remainder of their agreement.

1779. Among the most important principles of public policy which must be taken into account by parties to a distribution agreement are the rules regarding competition contained in the EC Treaty. The application of Article 81 of the EC Treaty to distribution agreements is beyond the scope of this book and will not be discussed.

§3. Termination of the agreement

1780. In Belgium, specific rules regarding the termination of distribution contracts are contained in the Law of 27 July 1961. However, these rules are limited to the unilateral termination of certain categories of distribution agreements. With regard to all other categories of distribution agreements, the general principles of contract law apply. According to such principles, it is appropriate to distinguish between agreements of indefinite duration and agreements of fixed duration.

1. Agreements of indefinite duration

1781. The essence of all agreements of indefinite duration, including distribution agreements, is that either side may give notice of termination at any time. The exercise of this right is not dependent upon the existence of a breach committed by the other party. It is a discretionary right which is the natural consequence of the public policy principle that parties may not be bound by a contract for life. Thus, in theory, the party giving notice of termination has the right to terminate with immediate effect and without having to pay any indemnity. In practice, however, the courts tend to temper the rigors of this principle by holding that the requirements of good faith require that sufficient notice be given. Consequently, an abrupt termination not justified by any shortcomings committed by the other party may give rise to an obligation to indemnify the terminated party. However, where there are serious shortcomings (such as payment arrears or a failure to meet agreed a minimum sales quota, for example), the termination may be effective immediately and without indemnity even if damage is suffered as a result of the termination.

1782. In cases of unilateral termination, the role of the courts is limited. Unilateral termination is not effectuated by the courts; it is declared by either party because they have the right to end an agreement of indefinite duration at any time. Where a party disputes the termination, the role of the courts is limited to evaluating whether the exercise of the right to terminate was faulty. Wrongful termination may give rise to an obligation to pay damages, but the decision to terminate cannot be undone by the courts.

1783. For the sake of completeness, in addition to the rules on unilateral contract termination, agreements of indefinite duration remain subject to the normal rules of contract termination. Hence, such agreements may also be rescinded, annulled, terminated for reasons of *force majeure*, and so on, if the circumstances permit such form of termination.

2. *Agreements of fixed duration*

1784. Unlike agreements of indefinite duration, agreements of fixed duration may not be terminated unilaterally. In principle, any unilateral termination prior to the agreed moment of expiry of the contract will amount to a breach of contract for which damages may be due. Therefore, distribution agreements of fixed duration are subject to the normal rules on contract termination. For example, in case of serious breach by one party, the other party may request that a court rescinds the agreement on the basis of Article 1184 of the Civil Code (*See*, paras. 1814 *et seq.*).

1785. In the absence of contractual provisions to the contrary, agreements of fixed duration terminate automatically on the expiration date set forth in the agreement, and no notice of termination is required. If the parties continue to perform the agreement after the expiry date, they will normally be considered bound by an agreement of indefinite duration in the absence of indications to the contrary. Such agreements of indefinite duration are governed by the rules on termination discussed in paragraphs 1798 *et seq.*

3. *Other issues*

1786. Until the notice period expires, all the provisions of the contract remain fully in effect. Therefore, in an exclusive distribution agreement, the supplier may not appoint a new distributor in the contract territory during the notice period. Similarly, if the distributor is bound by an obligation not to sell products or services competing with those of the supplier, he will remain bound by this obligation throughout the notice period. In practice, these obligations may give rise to problems because both the supplier and the distributor will have a clear interest in trying to find alternative contract partners during the notice period. Particular care should be given to these problems, because, during the notice period, immediate termination of the contract based on serious default remains possible for both the supplier and the distributor. Violation of an exclusive right or of a non-compete obligation would normally be deemed a serious fault.

1787. Certain case law has gone so far as to hold that there is a general obligation on the parties during the notice period not to make any unilateral changes to the contractual practice which would impose additional burdens on the other party or which would deprive it of certain advantages (Comm. Brussels, 29 June 1981, *J.T.*, 1981, 554). This case held that even in a non-exclusive distribution agreement, the supplier could not appoint an additional distributor during the notice period if he had refrained from doing so prior to giving notice.

1788. A further issue which almost invariably surfaces after the termination of a distribution agreement concerns the dispersal of the stock of contract products which is still held by the distributor. If the parties have addressed this issue in their original contract, such arrangements will prevail. However, in the absence of specific contractual provisions, the case law almost unanimously holds that there is an obligation for the supplier to take back any unsold stock at the distributor's request. Several legal grounds are invoked to justify the existence of such an obligation. However, none of them is entirely satisfactory. The most commonly used justification is that each sales agreement is entered into under the (tacit) condition (*ontbindende voorwaarde/condition résolutoire*) that it will be cancelled in case of termination of the framework distribution agreement.

C. Law of 27 July 1961 on the Unilateral Termination of Certain Categories of Distribution Agreements

§1. Scope of application

1789. The Law of 27 July 1961 has a limited scope. It covers only those distribution agreements which fall within one of the categories specified in the Law of 27 July 1961. Moreover, the Law of 27 July 1961 only addresses problems related to the termination of these agreements. Issues such as the formation of the contract and the content of the agreement are not covered by the Law of 27 July 1961. In this section, both the definition of distribution agreements for the purposes of the Law of 27 July 1961 and the categories into which a distribution agreement must fall in order to be covered by the Law of 27 July 1961 will be addressed.

1. Definition of distribution agreements

1790. Article 1, para. 2, of the Law of 27 July 1961 defines a distribution agreement (*verkoopconcessie/concession de vente*) as:

> "*any agreement by which a supplier grants to one or more distributors the right to sell in their own name and for their own account products which the former manufactures or distributes.*"

1791. In order to develop an understanding of the agreements falling within the scope of the Law of 27 July 1961, each of the constituent elements of this definition are analysed below:

(i) *"any agreement"*: the Law of 27 July 1961 covers written, oral and even tacit agreements. In addition, the characterisation of a contractual relationship as a distribution agreement does not depend on compliance with any formal requirements or on the characterisation given to the agreement by the parties. In the absence of a written contract, the existence of a distribution agreement may be derived from the nature of the dealings between the parties concerned (Cass., 12 June 1986, *Pas.*, 1986, I, 1254);

(ii) *"by which a supplier grants a right to sell"*: a mere agreement to successive sales transactions does not satisfy this condition. For this condition to be met, the supplier must grant special rights to the distributor. The supplier must reserve for the distributor the right to sell the contract goods on a continuous and organised basis. For his part, the distributor must undertake to comply with specific rules of distribution imposed by the supplier.

1792. This part of the statutory definition also makes it clear that the Law of 27 July 1961 only covers distribution agreements which address the resale of products. Hence, licensing arrangements or supply agreements whereby the supplier sells products subsequently used by the purchaser to manufacture his own products fall outside the scope of the Law of 27 July 1961. Similarly, the Law of 27 July 1961 does not in principle, cover the supply of products for use in service contracts or in service franchises;

(i) *"to one or more distributors"*: besides exclusive distribution agreements, the scope of the scope of the Law of 27 July 1961 may also include agreements where the supplier has appointed several distributors in the same territory;

(ii) *"in their own name and for their own account"*: since the Law of 27 July 1961 applies only to traders acting in their own name and on their own account, commercial agents and commercial representatives cannot benefit from its protection;

(iii) *"products which the supplier manufactures or distributes"*: the distribution agreement must relate to products manufactured or distributed by the supplier. This part of the statutory definition clarifies the fact that agreements for the provision of services do not fall within the scope of the Law of 27 July 1961.

1793. The statutory definition of distribution agreements results in the exclusion of certain types of agreements from the scope of the Law of 27 July 1961. Some major exclusions are:

    (i) *occasional sales agreements:* these agreements lack the required continuous and organised nature of a distributorship;

    (ii) *service distribution agreements:* only distribution agreements for the resale of products are covered;

    (iii) *licensing agreements or other agreements pursuant to which the distributor manufactures the contract products*: such agreements are not confined to the resale of products manufactured or distributed by the supplier;

    (iv) *commercial agency and commercial representation agreements:* commercial agents and commercial representatives do not act in their own name and on their own account.

  2. *Specific categories of distribution agreements covered by the Law of 27 July 1961*

1794. Besides meeting the statutory definition of a distribution agreement, such an agreement must fit within one of the categories specifically included in the Law of 27 July 1961 in order to be subject to the Law of 27 July 1961. Pursuant to Article 1, para. 1, the Law of 27 July 1961 applies to the following distribution agreements:

    (i) exclusive distribution agreements;

    (ii) quasi-exclusive distribution agreements; and

    (iii) distribution agreements which impose certain onerous obligations upon the distributor.

1795. In practice, these categories cover the most common types of distribution agreements. They are discussed further in the following sections.

    (i) *Exclusive distribution agreements:* an agreement of this sort does not necessarily grant an exclusive right to only one distributor to sell the supplier's products within a defined area. This right may be granted to several distributors (shared exclusivity) and the supplier may also reserve the right to distribute the products himself (Cass., 23 February 1995, *J.L.M.B.*, 1995, 1356). Nor is it necessary that the distributor benefit from "absolute" territorial protection, which would result, for example, from a prohibition imposed on all distributors located in other territories from supplying products in the distributor's contract territory. In fact, such absolute territorial protection may give rise to serious problems under EC competition law. So-called "relative" territorial protection, such as protection against direct sales by the principal in the distributor's contract territory, is sufficient to bring a distribution agreement within the purview of the Law of 27 July 1961 (Cass., 10 September 1987, *Pas.*, 1988, I, 31).

    (ii) *Quasi-exclusive distribution agreements:* in order to fall within this category, the distributor must sell nearly all of the contract products in his territory. The Law of 27 July 1961 does not specify what must be understood by "nearly all of the products". Case law indicates that figures of 30 to 35 per cent are insufficient, while a share of 80 per cent in a particular territory was held to meet the test (Comm. Namur, 17 March 1997, general docket No. 1938/91, *not published*).

(iii) *Distribution agreements imposing onerous obligations upon the distributor*: the third category of distribution agreements covered by the Law of 27 July 1961 are those under which the supplier imposes "important" obligations upon the distributor which are closely and specifically related to the distribution agreement and the burden of which is such that the distributor would suffer serious prejudice if the agreement were terminated. Ascertaining whether or not certain obligations are sufficiently important to be covered by this category is left to the courts. To be considered "important", an obligation cannot be naturally bound to the activity of the distributor, nor spontaneously performed by the latter (Comm. Liège, 21 October 1994, *R.D.C.*, 1995, 900). By contrast, obligations related to issues such as quotas, exclusive supply, training of the technical staff, purchase of specific equipment, after-sale services, and promotional expenses have been considered sufficiently important for the Law of 27 July 1961 to apply.

1796. By way of illustration, the following set of obligations imposed on a motor vehicle distributor was considered onerous (Comm. Brussels, 24 October 1977, *B.R.H.*, 1978, 228):

   (i) the obligation to install or organise distributorship outlets according to criteria fixed by the supplier;

   (ii) the obligation to hire a sufficient number of skilled personnel in order to be able to carry out repair and maintenance work at all times;

   (iii) the obligation to apply prescribed repair and maintenance methods and to use special tools for these purposes;

   (iv) the obligation to print the name of the manufacturer on all company documents and advertising materials;

   (v) the obligation to have an agreed number of demonstration vehicles;

   (vi) the obligation to have a sufficient stock of cars and spare parts;

   (vii) the obligation not to sell outside a particular area; and

   (viii) the obligation not to sell competing products.

§2. *Rules governing agreements of fixed duration*

1797. Specific rules for the termination and the renewal of distribution agreements of fixed duration were introduced by a law adopted on 13 April 1971. These rules have been incorporated into Article *3bis* of the Law of 27 July 1961, thus amending its scope of application. Previously, the Law of 27 July 1961 only provided protection to distributors operating under an agreement concluded for an indefinite period. Article *3bis* of the Law of 27 July 1961 has been inserted to protect distributors bound by successive agreements of a short duration which the supplier, upon termination, could renew or refuse to renew, at his own discretion.

1. Termination

1798. As explained above (*See*, para. 1785), agreements of fixed duration normally terminate automatically at the end of the agreed period. By contrast, Article *3bis* of the Law of 27 July 1961 provides that unless the agreement has been terminated in accordance with certain formalities, it will automatically be renewed. This rule has been introduced in the interest of the distributor.

1799. For such termination to be valid, notice of termination must be given. The party which seeks to terminate a distribution agreement of fixed duration must provide notice by registered letter between 3 and 6 months before the expiry of the agreed contract term. If no valid notice of termination is given, the agreement will be renewed automatically.

2. Renewal

1800. Where the parties have not expressly provided for any renewal arrangements in their agreement, or where the agreement does not indicate the duration of the renewed agreement, Article *3bis* of the Law of 27 July 1961 provides that the agreement will automatically be renewed for an indefinite period of time. Moreover, Article *3bis* stipulates that in cases where a distribution agreement of fixed duration has been renewed twice, any subsequent renewal of the agreement will automatically result in the prolongation of the agreement for an indefinite period. Consequently, such agreements will be governed by the termination rules applicable to agreements of indefinite duration.

1801. The rule providing for the automatic renewal of the agreement for an indefinite period after the original contract term has been renewed more than twice applies even when clauses of the original contract have been modified by the parties.

§3. Rules governing agreements of indefinite duration

1. Forms of termination

1802. Agreements of indefinite duration can be terminated under the following circumstances: by giving reasonable notice or by paying an indemnity in lieu of notice (*See*, point (i) below); in case of a serious failure on the part of one of the parties to honour his obligations (*See*, point (ii) below); and, in case one party does not fulfil his obligations, the other party may also claim rescission of the contract with damages (*See*, point (iii) below).

i. Reasonable notice period

(a) *General principle:* Article 2 of the Law of 27 July 1961 provides that either party may terminate a distribution agreement of indefinite duration by giving reasonable notice or by paying an indemnity in lieu of notice. Strictly speaking, paying an indemnity is not an alternative to providing reasonable notice but is rather a countervailing obligation to the unfulfilled obligation to give such notice (Cass., 6 November 1987, *T.B.H.*, 1988, 182). In practical terms, however, an indemnity does provide an alternative for the party intending to terminate the agreement. Since a decision to terminate the agreement with immediate effect or to give insufficient notice is irrevocable (*See*, para. 1807), the terminating party can make a deliberate choice between giving reasonable notice or paying an indemnity. Neither the court nor the terminated party may impose a different choice on the terminating party.

(b) *Length of the reasonable notice period:* The length of the reasonable notice period can be determined either by an agreement between the parties or by the courts.

1803. It is only after one party has notified the other party of its intent to terminate the agreement that the parties can negotiate and agree to the length of the notice period. Prior to the notification of the termination of the agreement, the parties are not in a position to enter into a valid arrangement relating to this matter. Hence, provisions in the distribution agreement governing the required length of the notice period are in principle unenforceable. Such unenforceability cannot be cured by a unilateral ratification made after the notification of termination (Cass., 22 December 1988, *J.T.*, 1989, 458).

1804. If the parties do not agree on the notice period, it will be for the courts to decide the matter in equity, taking account of applicable customs.

1805. Case law suggests that when assessing the required length of the notice period, the courts typically consider the time needed by the terminated party to find a comparable situation. In this assessment, courts often take account of the following factors:

(a) the duration of the contractual relations;
(b) the level and the evolution of the terminated party's turnover;
(c) the relative importance of the business concerned for the whole of the activities of the terminated party;
(d) the extent of the contract territory;

(e) the nature of the products concerned and the renown of the trademark (if any); and

(f) the investments made and the nature of the obligations assumed by the terminated party.

1806. Determinations by the courts are often generous to the party which is terminated and vary from several months to three years or more.

1807. It may be useful to emphasise that the statutory requirement either to provide reasonable notice or to pay an indemnity, is not only incumbent on suppliers but also on distributors. Where the agreement is terminated by the distributor, the purpose of the notice period is to enable the supplier to find a comparable distributor. Whereas the courts seem to be inclined to grant shorter notice periods in cases where it is the distributor who terminates the contractual relations (Comm. Brussels, 7 March 1989, *T.B.H.*, 1990, 697), one could imagine instances where it would be difficult for the supplier to replace his former distributor by a comparable new one. Under those circumstances, a longer notice period could be justified.

(a) *Form of the notice:* the Law of 27 July 1961 does not impose specific requirements as to the form the notice takes. If the party receiving the notice is fully aware of the other party's intention to terminate the agreement, the notice will be deemed valid. Accordingly, oral notice could be sufficient, even though it may raise evidentiary problems.

(b) *Irrevocable nature of the notice:* if a party decides to terminate a distribution agreement by giving notice, it is bound by its decision and cannot unilaterally extend or reduce the notice period. Likewise, if the contract is terminated by one of the parties with immediate effect, that party cannot subsequently give notice in order to avoid the payment of an indemnity. The irrevocable nature of the notice further implies that the courts cannot order or grant an extension where the notice period is insufficient (Cass., 24 April 1998, *J.T.*, 598). The only remedy at the disposal of the courts under these circumstances is an indemnity in lieu of notice. Case law is divided as to whether the President of the Commercial Court, acting in the context of interim or summary proceedings, is also bound by this principle or whether he may order specific performance and require that the parties continue their dealings pending the outcome of the case. Also, once a party opts to terminate the distribution agreement by giving notice, it cannot later invoke a serious fault previously committed by the other party in the performance of its contractual obligations in order to terminate the agreement with immediate effect. The only exception to this principle is where the serious fault is committed in the course of the notice period. In that case, the serious fault may be relied upon to terminate the agreement with immediate effect regardless of the previously binding notice period.

(c) *Position of the parties during the notice period:* the legal situation of the parties during the notice period is identical to that described in paragraphs 1786 *et seq.*

ii. Serious failure

1808. Although a distribution agreement which is subject to the Law of 27 July 1961 may only be terminated unilaterally upon reasonable notice or the payment of an indemnity in lieu of notice to the other party, the Law of 27 July 1961 itself provides for an exception to this rule. Pursuant to Article 2 of the Law of 27 July 1961, neither notice nor indemnity will be due in case of a serious failure on the part of one of the parties to honour his obligations.

1809. The Law of 27 July 1961 does not define the notion of "serious failure". In the case law "serious failure" is typically understood to mean behaviour by one party which is not merely contrary to the provisions of the agreement, but which makes it impossible for the other party to continue performing the agreement.

1810. Case law provides numerous examples of "serious failure" which give rise to immediate termination of the agreement. The following list of serious failures by distributors is certainly not exhaustive. Moreover, it should be borne in mind that the outcome in each case depends on all of the surrounding circumstances and not just the identified factor:
    (a) the failure to pay a significant number of outstanding invoices;
    (b) a very poor performance of the contract in general;
    (c) an infringement of exclusive purchasing obligations;
    (d) the failure to meet contractual minimum sales quotas; or
    (e) an infringement of a contractual non-competition obligation.

1811. A "serious failure" by the supplier allows the distributor to terminate the agreement immediately, without paying an indemnity, where the distributor established:
    (a) an infringement by the supplier of the distributor's exclusivity;
    (b) a refusal to supply;
    (c) delays in supply;
    (d) a supply of defective products;
    (e) the assignment of the agreement; or
    (f) the removal of a part of the territory granted to the distributor.

1812. There are no compulsory requirements to be satisfied before terminating a distribution agreement for serious failure. It is clear, however, that the party terminating the agreement should be prepared to prove at a later stage that he terminated the contract and that the nature of the fault committed by the other party was such that termination without notice or indemnity in lieu of notice was justified. Therefore, it is advisable for the terminating party to inform the terminated party of the termination by registered letter, stating the reasons for which he considers termination to be justified.

1813. No intervention by a judge is required. However, the case will be brought before a court if the terminated party contests the allegations of serious failure. If the court considers that the alleged fault has not been committed or was not sufficiently serious to justify immediate termination without indemnity, the terminated party will be entitled to damages. The court may not order specific performance of the terminated agreement. Most courts conclude that termination for serious failure implies that all further co-operation between the parties within the framework of the distribution agreement has become impossible, and that the agreement should therefore be terminated with immediate effect. However, legal commentators admit that, in specific cases, a termination for serious failure does not prevent a brief maintenance of the agreement if the maintenance can limit the loss suffered by the terminated party. As a result, granting any notice would normally indicate that the failure by the terminated party was not sufficiently "serious" within the meaning of the Law of 27 July 1961. Case law has even held that by granting a notice period of only a few weeks, the terminating party waived his right to invoke serious failure. Under these circumstances, the terminating party risks being compelled to pay compensation to the terminated party.

iii. Rescission

1814. Article 1184 of the Civil Code provides that, in the case of contracts containing reciprocal obligations, if one party does not fulfil his obligations, the other party may either compel performance of the contract or claim rescission of the contract with damages. Rescission may only be sought through the courts, and the judge may grant a delay to the defendant depending on the circumstances. Rescission will only be granted if the alleged failure to perform the contract is sufficiently serious.

1815. Case law has made it clear that the mandatory rules on unilateral termination contained in the Law of 27 July 1961 are not exclusive of other forms of contract termination such as rescission based on Article 1184 of the Civil Code (Cass., 22 October 1993, *Pas.*, 1993, I, 851). Therefore, this proceeding may sometimes be a safe alternative for parties who are not sure about the seriousness of the fault committed by the other party and do not wish to terminate the agreement for serious fault without the prior intervention of a court. In contrast to unilateral termination for serious failure, where rescission is sought the agreement remains in effect until a judgement pronouncing the rescission has been granted. Therefore, unless there are valid reasons to suspend the performance of the contract (*"exceptio non adimpleti contractus"*), the party requesting the rescission of the distribution agreement must continue performing the agreement. However, if the court rejects the requested rescission the claimant does not run the risk of being compelled to pay an indemnity.

1816. Examples of cases where a distribution agreement may be rescinded on the basis of Article 1184 of the Civil Code are similar to those listed under paragraphs 1818 *et seq.* with regard to termination for serious failure.

1817. Even if a distribution agreement is covered by the Law of 27 July 1961, parties may include in the agreement clauses that specifically define those breaches which will result in the rescission of the agreement. If the agreement provides that the rescission will be automatic (*van rechtswege/de plein droit*), the role of the court is limited to verifying whether or not the breach has actually occurred without the possibility of evaluating whether the gravity of the breach is sufficient to justify the rescission.

1818. There are numerous examples of such defined breaches in the case law:
- (a) termination with 30 days notice if the distributor has not ordered a certain number of units having a certain value by the end of the year;
- (b) termination if the distributor has not placed any order with the supplier during a period of 3 months;
- (c) termination in the event of non-payment on the due date of a bill of exchange; and
- (d) termination if the dealer fails to purchase at least 90 per cent of the mutually agreed sales target from the supplier.

1819. The Supreme Court has also upheld the validity of a clause which provided the possibility to terminate the agreement by the occurrence of a condition regardless of any failure of the terminated party, arguing that such a clause is not covered by the Law of 27 July 1961 (Cass., 30 June 1995, *R.W.*, 1995-1996, 829). Clearly, the enforceability of such clauses makes it easier for suppliers to terminate distribution agreements covered by the Law of 27 July 1961 without having to grant a notice period or pay an indemnity. Precisely for that reason, the case law allowing the use of such clauses has been criticised.

2. Indemnities

1820. The Law of 27 July 1961 provides for two types of indemnities: (i) an indemnity in lieu of notice and (ii) a supplementary indemnity. The indemnity in lieu of notice seeks to compensate the terminated party for the failure of the other party to provide reasonable notice. The supplementary indemnity seeks to compensate the distributor mainly for the surplus value which he generated and which will be retained by the supplier upon termination. Whereas the indemnity in lieu of notice can be claimed by distributors or suppliers who are terminated, the supplementary indemnity is only available to distributors.

i. Indemnity in lieu of notice:

1821. Article 2 of the Law of 27 July 1961 requires the payment of an indemnity if, in the absence of a serious fault, a distribution agreement of indefinite duration is terminated unilaterally without providing reasonable notice. Thus, the statutory obligation to pay the indemnity provided in Article 2 arises only if the terminating party has failed to grant any notice at all, or has granted notice of an insufficient period of time.

1822. The indemnity in lieu of notice compensates the economic disadvantages resulting from the failure to give reasonable notice. Therefore, the indemnity must be equivalent to the economic advantages which would have resulted from such notice (Cass., 28 June 1979, *Pas.*, 1979, I, 1260). It is for the terminated party to provide evidence of the economic disadvantages that were caused by the absence of a reasonable notice period. If a notice period would not have been to the economic benefit of the terminated party (for example, where the distributorship was operated at a loss), no indemnity in lieu of notice will be due (Brussels Court of Appeal, 1 October 1975, *R.W.*, 1975-1976, 2150).

1823. Article 2 of the Law of 27 July 1961 states that the indemnity in lieu of notice must be "equitable", but does not provide any details regarding its calculation. It is for the parties to the contract to agree upon the level of the indemnity in lieu of notice following the notification of the termination of the agreement. If the parties fail to do so, the indemnity in lieu of notice will be determined by the courts. For that purpose, the courts typically consider that the indemnity should be based on the net profits generated by the distributorship increased by the unrecoverable fixed costs attributable to the terminated distributorship.

1824. The net profits generated by the distributorship are normally calculated on the basis of the average pre-tax net profits during a reference period preceding the termination of the agreement. Although the courts have used various reference periods, the average is a period of 2 or 3 years preceding the termination of the distributorship. Obviously, only the net profits relating to the terminated distributorship are taken into account. Profits resulting from other activities are disregarded. If the supplier breaches the exclusivity granted to the distributor and distributes the products concerned himself or appoints a new distributor, the net profits generated by the supplier or the new distributor will be taken into account for the calculation of the indemnity in lieu of notice (Brussels Court of Appeal, 1 October 1996, General docket No. 1995/AR/702, *not published*).

1825. Costs pursuant to the distribution agreement which are incurred despite the termination will be added to the net profits. These fixed costs can include such items as rental charges, heating, lighting and maintenance charges, salaries and social security contributions. If these are not exclusively incurred for the purposes of the distributorship, only a fraction of these fixed costs will be included in the calculation of the indemnity in lieu of notice. Generally, the percentage which the distributorship represents in the total turnover of the distributor's business will be applied to the total of the fixed costs.

1826. Although Article 2 of the Law of 27 July 1961 simply provides that the indemnity in lieu of notice must be equitable, the courts will not limit their assessments to considerations of fairness when a party fails to observe a reasonable notice period. The courts will calculate the economic factors referred to above and, only when they encounter difficulties in assessing some of these factors, they will refer to equitable grounds.

ii. Supplementary indemnity:

1827. Article 3 of the Law of 27 July 1961 provides that the distributor shall be entitled to an equitable supplementary indemnity if his distributorship is terminated unilaterally for reasons other than a serious failure on his part, or if he terminates the distributorship as a result of a serious failure by the supplier. This can only be claimed by distributors who are a party to a distribution agreement of indefinite duration within the meaning of the Law of 27 July 1961. Thus, the supplementary indemnity cannot be claimed by a supplier who is being terminated, nor can it be claimed by a distributor who is bound by a distribution agreement of a fixed duration.

1828. Article 3 of the Law of 27 July 1961 makes it clear that a distributor can only claim a supplementary indemnity if the termination is not attributable to him. Thus, whenever a supplier unilaterally terminates a distributorship in the absence of a serious failure by the distributor, the supplementary indemnity will be due. The fact that the distributor has been given reasonable notice or an adequate indemnity in lieu of notice is irrelevant.

The level of the supplementary indemnity may be agreed upon between the parties following the notification of the termination of the agreement. If the parties are not able to reach an agreement, the courts will decide the matter. In doing so, the courts will take account of the elements listed in Article 3 of the Law of 27 July 1961. It is generally accepted that this list is exhaustive, so no other elements will be considered. The following 3 elements are included in the list:

1829. *The notable surplus value associated with clientele brought in by the distributor that remains with the supplier after the termination:* in determining whether the distributor has generated a "notable surplus value", the courts have a significant amount of discretion. In this respect, the turnover or sales figures realised by the distributor at the commencement and termination of the contract and the evolution of the number of customers are often decisive. The duration of the period during which an increase in turnover or sales has been realised is also taken into consideration. An increase may be considered "notable" if it is reached over a period of, say, 2 or 3 years, but the same increase would not be notable if it were realised after, say, 10 years. Increasing or decreasing trends in sales for the period immediately before the termination of the contract are of particular relevance. A notable surplus value may not be found where there has been a decrease (or even stabilisation) in sales in the years immediately preceding the termination, even if clientele has increased over the full term of the contract (Comm. Brussels, 21 March 1972, *J.T.*, 1972, 447).

1830. *The surplus value in clientele must be the result of the distributor's efforts.* The burden of proof for this rests with the distributor (Cass., 28 October 1971, *Pas.*, 1972, I, 209). Facts such as sales results that are superior to those of other distributors in the same network, or increases in market share, may serve as evidence of the contribution of the distributor.

1831. *Furthermore, compensation will be granted only for that part of the clientele which remains with the supplier after the termination of the agreement.* On the one hand, the courts believe that a distributor will retain his clientele if he sells under his own brand name and simply continues such sales after termination with products of another supplier. On the other hand, the courts assume that the clientele will remain with the supplier if products are sold under the supplier's brand and purchases of the products are inspired by the specific qualities of the brand. Other factors which the courts may consider are the nature of the products concerned, the nature of the relationship between the distributor and his clientele, and the extent of the principal's access to the clientele.

1832. In the event that a distribution agreement follows a "commercial intermediaries" agreement of another type between the same parties, the surplus value associated with the clientele brought in by the distributor will be taken into consideration as from the conclusion of the distribution agreement, and not as from the beginning of the commercial relationship between the parties (Brussels Court of Appeal, 7 March 1991, *J.L.M.B.*, 1991, 1392). It should however be noted that the Law of 13 April 1995 regarding Commercial Agency Agreements (*Wet betreffende de handels-agentuurovereenkomst/Loi relative au contrat d'agence commerciale* – the "Agency Law") now also provides for an indemnity in case of termination of the agreement by the principal (*See*, paras. 1771 *et seq.*). It is thus doubtful whether this case law still stands when, for instance, a distribution agreement follows an agency agreement.

   (i) *The expenses incurred by the distributor in developing the distributorship from which the supplier benefits after the termination of the distributorship*: case law is scarce regarding the expenses to be included in the supplementary indemnity, and it focuses mainly on the question of whether or not such expenses could be considered to benefit the supplier after the termination of the distributorship. Advertising expenses, investments in immovable property and rental charges are typical areas where it has been difficult for the distributor to establish that the supplier benefits from the expenses. For instance, promotional expenses will only be taken into account if the advertising continues to have an impact after the termination of the distributorship and if the nature of the advertising is such that it entails benefits to the supplier. Such benefits will be considered to exist, for example, if the advertising focuses on the supplier's brand name.

   (ii) *Indemnities payable by the distributor to employees whose employment contract had to be terminated as a result of the termination of the distributorship:* if the distributor is obliged to terminate certain employment contracts because of the termination of the distributorship, he will be entitled to include the redundancy payments in the supplementary indemnity. When calculating this indemnity, no account may be taken of the notice period to be provided to the employees which coincides with the reasonable notice period granted to the distributor pursuant to Article 2 of the Law of 27 July 1961 (*See*, paras. 1803 *et seq.*). Thus, if the notice period for the employees is shorter than the notice period which is granted to the distributor pursuant to Article 2 of the Law of 27 July 1961, no costs for such employees may be included in the supplementary indemnity. Likewise, expenses relating to the termination of employment contracts which are already covered by the indemnity in lieu of notice cannot be taken into consideration for calculating the supplementary indemnity. A review of the case law suggests that only in rare cases are costs relating to the termination of employees' contracts included in the supplementary indemnity.

1833. Although Article 3 of the Law of 27 July 1961 lists 3 different elements to be taken into account for the calculation of the supplementary indemnity, judgements most often only specify one total figure and refrain from providing separate calculations. In addition, the supplementary indemnity in most cases is determined *ex aequo et bono*, *i.e.*, on the basis of fairness considerations.

§4. Sub-distributors

1834. Distributors may appoint one or more sub-distributors. Since there is no direct contractual relationship between the supplier and the sub-distributors, the latter normally can not make any direct claims against the supplier (*"res inter alios acta nec nocet, nec prodest"*). Article 5 of the Law of 27 July 1961 modifies this general principle in certain cases where sub-distributorships which were entered into for an indefinite duration, are terminated.

1835. Article 5(1) of the Law of 27 July 1961 establishes that those parts of the Law of 27 July 1961 which apply to the relationship between suppliers and distributors also apply to the agreements between distributors and sub-distributors. For example, if a distributor terminates a sub-distributorship agreement which meets the conditions of Article 1 of the Law of 27 July 1961 (*See*, paras. 1790 *et seq.*), the sub-distributor is entitled, in principle, to a reasonable notice period or an indemnity in lieu thereof (*See*, para. 1802) and he may claim a supplementary indemnity (*See*, 1827 *et seq.*) from the distributor. However, the sub-distributor must address his claims to the supplier in cases where the termination of the sub-distributorship is caused by the termination of the distributorship and the termination of the main distributorship is not attributable to the distributor (Art. 5(2) of the Law of 27 July 1961). The termination of the distributorship is not attributable to the distributor if he has terminated the agreement because of a serious fault by the supplier or if the supplier has done so without relying on a serious fault by the distributor.

1836. Where the length of a sub-distributorship is fixed, the distributor must respect the rules contained in Article *3bis* of the Law of 27 July 1961 (*See*, paras. 1797 *et seq.*). However, Article 5(3) of the Law of 27 July 1961 contains an exception. If a sub-distributorship of fixed duration expires on the same date as the main distribution agreement, the distributor who receives notice from the supplier shall have, in any event, 14 days to grant notice to the sub-distributor. In practice, this means that if the supplier provides notice of termination close to 3 months prior to the expiry of the main distribution agreement, the distributor, without infringing Article *3bis* of the Law of 27 July 1961, can provide notice to the sub-distributor as long as he does so within 14 days of having received his own notice of termination.

§5. *Territorial competence, applicable law and arbitration*

1837. Since the provisions of the Law of 27 July 1961 are generally deemed to be highly favourable to distributors, suppliers have considered various ways of trying to avoid its application by inserting in the distribution agreement appropriate clauses regarding choice of law, choice of forum and arbitration. On the other hand, the Law of 27 July 1961 itself contains certain rules which aim to ensure that its mandatory provisions are not evaded. The cornerstones of the Law of 27 July 1961 regarding jurisdiction and applicable law are contained in Articles 4 and 6.

1838. Article 4 of the Law of 27 July 1961 establishes that, if a distributor has suffered damage as a result of the termination of a distribution agreement which produced effects in Belgium, he may initiate legal proceedings before the courts in Belgium, either before the court of his own domicile or before the court of the domicile or the business seat of the supplier. Furthermore, this Article provides that the Belgian courts must exclusively apply Belgian law in such cases.

1839. Article 6 of the Law of 27 July 1961 states that the provisions contained in the Law override any contrary contractual stipulations which have been agreed upon prior to contract termination.

1840. In the absence of conflicting rules derived from international treaties or conventions, the provisions contained in Articles 4 and 6 of the Law of 27 July 1961 have the following consequences:
   (i) a choice of forum clause entered into before the termination of the agreement will be null and void if it refers the case to a foreign jurisdiction;
   (ii) a choice of law clause agreed upon before contract termination will be null and void if it leads to the application of foreign law; and
   (iii) an arbitration clause entered into before contract termination will be null and void if it leads to the application of foreign law (Cass., 28 June 1979, *Pas.*, I, 1260).

1841. Since the above rules may have far-reaching consequences, it is important to define their exact scope of application, which is subject to 3 different limitations. First, the wording of Article 6 of the Law of 27 July 1961 clearly establishes that the distributor can only benefit from special protection until the moment the contract is terminated. If he enters into any arbitration agreements, choice of forum clauses, or any other agreement which deviates from the Law of 27 July 1961 after contract termination has occurred, these agreements will be valid and enforceable. Secondly, choice of law clauses, choice of forum clauses and arbitration agreements, which result in a foreign court having jurisdiction or the application of foreign law, are valid and enforceable when the dispute between the parties does not relate to contract termination, since the scope of application of the Law of the Law of 27 July 1961 is limited to issues of contract termination. Finally, the mandatory rules on choice of forum and applicable law apply only where the distribution agreement has effect in Belgium (Art. 4 of the Law of the Law of 27 July 1961). This restriction has been interpreted to mean that, if the contract territory is located – partly or totally – outside Belgium, the mandatory protection regime from which the distributor benefits ceases to apply, at least for the part of the territory located abroad (Ghent Court of Appeal, 12 September 1996, general docket no 3383/91, *not published*).

1842. The above rules only apply to the extent that they do not contradict any provisions contained in international treaties or conventions. For example, EC Council Regulation No 44/2001 of 22 December 2000 on Jurisdiction and the Recognition and Enforcement of Judgements in Civil and Commercial Matters (the "Brussels Regulation" – O.J. [2001] L 012/1), which has recently replaced the Brussels Convention of 27 September 1968 on Jurisdiction and the Enforcement of Judgments in Civil and Commercial Matters, contains various rules on jurisdiction which override the principles contained in Articles 4 and 6 of the Law of 27 July 1961. If the Brussels Regulation applies in any given case, issues of jurisdiction will have to be decided in accordance with the specific provisions contained in the Brussels Regulation. Likewise, the United Nations Convention on the Recognition and Enforcement of Foreign Arbitral Awards of 10 June 1958, if applicable, supersedes Articles 4 and 6 of the Law of 27 July 1961 in so far as they have a bearing on problems of arbitration. The application of international treaties and conventions to distribution agreements covered by the Law of 27 July 1961 has given rise to extensive case law which will not be analysed within the framework of this book.

III. COMMERCIAL AGENTS

A. Introduction

1843. The Law of 13 April 1995 regarding Commercial Agency Agreements (*Wet betreffende de handelsagentuurovereenkomst/Loi relative au contrat d'agence commerciale* – the "Agency Law") implements EC Council Directive No. 86/653 on the Co-ordination of the Laws of the Member States relating to Self-employed Commercial Agents (the "Agency Directive" – O.J. [1986] L 382/17). Before the Agency Law came into force, the absence of legal provisions on agency contracts often led to legal uncertainty and a lack of legal protection of the agent. Jurisprudential and doctrinal solutions partially compensated for this lack of legal provisions.

1844. The Agency Law both implements and supplements the provisions of the Agency Directive. It contains a complete set of mostly mandatory rules (*i.e.*, rules that may not be superseded by contracts) governing the profession.

B. Definition of the agency agreement

1845. The Agency Law applies to agreements "*whereby one party, the commercial agent, acting independently and for payment, is charged on a regular basis by the other party, the principal, to negotiate and possibly to conclude business transactions in the name and on behalf of the principal*" (Art. 1 of the Agency Law).

1846. Commercial agents should be distinguished from commercial representatives (*handelsvertegenwoordigers/représentants de commerce*) and distributors (*concessiehouders/concessionnaires*). While both commercial agents and commercial representatives have an enduring working relationship with the principal and act in his name and on his behalf, their relationships with the principal differ: commercial agents are independent intermediaries whereas commercial representatives operate in subordination to the principal. One important consequence of this distinction is that commercial representatives are subject to Belgian labour law, whereas commercial agents are expressly excluded from the scope of Belgian labour law (Art. 4(3) of the Law of 3 July 1978 on Employment Agreements). When examining specific cases, the courts have to determine whether a relationship of subordination exists.

1847. The main distinction between commercial agents and distributors is that the former act in the name and on behalf of their principal, while distributors act in their own name and on their own behalf. The economic risk is the determining factor to distinguish distributors from commercial agents. When the intermediary acts in his own name, on his own behalf and is in charge of stocks, sales promotion and product distribution, the Law of 27 July 1961 will apply (*See*, paras. 1789 *et seq.*). When a person acts both as a commercial agent and distributor, courts typically compare the volume of business generated in the person's capacity of commercial agent with the volume of business generated as a distributor, in order to assess which activity is dominant. It is not excluded, however, that an intermediary may combine both capacities for different parts of his activities.

1848. The commercial agent is charged by the principal with the task of negotiating and possibly concluding "business transactions" (Art. 1 of the Agency Law). "Business transactions" is a much broader concept than the "sale or purchase of goods" referred to in Article 1.2 of the Agency Directive. Agency contracts pertaining to sub-contracting, leasing, services (advertising, travel, transport) and immovable goods therefore also fall within the scope of the Agency Law.

C. Mandatory provisions

1849. In light of the fact that the Agency Law seeks to provide maximal legal protection to the commercial agents, its provisions are mandatory law, except for certain provisions from which parties are allowed to derogate in writing. The only non-mandatory provisions are Article 4 (3) (performance of agency agreement for a definite term after expiration of the initial term), Article 7 (possibility to designate sub-agents), Article 15 (3) (basis and mode of calculation of the commission), Article 17 (fixed remuneration payable at the end of each month), Article 18, §2 (coincidence of the end of the notice period with the end of the calendar month), and Article 25 (2) (scope of the agent's liability in case of a del credere provision) of the Agency Law. Parties may only derogate from these provisions in writing.

D. Formation of the agency agreement

1850. There are no specific formal requirements which must be fulfilled in order to conclude a valid commercial agency agreement. However, written agreements are preferable to oral agreements, as the former allow for the insertion of non-compete clauses or *del credere* provisions. Moreover, written agreements provide increased legal certainty. The Agency Law specifies that "*each party shall be entitled to receive from the other party on request a signed written document setting out the terms of the agency agreement including any subsequent changes*" (Art. 5 of the Agency Law).

E. Term of the agency agreement

1851. Agency agreements can be concluded for a fixed term or for an indefinite term (Art. 4 (1) of the Agency Law). If an agency agreement for a definite term is still performed by the parties after the expiration of the term, the expired agency agreement is assumed to have been initially concluded for an indefinite term (Art. 4 (3) of the Agency Law). On this point, parties may nevertheless agree otherwise in writing. Oral agreements are automatically assumed to be concluded for an indefinite term (Art. 4 (2) of the Agency Law).

F. Duties of the parties

§1. Duties of the commercial agent

1852. While performing his activities, a commercial agent must look after his principal's interests and act dutifully and in good faith (Art. 6 (1) of the Agency Law). His obligation also holds *vis-à-vis* the principal's customers. This general obligation underlies the following more specific obligations of the commercial agent to:
    (i) make proper efforts to negotiate and, where appropriate, conclude the transactions for which he is responsible (Art. 6 (2), 1° of the Agency Law);
    (ii) communicate to his principal all the necessary information available to him (Art. 6 (2), 2° of the Agency Law). This obligation covers both information pertaining to the activities of the agent (concluded transactions, insolvency risk of customers, customer complaints) and general information such as market developments in the sector and customer demands. If, however, the principal requires the intermediary to provide detailed reports on his activities, the courts could consider that there is a relationship of subordination between the parties, and that, consequently, the intermediary is a commercial representative and not an agent;
    (iii) comply with reasonable instructions given by the principal (Art. 6 (2) 3° of the Agency Law). The agent only has to comply with general instructions pertaining to the general conditions of sale and the commercial strategy of the principal. In case of detailed instructions (for example specific working hours, specification of clientele which must be canvassed, *etc.*) the courts could again decide that there is a relationship of subordination, and that, consequently, the intermediary is a commercial representative and not an agent.

§2. Duties of the principal

1853. The Agency Law requires the principal to act dutifully and in good faith in the framework of his relations with the commercial agent (Art. 8 (1) of the Agency Law). In particular, the principal must:
    (i) provide the commercial agent with the necessary documentation relating to the business concerned (Art. 8 (2), 1° of the Agency Law);
    (ii) provide the commercial agent with the information necessary for the performance of the agency contract, and in particular notify the commercial agent within a reasonable period when he anticipates that the volume of commercial transactions will be significantly lower than that which the commercial agent could normally have expected (Art. 8 (2), 2° of the Agency Law);

(iii) inform the commercial agent within a reasonable period of his acceptance, refusal or non-execution of a commercial transaction negotiated by the commercial agent (Art. 8 (2) 2° of the Agency Law);

(iv) remunerate the commercial agent (*See*, paras. 1854 *et seq.*).

G. Remuneration of the commercial agent

§1. General

1854. The Agency Law sets forth detailed provisions on the remuneration of the commercial agent. These provisions address the following issues:

  (i) the level and calculation of the remuneration (Art. 15 of the Agency Law);
 (ii) the different types of remuneration (Art. 9 of the Agency Law);
(iii) the entitlement to a commission on transactions concluded during the period covered by the agency agreement (Art. 10 of the Agency Law);
(iv) the entitlement to a commission on transactions concluded after the termination of the agency agreement (Art. 11 of the Agency Law);
 (v) the moment at which the commission becomes due (Art. 13 of the Agency Law);
(vi) the extinction of the right to a commission (Art. 14 of the Agency Law); and
(vii) the information obligations of the principal (Art. 16 of the Agency Law).

1855. These provisions are described below.

§2. Level and calculation of the remuneration (Art. 15 of the Agency Law)

1856. As a general rule, the principal and the commercial agent are free to agree upon the level of the agent's remuneration. The level of the remuneration can for instance vary according to the categories of customers the agent is expected to seek, the type of products or services involved, or the role of the commercial agent in the transaction. Parties can also decide on specific remuneration for a transaction of particular importance (Art. 15 (1) of the Agency Law).

1857. In the absence of an agreement between the parties and in the absence of elements from which the implicit will of the parties can be deduced, the level of remuneration granted to the commercial agent is determined in accordance with the customary remuneration practices for similar transactions in the economic sector and the geographical area in which the commercial agent is active. If no such customary remuneration practices exist or if they cannot be determined, the commercial agent is entitled to a fair percentage of the deals he negotiates taking into account all the aspects of the transaction (Art. 15 (2) of the Agency Law).

1858. Unless otherwise provided, the remuneration of the commercial agent is based on the gross amount invoiced to the customer. Taxes and duties are excluded from the basis on which the remuneration is calculated. On the contrary, additional costs invoiced separately to the customers, such as transport, insurance, and packaging costs, are in principle included in the basis (Art. 15 (3) of the Agency Law). Parties can derogate from the legal calculation method for the remuneration of the agent, but cannot exclude from the basis fidelity premiums or discounts which the principal grants to customers without consulting or obtaining the consent of the agent (Art. 15 (4) of the Agency Law).

1859. The unilateral modification by the principal of the initially agreed remuneration amounts in principle to a unilateral termination of the agency agreement, unless the commercial agent has accepted for a certain period commissions based on the reduced calculation basis without making any reservation (Art. 15 (5) of the Agency Law).

§3. The different types of remuneration (Art. 9 of the Agency Law)

1860. The remuneration of a commercial agent may consist of either a fixed amount or commissions, or a combination of both. The Agency Law adds that all elements of the remuneration which vary according to the number or the value of the transactions concerned are considered to be commissions (Art. 9 (2) of the Agency Law).

§4. Entitlement to a commission on transactions concluded during the period covered by the agency agreement (Art. 10 of the Agency Law)

1861. The commercial agent shall be entitled to a commission on commercial transactions concluded during the period covered by the agency contract:
  (i) where the transaction is concluded as a result of his activities;
  (ii) where the transaction is concluded with a third party whom the commercial agent had previously acquired as a customer for transactions of the same nature; or
  (iii) where the commercial agent has an exclusive right to a specific geographical area or group of customers and where a transaction has been entered into with a customer belonging to that area or group.

§5. Entitlement to a commission on transactions concluded after the termination of the agency agreement (Art. 11 of the Agency Law)

1862. The agent is also entitled to a commission for transactions concluded after the termination or expiry of the agency agreement, if one of the following conditions is met:

    (i) the transaction is mainly attributable to the commercial agent's efforts during the period covered by the agency agreement and the transaction is entered into within a period of 6 months after the termination of that agreement; or

    (ii) in accordance with the conditions set forth in Article 10 of the Agency Law, the order of the customer reached the principal or the commercial agent before the agency contract expired or was terminated.

1863. This possibility for a relieved agent to request a remuneration after the expiry or termination of the agency agreement implies that a situation could arise in which the previous agent and the new agent both claim entitlement to remuneration for the same transaction, the former under Article 10 of the Agency Law and the latter under Article 11 of the Agency Law. In such cases, Article 12 of the Agency Law provides that priority shall be given to the previous agent, unless the circumstances dictate that the commission should be shared between the previous and the new agent.

§6. The moment at which the agent may claim the remuneration (Art. 13 of the Agency Law)

1864. The commission of the commercial agent becomes due as soon as, and to the extent that, one of the following circumstances arises:

    (i) the principal has executed the transaction or should have executed the transaction according to his agreement with the customer; or

    (ii) the customer has executed the transaction.

1865. The commission becomes due at the latest when the customer has executed his part of the transaction (or when he would have done so if the principal had duly executed his part of the transaction).

1866. It is mandatory law (*i.e.*, the parties may not agree otherwise) that the commission must be paid not later than on the last day of the month following the quarter in which it became due. The fixed remuneration to which the agent is entitled, if any, is paid out on a monthly basis, unless the parties have agreed otherwise (Art. 17 of the Agency Law).

§7. Agreement on the extinction of the right to the commission (Art. 14 of the Agency Law)

1867. Parties may agree in the agency contract that the right to a commission will be extinguished:

    (i) if and to the extent that the customer does not perform his obligations, except when the non-performance is due to circumstances imputable to the principal;

(ii) if the execution of the transaction has become impossible, unless this impossibility is imputable to the principal;

(iii) if the execution of the transaction cannot reasonably be imposed on the principal, especially when there are serious reasons imputable to the customer which justify the non-execution by the principal of its contractual obligations.

1868. When the parties have validly agreed that the right to the commission will be extinguished and one of the scenarios mentioned above materialises, the agent must reimburse any commission already paid to which he was not entitled.

§8. Information obligations of the principal (Art. 16 of the Agency Law)

1869. The principal shall supply his commercial agent with a statement of the commission due, not later than the last day of the month following the quarter in which the commission becomes due.

1870. Such a statement shall allow the agent to verify the amount of commission to which he is entitled. Furthermore, the commercial agent may request that he be provided with all the information which is available to the principal and which he needs in order to check the amount of commission due to him (such as, in particular, an extract of the accounting books). This right is both specific and limited, *i.e.*, it only covers information which the agent needs in order to check the amount of commission due and it does not confer on the agent a general right of access to the books of the principal.

H. Termination of the agency agreement

§1. Obligation to observe a notice period (Art. 18, para. 1 of the Agency Law)

1871. The Agency Law has introduced a mandatory minimum notice period (or, alternatively, an indemnity in lieu of notice) which must be observed by the terminating party in case of termination of either an agency agreement for an indefinite duration or an agency agreement for definite duration which foresees the possibility of termination before the term is reached (*See*, para. 1872). However, this obligation to observe a notice period (or to pay an indemnity in lieu of notice) does not apply – and thus an immediate termination of the agency agreement is possible – where exceptional circumstances render any future co-operation between the parties impossible or when one party seriously fails to perform his obligations (*See*, para. 1878).

§2. Length of the notice period (Art. 18, para. 1 of the Agency Law)

1872. The minimum notice period laid down by law amounts to one month for every commenced year of performance of the agency agreement, up to a maximum of 6 months.

1873. However, the parties are free to agree on longer notice periods. In such a case, the notice period which the principal must observe cannot be shorter than the notice period which the commercial agent must observe.

§3. Formal requirements (Art. 18, para. 2 of the Agency Law)

1874. Notice is given by handing over a written statement which indicates the beginning and the length of the notice period. Alternatively, this written statement may also be sent by registered mail, in which case it will have effect 3 days after the date on which it was posted. A third possibility is to serve the written statement by a bailiff's writ.

1875. Unless otherwise agreed by the parties, the end of the notice period must coincide with the end of a calendar month.

§4. Indemnity in lieu of notice (Art. 18, para. 3 of the Agency Law)

1876. The party who terminates the agency agreement without observing the minimum notice period and without relying on one of the grounds for immediate termination mentioned in Article 19 of the Agency Law (*See*, para. 1878), must pay an indemnity in lieu of notice. The amount of this indemnity will correspond to the remuneration which would have been due if the notice period had been observed.

1877. If the commercial agent is entitled to an indemnity in lieu of notice and is paid partially or wholly by way of commissions, the indemnity will be calculated on the basis of the average amount of commission received per month during the 12 months prior to the termination (or during the months preceding the termination if the agency lasted less than 12 months).

§5. Termination with immediate effect (Art. 19 of the Agency Law)

1878. As mentioned above, the agency agreement may be terminated with immediate effect in 2 cases: (i) when exceptional circumstances arise which render any future co-operation between the parties definitely impossible, and (ii) when one party seriously fails to carry out his obligations.

1879. Examples of the "exceptional circumstances" referred to in Article 19 include:
    (i) a serious or long-lasting disagreement between the principal and the agent;

   (ii) the sustained poor financial situation or possible bankruptcy of the principal or the agent;

  (iii) the illness or death of the agent;

  (iv) a judicial decision against the agent for facts which may cause the principal to lose his trust in the agent;

   (v) the take-over of the agency by a direct competitor of the principal; or

  (vi) the closing of operations of production or distribution.

1880. If a fault of the terminated party can be proven, the terminating party may introduce an additional claim for damages before the courts.

1881. Examples of "serious failure" under Article 19 of the Agency Law include:

   (i) acceptance of bribes by the agent;

  (ii) violation of contractual provisions prohibiting the conclusion of transactions by the agent on his own behalf;

  (iii) violation of contractual provisions prohibiting the conclusion of transactions on behalf of competitors;

  (iv) appointment of a second commercial agent where the agency agreement conferred exclusivity on the original commercial agent;

   (v) circumstances in which the commercial agent makes no effort whatsoever to look after the principal's interests.

1882. In contrast to the termination with immediate effect for exceptional circumstances, the immediate termination for serious failure implies the existence of a fault. Therefore, it will always be possible for the terminating party to introduce an additional claim for damages before the courts.

1883. If the terminated party disputes the existence of exceptional circumstances or serious failure, the court will assess *a posteriori* whether such circumstances or failure were present. The terminating party bears the burden of proof, hence the obligation to notify a termination for exceptional circumstances or serious failure by registered letter or bailiff's writ (Art. 19 (3) of the Agency Law). In case the court finds no exceptional circumstances or serious failure, the terminating party will have to pay an indemnity in lieu of notice calculated on the basis of Article 18, point 3 of the Agency Law (*See*, para 1878).

1884. The Agency Law sets forth 2 important conditions with regard to the right to terminate the agency agreement with immediate effect for exceptional circumstances or serious failure. Article 19 (2) of the Agency Law provides that the fact, which justifies an immediate termination, must not have been known to the terminating party for 7 working days or more before the termination. Article 19 (3) of the Agency Law provides that the notification of the exceptional circumstance or the serious failure must be communicated by registered mail or bailiff's writ within 7 working days after the termination.

§6. Clientele indemnity (Art. 20 of the Agency Law)

1885. A significant feature of the new Agency Law is that the agent is now entitled to request an indemnity for the clientele which he attracted to the principal's business during the agency. This right exists for agents with an agency contract regardless of whether the contract is for a definite or an indefinite duration. Parties may not derogate from the provisions on the "clientele" indemnity to the detriment of the agent before the termination or expiry of the agency agreement.

1886. The commercial agent is entitled to an indemnity if the following conditions are met:
    (i) the agent has brought in new customers to the principal or has significantly increased the volume of business with existing customers; and
    (ii) the principal continues to derive substantial benefits from the business with such customers.

1887. Unless proven otherwise by the principal, it is assumed that the principal continues to derive substantial benefits from the business brought in by the agent if the agency agreement contains a restraint of trade clause (Art. 20 (2) of the Agency Law).

1888. If the parties do not reach an agreement on the amount of the clientele indemnity, the amount will be determined by the courts. This indemnity may not exceed the remuneration for 1 year calculated on the basis of the agent's average annual remuneration over the preceding 5 years (Art. 20 (4) of the Agency Law).

1889. Under Article 20 (5) of the Agency Law, the agent shall not be entitled to an indemnity:
    (i) where the principal has terminated the agency contract because of a serious failure by the agent, as defined in Article 19 (1) of the Agency Law;
    (ii) where the commercial agent has terminated the agency contract, unless such termination is due to a serious failure or exceptional circumstances attributable to the principal as determined in Article 19 (1) of the Agency Law, or unless the termination is due to age, infirmity, or illness of the commercial agent; or
    (iii) where, with the agreement of the principal, the commercial agent or his heirs assign the rights and duties under the agency contract to a third party.

1890. The agent will lose his right to a "clientele" indemnity if he fails to inform the principal, within one year following the termination of the agency agreement, that he intends to request such an indemnity (Art. 20 (6) of the Agency Law). More-over, Article 26 of the Agency Law provides that all legal actions arising out of the agency agreement must be initiated within 1 year after the termination of the agency agreement or within 5 years after the occurrence of the facts which give rise to the action, provided the latter term does not exceed 1 year after the termination of the agency agreement. Therefore, it could be argued that a mere notification on the part of the agent of his intention to request a clientele indemnity will not suffice to safeguard his rights. Some authors suggest that the agent has one year from the notification to the principal that he intends to request a "clientele" indemnity to initiate legal action with regard to that indemnity.

1891. When the clientele indemnity to which the agent is entitled does not cover all of the injury which the agent has suffered, the latter may request additional damages. These damages correspond to the difference between the damage actually incurred by the agent and the amount of the clientele indemnity. The agent bears the burden of proof as regards those additional damages.

§7. Restraint of trade clause (Art. 24 of the Agency Law)

1892. Parties may include a clause restricting the possible business activities of a commercial agent after the termination of the agency agreement (a so-called "restraint of trade" clause).

1893. A restraint of trade clause is valid only if and to the extent that:
   (i) it is provided for in writing;
   (ii) it relates to the type of transactions the commercial agent was in charge of;
   (iii) it is limited to the geographical area or to the group of customers of the geographical area entrusted to the commercial agent;
   (iv) it is limited to 6 months after the termination of the agency agreement.

1894. Moreover, the restraint of trade clause will not be enforceable when:
   (i) the principal terminates the agency agreement for reasons other than exceptional circumstances or serious failure pursuant to in Article 19 (1) of the Agency Law; or
   (ii) the agent terminates the agency agreement invoking exceptional circumstances or serious failure referred to in Article 19 (1) of the Agency Law.

1895. The parties may agree on a lump sum which shall be payable if the agent breaches the restraint of trade clause. Such a lump sum may not exceed the remuneration for 1 year calculated on the basis of the agent's average annual remuneration over the preceding 5 years (Art. 24, §4 of the Agency Law). Nevertheless, if the principal proves that the damage which he suffered is higher than the amount mentioned above, he may claim a greater amount of compensation.

I. Contractual extension of the agent's liability (Art. 25 of the Agency Law)

1896. The agent may vouch for the solvency and the contractual performance of his customers (a so-called "*delcredere*" provision). Such a voucher is only valid if the following conditions are met:
  (i) it is agreed upon in writing;
  (ii) it pertains to transactions which the agent has personally concluded or nego-tiated;
  (iii) the principal does not unilaterally change the payment or delivery conditions; and
  (iv) the voucher is limited to the amount of the agreed commission, unless it per-tains to a specific transaction or to transactions which the agent has con-cluded in the name of the principal.

J. Prescription

1897. As already mentioned, legal actions arising out of an agency agreement must be initiated within 1 year after the termination of the agency agreement or within 5 years after the occurrence of the facts which give rise to the action, provided that the latter term does not exceed 1 year after the termination of the agency agree-ment (Art. 25 of the Agency Law).

K. The conflicts of laws

§1. Introduction

1898. Agency contracts very often have links with different countries (nationality or domi-cile of the parties, country of formation of the contract, country of performance, *etc.*). Therefore, questions may arise regarding the law applicable to the contract and the competent jurisdiction. These questions are generally governed by interna-tional or multilateral conventions or agreements, but they can also be subject to national legislation.

1899. Article 27 of the Agency Law protects the commercial agent whose principal place of business is located in Belgium. According to this provision, all disputes involving an agent located in Belgium will be subject to Belgian jurisdiction and to Belgian law. However, Article 27 specifically states that it does not affect the application of international agreements. This means that, in practice, the scope of Article 27 will be very limited with regard to agency contracts involving international aspects.

1900. Conflicts of laws regarding the applicable law for agency contracts are governed by the Rome Convention on the Law Applicable to Contractual Obligations of 19 June 1980 (the "Rome Convention", consolidated version – O.J. [1998] C 027/34). EC Council Regulation No 44/2001 of 22 December 2000 on Jurisdiction and the Recognition and Enforcement of Judgements in Civil and Commercial Matters (the "Brussels Regulation" – O.J. [2001] L 012/1), which entered into force on 1 March 2002 and replaced the Brussels Convention on Jurisdiction and the Enforcement of Judgements in Civil and Commercial Matters of 27 September 1968, governs conflicts of laws with regard to jurisdiction.

§2. Competent jurisdiction

1901. The Brussels Regulation applies in both civil and commercial matters. With respect to disputes concerning agency contracts, the Brussels Regulation only applies if the defendant is domiciled in an EC Member State, *i.e.*, any EC Member State, with the exception of Denmark (Art. 5 (5) of the Brussels Regulation). Denmark, in accordance with Articles 1 and 2 of the Protocol on the Position of Denmark annexed to the Treaty on European Union and to the Treaty establishing the European Community, did not participate in the adoption of the Brussels Regulation and is therefore not bound by it nor subject to its application.

1902. In general, the competent forum is the court of the EC Member State where the defendant is domiciled (Art. 2 of the Brussels Regulation) or, in matters relating to a contract, the court of the place where the contractual obligation in question is performed (Art. 5 (1) of the Brussels Regulation). In the case of the sale of goods and unless otherwise agreed, the place of performance of the obligation in question is the place in an EC Member State where, under the contract, the goods were delivered or should have been delivered. In the case of the provision of services and unless otherwise agreed, the place of performance of the obligation in question is the place in an EC Member State where, under the contract, the services were provided or should have been provided (Art. 5 (1) b of the Brussels Regulation).

1903. The place of performance of the contractual obligation in question is determined according to the applicable law. Parties may also agree upon the place of performance in a contractual clause.

1904. Belgian courts have *inter alia* accepted competence in the following cases:
(i) when an agency agreement is unlawfully terminated by the principal;

(ii) when the dispute concerns a commercial agent's remuneration which has been deposited into a Belgian bank account;

(iii) when the dispute concerns the "clientele" indemnity (*See*, paras. 1885 *et seq.*);

(iv) when an additional indemnity is claimed. Such a claim can be brought before a Belgian court in application of the general principle *"accessorium sequitur principale"*, according to which the dominant obligation involved in the dispute should be decisive.

1905. A Belgian court will also be competent if the defendant is not domiciled in a EC Member State but the commercial agent is domiciled in Belgium. In that case, Article 27 of the Agency Law will apply (*See*, para. 1899).

1906. Parties are allowed to agree upon the competent jurisdiction, provided that at least one of the parties is domiciled in an EC Member State and provided that jurisdiction is allocated to a court within an EC Member State (Art. 23 of the Brussels Regulation). However, the following conditions are imposed:

(i) the agreement must be in writing or evidenced in a writing; or

(ii) the agreement must be in a form which accords with practices which the parties have established between themselves; or

(iii) in international trade or commerce, the agreement must be in a form which accords with a usage of which the parties are or ought to have been aware and which in such trade or commerce is widely known to, and regularly observed by, parties to contracts of the type involved in the particular trade or commerce concerned.

1907. A written agreement is preferable to an unwritten agreement. Any agreement on jurisdiction must specifically concern the agency agreement in question. A choice of forum in any subsequent sales agreements, concluded by the principal will not bind the agent, but only the buyer.

§3. Applicable law

1908. The Rome Convention applies to disputes concerning choice of law obligations (Art. 1). The nationality of the parties or their domiciles do not influence the application of the Convention. The rules of the Rome Convention with respect to conflicts of laws may lead to the application of the law of a non-contracting State (Art. 2).

1909. The Rome Convention explicitly excludes from its application *"the question whether an agent is able to bind a principal to a third party"* (Art. 1.2 (f) of the Rome Convention). Issues of this nature are, according to current legal commentators, governed by the law of the place where the commercial agent has acted.

1910. In general, the parties are allowed to determine the law governing their contractual relationship. Their choice can be expressed or demonstrated by the terms of the contract or the circumstances of the case (Art. 3.1 of the Rome Convention). The parties have the right to make or alter their choice at any time (Art. 3.2 of the Rome Convention). Nevertheless, the parties' freedom to choose the applicable law may be restricted by mandatory rules, *i.e.*, rules from which the parties may not derogate. This will be discussed further in the following paragraphs.

1911. If the applicable law has not been chosen by the parties in accordance with Article 3 of the Rome Convention, the law of the country having the closest connection with the contract applies (Art. 4.1 of the Rome Convention). A contract is presumed to be most closely connected with the country where the party carrying out the characteristic performance has its habitual residence at the time the contract is concluded or, in the case of a body corporate or unincorporate, its central administration (Art. 4.2 of the Rome Convention). This presumption can be rebutted if the characteristic performance cannot be determined or if it appears that the contract is more closely connected to another country (Art. 4.5 of the Rome Convention). In case of an agency contract it is usually accepted that the characteristic performance is fulfilled by the commercial agent. Therefore, the applicable law will usually be the law of the country where the commercial agent is domiciled.

1912. As noted, the choice of the parties regarding the applicable law may be limited by mandatory rules. In certain circumstances these rules may apply to the contract irrespective of the law chosen by the parties. This may occur when:
  (i) the competent forum gives effect to the mandatory rules of another country, with which the situation has a close connection. This is only possible if and to the extent that, under the law of that country, those rules must be applied whatever the law applicable to the contract (Art. 7.1 of the Rome Convention); or
  (ii) the rules of the law of the forum are mandatory, irrespective of the law otherwise applicable to the case (Art. 7.2 of the Rome Convention).

1913. In this respect, it must be recalled that most of the provisions of the Agency Law are mandatory (*See*, para. 1849).

§4. Arbitration

1914. Finally, it should be noted that Article 27 of the Agency Law does not preclude the possibility that international agency contracts may be subject to arbitration. In some cases, this may even be more convenient, as the execution of arbitration decisions in foreign countries is often less cumbersome than the execution of judicial decisions.

IV. COMMERCIAL REPRESENTATIVES

A. Definition

§1. Constituent elements

1915. Pursuant to Article 4, paragraph 1 of the Law of 3 July 1978 on Employment Contracts (*Wet betreffende de arbeidsovereenkomsten/Loi relative aux contrats de travail* – the "Law of 3 July 1978") a commercial representation agreement is defined as an agreement whereby a white-collar employee, the commercial representative (*handelsvertegenwoordiger/représentant de commerce*), agrees to solicit potential customers for payment with a view to negotiating and/or concluding transactions under the authority, for the account, and in the name of one or more employers. The constituent elements of a commercial representation agreement are examined briefly below.

1. White-collar employee

1916. A commercial representative is an employee working under the authority of his employer. As a result, legal entities cannot qualify as commercial representatives (Ghent Labour Court, 12 March 1973, *R.W.*, 1973-1974, 166). Article 87 of the Law of 3 July 1978 indicates that the specific rules governing white-collar employees are applicable to commercial representation agreements.

2. Solicitation of potential customers

1917. Article 4 of the Law of 3 July 1978 states that the business of a commercial representative consists of seeking out and visiting potential customers. This implies an active effort on the part of the commercial representative but does not exclude the possibility that the commercial representative may only contact potential customers who reacted to previous advertisements or may limit himself to approaching potential customers listed by the employer. The activities of a commercial representative are typically carried on outside of the premises of the employer of the commercial representative.

3. Aim: negotiation and conclusion of transactions

1918. Article 4 of the Law of 3 July 1978 states that the activity of a commercial representative is characterised by a specific goal: the negotiation and conclusion of transactions. An individual whose task consists merely of visiting customers and advertising certain products or services will not qualify as a commercial representative. Similarly, an individual charged with supervising sales operations without actually negotiating or making sales will not fall within the scope of the rules governing commercial representation.

1919. One example of representatives who often do not meet the "negotiation and con-clusion" condition are representatives visiting medical doctors on behalf of phar-maceutical companies. Since the purpose of their visits is limited to promoting the usefulness of pharmaceutical products and does not include the negotiation or con-clusion of transactions with the doctors themselves, these representatives do not qualify as "commercial" representatives within the meaning of the Law (Cass., 8 January 1970, *Pas.*, 1970, I, 387). However, the conclusion of transactions does not necessarily imply the payment of a price by the customer. It may consist, for example, in the free placement of distributor machines restocked by a third party (Liège Labour Court, 18 September 2000, *J.T.T.*, 2001, 20).

1920. The transactions negotiated and concluded by commercial representatives may be for goods and services in all sectors of the economy. They may even relate to the services offered by a non-profit organisation.

1921. It should be noted that, although the insurance sector was initially excluded from the scope of the Law of 3 July 1978, the Belgian Arbitration Court recently de-cided that the exclusion of the insurance sector constitutes an infringement of the Constitution when the situation of the employee falls within the legal definition of a commercial representative (Arbitration Court, 17 June 1999, *Belgian Official Journal*, 1999, 33690).

4. *For the account and in the name of one or more employers*

1922. This condition distinguishes a commercial representative from an independent distributor. While commercial representatives act for the account and in the name of one or more employers, independent distributors typically act for their own account and in their own name (*See*, paras. 1769 and 1792).

5. *Under the authority of an employer*

1923. Since commercial representation agreements are employment contracts, it is essential that the employer be able to exercise a form of authority over his com-mercial representatives. However, commercial representation is an activity which implies a large degree of independent judgement. Therefore, an employer will generally be less able to give guidance to and exercise supervision over his commercial representatives than in ordinary employment relationships. Litigation regarding representation agreements often relates to the issue of whether the representative has acted under the authority of the other party.

1924. The abundant case law on this problem demonstrates that the courts routinely take a number of elements into account when establishing whether or not the repre-sentative acts under the authority of an employer. Such elements include: (i) whether or not the representative benefits from a guaranteed minimum income; (ii) whether the representative's costs are reimbursed; (iii) whether the representative's working hours are mandatorily fixed; (iv) whether the representative uses his own personnel; and (v) whether the representative is subject to detailed reporting requirements. Most courts examine a number of these elements and weigh the relative importance of each before reaching a conclusion. It follows that the presence of specific factors does not automatically lead to the same outcome in all cases and also that a number of elements are assessed in divergent manners by different courts.

6. On a continuous basis

1925. Article 88 of the Law of 3 July 1978 requires that for an employee to be a commercial representative, commercial representation must be his principal activity within the company. Commercial representation cannot be an activity subordinate to another function which the employee has in the same company. However, commercial representation can be done on a part-time basis if the employee exercises another function in another organisation or for another employer. In principle, it is accepted that a commercial representative may pursue a part-time activity as an independent distributor, for a different supplier, even if both activities are carried out in the same sector (Cass., 14 March 1994, *Pas.*, 1994, I, 252).

§2. Rebuttable presumption

1926. Article 4, paragraph 2 of the Law of 3 July 1978 provides that any agreement concluded between a principal and an intermediary will be deemed to be a commercial representation agreement until it is proven to be otherwise. This rebuttable presumption is valid irrespective of any explicit contractual clauses to the contrary and also applies in cases where the contract is silent on this issue. The rebuttable presumption contained in Article 4, paragraph 2 of the Law of 3 July 1978 is applicable as soon as a person is engaged in selling the products or services of another party as an intermediary. The presumption can be rebutted by demonstrating that one of the constituent elements of a commercial representation agreement is not present (*See*, paras. 1915 *et seq.*) or by showing that the relationship between the parties falls within one of the excluded categories mentioned in Article 4, paragraph 3 of the Law of 3 July 1978 (*See*, paras. 1928 *et seq.*).

1927. The legal presumption in favour of the existence of commercial representation agreements is important in that an intermediary claiming the applicability of the presumption will be able to benefit from the legal protection associated with employment agreements in general and commercial representation agreements in particular. As indicated above, litigation regarding the applicability of the rules governing commercial representatives often focuses on whether or not the principal is able to exercise authority over the intermediary.

§3. Excluded categories

1928. Article 4, paragraph 3 of the Law of 3 July 1978 lists a number of intermediaries which do not qualify as commercial representatives. None of these intermediaries acts under the authority of the principal, thereby ruling out the possibility that they may be bound by an employment agreement.

1929. The categories of intermediaries mentioned in Article 4, paragraph 3 of the Law of 3 July 1978 are the following:

    (i) the *commission agent (commissionair/commissionnaire):* an independent intermediary who acts for the principal but does so in his own name;

    (ii) the *broker (makelaar/courtier):* an independent intermediary who brings parties together, enabling these parties to negotiate and possibly to enter into an agreement;

    (iii) the *exclusive distributor (concessiehouder voor alleenverkoop/concessionnaire de vente exclusive):* an independent intermediary who acts in his own name and on his own account;

    (iv) the *intermediary*: a parry who is free to pass orders on to another party of his choice; and

    (v) the *commercial agent (handelsagent/agent commercial):* an independent intermediary who acts for the account and in the name of the principal in accordance with the Law of 13 April 1995 on Commercial Agency Agreements (*See*, paras. 1843 *et seq.*).

B. Formation of the agreement

1930. As in any employment agreement, a commercial representation agreement need not be in writing. However, some specific clauses, which are often included in commercial representation agreements, must be in written form in order to be valid. These clauses are:

    (i) non-competition provisions (Art. 104 *in fine* of the Law of 3 July 1978 – *See*, paras. 1952 *et seq.*); and

    (ii) *"delcredere"* provisions (Art. 107 of the Law of 3 July 1978 – *See*, para. 1946).

1931. In addition, the Law of 3 July 1978 requires that a clause providing for a probationary period, which is not typical of a commercial representation agreement, must be in writing in order to be valid (Art. 67, para. 1 of the Law of 3 July 1978).

1932. Finally, specific employment agreements, including specific commercial representation agreements, should always be in writing. These agreements are:
    (i) an agreement for a specified term (Art. 9 of the Law of 3 July 1978);
    (ii) an agreement regarding specified work (Art. 9 of the Law of 3 July 1978); and
    (iii) an agreement which provides for part-time employment (Art. 11*bis* of the Law of 3 July 1978).

C. Content of the agreement

§1. Applicable law

1933. A commercial representation agreement is generally governed by the same rules as those governing "white collar" employment agreements (Art. 87 of the Law of 3 July 1978). However, non-competition clauses in commercial representation agreements are not subject to these general provisions and are regulated by a separate set of rules (*See*, paras. 1952 *et seq.*). In addition, the Law of 3 July 1978 contains specific provisions concerning the remuneration of commercial representatives (*See*, paras. 1934 *et seq.*), "*delcredere*" clauses (*See*, para. 1946) and the termination of commercial representation agreements (*See*, paras. 1947 *et seq.*).

§2. Remuneration

1934. In principle, the level of a commercial representative's remuneration may be freely determined by the parties to the agreement. However, due regard should be given to any applicable local collective bargaining agreement (*collectieve arbeidsovereenkomst/convention collective de travail*), which may provide for mandatory minimum wages, indexation of fixed salaries and year-end bonuses.

1935. Pursuant to Article 89 of the Law of 3 July 1978, the remuneration of a commercial representative may consist of:
    (i) a fixed salary paid on a monthly basis (Art. 98 of the Law of 3 July 1978);
    (ii) commissions only; or
    (iii) a combination of a fixed salary and commissions.

1936. The Law of 3 July 1978 sets out specific rules governing the cases in which commission payments are due, as well as when they must be paid and the appropriate calculation method. These rules are discussed below.

1. Cases in which commissions are due

1937. A distinction must be drawn between direct and indirect commissions. Direct commissions relate to orders which have been passed on by the commercial representative to the employer. Indirect commissions concern orders placed with the employer by customers or from territories, which have been exclusively allotted to the commercial representative, but without the representative's direct intervention.

1938. Direct commissions are due during the term of the agreement for each order, which is accepted by the employer. For this mandatory rule to apply, it is not necessary that an actual sale is made unless the non-performance of the order is the commercial representative's fault. An order will be deemed not to have been accepted by the employer only if the employer expresses his refusal or reservation in writing within the term stated in the agreement or, in the absence of such a contractually agreed term, within one month following the placing of the order with the employer (Art. 90 of the Law of 3 July 1978). Contractual provisions cannot fix a ceiling for the payment of commissions (Cass., 27 November 1995, *Pas.*, I, 1071)

1939. Indirect commissions must be paid by the employer during the term of the agreement provided that the commercial representative can prove that he was granted the territory or clientele on an exclusive basis (Art. 93 of the Law of 3 July 1978). Contractual provisions cannot modify this mandatory rule. However, the Supreme Court has held that parties may agree that indirect commissions are only to be paid if the commercial representative has visited the customer concerned within a specific term prior to the order (Cass., 2 December 1966, *Pas.*, 1967, I, 421).

1940. If the agreement is temporarily suspended (in case of illness on the part of the commercial representative, for example), the commercial representative is entitled to claim direct commissions for orders placed before the period of suspension, even if the orders were accepted by the employer during that period (Art. 91 of the Law of 3 July 1978). In addition, the employer must pay direct commissions for orders placed during the period of suspension, provided that the commercial representative can prove that he had established direct contact with the customer during the term of the agreement which resulted in the orders concerned (Art. 92 of the Law of 3 July 1978). Finally, indirect commissions on transactions closed during the suspension of the agreement without the intervention of the commercial representative must be paid if the orders concerned were transmitted prior to the suspension of the agreement (Art. 93, para. 2 of the Law of 3 July 1978).

1941. Specific rules apply for commissions due after the termination of commercial representation agreements (*See*, paras. 1957 *et seq.*).

2. *When commissions must be paid*

1942. Unless otherwise stated in the agreement, commissions are payable 15 days following the delivery of the statement and documents relating to such commissions

(Art. 98 of the Law of 3 July 1978). The statement and documents, which should enable the commercial representative to calculate the commissions owed, must be provided by the employer on a monthly basis (Art. 97 of the Law of 3 July 1978).

1943. Parties may agree upon other arrangements for the payment of commissions. However, payment of commissions may not be made dependent on conditions whose fulfilment is uncertain. For example, an agreement may not provide that commissions are only payable after delivery or after payment for the goods is received (Antwerp Labour Court, 3 October 1978, *R.W.*, 1978-1979, 1663).

1944. After the termination of the agreement, mandatory rules concerning the payment of outstanding commissions apply (Art. 99 of the Law of 3 July 1978).

3. Calculation of commissions

1945. The calculation base for commissions is generally laid down in the agreement. In the absence of such contractual provisions, commissions are to be paid on:
  (i) the price stated on the order form in the document in which the employer accepts the order; or
  (ii) in the absence thereof, the price contained in relevant price lists; or
  (iii) in the absence thereof, the price actually charged to the customer (Art. 96 of the Law of 3 July 1978).

§3. Delcredere

1946. A *delcredere* clause is an express, written provision in the contract by which the parties may agree that the commercial representative will be responsible in case a customer is insolvent (Art. 107 of the Law of 3 July 1978). However, except in cases of serious fault or fraud on the part of the commercial representative, his liability in this respect may not exceed the amount of the commissions relating to the non-recoverable claims.

D. Termination of the agreement

§1. Applicable law

1947. Generally, the normal rules governing 'white-collar' employment contracts are applicable to the termination of commercial representation agreements. However, specific rules apply concerning "clientele" indemnities, non-competition provisions and commissions due after termination. These specific rules are discussed below.

§2. Clientele indemnity

1948. A "clientele" indemnity is given by an employer to compensate the commercial representative for damage incurred due to the loss of clientele brought to the employer. It does not indemnify the commercial representative for the loss of employment or remuneration (Cass., 15 December 1980, *Pas.*, 1981, I, 437).

1949. The right to a clientele indemnity is subject to the following 4 cumulative conditions (Art. 101 of the Law of 3 July 1978):

    (i) the agreement must have been terminated by the employer for reasons other than a serious breach of the contract by the commercial representative (*dringende reden/motif grave*) or by the commercial representative for a serious breach on the part of the employer. The Supreme Court has held that the unilateral modification of the terms of employment by the employer constitutes a unilateral termination of the commercial representation agreement by the employer, entitling the commercial representative to a clientele indemnity provided the other conditions outlined below are also met (Cass., 13 September 1972, *Pas.*, 1973, I, 50);

    (ii) the commercial representative must have introduced the customer in question to the employer. If the agreement contains a non-competition clause, the commercial representative is deemed to have brought clientele to the employer. This presumption is valid even if the non-competition provision is not effective in cases such as those where the agreement is terminated by the employer for reasons other than a serious breach of the commercial representative, or by the commercial representative for serious breach on the part of the employer (Cass., 26 March 1979, *Pas.*, 1979, I, 875) (*See*, paras. 1952 *et seq.*). The employer may, however, rebut this presumption (Art. 105 of the Law of 3 July 1978);

    (iii) the commercial representative must be disadvantaged by the termination of the agreement. According to the Supreme Court, the fact that the commercial representative has been able to keep his former clientele, such as by providing his new employer with the clientele he had brought to his former employer, constitutes proof that the commercial representative was not disadvantaged by the termination of the agreement (Cass., 21 December 1981, *Pas.*, 1982, I, 538 and *Cass.*, 26 April 1999, *J.T.T.*, 434); and

    (iv) upon termination of the agreement, the commercial representative must have been employed for a period of at least 1 year.

1950. The amount payable as a clientele indemnity is generally calculated on a lump-sum basis. If the employment period of the commercial representative ranges from 1 to 5 years, the clientele indemnity equals 3 months' remuneration. This amount is increased by 1 month's remuneration after 5 years and by an additional month's remuneration for each subsequent 5-year period. For example, a commercial representative who has been working for 6 years with the same employer is entitled to a clientele indemnity of 4 months' remuneration. Remuneration for the purposes of calculating the clientele indemnity includes fixed remuneration, commissions, and other advantages resulting from the agreement (year-end bonuses or group insurance, for example). The exact amount of the commissions is calculated by taking the monthly average of the commissions earned during the twelve months preceding the termination of the agreement (Art. 101 of the Law of 3 July 1978).

1951. Under one set of circumstances, the clientele indemnity may even exceed the lump-sum calculated in the manner described above. Where an agreement is terminated by the commercial representative for serious breach, and the commercial representative is able to prove that the lump-sum amount does not cover all damages which have been incurred, the representative may be granted an additional indemnity up to the amount of these additional damages (Art. 103 of the Law of 3 July 1978).

§3. Non-competition clauses

1952. Non-competition clauses in commercial representation agreements are governed by specific legal rules (Arts. 104 through 106 of the Law of 3 July 1978) which partially diverge from the provisions generally applicable to "white-collar" employment contracts.

1953. A commercial representative who earns less than € 25,921 (amount on 1 January 2003, subject to indexation) may not be bound by a non-competition clause. If the commercial representative earns more than this amount, a non-compete clause will only be valid if the restriction:
   (i) relates to activities similar to those conducted on behalf of the employer;
   (ii) does not exceed 12 months following the termination of the agreement; and
   (iii) relates to the territory in which the commercial representative carried out his activities.

1954. Moreover, non-competition provisions must be in writing.

1955. Non-competition clauses are not effective if the agreement is terminated:
   (i) during the trial period;
   (ii) by the employer for reasons other than a serious breach on the part of the commercial representative; or
   (iii) by the commercial representative on the basis of a serious breach committed by the employer.

1956. The agreement may provide for a lump-sum indemnity to be paid by the commercial representative in the event of a breach of the non-competition obligation, provided that this indemnity does not exceed 3 months' remuneration. However, the employer may obtain a higher indemnity if he can prove the actual level of damage incurred.

§4. Commissions due after termination

1957. The employer owes direct commissions to the commercial representative for orders placed prior to termination of the agreement, even if they were accepted after the termination (Art. 91 of the Law of 3 July 1978). The commercial representative is also entitled to receive direct commissions for orders placed during a period of 3 months following the termination of the agreement provided the commercial representative proves that he had established direct contact with the customer which resulted in the placement of the orders concerned (Art. 92 of the Law of 3 July 1978).

1958. In addition, indirect commissions are due for transactions entered into after the termination of the agreement, provided that the orders concerned were transmitted prior to the termination of the agreement (Art. 93(2) of the Law of 3 July 1978).

1959. If orders accepted prior to the termination of the agreement relate to staggered deliveries, the commercial representative is entitled to claim commissions for deliveries made during a 6-month period following the termination of the agreement (Art. 94 of the Law of 3 July 1978). According to the Supreme Court, the 6-month limitation only applies to framework agreements performed in accordance with the instructions of the customer (Cass., 4 June 1970, *Pas.*, 1970, I, 876). Therefore, orders whereby the customer is not entitled to cancel future deliveries are not caught by the 6-month limitation. Commercial representatives may claim a full commission for such firm orders placed prior to the termination of the agreement, even for deliveries extending beyond 6 months.

1960. Finally, the successor to a commercial representative will not be able to claim commissions to which his predecessor is entitled by virtue of the rules set out above (Art. 95 of the Law of 3 July 1978).

V. FRANCHISEES

A. Introduction

§1. Definition

1961. Franchisees can be defined as legally and financially independent commercial intermediaries acting in their own name and on their own behalf but entering into a particular form of business partnership based upon a close and ongoing collaboration with a franchisor. Together, the franchisor and the individual franchisees form the franchised network. The franchisor grants its individual franchisees the right, and imposes the obligation, to conduct a business in accordance with the franchisor's concept. To do so, the franchisor transfers to its franchisees a package of industrial and/or intellectual property rights (relating to trade marks, trade names, service marks, shop signs, utility models, designs, copyrights, know-how, patents, *etc.*) and a continuous commercial, legal and technical assistance.

1962. However, the definition above is not specific to franchises in Belgium. Indeed, no specific definition exists in Belgian law. Rather, the definition above has been inspired by the definition contained in Article 1 of the European Code of Ethics for Franchising as well as definitions found in paragraph 199 of the European Commission's Guidelines on Vertical Restraints (the "Vertical Restraints Guidelines" – O.J. [2000] C 291/1) and in the now-repealed European Commission block exemption Regulation No. 4087/88 of 30 November 1988 on the Application of Article 85(1) [now 81(1)] of the EC Treaty to Categories of Franchise Agreements (O.J. [1998] L 359/46). Belgian courts often rely on these definitions when confronted with franchise agreements.

§2. Different types of franchises

1963. Several types of franchises can be distinguished according to their object. For instance, industrial franchises concern the manufacture of goods, distribution franchises concern the sale of goods, and services franchises concern the supply of services. According to their object, certain legal rules will or will not apply to different types of franchise agreements. Furthermore, so-called "master franchises" are agreements whereby the franchisor grants the "master franchisee" the right to exploit a franchise for the purposes of concluding franchise agreements with third parties, the ultimate franchisees. The features of master franchises are often very different from these of normal franchises. In particular, the master franchisee should make sure that it does not transfer more rights to the franchisees than it actually receives from the master franchise agreement.

§3. Essential elements

1964. A franchise relationship shall, in principle, include at least the following elements and characteristics:
   (i) a contract between legally and financially separate and independent undertakings;
   (ii) a transfer of all relevant know-how by the franchisor to the franchisee;
   (iii) the licensing of intellectual property rights relating to trade marks or signs;
   (iv) the provision of commercial, technical and legal assistance by the franchisor to the franchisee;
   (v) the exploitation of the franchise in conformity with the franchisor's concept; and
   (vi) the use of a common name or shop sign and a uniform presentation of contract premises and/or means of transport.

1965. These elements are important as they summarise the distinctive elements of franchising compared to other forms of associated businesses. Where these elements are not included, it is not uncommon for Belgian courts, after an analysis of the parties' rights and obligations, to regard their agreement as being a contract but not a franchise agreement. Under Article 1156 of the Civil Code, the real intention of the parties prevails over the strict language of the contract, and judges may disregard the parties' characterisation of a contract if it is contradicted by its content and/or execution.

1966. For example, on 22 November 1995, the Commercial Court of Charleroi considered that the alleged franchise contract did not include a close and ongoing collaboration between the parties and consequently re-classified the contract as an exclusive distribution agreement which included a licence to use the trade name of the supplier (Comm. Charleroi, *J.L.M.B.*, 1997, 1668). In other circumstances, the courts may consider that the control and the obligations imposed on the franchisees (*e.g.*, opening times, prices, selection of the staff, control of the accounts) are such that no independence exists between the parties and may conclude that the franchisees are in fact employees, and that consequently all the provisions of Belgian labour law apply, including the obligation to pay social contributions (Cass., 10 November 1984, *J.T.*, 1985, 244). The Belgian courts may also consider that, given the absence of a transfer of know-how, a contract must be re-classified as the licence of a trademark, a distribution agreement or a supply agreement.

§4. Legal framework

1967. Although the Belgian Federal Parliament recently reviewed and discussed 3 legislative projects (House of Representatives, parliamentary doc. 50, No. 1190/001, of April 2001; House of Representatives, parliamentary doc. 50, No. 1307/001, of 15 June 2001; House of Representatives, parliamentary doc. 50, No. 1599/001, of 18 January 2002), at the end of 2002 Belgium still had no specific legislation as regards franchise agreements.

1968. Franchise agreements are thus regulated by general Belgian contract law. In addition, certain specific laws may apply to some aspects of the contractual relationship between the franchisor and the franchisees.

1969. For instance, all competition aspects of a franchise will be subject to the Law of 5 August 1991 on the Protection of Economic Competition co-ordinated on 1 July 1999 (the "Competition Law"), as well as the Law of 14 July 1991 on Trade Practices and Consumer Information Protection (the "Law on Unfair Trade Practices"). All intellectual property aspects will be construed in accordance with the relevant Belgian intellectual property legislation and, in certain circumstances, the termination of franchise agreements may be governed by the Law of 27 July 1961 on the Unilateral Termination of Certain Categories of Distribution Agreements, as modified on 1 April 1971 (the "Law of 27 July 1961") (*See*, paras. 1789 *et seq.*).

1970. Given the absence of any specific legislation as regards franchises, the written agreement between the franchisor and franchisee will constitute the main source of law between the parties and should therefore cover all of the different and numerous aspects of the franchise.

§5. European Code of Ethics

1971. Besides strict legal provisions, the European Franchise Federation, composed of 17 national franchise federations (including the Belgian Franchise Federation), has defined and upheld a "European Code of Ethics for Franchising" (hereinafter the "Code of Ethics"). Each member of the national federations is committed to the principles laid down in the Code of Ethics, and before entering into a contract with a franchisor, candidate franchisees should verify that the franchisor belongs to one of the 17 national federations. Although the Code of Ethics only lays down general principles, it has proved very useful for regulating the practice of franchising on European markets, and the Belgian courts have often considered that the parties referred to it as part of their agreement. It must be noted, however, that the Code of Ethics only applies to the relationship between a franchisor and individual franchisees and to the relationship between a master franchisee and individual franchisees but not the relationship between a franchisor and a master franchisee (Art. 6 of the Code of Ethics).

B. Pre-contractual relationship

§1. Pre-contractual negotiations

1972. Franchise agreements often require long negotiations. The drafting of a pre-contract before the signing of the final agreement may be appropriate. In Belgium, the general principles of the Civil Code apply to the negotiation and conclusion of franchise agreements. For example, Articles 1109 and 1116 of the Civil Code may sanction a franchisor for a mistake (*dwaling/erreur*) or misrepresentation (*bedrog/ dol*) which has led a franchisee to sign a franchise agreement on the basis of false information. Similar sanctions would apply to a franchisee for the same reasons.

§2. Pre-contractual information

1973. In Belgium, no specific legal obligation requires the franchisor to provide pre-contractual information to candidate franchisees. However, prior information is vital so that candidate franchisees are aware of all the implications of the business, *e.g.*, the current situation and future perspectives of the sector in question, the location of the premises, the expected profits and expenses of the franchise. Hence, a pre-contractual obligation to provide the candidate franchisees with full information could stem from the general obligation of good faith and loyalty imposed on the parties in the course of the negotiation of a contract. Such a pre-contractual obligation could also stem from the Code of Ethics, which compels franchisors to provide a *"full and accurate disclosure of information material to the franchise relationship, within a reasonable time prior to the execution of [the] binding documents"* (Art. 3.3 of the Code of Ethics).

1974. Where the franchisor has not provided sufficient pre-contractual information, it is possible for the franchisees to invoke the franchisor's tort liability under Articles 1382 and 1383 of the Civil Code for any wrongful act or negligence during the pre-contractual period which caused injury to the franchisees (*culpa in contrahendo*, or *buitencontractuele fout/faute extracontractuelle*). The franchisees could also rely on the above-mentioned Articles 1109 and 1116 of the Civil Code.

1975. The case law indicates that the franchisor's pre-contractual behaviour is often more severely sanctioned than the franchisees' pre-contractual behaviour. This is due to the franchisor's stronger economic position and the obligatory adherence of the franchisees to the provisions of the agreement (standard agreement for all the franchisees). However, the franchisees cannot simply and blindly rely on the franchisor's information. They must also take all necessary measures to be properly informed.

§3. Selection of individual franchisees

1976. Franchise agreements are *intuitu personae* contracts, i.e., contracts concluded taking into consideration the identity and essential characteristics of the contracting partner. Accordingly, the selection of franchisees is the franchisor's right. Obviously, the franchisor is entitled to verify that the candidate franchisee will be able to conduct the activities under the common brand name without damaging the reputation of the franchised network.

1977. Nevertheless, it is possible that the franchisor's refusal to conclude a franchise agreement with a candidate franchisee may constitute an "abuse of right" (*abus de droit/rechtsmisbruik*) if the refusal is subjective and arbitrary.

C. Contractual relationship

§1. Content of the agreement – ICC model international franchising contract

1978. Franchises are increasingly developed on an international basis and, to overcome the difficulties caused by a lack of uniform international rules in this field, the International Chamber of Commerce ("ICC") has published a model contract on international franchising agreements. This ICC model contract is intended to facilitate international franchising by offering franchisors and franchisees a framework agreement within which their rights and responsibilities can be determined and protected.

1979. The ICC model contract is very useful, as it takes into account the most commonly used clauses in franchise agreements and suggests alternative clauses for specific franchise agreements. The ICC model contract also strikes a fair balance between the interests of the franchisor and franchisees.

1980. However, in drafting their own agreement, the parties should bear in mind that the ICC model contract only applies to international franchise agreements and for the distribution of goods or provision of services. As such, it is not necessarily suitable for strict national franchises, industrial franchises, or master franchise agreements.

§2. Formation

1981. Franchise agreements need not fulfil any specific conditions to be validly formed. However, given the complexity of franchise relationships, it is difficult to envisage an oral franchise agreement. Also, the know-how transferred by the franchisor to the franchisees requires a clear description and will thus most likely be put in writing.

§3. *Duration*

1982. The parties are free to determine the duration of the franchise. The Code of Ethics indicates that the duration of franchise agreements should be long enough to allow the franchisees to recoup the initial investments, which are specific to the franchise (Art. 5.4).

1983. Often, franchise agreements are concluded for a fixed period of time but are renewable as per the modalities set forth in the contract. Some franchise agreements tie the duration of the franchise to the duration of the lease contract for the buildings occupied by the franchisee. It is important to specify the basis for any renewal or termination of the contract.

§4. *Fees and royalties*

1984. The franchisees pay the franchisor a fee and/or royalties, or a combination of fees which often include an entrance fee and a fixed percentage of the franchisee's annual turnover. The fees and/or royalties may be freely determined by the parties.

§5. *Lease contracts*

1985. Although it is not very frequent, it may happen that a franchise is run from a commercial property owned by the franchisor and leased to the franchisee under a commercial lease contract. However, this situation is not recommended, as it may create problems. In particular, a possible conflict may arise between the mandatory provisions of the Law of 30 April 1951 on Commercial Lease Agreements (*Regels betreffende de handelshuur in het bijzonder/Règles particulières concernant les baux commerciaux*) and the clauses of the franchise agreement, especially insofar as the duration of the franchise and commercial lease contracts are concerned. In case of termination of the franchise, the franchisee may wish to continue the lease contract regardless of the termination. Furthermore, Belgian courts could possibly rely on the franchisor's obligation to provide a continuous assistance to its franchisees, to condemn a franchisor who did not remind a franchisee to renew its commercial lease agreement.

§6. *Competition restrictions*

1986. Franchise agreements most often include restrictions on the parties' freedom to conduct the franchise business. These restrictions must, however, be in conformity with Belgian competition law, that is, Articles 2 and 3 of the Competition Law. The Law on Unfair Trade Practices is also designed to protect fair competition.

1987. Articles 2 and 3 of the Competition Law mirror Articles 81 and 82 of the EC Treaty. Furthermore, Belgian courts apply and construe Articles 2 and 3 of the Competition Law in light of the EC Treaty and EC legislation.

1988. It is recalled that, at the European level, franchises are regulated not only by Articles 81 and 82 of the EC Treaty but also by block exemption Regulation No. 2790/99 of 22 December 1999 on Vertical Restraints (O.J. [1999] L 336/21 – the "Vertical Restraints Block Exemption"), which replaced block exemption Regulation No. 4087/88 on Franchise Agreements. Although the 1999 block exemption Regulation on Vertical Restraints does not expressly refer to franchise agreements anymore, the European Commission has provided some guidance with respect to franchise in the Vertical Restraints Guidelines (O.J. [2000] C 291/1).

1989. As under European competition law, franchises which do not have a significant impact on the market fall outside the scope of the prohibition contained in Article 2 of the Competition Law.

1990. However, certain clauses or practices will always be prohibited. These include fixing prices, prohibiting franchisees from using know-how that has become common knowledge, cartels, and prohibiting franchisees from contesting the validity of the franchisor's intellectual or industrial property rights. As regards such "no-challenge" clauses, it should be added that, where EC law applies, a franchisor licensing its know-how to a franchisee may reserve the right to validity of the licensed know-how.

1991. It should be noted that the Belgian Competition Council, which is the body primarily responsible for competition matters in Belgium, has rendered very few decisions following a request for an individual exemption under Article 2(3) of the Competition Law (*i.e.*, the equivalent of Article 81(3) of the EC Treaty). Hence, there is very little legal certainty for franchisors and franchisees in this field.

1. Exclusive supply

1992. Distribution franchise agreements often include an exclusive supply clause whereby the franchisee is obliged to purchase the products exclusively (or almost exclusively) from the franchisor or a supplier designated by the franchisor. Such a clause is by nature anti-competitive, but it is sometimes necessary to allow the homogenous development of the franchised network.

1993. On 4 October 1996, the Commercial Court of Charleroi ruled on the termination of a franchise agreement whereby the franchisor had obliged his franchisees to be supplied exclusively by him (Comm. Charleroi, *R.D.C.*, 1999, 283). The franchisor's deliveries were delayed, but the franchisor maintained that the franchisees were responsible for the delays given their late payments. The Commercial Court of Charleroi ruled that franchisors are responsible for the exclusive deliveries and may be liable if they put their franchisees at risk by delaying or refusing to deliver the contract products.

2. Prices

1994. As with European competition law, under Belgian law the franchisor cannot restrict the franchisee's ability to determine its sale price. On the other hand, a franchisor generally may impose a maximum sale price or recommend a sale price, provided that this price does not amount to a fixed or minimum sale price as a result of a pressure from, or incentives offered by, any of the parties.

3. Non-compete clauses

1995. Franchise agreements may prevent franchisees from competing with the franchisor or other members of the franchised network during the period of the contract and/ or during a reasonable period after the termination of the contract. Such clauses aim at safeguarding the know-how developed and communicated by the franchisor and are often considered as valid, provided that they are limited in scope, time and location.

1996. By virtue of Article 5(a) of the Vertical Restraints Block Exemption, direct or indirect non-compete obligations effective during the franchise agreement may not be concluded for an indefinite period of time or a period exceeding 5 years. However, the time limitation of 5 years does not apply where the contract goods or services are sold by the franchisee from premises and land owned by the franchisor or leased by the franchisor from third parties not connected with the franchisee, provided that the duration of the non-compete obligation does not exceed the period during which the franchisee occupies such premises and land.

1997. The Vertical Restraints Block Exemption does not allow any non-compete obligation after the termination of the franchise agreement. However, there can be a derogation from this general prohibition whenever such a non-compete obligation is necessary to protect the know-how transferred by the franchisor to the franchisees. In that case, the non-compete obligation can have a duration of maximum 1 year, provided it is limited to the products or services competing with the contract products or services, and so long as the obligation is limited to the premises and land from which the franchisee has operated during the contract period.

§7. Intellectual and industrial property rights

1998. As mentioned above, franchises include the transfer of all necessary know-how (*e.g.*, technical methods, procedural systems, or other methods) by the franchisor to the franchisees, as well as the licensing of intellectual property rights related to the franchisor's distinctive signs, trade name, trademarks, store sign, logo or other distinguishing identification.

1999. As defined by the Belgian Franchise Federation in the annex to the European Code of Ethics, the know-how must be *secret*, *substantial* and *identified*:

> *"(a) 'secret' means that the know-how, as a body or in the precise configuration and assembly of its components, is not generally known or easily accessible; it is not limited in the narrow sense that each individual component of the know-how should be totally unknown or unobtainable outside the Franchisor's business;*
>
> *(b) 'substantial' means that the know-how includes information which is of importance for the sale of goods or the provision of services to end users, and in particular for the presentation of goods for sale, the processing of goods in connection with the provision of services, methods of dealing with customers, and administration and financial management; the know-how must be useful for the Franchisee by being capable, at the date of conclusion of the agreement, of improving the competitive position of the franchisee, in particular by improving the franchisee's performance or helping it to enter a new market;*
>
> *(c) 'identified' means that the know-how must be described in a sufficiently comprehensive manner so as to make it possible to verify that it fulfils the criteria of secrecy and substantiality; the description of the know-how can either be set out in the franchise agreement or in a separate document or recorded in any other appropriate form."*

2000. Franchisors and franchisees should be aware that the transfer of all know-how and the licensing of intellectual property rights are essential elements of franchise agreements.

2001. Franchisors should obviously pay particular attention to protecting their know-how and intellectual property rights in the most appropriate way. The know-how does not benefit from any intellectual property right protection as such, but the franchisor can protect the know-how in the franchise agreement itself. Often, franchise agreements set forth that the franchisee is only entitled to use the know-how for the purpose of the franchise and for the duration of the contract. At the expiry of the franchise, the franchisee is usually obliged to return all documents and equipment containing the know-how.

2002. The above-mentioned ICC model international franchising contract envisages all aspects related to the transfer and protection of know-how and intellectual property rights and constitutes a useful reference for the drafting of any franchise agreement.

D. Termination of the contractual relationship

§1. Application of general principles of contract law

2003. In Belgium, given the absence of any specific legislation as regards franchises, the general principles of contract law apply to the termination of franchise agreements. Franchises will always be concluded for a fixed period of time.

2004. According to the general principles above, agreements of fixed duration may not be terminated unilaterally and, in principle, any unilateral termination prior to the agreed date of expiry will amount to a breach of contract. In the absence of contractual provisions to the contrary, agreements of fixed duration terminate automatically on the expiration date set forth in the franchise agreement.

§2. Application of the Law of 27 July 1961

2005. In certain circumstances, termination of franchises may be governed by the Law of 27 July 1961 (*See*, paras. 1789 *et seq.* for a full analysis of the Law of 27 July 1961). However, the scope of the Law of 27 July 1961 is limited and only covers the unilateral termination of the categories of distribution agreements specified in the Law of 27 July 1961. The application of the Law of 27 July 1961 is nevertheless important as it provides considerable protection for distributors in case of unilateral termination of the distributionship.

2006. The application of the Law of 27 July 1961 to the termination of franchises is not automatic and raises some problems in Belgium. On 11 April 1997, the Brussels Court of Appeal rejected the application of the Law of 27 July 1961 to a franchise agreement after determining that the agreement conformed with the essential characteristics of franchises, *i.e.*, the transfer of a know-how, a reputation and a common business (Brussels Court of Appeal, *R.D.C.*, 1999, 264). The Brussels Court of Appeal also pointed out that the franchisees paid royalties for a licence, that a common image of the franchised network appeared on advertisements, and that the franchisor provided technical and economic assistance.

2007. However, the case law and doctrine are not settled on this issue. On 12 October 1994, the Ghent Court of Appeal considered that the Law of 27 July 1961 was applicable to a franchisee which distributed electrical appliances (Ghent Court of Appeal, *R.D.C.*, 1995, 501). The Ghent Court of Appeal noted that the franchisor delivered the goods to the franchisee, and that the franchisee resold them in his own name and on his behalf. The franchisee had been granted territorial exclusivity and was obliged to purchase the goods from the franchisor or suppliers accepted by the franchisor.

2008. It may also happen that, given the absence of one or several essential elements of a franchise agreement, courts will re-classify the contract and will consequently be able to apply the Law of 27 July 1961.

2009. In the light of the unsettled case law, it would seem that each contract must be examined on a case-by-case basis and that the courts will examine the obligations of the parties to determine the applicability of the Law of 27 July 1961. In practice, important differences exist between the negotiation and execution of franchises and distribution contracts covered by the Law of 27 July 1961, although franchise agreements do cover some of the same terms and conditions found in distribution contracts.

E. Legislative projects

2010. Often, national legislation only partially regulates franchises. For example, national laws may simply require an exchange of information between the parties prior to signing the contract. In certain countries, like in Spain, franchise agreements must be registered with a particular authority that analyses the clauses of the franchise agreements. Restrictive clauses are annulled.

2011. In Belgium, 3 draft laws are currently under discussion before the Federal Parliament. The authors of the projects all agree that, most often, franchisees do not have any bargaining power to negotiate the conditions of the franchise agreement and that, therefore, there is an imbalance between the rights and obligations of the franchisor and franchisee.

2012. The first draft law, dated 9 April 2001, has been proposed to regulate: (i) pre-contractual information; (ii) the transfer of the franchise agreement; (iii) the nullity of certain clauses; (iv) a pre-emption right for the franchisor; (v) duration; and (vi) termination. This project also suggests the creation of a committee which would render an opinion in case of arbitration. The second draft law, dated 15 June 2001, would establish protective measures in favour of franchisees related to: (i) pre-contractual information; and (ii) the execution and termination of the franchise. The third draft law, dated 18 January 2002, aims solely at imposing an obligation of pre-contractual information on the parties to allow for a clear understanding of the envisaged franchise agreement. The pre-contractual information would concern not only all the implications of the franchise but also the nature and importance of the franchisor's activity. Any breach of this obligation of pre-contractual information would be sanctioned by the nullity of the contract, provided that the failure to provide such information relates to an essential element of the franchise and provided the resulting incomplete information was relied on by one of the parties when that party consented to the agreement.

11. E-COMMERCE

I. INTRODUCTION

2013. There is no general definition of e-commerce (electronic commerce). E-commerce generally refers to:
    (i) the use of Internet applications in order to reach consumers or suppliers, the placing of on-line orders and the making of on-line payments;
    (ii) the trading of electronic goods and services; and
    (iii) financial transactions over the Internet.

2014. E-commerce is growing world-wide. Though there has been a slight increase of the use of e-commerce in Belgium, it still remains quite limited. According to the 2002 "e-readiness" report of the Economist Intelligence Unit (the "EIU"), Belgium has moved up from the nineteenth position to the sixteenth position on the top twenty e-maturity list. This list reflects several factors, such as telephone penetration, on-line security and protection of intellectual property.

2015. In recent years, the use of Internet in Belgium has been low compared to other European countries. This was mainly due to the fact that the telecommunications sector, which kept telephone rates relatively high, was only fully liberalised in 1998. Belgium has, however, recovered from its relative backlog. According to a study performed by Insites Consulting in 2002, there are over 3.2 million regular Internet users, a number which is expected to increase up to 3.6 million users in 2003. Internet users now represent practically all categories of the Belgian population. Another important change over the past few years is the increased use of broadband connections instead of traditional copper telephone lines.

2016. The Internet is mostly used for websites that are not related to e-commerce. Currently, more than 80 per cent of Belgian companies have their own website. These websites are mainly of an informative character and are not designed for commercial transactions. Research has demonstrated that only one out of 5 Belgian companies actually provide e-commerce applications. The use of electronic market places also remains quite limited in Belgium.

2017. In this chapter, different aspects of e-commerce will be dealt with. First, Section II will address the competent jurisdiction and applicable law in e-commerce disputes (*See*, paras. 2018 *et seq.*). Section III will deal with contracting on the

Internet (*See*, paras. 2033 *et seq.*). Section IV will examine the E-commerce Directive (as defined below; *See*, paras. 2055 *et seq.*). Section V will review electronic signatures (*See*, paras. 2066 *et seq.*). The liability of intermediaries in the field of e-commerce is addressed in Section VI (*See*, paras. 2082 *et seq.*). The registration of domain names and conflicts between domain names and trademarks form the subject of Section VII (*See*, paras. 2096 *et seq.*). Section VIII will be devoted to codes of conduct (*See*, paras. 2108 *et seq.*). Finally, Section IX will address the application of the competition rules to e-commerce (*See*, paras. 2114 *et seq.*).

II. JURISDICTION AND APPLICABLE LAW

A. Jurisdiction

§1. Belgian law

2018. National rules governing jurisdiction will only apply if there are no international rules defining the rules of competence. Belgian law contains several provisions dealing with this issue. According to Article 624 of the Judicial Code, the plaintiff is entitled to choose a competent court based on 4 grounds of jurisdiction, provided that the law does not specifically prescribe a basis for jurisdiction in a particular case. Generally, under Article 624 of the Judicial Code, the competent court will be that of the place of residence of the defendant, the place where the obligations giving rise to the dispute originated or the place where these obligations are or have to be executed.

2019. Furthermore, a number of provisions address special questions of jurisdiction. Article 15 of the Civil Code states that a Belgian citizen can be sued before a Belgian court for obligations contracted abroad or with a foreigner. Article 635 of the Judicial Code mentions different situations in which foreigners can be sued before a Belgian court by either a Belgian or a foreign plaintiff, such as the case where an obligation, which is the subject of dispute, is, has been or should have been performed in Belgium. If it is impossible to determine the competence of the Belgian courts with respect to foreigners on the basis of the aforementioned provisions, a Belgian plaintiff is allowed to bring the case before the court of his domicile or residence (Art. 638 of the Judicial code).

§2. Regulation No. 44/2001

2020. The Convention of 27 September 1968 on Jurisdiction and the Enforcement of Judgements in Civil and Commercial Measures (the "1968 Brussels Convention") (O.J. [1990] C 189/2) has been replaced by EC Council Regulation No. 44/2001 of

22 December 2000 on Jurisdiction and the Recognition and Enforcement of Judgements in Civil and Commercial Matters ("Regulation No. 44/2001" – O.J. [2001] L 12/1), which entered into force on 1 March 2002 and is directly applicable in the EC Member States.

2021. Regulation No. 44/2001 only applies to civil and commercial matters. It aims to harmonise the rules of international private law in the different EC Member States and to ensure the recognition and execution of judgements. Furthermore, Regulation No. 44/2001 seeks to adopt the existing European jurisdictional rules to the new questions posed by the advent of Internet and e-commerce. The modifications entail significant consequences for on-line contracts and the development of e-commerce.

2022. As a basic principle, Regulation No. 44/2001 provides that jurisdiction is determined by the country of domicile of the defendant (Art. 2). If the defendant is a company or other legal entity, its domicile is considered to be the place of its statutory seat, its central administration or its principal place of business (Art. 60). If the defendant is not domiciled in an EC Member State, jurisdiction will be determined by the law of the EC Member State where jurisdiction is sought (Art. 4).

2023. Like the 1968 Brussels Convention, Regulation No. 44/2001 provides that for contracts, jurisdiction is determined by the place of performance of the contract (Art. 5, para. 1). In order to avoid any doubt, the place of performance is defined as the place where the goods or services were or should have been delivered or provided.

2024. The provisions relating to consumer contracts have been subject to considerable modifications. The circumstances in which consumers can sue in their home country have been extended. As a general rule, Article 16 of Regulation No. 44/2001 states that consumers can choose to sue either in their own home country or in the EC Member State where the seller is domiciled. The newly incorporated Article 15 of Regulation No. 44/2001 considerably broadens the circumstances in which consumers can sue in their home country. This is allowed if "*the contract has been concluded with a person who pursues commercial or professional activities in the Member State of the consumer's domicile, or, by any means, directs such activities to that Member State or to several States including that Member State*". This provision seeks to protect consumers engaging in cross-border transactions, including those conducted via the Internet, by enabling them to bring an action arising from contracts concluded via the Internet in their own country of domicile. It is irrelevant whether the defendant is a European or third country business. In contrast, the seller can only file an action against a consumer in the consumer's country of domicile. Another modification introduced by Regulation No. 44/2001 concerns the abolishment of the rule that consumers must have taken the necessary steps for the conclusion of the contract in their EC Member State in order to be able to initiate proceedings in their home country.

2025. Regulation No. 44/2001 is likely to have a considerable impact on e-commerce. Regulation No. 44/2001 has, from the beginning, given rise to strong criticism, mainly from the business community, because it imposes a significant burden on e-commerce. This criticism concerns, in particular, the broad wording of the new Article 15 of Regulation No. 44/2001 ("[…], *by any means directs such activities to* [...]"). This wording seems to imply that the mere fact that a consumer has access to a business's website from its home country entails that a business will be considered to have directed its activities to the consumer's country, regardless of the business's intent to target consumers in that country. It is feared that this provision may discourage small businesses from using the Internet to conduct business, as it may give rise to claims from all over Europe.

B. Applicable law

§1. Rome Convention

2026. The EC Convention on the Law Applicable to Contractual Obligations of 19 June 1980 (the "Rome Convention" – O.J. [1980] L 266/1) determines the applicable law in contractual disputes. Following Article 1, paragraph 1, the Rome Convention applies to "*contractual obligations in any situation involving a choice between the laws of different countries*". Under the Rome Convention, any law can be applied, regardless of whether this is the law of an EC Member State (Art. 2). The provisions also apply to contracts concluded over the Internet.

2027. As a basic principle, the Rome Convention entitles parties to choose the applicable law (Art. 3, para. 1). In the absence of a choice of law by the contract parties, it is the law of the country that is most closely connected to the contract that will apply. Article 4, paragraph 2 of the Rome Convention provides that, "*Subject to any material qualification it shall be presumed that the contract is most closely connected with the country where the party who is to effect the performance which is characteristic of the contract has, at the time of the conclusion of the contract, his habitual residence or, in case of a body corporate or incorporate, its central administration.*"

2028. The Rome Convention also contains specific provisions governing consumer contracts (Art. 5). A consumer contract is defined as "*a contract the object of which is the supply of goods or services to a person ("the consumer") for a purpose which can be regarded as being outside his trade or profession, or a contract for the provision of credit for that object"*. As a principle, contracting parties can freely choose the governing law of the contract. Article 5, paragraph 2 of the Rome Convention, as a derogation to this principle, offers consumers the protection of the mandatory laws of their own country if:

   (i) the conclusion of the contract has been preceded in the consumer's country by a special proposal or form of advertising and the consumer has taken all actions necessary to conclude this contract in its home country; or

   (ii) the other party or its representative has received the consumer's order in this country.

2029. In an e-commerce context it is very often difficult to determine whether the above conditions have been fulfilled. The majority of legal doctrine has more or less accepted that the first condition will be satisfied if a consumer concludes a contract on the Internet by completing, for instance, a form on the website of a provider. However, a consumer surfing on the Internet, accessing a provider's website by chance and thereupon deciding to conclude a contract will not be able to benefit from the application of Article 5, paragraph 2 of the Rome Convention. This is explained by the "passive" attitude of the provider. By contrast, unsolicited offers by e-mail from providers do fall within the scope of this provision. Needless to say, the distinction between "active" and "passive" sales will often be a fine line.

2030. If the parties have failed to choose the applicable law, Article 5, paragraph 3 of the Rome Convention provides that the law of the country where the consumer is domiciled applies, provided that the conditions of Article 5, paragraph 2 of the Rome Convention providing for the protection of the mandatory law of the consumer's country of residence are satisfied.

§2. Preliminary Draft of the Rome II Regulation

2031. On 3 May 2002, the EC Commission unveiled a consultation paper on a Preliminary Draft Proposal for a Council Regulation on the Law Applicable to "Non-Contractual Obligations" (the "Preliminary Draft"). The Preliminary Draft is meant to serve as a basis for discussions leading to a formal proposal for a Regulation (the "Rome II Regulation"). The Preliminary Draft seeks to harmonise the rules of EC Member States governing the applicable law to non-contractual disputes, such as unfair marketing practices, defamation, product liability and environmental pollution. The Preliminary Draft is based on the "country of destination principle", which implies that cross-border non-contractual claims will be governed by the law of the country where the injury occurred, regardless of where the harmful event took place. However, on-line activities, such as e-commerce, would be governed by EC Directive No. 2000/31 of the European Parliament and the EC Council of 8 June 2000 on Certain Legal Aspects of Information Society Services, in particular Electronic Commerces, in the Internal Market (the "E-Commerce Directive" – O.J. [2000] L 178/1), which applies the "country of origin principle". This principle entails that information society service providers and their services should only comply with the laws of the country in which these service providers are established and from where they originate.

§3. Belgian law

2032. The applicable law concerning torts or harmful acts is not governed by any international convention. Therefore, conflicts regarding these issues will be subject to national conflict law. In Belgium, there is no uniform interpretation of which law should apply in case of torts or harmful acts. Some courts are of the opinion that, pursuant to Article 3, paragraph 1 of the Civil Code, the law of the place where the tort or harmful act was committed applies (the *lex loci delicti commissi),* whereas others uphold that the law of the place where the harmful consequences or damages have occurred (the *lex loci delicti)* should apply.

III. CONTRACTING ON THE INTERNET

A. Legal framework

§1. Distance Selling Directive

2033. EC Directive No. 97/7 of the European Parliament and of the EC Council of 20 May 1997 on the Protection of Consumers in respect of Distance Selling Contracts (the "Distance Selling Directive" – O.J. [1997] L 144/19) constitutes the European legal framework for the conclusion of distance contracts. The Distance Selling Directive defines a distance contract as *"any contract concerning goods or services concluded between a supplier and a consumer under an organised distance sales or service-provision scheme run by the supplier, who, for the purpose of the contract, makes exclusive use of one or more means of distance communication up to and including the moment at which the contract is concluded".* Contracts concluded over the Internet are distance contracts and are therefore governed by the Distance Selling Directive.

2034. The Distance Selling Directive seeks to protect consumers by offering them specific guarantees in order to increase their confidence in the Internet. The principal features of the Distance Selling Directive are as follows:

  (i) it contains an obligation on the supplier to provide specific information to the consumer before the conclusion of a distance contract and the obligation to confirm particular information;

 (ii) consumers are entitled to a withdrawal period of at least 7 working days without any penalty;

(iii) it provides for a time limit of 30 days for performance and refunds;

(iv) it introduces the requirement of prior consent of the consumer if the supplier uses automatic calling machines or faxes;

 (v) EC Member States are required to prohibit the supply of unsolicited goods or services to consumers in case of an unsolicited supply involving a demand for payment; and

(vi) where unsolicited goods are sent to a consumer, the absence of a response by the consumer cannot be construed as an acceptance of a contract.

§2. Belgian law on unfair trade practices

2035. The Distance Selling Directive has been implemented in Belgium in the Law on Unfair Trade Practices and on the Information and Protection of the Consumer of 14 July 1991 (*Wet betreffende de handelspraktijken en de voorlichting en bescherming van de consument/Loi sur les pratiques du commerce et sur l'information et la protection du consummateur* – the "Law on Unfair Trade Practices"). The Law on Unfair Trade Practices seeks to ensure fair competition and trade relations and to provide for consumer protection and the supply of sufficient and adequate information to the consumer. Article 9 of the Law on Unfair Trade Practices implements the Distance Selling Directive's provisions on distance selling contracts.

B. Formation of a Contract

2036. A valid contract under Belgian contract law is subject to 4 conditions: (i) consent, (ii) competence to act, (iii) a subject, and (iv) a permitted cause (Art. 1108 of the Civil Code). Belgian law does not make a distinction between "traditional" contracts and "electronic" contracts. As a result, the conditions of Article 1108 of the Civil Code also apply to contracts concluded over the Internet.

§1. Offer and acceptance

2037. When contracting on the Internet, it is very important to determine whether an offer has been made and by whom. Under Belgian law, an offer has to express the intention to conclude a contract and must be sufficiently clear. This means that the offeror must accept to be bound by the contract and that the offer must at least contain the essential characteristics of the goods or service, such as the price and subject. Acceptance of the offer by the consumer will constitute a contract, provided that the acceptance corresponds with the offer. Thus, in an e-commerce context, a website displaying products for sale and mentioning the essential elements pertaining to those products will constitute a valid offer and its acceptance by a customer will establish a contract.

§2. Place and time of formation of the contract

2038. A contract is considered to be formed at the moment the offeror obtains knowledge or could reasonably have obtained knowledge of the acceptance of his offer. It is thus not necessary that the offeror has actual knowledge of the acceptance of his offer. The fact that the acceptance of an offer reaches the service provider of the offerer's computer and that the offeror is able to have access to it, is thus sufficient for the conclusion of a contract.

2039. The place where a contract is formed is determined by the moment at which the contract has been formed. It is considered to be the place where the offeror was at the moment he obtained or should have obtained knowledge of the acceptance of his offer. In general, this place will be the location where the offeror is registered or domiciled.

§3. Obligation to provide information

2040. The Law on Unfair Trade Practices imposes specific obligations with respect to the information that must be provided to consumers by sellers. These obligations pertain to both the pre- and post contractual phase.

2041. When visiting a website offering products or services, the consumer must be able to find the following information in a clear and comprehensible way:
  (i) the identity of the supplier and his address;
  (ii) the main characteristics of the goods or services;
  (iii) the price of the products or services;
  (iv) delivery costs, where appropriate;
  (v) arrangements for payment, delivery or performance;
  (vi) the existence or absence of a right of withdrawal;
  (vii) the conditions under which goods can be returned or taken back, including, where appropriate, the cost thereof;
  (viii) the cost of using the means of distance communication;
  (ix) the period during which the offer or the price remains valid; and
  (x) where appropriate, the minimum duration of the contract.

2042. The supplier is also under an obligation to provide specific information after the consumer has placed an order. The supplier must confirm the information which the consumer has found on the website (such as the identity of the supplier, the price of the product or service and mode of payment) and also provide the following information:
  (i) if applicable, the consumer's right to withdraw from the contract. The supplier must specify under which conditions and according to which rules the consumer can exercise its right of withdrawal and incorporate a specific clause to this respect;
  (ii) in case there is no right to withdraw, an explicit clause should be incorporated mentioning the absence of a right to withdraw;
  (iii) the address of the supplier where the consumer is able to give notice of his complaints;
  (iv) the existing after sale services and commercial guarantees; and
  (v) the conditions under which the agreement can be cancelled if it concerns a contract of indefinite term or a contract for more than one year.

The consumer must receive this information:
  (i) when buying a product, at least at the moment of delivery; or
  (ii) where it concerns a service, before the agreement is executed or, if the execution was started before the expiration of the withdrawal period, during the execution of the agreement.

2043. The Law on Unfair Trade Practices allows the supplier to provide the required information by means of electronic mail, floppy-disc, CD-rom, post or fax.

2044. Finally, the Law on Unfair Trade Practices also provides for sanctions if the supplier has not complied with its obligation to provide information. The nature of these sanctions will depend on the information which the supplier has failed to provide.

C. Right of withdrawal

2045. With respect to distance selling contracts, the consumer has a right to refuse the goods or services that were ordered. The right of withdrawal seeks to protect consumers that have not been able to physically see the products or services bought. This right can be exercised without giving any reason and without any costs. The only costs that may be charged are direct costs for returning the goods, provided that this is foreseen by the contract.

2046. A period of at least 7 working days is offered to the consumer to withdraw from the contract. If the supplier has not complied with his obligation to provide postcontractual information, a withdrawal period of 3 months applies. If the supplier has failed to incorporate a specific clause with respect to the consumer's right of withdrawal, the consumer will be allowed to keep the products or services concerned without any payment, since it is considered that the products or services have been delivered without request.

2047. If a consumer exercises his right to withdrawal from the contract and has paid for the goods or services, the supplier must reimburse the consumer within a period of 30 days of the consumer's notice.

2048. Finally, the Law on Unfair Trade Practices provides for certain exceptions to the right of withdrawal. These include contracts:
 (i) for the provision of services if performance has begun, with the consumer's consent, before the end of the 7 working day withdrawal period;
 (ii) for the supply of goods made to the consumer's specifications or clearly personalised or which, by reason of their nature, cannot be returned or are liable to deteriorate or expire rapidly;
 (iii) for the supply of audio or video recordings or computer software that were unsealed by the consumer;
 (iv) for the supply of newspapers, periodicals and magazines; and
 (v) for gaming and lottery services.

D. E-payment

2049. The confidence of consumers in, and hence the success of, e-commerce depends heavily on the security and safety of payment systems. In the past few years, several types of e-payment have been developed. Currently 2 types of digital cash systems are emerging: "smart cards" and "E-cash".

2050. Smart cards contain a chip that makes it possible to store information. This enables the smart card to have multiple functions, such as the function of an "electronic purse". Advantages for consumers include security, convenience, flexibility and international use. The advantages for suppliers consist in efficiency and lower costs.

2051. Another system of e-payment is the E-cash system (also referred to as "digital coins"). The use of this method is based on a serial number attributed to a coin. This number enables the bank to effect payments. The use of digital coins is however not completely risk-free. These risks pertain mainly to the anonymity of the consumer and on-line verification (the supplier would have to check whether a coin has been previously spent which takes time and entails costs).

2052. On 17 August 2002, the Law on Transactions by Electronic Payment Instruments (*Wet betreffende de transacties uitgevoerd met instrumenten voor de elektronische overmaking van geldmiddelen/Loi relative aux opérations effectuées au moyen d'instruments de transfert électonique de fonds* – the "Law on Electronic Payments") was published in the *Belgian Official Journal*. This Law on Electronic Payments implements Commission Recommendation No. 97/489 of 30 July 1997 (O.J. [1997] L 208/52) concerning transactions by electronic payment instruments. The Law on Electronic Payments seeks to contribute to the development of e-commerce by enhancing consumers' trust in e-commerce and increasing its acceptance by the suppliers.

2053. The Law on Electronic Payments provides for an obligation on the supplier to furnish information concerning the terms and conditions of payment and the use of electronic payment instruments. Furthermore, it regulates the liabilities of the parties involved in a contractual relationship and also limits the consumer's liability in case of loss or theft.

2054. In this context it is also important to mention EC Directive No. 2000/46 of 18 September 2000 on the Taking Up, Pursuit of and Prudential Supervision of the Business of Electronic Money Institutions (O.J. [2000] L 275/39). This Directive, which had to be implemented by 27 April 2002, seeks to take account of the specific characteristics of e-money institutions and to harmonise EC Member States' regulations relating to these institutions. An e-money institution is defined as "*an undertaking or any other legal person (…) issuing means of payment in the form of electronic money*". The Directive regulates the activities that may be exercised by the e-money institutions. The Belgian government submitted a draft proposal for the transposition of this Directive to the Belgian Parliament on 13 November 2002. This draft proposal has not yet been implemented.

IV. EUROPEAN DIRECTIVE ON E-COMMERCE

A. Introduction

2055. The E-Commerce Directive intends to provide "*a clear framework to cover certain legal aspects of electronic commerce in the internal market*". Its main objective is to create a legal framework to stimulate the development of e-commerce within the internal market and to increase legal certainty, in particular with respect to consumers.

2056. The E-Commerce Directive addresses the following issues: (i) the introduction of an "internal market clause", (ii) the establishment of information society providers, (iii) commercial communications, (iv) on-line contracts, (v) the liability of intermediaries, and (vi) specific implementation issues such as codes of conduct and co-operation between EC Member States. Certain activities are explicitly excluded from the scope of application of the E-Commerce Directive, such as tax issues and questions relating to agreements or practices regulated by cartel law.

2057. In order to deal with the issue of the applicable law to on-line services, Article 3 of the E-Commerce Directive (the "internal market clause") introduces the "country-of-origin principle" (*See*, para. 2031). Information society services are defined by EC Directive No. 98/34 of the European Parliament and of the EC Council of 22 June 1998 laying down a Procedure for the Provision of Information in the Field of Technical Standards and Regulations (O.J. [1998] L 204/37) as *"any service normally provided for remuneration, at a distance, by means of electronic equipment for the processing (including digital compression) and storage of data and at the individual request of a recipient of a service."* This broad definition covers all on-line activities, including on-line transactions relating to the provision of goods and services. It also covers activities that are not remunerated by the addressee, such as on-line offers of information and commercial communications. It is however unclear how the country-of-origin principle should be reconciled with the conflict rules of the Rome Convention. It seems that this is an issue that will need to be clarified by the European Court of Justice.

2058. Article 2 of the E-Commerce Directive defines the place of establishment as the place where a service provider effectively pursues an economic activity through a fixed establishment for an indefinite period. This provision explicitly states that the presence and use of technical means and technologies required to provide the service do not constitute an establishment. Therefore, the place of establishment does not involve the place where a website or server is situated or accessible. The advantage of this principle is that information society providers no longer have to comply with the laws of different EC Member States, but only the EC Member State where they are established. It should, however, be noted that the country of origin principle does not apply to information society service providers established outside the European Community, which may therefore be subjected to the separate laws of all the EC Member States. In addition, the country-of-origin principle does not apply to, *inter alia,* intellectual property rights, the choice of applicable law and contractual obligations regarding consumer agreements, which can be defined as agreements involving natural persons acting for purposes outside their trade, business or profession.

2059. The E-Commerce Directive imposes disclosure and information requirements on Internet service providers and on-line communications. The E-Commerce Directive requires Internet service providers to provide information on their identity, such as their name, place of business and electronic e-mail address. On-line communications must disclose the commercial nature of the electronic message and the intended purpose of the message. In the case of contracts, the applicable contractual clauses and characteristics of the goods or services must be disclosed.

2060. Moreover, the E-Commerce Directive establishes certain requirements with respect to unsolicited commercial communications. EC Member States allowing unsolicited e-mail communications must ensure that these communications, when originating from a service provider established in their territory, are "identifiable clearly and unambiguously". The E-Commerce Directive seeks to protect personal data by limiting unsolicited commercial e-mails (commonly known as "spamming"), by means of an "opt-out" system. This means that individuals are able to notify service providers that they do not wish to receive unsolicited commercial e-mail. In addition, EC Member States are authorised to prohibit spamming by national legislation.

2061. Special attention is paid to the way in which on-line contracts should be concluded. The E-Commerce Directive introduces the principle of non-discrimination between contracts entered into on-line and written contracts. EC Member States should adjust their national legislation in such a way as to fully allow the conclusion of on-line contracts. EC Member States should also ensure that specific information with respect to on-line contracting is provided by service providers. This obligation mainly refers to "business to consumers" (B2C) contracts. Furthermore, the E-Commerce Directive sets rules relating to the placing of on-line orders with respect to contracts involving consumers. For example, service providers should acknowledge receipt of an electronic order without delay. Moreover, the order and acknowledgement of receipt are deemed to be received when the recipients have access to them.

2062. The issue of liability of intermediary service providers is also regulated by the E-Commerce Directive. As a basic principle, the E-Commerce Directive exempts technical or intermediary service providers from liability as regards the content of messages. In this respect a distinction is made between different types of technical intermediary activities: "mere conduit", which refers to service providers whose service consists of the transmission in a communication network of information provided by a recipient of the service, or the provision of access to a communication network, "caching and hosting". The exemption of mere conduit, relates to service providers that have not initiated the transmission; that have not selected the receiver of the transmission; and that have not selected or modified the information contained in the transmission. With respect to caching and hosting, the E-Commerce Directive provides, under certain conditions, for an exemption of the liability of service providers for storing information at the request of a recipient. Nevertheless, actual knowledge of an illegal activity or information or a failure to act against a notice of illegal content may deprive a service provider of its exemption.

2063. The E-Commerce Directive addresses specific implementation issues. It encourages EC Member States to draft codes of conduct, in particular by trade, professional and consumer associations or organisations, in order to contribute to the proper implementation of the E-Commerce Directive. Specifically, codes of conduct relating to the protection of minors and human dignity are encouraged. EC Member States should encourage and facilitate out-of-court dispute settlement, by ensuring that their national legislation does not hamper the use of out-of-court schemes. Finally, the E-Commerce Directive contains a provision dealing with the co-operation between different EC Member States.

B. Implementation of E-Commerce Directive in Belgium

2064. EC Member States were required to implement the E-Commerce Directive by January 2002. However, several EC Member States, including Belgium, failed to do this. The Belgian Council of Ministers adopted a draft proposal on 30 November 2001. This draft law is still to be voted upon by the Belgian Parliament.

2065. In general, the draft proposal copies the provisions of the E-Commerce Directive, even though there are some differences. The most remarkable deviation concerns the opt-in system for non-solicited electronic mail. Providers may only send unsolicited e-mails to persons who have given their prior explicit consent to this. The system adopted by Belgian law is thus more protective to individuals than the opt-out system adopted by the E-Commerce Directive.

V. ELECTRONIC SIGNATURES

A. Introduction

2066. EC Council Directive No. 1999/93/EC on a Community Framework for Electronic Signatures (the "E-Signature Directive" – O.J. [2000] L 13/12) provides for a harmonised regime applicable to the recognition of electronic signatures throughout the European Community.

2067. The E-Signature Directive achieves the recognition of electronic signatures in 2 different manners. First, it provides for the admissibility of electronic signatures as evidence in judicial proceedings. Second, it puts electronic signatures meeting certain security requirements on the same footing as hand-written signatures.

2068. On 20 December 2000, the Belgian Parliament adopted a Law Recognising the Probative Value of Electronic Signatures (the "E-Signature Law"). This law implements the provisions of the E-Signature Directive dealing with the admissibility of electronic signatures as evidence in judicial proceedings. The other part of the E-Signature Directive was implemented by the Law on Electronic Signatures and Certification Services of 9 July 2001 (*Wet houdende vaststelling van bepaalde regels in verband met het juridisch kader voor elektronische handtekeningen en certificatiediensten/Loi fixant certaines règles relatives au cadre juridique pour les signatures électroniques et les services de certification* – the "Certification Law"), recognising advanced electronic signatures in Belgium.

B. The E-Signature Law – Probative Value of Electronic Signatures

2069. The E-Signature Law created a new paragraph in Article 1322 of the Civil Code. The new rule accepts, in judicial proceedings, electronic signatures allowing the identification of the author of the signature and establishing the inalterability of the signed document. Unlike the situation applicable previously, courts are now obliged to examine the electronic signature relied upon by the parties and assess its probative value. Article 1322, paragraph 2 of the Civil Code only applies to private deeds (*onderhandse akten/actes sous-seing privé*) and not to notarial deeds (*authentieke akten/actes authentiques*).

C. The Law of 9 July 2001 Creating the Legal Framework for the Recognition of Advanced Electronic Signatures (the "Certification Law")

2070. The Certification Law is a faithful implementation of the relevant provisions of the E-Signature Directive. Its objective is to afford the same probative value to advanced electronic signatures based upon a qualified certificate as that attributed to hand-written signatures. The E-Signature Directive creates the legal framework necessary for the creation of these advanced electronic signatures.

2071. Article 2 of the Certification Law defines an "electronic signature" as a set of data in electronic form, affixed to or logically associated with other electronic data, that are used as a means of verification. An "advanced electronic signature" has to satisfy the following additional requirements. It must (i) be linked in a unique way to the signer; (ii) make it possible to identify the signer; (iii) be created with means that the signer can keep under his exclusive control; and (iv) be linked in such a way to the underlying data that any later modification of such data can be traced.

2072. Since advanced electronic signatures based upon a qualified certificate are considered to be as safe as hand-written signatures, the courts will have to accept their probative value without being able to review their secure nature.

D. Equality with hand-written signatures

2073. Article 4, paragraph 4 of the Certification Law provides that an advanced electronic signature based on a qualified certificate and created by a secure signature creation device is considered to be a signature in the sense of Article 1322 of the Civil Code.

§1. Secure signature-creation device

2074. Any code or private cryptography key used by a signatory to create an electronic signature constitutes signature-creation data. Configured software and hardware used to implement this data are signature-creation devices. In order to be secure, such devices will have to meet the requirements set out in Annex III of the Certification Law. These requirements are (i) that the device should not alter in any way the content of the data to be signed or prevent such data from being presented to the signatory prior to the signature process; (ii) that the device should, by appropriate technical and procedural means, ensure that the signature-creation data is sufficiently secure (this data must be unique and secret; it should not be liable to be derived or forged, and the signatory must be able to prevent it from being used by others).

§2. Certification Service Provider.

2075. A Certification Service Provider ("CSP") is defined as any natural person or legal entity delivering and administering certificates or providing other services in relation to electronic signatures.

§3. Qualified Certificate.

2076. Any electronic attestation which links signature-verification data to a person and confirms the identity of that person is a certificate. In order to qualify, this certificate must include the information listed in Annex I of the Certification Law and be issued by a CSP that fulfils the requirements laid down in Annex II.

E. Free Movement

2077. All products and services linked to electronic signatures can circulate freely within the European Economic Area ("EEA"). They are regulated by the law of the country of origin of the CSP. In addition, the provision of certification services cannot be made subject to a prior authorisation (Art. 4, para. 2 of the Certification Law).

F. International Dimension

2078. Certificates emanating from CSPs located outside the EEA can also be recognised in Belgium if:
   (i) these CSPs satisfy the requirements laid down in the Directive and have been recognised under a voluntary scheme established in one of the EC Member States;
   (ii) a qualified CSP within the EEA guarantees the certificate; or
   (iii) the certificate or the CSP is recognised under a bilateral or international agreement.

G. Liability of the CSP

2079. By issuing or guaranteeing a qualified certificate to the public, CSPs will generally be responsible for certification services (Art. 14 of the Certification Law) and, more specifically, for the accuracy of the information contained in the certificate at the time of issuance. However, a CSP can restrict the use of its certificate to specific purposes or place a limit on the value of the transactions for which the certificate can be used. If this is advertised in a fashion recognisable for third parties, CSPs will not be liable for any use in excess of such limitations.

H. A Neutral Framework

2080. The wording of the Certification Law allows for the recognition of electronic signatures irrespective of the technology involved.

I. Voluntary Accreditation Scheme (Art. 17 of the Certification Law)

2081. Any CSPs that fulfil the requirements laid down in Annex II, issue qualified certificates including the information listed in Annex I and use signature creation devices complying with the requirements of Annex III can apply for a certification by the authorities. Although such certification is not compulsory, certified CSPs will probably be perceived by the general public as more trustworthy than others. However, for an electronic signature to have the same value as a hand-written signature, it does not matter whether the CSP issuing the certificate was certified or not.

VI. INTERMEDIARY LIABILITY

A. Legislative Framework

2082. Belgium does not have any specific rules dealing with the issue of liability of on-line providers acting as intermediaries. Therefore, the general principles of civil liability apply. Service providers may also be held liable on the basis of the general principles of criminal law.

2083. It is accepted that service providers spreading illegal or wrongful information may be held liable for this on the basis of the rules on torts and harmful acts, *i.e.*, the so-called "civil liability" (Arts. 1382 and 1383 of the Civil Code). As a general rule, whoever causes injury by action or inaction is liable to compensate for the damage inflicted. The liability of intermediaries for material that is spread by third parties on the Internet through their facilities is generally determined by the question whether the intermediaries had or should have had any knowledge of the existence of the illegal or infringing material and whether they failed to remove or prevent access to this material, although they were in the possession of the necessary technical means to do so. The specific circumstances of the case and their appreciation by the courts will therefore be decisive.

2084. Service providers may be held criminally liable for spreading or having spread illegal information through their servers. In order to establish this criminal liability, there should be guilt. The level of liability will depend on the level of involvement of the service provider.

B. Belgian case law on liability

2085. Belgian case law regarding the liability of on-line intermediaries is still very limited. The scarce cases dealing with the liability of intermediaries, such as service and content providers, are discussed below:

§1. IFPI & Polygram Records vs. Belgacom Skynet

2086. The *Skynet*-case concerned a Belgian Internet service provider (Skynet), hosting websites which included links to certain sites containing illegal MP3-files. IFPI Belgium (a representative organisation of record producers and distributors in Belgium) initiated legal proceedings against Skynet, because it had failed to respond to IFPI's request to remove these links from its websites.

2087. The President of the Court of First Instance of Brussels sided with IFPI (Pres. Comm. Brussels, 2 November 1999, *Computerrecht*, 2000, 36). The court held that, given the fact that Skynet had regularly been requested to remove the links and that the Internet service provider had access to file scanners to identify MP3-files, it had acted contrary to fair trade practices as mentioned in Article 93 of the Law on Unfair Trade Practices by not removing the links. The court ordered Skynet to immediately cease this unfair practice.

2088. The Brussels Court of Appeal overturned the decision of the Court of First Instance (Brussels Court of Appeal, 13 February 2001, *Computerrecht*, 2001, 144). According to the Brussels Court of Appeal, Skynet had not acted in a manner contrary to what a diligent and prudent ISP would have done under similar circumstances. The court considered that a diligent and prudent Internet service provider is obliged to remove hyperlinks referring to illegal MP3-files, or make them inaccessible, only under the following conditions:
  (i) the claimant must notify the service provider by e-mail about the presence of the links. The notification must provide details regarding the illegal links and the web-page(s) on which the links appear and the illicit downloadable music copies. The notification must include a specific request to prevent access, remove the hyperlinks or make them inaccessible and provide evidence convincing the service provider that the files to which the links refer are likely to be illegal;
  (ii) the identified links must be removed by the service provider within 3 working days upon receipt of the notification, unless it is proved that the files to which the links refer are legal; and
  (iii) the claimant must explicitly accept to take full responsibility for the removal of or prevention of access to the links concerned. The claimant must indemnify the service provider for any claims brought by the provider's customers.

2089. The Brussels Court of Appeal held that since IFPI had not followed the above steps, Skynet could not be held liable.

§2. IFPI vs. Beckers

2090. This case concerned the liability of a student who, as a provider, owned a website containing more than 25,000 hyperlinks to illegal MP3 music files. The IFPI initiated proceedings against Beckers in order to have his website closed down. According to the IFPI, the fact that Beckers' website contained hyperlinks to illegal music files constituted a wrongful act which caused injury to its members. Beckers argued that he was only referring Internet users to information offered by others.

2091. The Court of First Instance of Antwerp (Pres. Court of First Instance Antwerp, 21 December 1999, *A.M.*, 2000, 296) sided with the IFPI and ordered Beckers to close his website. The court held that Beckers had consciously established hyperlinks to illegal files and was therefore liable for committing a wrongful act.

§3. IFPI vs. Innet Belgium & Innet Luxemburg

2092. This case concerned the liability of two hosting service providers, Innet Belgium and Innet Luxemburg, for hosting a website of "Magic Com", a company selling illegal recordings and bootlegs over the Internet. IFPI decided to bring an action against these companies before the President of the Court of First Instance of Namur on the basis of Article 87 of the Copyright Law (a cease-and-desist action). IFPI requested that the defendants be prohibited from providing access or services to Magic Com. IFPI also asked for the disclosure of the number of consultations of the Magic.com site.

2093. The President of the Court of First Instance of Namur decided to dismiss the claims of IFPI (Pres. Court of First Instance Namur, 11 February 1997, *not published*). The claim against Innet Belgium was rejected on the ground that Innet Belgium was not related in any way to Magic.com, as there was only an agreement between Innet Luxemburg and Magic.com. The claim against Innet Luxemburg was rejected on the basis of a lack of urgency.

§4. Easy Computing vs. Ad Valvas

2094. Ad Valvas provided the free service of "wanted ads". This service was used by a specific Internet user in order to place free ads for illegal copies of copyright protected software sold by him. Easy Computing was the copyright owner of some of this software and filed an application for a temporary injunction on the basis of the FTP and the Copyright Law. In its decision, the President of the Court of First

Instance of Kortrijk accepted the claim of Easy Computing. However, the action being in summary proceeding, the President did not address Easy Computing's arguments but based its decision on a *prima facie* assumption (Pres. Comm. Kortrijk, 10 September 1998, *Computerrecht*, 1998, 30).

§5. Novell vs. X.

2095. In this case, the provider of a "Bulletin Board Service" was held liable by the Court of First Instance of Hasselt for the presence on its server of illegal copies of software owned by Novell (Criminal Court Hasselt, 16 February 1999, *not published*). The Court of First Instance held that the provider was responsible for the content of the Bulletin Board Service and, as a consequence, was obliged to check the software that was placed thereon by Internet users.

VII. DOMAIN NAMES

A. International registration of domain names

2096. ICANN, the Internet Corporation for Assigned Names and Numbers, is an international non-profit private sector body. ICANN was created in 1988 by a coalition of different Internet business, technical, academic and user communities and is responsible for the global co-ordination of key Internet functions. Its most important aims are preserving operational stability of the Internet, promoting competition, achieving broad representation of global Internet communities and developing policy. More specifically, ICANN is responsible for co-ordinating the assignment of:
   (i) Internet domain names;
   (ii) IP address numbers; and
   (iii) Protocol parameter and port numbers.

B. Domain names and intellectual property rights

2097. Most of the conflicts between domain names and intellectual property rights relate to trademarks. This is a legal issue that still needs to be developed. In general, the abusive registration of trademarks as domain names can be restricted by subjecting such registration to specific rules. In some countries, domain names will only be granted after it has been verified whether the applicant of the domain name is entitled to the name in question. However, in an increasing number of countries, domain names are registered on a "first come first served" basis. This system has been the source of numerous infringements of trademark rights. For this reason, several bodies, such as the WIPO, have developed procedures for the resolution of disputes related to domain names, as well as guidelines and codes of conduct with respect to the registration of domain names.

2098. In order to deal with "domain name grabbing", the Belgian government submitted a proposal to the Parliament on 29 January 2001 regarding the abusive registration of domain names. The proposal, which has not yet been adopted by the Parliament, defines abusive domain registration broadly. It states that the registration, with the purpose to damage third parties or obtain illegal advantage, of a domain name which is identical or similar in such a way as to create a risk of confusion with a trade mark of products or services or a commercial name belonging to a third party is prohibited.

2099. Contrary to trademarks, which have a special status defined by law, domain names are not subject to any specific legislation. It is, however, accepted that the registration of a domain name can constitute an infringement of a registered trade mark or trade name. The issue of domain names conflicting with trade names has been addressed several times by the courts. However, the legal basis for curbing such behaviour has varied from case to case.

2100. One of the first cases addressing this issue was the *Tractebel*-case (Brussels Court of Appeal, 1 April 1998, *Computerrecht*, 1998, 176). It involved the registration of a domain name corresponding to a trade name without opening a website. The Brussels Court of Appeal held that the registration of a domain name corresponding to the trade name of a third party constituted a breach of the Law on Unfair Trade Practices. The Court of Appeal based its decision on 3 elements:
  (i) the trade name formed part of the domain name;
  (ii) the registration prevented the owner of the trade name from using the trade name; and
  (iii) the registering party had offered to sell the domain name to the owner of the trade name.

2101. In the *Cockerill-Sambre* case, which related to the same issues as the *Tractebel* case, the court decided that the registration of the domain name corresponding to a trade name did not constitute an infringement of the FTP (Pres. Comm. Brussels, 27 November 1997, *Computerrecht*, 1998, 26). The court added, however, that the registration of a domain name for the purpose of selling that domain name at a high price constituted, in that case, an abuse of a dominant position.

2102. An example of a case regarding domain names infringing trademarks, is the *Blue Box*-case. In this case, the registered domain name corresponded to a trade mark owned by another company. After having agreed to end the use of the domain name by closing the website, the registering company decided to keep the domain name concerned. The court found this behaviour to constitute an infringement of Article 93 of the Law on Unfair Trade Practices, since by keeping the domain name, the trade mark owner was prevented from using its trademark (Pres. Comm. Brussels, 3 January 1997, *D.I.T.*, 1997, 37).

C. Registration of domain names in Belgium

2103. In Belgium, domain names are administered by a non-profit registration company, DNS Belgium. In December 2000, DNS Belgium made the rules for domain registration more flexible. They no longer require that the applicant of a domain name should have a link with the domain name for which it applied. Furthermore, it has become possible to obtain a ".be"-domain name for individual persons. On 30 October 2001, DNS announced further modifications. The most important modification concerns the enlargement of the alternative dispute resolution procedures.

2104. Registration takes place according to the "first come first served" rule. This means that a domain name can only be registered if it has not been registered before. According to the terms and conditions of DNS Belgium, the following domain names will not be registered:
   (i) names already registered will be put on hold. This will be the case if proceedings are in progress over the domain name concerned or if DNS has requested the domain name holder to replace his registered domain name or in case the registrar's contract with DNS is terminated;
   (ii) names having less than 2 characters; and
   (iii) names consisting of other characters than "A-Z", "0-9" and "–", starting or ending with "–".

2105. Since 15 October 2002, licensees are allowed to transfer domain names. Previously, domain names were considered to be personal and non-transferable. The procedure for the transfer of domain names is as follows:
   (i) the buyer, after having concluded the sale of a domain name, should request its agent to initiate the transaction for the transfer of the domain name.
   (ii) once the transaction has been initiated, both parties will receive an e-mail requesting the parties to confirm their agreement.
   (iii) the transfer will be completed upon the explicit confirmation of both parties. If no reply is received within a period of 8 days, an additional period of 8 days will be granted to the parties for a confirmation by fax. If this period has expired without any proper confirmation, the transaction will be annulled.

2106. DNS has charged the Belgian arbitration and mediation centre (*CEPINA/ CEPANI*) with the settlement of disputes over domain names. This procedure is generally much shorter than judicial proceedings. Furthermore, the procedure takes place on-line and does not require the parties to appear before the arbitrator. The final decision is published on the CEPINA/CEPANI website and forwarded to DNS Belgium, which will carry out the decision by, for instance, removing a specific domain name or modifying the name of a domain name holder.

D. Introduction of ".EU"-domain names

2107. In March 2002, the European Parliament approved the introduction of a new .eu domain extension. The new ".eu"-domain name will complement existing Internet Top Level Domains (TLDs) such as ".com", ".org" and national TLD´s such as ".be". The new ".eu"-domain name can be obtained by both businesses and individuals living within the European Community. The ".eu"-domain name provides a Pan-European domain name and e-mail address. The European Commission has been charged with establishing the infrastructure for the ".eu"-domain name. This task will involve the selection of an organisation to manage .eu registrations, defining rules preventing cybersquatting and the development of a dispute settlement procedure. It is foreseen that the registration of .eu domain names will be effective as from the beginning of 2003.

VIII. CODES OF CONDUCT AND THE OBSERVATORY OF INTERNET RIGHTS

A. Codes of conduct

2108. A code of conduct constitutes a set of commitments that is undertaken voluntarily, without any legal obligation. In general, such commitments are undertaken by companies, associations and other institutions in order to influence or rule commercial activities. Therefore, they can be very useful in order to supplement existing laws and offer more protection to certain parties, such as consumers or citizens. Generally, conduct codes can be found in different sectors and may also serve different objectives.

2109. The Belgian Federation of Enterprises (*Verbond van Belgische Ondernemingen/ Fédération des Entreprises de Belgique*) has established a code of conduct with respect to e-commerce in order to increase the confidence of users and facilitate the development of e-commerce in Belgium. The advantage of such a code is its flexibility, as it can easily be adapted to new technological developments. In addition, it offers a reference to enterprises as to how they should carry out their e-commerce activities. The code of conduct aims at serving all kinds of activities and is therefore of a general character. By signing the code of conduct, an enterprise undertakes to apply these rules in all its e-commercial activities. The code of conduct consists of 2 main parts: a general part, applying to all activities and a second part which only applies to "business-consumer" relationships. The general part contains requirements regarding the access to specific information on the enterprise, pre-contractual information, commercial communications, safety of transactions, links to other sites and complaints and disputes. The part with respect to consumer relations contains provisions on the conclusion and execution of a contract, the right of withdrawal, payment and data protection.

2110. As regards the way in which or to what extent the supplier is bound by the code of conduct, there are various possibilities. Usually, this is regulated by the code of conduct in question. Certain codes of conduct provide, for example, that a third party can submit a complaint with the association or institution concerned in the event that the code of conduct is not respected. In general, the consequence of the non-compliance of a supplier will be that a procedure will be initiated and sanctions imposed.

2111. Another possibility is to initiate legal proceedings before the competent court. In such a case, it will be of importance for establishing liability whether or not the supplier in the contract has expressly referred to the code of conduct. If an agreement does not contain any express reference to a conduct code, the code will probably not be binding. If, in contrast, an agreement explicitly refers to the code of conduct, the code of conduct will form an integral part of the agreement. This code of conduct is available in Dutch or in French on the following address: www.vbofeb.be/vbosite/home.asp.

B. Observatory of Internet Rights

2112. On 18 December 2001, a notice providing for the creation of the "Observatory of Internet Rights" (*Observatorium van de Rechten op het Internet/L'Observatoire des Droits sur Internet* – the "Observatory") was published in the *Belgian Official Journal*. This new body was established at the initiative of the Ministry of Economic Affairs to address the problems raised by the development of e-commerce and the use of new information and communication technologies. The Observatory also constitutes a forum where individuals are able to express their opinions and obtain information with respect to decisions in the information and communication technology ("ICT") field. Its activities include:

(i) issuing opinions on economic problems resulting from the use of new information and communication technologies;

(ii) organising a dialogue between the economic actors concerned; and

(iii) informing and heightening public awareness of new technologies.

2113. The Observatory is composed of experts in the field of new technologies, business representatives and representatives of ICT users. The Minister of Economic Affairs holds an observer seat, as does the Minister for Small and Medium-Sized Enterprises.

IX. E-COMMERCE AND COMPETITION LAW

A. Distribution Agreements

2114. Distribution agreements concluded over the Internet may come within the scope of Article 81 of the EC Treaty. Nevertheless, they may benefit from European Commission Regulation No. 2790/1999 on the Application of Article 81, paragraph 3 of the Treaty to Categories of Vertical Agreements and Concerted Practices (the "Vertical Restraint Block Exemption" – O.J. [1999] L 336/21). Sales on the Internet may fall under the scope of the Vertical Restraint Block Exemption if the market share of the supplier does not exceed 30 per cent of the relevant market and if the agreement does not contain any hard-core restrictions banned by the Block Exemption Regulation. For example, a clause restricting the distributors' freedom to determine the prices to be charged over the Internet ("resale price maintenance") or a clause restricting the territory into which, or customers to whom a supplier's distributors may sell, constitute hard-core restrictions and are therefore prohibited.

2115. The European Commission has furthermore held that restrictions preventing distributors from using the Internet as a distribution mechanism will violate Article 81 of the EC Treaty. The European Commission holds the opinion that suppliers can adopt less restrictive measures to protect the quality of websites and ensure service levels for Internet sales.

B. B2B market places

2116. B2B-market places are on-line market places in which businesses are able to trade or procure goods or services. They offer the framework for the vast majority of business transactions conducted over the Internet. The use of B2B-market places may bring important benefits, such as a reduction in transaction costs. Furthermore, they may create market efficiencies by reducing research and information costs and improving inventory management, resulting in lower prices for consumers. Nevertheless, B2B-market places are also able to endanger competition within the internal market.

2117. In order to be permitted under EC law, B2B-market places must comply with Articles 81 and 82 of the EC Treaty. B2B-exchanges, depending on the structure they have, may also need to be notified under EC Council Regulation No. 4064/89 of 21 December 1989 on the Control of Concentrations between Undertakings (the "Merger Regulation" – O.J. [1989] L 395/1).

2118. When assessing the compatibility of B2B market places with the EC competition rules, the European Commission will consider different issues. In the first place it will assess whether the B2B-market place could have market power that could be exercised in an abusive manner. Secondly, the European Commission will examine whether the B2B-market place could be operated to co-ordinate behaviour among competitors. Another point of concern is whether the B2B-market place is liable to exclude specific competitors from the market place without any objective reason. The exchange of sensitive business information among competitors may also be problematic. Finally, the European Commission will be wary of a concentration of buyer power.

2119. The European Commission has cleared several B2B market places, both under Article 81 of the EC Treaty and the Merger Control Regulation. In general, the European Commission has adopted a positive attitude towards them, mainly because of the fact that they may increase competition.

12. INTELLECTUAL PROPERTY

2120. This chapter reviews the law governing copyright and neighbouring rights, data-bases, patents, trade marks, designs and models, know-how, topographies of semi-conductor products and plant variety rights. The principal focus will be on the Belgian rules that provide the basis for these rights. Where necessary, references will be included to the many international conventions of which Belgium is a sig-natory. In addition, a cursory review will be given of the multiple ways in which EC law affects the protection afforded by Belgian intellectual property law.

I. COPYRIGHT AND NEIGHBOURING RIGHTS

A. Applicable law

2121. The Belgian Law on Copyright and Neighbouring Rights *(Auteurswet/Loi sur le droit d'auteur* – the "Copyright Law") was enacted on 30 June 1994. This law replaced the old copyright law of 22 March 1886 (the "Old Copyright Law"). Other important pieces of legislation in the copyright field are:
   (i) The Law of 30 June 1994 on the Protection of Computer Programs, implemen-ting EC Council Directive No. 91/250 of 14 May 1991 on the Legal Protec-tion of Computer Programs (O.J. [1991] L 122/42);
  (ii) The Royal Decree of 28 March 1996 on Private Copying, implementing Arti-cle 55 of the Copyright Law, which states that the authors, performers and producers of phonograms and audiovisual works are entitled to remuneration for the private copying of sound or audiovisual works. This Royal Decree lays down the terms of such remuneration.
 (iii) The Royal Decree of 30 October 1997 on Reprography, implementing Arti-cles 59 and 60 of the Copyright Law which states that authors and publishers are entitled to remuneration for the reproduction of their works. The remu-neration must be paid by the producer, importer or (intra-Community) ac-quirer of equipment that is used for the reproduction (*i.e.*, copying) of protected works. Remuneration is also due from the persons copying works in propor-tion to the number of copies made or from the persons putting a copying

machine at the disposal of third parties. This Royal Decree lays down the modalities of such remuneration.

(iv) The Royal Decree of 8 July 1998 on the Resale Right (*volgrecht/droit de suite*), implementing Articles 11 *et seq.* of the Copyright Law, which grant an inalienable resale right to authors on their works of plastic art (*See*, para 2141).

2122. Further, the Law of 26 June 1951 made the Berne Convention for the Protection of Literary and Artistic Works (the "Berne Convention") applicable in Belgium (the Berne Convention has been revised many times. The Law of 26 June 1951 relates to the Brussels Revision of 1948). By the Law of 26 September 1974, Articles 21 to 38 of the Stockholm revision (1967) to the Berne Convention were approved. In fact, pursuant to the TRIPS Agreement (*See*, para. 2125), the Paris revision has applied in Belgium since 1996. Indeed, the contracting states to the TRIPS Agreement undertook to apply Articles 1 through 21 (with the exception of Article 6*bis*) and the Annex to the Paris Act. The Paris Act of 24 July 1971 was only approved officially by the Law of 25 March 1999.

2123. Belgium is also a member of the Universal Copyright Convention ("UCC") of 6 September 1952, which was implemented by the Law of 20 April 1960. It is unlikely, however, that Belgium will ever approve the 1971 Paris revision of the UCC.

2124. Belgium also ratified the International Convention for the Protection of Performers, Producers of Phonograms and Broadcasting Organisations of 26 October 1961 (the "Rome Convention") by the Law of 25 March 1999. The Rome Convention entered into force on 20 November 1999.

2125. The Agreement on Trade-Related Aspects of Intellectual Property Rights (the "TRIPS" Agreement), annexed to the GATT agreement of 15 April 1994, aims at, on the one hand, the further extension of the geographical scope of the classic intellectual property conventions and, on the other hand, an improved enforcement of intellectual property rights. The TRIPS Agreement was approved by the Law of 23 December 1994 and entered into force on 1 January 1996.

2126. Finally, it should be noted that Belgium was initially not a signatory of the 2 World Intellectual Property Organization ("WIPO") Treaties, more particularly, the WIPO Copyright Treaty (the "WCT") and the WIPO Performances and Phonograms Treaty (the "WPPT"). However, the EC Council of Ministers issued a decision on 16 March 2000 on the approval, on behalf of the European Community, of those treaties with regard to matters within its competence (O.J. [2000] L 89/6).

2127. At the European level, the following legislative instruments, which have not yet been implemented in Belgium, must be mentioned:

– EC Directive No. 2001/29 of 22 May 2001 on the Harmonisation of Certain Aspects of Copyright and Related Rights in the Information Society (O.J. [2001] L 167/10) (Belgium has not yet implemented the provisions of this Directive, although the deadline for doing so passed on 22 December 2002); and

– EC Directive No. 2001/84 of 27 September 2001 on the Resale Right for the Benefit of the Author of an Original Work of Art (O.J. [2001] L 272/32).

B. Copyright

§1. Definition

2128. Copyright *(auteursrecht/droit d'auteur)* is a temporary and exclusive right relating to a literary or artistic creation. The Copyright Law does not define the terms "literary or artistic creation". However, Article 2 of the Berne Convention provides a non-exhaustive list of protected works including, *inter alia*, materials, books, pamphlets, lectures, dramatic works, musical compositions, cinematographic works, works of drawing, painting and architecture, works of applied art, geographical charts, plans and certain plastic works. Furthermore, Article 2 of the Berne Convention states that translations, adaptations, arrangements of music and other alterations of a literary or artistic work qualify for copyright protection. This also applies to collections of literary or artistic works.

2129. Article 1 of the Law of 30 June 1994 implementing the EU Directive of 14 May 1991 on the Legal Protection of Computer Programs affords copyright protection to computer programs (*See*, paras. 2209 *et seq.*). In Belgium, databases are protected by a *sui generis*-right (*See*, paras. 2219 *et seq.*).

2130. Works that do not qualify for copyright protection include official texts of the various branches of government (Art. 8, para. 2 of the Copyright Law), certain forms of public speeches (Art. 8, para. 1 of the Copyright Law) and news items (Art. 9(3) of the Berne Convention).

§2. Substantive requirements

2131. The Copyright Law does not contain any explicit substantive requirements for copyright protection to apply. However, legal commentators have discerned 2 requirements in the wording of Article 1, paragraph 1 of the Copyright Law, which reads as follows:

> "Only the author of a work of literature or art is entitled to copy the work by any method and in any form and to authorise such copying."

2132. The notions of "author" and "work" have caused most commentators to agree that copyright protection for a work requires both the expression in a certain form and originality, marked by the personality of the author.

1. Expression

2133. This requirement reflects the traditional notion of copyright, as recognised in most jurisdictions, that a copyright should protect against unauthorised copying of an author's "expression", but not against the copying of the "ideas" contained in the work.

2. Originality

2134. The Belgian Supreme Court has clarified the originality requirement (Cass., 27 April 1989, *Pas.*, 1989, I, 908; Cass., 25 October 1989, *Pas.*, 1990, I, 239; Cass., 2 March 1993, *Ing.-Cons.*, 1993, 145). According to the Supreme Court, a work will be considered original if it is the result of an intellectual effort and if it reflects the personality of the author.

2135. These Supreme Court judgements also confirm 2 important principles on which most commentators had been in agreement for some time, but which had divided lower courts. First, copyright protection does not require the work to present some artistic value. Second, copyright is not concerned with rewarding the efforts that went into the creation of a work.

§3. Procedural requirements

2136. There are no procedural requirements for copyright protection to apply.

§4. Rights of the author

2137. Article 6 of the Copyright Law provides that the first right holder is the *natural* person who has created the work. In view of the important moral component of the copyright (*See*, paras. 2148 *et seq.*) and its originality requirement, only the natural person whose personality is reflected in the work can be the first right owner.

2138. The economic rights of the original right holder may of course be transferred to a third party, without prejudice to the author's moral rights. As regards works that are created in execution of an employment agreement, Article 3, paragraph 3 of the Copyright Law provides that the author's economic rights are transferred to the employer provided such transfer has explicitly been agreed upon and provided the creation of the work is included in the scope of the employment agreement.

2139. As noted above, owning copyright in a work affords two fundamental categories of rights: economic rights and moral rights.

1. Economic Rights

2140. The economic rights of an author comprise 2 basic sub-categories: (i) the right to reproduce the work and (ii) the right to represent the same. Both rights will be discussed in this section.

2141. The so-called "resale right" *(volgrecht/droit de suite)*, which is characteristic of works of plastic art *(werken van beeldende kunst/les oeuvres plastiques)* and which entitles an artist to an interest in any sale of his work at a public auction, is governed by Articles 11 through 13 of the Copyright Law. This right is inalienable but the author, his heir or legatee, can collect proceeds from the resale right through the intermediary of a collective management society. At the European level, the EC Council of Ministers and Parliament has adopted Directive No. 2001/84 of 19 July 2001 on the Resale Right for the Benefit of the Author of an Original Work of Art (O.J. [2001] L 272/32), which aims at harmonising the legislation on this matter in the different EC Member States. This Directive must be implemented by 1 January 2006.

2142. Mention should also be made of the rights associated with a "discovered" work. Article 2, paragraph 6 of the Copyright Law confers a protection equivalent to the author's economic rights to anyone who, after the expiry of the copyright protection, lawfully publishes or communicates to the public a work that has not been published before. The duration of this protection is 25 years as from the moment at which the work is first lawfully published or communicated to the public.

i. Right to Reproduce a Work

2143. The author of a work has the exclusive right to reproduce such work by any method and in any form and to authorise such reproduction (Art. 1, para. 1 of the Copyright Law). The scope of this right is broadly construed. This is borne out by the reference in the Copyright Law, as an example, to the author's right to adapt the work or make a translation of it (so-called "intellectual reproductions", which may give rise to a distinct copyright for the author of the adaptation or the translation; Art. 1, para. 1, second sentence of the Copyright Law) and to his rental and lending rights (Art. 1, para. 1, third sentence of the Copyright Law). The exclusive right of the author also extends to partial reproductions, and, more generally, any reproduction of the elements of the work which give it its originality. As regards motion pictures, for example, the right to reproduce extends to a copy which only contains certain characteristics or essential elements of the original work, such as the plot, the characters and the scenario.

2144. However, the Copyright Law places limits on the author's exclusive right to reproduce the work the author's exclusive right is also limited as a result of EC law (*See*, para. 2196). Article 21 of the Copyright Law allows the use of short quotations for critical, polemic or educational purposes, or in the framework of scientific activities, provided that fair professional practices are observed and provided such quotations are justified by the intended purpose. These quotations must mention the source and the name of the author. This exception applies not only to literary works but to copyrighted works in general. Under certain circumstances, the author cannot oppose the reproduction or communication of his copyrighted works. Article 22 of the Copyright Law sets out these exceptions to the exclusive right to reproduce (*e.g.*, reproduction of short fragments in a news report with a view to providing information; private communication in the family circle; reproduction for educational or private purposes; caricature or parody). These exceptions apply notwithstanding any contractual clause to the contrary but must be interpreted restrictively.

ii. Right to Communicate Work to the Public

2145. The author has the exclusive right to communicate his work to the public. Accordingly, the author controls all acts which involve communication of the work to the public by any process whatsoever. It is not required, for the act of communication to fall foul of the author's exclusive right, that the organiser of the communication actively participate in the communication. Nor is it necessary for the author to have the intent to communicate the work or to charge any entrance fee to the public. The legislator has limited the scope of the exception to the author's right to any communication in the family circle. The question arises whether or not a communication outside of the family circle would necessarily be deemed to constitute a communication to the public. However, some commentators argue that a communication to a closed group of people that is socially interlinked should fall outside the scope of the author's exclusive right.

2146. Articles 51 through 54 of the Copyright Law, implementing EC Council Directive No. 93/83 of 27 September 1993 (O.J. [1993] L 248/15), regulate certain forms of cable distribution, which is a specific process of communication to the public. Articles 48 through 50 of the Copyright Law deal with communication to the public via satellite.

2147. Every single communication to the public creates an entitlement to a royalty. For example, if a broadcasting company broadcasts a film which is subsequently distributed by a cable operator and ultimately received by a television set located in a pub, the owners of the copyright in the film will be entitled to royalties from the broadcasting company, the cable operator and the pub owner.

2. *Moral Rights*

2148. The protection of certain moral rights was first enshrined in Article 6*bis* of the Berne Convention. The first paragraph of that provision states that:

> "*[i]ndependently of the author's economic rights, and even after the transfer of the said rights, the author shall have the right to claim authorship of the work and to object to any distortion, mutilation, or other modification of, or other derogatory action in relation to, the said work which would be prejudicial to his honour or reputation.*"

2149. The second paragraph of Article 6*bis* of the Berne Convention provides that the moral rights shall be maintained after his death and at least until the expiry of the economic rights. Although the Old Copyright Law did not explicitly provide for moral rights of the author, such rights were recognised by both the courts and commentators. Article 1, paragraph 2 of the Copyright Law now specifically states that the author of a work of literature or art has an inalienable moral right in his work. It is not possible for an author to make a blanket waiver of his moral right for the future.

2150. The Copyright Law regulates the 3 following moral rights.

i. Right of First Publication

2151. The right of first publication enables an author to decide if, when and under what form(s) the work will be brought to the public's knowledge.

2152. The right of first publication has important economic implications for the author. Pursuant to Article 1, paragraph 2, fourth sentence of the Copyright Law, works are not subject to seizure by creditors as long as they have not been published. Moreover, the right is irrevocable: once exercised, the right is extinguished.

2153. Without limitation, the author must not renounce the exercise of the right of first publication in the future work, or assign it. But he can validly undertake to bring the work to the public's knowledge when it has acquired specifically defined characteristics.

ii. Right of Paternity

2154. The right of paternity is the right which enables an author to claim authorship of his work, or, on the contrary, to refuse authorship (right to anonymity). This right survives any transfer of title to the copyright. However, leading commentators accept that the author may contractually give up his right of paternity for the past.

iii. Right of Integrity

2155. The right of integrity is the right of an author to receive respect for his work and, therefore, the right to object to any modification of his work (Art. 1, para. 2, sixth sentence of the Copyright Law). In other words, any modification of the work requires the permission of the author. Such modifications must be defined or reasonably determinable. Notwithstanding any renunciation, the author moreover maintains the right to oppose any distortion, mutilation or similar alteration of his work or any other derogatory action in relation to the work that would be prejudicial to his honour or reputation (Art. 1, para. 2, seventh sentence of the Copyright Law). The right to oppose any distortion and similar acts persists, notwithstanding contractual provisions to the contrary, whereas the right to oppose a modification of the work can be waived.

§5. Duration of copyright protection

2156. Pursuant to Article 2 of the Copyright Law, copyright protection is in general afforded during the life of the author and 70 years thereafter. Under the Old Copyright Law, protection was only afforded for 50 years after the death of the author but this term was extended pursuant to EC Council Directive No. 93/98 of 29 October 1993 Harmonising the Terms of Copyright and Certain Related Rights (O.J. [1993] L 290/9), which has harmonised this matter in the different EC Member States.

2157. The Copyright Law contains specific provisions that govern the duration of copyright protection for works of joint authorship, audiovisual works, anonymous or pseudonymous works, works that consist of several volumes, parts, episodes *etc.*, and works that are published for the first time after the death of the author.

2158. Even though the Copyright Law does not specifically regulate the duration of protection of the author's moral rights, legal commentators seem to accept that the Copyright Law should be interpreted as affording the same duration of protection for moral rights as it does for the copyright itself, *i.e.*, 70 years after the death of the author.

C. Neighbouring rights

§1. Introduction

2159. The Copyright Law grants neighbouring rights to 3 categories of beneficiaries: (i) performers, (ii) producers of phonograms or of first fixations of films, and (iii) broadcasting organisations.

§2. Relationship between copyright and neighbouring rights.

2160. Article 33 of the Copyright Law provides that the chapter on neighbouring rights does not affect the rights of authors. Although some read this article as the confirmation of a hierarchy between superior copyright and inferior neighbouring rights, the literature predominantly regards them as cumulative and competitive rights. Notwithstanding the foregoing, there is in fact a hierarchy between the author and the performer as regards moral rights. On the other hand, the economic rights of an author cannot prevent a performer from exercising his/her own economic rights.

§3. Performer

1. Definition

2161. Although the Copyright Law does not define the concept of "performer", the preparatory works of the Copyright Law refer to the definition drawn up by the Rome Convention. The Convention defines performers as the *"actors, singers, musicians, dancers, and other persons who act, sing, deliver, declaim, play in, or otherwise perform literary or artistic works"* (Art. 3 (a) of the Rome Convention).

2162. The Copyright Law makes 2 adjustments to this definition:
(i) it extends the scope of application of the neighbouring rights to circus acts and variety shows, which are rarely considered as artistic works; and
(ii) it excludes from the definition dubbing performers as well as extras and bit parts-comedians.

2163. A performance may be protected by the neighbouring rights even if the copyright protection has already expired (*e.g.*, the performance of traditional dances).

2164. It must be noted that, although performances of a sportsman do not constitute artistic works, figure ice skating, synchronized swimming or eurhythmics may constitute artistic works.

2. Economic rights of the performer

2165. As is the case for an author, the economic rights of a performer include both the right to reproduce the performance and the right to communicate it to the public.

To these rights must be added the resulting entitlement to remuneration (Arts. 40, 42, 55 and 62 of the Copyright Law).

i. Right of Reproduction of the Performance

2166. The performer of an artistic or literary work has the exclusive right to reproduce or authorise the reproduction of the performance (Art. 35, para. 1 of the Copyright Law). The reproduction includes the right to fix an unfixed performance and the right to reproduce the fixed performance.

2167. Article 46 of the Copyright Law provides some exceptions to the right of the performer to reproduce a performance (short quotations, news reports, private communications in the family circle, *etc.*).

ii. Right to Communicate to the Public

2168. The performer of an artistic or literary work has the exclusive right to the communication (or the reproduction, whether or not authorised) of his performance. As the description of this right corresponds fully to the equivalent right of the author, we refer to the comments on the author's rights of communication to the public (*See*, paras. 2145 *et seq.*).

3. Moral Rights of the Performer

2169. The moral rights attributed to the performer by the Copyright Law are less numerous and less extensive than the moral rights granted to the author. For example, the performer does not benefit from a right of first publication. Moreover, the paternity right (Art. 34, para. 3 of the Copyright Law) and the right of integrity (Art. 34, para. 4 of the Copyright Law) are more limited than the corresponding rights of the author.

4. Duration of Protection

2170. Pursuant to Article 38, paragraph 1 of the Copyright Law, the protection of the neighbouring rights starts at the date of the performance and expires after a period of 50 years as from the first day of the year following the performance of the artistic or literary work. Nevertheless, the starting date may be postponed in the event that the performance is subject to a lawfully published fixation or a fixation communicated to the public afterwards. In these cases, the starting date will be the date of publication.

§4. *Producers of Phonograms or of First Fixations of Films*

1. *Definition*

i. The producer of phonograms

2171. The Rome Convention defines the producer of phonograms as *"the person who, or the legal entity which, first fixes the sounds of a performance or other sounds"* (Art. 3 (c) of the Rome Convention). EC Directive No. 92/100 of 19 November 1992 on Rental Right and Lending Right and on Certain Rights Related to Copyright in the Field of Intellectual Property (O.J. [1992] L 346/61) ("EC Directive No. 92/100") adds that this person or legal entity is the one that takes the initiative or has the responsibility for the first fixation. It results from these definitions that the producer is the person or legal entity that bears the responsibility for the fixation process in its financial and technical aspects.

2172. The phonogram corresponds to a fixation of sounds. It is immaterial whether the sounds are part of an artistic work. For example, bird songs or street noises may benefit from neighbouring rights.

2173. The protected performance is the first fixation. However, a new fixation of sounds, adding sounds or adapting the first fixation, is also protected.

ii. The producer of first fixations of films

2174. Neither the Copyright Law nor the Rome Convention defines the concept of "producer of first fixations of films". For the purpose of EC Directive No. 92/100, the term "film" designates *"a cinematographic or audiovisual work or moving images, whether or not accompanied by sounds"* (Art. 2, 1° of EC Directive No. 92/100). One image or a succession of fixed images could suffice. It is not material whether the images constitute an artistic work.

2. *Economic and moral rights of the producer*

2175. The economic rights of the producer (of phonograms or first fixations of films) are identical to those of a performer or of an author: these are the rights of reproduction and of communication to the public. As is the case for the performer and the author, the rights are exclusive. To these exclusive rights must be added the resulting right to remuneration (Arts. 40, 42, 55 and 62 of the Copyright Law).

2176. The exceptions to the right of the performer also apply to the producer.

2177. The Copyright Law grants no moral right to the producer of phonograms or first fixations of films. However, a producer can always command respect for its reputation and protect its moral rights by means of general principles of law.

3. Duration of the protection

2178. With respect to the duration of protection, we refer to our comments relating to the duration of the right of the performer (*See*, para. 2170).

§5. Broadcasting organisations

1. Definition

2179. The only useful definition relation to broadcasting organisations is found in the Rome Convention, which simply refers to "broadcasting". The Rome Convention defines broadcasting as *"the transmission by wireless means for public reception of sounds or of images and sounds"*. However, this definition omits the transmission of texts or images alone. Moreover, the definition only covers the transmission by wireless means although it is generally accepted that the means, of transmission is not decisive for the determination of whether a broadcasting organisation may benefit from the neighbouring rights.

2. Economic and moral rights of the broadcasting organisation

2180. Broadcasting organisations do not have any moral rights. Furthermore, their economic rights are restricted compared to other rightholders.

i. Right of Reproduction

2181. The right of reproduction enjoyed by broadcasting organisations is similar to the right of reproduction granted to authors, performers and producers. However, the Copyright Law did not grant rental and lending rights to broadcasting organisations.

ii. Right to Communicate to the Public

2182. The broadcasting organisation has no general right of communication to the public. However, Article 44, paragraph 1 of the Copyright Law provides 2 specific rights:
   (a) an exclusive right of simultaneous or recorded broadcast;
   (b) an exclusive right to oppose the communication of broadcasts in places accessible to the public against an entrance fee.

3. Duration of the protection

2183. As regards the duration of the protection enjoyed by broadcasting organisations, we refer to our comments relating to the duration of the right of the performer (*See*, para. 2170).

D. Exploitation of the economic rights

§1. Domestic

1. Contracts and licences

2184. As regards both the author's economic rights and the neighbouring rights, the Copyright Law specifically states that they are transferable in whole or in part and assignable in conformity with the rules of the Civil Code. The parties' contractual freedom is limited only by legal provisions in the broad sense, *inter alia*, the provisions of EC law governing competition (Arts. 81 and 82 of the EC Treaty) and the free movement of goods (Arts. 28 and 30 of the EC Treaty) (*See*, paras. 2193 *et seq.*). The limits to the contractual freedom which apply to copyright contracts in general will be discussed hereafter. Next to these general principles, specific provisions apply to, *inter alia*, employment agreements and works for hire (Art. 3, para. 3 of the Copyright Law), plastic works (Art. 9 of the Copyright Law), audio-visual works (Arts. 17 through 20 of the Copyright Law), publishing agreements (Arts. 25 through 30 of the Copyright Law) and staging agreements (Arts. 31 and 32 of the Copyright Law).

i. Written proof *vis-à-vis* the author

2185. Article 3, paragraph 1 of the Copyright Law provides that all contracts must be proven *vis-à-vis* the author by a written document (however, the requirement of written proof does not apply with regard to the producers' and radio broadcasters' neighbouring rights). The Copyright law does not require that all contracts be in writing. The author may waive the requirement of written proof: he may himself acknowledge that he has contracted orally with an editor. *Vis-à-vis* third parties, the contract is a legal fact that can be proven by any means.

ii. Restrictive interpretation

2186. The contractual provisions concerning copyright must be restrictively interpreted in the author's favour. Article 3, paragraph 1 of the Copyright Law also expressly stipulates that the transfer of an object incorporating the work does not imply the transfer of the right to exploit this work.

iii. Specific provisions in the author's favour

2187. For every exploitation method, the author's remuneration, the scope and the duration of the transfer must be expressly provided for in the contract. Also, the transfer of rights as regards yet unknown forms of exploitation is void.

iv. Transfer of rights with regard to future works

2188. The transfer of rights regarding works that have not yet been created is valid only if it applies to works that are created within a certain period of time and only if those works belong to a specific genre.

v. Obligation to exploit the work according to fair practices characteristic of the profession

2189. The author's contracting party will always have the obligation to exploit the work according to fair practices characteristic of the profession. Any contractual clause to the contrary will be deemed void.

2190. As explained above (*See*, para. 2144), the Copyright Law provides for certain exceptions to the author's exclusive right (*e.g.*, the copy for educational or scientific purposes, public lending). As a corollary to these exceptions, the Copyright Law provides for remuneration in order to compensate the author for the loss of income resulting from the statutory exceptions to his exclusive right. This system is also referred to as a system of "legal licences", because it deals with situations in which the copyrighted work is exploited without the author having consented to such exploitation.

2. *Collective management*

2191. Since authors, performers and producers are incapable of controlling the distribution of their works and performances and of collecting the remuneration related to their works and performances, companies of collective management have been created. In some cases, the intervention of such collective management companies has even become mandatory under the Copyright Law (*e.g.*, as regards the collection of contributions for private copying, cable transmission rights).

2192. The Copyright Law has put into place – sometimes quite burdensome – rules on the organisation and control of the activities of these collective management companies. These rules find their justification in the increasing importance of copyright management societies and the fact that they have, each with regard to their field of activities, a monopoly position.

§2. *Impact of EC law*

2193. Contracts involving a Belgian copyright should be drafted with due regard to the provisions of EC law governing competition (Arts. 81 and 82 of the EC Treaty) and the free movement of goods (Arts. 28 and 30 of the EC Treaty).

1. Competition law

2194. Contract clauses that confer a form of exclusivity on the licensee may, depending on the circumstances, run counter to Article 81(1) of the EC Treaty, if the general conditions of application of Article 81(1) are satisfied. Case law of the EC Commission (*e.g.*, O.J. [1989] L 284/36, *Film purchases by German television stations*; *See*, also, *XXVIth Report on Competition Policy*, 1996, No. 83; O.J. [1993] L 179/23, *U.E.R. – system of Eurovision*; on appeal: CFI, 11 July 1996, Joined Cases T-528, 542, 543 and 546/93, *Métropole télévision S.A. et alii* v. *EC Commission*, [1996] ECR II-649; O.J. [1989] L 226/25, *MGM/UA-UIP*), the European Court of First Instance (CFI, 12 June 1997, Case T-504/93, *Tiercé Ladbroke S.A.* v. *EC Commission*, [1997] ECR 923) and the European Court of Justice (ECJ, 6 October 1982, Case 262/81, *Coditel S.A. et alii* v. *Ciné-Vog Films S.A.* ("*Coditel II*"), [1982] ECR 3381) would seem to indicate that relevant factors in this respect might include the forms of copyright exploitation covered by the licence, the geographic area of the licence, the duration of the licence and the special characteristics of the industry in which the licence will operate.

2195. Export bans on copyrighted works will usually fall under Article 81(1) of the EC Treaty (*See, e.g.*, *STEMRA/Viditone, Eleventh Report on Competition Policy*, No. 98*)*, as will non-competition clauses, provisions requiring payment of royalties on products that are not protected by copyright and contract clauses requiring the transfer by the licensee to the licensor of all rights in the improvements to the product that was originally licensed (*Neilson-Hordell/Richmark, Twelfth Report on Competition Policy*, Nos. 88 and 89).

2196. Landmark case-law (CFI, 10 July 1991, Cases T-69/89, T-70/89 and T-76/89, *Radio Telefis Eireann and others* v. *Commission*, [1991] ECR II-485, II-535 and II-575, on appeal: ECJ, 6 April 1995, Joined Cases C-241 and 242/91P, *Radio Telefis Eireann and Independent Television Publications* v. *EC Commission* ("*Magill*"), [1995] ECR 743) suggests that a copyright holder (as well as owners of other intellectual property rights) may be required under Article 82 of the EC Treaty to accept compulsory licences if a third party can demonstrate that a new product which it intends to develop on a market different from that on which the copyright holder is active requires the use of technology or information protected by the copyright and if the refusal by the copyright holder to allow the use of such technology or information is inspired by a desire to maintain a dominant position on a given market. A broad interpretation of the concept of "abuse of a dominant position" has recently led the EC Commission to compel that a copyright holder grant a licence to its direct competitor (EC Commission Decision of 3 July 2001, *NDC Health/IMS Health*, O.J. [2002] L 59/18). The EC Commission's interim measures were, however, suspended by the President of the European Court of First Instance (CFI, 26 October 2001, Case T-184/01 R, *IMS Health Inc.* v. *EC Commission*, [2001] ECR II-3193, upheld by the President of the European Court of Justice, ECJ, 11 April 2002, Case C-481/01 P(R)), *NDC Health Corporation et alii* v. *IMS Health Inc. and EC Commission*, [2002] ECR I-3401). It remains to be seen whether the decision of the EC Commission will be upheld on the merits. In any event, the guiding legal principle remains that the circumstances in which the exercise of a copyright could be regarded as abusive under Article 82 of the EC Treaty must be "exceptional". For example, a refusal to license a third party could be found to be abusive if there is an anti-competitive element additional to the normal use of the intellectual property right in question (*See*, also, CFI, 12 June 1997, Case T-504/93, *Tiercé Ladbroke S.A.* v. *EC Commission*, [1997] ECR II-927).

2. *Free movement of goods*

2197. The rules governing the so-called "Community-wide exhaustion" of intellectual property rights affect to a considerable extent the possibilities for the owner of a Belgian copyright to stop the importation of goods protected by that copyright. Under the exhaustion doctrine, the Belgian copyright owner will be prevented from relying on his copyright to stop the importation of products that were sold by himself, an affiliated company or a licensee in another EC Member State (*e.g.*, ECJ, 8 June 1971, Case 78/70, *Deutsche Grammophon GmbH* v. *Metro-SB-Großmärkte GmbH & Co KG* [1971] ECR 487 and ECJ, 20 January 1981, Joined Cases 55 and 57/80, *Musik-Vertrieb Membran GmbH et alii* v. *GEMA* [1981] ECR 147). By contrast, the exhaustion doctrine will not apply if the product was legally placed on the market in a Member State where the period of copyright protection had already expired, and if that product's entry into Belgium is sought thereafter. In that case, the Belgian copyright owner will be able to block the imports (ECJ, 24 January 1989, Case 341/87, *EMI Electrola GmbH* v. *Patricia Im-und Export and others* [1989] ECR 79).

2198. The exhaustion doctrine generally applies only to imports from EC Member States The following provisions of the Copyright Law lay down the exhaustion doctrine: Article 35 (with regard to performers), Article 39 (with regard to producers of phonograms and of first fixations of films) and Article 44 (with regard to broadcasters). Imports from non-EC countries do not fall under its scope. However, the exhaustion doctrine also applies to imports into the Community from the former EFTA countries, provided the imported goods originated in an EC Member State of the EEA (Arts. 8(2) and 13, EEA Agreement and Article 2 of Protocol 28, EEA Agreement).

E. Infringements and remedies

§1. Civil remedies

2199. All claims involving copyright should be brought before the Court of First Instance *(Rechtbank van Eerste Aanleg/Tribunal de Première Instance)* even if the dispute arises between commercial parties, provided the amount at stake exceeds € 1,860 (Art. 569(7) of the Judicial Code). Claims involving less than € 1,860 should be brought before the Justice of the Peace *(Vredegerecht/ Justice de paix)*.

2200. If the dispute involves alleged acts of counterfeiting, the action should be brought before the Court of First Instance that has jurisdiction over the place where the counterfeiting took place (Art. 627(5) of the Judicial Code). In cases of urgency, the President of the Court of First Instance may hand down a decision following summary proceedings. Such a decision may provide for periodic penalty payments.

2201. Articles 1481 through 1488 of the Judicial Code provide for a special and useful procedure *(beslag inzake namaak/saisie en matière de contrefaçon)*, which enables the copyright owner to obtain an inventory of relevant items in premises where it is alleged that acts of counterfeiting took place and to seize specific goods in such premises. This procedure is also open to owners of a patent right, a plant variety right, a neighbouring right and a *sui generis*-database right. According to this procedure, one or more court-appointed experts may be empowered to describe all goods thought to be counterfeited, as well as all plans, documents, calculations and writings that bear evidence of the alleged acts of counterfeiting. These documents may include the books of the company (Brussels Court of Appeal, 28 February 1985, *Computerrecht*, 1986, 50). In addition to appointing one or more experts, a judge may prohibit the keepers of allegedly counterfeit goods from disposing of the same. The judge may also appoint a special caretaker, affix seals on certain goods and seize money generated by the alleged acts of counterfeiting. A major advantage of this procedure is the element of surprise. The authorisation from the Court to proceed with the inventory can be obtained through *ex parte*-filings. Any resistance to submit to an investigation can, if necessary, be overcome with the help of the police (Arts. 1485 and 1504 of the Judicial Code). Article 1488 of the Judicial Code requires the plaintiff to initiate proceedings on the merits within one month of the communication of the expert's report to the different parties involved or within one month of the seizure of moneys.

2202. Article 87 of the Copyright Law allows any interested party to introduce a claim for a cease-and-desist order before the President of the Court of First Instance. In contrast, the commercial cease-and-desist order (*i.e.*, on the basis of Article 96 of the Law on Unfair Trade Practices) does not apply to counterfeit acts even if the case is initiated by a person other than the right holder, and even if the infringement also constitutes an unfair trade practice.

§2. Criminal sanctions

2203. Article 80, paragraph 1 of the Copyright Law provides that any malicious or fraudulent breach of a copyright constitutes a criminal offence. The same goes for the malicious or fraudulent use of the author's name (*i.e.*, signing the work of another individual with fraudulent intent; *See*, Art. 80, para. 2 of the Copyright Law). Article 80, paragraph 3 of the Copyright Law prohibits the acts of knowingly selling, leasing, exhibiting for sale or lease, keeping in a warehouse with the purpose of selling, or importing into Belgium counterfeit goods.

F. International protection

2204. Article 79 of the Copyright Law states, as a general principle of law, that foreign nationals will benefit from the same copyright protection as Belgian nationals for a period that does not exceed the duration of the protection which applies in Belgium. If the copyright expires in the author's country of origin, then the protection under the Belgian law will expire simultaneously. If the Belgian authors are protected to a lesser extent in a foreign country, then the nationals of that country will only be granted copyright protection in Belgium to a similar extent.

2205. If the protective rules of international conventions are more favourable, then the latter will apply (with, to a certain extent, an exception for remuneration for private copying or for educational or scientific use).

2206. The Berne Convention requires its members to apply the principle of national treatment, rather than reciprocity, to works from nationals of a member of the Berne Convention (Art. 3, para. 1 of the Berne Convention). The Berne Convention as a rule also requires its members to apply the principle of national treatment to authors who are not nationals of a member of the Berne Convention but who publish their work for the first time in a member country, or simultaneously in a country outside the (Berne Convention) Union and in a member country (Art. 3, para. 2 of the Berne Convention; but *See*, Art. 6, para. 1, which allows for a form of reciprocity where the country which is not a member of the Berne Convention affords insufficient protection to the nationals of the country of the Berne Convention where protection is sought).

2207. The principle of national treatment bears an exception with respect to the term of protection. Article 7, paragraph 8, of the Berne Convention provides that the term of protection shall be governed by the law of the country where protection is claimed, but shall not exceed the term fixed in the country of origin of the work.

2208. The TRIPS Agreement also provides for the principle of national treatment. More specifically, Article 2 states that, as a rule, each EC Member State shall accord to the nationals of other EC Member States treatment no less favourable than that granted to its own nationals with regard to the protection of intellectual property. However, the TRIPS Agreement does not apply to moral rights (Art. 9, para. 1 of the TRIPS Agreement). Moreover, the principle of "national treatment" is limited as regards neighbouring rights (Arts. 3 and 4 of the TRIPS Agreement). As regards the nationals of a country other than an EC Member State, Article 4 of the TRIPS Agreement establishes the principle of "most-favoured-nation treatment" (subject to certain exceptions): with regard to the protection of intellectual property, any advantage, favour, privilege or immunity granted by an EC Member State to the nationals of any other country shall be accorded immediately and unconditionally to the nationals of all other EC Member States.

G. Computer programs

2209. On 30 June 1994, a second law in the field of copyright was enacted, more specifically, the law by which EC Council Directive No. 91/250 of 14 May 1991 on the Legal Protection of Computer Programs (O.J. [1991] L 122/42) was transposed to Belgian law (the "Law on the Protection of Computer Programs"). The Directive offers copyright protection to computer programs by providing in its Article 1 that *"Member States shall protect computer programs* (including the preparatory design material), *by copyright, as literary works within the meaning of the Berne Convention"*. The EC Commission recently issued a proposal for a Directive on the *patentability* of computer-implemented inventions (COM (2002) 92 final). This proposal will be discussed in the section dealing with patents.

§1. Scope of the Law on the Protection of Computer Programs and conditions for protection

2210. Protection applies to the expression in any form of a computer program. However, the underlying ideas and principles are not protected (Art. 2 of the Law on the Protection of Computer Programs). In order to be protected by copyright, the computer program must be the author's own intellectual creation. No other criteria than the criterion of "originality" will be applied to determine its eligibility for protection and no tests as to the qualitative or aesthetic merits of the program will have relevance. There are no procedural requirements for copyright protection to apply.

§2. *Rightholders*

2211. The author(s) of the computer programs will also be the owners of the copyright. However, Article 3 of the Law on the Protection of Computer Programs creates the following presumption: where a computer program is created by an employee in the execution of his duties or following the instructions given by his employer, the latter shall be deemed to be the rightholder of all economic rights in the program, unless otherwise provided for by contract. This presumption does not apply to the moral rights in the computer programs, nor to "related works", such as manuals.

§3. *Economic rights: scope and exceptions*

2212. Article 5 of the Law on the Protection of Computer Programs lists the economic rights of the author of a computer program. First, the right of reproduction includes the right to authorise or to prohibit:
   (i) the so-called "material" reproduction of the program (*i.e.*, the reproduction of the computer program as such, *e.g.*, downloading), in whole or in part, temporary or permanent, by any means and in any form;
   (ii) the "intellectual" reproduction of the program (*e.g.*, the translation, adaptation, arrangement and any other alteration of a computer program); and
   (iii) any form of distribution to the public of the computer program (or of copies thereof).

2213. The rightholder also has the exclusive right of communicating the computer program to the public by virtue of Article 1, paragraph 1 of the Copyright Law.

2214. The exceptions to the exclusive right are listed at the end of Article 5 and in Articles 6 through 8 of the Law on the Protection of Computer Programs. In addition, the exceptions provided for by the Copyright Law are deemed to apply to the copyright protection of computer programs, unless such exception is specifically regulated by the Law on the Protection of Computer Programs. For example, the exception of "private copying" is specifically regulated by the Law on the Protection of Computer Programs: it supersedes Article 22 of the Copyright Law, which regulates this issue for copyrighted works in general.

2215. The following exceptions apply:
   (i) Article 5 *in fine* of the Law on the Protection of Computer Programs states that the first sale in the Community of a copy of a program by the rightholder or with his consent shall exhaust the distribution right within the Community of that copy, with the exception of the right to control further rental or lending of the program or a copy thereof (*i.e.*, the "exhaustion of right" principle);

(ii) Unless otherwise provided for by contract, the person who is entitled to use the program may reproduce it if such reproduction is required for the use of the program in accordance with its intended purpose, including for error correction (Art. 6, para. 1 of the Law on the Protection of Computer Programs);

(iii) The lawful user of the computer program is allowed to make a back-up copy of that program in so far as the copy is necessary for that use (Art. 6, para. 2 of the Law on the Protection of Computer Programs);

(iv) The lawful user of a copy of the computer program may also observe, study or test the functioning of the program in order to determine the ideas and principles that underlie any element of the program if he does so while performing any of the acts of loading, displaying, running, transmitting or storing the program which he is entitled to do (Art. 6, para. 3 of the Law on the Protection of Computer Programs);

(v) Decompilation is authorised in so far as it is aimed at the creation of a new compatible program, *i.e.*, if necessary to achieve the interoperability of an independently created computer program with other programs. The scope of the exception is limited: decompilation for the mere analysis of the program is not authorised. Moreover, it is subject to several conditions (Art. 7 of the Law on the Protection of Computer Programs).

§4. Moral rights

2216. The moral rights in a computer program are regulated in accordance with Article 6*bis*, paragraph 1 of the Berne Convention (Art. 4 of the Law on the Protection of Computer Programs). The Berne Convention only grants the rights of paternity and integrity. The right of first publication therefore seems to be excluded from the scope of the Law on the Protection of Computer Programs. The moral rights cannot be transferred.

§5. Sanctions

2217. Infringing the copyright on a computer program gives rise to the same civil or criminal sanctions as infringements of other copyrighted works. The Law on the Protection of Computer Programs specifies two other types of (criminal) infringements:

(i) Any act of putting into circulation, or the possession for commercial purposes of a copy of a computer program with actual or constructive knowledge that it is an infringing copy;

(ii) Any act of putting into circulation, or the possession for commercial purposes of any means the sole intended use of which is to facilitate the unauthorised removal or circumvention of any technical device that may have been applied to protect a computer program.

2218. In civil cases, the Courts of First Instance (*Rechtbank van Eerste Aanleg/Tribunal de Première Instance*) are exclusively competent, irrespective of the value of the litigation. As regards territorial competence, only the courts of Antwerp, Brussels, Ghent, Liège and Mons have jurisdiction.

II. THE LEGAL PROTECTION OF DATABASES

A. General Overview

2219. The legal protection of databases is regulated partly by the Copyright Law and partly by the Law of 31 August 1998 (the "Database Law"). The Database Law implements into Belgian law the EC Directive of 11 March 1996 on the Legal Protection of Databases (the "Database Directive" – O.J. [1996] L 77/20). The section of the Copyright Law dealing with databases and the Database Law together constitute a relatively faithful implementation of the Database Directive.

2220. A database is defined in the Database Directive, the Copyright Law and the Database Law as "*a collection of independent works, data or other materials arranged in a systematic or methodical way and individually accessible by electronic or other means*".

2221. The Database Directive provides for 2 different forms of legal protection of databases. The first form of protection is a copyright protection of databases which, by reason of the selection or arrangement of their contents, constitute the author's own intellectual creation. This copyright protection does not extend to the contents of the database, and is without prejudice to any rights subsisting in such contents (Art. 3 of the Database Directive). The second form of protection consists of a *sui generis*-right for the maker of the database (*i.e.*, the person who has invested in its production) to prevent certain acts in relation to the use of the contents of the database (Art. 7 of the Database Directive).

2222. The Database Directive thus requires the recognition of 2 separate rights, namely the copyright in the database as such, and the maker's *sui generis*-right. The Copyright Law contains a separate section dealing with the copyright protection of databases. The Database Law in turn deals with the maker's *sui generis*-right.

B. Database Copyright

§1. Scope of protection

2223. Articles 20*bis* through 20*quater* of the Copyright Law contain specific provisions with regard to the database copyright. In addition to these specific provisions, the general copyright regime applies to databases. According to Articles 569, 7° and 1481 of the Judicial Code the database copyright is qualified as a neighbouring right to copyright (*naburig recht/droit voisin*).

2224. As noted, Article 20*bis* of the Copyright Law provides that databases which, by reason of the selection or arrangement of their contents, constitute the author's own intellectual creation, are protected as such by copyright.

2225. The beneficiary of the copyright protection is the author of the database. The author of the database can be a person other than the maker of the database, who is the beneficiary of the protection of a database by the *sui generis*-right (*See*, paras. 2231 *et seq.*).

§2. Exceptions to the database copyright

2226. In addition to the general exceptions to copyright, certain additional exceptions to the database copyright exist in favour of lawful users of databases. A lawful user is defined as the person who performs acts that are permitted by the author of the database or by law (Art. 20*quater* of the Copyright Law).

2227. The lawful user of a database or of a copy thereof can perform, without the authorisation of the author of the database, any of the acts provided for in Article 1, paragraph 1 of the Copyright Law (*i.e.*, the right to reproduce the database in whatever manner or whatever form) that are necessary for the purposes of gaining access to the contents of the database and for the normal use of such contents. To the extent that the lawful user uses only part of the database, the exception solely applies to that part. This exception is a provision of mandatory law (Art. 20*quater* of the Copyright Law).

2228. Furthermore, the author of the database that has legally been made available cannot prevent:
   (i) the reproduction for private purposes of databases that are recorded on a graphic or similar carrier (non-electronic databases);
   (ii) the reproduction of databases that are recorded on a graphic or similar carrier (non-electronic databases) for the purposes of illustration for teaching or scientific research, to the extent justified by the non-commercial purpose to be achieved and without prejudice to the normal exploitation of the database;

(iii) the reproduction of databases that are recorded on carriers other than a graphic or similar carrier (electronic databases) for the purposes of illustration for teaching or scientific research, to the extent justified by the non-commercial purpose to be achieved and without prejudice to the normal exploitation of the database;

(iv) the communication of a database for the purposes of illustration for teaching or scientific research by institutions officially recognised or created for these purposes by the public authorities, to the extent the communication is justified by the non-commercial purpose to be achieved, and provided that it takes place within the framework of the normal activities of the institution and does not prejudice the normal exploitation of the database;

(v) the reproduction or communication to the public of a database for the purposes of public security or an administrative or judicial procedure and without prejudice to the normal exploitation of the database.

2229. When the database is reproduced or communicated for the purposes of illustration for teaching or scientific research, the name of the author and the name of the database have to be indicated (Art. 22*bis* of the Copyright Law).

§3. Presumption of transfer of rights in the case of an employment contract

2230. Except in case of a contrary provision in an employment contract or in the by-laws of a company, the employer is presumed to be the only beneficiary of the economic rights in respect of databases that are not made in the cultural industry by one or more employees or officials during the execution of their duties or in accordance with the instructions of their employer (Art. 20*ter* of the Copyright Law).

C. Maker's *sui generis*-right

§1. Scope of protection

2231. The maker of a database is defined in Article 2, 5° of the Database Law as the natural person or legal entity who takes the initiative and the risk of the investment through which the database has come into existence.

2232. The makers of databases have the right to prevent extraction or re-utilisation of the whole or of a substantial part, evaluated qualitatively and/or quantitatively, of the contents of their databases (Art. 4 of the Database Law). This *sui generis*-right applies to databases in any form which show that there has been – qualitatively and/or quantitatively – a substantial investment in either the acquisition, verification or presentation of the contents. Furthermore, the maker's right applies irrespective of the eligibility of the database or the contents thereof for protection by copyright or other rights. The protection of a database under the *sui generis*-right does not prejudice the rights existing in respect of its contents (Art. 3 of the Database Law).

2233. "Extraction" means the permanent or temporary transfer to another medium of all or a substantial part of the contents of a database by any means or in any form. "Re-utilisation" means any form of making available to the public all or a substantial part of the contents of a database by the distribution of copies, by renting, by on-line or other forms of transmission. Public lending is not an act of extraction or re-utilisation (Art. 2, 2° and 3° of the Database Law).

2234. The repeated and systematic extraction and/or re-utilisation of insubstantial parts of the contents of the database implying acts inconsistent with a normal exploitation of that database, or which unreasonably prejudice the legitimate interests of the maker of the database, are not permitted. The first sale of a copy of a database within the European Community by the rightholder or with his consent exhausts the right to control resale of that copy within the European Community (Art. 4 of the Database Law).

§2. *Term of protection*

2235. The database maker's right expires fifteen years as from the first of January of the year following the date of completion. In case of a database which is made available to the public in whatever manner before the expiry of the 15-year period, the term of protection expires 15 years as from the first of January of the year following the date when the database was first made available to the public.

2236. Any substantial change to the contents of the database that would result in the database being considered as a substantial new investment will confer on this new database its own term of protection (Art. 6 of the Database Law).

§3. *Exceptions to the sui generis-right*

2237. Certain exceptions to the database maker's right exist in favour of lawful users. A lawful user is defined as the person who extracts and/or re-utilises the database in a way permitted by the maker of the database or by law (Art. 2, 5° of the Database Law).

2238. The lawful users of a database which is made available to the public in whatever manner may, without the authorisation of its maker:
  (i) in case of extraction exclusively for private purposes, extract a substantial part of the contents of a non-electronic database;

(ii) in case of extraction for the purposes of teaching or scientific research, extract a substantial part of the contents of a database to the extent justified by the non-commercial purpose to be achieved;

(iii) in case of extraction or re-utilisation for the purposes of public security or an administrative or judicial procedure, extract and/or re-utilise a substantial part of the contents of a database (Art. 7 of the Database Law).

§4. Rights and obligations of lawful users

2239. The maker of a database which has been made available to the public in whatever manner may not prevent a lawful user of the database from extracting and/or re-utilising insubstantial parts of its contents for any purposes whatsoever. Where the lawful user is authorised to extract and/or re-utilise only part of the database, this right only applies to that part (Art. 8 of the Database Law).

2240. The lawful user of a database which has been made available to the public in whatever manner may not perform acts inconsistent with the normal exploitation of the database or unreasonably prejudice the legitimate interests of the maker of the database (Art. 9 of the Database Law).

2241. The lawful user of a database which has been made available to the public in whatever manner may not cause any prejudice to the holder of a copyright or a neighbouring right in respect of the works or subject matter contained in the database (Art. 10 of the Database Law).

2242. The provisions of Articles 7 through 10 of the Database Law are of a mandatory character.

III. PATENTS

A. Applicable law

2243. The primary source of legislation in relation to patents is the Law of 28 March 1984 on Inventor's Patents, as amended by the Law of 28 January 1997 (hereinafter referred to as the "Patent Law"). A second important piece of legislation is the Law of 8 July 1977. This Law caused Belgium to adopt 4 international conventions, namely the Strasbourg Convention on the Unification of Certain Points of Substantive Patent Law of 27 November 1963, the Patent Co-operation Treaty ("PCT") of 19 June 1970, the European Patent Convention ("EPC") of 5 October 1973 (as well as the Implementing Regulations to this Convention and 4 Protocols) and the Community Patent Convention ("CPC") of Luxembourg of 15 December 1975. It should be mentioned that the CPC did not enter into force because of a lack of a sufficient number of deposited instruments of ratification.

2244. Belgium adopted the Paris Industrial Property Convention of 1883 (the "Paris Convention") (1967, Stockholm version) by Law of 26 September 1974. Belgium also adopted the 1971 Strasbourg Convention concerning the International Patent Classification by Law of 22 January 1975. Belgium is furthermore a member country of the 1977 Budapest Treaty on the International Recognition of the Deposit of Microorganisms for the Purposes of Patent Procedure, which has been approved by Law of 15 December 1983. Finally, as a member of the WTO, Belgium adopted the Agreement on Trade-related Aspects of Intellectual Property Rights (the "TRIPS Agreement"), which has been approved by Law of 23 December 1994.

2245. The regulatory framework resulting from the combination of the Patent Law and the international conventions, as implemented by Belgian law, is as follows.

2246. The Paris Convention ensures free access to the Belgian patent system for nationals or residents of other member countries. It requires Belgium to apply the principle of national treatment on the basis of nationality, domicile or place of business (Arts. 2 and 3 of the Paris Convention) and to establish a system of Convention priority, under which an application in one of the member countries gives this applicant a priority period of 12 months to pursue an application in Belgium (Art. 4(c)(1) of the Paris Convention). The PCT facilitates the application for a patent in relation to the same invention in more than one jurisdiction. It also provides for the possibility to have an international search and a preliminary examination carried out in relation to an application. The member countries nonetheless retain their independence deciding whether to grant or deny a patent.

2247. The EPC not only establishes a streamlined application procedure but also creates a unified set of rules governing the grant of a patent. It has a great practical significance: most, if not all, major Belgian patents are derived from an EPC patent. The substance and scope of the patent acquired in Belgium as a result of a PCT or EPC application remain governed by the Patent Law. It follows that the rights enjoyed by a patent owner in Belgium may differ to some extent from those enjoyed by that same party in other countries, although the patents in the different jurisdictions were obtained by a single application (such as a PCT application) or were granted following a single patent application review procedure (in relation to an EPC application). In sum, the 3 forms of patent protection (Belgian patent, PCT patent and EPC patent) constitute, as far as their operation in Belgium is concerned, 3 different avenues to obtain the same result: patent protection afforded by Belgian patent law.

2248. On 5 July 2000, the EC Commission proposed the creation of a Community Patent which offers inventors the possibility of obtaining a single patent legally valid throughout the European Community (Commission proposal of 1 August 2000 for a Regulation of the Council on the Community Patent; *See*, COM (2000) 412 final). The proposal has not been adopted so far, owing mainly to conflicts regarding the possible creation of an *ad hoc* Court at the European level. However, it is expected that the Community Patent Regulation proposed by the Commission will be adopted soon.

2249. The Belgian regulatory framework is completed by a large number of Royal Decrees. Important Royal Decrees include those on the filing of an EPC application (Royal Decree of 27 February 1981), the filing of a PCT application (Royal Decree of 21 August 1981) as well as the filing of a national patent application, the grant of a national patent and the maintenance of such national patens (Royal Decree of 2 December 1986).

2250. Patents on medicinal products are governed by EC Council Regulation No. 1768/92 of 18 June 1992 concerning the Creation of a Supplementary Protection Certificate ("SPC") for Medicinal Products (O.J. [1992] L 182/1) which has been implemented by the Law of 29 July 1994. The Regulation intends to compensate pharmaceutical manufacturers for the period of patent protection which is lost while awaiting authorisation for marketing a medicinal product. The SPC affords the same rights as those afforded by the patent which protects a medicinal product. According to Article 13 of the SPC Regulation, the SPC takes effect at the end of the term of protection afforded by the patent for a period equal to the period which elapsed between the date on which the application for a patent was lodged and the date of the first marketing authorisation in the Community, reduced by a period of 5 years. The duration of the SPC will in any case be limited to 5 years.

2251. Similar additional protection applies to plant protection products pursuant to EC Regulation No. 1610/96 of the European Parliament and of the EC Council of 23 July 1996, which was implemented by the Law of 5 July 1998.

B. Definition

2252. A patent (*octrooi/brevet*) is a temporary and exclusive right to exploit an invention, which is a product or a process that provides a new way of doing something, or offers a new technical solution to a problem.

C. Substantive requirements

2253. Articles 2 and 4 of the Patent Law contain 5 conditions that must be satisfied in order for an invention to qualify for patent protection. These conditions mirror the requirements for patentability contained in Articles 52 through 57 of the EPC and are as follows:
    (i) there must be an invention;
    (ii) the invention has to be susceptible of industrial application;
    (iii) the invention must be new;
    (iv) the invention must be the result of an inventive step;
    (v) the invention must not be contrary to morality or public policy.

2254. These are discussed in the following sections.

§1. Invention

2255. The notion of "invention" is not defined in the Patent Law, but relates to the creation of a product, a process or a tool. Article 3 of the Patent Law further specifies that a number of concepts will "as such" not be considered to be an invention:
    (i) discoveries, scientific theories and mathematical methods;
    (ii) aesthetic creations;
    (iii) schemes, rules and methods for performing mental acts, playing games or doing business;
    (iv) presentation of information.

2256. Under Article 3 of the Patent Law and Article 52(2) of the EPC, computer programs as such are not regarded as inventions and are thus excluded from patentability. However, since more than 30,000 patents have in practice been granted in relation to computer programs, the EC Commission tabled a proposal that would create patent protection for computer-implemented inventions (Proposal of 20 February 2002 for a Directive on the Patentability of Computer-implemented Inventions; *See*, COM (2002) 92 final). The proposal aims at harmonising the discrepancies between the case law of the EPO and the Courts of the EC Member States by adopting a patent system that meets the need for protection of inventions on the basis of the general principles of European patent law. As a general rule, an invention must make a technical contribution to the state of the art in order to be patentable. Unlike the US patent system, the proposed EC Directive should ensure that patents will not be granted for "pure" business methods or, more generally, social processes since they do not meet the strict criteria including the need for technical contribution. Article 4 of the Patent Law lists a number of areas that are excluded from the scope of the Patent Law for purposes of purely substantive delimitation. As a result, it is not possible to obtain a patent for plant varieties protected by the Plant Variety Law, animal varieties and essentially biological processes for the production of plants or animals. Article 4 specifies that the exclusion pertaining to biological processes does not cover microbiological processes or the products thereof.

2257. Patents covering biotechnological inventions are governed by EC Directive No. 98/44 of the European Parliament and of the Council of 6 July 1998 on the Legal Protection of Biotechnological Inventions (O.J. [1998] L 213/13 – "EC Directive No. 98/44"). The EC Directive No. 98/44 provides that biological material may be the subject of an invention and that biological inventions can, under certain conditions, be patentable, even if they concern a product consisting of or containing biological material or a process by means of which biological material is produced, processed or used. The Directive maintains the distinction between plant and animal varieties (which are not patentable) and inventions which concern plants or animals (which are). Further, the distinction between invention and discovery is unfortunately insufficiently clarified. As regards its ethical provisions, the Directive is innovative. Although EC Directive No. 98/44 had to be implemented by 30 July 2000, Belgium has not yet done so.

§2. Susceptible of industrial application

2258. An invention is considered to be susceptible of industrial application if it can be made or used in any kind of industry, including agriculture (Art. 7, para. 1 of the Patent Law). Methods for treatment of the human or animal body by surgery or therapy as well as diagnostic methods are not considered to be inventions susceptible of industrial application (Art. 7, para. 2 of the Patent Law). However, this exclusion does not apply to products for use in any of these methods.

§3. Novelty

2259. A new invention is an invention that does not form part of the state of the art (Art. 5, para. 1 of the Patent Law). The state of the art comprises everything made available to the public by means of a written or oral description, by use or in any other way before the date of filing of the patent application (Art. 5, para. 2 of the Patent Law). By contrast, the state of the art does not include any disclosure of an invention within a period of 6 months prior to the patent application which is the result of an evident abuse in relation to the applicant or which follows from the divulging of the invention at an official international exhibition (Art. 5, para. 5 of the Patent Law).

§4. Result of an inventive step

2260. An invention is considered to involve an inventive step if it is not obvious to a person skilled in the art when considering the state of the art (Art. 6 of the Patent Law).

§5. Not contrary to morality or public policy

2261. Inventions whose publication or exploitation would be contrary to morality or public policy, including inventions protecting human and/or animal health, as well as inventions protecting the environment, are not patentable (Art. 4, para. 2 of the Patent Law). However, the invention would not be considered unpatentable for the mere fact that its exploitation is prohibited by law or regulation (*Ibid.*).

2262. EC Directive No. 98/44 allows the patenting of biotechnological inventions, including processes for the modification of the genetic identity of plants or animals, unless these processes are likely to cause suffering without any substantial medical benefit to man or animal.

2263. Furthermore, the Biodiversity Convention concluded at United Nations level on 5 June 1992 in Rio de Janeiro and approved by Belgium also allows the patenting of biotechnological inventions, provided that the benefits arising out of the use of genetic resources are fairly shared, in particular through appropriate access to genetic resources and appropriate transfer of relevant technologies among the contracting States.

D. Procedural requirements

2264. The following paragraphs are limited to a discussion of the procedural aspects of an application for a Belgian patent. A patent application form must be submitted to the Department of Industrial Property of the Ministry of Economic Affairs by the applicant or by his duly authorised proxy or attorney-at-law (Art. 55 of the Patent Law). According to Article 15 of the Patent Law, the application should contain:
  (i) a request for the grant of a patent (*verzoek/requête*);
  (ii) a description of the invention (*beschrijving/description*) which must be sufficiently precise and complete so that a normally skilled professional can obtain the described result;
  (iii) one or more claims (*conclusies/revendications*) describing the new technical features for which patent protection is sought;
  (iv) any drawings referred to in the description or the claims; and
  (v) an abstract of the invention (*uittreksel/abrégé*).

2265. A patent application is subject to the payment of a filing fee.

2266. The application is officially recorded. The official record mentions the date and hour on which the application was lodged. The validity of the official record is not affected by the fact that specific documents attached to the application present deficiencies. These deficiencies can be cured within a regularisation period, subject to the payment of additional fees (Art. 20 of the Patent Law), provided that the initial application contains the following essential elements:
   (i) the request for the grant of a patent;
   (ii) data revealing the identity of the applicant; and
   (iii) a description of the invention as well as one or more claims (Art. 16, para. 1 of the Patent Law).

2267. Subject to the payment of an additional fee, the application is normally followed by a search which is carried out by the European Patent Office. The resulting report contains the relevant elements of the state of the art which should be considered in the assessment of the novelty of the invention and the existence of an inventive step (Art. 21 of the Patent Law).

2268. The search report has no decisive significance. Its purpose is limited to the supply of information. The search report does not authorise the competent authorities to deny the grant of a patent. This explains the wording of Article 22, paragraph 3 of the Patent Law which states that a patent is granted at the peril of the applicant and does not confer any guarantee on its owner as to its validity. It is therefore the exclusive task of the courts to apply and construe the Patent Law in relation to any dispute regarding the validity of a patent.

2269. In addition, a formal search is not even mandatory. The failure to carry out a search would result only in a reduced term of protection for the patent, that is, 6 years rather than 20 (Art. 39, para. 2 of the Patent Law).

2270. Patents are granted by Ministerial Decree (Art. 22, para. 1 of the Patent Law). The patent is registered and published in the Register of Patents (*Register der uitvindingsoctrooien/Registre des brevets d'invention*) and in the Collection of Patents (*Verzameling der uitvindingsoctrooien/Recueil des brevets d'invention*). The complete application file is also made available to the public. No publication will be made if the invention relates to state security or nuclear energy.

2271. When an EPC patent, which is delivered by the European Patent Office, includes Belgium among the countries covered by the patent and if the EPC patent concerned has not been presented in either French, Dutch or German, the applicant must submit to the Department of Industrial Property of the Ministry of Economic

Affairs a translation of the specification within 3 months as from the grant. Failing such translation, the patent concerned will be deemed not to produce any effect in Belgium (Art. 5 para. 2 of the Patent Law and Art. 6 of the Royal Decree of 27 February 1981).

E. Rights of the patent owner

2272. The patent owner has the exclusive right to exploit the invention. This implies also that the patent owner is entitled to sue any third party interfering with this exclusive right (Art. 27 of the Patent Law). Article 28 of the Patent Law provides for a number of exceptions to the exclusive right of the patent owner. Accordingly, an invention can be exploited legitimately by third parties if used for, *inter alia*, private non-commercial purposes, experimentation or preparations made on request and based on medical prescriptions. Furthermore, any third party who, in good faith, had the invention in his possession in Belgium before the date of patent application will enjoy the benefit of the "exception of prior use or personal possession" (Art. 30 of the Patent Law). He may continue to exploit the invention for his own personal use (*Ibid.*).

2273. The status of inventions made by employees is governed by the wording of the employment agreement rather than by the provisions of the Patent Law. It is generally accepted that the employer is entitled to the invention made in the course of employment by an employee hired to make inventions or carry out research in a given domain. Inventions of this kind are known as "inventions performed during professional duties" (*dienstuitvindingen/inventions de service*). Unless otherwise provided for in the employment contract, the employee is not entitled to additional remuneration for transferring the patent to his employer (Brussels Court of Appeal, 25 May 1994, *R.W.* 1996-1997, 888). There is, on the other hand, a consensus that inventions that were not made during working hours with the administrative and research facilities of the employer belong to the employee. Inventions of this form are known as "personal inventions" (*vrije uitvindingen/inventions personnelles*). Nevertheless, the Belgian courts are divided on the issue of inventions made with the employer's administrative and research facilities but not in the course of employment. These are the so-called "mixed inventions" (*afhankelijke uitvindingen/inventions dépendantes*). There seems to be a tendency to grant the right in such inventions to the employer (Labour Court of Ghent, 18 May 1987, *T.G.R.*, 1987-1988, 89).

F. Duration of patent protection

2274. The exclusive right of the patent owner becomes operative on the day the patent is made available to the public (Art. 24 of the Patent Law). The period of patent protection starts running on the date of the patent application and expires 20 years thereafter (Art. 39, para. 1 of the Patent Law). However, if no search is carried out, the patent protection expires after 6 years.

2275. The continued protection afforded by the patent is subject to the payment of a progressive annual fee from the third year after the patent application onwards (Art. 40 of the Patent Law). Failure to pay this fee results in forfeiture of the patent after 6 months following the anniversary of the date of patent application.

2276. A supplementary protection certificate extends the protection period up to a maximum of 5 years for medicinal products and plant production products (*i.e.*, for a period equal to the period which elapsed between the date on which the application for a basic patent was lodged and the date of the first authorisation to place the product on the market in the Community, reduced by a period of 5 years), provided that the product concerned is already covered by a basic patent and provided that a marketing authorisation has been granted by the relevant administrative authorities.

2277. A specific application form requesting the grant of the supplementary protection must be deposited with the Department of Industrial Property of the Ministry for Economic Affairs within 6 months as from the date of the first authorisation to place the product on the market in the Community. In case the patent owner and the holder of the aforementioned authorisation are two different persons, the supplementary protection certificate will not be granted to the patent owner if the holder cannot provide evidence of the marketing authorisation (ECJ, 23 January 1997, Case C-181/95, *Biogen Inc.* v. *Smithkline Beecham Biologicals S.A.*, judgement of 23 January 1997, [1997] ECR-I 357).

G. Assignments and licences

§1. Domestic law

2278. A patent can be assigned in whole or in part like any other asset of the patent owner. Such an assignment can result from the conclusion of a sales contract, an exchange contract, a voluntary settlement, *etc.* The assignment must be made in writing and requires registration with the Department of Industrial Property of the Ministry of Economic Affairs in order to be enforceable against third parties (Art. 44 of the Patent Law).

2279. Alternatively, a patent can be licensed in whole or in part. Licence agreements must also be in writing and their existence must likewise be reported to the Department of Industrial Property of the Ministry for Economic Affairs in order to be enforceable against third parties (Art. 45 of the Patent Law).

2280. Articles 31 through 38 of the Patent Law contain detailed provisions regarding compulsory licences. According to Article 31 of the Patent Law, the Minister for Economic Affairs may, under specific conditions, require a patent owner to grant a licence to a third party if an invention has not been sufficiently exploited in Belgium without valid reason, or if the exploitation of a technically important patent is dependent on the acquisition of a licence for another patent. The Patent Law succinctly describes the procedure that will lead to the grant of such a licence. Compulsory licences cannot be exclusive. They may be limited in time or restricted to a particular part of an invention. A compulsory licence cannot be transferred or sub-licensed unless combined with the part of the business that is used for the exploitation of that licence.

2281. A patent can also constitute a contribution to a company's assets. This contribution can take the form of either an assignment of the patent or a licence granted to the company. The patent can likewise be used as a pledge for a debt or be seized like any other asset owned by the patent owner.

§2. *Impact of EC law*

2282. Parties are free to determine the contents of their assignment or licensing agreement in accordance with the general rules of contract law. However, patent licensing agreements should be drafted with due regard to the principles of EC competition law contained in Articles 81 *et seq.* of the EC Treaty and in EC Commission Regulation No. 240/96 of 31 January 1996 on the Application of Article 81(3) of the EC Treaty to Certain Categories of Technology Transfer Agreements (the "Technology Transfer Block Exemption" or the "TTBE"; *See*, O.J. [1996] L 31/2). The TTBE covers certain patent licences and know-how licences. Patent licensing agreements listed in Article 1 of the TTBE are automatically exempted from the prohibition of Article 81(1) without prior notification to the EC Commission. Article 2 of this Regulation sets out a list of "white clauses", which are allowed in patent licensing agreements, as well as a list of "black clauses" which are subject to the general prohibition laid down in Article 81(1) of the EC Treaty. The EC Commission has started a review process of the TTBE. This process is expected to culminate in a new Regulation that is less formalistic and more in tune with economic reality.

2283. Article 82 of the EC Treaty prohibiting the abuse of a dominant position also applies to specific types of behaviour by patent owners. In the pharmaceutical sector, for instance, the EC Commission scrutinises whether or not the patent owners extend their monopoly right in an abusive manner in order to prevent potential newcomers from entering the market.

2284. As is the case for other intellectual property rights, the European Court of Justice has established rules concerning the "Community-wide exhaustion doctrine" which significantly affects the possibilities for the owner of a Belgian patent to stop the import of goods protected by that patent. Under the exhaustion doctrine, the patent owner cannot prevent the use of a potential invention within the European Union territory, once he has marketed the concerned patented invention in any of the EC Member States (ECJ, 31 October 1974, Case 15/74, *Centrafarm B.V. et alii* v. *Sterling Drug Inc.* [1974] ECR 1147). The exhaustion rule only applies if the product was put on the market of any EC Member State by the patent owner or with his consent (ECJ, 5 December 1996, Joined Cases C-267/95 and C-268/95, *Merck & Co. and Others* v. *Primecrown Ltd. and Others* and *Beecham Group plc.* v. *Europharm of Worthing Ltd.*, [1996] ECR 6285). In contrast, the exhaustion doctrine does not apply to products that were manufactured in another EC Member State by the holder of a compulsory licence granted in respect of a parallel patent held by the same proprietor (ECJ, 9 July 1985, Case 19/84, *Pharmon* v. *Hoechst* [1985] ECR 2281). Likewise, a patent owner can enforce his patent right against the import of infringing products first marketed without his consent in another Member State where patent protection was not available (ECJ, 30 June 1988, Case 35/87, *Thetford Corporation and Another* v. *Fiamma SpA and Others* [1988] ECR 3585).

H. International protection

2285. The body of patent law which governs the acquisition, existence and exercise of patent rights in Belgium results from the combined application of the Patent Law and a number of international conventions. A brief discussion of the impact in Belgium of the major international conventions is contained in paragraphs 2243 *et seq.*

I. Infringements and remedies

§1. Civil remedies

2286. All claims based on patent infringement (*inbreukvordering/action en contrefaçon*) should be brought before the Court of First Instance (*Rechtbank van Eerste Aanleg/*

Tribunal de Première Instance) attached to the Court of Appeal which has jurisdiction over the place where the counterfeiting act took place or over the place of residence of the defendant, irrespective of the amount at stake (Art. 73, para. 1 and 2 of the Patent Law). These rules do not preclude the possibility of submitting disputes involving patents to arbitration (Art. 73, para. 6 of the Patent Law). Nonetheless, the claims listed in Article 73, paragraph 5 must be exclusively brought before the Court of First Instance that has jurisdiction over the place of residence of the defendant.

2287. Acts of counterfeiting are detailed in Article 27 of the Patent Law.

2288. The limitation period for an infringement action against the counterfeiter is 5 years as from the day on which the infringement took place.

2289. Counterfeiting acts may result in a cease-and-desist order, an award of damages, a publication of the judgment awarding the damages and a confiscation of counterfeit goods as well as any tools used to produce the counterfeit goods (Arts. 52 and 53 of the Patent Law).

2290. The patent owner may also issue a writ of summons in summary proceedings based on patent infringement in order to obtain an injunction before the President of the Court of First Instance. The judge will be requested to evaluate the evidence on a *prima facie*-basis and issue a cease-and-desist order against the infringer as regards the production, use, exhibition and commercialisation of all infringing materials. In principle, such a judgement is provisional in nature until the final judgement on the merits of the case has been rendered by the Court of First Instance.

2291. Furthermore, Arts. 1481 through 1488 of the Judicial Code contain a specific procedure (*beslag inzake namaak/saisie-description*) allowing the patent owner to obtain an inventory of the relevant items located in the premises where the alleged acts of counterfeiting took place and to seize specific goods in such premises.

2292. In derogation of the principle of the territoriality of patent protection, the Belgian Supreme Court has allowed, on the basis of Article 24 of the Brussels Convention on Jurisdiction and the Enforcement of Judgements in Civil and Commercial Matters (the "1968 Brussels Convention" – now: Art. 31 of the EC Regulation No. 44/2001 of 22 December 2000 on Jurisdiction and the Recognition and Enforcement of Judgements in Civil and Commercial Matters – the "Brussels Regulation"), the owner of a foreign patent to initiate the specific procedure described above before a Belgian Court (Cass., 3 March 1999, *R.D.C.*, 2000, 128).

2293. Finally, with respect to cross-border injunctions, recent case law in "Belgian torpedo matters" indicates that cross-border jurisdiction for declaratory claims of non-infringement will be accepted by the Belgian Courts only in very precise and narrow circumstances (Brussels Court of Appeal, 20 February 2001, *I.R.D.I.*, 2001, 168). The so-called "torpedo" tactic consists of the attempt by a plaintiff, who fears being sued for patent infringement in an EC Member State where proceedings are known to proceed swiftly, *e.g.*, in the Netherlands, to seize a (purportedly slow-moving) Belgian Court in order to obtain a declaration of non-infringement applying in Belgium and abroad. Articles 21 and 22 of the 1968 Brussels Convention (now Arts. 27 and 28 of the Brussels Regulation) require that a later seized court stay its proceedings in favour of an earlier seized court. In other words, the plaintiff seizes the Belgian Court, thereby speculating on the lengthy character of the proceedings, in an attempt to block a possible infringement action in another EC Member State until a judgement is handed down by the Belgian Court. The Belgian Courts have labeled such actions as abusive on several occasions, which has caused the "torpedo"-action to lose its attractiveness to *male fide*-plaintiffs.

§2. Criminal sanctions

2294. The Patent Law does not provide for any criminal sanctions.

IV. DESIGNS AND MODELS

A. Applicable law

2295. The primary source of legislation in relation to designs and models is the Uniform Benelux Law of 25 October 1966 regarding Designs or Models (*Eenvormige Beneluxwet inzake tekeningen of modellen/Loi uniforme Benelux en matiere de dessins ou modèles* – the "Designs and Models Law"). The Designs and Models Law entered into force on 1 January 1975 and was the result of the Benelux Treaty that was signed in Brussels on 25 October 1966. For purposes of the Designs and Models Law, the territories of Belgium, the Netherlands and Luxembourg constitute a single jurisdiction.

2296. Of continued relevance is the previous system of protection of industrial designs and models established by Royal Decree No. 91 of 29 January 1935. Rights acquired in Belgium under this Royal Decree (the "Old Design Rights") remain, under certain conditions, valid after the entry into force of the Design and Models Law (Arts. 25 and 26 of the Designs and Models Law).

2297. The Benelux countries are signatories of the Hague Agreement concerning the International Deposit of Industrial Designs of 28 November 1960 (which entered into force on 1 August 1984 – the "Hague Agreement"). The Benelux countries further adopted the Paris Industrial Property Convention of 1883 (the "Paris Convention") (1967, Stockholm version).

2298. In addition to the protection afforded by these rules, designs and models may also qualify for copyright protection (Art. 21 of the Designs and Models Law – *See*, Chapter 12, III, C).

2299. The Belgian legal framework regarding designs and models is completed by a number of Royal Decrees pertaining to, among other things, the so-called "confirmatory registration" required for Old Design Rights by Article 26 of the Designs and Models Law (Royal Decree of 27 December 1974) and various regulations implementing the Designs and Models Law (Royal Decrees of 28 April 1989 and 31 May 1989).

2300. On 13 October 1998, the European Parliament and the Council adopted Directive No. 98/71/EC on the Legal Protection of Designs (O.J. [1998] L 289/28 – the "Design Directive"). The implementation of the Design Directive should have been completed by 28 October 2001 and requires substantive changes to the Designs and Models Law.

2301. On 22 December 1994, the EC Council adopted Regulation No. 3295/94 laying down Measures to Prohibit the Release for Free Circulation, Export, Re-export Or Entry for a Suspensive Procedure of Counterfeit and Pirated Goods ("Regulation No. 3295/94 " – O.J. [1994] L 341/8). This Regulation was amended by Regulation No. 241/1999 of 25 January 1999 ("Regulation No. 241/1999" – O.J. [1999] L 27/1).

B. Definition

2302. The right in a design (*tekening/dessin*) or model (*model/modèle*) is temporary and exclusive, pertaining to the new appearance (*nieuw uiterlijk/aspect nouveau*) of a product with a utilitarian function.

C. Substantive requirements

2303. Four conditions must be satisfied in order to qualify for protection under the Designs and Models Law:
    (i) there must be an appearance;
    (ii) the appearance must be new;
    (iii) it must pertain to a product with a utilitarian function; and
    (iv) it must be in a permissible form.

§1. Appearance

2304. The Designs and Models Law does not define the term "appearance" but it excludes in Article 2(1) any feature that is indispensable to obtaining a technical result. According to the Benelux Law, only the appearance of a product in a materialised form, and not an underlying principle, theory or system, is eligible for protection.

§2. Novelty

2305. According to Article 4(1) of the Designs and Models Law, a design or model lacks novelty if:
   (i) at any time during the 50 years preceding the date of registration (or the date of priority under the Paris Convention), a product identical in appearance to the design or model, or differing only in minor respects, is *de facto* known in the relevant industrial or commercial circles in the Benelux territory. In this respect it is not necessary for the design or model to be known in the entire Benelux territory. However, according to Article 4*bis* of the Designs and Models Law, this is not the case when creation by the depositor or by a third party that gained knowledge of the creation directly or indirectly from the depositor within 12 months preceding the date of registration (or the date of priority under the Paris Convention) is *de facto* known due to publication of this creation. This is an important exception because it provides for a 1-year test period during which a designer has the opportunity to test the success of a design or model. Afterwards the designer can decide whether the design or model was successful enough to be protected from counterfeiting as a registered design. This could be particularly important to fashion designers;
   (ii) an identical design or model, or a design or model differing only in minor respects, has been the subject of a registration followed by a publication.

§3. A product with a utilitarian function

2306. The requirement that the product should have a utilitarian function implies that products with an exclusively ornamental value will not qualify for protection under the Designs and Models Law.

§4. Permissible form

2307. The appearance should not be contrary to morality or public policy.

2308. According to Article 21(1) of the Designs and Models Law, designs or models with a markedly artistic character (*duidelijk kunstzinnig karakter/caractère artistique marqué*) may simultaneously qualify for protection under the Designs and Models Law and the Copyright Law, provided that the conditions for the application of both laws are satisfied. Designs or models without a markedly artistic character are excluded from copyright protection (Art. 21(2) of the Designs and Models Law). In an important 1987 judgment, the Benelux Court of Justice held that the phrase "markedly artistic character" does not require the design to have a specific artistic value. The Benelux Court of Justice added that these words simply reiterate the general requirement of copyright protection, namely that the design should present a form of originality marked by the personality of the author (Benelux Court of Justice, *Screenoprints/Citroën Nederland*, 22 May 1987, Jur., 1987, 13).

2309. Designs or models can also enjoy protection under trademark law provided the design or model serves to distinguish goods or services (Art. 1 of the Uniform Benelux Law regarding Trademarks of 30 June 1969; *See*, paras. 2355 *et seq.*). This was confirmed by the Brussels Commercial Court which decided that the only requirement for a design or model to benefit from trademark protection is that it must allow the public concerned to recognise that a certain good originates from a particular company (*Comm. Brussels*, 25 October 1996, *Ing. Cons.* 1996, 409).

D. Procedural requirements

2310. A right to a Benelux design or model is acquired by the registration of the design or model with the Benelux Designs and Models Office in The Hague or in Brussels with the Belgian Ministry of Economic Affairs (Department of Industrial Property). A third possibility consists of filing an international registration under the Hague Agreement with the International Office for the Protection of Industrial Property in Geneva.

2311. A Benelux registration file should contain the identity of the applicant, a photographic or graphic image of the product and an indication as to the type of product in which the "appearance" will be incorporated. The implementing regulations contained in the Royal Decree of 31 May 1989 (Art. 1(6)) specify that, for purposes of product description, it is preferable to use the terminology of the alphabetical list of the international classification established by the Locarno Agreement of 8 October 1968. In addition, the registration file should contain the means of reproduction with which the image pertaining to the appearance was made, *e.g.*, photographs. It is possible to include a claim regarding the colours of the design. The file may also contain a description of the characteristic features of the design.

One registration may pertain to a maximum of 50 designs or models. The registration and ensuing publication of a design are subject to the payment of fees.

2312. The registration does not give rise to an examination of the contents of the design by the registration authorities (Art. 9(1) of the Designs and Models Law). It is the exclusive task of the courts to apply and construe the Benelux Law in relation to any dispute regarding the validity of a design.

E. Rights of the design owner

2313. A model or design created by an employee in the course of his employment shall be considered to be the creation of his employer, unless the employment agreement provides otherwise (Art. 6(1) of the Designs and Models Law). Similarly, a design or model created under a contract for services will be considered to be created by the party who commissioned the design or model, unless the contract provides otherwise and provided the product incorporating the design or model is intended to be put to commercial or industrial use (Art. 6(2) of the Designs and Models Law).

2314. Pursuant to Article 14(1) of the Designs and Models Law, the owner of the exclusive right in a design or model is entitled to prevent a number of acts from being performed for commercial purposes with respect to products which are identical in appearance with the design or model, or which differ only in minor respects. The acts that can be prevented are listed in Article 14(1) of the Designs and Models Law, namely the manufacturing, importation, exportation, sale, offering for sale, renting, offering for rent, exhibition, supply and use of the infringing product as well as the stocking of infringing products with the intent of committing any of these acts.

2315. Article 17 of the Designs and Models Law provides for an exception to the exclusive right of the owner of a registered design or model by recognising a right of prior use for a party who created products identical in appearance to the registered design or model or differing only in minor respects prior to the date of registration of that design or model.

F. Duration of design protection

2316. The registration of a Benelux design or model is valid for 5 years. Subject to the payment of the appropriate fees, two extensions of 5 years each can be obtained, leading to a total maximum period of protection of 15 years (Art. 12 of the Designs and Models Law).

G. Assignments and licences

§1. Domestic law

2317. A design or model can be assigned, provided that the assignment agreement is in writing and pertains to the entire Benelux territory (Art. 13(1) of the Designs and Models Law). Non-compliance with either of these requirements nullifies the agreement. Moreover, the pertinent part of the agreement, or a declaration signed by the contracting parties which evidences the assignment, should be registered in order to make the assignment enforceable as against third parties.

2318. A design or model can also be licensed. Parties are free to determine the contents of their licensing agreement. However, according to Article 13(2) of the Designs and Models Law, any restriction with regard to the licence other than a restriction regarding its term will not have any effect under the Designs and Models Law. It follows that, for example, the imposition of territorial restrictions on a licensee that would carve out a part of the Benelux territory will not be operative under the Designs and Models Law. Leaving aside EC or national competition law considerations, it would nonetheless be possible for a licensor to bring an action against his licensee for breach of contract if the licensee did not comply with the territorial restrictions contained in the licensing agreement.

2319. A licensing agreement also requires registration in order to be enforceable against third parties.

§2. Impact of EC law

2320. There is no precedent under EC competition law for the assessment of design right licensing agreements. However, it would seem that some of the principles that govern copyright licences may also apply to design right licences. In addition, it is clear that the owner of a registered design may block the importation of products identical in appearance to the registered design without infringing Arts. 28 and 30 of the EC Treaty provided that:
   (i) the products at issue were not marketed with the consent of the owner of the registered design himself, or a licensee or affiliate;
   (ii) there are no anti-competitive agreements among the parties; and
   (iii) the respective design rights that were acquired in various EC Member States by different persons originated independently of one another (ECJ, 14 September 1982, Case 144/81, *Keurkoop B.V.* v. *Nancy Kean Gifts B.V.*, [1982] ECR 2853 involving a design for ladies' handbags registered under the Designs and Models Law).

H. International protection

2321. The Paris Convention ensures the free access of nationals or residents of other member countries to the Benelux system for the protection of designs and models. These parties receive national treatment for their registrations (Arts. 2 and 3 of the Paris Convention) and benefit from a priority right of 6 months to pursue a Benelux application after having registered a design in another member country (Art. 4(c) 1 of the Paris Convention).

2322. An international design registration made abroad under the Hague Agreement will have the same effect as a Benelux registration if the Benelux countries were identified in the application as a territory where protection is sought (Art. 7 of the Hague Agreement).

I. Infringements and remedies

2323. In Belgium, all claims involving design rights should be brought before the Court of First Instance *(Rechtbank van Eerste Aanleg/Tribunal de Première Instance)* (Art. 568 of the Judicial Code), even if the dispute arises between commercial parties (Art. 16 of the Designs and Models Law), provided the value of the claim exceeds € 1,860 (Art. 590 of the Judicial Code). Claims of less than € 1,860 are handled by the Justice of the Peace *(Vredegerecht/Justice de paix)*.

2324. According to Article 29 of the Designs and Models Law, parties may freely agree on the court in which a dispute involving a registered design or model will be heard. In the absence of a contractual arrangement, an action may be initiated before the court with jurisdiction over the place where the defendant resides, or with jurisdiction over the place where the obligation at issue arose, was performed or was due to be performed. If these rules are not sufficient to determine a territorially competent court, the action may be brought before the court with jurisdiction over the place of residence of the plaintiff or, if the plaintiff does not have a place of residence in a Benelux country, before the Court of First Instance of either Brussels, Luxembourg or The Hague.

2325. The Designs and Models Law does not provide for any penalties for infringements of registered design or model rights. According to the general rules contained in the Judicial Code, the court may issue a cease-and-desist order, award damages and impose a periodic penalty payment. It would also appear that a court may order the destruction of infringing products and of the tools used to make the infringing products.

2326. Damages can only be obtained as of the date of publication of the characteristic features of the registered design, unless the infringing party knew that the design or model had been registered (Art. 14(3) of the Designs and Models Law).

2327. As noted, on 22 December 1994 the EC Council adopted Regulation No. 3295/94 laying down measures to prohibit the release for free circulation, export, re-export or entry for a suspensive procedure of counterfeit and pirated goods. This Regulation was amended by Regulation No. 241/1999 of 25 January 1999.

2328. The purpose of Regulation No. 3295/94 is to prevent, to the extent possible, the placing on the market in the Community of counterfeit goods imported from third countries and to prevent the exportation and re-exportation of these goods from the Community. To this end, Regulation No. 3295/94 empowers the customs authorities of the EC Member States to intervene either at the request of the trademark owner or, in certain cases, at their own initiative. The customs authorities can block the goods during a limited period of time, allowing the trademark owner to enforce his rights in court. Regulation No. 241/1999 introduced a centralised procedure allowing the owners of Community trademarks to request intervention by the relevant authorities. Consequently, owners of Community trademarks do not have to address a request for intervention to the customs authorities of every EC Member State.

2329. In conjunction with or instead of the action for damages, the owner of the exclusive right can bring an action for payment of profits made following the performance of one of the prohibited acts listed in Article 14(1) of the Designs and Models Law.

2330. Article 14*bis* of the Designs and Models Law grants the holder of the exclusive right the competence to remove counterfeit products from circulation or to demand their destruction in case of counterfeiting in bad faith. The owner of the exclusive right can also demand that the infringing person reveal all information about the origin of the counterfeit products. This action is only possible if the infringement has been established by a court.

2331. The Designs and Models Law does not contain criminal sanctions, but if the design or model has a markedly artistic character (*See*, paras. 2303 *et seq.*), the criminal sanctions of the Copyright Law may apply.

2332. Any questions relating to the interpretation of the Designs and Models Law may be submitted by a national court to the Benelux Court of Justice *(Benelux Gerechtshof/Cour de Justice Bénélux)* for a preliminary ruling.

J. Impact of EC law

2333. Both the licensing and exercise of design rights may be influenced by the rules of EC law governing competition (Arts. 81 and 82 of the EC Treaty) and the free movement of goods (Arts. 28 to 30 of the EC Treaty) (*See*, para. 2320).

2334. As noted, the European Parliament and the EC Council adopted on 13 October 1998 the Design Directive. The 2 main aspects of the Design Directive are: first, a process of limited harmonisation of design laws in Member States; second, the creation of a unitary definition of the requirements with which a registered design right must comply. As will be explained below, implementation of the Design Directive requires substantive changes to the Designs and Models Law as it presently stands. In addition, the Regulation on Community Design will be briefly discussed.

§1. The Design Directive

1. Scope

2335. The Design Directive applies only to registered designs. Article 1 of the Design Directive defines a design as *"the appearance of the whole or part of a product resulting from the features of, in particular, the lines, contours, colours, shape, texture and/or materials of the product itself and/or its ornamentation."*

2336. The Design Directive provides a broad definition of a "product" without referring to a utilitarian function. Thus, purely decorative models can also enjoy protection. Another difference compared to the Benelux law is that, pursuant to the Design Directive, one deposit suffices to protect products with different purposes of use. The scope of protection of the Design Directive is therefore broader than that of the Designs and Models Law because a single deposit is valid for different uses.

2. Novelty

2337. According to Article 3 of the Design Directive, designs must be new and have individual character. Parts of complex products can only be considered to have a new and individual character if these parts remain visible during the normal use of the complex product and if the visual features themselves are new and have individual character. This is intended to exclude "under the bonnet" spare parts from protection. "Normal use" is understood to be use by the end user and not by a person maintaining, repairing or servicing the complex product.

2338. The novelty of a design is judged by whether an identical design has been made available to the public before the date of filing the application for registration or, if priority is claimed, the date of priority. Designs are considered to be identical if their features differ only in immaterial details (Art. 4(1) of the Design Directive).

3. Individual character

2339. According to Article 5 of the Design Directive, a design is considered to have individual character if the overall impression that it gives informed users is different from the overall impression created by a design that was made available to the public before the date of filing (or priority date). The degree of design freedom must be considered in assessing whether the design has an individual character. Recital 13 of the Design Directive states that this assessment should be based on whether the overall impression on an informed user viewing the design clearly differs from the impression that the design corpus gives him, taking into consideration the nature of the product to which the design is applied or in which it is incorporated, and, in particular, the industrial sector to which it belongs and the degree of freedom of the designer in developing the design. The Designs and Models Law does not contain this requirement of an individual character, which is a subjective criterion.

2340. The requirement that a design must have "individual character" under the Design Directive closely resembles the requirement of originality required under copyright law. Indeed, if a design or model meets the individual character requirement, it will also qualify for copyright protection. Therefore, the combined protection of design and copyright will, in principle, always be possible (Art. 17 of the Design Directive). However, such combined protection seems inconsistent with the current wording of Article 21 of the Designs and Models Law, which limits the protection to models with a markedly artistic character. The wording of the Design Directive confirms the Benelux Court's *Screenoprints* judgement of 22 May 1987, referred to above, in the sense that the criterion of "markedly artistic character" of the Designs and Models Law should be interpreted as meaning that the design should have "individual character".

4. Publicly available

2341. Article 6(1) of the Design Directive stipulates that a design is deemed to have been made available to the public if it has been published, exhibited, used in trade or otherwise disclosed. The provision identifies 2 exceptions to this rule. First, the rule would not apply in cases where the design could not reasonably have become known in the normal course of business in the sector concerned. The second exception is where the disclosure to a third person was done under conditions of confidentiality.

5. *Exceptions*

2342. Article 7 of the Design Directive states that a design right shall not be granted to features of appearance that are solely dictated by its technical function. Designs contrary to public policy or accepted principles of morality are also excluded from the scope of the Design Directive (Art. 8 of the Design Directive).

2343. The protection offered by the Design Directive extends to any design which does not make a different overall impression on the informed user, again taking design freedom into consideration (Art. 9 of the Design Directive).

2344. Article 11 of the Design Directive exhaustively lists cases in which a design cannot be registered or, if registered, may be declared invalid. This occurs when:
 (i) the design does not fall within the definition of design;
 (ii) the design is not new or does not have an individual character;
 (iii) the design relates to technical functions or interconnecting features;
 (iv) the design is contrary to public policy or accepted principles of morality;
 (v) the applicant or holder is not entitled to the design under the law of the EC Member State; or
 (vi) where the design conflicts with an existing design.

2345. The protection offered by the Design Directive does not extend to products put on the market by the holder of the registered design or with his consent (Art. 15 of the Design Directive).

6. *Use*

2346. The holder of a registered design will have the exclusive right to use it and to prevent any third party from copying or using it. Use covers, in particular, the making, offering, putting on the market, importing, exporting or use of a product in which such a design is incorporated or to which it is applied, or importing, exporting or stocking such a product for those purposes (Art. 12 of the Design Directive).

2347. According to Article 13 of the Design Directive, a design right is deemed not to be infringed in the case of:
 (i) acts done for private and non-commercial purposes;
 (ii) acts done for experimental purposes;
 (iii) reproduction for quotation or teaching purposes (provided this is compatible with fair trade practice and does not unduly prejudice the normal exploitation of the design); or

(iv) equipment on ships and aircraft that are temporarily in the EC Member State, but registered in another country, as well as the importation of spare parts and accessories for repairing such craft.

2348. The transitional provision in Article 14 of the Design Directive states that, as regards the use of the design of a component part used for the purpose of the repair of a complex product to restore the original appearance, national law remains in force until amendments to the Design Directive have been adopted. The EC Commission can propose amendments to the Design Directive until 28 October 2005.

2349. Pursuant to Article 10 of the Design Directive, initial registration will offer protection for one or more periods of 5 years. This period is renewable in 5-year periods up to a maximum of 25 years.

7. National law

2350. The implementation of the Design Directive in the EC Member States' national law was due by 28 October 2001 (Art. 19 of the Design Directive). The Benelux countries currently anticipate implementing the Design Directive in the Designs and Models Law by the end of 2003.

§2. Community Design Regulation

2351. On 12 December 2001, the EC's Council of Ministers adopted Regulation No. 6/ 2002 introducing a single Community system for the protection of designs. Pursuant to this Regulation, designs can be registered with the EC's Office for Harmonisation in the Internal Market in Alicante, Spain. The Community system will exist in parallel with national systems in the EC Member States, and companies can continue registering designs under national law.

2352. The Regulation provides for two types of design protection, directly applicable in each EC Member State: the Registered Community Design and the Unregistered Community Design. Both designs are only eligible for protection if they are new and have an individual character.

2353. Holders of a Registered Community Design will be granted exclusive rights to use the design concerned and to prevent any third party from using the design in the European Union for a period of maximum 25 years in successive 5-years periods. The Unregistered Community Design right will last for 3 years beginning on the date on which products incorporating the design or based on the design were first made available to the public.

2354. On 21 October 2002, the EC Commission adopted a Regulation implementing the above-mentioned Regulation No. 6/2002. This Regulation allows the office in

Alicante to begin registering Community Designs. Applications for registration will be considered by the office in Alicante as from 1 April 2003, but actual filings can already be made as from 1 January 2003.

V. TRADEMARKS

A. Applicable law

2355. By Law of 30 June 1969 Belgium adopted the Uniform Benelux Law regarding Trademarks (*Eenvormige Beneluxwet op de merken/Loi uniforme Bénélux sur les marques* – the "Trademark Law") annexed to the Benelux Treaty regarding Trademarks of 19 March 1962 (the "Benelux Treaty"). The Trademark Law entered into force on 1 January 1971. The Benelux Treaty and the Trademark Law originally applied only to products and not to services. By a separate Protocol of 10 November 1983, which entered into force in Belgium on 1 January 1987, a chapter dealing with service marks was added to the Trademark Law (Arts. 39 and following of the Trademark Law). For the purposes of the Trademark Law, the territories of Belgium, the Netherlands and Luxembourg constitute one territory. The old Belgian Law regarding Industrial and Commercial Marks of 1 April 1879 (the "Old Trademark Law") is still applicable as regards its criminal provisions (Arts. 8 to 15).

2356. The Benelux countries have adopted the Paris Industrial Property Convention of 1883 (the "Paris Convention") (1967, Stockholm version). They are also members of the Madrid Agreement concerning the International Registration of Marks (1967, Stockholm version) (the "Madrid Agreement") and the Nice Agreement concerning the International Classification of Goods and Services for the Purposes of the Registration of Marks (1977, Geneva version).

B. Definition

2357. A trademark right is a temporary and exclusive right to distinguish products or services by using a specific sign. An individual trademark identifies one or more characteristics that are common to products or services of a single business. A collective trademark identifies one or more characteristics that are common to products or services of different businesses.

2358. A trademark may consist of words (including personal names), designs, single colours, colour combinations, stamps, letters, numerals, the shape of a good or its packaging, or a combination of some of these elements. In general, a trademark is a sign which is capable of distinguishing the goods or services of one company from those of another (Art. 1 of the Trademark Law).

2359. Excluded from trademark protection are shapes which result from the nature of the goods themselves, shapes which give substantial value to the goods, and shapes which are necessary to obtain a technical result (Art. 1 of the Trademark Law).

C. Substantive requirements

2360. A sign may benefit from protection under the Trademark Law if it is distinctive and new. In addition, it should not be registered in bad faith, should not be contrary to morality or public policy and its use should not induce the public into error. These requirements are discussed below.

§1. Distinctiveness

2361. In the *Baby-Dry*-case (ECJ, 20 September 2001, Case C-383/99 P, *Procter & Gamble Company* v. *OHIM*, [2001] ECR I-6251), the European Court of Justice cast new light on the requirement of distinctiveness by annulling the judgment of the European Court of First Instance of 8 July 1999 which had upheld the decision of the First Board of Appeal of the Office for Harmonisation in the Internal Market ("OHIM") of 31 July 1998 refusing to register "Baby-Dry" as a Community trademark for babies' nappies. (CFI, 8 July 1999, Case T-163/98, *Procter & Gamble Company* v. *OHIM*, [1999] ECR II-2383).

2362. The European Court of Justice held that the OHIM and the European Court of First Instance had interpreted the absolute grounds for refusal to register a sign as Community trademark, contained in Art. 7(1)(b) and (c) of the Community Trade Mark Regulation (the "CTM Regulation"), too broadly. The Court explained that the purely descriptive signs referred to in Art. 7(1)(c) of the CTM Regulation are only those which may serve in normal usage, from a consumer's point of view, to designate, either directly or by reference to one of their essential characteristics, goods or services such as those in respect of which registration is sought.

2363. As regards trademarks composed of words, such as "Baby-Dry", the European Court of Justice explained that descriptiveness must not only be determined in relation to each word taken separately, but also in relation to the combination which they form.

2364. In applying this test, the European Court held that each of the two words in the combination "Baby-Dry" may form part of expressions used in everyday speech to designate the function of babies' nappies. The European Court of Justice added, however, that their syntactically unusual juxtaposition is not a familiar expression in the English language, either for designating babies' nappies or for describing their essential characteristics. The European Court of Justice concluded that word combinations like "Baby-Dry" cannot be regarded as exhibiting a descriptive character as a whole.

2365. Although the European Court of Justice in the *Baby-Dry* case apparently broadened the scope of trademarks that can be considered to have a descriptive character, it set limits to the registration of combinations of descriptive words, in a more recent judgment.

2366. In the *Companyline* case (ECJ, 19 September 2002, Case C-104/00 P, *DKV Deutsche Krankenversicherung AG* v. *OHIM, not yet published*), the European Court of Justice concluded that the term "Companyline" lacks distinctive character. In the view of the European Court of Justice, word combinations, such as "company line", which consist exclusively of 2 words that are customary in English-speaking countries, cannot be protected.

2367. It would appear that the European Court of Justice distinguished the *Companyline* case from the *Baby-Dry* case, since the latter was considered to have a distinctive character on the basis of the unusual combination of the words "baby" and "dry", while the coupling of the words "company" and "line" does not confer an additional characteristic on them.

§2. Novelty

2368. A trademark will be considered to be new unless there has been a prior use of an identical or substantially similar sign with regard to identical or similar goods or services.

2369. The novelty of a trademark will, in principle, be judged in relation to identical or similar goods or services. A 1975 judgement of the Benelux Court of Justice appeared to suggest that trademarks with a certain renown could block the use of an identical or similar sign in other sectors of the economy. However, the Benelux Court of Justice indicated that this would be the case where the use of the competing sign in another sector of the economy would prevent the first trademark from continuing to create, in the minds of potential customers, an instant association with the goods or services for which the trademark was registered and used (Benelux Court of Justice, 1 March 1975, *Colgate-Palmolive* v. *Distilleerderijen K Bols* ("*Klarein/Claeryn*"), *R.W.*, 1974-1975, 2059). However, the Court's decision was overruled by the European Court of Justice in the *Sabel* case (ECJ, 11 November 1997, Case C-251/95, *Sabel B.V.* v. *Puma A.G., Rudolf Dassler Sport*, [1997] ECR I-6191), which will be discussed below.

2370. Prior use that will prevent a trademark from being new may consist of:

    (i) an earlier registration of an identical trademark for identical goods or services that has not yet expired (Art. 3(2)(a) of the Trademark Law);

    (ii) an earlier registration of an identical or similar trademark for identical or similar goods or services that has not yet expired, if there exists a likelihood of association with the earlier sign on the part of the public (Art. 3(2)(b) of the Trademark Law);

However, in its *Sabel* decision, the European Court of Justice found this provision to be inconsistent with Article 4(1)(b) of the Trademark Directive, which contains the criterion of "*a likelihood of confusion, including a likelihood of association*". The European Court of Justice held this criterion to be stricter than the requirement of a mere likelihood of association provided for by the Trademark Law. It was held that a mere association which the public might make between two trademarks as a result of their analogous semantic content is not, *per se*, a sufficient ground for concluding that there is a likelihood of confusion within the meaning of the Trademark Directive. The decision confirmed that the likelihood of association does not provide an alternative, but merely a possible element of the likelihood of confusion. In the view of the European Court of Justice, Article 4(1)(b) of the Trademark Directive cannot be applied where there is no likelihood of confusion on the part of the public. The likelihood of confusion must be assessed "globally", taking into account all factors relevant to the circumstances of each case. The "global appreciation" of the visual, aural and conceptual similarity of the trademarks has to be based on the overall impression given by the trademarks, bearing in mind any distinctive and dominant components.

In the opinion of the European Court of Justice, the likelihood of confusion covers 2 possible situations. In the first case, the public confuses the trademarks and believes that the goods or services concerned are coming from the same company ("likelihood of direct confusion"). In the second case, the public establishes a link between the owners of the trademarks and believes that the goods or services concerned are coming from economically linked companies ("likelihood of indirect confusion"). A mere association does not suffice. The Trademark Law will therefore have to be interpreted in accordance with the precepts of the European Court of Justice.

The European Court of Justice later confirmed the *Sabel* decision in *Canon Kabushiki Kaisha* v. *Metro-Goldwyn-Mayer Inc.* (ECJ, 29 September 1998,

Case C-39/97, [1998] ECR I-5507) and *Marca Mode C.V.* v. *Adidas A.G. and Adidas Benelux B.V.* (ECJ, 22 June 2000, Case C-425/98, [2000] ECR I-4861);

(iii) an earlier registration of a similar trademark for dissimilar goods or services that has not yet expired, if, or to the extent that, the earlier trademark is widely known in the Benelux territory and the use of the later sign without due cause would take unfair advantage of, or be detrimental to, the distinctive character or the reputation of the earlier trademark (Art. 3(2)(c) of the Trademark Law);

(iv) an earlier registration by a third party of an identical trademark for similar goods or services that expired within a period of 2 years prior to the registration of the new trademark, unless the third party had given its consent or the expiry was the result of non-use of the earlier trademark (Art. 4(4) of the Trademark Law);

(v) under specific circumstances, an earlier use of a generally known sign that was never registered (Art. 6*bis* of the Paris Convention); or

(vi) prior use abroad of a generally known sign that is owned by a third party (Art. 6*bis*, Paris Convention and Art. 4(5) of the Trademark Law).

§3. No registration in bad faith

2371. According to Article 4(6) of the Trademark Law, the registration of a trademark in bad faith does not create a trademark right.

§4. No contradiction with morality or public policy

2372. Article 4(1) of the Trademark Law stipulates that the registration of a trademark that is contrary to morality or public policy in one of the Benelux countries does not create a trademark right.

§5. No deceptive link

2373. Article 4(2) of the Trademark Law prohibits the registration of a trademark for goods or services where the use of the trademark could induce the public into error.

D. Procedural requirements

2374. A Benelux trademark is acquired by registration of the sign with the Benelux Trademark Office in The Hague or with the Belgian Ministry for Economic Affairs (Department of Industrial Property) in Brussels. A third possibility consists of filing an international registration under the Madrid Agreement with the International Bureau of the World Intellectual Property Organisation ("WIPO") in Geneva.

However, such an international registration requires that the applicant has already obtained a registration in one of the member countries of the Madrid Agreement.

2375. A current proposal, which is anticipated to become effective in the beginning of 2004, aims to include a new Article 6*quater* in the Trademark Law. Art. 6*quater* will grant a right of opposition to the holder of an existing trademark or to the applicant of a new trademark against a trademark which is in order behind their trademark, or against a trademark which can create confusion. According to the proposal, an opposition procedure can be initiated within 2 months following the publication of the registration of the trademark.

2376. Persons or companies wishing to oppose a trademark, but without physical presence in the EEA, must be represented by an authorised person. Companies with a physical presence within the EEA can authorise an employee to initiate the opposition procedure on its employer's behalf.

2377. The Benelux Trademark Office will consider the opposition within a reasonable time period. The Office's decision can be appealed before a court.

E. Rights of the trademark owner

2378. The owner of a trademark has the exclusive right to use the trademark. This exclusive right implies that he also has the right to defend his trademark against any third party interfering with this right.

2379. The exclusive right of the trademark owner extends to any use of the trademark on goods or services identical or similar to those for which he uses the trademark. Under specific conditions, the owner may even prevent the use of his trademark in other sectors of the economy.

2380. The registration of a collective trademark covers the use of all goods and services, without distinction. The owner of a collective trademark is not entitled to use the trademark for his own goods or services (Art. 19 of the Trademark Law).

F. Duration of trademark protection

2381. A trademark is valid for a period of 10 years from the date of its registration (Art. 10 of the Trademark Law). The registration may be renewed indefinitely. An international registration under the Madrid Agreement is, in principle, valid for 20 years and can also be renewed (Art. 6 of the Madrid Agreement).

2382. A trademark owner is required to use his trademark. Failure to make "normal" use of the trademark, without a valid reason, for an uninterrupted period of 5 years, may result in the forfeiture of the trademark right (Art. 5(2)(a) of the Trademark Law).

G. Assignments and licences

§1. Domestic law

2383. A trademark can be assigned, provided that the agreement is in writing and pertains to the entire Benelux territory (Art. 11A of the Trademark Law). Non-compliance with either of these requirements nullifies the agreement. Moreover, the pertinent part of the agreement, or a declaration signed by the contracting parties which evidences the assignment, should be registered with the Benelux Trademark Office in The Hague or with the Department of Industrial property of the Ministry of Economic affairs in Brussels, in order to make the assignment enforceable against third parties (Art. 11C of the Trademark Law).

2384. A trademark can also be licensed. A licensing agreement must be in writing. Non-compliance with this requirement renders the agreement void.

2385. Parties are free to determine the content of their licensing agreement. According to Article 11B of the Trademark Law, a trademark owner can invoke his exclusive right against a licensee who infringes the provisions of the licence agreement regarding its duration, the ways in which the trademark can be used, the categories of goods for which it can be used, the territory in which the trademark can be used or the quality of the goods commercialised by the licensee.

§2. Impact of EC law

2386. Contract clauses conferring an exclusive right on the licensee of the trademark may be found to infringe Art 81(1) EC Treaty (*See*, *Campari*, O.J. [1978] L 70/69). A similar fate will befall non-competition clauses and prohibitions imposed on the licensee against active sales outside the territory (*Ibid*; *See*, also as regards prohibitions of active sales *Moosehead/Whitbread*, O.J. [1990] L 100/32). However, these clauses are capable of exemption under Article 81(3) of the EC Treaty.

2387. The doctrine of "Community-wide exhaustion" (*See*, paras. 2197 *et seq.*) also applies to trademarks. It follows that a Benelux owner of a trademark will be prevented from relying on his trademark to stop the importation of products which were sold by himself, or with his consent by an affiliated company or a licensee in another EC Member State (ECJ, 31 October 1974, Case 16/74, *Centrafarm B.V. and Adriaan de Peijper* v. *Winthrop B.V.*, [1974] ECR 1183). In contrast, the Benelux owner of a trademark can stop the importation of goods from a third country into the Community, even if these goods were put on the market in that third country by the trademark owner or with his consent. What constitutes "consent" was addressed by the European Court of Justice in its judgement of 20 November 2001 (ECJ, 20 November 2001, Joined Cases C-414/99, *Zeno Davidoff S.A.* v. *A&G Imports Ltd.* and *Levi Strauss & Co* and *Levi Strauss (UK) Ltd.* v. *Tesco Stores Ltd. et alii* – [2001] ECR I-8691). According to the European Court of Justice, consent must be expressed in such a way that an intention to renounce those rights is unequivocally demonstrated. It follows that consent must be expressed positively. Implied consent to the marketing within the EEA of goods put on the market by the trademark owner outside the EEA cannot be inferred from the mere silence of the trade mark owner.

H. International protection

2388. The Paris Convention ensures the free access of nationals or residents of other member countries to the Benelux system for the protection of trademarks. These parties receive national treatment for their registrations (Arts. 2 and 3 of the Paris Convention) and benefit from a priority right of 6 months to pursue a Benelux application after having registered a trademark in another member country (Art. 4(c) 1 of the Paris Convention). However, this right of priority is not obtained automatically and must be expressly applied for when the trademark is being registered, or within 1 month following that registration (Art. 6D of the Trademark Law).

2389. An international trademark registration made abroad under the aegis of the Madrid Agreement with the International Bureau of the WIPO will have the same effect as a Benelux registration if the Benelux countries were designated in the application as a territory where protection is sought (Art. 4 of the Madrid Agreement).

I. Infringements and remedies

§1. Jurisdiction of the courts

2390. In Belgium, all claims involving trademark rights must be brought before either the Court of First Instance (*Rechtbank van Eerste Aanleg/Tribunal de Première Instance*) (Art. 568 of the Judicial Code) or the Commercial Court (*Rechtbank van Koophandel/Tribunal de Commerce*) (Art. 573 of the Judicial Code), depending on whether or not the dispute arises between commercial parties. However, claims of less than € 1,860 are adjudicated by the Justice of the Peace (*Vredegerecht/ Justice de paix*).

2391. According to Article 37 of the Trademark Law, parties may agree on the territorial jurisdiction of the court before which a dispute involving a trademark will be brought. In the absence of a contractual arrangement, an action may be initiated before the court with territorial jurisdiction over the place where the defendant resides or with territorial jurisdiction over the place where the obligation at issue arose, was performed or was due to be performed. If these rules are not sufficient to determine the territorially competent court, the action may be brought before the court with territorial jurisdiction over the place where the plaintiff resides or, if the plaintiff does not have a place of residence in a Benelux country, before the competent court in either Brussels, Luxembourg or The Hague.

2392. Any questions regarding the interpretation of the Trademark Law may be submitted by a national court to the Benelux Court of Justice (*Benelux Gerechtshof/Cour de Justice Bénélux*) for a preliminary ruling.

§2. Remedies

1. Use

2393. Article 13A(1) of the Trademark Law authorises a trademark owner to defend his trademark against unlawful use by third parties.

2394. Under Article 13A(1)(a) of the Trademark Law, a trademark owner is able to oppose the use of his trademark on goods or services that are identical to those for which the trademark is registered.

2395. Under Article 13A(1)(b) of the Trademark Law, a trademark owner is able to oppose the use made of his trademark or a similar sign on goods or services that are identical or similar to those for which the trademark is registered, provided there is a likelihood of confusion among the public between the trademark and the sign. This provision also needs to be interpreted in light of the case law of the European Court of Justice (ECJ, 11 November 1997, Case C-251/95, *Sabel B.V.* v. *Puma A.G., Rudolf Dassler Sport*, [1997] ECR I-6191; ECJ, 29 September 1998, Case C-39/87, *Canon Kabushiki Kaisha* v. *Metro-Goldwyn-Mayer Inc*, [1998] ECR I-5507; ECJ, 22 June 2000, Case C-425/98, *Marca Mode cv* v. *Adidas A.G. and Adidas Benelux B.V.*, [2000] ECR I-4861) which establishes that a likelihood of association is not sufficient to establish a likelihood of confusion within the meaning of the Trademark Directive.

2396. Furthermore, Article 13A(1)(c) of the Trademark Law allows a trademark owner to prevent the use by third parties of his trademark or a similar sign on goods or services that are not similar to those for which the trademark is registered, where such use of the trademark would, without a valid reason, take unfair advantage of, or be detrimental to, the distinctive character or reputation of the trademark. Finally, Art 13A(1)(d) of the Trademark Law allows a trademark owner to prevent the use by third parties of his trademark or a similar sign other than for the purpose of distinguishing goods or services, where such use of the trademark would take unfair advantage of, or be detrimental to, the distinctive character or reputation of the trademark.

2397. Article 13A(2) of the Trademark Law contains a non-exhaustive list of what is understood by the use of a trademark or an identical sign:
   (i) affixing the sign to the goods or the packaging of the goods;
   (ii) offering the goods, or putting them on the market or storing the goods for these purposes under that sign;
   (iii) importing or exporting the goods under that sign; or
   (iv) using the sign on business papers and in advertising.

2. Damages

2398. According to Article 13A(4) of the Trademark Law, the trademark owner can claim damages under the same conditions as mentioned in Article 13A(1) of the Trademark Law.

2399. In combination with or instead of the action for damages, the trademark owner can bring an action to recover profits that result from the use of the trademark (Art. 13(A)(5) of the Trademark Law).

2400. Courts may issue cease-and-desist orders and may order the payment of damages. It is generally accepted that temporary relief can be obtained in summary proceedings. In addition, the courts may impose periodic penalty payments.

3. Other

2401. While the rights of the trademark owner are exhausted once the goods have been put on the market within the Community by the owner himself or with his consent, he will nonetheless be able to oppose the use of the trademark on such goods if the state of the goods has changed or deteriorated (Art 13A(9) of the Trademark Law).

2402. Article 13B of the Trademark Law expressly provides that the classification of goods or services made at the time of the registration of the trademark is not binding for a court which has to determine whether or not goods or services are identical or similar.

2403. The Trademark Law contains provisions that enable the public prosecutor and every interested third party to invoke the nullity of a trademark or its forfeiture (Art. 14 of the Trademark Law).

4. *Criminal sanctions*

2404. Article 8 of the Old Trademark Law contains criminal provisions that punish the acts of counterfeiting, the fraudulent use of a counterfeit trademark, the fraudulent use of an authentic trademark by a party who is not the owner of that trademark and the intentional sale, offering for sale or putting on the market of counterfeit trademarks.

J. Impact of EC law

§1. *EC Competition Law and the Counterfeit Regulations*

2405. Both licensing and the exercise of trademark rights may be influenced by the rules of EC competition law (Arts. 81 and 82 of the EC Treaty) and the free movement of goods (Arts. 28 through 30 of the EC Treaty).

2406. On 1 December 1986, the EC Council of Ministers adopted Regulation No. 3842/86 Laying Down Measures to Prohibit the Release for Free Circulation of Counterfeit Goods (O.J. [1986] L 357/1; corrigendum: O.J. [1987] L 33/18 – "Regulation No. 3842/86"). Regulation No. 3842/86 was implemented by Commission Regulation No. 3077/87 of 14 October 1987 (O.J. [1987] L 291/19). On 22 December 1994, Regulation No. 3842/86 was replaced by EC Council Regulation No. 3295/94 Laying Down Measures to Prohibit the Release for Free Circulation, Export, Re-export or Entry for a Suspensive Procedure of Counterfeit and Pirated Goods (O.J. [1994] L 341/8 – "Regulation No. 3295/94"). Regulation No. 3295/94 was amended by Regulation No. 241/99 of 15 January 1999 (O.J. [1999] L 27/1). The implementation of this Regulation was regulated by Commission Regulation No. 1367/95 of June 1995 (O.J. [1995] L 133/2). This Regulation was amended by Regulation No. 2549/99 of 1 December 1999 (O.J. [1999] L 308/16). Regulation No. 3295/94 as amended and its implementing Regulation aim to discourage trade in counterfeit goods. They lay down the conditions under which customs authorities of the EC Member States must intervene with regard to goods that are suspected of being counterfeit. In addition, these Regulations determine the measures that may be taken by the customs authorities once it is established that specific goods are indeed counterfeit. The EC Commission will shortly table a proposal providing for radical overhaul of Regulation No. 3295/94.

§2. *The Trademark Directive*

2407. On 21 December 1988, the EC Council of Ministers adopted the First Directive No. 89/104 to Approximate the Laws of the EC Member States relating to Trademarks (O.J. [1989] L 40/1) (the "Trademark Directive"). The Trademark Directive was intended to remove a number of disparities between national trademark laws. The scope of the Trademark Directive is limited to rules of substantive trademark law. The Trademark Directive does not address procedural questions relating to the acquisition, maintenance or cancellation of trademarks. The Trademark Law did not require major amendments to bring it into line with the Trademark Directive.

§3. The Community Trademark

2408. In addition to harmonising existing national trademark legislation, the EC Council of Ministers adopted Council Regulation (EC) No. 40/94 of 20 December 1993 on the Community Trademark (the "CTM Regulation") (O.J. [1994] L 11/1). The CTM Regulation was amended by Regulation No. 3288/94 of 22 December 1994 for the implementation of the agreements concluded in the framework of the Uruguay Round (O.J. [1994] L 349/83). The CTM Regulation has direct effect in the EC Member States and is therefore directly applicable before the national courts.

2409. The CTM Regulation introduces the Community Trademark ("CTM"), affording uniform trademark protection for the entire territory of the Community. Article 1 of the CTM Regulation provides that a CTM will have a unitary character and equal effect throughout the Community. The CTM system is largely similar to the system established by the Trademark Directive. The CTM system is administered by the Office for Harmonisation in the Internal Market (the "OHIM"), which was established in Alicante (Spain) in 1994. It has been possible to file CTM applications since 1 January 1996. Applicants have the choice of filing a CTM application at the OHIM or at the central industrial property office of an EC Member State.

VI. KNOW-HOW

A. Applicable law

2410. There is no comprehensive set of rules governing know-how under Belgian law. Limited forms of protection are afforded to particular types of know-how under specific circumstances. Relevant statutory provisions include Article 309 of the Criminal Code, Article 17(3)(a) of the Law of 3 July 1978 on Employment Agreements, Article 1382 of the Civil Code and Article 93 of the Law of 14 July 1991 on Unfair Trade Practices.

B. Definition

2411. Under Belgian law, know-how is not a recognised intellectual property right. It follows that a statutory definition of the concept of know-how does not exist. Several legal commentators have put forward a definition of what they consider to be know-how. The Supreme Court requires the courts to define know-how and trade secrets according to the "usual meaning" of these terms (Cass., 26 June 1975, *R.C.J.B*, 1976, 351).

2412. A workable definition is contained in EC Commission Regulation No. 240/96 of 31 January 1996 on the Application of Article 85(3) of the EC Treaty (now: Art. 81(3)) to Certain Categories of Technology Transfer Agreements ("Technology Transfer Block Exemption" or "TTBE"), which covers the transfer of technology, both patented and unpatented (O.J. [1996] L 31/2). According to Article 10 of the TTBE, know-how is a body of technical information that is secret, substantial and identified in any appropriate form.

C. Substantive requirements

2413. In the absence of a clear definition of the notion of know-how, elaborate substantive requirements for its protection do not exist. It is, however, generally accepted that the requirement of secrecy is not absolute. Know-how is generally thought to retain its confidential character as long as it is not readily accessible (Cass., 26 June 1975, *R.C.J.B.*, 1976, 351).

D. Procedural requirements

2414. There are no procedural requirements in order for know-how to benefit from protection under the relevant statutory provisions.

E. Rights of the owner of know-how

2415. The rights of the owner of know-how will vary according to the rules on which he intends to rely. One important category of rights comprises the contractual rights derived from a variety of agreements involving the use of know-how. In addition, owners of know-how may benefit from specific statutory rights under particular circumstances. This is the case for an employer in his relationship with his employees. Pursuant to Article 17(3)(a) of the Law on Employment Agreements, employees have a secrecy obligation regarding technical know-how, commercial know-how and confidential information regarding personal or sensitive matters of which they became aware during their employment. This secrecy obligation also continues after the employment agreement has come to an end. Failure to observe this obligation may constitute a serious breach of the employment agreement justifying instant dismissal.

F. Assignments and licences

2416. Assignments and licences of know-how are not subject to any procedural requirements. Moreover, parties are free to determine the contents of their assignment or licensing agreement in accordance with the general rules of contract law.

2417. Know-how licensing agreements should be drafted with due regard for the provisions of EC competition law contained in the TTBE. Know-how licensing agreements that satisfy the conditions set out in the TTBE are automatically exempted from the prohibition of Article 81(1) of the EC Treaty without prior notification to the Commission. The TTBE contains detailed rules governing exclusivity, territorial restrictions, field-of-use restrictions, customer restrictions, post-term use bans, grant-back clauses, non-competition clauses, sub-licences, output restrictions and royalties. The TTBE is currently under review by the Commission and is expected to undergo substantial amendments.

G. Infringements and remedies

§1. Civil remedies

2418. The employer has a right of action against his employee for a breach of the latter's secrecy obligation with regard to the employer's know-how (Art. 17(3) (a) of the Law on Employment Agreements).

2419. In exceptional circumstances, the owner of know-how may rely on general principles of tort law (Art. 1382 of the Civil Code) or Article 95 of the Law on Unfair Trade Practices. Under the latter provision, a right of action is available to a victim of the conduct of competitors which is contrary to good commercial practice.

§2. Criminal sanctions

2420. Pursuant to Article 309 of the Criminal Code, the communication to third parties of an employer's technical know-how by a former or current employee with a malicious or fraudulent intent may carry a fine and/or a prison term.

VII. SEMICONDUCTOR TOPOGRAPHIES

A. Applicable law

2421. The Law of 10 January 1990 on the Legal Protection of Topographies of Semiconductor Products (*Wet betreffende de rechtsbescherming van topografieën van halfgeleiderprodukten/Loi concernant la protection juridique des topographies de produits semi-conducteurs* – the "Semiconductor Law") created a *sui generis* intellectual property right in respect of topographies of semiconductor products. The Semiconductor Law implements EC Council Directive 87/54 of 16 December 1986 on the Legal Protection of Topographies of Semiconductor Products (the "Semiconductor Directive" – O.J. [1987] L 24/36).

B. Definition

2422. The right in the topography of a semiconductor product is an exclusive and temporary right of reproduction and commercial exploitation (Art. 1 of the Semiconductor Law). The terms "semiconductor product" and "topography" are defined by an explicit reference to the Semiconductor Directive.

2423. Article 1(1)(a) of the Semiconductor Directive defines a "semiconductor product" as "the final or an intermediate form of any product:
   (i) consisting of a body of material which includes a layer of semiconducting material;
   (ii) having one or more other layers composed of conducting, insulating or semiconducting material, the layers being arranged in accordance with a predetermined 3-dimensional pattern; and
   (iii) intended to perform, exclusively or together with other functions, an electronic function."

2424. Article 1(1)(b) of the Semiconductor Directive defines the "topography" of a semiconductor product as "a series of related images, however fixed or encoded:
   (i) Representing the 3-dimensional pattern of the layers of which a semiconductor product is composed; and
   (ii) in which series each image has the pattern or part of the pattern of a surface of the semiconductor product at any stage of its manufacture."

C. Substantial requirements

2425. The topography of a semiconductor product will benefit from protection under the Semiconductor Law if the following conditions are satisfied:

(i) the topography is the result of the creator's own intellectual efforts;

(ii) the topography is not commonplace in the semiconductor industry; and

(iii) the topography is fixed or encoded.

D. Procedural requirements

2426. The Semiconductor Law does not contain any procedural requirements in order for protection to apply.

E. Rights of the creator

2427. The Semiconductor Law contains an explicit provision whereby a topography created by an employee in the course of his employment will be considered to be the creation of his employer, unless the employment agreement provides otherwise (Art. 4, para. 1 of the Semiconductor Law). Similarly, a topography created under a contract for services will be considered to be created by the party who commissioned the topography, unless the contract provides otherwise (Art. 4, para. 2 of the Semiconductor Law).

2428. Pursuant to Article 1 of the Semiconductor Law, the creator of a topography of a semiconductor product has the exclusive right of reproduction and commercial exploitation. There are 2 important exceptions to this exclusive right (Arts. 10 and 11 of the Semiconductor Law):

(i) the holder of the right is not entitled to prevent any reproduction of the protected topography if done for the purpose of analysing, evaluating or teaching the topography, or the concepts, processes, systems or techniques embodied in the topography. In addition, if the analysis or evaluation of an existing topography results in the creation of a new topography which satisfies the general criteria for protection, the creator of the new topography will have an exclusive right of his own in that new topography;

(ii) a party who, when it acquires a semiconductor product, does not know, or has no reasonable basis to believe, that the topography of that product is protected by an exclusive right must not be prevented from exploiting that product. This so-called "exception of innocent infringement" nevertheless requires the *bona fide* infringing party to pay royalties to the rightholder from the moment it knows, or has reasonable grounds to believe, that the topography of the semi-conductor product is protected by an exclusive right.

F. Duration of the exclusive right

2429. The exclusive right expires 10 years after the end of the calendar year during which the topography was first commercially exploited in any part of the world (Art. 9, para. 2 of the Semiconductor Law). If such commercial exploitation does not take place, the period of protection expires 15 years after the topography was first fixed or encoded (Art. 9, para. 3 of the Semiconductor Law).

G. Assignments and licences

2430. Assignments and licences of the exclusive right to the topography of a semiconductor product are not subject to any procedural requirements. Moreover, parties are free to determine the content of their assignment or licensing agreement in accordance with the general rules of contract law.

H. International protection

2431. According to Article 6 of the Semiconductor Law, the right to protection applies in favour of natural persons who are nationals of an EC Member State, or who habitually reside in the territory of such an EC Member State. Similarly, the exclusive right will also be available to companies or other legal persons that have a real and effective industrial or commercial establishment in the European Community.

2432. Pursuant to Article 8 of the Semiconductor Law, the right to protection will also apply in favour of parties who first commercially exploit a topography within an EC Member State, which has not yet been commercially exploited anywhere in the world, provided that such parties were exclusively authorised to commercially exploit the topography throughout the EC by the party entitled to grant such rights.

2433. Finally, Article 7 of the Semiconductor Law provides for the possibility that nationals or companies of non-EC countries would also benefit from the protection afforded by the Semiconductor Law as a result of the requirements of an international convention or a decision by the EC Council of Ministers.

2434. On 9 October 1990, the EC Council adopted 2 decisions establishing a permanent system regarding the extension of legal protection of topographies created by third country nationals. The first decision extends the protection unconditionally and permanently to nationals of third countries which themselves are regarded by the Council as applying similar protection arrangements to all EC Member States (O.J. [1990] L 285/29). Third countries in this category include Australia, Japan and Sweden. The second Council decision grants limited protection over time which is subject to a number of conditions of reciprocity (O.J. [1990] L 285/31). The EC

Council instructed the EC Commission to ascertain whether the countries listed in an annex to the second decision satisfy these conditions of reciprocity. To date, the EC Commission has identified, *inter alia*, Hong Kong, Norway, the United States of America and Switzerland as fulfilling the necessary reciprocity requirements. By decision of 22 December 1994, the EC Council extended the protection to all the WTO countries (O.J. [1994] L 349/201).

I. Infringements and remedies

2435. All claims regarding rights to topographies should be brought before the Court of First Instance (*Rechtbank van Eerste Aanleg/Tribunal de Première Instance*) even if the dispute arises between commercial parties (Art. 569(23) of the Judicial Code and Art. 16, para. 1 of the Semiconductor Law). The plaintiff can choose to bring his action before the court attached to the Court of Appeal with jurisdiction over the place where the alleged infringement occurred or with jurisdiction over the place where the defendant resides. If the defendant does not reside in Belgium, the claim can be brought before the court with jurisdiction over the place where the plaintiff resides (Art. 16, para. 2 of the Semiconductor Law). These rules cannot be altered by contract although the Semiconductor Law does allow for arbitration (Art. 16, para. 3 of the Semiconductor Law).

2436. The court may issue a cease-and-desist order with respect to infringements and may award damages resulting from such infringements. If the infringements were in bad faith, the court may confiscate the infringing semiconductor products, as well as the instruments that were especially intended for the production of the illegal products. If the semiconductor products have already been sold by the infringer, the court will order the payment of an amount equal to the price or value of the semiconductor products sold (Arts. 13 and 14 of the Semiconductor Law).

2437. The limitation period for an infringement action is 5 years from the day on which the infringement took place (Art. 15 of the Semiconductor Law).

VIII. PROTECTION OF PLANT VARIETIES

A. Applicable law

2438. The protection of plant varieties is governed by the Law of 20 May 1975 on the Protection of Plant Varieties (*Wet tot bescherming van kweekprodukten/Loi sur la protection des obtentions végétales* – the "Plant Variety Law"). Furthermore,

Belgium is a member of the International Union for the Protection of New Varieties of Plants (*Union internationale pour la Protection des Obtentions Végétales –* "UPOV"). Belgium ratified 2 international agreements that were adopted under the auspices of UPOV, namely the International Convention for the Protection of New Varieties of Plants of 2 December 1961 (the "UPOV Convention") (implemented by the Law of 5 December 1976) and the Additional Act modifying the UPOV Convention of 10 November 1972 (implemented by the Law of 29 December 1976).

2439. Belgium did not become a party to the 1978 revision of the UPOV Convention. It did, however, sign the 1991 amended version. A new law intended to implement this revision is now being prepared and is expected to supersede the Plant Variety Law.

2440. A number of Royal Decrees implementing the Plant Variety Law regulate the registration procedure (Royal Decree of 22 July 1977), the fees payable in order to benefit from protection (second Royal Decree of 22 July 1977) and the list of categories of plant varieties that are eligible for protection (Royal Decree of 12 March 1991).

B. Definition

2441. A plant variety right is an exclusive and temporary right to produce and commercialise a new plant variety. The term "plant variety" covers any clone, line, stock or hybrid which is capable of cultivation, as well as any cultivar.

2442. The protection afforded by the Plant Variety Law excludes the possibility of obtaining patent protection.

C. Substantial requirements

2443. A plant variety must satisfy the following conditions in order to benefit from protection:
  (i) the variety must be new;
  (ii) the variety must be sufficiently uniform;
  (iii) the variety must be stable;
  (iv) the variety must belong to a genus or species that is listed in the annex to the Royal Decree of 12 March 1991; and
  (v) the variety must have a designated name.

§1. *Novelty*

2444. According to Article 4 of the Plant Variety Law, a variety is new when it can be clearly distinguished, through a number of important characteristics, from any other variety whose existence is commonly known at the time of application. This common knowledge may result from prior cultivation or commercialisation, the registration or the application for a registration in an official register, the inclusion of the variety in a collection which serves as a reference, or the accurate description of the variety in a publication. The characteristics which cause a variety to be distinct from other varieties may be of a morphological or physiological nature.

§2. *Sufficient uniformity*

2445. Pursuant to Article 5 of the Plant Variety Law, the uniform nature of a variety will be assessed with regard to the particular features of the variety's sexual reproduction or vegetative propagation.

§3. *Stability*

2446. According to Article 6 of the Plant Variety Law, the variety will be deemed to have the required stability if it remains true to its description after repeated reproduction or propagation. If the applicant specifies a particular cycle of reproduction, the variety should maintain its characteristics at the end of each cycle.

§4. *Predetermined genus or species*

2447. The variety must belong to a genus or species that is listed in the annex to the Royal Decree of 12 March 1991 (Art. 1 of the Plant Variety Law).

D. Procedural requirements

2448. In order to benefit from protection under the Plant Variety Law, an application for protection should be filed with the department for the protection of plant varieties of the Ministry of Agriculture (*Dienst tot bescherming van kweekprodukten/ Service de la protection des obtentions végétales*). This department will be transferred to the Ministry for Economic Affairs in the near future. The application is then entered onto a specific register of applications. The filing of an application implies the payment of a fee.

2449. The department referred to above will determine whether the variety satisfies all substantial requirements for protection. The examination may be carried out by an expert appointed by the department. A special council may be consulted for advice on any given application.

2450. A successful application will result in the grant of a breeder's certificate (*kwekers-certificaat/certificat d'obtention*). The certificate is published in 2 official registers.

2451. The holder of a breeder's certificate is required to pay an annual fee. Failure to pay the fee results in the forfeiture of the exclusive right to the plant variety (Art. 33, para. 2 of the Plant Variety Law).

E. Rights of the holder of a breeder's certificate

2452. The Plant Variety Law contains a provision whereby a variety created by an employee in the course of his employment will be considered to be the creation of his employer, unless it is agreed otherwise (Art. 26 of the Plant Variety Law).

2453. The holder of a breeder's certificate has the exclusive right to produce for commercial purposes and to commercialise the reproductive material of the plant variety (Art. 21 of the Plant Variety Law; *See* also, Art. 35 of the Plant Variety Law, which lists acts of counterfeiting). This exclusive right does not entitle the holder of the right to prevent the production or maintenance of reproductive material for scientific purposes or for the creation of a new variety (Art. 22 of the Plant Variety Law). However, if such a new variety is used repeatedly to produce another variety for commercial purposes, this use will require the authorisation of the original holder of the right.

F. Duration of the plant variety protection

2454. The duration of the protection afforded to a specific variety depends on the genus or species to which it belongs (Art. 11 of the Plant Variety Law). The periods of protection afforded to the various genera and species are contained in the Royal Decree of 12 March 1991. They vary between 15 and 25 years. The protection period starts from the date the breeder's certificate is granted.

G. Assignments and licences

2455. The right holder is authorised to license his right (Art. 23 of the Plant Variety Law) or to assign it in whole or in part (Art. 32 of the Plant Variety Law). Both licences and assignments have to be registered in the register of varieties. An assignment of a plant variety right must be in writing.

2456. Licences of plant variety rights should be drafted with due regard for the provisions of EC law governing competition (Arts. 81 and 82 of the EC Treaty). The European Court of Justice held in the *Nungesser* case (ECJ, 8 June 1982, Case

258/78, L.C., *Nungesser K.G.* and *Kurt Eisele* v. *Commission*, [1982] ECR 2065, at p. 2065), that it is "*not correct to consider that breeders' rights are a species of commercial or industrial property right with characteristics of so special a nature as to require, in relation to the competition rules, a different treatment from other commercial* and *industrial property rights.*"

2457. It follows that contract clauses providing for exclusivity, specific forms of territorial protection, sale and export restrictions, price-fixing, output restrictions and non-competition will often be found to violate Article 81 of the EC Treaty. However, the European Court of Justice concluded in the *Nungesser* case, that an open exclusive licence of an innovative product is not in itself incompatible with Article 81(1) of the EC Treaty. In another context, the European Court of Justice ruled that sale and export restrictions imposed on a licensee with regard to basic seed did not violate Article 81(1) of the EC Treaty in so far as these were necessary to enable the breeder to select the growers who were to be his licensees (ECJ, 19 April 1988, Case 27/87, *Sprl. Louis Erauw Jacquery* v. *S.C. La Hesbignonne*, [1988] ECR 1919, at p. 1939).

2458. Arts. 24 and 25 of the Plant Variety Law provide for a system of compulsory licensing where the exclusive right is considered to be insufficiently exploited or deemed to be offered for licence against "unjust prices".

H. International protection

2459. The Plant Variety Law offers national treatment to varieties developed abroad that require protection under the UPOV Convention or under another international agreement (Art. 9, para. 1 of the Plant Variety Law). Under the conditions articulated in Article 10 of the Plant Variety Law, varieties created in a UPOV country benefit from a priority right in Belgium during a period of 12 months from the day the application for protection was lodged in the country of origin of the variety.

2460. Varieties developed abroad that do not qualify for national treatment may benefit from protection under the Plant Variety Law if there is reciprocal treatment for Belgian varieties in the country where the foreign variety was created (Art. 9, para. 2 of the Plant Variety Law). Even in the absence of any such reciprocal treatment for Belgian varieties, a variety developed abroad may acquire protection under the Plant Variety Law as a result of a decision of the Minister responsible for plant varieties (Art. 9, para. 3 of the Plant Variety Law).

I. Infringements and remedies

2461. The Court of First Instance (*Rechtbank van Eerste Aanleg/Tribunal de Première Instance*) has exclusive jurisdiction over disputes falling under the scope of the Plant Variety Law (Art. 38, para. 1 of the Plant Variety Law). Article 36 of the Plant Variety Law empowers the court to confiscate counterfeit varieties, to issue cease-and-desist orders and to award damages.

J. EC Law

2462. Pursuant to Regulation No. 2100/94, adopted by the EC Council of Ministers on 27 July 1994, parties can apply for a Community industrial property right for plant varieties (O.J. [1994] L 227/1). This Community-wide industrial property right is without prejudice to the right of the Member States to grant national property rights for plant varieties. It is, therefore, possible for a party to hold simultaneously a Belgian and a Community industrial property right for a specific plant variety.

2463. A party wishing to obtain a Community right must file an application with either the Community Plant Variety Office (the "Office") in Angers, France, or with one of its sub-offices or national agencies. An application can be filed by any natural or legal person that meets the conditions set out in the Regulation. The Office charges fees for its official acts provided for under the Regulation as well as for each year of the duration of a Community plant variety right.

2464. The term of the Community plant variety right runs until the end of the twenty-fifth calendar year or, in the case of varieties of vine and tree species, until the end of the thirtieth calendar year, following the year in which the right was granted. In respect of certain genera or species, the duration of the validity of the right can be extended by a maximum of 5 years.

13. ANTITRUST

I. INTRODUCTION

2465. The Law of 5 August 1991 on the Protection of Economic Competition (*Wet tot bescherming van de economische mededinging/Loi sur la protection de la concurrence économique* – the "Competition Law") marked an important step in the development of the rules of Belgian competition law.

2466. The Competition Law is, in most respects, modelled on the EC competition rules and draws heavily on the relevant EC Treaty provisions and implementing regulations for both substantive and procedural matters. According to its legislative history, the case law developed by the European Court of Justice and the EC Commission is relevant for the purpose of interpreting the Competition Law.

2467. However, soon after its entry into force in 1993, it became clear that many legal problems remained to be solved: the Belgian competition authorities (essentially the Competition Service (*Dienst voor de Mededinging/Service de la Concurrence*) and the Competition Council (*Raad voor de Mededinging/Conseil de la Concurrence*) suffered from a lack of institutional transparency regarding the delimitation of their respective tasks. Adding to this, the lack of adequate funding and the fact that the Competition Council's President did not function on a full-time basis led to an inability of the institutions to effectively deal with proceedings regarding restrictive practices. For several years, the Competition Council's activities were essentially limited to merger control. Regarding this, the relevant merger thresholds caused even more problems, as their application brought many concentrations with little effect on competition in Belgium within the scope of the Competition Law, thus increasing the already heavy workload of the competition authorities.

2468. These issues led to a lengthy legislative process of amending the Competition Law, which culminated in two Laws of 26 April 1999 (one dealing with institutional aspects, the other with material issues). The entire Competition Law was subsequently co-ordinated by Royal Decree of 1 July 1999. The new Laws mainly introduced important institutional and procedural changes (*See*, paras. 2566 *et seq.*), as well as new merger thresholds (*See*, para. 2531).

2469. In its Annual Report of 2001 (Competition Council, Annual Report 2001, point 3.2, p.16), the Competition Council expressed its concern that the new merger thresholds were still too low to stop the influx of an excess of notifications, dealing with concentrations which had no real effect on the relevant Belgian markets at all. Indeed, also in recent years, the number of decisions concerning anti-competitive agreements or abuses of dominant positions pales in comparison to the sheer number of merger cases, most of which are eventually approved without conditions (*See*, para. 2554 *et seq.*) as the relevant market shares involved do not exceed 25%. For this reason, the Competition Council has recently adopted a simplified notification procedure, applicable to mergers that, based on certain criteria, *prima facie* do not appear to infringe Belgian merger law.

2470. The analysis of the Competition Law provided in this chapter is divided into 3 parts:
    (i) first, the substantive rules regarding restrictive practices (agreements, concerted practices, abuses of a dominant position) and merger control are examined;
    (ii) secondly, an overview is given of the different institutions, both administrative and judicial, that are involved in competition control in Belgium; and
    (iii) finally, the procedures regarding restrictive practices and concentrations are discussed.

II. SUBSTANTIVE RULES

A. Agreements, decisions and concerted practices

2471. Article 2(1) of the Competition Law, which is phrased in terms very similar to Article 81(1) of the EC Treaty, prohibits all agreements between undertakings, decisions by associations of undertakings and concerted practices which have as their object or effect the prevention, restriction or distortion to an appreciable extent of competition within the relevant Belgian market, or a substantial part thereof. While the Competition Law provides little guidance as to the proper interpretation of the key concepts contained in Article 2(1), the case law of the EC Commission and the European Court of Justice is of assistance in this respect.

§1. Principle – Article 2 of the Competition Law

1. Undertaking

2472. Article 2(1) of the Competition Law applies only to undertakings. The concept of "undertaking" must be given the same broad meaning as under EC competition law, and covers all natural persons and legal entities which pursue an economic objective on a lasting basis (Art. 1(a) of the Competition Law). The broad definition of "undertaking" contained in the Competition Law implies that the nationality or domicile of the natural person or legal entity will have no bearing on the application of Article 2(1).

2473. As an example of the broad definition of the concept of undertaking for the purpose of Article 2(1) of the Competition Law, on 7 May 1999 (Cass., 7 May 1999, *Pas.*, I, 270), the Belgian Supreme Court considered that pharmacies, although they do not qualify as traders under Article 1 of the Belgian Commerce Code and have a social function, carry out an activity related to the exchange of products and services. They have an economic objective which they exercise in a durable manner and therefore can generally be defined as enterprises within the meaning of Article 2(1) of the Competition Law. Furthermore, the Supreme Court acknowledged that the Order of pharmacists, *i.e.*, the professional associations regrouping individual pharmacies, constitutes an association of undertakings within the meaning of Article 2(1) of the Competition Law and that its decisions must be assessed under the competition legislation and regulation.

2474. As another example of the broad definition of undertakings and associations of undertakings, the Competition Council ruled, on 8 January 2002 (Comp. Council, 23 July 2002, *Raphaël Tambue*, No. CONC-VMP-96/0001, *Belgian Official Journal*, 8 January 2002, 32,875), on a case brought by a trainee at the Arlon Bar (*l'ordre des avocats du Barreau d'Arlon*), against certain rules and practices of the said Bar (including the obligatory exams in order to obtain a certificate of competence (*certificat d'aptitude à la profession d'avocat* or "CAPA"), which he considered to be restrictive of competition within the meaning of Article 2 of the Competition Law. A question in this respect had also been submitted to the Court of Arbitration (*Arbitragehof/Cour d'Arbitrage*) which has the power to review laws against certain Articles of the Constitution. On 30 April 1997, the Court of Arbitration ruled that the fact that, on certain issues (as described in the Judicial Code), the Competition Council was not competent with regard to the bar associations, did not make the ruling unconstitutional. According to the Competition Council, the Court of Arbitration, however, did not rule out the Competition Council's competence altogether. The Competition Council concluded that it remains competent to assess whether the contested regulations constitute a competition law infringement or not. The Competition Council then considered the question whether the rules and regulations of these associations are to be qualified as "decisions of associations of undertakings" within the meaning of Article 81 of the EC Treaty and Article 2 of the Competition Law. The Competition Council first ruled that it can no longer be doubted that a lawyer constitutes an undertaking within the meaning of Article 2 of the Competition Law, the economic nature of the profession's activity being obvious. With regard to the bar associations, the Competition Council took into account the fact that these associations at least partly serve the public interest, but that they are concerned with economic activities as well. The Competition Council concluded that these 2 functions must not be artificially separated and that the bar associations are therefore to be regarded as "associations of undertakings". Their rules and regulations are thus decisions of such associations of undertakings and may be found to infringe competition law if they prevent, restrict or distort competition on the market to any appreciable extent. With regard to the CAPA, the Competition Council concluded that *"it may be held that the access to the lawyer profession is restricted, or even impeded, by the requirement of passing the CAPA exams and that the contested regulation constitutes a restriction of competition"*. However, the Competition Council also took note of the fact that the success rate with regard to the CAPA exams is very high (more than 99% of the trainees pass these exams), leading to the conclusion that the restriction of competition does not have an "appreciable extent". On this ground, the Competition Council rejected the plaintiff's case.

2. Agreement, decision of an association or concerted practice

2475. The concepts "agreement", "decision of an association" and "concerted practice" cover a wide range of actions involving at least 2 independent undertakings acting in concert. As the case law relating to Article 81 of the EC Treaty indicates, agreements within the meaning of Article 2(1) of the Competition Law need not necessarily be legally binding contracts. The reference in Article 2(1) of the Competition Law to decisions of associations or undertakings indicates that the prohibition can also apply to situations where undertakings do not enter into direct agreements, but instead act in concert through the intermediary of an association. The notion of concerted practices refers to collusive behaviour whereby the undertakings concerned replace their independent behaviour with a form of practical co-operation or co-ordination. It should be noted that, especially with regard to concerted practices, the distinction between legitimate market behaviour and an infringement of Article 2(1) of the Competition Law is often difficult to make.

3. Effects on competition

2476. Article 2(1) of the Competition Law contains the following non-exhaustive list of practices which prevent, restrict or distort competition:
  – directly or indirectly fixing purchase or selling prices or any other trading conditions;

- limiting or controlling production, markets, technical development or investment;
- sharing markets or sources of supply;
- applying dissimilar conditions to equivalent transactions with other trading parties, thereby placing them at a competitive disadvantage; and
- making the conclusion of contracts subject to acceptance by the other parties of supplementary obligations which, by their nature or according to commercial usage, have no connection with the subject of such contracts.

2477. This is the same list as that which is included in Article 81(1) of the EC Treaty. It is however also not exhaustive: hence, for the purposes of the application of Article 2(1) of the Competition Law, this list must be supplemented by those practices which have been considered to restrict competition within the meaning of Article 81(1) of the EC Treaty.

4. De Minimis

2478. The prohibition contained in Article 2(1) of the Competition Law applies only to practices which restrict competition to an appreciable extent. In other words, restrictions of competition which are *de minimis* are not caught by the prohibition in the Competition Law. This stems from the wording of Article 2(1) of the Competition Law.

2479. It can be noted that before the Competition Law was amended in 1999, Article 5 used to establish a presumption that restrictive practices were *de minimis* if they were entered into by Small and Medium-Sized Enterprises ("SMEs"). These agreements were therefore not caught by the prohibition laid down in Article 2(1) of the Competition Law. In 1999, Article 5 of the Competition Law was amended and said presumption abrogated.

5. Exemption from notification for individual exemptions

2480. As a general rule, like under EC competition law, there is no obligation, under Belgian competition law, for undertakings to notify their agreements to the Competition Council. They must only do so if their agreement is deemed to fall within the prohibition of Article 2(1) of the Competition Law and they wish to obtain an individual exemption (under Art. 7(1) of the Competition Law).

2481. However, the new wording of Article 5 of the Competition Law sets forth that undertakings which fulfil certain conditions as laid down in Article 12(2) of the Law of 17 July 1975 on the Annual Accounts of Undertakings (*Wet met betrekking tot de boekhouding van de ondernemingen/Loi relative à la comptabilité des* enterprises) *i.e.*, the so-called SMEs, are exempted from this very obligation to notify their agreements in order to obtain an individual exemption. It is to be noted that, although Article 5 of the Competition Law refers to Article 12(2) of the Law of 17 July 1975 on the Annual Accounts of Undertakings, in reality, Article 12(2) of the Law of 17 July 1975 has been abolished. The above-mentioned conditions are now included in Article 15 of the Belgian Company Code (*Wetboek van Vennootschappen/Code des Sociétés*).

2482. Article 5 of the Competition Law may seem to provide a more favourable treatment to SMEs but SMEs should not rely too heavily on it for at least 2 reasons. Firstly, Article 5 does not grant an automatic exemption from the prohibition laid down in Article 2(1), so agreements entered into by SMEs could still be considered anti-competitive and could still be challenged by interested parties. Secondly, Article 5 only applies in relation to restrictive practices regulated by Article 2 of the Competition Law. This was expressly confirmed by the Antwerp Court of Appeal on 17 January 2000 and 11 September 2000 (Antwerp Court of Appeal, 17 January 2000, *Jaarboek Handelspraktijken en Mededinging/Annuaire Pratiques du Commerce et Concurrence*, 2000, 612; Antwerp Court of Appeal, 11 September 2000, *ibidem*, 620). In relation to Article 3 of the Competition Law (abuse of a dominant position), the Antwerp Court of Appeal made it clear that, given the wording of Article 5, the size of the enterprises did not play a role in the application of Article 3. In other words, Article 3 also applies to SMEs. The practical effect of the new wording of Article 5 is that it may lead SMEs to claim that no fines should be imposed on them because of restrictive agreements entered into between them since SMEs are explicitly exempted from individual requests for exemptions.

2483. Undertakings will benefit from Article 5 of the Competition Law whenever they do not, individually, exceed more than one of the following thresholds:
  – average number of employees during the relevant period: not in excess of 50;
  – annual turnover, excluding value added tax: not in excess of € 6,250,000;
  – balance sheet total: not in excess of € 3,125,000.

2484. However, if the average number of employees during the relevant period exceeds 100, then Article 5 of the Competition Law does not apply. The annual turnover referred to in the second criterion must be calculated on the basis of the total turnover achieved during the relevant period on export markets as well as the Belgian domestic market (Art. 46(1) of the Competition Law).

6. Defining the relevant market

2485. Article 2(1) of the Competition Law applies to practices which prevent, restrict or distort competition on the relevant Belgian market or a substantial part thereof. In other words, Article 2(1) is only concerned with the anti-competitive impact of certain practices within Belgium and cannot be invoked in order to prohibit conduct, the anti-competitive effects of which are only felt outside of Belgium. Article 2(1) of the Competition Law refers not only to the relevant Belgian market, but also to a substantial part of that market. Legislative history indicates that the determination of the relevant geographic and product market within which competition is being restricted must be made in accordance with the rules developed by the European courts and the EC Commission. Legislative history further indicates that a city, and certainly a province, may qualify as a substantial part of Belgium for the purposes of the application of Article 2(1) of the Competition Law.

7. Negative clearance

2486. At the request of the undertakings or associations of undertakings concerned, the Competition Council may issue a decision stating that, on the basis of the information available to it, there is no ground for taking action pursuant to Article 2(1) of the Competition Law (Art. 6(1) of the Competition Law). Such a decision – which is referred to as a negative clearance – implies a finding that one or more constitutive elements of Article 2(1) are not present in the situation reviewed by the Competition Council. The Competition Council must provide reasons in the decision granting negative clearance (Art. 30 of the Competition Law).

8. Exemption

2487. There are 3 ways in which a restrictive practice within the meaning of Article 2(1) of the Competition Law can escape the prohibition contained in that provision: (i) through an individual exemption by the Competition Council, (ii) through the application of a group exemption issued by Ministerial Decree and (iii) upon the application of an exemption pursuant to Article 81(3) of the EC Treaty.

i. Individual exemption

2488. Individual exemption by the Competition Council depends on the following.

(a) Conditions

2489. An exemption from the prohibition contained in Article 2(1) of the Competition Law can be obtained if a restrictive practice meets all of the following conditions, which are listed in Article 2(3):
   (i) the practice must contribute to improving the production or distribution of goods or to promoting technical or economic progress, or it must offer small and medium-sized undertakings the possibility of strengthening their competitive position on the relevant market or on the international market;

    (ii) the practice may not entail the imposition of restrictions on the undertakings concerned which are not indispensable to the attainment of these objectives;

   (iii) consumers must obtain a fair share of the resulting benefits; and

   (iv) the practice may not afford such undertakings the possibility of eliminating competition in respect of a substantial part of the products in question.

2490. With the exception of the reference to the strengthening of the competitive position of small and medium-sized undertakings, the conditions for an exemption pursuant to Article 2(3) of the Competition Law are identical to those contained in Article 81(3) of the EC Treaty. Consequently, the relevant EC case law will be the principal guide in the interpretation of the conditions set forth in the Competition Law.

  (b) Notification requirement

2491. In principle, an individual exemption cannot be granted by the Competition Council on its own initiative. In order to obtain an individual exemption pursuant to Article 2(3) of the Competition Law, the restrictive practice must be notified (Art. 7(1) of the Competition Law).

2492. No fines may be levied for acts that take place between the time of notification of a restrictive practice with a view to attaining an exemption and the adoption of a decision by the Competition Council, provided these acts are within the limits of what is described in the notification (Art. 39 of the Competition Law) (*See*, para. 2634).

2493. By way of exception, Article 7(2) of the Competition Law lists a number of practices which need not necessarily be notified in order to obtain an exemption pursuant to Article 2(3). The undertakings concerned are, however, entitled to notify these practices should they so desire. The practices listed in Article 7(2) of the Competition Law are those:

   (i) to which not more than 2 undertakings are party and which have as their sole effect:

    (a) to restrict the freedom of one party in determining the prices or conditions of business upon which the goods which it has obtained from the other party to the contract may be resold; or

    (b) to impose restrictions on the exercise of the rights of the assignee or user of industrial property rights – in particular patents, utility models, designs or trade marks – or of the person entitled under a contract to the assignment, or grant, of the right to use a method of manufacture or knowledge relating to the use and to the application of industrial processes; or

(ii) which have as their sole object:

    (a) the development or uniform application of standards or types; or

    (b) joint research and development concerning technical improvements provided that all the parties have access to the results and are free to exploit such results.

2494. Since the EC Commission and the European Court of Justice have adopted a narrow construction of a similar list of practices contained in Article 4(2) of EEC Council Regulation No. 17: First Regulation implementing Articles 85 and 866 of the Treaty (O.J. [1962] P 13/204) ("Regulation No. 17/62"), now replaced by EC Council Regulation No. 1/2003 of 16 December 2002 on the implementation of the rules on competition laid down in Articles 81 and 82 of the Treaty (O.J. [2003] L 1/1), it is advisable not to rely too heavily on the exemption from notification provided in Article 7(2) of the Competition Law.

2495. In addition to the exceptions at Article 7(2) of the Competition Law, it is recalled that Article 5 of the Competition Law exempts undertakings which qualify as SMEs from the obligation to notify their agreements.

(c) Notification formalities

2496. Notification of a practice for the purposes of obtaining an individual exemption must be made to the Competition Council (Art. 7(1) of the Competition Law). The rules of notification to be followed by the applicants are further detailed in a Royal Decree dated 23 March 1993 (as last amended on 28 December 1999). Applicants will be careful to fill in an "Application Form CONC E/A – 1" as annexed to the Royal Decree.

(d) Decision

2497. An individual exemption pursuant to Article 2(3) of the Competition Law can only be obtained by way of a decision adopted by the Competition Council. The Competition Council is the only body which has the authority to make such a decision. As under EC competition law, the Competition Law does not define any time limits within which the Competition Council must adopt its exemption decisions. The Competition Council has the authority to grant an individual exemption subject to certain conditions or obligations (Art. 29(2) of the Competition Law). Individual exemptions may not be given for an indefinite period of time. The Competition Council must fix the term for which an individual exemption is granted, as well as the date from which this starts running (Art. 29(3) of the Competition Law). This date may not be earlier than the date of the notification. At the request of the undertakings concerned, the Competition Council may extend an individual exemption upon its expiry, provided the conditions of Article 2(3) of the Competition Law continue to be satisfied. Article 29(2)(2) of the Competition Law entitles the Competition Council to withdraw or alter an individual exemption under circumstances similar to those under which the EC Commission may withdraw or alter an exemption decision taken pursuant to Article 81(3) of the EC Treaty (Art. 8(3) of Regulation No. 17/62). Such a withdrawal or alteration is possible:

(i) where there has been a change in any of the circumstances which were central to the making of the decision;
(ii) where the parties commit a breach of any obligation attached to the decision;
(iii) where the decision is based on incorrect information or was induced by fraud; or
(iv) where the parties abuse the exemption granted to them.

ii. Group exemption

2498. Pursuant to Article 28(1) of the Competition Law, Royal Decrees can be adopted to provide for an automatic exemption of certain categories of practices. The Minister acts on his own initiative following consultation with the Competition Council and the Competition Commission, or upon a proposal from the Competition Council (*e.g.*, upon reception of a reasoned regulation proposal from a Rapporteur). The group exemptions referred to in Article 28 of the Competition Law are similar to the block exemption regulations which exist in EC competition law. The most important feature of such group exemptions is that practices which meet their requirements need not be notified to the Competition Council. They benefit from an automatic exemption pursuant to Article 2(3) of the Competition Law. However, it should be noted that no such group exemption has yet been adopted.

iii. Application of Article 81(3) of the EC Treaty

2499. The prohibition contained in Article 2(1) of the Competition Law is inapplicable to practices which benefit from an exemption pursuant to Article 81(3) of the EC Treaty. It is immaterial whether the exemption stems from an individual decision rendered by the EC Commission or from the application of a block exemption regulation. Practices to which an EC block exemption applies therefore need not be notified under the Competition Law and the Competition Council must refrain from reviewing them (Arts. 8 and 32 of the Competition Law).

2500. That being said, Article 53 of the Competition Law, as amended by Royal Decree of 10 August 2001, gives effect to Article 7 of EC Commission Regulation No. 2790/1999 of 22 December 1999 on the Application of Article 81(3) of the Treaty to Categories of Vertical Agreements and Concerted Practices (O.J. [1999] L 336). This Article states that where in any particular case vertical agreements (to which the vertical restraints block exemption applies) have effects incompatible with the conditions laid down in Article 81(3) of the Treaty in the territory of an EC Member State, or in a part thereof, which has all the characteristics of a distinct geographic market, the competent authority of that EC Member State may withdraw the benefit of application of this Regulation No. 2790/1999 in respect of that territory.

§2. *Case law*

2501. Belgian case law on Articles 2 and 3 of the Competition Law (barring provisional measures) is scarce. This is at least partly due to internal problems regarding the proper functioning of the Competition Council as mentioned above (*See*, para. 2467). Also, in quite a few cases, the Competition Council had to conclude that prescription of the facts had occurred or that the facts had changed, leaving the pending case without object.

2502. In *Touring Verzekeringen* (Comp. Council, 28 June 2000, No. 2000-E/A-23, *Touring Verzekeringen*, *Belgian Official Journal*, 28 November 2000, 39,714), the Competition Council investigated the effect on competition of networks of inter-dependent undertakings and agreements. The case concerned exclusive co-opera-tion agreements between Touring and certain garages. Whereas the individual market shares of the undertakings concerned were too low for these agreements to individually affect competition on the relevant market, the Competition Council examined whether there was a network effect because of similar agreements being concluded between various insurance companies and garages. In this case, the Competition Council ruled that the existence of such network was not proven.

2503. Some cases brought before the President of the Competition Council in order to obtain provisional measures have proven interesting also on the merits of the case: for instance, in *ETE-Kilt v. ASAF* (Comp. Council, 6 December 2000, No. 2000-V/ M-39, *ETE-Kilt/ASAF*, *Belgian Official Journal*, 27 February 2001, 6113), the association of enterprises ASAF was deemed to have infringed Article 2 of the Competition Law. ASAF is an association that organises carting races among other activities. In order to be able to participate in these races, drivers must have tires, not only complying with certain qualifications, but also of a particular brand (Dunlop). Although the President acknowledged ASAF's concern for equality be-tween drivers on a sportive level (which would be obtained if all had similar tires), the imposition of a particular brand was deemed *prima facie* disproportionate.

B. Dominant Positions

§1. *Principle – Article 3 of the Competition Law*

2504. Article 3 of the Competition Law provides that any abuse by one or more undertakings of a dominant position on the relevant Belgian market or a substantial part thereof is prohibited. The wording of Article 3 of the Competition Law is very similar to that of Article 82 of the EC Treaty. As in EC competition law, it is not a dominant position in itself, but rather the abuse of such a position that constitutes an infringement.

1. *A dominant position*

2505. Article 3 of the Competition Law only applies to undertakings which occupy a dominant position. Any finding of dominance requires the prior definition of a relevant market, both in relation to the product or service involved and from a geographical point of view.

i. Relevant product market

2506. In order to determine the relevant product market, the issue of product substitutability must be examined:
  (i) *demand side substitutability*: if from a customer's point of view products are substitutable or interchangeable because of their nature, price and use, those products will in principle be considered to belong to the same product market.
  (ii) *supply side substitutability*: even if there is little demand side substitutability between certain products, they may still belong to the same product market in so far as market entries by new producers or "switches" by producers from making one product to making another are not prevented by any "barriers to entry" (commercial, technical, financial or otherwise).

ii. Relevant geographical market

2507. The relevant geographical market is the territorial area in which the effects of an abuse of a dominant position are felt and in which market conditions for competitors are identical.

2508. For the notion of "Belgian market" or a substantive part thereof, *See*, para. 2485.

iii. Dominance

2509. The economic strength of the undertaking concerned must then be assessed within the market as it is defined. The legislative history makes it clear that the market definition and the dominance assessment required under the Competition Law must be done in accordance with the relevant principles applicable under EC competition law.

2510. For that reason, market share figures are bound to play an important role. If the case law developed in relation to Article 82 of the EC Treaty were to be followed in this respect, a market share of 35-40 per cent or more would constitute a strong indication of dominance for the application of Article 3 of the Competition Law.

2511. However, market shares are not the only possible indicators of the existence of a dominant position: many others exist (*e.g.,* high entry costs, vertical integration, financial powers, economic dependency).

2512. In general, a company may be said to have a dominant position on a certain relevant market if it can act independently upon that market, that is without having to take account of the actions of its competitors (if any) or customers. In a decision dated 15 November 1999, the President of the Commercial Court of Kortrijk took the view that it was not sufficient for an undertaking to be economically dependent on another to establish the existence of a dominant position. (Pres. Comm. of Kortrijk, 15 November 1999, *Jaarboek Handelspraktijken en Mededinging/Annuaire Pratiques du commerce et Concurrence*, 1999, 757)

2. Abuse

2513. Abuse is an objective concept: it does not imply an intent to harm or even a morally reprehensible behaviour. Any means by which the dominant party acts on the market, save by its own merits, may constitute an abuse (theory of "competition on the merits"). No causal link between the existence of a dominant position and its abuse is required.

2514. Article 3 of the Competition Law contains the following non-exhaustive list of abusive conduct:
   (i) directly or indirectly imposing unfair purchase or selling prices or other unfair trading conditions;
   (ii) limiting production, markets or technical development to the prejudice of consumers;
   (iii) applying dissimilar conditions to equivalent transactions with other trading parties, thereby placing them at a competitive disadvantage; or
   (iv) making the conclusion of contracts subject to acceptance by the other parties of supplementary obligations which, by their nature or according to commercial usage, have no connection with the subject of such contracts.

2515. As indicated, the list of practices referred to in Article 3 of the Competition Law is not exhaustive. Other practices may also amount to abuses of a dominant position.

In this respect, EC competition law will, in all likelihood, serve as a basis for the interpretation of Article 3 of the Competition Law.

2516. Examples of condemned abuses that can be found in the rich body of EC case law include:
(i) in vertical relations:
  - imposing unfair conditions or excessive prices on buyers
  - refusals to supply
  - discriminatory practices, especially as regards prices (on the basis of nationality/residence)
  - market segmentation
  - imposing market policy of dominant undertaking on other market players
  - fidelity rebates
  - predatory pricing
(ii) in horizontal relations:
  - refusing access to essential facilities
  - acquiring a competitor (see also: concentrations)
  - selling below costs
  - (in some circumstances) acquiring an exclusive license
  - imposing market share agreements on new market entrants

3. Negative clearance

2517. Undertakings are entitled to request the Competition Council to confirm that a particular practice does not constitute an abuse of a dominant position. Any negative clearances by the Competition Council must be granted by way of a reasoned decision (Arts. 6 and 30 of the Competition Law).

2518. It should be noted that Article 3 of the Competition Law does not foresee as an option to apply for an exemption, whether individual or collective: if Article 3 is deemed to apply, no such exemption may be granted and the infringement will be penalised.

§2. Case law

2519. A general note to be made regarding the Competition Council's case law concerning Article 3 of the Competition Law is that the Competition Council tends to define the relevant market very narrowly, which leads to a finding of the existence of a dominant position in the majority of cases.

2520. An important ruling was delivered in January 1999 with regard to certain practices of official importers of motorcycles (Comp. Council, 21 January 1999, *Occasie-markt "De Zwarte Arend" bvba v. Honda Belgium NV, Belgian Official Journal*, 13 March 1999, 8268-8284). This case concerned the complex Belgian system of "certificates of conformity". According to Belgian law, motorcycle constructors or their representatives are authorised to hand down the certificates warranting that a particular motorcycle conforms to an approved type. In principle, independent importers need to petition to obtain such certificates from the constructor (or their representative), the public authorities having limited their own intervention in the field to the exceptional granting of certificates in singular cases. In Belgium, certain constructors are thereby represented by their "official importers". In the case at hand, independent importers brought a complaint that some of those official importers abused their dominant position by exercising their authority to grant certificates in a way that restricts competition to the detriment of independent companies.

2521. First of all, the Competition Council confirmed that the official importers held a dominant position within the meaning of Article 3 of the Competition Law. It rejected the defendants' argument that they only acted in a capacity which was regulated by law. It also refused to heed the observation that the "exceptional" procedure by which the public authority acted in "singular" cases was in fact extensively used by independent importers in order to circumvent the more costly regular certification process. The Competition Council deemed that this use of a procedure *contra legem* could not lead to a wider definition of the relevant market, as the defendants argued.

2522. The Competition Council then proceeded to examine the arguments brought by the plaintiffs and the Competition Service regarding the existence of an abuse. Whereas it rejected the Service's allegation that the price charged by the official importers for certification duties was excessive (the real costs of these duties are difficult to estimate) and that the defendants "unduly" required that the independent importers delivered the motorcycles to them for an entire day (a custom in the sector, which was based on objective reasons of organisation of the work), it judged that an abuse of the dominant position did exist in that one of the defendants demanded the intervention of his own official dealer in processing the certification request and for the delivery and placement of spare parts. Also the limitation of the number of certification days to 2 each week and the requirement that the motorcycles were delivered in "ready-to-drive" condition were ruled to be abusive. Finally, the implementation of a sound test, where such a test was not legally required, was also condemned.

2523. In *Way Up S.A. v. Belgacom* (Comp. Council, 22 April 1999, No. 1999-VMP-7, *Way Up S.A. v. Belgacom S.A.*, *Belgian Official Journal*, 18 August 1999, 30,795), the Competition Council examined whether an abuse of a dominant position could be justified by the fact that it was imposed by law. Way UP (a press agency) complained to the Competition Council regarding Belgacom's practice of granting a 50% discount on its telephone tariffs to the press agency Belga and to certain newspaper agencies. However, according to Belgacom, Way Up was not eligible for such a discount as these discounts were foreseen in a restrictive way in the management contract between Belgacom and the Belgian State (a contract with the enforceability of a law). The Competition Council ruled that the existence of a legal obligation could justify an abuse of a dominant position. It thereby ruled against the case law of the European Courts on the subject, which had indicated that a legal obligation may not justify such an abuse. In another decision by the Brussels Court of Appeal on 9 June 1998, Belgacom was found to have abused its dominant position by accepting to provide information on individuals only at inequitable and discriminatory prices to a publisher of telephonic repertories. (Brussels Court of Appeal, 9 June 1998, *Jaarboek Handelspraktijken en Mededinging/ Annuaire Pratiques du commerce et Concurrence*, 1998, 720)

2524. In its judgment of 9 June 2000, the Belgian Supreme Court confirmed that a judge may not rule on the existence of a dominant position without duly examining the relevant market. It may be retorted that a judge is often ill-disposed to evaluate the market context thoroughly and independently as all the information the judge obtains regarding the relevant market is offered by the parties concerned. (Belgian Supreme Court, 9 June 2000, *Arresten van het Hof van Cassatie,* 2000, 354; *Pas.*, 2000, I, 354)

2525. In *ASA Systems v. UPEA* (Comp. Council, 28 June 2000, No. 2000-V/M-22, *ASA Systems v. UPEA, Belgian Official Journal*, 23 November 2000, 39,086) and *Source v. IMS* (Comp. Council, 27 October 2000, No. 2000-V/M-34, *Source v. IMS, Belgian Official Journal*, 21 February 2001, 5182), the President of the Competition Council, after a thorough examination of the facts, gave strong indications of what was to be considered as an abuse of a dominant position, although these cases concerned provisional measures and therefore any conclusions regarding the grounds of the matter were given *prima facie* and notwithstanding further examination by the Competition Council on the merits.

2526. In *ASA Systems v. UPEA*, the President of the Competition Council judged it reasonable to accept that UPEA (a professional organisation of insurance companies) had abused its dominant position in its conduct *vis-à-vis* ASA Systems. UPEA had composed a list of insurance companies which complied to its standards with regard to the placement of burglary alarm installations. This list, as well as the certificates that UPEA granted were of importance, as they were looked upon by customers as a clear sign of quality. The President of the Competition Council concluded from the facts at hand that UPEA had not followed its own rules regarding inclusion and exclusion of certain companies of its list and that its relationship with ASA Systems showed signs of an arbitrary approach. The President took particular offence at the way in which UPEA formally re-included ASA Systems in its list, while at the same time refusing to grant it the certificates it needed to conduct its business as a member of the UPEA-system.

2527. In *Source v. IMS*, the President of the Competition Council examined at some length the allegations that IMS, in determining the price at which it sold its products, abused its dominant position. IMS constructed its prices on the basis of a Common Part (covering the production costs and payable only once by a customer who desires to purchase several Products) and a Specific Part (per product). Above all, access to the valuable MIDAS information database, held by IMS, was restricted to subscribers to the LMPB product range. According to Source, this pricing system removed the customer's incentive to buy products elsewhere, once an initial purchase has been made at IMS, and constituted a form of tying. The President of the Competition Council shared this view.

C. Concentrations

§1. Principle

2528. The Competition Law prohibits, subject to certain exceptions, concentrations which create or strengthen a dominant position, that significantly hinder effective competition within the relevant market (Art. 10).

1. Concentration

2529. According to Article 9(2) of the Competition Law, a concentration results when:
  (i) 2 or more previously independent undertakings merge; or
  (ii) one or more persons who control at least one undertaking acquire control of the whole or parts of one or more other undertakings; or
  (iii) a joint venture is created which performs on a lasting basis all the functions of an autonomous economic entity.

2530. "Control" shall be deemed to arise when one or more persons, through rights, contracts or any other means, are able to exercise a decisive influence on an undertaking. This influence can take the form of the ownership or the right to dispose of all or part of the assets of the controlled undertaking or the rights that confer a decisive influence on the composition, voting and resolutions of the organs of an undertaking, *i.e.*, the general shareholders meeting and the board of directors.

2. *Merger thresholds*

2531. Like most EC Member States, Belgium has a system of mandatory pre-merger notification (Art. 12 of the Competition Law). Mergers, acquisitions, take-overs and joint ventures of the type described above are subject to control in Belgium only when the following quantitative thresholds are met:
  (i) the combined Belgian turnover of the companies concerned (including their affiliates) must exceed € 40 million; and
  (ii) at least 2 of the companies concerned, including their affiliates, each have a Belgian turnover exceeding € 15 million (Art. 11(1) of the Competition Law).

In addition to meeting the above thresholds, the concentration must not meet the thresholds of the EC Merger Regulation (EEC Council Regulation No. 4064/89) of 21 December 1989 on the control of concentrations between undertakings (O.J. [1989] L 395/1). Any concentration that must be notified to the EC Commission cannot be notified in Belgium and is outside the jurisdiction of the Belgian merger control authorities to review.

2532. The Belgian turnover is calculated on the basis of the income resulting from the sales of products and/or the provision of services to undertakings and consumers located in Belgium during the previous financial year. Article 46 of the Competition Law provides that the turnover set forth in Article 11(1) of the Competition Law must be determined in accordance with the latest consolidated annual accounts of the undertaking concerned.

2533. For banks and other financial institutions the turnover figure is replaced by one-tenth of the total balance sheet, and for insurance companies, by the gross value of premiums owned.

3. *Scope*

i. Material

2534. The Competition Law requires the Competition Council to allow a merger when it finds that the undertakings concerned jointly control less than 25 per cent of the relevant market (Art. 33(2)(a)). As indicated above, the relevant product market includes all the products and/or services which are regarded as interchangeable or substitutable by customers or suppliers by reason of product characteristics, prices and intended use. The relevant geographic market includes the territory inside Belgium in which the undertakings concerned are supplying the products or services concerned and where the conditions of competition are sufficiently homogeneous.

2535. Financial institutions or insurance companies holding securities on a temporary basis with a view to reselling them are not subject to merger control with respect to the securities so acquired. This exception requires that the institutions do not exercise voting rights on matters affecting the competitive conduct of the company concerned and that the resale of the securities purchased under the exception takes place within one year of their acquisition.

2536. In defining the relevant market, the Competition Council appears to have ceased including all kinds of neighbouring markets which were (often only indirectly) linked. In recent cases, the Competition Council has only taken into account markets with a direct (horizontal or vertical) link to each other.

ii. Territorial

2537. Belgium applies an effects test, so that mergers of foreign-based companies are subject to Belgian merger control, provided that the Belgian turnover thresholds for review are exceeded.

2538. As explained above, if the same merger is subject to scrutiny by the EC merger control authorities, the Belgian merger control provisions will no longer apply.

4. Assessment by the Competition Council

2539. The Belgian Competition Law enumerates factors to be considered by the Competition Council when it makes a decision on a proposed merger pursuant to Article 10(1). When appraising the restrictive effect on competition, the Competition Council shall consider:
   (i) the need to preserve and develop effective competition on the national market;
   (ii) the position of the companies concerned in the relevant market, their economic and financial power;
   (iii) the choice left for suppliers and users, their access to supply sources or to prospective markets;
   (iv) the evolution of supply and demand for the products or services concerned; and
   (v) the technical and economic progress regarding whether it is in the interest of the consumer and does not hinder effective competition (Art. 10(2) of the Competition Law).

5. Notification

i. General rule

2540. Whenever the thresholds are met, a proposed concentration must be notified to the Competition Council, using Form CONC C/C-1. Although the information to be provided in Form CONC C/C-1 is considerable, the Competition Council may waive the supply of certain information if it appears to be unnecessary for the appraisal of a proposed transaction.

2541. The notification must be filed within one month from either the conclusion of the agreement, the announcement of the public bid, or the acquisition of a controlling interest (Art. 12(1) of the Competition Law). If the concentration results from an agreement, the obligation to notify rests jointly on all parties. In all other instances, it is the party acquiring control that is to notify the transaction (Art. 12(2) of the Competition Law).

2542. Substantial fines may be imposed on parties putting a concentration into effect without prior notification (Art. 37(2) of the Competition Law). In addition, fines may be imposed if, prior to the adoption by the Competition Council of its decision on the admissibility of the concentration, the companies concerned take measures impeding the reversibility of the merger or causing a lasting change in the market structure (Art. 38 of the Competition Law).

2543. Failure to notify may also cause the enforceability of the transaction to be challenged. If notification is required but is not made, the transaction is not automatically void. However, an unnotified transaction may be subject to an investigation by the Competition Service and the College of Rapporteurs at any time; this investigation may possibly result in the transaction being opposed by the Competition Council.

2544. Also an individual third party may act in case the parties involved in a merger fail to duly notify their merger agreement:
(a) pursuant to Article 23 of the Competition Law, a third party could file a complaint with the Competition Council if the relevant parties fail to notify when obliged to do so in accordance with Article 12 (1) of the Competition Law;
(b) if a particular planned merger constitutes an abuse of a dominant position under Article 3 of the Competition Law, interested parties may request the ordinary courts to prohibit this transaction or impose conditions necessary to restore effective competition (including the divestiture of certain undertakings or assets), regardless of whether the transaction has been properly notified;

(iii) where a merger has been implemented without prior notification, it is conceivable that a third party having standing could bring a claim for damages before an ordinary court in relation to the merger or request the court to rule that it is not obliged to recognize the existence of the merged entity, *e.g.*, in respect of any contractual obligations it may have with the merged entity.

2545. The confidentiality of the information filed with the authorities is guaranteed by criminal sanctions (Arts. 44 and 45 of the Competition Law).

ii. Simplified notification procedure

2546. As noted before, the case law of the Competition Council shows that certain categories of concentrations are usually approved without having given rise to any real concern. In order to improve merger control, the Competition Council has introduced a "simplified notification procedure". (Joint declaration of the Competition Council and of the College of Rapporteurs concerning a simplified procedure for dealing with certain concentrations, *Belgian Official Journal*, 11 December 2002)

2547. The objective is that, if all relevant conditions are complied with and in so far as no special circumstances arise, the Competition Council shall endeavour to reach a decision of approval within 25 days upon notification.

2548. Also the notification form itself is simplified, whereby the emphasis lies on market definition and market information. Pre-notification contacts between the companies involved and the College of Rapporteurs are actively encouraged.

2549. The simplified notification procedure shall apply to the following categories of concentrations:
    (a) 2 or more undertakings acquire joint control over a joint venture, if (i) the Belgian turnover of the joint venture and/or the Belgian turnover of the branch of activities incorporated therein do not exceed € 15 million and (ii) the total value of the assets transferred to the joint venture does not exceed € 15 million for Belgium;
    (b) 2 or more undertakings merge, or one or more undertakings acquire sole or joint control over another undertaking, if none of the parties involved are active on the same product or geographical market or on a product market which is upstream or downstream from a product market on which the other party to the concentration is active;
    (c) 2 or more undertakings merge, or one or more undertakings acquire sole or joint control over another undertaking, (i) and 2 or more parties to the concentration are active in the same product and geographical market or

(ii) one or more of them are active on the same product or geographical market or on a product market which is upstream or downstream from a product market on which the other party to the concentration is active, (iii) in so far as their aggregate market share does not exceed 25%.

(d) The notifying parties are active on so-called "small markets", "emerging markets" and "innovative markets". It should be noted that the Competition Council has yet to define these concepts.

2550. The Competition Council and its College of Rapporteurs reserve the right to evaluate in each individual case whether the market conditions and factual circumstances are so to effectively warrant the use of a simplified procedure. If some factors would suggest the need of a full investigation by the College of Rapporteurs, the latter may reject the option of the simplified notification procedure.

6. Ancillary restraints

2551. Before the Competition Law was amended in 1999, Article 10(3)(a) and (b) set forth that the Competition Council could not authorise a concentration if restrictions were imposed on the undertakings concerned that were not indispensable for the concentration or that afforded the undertakings concerned the possibility of restricting competition in respect of a substantial part of the products or services in question. In 1999, the Belgian Parliament amended this provision but did not include it elsewhere in the Competition Law. As a result, the Competition Law is silent on this issue of so-called "ancillary restraints" in merger notifications. Whereas the relevant section of the notification form (section 9) dealing with ancillary restraints was maintained despite the amendment of the corresponding article of the Law, the competition authorities have published a note on the on-line version of this form, stating that this constitutes an error.

2552. This can be distinguished from EC merger control law, where the existence of restrictions that are not indispensable to the merger do not necessarily affect the legality of the merger itself, but simply the legality of the side restrictions.

2553. However, in its *CRH plc/NV Schelfhout C.* case (Comp. Council, 13 December 2000, No. 2000-C/C-41, *CRH plc/N.V. Schelfhout C., Belgian Official Journal*, 3 May 2001, 14383), the Competition Council has stated that: "*it is incorrect to claim that a non-compete clause, being an ancillary restraint, does not directly relate to the implementation of a concentration*" (emphasis added). This would seem to indicate that, at the very least, non-compete clauses should still be notified. This case law was rendered before the EC Commission adopted a new position on this issue in its Notice on Restrictions Directly Related and Necessary to Concentrations (O.J. [2001] C 188/5). Given that Belgian law is to be interpreted in the light of EC law, it is expected that clearance should no longer be sought or obtained for ancillary restraints.

§2. Case law

2554. The 1999 merger thresholds were conceived in order to reduce the inflow of notifications received by the Competition Council. However, the first years of operation of these new provisions show that the number of notifications has barely decreased. Today, merger control still accounts for the vast majority of the Competition Council's jurisprudence.

2555. It is also noteworthy that in a large majority of these cases, the Competition Council has merely stated that the concentration resulted in a market share of less than 25 percent. In only a handful of cases has the Competition Council refused to clear a concentration.

2556. In *Douglas/Ici Paris XL* (Comp. Council, 18 May 1994, No. 94-C/C 14, *Parfumerie Douglas GmbH/Compartilux SA*, *Belgian Official Journal*, 12 July 1994, 18412), the Competition Council blocked a merger in the perfume retailing business which, through an elaborate system of selective distribution (*i.e.*, excluding department stores, drugstores and beauty parlours), would have led to a dominant position on the relevant market, to the detriment of small and independent distributors.

2557. Clearance was also refused in *Callebaut/Barry* (Comp. Council, 3 June 1997, No. 97-c/c 11, *Callebaut A.G./Barry*, *Belgian Official Journal*, 14 June 1997, 16060), as the combined market share of the two companies on the open market of industrial chocolate in Belgium would reach approximately 85 percent. However, in June 1997, the Brussels Court of Appeal declared the decision of the Competition Council null and void for procedural reasons, and held that the Callebaut's acquisition of Barry was deemed approved (Brussels Court of Appeal, 25 June 1997, *Annuaire Pratiques du commerce & Concurrence* 1997, 1998, 719).

2558. The acquisition by IMS Health Incorporated ("IMS") of all European and Japanese activities of Pharmaceutical Marketing Services Inc. ("PMSI") was blocked (Comp. Council, 14 December 1998, No. 98-c/c-16, *IMS Health Incorporated/ Pharmaceutical Marketing Services inc. (PMSI)*, *Belgian Official Journal*, 9 March 1999, 7446) as the proposed merger would have strengthened the dominant position of IMS on the relevant market by allowing IMS to provide both quantitative and qualitative studies (*i.e.*, the company would have considerably reinforced its presence by providing an integrated service at a lower cost than its competitors).

2559. In its decision in *The Coca-Cola Company/Cadburry Schweppes* (Comp. Council, 26 April 1999, No. 99-C/C-04, *The Coca-Cola Company/ Cadburry Schweppes plc, Belgian Official Journal,* 7 July 1999, 25,512), the Competition Council denied clearance of the transaction (licensing of Cadbury Schweppes trademarks) primarily on the grounds that the Belgian operations of Cadbury would be heavily dependent on Coke's technical and logistical support. The Competition Council thus confirmed the theory of dominance through economic dependency in the context of merger control. This ruling followed a modification by the parties of an earlier notification, in which not only the licensing of trade marks, but also the transfer of certain production facilities was foreseen. In Kinepolis (Comp. Council, 17 November 1997, No. 97-C/C-25, *Kinepolis Group/Group Bert/Group Claeys, Belgian Official Journal,* 5 February 1998, 3276), the approval of a concentration was made subject to certain conditions to be fulfilled and guaranteed by the merging entities (*See*, Art. 32*quarter* of the Competition Law): the Competition Council granted an approval on the condition that the group emerging from the proposed concentration would not, among other things, (i) demand or request from distribution companies exclusive rights for the release of films in its cinemas, (ii) limit the release of the films it distributes to its own complex of cinemas, (iii) demand or request any priority rights for the exclusive release of a film during a specific period, and (iv) end the existing agreements with independent operators.

2560. In 3 decisions dated 12 November 2002 (Comp. Council, Nos. 2002-C/C-81 (*Electrabel Customer Solutions S.A./Sedilec S.c.r.l.*), 2002-C/C-82 (*Electrabel Customer Solutions S.A./Simogel S.c.r.l.*) and 2002-C/C-83 (*Electrabel Customer Solutions S.A./Intermosane 2*), the Competition Council prohibited a take-over by Electrabel Customer Solutions (a subsidiary of Electrabel, a firm which, until recently, had a monopoly on the Belgian electricity market) of the customers of certain intermunicipalities (*intercommunales*), which until then had been responsible for the distribution of electricity to the end customers. The mergers were planned in the context of the liberalisation of the Belgian electricity market, which precluded the intermunicipalities from operating the distribution grid and distributing electricity to customers at the same time. The 3 transactions were part and parcel of a *"Memorandum of Understanding"* between Electrabel and all intermunicipalities (associated in the Intermixt Wallonie group). The Competition Council judged that the 3 mergers would only serve to consolidate the already dominant position of Electrabel on the Belgian market. It is interesting to note that, only a few months earlier (Comp. Council, No. 2002-C/C-60 (*Electrabel Customer Solutions S.A./Ideg S.c.r.l*) and 2002-C/C-61 (*Electrabel Customer Solutions S.A./Interlux S.c.r.l.*) of 30 August 2002, *Revue Trimestrielle de Jurispru-*

dence, 2002/02, 94-110), the Competition Council had approved similar transactions whereby Electrabel Customer Solutions would take over the customers of two other intermunicipalities, albeit subject to severe conditions regarding contract flexibility and information toward the customers of their right to choose another distributor. The decisions of 12 November 2002 represented a new, more strict view of the Competition Council with regard to the competition issues involved in liberalising the Belgian energy markets.

2561. Cases like *Fortis Banque S.A./Heller International Group, Inc.* (Comp. Council, 25 January 2000, No. 2000-C/C-1, *Fortis Banque S.A./Heller International Group, Inc., Belgian Official Journal,* 9 March 2000, 7132) and *Canal+ Benelux B.V./ S.A. Deficom Group* (Comp. Council, 7 April 2000, No. 2000-C/C-9, *Canal+ Benelux/Deficom Group S.A., Belgian Official Journal,* 20 June 2000, 21585) show that also the shifting of shareholdings between existing shareholders of a company may constitute a concentration, in so far as such a shift results in an effective change of control over that company.

2562. The Competition Council has not in all cases displayed consistency in the application of the definition of a "concentration": in *Concentra*, the shares of the target company were equally divided among the 3 shareholders, yet there was no joint control, as all major decisions were taken by a board that acted by simple majority voting. The Competition Council nevertheless defined the transaction as a concentration, without indicating its reasons to do so. (Comp. Council, 19 May 2000, No. 2000-C/C-14, *N.V. Concentra Holding/N.V Concentra Grafische Groep/N.V Roularta Media Group/N.V Mercator Holding, Belgian Official Journal,* 30 September 2000, 33533)

2563. As stated above regarding the calculation of turnover, the basic rule is that only the turnover generated with respect to Belgian customers is taken into account (as it is surmised that the seat of the customer is the place where contracts are concluded and where competition with other suppliers occurs). Whereas the Competition Council has generally held to this approach, an exception was made in, *e.g.*, the *Ashton Mining*-cases (Comp. Council, 18 October 2000, No. 2000-C/C-30, *Rio Tinto Ltd./Ashton Mining Ltd., Belgian Official Journal,* 9 January 2001, 480 and Comp. Council, 18 October 2000, No. 2000-C/C-31, *De Beers Australia Holdings Pty Ltd./Ashton Mining Ltd., Belgian Official Journal,* 3 May 2001, 14,375). These cases concerned the diamond industry: although Antwerp is an obvious centre of this activity, most products are intended for customers located in India (where the diamonds are processed). The Competition Council disregarded the location of the customers in considering that the relevant turnover was, in fact, generated in Antwerp (*i.e.,* the location of the service rendered). The Competition Council explained its reasoning in *N.V. P&O Ports Holdings/N.V. Antwerp Combined Terminals* (Comp. Council, 8 November 2000, No. 2000-C/C-35, *N.V. P&O Ports Holdings/N.V. Antwerp Combined Terminals, Belgian Official Journal,* 3 May 2001, 14379): it cited the difficulty in verifying the location of relevant customers as well as the absence of geographic allocation of turnover in the company's books.

2564. In *C & N Touristic Belgium NV/City Bird Holding SA/City Bird SA* (Comp. Council, 19 September 2001, No. 2001-C/C-48, *C & N Touristic Belgium NV/City Bird Holding SA/City Bird SA, Belgian Official Journal,* 4 April 2002, 13908), the Competition Council applied the principle of the "failing company defense". This means the transfer of a company which would otherwise face bankruptcy.

2565. Whereas market shares no longer figure as criteria in order to determine the merger thresholds, the Competition Council relies heavily on them to determine whether a dominant position would be created or strengthened by a given concentration (*See, supra, e.g., Coca-Cola Company/Cadbury Schweppes plc* and the *Ashton Mining-*cases).

III. INSTITUTIONS

A. The Competition Service

§1. Composition

2566. According to the text of Article 14 of the Competition Law, 3 divisions may be distinguished within the Competition Service:
  (i) the Service itself;
  (ii) the Competition Council's Secretariat; and
  (iii) the College of Rapporteurs.

§2. Role and Competences

1. The Competition Service

2567. The Competition Service is a service within the Ministry of Economic Affairs. It is mainly responsible for investigating the cases covered by the Competition Law and ensuring that any decisions adopted pursuant to the Competition Law are properly enforced.

2568. Since the 1999 amendment of the Competition Law, the Competition Service exercises this competence under the control and according to the instructions of the College of Rapporteurs, which holds the right of initiative in competition procedures.

2569. The functionaries of the Competition Service also have the option to start a general or sectoral investigation *propriu motu* (*i.e.*, at their own initiative) in case of serious indications of the existence of prohibited restrictive practices.

2. *The Secretariat*

2570. The Secretariat serves as a registrar for the Competition Council. It is also a link between the administration, the Competition Council and the Ministry.

2571. It should be noted that Article 14 of the Competition Law merely states that the Ministry of Economic Affairs is responsible for the Secretariat. It is therefore no longer so that the functionaries of this Secretariat are chosen exclusively from the Competition Service. As it remains an important administrative tool, the Secretariat is none the less mentioned here as a functionally inherent component of said Service.

3. *The College of Rapporteurs*

2572. The College of Rapporteurs (*korps van verslaggevers/collège des rapporteurs*) was added to the Competition Service by the 1999 amendment of the Competition Law. Members are appointed by Royal Decree as a result of a comparative selection. Although they are members of the Competition Service, the Competition Law refers to an administrative and financial statute designed to provide for the necessary independence to fulfil their tasks.

2573. There is an equal number of Dutch-speaking and of French-speaking Rapporteurs. They select among each other a Chief Rapporteur for a 3-year term.

2574. The first Rapporteurs are functionaries of the Ministry of Economic Affairs, which were selected on an interim basis by Royal Decree.

2575. The College of Rapporteurs was created in response to difficulties in the delimitation of competences between the Competition Council and the Competition Service. The intention is to provide an independent link between these two institutions, to the greater efficiency of both.

2576. Article 14(2) of the Competition Law mentions the competences of this College:
   (i) leading and organising the investigations;
   (ii) giving orders to members of the Competition Service; and
   (iii) reporting on investigations to the Competition Council.

2577. Thus, the College of Rapporteurs serves as a medium between the investigation phase and the decision phase of a competition procedure (*See*, paras. 2597 *et seq.*).

2578. The Rapporteurs may act alone, unless the Competition Law provides that the College must act as a body.

B. The Competition Council

§1. Composition

2579. The composition of the Competition Council has been changed by the 1999 amendment to the Competition Law. The new Law foresees 20 effective members, rather than 12 effective members and 12 reserve members. Also the principle that half of the Competition Council's members should be magistrates has been abandoned.

2580. Aside from the President and the Vice-President, who are magistrates, 8 members are selected among magistrates, lawyers or university professors and 10 members are chosen because of their expertise in the field of competition. At least 4 of the members with legal professions should be magistrates.

2581. Another significant change from the past is that 4 of the Competition Council's members are appointed on a full-time basis, among which its President and Vice-President. These 4 members are in principle forbidden to exercise another profession during the term of their mandate. The magistrates among them will be replaced in their function as judges by newly appointed magistrates, so as not to disrupt the judiciary system.

2582. According to a new Article 18*bis* of the Competition Law, the members of the Competition Council are held to a strict duty of confidentiality.

§2. Role and Competition Competences

2583. The Competition Council is essentially an administrative tribunal. It is mainly responsible for adopting decisions pursuant to the Competition Law (negative clearances, exemption decisions and decisions relating to concentrations), and has broad advisory powers. It must also submit an annual report on the application of the Competition Law to the Minister of Economic Affairs.

§3. The President of the Competition Council

2584. As indicated above, the President of the Competition Council is a magistrate who is a member of the judiciary. Apart from his role as President of the Competition Council, he also may order interim measures with respect to cases which are being investigated under the Competition Law (Art. 35). In such case, the President is authorised to impose periodic penalty payments.

C. The role of the Belgian commercial courts

§1. The Commercial Court

2585. As a proceeding before the Belgian competition authorities has in the past proven to be rather lengthy, it comes as no surprise that private parties often prefer to bring their case before the commercial courts, who are competent to apply both national and EC competition law. Hence, often summary proceedings are brought in order to limit as much as possible the delay in obtaining a ruling which may counter the negative effects of the alleged infringement in the field.

2586. Legal confusion and uncertainty may be caused by the fact that 2 different and separate sets of proceedings (administrative and judicial) may be applied to the same facts at approximately the same time. Apart from this, it is understandable that a commercial court is disposed to pay more attention to the private interests at hand, especially where commercial practices are at issue, than to a more general concept of market order.

2587. It is however important to note that, whereas the commercial courts have competence to apply Articles 2(1) and 3 of the Competition Law, they are not entitled to grant individual or collective exemptions under Article 2(3) or a negative clearance under Article 6 of the Competition Law (Comp. Council, 25 January 2002, No. 2002-V/M-02, *S.A. Clear Channel Belgium/S.A. JC Decaux Belgium Publicité, Belgian Official Journal.*, 23 July 2002). By virtue of a recent decision of the Belgian Supreme Court (Cass., 7 January 2000, *T.B.H.*, 2000, 369), a trade practice restraining competition that is targeted yet permitted by both EC and Belgian competition law can only be prohibited under Article 93 of the Law on Unfair Trade Practices (*Wet van 14 juli 1991 betreffende de handelspraktijken en de voorlichting en de bescherming van de consument/Loi du 14 juillet 1991 sur les pratiques du commerce et sur l'information et la protection du consomateur*) if the alleged violation of Article 93 does not solely consist in the fact that this practice is restrictive of competition within the meaning of EC and Belgian competition law. It is noteworthy that this theory has been clarified in a later decision rendered by the Supreme Court (Cass., 25 October 2001, *A.J.T.*, 2001-02, 609-613). In this case, the Supreme Court explicitly ruled that sales at a loss by an undertaking that does not hold a dominant position on the relevant market could in certain circumstances constitute a violation of Article 93 of the Law on Unfair Trade Practices.

2588. In *VZW Radio Tienen/SABAM* (Comp. Council, 30 August 2000, No. 2000-V/M-27, *VZW Radio Tienen/C.V.B.A. SABAM, Belgian Official Journal,* 9 January 2001, 473), the Competition Council made it clear that it does not consider itself bound by a court decision on the basis of Article 2 or 3 of the Competition Law, as the objectives of the court in applying these Articles are entirely different from those of the Competition Council: whereas the court intervenes and judges on the basis of private interests of the parties involved, the Competition Council is concerned with general market conditions and the public interest. Both objectives require a different approach.

2589. Furthermore, unlike the Competition Council, the commercial courts do not have competence to rule on the admissibility of a concentration under Article 10 of the Competition Law. They will, however, refuse to grant any legal consequence to a concentration that was declared inadmissible by the Competition Council.

§2. The Brussels Court of Appeal

2590. The Brussels Court of Appeal is responsible for hearing appeals against decisions taken by the Competition Council and its President. It will also give preliminary rulings on issues of law concerning the Competition Law at the request of other courts and tribunals.

§3. The Supreme Court

2591. In reviewing last resort judgements rendered on appeal as well as the preliminary rulings by the Brussels Court of Appeal, the Supreme Court gives the ultimate explanation of the Competition Law.

D. The Competition Commission

2592. The Competition Commission is a joint committee which forms part of the Central Economic Council (*Centrale Raad voor het Bedrijfsleven/Conseil Central de l'Economie*). It has powers to advise on any draft decision where the Competition Law requires such consultation, on issues of general competition policy, amendments to the Competition Law and the adoption of group exemption regulations (Art. 21 of the Competition Law). The Competition Commission will act either upon its own initiative or at the request of the King, the Minister of Economic Affairs or the Competition Council. The Competition Commission must answer a request for an opinion by the deadline stipulated by the Minister, which must not be shorter than 15 working days. If the Competition Commission does not provide its opinion within the deadline imposed by the Minister, the opinion is no longer required.

E. The Competition Council of Ministers

2593. One of the main 1999 reforms of the Competition Law concerns the new powers granted to the Competition Council of Ministers, more particularly with regard to merger control (the so-called "third phase").

2594. Essentially, this third phase grants the Competition Council of Ministers the power to authorise a concentration deemed unacceptable by the Competition Council, if such is demanded by the public interest. By the same token, the Competition Council of Ministers may remove any conditions attached to an approval given by the Competition Council.

IV. RULES OF PROCEDURE

A. General

§1. Procedure

1. Initiation of proceedings

2595. Investigations by the College of Rapporteurs of anti-competitive practices may start as a result of one of the following acts:

  (i) requests by the undertakings or associations of undertakings concerned for a negative clearance or an exemption decision;
 (ii) complaints lodged by interested parties demonstrating a direct and immediate interest;
(iii) requests by the Minister of Economic Affairs or the Competition Council where there are strong indications of a restrictive practice (in violation of Art. 2(1) and/or Art. 3 of the Competition Law) or in connection with a proposal for a group exemption. The College of Rapporteurs may also start an investigation on its own initiative;
 (iv) requests by the Minister for Small and Medium-Sized Businesses of a public institution charged with the supervision of a particular economic sector in cases of restrictive practices (in violation of Art. 2(1) and/or Art. 3 of the Competition Law);
  (v) requests by the Brussels Court of Appeal within the framework of a request for a preliminary ruling.

2596. The rules to be followed by all interested parties to lodge a request or a complaint are further defined in 2 Royal Decrees dated 23 March 1993 and 22 January 1998.

   2. Investigative powers

2597. The College of Rapporteurs has wide investigative powers, comparable to those of the EC Commission. Pursuant to Article 23 of the Competition Law, the Rapporteurs may request undertakings and associations of undertakings to provide information. If the undertakings or associations do not provide the requested information within the time limit specified by the Rapporteur in charge of the case or if the information they provide is inaccurate, incomplete or distorted, the College of Rapporteurs can order, by a reasoned decision, that the information be supplied. Article 37 of the Competition Law gives the Competition Council the power to impose fines ranging from € 500 to € 25,000 if the information is not given accurately or within the time limit set for reply. Moreover, periodic penalty payments of up to € 6,200 per day may be imposed in the event that undertakings or associations do not comply with decisions requiring them to supply certain information. The Rapporteurs may also collect all information, take written or oral testimonies, obtain all necessary documents or information and make all necessary on-the-spot findings. They may conduct a search at the undertaking's premises in order to examine the books and other business records and take copies thereof. Also provided they have obtained the prior authorisation of a judge, they may conduct searches (between 5.00 am and 9.00 pm) at the houses of company managers, directors and staff, as well as all other internal and external persons charged with the commercial, accounting, administrative, financial and fiscal management of the undertaking. In the fulfilment of their task, they can effect seizure on the spot and seal off a premises for a period which cannot exceed 48 hours. These measures must be recorded in a written report, a copy of which must be handed to the person against whom these measures are taken. The Rapporteurs can appoint experts whose advisory task must be laid down by them.

2598. Investigations carried out by the College of Rapporteurs may only take account of facts which took place within a period of 5 years before the date on which the Competition Service decided to initiate an investigation, or was requested to do so. The statute of limitations is tolled by any investigations made during that period. These investigations cause a new 5-year limitation period to start. A limitation period, of 5 years, which is tolled by acts of enforcement, is also applicable to the payment of fines and periodic penalty payments.

3. Procedure before the Competition Service and the Competition Council

2599. Applications and complaints relating to practices restricting competition must be brought before the Competition Council, which will forward them to the College of Rapporteurs. The College of Rapporteurs will examine, prior to starting its investigation, whether the request is admissible (Art. 24 (2) of the Competition Law). If it concludes that the request is inadmissible, it will propose to the Competition Council that it does not act upon the request. If the request is deemed admissible by the Rapporteur, or if the Competition Council rejects the conclusion of inadmissibility reached by the Rapporteur, the Rapporteur will start its investigation. At the end of its investigation, and prior to drafting its report – which must indicate the grounds on which it is based – the Rapporteur will communicate its statement of objections to the enterprises concerned and must grant them an opportunity to present their observations (Art. 24(3) of the Competition Law). The Rapporteur then submits its report to the Competition Council. The report will include a proposed decision (Art. 24(4) of the Competition Law). Complementary investigative measures can be requested by the Competition Council (Art. 24(5) of the Competition Law).

2600. Upon receipt of the report from the Rapporteur, the Competition Council must inform the undertakings whose activities were investigated of the report's completion. It must send a copy of the report to them and, if deemed appropriate, also to the complainant. This must be done at least one month before the hearing at which the case will be examined. The addressees of the report must also be given the opportunity to consult a non-confidential version of the administrative file held by the Competition Council and obtain copies thereof.

2601. In *VT4 v. VTM* [Comp. Council, 23 April 2001, No. 2001-P/K-21, *VT4 v. VTM*, *Belgian Official Journal*, 21 September 2001, 31,739], the Competition Council refused to grant the complainant access to a report by an inspection body in the media sector that was filed as an exhibit to the Competition Council. This decision was motivated by the fact that this report still contained "business secrets" and that the confidentiality of such data had not yet been the subject of debate with the parties involved. This motivation is not directly based on the Competition Law, but emanates from the discretionary powers of the Competition Council in such matters.

2602. The parties may also submit written observations. The Competition Council will examine the case at a hearing where the undertaking whose activities have been investigated will be heard, as well as the complainant, should he so request. Other persons or undertakings may also be heard by the Competition Council.

The Competition Council can ask the Rapporteur to lodge a supplementary report and must specify the matters to which it must be related. This report must be communicated to the parties by the Rapporteur and lodged with the Competition Council (Art. 27(2)(6)). In any event, a decision must be made within 6 months of the initial report. The rules of procedure to be followed by the Competition Council are further defined in a Royal Decree dated 15 March 1993.

4. Provisional measures

2603. Article 35 of the Competition Law empowers the President of the Competition Council to adopt provisional measures in order to suspend the restrictive practices under investigation when this is necessary to avoid serious, immediate and irreparable damage to the undertakings whose interests are affected by these practices, or harm from being done to the general economic interest. The President will request the College of Rapporteurs to submit a report containing the measures the College of Rapporteurs considers necessary to suspend the restrictive practices. This report must be submitted to the President within the time limit fixed by the President himself. The President takes a reasoned decision on the granting of provisional measures. Before the Competition Law was amended in 1999, this decision had to be reached within a period of 15 days after the submission of the report. However, no time limit is fixed anymore in the amended Competition Law. All parties to the proceeding must be given access to the report and an opportunity to make their views known. The decision will be notified to the undertaking concerned and to the complainant. If the President of the Competition Council finds it necessary to inform interested third parties for the full effectiveness of the application of the provisional measures, the President of the Competition Council may decide to inform third parties about the decision. To inform third parties about the decision, it is possible that the President of the Competition Council imposes that the decision be referred to on the web site of the undertaking concerned. In the event that the provisional measures are not respected, the President of the Competition Council may impose periodic penalty payments of up to € 6,200 per day.

2604. The President of the Competition Council can grant provisional measures provided that 3 cumulative conditions are respected. These conditions, which have been established by the case law of the Competition Council, are: (i) the existence of a complaint; (ii) a *prima facie* infringement of Articles 2(1) or 3 of the Competition Law; and (iii) an irreparable prejudice to the complainant. The first condition allows to distinguish between a request for provisional measures before the President of the Competition Council and an action for summary proceedings before the ordinary courts, where the action can be lodged without a prior complaint. The second condition refers to infringements to the Competition Law and not to contractual breaches or infringements to the Law on Unfair Trade Practices. As to the third condition, it must be noted that a late request for provisional measures (*i.e.,* months or years after the complaint) may be interpreted as a presumption that there is no irreparable damage to the complainant.

2605. The President of the Competition Council has autonomous powers and he is therefore not bound by decisions of the ordinary courts raised before him by the parties in the case (*e.g.,* either an action for summary proceedings or a cease-and-desist action) (Comp. Council, 25 January 2002, No. 2002-V/M-02, *S.A. Clear Channel Belgium/S.A. JC Decaux Belgium Publicité, Belgian Official Journal,* 23 July 2002).

§2. Appellate procedure

2606. Appeal may be lodged against the decisions taken by the Competition Council, or its President, at the Brussels Court of Appeal within 30 days from the date of notification of the decision, or the date of publication of the decision in the *Belgian Official Journal.*

2607. Decisions by which the Competition Council refers a matter to the Rapporteur and decisions by which the chairman of the Competition Council extracts items from the dossier may not be the subject of a separate appeal.

2608. The appeal may be lodged by the undertakings that were subject to the investigation, by the complainant, by the Minister for Economic Affairs and by any parties that appeared before the Competition Council.

2609. The new provisions set forth that the appeal must be lodged against the decision and no longer against the Belgian State as represented by the Minister for Economic Affairs.

2610. The Competition Council and the Minister of Economy can submit written observations before the Brussels Court of Appeal (Art. 43*bis*, para. 2 *in fine* of the Law). They can also have access to the file but they cannot remove it.

2611. The appeal has no suspensive effect, although the court may, upon request, suspend the obligation to pay fines or penalties until the date of its judgment on the merits.

2612. The decision of the Brussels Court of Appeal is published in the *Belgian Official Journal.*

§3. Prejudicial questions to the Brussels Court of Appeal

2613. The new provisions on prejudicial questions are to a large extent inspired by the procedure before the Belgian Court of Arbitration.

2614. Article 42 and 42*bis* of the Competition Law provide that any court or tribunal with the exception of the Supreme Court, if it considers that a decision on the compatibility of a practice with the Competition Law is necessary in order to enable it to give judgment, may suspend the case and request the Brussels Court of Appeal to give a preliminary ruling.

2615. However, the court in which proceedings are brought is not obliged to stay the proceedings and to refer the matter to the Brussels Court of Appeal if:
    (i) the action is inadmissible on procedural grounds deriving from rules which are not themselves the subject of the reference for a preliminary ruling; or
    (ii) the Brussels Court of Appeal has already ruled on a question or on an appeal with the same subject matter; or
    (iii) an answer to the question referred for a preliminary ruling is not essential in order for the court to pronounce its decision; or
    (iv) the competition practice is manifestly unlawful.

2616. The registrar of the Court of Appeal will immediately inform the parties of the prejudicial question and invite them to make their written observations within one month.

2617. The Court of Appeal may ask the College of Rapporteurs to conduct an investigation in order to enable it to give its preliminary ruling.

2618. The new provisions of the Competition Law enable the Competition Council, the Rapporteurs and the Minister of Economy to intervene before the Brussels Court of Appeal. They can submit written observations and have access to the file. However, Article 42*bis*, paragraph 4 of the Competition Law stipulates that access to file must be exercised without removing the file. This would mean that no copies can be made.

2619. The ruling of the Brussels Court of Appeal is not subject to appeal and is, as to the legal issue that it addresses, binding upon the court or tribunal that made the request. However, as has been stated before, the Belgian Supreme Court gives the ultimate explanation of the Competition Law, although it may not re-examine the facts of the issue at hand.

B. Merger Control

§1. Procedure

1. Initiation of proceedings

2620. Investigations by the College of Rapporteurs of concentrations may start as a result of the following acts:

   (i) notification of concentrations by the parties;

   (ii) requests by the Minister of Economic Affairs or the Competition Council when a concentration has not been notified contrary to Article 12(1) of the Competition Law, or a decision taken by virtue of Articles 12(5), 33 or 34 of the Competition Law has not been respected;

   (iii) requests by the Minister for Small and Medium-Sized Businesses or a public institution charged with the supervision of a particular economic sector in case a concentration has not been notified contrary to Article 12(1) of the Competition Law.

2. First stage

2621. Following notification, the Competition Council is obliged to adopt a decision (which may include a decision to take its inquiry to a "second stage" investigation) within 45 days after notification of a concentration (Art. 33(2),2 of the Competition Law). If it fails to do so, the proposed concentration is deemed to be cleared (Art. 33(2),3 of the Competition Law).

2622. Time limits may be extended by agreement of all concerned. Failure to reply to an information request does not automatically stay the applicable time-limits. However, if information is not provided during the initial 45-day period, the Competition Council is likely to initiate a second stage investigation. The investigation process may only cover facts pre-dating the merger by 5 years or less.

2623. Upon receipt of a notification, the Competition Council immediately transmits the file to the College of Rapporteurs. The latter will appoint one of its members for the handling of the case. This assignment commences the investigative process.

2624. The first stage is to be completed within 45 days of receipt of a complete notification.

2625. The powers of discovery of the College and of the Service are considerable. In addition to the right to request information, they include the right to carry out on-the-spot investigations at the private dwellings of executives, employees and experts of the companies concerned, provided a prior authorisation is obtained from an examining magistrate. The power of the appointed Rapporteur to request information extends to third parties. The normal investigation process leads to the preparation of the Rapporteur's report, which contains its recommendations to the Competition Council. At the first level of investigation, the options are to approve the merger or to proceed to a second-stage investigation.

2626. The report prepared by the Rapporteur for the Competition Council must be sent to the parties at least 15 days before the proposed hearing date (Art. 32*bis*(3) of the Competition Law). The file of the investigation must also be made available for inspection. However, confidential information must first have been removed from the file (Art. 32*ter* of the Competition Law).

2627. Article 12(4) of the Competition Law requires parties to the transaction to refrain from taking any actions which could hinder the reversibility of the transaction until the Competition Council has made its decision on the proposed merger. This provision does not prohibit a merger from being completed prior to a final ruling of the Competition Council. However, parties bear the risk and possible costs of completing a transaction that subsequently may be dissolved by the Competition Council.

3. Second stage

2628. Where the Competition Council has decided to initiate a second stage investigation it must reach a decision within 60 days from the initiation of this second stage proceeding (Art. 34(1) of the Competition Law). Failure to do so will result in the proposed merger being tacitly approved (Art. 34 of the Competition Law).

2629. The Competition Council, following a second stage proceeding may order that the merger be prohibited as it creates or strengthens a dominant position which significantly hinders effective competition within the relevant market.

2630. If the merger has been consummated prior to its decision, the Competition Council may order a complete or partial dissolution or divestiture of the combined undertakings or assets with a view to re-establishing effective competition (Art. 33(4) of the Competition Law). The ability to make conditional orders is not limited. The Competition Council may give a conditional approval where the parties have entered into an agreement that is likely to restrict competition. The Competition Law does not limit the types of conditions which the Competition Council may impose on the parties.

§2. Appellate procedure

1. The Brussels Court of Appeal

2631. The decision of the Competition Council is subject to appellate review before the Brussels Court of Appeal. An appeal must be filed within 30 days from the day of publication of the decision of the Competition Council in the *Belgian Official Journal* (Art. 41(2)). The Brussels Court of Appeal has full powers of review (*i.e.,* it may go beyond a mere review of the legality of the decision involved in order to examine the facts of the case).

2. The Competition Council of Ministers

2632. The Competition Council of Ministers, at the request of the notifying parties or on its own, may approve the execution of a proposed transaction initially banned by the Competition Council within 30 days from the day of publication of the decision of the Competition Council in the *Belgian Official Journal*, on the ground that the restrictions to competition, identified by the Competition Council, are outweighed by reasons of general interest. The Competition Council of Ministers may even lift, partially or totally, the conditions and charges set by the Competition Council.

C. Fines

2633. The Competition Council may impose fines upon each of the undertakings concerned of up to 10 per cent of their annual turnover in the following cases:
   (i) when it finds a restrictive practice;
   (ii) when a condition or obligation attached to an exemption decision is breached;
   (iii) when an exemption decision was obtained on the basis of incorrect information or by fraud;
   (iv) when the parties abuse the exemption which was granted to them;
   (v) when a condition or obligation attached to an approval decision is breached;
   (vi) when the undertakings concerned, prior to the adoption of a decision by the Competition Council on the compatibility of a concentration with the Competition Law, take measures which hinder the reversibility of the concentration or that bring about a protracted change in the market structure.

2634. No fines may be levied for acts that take place between the time of notification of a restrictive practice with a view to attaining an exemption and the adoption of a decision by the Competition Council, provided these acts are within the limits of what is described in the notification (Art. 39 of the Competition Law). Of course, notification cannot be used in order to circumvent the imposition of fines for a blatant competition law infringement. On a literal reading of Article 39 of the Competition Law, it would seem that the immunity of fines only applies to mere notifications for an individual exemption (under Article 7(1) of the Competition Law), with the exception of notifications for a negative clearance (under Article 6 of the Competition Law). However, this is only very theoretical as, in practice, companies notifying with the Competition Council will most likely request an individual exemption at the same time as their request for a negative clearance. The Competition Council may also impose fines of between € 500 and € 25,000 upon persons, undertakings and associations of undertakings in the following cases:

   (i) when incorrect or misleading information is supplied in a notification or in reply to a request for information;

  (ii) when information supplied is incomplete;

 (iii) when information is supplied late;

 (iv) when the investigations by the Competition Service are hindered (*See*, Comp. Council, 16 February 2000, No. 2000-C/C-2, *Morgan Grenfeld Private Equity Ltd./Bambino Holdings Ltd., Belgian Official Journal,* 18 April 2000, 11,877); and

  (v) when a concentration is put into effect without prior notification.

2635. In practice, so far, the maximum fine imposed by the Competition Council in circumstances where the parties were late in notifying the planned operation is BEF 100,000 (*i.e.,* € 2,478.94) (Comp. Council, 29 September 1994, No. 1994-C/C-31, *N.V. Westimex Belgium/Dalgety Holland B.V., Belgian Official Journal,* 19 November 1994, 28762; Comp. Council, 15 September 1997, No. 1997-C/C-20, *De Post/N.V. Hagefin/R. Ketels/A. Boodts, Belgian Official Journal,* 22 October 1997, 28124. See, also, Comp. Council, 4 April 2001, 130. 2001-I/0-16, SA Daimler Chrysler Belgium Luxemburg/NV Van Steen, *Belgian Official Journal,* 19 July 2001, 29563). The Competition Council also once imposed a fine of BEF 1 million (*i.e.,* € 24,789.35) on undertakings which had appointed new executives prior to the decision to allow the operation and had thereby taken a measure impeding the reversibility of the concentration (Comp. Council, 26 May 1998, No. 1998-C/C-10, *Bodycote International Plc/HIT S.A., Belgian Official Journal,* 1 July 1998, 21626). In that case, the parties were also late by 7 weeks to notify the planned concentration but the Competition Council accepted that the parties (as well as the Competition Service) encountered difficulties in gathering the information on the Belgian market and their shares on that market. As a result, the Competition Council did not impose any fine in that regard. The Competition Council decided not to oppose the concentration.

2636. In case *NV BATC (now: NV BIAC)/NV Restair* [Comp. Council, 30 March 2001, No. 2001-E/A-14, *NV BATC (now: NV BIAC)/NV Restair, Belgian Official Journal*, 3 October 2001, 33517, the Competition Council imposed fines on the parties concerned due to the fact that they were late in notifying their agreement (a vertical agreement regarding exploitation of V.I.P. Lounges). This decision was criticized, as the Competition Law only foresees the imposition of a fine for tardive notifications with regard to concentrations (Art. 12, para. 1 of the Competition Law). Eventually, the Court of Appeal suspended the ruling and ordered the reimbursement of the fines, as it deemed that the parties involved had not had an opportunity to conduct a proper defense with regard to the imposition of these fines.

2637. In case *Occassiemarkt "De Zwarte Arend" bvba v. Honda Belgium NV (See,* para. 2520), the Competition Council imposed a record fine of BEF 45,800,000 (€ 1,135,352), of which BEF 30 million (€ 743,680) was on Honda alone.

2638. Finally, periodic penalty payments of up to € 6,200 per day may be imposed by the Competition Council or by its President in several situations described in the Competition Law.

14. UNFAIR TRADE PRACTICES

I. INTRODUCTION

2639. The law on unfair trade practices is designed to protect free competition. Its fundamental principle is that everyone is free to enter into the business of his choice and to compete in Belgium in any market at his discretion. A trader may thus lawfully attempt to attract the customers of his competitors. However, certain methods of competing and attracting clients are prohibited in Belgium under a theory of unfair trade practices. This means that persons engaged in trade or business must comply with certain rules of "fair play", and, more specifically, "fair trade practices".

2640. The law on unfair trade practices is governed by the Law of 14 July 1991 on Trade Practices and Information to and Protection of the Consumer (*Wet betreffende de handelspraktijken en de voorlichting en bescherming van de consument/Loi sur les pratiques du commerce et sur l'information et la protection du comsommateur* – the "Law on Unfair Trade Practices"). The Law on Unfair Trade Practices replaced the Law of 14 July 1971 and came into effect on 29 February 1992. Whereas under the Law of 14 July 1971 only the interests of competitors and other traders were protected, the Law on Unfair Trade Practices, for the first time, also protects the interests of consumers.

2641. Several changes have been made to the Law on Unfair Trade Practices since its entry into force. Two laws of 25 May 1999 have incorporated the provisions of 2 EC Directives into the Law on Unfair Trade Practices and updated the provisions of the Law on Unfair Trade Practices. The first law (Law of 25 May 1999 Amending the Law of 14 July 1991 on Trade Practices and the Information to and Protection of the Consumer – the "Law on Comparative Advertising") incorporated the provisions of EC Directive No. 97/55 on Comparative Advertising (Directive No. 97/55 of the European Parliament and the Council of 6 October 1997 Amending Directive No. 84/450 Concerning Misleading Advertising so as to Include Comparative Advertising, O.J. [1997] L 290/18 – the "Comparative Advertising Directive") into the Law on Unfair Trade Practices. The second law (Law of 25 May 1999 Amending Arts. 97 and 117 of the Law of 14 July 1991 on Trade Practices and the Information to and Protection of the Consumer – the "Law on Distance Selling") implemented the provisions of Directive No. 97/7 of the European Parliament of 20 May 1999 on the Protection of the Consumer in Contracts

Concluded at a Distance (O.J. [1997] L 144/19 – the "Distance Selling Directive"). The Law on Unfair Trade Practices as it stands today entered into force on 1 October 1999.

2642. The provisions of the Law on Unfair Trade Practices and some of its implementing Royal Decrees will be discussed below. First, the rules governing the information that traders must give to consumers will be discussed. Secondly, several regulated trade practices will be discussed. Thirdly, the treatment of unfair terms in consumer contracts will be examined. Finally, general prohibition of unfair trade practices contained in the Law on Unfair Trade Practices will be discussed.

2643. However, the Law on Unfair Trade practices did not fully implement the above-mentioned EC Directives. The Belgian provisions were restricted to any person engaged in trade or business, whereas the rules prescribed by the EC Directives were meant to apply to any seller or supplier, meaning any natural or legal person acting for the purposes relating to his trade, business or profession. This regulatory lack has been remedied by the enactment of the Law of 2 August 2002 on Misleading and Comparative Advertising, Unfair Contract Terms and Distance Selling, regarding Liberal Professions (*Wet betreffende de misleidende en vergelijkende reclame, de onrechtmatige bedingingen, en de op afstand gesloten overeenkomsten inzake de vrije beroepen/Loi relative à la publicité trompeuse et à la publicité comparative, aux clauses abusives et aux contrats à distance en ce qui concerne les professions libérales* – the "Law on Unfair Trade Practices in Liberal Professions"). The Law came into effect on 30 November 2002. Under the current Belgian law attorneys, accountants, auditors and tax advisers are still considered as persons engaged in liberal professions.

2644. 5 issues are addressed by the Law on Unfair Trade Practices in Liberal Professions. Firstly, it ensures consumers' contracts concluded with persons engaged in liberal professions adequate protection against comparative and misleading advertising, distance selling and unfair contract terms. It also provides for the appropriate enforcement tools and remedies. Most of these rules consist in a mere duplicate of the parallel provisions of the Law on Unfair Trade Practices; other provisions show slight differences.

II. INFORMATION TO THE CONSUMER

A. Indication of prices

§1. General principles

2645. Except in the case of public auctions, any trader who offers a product for sale to consumers must indicate its price unambiguously and in writing. When products are displayed for sale to consumers, the price must be clearly and conspicuously indicated (Art. 2, para. 1 of the Law on Unfair Trade Practices). Likewise, traders who offer services to consumers must also indicate the applicable price in writing in an unambiguous, legible and conspicuous fashion (Art. 2, para. 2 of the Law on Unfair Trade Practices).

2646. In order to inform the consumer fully of the price for products or services, the actual price or tariff payable must be indicated, including VAT, all other taxes and all charges for additional services which the consumer is obliged to pay (Art. 3 of the Law on Unfair Trade Practices).

2647. Article 4 of the Law on Unfair Trade Practices deals with the currency in which the prices must be expressed. This has been modified by the Law of 12 December 2001 concerning the Euro. It now provides that all prices and tariffs have to be indicated in Euro.

§2. Announcement and publication of price reductions

2648. The Law on Unfair Trade Practices contains specific rules governing announcements of price or tariff reductions (Arts. 42 through 45). Any trader announcing a price or tariff reduction must refer to the prices or tariffs he previously consistently charged for identical products or services in the same establishment (Art. 43, para. 1 of the Law on Unfair Trade Practices).

2649. To ensure that traders comply with this requirement, Article 5 of the Law on Unfair Trade Practices prescribes specific ways in which actual price or tariff reductions may be presented. Such presentation must take one of the following four forms:
- (i) the new price must be placed adjacent to the old price, through which a line must be drawn;
- (ii) the words new price (*nieuwe prijs/nouveau prix*) and old price (*oude prijs/ ancien prix*) must be placed adjacent to the respective amounts;
- (iii) the percentage reduction represented by the new price must be placed adjacent to the old price through which a line is drawn; or

(iv) the trader must publish a uniform percentage reduction applicable to all products and services or categories of products and services to which the publication refers.

2650. A trader may not offer a consumer a price reduction for a product or a service as a free offer of a quantity of a product or part of a service.

2651. The announced price reductions have to be real. Except for products that are subject to a rapid decrease in value, no price or tariff can be considered as the normal price if it has not been applied for an uninterrupted period of one month immediately prior to the date from which the reduced price will be applied. The date from which the reduced price will be applied must be indicated during the whole sales period. Except for clearance sales, this period cannot be longer than one month, and, except for products which cannot be kept longer, cannot be shorter than one whole sales day (Art. 43, para. 2 of the Law on Unfair Trade Practices).

2652. Article 43, paragraph 4 of the Law on Unfair Trade Practices was amended by Article 10 of the Law on Comparative Advertising. It provides that, with the exception of comparative advertising allowed for in Article 23*bis* of the Law on Unfair Trade Practices, the trader can only refer to other prices if he announces it in an unambiguous, legible and conspicuous fashion and if it concerns a retail price that is regulated by a law. In that case he cannot proceed to the forms of indication of a price reduction described in Article 5 of the Law on Unfair Trade Practices (*See*, para. 2649).

B. Indication of quantities

2653. The purpose of the provisions of the Law on Unfair Trade Practices concerning the indication of quantities (Arts. 7 through 12) is to provide consumers with correct information relating to quantities being purchased. Any product packaged for retail sale must bear on its packaging, or on the product itself where the product is sold without packaging, an unambiguous, legible and conspicuous indication of quantities in legal units (kilogramme, litre, metre or square metre), so that no doubt remains as to the quantity of the product sold.

C. Labelling of products and the use of languages on labels

§1. Rules of the Law on Unfair Trade Practices

2654. Article 13 of the Law on Unfair Trade Practices governs the use of languages on labels. It provides that the indications, which according to the Law on Unfair Trade Practices or its implementing Royal Decrees, must be inserted on the product label, the instructions on the use of the products and the warranties, are drafted at least in the language or languages of the language area where the products or services are put on the market.

2655. The expression "language area" refers to Article 4 of the Belgian Constitution. There are 4 language areas in Belgium: the monolingual (Dutch) area Flanders, the bilingual (French and Dutch) area Brussels, the monolingual (French) area Wallonia (except for the East Cantons), and the monolingual (German) area of the East Cantons. This means that a company that wants to commercialise its products in the whole country should preferably affix labels or use instructions in all 3 national languages.

§2. Compatibility with EC law

2656. The European Court of Justice has found the Belgian compulsory language requirements to be in violation of Article 14 of EC Council Directive No. 79/112 of 18 December 1979 on the Harmonization of the Laws of the Member States concerning the Labeling and Presentation of Foodstuffs Destined at the End User and concerning the Advertising in This Respect (O.J. [1979] L 33/1 – "Directive No. 79/112") and Article 28 [*ex* Article 30] of the EC Treaty on several occasions. This occurred in the *Peeters I* case (ECJ, 18 June 1991, Case 369/89, [1991] *ECR* I-2971), the *Meyhui* case (ECJ, 9 August 1994, Case 51/93, [1994] *ECR* I-3879) and the *Peeters II* case (ECJ, 12 October 1995, Case 85/94, [1995] *ECR* I-2955). In these cases, it was held that the applicable EC legislation provides that indications must be drafted in a language easily understood by consumers. In the opinion of the European Court of Justice, however, words of a language other than the language of the language area and signs, symbols, *etc.* can satisfy this requirement.

2657. These cases were confirmed by the European Court of Justice in its decision in the 1998 *Goerres* case (ECJ, 14 July 1998, Case 385/96, [1998] *ECR*, I-4431). This case concerned the German legislation that imposes the use of a certain language for the labelling of foodstuffs, but alternatively allows the use of a language that is easily understood by the purchaser. The Court found this legislation to be in accordance with Directive No. 79/112 because it did not impose a more stringent requirement than the obligation to use a language that is easily understood.

2658. For many products there is at present no harmonisation or only a partial harmonisation under EC law. It could be concluded from the *Peeters I* case that the same rules apply to those products as those that apply to foodstuffs, *i.e.*, the obligation to use a language that is easily understood by the consumer. This interpretation is based on the fact that the *Peeters I* case was not only based on Directive No. 79/112 but also on Article 28 of the EC Treaty.

2659. The decision in the recent *Colim/Bigg's Continent Noord* case (ECJ, 3 June 1999, Case 33/79, [1999] *ECR* I-3175) confirms this interpretation. The European Court of Justice decided that in respect of products for which there exists no or only partial harmonisation, EC Member States can impose additional language requirements. However, since these requirements restrict the free movement of products within the Community, they have to be proportionate to the pursued aim. In the opinion of the European Court of Justice, this means that a national rule that imposes the use of a certain language, cannot exclude alternatives such as words of another language that are easily understood, drawings or symbols. On that basis, the European Court of Justice found Article 13 of the Law on Unfair Trade Practices to be in violation of Article 28 of the EC Treaty.

D. Appellations of origin

§1. Concept

2660. Articles 16 through 21 of the Law on Unfair Trade Practices regulate the use of appellations of origin. Article 16 of the Law on Unfair Trade Practices reproduces the definition of the Lisbon Agreement for the Protection of the Appellations of Origin and their International Registration, to which Belgium is not a signatory. The concept of "appellation of origin" is defined as the geographical name of a country, region, or locality which serves to designate a product originating therein and the quality and characteristics of which are due exclusively or essentially to the geographical environment, including natural and human factors.

2661. Article 16 of the Law on Unfair Trade Practices makes it clear that not every indication of the place of origin may be referred to as an appellation of origin. Qualified and simple indications of source do not fall within the scope of Article 16. An indication of a place of origin may be referred to as an appellation of origin only if the following criteria are met:
(i) the appellation must be the geographical name of a country, region or locality;
(ii) the appellation of origin must serve to designate a product originating in the country, region or locality referred to;
(iii) there must be a qualitative link between the product and the geographical area. The quality and characteristics of a product must be due exclusively or essentially to the geographical environment. If the quality and characteristics of a product are due only to a limited extent to the geographical environment, the name of the product is not an appellation of origin but merely an indica-

tion of source, or even a generic name. The concept of geographical environment includes natural and human factors, such as the professional traditions of the producers established in the geographical area concerned; and

(iv) the appellation of origin must be established by Royal Decree at the national level. The regional legislative bodies may enact specific rules concerning the recognition and protection of regional appellations of origin (*e.g.*, the Decree of the Walloon Regional Council of 7 September 1989).

§2. Procedure

2662. At the national level, an appellation of origin is protected by Royal Decree (Art. 17 of the Law on Unfair Trade Practices). The procedure leading to the enactment of a Royal Decree protecting a specific appellation of origin is as follows: the Minister for Small and Medium-Sized Enterprises publishes an announcement in the *Belgian Official Journal* (*Belgisch Staatsblad/Moniteur belge*) inviting any interested person or association to comment, within a month, on the proposition to designate an indication of a place of origin as an appellation of origin (Art. 18 of the Law on Unfair Trade Practices).

2663. Following the proposition of the Minister, the Government enacts a Royal Decree designating the names which shall be considered as appellations of origin and determining the conditions which products must comply with in order to be manufactured, offered for sale or sold under a particular appellation of origin.

§3. Scope of protection

2664. The scope of protection granted to an appellation of origin established by Royal Decree pursuant to Articles 17 and 18 of the Law on Unfair Trade Practices, is very extensive. The general rule is that any usurpation or imitation of the appellation is prohibited.

2665. The Law on Unfair Trade Practices prohibits the use of an appellation of origin when this appellation of origin has not been established by Royal Decree (Art. 20, 1° of the Law on Unfair Trade Practices). It also prohibits the manufacture, offer for sale or sale of products under a specific appellation of origin where those products do not comply with the conditions laid down in the Royal Decree establishing that appellation of origin (Art. 20, 2° and 3° of the Law on Unfair Trade Practices).

2666. According to Article 21 of the Law on Unfair Trade Practices, the usurpation or imitation of an appellation or origin is prohibited, even where:

(i) the true origin of the product is indicated; or

(ii) the appellation of origin is qualified by terms such as "kind", "type", "fashion", "similar" or the like; or

(iii) words of a foreign language are used, if these words are merely a translation of the appellation of origin or if they can create confusion with an appellation of origin.

E. Advertising

2667. Articles 22 through 29 of the Law on Unfair Trade Practices deal with advertising. Their purpose is to protect the public in general, namely, consumers and persons carrying on a trade or business, against misleading advertising. It is this part of the Law on Unfair Trade Practices that has felt the greatest impact from recent legislative changes. The Law on Comparative Advertising has amended Articles 22 and 23 and has inserted a new Article 23*bis* into the Law on Unfair Trade Practices so as to allow for comparative advertising under certain conditions that are modelled on the Comparative Advertising Directive. Before the adoption of the Law on Comparative Advertising, comparative advertising was prohibited except in cases where it was absolutely necessary. The courts were very restrictive in their interpretation of this exception and almost never allowed comparative advertising.

§1. Definitions

2668. Article 22 of the Law on Unfair Trade Practices defines advertising very broadly as "*any communication that is directly or indirectly intended to promote the sale of products or services, including real estate, intangible rights and obligations, regardless of the place or the means of communication*".

§2. Prohibited advertising

2669. Article 23 of the Law on Unfair Trade Practices contains a number of prohibitions to which any kind advertising that meets the requirements of the definition is subject. The following types of advertising are prohibited:

(i) advertising containing allegations, indications or statements that are misleading as to the identity, nature, composition, origin, quantity, availability, method and date of manufacture, the characteristics and the environmental impact of the products concerned;

(ii) similar misleading advertising relating to the provision of services;

(iii) advertising that is misleading as to the identity or qualities of the trader of a product or service;

(iv) advertising whereby a trader omits essential information with the intention of misleading the consumer;

(v) any advertising that cannot be clearly recognised as such and does not clearly and unambiguously bear the word advertising (*reclame/publicité*). For instance, the advertising should be separated from the content of a newspaper. The practice of using the neutral term communication (*mededeling/communiqué*) is prohibited. Furthermore, the second sentence of this section – inserted by the Law on Comparative Advertising – provides that unsolicited advertising via e-mail must be clearly and unambiguously recognisable as such by the recipient;

(vi) advertising containing disparaging statements with respect to another trader, its products, services or activities, with the exclusion of comparative advertising allowed for under the conditions set out in Article 23*bis* of the Law on Unfair Trade Practices. Disparaging allegations are prohibited even when they are correct or truthful. The fact that the person making the disparaging allegations acts in good faith is irrelevant. Thus, allegations that a trader is dishonest, negligent or charges excessive prices, even if these allegations are correct, have been consistently condemned;

(vii) with the exclusion of comparative advertising allowed for under the conditions set out in Article 23*bis* of the Law on Unfair Trade Practices, advertising containing dishonest or disparaging comparisons or making it possible to unnecessarily identify one or more traders. The conditions of Article 23*bis* for comparative advertising to be permitted are discussed below. As mentioned above, this is one of the major changes made to the Law on Unfair Trade Practices;

(viii) advertising containing elements likely to create confusion in relation to a trader, its products, services or activities, with the exclusion of comparative advertising allowed for under the conditions set out in Article 23*bis* of the Law on Unfair Trade Practices;

(ix) advertising campaigns for "loss leaders" where the trader does not have a sufficient stock of the advertised products or cannot materially provide the advertised service so as to meet the demand that normally can be expected given the extent of the advertising campaign. Hence, the Law on Unfair Trade Practices provides for protection against the practice of advertising "loss leaders". A loss leader is a product sold or service provided on special conditions with the intention of enticing customers into a store and to sell them other products that generate a substantial profit margin;

(x) advertising giving consumers the hope or the certainty of having won or possibly winning a product, service or any advantage as a matter of chance. The prohibition does not apply to the advertising of officially permitted lotteries and of (free) offers of tickets to such lotteries;

(xi) advertising promoting behaviour that contravenes the Law on Unfair Trade Practices. For example, if a joint offer that contravenes the provisions of the Law on Unfair Trade Practices is advertised, the advertisement itself will amount to a violation of the Law on Unfair Trade Practices and may be prohibited on this ground;

(xii) advertising that refers to comparative tests made by consumer organisations;

(xiii) advertising concerning products or appliances that are not medicines and which are unjustifiably presented as improving the medical condition of the consumer; and

(xiv) with the exception of cases of permitted joint offers, advertising concerning the free offer of products or services or any other advantage if the question to obtain them is not separated from any order coupon for products or services. This last prohibition is new and has been inserted by the Law on Comparative Advertising.

2670. Article 4 of the Law on Unfair Trade Practices in Liberal Professions prevents any person engaged in a liberal profession from misleading advertising. Although the misleading nature of a specific advertisement is to be decided on a case by case basis, the deciding judge should consider following directives (Art. 5 of the Law on Unfair Trade Practices in Liberal Professions):

(i) any indication concerning the supplied goods and services regarding their availability, finish or execution, composition, quantity, specifications, fitness for purpose, geographic or commercial origin, expectations regarding a particular use, outcomes and essential characteristics of tests and inspections, or the omission of such information;

(ii) the price or method of price calculation, as well as the conditions under which the goods have been delivered, the services supplied; and

(iii) the skills, qualification and rights of the advertiser, including his identity, competencies, proficiency and his industrial, commercial or intellectual property rights, or his awards and honours.

§3. Comparative advertising

2671. As mentioned above, Article 23*bis* of the Law on Unfair Trade Practices allows for comparative advertising under certain conditions. This Article has been inserted by the Law on Comparative Advertising, which implemented the provisions of the Comparative Advertising Directive. This is one of the major changes to the Law on Unfair Trade Practices since it came into existence. The prohibition set out in Article 22*bis* of the Law on Unfair Trade Practices has been fully reproduced in Article 6 of the Law on Unfair Trade Practices in Liberal Professions. Thus, the same prohibition applies to contracts entered in with persons engaged in liberal professions.

1. Definition

2672. Comparative advertising is defined in Article 22 of the Law on Unfair Trade Practices as any form of advertising that explicitly or implicitly mentions a competitor or the products or services offered by a competitor. This is a literal copy of the definition contained in Article 2*bis* of the Comparative Advertising Directive.

2. Conditions

2673. According to Article 23*bis*, paragraph 1 of the Law on Unfair Trade Practices, comparative advertising is allowed if it satisfies 2 positive and 6 negative conditions that apply cumulatively. Comparative advertising is permitted provided that (i) it compares comparable (*i.e.*, substitutable from a buyer's perspective) products or services; (ii) it involves an objective comparison of one or more material, relevant, verifiable and representative characteristics of those products or services, which may include the price; (iii) it is not misleading, confusing or destructive; (iv) it does not dishonestly benefit from another business' reputation (parasitic comparison); (v) it does not present products or services as an imitation or counterfeit of products or services covered by a protected trademark or trade name; and (vi) it does not contain a comparison of products with different appellations of origin. These conditions are a faithful implementation of the Comparative Advertising Directive.

2674. Any advertising that explicitly or implicitly mentions a competitor or the products or services offered by a competitor and does not fulfil these 8 conditions is still prohibited under Article 23, 7° of the Law on Unfair Trade Practices. In this respect, a trader who uses a competitor's trademark as a metatag for his website in order to inform potential customers of his existence and his products only identify this competitor in his advertising without due comparison, therefore infringes Article 23, 7° of the Law on Unfair Trade Practices (Pres. Comm. Antwerp, 16 March 2000, *Jaarboek Handelspraktijken/Annuaire Pratiques du commerce* 2000, 101).

3. Special offers

2675. Article 23*bis*, paragraph 2 of the Law on Unfair Trade Practices deals with comparisons referring to special offers. It provides that any comparison referring to a special offer shall indicate in a clear and unequivocal way the date on which the offer ends, and, where the special offer has not yet begun, the date of the start of the period during which the special price or other special conditions shall apply or, where appropriate, that the special offer is subject to the availability of the products and services.

2676. This provision will change the judicial interpretation of the prohibition on advertising for sale without a sufficient stock contained in Article 23, 9° of the Law on Unfair Trade Practices (*See*, para. 2269) in relation to comparisons. The courts have previously interpreted this prohibition in the sense that traders could not exonerate themselves by the indication that the offer is subject to the availability of the products and services. The new provision on comparative advertising now provides that a comparison that refers to a special offer is permitted if it indicates, apart from the relevant date, that the offer is subject to the availability of the products and services.

2677. Article 23*bis*, paragraph 3 of the Law on Unfair Trade Practices repeats that all comparative advertising that does not comply with the conditions set out in paragraphs 1 and 2 is prohibited.

4. Influence on other provisions of the Law on Unfair Trade Practices

2678. As mentioned above, a *proviso* had to be added to Article 43, paragraph 4 of the Law on Unfair Trade Practices that deals with price comparisons. This Article does not apply to the types of comparative advertising that are allowed under Article 23*bis* of the Law on Unfair Trade Practices. The Comparative Advertising Directive and the Law on Unfair Trade Practices explicitly mention the price of a product or service as a material, relevant, verifiable and representative characteristic. Therefore, price comparisons that comply with the other conditions of Article 23*bis* are allowed and are not subject to Article 43, paragraph 4 of the Law on Unfair Trade Practices.

2679. The Comparative Advertising Directive is very favourable towards price comparisons because they increase competition. The Preamble to the Comparative Advertising Directive submits price comparisons only to the condition of not being misleading. If this interpretation were to be followed by Belgian courts, price reductions would not have to comply with the other conditions of Article 23*bis* of the Law on Unfair Trade Practices.

2680. Furthermore, a *proviso* had to be added to several of the prohibitions on certain forms of advertising set out in Article 23, *i.e.*, Article 23, 6°-8° of the Law on Unfair Trade Practices (*See*, para. 2269). In these prohibitions an exception is made for comparative advertising allowed under the conditions set out in Article 23*bis* of the Law on Unfair Trade Practices. Comparative tests that fulfil the requirements of Article 23*bis* of the Law on Unfair Trade Practices can no longer be prohibited.

§4. Verification of advertising

2681. Article 24 of the Law on Unfair Trade Practices provides that the competent Minister may compel a trader to prove within a period of 1 month that certain measurable and verifiable elements mentioned in his advertising are objectively correct. These measurable and verifiable elements are:
   (i) the identity;
   (ii) the quantity;
   (iii) the composition;
   (iv) the price;
   (v) the origin;
   (vi) the date of production or expiry;
   (vii) the conditions of sale, hire, lease, supply or warranty of the products or services that are the subject of the advertising;
   (viii) the modalities of use; and
   (ix) the availability and the existence of the offered products or services.

2682. In addition, any contracts or conditions of sale relating to products or services may be interpreted in the light of the elements mentioned in the corresponding advertising.

§5. Specific statutes

2683. Besides the Law on Unfair Trade Practices there are a number of statutes that provide specific rules with regard to advertising for certain products, services or professions. For example, Article 9 of the Law of 25 March 1964 on Pharmaceutical Products (*Wet op de geneesmiddelen/Lois sur les médicaments* – the "Law on Pharmaceutical Products") prohibits all forms of advertising for non-registered pharmaceutical products and advertising to the general public for pharmaceutical products that are subject to a doctor's prescription. The provisions of the Law of 25 March 1964 concerning advertising are implemented in a comprehensive and detailed way by the Royal Decree of 7 April 1995 on the Information on and Promotion of Pharmaceutical Products for Human Use (*Koninklijk Besluit betreffende de voorlichting en de reclame inzake geneesmiddelen voor menselijk gebruik/Arrêté Royal relatif à l'information et à la publicité concernant les médicaments à usage humaine*).

§6. Self-regulatory practices

2684. Mention should also be made of the activities of the "Advertising Ethics Jury" (*Jury voor Eerlijke Praktijken inzake Reclame/Jury d'éthique publicitaire*). The Advertising Ethics Jury is a self-regulatory body that issues non-binding recommendations to the media on the conformity of an advertisement with Belgian advertising law or with the Code on Advertising Practices of the International Chamber of Commerce. When an advertisement violates either Belgian law or the Code on Advertising Practices, the Advertising Ethics Jury may recommend the suspension of the advertising.

2685. A recommendation by the Advertising Ethics Jury is considered to be an effective means of stopping misleading and unfair advertising, since most of the media have agreed to follow the Jury's recommendations.

F. General obligation to inform the consumer

2686. Article 30 of the Law on Unfair Trade Practices requires the trader to disclose to the consumer correct and useful information relating to the characteristics of the product or service and the conditions of sale. The trader must fully inform the consumer, at the latest at the time of conclusion of the sale contract. In this respect, the trader must take into account (i) the extent to which the consumer expressed a need to obtain information, and (ii) the use to which the consumer has declared he will put the products or services to their reasonably foreseeable use.

G. Obligation to deliver an order form

2687. Article 39 of the Law on Unfair Trade Practices requires traders to issue an order form to the consumer whenever the delivery of a product or the supply of a service is postponed and an advance payment has been made by the consumer. The Law on Unfair Trade Practices empowers the Government to set out the elements the order form should contain. Article 39 of the Law on Unfair Trade Practices provides that these elements are binding on the trader who provided the order form and supersede all other contractual terms contained in general or particular conditions of sale.

III. REGULATED SALES METHODS

A. Sales at a loss

2688. Article 40 of the Law on Unfair Trade Practices prohibits any offer for sale or sale at a loss. A sale at a loss is defined *"as any sale at a price that is not at least equivalent to the price invoiced to the trader himself when he purchased the product or would repurchase the product"*. The Law on Unfair Trade Practices also defines a sale at a loss as *"any sale that provides the trader with an extremely small net profit margin"*. A small margin may be justified, however, in certain circumstances, such as when there is a substantial sales volume.

2689. However, products may be sold at a loss in specific situations enumerated in Article 41 of the Law on Unfair Trade Practices. These include the following:
  (i) seasonal and clearance sales;
  (ii) the sale of products that are subject to a fast decrease in value and which therefore can no longer be held in stock;
  (iii) the sale of products that were offered in response to a short-term trend and that, as a result of the decline of the trend, can no longer be sold under normal commercial conditions;
  (iv) the sale of products of which the commercial value is significantly reduced as a result of deterioration, reduced uses to which they may be put or a marked technological change; and
  (v) cases where the loss-making price corresponds to the price generally charged by other traders so that the competition forces the trader to use such a low price.

B. Clearance sales

2690. Clearance sales are sales announced under the names of *"liquidation, uitverkoop, Ausverkauf"* or similar names, that are held to accelerate the disposal of an inventory or of an assortment of products. Article 46 of the Law on Unfair Trade Practices provides that clearance sales may only be held in specific cases, such as, for example:
  (i) pursuant to a court order;
  (ii) the winding up of a business;
  (iii) the renovation or alteration of the business facilities that takes longer than 20 working days;
  (iv) the moving of the business premises from one place to another, provided the premises were exploited by the same trader for at least 1 year; and
  (v) serious damage caused to the entire inventory or to part of it.

2691. Prior to any sale or announcement of a clearance sale, a trader must inform the Ministry for Economic Affairs by registered mail of its intention to hold a clearance sale and the reasons for holding such sale. The trader may not proceed with the sale until ten working days after the registered letter has been sent. A clearance sale may not last longer than 5 months, with one exception. If the trader ceases his business activities because of retirement, the clearance sale can last for 12 months (Art. 48, para. 1 of the Law on Unfair Trade Practices).

C. Seasonal sales

2692. Seasonal sales are defined in Article 49 of the Law on Unfair Trade Practices as including all sales to consumers, at reduced prices, aimed at a seasonal replenishment of the trader's inventory. Seasonal sales must meet certain conditions. All seasonal sales must be announced under the names of "*soldes, opruiming, solden or schlussverkauf*".

2693. For clothing, leather item and shoes, seasonal sales may only take place from 3 to 31 January and from 1 to 31 July of each calendar year. If 3 January or 1 July of a particular calendar year is a Sunday, the seasonal sales may commence one day earlier (Art. 52, para. 1 of the Law on Unfair Trade Practices). For other products or categories of products the same period applies, unless the Government fixes another period by Royal Decree (Art. 52, para. 2 of the Law on Unfair Trade Practices).

2694. Seasonal sales must be held at the premises where the products on sale or identical products are usually sold (Art. 51, para. 1 of the Law on Unfair Trade Practices). Only products that were in the possession of the trader at the beginning of a seasonal sale and that were normally sold by the trader prior to the seasonal sale may be offered as part of the seasonal sales campaign (Art. 51, para. 2 of the Law on Unfair Trade Practices). Products that are sold during a seasonal sales campaign must be sold at a reduced price. The price reduction must be real in comparison to the prices previously and usually asked for the same products, that is, the price asked for identical products sold in the same premises during a period of at least one month preceding the price reduction (Art. 51, para. 3 of the Law on Unfair Trade Practices).

D. Combined offers of products and services

2695. The Law on Unfair Trade Practices contains a general prohibition on tying of products or services that are offered to consumers. A combined offer exists when the acquisition, whether for free or not, of products or services, any other advantages or vouchers for future premiums is conditional on the acquisition of other, even identical, products or services (Art. 54 of the Law on Unfair Trade Practices).

2696. Exceptions to this rule are as follows:

(i) the joint offer for a single price of products or services that constitute a single unit (Art. 55(1) of the Law on Unfair Trade Practices). Belgian case law is not very generous in its interpretation of what constitutes a single unit. The exception only applies if consumers have developed the habit of buying the separate products or services at the same time. This means that their decisions will not be substantially influenced by the fact that the products or services are offered together and that they cannot obtain a promotional advantage from the joint offer. For example, the offer of a mobile phone with a free SIM card and a subscription at half price during 3 months is not covered by the exception and therefore prohibited (Pres. Comm. Antwerp, 13 November 1997, *Jaarboek Handelspraktijken/Annuaire Pratiques du Commerce* 1997, 333). The same applies to the joint offer of a mobile phone and a subscription to a particular mobile telephony operator (Brussels Court of Appeal, 13 June 2000, *Jaarboek Handelspraktijken/Annuaire Pratiques du commerce* 2000, 320).

(ii) the joint offer for a single price of identical products or services, provided that the products or services are separately available at their usual price, the consumer is properly informed of the price and the fact that each product or service may be obtained separately, and the price reduction that results from the joint offer does not exceed one third of the full price the consumer would have to pay at the usual rate (Art. 55(2) of the Law on Unfair Trade Practices). Belgian case law construes the concept of "identical products or services" narrowly. Only products or services which are identical with respect to their form, dimension, quality, measures and characteristics are considered to be identical; products that are merely similar are not. For example, the joint offer of 2 books having a different title is not covered by the exception (Pres. Comm. Brussels, 23 May 1981, *J.C.B.*, 1982, 57). Likewise, a joint offer of 2 pairs of glasses, one pair having a value of BEF 350 (*i.e.*, about € 8.68) and the other pair having a value of BEF 245 (*i.e.*, about € 6.07) was held to violate the tying prohibition (Antwerp Court of Appeal, 10 May 1979, *R.W.*, 1979-80, 654);

(iii) the offering for free, together with a principal product or service, of accessories to the product, packaging, small products or services accepted by the trade, including delivery, installation, control and maintenance of the products sold, samples (to the extent that they are offered in quantities necessary to check the quality of the product), pictures and other print of minimal commercial value, vouchers granting participation in lotteries authorised by law and promotional articles that bear a non-erasable message provided that their value does not exceed 5 per cent of the price of the main article (Art. 56 of the Law on Unfair Trade Practices). The exception of the free offer of accessories to the product implies that the main product can be used without the accessories. For example, the offer of a mobile phone with a free subscription is not covered by the exception (Pres. Comm. Dendermonde, 21 January 1998, *Jaarboek Handelspraktijken/Annuaire Pratiques du Commerce* 1998, 318);

(iv) the free issue, together with a principal product or service, of vouchers entitling the consumer to a discount or a premium provided the specific requirements laid down in Article 57 of the Law on Unfair Trade Practices are complied with. In this respect, the offer by a chain of supermarkets of a free Christmas tree to consumers who had purchased at least 4 different and unrelated items completely for a minimum total amount of BEF 500 (*i.e.*, about € 12.39) was held to be contrary to Article 57(4) of the Law on Unfair Trade Practices (Comm. Brussels, 15 December 1995, *Jaarboek Handelspraktijken/ Annuaire Pratique du Commerce*, 1995, 278). This Article only allows the offering of vouchers, consisting of documents, that entitle the consumer after the purchase of a certain number of products or services to a free offer upon the purchase of a similar product or service. It was held that none of the products of which the varied choice of a consumer consists can be considered as a "similar" product. A trader issuing certain types of vouchers must be registered with the Ministry for Economic Affairs (Art. 59 of the Law on Unfair Trade Practices).

E. Free offer of vouchers

2697. Articles 63 through 68 of the Law on Unfair Trade Practices deal with the free offer of vouchers by a trader, producer or importer. The purpose of the Law on Unfair Trade Practices is to ensure that the obligations arising out of the issue of vouchers are honoured.

2698. To that end, vouchers must expressly mention the essential conditions of the offer: (i) the value of the voucher, (ii) the products or services to which the offer relates, (iii) the places where the voucher can be used, (iv) the term of the offer, and (v) the identity of the issuer (Art. 64 of the Law on Unfair Trade Practices) and they must be accepted by the traders concerned. Such traders must be reimbursed by the issuer within a reasonable period of time (Art. 66 of the Law on Unfair Trade Practices). The Law on Unfair Trade Practices gives the Government broad powers to regulate the issue of vouchers.

F. Public auctions

2699. Articles 69 through 75 of the Law on Unfair Trade Practices regulate public auctions. The general rule is that sales of new products at public auctions are prohibited, except in the situations provided by the Law on Unfair Trade Practices such as:
   (i) non-commercial auctions;
   (ii) auctions exclusively aimed at traders;
   (iii) auctions of works of art or collections;
   (iv) auctions in execution of a law or a judgement; or
   (v) winding-up sales.

G. Unsolicited products and services

2700. Article 76 of the Law on Unfair Trade Practices and Article 17, paragraph 1 of the Law on Unfair Trade Practices in Liberal Professions lay down the rules related to the unsolicited supply of products and services. They prohibit the forwarding to anyone, without prior request on his part, of any product with the invitation to purchase the product against payment of the price or, alternatively, to return the product to the sender, even free of charge. The same prohibition applies to unsolicited services. In the situation where a product or service is sent without the consent of the addressee, the addressee is entitled to consider the unsolicited product or service as a free gift and he cannot be required to make any payment. The Minister can make an exception to this prohibition in respect of offers with a charitable purpose.

H. Distance selling

2701. It is in this part of the Law on Unfair Trade Practices that the second major change was introduced in 1999 by the Law on Distance Selling, implementing the provisions of the Distance Selling Directive.

2702. The changes made to Articles 77 through 83 of the Law on Unfair Trade Practices are not very revolutionary since the Law on Unfair Trade Practices already contained a detailed set of innovating rules in this respect. The existing protection of the consumer concerning sales at a distance has been extended to all contracts concluded at a distance, with the exception of financial services. Recent developments relating to electronic commerce and electronic payment systems were also taken into account. Contracts concluded at distance with persons engaged in liberal professions are equally well protected, as Articles 11 through 17 of the Law on Unfair Trade Practices in Liberal Professions roughly reproduce the aforementioned provisions.

§1. Definitions

2703. Article 77, paragraph 1 of the Law on Unfair Trade Practices contains several definitions:

   (i) *distance contract*: this is any contract concerning products or services concluded between a trader and a consumer under organised distance sales or service-provision schemes run by the trader, who, for the purposes of the contract, makes exclusive use of one or more means of distance communication up to and including the moment at which the contract is concluded. This definition does not mean that the execution of the contract must happen at a distance;

  (ii) *means of distance communication*: any means which, without simultaneous physical presence of the trader and the consumer, may be used for the conclusion of a contract between those parties. The Distance Selling Directive contains in its Annex I an indicative list of means of distance communication, such as printed paper with or without address, press advertising with order form, catalogue, phone with human intervention or without human intervention (automatic calling machine, audiotext), videotext (micro-computer, television screen with keyboard or touchable screen), electronic mail, telefax and sales by television (teleshopping, telesales). However, it results from the general wording of the definition that all means of distance communication are covered by the specific legislation;

 (iii) *operator of a means of communication*: any public or private natural person or legal entity whose trade, business or profession involves making one or more means of distance communication available to traders;

  (iv) *financial services*: a number of banking, insurance, credit or investment services.

2704. Distance selling therefore falls within the scope of the Law on Unfair Trade Practices if a consumer receives an offer through a means of distance communication in the absence of a simultaneous physical presence of the trader and the consumer, and the sale is concluded without the physical presence of the trader and the consumer, *i.e.*, the consumer accepts the offer by using a means of distance communication. Thus, the contract must be concluded between a trader and a consumer who are simultaneously present neither for the offer nor for the acceptance.

2705. Article 77, paragraph 2 of the Law on Unfair Trade Practices provides that the rules on distance selling do not apply to contracts concerning financial services.

2706. As Article 11 of the Law on Unfair Trade Practices in Liberal Professions does not provide for any specific definition, the above-mentioned definitions also apply to Articles 11 through 17 of the Law on Unfair Trade Practices regarding Liberal Professions. Pursuant to Article 11, said Law also excludes financial services.

§2. Compulsory information

2707. When receiving an offer via a means of distance selling, the consumer should be clearly and unambiguously informed, so that no doubt remains regarding the following elements:
   (i) the identity and address of the trader;
   (ii) the most important characteristics of the product or service;
   (iii) the price of the product or service;
   (iv) the costs of delivery, if any;
   (v) the means of payment, delivery or execution of the contract;
   (vi) the cooling-off period;
   (vii) how to reject a product and how to return a product (including a listing of any applicable return charges);
   (viii) the costs of use of a means of distance communication when calculated on a different basis than the standard rates; and
   (ix) the validity period of the offer.

2708. In case of a telephone conversation, the trader must mention his identity and the commercial purpose of the phone call explicitly at the beginning of the conversation (Art. 78 of the Law on Unfair Trade Practices).

2709. Said provisions are extended to contracts concluded with persons engaged in liberal professions, as the wording of the provision set out in Article 12 of the Law on Unfair Trade Practices in Liberal Professions is identical to the wording of Article 78 of the Law on Unfair Trade Practices.

§3. Confirmation of information

2710. According to Article 79 of the Law on Unfair Trade Practices and Article 13 of the Law on Unfair Trade Practices in Liberal Professions, certain information must be confirmed to the consumer in writing or via another medium at his disposal and accessible by him.

§4. Cooling-off period

2711. A distance contract is only definitively concluded after a cooling-off period of at least 7 working days within which the consumer has the right to reject the contract without giving any reason. Only the direct costs of sending back the ordered items can be charged to the consumer. However, these costs cannot be charged to the consumer if the trader did not comply with his obligation to inform the consumer as contained in Articles 78 and 79, paragraph 1 of the Law on Unfair Trade Practices or Article 13 of the Law on Unfair Trade Practices in Liberal Professions.

2712. The duration and calculation of the cooling-off period depend on whether or not the trader complied with his obligation to inform the consumer contained in Article 79, paragraph 1 of the Law on Unfair Trade Practices or Article 13 of the Law on Unfair Trade Practices in Liberal Professions. The cooling-off period always starts running on the day following the triggering event:

(i) If the trader complied with his obligation to inform, the cooling-off period is 7 working days and starts running:
   (a) for products: from the moment of delivery; and
   (b) for services: from the moment of entering into the contract or from the moment of compliance with the obligation to inform (Art. 80, para. 1 of the Law on Unfair Trade Practices and Article 14, para.1 of the Law on Unfair Trade Practices in Liberal Professions).
(ii) If the trader did not comply with his obligation to inform, the cooling-off period is 3 months and starts running:
   (a) for products: from the moment of delivery;
   (b) for services: from the moment of entering into the contract.

However, if the information is provided within the 3-month period, the cooling-off period of 7 working days will nevertheless start running (Art. 80, para. 2 of the Law on Unfair Trade Practices and Art. 14, para.1 of the Law on Unfair Trade Practices in Liberal Professions).

2713. The rejection of the offer is valid if the consumer "notifies" the trader of his rejection before the end of the cooling-off period. The Law on Unfair Trade Practices does not specify how this notification should occur, but the consumer will have to provide proof of this notification. However, in case of dispute, the burden of proof of a timely notification rests on the trader (Art. 82, para. 1 of the Law on Unfair Trade Practices and Art. 16 of the Law on Unfair Trade Practices in Liberal Professions).

2714. Without prejudice to the application of Article 45, paragraph 1 of the Law of 12 June 1991 concerning Credit to Consumers (*Wet op het consumentenkrediet/ Loi relative au crédit à la consommation*), no advance payment or payment can be demanded from the consumer during the cooling-off period of 7 working days described in Article 80, paragraph 1 of the Law on Unfair Trade Practices. This prohibition does not apply, however, if the trader provides proof that he has respected the rules specified by Royal Decree allowing reimbursement of amounts paid by the consumer. In case of exercise of the rejection right described in Article 80, paragraphs 1 and 2 or Article 14 of the Law on Unfair Trade Practices in Liberal Professions, the trader is obliged to reimburse free of charge the amounts paid by the consumer. The reimbursement has to be carried out within thirty days following the rejection (Art. 80, para. 3 of the Law on Unfair Trade Practices; Art. 14, para. 3 of the Law on Unfair Trade Practices in Liberal Professions).

2715. Unless otherwise agreed between the parties, the consumer cannot exercise the rejection right described in Article 80, paragraphs 1 and 2 of the Law on Unfair Trade Practices for contracts and Article 14, paragraph 3 of the Law on Unfair Trade Practices in Liberal Professions concerning:

    (i) the supply of services the execution of which has started with the approval of the consumer before the end of the cooling-off period of 7 working days described in Article 80, paragraph 1 of the Law on Unfair Trade Practices;

    (ii) the delivery of products manufactured according to the specific instructions of the consumer or having an obvious personal character, or that cannot be sent back or can rapidly go off or by their nature become outdated;

    (iii) the supply of audio or video recordings and computer programming tools the seals of which have been broken by the consumer;

    (iv) the supply of newspapers, periodicals and magazines; and

    (v) gambling and lotteries (Art. 80, para. 4 of the Law on Unfair Trade Practices).

2716. The consequences of the exercise of the rejection right are set out in Article 81, paragraphs 3 and 4 of the Law on Unfair Trade Practices. Upon rejection, the possible costs of sending back cannot be charged to the consumer if the delivered product or the supplied service do not match the description of the offer or if the trader did not comply with his obligation to inform the consumer contained in Articles 78 and 79, paragraph 1 of the Law on Unfair Trade Practices.

2717. Upon rejection of a contract financed by a credit agreement, the consumer can reject the credit agreement free of charge, provided that:

    (i) the credit agreement was entered into with the trader or supplied by a third party, to the extent that there exists an agreement between this third party and the trader with the purpose of ensuring the financing of the sale by the latter, and

    (ii) the rejection of the credit agreement occurs within the periods and in accordance with the terms contained in Article 80 of the Law on Unfair Trade Practices and Article 14 of the Law on Unfair Trade Practices in Liberal Professions.

§5. *The execution of the contract*

2718. Unless the parties have agreed otherwise, the trader must execute the order within 30 days following the order, to be calculated from the day following the day on which the consumer sent his order to the trader. With the exception of *force majeure*, the contract will be dissolved automatically in case of non-execution by the trader, without prejudice to the possibility of the customer claiming damages.

2719. Upon expiry of the execution period of 30 days, the parties can agree to an extension of this period. No fees or costs originating from the dissolution can be charged to the consumer. The amounts that the consumer might already have paid must be reimbursed to him within 30 days (Art. 81, para. 1 of the Law on Unfair Trade Practices).

2720. The sending of products and titles representing services occurs at the risk of the trader (Art. 81, para. 2 of the Law on Unfair Trade Practices). This means that the risk of loss or destruction resting on the consumer as the owner, from the moment of the entering into the contract, is seriously limited during transportation in case of distance selling.

2721. Article 15, paragraph 1 of the Law on Unfair Trade Practices in Liberal Professions sets out an equivalent provision.

§6. *Electronic payment*

2722. Article 81, paragraph 5 of the Law on Unfair Trade Practices deals with protection measures for consumers who use an instrument for electronic transfer of money in case of a distance contract. According to the Explanatory Notes (*Memorie van Toelichting/Exposé des Motifs*) of the Law on Unfair Trade Practices, these instruments include all means of payment that allow the holder to transfer money to the addressee using a pin code or another proof of identification.

2723. The issuer of an instrument for electronic payment must provide the consumer with appropriate means of declaration in case of loss, theft or fraudulent use of such an instrument. The issuer will usually be a bank or a credit card company, but can also be a company that handles the "merchant acquiring" of a credit card company (*e.g.*, Bank Card Company handles the merchant acquiring of Visa/Mastercard/Eurocard in Belgium).

2724. As soon as the consumer becomes aware of (i) the loss or theft of the instrument or the means that allow its use or (ii) any fraudulent use of the instrument, he should declare this to the issuer or to the entity appointed by the issuer. Until this declaration, the consumer is liable for the consequences of the loss, theft or fraudulent use of the instrument by a third party for any amount of up to € 150, except if (i) the consumer acted with serious negligence, in which case he will be liable for the amount to be determined by Royal Decree, or if (ii) the consumer acted fraudulently, in which case he will be liable without limitation. After the declaration, the consumer who did not act fraudulently will no longer be liable for the consequences of the loss, theft or fraudulent use of the instrument by a third party.

2725. Contrary to the liability regime mentioned above, the consumer is not liable in case of use of the instrument without physical presentation or electronic identification of the instrument. These are the cases of on-line payment. As this kind of payment is currently not yet secured, it is logical that the issuer carries the risk. In this hypothesis, the consumer can demand the annulment of the payment in case of fraudulent use of the instrument. The issuer must reimburse the consumer the amounts that have already been paid within 30 days. If the consumer acted fraudulently, an amount to be determined by Royal Decree can be deducted from the payments the issuer has to reimburse.

2726. Pursuant to Article 15 of the Law on Unfair Trade Practices in Liberal Professions, Article 81, paragraph 5 of the Law on Unfair Trade Practises also applies to contracts concluded by consumers with persons engaged in liberal professions.

§7. Burden of proof

2727. The burden of proof of the existence of the compulsory information, the confirmation thereof, the compliance with the time limits and the consent of the consumer rests on the trader (Art. 82, para. 1 of the Law on Unfair Trade Practices and Art. 16 of the Law on Unfair Trade Practices in Liberal Professions). This regime of proof considerably mitigates the previous regime of proof under which it was impossible to use presumptions. The relaxation was necessary in the light of technological evolution that encourages the consumer to consent other than in writing.

§8. Requirement of consent of the consumer for the use of certain means of communication

2728. In relation to distance contracts, the use of the following means of communication requires the consent of the consumer:
(i) automated retrieval systems without human intervention (retrieval automation), e.g., answering machines displaying options to buy products or services and on-line contracting; and
(ii) fax.

2729. This list can be extended by Royal Decree.

2730. Other means of communication can only be used in the absence of an apparent objection of the consumer. No charges can be made to the consumer for the exercise of his right to object. The means of exercise of this opposition right will be determined by Royal Decree (Art. 82, para. 2 of the Law on Unfair Trade Practices and Art. 17, para. 2 of the Law on Unfair Trade Practices in Liberal Professions).

I. Illicit sales practices

2731. Article 84 of the Law on Unfair Trade Practices prohibits dishonest sales practices, such as pyramid sales (*i.e.*, sales through a hierarchy structured network, where the gain is not meant to arise from the benefit margin of the sale to the consumer, but mainly from the benefit margin of the sale to the resellers, whether professionals or not) and snowball sales (*i.e.*, sales to consumers whereby a consumer's hope arises that he will be offered the chance to get certain products or services for free or below their value, if he incites a number of other consumers, who are not already involved, to purchase the products or services concerned).

2732. Article 85 of the Law on Unfair Trade Practices prohibits sales practices that make misleading references to philanthropic or humanitarian causes.

J. Consumer sales concluded outside the business premises of the trader

2733. Articles 86 through 92 of the Law on Unfair Trade Practices deal with consumer sales concluded outside the business premises of the trader. These provisions of the Law on Unfair Trade Practices incorporate into Belgian law the principles of the EC Council Directive of 20 December 1985 to Protect the Consumer in Respect of Contracts Negotiated Away From Business Premises (O.J. [1985] L 372/31).

§1. Scope of application

2734. The sales contracts in question are those in which a trader supplies products or services to a consumer and that are concluded:
   (i) at the consumer's home, at the home of another consumer, or at the consumer's place of work;
   (ii) during an excursion organised by or for the trader; or
   (iii) during a commercial fair or an exhibition, provided in such case that payment of the entire amount is not made on the spot and the price exceeds € 200 (Art. 86 of the Law on Unfair Trade Practices).

2735. The scope of application of the relevant consumer protection rules do not apply, *inter alia*, to:

(i) contracts concluded at the consumer's home, at the home of another consumer or at the consumer's place of work, when the consumer has expressly requested the visit of the trader in order to negotiate the purchase of a product or service. The Law on Unfair Trade Practices provides that, where a trader offers by telephone to visit the consumer, the consent of the consumer to such offer does not constitute a preliminary request;

(ii) contracts for the supply of foodstuffs, beverages and household articles supplied by regular roundsmen;

(iii) public auction sales;

(iv) distance sales; and

(v) insurance contracts (Art. 87 of the Law on Unfair Trade Practices).

§2. Compulsory information

2736. Consumer sales concluded outside the business premises of the trader must be concluded in writing in as many originals as there are contracting parties with separate interests. The written contract must be executed at the latest at the time of delivery. The contract must mention the following elements: (i) identity and address of the trader, (ii) date and place of conclusion of the contract, (iii) identification of the product or service and of its main characteristics, (iv) delivery conditions, price and modalities of payment, and (v) a renunciation clause conspicuously inserted in heavy print on the first page of the contract. This renunciation clause mentions the right of the consumer to renounce the sale by registered letter free of charge within seven working days as of the day following the day of the signing of the contract (Art. 88 of the Law on Unfair Trade Practices).

§3. Cooling-off period

2737. The sales of products and services concluded outside the business premises of the trader are only concluded after a cooling-off period of 7 working days as of the day following the day of the signing of the contract. During this period the consumer has the right to inform the trader by registered letter that he renounces the sale. No supply of services can take place until this cooling-off period has expired. With the exception of sales concluded during a commercial fair or exhibition, no advance payment or payment in any form can be demanded or accepted from the consumer before the expiry of the cooling-off period.

IV. UNFAIR TERMS IN CONSUMER CONTRACTS

2738. The adoption of the Law on Unfair Trade Practices marks an important step in the development of the rules protecting consumers against unfair terms in contracts. Prior to the adoption of the Law on Unfair Trade Practices, Belgium lacked comprehensive legislation relating to unfair terms in consumer contracts. Chapter V of the Law on Unfair Trade Practices introduced into Belgian law the first comprehensive statutory provisions on unfair terms in consumer contracts. After the adoption of the Law on Unfair Trade Practices, several changes have been made to the provisions governing unfair terms in consumer contracts. Most of the changes were additions to the list of blacklisted terms. Chapter III of the Law on Unfair Trade Practices in Liberal Professions contains the rules regarding unfair terms in contracts entered in by consumers with persons engaged in liberal professions.

A. Scope of application

2739. The scope of application of Chapter V of the Law on Unfair Trade Practices is confined to contracts concluded with consumers. A "consumer" is defined as *"any physical person or legal entity who acquires or uses products or services exclusively for non-professional purposes"* (Art. 1(7) of the Law on Unfair Trade Practices). Article 31, paragraph 2 of the Law on Unfair Trade Practices provides that for the purposes of the section of the Law on Unfair Trade Practices dealing with unfair terms in consumer contracts, "trader" and "products" have a different meaning than in the other parts of the Law on Unfair Trade Practices. A "trader" means *"any natural person or legal entity that acts within the boundaries of its professional activity in the conclusion of a contract with a consumer, with the exception of self-employed persons"*. "Products" include not only physical movable goods, but also immovable goods, rights and obligations. On the contrary, Chapter III of the Law on Unfair Trade Practices in Liberal Professions does not provide for a particular scope of application.

2740. Article 31, paragraph 1 of the Law on Unfair Trade Practices and Article 7, paragraph 2 of the Law on Unfair Trade Practices in Liberal Professions provide that a contractual term is unfair if, alone or in combination with another term or terms, it causes a significant imbalance in the contracting parties' rights and obligations. For the purposes evaluating the unfair character of a contractual term, all circumstances surrounding the conclusion of the contract and all the other terms of the contract or of another contract on which the contract depends at the moment of its conclusion should be taken into account, having regard to the products or services to which the contract relates. The assessment of the unfair character of a contractual term does not relate to the determination of the proper subject of the contract, nor to the equivalence of the price or fee on the one hand and the products to be delivered or the services to be supplied on the other hand, to the extent that these terms are formulated clearly and unambiguously (Art. 31, para. 3 of the Law on Unfair Trade Practices and Art. 8 of the Law on Unfair Trade Practices in Liberal Professions).

2741. If some or all of the contractual terms are written, they must be set out clearly and unambiguously. In case of doubt about the meaning of a term, the interpretation that is most favourable towards the consumer prevails. However, this rule does not apply to a cease-and-desist order on the basis of Article 95 of the Law on Unfair Trade Practices (Art. 31, para. 3 of the Law on Unfair Trade Practices and Art. 9 of the Law on Unfair Trade Practices in Liberal Professions).

2742. Article 33 of the Law on Unfair Trade Practices provides that if some of the terms of a contract are considered to be unfair and therefore void, the remainder of the contract is still binding on the parties provided that it can continue to exist without the void terms. Article 32 of the Law on Unfair Trade Practices contains a "blacklist" of prohibited terms in consumer contracts, that is, terms that are always void. Similarly, Article 7, paragraph 4 of the Law on Unfair Trade Practices in Liberal Professions prohibits the terms "blacklisted" in the Annex to the Law on Unfair Trade Practices in Liberal Professions.

B. Blacklisted provisions

§1. Performance

2743. The following clauses relating to contracts between a trader and a consumer are always void:
   (i) provisions whereby the consumer is immediately and definitively bound at the time of the signing of the contract, while the trader's or professional's commitment is subject to a condition the fulfilment of which is within the trader's or professional's sole discretion (Art. 32(1) of the Law on Unfair Trade Practices and Section 1(c) of the Annex to the Law on Unfair Trade Practices in Liberal Professions);
   (ii) provisions that grant the trader or professional the right to change the characteristics of the product or service unilaterally in cases where the trader has been informed that the characteristics of the product or service are essential to the consumer or where such characteristics are essential for the purpose served by the product or service (Art. 32(3) of the Law on Unfair Trade Practices and Section 1(k) of the Annex to the Law on Unfair Trade Practices in Liberal Professions);

(iii) provisions that entitle the trader to fix or to modify, at his sole discretion, the performance period (Art. 32(4) of the Law on Unfair Trade Practices) and Section 1(j) of the Annex to the Law on Unfair Trade Practices in Liberal Professions);

(iv) provisions whereby the trader reserves the right to decide, at his sole discretion, whether the products delivered or the services supplied are in conformity with those contractually agreed upon, or whereby the trader reserves the exclusive right to interpret any clause of the contract (Art. 32(5) of the Law on Unfair Trade Practices and Section 1(m) of the Annex to the Law on Unfair Trade Practices in Liberal Professions);

(v) provisions providing that the consumer must perform his obligations, even though the trader has not performed his obligations or fails to perform his obligations (Art. 32(8) of the Law on Unfair Trade Practices and Section 1(o) of the Annex to the Law on Unfair Trade Practices in Liberal Professions); and

(vi) provisions irrefutably determining the consumer's consent to terms the content of which could not actually be checked before concluding the contract (Art. 32(23) of the Law on Unfair Trade Practices and Section 1(i) of the Annex to the Law on Unfair Trade Practices in Liberal Professions).

§2. Price

2744. Following price stipulations in consumers' contracts with persons engaged in liberal professions are void (Section 1(1) of the Annex to the Law on Unfair Trade Practices in Liberal Professions). Firstly, a clause according to which the price of goods will be determined at the time of delivery without giving the consumer the equivalent right to cancel the contract if the final price is too high in relation to the price agreed when the contract was concluded. Secondly and under the same conditions, a clause allowing a seller of goods or supplier of services to increase their price once the contract has been concluded.

§3. Termination

2745. The following termination-related provisions are void:

(i) According to both the Law on Unfair Trade Practices and the Law on Unfair Trade Practices in Liberal Professions:

(a) provisions binding the consumer for an indefinite period without clearly mentioning a reasonable period of notice to terminate the contract (Art. 32(16) of the Law on Unfair Trade Practices and Section 1(g) of the Annex to the Law on Unfair Trade Practices in Liberal Professions);

    (b) provisions extending the contract for an unreasonable period if the con-
sumer fails to terminate the contract in time, or automatically extending
a contract of fixed duration in the absence of notification to the contrary
by the consumer where the ultimate date stipulated for notification by the
consumer of his decision not to extend the contract is too remote from
the end of the contract (Art. 32(17) of the Law on Unfair Trade Practices
and Section 1(h) of the Annex to the Law on Unfair Trade Practices in
Liberal Professions);

(ii) Pursuant the Law on Unfair Trade Practices:

    (a) provisions preventing the consumer from terminating the contract in case
the trader fails to perform his obligations (Art. 32(6) of the Law on Unfair Trade Practices);

    (b) with the exception of *force majeure* cases, provisions enabling the trader
to terminate or modify the contract unilaterally without compensation for
damages to the consumer (Art. 32(9) of the Law on Unfair Trade Practices);

    (c) provisions only allowing the consumer to terminate the contract against
payment of damages, even in cases of *force majeure* (Art. 32(10) of the
Law on Unfair Trade Practices);

    (d) provisions entitling the trader to terminate the contract because of the
introduction of the Euro. However, this prohibition does not apply to
contracts that have been the subject of individual negotiations, the burden of proof of which rests on the trader. A contractual term is irrebuttably
presumed not to have been the subject of an individual negotiation if it
has been drawn up before the conclusion of the contract and the consumer therefore did not have any influence on its contents (Art. 32(22) of
the Law on Unfair Trade Practices);

(iii) Pursuant the Law on Unfair Trade Practices in Liberal Professions:

    (a) provisions enabling the professional to terminate the contract, where the
same facility is not granted to the consumer (Section 1(f) of the Annex to
the Law on Unfair Trade Practices in Liberal Professions); and

    (b) provisions permitting the professional to retain the advances paid by the
consumer where it is the professional himself who terminates the contract (*Ibid.*).

§4. Warranties

2746. The following warranty-related provisions are void:

    (i) provisions restricting the consumer's right to terminate the contract in case
the trader fails to repair or replace a defective product within a reasonable
period (Art. 32(7) of the Law on Unfair Trade Practices);

(ii) provisions excluding or restricting the statutory warranty in respect of hidden defects (Art. 32(12) of the Law on Unfair Trade Practices);

(iii) provisions imposing a duty on the consumer to give notice of defects within an unreasonably short period (Art. 32(13) of the Law on Unfair Trade Practices);

(iv) provisions allowing the trader or professional to keep the amounts paid by the consumer in case the latter decides not to conclude the contract, without providing that the consumer may receive an equal amount in damages in case the trader decides not to conclude the contract (Art. 32(24) of the Law on Unfair Trade Practices and Section 1(d) of the Annex to the Law on Unfair Trade Practices in Liberal Professions);

(v) provisions allowing the trader or professional to keep the advance payments made by the consumer in case the former terminates the contract (Art. 32(25) of the Law on Unfair Trade Practices and Section 1(f) of the Annex to the Law on Unfair Trade Practices in Liberal Professions);

(vi) provisions excluding or limiting in an improper way the statutory rights of the consumer against the trader, the professional or another party in case of complete or partial non-performance or defective performance of his obligations by the trader (Art. 32(27) of the Law on Unfair Trade Practices and Section 1(b) of the Annex to the Law on Unfair Trade Practices in Liberal Professions);

(vii) provisions enabling the trader to transfer the contract without his consent, if this might reduce the consumer's warranties (Art. 32(28) of the Law on Unfair Trade Practices Section 1(p) of the Annex to the Law on Unfair Trade Practices in Liberal Professions);

§5. Liability

2747. The following liability-related provisions are void:

(i) provisions excluding the trader's liability for damages resulting from an intentional or serious breach committed either by the trader or by his employees or agents (Art. 32(11) of the Law on Unfair Trade Practices);

(ii) provisions excluding the trader's liability for damages resulting from the failure to perform an essential obligation of the contract (*Ibid.*);

(iii) provisions depriving the consumer of the right to take legal action against the trader or professional (Art. 32(19) of the Law on Unfair Trade Practices and Section 1(q) of the Annex to the Law on Unfair Trade Practices in Liberal Professions);

(iv) provisions excluding or limiting the statutory liability of the trader or professional in case of the death or physical injury of the consumer due to an action or omission of the trader (Art. 32(22*bis*) of the Law on Unfair Trade Practices and Section 1(a) of the Annex to the Law on Unfair Trade Practices in Liberal Professions); and

(v) provisions limiting the obligation of the trader or professional to comply with the obligations entered into by his proxyholders or making the trader's or professional's obligations dependent on compliance with a special formality (Art. 32(26) of the Law on Unfair Trade Practices and Section 1(n) of the Annex to the Law on Unfair Trade Practices in Liberal Professions).

§6. Penalties

2748. Regarding contracts entered in with traders, the following provisions relating to penalty payments are void:

(i) provisions whereby a penalty payment is imposed on the defaulting consumer, but a similar penalty is not imposed on the defaulting supplier (Art. 32(15) of the Law on Unfair Trade Practices); and

(ii) provisions that impose on the consumer penalties or liquidated damages that substantially exceed the foreseeable amount of damages (Art. 32(21) of the Law on Unfair Trade Practices).

2749. Similarly, pursuant to Section 1(e) of the Annex to the Law on Unfair Trade Practices in Liberal Professions, provisions whereby an unreasonably high penalty payment is imposed on the defaulting consumer are void.

§7. Right to set-off

2750. Provisions eliminating the consumer's right to set-off claims against the trader or professional are void (Art. 32(14) of the Law on Unfair Trade Practices and Section 1(b) of the Annex to the Law on Unfair Trade Practices in Liberal Professions).

§8. Evidence

2751. Provisions restricting the evidentiary means the consumer is entitled to avail himself of are void (Art. 32(18) of the Law on Unfair Trade Practices and Section 1(q) of the Annex to the Law on Unfair Trade Practices in Liberal Professions). Following the Law on Unfair Trade Practices, however, contracts entered in with traders can provide for an agreement on the burden of proof.

§9. Venue

2752. Pursuant to Article 32(20) of the Law on Unfair Trade Practices, provisions conferring jurisdiction on courts other than those which are normally competent, are void. Section 1(q) of the Annex to the Law on Unfair Trade Practices in Liberal

Professions only prohibits arbitration clauses conferring exclusive jurisdiction to tribunals that have not been expressly recognised by the legislator.

2753. The Law on Unfair Trade Practices prevents the consumer from renouncing the rights conferred on him with regard to unfair contractual terms (Art. 33(3) of the Law on Unfair Trade Practices). The Law on Unfair Trade Practices also empowers the Government, for particular sectors or for particular products or services, to require or to prohibit the inclusion of certain terms in consumer contracts. The government may also require the use of standard forms. In addition, a Commission for Unfair Terms (*Commissie voor Onrechtmatige Bedingen/Commission des Clauses Abusives*) has been set up which can provide the Government, consumer and professional organisations and groups of companies, upon their request, with appropriate recommendations (Arts. 35 and 36 of the Law on Unfair Trade Practices and Art. 10 of the Law on Unfair Trade Practices in Liberal Professions).

V. THE "CATCH-ALL" PROVISIONS OF THE LAW ON UNFAIR TRADE PRACTICES: THE GENERAL PROHIBITION ON UNFAIR TRADE PRACTICES

A. Introduction

2754. Articles 93 and 94 of the Law on Unfair Trade Practices are of considerable importance in that they constitute 2 general "catch-all" provisions prohibiting any unfair trade practices. Article 93 of the Law on Unfair Trade Practices prohibits any act contrary to fair trade practices whereby a trader injures or attempts to injure the professional interests of one or more other traders. Article 94 of the Law on Unfair Trade Practices prohibits any unfair trade practices whereby a trader injures or attempts to injure the interests of one or more consumers. Unlike the competition rules outlined in Chapter 13, Articles 93 and 94 of the Law on Unfair Trade Practices are not concerned with the maintenance of competition in Belgium, but rather with the protection of specific competitors and consumers against unfair competition.

2755. Articles 93 and 94 of the Law on Unfair Trade Practices confirm and to some extent enlarge the general prohibition against unfair trade practices contained in Article 54 of the Law of 14 July 1971 and in Article 1 of the Royal Decree No. 55 of 23 December 1934. Unlike Royal Decree No. 55 and the Act of 1971, however, the Law on Unfair Trade Practices aims at protecting not only traders but also consumers against unfair trade practices.

B. Scope of application

§1. Personal scope of application

2756. Articles 93 and 94 of the Law on Unfair Trade Practices prohibit unfair trade practices whereby a trader injures or attempts to injure the professional interests of one or more traders or the interests of one or more consumers. The unfair trade practices concerned are only those committed by traders. The Law on Unfair Trade Practices, however, defines the concept of trader broadly. Article 1(6) of the Law on Unfair Trade Practices defines a trader as:

   (i) any natural person or legal entity who offers or sells products or services, respectively, in the context of his professional activities or in pursuance of its corporate objective;

  (ii) any public institution or legal entity in which the public authorities have a significant interest, that exercises a commercial, financial or industrial activity and that offers or sells products or services; or

  (iii) any person who, even without the objective of making profit, in his own name or in the name of a third party, exercises a commercial, financial or industrial activity and offers or sells products or services.

2757. For the purpose of the application of Articles 93 and 94 of the Law on Unfair Trade Practices, the corporate form used by a trader in order to pursue his activities is irrelevant. It is the nature of the activities carried out that determines whether or not a "trader" is involved. A self-employed person, for example a public notary, who has organised his activities in a commercial partnership, is not a "trader" within the meaning of Article 1(6) of the Law on Unfair Trade Practices (Pres. Comm. Antwerp, 18 February 1999, *Jaarboek Handelspraktijken/Annuaire Pratiques du Commerce* 1999, 808). Articles 93 and 94 of the Law on Unfair Trade Practices apply to both Belgian and foreign traders.

§2. Territorial scope of application

2758. Unfair trade practices committed in Belgium and having their effects in Belgium clearly fall within the scope of application of Articles 93 and 94 of the Law on Unfair Trade Practices. However, acts committed abroad having effects within Belgium may also fall within the scope of application of Belgian law on unfair trade practices (Brussels Court of Appeal, 29 February 1956, *Jur. Comm. Brussels*, 1956, 152; Pres. Comm. Brussels, 15 September 1999, *Jaarboek Handelspraktijken/ Annuaire Pratiques du Commerce* 1999, 722.). Similarly, unfair trade practices committed in Belgium, having effects within a foreign country are covered. Belgian courts consider that the scope of application of the Belgian law on unfair trade practices is not limited to the protection of the Belgian internal market, but that it also extends to the prohibition of all unfair trade practices committed within Belgium even though the effects of such practices are felt abroad (Pres. Comm. Brussels, 31 December 1952, *J.T.*, 1953, 89).

C. Substantive elements of Articles 93 and 94 of the Law on Unfair Trade Practices

§1. General

2759. As stated, Articles 93 and 94 of the Law on Unfair Trade Practices prohibit any unfair trade practices whereby a trader injures or attempts to injure the professional interests of one or more traders or the interests of one or more consumers. Articles 93 and 94 of the Law on Unfair Trade Practices thus prohibit in broad terms all unfair trade practices. All unfair trade practices that are not specifically prohibited by other provisions of the Law on Unfair Trade Practices may be covered by Articles 93 and 94 of the Law on Unfair Trade Practices.

§2. Unfair trade practices

2760. The concept of "unfair trade practices" was introduced into Belgian law by Royal Decree No. 55 of 23 December 1934. The Law on Unfair Trade Practices, however, does not provide any definition of the concept. Hence, the courts must determine, on a case-by-case basis, which acts constitute unfair trade practices. Some courts have attempted to define "fair trade practices" as the rules of commercial ethics to be followed by traders in the exercise of their activities (Antwerp Court of Appeal, 29 May 1990, *Jaarboek Handelspraktijken/Annuaire Pratiques du Commerce* 1990, 258). However, this definition does not provide any guideline as to which acts are deemed to be unfair trade practices.

2761. The practices prohibited by Articles 93 and 94 of the Law on Unfair Trade Practices cover a wide spectrum. The following examples of practices that constitute unfair trade practices are further commented upon in the following paragraphs:
- breaches of the law;
- third party interference with contract;
- interference with the functioning of a business;
- passing off;
- disparagement;
- misrepresentations as to the origin of products; and
- misrepresentations or exaggerations.

1. Breaches of the law

2762. Breaches of the law by traders (breaches of the social security and tax laws (Antwerp Court of Appeal, 19 February 1999, *Jaarboek Handelspraktijken/Annuaire Pratiques du Commerce* 1999, 531), price regulations (Pres. Comm. Brussels, 7 July 1980, *Ing. Cons.*, 1981, 82), national and EC competition rules (Comm. Brussels, 6 June 1986, *Jaarboek Handelspraktijken/Annuaire Pratiques du Commerce* 1986, II, 160; Ghent Court of Appeal, 3 February 1999, *Jaarboek Handelspraktijken/Annuaire Pratiques du Commerce* 1999, 859) have consistently been held to constitute unfair trade practices.

2763. However, the breach of a rule of Belgian law that is contrary to an international treaty has been held not to constitute an unfair trade practice. In one case, for example, the President of the Commercial Court of Liège held that the violation by a trader of Article 58 of the VAT Code did not constitute an unfair trade practice, because Article 58 of the VAT Code violated Article 28 [*Ex* Article 30] of the EC Treaty (Pres. Comm. Liege, 25 April 1984, *J.T.*, 1984, 459). Moreover, the Belgian Supreme Court recently held that a trade practice in restraint of competition cannot constitute an unfair trade practice, provided that this restraint is allowed under EC and Belgian competition law (Cass., 7 January 2000, *T.B.H.*, 2000, 369). The fact that a public inspection tolerates a breach of a rule of Belgian law is irrelevant to its qualification as an unfair trade practice (Pres. Comm. Turnhout, 14 March 1997, *Jaarboek Handelspraktijken/Annuaire Pratiques du Commerce* 1997, 470).

2. Third-party interference with a contract

2764. Third-party interference with a contract (*derde medeplichtigheid/tierce complicité*) refers to practices whereby a trader induces a party who has a contractual relationship with another trader to breach his contractual commitment. A trader may commit an unfair trade practice when, knowing of the existence of a contract between 2 parties, he induces one of the parties to breach such contract. 3 conditions must be met to constitute an interference with contract : (i) the occurrence of a breach of contract, (ii) the participation of the trader in the breach, and (iii) the trader knows (or ought to know) that he is participating in a breach of contract (Ghent Court of Appeal, 5 May 1999, *Jaarboek Handelspraktijken / Annuaire Pratiques du Commerce* 1999, 528).

2765. Even though it was established case law that a third party who induces a breach of contract by another may commit an unfair trade practice (Cass., 17 June 1960, *Ing. Cons.*, 1960, 442; Cass., 3 November 1961, *Ing. Cons.*, 1961, 413), there remained considerable uncertainty, until the Supreme Court decision of 22 April 1983 (Cass., 22 April 1983, *R.W.*, 1983-1984, 427), as to what conduct by a third party would be deemed to constitute an unfair trade practice. The case law of the Supreme Court indicates that the mere knowledge of the existence of a contract is not sufficient to turn dealings with a party, who is prohibited by that contract from entering into another contract with one of the contracting parties, into an unfair trade practice. The trader would also have knowingly to collaborate in the breach of the other party's contractual commitments. Whereas a trader may not knowingly collaborate in the breach by a party of his contractual commitments, the trader may induce a party to a contract to deal with him upon termination of such contract.

3. Interference with the functioning of a business

2766. Any act designed to interfere with the functioning of the business of a competitor is prohibited as an unfair trade practice. Examples of illegal interference with the functioning of a competitor's business include the hiring of a competitor's employee with the intention of disrupting the competitor's business or attempts to induce a competitor's employees to go on strike (Brussels Court of Appeal, 18 June 1986, *R.D.C.B.*, 1986, 735). Nevertheless, in principle there is nothing wrong in hiring a competitor's employee provided there is no fraudulent intention. It is not allowed, for example, to hire a competitor's employee in order to obtain confidential information or to create confusion between 2 competitors (Pres. Comm. Antwerp, 3 December 1998, *Jaarboek Handelspraktijken/Annuaire Pratiques du Commerce* 1998, 587).

4. Passing off

2767. Practices tending to create confusion with the products or services of another trader can be prohibited as unfair trade practices either on the basis of Article 23 of the Law on Unfair Trade Practices (*See*, paras. 2669 *et seq.*), which prohibits advertising containing elements likely to create confusion with a trader, its products, services or activities, or on the basis of Article 93 of the Law on Unfair Trade Practices. Practices likely to cause confusion that do not fall under Article 23 of the Law on Unfair Trade Practices may still be prohibited under Article 93 of the Law on Unfair Trade Practices.

2768. Confusion with another trader's products or services is most likely to occur when there is a similarity in the following areas:

i. Similarity of trade names

2769. The use by a trader of trade names or terms similar to another trader's trade name is prohibited where such use deceives consumers into believing that the trader's products or services are those of the other trader. No violation of the Law on Unfair Trade Practices will occur where no deception or confusion between similar trade names is likely to occur.

2770. Where products or services are sufficiently dissimilar so that consumers can distinguish one product from another without any probability of confusion, no violation of the Law on Unfair Trade Practices occurs even though similar names are used. Similarly, there will be no violation of the Law on Unfair Trade Practices when a trader in his advertising uses the trade name of another trader to define the purpose of his own products or services. For instance, the Brussels Court of Appeal held that a manufacturer of spare parts for cars may indicate the makes of cars for which the spare parts are intended (Brussels Court of Appeal, 3 March 1948, *Pas.*, 1949, Il, 83). Case law indicates, however, that, in referring to the trade name of the other manufacturer, the trader must refrain from creating the impression that he is selling the manufacturer's products (Pres. Comm. Liege, 29 October 1990, *Jaarboek Handelspraktijken/Annuaire Pratiques du Commerce* 1990, 502). The fact that one trader owns a chain of stores and the other trader only one is irrelevant when both traders are working in the same economic field (Antwerp Court of Appeal, 1 March 1999, *Jaarboek Handelspraktijken/Annuaire Pratiques du Commerce* 1999, 498).

ii. Cybersquatting

2771. Since 1998, it is established case law that a trader who registers a trade name of another trader as a domain name (*i.e.*, the characteristic part of a URL: the domain name in www.vanbaelbellis.com is "vanbaelbellis") without the latter's permission, in order to prevent him from building a site on the Internet under his own trade name, or to sell him the domain name for an inflated price, commits an unfair trade practice (Brussels Court of Appeal, 1 April 1998, *Jaarboek Handelspraktijken/ Annuaire Pratiques du Commerce* 1998, 467; Pres. Comm. Antwerp, 7 January 1999, *Jaarboek Handelspraktijken/Annuaire Pratiques du Commerce* 1999, 565). This practice is known as "cybersquatting" or "domain grabbing". Furthermore, the use of a domain name which is identical to or closely resembles another trader's trade name which is also a registered trademark, may constitute a trademark infringement. Therefore, the use of another trader's registered trademark as a domain name can be brought before the courts on the basis of both Article 93 of the Law on Unfair Trade Practices and Article 13 A.1.d of the Uniform Benelux Law regarding Trademarks (*Eenvormige Beneluxwet op de Merken/Uniforme Loi Bénélux sur les Marques*).

iii. Similarity of signs

2772. The use by a trader of a sign similar to that used by another trader to designate his establishment is prohibited under the Law on Unfair Trade Practices where such similarity may deceive a potential purchaser. Case law indicates that whether the traders are competitors is irrelevant (Pres. Comm. Brussels, 25 March 1974, *J.C.B.*, 1974, 608). The use of similar signs will be held to constitute an unfair trade practice if such similarity of signs brings about a reasonable risk of confusion between the 2 traders. Where the products or services sold by the 2 traders concerned differ widely, the risk of confusion is unlikely to occur (Antwerp Court of Appeal, 19 November 1990, *Jaarboek Handelspraktijken / Annuaire Pratiques du Commerce* 1990, 274).

iv. Similarity of labels

2773. The use by a trader of labels similar to those of another trader constitutes an unfair trade practice where such similarity may deceive a potential purchaser. For instance, a manufacturer commits an unfair trade practice where he imitates the form, design or colour of another's labels and packaging to the extent that such imitation may induce consumers to purchase his products in the belief that they are buying the competitor's products. For example, in a case where a manufacturer had sold chocolate spread in a package having a similar shape and colour as that used by a well-known competing manufacturer, the Brussels Commercial Court held that such similarity could confuse consumers (Pres. Comm. Brussels, 5 May 1980, *J.T.*, 1981, 538).

2774. Case law indicates, however, that where the package used by the competitor presents no sufficiently distinctive character, the similarity will not be prohibited. For instance, an action against a trader of salad oil who had imitated plastic bottles used by the plaintiff was dismissed on the ground that the various brands of salad oil were all sold in bottles having the same appearance and that there was, thus, no risk of confusion (Court of First Instance Ieper, 21 December 1966, *R.W.*, 1966-1967, 1248).

v. Similarity of other characteristic elements

2775. The imitation by a trader of other elements characterising the business, products or services of another trader, such as appearance or design of such trader's premises, may also constitute an unfair trade practice. The criterion used by courts in assessing whether the imitation by a trader of other characteristic elements of another trader constitutes an unfair trade practice is the likelihood that such imitation will create a confusion between the business, products or services of both traders.

5. *Disparagement*

2776. Disparaging statements about another trader, his products or services constitute an unfair trade practice and can be prohibited under either Article 23 or Article 93 of the Law on Unfair Trade Practices. All denigrating statements are regarded as disparaging when they are capable of affecting the reputation of another trader, his products or services. Even if true, disparaging statements are illegal if they are directed against an identified or identifiable trader or group of traders. In contrast, general disparaging statements about competitors are not prohibited provided that they do not designate, directly or indirectly, a given trader or a given group of traders.

2777. For instance, the following statements have been held as constituting illegal disparagement by Belgian courts: statements that a given competitor is a slow payer and that he has frequent quarrels with his associates (Brussels Court of Appeal, 26 June 1970, *Pas.*, 1971, II, 26); and that the products of a competing firm are sold at excessive prices or that they are of poor quality (Pres. Comm. Brussels, 6 April 1979, *Ing. Cons.*, 1979, 170).

2778. In order to constitute a prohibited trade practice, disparagement must be directed against identified or identifiable traders. This condition is clearly satisfied when the disparaging statements expressly refer to the name or marks of a specific trader. Even if the name of another trader is not expressly mentioned in the disparaging statements, the statements will be illegal if it is possible to identify the trader who is the subject of the disparagement. The criterion is whether the buying public can reasonably be expected to determine against which trader the disparagement is aimed. In a recent case, the Irish low-cost carrier "Ryanair" was convicted for disparaging statements concerning the fares of the Belgian flag-carrier "Sabena" in a publicity campaign. In this case, "Sabena" was expressly mentioned as being a former monopolist charging very high fares (Pres. Comm. Brussels, 10 July 2001, *T.B.H.*, 2002, 311).

2779. Disparaging statements may be directed not only against one or more competitors but also against an identified or identifiable group of competitors. Any member of the group of competitors affected by the disparagement may bring an action against the author of the disparagement. For instance, the Brussels Court of Appeal held that critical comments about the prices charged by Brussels jewellers made by a mail-order house constituted illegal disparagement actionable by any Brussels jeweller or their trade association (Brussels Court of Appeal, 6 December 1958, *Ing. Cons.*, 1959, 377).

2780. In contrast, no charge of disparagement is possible for statements so vague or so general that the public cannot identify the trader in question. For instance, the case law has considered the following advertisement too vague to constitute illegal disparagement: "*No fake price reduction*" (Pres. Comm. Brussels, 16 October 1962, *J.T.*, 1963, 85). Unflattering comments about other traders are, thus, permissible when they are phrased in general terms and there is no clue enabling the buying public to identify the trader or traders alluded to.

6. Misrepresentations as to the origin of products

2781. Misrepresentations as to the geographical origin of a product have frequently been found to constitute acts contrary to fair trade practices. For instance, the use of a trademark evoking a Scottish origin, creating the impression that a brand of whisky actually manufactured in Belgium was imported from Scotland, was held by the Brussels Court of Appeal to constitute an act contrary to fair trade practices (Pres. Comm. Brussels, 24 September 1990, *Jaarboek Handelspraktijken / Annuaire Pratiques du Commerce* 1990, 466).

7. Misrepresentations or exaggerations ("puffing")

2782. In many instances, a trader will exaggerate the virtues of his products or services. If a representation states in general terms that a product or service is superior or of a high quality, it is only "puffing" and not an unfair trade practice. Hence, representations that do not go beyond general praise of a product or service do not constitute acts contrary to fair trade practices. Words such as "perfect", "the best" or "excellent" are similarly regarded as mere "puffing" upon which no charge of deception can be based.

2783. On the other hand, where a trader makes claims about his products or services that are misleading and false, he may commit an unfair trade practice. The line of demarcation between "puffing" and false claims is the point at which a manufacturer no longer speaks generally of his products' high quality, but turns to specific claims that are false. Thus, a trader may not represent his products or services as having qualities that they do not in fact possess. For instance, unsupported advertisements suggesting that public authorities have recognised the superior value of a product (Comm. Brussels, 15 October 1962, *J.T.*, 1963, 85), that a company has been manufacturing beer since 1919 whereas in fact it first started manufacturing beer in 1961 (Comm. Brussels, 22 February 1962, *Ing. Cons.*, 1963, 381), or that a hair lotion will stop hair-loss with a 100 per cent efficiency (Comm. Brussels, 3 September 1974, *J.T.*, 1975, 121) have been held by the courts to constitute unfair trade practices.

§3. Injury requirement

2784. Unfair trade practices prohibited by Articles 93 and 94 of the Law on Unfair Trade Practices are those whereby a trader injures or attempts to injure the professional interests of one or several other traders or the interests of one or several consumers. Even though the existence of some form of injury is a necessary condition for the existence of an unfair trade practice within the meaning of Articles 93 and 94 of the Law on Unfair Trade Practices, such injury does not need to have actually occurred. Articles 93 and 94 may be relied upon to enjoin imminent or threatened unfair trade practices. The absence of a requirement of actual damage constitutes for plaintiffs one of the main advantages of special summary proceedings (*vordering tot staking/action en cessation*) compared to the tort action of Article 1382 of the Civil Code, which requires the proof of actual damage (Cass. 28 November 1997, *Arr. Cass.*, 1997, 1243).

D. Article 94*bis* of the Law on Unfair Trade Practices

2785. Article 94*bis* of the Law on Unfair Trade Practices states that it is forbidden for a consumer to sign a bill of exchange to guarantee his obligations *vis-à-vis* a trader, unless it is allowed under a particular law.

E. Examples of acts that cannot be prohibited on the basis of the Law on Unfair Trade Practices

§1. Infringement of intellectual property rights

2786. Article 96 of the Law on Unfair Trade Practices excludes from the scope of the cease-and-desist order infringements sanctioned by the laws on patents, trademarks relating to products or services, designs or models and copyrights. Hence, Article 96 of the Law on Unfair Trade Practices refers to intellectual property rights that are protected by special statutory provisions.

2787. A Supreme Court ruling of 16 March 1939 (Cass., 16 March 1939, *Pas.*, I, 1939, 208), established that actions against infringements of intellectual property rights must be based on the specific statutory provisions ensuring legal protection of the intellectual property right in question. Thus, if a trader sought, for instance, to create confusion with the products of another trader through imitation of the other trader's trademark, the practice was actionable only under trademark law and not under the Law on Unfair Trade Practices. Actions based on the Law on Unfair Trade Practices could not be brought even in cases where protection under, for example, the trademark law or the patent law was not available because the trademark had not been registered or the invention had not been patented (Pres. Comm. Brussels, 7 July 1980, *J.T.*, 1980, 536). The rule was that where the practice complained of qualifies as an infringement of an intellectual property right, the plaintiff is precluded from relying on the law of unfair trade practices.

2788. In respect of trademarks, this means that it was not possible to rely on the Law on Unfair Trade Practices for the kind of trademark infringements provided under Article 13, A, 1a and b of the Uniform Benelux Trademark Law because these kinds of infringements relate to the use of a trademark for identical or similar goods or services (*daden van merknamaak/actes de contrefaçon de marques*). These kinds of infringements therefore relate to the specific function of the trademark, *i.e.*, an indicator of origin. On the other hand, Article 13, A, 1, c and d of the Uniform Benelux Trademark Law deal with the use of a trademark for dissimilar goods or services and for purposes other than distinguishing goods or services. These kinds of infringements relate to the distinctiveness and attractive power of famous trademarks and not to the specific function of the trademark. Therefore, the courts have always accepted that infringements of Article 13, A, 1, c and d of the Uniform Benelux Trademark Law could also be curtailed under the catch-all provisions of the Law on Unfair Trade Practices. However, in a recent judgement of 9 January 2002, the Belgian Court of Arbitration held that this distinction between the 2 above-mentioned kinds of trademark infringement violates the principle of equality of Articles 10 and 11 of the Belgian Constitution (Court of Arbitration, 9 January 2002, *T.B.H.*, 2002, 842). Therefore, it would seem that all trademark infringements under Article 13.A.1 of the Uniform Benelux Trademark, including those described under Article 13.A.1a and b, can now also be challenged on the basis of the Law on Unfair Trade Practices. However, it should be noted that the President of the Antwerp Commercial Court has held that the judgement of the Court of Arbitration stating that Article 96 of the Law on Unfair Trade Practices violates Articles 10 and 11 of the Constitution only applies to the case in which the preliminary question to the Court of Arbitration was raised and between the parties involved. The Court of Arbitration has not abolished Article 96 of the Law on Unfair Trade Practices. As a result, the President of the Antwerp Commercial Court has applied Article 96 of The Law on Unfair Trade Practices without taking into account the judgement of the Court of Arbitration and without raising a preliminary question with the Court of Arbitration (Pres. Comm. Antwerp, 20 June 2002, *T.B.H.*, 2002, 848). It will therefore be a task for the legislator to clarify this issue and amend the Law on Unfair Trade Practices to the extent necessary.

2789. In contrast, an action based on the Law on Unfair Trade Practices is available when the infringement of the intellectual property right complained of is accompanied by unfair trade practices. In such a case, the plaintiff does not seek to enjoin acts falling solely within the scope of application of the laws relating to intellectual property rights, but seeks to enjoin the unfair practices that accompany the infringement of such intellectual property rights (Brussels Court of Appeal, 17 May 1984, *Ing. Cons.*, 1984, 341).

§2. Breach of contract

2790. It is established case law of the Supreme Court (Cass., 25 November 1943, *Pas.*, 1944, 1, 70 and Cass., 25 November 1943, *Pas.*, 1944, 1, 72) that contracting parties cannot rely on the Law on Unfair Trade Practices to challenge pure breaches of contract. In the first case cited above, which involved the breach by an employee of a non-competition covenant included in an employment contract, the Supreme Court held that the scope of Royal Decree No. 55 (superseded by Art. 93 of the Law on Unfair Trade Practices) is limited to acts based on tort, and excludes acts that, not being unfair trade practices, are prohibited only by virtue of a contract. The Supreme Court upheld the same reasoning in the second case cited above concerning a dispute between 2 partners, where one partner was accused by the other of unfair acts against the partnership.

2791. In contrast, practices that would be prohibited as unfair trade practices independently of the existence of a contract are actionable under Article 93 of the Law on Unfair Trade Practices even if they also constitute a breach of contract. In such a case, the plaintiff may at his option either bring an action for breach of contract or petition the President of the Commercial Court for a cease-and-desist order on the basis of the Law on Unfair Trade Practices. The issue of whether or not the plaintiff may both bring an action in contract and petition the President of the Commercial Court for a cease-and-desist order on the basis of the Law on Unfair Trade Practices is controversial. In a case where the defendant had signed a covenant not to establish a business similar to the business he was selling to the plaintiff in the neighbourhood and the defendant had established the same business in the building occupied by the plaintiff, the Brussels Court of Appeal held that the action brought on the basis of the Law on Unfair Trade Practices was proper because, even though the defendant's conduct constituted a breach of a contractual undertaking, it was also contrary to fair trade practices (Brussels Court of Appeal, 2 June 1961, *Ing. Cons.*, 1961, 232).

F. Enforcement and remedies

§1. Cease-and-desist orders

2792. Pursuant to Article 95 of the Law on Unfair Trade Practices, a party seeking relief against an unfair trade practice may apply to the President of the Commercial Court for a cease-and-desist order. Such an order must be granted, following a special summary proceeding (*vordering tot staking/action en cessation*), if the following conditions are met:
   (i) the petitioner must have a personal interest in the termination of the practice complained of. Article 98 of the Law on Unfair Trade Practices provides that the following persons or entities may also apply for a cease-and-desist order:
      (a) the Minister for Economic Affairs (with the exception of acts covered by Art. 93 of the Law on Unfair Trade Practices);
      (b) trade associations, provided that they have legal personality and they have an interest in obtaining the termination of the alleged unfair trade practice (with the exception of acts covered by Art. 94 of the Law on Unfair Trade Practices); and
      (c) consumer associations, provided that they have legal personality and that they are represented at the Consumer Council (*Raad voor het Verbruik/ Conseil de la Consommation*) (with the exception of acts covered by Art. 93 of the Law on Unfair Trade Practices); and
   (ii) the activity alleged to constitute an unfair trade practice must not have been discontinued prior to the time when the action was brought, unless such practice is capable of being repeated. Nonetheless, Article 95, paragraph 2 of the Law on Unfair Trade Practices provides that the President of the Commercial Court may forbid a misleading advertisement that has not yet been published but the publication of which is imminent.

2793. Pursuant to Article 18, a consumer seeking relief against an infringement on the Law on Unfair Trade Practices in Liberal Professions may apply to the President of the Civil Court for a similar cease-and-desist order, following the same special summary proceeding.

2794. Additionally to persons considered to have a personal interest, following persons or organisations may also apply for cease-and-desist orders against infringements on the Law on Unfair Trade Practices in Liberal Professions:
   (i) profession regulating authorities, inter-professions associations or profession's associations that have legal personality;
   (ii) consumers associations, under the above-mentioned conditions;

(iii) a recognised sickness insurance funds or a recognised health service; and

(iv) the Minister(s) in charge of the underlying matter.

2795. The Commercial or Civil Court territorially competent to hear the case is that of the domicile of the defendant or that of the place where the alleged unfair trade practice took place (Art. 624 of the Judicial Code). Where the President of the Commercial or Civil Court determines that an unfair trade practice has been committed or attempted, he may enjoin the commissioning of such an act in the future. In addition, the President's cease-and-desist order may be accompanied by the imposition of periodical penalty payments (*dwangsom/astreinte*) if the cease-and-desist order is not complied with. However, the President is not entitled to award damages. Decisions delivered by the President of the Commercial or Civil Court may be appealed to the Court of Appeal within 1 month following the formal notification of the judgment enjoining the unfair trade practice.

§2. Publication of judgment

2796. The President of the Commercial Court or Civil issuing a cease-and-desist order may order the posting of the judgment within or outside the premises of the offender and/or the publication of the judgment in newspapers or in any other way at the offender's expense. In some recent cases, the President of the Commercial Court also ordered a publication on the website of the offender (Pres. Comm. Brussels, 10 July 2001, *T.B.H.*, 2002, 311). Such posting or publication may be ordered only when such measure is likely to contribute to the termination of the challenged act or of its effects (Art. 99 of the Law on Unfair Trade Practices and Art. 24 of the Law on Unfair Trade Practices in Liberal Professions).

§3. Criminal sanctions

2797. The violation of a cease-and-desist order issued by the President of the Commercial or Civil Court constitutes in itself an offence punishable by a fine of € 1,000 to € 20,000 (to be multiplied by 5) (Art. 104 of the Law on Unfair Trade Practices and Art. 26 of the Law on Unfair Trade Practices in Liberal Professions). Article 103 of the Law on Unfair Trade Practices provides that persons who maliciously infringe the provisions of the Law on Unfair Trade Practices are exposed to fines ranging from € 500 to € 20,000 (to be multiplied by 5). Article 102 of the Law on Unfair Trade Practices lists, in addition, infringements of specific provisions of the Law on Unfair Trade Practices which are punishable by fines ranging from between € 250 and € 10,000 (to be multiplied by 5).

2798. Similarly following Article 25 of the Law on Unfair Trade Practices in Liberal Professions, persons engaged in liberal professions selling products or supplying services through distance contracts who do not provide the consumer with crucial information, as well as persons offering unsolicited products and services are exposed to fines ranging from € 250 to € 10,000 (to be multiplied by 5).

§4. Warning procedure

2799. Article 101 of the Law on Unfair Trade Practices provides for a warning procedure (*waarschuwingsprocedure/procedure d'avertissement*), whereby the Minister for Economic Affairs may formally notify a trader that he is breaching the Law on Unfair Trade Practices and that, if the trader does not cease the violation, the Minister for Economic Affairs will institute legal proceedings against the alleged offender.

§5. Investigation

2800. Officers of the General Economic Inspection (*Algemene Economische Inspectie/ Inspection Générale Economique*) appointed by the Minister for Economic Affairs (*Minister van Economische Zaken/Ministre des Affaires Economiques*) are empowered to investigate infringements of the Law on Unfair Trade Practices which may entail criminal sanctions (Art. 113 of the Law on Unfair Trade Practices). To that end, they may conduct on-the-spot investigations (*Ibid.*). Officers appointed by the Minister for Economic Affairs other than the officers of the General Economic Inspection may, on the basis of the reports of the investigation, make administrative settlement offers. Such an administrative settlement prevents a criminal case from being brought in relation to the infringement concerned (Art. 116 of the Law on Unfair Trade Practices).

15. REAL ESTATE

2801. Belgian legislation and case law regarding immovable assets or realty (*onroerende goederen/immeubles*) are extensive and detailed.

2802. The concept of realty itself is threefold in Belgian law: it concerns (i) immovable assets by nature (Art. 523 of the Civil Code), (ii) immovable assets by destination (Art. 522 of the Civil Code) and (iii) immovable assets by reason of the object to which they relate. The latter 2 of these elements (ii and iii) are always linked to the former (i): movable assets (*roerende goederen/meubles*) achieve a realty status because of their being permanently affected to a realty in kind by its proprietor whereas certain intangible assets may be deemed real because of the nature of their object.

2803. For purposes of this chapter, real estate is defined as immovable assets by nature, meaning the ground and every building or construction which is incorporated therein. Case law has given an increasingly extensive interpretation of the notion of incorporation: anything which is somehow attached to the ground, even in a haphazard or provisional manner, is considered realty (*e.g.*, a house, a building, a wooden shed or even a caravan without wheels).

2804. Below, we will discuss (i) the acquisition of real estate, (ii) 2 particular rights pertaining to real estate (construction right and long term lease), (iii) the different regimes regarding lease of real estate and (iv) expropriation.

I. ACQUISITION OF REAL ESTATE

2805. A distinction must be made between (i) the general principles governing the purchase of land or the acquisition of existing buildings and (ii) the specific legislation on the acquisition of buildings under construction, *i.e.*, the Law of 9 July 1971 on the Construction and the Sale of Housing to be Constructed or in the Process of Being Constructed (*Wet tot regeling van de woningbouw en de verkoop van te bouwen of in aanbouw zijnde woningen/Loi réglementant la construction et la vente d'habitations à construire ou en voie de construction* – the Law "Breyne").

A. Purchase of land – Acquisition of existing buildings

§1. Agreement between seller and purchaser

2806. The purchase of land is typically the subject of a written contract between the seller and the purchaser in which the conditions of the sale are set out. In general, the written contract should at least contain the purchase price, the payment procedure, the date of the transfer of title and a sufficiently detailed description of the land and (if applicable) building.

2807. In order to give a proper description of the land and building and also to obtain information on the identity of the present owner, it is useful to request an excerpt of the relevant documents kept by the regional offices of the Ministry of Finance responsible for the land registry (*kadaster/cadastre*). Application forms can be obtained from the offices of the land registry or the municipal authorities.

2808. In addition, the contract will include clauses dealing with the appointment of the notary public who will attest the authentic deed, the date by which the authentic deed must be attested, the applicable zoning and planning requirements, the existence of pre-emption or similar rights and the existence of easements.

2809. The contract may also provide for "conditions precedent". A condition precedent suspends the entry into force of the contract until such time as the condition has been fulfilled. With regard to the purchase of land or buildings, it is customary to include the grant of a favourable zoning and planning certificate (allowing for construction of the envisaged building on the site) or of the required financial support (a loan or credit facility) as conditions precedent.

2810. Written contracts relating to the purchase of land or building are subject to a registration formality (Art. 19(2) of the Registration and Mortgage Tax Code). This formality must be complied with within 4 months following the date of execution of the contract (Art. 32(4) of the Registration and Mortgage Tax Code). The registration requirement does not affect the validity of the contract.

2811. The amount of registration fees, originally fixed by federal law, is presently a matter of regional competence. In Flanders, the base percentage is 10 per cent of the purchase price, with a reduced fee of 5 per cent for small properties and modest houses. In Wallonia, the base percentage is 12.5 per cent and the reduced fee amounts to 6 per cent. Brussels does not have a reduced tariff. The base percentage is here also 12.5 per cent, although realty agents benefit from a slightly lower tariff (8 per cent).

§2. Notarial deed

2812. The involvement of a notary public in any transaction involving the purchase of land or buildings is mandatory since only notarial deeds may be registered (Art. 1 of the Law of 16 December 1851). In practice, the purchaser and the seller will therefore not register the contract themselves. The notary public will normally take care of the necessary registration tax and mortgage register formalities. The involvement of a notary public in the purchase of land or buildings also constitutes an added security for the parties involved, since the notary has a duty to thoroughly investigate the legal status of the realty concerned. In case the provisions of the authentic deed do not match reality, the notary may be held professionally liable for ensuing damages.

B. Acquisition of buildings under construction

2813. The acquisition of buildings under construction is governed by the Law "Breyne". The Law "Breyne" was amended by the Law of 3 May 1993 (implemented by Royal Decree of 21 September 1993) in order to provide for better protection and more guarantees for the purchaser.

2814. In order to fall within the scope of application of the Law "Breyne", the conditions discussed below must be met. These include the kind of agreement to be used, the type of building to be constructed and the payment modalities.

§1. Nature of the agreement

2815. The agreement must concern either the transfer of ownership (such as a sales agreement) or the construction or management of a construction project.

§2. Type of building

2816. The building must be constructed either exclusively for housing purposes or partly for housing and partly for professional purposes. If the building is to be used for professional reasons, the part which will be used for housing must at least be of equal importance to that which will be put to professional use.

2817. Article 1 of the Law "Breyne" provides that only buildings to be constructed or still under construction are within its scope. The Law "Breyne" does not apply to completed buildings. A building will be deemed completed if the purchaser can make normal use of it. In other words, the fact that certain minimal finishing works may still have to be done does not necessarily prevent the building from being deemed completed.

2818. Since 1993, the scope of the Law "Breyne" is extended to include renovation or enlargement contracts for a total amount exceeding € 18,600, provided that this amount exceeds 80 per cent of the sales price of the realty concerned.

§3. Payment conditions

2819. The Law "Breyne" applies only if the purchaser or developer is required to make one or more payments prior to the completion of the works.

§4. Excluded agreements

2820. Even if the aforesaid conditions are all met, the Law "Breyne" will not apply to agreements entered into by the following parties:
  (i) certain social housing companies (Art. 2, 1);
  (ii) municipalities or inter-municipal associations (Art. 2, 2);
  (iii) a purchaser or developer whose regular activities consist of constructing housing or conducting construction management projects and the subsequent resale of the buildings concerned (for example real-estate promoters or building contractors) (Art. 2, 3).

2821. Likewise, the Law "Breyne" will not apply to mere studies relating to construction works (Art. 2, 3) insofar as the cost of such a study does not exceed 2 per cent of the estimated construction cost and if the study agreement contains a description of the pertaining construction works and allows for a 7-day reflection period on behalf of the acquiror.

§5. Special conditions imposed by the Law "Breyne"

2822. The Law "Breyne" provides for a number of conditions, which primarily aim to protect the purchaser. These include, among others, rules with regard to the transfer of ownership and risk, formal requirements, liability for defects, payment conditions and guarantees.

1. Transfer of ownership

2823. The transfer of ownership takes place on the date of the execution of the agreement (Art. 4 of the Law "Breyne"). The ownership of parts which must still be constructed at the time the agreement is executed is transferred upon the laying of the foundations in the soil or the incorporation of the parts into the already existing parts of the building (Art. 5 of the Law "Breyne"). Retention of title clauses delaying the transfer of ownership cannot be validly included in the agreement.

2. Transfer of risk

2824. The transfer of risk for the loss of the property (due to a fire, for example) cannot take place prior to the date of the provisional acceptance of the works (Art. 5 of the Law "Breyne").

3. Liability for substantial defects

2825. Liability for substantial defects applies not only to the building contractor and the architect, but also to the party selling a building by virtue of an agreement falling within the scope of application of the Law "Breyne". Not only does the initial purchaser of the building benefit from it, but so, too, will subsequent purchasers. The liability claim can, however, only be lodged against the initial seller (Art. 6 of the Law "Breyne"). Liability is limited to 10 years.

4. Formal requirements

2826. The agreements subject to the Law "Breyne" must comply with the following formal requirements (Art. 7):
    (i) the agreements must be in written form;
    (ii) the agreements must mention (i) the identity of the owner of the land; (ii) the date on which the construction permit has been granted; (iii) the conditions attached to the construction permit; (iv) a detailed description of the common and the private parts of the building; (v) the total price and method of payment; (vi) whether the price can be revised; (vii) whether there is a condition precedent to the entry into force of the contract (no longer than 3 months as of the date of the agreement) or to the delivery of a construction permit; (viii) the date on which the construction works will start; (ix) the term within which the works will be completed; (x) the penalty in case of delay (which must at least be equal to a standard rent); (xi) the procedure relating to the acceptance of the works by the developer; and (xii) a statement from the parties that they have had knowledge of the data and documents referred to in Article 7 of the Law "Breyne" for at least 15 days.
    (iii) detailed plans and related documents signed by an architect and, in the case of apartments, the notarial deed including the regulation governing the co-ownership, must be annexed to the agreements.

2827. In any case, the agreements should contain a specific notice that the buyer or the developer has the right to invoke the nullity of the agreement (or any part thereof) if it constitutes an infringement of the provisions of the law regarding formalities (Art. 7 of the Law "Breyne") and regarding the use of recognised construction workers (Art. 12 of the Law "Breyne").

5. Acceptance of the works by the developer

2828. The acceptance of the works by the developer or purchaser must take place in 2 stages: *i.e.*, the provisional and the definitive acceptance. There must be at least one year between the provisional and the definitive acceptance. In addition, definitive acceptance of an apartment may not take place until such time as the definitive acceptance of the most important common parts has occurred (Art. 9 of the Law "Breyne").

6. Payment conditions

2829. Article 10 of the Law "Breyne" contains strict requirements as to the payment procedures. The seller or constructor may not demand or accept payment before the written agreement has been signed. This prohibition includes value papers such as cheques bills of exchange or orders. A provision to be paid at that time may not exceed 5 per cent of the total price. At the occasion of the signing of the notarial deed, payment may only be demanded in relation to the price of the grounds and the works that have already been finished, under deduction of the provision. After this, the rest of the price becomes due "piece-meal", as the works progress.

7. Guarantees

2830. Article 12 of the Law "Breyne" obliges the building contractor or the seller to provide the purchaser with certain financial guarantees. The nature of these guarantees differ depending on whether a registered or a non-registered contractor or seller is involved.

8. Sanctions

2831. The Law "Breyne" provides for 2 types of sanctions, namely contractual and criminal sanctions. Failure to comply with the conditions of the law entitles the purchaser to claim the nullity of the clause concerned. Failure to comply with the formal requirements of Article 7 of the Law "Breyne", the requirement to provide a guarantee included in Article 12 of the Law "Breyne" and the rules governing the acceptance procedure may, at the discretion of the purchaser, even result in the nullity of the agreement as a whole. The nullity claim must be brought by the purchaser either prior to the date on which the authentic deed is notarised or, in the case of a construction agreement, prior to the provisional acceptance of the works (Art. 13 of the Law "Breyne"). If the seller or the contractor infringes the pricing rules of Article 10 of the Law "Breyne", he may incur criminal liability (Art. 14 of the Law "Breyne").

II. CONSTRUCTION RIGHT AND LONG TERM LEASE

2832. Also certain rights may be considered to be immovable. Their realty nature is due to the fact that their object is a (tangible) immovable asset. Among the oldest of these "untangible" immovables are the construction right (*opstal/superficie*) and long term lease (*erfpacht/emphyteose*).

A. Construction right

§1. Nature of the construction right

2833. Article 1 of the Law of 10 January 1824 on the Construction Right (*Wet over het recht van opstal/Loi sur le droit de superficie* – the "Construction Right Law") states that, "*the right to construct gives the right to own buildings, works or plantations on land that is owned by another.*" Thus, this right constitutes a derogation from Articles 552 and 553 of the Civil Code, which essentially hold that constructions, plantations and works belong to the proprietor of the ground.

The owner of the buildings and the plantations is called the rightholder (*opstalhouder/superficiaire*), whereas the owner of the land is called the land owner (*eigenaar/tréfoncier*).

2834. The construction right is immovable because of the object to which it relates (*i.e.*, the building or plantation). It is also temporary: it may not last longer than 50 years. However, a possibility exists to renew the right an indefinite number of times.

§2. Acquiring the construction right

2835. The construction right may be obtained by means of a title (an agreement, a will, *etc.*). Yet even if a false ownership title exists, the holder may obtain the right by means of acquisitory prescription after 10 or 20 years (depending on whether or not the real owner lives in the district of the Court of Appeal where the ground is located).

§3. Causes of termination

2836. The construction right may be terminated due to many reasons. We name but a few.

1. End of duration

2837. In case of a contractual construction right, the expiring of the contract's term is the most obvious way in which the right may come to an end. Tacit renewal of the right is not possible under Belgian law.

2. Merging

2838. If the construction right and the ownership of the ground are rejoined in one person, the construction right is effectively terminated, although rights acquired by third parties must still be respected.

3. Destruction of the ground

2839. Only a complete destruction of the ground (for instance, by an Act of God, such as an earthquake) on which the buildings or plantations are located results in a termination of the construction right. Mere co-incidental destruction of buildings or plantations themselves does not suffice, since the rightholder can always erect new constructions.

4. 30 year prescription

2840. If the rightholder does not exercise his right during 30 consecutive years, the construction right to building expires due to disuse (*non usus*, Article 9, 3 of the Construction Right Law).

5. Expropriation

2841. A rightholder is entitled to compensation in the event of expropriation of the ground by the State (*See*, paras. 2933 *et seq.*).

6. Other possibilities

2842. The Construction Right Law provides for several other ways to end a construction right, such as a judicial annulment of the rightholder's title, the dissolution or annulment of the rights of the land owner, waiver of rights by the rightholder, *etc.*

2843. Death of the rightholder or of the land owner in no way alters the existence of the construction right. The relevant rights and duties become an integral part of the deceased party's inheritance.

2844. There is some discussion concerning the validity of a tacit termination clause in a contract with regard to a construction right. Jurisprudence is divided on the matter, but it would secure at least that such a clause can only be valid in a reciprocal agreement (*i.e.*, where the construction right is for consideration).

§4. Fate of constructions upon termination

2845. At the moment of termination of the construction right, the ownership of the building or the plantation is transferred to the land owner, who will have to compensate the rightholder for the actual value of the realty transferred. The latter has a right of retention on the assets until he is properly compensated.

The land owner cannot prevent the rightholder from destroying the buildings he constructed, on the condition that the land is returned in the state in which it was before construction took place.

B. Long term lease

§1. Nature of the long term lease

2846. According to the Law of 10 January 1824 on the Long Term Lease (*Wet over de erfpacht/Loi sur le bail emphytéotique* – the "Long Term Lease Law"), the right of long term lease is a *"real right, granting the use of an immovable asset which is owned by another person, on the condition of paying this other person a yearly fee, be it in money or in kind, as recognition of his ownership right"*. (Art. 1 of the Long Term Lease Law). The rightholder is called the "lessee" and the owner the "lessor".

2847. The long term lease may not exceed a duration of 99 years, nor may it be shorter than 27 years.

§2. Rights of the lessee

1. Rights of the lessee regarding the object of the long term lease

2848. According to Article 3 of the Long Term Lease Law, the lessee exercises *"all the rights attached to the ownership of the realty"*. This means that the lessee effectively enjoys all rights attached to the use of the asset (*i.e.*, he may act as if he were the realty's owner). For instance, the lessee may let the realty to a third party. He may also burden it with servitudes for as long as his own right lasts (Art. 6 of the Long Term Lease Law).

2. Rights of the lessee regarding the long term lease

2849. The lessee is entitled to transfer his right of long term lease to a third party. He may also submit it to a mortgage (Art. 6 of the Long Term Lease Law). Upon the death of the lessee, his rights and duties are transferred to his inheritors.

§3. Duties of the lessee

2850. The lessee should take the necessary steps to preserve the realty, including day-to-day management and daily repairs (Art. 5 of the Long Term Lease Law). He should abstain from doing anything which would diminish the value of the property (Art. 3, first alinea of the Long Term Lease Law). Likewise, he is to ensure the conservation of the lessor's ownership right (Art. 13, *in fine* of the Long Term Lease Law).

In exchange for his rights of use, the lessee must also pay any imposition or tax due with regard to the realty (Art. 9), as well as an annual fee (*canon*) to the lessor (Art. 1). As stated above, this fee is not so much a rent, but rather a periodic manifestation of the lessee's recognition of the lessor's ownership right. It therefore does not have a necessary link of equivalence to the fruits of the property.

§4. Acquiring the long term lease

2851. Like the construction right, the right of long term lease may be the object of a contract or a will (albeit that the latter possibility occurs seldom in practice). The right may also be obtained as a result of prescription.

§5. Causes of termination

2852. The long term lease expires because of the same causes as those stated with regard to the termination of the construction right (*See*, paras. 2833 *et seq.*).

A specific reason for ending the long term lease is the abuse of the right. A court may decide, by applying Article 15 of the Long Term Lease Law, to terminate the right of the lessee when the latter has inflicted "noticeable damage" to the property. Apart from termination, the lessor is entitled to an indemnity, unless the lessee repairs the damage (Art. 16 of the Long Term Lease Law).

§6. Fate of constructions upon termination

2853. The lessee may remove constructions or plantations from the land. If he decides to leave them, the lessor becomes their rightful owner on a gratuitous basis (Art. 8 of the Long Term Lease Law).

III. TYPES OF LEASE AGREEMENTS

A. Common lease agreements

§1. Applicable law

2854. The general rules and principles regarding the lease of realty under Belgian law are laid down in Articles 1714 to 1762*bis* of the Civil Code. These Articles set out the rules with regard to the lease of realty in cases where the lease does not fall within the scope of application of special regimes, such as residential or commercial leases (*See*, paras. 2868 *et seq.*). They also serve as a general regulation supplementing residential and commercial lease law. It is therefore wise to keep in mind the general rules as set out in the Civil Code when considering a residential or commercial lease agreement. They should be regarded as fundamental principles of lease law. We will describe these principles schematically.

§2. Definition of a lease

2855. Article 1709 of the Civil Code defines a lease agreement as "*an agreement by which one party agrees to give the other party the use and enjoyment of an asset during a certain period and in exchange for a certain fee (rent) which the latter agrees to pay.*"

§3. Creating a lease agreement

2856. Both oral and written agreements are acceptable according to Article 1714 of the Civil Code. However, in case of a purely verbal agreement, Article 1715 of the Civil Code imposes a rather heavy burden of proof with regard to the existence of the agreement (in court or against third parties). Only judiciary oath or confession will be accepted as sufficient proof. In view of these difficulties of proving the existence, but also the terms and conditions of a verbal agreement, parties are encouraged to conclude a written agreement.

However, in case the duration of the agreement exceeds 9 years, the parties are not only obliged to draft a written agreement, also a notary deed must be drawn up. This deed has to be transcribed in full at the local mortgage registry in order to be enforceable to third parties.

§4. Duration and termination of lease agreements

1. Notice of Termination

2857. If a written agreement is reached to lease a realty for a certain (fixed) period, this agreement ends on the day that this period expires. In such a case, there is no need for a notice of termination (Art. 1737 of the Civil Code). Written lease contracts for an undetermined period of time and oral agreements may be terminated unilaterally by either party provided they give due notice.

2. Mutual consent

2858. The parties may at any time agree to end the agreement by mutual consent (Art. 1134 of the Civil Code). There are no formal requirements to such consent. However, again for reasons of legal certainty, parties are advised to confirm their agreement in writing.

3. Breach of contract

2859. In the event that a party does not comply with its obligations under the lease agreement, the other party is entitled to request the termination of the agreement in court (Articles 1184 and 1741 of the Civil Code).

4. Destruction of realty

2860. If the realty which is the object of the lease agreement is destroyed in its entirety by an Act of God during the course of the lease, the lease ends automatically. If the destruction of the property is only partial, the lessee has a choice to obtain either a reduction of the rent or the termination of the agreement (Art. 1722 of the Civil Code).

5. Instances that do not bring about termination

2861. Parties should be aware that the following instances or occurrences do *not*, in principle, result in the end of a lease agreement:
- death of a party (Art. 1742 of the Civil Code) – rights and duties under the agreement are transferred onto the heirs of the deceased;
- insolvency of a party;
- an explicit cancellation clause in the contract (which would allow a party to unilaterally end the lease if he considers the other party to be in breach of contract) – according to Article 1762*bis* of the Civil Code, such a clause is null and void: cancellation in case a party violates the stipulations of a lease agreement is a matter which, under Belgian law, needs to be resolved in court; and

– the sale of the realty.

§5. Rent

2862. There can be no lease without rent being due: the payment of rent is an essential element in any lease agreement.

2863. Although rent is most often payable in money, there is no requirement that the consideration consists indeed in money. Periodic payments in kind or even by means of services rendered may also be agreed upon.

2864. As rent constitutes an essential element in a lease agreement, the rent due must be determined in that agreement or, at the very least, be determinable on the basis of its clauses.

2865. Contracting parties are essentially free to determine the rent by mutual consent. This also holds true in case of extension of an existing lease: a new rent may be determined at this occasion. Parties are equally free to determine when the rent will be due. Most landlords insist on the rent being paid monthly and in advance.

§6. Registration of lease

2866. Written lease agreements are usually drawn up in 3 original copies and must be registered within 4 months of their execution. One original copy must be filed with the Registration Office, while the tenant and the landlord each keep one original. Registration is a fiscal obligation which entails the payment of a charge.

Registration is important not only because it represents a legal obligation (non-compliance is subject to fines), but also because it is the easiest method for the tenant to protect his rights *vis-à-vis* the landlord and third parties in case of a subsequent sale of the leased premises. The lease normally provides that the tenant shall take care of the registration formalities and pay the registration fee.

§7. Sublease and transfer of lease

2867. Subleasing and transferring the lease are allowed unless the lease agreement states otherwise (Art. 1717 of the Civil Code).

Apart from contractual limitations, the lessee is also constrained by legal limitations to his right to transfer or sublease: a lessee who does not have his principal place of residence in the leasehold may not transfer or sublease it to a sub-lessee who would take his principal residence there (Art. 1717 of the Civil Code) (*See*, para. 2896).

B. Residential lease agreements

§1. Applicable law

2868. The rules governing the lease of realty which the lessee will use as his principal place of residence are set forth in the Law of 20 February 1991, as substantially amended by the Law of 13 April 1997 (*Regels betreffende de huurovereenkomst met betrekking tot de hoofdverblijfplaats van de huurder in het bijzonder/Loi modifiant et complétant les dispositions du Code Civil relatives aux baux à loyer* – the "Residential Lease Law").

2869. The ongoing changes and amendments to the Residential Lease Law have prompted the legislator to provide for a rather complex system of transitory measures, depending primarily on the date of the lease agreement. A detailed analysis of this system goes beyond the scope of this section. Hereinafter, we will therefore exclusively deal with the law as it stands and as it is applicable to new lease agreements.

§2. Definition of residence

2870. By the Law of 24 December 2002, a definition of what constitutes a "residence" was added to the residential lease law. Until then, this notion remained implicit. Article 1, paragraph 1 of the Residential Lease Law presently states that a residence is any movable or immovable asset, or any part thereof, which serves as a place of principal residence to the lessee. This definition broadens the scope of application of the Residential Lease Law (and the protection if offers to lessees).

§3. Creating a residential lease agreement

2871. Lease agreements need not be in writing in order to be valid. However, in view of the difficulties of proving the existence and the terms and conditions of a verbal agreement, it is strongly recommended that tenants insist on a written lease agreement which clearly defines, *inter alia*, the property let, the duration of the lease, the amount of rent, the charges payable and the conditions of termination. For foreigners, it may be advisable to obtain a translation of the lease contract before signing it. Prospective tenants should be encouraged to negotiate alterations to standard leases which almost invariably favour the landlord.

§4. Duration and termination of residential lease agreements

2872. Lease agreements may be terminated at any time upon mutual consent of the landlord and the tenant. The Justice of the Peace (*Vredegerecht/Justice de Paix*) may also pronounce the rescission of a lease agreement if one of the parties commits a serious breach of his obligations imposed by the law or the lease agreement (*See,* para. 2859). In addition, the parties may under specific conditions, terminate the lease agreement unilaterally. In this respect a distinction should be drawn between agreements with a duration of 9 years, agreements with a duration of 3 years or less and agreements with a duration of more than 9 years.

1. Lease agreements with a duration of 9 years

2873. Under Belgian law, verbal lease agreements, written lease agreements without a fixed duration, and written lease agreements with a fixed duration of between 3 to 9 years are deemed to have been entered into for a duration of 9 years.

2874. Upon expiry of the 9-year term the landlord or the tenant is entitled to terminate the agreement, without giving any reason and without paying any indemnity, provided the terminating party gives notice of termination 6 months prior to expiry. Where neither of the parties serves such notice, the lease agreement will be tacitly renewed for successive periods of 3 years. In that case, each party has the right to terminate the agreement every 3 years, without giving a reason and without indemnity, provided the terminating party gives a 6 months' notice prior to the expiry of the agreement.

2875. During the 9-year term, the landlord has the right to terminate the lease agreement in the following cases:
- (i) the landlord or any of his/her family members intends to personally occupy the rented premises. In such a case, the landlord should provide 6 months' notice of termination (the cancellation term starts on the first day of the month following the month in which said notice was given) and identify to the tenant the person who will occupy the rented premises. If the identified person does not personally occupy the rented premises within one year from the end of the cancellation term (or, in case of extension, from the restitution of the realty by the lessee) for a period of at least 2 years, an indemnity of 18 months' rent will be due from the landlord, unless exceptional circumstances exist. An exception is made regarding termination for private use by a third degree relative: in this case, the cancellation term will not expire before the end of the first 3-year period;
- (ii) the landlord intends to rebuild or renovate the rented premises. A termination of the lease agreement on this ground can only be effective upon expiry of each period of 3 years and provided that a notice of 6 months is given. The tenant should also be informed about the nature of the proposed rebuilding and the compliance with legal requirements. In addition, the landlord must demonstrate that the proposed rebuilding relates to the habitable part of the rented premises and that the rebuilding costs exceed the amount of 3 (or in

some instances 2) years of rent. It should be noted that lease agreements may restrict or exclude the right of the landlord to terminate the agreement on grounds of renovation of the rented premises. The 1997 amendment of the Residential Lease Law has led to greater flexibility in favour of the lessor: if a lessor owns several leased residences in the same building, he may at any moment cancel those lease agreements because of renovation or reconstruction works, subject to the condition that such termination does not occur during the first year of lease; and

(iii) at the expiry of each term of 3 years the landlord has the right to terminate the agreement without reason upon providing 6 months' notice and subject to the payment of an indemnity. This indemnity amounts to 9 or 6 months of rent depending on whether the notice is served at the end of the first term of 3 years or at the end of the subsequent term of 3 years. Lease agreements may limit or exclude the possibility for the landlord to terminate the agreement without reason.

2876. When faced with a notice of termination by his lessor, the lessee has a right to give a counter-notice in order to end the lease within a month. This term starts on the first day of the month following the month of the lessor's original notice. In case of a valid counter-notice, the lessee cannot be required to pay any indemnification, even if the lease agreement ends before the expiry of the first 3-year period.

2877. Unlike the landlord, the tenant is entitled to terminate the lease agreement at any time and without reason provided he gives 3 months' notice. However, during the first 3 years of the agreement he will be required to pay an indemnity to the landlord which amounts to 3, 2 or one months' rent depending on whether he terminates the agreement during the first, second or third year respectively.

2. *Lease agreements with a duration of 3 years or less*

2878. Parties may enter into a short term lease agreement with the option of one extension, the total duration of which does not exceed 3 years. These agreements must be in writing, otherwise the agreement is deemed to have been entered into for 9 years.

2879. The extension is in itself subject to the following conditions:
   (i) it must be in written form;
   (ii) the conditions of the lease must remain unaltered, apart from the duration; and
   (iii) the total duration (of lease and renewal) may not exceed 3 years

2880. Written lease agreements with a duration which does not exceed 3 years cannot be unilaterally terminated prior to the expiry of the initial term. However, each party is entitled to terminate the agreement by serving 3 months' notice before the expiry of the term . If no notice is served during a period of 3 years as of the date of the initial agreement, and the tenant still occupies the rented premises after such term, the lease agreement is deemed to have been entered into for a period of 9 years with effect from the date of the original agreement. In this case the termination of the lease agreement is subject to the same rules as those governing the termination of lease agreements with a duration of 9 years.

3. Lease agreements with a duration of more than 9 years

2881. Parties may enter into lease agreements with a duration of more than 9 years. If such agreements are not made in writing, they are deemed to have been concluded for a term of 9 years. As Article 1 of the Registration and Mortgage Law imposes the registration of all lease agreements the term of which exceeds 9 years, a deed by a notary public will be required (*See*, para. 2856).

2882. Such agreements may be terminated upon expiry of the contractually agreed term provided the terminating party respects a notice period of 6 months. If no notice is served within that term, the agreement is automatically extended under the same conditions for successive periods of 3 years.

2883. The parties may terminate the agreement before the end of the contractually agreed term under the same conditions as those applicable to agreements with a duration of 9 years. The indemnity which the landlord is required to pay if he terminates the agreement without reason at the expiry of the third or any successive term of 3 years amounts to 3 months' rent.

4. Lease for life

2884. The option of a lease that lasts as long as the lessee lives was incorporated into the Residential Lease Law in 1997. In order to create a lease for life, a written contract is required. Although there are no further formal requirements, it is wise to make up the agreement before a notary public and to register it with the mortgage registry.

The lease term ends automatically when the lessee dies. Nevertheless, the lessee has an option to end the agreement at any time on the condition of respecting 3 months' notice. The lessor, on the other hand, has no right to terminate the contract, except if such a right is provided explicitly in the lease agreement itself.

This section of the Residential Lease Law only applies to lease agreements concluded from 31 May 1997.

5. Formalities regarding termination

2885. The Residential Lease Law is silent with regard to any formalities concerning the termination of the lease.

2886. Lease agreements may provide that notice of termination be given by registered letter. Even in the absence of such a provision, it is advisable to give notice by registered letter in order to avoid difficulties of proof. Failure to give notice in the required form at the appropriate time may lead to the extension of the parties' obligations. Upon vacating the premises, it is advisable to have the landlord sign a dated receipt for the keys.

§5. Survey, guarantee and fire insurance

2887. In Belgium, it is standard practice to have a survey *(plaatsbeschrijving/état des lieux)* done upon taking possession of the leased premises and upon departure. The purpose of such survey is to describe in some detail the state of the leased premises. Where such a survey is drawn up, the tenant will have to return the premises in the initial condition, except for damage due to *Acts of God* and normal wear and tear. Often both parties agree to have the survey done by a real estate expert whose fee is shared equally by the tenant and the landlord.

2888. If no survey has been done upon taking possession of the premises, the law provides that, in the absence of proof to the contrary, the tenant is deemed to have received the premises in the same condition as they are at the expiry of the agreement. In other words, if no survey has been drawn up, the landlord bears the burden of proof that the tenant is responsible for damage, if any, to the leased premises. This provision, which is to the benefit of the tenant, applies notwithstanding any clause to the contrary in the lease agreement.

2889. It is also standard practice (though not a legal requirement) that, at the time of signature of the lease agreement, the landlord requires the deposit of a guarantee. Usually the guarantee takes the form of a sum of money which legally may not exceed 3 months' rent. The landlord is not entitled to receive cash payment of the guarantee, nor payment of such sum on his bank account. Such guarantees must be paid into a blocked interest-bearing account opened in the name of the tenant and may be released only upon agreement of the tenant and the landlord or pursuant to a court decision. Contractual provisions to the contrary are null and void. The interest accrues to the benefit of the tenant.

2890. Finally, tenants should note that it is essential to obtain sufficient insurance coverage for fire damage. Belgian law contains very stringent rules on the liability of tenants for fire damage. The fact that the landlord also holds fire insurance in no way renders the tenant's coverage dispensable, since the risks covered are different (property insurance as opposed to liability insurance).

§6. Rent

2891. Each time a new lease agreement is entered into, the rent may be freely agreed upon between the landlord and the tenant. However, and in contrast with general lease law, if a lease agreement has not been terminated but extended between the same parties, the rent cannot generally be modified.

2892. Unless otherwise provided in the lease agreement, the rent may be subject to indexation. Indexation means that the amount of rent rises in accordance with the increases of the official consumer price index which is published on a monthly basis. Indexation of rent is allowed only once per year upon written request of the landlord and may not take place before the first anniversary date of the entry into force of the lease agreement. The request for indexation has retroactive effect for 3 months. The increased rent may not exceed the amount resulting from the application of the following formula:

$$\text{new rent} = \frac{\text{base rent x new index}}{\text{base index}}$$

2893. The base rent is the rent which was agreed upon in the lease agreement excluding any additional charges. The base index is the official consumer price index of the month preceding the month in which the lease agreement was concluded. The new index is the official consumer price index of the month preceding the month of the anniversary date of the entry into force of the agreement. The official consumer price index is announced each month by the Ministry of Economic Affairs *(Ministerie van economische zaken/Ministère des affaires économiques)* and is published in most newspapers.

2894. During the ninth and the sixth month preceding the expiry of each term of 3 years, the landlord or the tenant may request the other party to revise the rent (upwards or downwards). If the parties fail to agree, each party may request the court (Justice of the Peace) to revise the rent, provided such request is made during the sixth and the third month preceding the expiry of each term of 3 years. The Court (Justice of the Peace) may accept such revision of the rent in the following circumstances:

   (i) due to new circumstances, the normal rent of the rented premises is more than 20 per cent higher or lower than the rent payable at the time of the submission of the request for revision; or

(ii) due to renovation works financed by the landlord, the normal rent of the rented premises exceeds the rent payable at the moment of the submission of the request for revision by more than 10 per cent.

2895. Lease agreements will also typically contain provisions relating to additional charges, such as maintenance fees, electricity, heating, water and so on. With respect to these additional charges, it should be noted that the real estate withholding tax may no longer be contractually imposed on the tenant. If the lease agreement provides for a lump-sum amount for the additional charges, each party may request the court (Justice of the Peace) to revise the amount or to substitute the lump-sum amount by a system based on the effectively incurred expenses. As with the revision of the base rent, such requests for revision of the charges must be submitted during the sixth and the third month preceding the expiry of each term of 3 years.

§7. Transfer of lease and sublease

1. Transfer of Lease

2896. As stated above (*See*, para. 2867), a lessee who does not use the realty as his principal place of residence may not transfer his lease agreement to a third party (sub-lessee) who would take his principal residence there.

2897. However, a lessee who does have his principal place of residence in the realty, may transfer his lease agreement to a third party, but only on the condition that the lessor explicitly consents in advance to such transfer. In this case, the lessee can no longer be held liable for the lease as of the date of the transfer, unless the consent of the lessor is qualified in this respect (*e.g.*, shared responsibility by the transferror and the transferree as a precondition to consent).

2898. If a lessee decides to transfer his lease agreement without obtaining the lessor's required consent, he remains liable for any costs or damages *vis-à-vis* the new lessee and the lessor.

2. Sublease

i. The lessee does not have his principal place of residence in the realty

2899. As a rule, a lessee who does not have his principal place of residence in the realty which he leases, may not sublease the said realty to a third party (sub-lessee) who would take his principal residence there.

2900. The 1997 amendment to the Residential Lease Law has introduced 2 important exceptions to this rule:

(i) a legal entity (municipality, non-profit organisation, social service, *etc.*) may sublease property to persons in need of social assistance. In such case, the realty will exclusively serve as the person's principal residence. Prior consent of the lessor is required and not only the sublease, but also the lease by the legal entity itself is subject to the provisions of the Residential Lease Law; and

(ii) a lessee who leases the realty under the terms of a commercial lease agreement may sublease a part of the property to a sub-lessee who takes his principal residence there. Such a sublease is only valid to the extent that the principal (commercial) lease agreement does not contain a prohibition on subleasing. Only a part of the realty may be subleased and the (principal) lessee must continue his commercial activity in the premises.

ii. The lessee has his principal place of residence in the realty

2901. A lessee who has his principal place of residence in the realty may not sublease the totality of this realty. He may only sublease a part of it, on the condition that he keeps his principal residence in the remaining part.

2902. The subleased part of the property may or may not serve as a principal residence for the sub-lessee. If the former is the case, the agreement between the lessee (sub-lessor) and the sub-lessee is, in principle, governed by the Residential Lease Law, notwithstanding the following exceptions:

(i) the duration of the sublease agreement is limited to that of the lease agreement;

(ii) the lessee (sub-lessor) is obliged to inform the sub-lessee of the extent of his own rights regarding the realty;

(iii) upon termination of the agreement, the sub-lessee may not petition for an extension due to exceptional circumstances;

(iv) if the principal lessor should decide to terminate the lease agreement, the principal lessee should inform his sub-lessee within 15 days upon reception of the cancellation notice; he should likewise inform the sub-lessee that the sublease agreement will also end on the date of termination of the principal lease; and

(v) if the principal lessee (sub-lessor) should decide to terminate the principal lease agreement before its contractual term has ended, the sub-lessee is entitled to a 3 month cancellation period and a compensation fee amounting to 3 months' rent.

C. Commercial lease agreements

§1. Applicable law

2903. Commercial lease agreements are governed by the Law of 30 April 1951 on Commercial Lease Agreements (*Regels betreffende de handelshuur in het bijzonder/de règles particulières aux baux commerciaux* – the "Commercial Lease Law").

The Commercial Lease Law is applicable to the lease of unmoveable assets (or parts thereof) which, either explicitly or implicitly at the moment of taking possession of the realty by the lessee, by means of an explicit agreement or during the course of an existing lease agreement, are affected primarily for the exercise of a retail business or a craftsman's profession in direct contact with the public.

§2. Creating a commercial lease agreement

2904. As is the case with lease agreements subject to general law (*See*, para. 2856), it is, in principle, not required that the lease agreement take the form of a written contract. However, should a written agreement be made up, there is a fiscal obligation to register this document. The advantages of such registration have been described above (*See*, para. 2866).

In case of a lease exceeding 9 years, a written contract, authenticated by a notary public, is required.

2905. Certain leases are excluded from the application of the Commercial Lease Law. These are:
   (i) a lease which is normally granted for no more than one year, due to the nature or the destination of the realty (*e.g.*, a hastily constructed shed near a sporting stadium);
   (ii) the lease of public assets, which are exempt from real estate taxes;
   (iii) a lease by guardians in the context of the exercise of their custodial function (*e.g.*, in cases of insanity, incarceration or internment);
   (iv) the lease of low-value realty; and
   (v) a lease which is authorised by a public authority.

§3. Conditions for validity of commercial lease agreements

2906. Any natural person (older than 18 years) or legal entity (association or company) with legal capacity to act may conclude a commercial lease agreement. Article 1418 of the Civil Code states that in case of married individuals, the consent of both spouses is needed.

The object of the lease is to be defined by the parties. When drafting the lease agreement, parties should take special care that this description is sufficiently precise in order to avoid disagreement on this topic afterwards.

The cause of the lease should be permissible (*e.g.*, no house of ill repute or gambling den).

§4. Duration and termination of commercial lease agreements

1. Nine-year term

2907. The duration of the lease may not be shorter than 9 years. This term starts at the moment when the lessee takes possession of the realty (and not at the moment of the signing of the contract). (Art. 3 of the Commercial Lease Law) If no duration has been foreseen or if a shorter term than 9 years has been stated in the lease agreement, the agreement is not void but the lease is automatically extended to 9 years. Parties are free to provide for a longer duration than 9 years, subject to the requirement of registering the agreement in order to make it legally binding toward third parties.

2908. In case of subtenancy, the same rule of a 9-year lease applies. However, the sublease may not last longer than the duration of the main lease.

2. Cancellation by the lessee

2909. The lessee may cancel the lease at the end of each 3-year period, subject to the condition of giving advance notice no later than 6 months before the end of such period. The lessee has this option by force of law, even in the absence of a contractual clause providing for it. That being said, the lease agreement may provide a clause which is more beneficial to the lessee (*e.g.*, a yearly cancellation option or a shorter period for advance notice). The cancellation notice must be given by registered letter or a server writ.

3. Cancellation by the lessor

2910. The lessor may also cancel a lease agreement before its time. He can do so at the end of each 3-year period, provided that:
   (i) such option is explicitly provided for in the lease agreement; and
   (ii) one of the following reasons for ending the agreement is present:
      (a) the lessor wishes to conduct his own business on the premises;
      (b) the lessor wishes to allow his wife or relatives (ascendants or descendants) to conduct a business on the premises; or
      (c) the lessor wishes to allow his or his family's association to conduct a business on the premises

2911. The lessor should give advance notice of at least one year. The cancellation notice must be given by registered letter or a server writ.

4. Cancellation by mutual consent

2912. Likewise, the parties may agree to terminate the agreement. Such consent must take the form of an authentic act or a declaration by the Justice of the Peace.

§5. Rent

1. Fixing a rent

2913. Parties are at liberty to fix the rent for the commercial lease. This is equally so in the case of lease renewal. If the parties are unable to reach agreement, the judge will fix the rent in equity, taking into account the rents which are in force with regard to similar realty in the same neighbourhood and other factual circumstances, such as the tax value of the premises, its sales value, the consumption index, any revenue from subleases, *etc*. However, the judge may not fix the rent above what was demanded by the lessor or below what was offered by the lessee. Likewise, he may not take into account any added or reduced value which is due solely to the lessee.

2. Three-yearly review of the rent

2914. At each 3-year anniversary of the entry into force of a commercial lease, each party may, under certain circumstances, ask for an increase or reduction of the rent at the Justice of the Peace (Art. 6 of the Commercial Lease Law).

2915. A request for increase or reduction of the rent may only be addressed to the judge if the normal rental value of the premises
    (i) is 15 per cent higher or lower as compared to the rent provided for in the lease or fixed at the last revision; and
    (ii) further to new circumstances which are extraneous to the parties.

2916. In addition, the request must be addressed to the Justice of the Peace in the course of the last 3 months preceding the expiration of the concerned 3-year time period. The judge will decide in equity.

2917. Parties may only depart from this rule in order to make the revisions easier, for example, by increasing the frequency of the revision or in reducing the 15 per cent legal variation rate. The revision, however, remains subject to "new circumstances" (alternation in the costs of repairs, real estate market in general, *etc*.) and to a judge's decision.

§6. Sublease and transfer of lease

2918. Articles 10 and 11 of the Commercial Lease Law deal with the possibility for a lessee to sublease the premises or to transfer his leasehold.

2919. The ruling principle is that both (full or partial) sublease and transfer of the lease are allowed in the absence of a prohibition thereto in the main lease agreement. It is, thus, possible for the parties to agree to exclude the possibility of sublease or transfer. However, this option is limited by one exception: a contractual prohibition must not prevent a sublease or transfer of the lease which coincides with the transfer or lease of the business as such and all rights pertaining thereto. In this event, only the fact that the lessor or his family inhabits part of the realty would uphold the contractual prohibition.

2920. Whereas the main consequence of a sublease or transfer of the lease is the establishment of a link between the sub-lessee or transferee and the main lessor, the main lessee/sub-lessor/transferor should bear in mind that he remains jointly responsible with regard to all duties concerning the main lease until this main lease expires or is renewed by the sub-lessee or transferee.

2921. In case no transfer of business occurs, the main lessee retains his status of "lessee" *vis-à-vis* the main lessor and the 3-party relationship is continued.

§7. Renewal

2922. In principle, the lessee has the right to ask for 3 successive 9-year extensions of the commercial lease (Art. 13 of the Commercial Lease Law). Of course, the lessee's request must comply with the formal conditions provided for by the Law.

2923. On receipt of such a request the lessor has a number of alternatives which can be briefly summarised as follows:
(i) in the absence of a reply by registered letter within 3 months from the receipt of the lessee's request for renewal, the lessor is deemed to have accepted the renewal;
(ii) the lessor can accept the renewal under different terms and conditions. In case of a dispute on these terms and conditions, the issue will be referred to the judge, who will decide in equity;
(iii) the lessor can only oppose the lessee and accept a better financial offer from a third party in case this offer (i) is binding for at least 3 months and (ii) includes the undertaking of the third party to pay to the lessee the indemnity for ejectment provided for in the Commercial Lease Law. The lessee moreover disposes of the right to make an equivalent offer, in which case its offer takes precedence; and

    (iv) the lessor is entitled to refuse the renewal of the lease, in which case he will, under specific circumstances, be liable for the payment of an indemnity, amounting to 3 years' rent, possibly increased by any sum necessary to compensate the lessee's damage in full.

2924. No indemnity will be due to the lessee if the lessor refuses the renewal for one of the following reasons:
    (i) he intends to personally occupy the rented premises for private purposes or in order to run a different business;
    (ii) a serious breach by the lessee of its obligations;
    (iii) a better offer from a third party (without an equivalent offer from the lessee); or
    (iv) the absence of a legitimate interest on the part of the lessee in a renewal.

2925. In case of a refusal for the following reasons, an indemnity will be due, the amount of which will vary according to the circumstances of the case, but usually will be equal to at least 1 year of rent:
    (i) the personal occupation by the lessor to operate the same kind of business;
    (ii) the lessor intends to put an end to the commercial purpose of the premises; or
    (iii) the lessor intends to rebuild part or all of the premises (costs exceeding 3 months' rent).

§8. Transfer of the realty

2926. If the lessor decides to sell or otherwise transfer the ownership of the leased realty, this will, of course, greatly affect the position of his lessee. This eventuality is governed by article 12 of the Commercial Lease Law.

2927. Without going into detail, the lessee should be advised to ensure that the commercial lease agreement has a fixed date. This fixed date ensures the lessee's rights *vis-à-vis* the new owner of the realty, at least on a temporary basis. If the new owner wishes to terminate a lease with a fixed date, he will have to abide by certain formalities, including (but not limited to) a notice of at least one year.

2928. An agreement has a fixed date if drafted as an authentic act or, in the case of a non-authentic act, as of the date of its registration (*See*, para. 2866).

IV. EXPROPRIATION

A. Introduction

2929. Article 16 of the Constitution provides that nobody may be deprived of the real estate which he owns unless such expropriation is made in the general interest, with the provision of a fair and prior indemnification and in accordance with the principles provided by law. The following key concepts of Belgian expropriation law will be discussed below:

   (i) the general interest;

   (ii) fair and prior indemnification; and

   (iii) the Law governing expropriation procedures.

B. General interest

2930. Expropriation of real estate is only permitted if it is in the general interest. The concept of general interest must be given a fairly broad interpretation. For instance, the expropriation of real estate will be deemed to be in the general interest if it serves to implement the plans established for zoning and planning purposes. On the contrary, if a public authority acquires real estate which will not be used and is not intended to be used for the performance of its tasks in the general interest, expropriation is not the proper method of obtaining ownership of such real estate. The acquisition will require the agreement of the owner.

C. Fair and prior indemnification

2931. The expropriation of real estate requires the payment of a fair indemnification. The indemnification may amount to more than an objective purchase price. It includes, in addition to the objective value of the expropriated real estate, compensation for the damage caused by the expropriation. For instance, the indemnification may also encompass a reinvestment compensation or compensation for the fact that neighbouring land of the same owner will undergo a reduction in value as a result of the expropriation. The indemnification will only be deemed fair if it includes full compensation for all the damage resulting from the expropriation.

2932. The requirement of prior indemnification means that possession of the expropriated goods may only be taken following payment of the necessary compensation. In this context, it is important to distinguish between the taking of possession and the transfer of ownership. The transfer of ownership may indeed occur prior to the payment of the indemnification.

D. Law governing expropriation procedures

2933. The most important rules governing expropriation are contained in the Law of 17 April 1835 and 27 May 1870 (*Wet op de onteigening ten algemene nutte/Loi sur l'expropriation pour cause d'utilité pubique* – ordinary expropriation procedure) and the Law of 26 July 1962 (*Wet betreffende de rechtoplegging bij hoogdringende omstandigheden inzake ontreiniging ter algemenen nutte/Loi relative à la procedure d'extrême urgence en matière d'expropriation pour cause d'utilité publique* – expropriation procedure in urgent cases).

2934. What is common to both regimes is that, in the first instance, the agreement of all parties (the authorities and the real estate owners) is sought regarding the specifics of the expropriation, including the indemnification to be granted. If no such agreement can be reached, this administrative phase will be followed by a judicial phase.

2935. The judicial phase differs depending on whether the ordinary or the urgent expropriation procedure is to be followed. In the former case, the court of first instance will rule on whether the parties have complied with all required formalities. It will also decide on the level of indemnification, and the authorities may only take possession of the real estate at the moment that this indemnification is fully paid. In the latter case, the Justice of the Peace will rule on the expropriation and impose a provisional indemnity (a rough estimate of the final indemnification to be paid). Possession of the realty may be taken as soon as the expropriating party has provided all the other parties with a copy of the judgment setting out the amount of the provisional indemnity, evidence of the required payments and a copy of the description of the goods concerned provided by the expert appointed by the Justice of the Peace. In addition, the expropriating party must obtain a specific judicial order entitling him to take possession of the goods concerned. The final indemnification is the subject of a subsequent judgement by the Justice of the Peace.

2936. Ownership (as opposed to possession) is transferred on the date of an agreement thereto or on the date of the competent court's judgement confirming compliance with the applicable legal provisions.

2937. Mention must be made of the fact that an option of expropriation has also been foreseen in several federal laws or regional decrees. Although such regulations often contain minor adaptations to or specifications of the general expropriation procedure, the essence of the said procedure and the principles on which it is founded remain unabridged.

16. ENVIRONMENTAL LAW

I. INSTITUTIONAL FRAMEWORK

A. Regionalisation

§1. Attribution to the regions

2938. In Belgium, the power to adopt and enforce environmental laws has gradually been transferred from the national to the regional level. The constitutional reforms of 1980, 1988, 1993 and 2001, which transformed Belgium into a federal state, gave the Flemish, Walloon and Brussels-Capital Regions legislative power with respect to many environmental issues, while the powers at federal level have been limited to aspects of environmental policy with a transnational or inter-regional character. Consequently, environmental policy in Belgium has to a very large extent been attributed to the regions. All together, there are 5 environmental policies in Belgium, *i.e.*, the federal, Flemish, Brussels-Capital, Walloon and European environmental policies.

§2. Division of competencies

2939. The division of competencies between the Federal Government and the regions is laid down in Article 6(1) of the Special Institutional Reform Law of 8 August 1980, as amended (*Bijzondere wet tot hervorming der instellingen/Loi spéciale de réformes institutionnelles* – the "Special Law"). It can be noted that, although Article 6(1) seems to provide a clear-cut division of competencies between the federal and regional governments, in practice, federal and regional competencies sometimes clash and the division of powers has often been disputed.

1. Federal state

2940. In broad terms, the division of environmental powers in Belgium is divided as follows. By virtue of Article 6(1) of the Special Law, the Federal Government is competent to set product standards, to provide protection against ionising radiation, including uranium extraction and disposal of radio-active waste, and to supervise the transit of waste. Besides these explicit environmental competencies, the Federal Government is also competent to impose product taxes, to award eco-labels, to protect the North Sea, to protect the health and safety of workers, to provide civil protection, to co-ordinate the preparation and follow-up of the implementation of the European environmental policy at national and regional level, and to exercise a substitution power where the regions have failed to respect environmental commitments on a European or international level.

2. Regions

2941. The regions are exclusively competent for the protection of the environment *sensu stricto* (soil, subsoil, water, air and noise), waste policy (apart from radio-active waste and the regulation of the transport of waste which remain federal), the environmental supervision of enterprises (other than the supervision of health and safety at work which remains an exclusively federal competence), water policy, zoning planning policy (*e.g.*, the granting of building permits), nature conservation policy (except the import, transport and export of exotic plants and living or dead animals), natural resources policy, and some aspects of energy policy. Besides these explicit environmental competences, the regions are also competent in some aspects of environmental criminal law, environmental tax law, and European and international environmental law.

3. Provinces and communes

2942. The provinces and communes have only limited environmental powers. These powers mainly consist of administrative and supervisory competences (including the tracing and establishment of breaches of environmental legislation), often delegated to them by the regional governments. The provinces and communes may intervene only to protect a provincial or communal interest, which mostly implies intervention to protect public health.

B. Competent authorities

2943. Enterprises active in Belgium may find that contacting the right administration or competent body turns out to be a rather difficult task. Indeed, in Belgium, the main bodies responsible for environmental policy are the federal, regional, provincial and municipal executives, but these bodies are also assisted by several specialised public/regional agencies charged with the enforcement of environmental laws. Also, many private companies or associations often take part in environmental management in their region.

§1. Federal State

2944. There are currently 9 federal departments or public services with competence in environmental policy matters. These include the Ministry for Social Affairs,

Public Health and Environment; the Ministry for the Middle Class and Agriculture; the Ministry for Economic Affairs; the Ministry for Employment and Labour; the Ministry for Traffic and Infrastructure; the Ministry for Internal Affairs; the Ministry for Defence; the Services of the Prime Minister; the Ministry for Foreign Affairs; Foreign Trade and Development Co-operation. Inter-departmental co-ordination is achieved through the Ministerial Committee for the Environment. Consultation between the federal and regional levels is organised through working groups installed by the Inter-Ministerial Conference for the Environment (*Interministeriële Conferentie Leefmilieu (ICL)/Conférence Interministérielle de l'Environnement (CIE)*). In addition, there are a number of important authorities and institutions which provide support on environmental policy, such as the Federal Planning Bureau (*Federaal Planbureau/Bureau fédéral du plan*), the Federal Council for Sustainable Development (*Federale Raad voor duurzame Ontwikkeling/ Conseil fédéral du Développement durable*), the Inter-regional Cell for the Environment ("Irceline" – *Intergewestelijke Cel voor het Leefmilieu/Cellule Interrégionale de l'Environnement*), and the Federal Office for Scientific, Technical and Cultural Affairs (*Federale Diensten voor Wetenschappelijke, Technische en Culturele Aangelegenheden/Services fédéraux des Affaires scientifiques, techniques et culturelles*).

§2. Flemish Region

2945. In the Flemish Region, the Environmental Directorate of the Flemish Executive, commonly known as AMINAL (*Administratie Milieu, Natuur- en Landinrichting*) consists of 6 departments: (i) general environmental policy, (ii) environmental investments, (iii) environmental permits, (iv) environmental inspection, (v) nature conservation/development, and (vi) land use/management. The departments responsible for environmental permits and environmental inspections also have branches in each of the 5 Flemish provinces.

2946. In addition to AMINAL, several specialised, semi-independent governmental agencies have been set up in the Flemish region to deal with environmental issues. These include:
   – OVAM (*Openbare Vlaamse Afvalstoffenmaatschappij*) which is entrusted with significant powers in the field of waste disposal, such as the development of waste management plans, the receipt of notifications concerning the removal of waste and the registration of polluted sites. The enforcement powers of OVAM are particularly important. OVAM has, *inter alia*, the power to order the removal of waste as well as the power to order the clean-up of contaminated sites.

– VMM (*Vlaamse Milieumaatschappij*), the Flemish Environmental Company which carries out various administrative tasks concerning pollution of surface water and the air, such as the development of annual water purification programmes, the drafting of annual reports on the emission of polluting substances into the air, and the creation and operation of a network for the systematic measuring of water and air quality.

§3. Brussels-Capital Region

2947. The Executive of the Brussels-Capital Region is responsible for the specific environmental policy of this region but has delegated most of its powers to the Brussels Institute for Environmental Management (*Brussels Instituut voor Milieubeheer (BIM)/Institut Bruxellois pour la Gestion de l'Environnement (IBGE)*). This is a semi-independent agency with particularly broad advisory, management and enforcement powers with respect to a wide range of environmental issues, including waste, air, noise, nature, soil, water and energy. It is structured into several divisions and departments dealing directly with enterprises. Enterprises doing business in Belgium can obtain all relevant information from the Brussels Regional Development Agency (*Gewestelijke Ontwikkelingsmaatschappij voor Brussel (GOMB)/Société de Développement Régional de Bruxelles – Guichet ECOBRU (SDRB)*).

§4. Walloon region

2948. The Ministry of the Walloon Region is composed of 8 Directorates-General among which the Directorate-General for Natural Resources and Environment (*Direction Générale des Ressources Naturelles et de l'Environnement (DGRNE)*) is the main body in charge of environmental policy. Other Directorates-General are also concerned with environmental issues: the Directorate-General for Zoning Planning, Lodging and Patrimony (*Direction Générale de l'Aménagement du Territoire, du Logement et du Patrimoine*) and the Directorate-General for Economy and Labour (*Direction Générale de l'Economie et de l'Emploi*).

2949. DGRNE is itself divided into 5 administrative divisions: (i) Nature and Forests, (ii) Prevention and Authorisations, (iii) Waste (the Walloon Office for Waste) (*Office wallon des déchets (OWD)*), (iv) Water, and (v) Police of the Environment. The OWD has enforcement powers with respect to waste disposal which are similar to, although more limited than, those of OVAM in the Flemish region. DGRNE is assisted by several public bodies such as the Scientific Institute of Public Service (*Institut Scientifique de Service Publique*), the Public Company for Environmental Quality (*Société Publique d'Aide à la Qualité de l'Environnement*), the Public

Company for Water Management (*Société Publique de Gestion de l'Eau*), and the Walloon Environmental Council for Sustainable Development (*Conseil Wallon de l'Environnement pour le Développement Durable*), which is part of the Economic and Social Council of the Walloon region (*Conseil Economique et Social de la Région Wallonne (CESRW)*).

C. Co-ordination and external relations

§1. Means of co-ordination

2950. Given the existence of 5 environmental policies resulting from the regionalisation of Belgian environmental law and the cross border dimensions of the environment, some mechanisms had to be put in place to provide for internal as well as external co-ordination between all the responsible bodies. Therefore, to avoid conflicting or different regulations for matters common to all 3 regions, Article 92*bis* of the Special Law provides for the possibility, and, in some cases, obligation, for the Federal State and the federated entities to conclude co-operation agreements between themselves. Furthermore, inter-regional conferences and the Inter-Ministerial Conference for the Environment in particular have been established since 1993 to provide a forum for discussion between all the institutions concerned.

§2. External relations

2951. Belgium's external relations traditionally remain a federal competence. However, since 1993, Article 167(1) of the Constitution provides that the regions and communities can engage in international co-operation, including the conclusion of treaties, on matters falling within their competence. The Belgian Constitution foresaw the conclusion of 2 co-operation agreements between the Federal State and the federated entities. The first one, dated 8 March 1994, concerns the representation of Belgium in the Council of Ministers of the European Union. The basic rule is that the Belgian actors must co-operate to find a common position. Belgium is then represented in the Environmental Council of Ministers by a federal delegate, assisted by one regional delegate who changes every 6 months. The second obligatory co-operation agreement, dated 30 June 1994, concerns international organisations carrying out activities which constitute shared competences between the Federal State and the federated entities. Given the specific characteristics of the environmental sector, the Federal State and the 3 regions concluded, on 5 April 1995, a further distinct Co-operation Agreement on International Environmental Policy. This Co-operation Agreement set up a Co-ordination Committee for International Environmental Policy (*Coördinatiecomité Internationaal Milieubeleid*

(CCIM)/Comité de Coordination de la Politique Internationale de l'Environnement (CCPIE)) within the Inter-Ministerial Conference for the Environment mentioned above. This Committee is made up of federal and regional representatives and is responsible for the adoption of a coherent common position between all Belgian actors in relation to Belgium's international commitments.

2952. It is noted that the Special Law, as amended in 1993, provides for a "substitution power" for the Federal State. Article 16(3) of the Special Law stipulates that when the Belgian State has been charged with a violation of duties under international or supranational law concerning matters which in fact fall within the competences of the regions, the Belgian State has, under very strict conditions, the right to regulate in the negligent region's place.

D. Policy instruments

§1. Overview

2953. Once a government has defined its environmental goals, it can execute its environmental policy by using different instruments. These instruments have been developed over the years. Traditionally, from the 1960s to the 1980s, governments made use of so-called "direct regulation instruments". That is to say, they regulated the field by imposing restrictions, requirements, prohibitions, the use of a permit, and all kinds of control such as on quality, emissions, *etc.* The adoption of such measures is, however, a particularly difficult exercise as, by definition, they run behind technological development. Governments in Belgium, as well as across Europe, needed a broader range of instruments to tackle even more diffuse sources of environmental pressures. Nowadays, besides instruments of direct regulation, governments use various social regulation instruments (*e.g.*, environmental education, labels, impact reports, environmental care systems, environmental policy agreements), financial aid instruments (*e.g.*, subsidies, fiscal incentives), planning instruments, and market regulation instruments (*e.g.*, liability rules, enforcement incentives). More and more attention is paid to the use of these last instruments. This is certainly the case for the environmental policy and legislation developed by the Flemish Region.

§2. Planning instruments

2954. As regards planning instruments, they allow governments to establish long-term general and/or sectoral environmental targets, priorities, and methodologies, and to co-ordinate the different aspects of their environmental policies, on the basis of analyses of the environmental situation. In addition, they provide a certain transparency to citizens and enterprises. However, planning instruments are also criticised as giving citizens the impression that the public authority is concerned about the environment while, in effect, planning instruments often lack the means to achieve ambitious environmental objectives. The use of planning instruments is at the discretion of governments, although it can sometimes be rendered compulsory by virtue of European Directives. For instance, since 1975, Member States of the European Community have been obliged to elaborate plans for the management of waste. In this regard, European Directives indicate the measures to be developed in such plans (*e.g.*, type, quantity and origin of the waste to be managed). The Federal State and the 3 regions have adopted legal frameworks enabling them to periodically set up plans for sustainable development. These are the federal Law of 5 May 1997 on the Co-ordination of Federal Policy for Sustainable Development (*Wet betreffende de coördinatie van het federale beleid inzake duurzame ontwikkeling/Loi relative à la coordination de la politique fédérale de développement durable*), the Walloon Decree of 21 April 1994 concerning Environmental Planning for Sustainable Development (*Décret relatif à la planification en matière d'environnement dans le cadre du développement durable*), Articles 2.1.1 to 2.2.8 of the Flemish Decree of 5 April 1995 (*Decreet houdende algemene bepalingen inzake milieubeleid*) referring expressly to planning, and Articles 16 to 23 of the Brussels-Capital Ordinance of 29 August 1991 on Planning and Urbanism (*Ordonnantie houdende organisatie van de planning en de stedebouw/Ordonnance organique de la plannification et de l'urbanisme*).

2955. Environmental plans are not legally binding for citizens and enterprises but they are for the public authorities which must execute and justify their decisions by referring to the plans.

II. LEGISLATIVE FRAMEWORK

A. Characteristics of Belgian environmental law

§1. Impact from international and European Law

2956. Environmental law in Belgium, as in the other Member States of the European Community, is to a very large extent influenced by international and European norms, and the federal and regional governments are often compelled to implement supranational requirements. Enterprises concerned with environmental issues in Belgium should not, therefore, apply Belgian environmental law separately from international and/or European environmental law.

§2. Multiple legislative systems – multiple sectoral and non-sectoral laws

2957. As already mentioned, Belgian environmental law is characterised by the regionalisation of environmental policy since 1980, with the consequence that there is not only one but 5 environmental legal systems in Belgium: Flemish, Walloon, Brussels, federal and European environmental legislation. This already suggests a certain degree of complexity for companies who wish to understand their environmental rights and obligations. Also, in 1980, the Flemish and Walloon Regions immediately started using their newly granted on powers and, have, since then, made extensive use of them. The Brussels-Capital Region only became active in the 1990s. As for many other countries, the regions adopted environmental provisions one after another to face the environmental problems of the moment and, over the years, Belgian environmental law has developed very rapidly. Indeed, decrees and ordinances have been adopted, replaced and/or amended at a very high speed. As a result of this evolution, environmental law in Belgium has developed into a rather complex set of sectoral measures which make it difficult to get a clear picture.

§3. Future developments

2958. In the light of this complexity, the regional and the federal governments are aware that efforts must be made to harmonise, simplify and codify their environmental legislation. Regional environmental decrees and ordinances are still very "sectoral" and should be more "general". In other words, topics which arise in all the various sectoral environmental legislation should be harmonised or co-ordinated as much as possible. The most important legislative revision so far is in the field of environmental permits where, as will be explained below, every region has adopted a single environmental permit for all environmental sectors. This is a first step towards a certain co-ordination of environmental law in Belgium. It is noted that, compared to the Walloon and Brussels-Capital Regions, the Flemish Region appears to have adopted the most radical approach in this co-ordination and harmonisation process. In the Flemish region, the complexity of the environmental law system led the Flemish Minister for the Environment to set up, on 5 July 1989, the "Interuniversity Commission for the Reform of the Environmental Legislation in the Flemish Region" (*Besluit van de Vlaamse Executieve houdende oprichting van een interuniversitaire Commissie tot herziening van het milieurecht in het Vlaamse Gewest*). 5 years after its foundation, this commission proposed a draft "framework decree on environmental policy". This text tackles horizontal subjects as well as new rules regarding the decision-making process (*e.g.*, planning, authorisations), compliance with the legislation (*e.g.*, monitoring, administrative and criminal sanctions), safety measures and liability rules. A few decrees have already been adopted on the basis of this draft framework decree and one can expect that further new non-sectoral decrees will be adopted in the near future.

The Walloon Government in turn has announced its objective to adopt a Walloon Code of Environmental law (*Code wallon du droit de l'environnement*). This codification is not expected to be completed in the near future.

§4. "Greening" of the law

2959. A relatively new characteristic of Belgian environmental law is the so-called "greening" of the law, that is to say the introduction of ecological elements into the classical branches of law (*e.g.*, constitutional law, administrative law, tax law, civil liability law, criminal law, insurance law, company law, economic law, labour law, judicial private law, accountancy law, and European law). Governments in Belgium seem to be willing to introduce more ecological concerns into the other branches of law. It is expected that this approach will become more important in the light of the development of this "greening" effect encouraged by the EC Commission at the European level.

B. Legal bases

2960. The main source of Belgian environmental law is legislative. So far, the case law on this subject is extremely limited.

§1. Article 23 of the Constitution

2961. Article 23 of the Belgian Constitution recognises "the right to the protection of a healthy environment" and therefore the obligation on the government to protect the environment. It is noted that this constitutional provision cannot be directly enforced by private individuals.

§2. Article 6 of the Special Law of 1980

2962. Article 6 of the Special Law provides for the division of powers between the Federal Government and the regional executives.

2963. The core of the legislation is, however, found in federal laws, regional decrees and ordinances and their executive decisions. These pieces of legislation are far too numerous and change too rapidly to cite them all. Only some (of the) important ones will be mentioned.

§3. Flemish Region

2964. In the Flemish Region, the Flemish Council adopted a Decree on 28 June 1985 on environmental permits (*Decreet betreffende de milieuvergunning*). On the basis of that Decree, the Flemish government adopted a Decision of 6 February 1991 to draft a Flemish Regulation on environmental permits (*Besluit van de Vlaamse Executieve houdende vaststelling van het Vlaams reglement betreffende de milieuvergunning*) ("VLAREM I"), and a Decision of 1 June 1995 containing general and sectoral regulations concerning environmental health and safety (*Besluit van de Vlaamse regering houdende algemene en sectorale bepalingen inzake milieuhygiëne*) ("VLAREM II"). The Flemish Council also adopted an important Decree of 5 April 1995 concerning general regulations in the matter of environmental policy, which states the goals and principles of Flemish environmental policy.

§4. Brussels-Capital Region

2965. The Brussels-Capital Region adopted an Ordinance of 5 June 1997 on Environmental Permits (*Ordonnantie betreffende de milieuvergunning/Ordonnance relative aux permis d'environnement* – the "Ordinance of 5 June 1997) (amending the Ordinance of 30 July 1993), followed by a Regulation of 4 March 1999 establishing the list of establishments belonging to Classes IB, II, and III and an Ordinance of 22 April 1999 establishing the list of the establishments belonging to Class IA.

§5. Walloon Region

2966. In the Walloon Region, a Decree on Environmental Permits was adopted on 11 March 1999 (*Décret relatif au permis d'environnement*) (as last amended by a Decree of 19 September 2002). This Decree only took effect on 1 October 2002, after the Walloon Government adopted executive decisions implementing it. 4 executive decisions were adopted on 4 July 2002 regarding: (i) the list of projects subject to an impact assessment and the list of classified installations and activities, (ii) the procedure for granting environmental permits, (iii) environmental impact assessments, and (iv) general exploitation conditions.

§6. Environmental agreements

2967. Another, albeit contested, source of law results from the practice, started by public authorities, in the 1980s, of concluding so-called "environmental agreements" or environmental policy agreements with companies, industries or representative organisations of companies. These environmental agreements aim to prevent environmental pollution, limit or avoid its consequences or promote more effective environmental management. However, they do raise legal issues, especially as regards the power of public authorities to use their regulatory power in a contractual way. To remedy this situation, the Flemish Region adopted a Decree of 15 June 1994 on Environmental Agreements (*Decreet betreffende de milieubeleidsovereenkomsten*) which defines the scope and limits of the use of such instruments. This decree provides that an environmental policy agreement cannot replace or be less stringent than the prevailing legislation and may not last for more than 5 years. No similar general legal framework for the adoption of environmental agreements has been adopted in the other regions of the country. A proposal for similar legislation from the Walloon Region was rejected by the legislative section of the Council of State (*Raad van State/Conseil d'État*). The Federal Parliament included a provision in a Law of 21 December 1998 on Product Standards (*Wet betreffende de productnormen ter bevordering van duurzame productie- en consumptiepatronen en ter bescherming van het leefmilieu en de volksgezondheid/Loi relative aux normes de produits ayant pour but la promotion de modes et de consommation durables et la protection de l'environnement et de la santé*), which allows the government to conclude agreements with representative organisations for the commercialisation of products less harmful to the environment.

III. DIRECT REGULATION INSTRUMENTS

A. Overview

2968. Direct regulation instruments include all environmental restrictions and requirements imposed on companies, either in laws and/or in environmental permits. Importantly, these restrictions and requirements may vary from region to region, while old national legislation may still be applicable. To complicate matters further, environmental law in Belgium is in a state of flux because, as in other EC Member States, this body of law is still, to a large extent, new and untested. In addition, in some cases, important legislation is still on the table. Companies doing business in Belgium are thus well advised to investigate thoroughly for themselves environmental issues, including the requirements that must be met for the issue of permits and liability for the breach of the relevant rules, and to avoid relying on second-hand accounts of other companies' experiences. The main and most important instrument of direct regulation is the environmental permit. The regimes applicable to environmental permits are described below. Other instruments of direct regulation, such as sectoral legislation on water, air, waste, *etc.* are beyond the scope of this book.

B. Gradual consolidation of environmental permits

2969. The environmental permit is an authorisation issued by the competent authorities, which contains the technical norms and obligations that the operator of an installation must respect in order to reduce the potential environmental nuisance inherent to the installation and which may constitute a risk for the neighbourhood and the environment. The issue of environmental permits is an exclusive competence of the regions. In the past, companies doing business in Belgium have been faced with the problem of having to obtain many environmental permits and licences for different nuisances and from different public authorities. For instance, separate licences were required for the discharge of waste into surface water, ground water, the disposal of toxic waste and the disposal of non-toxic waste. In addition, only a minimal co-ordination of the procedures to obtain the various environmental permits had been achieved. Environmental licences granted by the regions are now global, that is to say, they encompass all environmental aspects of the operations and provide for a single, although complex, procedure.

2970. As described below, all 3 regions have now adopted legislation for a single environmental permit. The regional rules of the Flemish, Brussels-Capital and Walloon Regions are rather similar in their principles, while their details (*e.g.*, terminology, time limits, periods, and competent authorities) may be different. The main procedural steps common to all 3 regions are the verification of the admissibility and completeness of the application, the public inquiry, the advice, the decision, and the publicity. The regional rules have territorial application and the place of the plant or establishment determines which of the 3 sets of rules is applicable. Attention must be drawn to the fact that, before applying for an environmental permit, enterprises should verify that the activity can be carried out in the place envisaged. To know which activities can be carried out in one particular area, enterprises should contact the planning services of the municipality concerned. Enterprises should also contact the planning services in the event of a planning (or building) permit being required (in most cases) in addition to an environmental permit. Besides environmental and building permits, specific permits may in limited circumstance still be required for certain specific activities. For example, the Flemish Region requires a specific permit in relation to radioactive material. The Walloon

Region requires specific permits for mining concessions. However, these permits will not be analysed in this chapter.

C. Environmental impact assessment as a condition to obtaining environmental permits

2971. In many cases, it is necessary to carry out an environmental impact assessment before an environmental permit may be obtained.

§1. EC Directive No 85/337

2972. This obligation results from the implementation, in all 3 regions, of EC Council Directive No. 85/337 of 27 June 1985 concerning the Assessment of the Effects of Certain Public and Private Projects on Environment (O.J. [1985] L 175). It should be noted that the draft of an environmental impact report may be required for purposes other than the issue of an environmental permit (*e.g.*, for a building permit).

§2. Flemish Region

2973. In the Flemish Region, the Regulation of the Flemish Government of 23 March 1989 concerning the Environmental Impact Assessment of Certain Categories of Classified Installations (*Besluit van de Vlaamse Executieve houdende organisatie van de Milieu-effectbeoordeling van bepaalde categorieën van hinderlijke inrichtingen*) (as amended) requires that an "environmental impact report" must be filed together with the application for a licence if it concerns one of the classified installations indicated in Article 3 of the Decree. A similar regulation exists in Articles 7 to 16 of the Decision of 6 February 1991 ("VLAREM I") for the drafting of a "safety report", which must be added to the application for an environmental permit for facilities containing dangerous substances, as mentioned in the annex to this Decision.

§3. Brussels-Capital Region

2974. The Ordinance of 5 June 1997 provides that an "environmental study" is required for all applications for a Class IA environmental permit or certificate, while an "environmental report" is required for all applications for a Class IB permit or certificate. The Brussels-Capital Region handles, on average, no more than 20 applications for a Class IB permit per year. The filing of Class IB permit applications requires that the environmental impact assessment is carried out by an independent registered experts office, which is aware of all the various details of the regulation concerning environmental impact assessments.

§4. Walloon Region

2975. In the Walloon Region, by virtue of the Decree of 11 March 1999 on Environmental Permits (as last amended by a Decree of 19 September 2002), every application for an environmental permit has to either contain an "environmental impact assessment notice" (*notice d'évaluation des incidences sur l'environnement*), or an "environmental impact study" (*étude d'incidences sur l'environnement*). An environmental impact study, carried out by an independent registered expert, is requested for all projects listed in one of the 4 executive regulations adopted by the Walloon Government on 4 July 2002 to implement the Decree of 11 March 1999 on Environmental Permits. An environmental impact assessment notice is required in all other cases but the Decree provides that the government can consider that the application for an environmental permit constitutes the environmental impact assessment notice. No environmental impact assessment or notice is required for Class III activities or facilities.

2976. The following sections describe the environmental permits that are compulsory for classified installations prior to the commencement or change of any activities and/or the use or transformation of any facilities.

D. Environmental permits: EC Directive No. 96/61

2977. On 24 September 1996, the EC Council adopted Directive No 96/61 concerning Integrated Pollution Prevention and Control (O.J. [1998] L 19/83). Among the conditions to be imposed on the holder of an environmental permit, the Directive requires that the reduction and treatment of the waste produced by the activity, the rational use of energy, and the cleaning up of the site after cessation of the activity are included. On the basis of the Directive, the authorisation must also take into account the risk of pollution to air, water and soil, and fix limits for polluting emissions, by reference to the best available techniques, taking into account the long-term effects of the activities. Since 30 October 1999, all the conditions for running a facility must be integrated in an environmental permit prior to the operation of the facility. Furthermore, the conditions imposed on facilities already authorised must be adapted, even before the expiration of the permit.

E. Flemish region

2978. In the Flemish Region, the Regulation of 6 February 1991 (*Besluit van de Vlaamse Executieve houdende vaststelling van het Vlaams reglement betreffende de milieuvergunning*) which implemented the Decree of 28 June 1985 on Environmental Permits (*Decreet betreffende de milieuvergunning*), has led to the consolidation of various environmental permits into one comprehensive permit. This comprehensive permit is issued as a result of a single procedure provided for in VLAREM I. VLAREM I is supplemented by a Decision of 1 June 1995 ("VLAREM II") providing for a comprehensive compilation of technical standards which are inserted as conditions of environmental permits. In addition, very strict noise standards are imposed by VLAREM II.

2979. As of 1 September 1991, the following permits and procedures were consolidated by VLAREM I into a comprehensive environmental permit (*milieuvergunning*) and a single procedure was established for granting these permits:
  (i) the operating permit for hazardous facilities;
  (ii) the drainage permit for the discharge of substances into surface water;
  (iii) the permit for the drainage of certain pollutants into ground water;
  (iv) the operating permit for disposal of toxic waste; and
  (v) the operating permit for disposal of non-toxic waste.

2980. The duration of existing permits, issued on the basis of the former procedures, may not exceed 20 years (starting from 1 September 1991).

2981. VLAREM I also introduced a reciprocal suspension system for the environmental permit and the building permit. That is to say, the building permit does not come into effect if the environmental permit has not been obtained and *vice versa*.

2982. VLAREM I generally distinguishes between 3 kinds of hazardous facilities:
  (i) Class I facilities which require a permit from the provincial authorities, *i.e.*, the Deputation of the Province (*Bestendige Deputatie/ Députation Permanent*);
  (ii) Class II facilities which require a permit from the municipal authorities, *i.e.*, the College of Mayor and Aldermen (*College van Burgemeester en Schepenen/ Collège des Bourgmestre et Echevins*); and
  (iii) Class III facilities which merely require that the municipal authorities be notified.

2983. It should be noted that the municipal authorities have the authority to issue permits for temporary facilities.

2984. VLAREM I provides detailed rules and model forms dealing with the content of applications for environmental permits and the documents that need to be provided in support of such applications. An application typically requires information relating to items such as the number of employees, turnover, existing environmental protection devices and the method of drainage. Supporting documents may include the following:

    (i) an environmental impact assessment report for facilities that are listed in the Flemish Regulation of 23 March 1989; and

   (ii) a safety report on facilities that store or use in their production process (as a raw material, input product, final product or waste) a dangerous substance listed in an annex to VLAREM I. The safety report is drawn up by a panel of one or more certified experts, possibly assisted by one or more non-certified experts selected by the applicant.

2985. The procedure to be followed in order to obtain an environmental permit is cumbersome and essentially consists of the following steps:

    (i) within 14 days of filing the application, the competent authority must inform the applicant in writing as to the admissibility and completeness of the application. If the application is considered to be inadmissible or incomplete, the reasons for the decision must be explained;

   (ii) a 30-day period for public comment during which the application and supporting documents are made available to the public, and notices are posted at the facility. With respect to Class I facilities, more stringent publicity requirements apply, in that notices must be placed in at least two local daily or weekly publications. In addition, adjoining landowners must be notified and a public meeting must be held; and

  (iii) advisory opinions must be obtained from the competent authorities:

      (a) with respect to Class I facilities, a number of regional advisory committees as well as the local municipal authority must, within 60 days, issue an opinion on the application; and

      (b) with respect to Class II facilities, only the local municipal authorities must, within 30 days, issue an opinion on the application. If the authority concerned fails to issue its opinion within the prescribed time limits, the opinion is deemed to be affirmative;

   (iv) co-ordination between the authorities ruling on the application and the advisory committees is the responsibility of provincial permit commissions. These commissions forward applications to the competent advisory committees and transmit the opinions to the authority which rules on the application. In addition, these commissions must also give an opinion on applications covering Class I facilities;

    (v) within 4 months (Class I facilities) or 3 months (Class II facilities) from the date the application was declared admissible and complete, the competent authority must decide on the application. If no decision is taken within these time limits, the applicant may lodge an appeal with the competent authority. The decision is publicised by posting it at the facility and is available for inspection by the public. The permit is granted for a maximum period of 20 years, but may be withdrawn if the conditions imposed by the permit are breached or if any laws are broken;

(vi) it should also be emphasised that, if the terms of a permit are, at a later stage, found to provide unsatisfactory protection for the environment, the administration may impose additional measures; and

(vii) appeals against decisions refusing a permit must be lodged within 30 days with either the provincial authorities (with respect to decisions by municipal authorities) or the regional authorities (with respect to decisions by provincial authorities).

2986. VLAREM I also provides rules concerning, *inter alia*, the following issues:

(i) free access of persons to information on the environment, without these persons having to show an interest. Requests for access to environmental data are dealt with by the provincial authorities (implementation of the EC Directive No. 90/313 of 7 June 1990 on Freedom of Access to Information on the Environment – O.J. [1990] L 158/56);

(ii) operating conditions attached to the permit are spelt out in considerable detail. Operating conditions may be amended at any time. VLAREM I also imposes a general obligation on operators to take all measures necessary in order to prevent damage or nuisance;

(iii) if a permitted facility is acquired by another operator, the permit remains valid for the remaining period of its duration, provided that, 10 days prior to the acquisition, the new operator notifies the take-over to the authority that issued the permit;

(iv) supervision (for example, taking of samples) and enforcement (such as closure by the local mayor of facilities infringing the terms of a permit or regulatory requirements) by the competent enforcement officials; and

(v) provisions that contain rules with respect to permits covering specific environmental hazards, for example, permits allowing the discharge of certain dangerous substances in surface and ground water are subject to a new examination every 4 years.

F. Brussels-Capital Region

2987. The Brussels-Capital Region replaced the previous operating permit by a single environmental permit encompassing all potential environmental nuisances resulting from the running of a facility. The Brussels-Capital Region adopted an Ordinance of 30 July 1992 on environmental permits, but the system of unique environmental permits was only put into force on 1 December 1993 due to the adoption of an Ordinance of 23 November 1993 amending the 1992 Ordinance. On 5 June 1997, the region adopted a new Ordinance amending the 1993 Ordinance. It also took a Regulation of 4 March 1999 and another Ordinance of 22 April 1999 establishing the list of 4 classes of hazardous facilities according to the nature and the importance of the dangers and nuisances they cause:

   (i) Class IA facilities which require a permit from the Brussels Institute for Environmental Management (BIM);

  (ii) Class IB facilities which require a permit from the BIM;

 (iii) Class II facilities which require a permit from the municipal authorities, *i.e.*, the College of Mayor and Aldermen (*College van Burgemeester en Schepenen/ Collège des Bourgmestre et Echevins*);

 (iv) Class III facilities which merely require that the municipal authorities be notified; and

  (v) As in the Flemish Region, an environmental permit can be issued for temporary facilities.

2988. An "environmental certificate" can be granted for Class IA and IB facilities. This certificate does not free the facility from the obligation to obtain an environmental permit. It can be issued by BIM, prior to the issue of an environmental permit, and gives an indication to the applicant of whether, and under which conditions, an environmental licence is likely to be delivered if an application for a licence were made. The information that has to be provided is less demanding than for an environmental licence and therefore less expensive. The environmental certificate also presents the advantage of allowing the applicant to better prepare its future application for a permit.

2989. When a facility belongs to one of the categories mentioned above, an environmental permit is required in various situations:

   (i) a project to run a new facility or activity;

  (ii) when the environmental licence is about to expire;

 (iii) when the authorisation is no longer valid; and

 (iv) for changes to the facility.

2990. All applications for an environmental permit must be lodged with the municipal authorities. This is the so-called principle of a single "window", which is particular to the Brussels-Capital Region. A standard application form can be obtained from the municipal authorities or can be directly downloaded from the BIM Internet web site. Steps of the procedure vary according to the classification of the hazardous facility in question. Indeed, a specific procedure is defined for each classification of facility. When several facilities or activities belong to different classes, the application is lodged according to the rules applicable to the facility belonging to the stricter class. The procedure for "mixed projects", *i.e.*, projects requiring both a Class IA or IB environmental permit and a planning permit, must be introduced and handled simultaneously by BIM and the authority in charge of planning.

2991. All these different procedures are described in "An Administrative and Technical Guide on the Environmental Permit" (*Administratieve en Technische Gids voor de Private Aanvrager/Guide Administratif et Technique du Permis d'Environnement à l'Usage du Demandeur Privé*), which is strongly recommended as a reference for extensive explanation and guidelines. In broad terms, however, most procedures follow similar steps:

   (i) examination of the application and visit to the site by a delegate of BIM and/ or of the commune. A dialogue is launched with the owner of the site to clarify the environmental nuisances which could be caused by the facility and how to remedy them. The procedure continues only if the file is complete.

   (ii) The application is subject to a public inquiry, allowing residents to communicate their opinions.

   (iii) For Class IA and IB licences, the opinion of the residents and of the owner of the site are dealt with by the Consultation Commission (*Overlegcommissie/ Commission de Concertation*), which is composed of representatives of the municipality, and the regional administrations for urbanism, environment, economic development and buildings and sites. This Consultation Commission produces an advice. This advice, although not binding on BIM or the municipal authorities, in practice often determines the final decision.

   (iv) An environmental permit is issued after consultation of all the various authorities such as the fire brigade, the zoning authorities etc., and on the basis of the advice of the Consultation Commission. Provided that all security measures required are present, an environmental permit will be granted. If the nuisance, which may potentially be caused by the activity, is such that the operating conditions do not allow it to be reduced to acceptable proportions, the licence may be refused. This is a delicate matter of evaluation of the interests of the operator and the neighbours.

2992. Class IA, IB and II licences are valid for a maximum period of 15 years following the start of the operations. The authorities fix the time period within which the activities covered by the permit must be started. This time period may not exceed 2 years from the date of the notification of the decision. Class III facilities can be operated for an unlimited period of time.

G. Walloon Region

2993. Since 1 October 2002, the issue of environmental permits in the Walloon Region has been regulated by the Decree of 11 March 1999 on Environmental Permits (*Décret relatif au permis d'environnement*) as well as by 4 executive decisions, which have all been adopted by the Walloon government on 4 July 2002.

2994. Before the Decree of 11 March 1999 entered into force, the area was regulated by the old national legislation, that is to say the national General Regulation for the Protection of Employees (*Algemeen reglement voor de arbeidsbescherming(ARAB)/ Règlement général pour la protection du travail (RGPT)*).

2995. In contrast to the Flemish and Brussels-Capital legislation, the Walloon Decree of 11 March 1999 lays down a single permit for so-called "mixed projects", *i.e.*, projects requiring both an environmental and a building permit. In other words, a single environmental and building permit will be issued following a single procedure. Explanation on this procedure can be found on the website of the Walloon Region. It is also expected that, in the long term, the Directorates General for Environment and Urban Development will merge.

2996. As it has already been mentioned, although the environmental permit in the Walloon Region is global and covers all potential environmental nuisances, separate permits are nonetheless still required for the valorisation of tips and mining concessions.

2997. Besides the existence of Class I and II facilities, the Walloon Decree of 11 March 1999 establishes a Class III facility, for which only a declaration to the authorities is required. Although the Decree distinguishes between Class I and II facilities, applications for Class I and II facilities permits are all lodged with the College of Mayor and Aldermen (*Collège des Bourgmestre et Echevins*) and all reviews are brought before the regional government. As for all administrative acts, the decision to deliver or to refuse to deliver a permit may be challenged before the Belgian Council of State.

2998. One of the objectives of the Decree on environmental permits is to simplify the procedure, which can be broadly outlined as follows:
   (i) an environmental impact assessment is required for all activities and facilities subject to an environmental permit (Class I and Class II) listed in the executive decision of the Walloon Region dated 4 July 2002. The environmental impact assessment takes place at the very beginning of the procedure, even before the application for an environmental permit. Activities and facilities which are subject to an environmental permit but for which no environmental

impact assessment is required are only subject to a notice. However, this requirement is fulfilled by simply filling in the application form for an environmental permit. Activities and facilities belonging to Class III which are not subject to an environmental permit but only to a declaration do not require an environmental impact assessment;

(ii) a public consultation is organised prior to the environmental impact assessment;

(iii) the application for an environmental permit is made directly on an application form issued by the municipality or a regional authority. Enterprises required to obtain an environmental permit should pay attention to the careful completion of this application form;

(iv) a public inquiry is organised;

(v) a *fonctionnaire technique* is in charge of examining the application, collecting the different opinions of different public authorities, drafting a report on all steps of the procedure and submitting a draft decision to the College of Mayor and Aldermen (*Collège des Bourgmestre et Echevins*). The *fonctionnaire technique* is a person belonging to the DGRNE;

(vi) the applicant has a right to know about the status of his application at all stages of the procedure; and

(vi) in principle, an environmental permit for a Class II activity or facility will be issued at the latest 70 to 100 days after the *fonctionnaire technique* has communicated his decision on the completeness and admissibility of the file, or, if he does not communicate any decision, the day following the deadline imposed for the communication of that decision. For Class I activities or facilities, an environmental permit will be delivered after 130 to 170 days.

IV. LIABILITY FOR ENVIRONMENTAL DAMAGE

A. Introduction

2999. In Belgium, a clear tendency exists towards stricter enforcement of environmental rules. Public prosecutors, environmental groups and the public at large are becoming more tenacious when confronted with environmental infringements. This tendency also reflects growing concerns about the environment on a world-wide scale. Companies doing business in Belgium must, therefore, be mindful of two kinds of liability for environmental damage: "public" liability and civil liability.

3000. Although only substantive environmental liability law will be briefly discussed and not the way that environmental law can be enforced in courts, prior to discussing the various kinds of environmental liability, mention should be made of (i) the on-going general debate in Belgium as to whether or to what extent environmental non-profit associations have any authority in environmental matters, and (ii) the possibility of summary proceedings, either before the administrative and/or judicial authorities. Issues such as the liability of the state or other public authorities for environmental pollution will not be discussed.

B. Standing of environmental non-profit associations

§1. In judicial proceedings

3001. In judicial proceedings, a claim can only be filed by the person who has directly suffered harm. This requirement for personal damage causes problems in cases of "ecological" damage, when non-profit organisations may want to file a claim. The Belgian Supreme Court has held that non-profit environmental associations do not have standing to challenge activities with an adverse impact on the environment, unless the action involves property actually belonging to or managed by those associations (Cass., 19 September 1996, *R.C.J.B.*, 1997, 110). Several lower civil courts have taken a more liberal stance and held that environmental organisations have standing to request so-called "cease-and-desist" orders. The situation has, to some extent, been clarified by the federal Law of 12 January 1993, which has granted non-profit environmental associations the right to apply for cease-and-desist orders where the underlying legal issue relates to the objectives of the association (*Wet betreffende een vorderingsrecht inzake bescherming van het leefmilieu/ Loi concernant un droit d'action en matière de protection de l'environnement* – the "Law of 12 January 1993").

3002. As regards the general standing of non-profit environmental organisations in judicial proceedings, the international Convention on Access to Information, Public Participation in Decision-making and Access to Justice in Environmental Matters, signed in Aarhus (Denmark) on 25 June 1998 should be mentioned, even if, thus far, it has not been ratified by Belgium. This Convention clearly states that non-governmental organisations promoting environmental protection and meeting any requirements under national law are to be deemed to have an interest (Art. 2, para. 5). It would seem that this provision is sufficiently clear and does not require any legislative intervention to be applied. Consequently, non-profit environmental organisations fulfilling the conditions of the law of 27 June 1921 granting civil personality to non-profit associations should have standing without showing anything other an interference with their social object.

§2. In administrative proceedings

3003. In administrative proceedings, the Council of State (*Raad van State/Conseil d'Etat*) is more lenient in accepting the standing of non-profit associations and considers that environmental organisations may request the annulment and suspension of unilateral administrative acts affecting the environment, even if such acts do not relate to personal property of these organisations (Council of State, 19 October 1982. *R.W.*, 1982-83, 2549).

C. Summary proceedings – suspension – cease-and-desist orders

§1. Administrative proceedings

3004. In principle, any (environmental) administrative decision can be challenged before the Council of State, which is an administrative court with the task, when all conditions are fulfilled, of judging the legality of administrative acts in general. On the basis of the Co-ordinated Laws on the Council of State, the Council of State is competent to annul administrative acts as well as to suspend their implementation because the consequences may be serious. This means that as soon as an appeal for annulment is presented, an appeal for suspension can be presented. Suspension is only possible when the following conditions are met:
  (i) the specified act, permit or administrative regulations must be capable of annulment; and
  (ii) serious consequences which would be difficult to remedy and which seem to result from the immediate implementation of the act or regulation must be put forward.

3005. The Council of State also has the competence to order all necessary measures to secure the interests of the parties or of the persons who have an interest in the conclusion of the case. The measures do not concern the civil rights of the parties but only measures against the acting government.

3006. It must be noted that, although administrative decisions about building permits or environmental permits are decisions which may be suspended and annulled by the Council of State, this can only occur once the organised procedure laid down in the regulations has been followed.

§2. Judicial proceedings

1. General rules

3007. As a general rule, civil matters can be referred before the President of the Court of First Instance (*Rechtbank van Eerste Aanleg/Tribunal de Permière Instance*) provided that 2 conditions are met: (i) urgency, and (ii) the provisional character of the request.

2. *The Law of 12 January 1993 granting Legal Access to Environmental Protection Groups (the "Law of 12 January 1993")*

3008. The Law of 12 January 1993 allows recognised environmental groups, albeit under certain conditions, to obtain an injunction against third parties ordering them to cease environmental infringements or to prevent future actions with an adverse effect on the environment. According to the case law of the Belgian Supreme Court, such an injunction may also consist of a repair order. The cease-and-desist action must be initiated before the President of the Court of First Instance, provided that 2 conditions are met: (i) only the public prosecutor, an administrative authority or a non-profit environmental association is entitled to act before the President of the Court of First Instance, and (ii) the activities must constitute a manifest violation or a serious threat of violation of one or more legal provisions. The concept of "manifest violation" is subjective and has been subject to divergent interpretations.

D. Public liability

3009. "Public" liability refers to liability resulting from the infringement of public rules or conditions attached to an environmental permit. Public liability encompasses both criminal liability and administrative action and sanctions. It may be distinguished from civil liability in that the plaintiff is a public authority, *i.e.*, an enforcement agency or the public prosecutor's office.

§1. Criminal sanctions

3010. In Belgium, criminal sanctions are sanctions that are laid down in various sectoral and non-sectoral regulations. They have traditionally been the principal means of enforcing environmental legislation. Typically, criminal sanctions are imposed when soil is contaminated or when substances are discharged in violation of a permit or without any permit at all. It is worth noting that a discharge may be illegal even if the substance involved is not hazardous or toxic.

1. Criminal liability

3011. Until recently, companies could not be held criminally liable for infringements of environmental legislation because, under Belgian criminal law, a legal entity was not deemed capable of committing a fault, one of the constitutive elements of a crime. However, the situation has changed with the adoption of the Law of 4 May

1999 establishing Criminal Liability for Legal Entities (*Wet tot invoering van de strafrechtelijke verantwoordelijkheid van rechtspersonen/Loi instaurant la responsabilité pénale des personnes morales*) (Art. 5 of the Criminal Code). Article 7*bis* of the Criminal Code now fixes criminal sanctions such as fines, confiscation, publicity of the sentence, prohibition of the exercise an activity, the temporary or permanent closing of installations and the dissolution of the legal entity. Article 91 of the Code of Criminal Procedural, as amended by the Law of 4 May 1999, allows the instructing judge to take provisional measures like the prohibition to undertake transactions leading to insolvency, the suspension of the dissolution or liquidation procedure, and the payment of a bail.

3012. As to individual people, the public prosecutor and the courts attempting to hold them criminally liable are faced with the task of identifying people within the company who actually committed the act or omission leading to the infringement. This means that they must examine the articles of incorporation, internal corporate guidelines and any other relevant corporate documents in an effort to identify the person actually responsible for environmental matters in the company concerned. Moreover, this person must have actually assumed this responsibility and he must have the actual power and means (such as control over financial resources) to take the decisions which resulted in the pollution.

3013. The responsible person may be a director, an employee responsible for the company or even a person who has no contractual relationship with the company (Cass., 23 May 1990, *Arr. Cass.*, 1989-90, 1213). Directors of companies may avoid liability by delegating environmental compliance, provided that the delegation is clearly defined and that the director could reasonably count on the designated employee to take all necessary supervisory and safety measures. It is noted that, in the Flemish Region, following the introduction of the obligation to appoint an environmental co-ordinator in every Class I installation, there will be more opportunity to prosecute either the environmental co-ordinator or the company directors, or other leading persons in the company for environmental crimes committed by that company.

3014. The person identified as being responsible for environmental compliance in a company will only be criminally liable if it is established that, with respect to the specific instance of pollution at issue, the person was at fault for purposes of the criminal law. That is, he was responsible for the acts or omissions that actually caused the pollution (Cass., 10 April 1979, *Pas.*, I, 951). It should be noted that the standard of fault in these cases is relatively low because, as a general rule, the element of intent only requires the plaintiff to establish criminal negligence as opposed to criminal intent. For instance, Article 2 of the Law of 26 March 1971 on the Protection of Surface Water provides for criminal sanctions with respect to the unlawful discharge of substances or objects into surface water. It is irrelevant whether this discharge is caused by a deliberate act or mere negligence (such as the failure to supervise employees properly) (Criminal Court of Arlon, 2 February 1987, *T. Aann.*, 1988, 86; confirmed by Liège Court of Appeal, 29 March 1988, *T. Aann.*, 1988, 88).

3015. A company director may be able to avoid criminal liability on the grounds that compliance with a specific environmental regulation would impose undue financial hardship on the company. In one widely debated judgment, the Ghent Court of Appeal acquitted a director because the court considered it reasonable for the director to have chosen to commit a minor environmental offence rather than risk bankrupting the company by complying with the rules which, in that case, would have necessitated major investments in a water-purifying facility (Ghent Court of Appeal, 27 June 1985, *R.W.*, 1986-87, 1691).

3016. It should be noted that a number of environmental laws hold a company liable under civil law to pay damages, criminal penalties and costs which were judicially imposed on its agents or employees acting within the scope of their authority.

2. Investigation and establishment of criminal infringements

3017. Infringements of environmental laws often require the intervention of specialised agents and adequate investigation means. The Code of Criminal Procedure and the Criminal Code are not well equipped to deal with specific environmental violations, so that the regions have included, in their decrees and ordinances, provisions relating to the investigation and establishment of criminal infringements. Most such provisions vary from one piece of legislation to another, with the exception of the Brussels-Capital Region where the Ordinance of 25 March 1999 on the Investigation, Establishment, and Punishment of Environmental Infringements (*Ordonnantie betreffende de opsporing, de vaststelling, de vervolging en de bestraffing van misdrijven inzake leefmilieu/Ordonnance relative à la recherche, la constatation, la poursuite et la répression des infractions en matière d'environnement*) is applied as one harmonised piece of legislation. In broad terms, the different investigative powers of the specialised agents which are laid down in specific legal provisions are as follows:
  (i) entry onto plants and installations which are not private residences;
  (ii) questioning people;
  (iii) the right to be supplied with documents and to take copies;
  (iv) drawing up a report;
  (v) fixing seals;

(vi) levying seizure; and

(vii) taking samples.

3018. Criminal provisions punish those who seek to oppose or hinder the implementation of these measures. While the specialised agents are unable to use actual coercion, it is generally foreseen that they can request the assistance of the federal police.

3. Criminal enforcement of environmental laws

3019. Effective criminal enforcement of environmental laws has proven problematic. Criminal sanctions for violations of environmental laws have often been criticised because the penalties and prison terms are generally considered to be too lenient. In addition, public prosecutors have dropped the vast majority of cases in the course of the investigation for a number of reasons:

(i) the intricacy of the legislation which is a patchwork of old national and new regional laws that are, at times, inconsistent; for instance the definition of "waste" is different in federal, Brussels, Flemish and Walloon legislation;

(ii) the difficulty of identifying the management ultimately responsible for the infringement, a problem that is particularly difficult where the company has ceased to exist or has been restructured, or where the internal management structure and division of responsibilities have changed;

(iii) the lack of expertise and resources, especially at the regional and municipal level, to resolve technically complex environmental problems; and

(iv) the difficulties of submitting convincing evidence.

3020. The failure of the courts to deal in an effective manner with infringements of environmental laws has given rise to strong public criticism. Public prosecutors are gradually becoming more active in the area of criminal enforcement of environmental legislation. In industrialised cities, such as Antwerp, a number of public prosecutors have special responsibility for environmental matters and a specialised chamber of the court deals exclusively with environmental issues.

3021. Those who believe that they have sustained personal and individual damage, stemming directly from an act which constitutes an infringement of a criminally sanctioned environmental law or regulation, may initiate a criminal procedure by simultaneously lodging a complaint with the instructing judge (*onderzoeksrechter/ juge d'instruction*) and intervening as a civil party (*burgerlijke partijstelling/constitution de partie civile*) in which they claim damages under the relevant rules of civil law. The advantage for the injured party of following this course of action is that the public prosecutor must open the case and that fault, once established in the criminal proceeding, will be conclusive evidence for civil purposes of a breach of the duty of care. The Walloon Region regularly intervenes as a civil party in order to recover the costs which it incurred in cleaning up polluted sites. It may also be recalled that the Supreme Court has consistently held that non-profit environmental organisations do not have, as a general rule, the authority to intervene as a civil party before the criminal courts.

§2. Administrative sanctions

3022. Administrative sanctions are sanctions that are laid down in the various sectoral and non-sectoral regulations and which are applied unilaterally by administrative bodies without the prior intervention of the courts.

3023. Administrative sanctions cover a wide array of measures including the withdrawal or modification of permits, injunctions, the closing of companies, the interruption of activities, the sealing of an establishment and the removal of dangerous materials. Moreover, certain decrees provide that the competent administration can impose administrative fines (as distinguished from criminal fines). More and more often, the legislators tend to make use of administrative fines to compensate for the inefficiency of criminal proceedings. For example, the Brussels-Capital Ordinance of 25 March 1999 sets forth that the general director of BIM is to communicate reports to the public prosecutor who is given 6 months to make clear his intentions of proceeding further or not. In the event he does not, the general director can propose that the enterprise pay an administrative fine. It is then up to the enterprise to contest the fine.

3024. Administrative sanctions may be imposed by different authorities such as the mayor of a commune, the governor of a province, the environmental ministry (such as AMINAL) or a specialised agency (such as OVAM or BIM). It is noted that if the European environmental chapter of the EC Treaty is modified, which may be possible in the medium term, the EC Commission might be entrusted with the power to impose administrative fines, the same way as it already does for infringements of EC competition law. Increasing the powers of the EC Commission would, however, require a better harmonisation of environmental law in the European Union.

3025. Specific administrative procedures (*e.g.*, competent authorities, the opportunity to appeal) have been developed in all 3 regions of the country and differ from one sectoral legislation to another.

E. Civil liability

§1. General principles of tort liability

3026. This section focuses on those aspects of the general rules of tort liability laid down in the Civil Code that are of particular importance in the context of environmental damage. Specific strict or no-fault liability systems for environmental damage, which aim to alleviate the burden of proof on the victim, will be analysed separately.

3027. As a general rule, tort liability for environmental damage only accrues if the plaintiff establishes that he suffered personal injury caused by the breach of a duty of care by the defendant (Art. 1382 *et seq.* of the Civil Code). In cases where conditions for civil liability are fulfilled (negligence, damage, causal link between the negligence and the damage), the judge can order restoration of the original situation or the payment of an indemnity. In environmental matters, the requirement for the claimant to establish a breach of a duty of care is generally not problematic because most pollution activities are specifically prohibited by statute and, in Belgium, a breach of a statutory duty is conclusive proof of a breach of the duty of care, in contrast to the systems of tort law in many countries.

3028. The duty of care, laid down in Article 1382 *et seq.* of the Civil Code, may also be breached if the claimant can prove that a company, while not infringing an express statutory provision, does not abide by the general duty of care applicable in environmental matters. In other words, a person may be liable for damages under Article 1382 *et seq.* of the Civil Code, even if he acts in strict conformity with an environmental permit, if this person's conduct does not conform with the general duty of care. The Antwerp Court of Appeal has described the general duty of care in environmental matters as the reasonable and normal care which an operator of undertakings of the kind must observe, taking into account all factual circumstances such as the size of the undertaking, its location and surroundings, the climate and the current state of the art and technology (Antwerp Court of Appeal, 17 February 1988, *R.W.*, 1989-90, 50).

3029. As a practical matter, the power of the courts when there are breaches of environmental laws is limited. As a general rule, courts do not have the power to order that a facility, operated pursuant to a permit, be shut down, nor can they generally impose conditions which run counter to those attached by the administration to the permit in question (Cass., 26 November 1974, *R.W.*, 1974-75, 1708).

§2. Strict liability

3030. In a number of instances, a regime of strict liability (liability without fault) has been laid down by the courts (Art. 1384, para. 1 of the Civil Code) or in specific laws, aimed at alleviating the claimant's burden of proof. In a system of strict liability, the claimant must prove that he has sustained specific injury and that this injury was caused by the defendant. The victim is not required, however, to prove that a duty of care was breached by the defendant. In order to facilitate the identification of the actual responsible person, some laws channel liability to a certain class of person or undertaking, such as the producer of toxic waste.

1. Article 1384, para.1 of the Civil Code

3031. A person having responsibility for a product or using it on his own account, whether it be the owner, operator or lessor, may be liable under Article 1384, para. 1 of the Civil Code for damages resulting from a "defect", that is, an intrinsically abnormal characteristic, of the product concerned. This ground of liability is of particular importance with respect to accidental environmental damage, such as damage caused as a result of a defect of a machine or the breaking of a cable.

3032. The question of whether or not a product is affected by an intrinsically abnormal characteristic may be difficult to answer in any given instance of pollution. The Supreme Court has held that an industrial facility is not defective, within the meaning of Article 1384, para. 1 of the Civil Code, by the mere fact that this facility generates air pollution because it is normal that industrial facilities generate some pollution (Cass., 18 September 1980, *R.W.*, 1981-82, 29).

3033. Purchasers of polluted sites may also, in certain circumstances, be held liable on the basis of Article 1384, para. 1 of the Civil Code for damages caused by a source of pollution located on such sites. A person held liable for environmental damage on this basis may, depending on the circumstances, be able to start proceedings against the following persons:
   (i) the person who actually caused the damage;
   (ii) the seller on the basis of Article 1643 *et seq.* of the Civil Code, that is, the implied warranty for hidden defects in contracts of sale;
   (iii) the lessor on the basis of Article 1721 of the Civil Code, that is, the implied warranty for hidden defects in lease contracts; and
   (iv) the producer of toxic waste on the basis of Article 7 of the Law of 22 July 1974 on Toxic Waste (*Wet op de giftige afval/Loi sur les déchets toxiques*).

2. Other specific systems of strict environmental liability

3034. The following specific systems of strict environmental liability should also be mentioned:

(i) *Toxic waste*: Article 7 of the Law of 22 July 1974 on Toxic Waste, which is still in force in the 3 regions, provides that a producer is strictly liable for all damages caused by the toxic waste which it has produced. It should be mentioned that the producer remains liable even if it hands the toxic waste over to a licensed transport company or processor. It is noted that this example of strict liability is an application of the general "polluter pays" principle.

(ii) *Oil pollution of the sea*: the owner of a seagoing vessel is liable for all damage caused by oil spilled by such a vessel (*Wet houdende goedkeuring en uitvoering van het Internationaal Verdrag inzake de burgerlijke aansprakelijkheid voor schade door verontreiniging door olie, en van de Bijlage opgemaakt te Brussel op 29 november 1969/Loi portant approbation et exécution de la Convention internationale sur la responsabilité civile pour les dommages dus à la pollution par les hydrocarbures, et de l'Annexe, faites à Bruxelles le 29 novembre 1969* – Law of 20 July 1976).

(iii) *Ground water extraction*: an *operator* of a plant in which ground water is extracted is liable for damages caused by this activity above the ground regardless of any fault committed by the operator (the Flemish Decree of 24 January 1984; the Walloon Decree of 11 October 1985, and the federal Law of 10 January 1977 (*Wet houdende regeling van de schadeloosstelling voor schade veroorzaakt door het winnen en het pompen van grondwater/Loi organisant la réparation des dommages provoqués par des prises et des pompages d'eau souterraine*), which is still applied in the Brussels-Capital Region and which was transposed in the Flemish Decree of 1984.

(iv) *Nuclear facilities*: the operator of a nuclear facility is liable for all damages caused by a nuclear accident or by the transport of radioactive materials emanating from such a facility (*Wet betreffende de wettelijke aansprakelijkheid op het gebied van kernenergie/Loi sur la responsabilité civile dans le domaine de l'énergie nucléaire* – Law of 22 July 1985).

(v) *Contaminated ground*: Article 25 of the Flemish Decree of 22 February 1995 on the Cleaning up of the Soil (*Decreet betreffende de bodemsanering* – the "Soil Clean-up Decree") lays down presumptions of liability of the person who generated the pollution or the operator of a classified installation.

(vi) *Sea protection*: Article 37, paragraph 1 of the Law of 20 January 1999 on the Protection of the Sea (*Wet ter bescherming van het mariene milieu in de zeegebieden onder de rechtsbevoegdheid van België/Loi visant la protection du milieu marin dans les espaces marins sous juridiction de la Belgique*) (to the extent that Belgium has jurisdiction), obliges those who caused damages to the sea to repair the damages regardless of any fault they have committed.

F. Nuisance

3035. In 2 landmark judgements of 6 April 1960, the Supreme Court held that Article 544 of the Civil Code – the general provision stating that property entails a right to the most extensive use of a good which is compatible with the law – implies a duty on adjoining landowners to abstain from "nuisance" and to pay a reasonable compensation if such nuisance occurs (Cass., 6 April 1960, *Pas.*, 1960, I, 920).

3036. Nuisance is defined as the use or enjoyment of one's property which, regardless of whether it is in itself wrongful, results in an interference (including noise, odours and so on) in the use or enjoyment of adjoining property by another person which exceeds the bounds of the normal inconveniences which the latter person, taking all specific circumstances into account, must reasonably be expected to suffer.

3037. For instance, the owner of land, on which a facility for the cleaning of stones was located, was held liable to pay compensation to adjoining landowners for the dust and traffic problems caused by the continuous entrance and exit of heavy trucks from this facility, even though the owner had previously obtained an operating permit and did not own the trucks (Antwerp Court of Appeal, 30 May 1989, *Limb. Rechtsl.*, 1989, 126).

V. ENVIRONMENTAL ISSUES IN MERGERS AND ACQUISITIONS

A. Checklist

3038. In the event of a merger or acquisition, enterprises should check that the merging company or company to be acquired complies with all environmental rules. In this regard, particular attention should be paid, for instance, to:
  (i) environmental permits;
 (ii) sectoral environmental arrangements:
    (a) waste disposal arrangements, including toxic waste; and
    (b) ground water capture arrangements;
(iii) existence of pollution:
    (a) soil pollution of land presently owned or controlled, or of land previously owned or controlled; and

     (b) contaminated buildings (*e.g.*, asbestos, PCBs);
  (iv) compliance with rules on:
     (a) environmental co-ordination; and
     (b) environmental reporting;
  (v) existence of claims for damages.

3039. It is recalled that in case, following the concentration, new activities are to be carried out on the site of the acquired company, a new environmental permit may be necessary, with possibly new environmental obligations imposed by the regional authorities.

3040. In practice, a thorough due diligence exercise on environmental issues should be performed. Some recommend that inquiries with local plant operators are often more useful than a full review of the data room. Analyses, tests, studies and other check-outs are also strongly recommended. Furthermore, as site pollution and rehabilitation may turn to be a rather costly operation, acquiring companies are advised to draw up a chronological overview of all the activities carried out on the site. Polluting activities as well as potential pollution can be determined in this way. As a general remark, when planning to acquire or merge with another company, typically, the acquirer will seek protection through representations and warranties in the acquisition agreement.

3041. In the light of the so far lenient attitude of public authorities, it is not rare that companies in Belgium often infringe either the applicable statutes or the conditions of their environmental permits. However, enterprises are advised against these practices, as enforcement of environmental law in Belgium is becoming stricter and public authorities could also take advantage of the concentration to change their attitude.

B. Parenthesis: Applicable legislation on soil clean-up obligations

3042. Enterprises doing business in Belgium and planning to merge or acquire another company should be aware that soil pollution of the land to be acquired may have significant legal consequences on the merger or acquisition operation. In particular, the Flemish Decree of 22 December 1995 on Soil clean-up (*Decreet betreffende de bodemsanering* – the "Soil Clean-up Decree") provides that in case of soil contamination, the contract of acquisition can be declared void. No specific legislation on soil clean-up exists to date in the Walloon and Brussels-Capital Regions. It should, however, be noted that the Walloon Region is currently working on adopting a decree which is expected to be worded in terms similar to the Flemish Soil Clean-up Decree.

3043. In the Flemish Region, soil pollution is regulated by the Soil Clean-up Decree which came into force on 29 October 1995. It is supplemented by a Decision of the Flemish Government of 5 March 1996 ("VLAREBO").

3044. By virtue of the Soil Clean-up Decree, contaminated sites may be discovered in the event of: (i) a transfer of assets, (ii) a closure of facilities, or (iii) on the investigation by the Public Flemish Waste Agency (OVAM). Polluted sites are then registered by OVAM in a register. Potential buyers can consult this register and obtain a certificated extract of the register with detailed information on the polluted sites.

3045. The Soil Clean-up Decree makes an important distinction between "historical" and "new" soil pollution. Historical soil pollution originated before the coming into force of the Soil Clean-up Decree, while new soil pollution originated after the coming into force of the Soil Clean-up Decree. The Soil Clean-up Decree makes another important distinction between the person who has the obligation to clean-up the polluted soil (cleaning-up obligation) and the person who is liable for the pollution and who has to ultimately pay the financial costs for the cleaning-up (final allocation of the financial burden).

1. New pollution

3046. An obligation to clean-up new polluted sites is imposed by the Soil Clean-up Decree as soon as the benchmark standards established by the Flemish Government are exceeded. These standards take into consideration the characteristics of the soil as well as its function. In case no standards exist for a particular type of soil pollution, a cleaning-up obligation is imposed only when the pollution presents a "serious threat". It is important to note that, as far as new pollution is concerned, this obligation exists automatically, without the need for an order from the Flemish Government.

3047. The person who has the obligation to clean up the polluted soil is the operator of the site and not the owner of the site. However, in some specific cases, this obligation is imposed on the owner of the site unless he can prove that the site is under the control of someone else.

3048. The person who has cleaned the site can then have recourse against the person responsible for the pollution and obtain the reimbursement of the cleaning costs. The Soil Clean-up Decree introduced a non-retroactive strict liability rule by virtue of which the person responsible for the pollution is the one who caused it. It should be noted that this liability is restricted to the costs for the cleaning-up of the site and does not cover damages to persons caused by the pollution.

3049. An exception to the cleaning-up obligation is made for "innocent landowners". The owner or operator of a polluted site is not obliged to carry out the cleaning-up of the site if he can prove that: (i) he did not cause the pollution himself (by his fault or otherwise), (ii) when acquiring the property, he was not and should not have been aware of the pollution, and (iii) no suspected facilities or activities were established or performed on the soil since 1 January 1993. Furthermore, his liability is limited to the costs necessary to prevent the pollution spreading any further or becoming an immediate danger.

2. Historical pollution

3050. For information purposes only, a list of all polluted sites has been drawn up by the Flemish Government. An obligation to clean up historical pollution depends on the existence of a "serious threat" to human beings and the environment. The actual danger is based on a risk-assessment approach.

3051. The person who has the obligation to clean up the polluted soil is the operator of the site. However, contrary to the situation for new pollution, the obligation to clean up historical pollution is not automatic but requires an order from the Flemish Government.

3052. As far as liability for historical pollution is concerned, it is not determined on the basis of the non-retroactive strict liability rule mentioned above, but is governed by the rules in effect before the Soil Clean-up Decree came into force, *i.e.*, the Belgian Civil Code.

3053. The "innocent landowners" rules also apply to historical pollution, albeit under less strict conditions. The owner of a polluted site is not obliged to carry out the cleaning-up of the site if he proves that: (i) he did not cause the pollution himself, and (ii) when acquiring the property, he was not and should not have been aware of the pollution. Moreover, in case the "innocent landowner" did know or should have been aware of the historical pollution, he will not have to clean up the site if the polluted land was acquired prior to 1993 and was since then exclusively used for non-professional purposes.

3. Transfer of assets

3054. The Soil Clean-up Decree aims, in particular, at protecting buyers of polluted sites and provides specific rules for the transfer of assets. As has already been mentioned, the establishment of a register of polluted sites allows potential buyers to be informed about the pollution of the land to be acquired.

3055. The Soil Clean-up Decree sets forth general rules applicable to agreements on the transfer of all property and specific rules applicable to the transfer of suspected property. As a general rule, the owner of a site is required, prior to certain real estate transactions, to submit a soil certificate to the potential contractual party. This certificate is issued by OVAM, in principle one month after the application was made.

3056. Specific rules apply when the transfer of suspected property is at stake. According to the Soil Clean-up Decree, susceptibly polluted property cannot be transferred if no exploratory investigation has been performed. This investigation is financed by the seller and is carried out under the direction of a soil sanitation expert. OVAM must thus be notified of every envisaged transfer together with the report following the exploratory investigation. OVAM may decide whether further investigations and possibly a cleaning-up are required.

3057. Significantly, if the provisions described above are ignored, the contract of acquisition may be declared void.

4. Competent authority and procedure

3058. The procedure set out in the Soil Clean-up Decree can be divided into 4 phases:
   (i) a first phase is the *exploratory investigation.* This investigation has the purpose of establishing whether or not there are serious grounds for believing that soil contamination has taken place on certain land.
   (ii) The second phase consists of the *descriptive soil examination.* This examination is conducted in order to establish the seriousness of the soil contamination. Before carrying out any descriptive soil examination, an examination proposal is drawn up under the direction of an officially recognised soil sanitation expert. OVAM issues a compliance certificate, if the study is satisfactory.
   (iii) Once the investigations are finalised a *soil sanitation plan* is drafted. This plan determines the manner in which the soil sanitation is to be carried out. It is drawn up by and carried out under the direction of officially recognised soil sanitation experts under the supervision of OVAM.
   (iv) A final phase consists of the actual *soil sanitation operations.* These operations aim at decontaminating the land and are carried out under the direction of a soil sanitation expert. They also include an after-care phase. If soil pollution is discovered, it may be necessary to take *precautionary and safeguard measures* prior to actually carrying out any cleaning-up operation.

5. Sanctions

3059. Apart from the sanction of nullity mentioned above, the Soil Clean-up Decree provides for criminal sanctions in case the provisions of the Decree are not respected.

17. SUBSIDIES

I. INTRODUCTION

3060. The incentives made available by the Belgian public authorities are of great importance to investors contemplating the establishment of business operations or the
expansion of existing facilities in Belgium. A central geographical location, a
favourable standard of living, and the availability of skilled and multilingual
labour are among the major factors that have attracted considerable foreign capital
to Belgium in the past. Over the past 40 years, Belgium pursued an active policy
of encouraging foreign investment through very favourable incentives and, consequently, used to rank high among the preferred investment areas within the
European Community.

3061. However, many national aid schemes and other public incentives have been abolished, amended, reduced or suspended due to stricter enforcement by the EC
Commission of the EC rules on state aid. Today, the majority of public incentives
are granted by the regional governments rather than the Federal Government. As a
result of the stricter enforcement practice of the EC Commission, the regulatory
framework governing public incentives in the Flemish, Walloon and Brussels-
Capital Regions has been modified significantly over the past few years and is
expected to change again in the near future.

3062. In the Flemish Region, the Flemish Government recently adopted a new draft framework decree (the "Framework Decree") that will govern the economic incentives
policy for that region. This new decree, once it is adopted by the Flemish Parliament, will be the first important step in the re-orientation of the existing economic
expansion policy and will, in the long run, replace the existing federal and Flemish
regulations applicable in the Flemish Region. The draft Framework Decree has
3 main objectives: (i) to simplify the existing regulations and make them more
transparent; (ii) to ensure that the Flemish regulatory framework is fully compliant
with the applicable EC rules on state aid; and (iii) to adapt the existing public
incentives policy to the current needs of the industry in Flanders.

3063. In the Walloon Region, the government is considering a new draft decree (the
"Draft Decree") that will replace the existing regulatory framework on economic
expansion. The Draft Decree covers 4 main areas: (i) small and medium-sized
enterprises; (ii) large enterprises; (iii) the environment; and (iv) the development

of infrastructures by mixed public/private enterprises (*infrastructures d'accueil*). No major legislative developments in the area of public incentives are expected to take place in the Brussels-Capital Region in the near future.

3064. This chapter will provide a concise overview of public incentives that are currently available to Belgian and foreign companies operating in Belgium. First, a brief survey of the different sources of public incentives is provided (*See*, Section II, para. 3065). Second, the various types of incentives available are outlined and the possibility of accumulating these various categories of incentives is discussed (*See*, Section III, paras. 3066 *et seq.*). Finally, the general application procedure is outlined (*See*, Section IV, paras. 3162 *et seq.*).

II. SOURCES OF AID

3065. Public incentives are granted by a number of different institutions. The governments of the Brussels-Capital, Flemish and Walloon Regions are primarily responsible for granting financial incentives to individuals and companies. However, some types of incentives may also be granted by the Federal Government. In addition, various public institutions and funds, as well as local administrations, may provide aid. Specific investment projects in Belgium may also benefit from aid provided by the European Community.

III. TYPES OF AID

A. Introduction

3066. The various public incentives currently available in Belgium may be classified into general investment incentives (*See*, paras. 3068 *et seq.*) and specific investment incentives (*See*, paras. 3105 *et seq*). Among the many specific investment incentives, individuals and companies operating in Belgium should be aware of the following schemes: research and development incentives (*See*, paras. 3105 *et seq.*), employment and training incentives (*See*, paras. 3114 *et seq.*), tax incentives (*See*, paras. 3126 *et seq.*), incentives granted by various investment companies (*See*, paras. 3139 *et seq.*), export incentives (*See*, paras. 3141 *et seq.*) and environmental incentives (*See*, paras. 3154 *et seq.*).

3067. As the governments of the Brussels-Capital, Flemish and Walloon Regions have, to a large extent, been entrusted with industrial policy matters, the terms and conditions of the various aid schemes available to individuals and companies will differ depending on the location of the proposed investment. Most of the enterprises active in Belgium have been established with direct financial assistance and or tax incentives granted by Belgian public authorities.

B. General investment incentives

§1. Regional aid under the Law of 30 December 1970

1. Introduction

3068. Aids for general investments are governed by the federal Law of 30 December 1970 on Economic Expansion (*Wet betreffende de economische expansie/Loi sur l'expansion économique* – the "Law of 30 December 1970"). Over the years, the Law of 30 December 1970 has been amended by several decrees adopted by the regional governments. Enterprises doing business in Belgium should thus examine the particularities of regional aid schemes in each region. This will become even more relevant once the Flemish and Walloon Regions will have adopted new legislation on economic expansion.

3069. In the Flemish Region, the current applicable regulatory framework consists of the Law of 30 December 1970 and a Decree of 15 December 1993 on the Enhancement of Economic Expansion (*Decreet tot bevordering van de economische expansie* – the "Flemish 1993 Decree"). The Flemish 1993 Decree applies in all instances where the Law of 30 December 1970 does not apply. It should be recalled that a draft framework decree is being considered that will replace all legislation on economic expansion, including the Law of 30 December 1970 and the Flemish 1993 Decree.

3070. In the Walloon region, the applicable regulatory framework consists of the Law of 30 December 1970 and a Decree of 25 June 1992 (the "Walloon 1992 Decree"). However, like the Flemish Region, the Walloon Region is in a process of adopting new legislation on economic expansion.

3071. As will be further explained below, the Law of 30 December 1970 does not apply in the Brussels-Capital Region.

2. Scope of the Law of 30 December 1970

3072. The Law of 30 December 1970 aims at promoting investment that will create jobs in so-called "development zones". These geographical areas are defined in implementing regional regulations in accordance with the applicable EC legislation (Guidelines on national regional aid – O.J. [1998] C 74/6) and cover large parts of the Walloon Region, and some parts of the provinces of Limbourg, West Flanders, East Flanders and Antwerp in the Flemish region. No development zones are located in the Brussels-Capital Region, which only grants general investment incentives to small and medium-sized enterprises ("SMEs") under the federal Law of 4 August 1978 on Economic Reorientation (*Wet tot economische herorientering/Loi de réorientation économique* – the "Law of 4 August 1978") and an Ordinance of 1 July 1993 on the Promotion of Economic Expansion (*See,* para. 3087). The following discussion does not, therefore, apply to the Brussels-Capital Region.

3073. While the Law of 30 December 1970 is theoretically applicable to all types of companies, its application is, in practice, generally restricted to companies other than SMEs, that is, companies that do not fall within the scope of the Law of 4 August 1978 (*See,* paras. 3085 *et seq.*).

3074. Under the Law of 30 December 1970, aid may be granted for investment in tangible or intangible assets that contribute to the creation, expansion, reconversion or modernisation of industrial, handicraft and service companies. Implementing legislation and guidelines issued by the Flemish and Walloon Regional Governments provide for minimum thresholds which must be reached in order for the investments to benefit from aid (varying between € 125,000 and € 625,000 in the Flemish Region and € 500,000 in the Walloon Region), as well as a list of specific sectors and investments which are excluded from the scope of the Law of 30 December 1970.

3075. Investment incentives under the Law of 30 December 1970 may be characterised as either direct financial assistance, given in the form of interest subsidies, capital grants, investment grants, guarantees or tax advantages. As a general rule, enterprises wishing to benefit from tax incentives may only benefit from such incentives if they have already applied for or benefit from direct financial assistance.

3. Direct financial assistance

3076. Direct financial assistance for promoting investment may be granted in various forms, the most important of which are interest subsidies and capital grants in the Flemish Region and investment grants in the Walloon Region. It is recalled that the Brussels-Capital Region does not grant any general investment incentives to large enterprises.

3077. *Interest subsidies:* Interest subsidies are granted by the Flemish Region on loans obtained by the recipient from accredited lending institutions in Belgium (Art. 6, para. 1 of the Law of 30 December 1970) or on bonds issued by the recipient but subscribed to, or acquired by, an approved private or state lending institution or a specific public investment corporation (Art. 6, para. 2 of the Law of 30 December 1970). Implementing regulations of the Flemish Regional Government provide that, in addition to classic investment loans, roll-over credits and financing in the form of accredited leasing operations may benefit from interest subsidies. The subsidy consists of a percentage of the amount of the investment that has been financed by external funds. The rate of the interest subsidy depends on the location and type of investment involved. With respect to the interest subsidy to be granted, the Flemish Regional Government has also established guidelines aimed at assuring greater flexibility in attracting foreign investment. Thus, investments are now rated with differing priorities. Great importance and, therefore, higher interest subsidies will be given to investments that involve projects of a strategic interest for the Flemish Region (increase up to 10 per cent), or that contribute to achieving environmental objectives (increase up to 12 per cent). In the past, higher interest subsidies (increase up to 9 per cent) were also granted for investments that were highly labour-intensive, but these measures have been suspended since 28 April 2001 (and will remain suspended until 31 December 2003). An application for an interest subsidy should be addressed to the Flemish Regional Government by the financial institution which grants the credit. Interest subsidies are paid by the region directly to the financial institution involved on a bi-annual basis.

3078. *Capital grants:* In the Flemish Region, to the extent that the recipient uses its own funds for financing the investment, the interest subsidy may be replaced in whole or in part by a capital grant of an amount equal to the interest subsidy which would have otherwise been paid (Art. 9 of the Law of 30 December 1970). In principle, the rules applicable to interest subsidies also apply to capital grants, although small differences exist between these 2 types of incentives. Capital grants are paid directly by the Flemish Regional Government to the recipient, and are payable in 2 or 3 instalments, depending on the amount of the subsidy. An application for a capital grant should be addressed to the Flemish Regional Government by the investor himself.

3079. *Investment grants:* In the Walloon Region, a uniform type of investment incentive has been created which takes the place of classic interest subsidies and capital grants. This investment incentive is called an "investment grant". The investor himself must be an individual, a commercial company, or an "independent technical unit" which belongs to a commercial company. The investor must not be a small or medium-sized enterprise. The investment grant is calculated as a percentage of the total investment. The amount of the premium depends on the importance attributed by the Walloon Regional Government to the investment on the basis of the following criteria: (i) the effect of the investment on employment (0 to 10 per cent) and (ii) the importance of the activity (0 to 8 per cent). The basic aid granted amounts to at least 3 per cent of the total investment. The investor may request a first instalment of 40 per cent of the grant once 25 per cent of the investment programme is completed. A second instalment of 40 per cent of the grant may be paid once 75 per cent of the investment programme is completed. The rest of the grant may be requested after full completion of the investment programme and the achievement of the objective of employment, provided that the beneficiary respected all applicable fiscal, labour, and environmental regulations. An application for an investment grant should be addressed to the Walloon Regional Government by the investor himself prior to starting the programme.

4. Guarantees

3080. In negotiating the terms and conditions of investment loans with banks, an investor may wish to take advantage of a public guarantee for the repayment of the principal amount, interest and additional costs of the investment loan (Arts. 19 to 21 of the Law of 30 December 1970). The guarantee, which is provided by the regional governments, amounts to up to 75 per cent or 100 per cent of the loan, depending on whether the loan has been granted by a private or public lending institution (Art. 19, para. 2 of the Law of 30 December 1970).

5. Investment tax incentives

3081. The Law of 30 December 1970 also provides for specific tax incentives designed to stimulate investment. The various types of incentives include temporary exemptions from real property taxes (Art. 16 of the Law of 30 December 1970) and accelerated depreciation (Art. 15 of the Law of 30 December 1970).

3082. An exemption from real property taxes may be granted for a period of up to 5 years provided that the employment in the company concerned increases with a certain minimum percentage (more than 30 per cent for the Flemish Region and more than 20 per cent for the Walloon Region). This exemption covers land, buildings and equipment and tools, and applies as of the beginning of the year following the start-up of the operation (Art. 16 of the Law of 30 December 1970).

3083. With respect to investment in industrial buildings, plants, equipment, and so on, the investor may be authorised to apply the double depreciation method (twice the straight-line depreciation) for a maximum period of 3 years. However, use of this accelerated depreciation method is limited to certain development zones (for instance, certain areas in the province of Limburg in the Flemish Region).

3084. An application for the property tax exemption and the use of accelerated depreciation must be made together with the application for interest subsidies and/or capital grants.

§2. *Aid for small and medium-sized enterprises ("SMEs")*

1. *Introduction*

3085. Aids for SMEs are currently governed by the federal Law of 4 August 1978 on Economic Reorientation (*Wet tot economische herorientering/Loi de réorientation économique* – the "Law of 4 August 1978"), as well as by regional legislation. The Law of 4 August 1978 provides for aid to SMEs located anywhere in Belgium. Over the years, the Law of 4 August 1978 has been amended by several Decrees or Ordinances adopted by the regional Governments of the Flemish, Walloon and Brussels-Capital Regions.

3086. In the Flemish Region, the Law of 4 August 1978 applies to small enterprises and the self-employed. It should be recalled that the Flemish Region is about to adopt a new Framework Decree to replace all legislation on economic expansion, including the Law of 4 August 1978.

3087. In the Brussels-Capital Region, aids for SMEs are granted under the Law of 4 August 1978, as explained by Ministerial Guidelines, and under an Ordinance of 1 July 1993 on the Promotion of Economic Expansion (*Ordonnantie betreffende de bevordering van de economische expansie/Ordonnance concernant la promotion de l'expansion économique* – the "Brussels 1993 Ordinance"). While the Law of 4 August 1978 applies to aids granted to small enterprises, the Brussels 1993 Ordinance only applies to medium-sized enterprises.

3088. In the Walloon Region, the Law of 4 August 1978 applies together with a Decree of 25 June 1992 (the "Walloon 1992 Decree"), as well as all implementing regulations. It should be recalled that the Walloon Region is about to adopt a new Decree to replace the existing legislation on economic expansion.

3089. Since the Law of 4 August 1978 is still currently applied in all 3 regions, it is further discussed below, taking into account the different current modalities in the regions.

2. Scope of the Law of 4 August 1978

3090. The Law of 4 August 1978 provides for various investment incentives for SMEs located in Belgium. An enterprise is an SME if each of the following conditions is met:
- In the Flemish Region, the Law of 4 August 1978 applies only to small enterprises and the self-employed. A small enterprise is an enterprise that has less than 50 employees and an annual turnover not exceeding € 7 million or a total value of assets not exceeding € 5 million. Additionally, the criterion of "independence" must be satisfied, *i.e.*, one or more large enterprises may not hold more than 25 per cent of the capital or voting rights of small enterprises.

- In the Brussels-Capital Region, the Law of 4 August 1978 only applies to enterprises that employ less than 40 persons (for commercial enterprises) or less than 50 persons (for handicraft, industrial and service enterprises). Medium-sized enterprises may receive aids on the basis of the Brussels 1993 Ordinance, provided that they employ a maximum of 250 persons and their annual turnover does not exceed € 40 million or the total value of their assets does not exceed € 27 million. In addition, in order to be eligible for aid, no more than 25 per cent of the capital of medium-sized enterprises may be held by enterprises other than SMEs which are not public investment companies or venture capital enterprises.

- In the Walloon Region, an SME is, for the purpose of this aid, an enterprise which employs less than 250 persons and has an annual turnover not exceeding € 40 million or a total value of its assets not exceeding € 27 million. Moreover, no more than 25 per cent of the capital of the enterprise may be held by enterprises other than SMEs which are not public investment companies or venture capital enterprises.

- The enterprise does not belong to a sector which is excluded by the Royal Decree of 10 October 1978 implementing the Law of 4 August 1978 (for example, banking, insurance, or real estate) or by the regional implementing regulations. Moreover, some types of investments and some categories of activities are excluded by these regulations, such as investments made by financial institutions in the Walloon Region. In the Flemish Region, the guidelines to the Law of 4 August 1978 also contain a list of excluded types of investments such as investments related to the transport of goods and persons, and the acquisition of airplanes.

3091. The Law of 4 August 1978 and the regional implementing legislation also limit the types of investment that may benefit from state aid. The investment must generally relate to tangible or intangible assets and contribute to the creation, expansion,

743

conversion or modernisation of the SME concerned (Art. 4 of the Law of 4 August 1978). The implementing legislation of the regional governments generally imposes minimum thresholds for the investment to benefit from aid (as a general principle, € 62,500 in the Flemish Region, between € 6,200 and € 25,000 in the Brussels-Capital Region and between € 31,000 and € 500,000 in the Walloon Region).

3092. The categories of investment incentives available under the Law of 4 August 1978 are, to a large extent, similar to those provided for under the Law of 30 December 1970. They include various forms of direct financial assistance, such as interest subsidies, capital grants, investment grants and grants from the Participation Fund (*Participatiefonds/Fonds de Participation*), as well as guarantees and tax incentives. As a general rule, enterprises wishing to benefit from tax incentives may only benefit from such incentives if they have already applied for or benefit from direct financial assistance.

3. Direct financial assistance

3093. Under the Law of 4 August 1978, SMEs may benefit from direct financial assistance in the form of interest subsidies, capital grants, investment grants and grants from the Participation Fund.

3094. As under the Law of 30 December 1970, interest subsidies and capital grants are not granted in the Walloon Region, since these have been replaced by a single investment grant. In the Brussels-Capital Region, direct financial assistance is provided to SMEs through investment grants. Small enterprises established in Brussels may also benefit from interest subsidies, in addition to or instead of investment grants.

i. Interest subsidies

3095. Loans to SMEs which are granted by accredited lending institutions may benefit from interest subsidies. The rules governing the determination of the available interest subsidies vary depending on whether the investment is located in the Brussels-Capital Region or the Flemish Region. One of the basic criteria in this respect is the nature of the activities carried out by the SMEs. Other criteria, such as the contribution of the investment to employment, industrial policy or environmental goals may also be relevant. It is recalled that in the Brussels-Capital Region, only small enterprises may benefit from interest subsidies, in addition to or instead of investment grants.

ii. Capital grants

3096. As under the Law of 30 December 1970, interest subsidies may be replaced in whole or in part by capital grants to the extent that the SME uses its own funds for financing the investment. The amount of capital grants is calculated on the same basis as for interest subsidies.

iii. Investment grants

3097. As under the Law of 30 December 1970, the Walloon Region has replaced interest subsidies and capital grants by so-called "investment grants". The Walloon Region draws a distinction between (i) small familial enterprises, (ii) enterprises employing between 21 and 50 persons, (iii) enterprises employing between 50 and less than 100 persons, (iv) enterprises employing between 100 and 150 persons, and, finally, (v) enterprises employing between 150 and 250 persons. As a general rule, the amount of the investment must exceed the average of the depreciation made during the 3 accounting years preceding the filing of the application or the authorisation to start the investment. This principle, however, does not apply to enterprises existing for less than 3 years or to small familial enterprises. For the small familial enterprises, the minimum investment required by the Walloon region is € 43,400. In all SMEs employing between 21 and 50 people, a minimum of € 125,000 should be invested. Above 50 employees, a minimum of € 125,000 per 50 additional employees is required. The level of the regional aid depends on the nature of the activity of the SME, that is: the effect of the investment on employment and the importance of the activity. The basic aid varies between 7.5 and 15 per cent.

iv. Small familial enterprises

3098. The aid may amount to 15 per cent (basic aid) and 0 to 6 per cent (importance of the activity).

v. SMEs employing between 21 and 49 persons

3099. The aid may amount to 11 per cent (basic aid), 0 to 8 per cent (employment), and 0 to 2 per cent (importance of the *activity*).

3100. *SMEs employing 50 or more persons:* the aid may amount to 7.5 to 10 per cent (basic aid), 0 to 8 per cent (employment), and 0 to 3 per cent (importance of the activity).

3101. In order to obtain an investment grant, the investor himself must make a request to that effect. The grant is payable in periodic instalments, the timing and amount of which vary according to the total amount of the investment. In the Brussels-Capital Region, the level of investment grant for small enterprises varies from

5 per cent to 15 per cent depending on whether the enterprises are newly created and on the type of their activities. For medium-sized enterprises, the aid depends on the level of the basic aid (3 per cent), the effect of the investment on employment (3 per cent) and the location of the enterprise (2.5 per cent). The maximum aid payable to medium-sized enterprises in Brussels is 7.5 per cent of the investment.

3102. *Grants from the Participation Fund:* the Participation Fund (*Participatiefonds/Fonds de Participation*), which aims to improve the financial structure of existing or newly created SMEs by increasing their assets, may grant aid in various forms. With respect to closely held corporations, the Participation Fund may acquire minority shareholding interests or purchase bonds. In addition, the Participation Fund may grant subordinated loans. The Participation Fund grants different types of loans to SMEs. A "starting loan" may be obtained by a job-seeker who wishes to establish himself or herself as a self-employed person or who wishes to establish or acquire an enterprise. A "creation" loan (*instaplening/prêt de création*) may be granted to SMEs operating for less than one year and searching for the most profitable way to start their businesses. A "progression" loan (*progressielening/prêt de progression*) serves to finance investment projects which are essential for the development of the enterprise. Finally, a "transfer" loan (*overdrachtlening/prêt de transmission*) is available for partially financing the acquisition of a SME with future perspectives. Applications can be submitted to the Participation Fund.

4. Guarantees from the Guarantee Fund

3103. In order to facilitate the grant of loans, the Guarantee Fund (*Waarborgfonds/Fonds de Garantie*) may provide public guarantees to SMEs (Arts. 12 through 27 of the Law of 4 August 1978). Such guarantees cover the reimbursement of the principal amount, interest and additional costs of loans granted by accredited lending institutions. As a result of the regionalisation, loans are granted by the regional Guarantee Funds (the Flemish, Brussels and Walloon Guarantee Funds) which apply their own regulations. In the Flemish Region, applications can be submitted by the lending institutions to the Flemish Guarantee Fund (*Vlaams Waarborgfonds*). In the Brussels-Capital and Walloon Regions, enterprises may only apply through the intervention of a bank. In the Walloon Region, the Walloon Region Guarantee Company (*Société de Garantie Régionale Wallonne (SGRW)*) has been replaced since 11 July 2002 by a new company, the *Société Wallonne de Financement et de Garantie des PME (SOWALFIN)*, which is now the only financial structure for SMEs (investment, guarantee, *etc.*) in Wallonia.

5. Investment tax incentives

3104. The Law of 4 August 1978 also provides for tax incentives designed to stimulate investment by SMEs. These incentives are similar to those provided for under the Law of 30 December 1970, and include temporary exemptions from real property taxes, accelerated depreciation and exemptions from capital registration tax with regard to capital subscriptions. The terms and conditions for obtaining beneficial tax treatment are specified in the implementing regional legislation. Applications for such tax incentives must be made together with applications for interest subsidies and/or capital grants. In the Brussels-Capital Region, the Brussels 1993 Ordinance provides for similar tax incentives.

C. Research and development incentives

§1. Introduction

3105. Various incentives are granted by the regions to promote research and development projects. These incentives are governed by regional regulations. In the Flemish Region, the Government adopted a Decision on 5 October 2001 concerning Aid to Technological Research and Development Projects (*Besluit van de Vlaamse Regering tot regeling van de steun aan de projecten van technologisch onderzoek en ontwikkeling van het bedrijfsleven in Vlaanderen*). In the Brussels-Capital Region, the Government recently adopted an Ordinance of 21 February 2002 on the Promotion and Financing of Scientific Research and Technological Innovation (*Ordonnantie betreffende de aanmoediging en de financiering van het wetenschappelijk onderzoek en de technologische innovatie/ordonnance relative à l'encouragement et au financement de la recherche scientifique et de l'innovation technologique* – the "Brussels 2002 Ordinance"), and a Regulation of 18 July 2002 implementing the Brussels 2002 Ordinance. In the Walloon Region, research and development aids are granted by virtue of a Decree on Subsidies from the Walloon Region for Research and Technologies of 5 July 1990 (*Décret relatif aux aides et aux interventions de la Région Wallonne pour la recherche et les technologies*).

3106. The main incentive schemes designed to promote research and development activities are direct subsidies, capital advances and the investment deduction mechanism. In recent years, the regional Governments have changed their policies on aid for research and development projects as a result of the stricter application of the EC rules on state aids.

3107. Incentives in the field of research and development are primarily divided into aid for basic industrial research and aid for the development of prototypes, new products and new manufacturing processes. Aid for a combination of both (basic industrial research and the development of prototypes, *etc.*) is available as well. Enterprises doing business in Belgium should be aware that, besides aid for basic industrial research and aid for the development of prototypes, new products and new manufacturing processes, various other incentives exist which are not examined in this chapter.

§2. *Basic industrial research*

3108. Basic industrial research means activities aimed at increasing the level of knowledge prior to the development of specific products or processes. The subsidy usually amounts to 50 per cent of the marginal costs directly related to the research work. For international research programmes, the percentage can increase to 65 per cent (in the Brussels-Capital Region). For SMEs, this percentage increases to 60 per cent (in the Flemish Region), 75 per cent (in the Brussels-Capital Region), or 70 per cent (in the Walloon Region). These maximum aid levels are higher than the levels permitted under the EC rules on state aid for research and development, but they are, nevertheless, still applied by the Brussels and the Walloon Regions (for a review of the EC restrictions of state aid for research and development, *See*, "Community framework for state aids for research and development", O.J. [1996] C 45/5).

3109. It should be noted that, in the Walloon region, the definition of an SME for research and development financial assistance differs from the definition of an SME for direct financial assistance. In the case of research and development, a company must meet the following criteria in order to be considered an SME:
  (i) it employs less than 250 persons;
  (ii) it has a yearly turnover of less than € 20 million, or the total value of its assets does not exceed € 10 million; and
  (iii) maximum one-fourth of its capital is owned by one or several large companies which are neither institutional investors not exercising any control, nor public companies with a participation, nor venture capital companies.

3110. In the Flemish Region, a company must meet the following criteria in order to be considered as an SME for research and development aid:
  (i) it employs less than 250 persons;
  (ii) it has a yearly turnover of less than € 40 million, or the total value of its assets does not exceed € 27 million; and

(iii) it has no more than one-fourth of its capital controlled by another company that is not itself an SME.

§3. Aid for the development of prototypes, new products and new manufacturing processes

3111. Aid for the development of prototypes, new products and new manufacturing processes is granted by the Walloon Region under the form of capital advances and by the Brussels-Capital Region under the form of capital advances or direct subsidies. Under this system, the risks taken in a development project are shared by the promoter and the region. The level of intervention varies from 25 per cent up to 65 per cent in specific circumstances in the Brussels-Capital Region and to 50 per cent in the Walloon Region (70 per cent for SMEs). In the Flemish Region, direct subsidies amount to 25 per cent (or 35 per cent for SMEs) of the accepted gross costs of the project. Aid for prototype-research may also be granted in the form of a subordinated loan, but the total amount of this additional financing mechanism combined with the direct subsidy must not exceed 80 per cent of the project costs.

3112. To promote the employment of young researchers in the enterprises, the Walloon Region has developed the "First-Enterprise" programme. First-Enterprise is financial aid that covers a percentage of the wage cost of a young researcher. This percentage amounts to 50 per cent when it is a large enterprise and 80 per cent when it is an SME, except when the researcher is already employed by the enterprise. The Walloon Region also grants complementary measures for the promotion of technological research by enterprises located in certain geographical areas, defined in so-called "Objective 1" and "Objective 2" programmes.

3113. Research and development investment may also benefit from tax incentives. For instance, research and development investment projects may benefit from the so-called "investment deduction" (*See*, para. 3127).

D. Employment and training incentives

§1. Introduction

3114. In order to stimulate employment, the national and regional governments have devised various grants for employment (*See*, paras. 3316 *et seq.*) and training incentives (*See*, paras. 3122 *et seq.*). It may be noted that, in addition, local entities and, more importantly, the EC have launched several aid programmes for the same purpose.

3115. The main incentive schemes designed to promote employment and training are employment subsidies, employment premiums, reductions in salary and social security payments, training subsidies, training cheques and training premiums.

§2. *Employment incentives*

3116. At the federal level, employment incentives are generally granted for hiring unemployed persons, especially those who have more difficulties being hired, such as elderly persons or persons who have been unemployed for a long period of time (*See, e.g.,* the Royal Decree of 19 December 2001). However, they can also be granted to stimulate employment when an enterprise is established or its business expanded.

3117. In addition to employment incentives at the federal level (which apply in all 3 regions), the regions have developed specific measures in order to improve employment.

3118. In the Flemish Region, employment incentives granted in the framework of the legislation on economic expansion (*See,* para. 3069) have been suspended by a decision adopted by the Flemish Government on 20 April 2001. However, the Flemish Government adopted several decisions on the grant of different types of premium. For example, so-called encouragement premiums are provided in the framework of a career break system. Furthermore, a premium (*Tegemoetkoming in het loon van moeilijk te plaatsen werklozen*) may be granted to enterprises for the recruitment of elderly persons, provided that their employment does not lead to the dismissal of another employee and is offered for an indefinite duration, and is at least on a part-time basis. The amount of the premium is € 371.84 per month for employees and € 2.23 per hour for workers. Finally, a premium (*Beroepservaringspremie*) is granted for the recruitment of persons who have been unemployed for more than 36 months, in order to offer them the opportunity to gain professional experience. They must be employed at least on a part-time basis for one year. The amount of the premium depends on whether employment is on a part-time or full-time basis and varies between € 247.89 and € 495.79. An additional premium of € 148.74 may be granted for persons who have been unemployed for more than 60 months.

3119. In the Brussels-Capital Region, higher investment subsidies are available on the basis of the Brussels 1993 Ordinance (*See,* para. 3087). Under the Brussels 1993 Ordinance, additional aid may be granted if investment is made in certain economic areas of revitalisation (*espaces de revitalisation économique*) or meets some objectives in terms of employment. Also, premiums may be granted to SMEs for the employment of certain categories of persons who are more difficult to hire (the so-called *"prime de transition professionnelle"*). The unemployed person must be registered with the Brussels Regional Office for Employment (*Brusselse Gewestelijke Dienst voor Arbeidsbemiddeling (BGDA)/Office Régional Bruxellois de l'Emploi (ORBEM)*.The *prime de transition professionnelle* may be granted for 12 months and varies between € 250 and € 500 depending on the category of the unemployed person and the type of employment contract (full-time/part-time).

3120. In the Walloon Region, there are currently 2 main aid schemes under a Decree of 19 May 1994 (the "Walloon 1994 Decree") and Royal Decree No. 258 of 31 December 1983. Under the Walloon 1994 Decree (replacing Royal Decree No. 123 of 30 December 1982), SMEs may be entitled to receive aid for recruiting up to 5 additional persons involved in projects for the development of new products or production processes, the promotion of exports outside the EC Community, the conservation of energy and raw materials, or the protection of the environment and the fulfilment of quality standards other than those imposed by the Walloon Region, the Federal Government or the EC Community. Under Royal Decree No. 258, another employment incentive may be granted to SMEs and self-employed persons providing services to SMEs. This incentive consists of the payment, during maximum 2 years, of part of the wages and social security contributions of the newly employed person.

3121. The Walloon Government has, however, recently adopted a new Decree of 25 April 2002, which establishes general principles for the reform of all programmes dealing with unemployment and is intended to abrogate the current system, including the Walloon 1994 Decree and Royal Decree No. 258. It is to be noted that the new Decree will only come into force when the Walloon Government has adopted the necessary implementing texts. Under the new Decree, employers will receive an annually fixed grant for each job-seeker that they employ. Certain sectors are, however, excluded from the scope of the Decree, such as banks, health, sports and entertainment. The amount of the aid is calculated by way of points. One point amounts to € 2,541 for a full-time worker.

§3. Training incentives

3122. The regional employment offices provide for an array of training incentives. For instance, financial assistance may be available for expenses incurred in hiring and training personnel in connection with the establishment or conversion of companies. In addition, regional employment offices possess their own training centres and organise training courses in close collaboration with companies.

3123. The training incentives granted in the Flemish Region include several subsidies for the training of employees, unemployed persons or self-employed persons in relation to innovation within the firm (*hefboomkredieten*). The amounts of the subsidies vary depending on the type of the subsidies and the corresponding conditions. Furthermore, managerial training projects (*peterschapsprojecten*) for large enterprises to supervise groups of small enterprises are encouraged. The subsidy granted for managerial training projects may cover up to 70 per cent of the costs of the project, with a maximum of € 99,157.41 per year. The Flemish Region also encourages individual professional training (*individuele beroepsopleiding*). This training enables unemployed persons, persons seeking employment and persons living with a minimum income to be trained for a period of between one to 6 months. During this period, the employer does not pay any wages or social security contributions, but only a productivity premium (*productiviteitspremie*). The employer is obliged to offer a contract of an indefinite duration to the person concerned. Furthermore, since the beginning of 2002, self-employed persons or enterprises can buy "training cheques" (*opleidingscheques*) for their employees, directors or active partners. 50 per cent of a training cheque is paid for by the enterprise and 50 per cent is paid for by the Flemish Government. This cheque can be used to pay for training courses received by employed persons of an enterprise. An enterprise can buy training cheques for a maximum amount of € 6,000 every year.

3124. Training incentives granted in Brussels include subsidies for the collective training of directors, executives or personnel of the enterprise. This aid may amount to 50 per cent of the cost of the project, with a maximum of € 6,197.34 per training action. Another training subsidy may be granted by the regional employment office to SMEs at the time of their establishment, expansion or conversion for the training of unemployed persons. This aid may amount to € 2,500 per person for a maximum duration of 6 months. Other incentives exist for specific language training.

3125. Various training incentives are granted by the Walloon Region, among which are premiums for employing persons of 16 to 25 years old who wish to work and study at the same time. These premiums may amount to € 1,239.47 for a training period of more than 12 months and to € 743.68 for a training period of 6 months to one year. Other incentives also exist for the training and recruitment of unemployed persons (the so-called *Plan Formation Insertion (PFI)*). By virtue of this plan, enterprises do not pay any wages but only an encouragement premium (*prime d'encouragement*) which is exempted from social security contributions.

E. Tax incentives

3126. In addition to the tax incentives provided for in the Law of 30 December 1970 and the Law of 4 August 1978, various tax incentives have been devised by the Federal Government for stimulating investment. These tax measures include the so-called "investment deduction" and favourable treatment for co-ordination centres, distribution centres and services centres (*See*, Chapter 5).

§1. Investment deduction

3127. The investment deduction acts to stimulate specific investments such as research and development and energy-saving projects, as well as investment by SMEs. It allows enterprises to deduct from their taxable income a percentage of qualifying investments in qualifying and newly acquired assets that are used for business purposes (*See*, paras. 696 *et seq.*).

§2. Co-ordination centres

3128. The Belgian co-ordination centre legislation provides for major tax incentives and other advantages for qualifying international groups which carry out financial and management services (*See*, paras. 715 *et seq.*). It must be pointed out that the Minister of Finance is examining new regimes which may replace the actual legislation on co-ordination centres by the year 2005.

3129. The establishment of a co-ordination centre is presently subject to government approval which is valid for 10 years and is renewable. A co-ordination centre should be set up as a Belgian subsidiary or branch of an international group of connected companies with a consolidated capital of at least € 24 million and a consolidated annual turnover of € 240 million. For members of this multinational group, the co-ordination centre may carry on authorised activities including, for example, factoring, reinvoicing, hedging exchange risks, accounting, data processing and research and development. In addition, the co-ordination centre should employ at least 10 full-time employees by the end of the second year of its operations in Belgium.

3130. The special tax treatment includes the taxation, for a 10-year period, on the basis of a tax base calculated as a percentage (generally 8 per cent) of the operating expenses incurred by such co-ordination centres except personnel costs and financial charges. The tax benefits also provide specific exemptions or reductions from registration duties and withholding taxes.

3131. Other advantages relate to the exemption from the obligation to obtain a work permit for foreign executives and researchers.

§3. Distribution centres

3132. In order to encourage foreign investors to set up regional distribution centres in Belgium, the Belgian tax administration has established specific rules on the taxation of so-called distribution centres (*See*, paras. 730 *et seq.*).

3133. The special tax rules on distribution centres apply only to Belgian companies and branches of foreign companies that carry on authorised activities exclusively for companies of the same international group. Authorised activities include the purchasing, storage, administration, packaging, transportation and delivery of raw materials, supplies, merchandise or finished products. The distribution centres are not allowed to transform or process the raw materials, supplies, merchandise or finished products and they are not entitled to sell these goods to third parties. Distribution centres need the approval of the tax administration.

3134. Unlike co-ordination centres, distribution centres do not benefit from special tax treatment. In particular, the taxable income of a distribution centre is generally the same as for all other companies. However, the tax administration has issued specific rules on transfer pricing. Basically, the tax authorities generally agree that distribution centres will not be considered to have granted abnormal advantages to connected companies provided that they have applied a profit margin of 5 per cent to their operating expenses. Raw materials and supplies may, without any profit, be resold to other companies of the group.

3135. Applications must be filed with the Tax Administration (*Hoofdbestuur der directe belastingen/Administration centrale des contributions directes*).

§4. Service centres

3136. The rules on the taxation of so-called service centres established in 1996 (*See*, paras. 739 *et seq.*) stem directly from those on the taxation of distribution centres.

3137. The special service centre tax regime only applies to companies that are part of a Belgian or foreign group of connected companies carrying on authorised activities exclusively for companies of the same international group. Independent companies which are not part of a group are excluded from the application of this regime. The authorised activities include preparatory activities, providing information to clients, activities contributing passively to sales activities and activities implying active intervention in sales. Strictly commercial activities and involvement in the production process are prohibited. Service centres, similarly to distribution centres, do not benefit from any special tax treatment. The service centres will, however, not be considered to have granted abnormal or well-disposed advantages to connected companies provided that the taxable profit for the services is not below a certain percentage.

3138. Applications must be submitted to the Department of Preliminary Decisions (*Dienst van Voorafgaande Beslissingen/Service des décisions préalables*) of the Ministry of Finance before the creation of the service centre or during the year preceding the year in which the service centre wishes to benefit from the regime.

F. Investment companies

3139. A national investment company (*Nationale Investeringsmaatschappij/Société Nationale d'Investissement*), assisted by regional investment companies, was created in order to promote the general interest of the Belgian economy. This national investment company has, however, been privatised, while the regional investment companies have continued to operate as state-owned companies. These regional investment companies are: the *Gewestelijke Investeringsmaatschappij Vlaanderen (GIMV), the Société Régionale d'Investissement Wallon (SRIW)* and the *Gewestelijke Investeringsmaatschappij Brussel/Société Régionale d'Investissement de Bruxelles (GIMB/SRIB)*. In addition, on 11 July 2002, the Walloon Region created a new financial company for SMEs, *i.e.*, the *Société Wallonne de financement et de garantie des PME (SOWALFIN)* which includes: (i) the *Financière wallonne des PMI (FWPMI)*, the branch of the SRIW specialised for SMEs; (ii) the *Société de garantie régionale wallonne (SGRW)*; and (iii) the *Invests* (*i.e.*, state-funded investment companies). SOWALFIN provides guarantees, subordinated loans, export credits and advance financing.

3140. The regional investment companies are responsible for the promotion of private and public economic initiatives. For this purpose, they are entitled to participate in the creation of companies, to take shares or interests in such companies and to contribute to their management. Participation may also occur through a Belgian subsidiary of a foreign company. Applications for intervention must be filed by the company with the relevant regional investment company.

G. Export incentives

3141. Export incentives in Belgium consist of credits, credit insurance, subsidies, interest subsidies and assistance granted by Belgian organisations (*See*, paras. 3142 *et seq.*), as well as certain tax incentives (*See*, para. 3153).

§1. Belgian organisations that can assist companies in their export operations

3142. Exports originating in Belgium may benefit from various incentives provided by the institutions described below.

1. Regional foreign trade offices

3143. Since the last reform of the federal structure of the Belgian State (the "*St Polycarpe agreement*"), the regions have become competent with regard to external trade relations. The Belgian Foreign Trade Office (*Belgische Dienst voor Buitenlandse Handel (BDBH)/Office Belge du Commerce Extérieur (OBCE)* thus no longer exists. Instead, a co-operation agreement between the 3 regions and the federal state is envisaged, which will set up a Foreign Trade Agency, to be located at the same address as the now defunct Belgian Foreign Trade Office.

3144. Regional governments have assumed responsibility for supporting prospective activities. Each region has its own foreign trade office. In the Flemish Region, the Flemish Foreign Trade Office (*Vlaamse Dienst voor Buitenlandse Handel (VDBH)* has been replaced by Export Flanders (*Export Vlaanderen*). *Export Vlaanderen* is entrusted with the power to grant export subsidies to enterprises, individuals and associations of enterprises. In the Walloon Region, the General Office of Foreign Relations and the Walloon Export Agency (*Direction Générale des Relations Extérieures (DARE)/Agence Wallonne à l'Exportation (AWEX)* promote the export of walloon products, technical developments and services. In the Brussels-Capital Region, the Foreign Trade Service (*Dienst voor de Buitenlandse Handel van het Brussels Hoofdstedelijk Gewest/Service du Commerce Extérieur de la Region de Bruxelles-Capitale*) is responsible for promoting regional exports. Only SMEs may benefit from the financial aids granted by the Brussels-Capital Region. The aid may not exceed 50 per cent of the admissible expenses and cannot be higher than € 200,000 per project.

2. Finexpo (former Copromex)

3145. Finexpo is the committee for the financial support of exports and is part of the Ministry of Foreign Trade. Finexpo may grant interest subsidies for loans used to finance the export of equipment to non-EC countries. Finexpo only grants interest subsidies to the extent that they are necessary to ensure that the interest charged is comparable to that being charged in competing industrial countries. Exporting enterprises filing applications must prove that they are competing with foreign suppliers and that there is a need for stabilisation of the interest rate in order to be able to compete. Such subsidies must be granted in accordance with Belgium's international obligations with regard to interest subsidies, in particular those set forth in the OECD's "*Arrangement on Guidelines for Officially Supported Export Credits (Consensus)*". Consequently, Finexpo primarily grants interest subsidies in the context of transactions with less-developed countries. Finexpo also grants roll-over credits involving foreign currencies. In these cases, Finexpo may guarantee a minimum fixed rate for the duration of the transaction. Accordingly, the exporter is able to propose to its foreign buyer a fixed exchange rate in connection with the financing of a transaction. These minimum rates (Commercial Interest Reference Rate or CIRR) are monthly determined by the OECD and are binding. Finexpo may also grant super-subsidies, guaranteeing a very low interest rate (lower than one per cent). Super-subsidies are only granted for projects (involving the export of equipment and investment goods) in developing countries. Applications for an interest subsidy must be submitted to Finexpo.

3146. Creditexport stopped its activities in August 1998. The Rediscounting and Guarantee Institute (*Herdisconterings- en Waarborginstituut (HWI)/Institut de Réescompte et de Garantie (IRG)* was dissolved in December 1998.

3. National Delcredere Office

3147. The National Delcredere Office (*Nationale Delcredere-dienst/Office National du Ducroire*) is an independent institution operating under the auspices of the state. Its main purpose is to insure the credit risks related to export transactions. The National Delcredere Office also covers political risks associated with Belgian investments abroad and those related to exchange rates.

3148. The following risks are covered:
   (i) where a debtor is incapable of performing his obligations or refuses to do so without a legitimate reason;
   (ii) political and similar risks which assume the nature of force majeure for the insured or the debtor (*e.g.*, war, revolution, natural disaster, shortage of foreign currency);
   (iii) cancellation of the contract by the foreign buyer before the goods are delivered or non-fulfilment of the conditions necessary to perform the contract; and
   (iv) non-payment of claims.

3149. Other risks may be covered such as sequestration or damage to engineering equipment and the unfair calling of bank guarantees.

3150. Export transactions are insured within the framework of an overall agreement, which the exporter and the National Delcredere Office have to negotiate. The scope of this agreement may vary depending on the nature of the exported goods.

4. The Belgian Enterprise for International Investments

3151. The Belgian Enterprise for International Investments (*Belgische Maatschappij voor Internationale Investeringen (BMI)/Société belge d'Investissement International (SBI)* is an investment company financing foreign investments by Belgian companies. The Belgian Enterprise for International Investments may grant loans and capital, and may offer legal and fiscal aid and other forms of assistance. In general, it grants capital to Belgian companies for:
  (i) the creation of subsidiaries or joint ventures; and
  (ii) the acquisition, restructuring, privatisation and/or expansion of existing companies.

3152. The Belgian Enterprise for International Investments operates at market conditions. Furthermore, the financial assistance received must be used for investments abroad. The eligibility criteria are: (i) feasibility, (ii) strong financial structure and profitability of the project, (iii) quality of the partner company, (iv) size of the project, (v) liquidity of the investment and (vi) the economic interest for Belgium and the host country. It must be noted that, unlike other financial institutions, it does not grant capital or loans to the Belgian parent company, but instead to the foreign subsidiary. The Belgian Enterprise for International Investments usually intervenes for a period of 5 to 10 years. The amount of aid varies between € 0.4 million and € 2.5 million.

§2. Tax measures

3153. As far as export transactions are concerned, VAT rebates as well as the exemption of excise duties may be granted.

H. Environmental Incentives

§1. Introduction

3154. Environmental incentives are granted by the national and regional Governments in order to stimulate enterprises to invest in an environmentally-friendly way.

3155. In the Flemish Region, aids for environmental investments are granted under the Law of 30 December 1970, the Law of 4 August 1978 and a Decision of the Flemish Government of 11 January 2002. In the Brussels-Capital Region, environmental incentives are granted by virtue of the Brussels 1993 Ordinance. The environmental incentives are granted in the Walloon Region on the basis of the Law of 30 December 1970 and the Law of 4 August 1978 as completed by the Walloon 1992 Decree.

3156. It must be recalled that the Flemish and Walloon Regions are currently discussing new Decrees intended to replace the existing regulations relating to economic expansion, including the Law of 30 December 1970 and the Law of 4 August 1978. One of the main sections of these decrees will create a new regime of specific aids for investments that promote the protection of the environment. The current environmental incentives will thus only be briefly described below. Environmental incentives granted by the national and regional governments currently include subsidies, interest-free advances, investment grants, exemption from real property taxes and the investment deduction mechanism.

§2. *Environmental incentives*

3157. In the Flemish Region, on 11 January 2002, the Flemish Government adopted a Decision concerning aid for environmental investments by enterprises. Eligible environmental investments are investments aimed at the conservation of energy, the conservation of raw materials or the reduction of environmental hazard. The relocation of an enterprise is in principle not an acceptable environmental investment. It is important to note that only additional charges of environmental investments may be subsidised. Additional criteria provide, as far as SMEs are concerned, that the environmental investments must either be intended to comply with new (EC) mandatory environmental standards or to apply standards that are stricter than the existing standards. Large enterprises can only obtain environmental incentives in order to apply standards that are stricter than the existing EC standards. The amount of aid differs depending on whether the aid is granted to comply with the new EC standards (15 per cent for small enterprises and 8 per cent for medium-sized enterprises) or whether the aid is granted to apply standards that are stricter than the existing standards (20 per cent for small enterprises and up to 12 per cent for medium-sized and large enterprises). Furthermore, in order to receive environmental aid, the use of so-called "black-list substances" (*zwartelijst-stoffen*) is prohibited. Environmental investments that can be recovered within 2 years are excluded.

3158. The Brussels-Capital Region grants environmental incentives for: investments pursuing a rational use of energy, water or raw materials, the adjustment to EC standards implying considerable investments, the protection of the environment and the adjustment of the company's equipment to the Euro. The incentives may amount to up to 20 per cent of the investment or part of the investments directly related to one of the goals mentioned above. In order to obtain an environmental incentive, the investment must meet the following criteria. It must:
  (i) lead to a considerable reduction of environmental pollution;

(ii) provide serious adjustment of the production process, increasing the durability or the possibility of recycling; or

(iii) lead to a considerable reduction of the amount of waste of every production unit or a considerable improvement of waste recycling.

3159. Incentives are granted in the form of investment grants. Enterprises may also be exempted from real property taxes for a period of up to 5 years.

3160. The Walloon implementing legislation currently imposes the requirement that investments must be of particular importance for the environment. The promotion of energy-saving and the reconstruction of polluted sites are examples of eligible environmental investments. Additional criteria provide that the investment must pursue the application of standards stricter than those imposed by the region, the State or the EC and must pursue the realisation of certain investment programmes. The incentive may amount to up to 20 per cent of the investment programme.

I. Combination of incentives

3161. The possibility of combining the different categories of incentives which are primarily granted by the regional Governments varies depending on the region where the investment is made. In the Walloon Region, for instance, investment grants and the specific aid granted in the field of research and development may not be combined. Moreover, it will be recalled that additional aid may be provided by EC, national and other sources.

IV. APPLICATIONS FOR AID

A. General investment aids

§1. Flemish Region

3162. Enterprises should be aware that applications for general investment aid must be made before the first invoice of the investment. Late applications may lead to a refusal of the whole project, unless the project consists of separate and clearly defined parts. Also, a minimum duration of 12 months is required between 2 applications for the same type of aid. The investment must be terminated 24 months after the registration date of the application. This timelimit can be extended for important projects or in special cases.

3163. Applications for general investment aids must be addressed to:

Ministerie van de Vlaamse Gemeenschap
Afdeling Economisch Ondersteuningsbeleid
Markiesstraat 1
1000 Brussels

Tel.: 32-(0)2/553.35.11

Fax: 32-(0)2/553.37.88

E-mail: economiesteun@vlaanderen.be

Web site: www.vlaanderen.be/subsidiewegwijzer or www.vlaanderen.be
(section "economics, labour & tourism")

§2. *Brussels-Capital Region*

3164. Enterprises should be aware that investments invoiced and paid more than 6 months
before the registration date of the file are not eligible for aid. Payment of the aid
will be made once the completed file has been processed by the administration,
depending on the available budget. According to the administration, this may take
up to one year.

3165. The applicant or his/her bank or credit institution (in case of investment credits)
should send the application form provided by the region, duly signed and completed,
to:

Service pour l'Expansion Economique de la Région de Bruxelles-Capitale
Boulevard du Jardin Botanique 20
1032 Brussels

Tel.: 32-(0)2/800.34.69

Fax: 32-(0)2/800.38.06

3166. The following documents should be annexed to the application form:
    (i) a copy of the registration of the company with the trade register;
    (ii) a copy of the articles of incorporation and shareholding information;
    (iii) a copy of the last annual accounts (unless the company is newly created);
    (iv) certificates from the tax and social security authorities stating that the company fulfilled its obligations under VAT, tax and social security law; and
    (v) a copy of the invoices relating to the investment for which aid is sought.

§3. Walloon Region

3167. Applications must be submitted before initiating any investment. The Walloon administration acknowledges receipt of the application within 15 days. Enterprises must then file a complete dossier within 6 months (under the Law of 4 August 1978) or 4 months (under the Law of 30 December 1970) of the date of acknowledgement of receipt.

3168. For information, "MIDAS" is a database of all public incentives granted in the Walloon region, including a detailed description of each aid and the relevant application forms. It can be found at the following web site address:

> http://mrw.wallonie.be/dgee/dpe/dia/fr/01Nouveau-Site/01DataBases/
> DB_Programmes/FR/Prog_Midas/index.cfm

3169. Application forms are available from the region and must be addressed to:

> Ministère de la Région Wallonne
> Direction générale de l'Economie et de l'Emploi
> Direction de l'Industrie
> Place de la Wallonie, 1, Bâtiment II
> 5100 JAMBES (Namur)
>
> Tel.: 32-(0)81/33.37.40
>
> Fax: 32-(0)81/33.39.33
>
> Web site: http://mrw.wallonie.be/dgee/dpe/dia/fr

B. Research and development aids

§1. Flemish Region

3170. The financing of research and development projects in the Flemish Region is done through the Institute for the Promotion of Innovation by Science and Technology in Flanders (*Instituut voor Innovatie door Wetenschap en Technologie in Vlaanderen (IWT)*. The Institute supports and stimulates industrial research and technology transfer within the Flemish industry. All requests for all the various types of aid must be submitted to the Institute. The information required includes, *inter alia*, the industrial and commercial implications of the planned project as well as its social and economic aspects (employment, energy-saving potential, *etc.*). Criteria that are of importance for the evaluation of the decision include scientific value, technical feasibility and valorisation potential of the project. 2 weeks after the application is submitted to the IWT, the applicant will be informed about the admissibility of the application. All applications are communicated to external experts for advice. The final decision is adopted on the basis of criteria such as the scientific value and potential valorisation of the project as well as other particular economic and financial factors. On average, a decision will be taken within 75 days following the submission of the application.

3171. The IWT can be contacted at:

IWT
Bischoffsheimlaan 25
1000 Brussels

Tel.: 32-(0)2/209.09.00

Fax: 32-(0)2/223.11.81

E-mail : info@iwt.be
Web site: http://www.iwt.be

§2. Brussels-Capital Region

3172. In the Brussels-Capital Region, requests by very small enterprises (*i.e.*, enterprises that employ maximum 10 persons) for aid for both basic industrial research and prototype development projects must be submitted to the Ministry of the Brussels-Capital Region whose Research and Innovation Department provides application forms. The Department can be reached at:

Service Research & Development
Boulevard du Jardin Botanique 20
1032 Brussels

Tel.: 32-(0)2/204.21.11

3173. Requests for aid for companies other than very small enterprises, with an annual turnover under € 300,000, may only be submitted on the basis of an invitation to tender. Invitations to tender are organised twice a year by the Research and Development Department of the Brussels-Capital Region.

3174. Applications should be submitted on the application form provided by the Research and Development Department of the Ministry. Applicants must also provide a detailed 2-year programme and budget, explain the general grounds of the project and its economic justification and provide a description of the resources employed. Upon receipt of the dossier, the Ministry will send an acknowledge-ment of receipt to the applicant. If the Research and Development Department considers that the application is admissible, it will inform the applicant. The ad-ministration has 50 working days (if the applicant is a very small enterprise) or 80 working days (in all other cases) to submit a report to the Government on the research project. The Government must take its decision within 10 working days from the notification of the report.

§3. *Walloon Region*

3175. Requests for aid for prototype development, basic industrial research and the "First-enterprise" programme in the Walloon Region must be filed and submitted according to the guidelines of the DGTR. Once the dossier is complete, an opinion (negative or positive) will be sent to the applicant within maximum 60 working days following the receipt of the dossier. This opinion is submitted to the Ministry which takes the final decision. If the decision is positive and the budget available, an agreement specifying the rights and obligations of both parties will immedi-ately be concluded.

3176. The DGTR can be contacted at:

Direction Générale des Technologies et de la Recherche (DGTR)
Division "Aides aux Entreprises"
Avenue Prince de Liège 7
5100 JAMBES (NAMUR)

Tel.: 32-(0)81/33.56.48

Fax: 32-(0)81/30.66.00

Web-site: http://mrw.wallonie.be/dgtre

C. Employment and training aids

§1. *Flemish Region*

3177. Training cheques can only be ordered via the Internet. Enterprises must communi-cate their VAT-number, Trade Registry number and social security number. In case an enterprise does not have these numbers, it must give its name and address. The Graydon database should then be consulted in order to see whether the enterprise is allowed to buy training cheques. This will be the case if the enterprise has its seat in the Flemish region, is active in an acceptable sector, and is not a non-profit organisation. If the application is admissible, the enterprise will receive an order form via e-mail mentioning the client number and the amount to be paid (50 per cent of the total value of the cheques). The cheques will be printed out and delivered to the company only if the payment is made within 14 days after the request.

Applications for encouragement premiums must be addressed to:

Ministerie van de Vlaamse Gemeenschap
Administratie Werkgelegenheid
Afdeling Tewerkstelling, Aanmoedigingspremies
Markiesstraat 1, 8ste verdieping
1000 Brussels

Tel.: 0800/90045 (green number)

Fax: 32-(0)2/553.44.22

E-mail: aanmoedigingspremie@vlaanderen.be

Web site: www.vlaanderen.be/subsidiewegwijzer or www.vlaanderen.be (section "economics, labour & tourism")

Applications for the premium for recruitment of elderly persons (*Tegemoetkoming in het loon van moeilijk te plaatsen werklozen*) and the permium for the recruitment of long-term unemployed persons (*Beroepservaringspremie*) must be addressed to:

Ministerie van het Vlaamse Gewest
Departement Economie, Arbeid en Binnenlandse Aangelegenheden
Markiesstraat 1
1000 Brussels

Applications for subsidies for the training of employees, unemployed persons or self-employed persons in relation to innovation within the firm (*Hefboomkredieten*) must be addressed to:

Ministerie van de Vlaamse Gemeenschap
Afdeling Europa Werkgelegenheid
Markiesstraat 1, 8ste verdieping
1000 Brussels

Tel.: 32-(0)2/553.44.34

Fax: 32-(0)2/553.44.25

E-mail: europa@vlaanderen.be

Web-site: http://www.vlaanderen.be

Further information concerning managerial training projects (*Peterschapsprojecten*) can be obtained from:

Ministerie van de Vlaamse Gemeenschap
Afdeling Europa Economie
Markiesstraat 1
1000 Brussels

Tel.: 32-(0)2/553.38.78 – 32-(0)2/553.38.79

Fax: 32-(0)2/502.47.02

E-mail: economie.europa@vlaanderen.be

Web site: www.vlaanderen.be/subsidiewegwijzer or www.vlaanderen.be (section "economics, labour & tourism")

Applications for professional individual training (*Individuele beroepsopleiding*) must be addressed to:

Vlaamse Dienst voor Arbeidsbemiddeling en Beroepsopleiding (VDAB)
Keizerslaan 7
1000 Brussels

Tel.: 32-(0)2/515.41.11

Fax: 32-(0)2/514.11.06

E-mail: info@vdab.be

Web-site: http://vdab.be

Further information with regard to training cheques (*Opleidingscheques*) can be obtained from:

Ministerie van de Vlaamse Gemeenschap
Cel Opleidingscheques
Afdeling Economisch Ondersteuningsbeleid
Markiesstraat 1
1000 Brussels

Tel: 32-(0)2/553.37.10

E-mail: opleidingscheques@vlaanderen.be

Web-site: http://www.vlaanderen.be/opleidingscheques

§2. Brussels-Capital Region

3178. The application form provided by the regional employment office must be sent by registered letter within 2 months of the date of hiring to:

> Brusselse Gewestelijke Dienst Arbeidsbemiddeling (BGDA)/Office
> Régional de l'Emploi (ORBEM)
> Boulevard Anspach, 65
> 1000 Brussels
>
> Tel.: 32-(0)2/505.14.11
>
> Fax: 32-(0)2/511.30.52
>
> Web-site: www.bgda.be

3179. Applicants should also submit the following information:
   (i) a copy of the statistical framework annexed to the declaration sent to the social security administration for the 4 terms preceding the hiring;
   (ii) a copy of the document provided by ORBEM to the job seeker which certifies that he or she meets the legal requirements; and
   (iii) a copy of the work contract of the person hired by the company requesting the aid.

§3. Walloon Region

3180. Regarding the employment premium granted under the 1978 Act, the application form (available online) must be submitted at the latest 18 months following the reference trimester (the trimester where jobs were created) and at the earliest in the thirteenth month after this trimester to:

> Ministère de la Région Wallone
> Direction Générale de l'Economie et de l'Emploi
> Division des P.M.E. et des Conseillers d'Entreprise
> Direction des P.M.E.
> Place de wallonie, 1, Bât. 3
> 5100 NAMUR (Jambes)
>
> Tel.: 32-(0)81/33.42.52

Fax: 32-(0)81/33.42.22

3181. Applications for other employment or training incentives should be addressed with a specific form available online to:

Ministère de la Région Wallonne
Direction Générale de l'Economie et de l'Emploi
Division de l'Emploi
place de la Wallonie 1 – Bâtiment II – 4ème étage
5100 JAMBES (NAMUR)

Tel.: 32-(0)81/33.43.43

Fax: 32-(0)81/33.43.22

D. Environmental aids

§1. Flemish Region

3182. Application for environmental aids must be made following a procedure similar to that for general investment aid and must be addressed to:

Ministerie van de Vlaamse Gemeenschap
Afdeling Economisch Ondersteuningsbeleid
Markiesstraat 1
1000 Brussels

Tel.: 32-(0)2/553.35.11

Fax: 32-(0)2/553.37.88

E-mail: economiesteun@vlaanderen.be

Web-site: www.vlaanderen.be/subsidiewegwijzer or www.vlaanderen.be (section "economics, labour & tourism")

§2. Brussels-Capital Region

3183. The applicant or his/her bank or credit institution (in case of investment credits) should send the application form provided by the region, duly signed and completed, to the same Service as applications for general investment aids. The documents required are the same as those required for the process of general investment aids. Upon receipt of the dossier, the administration will notify the enterprises of the registration date and file number. Investments invoiced before the registration date are not eligible for aid if: (i) they have been made more than 6 months before the registration date, or (ii) the investment exceeds € 2 million. Enterprises may, however, obtain aid for investments over € 2 million and for investments made more than 6 months before the date of registration by obtaining a prior authorisation from the administration. The applicant should send a letter to the authority, detailing the planned investment. The authorisation of the administration must then be annexed to the application form when the enterprise applies for the aid. The aid will be paid, depending in the budget, once the administration is in possession of the completed dossier and of proof that the investments have been made.

§3. Walloon Region

3184. Applications must be submitted with a specific form (available online) before investments are made. They must be addressed to:

Ministère de la Région Wallonne
Direction générale de l'Economie et de l'Emploi
Direction de l'Industrie
Place de la Wallonie, 1, bâtiment II
5100 JAMBES (NAMUR)
Tel.: 32-(0)81/33.43.43

Fax: 32-(0)81/33.43.22

18. PRODUCT LIABILITY

I. INTRODUCTION

3185. Until 1991, Belgium did not have any specific legislation dealing with product liability. To claim compensation for harm caused by defective products, plaintiffs thus relied on general tort principles or on an implied warranty theory based on principles of contract law. The concept of liability without fault, or strict liability, was not explicitly recognised in Belgian law, except in very specific legislation dealing, for example, with the transport of gaseous products through pipelines (Law of 12 April 1965), toxic waste (Law of 22 July 1974) and nuclear energy (Law of 22 July 1985). However, as the Belgian courts adopted an increasingly liberal interpretation of the provisions in the Belgian Civil Code regarding negligence and implied warranties, the Belgian product liability regime began to resemble one of strict liability.

3186. This situation changed with the incorporation into Belgian law of the EC Council Directive No. 85/374 of 25 July 1985 on the Approximation of the Laws, Regulations and Administrative Provisions of the Member States concerning Liability for Defective Products dealing with liability for defective products which is based on the principle of strict liability (O.J. [1985] L 210/29 – the "EC Product Liability Directive"). The Law of 25 February 1991 concerning Liability for Defective Products (*Wet betreffende de aansprakelijkheid voor producten met gebreken/Loi relative à la responsabilité du fait des produits défectueux*) (the "Law on Product Liability") incorporates the provisions of the EC Product Liability Directive into Belgian law. The Law on Product Liability applies to products put into circulation after 1 April 1991. The Law on Product Liability does not replace the existing product liability rules, but merely supplements them.

3187. This chapter will deal with the Law on Product Liability (*See*, Section II), the 1994 legislation on consumer safety (*See*, Section III) and the pre-existing rules on the subject, *i.e.*, implied warranty (*See*, Section IV) and tort liability (*See*, Section V). It will conclude with a brief overview of recent European legislation regarding the sale of consumer goods (*See*, Section VI).

II. THE LAW ON PRODUCT LIABILITY

3188. The Law on Product Liability is based on the principle that the producer is liable for any damage caused by a defect in his product (Art. 1) and that the injured person must prove the existence of the damage, the defect and the causal relationship between defect and damage (Art. 7). These principles refer to the following key terms which will be analysed in some detail: "product", "producer", "defect" and "damage". The defences, both legal and contractual, available to producers, and the time limits applicable to product liability claims, will also be examined.

A. Product

3189. Article 2 of the Law on Product Liability defines the term "product" as any movable object, regardless of how it was manufactured, even if it has been incorporated into another movable object or into an immovable object, or has become immovable by destination (for the term "immovable property by destination", *See*, Chapter 15). Thus, for example, a shock absorber incorporated into a motor vehicle, a beam used in the construction of a building, or equipment installed by a landowner for the purpose of servicing and exploiting a piece of land (*i.e.*, immovable property by destination within the meaning of Article 524 of the Civil Code) are all products within the meaning of the Law on Product Liability.

3190. The Law on Product Liability does not apply to services. It should be noted, however, that the distinction between product liability and damage due to a service is not always easy to make. For instance, a kitchen is bought and delivered to the buyer. The seller also agrees to install it. After a few days, a fire breaks out and the kitchen burns down. It is not unthinkable that the lack of safety in this case is not solely or entirely attributable to a defect in the product (*i.e.*, the kitchen), but rather to a combination of factors, including the installation (*i.e.*, a service).

3191. Prior to December 2000, agricultural products, game, stock-farming and fishery products were not considered products within the meaning of the Law on Product Liability, unless they had undergone initial processing. In compliance with EC Directive No. 1999/34 of the European Parliament and of the Council of 10 May 1999 amending EC Council Directive No. 85/374 on the Approximation of the Laws, Regulations and Administrative Provisions of the Member States concerning Liability for Defective Products (O.J. [1999] L 141/2) the Law on Product Liability was altered to include these products, effective as of 4 December 2000.

3192. Objects which are immovable by nature are excluded from the scope of the Law on Product Liability. Also intangible products (goodwill, intellectual property rights, *etc.*) are excluded. However, the Law on Product Liability explains that electricity constitutes a product within the meaning of the Law on Product Liability. Nuclear energy, on the other hand, has been explicitly excluded.

3193. As far as books and documents are concerned, we would contend that the Law on Product Liability only applies if the defect is inherent to the carrier (*i.e.*, the book or paper as an object) and not if damage is caused due to its content, which is an intangible (*e.g.*, a do-it-yourself book that describes a certain procedure which, when followed, results in damage). A similar position could be maintained in relation to software products, albeit that the special nature of such products, which are closely bound to their carriers and to computer hardware, should also be taken into account on a case-by-case basis.

B. Producer

3194. The term "producer" within the meaning of the Law on Product Liability is a complex notion. It covers not only the actual producer of the product but also the so-called "apparent" producer and, under certain conditions, the importer into the European Union and even the supplier of the product.

3195. Article 3 of the Law on Product Liability specifies in the first place that the manufacturer of the product, be it a finished product or a component part, will be considered as the producer within the meaning of the Law on Product Liability. The term "producer" also covers producers of raw materials. The place of establishment of the producer is immaterial for purposes of the Law on Product Liability.

3196. Apart from the actual producer or manufacturer of a product, the term "producer" also includes the "apparent" producer. This latter term refers to any person who, by putting his name, trademark or other distinguishing feature on a product presents himself as its producer (Art. 3 of the Law on Product Liability). Placing one's name or trademark on a product is generally not sufficient to be considered its apparent producer. For example, if a product indicates clearly the identity of its producer, the owner of the trademark, which may also be indicated on the product, will not be considered the apparent producer of the product. However, if no mention is made of the producer, the trade marks owner risks being considered as the apparent producer within the meaning of the Law on Product Liability. This may raise difficult problems, for example, for OEM (original equipment manufacturer) buyers or for owners of distribution trademarks.

3197. The importer of a product into the European Union will be deemed to be its producer, provided importation takes place in the course of the importer's business activities with a view to selling the product or transferring its use to a third party (Art. 4(1) of the Law on Product Liability). It should be stressed that Article 4(1) of the Law on Product Liability only applies to importers who ship the product into the European Union. Importers who ship the product from one EC Member State to another are not covered.

3198. The requirement in Article 4(1) of the Law on Product Liability that the product must be imported with a view to its sale or the transfer of its use to a third party excludes the application of the Law on Product Liability when a product is imported exclusively for the importer's own use. This will, for example, be the case when a manufacturer imports equipment exclusively for use in its own factory.

3199. The words *"transfer the use of the product to a third party"* which are used in Article 4(1) of the Law on Product Liability are not derived directly from the EC Product Liability Directive. Rather, Article 3(2) of the EC Product Liability Directive refers to *"hire, leasing or any other form of distribution"*. It is, however, believed that these notions are equivalent.

3200. Any liability incurred by an importer under Article 4(1) of the Law on Product Liability is without prejudice to the liability of the producer.

3201. A final category of potentially liable persons under the Law on Product Liability are the suppliers of products. Under Article 4(2) of the Law on Product Liability, the supplier of a product that has caused damage will be deemed its producer:
  (i) if, in the case of a product which has been manufactured in the European Union, the producer cannot be identified; or
  (ii) in the case of a product which has been imported into the European Union, the importer cannot be identified even if the name of the producer is indicated.

3202. In both cases, the supplier may escape liability if he informs the injured person within a reasonable time of the identity of the producer or, as the case may be, of the importer or of the person who supplied him with the product. What constitutes a "reasonable time" is likely to depend on the circumstances of each case.

3203. As the term "producer" covers several categories of potentially liable persons, it is likely that in any complex product liability litigation, the injured party will be able to pursue its claim against several defendants. Article 9 of the Law on Product Liability provides that in such cases all persons who are liable for the same damage are to be jointly and severally liable.

C. Defect

3204. A product is defective when, in view of all the circumstances, it does not provide the level of safety a person is entitled to expect (Art. 5 of the Law on Product Liability). The Law on Product Liability mentions 3 examples of such circumstances: (i) the presentation of the product, (ii) its normal use or the use to which it could reasonably be expected that the product would be put, and (iii) the time when the product was put into circulation. Article 5 of the Law on Product Liability further specifies that a product may not be considered defective for the sole reason that a better product is subsequently put into circulation.

§1. Presentation of the product

3205. The presentation of the product refers to the product's design, packaging, labeling, user instructions, and similar items. The presentation of a product could render the product unsafe if it fails to warn the user against certain risks inherent in using the product. Also advertising is an element of the presentation of a product. In cases where risks are widely known to the public at large, however, the failure to mention these risks would not necessarily render the product unsafe.

§2. Normal use of the product

3206. The normal use of the product, or the use to which it may reasonably be expected that the product will be put, is relevant to the assessment of the safety of the product. It allows an exclusion of the producer's liability in cases of misuse of the product or of use that is not reasonable under the factual circumstances at hand.

3207. The addition of the words "*the use to which it may reasonably be expected that the product will be put*" is important. It is intended to cover situations where a product is not being used in accordance with its intended use, but where the improper use is reasonably foreseeable. For example, a toy covered with toxic paint would be considered unsafe because it is reasonably foreseeable that small children may put the toy in their mouths while playing.

§3. Time when the product was put into circulation

3208. A product may not be considered defective for the sole reason that a better product is subsequently put on the market. In other words, whether a product is safe must be determined in accordance with the safety standards accepted at the time the product was put into circulation.

§4. The safety that a person is entitled to expect

3209. The Law on Product Liability does not specify which expectations are to be deemed legitimate and which are not. It is mainly up to the judge to evaluate this under the specific circumstances of the case.

3210. Of course, one may refer to the notions of "reasonableness" and "good faith" as guiding principles in this respect. This means that, on the one hand, the injured person may not rely on totally unreasonable safety expectations and that, on the other hand, the judge is in no way bound to safety norms proposed by the producer.

3211. Although the Law on Product Liability essentially introduced a strict liability regime, it cannot be entirely excluded that a judge, when evaluating the legitimate expectations of a person, also takes into account the issue of "fault" by either party.

3212. Another element to be taken into account is that the legitimate expectations to be evaluated should be those of an abstract person and not those of the injured individual in the case at hand. However, a nuance may be added: one should consider an abstract person belonging to the user group that the producer targets.

D. Damage

3213. Article 11 of the Law on Product Liability defines "damage" as damage caused to persons including pain and suffering and, subject to certain restrictions, damage to property.

3214. Article 11 of the Law on Product Liability does not elaborate upon the meaning of the phrase "damage caused to persons". Article 9 of the EC Product Liability Directive offers some guidance, however, as it uses the equivalent term "damage caused by death or personal injuries". Since the EC Product Liability Directive is without prejudice to national provisions relating to non-material damage, the Law on Product Liability, in keeping with traditional Belgian tort liability principles, specifies that damage includes pain and suffering *(morele schade/dommages moraux)*. Pain also includes esthetical damage, *i.e.*, the so-called *"pretium doloris"*.

3215. The restrictions relating to damage to property covered by the Law on Product Liability are stringent. Damage to property only gives rise to compensation if the item of property is ordinarily intended for private use or consumption and is used by the injured person mainly for his/her own private use or consumption. Both of these conditions must be met.

3216. The restrictions relating to private use or consumption are intended to exclude damage to items of property that are ordinarily intended, or which are mainly or exclusively used by the injured person, for business purposes. Given these restrictions, it appears that business enterprises will normally not be able to rely on the Law on Product Liability to obtain compensation for damage caused to property owned by them.

3217. A further important exception is that the Law on Product Liability does not cover damage to the defective product itself. This type of damage remains subject to the rules governing the sale of goods.

3218. For damage to property, the Law on Product Liability provides that the total compensation due is the amount remaining after a lump-sum deduction of € 500. Moreover, the EC Product Liability Directive (Art. 16) allows the Member States to impose a limit of no less than € 70 million on the producer's total liability for damage resulting from death or personal injury caused by identical items with the same defect. The Belgian Parliament decided against the imposition of such a cap.

3219. Finally, the Law on Product Liability does not apply to the following types of damage: damage covered by the Law of 22 July 1985 on Civil Liability in the Area of Nuclear Energy (*Wet betreffende de wettelijke aansprakelijkheid op het gebied van kernenergie/Loi sur la responsabilité civile dans le domaine de l'énergie nucléaire*) (Art. 15) and, under certain conditions, damage covered by social security compensation schemes (Art. 14). As to the latter exception, the question arises whether the EC Product Liability Directive leaves room for such an exception since it may limit the rights of the injured person in a way which, arguably, is not permitted by the EC Product Liability Directive.

E. Burden of proof

3220. Article 7 of the Law on Product Liability states that the injured party must prove:
  (i) a defect in the product;
  (ii) the damage suffered; and
  (iii) the causal link between defect and damage.

3221. The mere existence of the damage is not in itself sufficient evidence of a lack of safety in the product. Nonetheless, it may be derived *a contrario* from Article 8(b) of the Law on Product Liability that the injured party will not have to prove the existence of a defect at the moment when the product was put into circulation. This article indicates that it is for the producer to prove that it is reasonable to assume that there was no defect at that moment. (*See*, paras. 3222 and 3223.)

F. Legal defences

3222. When the injured person proves the existence of a defect, of damage and of a causal relationship between defect and damage, the producer will be held liable unless he can prove the existence of one of the circumstances listed in Article 8 of the Law on Product Liability:

   (i) that he did not put the product into circulation. Article 6 of the Law on Product Liability defines the notion "to put into circulation" as "*the first act which demonstrates the producer's intention to give to the product its intended destination by transferring it to third parties or by using it for the benefit of third parties*"; (for instance, the transfer of a product to an independent laboratory for further testing is not to be equated to putting this product into circulation);

   (ii) that, having regard to the circumstances, it is probable that the defect which caused the damage did not exist at the time when the product was put into circulation by him or that this defect came into being afterwards;

   (iii) that the product was neither manufactured by the producer for sale or any form of distribution for an economic purpose, nor manufactured or distributed by him in the course of his business;

   (iv) that the defect is due to compliance of the product with mandatory regulations issued by the public authorities;

   (v) that the state of scientific and technical knowledge at the time when the producer put the product into circulation was not such as to enable the existence of the defect to be discovered. Belgium has therefore not made use of the option left open by the EC Product Liability Directive to maintain the producer's liability in these circumstances (Art. 15(1)(b)); or

   (vi) in the case of a manufacturer of a component, that the defect is attributable to the design of the product in which the component has been fitted or to the instructions given by the manufacturer of the product.

3223. Other than on the above legal defences, the producer may not rely on any circumstance to escape liability towards the injured person.

G. Contractual defences

3224. Article 10(1) of the Law on Product Liability states the fundamental principle that the producer's liability towards the injured person may not be contractually limited or excluded. This prohibition does not affect the possibility for the producer to reduce or exclude his liability under other liability regimes (within the limits set by those regimes) and to provide contractual safeguards in his relations with parties other than the injured person. The Law on Product Liability does not affect the traditional rules governing contractual limitations of liability, indemnity clauses and the like in relations with persons other than the injured person.

H. Concurrent liability

3225. When several persons are liable for the same damage towards the injured person, their liability under the Law on Product Liability is joint and several (Art. 8). This is without prejudice to rights of recourse which they may exercise amongst themselves. Under Belgian law, among persons having committed faults which have caused the same damage, damages are due in proportion to their relative fault.

3226. That the damage to the injured person is caused both by a defect in the product and by the act or the omission of a third party does not enable the producer to reduce or exclude his liability towards the injured person (Art. 10(2) of the Law on Product Liability). Again, this is without prejudice to the right of recourse which the liable producer may have against the third party whose act or omission has contributed to the damage. If such an act or omission amounts to a fault, the third party will be required to pay damages in proportion to his relative fault.

3227. In cases where the damage is caused both by a defect in the product and by a fault of the injured person, or a person for whom the injured person is responsible, the producer's liability may be reduced or excluded. On this latter point (the possibility to exclude the producer's liability) the Law on Product Liability departs from traditional Belgian tort liability principles, which only allow a reduction of liability to take into account the relative fault of the producer and the victim.

3228. Liability under the Law on Product Liability may finally coincide with contractual fault or with liability under Article 1641 of the Civil Code (*See*, paras. 3278-3301): in such cases, the injured party may base its claim for damages on any or all applicable rules, the total amount of damages being limited to compensation for the actual damage sustained.

I. Time limits

3229. Article 12(2) of the Law on Product Liability provides that legal proceedings on the basis of the Law on Product Liability must be instituted within a period of 3 years as of the day the injured person became aware, or should reasonably have become aware, of the damage, the defect and the identity of the producer. The normal rules on interruption and suspension of limitation periods, which are contained in Articles 2242 *et seq.* of the Civil Code, are applicable.

3230. Article 12(1) of the Law on Product Liability provides that the rights of the injured person to obtain compensation from the producer on the basis of the Law on Product Liability are extinguished after a period of 10 years starting on the day on which the defective product was put into circulation. The product referred to is the actual product which caused the damage and not the first product in the series of products to which the defective product belonged. The phrase *"to put into circulation"* is defined in Article 6 of the Law on Product Liability (*See*, para. 3222). The injured person can prevent the extinction of his rights under the Law on Product Liability if he starts legal proceedings under the Act against the producer prior to the expiry of the period of 10 years.

III. PRODUCT LIABILITY AND CONSUMER SAFETY

A. The General Product Safety Directive

3231. EC Council Directive No. 92/59 on General Product Safety (O.J. [1992] L 228/24) (the "EC General Product Safety Directive") aims to ensure that consumer products placed on the internal market of the European Union present a high level of protection of safety and health. It is justified by the fact that differences in Member State product safety laws would (i) lead to disparities in consumer protection, (ii) distort competition and (iii) create barriers to intra-Community trade.

B. The Law on Consumer Safety

§1. Framework

3232. In Belgium, the EC General Product Safety Directive was implemented by the Law on Consumer Safety of 9 February 1994 (*Wet betreffende de veiligheid van de consumenten/Loi relative à la sécurité des consomateurs*) (the "Law on Consumer Safety").

3233. The Law on Consumer Safety establishes a duty on economic operators, which is enforceable by public authorities, to only place safe products on the market. This obligation complements the private law product safety obligation contained in the Law on Product Liability. To this end, it establishes a framework for product safety, set out in 4 chapters:
   (i) a general safety requirement;
   (ii) the creation of a Commission for Consumer Safety;

(iii) procedures for detection and verification of infringements;
(iv) sanctions and fines.

§2. General Safety Requirement

3234. The general safety requirement is briefly stated in Article 2, paragraph 1 of the Law on Consumer Safety: "*Producers shall be obliged to place only safe products (and services) on the market.*" As this chapter only deals with product liability issues, further references to services will be omitted.

3235. Regarding this general safety requirement, Article 7 of the Law on Consumer Safety obliges producers to spontaneously offer consumers the information they need in order to assess the risks related to a product. Producers also have to take the measures which are necessary in order to stay informed as to potential risks which are linked to their products (*e.g.*, by investigating complaints, conducting market research, *etc.*). The Law on Consumer Safety, by opting for an active information duty, takes the view that prevention is better than compensation.

3236. The distributor of the products is also subject to certain obligations. Article 2, paragraph 2 of the Law on Consumer Safety obliges the distributor to act with due care in order to help ensure that the product complies with the general requirement that it should be safe. In particular, distributors should not supply products which they know, either from information actually in their possession or because of their status as professionals, to be dangerous. They must monitor the safety of the products within the limits of their activity; they must pass any information they receive back to the producer; and they must co-operate with the producer whenever the producer takes action to eliminate a risk.

§3. Relevant Products

3237. Article 1, paragraph 1 of the Law on Consumer Safety specifies that the Law on Consumer Safety applies to products intended for consumers or likely to be used by consumers, as opposed to those used exclusively in the context of a trade or business. However, the Law on Consumer Safety does not apply to products which are already governed by another law, such as the machinery or toys regulations. Subject to certain exceptions, the safety requirement is applicable to all consumer products, whether new, used or reconditioned. The exceptions are second-hand products supplied as antiques.

§4. Definition of Producer

3238. Article 1, paragraph 3 of the Law on Consumer Safety defines who the producer is. It thereby makes it clear that manufacturers or importers are primarily responsible for a product's safety; but that other economic operators are also required to ensure the safety of the products within the limits of their activities. The article's definition of a producer is very broad and includes:

(i) the manufacturer of the product, when he is established in the Community (this is a factual question to be decided on a case-by-case basis);

(ii) any person holding himself out as the manufacturer by affixing his name, trademark or other distinctive marks on the product;

(iii) any person who reconditions the product;

(iv) the manufacturer's authorised representative, when the manufacturer is not established in the Community;

(v) if no such representative exists, the importer of the product;

(vi) other professionals in the supply chain, insofar as their activities may affect the safety properties of a product.

§5. Definition of Distributor

3239. It is important to note that Article 1, paragraph 4 of the Law on Consumer Safety distinguishes the producer from "distributors" who are professionals in the supply chain, and whose activity does not affect the safety properties of the product. In principle a distributor is not subject to the general safety requirement, but must (as mentioned above) nevertheless act with due care in order to help to ensure compliance with the general safety requirement, for example, by not supplying products which are known or presumed to breach the general safety requirements and by participating in monitoring the safety of products placed on the market.

§6. Definition of a safe product

3240. Pursuant to Article 2, paragraph 1 of the Law on Consumer Safety, a product is "safe" if it offers the guarantees which a consumer is entitled to expect regarding safety and protection of health, provided that it is used under normal conditions of use or other foreseeable conditions. Even if higher levels of safety are possible or other products which pose a smaller risk exist, these are not grounds for considering a product to be "unsafe" or "dangerous".

3241. When determining the safety of a product, the following points should, among others, be considered:

(i) the characteristics of the product, i.e., its composition, packaging, instructions for assembly and maintenance;

(ii) its effect on other products, if it is reasonably foreseeable that it will be used with other products;

(iii) the product's presentation, *i.e.*, the labelling, any instructions for its use and disposal and any other indication or information provided by the producer; and

(iv) the categories of consumers at serious risk when using the product, in particular children.

3242. Article 3 of the Law on Consumer Safety adds further criteria for judging whether a product complies with the general safety requirement:
  (i) EC or Belgian regulation;
  (ii) voluntary standards giving effect to a European standard or Community technical specifications;
  (iii) codes of good practice in respect of health or safety in the sector concerned;
  (iv) the state of the art in professional knowledge and technology; and
  (v) the level of safety which consumers are entitled to expect.

3243. However, if it appears that a product is dangerous, despite its conformity with the above-mentioned criteria, the competent authorities are nonetheless entitled to act accordingly.

3244. It should be noted that if the health and safety characteristics of the product in question are governed by specific legislation, the Law on Consumer Safety will not apply. (Art. 9 of the Law on Consumer Safety)

§7. *Monitoring of Products*

3245. Under Article 5 of the General Product Safety Directive, the EC Member States must establish authorities and give them the necessary powers to take measures to ensure that producers and distributors comply with the obligations imposed on them. The authorities should have the power to impose penalties on producers and distributors who are at fault. Manufacturers should be aware of this possibility when placing their products on the market.

3246. The Law on Consumer Safety gives the relevant powers to the King and the Minister responsible for consumer affairs: they can prohibit or regulate production, import, export, sale or distribution and even possession of products which are deemed to be dangerous. Such regulatory measures may concern conditions of production, labeling, packaging and information duties toward consumers. (Arts. 4, 5 and 6 of the Law on Consumer Safety)

3247. Article 8 of the Law on Consumer Safety obliges the competent authority to take into account the principle of proportionality when exercising these powers.

3248. The King and the Minister are to be assisted by a Commission for Consumer Safety, which is part of the Consumption Council (Art. 11 of the Law on Consumer Safety). The Commission considers all problems regarding the safety of products and issues motivated opinions, also at the request of a court or of any given natural or legal person. (Art. 13 of the Law on Consumer Safety)

3249. Articles 22 through 25 of the Law on Consumer Safety set out the sanctions to be imposed on producers who do not respect their legal obligations: apart from fines and the seizure of goods, these include the seizure of profits and revenues which were obtained from the infringement.

§8. The Law on Consumer Safety and the Law on Product Liability

3250. The safety test imposed by the Law on Consumer Safety appears to be substantially similar to the legitimate safety expectation test under the Law on Product Liability. The level of safety required by the Law on Consumer Safety would therefore be indicative of the standard below which a product is to be considered defective pursuant to the wording of Article 5 of the Law on Product Liability. Article 2 of the Law on Consumer Safety refers to guarantees which the consumer is *"entitled to expect"* with regard to safety and health protection. The General Product Safety Directive, on which the Law on Consumer Safety is based, indicates that a person is entitled to expect that a product will cause only *"the minimum risks compatible with the product's use, considered as acceptable and consistent with a high level of protection for the safety and health of persons"*. It must however be pointed out that the Law on Consumer Safety only takes into consideration the safety and health of persons, while the Law on Product Liability also refers to the safety of a person's private property.

3251. Article 3 of the Law on Consumer Safety establishes a link between the general safety requirement and the formulation of standards. When a product complies with EC or Belgian regulations or voluntary standards, that product is also presumed to meet the general safety requirement of the Law on Consumer Safety. However, this presumption can be rebutted where there is evidence that, despite the fact that the product complies with the standards, it is still dangerous. Therefore, it is evident that the product could also still be found to be defective under the Law on Product Liability if it had caused damage. This can be asserted even more strongly because the Preamble to the General Product Safety Directive makes clear that it does not affect "victims' rights" under the Product Liability Directive.

3252. Although the Laws on Product Liability and Consumer Safety present marked similarities, the most notable being that the definition of an "unsafe product" in the

Law on Consumer Safety is almost identical to the definition of "defective product" in the Product Liability Act, the 2 laws are nonetheless independent of each other in their effect. It is, however, probable that a court which has to decide whether a product is "defective" will also be inclined to consider the assessment criteria of the Law on Consumer Safety: if a product does not meet the safety requirement under the Law on Consumer Safety at the time when it is put into circulation, it will most likely be considered to be defective within the meaning of the Law on Product Liability; but a product may be "defective" in the sense of the Law on Product Liability even if it is considered "safe" under the relevant safety regulations because safety regulations only lay down minimal standards. In other words, an "unsafe" product is likely to be held to be "defective", in the sense of the Law on Product Liability; but the converse does not necessarily hold true: a "safe" product may still be "defective". However, if the product meets all state of the art standards which were, at the time that the product was put into circulation, commonly applied and recognised in the industry, it will, as a practical matter, be difficult for the claimant to demonstrate that the product was defective.

3253. The Law on Consumer Safety and the Law on Product Liability complement one another, forming different parts of an overall approach to ensure that only safe products are manufactured and placed on the market. The Law on Product Liability is a private law measure. Its aim is to provide compensation to individual victims who have suffered damage. Thus, it is an *ex post facto* measure, giving compensation after the event. It is aimed primarily at individual defective products; but the risk of having to pay damages will provide a strong incentive to ensure that an entire line of products is not defective. Its test for "defectiveness", while objective, is related to the circumstances surrounding the injury.

3254. The Law on Consumer Safety, on the other hand, is a public law measure concerned with prevention instead of compensation and public law instead of personal compensatory claims. It is aimed primarily at categories of products. Action is taken by the State, not individuals. The standard of what is "unsafe" is completely objective and the Law on Consumer Safety does not include defences for the producer as the Law on Product Liability does. It operates primarily as a preventive measure, being designed to ensure that dangerous products are withdrawn from the market before damage occurs. In this sense it can be said to operate in advance of the Law on Product Liability. However, it can also apply after the Law on Product Liability. Where an individual has suffered damage and brought a claim under product liability law, this may alert the appropriate national authority to the possibility that a product which it had not previously considered to be unsafe may in fact be so.

IV. IMPLIED WARRANTY

3255. A seller may be held liable for harm caused by a defective product on the basis of an implied warranty derived from general principles governing sales contracts. Article 1641 of the Civil Code holds the seller responsible for hidden defects in the product sold which render it unsuitable for the use for which it is intended, or which so diminish such use that the buyer would not have purchased it, or would have paid a lower price for it, had he known of them. Article 1643 of the Civil Code further specifies that the seller shall be liable for damage caused by hidden defects, even if he is unaware of their existence, unless he has contractually excluded his liability and stipulated that he would not be obligated for any guarantee.

A. Defect

3256. The term "defect" is defined in a broad manner in Article 1641 of the Civil Code as *"any defect which makes the product unsuitable for its intended use, or which diminishes this use to such an extent that, if the buyer had been aware of the existence of this defect, he would not have purchased the product or would only have paid a lower price"*. In short, the defect must be significant.

3257. Article 1641 of the Civil Code has been interpreted in the case law as including not only inherent or structural defects of products, but also so-called "functional defects", *i.e.*, defects which, even if they do not make the product inherently defective, render the product unfit for its intended use.

3258. A seller must be aware of the normal use and applications of the product (for example, ordinary use or use described in advertising) as well as of the specific use of the product, if this specific use was communicated by the buyer to the seller during the negotiations leading to the conclusion of the contract.

B. Existence of the defect prior to delivery

3259. A seller is, according to the traditional view, only liable for defects which existed prior to the conclusion of the sales contract, since it is at that point in time that the risks with respect to the goods are, as a general rule, passed on to the buyer. According to the dominant modern view, however, the point of reference is the delivery of the products rather than the conclusion of the agreement. The defect must have existed prior to the delivery of the goods to the buyer.

3260. It is sufficient that the essential elements of the defect existed in latent form prior to the delivery of the goods to the buyer. It is up to the buyer to prove that the defect existed, at least in a latent manner, at the moment that the contract was concluded or that the goods were delivered. The Belgian courts have, however, considerably reduced the burden of proof on the plaintiff by accepting that the plaintiff need only prove the probability of the existence of the defect at the moment that the contract was concluded or the goods were delivered.

3261. It will be recalled that under the Law on Product Liability the burden of proof is reversed on this particular point. The producer is deemed liable unless he proves that the defect did not exist at the moment he put the product into circulation (*See*, para. 3221).

C. Hidden defect

3262. The buyer may only initiate proceedings on the basis of Article 1641 of the Civil Code if he neither actually knew nor should have known of the defect. The buyer has no cause of action under Article 1641 of the Civil Code if the defect could, upon inspection of the goods or samples, be detected at the moment that the goods were delivered, or if the seller notified the buyer of the existence of the defect.

3263. According to case law on the subject, the buyer is deemed to know of defects which he could have detected by a *"diligent but normal examination of the goods immediately after delivery of the goods"*. In determining whether the buyer's examination of the goods was diligent, the technical knowledge which a buyer normally has on account of his professional expertise must be taken into account. "Normal examination" does not imply that the buyer must have recourse to unusual or onerous scientific testing.

3264. A defect will also be deemed hidden if the buyer did not have the practical opportunity to examine the goods upon delivery, provided the buyer was not negligent in any respect, or if the existence of the defect could only be ascertained after its use.

D. Remedies

3265. The remedies available to the buyer are very different depending on whether the seller was aware, or must be deemed to have been aware, of the defects at the time of the sale.

§1. Limited remedies if the seller was not aware of the defects ("good faith")

3266. If a seller is held liable on the basis of an implied warranty for hidden defects (Arts. 1641 and 1643 of the Civil Code), the buyer may request either that the contract be rescinded (reimbursement of the price paid to the buyer and return of the product to the seller), or opt to keep the product but receive reimbursement of part of the price to be determined by an expert (Art. 1644 of the Civil Code). If the sales contract is rescinded and the seller reimburses the sales price, he will also have to reimburse the buyer for the costs incurred by reason of the sales agreement (Art. 1646 of the Civil Code). These remedies are the only ones available to the buyer. For example, the buyer has no right to claim that the seller should repair or replace the defective product.

§2. Remedies if the seller was aware of the defects ("bad faith")

3267. A seller who knows or is, by operation of a legal presumption, deemed to know of the defect of the goods will, in addition to the remedies described above, be liable for all damage caused by the defective product (Art. 1645 of the Civil Code).

3268. In a well-established line of cases, the Belgian Supreme Court has held that professional sellers, such as manufacturers, importers, distributors, and retailers are presumed by law to be aware of the existence of any hidden defect affecting products which they sell (Cass., 9 October 1980, *J.T.*, 1981, 70; Cass., 28 February 1980, *R.W.*, 1980 – 1981, 2319). This presumption may be rebutted by the professional seller only if he can prove that it was absolutely impossible for him, given the state of technology, to know of the defect at the time of the sale of the product. Professional sellers rarely ever succeed in rebutting this presumption. The practical effect of the presumption is that professional sellers are under a duty to ensure that the goods which they market are free of defects.

3269. As indicated, if the seller was actually aware or presumed to be aware of the hidden defects, he will be held liable for all damages caused by the defect. The Supreme Court defines damages as *"every partial or total loss of a good that one owns or of an advantage that one could expect to obtain"* (Cass., 6 October 1961, *Pas.*, 1962, I, 153). Damage includes, *inter alia,* the following items: physical and emotional injury to a person, damage for the fact that the buyer could not use the product for a certain period of time, damage for the costs of repairing the product, loss of profit, damage to other products and damage for the cost of alternative transportation for the buyer.

§3. Remedies must be requested within a "brief period"

3270. Claims made on the basis of hidden defects must be brought within a "brief period" of time (Art. 1648 of the Civil Code). The law does not prescribe the exact length nor the starting point of this "brief period". Length and starting point will, in each particular case, be determined by the court, taking into account all the facts of the case (for example, the nature of the defect and the surrounding circumstances). The courts therefore enjoy a wide margin of discretion in this respect. For example, as to the starting point of the "brief period", this can either be the delivery date or the date of discovery of the defect. Given this margin of discretion, it is not possible to provide strict criteria on the acceptable length of the "brief period".

3271. It is accepted in the case law that, when there are extensive negotiations between the buyer and the seller regarding compensation for damage caused by a defect in the product, the "brief period" within which the buyer must institute legal proceedings is suspended. However, negotiations cannot suspend this period indefinitely. For example, a claim for damages was judged to have exceeded the time limit since it had been brought 15 months after it had become apparent that a settlement out of court could not be reached (Antwerp Court of Appeal, 5 December 1996, *A.J.T.*, 1997-1998, 78).

3272. The requirement of a "brief period" has been added in the interest of both the buyer and the seller: it should allow for an accurate assessment of the circumstances at the time of the sale and it reduces the possibility of (wrongfully) claiming that the defect originated only after the sale. (Antwerp Court of Appeal, 7 November 1995, *A.J.T.*, 1995-1996, 570)

E. Contractual defences

3273. Article 1643 of the Civil Code allows the seller to stipulate that he will not compensate or indemnify the buyer for hidden defects. However, such contractual exclusion of liability is valid only if the seller was not aware of the existence of the defects. Since professional sellers are deemed by law to be aware of the existence of defects in products (*See*, para. 3268), they may not exclude or otherwise limit their liability for hidden defects.

3274. This is a mandatory rule of law which is intended to protect the buyer and thus overrides any other contractual provision which is less advantageous for the buyer than the regime provided by the Civil Code (for example as regards the choice of remedies, the amount of damages and the time period within which the buyer must start legal proceedings). The parties may only validly deviate from the provisions of the Civil Code in a way which is detrimental to the buyer after the damage has occurred. The professional seller, at all levels of the distribution process, can only, by means of an express contractual clause to that effect, exonerate himself from responsibility for hidden defects in cases where it is absolutely impossible for him to know of the defects. In other words, the defect must be untraceable. This requirement is interpreted very strictly by the Belgian courts. For instance, in 1990, the Supreme Court decided that the untraceability of the defect must not depend on the technical means and competence of the particular seller (Cass. 7 December

1990, *Arr. Cass.*, 1990-91, 391). Thus, the relevant jurisprudence comes close to recognising the strict liability of the seller regarding hidden defects.

F. Direct claims against suppliers of the seller

3275. The case law has extended the scope of liability for hidden defects under Article 1641 to 1649 of the Civil Code so as to make them more suitable in the context of product liability claims by severely limiting the concept of privity of contract. It is accepted under Belgian law that a person who suffers damage caused by a product which he has bought not only has a cause of action against his immediate contracting party (the seller), but also has a direct claim against any previous seller of the defective product (Ghent Court of Appeal, 13 November 1978, *R.W.*, 1979 – 1980, 132; Brussels Court of Appeal, 27 November 1963, *Pas.*, 1965, II, 52). Thus, a consumer who has bought a defective product from a retailer may sue the wholesaler, the importer and even the manufacturer in addition to the retailer with which he has a direct contractual relationship.

3276. Foreign manufacturers should not rely too much on jurisdictional defences to escape liability since a Belgian court may entertain jurisdiction over foreign defendants if at least one of the co-defendants (for example, the Belgian importer) has been properly sued before that Belgian court (*See*, para. 3645).

G. Concurrent liability

3277. As has already been mentioned with regard to the Law on Product Liability (*See*, paras. 3225 *et seq.*), there exists a possibility of concurrent liability. Sometimes, one can identify different causes of the damage sustained, apart from a defect in the product at hand. This will in most cases lead to a division of liability for the damage.

V. TORT LIABILITY

3278. Product liability claims may also be based on general principles of tort law, which are found in Articles 1382 to 1386*bis* of the Civil Code. Articles 1382 and 1383 cover damage caused by negligence, Article 1384, paragraph 1 covers damage caused by defective products and Article 1386 covers damage caused by collapsing buildings.

A. Negligence (Arts. 1382 – 1383 of the Civil Code)

§1. Basic principles

3279. Anyone who through his negligence injures another person is liable for this injury. Article 1382 of the Civil Code applies this principle to negligent acts. Article 1383 of the Civil Code applies it to negligent omissions.

3280. To recover damages, the injured person must establish the existence of the following 3 elements:
  (i) a negligent act or omission;
  (ii) injury which he has sustained; and
  (iii) a causal relationship between the negligent act or omission and the injury.

§2. Application to defective products

3281. Producers and distributors may be negligent in various circumstances. The case law, especially in recent years, has held that manufacturers and professional sellers are under a strict obligation not to put into circulation a product which is liable to injure persons or property (Brussels Court of Appeal, 13 November 1987, *J.M.L.B.*, 1987, 1460). A breach of this safety obligation amounts to a fault within the meaning of Articles 1382 and 1383 (*ibid.*). Liability can only be avoided if evidence is put forward that the professional seller was absolutely unaware of the existence of the defect (*ibid.*). The victim must prove that the defect existed at the time the product was put into circulation (Cass., 7 September 1984, *Pas.*, 1985, I. 35). Thus, the standards of behaviour imposed by principles of tort liability on manufacturers or professional sellers of defective products are very similar to those imposed by the principles pursuant to which professional sellers are held liable for hidden defects (Arts. 1641 and following of the Civil Code, *See*, para. 3268). If a manufacturer does not respect technical or safety standards contained in a legal or regulatory provision, that will be in and of itself sufficient to establish the existence of negligence. If such negligence causes harm, the manufacturer will be held liable for the damage.

3282. Manufacturers may also be held negligent for not disclosing adequate information on the use of or the risks inherent in their products. The use of inadequate packaging materials may, in certain circumstances, also amount to negligence.

§3. Remedies

3283. A person who through his negligence has harmed another person is, in principle, held liable for all damage resulting from the negligence. As indicated earlier (*See*, para. 3269), damage is defined as any partial or total loss of a good that one owns or of an advantage that one could expect to obtain (Cass., 6 October 1961, *Pas.*, 1962, I, *153*).

§4. Time limits

3284. Actions based on Arts. 1382 or 1383 of the Civil Code are in principle only time-barred after a period of 5 years (*i.e.*, combined with a maximum prescription period of 20 years as of the moment that the damage is incurred) as of the moment that the party suffering damage has learned of this damage and of the identity of the negligent party.

B. Tort liability for defective products (Art. 1384(1) of the Civil Code)

§1. Basic principles

3285. Pursuant to Article 1384(1) of the Civil Code, the keeper of a product is liable for damage caused to third parties by a defect in the product.

3286. The injured person must prove the existence of:
   (i) a defect in the product;
   (ii) damage which he has sustained; and
   (iii) a causal relationship between the defect and the damage.

3287. Article 1384, paragraph 1 of the Civil Code imposes liability without fault in that the conduct of the keeper of the product has no bearing on the issue of liability.

3288. The mere existence of a defect in the product is enough to establish liability provided that the other 2 conditions are met.

§2. Application to defective products

3289. Article 1384(1) of the Civil Code applies to all products movable or immovable, except to animals and buildings which are governed respectively by Articles 1385 and 1386 of the Civil Code.

3290. The mere fact that a product has caused damage is not sufficient to conclude the existence of a defect within the meaning of Article 1384, paragraph 1 of the Civil Code (Cass., 18 September 1980, *R.W.*, 1981-1982, 29). This requires evidence showing the existence of an *"abnormal situation which is liable to cause damage"* (Cass., 6 March 1981, *R.W.*, 1981-1982, 31).

3291. Although specifically intended to apply to liability for damage caused by defective products, Article 1384(1) of the Civil Code, has not evolved into a broad standard governing all or most product liability situations. The main reason is that Article 1384(1) of the Civil Code applies to the keeper of a defective product, rather than to its producer or supplier.

3292. The keeper of a product within the meaning of Article 1384, paragraph 1 of the Civil Code is the person who, for his own account, uses the product and benefits from it, or who takes care of its maintenance and has the authority, supervision and control over the product (Cass., 11 September 1980, *R.W.*, 1981-1982, 27). Attempts made by some lower courts to extend the notion of keeper of the product to producers or suppliers have been resisted.

§3. Remedies

3293. The remedies available under Article 1384, paragraph 1 of the Civil Code are identical to those available under Articles 1382 and 1383 of the Civil Code. The keeper of the defective product will be held to compensate for all damage which is the necessary consequence of the defect.

C. Liability for collapsing buildings (Art. 1386 of the Civil Code)

3294. Pursuant to Article 1386 of the Civil Code, the owner of a building is liable for damage caused by the total or partial collapse of the building when this is due to a lack of maintenance or to a construction defect.

D. Time Limits

3295. The Law of 10 June 1998 introduced new time limits for procedures under the Civil Code to replace the existing general time limit of 30 years. The new rules apply (non-retroactively) from 27 July 1998 onward.

3296. The Law of 10 June 1998 essentially distinguishes between 2 kinds of claims:

§1. Personal claims

3297. Personal claims are those which aim at enforcing obligations (except those originating from tort), the enforcement of judgments and events of nullity. All personal claims are restricted in time to 10 years (Art. 2262*bis*, para. 1 of the Civil Code).

§2. Claims regarding tort liability

1. If the tortious act is not a criminal offence

3298. In this case, the claim expires after 5 years following the day on which the injured party learned of the damage or its increase and of the identity of the person responsible. In any case, the claim can only be brought within 20 years, following the day on which the fact that caused the damage took place.

2. If the torteous act is a criminal offence

3299. The same time limits apply, except for the fact that the civil claim can never expire before the criminal claim (Art. 26 of the Title Preceding the Code of Criminal Procedure). This may occur more frequently than one would think: Belgian authorities have in the past frequently extended the criminal offence of "involuntary wounding" to cases of unsafe product in case of bodily harm to the user.

E. Contractual limitation or exclusion of tort liability

3300. Under Belgian law, parties to an agreement may stipulate clauses that limit or exclude their liability. Such exoneration clauses are generally speaking perfectly legal, although they will be interpreted restrictively (Art. 1162 of the Civil Code). Thus, the courts have decided that an exoneration clause will not be deemed to include exoneration for a serious fault or for tort liability, unless the relevant clause is sufficiently specific on these issues.

3301. There are some exceptions to the general rule of validity of exoneration clauses:
    (i) a party may not exonerate himself/herself for his/her own deception or intentional fault;
    (ii) an exoneration clause must not have the effect of rendering the agreement devoid of meaning or purpose; and
    (iii) specific regulation may prohibit the application of exoneration clauses in certain sectors (*e.g.*, in the air transport sector the Warsaw Treaty).

VI. FUTURE LEGISLATION ON THE SALE OF CONSUMER GOODS

3302. On 7 July 2001, the European Parliament and EC Council Directive No. 1999/44 of 25 May 1999 on the Sale of Consumer Goods and Associated Guarantees was published in the *Official Journal of the European Communities* ("Directive No. 1999/44") (O.J. [1999] L 171/12). It must be implemented in the EC Member States by 1 January 2002.

A. Objectives

3303. The objectives of the Directive No. 1999/44 are: (i) to provide consumers (*i.e.*, any natural person who, in the contracts covered by Directive No. 1999/44, is acting for purposes which are not related to his trade, business or profession) with a uniform minimum level of legal rights to remedies in the event of non-conformity of a product with the contract of sale existing at the time of delivery, and (ii) to ensure that guarantees offered voluntarily by sellers and manufacturers are clearly understood by consumers.

B. Main features

§1. Conformity with the contract

3304. Sellers must deliver to the consumer only such goods as are in conformity with the contract of sale. A presumption that goods are in conformity will exist where the goods (i) comply with the seller's description; (ii) are fit for the purpose required by the consumer as made known by him to the seller; (iii) are fit for their normal intended purpose; and (iv) show the quality and performance normally expected of products of this type, taking into account considerations such as the nature of the goods.

3305. There will be no lack of conformity if the consumer knew, or ought reasonably to have known, of the lack of conformity, or if the lack of conformity came about as a result of materials supplied by the consumer himself. Moreover, although a seller must normally stand by any statements he has made to the consumer, he will not be bound by statements made (e.g., on his behalf) of which he was not himself aware, or if the statement were corrected in time, or if he can show that the consumer would not have been influenced by such a statement in any event.

3306. Any lack of conformity resulting from incorrect installation of the goods will be deemed lack of conformity of the goods themselves, if the installation was part of the contract of sale.

§2. The consumers' remedies

3307. The hierarchy of remedies for the consumer are as follows: in the first instance, the consumer is entitled to have the goods repaired or replaced, at no expense to the consumer, unless these remedies prove impossible or disproportionate. A remedy is considered to be "disproportionate" if it imposes costs on the seller which, in comparison with the alternative remedy, are unreasonable, taking into account the value of the goods, the significance of the defect and whether the alternative remedy could be completed without significant inconvenience to the consumer. In order to determine whether the costs are "unreasonable", the costs of one remedy should be "significantly higher" than the costs of the other remedy.

3308. In any case, repair or replacement must be carried out within a reasonable time and without significant inconvenience to the consumer.

3309. The consumer may ask for a price reduction or a refund in the following instances:
   (i) if the consumer is not entitled to require repair or replacement (*i.e.*, if such remedies are either impossible or disproportionate, as explained above);
   (ii) if the seller has not completed the repair or replacement within a reasonable time; or
   (iii) if the seller has not completed the remedy without significant inconvenience to the consumer.

3310. However, contractual rescission and refund will not be allowed if the lack of conformity with the contract is "minor".

§3. The seller's right of redress

3311. Where the final seller is liable to a consumer as a result of lack of conformity with the contract resulting from an act or omission of the producer or a previous seller, Directive No. 1999/44 entitles him to pursue remedies against the person or persons who are liable in the contractual chain. Directive No. 1999/44 leaves it up to national law to determine the claims that can be made, the person or persons who are liable, and the procedure.

§4. Time limits

3312. Directive No. 1999/44 grants all consumers, irrespective of where they purchase goods in the European Union, a legal guarantee of 2 years against the seller from the moment the goods are delivered.

3313. Member States may provide that in order for the consumer to benefit from these rights, the consumer must inform the seller of the lack of conformity within a period of 2 months from the date on which he detected the lack of conformity. If a Member State decides to avail itself of this option, it must notify the EC Commission.

3314. During the first 6 months, the consumer will not have to prove the lack of conformity with the sales contract; such lack of conformity is presumed to have existed at the time of delivery.

§5. The Commercial guarantee

3315. The provision or a commercial guarantee is voluntary but any guarantee offered by the seller or the producer must not mislead the consumer. Certain transparency requirements are set out: (i) the commercial guarantee must clearly state that the consumer has rights under national legislation and that those rights are not affected by it; (ii) it must set out in plain language the contents and the essential steps for making claims under the guarantee; and (iii) on request by the consumer, it must be made available in writing or feature in another durable medium available and accessible to him. Moreover, where goods are marketed on the national territory of an EC Member State, the latter can require that the guarantee be drafted in one or more specified languages of the European Union.

§6. Rights cannot be waived

3316. The consumer's rights which are provided by Directive No. 1999/44 cannot be waived by him in any contractual terms or agreements concluded with the seller before the lack of conformity is brought to the seller's attention.

§7. Second-hand goods

3317. EC Member States can provide, in the case of second-hand goods, that the seller and consumer may agree on a period shorter than 2 years for the liability of the seller. However, such period cannot be less than one year.

§8. Minimum protection

3318. EC Member States may adopt or maintain in force more stringent provisions (as long as they are compatible with the EC Treaty) to ensure a higher level of protection.

§9. Entry into force

3319. The EC Member States are required to ensure that Directive No. 1999/44 will be implemented and enter into force by 1 January 2001. The Commission is then required to review the application of this Directive no later than 7 July 2006.

C. Implementation into Belgian law

3320. At the time of publication, the Ministry of Justice has tabled a proposal of amendments to the Civil Code, intended to implement Directive No. 1999/44 into the Belgian legal system.

3321. Essentially, the proposed amendments (to date still a mere working document) consist of an addition to the present article 1604 of the Civil Code and the creation of a new sub-section in the chapter regarding the obligations of the seller (book III, title VI, chapter IV of the Civil Code).

3322. Article 1604 of the Civil Code defines the concept of "delivery" in the context of a sales contract. According to the proposal, it is to be supplemented with a clause stating that the seller is obliged to deliver to the buyer a good which is in conformity with the agreement.

3323. The new sub-section, consisting of articles 1649*bis* to 1649*octies* of the Civil Code, is a more or less literal transposition into Belgian law of the content of Directive No. 1999/44 as described above (*See*, paras. 3302 *et seq*.). It may however be noted that the present text does not include a strict 2 month time limit for the consumer in order to notify a lack of conformity to the seller (*See*, para. 3313). Rather, seller and consumer may agree upon the relevant notice period, yet the proposal explicitly provides for a *minimum* term of 2 months.

3324. Any infringement of this new sub-section will be cause for a cease-and-desist order pursuant to relevant provisions of Belgian commercial law (*e.g.*, Law on Unfair Trade Practices, Law of 2 August 2002 concerning Misleading and Comparative Advertising, unfair contract terms and long-distance agreements regarding independent professions). Also the relevant provisions of the Judicial Code and the Law on Consumer Safety will be amended.

19. DATA PROTECTION

I. INTRODUCTION

3325. The purpose of Belgian data protection law is to ensure that the processing of personal data involving an individual does not violate that individual's privacy or fundamental rights and freedoms.

3326. The first set of rules governing the processing of personal data was introduced in Belgium by the Law of 8 December 1992 on the Protection of Privacy with regard to the Processing of Personal Data (*Wet tot bescherming van de persoonlijke levensfeer ten opzichte van de verwerking van persoonsgegevens/Loi relative à la protection de la vie privée à l'égard des traitement de données à caractère personnel*) (the "Data Protection Law"). The EC Data Protection Directive 95/46 (the "Data Protection Directive") (O.J. [1995] L 281/31) was later adopted at the European level. The Data Protection Directive sets out a more comprehensive and protective data protection regime than that already in force under the 1992 version of the Data Protection Law. The Data Protection Law of 11 December 1998 modified the 1992 version of the Data Protection Law in order to implement the Data Protection Directive in Belgium. This new regime entered into force on 1 September 2001, together with the implementing Royal Decree of 13 February 2001 (the "Royal Decree" of 13 February 2001).

3327. In addition to this general data protection regime, another EC Directive, Directive 97/66/EC on Privacy in the Telecommunications Sector ("Directive No. 97/66") (O.J. [1997] L 24/1), creates additional rules supplementing the Data Protection Directive in the field of privacy in the telecommunications sector. The implementation of Directive No. 97/66 in Belgium took place through the modification of several pieces of legislation, such as the Law of 14 July 1991 on Trade Practices and the Information and Protection of Consumers (*Wet betreffende de handelspraktijken en de voorlichting en bescherming van de consument/Loi sur les pratiques du commerce et sur l'information et la protection du consommateur*) (the "Law on Unfair Trade Practices"), and the Law of 21 March 1991 reforming Certain Public Economic Undertakings (*Wet betreffende de hervorming van sommige economische overheidsbedrijven/Loi portant réforme de certaines entreprises publiques économiques*) (the "Law on Public Undertakings"). A new Directive No. 2002/58/EC on Privacy and Electronic Communications (the "Directive No. 2002/58") (O.J.

[2002] L 201/37), which was published on 31 July 2002 and will have to be implemented in Belgium by 31 October 2003, is due to replace Directive No. 97/66 in the near future.

3328. The processing of personal data can only take place in a number of specific situations listed in the Data Protection Law. Personal data cannot otherwise be processed. But even among the authorised forms of processing, only those complying with a set of fundamental principles will be considered legitimate.

3329. In Sections II and III below, the definitions and main actors of the Data Protection Law as well as the scope of the Data Protection Law will be described. Section IV will address the extensive list of situations in which the processing of personal data is permitted. A set of fundamental principles will be examined in Section V. Sections VI and VII will discuss 2 special situations, namely the processing of special categories of data and the conservation or further processing of personal data beyond the original purpose for which they were collected. The rights of data subjects and the obligations of data controllers will be reviewed in Sections VIII and IX. Section X will address the allocation of responsibility and the criminal sanctions provided for by the Data Protection Law. Section XI will briefly discuss rules applying to the processing of data by public authorities. Section XII will deal with the particular requirements applicable to the transfer of personal data to non-EC countries. Section XIII will address the public register of automatic processing. Lastly, Section XIV will discuss the special data protection rules applicable to specific sectors. The implementation in Belgium of Directive No. 97/66 and the changes brought about by Directive No. 2002/58 will also be addressed in this final section.

II. DEFINITIONS AND MAIN ACTORS IN THE PROCESSING OF PERSONAL DATA

A. Personal Data and Data Subject

3330. The Data Protection Law regulates the processing of "Personal Data". Personal Data are defined in the Data Protection Law as any information relating to an identified or identifiable natural person, *i.e.*, the "Data Subject". In contrast, the processing of data relating to a legal entity is not caught by the Data Protection Law.

3331. Data Subjects are granted specific rights in respect of the processing of their Personal Data. These rights are designed to guarantee the protection of the Data Subject's privacy (*See*, para. 3384 *et seq.*).

3332. A person will be "identifiable" as soon as there is an objective possibility to identify him or her directly or indirectly by any reasonable means (*e.g.*, through a third person, a social security number), be it by the holder of the data or by any other person.

3333. Conversely, data which do not make the identification of the Data Subject possible (anonymous data) will fall outside the scope of the Data Protection Law.

B. Processing

3334. The notion of "processing" is very comprehensive. It encompasses any operation or set of operations involving Personal Data, whether or not by automatic means, such as the collection, recording, organisation, storage, adaptation, alteration, retrieval, consultation, use, disclosure by transmission, dissemination or otherwise making available, alignment, combination, as well as blocking, erasure or destruction of Personal Data. The same regime applies to all these uses of Personal Data.

C. Controller

3335. The natural person or legal entity who determines, alone or jointly with others, the purposes and means of such processing will be the "Controller" of the Personal Data.

3336. As a corollary to the rights of the Data Subject, the Data Protection Law imposes a number of obligations and restrictions on the Controller (*See*, paras. 3394 *et seq.*).

D. Processor

3337. The person actually processing the information is the "Processor". This person could either be the Controller or another person, acting as a subcontractor on the Controller's behalf and under its authority.

E. Privacy Commission

3338. The Data Protection Law created an independent body responsible for ensuring compliance with its provisions, the Privacy Commission (*Commissie voor de bescherming van de persoonlijke levenssfeer/Commission de la protection de la vie privée* – Arts. 23 through 36 of the Data Protection Law). The Privacy Commission is mainly responsible for centralising the information that Controllers have to communicate to it prior to initiating a form of Data Processing; checking the legitimacy of the form of processing notified; and giving opinions on specific data protection issues (such as Opinion No. 37/2001 of 8 October 2001 on the data protection issues raised by the census organised by the National Office for Statistics).

III. SCOPE OF THE DATA PROTECTION LAW

A. Applicability of Belgian law

3339. The Data Protection Law only applies to Controllers having a permanent establishment in Belgium. A Controller located in another EC Member State is governed by the law of that EC Member State. When the Controller is established outside of the EC, the Data Protection Law will still apply if the Controller, for purposes of processing Personal Data, makes use of equipment situated in Belgium, unless such equipment is used only for the purposes of transit over Belgian territory (Art. 3*bis* of the Data Protection Law).

3340. Controllers based outside the European Union but using equipment situated in Belgium must designate a representative in Belgium.

B. Forms of processing specifically excluded

3341. Article 3 of the Data Protection Law specifically provides for several exemptions from all or part of its provisions.

3342. The processing of Personal Data carried out by a natural person in the course of purely personal or household activities is totally exempted.

3343. The processing of Personal Data carried out solely for journalistic purposes or for the purpose of artistic or literary expression is exempted from several important provisions of the Data Protection Law.

3344. The processing of Personal Data in the context of police, intelligence and national security activities is also exempted from the application of a range of important provisions. However, the Data Subject's rights (*See*, paras. 3384 *et seq.*) are protected indirectly through the supervision exercised by the Privacy Commission (*See*, para. 3425).

IV. PERMITTED FORMS OF PROCESSING

3345. Article 5 of the Data Protection Law lists the situations in which the processing of Personal Data is considered legitimate. There can be no processing that does not come under one of the following categories:

A. Consent

3346. Personal Data can first be processed if the Data Subject has unambiguously given his or her consent to such processing. The Data Subject's consent is defined as any freely given, specific and informed indication of an agreement to the processing of Personal Data.

B. Performance of a contract

3347. The processing of Personal Data will also be allowed when the processing is necessary for the performance of a contract to which the Data Subject is a party or in order to take steps at the request of the Data Subject prior to entering into a contract.

C. Compliance with a legal obligation

3348. The Controller can also process Personal Data when the processing is necessary for compliance with an obligation to which the Controller is subject by law, such as the processing of personal data by employers in order to comply with their social security obligations.

D. Protection of the Data Subject's vital interests

3349. The processing will equally be authorised in situations where it is necessary to protect the vital interests of the Data Subject. This only covers processing essential to the Data Subject's life (*e.g.*, in case of medical emergency).

E. Public interest

3350. The processing is furthermore allowed when it is necessary for the performance of a task carried out in the public interest or for the exercise of official authority vested in the Controller or in a third party to whom the Personal Data are disclosed. This covers the processing of Personal Data by the authorities and the public sector, or by private entities fulfilling a task of the competence of the public sector.

F. Legitimate interest of the Controller

3351. Finally, the Controller will have the right to process Personal Data where the processing is necessary for the purposes of the legitimate interests pursued by the Controller or by a third party to whom the data are disclosed, provided that the interests or fundamental rights and freedoms of the Data Subject should not prevail over those of the Controller. This is a residual category allowing controllers to process Personal Data even though such processing cannot be justified otherwise, *e.g.*, on the ground that it is necessary for the performance of a contract or required by law. The specific circumstances of each processing operation will determine whether the interests of the Controller override the rights of the Data Subject. For example, an employer could justify the processing of Personal Data in order to create badges restricting access to its premises, on the grounds that it has a legitimate interest to do so. However, security measures cannot be authorised under this exception if they are excessive or do not otherwise comply with the fundamental principles listed below (*See*, paras. 3352 *et seq.*).

V. DATA PROTECTION PRINCIPLES

A. Preliminary Observations

3352. As briefly explained in paragraph 3328 above, it is not enough for a form of processing to fall within one of the categories listed in order to be legal. The processing activities must also comply with a number of fundamental principles that seek to protect the Data Subject's privacy and fundamental rights and freedoms. These principles are enumerated in Article 4 of the Data Protection Law.

3353. It is the Controller's responsibility to ensure that these principles are complied with (*See*, paras. 3423 and 3424).

B. Fair and lawful processing

3354. Personal Data must be processed fairly and lawfully. The fairness requirement essentially refers to the necessity that the processing be carried out in a transparent manner. A form of processing will be lawful if it complies with all applicable legal requirements.

C. Data collected for a specified, explicit and legitimate purpose

3355. Personal Data can only be collected for specified, explicit and legitimate purposes and should not be further processed in a way incompatible with those purposes. Consideration should be had for all relevant factors, in particular the reasonable expectations of the Data Subject and applicable statutory and regulatory provisions. This is a principle holding significant practical consequences for Controllers. It implies that Controllers must know, before collecting Personal Data, the purposes for which these data are collected. In addition, once collected, the data cannot be processed for a purpose different from the original purpose.

3356. In case the Controller intends to process Personal Data in a way that is not compatible with the initial purpose, this is a new form of processing that must comply with all the requirements of the Data Protection Law (especially the obligations to inform the Data Subject (*See*, paras. 3394 through 3407) and to notify the Commission (*See*, paras. 3412 through 3420).

D. Data must be adequate, relevant and not excessive

3357. The Personal Data must be adequate, relevant and not excessive in relation to the purposes for which they are processed.

E. Data must be accurate and, if necessary, kept up-to-date

3358. The Personal Data must be accurate, and if necessary, kept up-to-date. Every reasonable step should be taken in order to ensure that inaccurate or incomplete data are erased or rectified.

F. Data cannot be kept for longer than is necessary

3359. Finally, the Personal Data cannot be kept in a form that permits identification of Data Subjects for longer than is necessary for the purposes for which they were collected or for which they are further processed. If the Controller wishes to retain Personal Data for a longer period of time, these data will have to be made anonymous.

VI. SPECIAL CATEGORIES OF DATA

A. Principle

3360. The Data Protection Law creates a more restrictive regime for certain categories of data the processing of which is considered to pose a greater threat to the privacy and fundamental rights and freedoms of the Data Subject. The processing of these data is as a general rule prohibited, subject to limited exceptions.

3361. When the processing of special categories of data is authorised, the information to be communicated to the Data Subject and to the Privacy Commission is more exhaustive and more detailed (*See*, paras. 3399 and 3400).

B. Sensitive Personal Data

3362. Article 6 of the Data Protection Law prohibits the processing of certain so-called "sensitive data". These are data revealing racial or ethnic origin, political opinions, religious or philosophical beliefs and trade-union membership, as well as data concerning sex life.

3363. However, in certain exceptional cases these data may be processed. These exceptional situations involve the written consent of the Data Subject, on the understanding that this consent may be withdrawn by the Data Subject at any time; the obligation to comply with labour law or social security law obligations; or the fact that the data had already been made public by the Data Subject.

C. Health-Related Personal Data

3364. According to Article 7 of the Data Protection Law, the processing of health-related Personal Data is also prohibited, except in a limited number of cases. The most important exceptions are: (i) the written consent of the Data Subject, on the understanding that this consent may be withdrawn at any time; (ii) the obligation to comply with labour law, social security law or other legal requirements stemming from important public interest concerns; (iii) scientific research; or (iv) situations where the processing is necessary for the medical treatment of the Data Subject.

3365. Health-related Personal Data have to be processed under the responsibility of a health professional, unless the Data Subject has agreed in writing that such processing can take place without it being supervised by a health professional (Art. 7, para. 4 of the Data Protection Law).

3366. Health-related Personal Data must be collected directly from the Data Subject. However, they can be collected from other sources if this is necessary to the purpose of the processing or if the Data Subject is incapable of procuring the data (Art. 7, para. 5 of the Data Protection Law).

D. Personal Data relating to judicial and administrative proceedings

3367. Article 8 of the Data Protection Law prohibits the processing of Personal Data related to judicial or administrative proceedings apart from a number of exceptional cases. The processing of Personal Data relating to judicial and administrative proceedings will for instance be authorised when such processing is required by law; is performed by or under the supervision of the authorities; or is performed by individuals or companies, or by their counsel, when dealing with litigation to which they are a party.

E. Impact of the dependent position of the Data Subject

3368. The Royal Decree of 13 February 2001 specifies that the Processing of sensitive, health-related or judicial Personal Data authorised in writing by the Data Subject will still be prohibited if the Data Subject was placed in a dependent position *vis-à-vis* the Controller (Art. 27 of the Royal Decree of 13 February 2001). This will be deemed to be the case if the Controller is the current or potential employer of the Data Subject. This prohibition is lifted if the purpose of the processing is to grant an advantage to the Data Subject.

VII. CONSERVATION AND FURTHER PROCESSING OF PERSONAL DATA FOR HISTORICAL, STATISTICAL AND SCIENTIFIC PURPOSES

A. Introduction

3369. Exceptionally, storage or further processing of Personal Data (*i.e.*, for another purpose than that declared to the Data Subject and the Privacy Commission – *See*, paras. 3394 through 3407 and 3412 through 3420) will be allowed if it takes place for historical, statistical or scientific purposes (Art. 4, para. 1, 2 and 5 of the Data Protection Law) and provided the data were collected in conformity with the fundamental principles discussed above (*See*, paras. 3352 *et seq.*). The original Controller will be allowed to process the Personal Data further, or to transfer them to another Controller for further processing. The conditions under which such processing and storage will be admitted are stipulated in Articles 2 through 24 of the Royal Decree of 13 February 2001.

B. Definitions

3370. The Royal Decree of 13 February 2001 distinguishes between non-coded Personal Data, coded Personal Data and anonymous data:
   (i) non-coded Personal Data involve any form of information relating to an identified or identifiable natural person;
   (ii) coded Personal Data are Personal Data which will only allow the identification of the Data Subject through the use of a code;
   (iii) anonymous data are data which cannot be used to identify the Data Subject and are therefore not Personal Data.

3371. Historical, statistical and scientific purposes relate to a broad range of activities, including pure scientific research, at one end of the spectrum, as well as customer behaviour studies carried out to establish general consumption patterns, at the other end.

C. Regime

3372. As a general principle, the further processing of Personal Data for historical, statistical and scientific purposes should be performed on Anonymous Data only (Art. 3 of the Royal Decree of 13 February 2001).

3373. However, if the processing of anonymous data is not sufficient in order to fulfil the purpose of the processing, coded Personal Data (Art. 4 of the Royal Decree of 13 February 2001) or even non-coded Personal Data (Art. 5 of the Royal Decree of 13 February 2001) can be used instead. The further processing of coded and non-coded Personal Data will be subject to similar requirements of notification to the Privacy Commission and communication of specific information to the Data Subject (*See*, paras. 3376 *et seq.*).

3374. The coding of the Personal Data has to be performed before any further processing (Art. 7 of the Royal Decree of 13 February 2001) or transfer to a third party (Art. 9 of the Royal Decree of 13 February 2001).

3375. Situations where there is more than one Controller and the coded Personal Data are transferred to one or more third parties for further processing pose a greater threat to data protection. In such situations, the coding of the Personal Data can only be performed by an intermediary. In this case, the intermediary (who is otherwise regarded by the Royal Decree of 13 February 2001 as being a subcontracting

Processor) will have to be independent and will be considered to be the Controller of the further processing and, as such, will be primarily liable for any breach of the Data Protection Law (Arts. 10 and 11 of the Royal Decree of 13 February 2001).

D. Obligations of the Controller and intermediary in case of further processing of non-anonymous data (Arts. 12 through 21 of the Royal Decree of 13 February 2001)

3376. The main obligations of the original Controller are, prior to the further processing or transfer to a third party, to notify the Privacy Commission of the intended further processing and to provide adequate technical and organisational safeguards to ensure that the coding of the Personal Data is effective.

3377. The original Controller, or the intermediary, can only communicate the coded Personal Data to those persons presenting to them the acknowledgement of receipt of a valid notification to the Privacy Commission. This ensures that the recipient of the data has complied with the notification requirement (*See*, paras. 3412 *et seq.*).

3378. The further processing of coded or non-coded health-related or judicial Personal Data for historical, statistical or scientific purposes will only be allowed if the Controller or the intermediary (whichever performs the coding of the Personal Data) has communicated specific information to the Data Subject and advised same of his or her right to object to the processing (*See*, paras. 3392, 3401 and 3402).

3379. In addition, the Data Subject must explicitly consent to the further processing of non-coded Personal Data (Art. 19 of the Royal Decree of 13 February 2001).

3380. However, if the original Controller or the intermediary considers that to inform the Data Subject of the envisaged processing would be impossible or require disproportionate efforts, they may refrain from doing so. The only requirement imposed on them is to communicate detailed information to the Privacy Commission, which can issue a non-binding recommendation within a period of 90 days. After the expiry of this 90-day period, the Controller may proceed with the processing.

3381. As regards sensitive, health-related or judicial Personal Data, the Controller will be exempted from informing the Data Subject of the envisaged processing if these data were made publicly available by the Data Subject or if these data are closely related to the public character of the Data Subject or to public events in which he or she was or is involved.

E. Publication of the results of the further processing (Art. 23 of the Royal Decree of 13 February 2001)

3382. The publication of the results of the processing must not allow for the identification of the Data Subject unless the Data Subject gave his or her explicit consent and the privacy of third parties is not affected; or the Personal Data being processed were made publicly available by the Data Subject or these data are closely related to the public status of the Data Subject or to public events he or she was or is involved in.

F. General exception (Art. 24 of the Royal Decree of 13 February 2001)

3383. The rules discussed above do not apply to Personal Data processed for historical, statistical and scientific purposes by armed forces, intelligence services and other departments linked to national security.

VIII. RIGHTS OF THE DATA SUBJECT

A. Right of access (Art. 10 of the Data Protection Law)

3384. The Data Subject has the right to obtain confirmation from the Controller as to whether Personal Data are being processed as well as information on the purposes of such processing, the categories of Personal Data concerned and the categories of recipients to whom the data are disclosed. Furthermore, the Data Subject has the right to obtain communication of such Personal Data and any information as to their source in an intelligible form. In case of automatic processing of Personal Data, the Data Subject has the right to be informed of the logic underlying the automation.

3385. The Data Subject has the right to be informed, either directly or with the help of a healthcare professional, of his health-related Personal Data that are being processed. However, the disclosure of those data can be postponed if the immediate disclosure would interfere with the research for which the data are being processed.

3386. The Controller or the Processor must communicate the requested information to the Data Subject within 45 days of the latter's request.

B. Right to have the data corrected or erased (Art. 12, sections 1 and 4 of the Data Protection Law)

3387. Any Data Subject has the right to obtain, free of charge, the rectification of inaccurate Personal Data.

3388. The Data Subject also has the right to obtain, free of charge, the erasure of all Personal Data. In addition, the Data Subject has the right to forbid the use of all Personal Data (i) that are incomplete or irrelevant in view of the purpose of the processing, (ii) the recording, communication or storage of which are prohibited, or (iii) that have been stored for longer than the authorised period of time. It is only inasmuch as the Personal Data are incomplete or not necessary in view of the purpose of the processing that the data will have to be erased or corrected. If, for instance, the processing is mandated by law, the Data Subject will only be able to have his or her Personal Data corrected or erased if these data are not necessary in order to fulfil such purpose.

3389. The Controller will have one month to rectify or erase the Personal Data upon reception of the Data Subject's request. Within this period, it will also have to notify the rectification or the erasure to the persons who received these Personal Data, if (i) it still has knowledge of the addressees of the communication and (ii) if such notification does not appear to be impossible or to involve a disproportionate effort (Art. 12, section 3 of the Data Protection Law).

C. Right to object (Art. 12, paras. 2 and 3 of the Data Protection Law)

3390. Data Subjects have the right to object to the processing of Personal Data for serious and legitimate reasons having regard to their specific situation. This applies to processing operations which would otherwise be lawful (*e.g.*, because they are necessary in order to perform a contract concluded with the Data Subject) but, given the specific situation of the Data Subject, may not be carried out.

3391. Furthermore, this right to object is unconditional for Personal Data processed for direct marketing purposes. In this case, Data Subjects must specifically be asked whether they wish to object to the envisaged processing (*See*, paras. 3408 *et seq.*).

3392. The right to object is also unconditional in case of further processing of sensitive, health-related or judicial Personal Data for historical, statistical or scientific purposes (*See*, paras. 3378 and 3401).

D. Exercise of rights (Arts. 32 and 33 of the Royal Decree of 13 February 2001)

3393. To exercise these rights, the Data Subject can either send a signed and dated request by regular mail or any other means of telecommunications to the Controller or the Processor; or deliver a signed and dated request directly to the Controller or the Processor. In the latter case, an acknowledgement of receipt of the request must be given to the Data Subject.

IX. OBLIGATIONS OF THE CONTROLLER

A. Inform the Data Subject

3394. Article 9 of the Data Protection Law provides that prior to any processing, the Controller has to provide the Data Subject with specific information, unless the Data Subject already has that information.

§1. Information to be provided in all cases

3395. If the data are obtained directly from the Data Subject, the Controller must inform him or her at least of its identity and the purposes of the processing.

§2. Additional Information to be provided in special situations

3396. The Data Protection Law and the Royal Decree of 13 February 2001 provide for a number of additional items to be communicated to the Data Subject in special situations.

3397. Where this is necessary to ensure a fair processing (*See*, para. 3354), taking into account the specific circumstances in which the data are obtained, the Data Subject must also be informed of (i) the (categories of) recipients of the Personal Data; (ii) his or her right of access and right to rectify; and (iii) whether it is compulsory to reply to the questions as well as the possible consequences of a failure to reply.

3398. Controllers wishing to process Personal Data for direct marketing purposes must inform the Data Subject of his or her right to object to such processing.

3399. The Controller who wishes to process sensitive, health-related or judicial Personal Data also has to inform the Data Subject of the regulatory basis for the processing (Art. 25, 4° of the Royal Decree of 13 February 2001).

3400. If, the Controller wishes to process sensitive, health-related or judicial Personal Data on the basis of the written authorisation of the Data Subject, it also has to advise the Data Subject of the reasons for such processing and of the categories of persons who will have access to these data (Art. 26 of the Royal Decree of 13 February 2001).

3401. In case of further processing for historical, statistical or scientific purposes of (i) non-anonymous health-related or judicial Personal Data (coded or non-coded), or (ii) of non-coded Personal Data, the Controller must provide the Data Subject with a more detailed indication of the purposes of the processing (a short description of the concrete research project). The Controller must furthermore indicate from whom the Personal Data were obtained, the recipients of these data, the existence of a right to access and rectify them, and the existence of a right to object to the processing (*See*, para. 3392).

3402. Finally, for further processing of non-coded Personal Data, the Data Subject will have to be informed that his or her prior consent is required.

§3. Personal Data not directly obtained from the data subject

3403. If Personal Data are not obtained directly from the Data Subject, the Controller has to provide the Data Subject with the above information at the time it registers the Personal Data or no later than when the first communication of the Personal Data to a third party takes place (Art. 9, para. 2 of the Data Protection Law).

3404. Article 9, para. 2, c, of the Data Protection Law specifies that when the Personal Data are not obtained directly from Data Subjects, they must be informed of their right to object to the processing of their Personal Data for direct marketing purposes before the transfer of their Personal Data to a third party or their use on a third party's behalf.

3405. The Data Protection Law and the Royal Decree of 13 February 2001 read together provide for several instances in which the obligation to inform is tempered or even done away with.

3406. Thus, the obligation to inform the Data Subject can be postponed until the first time the Data Subject is contacted by the Controller or the third party to which the Personal Data have been transferred if informing the Data Subject earlier would be impossible or imply disproportionate efforts. If the Controller considers that it will never be able to inform the Data Subject because this would be impossible or imply disproportionate efforts, it will have to indicate the reasons for its position in the notification to the Privacy Commission (Art. 9, para. 2, 2, a of the Data Protection Law; Arts. 30 and 31 of the Royal Decree of 13 February 2001) (*See*, paras. 3412 *et seq.*).

3407. Likewise, further processing of coded Personal Data (other than sensitive, health-related or judicial data) for historical, statistical and scientific purposes will be exempted from the obligation to inform under the conditions set out above (*See*, paras. 3380 and 3381)

B. Direct Marketing

3408. To give more effect to the right of the Data Subject to object to the processing of his or her Personal Data, the Royal Decree of 13 February 2001 requires the Controller to request the Data Subject whether he or she wishes to oppose the processing (Arts. 34 and 35 of the Royal Decree of 13 February 2001).

3409. This question will have to be asked either (i) directly on the document which is used to collect the Personal Data, if these data are collected in writing (this includes collection in the Internet); or (ii) on a separate document or through any other technical means allowing for the storage of proof that the Data Subject had the opportunity to object, no later than 2 months after the collection of these data; or (iii) in writing on a separate document and prior to any processing, if the Controller wishes to process Personal Data not obtained directly from the Data Subject for direct marketing purposes.

3410. The Data Subject should be able to indicate his or her objection by returning the document he or she received from the Controller. The way to object to the processing has to be clearly indicated.

3411. If the Data Subject does not answer the Controller's request, he or she will be deemed not to object.

C. Notification to the Privacy Commission

3412. Prior to processing Personal Data, the Controller has the obligation to notify such processing to the Privacy Commission (Art. 17 of the Data Protection Law). The notified information will allow the Privacy Commission to assess the legality of the processing.

§1. Information to be provided at all times

3413. Article 17, para. 3 of the Data Protection Law, outlines the information which the notification has to contain. This includes (i) the identity of the Controller; (ii) the purpose of the processing; (iii) the categories of Personal Data to be processed with a specific description of sensitive, health-related and judicial Personal Data; (iv) the (categories of) persons who receive the Personal Data; (v) the guarantees given for any communication of Personal Data to third parties; (vi) the manner in which the persons to whom the Personal Data relate are informed of the processing; (vii) the service where the right of access may be exercised; (viii) the measures taken to facilitate the exercise of that right; (ix) the period of time, after the expiration of which the data may no longer be stored, used or disclosed, where applicable; and (x) a general description permitting a preliminary assessment of the appropriateness of the security measures taken pursuant to the confidentiality and security requirements (*See*, paras. 3421 and 3422).

§2. Additional Information to be provided in special situations

3414. Controllers wishing to take advantage of the exemption from the application of part of the Data Protection Law for processing carried out for journalistic purposes or for the purpose of artistic or literary expression (*See*, para. 3343) will also have to add the grounds on which the Controller is relying for the application of this exemption.

3415. The original Controllers or the intermediary wishing to code sensitive, health-related or judicial Personal Data for historical, statistical or scientific purposes without informing the Data Subject (*See*, paras. 3380 and 3381) will have to submit (i) a more detailed description of the purpose of the processing; (ii) the categories of Data Subjects concerned by the processing; (iii) the reasons making the processing of sensitive, health-related or judicial Personal Data necessary; (iv) the reasons making it impossible or disproportionately difficult to inform the Data Subject; as well as (v) an indication of the person from whom the Personal Data were obtained (Art. 16 of the Royal Decree of 13 February 2001).

3416. Controllers of a form of further processing wishing to process non-coded Personal Data for historical, statistical or scientific purposes without informing the Data Subject and without obtaining his or her consent (*See*, paras. 3380 and 3381) will have to communicate the same information as that described under paragraph 3415 above.

§3. Exemptions from the obligation to notify

3417. Firstly, the obligation to notify the Privacy Commission does not apply to the processing which has as its sole purpose the keeping of a register that is intended by law to provide information to the public and is open to consultation either by the public in general or by any person demonstrating a legitimate interest.

3418. Secondly, Article 17, para. 8 of the Data Protection Law provides that certain categories of Data Processing may, under certain conditions, be exempted from the notification requirement. The Royal Decree of 13 February 2001 (Arts. 51 through 62) lists several forms of processing that do not require notification, provided that the Personal Data are not kept longer than necessary and are processed exclusively in conformity with the purposes listed in the Royal Decree of 13 February 2001. However, the processing of these categories of Personal Data can be inspected by the Privacy Commission at any time (Arts. 31 and 32 of the Data Protection Law).

3419. The categories of Personal Data exempted from the notification requirement are, essentially, (i) data necessary for payroll management by the employer; (ii) the data used by the employer exclusively for the management of staff; (iii) Personal Data necessary for the accountancy of the Controller; (iv) Personal Data necessary for the administration of shareholders and partners; (v) Personal Data indispensable for contacting the Data Subject; or (vi) Personal Data processed by public authorities when such processing is governed by specific data processing rules.

3420. The exemption from the obligation to notify the Privacy Commission for some of the above-listed purposes does not apply to the processing of sensitive, health-related and judicial Personal Data. Nor does it apply to transfers of the listed Personal Data to third parties or their acquisition from third parties.

D. Confidentiality and security

3421. The Controller must ensure the confidentiality and security of the processing. This means, for instance, that if the processing is entrusted to a Processor, the Controller must choose a Processor offering sufficient security guarantees. The potential liability of the Processor in case of breach must also be agreed to in a contract (Art. 16 of the Data Protection Law).

3422. The Controller will be held liable for any breach of security under the conditions detailed in paragraphs 3423 and 3424 below.

X. LIABILITY AND SANCTIONS

3423. According to Article 15*bis* of the Data Protection Law, the Controller will be liable for any damages resulting from an act in breach of the Data Protection Law, including acts of Processors. However, the Controller can escape liability if it proves that the act that caused the damage cannot be attributed to him.

3424. Articles 38 *et seq.* of the Data Protection Law provide for criminal sanctions in several situations where the Controller or its agents have not respected the applicable rules on the protection of Personal Data. Third parties can also be criminally liable in exceptional circumstances.

XI. PERSONAL DATA PROCESSED BY PUBLIC AUTHORITIES IN THE CONTEXT OF POLICE AND INTELLIGENCE ACTIVITIES

3425. Given the specific missions of general interest performed by these public authorities, Data Subjects are not granted the right to access their Personal Data directly, nor to have these data rectified or deleted, or to object to the processing. Instead, the Privacy Commission will exercise a diluted version of these rights on behalf of the Data Subjects (Art. 13 of the Data Protection Law and Arts. 37 through 46 of the Royal Decree of 13 February 2001).

XII. TRANSFERS OF PERSONAL DATA TO THIRD COUNTRIES

3426. In addition to the above set of rules applicable to the processing of Personal Data within Belgium, Controllers wishing to export Personal Data outside the European Economic Area ("EEA") (the EC plus Iceland, Liechtenstein and Norway) will have to comply with additional requirements.

A. Principle – adequate protection

3427. In accordance with the Data Protection Directive, Article 21 of the Data Protection Law prohibits the transfer of Personal Data to a country outside the European Union that does not offer an "adequate level of protection".

3428. The adequacy of the law of a third country is assessed on a case-by-case basis, in the light of all the circumstances surrounding the data transfer, including the nature of the Personal Data, the purposes of the processing, the country of origin and the country of final destination, the rules of law, both general and sector-based, in force in the country of destination as well as the professional rules and security measures that are observed in that country.

3429. Adequate protection can therefore be created by the parties to the transfer through contractual arrangements, provided such arrangements ensure an adequate level of protection to the transferred data within the meaning of Article 21 of the Data Protection Law.

B. Standard contractual clauses approved by the EC Commission

3430. Article 26, paragraph 4 of the Data Protection Directive empowers the EC Commission to decide that certain contractual clauses offer sufficient safeguards for transfers to third countries with respect to the protection of privacy and fundamental rights and freedoms of individuals and as regards the exercise of corresponding rights. Such a Commission decision is binding on all the Member States. Transfers between persons committing themselves to abide by these clauses will be considered to be safe.

3431. The EC Commission has adopted 2 decisions containing model clauses declared to provide adequate protection in case of a transfer of Personal Data to third countries. The first one covers transfers of Personal Data to Controllers (Decision No. 2001/497 – O.J. [2001] L 181/19), while the second one applies to transfers of Personal Data to Processors (Decision No. 2002/16 – O.J. [2002] L 6/52).

3432. These clauses seek to create for Personal Data transferred to third countries a form of contractual protection equivalent to the protection afforded by the Data Protection Directive within the EC.

3433. These standard clauses offer parties to a transfer of Personal Data to third countries the guarantee that, provided all the requirements set out in the clauses are met, the transfer is legal. However, the duties these standard clauses impose on the parties are quite burdensome and, in situations where adequate protection could be reached through the adoption of less restrictive *ad hoc* clauses, the parties may choose to trade this guarantee of legality for better suited and less onerous contractual terms.

C. Law of the country of destination deemed by the EC Commission to provide adequate protection

3434. Article 25, paragraph 6 of the Data Protection Directive provides that the EC Commission may determine which third countries offer an adequate level of protection. Such a decision is binding on the EC Member States.

3435. To date, the laws of 3 third countries have been found to provide an adequate level of protection under the meaning of Article 25 of the Data Protection Directive, *i.e.*, Canada, Hungary and Switzerland. The "Safe-Harbor" scheme of the United States is also deemed to provide an adequate level of protection. Finally, the law of Argentina is due to be considered as providing adequate protection to transferred personal data in the near future.

3436. Transfers of Personal Data to Canada, Hungary, Switzerland and to recipients having signed up to the US Safe-Harbor system, are subject to the same rules as transfers to recipients located within the EEA.

D. Authorised transfers in situations in which there is no adequate protection

3437. Article 22, paragraph 1 of the Data Protection Law provides for several exceptions to the requirement of adequacy. Transfers of Personal Data to third countries not providing an adequate level of protection may take place in several exceptional situations: (i) there is unambiguous consent of the Data Subject; or (ii) the transfer is necessary for the performance of a contract to which the Data Subject is a party, or concluded in the Data Subject's interest; or (iii) the transfer is necessary for safeguarding the Data Subject's vital interests; or (iv) the transfer is necessary or legally required on important public interest grounds, or (v) the transfer is necessary for the establishment, exercise or defence of legal claims; or, finally, (v) the transfer is made from data contained in a register accessible to the public.

XIII. REGISTER OF AUTOMATIC PROCESSING

3438. Article 18 of the Data Protection Law provides that the Privacy Commission is responsible for keeping a register of all forms of automatic processing of Personal Data (the "Register"). This Register can be consulted directly at the premises of the Privacy Commission or indirectly through a request for information addressed to the Privacy Commission. Anyone can mail or directly hand over to the Privacy Commission a written request to obtain an excerpt from the Register. The details of the Privacy Commission are as follows:

Name: Commissie voor de bescherming van de persoonlijke levenssfeer/
Commission de la protection de la vie privée

Mailing address: Waterloolaan 115 Boulevard de Waterloo B-1000 Brussels

Location: Hallepoortlaan 5-8 Porte de Hal, B-1060 Brussels

Tel: +32(0) 2 / 542.72.00

Fax: +32(0) 2 / 542.72.01 and +32 (0)2 / 542.72.12

E-mail: commission@privacy.fgov.be

Internet: http://www.privacy.fgov.be/

Opening hours: 9.00 am to 11.45 am and 2.00 pm to 4.00 pm.

XIV. SECTOR-BASED DATA PROTECTION RULES

A. The telecommunications and electronic communications sector

3439. As indicated above, Directive No. 97/66 translated the principles set out in the Data Protection Directive into specific rules for the telecommunications sector. Directive No. 2002/58 on privacy and electronic communications was adopted in order to modernise Directive No. 97/66 and adapt it to market and technological developments.

3440. Directive No. 97/66 was implemented in Belgium through the modification of several pieces of legislation, most importantly the Law on Unfair Trade Practices (*See,* Chapter 14) and the Law on Public Undertakings (*Ibid.*).

3441. *Unsolicited communications (spamming)*: Articles 82 of the Law on Unfair Trade Practices regulates the use of telecommunication techniques for direct marketing purposes. The use of automatic calling machines or facsimile machines for the purpose of direct marketing is only allowed in respect of subscribers who have given their prior consent. Other telecommunication techniques, including electronic messages, may be used until recipients specifically indicate that they oppose recourse to such methods.

3442. Article 82 of the Law on Unfair Trade Practices will have to be modified in order to reflect the change dictated by Article 13 of Directive No. 2002/58 towards a system where no unsolicited messages can be sent for direct marketing purposes without the prior consent of the recipient of such message (recipient must "opt-in").

3443. However, the current system, requiring recipients to opt-out, will remain applicable to direct marketing communications made by a company wishing to contact its customers in order to promote products or services similar to those already sold to these customers.

3444. *Security*: Articles 105*sexies*B of the Law on Public Undertakings requires telecommunications operators to provide adequate security safeguards and inform their subscribers in case there are specific risks that the security of their network might be compromised. Directive No. 2002/58 will not change this.

3445. *Traffic Data*: Article 105*nonies* of the Law on Public Undertakings requires telecommunications operators to make their subscribers' or users' Personal Data anonymous if these data are to be kept longer than is necessary for establishing the communication or for invoicing purposes. Directive No. 2002/58 does not change this. However, Article 6.4 of Directive No. 2002/58 creates a new obligation to inform subscribers or users of the type of traffic data that are processed and of the duration of the processing.

3446. *Cookies*: Article 5.3 of Directive No. 2002/58 regulates the use of cookies, *i.e.*, the storage of information on the computer of Data Subjects. Data Subjects must be provided with clear and adequate information in accordance with the Data Protection Directive and be offered the right to refuse the placing of cookies on their computers. Services may be made conditional on the acceptance by Data Subjects of the placing of cookies on their computers, provided these cookies are necessary to provide the service requested by the Data Subjects.

B. National registry of natural persons

3447. The Law of 8 August 1983 on the Organisation of a National Registry of Natural Persons (*Wet tot regeling van een Rijksregister van de natuurlijke personen/Loi organisant un registre national des personnes physiques*) creates a database centralising Personal Data relating to any natural person legally residing in Belgium or registered with Belgian consulates abroad. Each natural person is given a unique identification number. This number can only be used by those that have access to the national registry and for the purpose for which they are granted such access.

3448. Access to the registry is restricted to public authorities for carrying out the task assigned to them by law and to other organisations duly authorised by a Royal Decree that act in the public interest.

C. Personal Data processed by social security public authorities

3449. Specific data protection rules apply to Personal Data processed by the social security public bodies and pooled by these bodies under the Law of 15 January 1990 on the Pooling of Social Security Data (*Wet houdende oprichting en organisatie van een Kruispuntbank van de sociale zekerheid/Loi relative à l'institution et à l'organisation d'une banque carrefour de la sécurité sociale*). This law contains some specific data protection rules departing only slightly from the general principles contained in the Data Protection Law.

3450. The main differences between this specific regime and the general regime are:
(i) the creation in each of the public bodies concerned of a security officer in charge of monitoring the security of the Personal Data held by the public body concerned and transferred between these bodies;

(ii) the supervision of the processing of health-related Personal Data by a physician appointed in each of the public bodies involved; and

(iii) the indication in the Law of 15 January 1990 of the security means which must be implemented in order to ensure the security of the Personal Data.

D. Law on Consumer Credit

3451. Finally, the Law of 12 June 1991 on Consumer Credit (*Wet op het consumentenkrediet/Loi relative au crédit à la consommation*) also contains specific data protection rules. It creates a register of defaulting debtors accessible to certain financial institutions and public authorities. It lists the categories of persons having access to the Personal Data, the Personal Data that can be included in this register and the time during which the Personal Data can be held by those having access to the register. It also contains a specific duty to inform when defaulting debtors are included in the register.

3452. As from 1 June 2003, following the full entry into force of the Law of 10 August 2001 on the Credit Register for Individuals (*Wet betreffende de Centrale voor Kredieten aan Particulieren/Loi relative à la Centrale des Crédits aux Particuliers*) and of its implementing Royal Decree of 7 July 2002, this register will not only cover defaulting debtors but will record all consumer credit contracts as well as all mortgage contracts, regardless of whether or not there is a default. Any lender supplying money under a mortgage contract or a consumer credit contract will have to communicate specific data relating to the contract and the debtor to the register. Data Subjects are granted a right to be informed and a right to correct their Personal Data similar to those which they have under the Data Protection Law. A special committee will be created in order to supervise this new system.

20. JUDICIAL COMPOSITION AND BANKRUPTCY

I. INTRODUCTION

3453. This chapter details the rules governing companies in financial difficulties.

II. TRACING OF COMPANIES IN DIFFICULTY

A. Company monitoring at the administrative level

3454. The Flemish Commission for Company Surveillance (*Vlaamse Commissie voor Preventief Bedrijfsbeleid* – the "Surveillance Commission"), established by Decree of 27 June 1985, monitors the financial situation and market prospects of companies employing at least 50 people with premises in the Flemish Region (*Vlaams Gewest*), with the exception of banks and insurance companies. There are no equivalent institutions in the 2 other regions of Belgium.

The Surveillance Commission either acts on its own initiative or at the request of the company at issue, the Flemish Executive (*Vlaamse Executieve*) or, subject to some conditions, a company's works council (*See*, Chapter 8). The information relied on by the Surveillance Commission includes the companies' annual accounts, the records of capital reductions as well as any data provided by the Flemish Executive or by the company itself. The Surveillance Commission can initiate discussions with the company if the investigations show any potential financial problems. The discussions take place on a voluntary basis.

The recommendations issued by the Surveillance Commission are non-binding. Nevertheless, the company might become ineligible for government support if it fails to take these recommendations into account or fails to respond to them adequately.

Although the Surveillance Commission is still operational, recent figures show that its contribution to the monitoring of companies is rather limited.

3455. In addition to the work of this Surveillance Commission, companies in difficulty may also be traced through the control of subsidies, as it may be in specific cases that subsidies have been granted to meet the financial difficulties of these companies.

3456. Finally, specific administrative authorities, such as the Banking and Finance Commission (*Commissie voor het Bank- en Financiewezen/Commission bancaire et financière*), created by Royal Decree No. 185 of 9 July 1935, or the Insurance Control Office (*Controledienst voor de Verzekeringen/Office de Contrôle des Assurances*), established by the Law of 9 July 1975, control the financial situation of banks and insurance companies as part of the review of their business licence.

B. Judicial monitoring

3457. Pursuant to Article 84, paragraph 3 of the Judicial Code and Article 5 through 8 of the Law of 17 July 1997 on Judicial Composition (*Wet van 17 juli 1997 betreffende het Gerechtelijk Akkoord/Loi du 17 juillet 1997 concernant le Concordat Judiciaire* – "Judicial Composition Law", *See*, paras. 3461 *et seq.*), the chambers of commercial investigation established within the commercial courts collect and examine economic data of businesses under their jurisdiction and, if necessary, initiate judicial composition or bankruptcy procedures. Key indicators of financial instability include:
- attachments of assets;
- repeated summons for payment by creditors;
- default judgments against the company;
- judgments involving cases in which the company did not contest the principal amount claimed;
- annual accounts;
- press reports; and
- any information supplied by the social security and tax authorities.

3458. In addition, the statutory auditor of a company (*commissaris-revisor/commissaire-réviseur*) is, in some circumstances, entitled to inform the commercial court of the deteriorating financial situation of the company, without infringing his professional secrecy duties (Art. 138, para. 4 of the Company Code – *Wetboek van Vennootschappen/Code des Sociétés.*)

3459. As soon as the investigating judge learns of the deteriorating financial situation of a specific company, the latter will be invited to a hearing in chambers at the commercial court and will be requested to supply full information regarding its financial position. An account of the hearing and the conclusions of the investigating judge will be recorded in a report (*eindverslag/rapport des diligences accomplies*). If the financial instability proves to be of a temporary nature, the investigations will come to an end. Otherwise, the judge may consider that the conditions of judicial composition proceedings are met and accordingly forward the file to the Public Prosecutor (*Openbaar Ministerie/Ministère Public*). Alternatively, if the conditions for bankruptcy are satisfied, the investigating judge is obliged to transmit the file to the Public Prosecutor who may initiate bankruptcy proceedings.

C. Personal monitoring

3460. Last but not least, businesses can check the financial health of their business partners by consulting the records kept by the registrar of the commercial court or the annual accounts maintained at the Belgian National Bank, or any commercial reports available.

III. JUDICIAL COMPOSITION

3461. The Judicial Composition Law aims at creating a framework that allows companies facing temporary financial difficulties to turn around on a long-term basis and to achieve a sustained recovery. This is why investigation chambers closely monitor the enterprises in difficulty so that proceedings in judicial composition can be started before any specific enterprise qualifies for bankruptcy. The Judicial Composition Law takes both the creditors' and the trader's interests into consideration, but also the interests of the trader's suppliers, clients and workers as well as the general interest of the region where the enterprise of the trader is located.

3462. Judicial composition proceedings involve a provisional stay period during which the applicant is protected from its existing creditors and is required to prepare the recovery plan. They also encompass a definitive stay period.

3463. It should be noted that the present legal framework on judicial composition has been fiercely criticised and seems to have only limited success. Recent figures show that since the entry into force of the Judicial Composition Law in 1998 only 757 judicial compositions were granted. It has been argued that the specific position of fiscal creditors and social security institutions as well as the inequality between secured and unsecured creditors are mainly responsible for the limited success of this procedure. Moreover, it appears that companies applying for judicial composition are stigmatised and loose half of their turnover. Finally, the high costs relating to a judicial composition constitute another important barrier for companies facing financial difficulties.

A. Conditions of judicial composition

3464. Pursuant to Articles 2, 9 and 15 of the Judicial Composition Law, the 3 requirements to obtain the benefits of judicial composition are as follows:
 (i) the applicant must be a trader (*handelaar/commerçant*);
 (ii) the trader must be having financial difficulties leading to a likely definitive cessation of payments (*staking van betalingen/cessation de paiements*) or the business' continuity of the trader must be threatened; and
 (iii) there must be "no obvious bad faith" on the part of the trader.

§1. Applicant must be a trader

1. Individuals

3465. Article 1 of the Commercial Code (*Wetboek van Koophandel/Code du Commerce*) defines a trader as anyone whose main or supplementary profession is the performance of commercial acts. An exhaustive list of such commercial acts is set forth in Articles 2 and 3 of the Commercial Code. This includes: (i) purchasing merchandise for the purpose of resale or of renting; (ii) purchasing a business; (iii) operating any manufacturing business, public or private works business, supply business or transport business. To qualify as a trader the person must perform commercial acts as his profession, which implies the pursuit of financial gain (Cass., 7 April 1898, *Pas.*, 1898, I, 146). Being listed in the commercial register constitutes a rebuttable presumption that the person registered is a trader (Art. 3 of the Royal Decree of 20 July 1964). Certain liberal professions such as that of architects, lawyers and medical doctors are legally, or at least ethically, incompatible with the status of trader.

2. Companies

3466. Only companies that have a legal personality separate from their shareholders or members and that are commercial rather than civil in nature can apply for judicial composition. On an interpretation of its corporate purpose, a company is deemed to be either commercial or civil (Art. 1 of the Company Code). If the object of the company consists of the performance of commercial acts, it will be deemed to be a commercial company. The legal form of the company (Cass., 30 April 1945, *Pas.*, 1945, I, 150) and the possibility that it may in fact engage in activities other than those described in its corporate purpose are irrelevant.

3467. Companies with a civil purpose that have adopted the form of a commercial company must be deemed civil companies and are banned from applying for judicial composition. By contrast, companies with a social function (*vennootschap met een sociaal oogmerk/société à finalité sociale*) performing commercial activities pursuant to their corporate purpose can apply for judicial composition. However, universities or so-called intermunicipal companies, *i.e.*, local administrative authorities which are in charge of the distribution of water or electricity (*inter-communales/intercommunales*) cannot apply for judicial composition.

§2. Economic conditions

3468. Judicial composition may be granted to a trader who finds it temporarily impossible to pay his debts or whose business' continuity is threatened by a likely cessation of payments (Art. 9, para. 1 of the Judicial Composition Law), *i.e.*, for example, (i) the trader has temporary cash flow problems or (ii) the trading losses have reduced the net assets (*netto activa/actif net*) to less than the half of the subscribed capital (Art. 633 of the Company Code). The temporary character is to be understood as meaning that the financial difficulties cannot exceed the maximum period of the judicial composition proceedings (*See*, paras. 3485 and 3507). In addition, pursuant to Article 9, paragraph 2 of the Judicial Composition Law, the economic recovery of the enterprise must be possible. An uncertain prospect of economic recovery is not sufficient to meet the criterion. Relevant elements in relation to the possible recovery of the business activity include the optimisation of existing production lines, the reduction of the wage bill, the increase of assets for tax redemption, the quality of leading-edge technology, *etc.*

3469. The judge enjoys a wide discretion in the appraisal of these economic conditions. This has led to a varying treatment of applications from one jurisdiction to another.

3470. Finally, a trader who has been declared bankrupt by a judge cannot apply anymore for judicial composition. By contrast, in case a trader does not meet the conditions of judicial composition, the judge should check whether the conditions of bankruptcy are fulfilled.

§3. "No obvious bad faith" on the part of the trader

3471. The applicant must not be of "obvious bad faith". In the event of "obvious bad faith" on the part of the trader, the proceedings can, however, be resumed to the extent that the trader no longer takes part in the management of the company concerned. But if the trader is an individual of "obvious bad faith", the impossibility of removing him implies that the application for judicial composition must be rejected. The court can also order specific measures so that the creditors regain confidence in the trader.

B. Participants in the proceedings

3472. Judicial composition always implies the intervention of a court. The competent court is the commercial court (*rechtbank van koophandel/tribunal de commerce*) of the place, in the case of an individual, where the trader is registered and has his domicile or, in the case of a company, where the company has its principal administrative office.

3473. The suspension commissioner (*commissaris inzake opschorting/commissaire au sursis*) plays a key role during the proceedings. Appointed by the court, he assists the trader in the management of the enterprise during both the provisional and definitive stay periods (*See*, paras. 3480 *et seq.*). Experienced in company management, the suspension commissioner also assists the trader in drafting the recovery plan. The suspension commissioner reports to the court on a regular basis.

3474. The Public Prosecutor may initiate judicial composition proceedings (Art. 11, para. 2 of the Judicial Composition Law) and express his views on the trader's application and on a possible revocation of the stay.

3475. Workers' representatives have the right to express their views at several stages of the proceedings, but these views are not binding.

C. 2-tier procedure

3476. The procedure of judicial composition consists of a first period during which the payment of the trader's existing debts (*i.e.*, those preceding the granting of the provisional stay) are provisionally suspended (the "provisional stay"). This is followed, if applicable, by a second period during which the payment of these claims is definitively suspended (the "definitive stay"). Both periods are limited in time.

§1. Initiation of the proceedings

3477. The trader or the Public Prosecutor can apply to the court for judicial composition (Art. 11 of the Judicial Composition Law).

3478. The petition (*akkoordaanvraag/requête*) of the trader includes documents establishing the enterprise's financial and economic situation as well as proposals for its recovery and/or for the satisfaction of the creditors. If the trader does not apply for judicial composition, the Public Prosecutor can initiate the proceedings by means of a writ of summons (*dagvaarding/citation*). Creditors are not allowed to apply for judicial composition of their debtor. Moreover, the court cannot open such proceedings on its own initiative.

3479. The application for judicial composition is not made public. However, all creditors and other persons having an interest may request the court to be heard (Art. 13, para. 1 of the Judicial Composition Law and Arts. 812 through 814 of the Judicial Code). Contrary to what applies in case of bankruptcy, the Judicial Composition Law does not impose that the decision of the trader to apply for judicial composition is communicated to the workers' representatives. However, such an obligation may follow from Article 25 of the Royal Decree of 27 November 1973 and Article 11 of Collective Bargaining Agreement No. 11 of 9 March 1972. Both laws provide for criminal sanctions if the workers' representatives are not informed.

§2. Provisional stay

1. Decision of the commercial court

3480. A trader cannot be declared bankrupt as long as the judge has not ruled on the application. From the day of application to the day of the court decision, creditors lose their right to realise the trader's assets but they are still entitled to seize some assets (Art. 12 of the Judicial Composition Law).

3481. After having heard the trader, the Public Prosecutor, the creditors, and, if applicable, the statutory auditor, the court rules on the application within 15 days as from the date of application (Art. 14 of the Judicial Composition Law).

3482. In accordance with the conditions described above, the court either accepts or rejects the application and, accordingly, grants or refuses the benefit of the provisional stay (*voorlopige opschorting/sursis provisoire*). The documents submitted to the court in support of the application must be sufficiently reliable so that the court can assess whether the conditions of judicial composition are satisfied on a *prima facie* basis (Art. 15 of the Judicial Composition Law; Comm. Ieper, 8 December 2000, *T.R.V.*, 2001, 37).

3483. The judgment granting the provisional stay to the trader:
   (i) mentions the duration of the provisional stay period;
   (ii) appoints the suspension commissioner(s);
   (iii) invites the creditors to declare their debts and specifies the period within which this declaration should be done; and
   (iv) provides for the time and place of the decision on the definitive stay.

3484. The trader's ability to manage his business and dispose of his assets can be limited by a requirement that the suspension commissioner should approve of some or all trader's transactions (Art. 15, para. 1, section 3 of the Judicial Composition Law). If the trader violates this restriction, the relevant transactions cannot be enforced as against the creditors.

3485. The duration of the provisional stay, also called "observation period", cannot exceed six months (Art. 15, para. 1 of the Judicial Composition Law). A 3-month extension is however possible (Art. 23 of the Judicial Composition Law).

3486. The judgment accepting the application is made public in 3 ways. Firstly, excerpts of the judgment are published in the *Belgian Official Journal* (*Belgisch Staatsblad/ Moniteur Belge*) and in 2 local newspapers. The publication in the *Belgian Official Journal* is the starting point for the creditors to declare their debts and amounts to proper notification. Secondly, the suspension commissioner personally informs by registered mail the known creditors of the trader's situation. This letter points out that the creditors must declare their debts before the prescribed deadline. Finally, a judicial composition file, containing all relevant documents, is held with the registrar of the commercial court. Consultation of the file is open to the creditors of the trader as well as to anyone demonstrating "a legitimate interest", subject to the court's approval.

3487. The court can reject an application for judicial composition, as is the case for almost 50 per cent of the applications. Such a decision is immediately applicable even if it is subject to appeal. As a result, the protection against a declaration of bankruptcy disappears (Art. 3 of the Judicial Composition Law). The court that rejects the application can simultaneously declare the trader bankrupt, subject to the prior hearing of the trader (Art. 15, para. 2 of the Judicial Composition Law).

2. Impact of provisional stay on trader's and creditors' rights

3488. The suspension commissioner is supposed to provide assistance to the trader. The latter maintains his full capacity as to the enterprise's management, unless the judgment provided otherwise (*See*, para. 3484) in which case the trader and the commissioner act jointly. The powers conferred on the suspension commissioner may vary from one case to the other, depending upon the skills, past performance and failures of the trader.

3489. The creditors' right to pursue any enforcement action against the trader's movable and immovable assets is suspended as of the date of the judgment providing for the provisional stay (Art. 21, para. 1 of the Judicial Composition Law). The judgment effects a freeze on all actions initiated against the trader, thereby enabling him to elaborate a recovery plan while being temporarily protected from his creditors. The prohibition of enforcement affects all creditors, secured or not, regardless of their rank, and including the creditors who benefit from a retention of title clause. While the creditors may sue the trader to obtain an enforceable title, enforcement cannot take place during the judicial composition proceedings. Finally, pending attachment orders maintain in principle their preserving effects, but the suspension commissioner can ask the court to release them.

3490. There are some exceptions to the general freeze on enforcement actions (*e.g.*, enforcement actions against banking institutions or insurance companies). Moreover, the trader's guarantors and co-debtors do not benefit from the provisional and definitive stays (Art. 21, para. 2 of the Judicial Composition Law). Furthermore, the general freeze on enforcement actions does not cause a suspension of the interests that becomes due after the judgment allowing the provisional stay. If the trader is unable to pay these interests, full recovery rights are revested in the creditors of the underlying debts (Art. 21, para. 1 of the Judicial Composition Law). Finally, some types of creditors can ask the judge for additional security.

3. Impact of the provisional stay on existing agreements

3491. Article 28 of the Judicial Composition Law guarantees the survival of the trader's existing contracts, even if these contain a termination clause that applies in case of an application for judicial composition. On the other hand, if a contracting party fails to perform its contractual obligations properly, general contract law (including principles such as the *exceptio non adimpleti contractus*, *i.e.*, the right to suspend the performance of its contractual obligations as long as the other contracting party fails to perform its contractual obligations) will prevail. Therefore, the court will always have to verify whether a creditor terminated the contract solely because the trader applied for judicial composition or whether the creditor terminated the contract because the trader did not (properly) execute his contractual obligations. This is the reason why penalty clauses, setting forth the financial consequences resulting from the non-execution of contractual obligations, are inoperative during the provisional stay period.

3492. The fate of the so-called *intuitu personae* contracts, *i.e.*, contracts based on the identity of the contracting parties, is a controversial issue. Whereas some have argued that the deterioration of the trust inherent in such contracts would allow the other party to terminate the agreements, others maintain that such an outcome would contradict the very wording of Article 28 of the Judicial Composition Law. The case law seems to support the second viewpoint. Article 28 of the Judicial Composition Law also covers suspension clauses which in fact are equivalent to termination clauses.

3493. The above effect of the provisional stay does not affect the contracts entered into during the stay period. Debts resulting from contracts concluded during the stay period are to be considered as debts of the estate if bankruptcy is declared during the stay period (Art. 44, para. 2 of the Judicial Composition Law) (*See*, para. 3605).

4. Declaration and admission of debts

i. Declaration of debts

3494. All trader's debts must be declared, so that the suspension commissioner has a clear view of the trader's liabilities. The debts must be declared by all the creditors, including those benefiting from securities or guarantees, within the time-limit set forth in the judgment (Art. 17 of the Judicial Composition Law). If the creditors fail to observe this deadline, their debts are not void but will only be paid during the definitive stay period in so far as such payment does not hamper the execution of the recovery plan (*See*, paras. 3496 *et seq.*). The declaration of the debts is filed with the registrar of the commercial court and mentions the surname, first name, occupation and domicile of the creditor, the cause and the subject of the debt as well as any security or/and guarantee attached to it (Art. 25, para. 4 of the Judicial Composition Law). Because agreements cannot be terminated in response to an application for judicial composition, it is advisable to make a reservation in the declaration for the consequences of such agreements.

ii. Admission of debts

3495. The suspension commissioner, assisted by the trader, will compare the declared debts with the accounting books and will either admit their debts or contest them. In the latter case, the creditor will receive notice of the challenge and will be summoned, along with the trader, to appear before the court that will examine the disputed debts. Before a decision on these debts is given the debt is provisionally admitted for an amount determined by the judge (Art. 27, para. 3 of the Judicial Composition Law). This order cannot be contested.

5. Recovery plan

3496. The recovery plan forms a strategic part of the judicial composition proceedings. It consists of a descriptive and a prospective part.

3497. The descriptive part details the current state of the business and explains the nature and gravity of the difficulties that beset the business, as well as their causes (Art. 29, para. 2 of the Judicial Composition Law).

3498. The second part describes the measures which the trader intends to adopt and which are expected to bring about the long-term recovery of the enterprise (Art. 29, para. 3 of the Judicial Composition Law). It proposes terms of payment and debt reductions (*schuldvermindering/abattement de créance*). The trader can reschedule the interest payment, convert debt into shares or organise a differentiated settlement for specific categories of debts (Art. 29 of the Judicial Composition Law). This last possibility is aimed at the payment of debts of small amounts the rescheduling of which is impractical, or at the payment of unsecured debt which is considered as vital for the enterprise's business. Such a separate settlement departs from the principle of the equal treatment of the creditors.

3499. The prospective part of the plan further details the financial requirements for the enterprise's recovery. If the trader intends to dispose of the business or part thereof, the plan will mention this (*See*, paras. 3518 *et seq.*).

3500. If the debtor intends to reduce the payroll, the prospective part of the plan will contain a "social restructuring plan" (*sociaal herstructureringsplan/plan social de restructuration*). Workers' representatives must be heard. The law does not set forth the significance of the workers' opinion, nor the consequences of the failure to hold such a meeting. All rules governing worker dismissal (severance payment, notice duration, *etc.*) must be observed (*See*, paras. 1353 *et seq.*).

3501. Fiscal creditors as well as creditors benefiting from a mortgage, lien, retention of title clause or other securities on identified assets of the trader are also subject to the terms of the plan in so far as (i) the payment of their debts is not suspended for more than 18 months as from the approval of the plan by the court and (ii) the plan provides for the payment of the interest on their debts (Art. 30 of the Judicial Composition Law). In case, however, the 2 above conditions are not satisfied, the court can only render the plan compulsory for these creditors if they explicitly approve the plan. Moreover, the court may also grant "additional securities" to these creditors if it considers this appropriate.

3502. Finally, the descriptive part of the plan can provide for the replacement of the management or for the modification of their powers.

§3. Definitive stay

1. Procedure

3503. The decision to grant (or to refuse) the definitive stay (*definitieve opschorting/ sursis définitif*) results from both the creditors' vote and the court's approval.

i. Creditors' vote

3504. The judgment allowing the provisional stay mentions the day and place for the judgment on the definitive stay. Creditors may consult the recovery plan at the court registry. The suspension commissioner informs the workers' representatives of the content of the plan (Art. 32 of the Judicial Composition Law).

3505. The vote on the plan is subject to specific majorities: half of the creditors having declared their debts and taking part in the vote must vote in favour of the recovery plan (Art. 34, section 1 of the Judicial Composition Law). In addition, the total value of the debts represented by the positive votes must represent half of the total debts. The creditors not having declared their debts are not allowed to vote. Moreover, as mentioned above, the individual approval of some creditors benefiting from a privilege is in certain cases (*e.g.*, when the payment of debts is suspended for more than 18 months) required as well (Art. 30 of the Judicial Composition Law).

ii. Court's approval

3506. If the vote is positive, the court approves or rejects the definitive stay within the 2 following weeks. Excerpts of the decision are published in the *Belgian Official Journal* (Art. 33 of the Judicial Composition Law).

2. *Granting of the definitive stay*

3507. The duration of the definitive stay cannot exceed 24 months as from the judgment date (Art. 34, para. 2 of the Judicial Composition Law). A 12-month extension is however possible.

3508. The approved recovery plan is binding on all creditors, including those that have voted against the plan and those that have failed to declare their debts. Sellers benefiting from a retention of title clause, secured creditors on identified assets of the trader, creditors benefiting from a mortgage or lien and fiscal creditors who voted against the recovery plan are bound by it provided the plan provides for the payment of the interest on their debts and provided the payment of their debts is not suspended beyond the 18-month period (Art. 30, para. 1 of the Judicial Composition Law). These creditors can request additional securities. The payment of undeclared debts or a debt that was declared too late is only possible in so far as it is compatible with the plan and does not jeopardise the plan's execution.

3509. The full execution of the recovery plan completely and definitively discharges the trader from all declared and undeclared debts, with the exception of the debts disputed by the suspension commissioner (Art. 35 of the Judicial Composition Law). The discharge does not apply to new debts which are not covered by the stay (Art. 44 of the Judicial Composition Law). If a reduced debt (*See*, para. 3498) is paid during the definitive stay, the part that was left unpaid does not become payable after the judicial composition proceedings, unless this was otherwise provided for in the recovery plan.

3510. The execution of the recovery plan discharges the trader, but not any co-debtors or guarantors who are not entitled to invoke the recovery plan against the creditors. But if the trader's co-debtors or guarantees pay the creditors, their action against the trader is subject to the recovery plan.

3511. The suspension commissioner supervises the execution of the plan and reports regularly to the court. The report may contain a request to revoke the definitive stay. These reports are available for consultation at the registrar of the court.

3512. One month before the end of the definitive stay period the suspension commissioner reports to the court on the execution of the plan. The court pronounces the end of the stay period and discharges the suspension commissioner (Art. 40 of the Judicial Composition Law). Excerpts of the judgment are published in the *Belgian Official Journal*.

3. Refusal of the definitive stay

3513. The court can refuse the definitive stay, even if the creditors vote favourably, in case the recovery plan violates the public order or in case fair management cannot be guaranteed. If the court is of the opinion that the conditions for bankruptcy are met, it can declare the trader bankrupt after having heard the latter (Art. 33 of the Judicial Composition Law).

4. Modification of the definitive stay

3514. The recovery plan can be modified in the light of the company's interest or that of a creditor who voted negatively (Art. 38 of the Judicial Composition Law). If the modification weakens the position of the creditors of the initial recovery plan, a new vote on the modification must take place.

5. Revocation of definitive stay

3515. The suspension commissioner will ask for the revocation of the definitive stay if the plan is not carried out in part or in full. A creditor who has not been paid (or will not be paid in the future) according to the terms of the plan can also ask for its revocation by means of a writ of summons served on the trader.

3516. After having heard the suspension commissioner, the trader and his guarantors, the court can simultaneously revoke the definitive stay and declare the trader bankrupt. The court can also compel the suspension commissioner to call an extraordinary general meeting of the shareholders. At this meeting, the suspension commissioner can propose the voluntary winding-up of the company.

3517. A revocation implies that the definitive stay has never existed. Creditors return to their situation prior to the acceptance of the plan, subject to the deduction of the payments already made by the trader from this date onwards. Excerpts of the revocation judgment are published in the *Belgian Official Journal*.

D. Transfer of business

3518. The transfer of a business, or part of it, may occur at the initiative of the trader or the suspension commissioner. Such a transaction is subject to various rules involving labour law and social security. The following outline only focuses on the judicial composition.

3519. A "transfer" of a business means any transaction that causes the business to change hands, including a merger, demerger *etc*. A "business" consists of a discrete branch of activity that makes up a whole. A transfer limited to specific assets does not constitute a "transfer of a business" within the meaning of the rules governing judicial composition. Transferring a business, or part of it, often implies that the remaining part of the company will be liquidated or declared bankrupt. Although disputed by some authors, transferring part of the business may safeguard part of an enterprise for the benefit of both creditors and employees.

3520. The transfer of a business, and its terms, should be mentioned in the recovery plan. The plan is subject to a number of majorities pursuant to Article 34, paragraph 1 of the Judicial Composition Law.

3521. A transfer can also be carried out outside any plan at the initiative of the suspension commissioner who must be authorised by the court (Art. 41, para. 1 of the Judicial Composition Law). A partial transfer of a business may occur as of the granting of the provisional stay. By contrast, a transfer of the whole of a business can only take place after the verification of debts as specified in Article 27 of the Judicial Composition Law. The proposals made by potential rescuers are examined by the suspension commissioner "*in the light of the maintenance of a viable commercial activity*" and "*the consequences for the creditors*" (Art. 41, section 2 of the Judicial Composition Law). The proposals are discussed with management and the workers' representatives.

3522. The suspension commissioner will submit the best proposal to the court for approval. The court will hear representatives of the management and of the workers. In the event of the transfer of the full business, a creditors' vote is required (Art. 41, para. 5 of the Judicial Composition Law). The terms of the transfer relate to the maintenance of a certain level of employment as well as the reimbursement of the creditors (Art. 41, section 1 of the Judicial Composition Law). Preserving full employment is not required. Full reimbursement of the creditors is also not required: if full reimbursement were possible, the trader probably would not have applied for judicial composition.

IV. BANKRUPTCY

3523. The Law of 8 August 1997 on Bankruptcy (*Faillissementswet van 8 augustus 1997/ Loi sur les faillites du 8 août 1997* – the "Bankruptcy Law"), as amended by the Law of 4 September 2002, aims at quickly forcing out of the market traders without any economic future, while taking into consideration the competing interests at stake.

A. Conditions for bankruptcy

3524. Pursuant to Article 2 of the Bankruptcy Law, a person is declared bankrupt if:
    (i) he is a trader (*handelaar/commerçant*); and
    (ii) he is in a situation of a persistent cessation of payments; and
    (iii) the creditworthiness of that person is undermined.

§1. Person is a trader

1. Individuals

3525. Reference is made here to the definition of individual trade provided for in the section on judicial composition. (*See*, para. 3465)

3526. If a member of a so-called liberal professional (such as a medical doctor or a lawyer) disregards the applicable legal or ethical provisions preventing him from acting as a trader, he may be declared bankrupt as well (Brussels Court of Appeal, 18 March 1986, *Pas.*, 1986, II, 84).

3527. The requirement that only traders can be declared bankrupt implies that persons who do not professionally engage in commercial activities cannot be declared bankrupt. Civil insolvency rules are contained in the Law of 5 July 1998 on the Collective Settlement of Debts (*Wet van 5 juli 1998 betreffende de collectieve schul-denregeling en de mogelijkheid van verkoop uit de hand van de in beslag genomen onroerende goederen/Loi du 5 juillet 1998 relative au règlement collectif de dettes et à la possibilité de vente de gré à gré des biens immeubles saisis*).

3528. Persons who are no longer traders can still be declared bankrupt if they were trad-ers at the time of the cessation of payments (Art. 2, para. 2 of the Bankruptcy Law). Similarly, deceased traders can also be declared bankrupt posthumously until 6 months after the decease (Art. 2, para. 3 of the Bankruptcy Law). In the case of a deceased trader, the trader's successors represent the trader in all bankruptcy operations (Art. 56 of the Bankruptcy Law).

3529. The date of the cessation of payments may be determined in the judgment. In case the judgment does not specify the date of the cessation of payments, this date is considered to coincide with the date of the judgment declaring the bankruptcy. The date of the cessation of payments can in principle not be set earlier than 6 months prior to the bankruptcy judgment (Art. 12 of the Bankruptcy Law) (*See*, para. 3565 *et seq.*).

2. *Companies*

3530. Reference is again made to the analysis provided for in the section on judicial composition (*See*, paras. 3466 *et seq.*).

3531. Because non-profit-making associations cannot operate commercially, they cannot be declared bankrupt. However, if a non-profit-making association in fact operates commercially on a regular basis, the court may consider that such an association should be regarded as a civil company devoid of a distinct legal per-sonality. Such a finding allows the court to declare all the administrators of the non-profit-making association bankrupt.

3532. Additionally a legal entity, which has been wound-up, can be declared bankrupt within 6 months following its liquidation (Art. 2, para. 4 of the Bankruptcy Law).

§2. *Persistent cessation of payments*

3533. The trader must be in the situation of a persistent cessation of payments (Art. 2 of the Bankruptcy Law), *i.e.*, he no longer pays his debts as they become due. It is not necessary that the trader fails to meet all his outstanding payment obligations. On the other hand, temporary cash-flow problems do not amount to a persistent cessa-tion of payments as the payment problems must be persistent. Similarly, a state of insolvency, *i.e.*, when a trader's debts exceed his assets, does not necessarily cause a trader to qualify for bankruptcy, as long as the trader continues to benefit from credit facilities.

§3. Undermined creditworthiness

3534. The condition of "undermined creditworthiness" (*wankelend krediet/crédit ébranlé*) is generally construed as referring to the refusal of third parties to grant credit to the trader, *e.g.*, the withdrawal by bankers of credit facilities or the supply of goods only on a "cash on delivery" basis.

3535. The court will verify whether a trader who still pays some of his creditors does not do so on the basis of fictitious credit. Thus, a trader who purchases goods on credit and who resells them below the market price, or a trader who can only pay his suppliers by not paying other important creditors such as VAT or social security authorities, will be considered as benefiting from fictitious credit and could be declared bankrupt (Cass., 26 November 1970, *J.T.*, 1971, 258).

3536. This shows that, even though the persistent cessation of payments and the undermined creditworthiness constitute strictly speaking 2 separate conditions of bankruptcy, these 2 conditions are closely interrelated, *i.e.*, one may be the cause or the consequence of the other (Cass., 17 June 1994, *R.D.C.*, 1994, 876).

§4. Moment at which the conditions of bankruptcy must be satisfied

3537. The 3 conditions for bankruptcy must be fulfilled at the time of the judgment of bankruptcy. Therefore, if a bankrupt trader lodges an appeal against the judgment of bankruptcy, the appellate court will not take into account any improvement in the financial situation of the bankrupt trader. The appellate court must verify whether the conditions for bankruptcy were fulfilled at the time of the original judgment.

B. Participants in the proceedings

3538. Under Belgian law there is nothing like a factual state of bankruptcy. Bankruptcy must always be declared by a judgment of the commercial court. If the trader is an individual, the competent court is that of the place where the trader has his principal establishment, *i.e.*, where the trader is carrying out his business (Art. 631, para. 1, section 1 of the Judicial Code). The competent court is determined on the day of the application or of the filing for bankruptcy. In addition, the court competent for judicial composition is solely competent for declaring the trader bankrupt during the judicial composition proceedings (Art. 631, para. 2, section 2 of the Judicial Code).

3539. As far as companies are concerned, the competent court is the commercial court of the place where the company has its registered office. In the case of a fictitious registered office, the principal administrative office will be decisive (Cass., 2

December 1996, *R.D.C.*, 1997, 526). The competent court is determined on the day of the application or of the filing for bankruptcy. However, if the individual trader or the company has moved the registered office within one year before the application or the filing for bankruptcy, the bankruptcy can also be declared by the court where the trader was previously located. In this case, the competent court is the first court before which the case is brought.

3540. Other important protagonists in the bankruptcy proceedings are the bankruptcy trustee (*curator/curateur*), the supervising judge (*rechter-commissaris/juge commissaire*), the provisional administrator (*voorlopig beheerder/administrateur provisoire*) as well as the Public Prosecutor (*Openbaar Ministerie /Ministère Public*).

3541. The bankruptcy trustee manages the estate (*failliete boedel/masse faillie*) in which all assets and liabilities of the bankrupt trader are brought together, and liquidates the assets to pay off the creditors' debts with the proceeds thereof. Bankruptcy trustees, hereinafter also referred to as "trustees", are chosen from persons mentioned on a list that is drawn up by the general assembly of the commercial court. Only lawyers registered with a Belgian bar who have enjoyed a specific education and are able to give guarantees as to their competence in the field of liquidation proceedings can be mentioned on this list (Art. 27 of the Bankruptcy Law). In case the bankruptcy so requires, the trustees may be assisted by accounting practitioners experienced in the management of collective proceedings. The trustee represents both the trader's creditors and the bankrupt trader. He acts under the supervision of the supervising judge who is appointed by the court among the judges. Assisted by the clerk of the court, the supervising judge rules on urgent measures, overviews the winding-up, decides on a contingency plan, presides over the creditors' meetings and also reports regularly to the court. The Public Prosecutor can initiate bankruptcy proceedings. The role of the provisional administrator is discussed below.

C. Procedure

§1. Initiation of procedure

3542. The bankruptcy is pronounced by the commercial court following either a declaration by the trader himself, a request by one or more creditors or a request by the Public Prosecutor or the provisional administrator (Art. 6 of the Bankruptcy Law). Bankruptcies regularly ensue from judicial composition proceedings.

1. From judicial composition to bankruptcy

3543. The court that has ordered the judicial composition proceedings has the power to declare the trader bankrupt if (i) it rejects the application for judicial composition, (ii) the trader no longer satisfies the conditions for judicial composition, (iii) the court does not grant the definitive stay or (iv) the court revokes the definitive stay (Arts. 15, para. 2, 24, 33 and 37 of the Judicial Composition Law). In these cases the court must hear the trader specifically on the conditions of bankruptcy.

2. Declaration of bankruptcy by trader

3544. Every trader must, within one month of his cessation of payments, apply for bankruptcy by filing a declaration to this effect with the court registry (Art. 9 of the Bankruptcy Law). The trader must explain in detail his financial situation, identify his liabilities and assets and deposit with the court his accounting books, the personnel register and a list of clients and suppliers (Art. 10 of the Bankruptcy Law).

3545. Article 9 of the Bankruptcy Law does not apply to foreign traders having a branch of activity in Belgium (Art. 3, para. 1 of the Bankruptcy Law).

3546. Criminal sanctions are applicable if the trader does not declare the bankruptcy within the prescribed time (Art. 489*bis* of the Criminal Code). The trader can also be held liable for damages in tort owing to his negligence in declaring bankruptcy in due time (Brussels Court of Appeal, 24 February 2000, *R.P.S.*, 2000, 258).

3547. The trader should also inform the workers' representatives of the bankruptcy. However, this consultation is not a formal condition for bankruptcy proceedings.

3. Filing for bankruptcy by one or more creditor(s)

3548. Any Belgian or foreign creditor has the right to request the court to declare a debtor bankrupt. The creditor must be able to provide evidence that he owns a due and outstanding debt against the debtor and that the trader is in the situation of persistent cessation of payments. The debt does not need to be secured or backed by a court order. Individual creditors are not permitted to use this procedure as a means to force the debtor to honour the payment of a debt when other ways to obtain payment remain available. The court will, in any case, review the general financial situation of the debtor. Indeed, the debtor's refusal to pay a debt may well be based on grounds other than financial difficulties.

4. Filing for bankruptcy by Public Prosecutor

3549. The Public Prosecutor is entitled to apply for bankruptcy with the court. This often occurs following the sending of a file by the chambers of commercial investigation established within the commercial courts.

5. Filing for bankruptcy by provisional administrator

3550. The provisional administrator (*voorlopige beheerder/administrateur provisoire*), appointed by the court (*See*, para. 3561), manages the trader's assets in case of absolute necessity. If there are precise, serious and corroborating signs that the conditions for bankruptcy are met, he is also entitled to apply for bankruptcy with the court (Art. 8 of the Bankruptcy Law).

§2. Judgment of the court

1. Content of the judgment

3551. The court can stay the bankruptcy decision for 15 days in order to offer the trader the possibility to apply for judicial composition (Art. 7 of the Bankruptcy Law).

3552. In addition to the declaration of bankruptcy, the judgment provides for:
  (i) the appointment of one or more bankruptcy trustees, depending on the importance of the bankruptcy;
  (ii) the appointment of a supervising judge;
  (iii) the order to make an inventory of the assets;
  (iv) the determination of the time-limit during which creditors must inform the court of their debts against the bankrupt trader (this time-limit cannot exceed 30 days following the judgment of bankruptcy);
  (v) the determination of the date and hour at which the list of the outstanding debts will be closed; and
  (vi) the newspapers in which excerpts of the judgment must be published

3553. Moreover, the judgment declaring the bankruptcy may indicate the date of the cessation of payments. This date is relevant for the validity of the transactions carried out by the trader prior to the judgment of bankruptcy and has important consequences (*See*, paras. 3565 *et seq.*).

3554. Pursuant to Article 149 of the Belgian Constitution the reasoning behind a judgment, *i.e.*, why the court considers that all conditions of bankruptcy are satisfied, must be stated in the judgment.

3555. The commercial court can reject a petition for bankruptcy.

2. Publicity given to judgment

3556. The judgment is served on the trader at the trustee's request. It informs the trader (i) of the possibility to lodge an appeal or an application to set aside the judgment proceedings, and (ii) of the trader's requested presence when the list of outstanding debts will be closed.

3557. Excerpts of the bankruptcy judgment are in principle published in 2 local newspapers and in the *Belgian Official Journal* (Art. 38 of the Bankruptcy Law). The judgment is also referred to in the file held at the registry of the court (Art. 39 of the Bankruptcy Law).

3558. The creditors known to the trustee will be personally informed of the bankruptcy and requested to declare all their outstanding debts.

3. Provisional freezing of trader's assets

3559. Since *ex officio* bankruptcy proceedings, *i.e.*, bankruptcy proceedings initiated by the court, no longer exist, there is a danger that a trader's assets may disappear prior to the declaration or the filing for bankruptcy. For this reason the President of the Commercial Court can, even prior to any bankruptcy proceedings, order the provisional dispossession (*preventieve ontzetting/ dessaisissment provisoire*) of the trader's assets in an interlocutory ruling. This measure can be requested by any person establishing a sufficient interest, *e.g.*, the trader's creditors or employees. Additionally, provisional dispossession may also be decided *ex officio*, *i.e.*, upon the initiative of the court (Ghent Court of Appeal, 26 January 1998, *R.D.C.*, 1998, 122) by the President of the Commercial Court. The proceedings are conducted on an *ex parte* basis: the trader is not informed of his future dispossession in order to ensure the effectiveness of the court order.

3560. The conditions for the provisional dispossession are (i) the absolute necessity for doing so, which amounts to extreme urgency, and, (ii) the existence of precise, serious and corroborating evidence that the conditions of bankruptcy are met (Art. 8, para.1 of the Bankruptcy Law).

3561. The decision of the President of the Commercial Court triggers the provisional dispossession of the trader's assets and appoints a provisional administrator (*voorlopig beheerder/administrateur provisoire*) to manage the assets concerned. The latter is entitled to file for bankruptcy against the trader (Art. 6 of the Bankruptcy Law).

3562. As noted, the provisional dispossession proceedings take place prior to any bankruptcy declaration. The president's decision becomes null and void either if an application for bankruptcy is not filed with the court within 15 days following the president's decision or if the judgment of bankruptcy is not pronounced within 4 months following the initiation of the bankruptcy proceedings (Art. 8, paras. 5 and 6 of the Bankruptcy Law).

3563. The President's decision is not published. Therefore, the payment of the debts to third parties who are unaware of the President's decision is valid and enforceable against the bankrupt estate in the case of an ensuing bankruptcy, unless (i) these third parties knew of the trader's dispossession, or (ii) the payment falls within the suspicious period (*See*, paras. 3565 *et seq.*) (Art. 8 of the Bankruptcy Law). Payments made by third parties to the trader after his dispossession are only valid if these third parties were unaware of the president's decision (Art. 8 of the Bankruptcy Law).

3564. The trader can lodge an application to set aside the President's decision.

4. Date of cessation of payments –"Suspicious period"

3565. Before being declared bankrupt a trader may be keen to favour some creditors to the disadvantage of the others, thereby thwarting the principle of equal treatment of all creditors. For this reason, the payments made by the bankrupt trader between the date deemed to be the date of the cessation of payments of his debts to the date of the judgment of bankruptcy are non-enforceable as against the estate. This period is called the "suspicious period" (*verdachte periode/période suspecte*) (Arts. 17 and 18 of the Bankruptcy Law).

3566. The date of the cessation of payments is considered to coincide with the date of the judgment declaring the bankruptcy or, in the case of a deceased trader, the date of his death. However, the court may also fix this date prior to the judgment of bankruptcy if objective information dictates such a decision (Art. 12 of the Bankruptcy Law).

3567. The non-enforceability laid down by Article 17 of the Bankruptcy Law is compulsory. As a result, the judge is obliged to declare certain transactions as non-enforceable as against the estate. These are:
(i) any transfer of movable or immovable property without consideration, or equivalent transactions (settlement of a debt without consideration, offering to be a guarantor of debt without consideration, *etc.*) (Art. 17, 1° of the Bankruptcy Law);
(ii) any contract against consideration if the value of what is transferred by the bankrupt trader significantly exceeds the value of what he receives in return (Art. 17, 1° of the Bankruptcy Law);

> (iii) any repayments, in money or otherwise, of debts that are not yet due: this includes the delivery of goods by the trader prior to the delivery date (Art. 17, 2° of the Bankruptcy Law);
>
> (iv) any repayments of mature debts other than (i) in money or (ii) by way of negotiable instruments or (iii) contractual payment modes (Art. 17, 2° of the Bankruptcy Law); or
>
> (v) the grant of mortgages or liens on goods of the bankrupt trader for debts previously incurred.

3568. In addition, acts that are not listed in Article 17 of the Bankruptcy Law may be non-enforceable only if the trustee demonstrates that the following 3 conditions are satisfied:

> (i) the acts took place during the suspicious period (*See*, para. 3565);
>
> (ii) the third party who dealt with the bankrupt trader was aware of the cessation of payments by the trader – mere knowledge by the third party is sufficient and it is not necessary to provide evidence of bad faith on the third party's part; and
>
> (iii) the acts are detrimental to the property of the bankrupt trader (Art.18 of the Bankruptcy Law).

§3. Declaration and verification of debts against the estate

3569. The trustee and the creditors need to calculate the trader's total liabilities as soon as possible. Therefore, all creditors, including those benefiting from securities on specific assets, must declare their debt(s) *vis-à-vis* the bankrupt trader.

1. Information to creditors

3570. Excerpts of the judgment whereby the trader is declared bankrupt are published in the *Belgian Official Journal* and in principle in 2 local newspapers. The trustee shall identify the bankrupt trader's creditors and inform them by a circular letter of the bankruptcy and of the need to declare their debts (Art. 62, para. 2 of the Bankruptcy Law).

2. Place and time of declaration of debts

3571. The creditors must declare their debts with the registry of the commercial court that rendered the bankruptcy judgment. In practice, creditors sometimes address their declaration of debts to the trustee. The trustee is then under an obligation to file the debts with the court registry; failure to do so could entail his liability.

3572. The debts must be declared within the period specified in the judgment which cannot exceed 30 days as from the date of the bankruptcy judgment (Art. 11, para.

1 of the Bankruptcy Law). If the creditor declares his debt after the prescribed time, he is not entitled to any part in the proceeds already distributed (Art. 72 of the Bankruptcy Law). The creditor can still declare his debts before the meeting during which the bankruptcy books are closed (Art. 72, paras. 2 and 3 of the Bankruptcy Law). However, he will only be entitled to his part in the proceeds not yet distributed among the creditors. In such a case, the creditor can only claim for a part of the proceeds distributed after his late declaration, subject to the payment of additional legal costs. Late declarations are in principle only permitted within 3 years as from the judgment of bankruptcy (Art. 72, para. 3 of the Bankruptcy Law).

3573. Creditors benefiting from a privilege, *i.e.*, a form of security, on determined asset(s) of the trader are entitled to execute their privilege, subject to the admission of their debt by the court. Creditors benefiting from a retention of title clause can enforce their debt at any stage of the bankruptcy proceedings.

3574. After the closure of the bankruptcy proceedings, the creditor can claim payment of his debt from the trader, unless the trader has been discharged (*See*, para. 3634).

3. Form of declaration of debts

3575. The declaration of debts is done in writing and mentions the full name and address of the creditor, his professional activities, the amount of and the basis for his debt and the security interests, mortgages or liens attached thereto, as well as the deed on which the debt is based, *e.g.*, a contract or a letter of credit (Art. 63 of the Bankruptcy Law).

3576. The written declaration must be executed by the creditor or his proxy holder, in which case a copy of the proxy indicating the amount of the debt is attached to the declaration (Art. 63, para. 2 of the Bankruptcy Law).

3577. All pending court cases at the time of the bankruptcy involving the bankrupt trader are suspended during the period of the bankruptcy proceedings. If the trustee admits the debts, the court proceedings become irrelevant. If not, the trustee is deemed to resume the proceedings in lieu of the bankrupt trader (Art. 63*bis* of the Bankruptcy Law).

3578. Any creditor residing outside Belgium is advised to elect a domicile in Belgium for the purpose of the proceedings. This requirement is compulsory for non-EU creditors. If the creditor elects a domicile in Belgium, all communications will be addressed to that address. Failure to elect a domicile in Belgium means that all communications will be kept at the registry of the commercial court (Art. 64 of the Bankruptcy Law).

3579. The declaration of debts must be made in the language used by the commercial court. If the trader has been declared bankrupt by the Brussels Commercial Court, the declaration of debts – as well as the proxy – may be made in French or in Dutch. These language requirements do not apply to the documents on which the creditor's debt is based. These documents can even be in a language other than the official languages used in Belgium.

4. Verification of debts

3580. The trustee and the trader verify the debts. The verification process takes place within the period determined by the judge which varies between 5 and 30 days as from the deadline for the declaration of debts. The trustee either admits the non-disputable debts or contests them. In doing so, he checks whether the requirements as to the form of the declaration are met, examines the document incorporating the underlying transaction presented by the creditor and compares that transaction with the records of the bankrupt trader. The trustee can raise legal objections against any particular claim. If the trustee disputes the debt or its amount, he can admit it provisionally for a limited amount. The trustee must hear the trader as to the verification of the debts and the most appropriate realisation of the trader's assets (Art. 65 of the Bankruptcy Law).

3581. The bankruptcy judgment mentions the place and date of the hearing where the formal record of the verification of the debts is established. Pursuant to Article 71 of the Bankruptcy Law, a document containing all information about the debts and their admission (or not) is drawn up on behalf of the registrar and is held for consultation at the court registry. At the hearing, the trustee states whether he accepts or refuses the declared debts. A formal record reflecting these statements is drawn up.

3582. The debts that have been accepted by the trustee and that are not challenged by the bankrupt trader or other creditors, are definitively established and, in principle, can no longer be contested. The definitive establishment of a debt covers both its existence and its amount. This rule is however subject to limitations regarding fraud, public order and *force majeure*.

5. Disputes over verification of debts

3583. If the trustee refuses a debt, or refuses the security attached to it, he will inform the creditor. To that end, the trustee will send a letter by registered mail to the creditor informing him of the place and time of the hearing (Art. 68 of the Bankruptcy Law).

3584. A debt that has been accepted by the trustee can be challenged by the bankrupt trader or by another creditor. Creditors are entitled to challenge debts of other creditors provided that their own debts have been verified.

3585. Subsequent to the hearing at which the formal record of the verification of the debts is drawn up, the commercial court rules on all disputes relating to the verification. The date for this ruling is determined in a letter sent by registered mail to the concerned creditors. The Belgian Parliament intended these disputes to be handled by the commercial court in an expeditious way. Therefore, debts requiring an in-depth analysis are set apart and are dealt with pursuant to the ordinary procedure.

§4. Consequences for trader

1. Personal consequences

3586. The declaration of bankruptcy affects the trader's personal freedom and his professional activities. The bankrupt trader must remain at the disposal of the trustee and the supervising judge and must appear in person whenever he is summoned (Art. 53 of the Bankruptcy Law). All letters addressed to him will be sent to and opened by the trustee (Art. 50 of the Bankruptcy Law). Moreover, in the hypothesis that a bankrupt trader is sentenced, even conditionally, to 3 months in prison, Royal Decree No. 22 of 24 October 1934 (as amended) ("Royal Decree No. 22") prohibits the trader from acting either as a director (*bestuurder/administrateur* or *zaakvoerder/gérant*) or as a commissioner (*commissaris/commissaire*) in several types of companies, including Belgian branches of foreign companies. The bankrupt trader and the administrator of a bankrupt company receiving an identical sentence are prohibited from pursuing any trade activity for a period from 3 to 10 years (Art. 3*bis* of Royal Decree No. 22). Finally, the bankrupt trader is banned from exercising certain professions such as stock broking, banking, accounting and the like.

3587. Additionally, the bankruptcy of a legal entity can, under certain circumstances, be extended to the company manager if the property of the company and of the manager have been inextricably mixed (Cass., 1 June 1979, *Pas.*, I, 1130).

2. Dispossession (ontheffing van dagelijks bestuur/dessaisissement)

3588. As of the day of bankruptcy the trader is deprived by law of all his assets, *i.e.*, the rights to manage and to transfer the assets, including the ones that he will obtain during the insolvency procedure, in order to safeguard the creditors' base for reimbursement. All payments, acts or transactions carried out by the trader, and all payments made to the trader after the declaration of bankruptcy are non-enforceable against the estate. The declaration of bankruptcy thus results in a situation similar to that resulting from the seizure of all assets of the bankrupt trader.

3589. At the same time, the commercial court appoints a trustee to manage the estate in which all assets and liabilities of the bankrupt estate are brought together and to liquidate the assets in order to pay the creditors with the proceeds thereof. These measures are based on the principles of equal treatment and the safeguarding of the creditors' rights. They seek to prevent the bankrupt trader from giving preferential treatment to one or more of his creditors to the detriment of the others.

3590. The bankrupt estate includes, in principle, all of the trader's assets. For the trader, the loss of his right to manage the estate does not result in the loss of his ownership rights. The trader will therefore be deemed to be the seller when the trustee sells assets of the bankrupt estate. Moreover, there are 3 exceptions to the general rule that the trader must not manage any of his assets. The trader and his family members may first be granted goods for personal use as well as a minimal allowance (Art. 1408 of the Judicial Code). Likewise, part of certain benefits to which the bankrupt trader is entitled (such as salary, pension, and other allowances) cannot be seized (Arts. 1409 through 1412 of the Judicial Code). Finally, indemnities compensating bodily harm resulting from illegal acts are not covered by the dispossession.

3591. The bankruptcy judgment does not deprive the bankrupt trader of the right to engage in new business activities, subject to the exceptions stated above (Cass., 26 October 1987, *R.W.*, 1987-1988, 950). Goods acquired as a result of these new business activities form part, after deduction of the costs and charges incurred for their acquisition and of an allowance necessary for the support of the bankrupt trader and his family, of the bankrupt estate (Mons Court of Appeal, 13 December 1988, *J.L.M.B.*, 1989, 157).

3592. The bankrupt trader is also deprived of his right to engage in legal proceedings, either as a plaintiff or as a defendant (Art. 24 of the Bankruptcy Law). In court, he must be represented by the trustee, even if the proceedings started prior to the declaration of bankruptcy or if an appeal was lodged against a judgment rendered prior to the declaration of bankruptcy. However, the trader may institute actions or defend himself in strictly personal matters, *e.g.*, parenthood, divorce, libel. Likewise, he can defend himself in criminal proceedings and actions related to any new business activity. The trustee may intervene in these proceedings in order to safeguard the rights of the trader's creditors.

3. Non-enforceability of acts of bankrupt trader (niet-tegenstelbaarheid van de daden van de gefailleerde/inopposabilité des actes du failli)

3593. All payments or transactions made by, or made to, the bankrupt trader from the date of bankruptcy are non-enforceable as against the estate (Art.16 of the Bankruptcy Law). The relevant date is the date of the initiating event rather than the date of its consequences. For instance, the relevant date of a debt resulting from a tort is rather the date of the tort than the date of the court decision on this tort. Similarly, the relevant date of a conditional debt is rather the date of the debt than the date of the fulfilment of the condition attached.

§5. Consequences for creditors

1. All debts against the bankrupt trader become due

3594. As a result of the bankruptcy, all existing debts against the bankrupt trader, under civil or commercial law, secured or unsecured, become due (Art. 22 of the Bankruptcy Law).

3595. Only the debts against the bankrupt trader become due. The position of co-debtors or guarantors is not affected. However, if the bankrupt trader has signed a promissory note or accepted a bill of exchange (or drawn an unaccepted bill of exchange) the co-debtors must provide security that payment will be made on the due date or, failing that, pay immediately.

3596. Debts on which no interest is due, and which have a due date falling more than one year after the declaration of bankruptcy, will be admitted to the estate after deduction of a sum equal to the statutory interest calculated over the period between the bankruptcy and the due date (Art. 22, para. 3 of the Bankruptcy Law).

3597. With respect to the transactions on credit, leases, or loans, the entire amount of the transaction becomes due. Penalty clauses are valid within the limits of the law.

2. Interest ceases to accumulate

3598. The interest due on debts that are unsecured or secured with a general privilege ceases to accumulate as of the declaration of bankruptcy (Art. 23, para. 1 of the Bankruptcy Law). All types of interest are covered: statutory, contractual and judicial. For debts secured with a special privilege, pledge or mortgage, the interest due continues to accumulate until payment but can only be claimed from the proceeds of the goods covered by the special privilege (*Ibid.*). The rule that interest ceases to accumulate applies only for the purposes of calculating the amount of the debts admitted to the estate. It does not affect the claim against the co-debtors or guarantors, nor the claim against the bankrupt trader after the closing of the bankruptcy proceedings (*See*, paras. 3629 *et seq.*).

3. *Enforcement of individual legal actions is suspended (opschorting van individuele vorderingen/suspension des poursuites individuelles)*

3599. As of the date of the bankruptcy, the creditors lose the right to bring or pursue any action against the bankrupt trader. Any such action must be initiated against the trustee (Art. 24 of the Bankruptcy Law). Actions involving the bankrupt trader that are pending at the time of bankruptcy will be pursued by the trustee. The trader may however intervene. Attachment proceedings instituted prior to the bankruptcy cease to have an effect as of the bankruptcy, unless the proceedings have already reached their final stage (Art. 25, para. 2 of the Bankruptcy Law), *i.e.*, the public sale. In that case, the proceeds of the sale will benefit the estate (*Ibid.*).

3600. These rules concerning the attachment proceedings only apply to unsecured creditors and creditors benefiting from a general security, *i.e.*, a security which covers all the assets of the bankrupt estate. By contrast, creditors benefiting from a specific security or privilege on movable property are allowed to enforce their security or privilege only once the procedure relating to the verification of debts has been completed (Art. 26 of the Bankruptcy Law).

4. *Consequences of bankruptcy on existing agreements*

3601. In principle, the contracts in existence at the time of bankruptcy remain in force. However, contracts entered into specifically in view of the personal capacities of the bankrupt trader (so called *intuitu personae* contracts; *e.g.*, franchising agreements), will terminate automatically. Moreover, many agreements provide for the automatic termination of the agreement in case the contracting party is declared bankrupt. A clause to that effect is valid.

3602. Since the declaration of bankruptcy has, in principle, no bearing on the existence of contracts, the trustee will decide for each contract whether to continue performing it or not (Art. 46 of the Bankruptcy Law). His decision must be guided by the best interests of the estate.

3603. In case of *inertia* by the trustee, the co-contractor can, preferably by the means of a registered letter, force him to decide within 15 days whether or not to continue the agreement. If the trustee does not take a position on the question within the prescribed time limit, the contract is deemed to terminate at the expiry date of the 15-day period. The eventual claim for damages resulting from this termination is a debt in the estate (Art. 46, para. 2 of the Bankruptcy Law) (*See*, para. 3605).

3604. If the trustee decides not to continue performing a contract, the other party's claim for damages, if any, will be admitted as a debt in the estate. On the other hand, if the trustee decides to continue performing the pending contract, the debt of the other party arising as a result of the continuation of the performance of the contract, posterior to the bankruptcy, will not become a debt in the estate, but rather a debt of the estate (Art. 46, para. 3 of the Bankruptcy Law).

3605. The distinction between debts in the estate (*schulden in de massa/dettes dans la masse*) and debts of the estate (*schulden van de massa/dettes de la masse*) which has been established by case law is of primary importance for the distribution of the proceeds among the trader's creditors. Debts of the estate are paid out of the estate prior to the payment of other creditors (debts in the estate). The debts of the estate include the costs and expenses involved in the management of the estate, the fees owed to the trustee, all types of legal and administrative expenses incurred by the trustee on behalf of the estate as well as the debts resulting from new agreements or agreements that are in existence at the time of the declaration of bankruptcy and which the trustee chooses to continue. All the other debts will be debts in the estate.

   5. Action for recovery of property – Retention of title clause – Recall of goods in transit

3606. The action for recovery of property (*revendicatievordering/action en revendication*) is admitted at any stage of the proceedings prior to the formal recording of the verification of debts (Art. 101, para. 3 of the Bankruptcy Law). The bankruptcy does not hamper the action for recovery of property, unless the asset concerned is no longer within the bankrupt trader's hands.

3607. The retention of title clause is enforceable against the estate (Art. 101 of the Bankruptcy Law). The clause must be in writing and is only enforceable if the goods concerned are still in the bankrupt trader's hands. The retention of title clause cannot be extended by mutual agreement so as to cover previous deliveries of unpaid goods (Cass., 17 October 1996, *J.L.M.B.*, 1997, 520).

3608. The goods that were sent but have not yet been delivered at the time of the declaration of bankruptcy can also be recovered, unless the goods reached the bankrupt trader's premises.

   §6. Liquidation of the estate – Overview of priorities among creditors

3609. The realisation by the trustee is permitted as from the date of the closure of the formal recording of the verification of debts. An authorization of the court is not required. In addition, the trustee is always entitled to realise any asset that is subject to depreciation, such as food, or whose conservation costs are considered to be prohibitive.

3610. The trustee, guided by the best interests of the estate, chooses the most appropriate method of sale for movable property. He does not need the prior approval of the supervising judge or of the commercial court.

3611. Immovable property must be sold by public auction or by mutual agreement, respecting the formalities laid down in Articles 1190 *et seq.* of the Judicial Code. The supervising judge expresses his views on the sale of immovable property.

3612. Creditors benefiting from a first mortgage can pursue the forced realisation of the mortgaged property as from the date of the formal recording of the admitted or contested debts. In this case, the trustee can however request the court for a one year stay, if this is in the interest of the estate and does not jeopardise the claims of the creditors benefiting from the mortgage (Art. 100, para. 2 of the Bankruptcy Law).

3613. Subject to this exception of the creditors benefiting from a mortgage, the trustee is solely entitled to pursue the forced realisation of immovable property (Art. 100, para. 1 of the Bankruptcy Law). Forced sales that were started prior to the bankruptcy judgment can be resumed by the trustee, subject to the prior approval of the court (Art. 100, para. 4 of the Bankruptcy Law).

3614. The trustee is entitled to dispose of a part or the whole of the business during the liquidation proceedings. In such a case, the assets (but not the liabilities) are sold to a third party provided the sale is profitable to the creditors. This sale of the business as a going concern, organised under Article 75, paragraph 4 of the Bankruptcy Law, also comprises immovable assets. Such a transfer is subject to specific labour law rules (*See*, Chapter 8).

3615. The proceeds of the disposal must be deposited with a specific government-controlled financial institution (*Deposito- en Consignatiekas/Caisse des Dépôts et Consignations*) and are distributed among the creditors in proportion to the debts that were verified and accepted. However, such a distribution only takes place after deduction of the debts of the estate and the sums paid out to secured creditors (Art. 99 of the Bankruptcy Law).

3616. The proceeds of the realisation of assets covered by a specific security do not form part of the bankrupt estate and are therefore not subject to the rule of Article 99 of the Bankruptcy Law. The creditors benefiting from a specific security are paid directly with the proceeds of the realisation of the goods covered by the specific securities. If the proceeds prove to be insufficient, these creditors are admitted as unsecured creditors for the rest of their claims, provided that these claims were declared and accepted.

3617. After payment of the debts of the estate, the secured debts are paid out. This only concerns those debts that are covered by a general security. By contrast, the debts covered by a specific security are paid out directly from the proceeds of the goods affected by the specific security. If after the payment of the creditors benefiting from a general security there are still proceeds left, these will be paid out to the unsecured creditors in proportion to the value of their debts.

3618. The above description deliberately ignores the extremely complex issues that may arise from the existence of conflicting securities. The complexity of this matter, which is partly caused by a marked absence of coherence in the applicable legal provisions, has given rise to extensive case law the analysis of which falls outside the scope of this chapter.

§7. Application to set aside and appeal proceedings

3619. A judgment declaring a trader bankrupt or fixing the date of cessation of payments can be executed even if an application to set aside the judgment or an appeal has been lodged against it. The trustee will however take all of the required safeguard measures and liquidate the assets under the control of the supervising judge.

3620. The application to set aside the judgment or the appeal will only be upheld if, at the time of the declaration of bankruptcy, the statutory conditions for bankruptcy were not met.

3621. The application to set aside the judgment asks the court, which has rendered the bankruptcy judgment, to withdraw it. This action is initiated by the defaulting party (opposition) or by any person, meriting an interest, not party to the initial judgment (third-party opposition). By contrast, during an appeal procedure, the plaintiff requests a higher court, namely the court of appeal, to overrule the judgment of the commercial court.

1. Opposition and third-party opposition

3622. The trader who defended himself before the court is not allowed to oppose the judgment but must instead lodge an appeal with the court of appeal.

3623. The trader declared bankrupt ensuing judicial composition proceedings cannot oppose the judgment, unless he has not been specifically heard on the conditions of bankruptcy. If this is not the case, he must lodge an appeal with the court of appeal.

3624. But the trader who applied for bankruptcy is not considered as a party to the proceedings and can therefore oppose the judgment.

3625. A creditor who has not taken part in the initial proceedings is entitled to file a third-party opposition against the judgment.

3626. An opposition by the bankrupt trader must be filed within 15 days following the notice served on him, and the third-party opposition by any other interested person within 15 days following the publication of the excerpts of the judgment in the *Belgian Official Journal*. The opposition or third-party opposition is notified to all parties involved in the initial judgment, including the trader and the trustee, and indicates why the conditions of bankruptcy were not met. The opposition or third-party opposition is promptly investigated. At a party's request, the parties will argue the case within a month (Art. 15 of the Bankruptcy Law).

2. Appeal

3627. The parties to the judgment having an interest in being overruled must resort to an appeal procedure. However, if a creditor was not a party to the judgment, he must oppose it.

3628. The appeal must be notified to all parties in the original proceedings, *i.e.*, the trustee, the creditors on whose request the judgment was rendered, *etc.* The lodging of an appeal by the trader must take place within 15 days of the official notification of the bankruptcy judgment. For any other party, the fifteen days period starts as from the publication in the *Belgian Official Journal* (Art. 14, para. 4 of the Bankruptcy Law).

§8. Closure of bankruptcy proceedings

1. Different ways to close proceedings

3629. In principle, bankruptcy proceedings are closed after the realisation and distribution of the assets of the bankrupt trader. The trustee will then convene a creditors' meeting at which he will file a report in which his fees, the debts of the estate as well as the realisation of the assets and their distribution to the various creditors are spelled out (Art. 79 of the Bankruptcy Law). The bankrupt trader is invited to attend and can present his views. Creditors also present their observations concerning the trader's discharge (*See*, para. 3634).

3630. The commercial court rules on all disputes that have arisen over the distribution of the proceeds, if any, and orders the official closure of the bankruptcy proceedings. This judgment is notified to the bankrupt trader and, if the commercial court deems it appropriate, published in the *Belgian Official Journal*.

3631. In practice, when, prior to the creditors' meeting, it appears that the assets owned by the bankrupt trader will not be sufficient to cover the expected costs and expenses to be incurred for the management and the liquidation of the estate another procedure is followed (*summiere rechtspleging tot sluiting van het faillisement/ procédure sommaire de clotûre*). In that case, the commercial court will, after having heard both the trustee and the bankrupt trader, order the closure of the bankruptcy proceedings. This judgment will be suspended for a one-month period during which the bankrupt trader or any other interested party may intervene to demonstrate the existence of sufficient funds to cover the expenses to be incurred in the administration and liquidation of the estate or to deposit a sum sufficient for these purposes.

2. Consequences of closure – discharge

3632. The judgment on the closure of the bankruptcy proceedings puts an end to the trustee's appointment.

3633. In case the bankrupt trader is a legal person, the legal entity is wound up as a result of the judgment on the closure of the bankruptcy proceedings (Art. 83 of the Bankruptcy Law).

3634. In case the bankrupt trader is a natural person, the commercial court can in the closure judgment declare the discharge of the trader. If discharged, the trader can no longer be sued for the payment of his trading debts by the creditors (Art. 82, para. 1 of the Bankruptcy Law). If the natural person is not declared discharged, the trader regains the right to manage his goods, whereas the creditors recover their rights of enforcement of their debts against the trader. Discharge is automatically rejected if the trader is convicted of theft, fraud and so on (Art. 489*ter* of the Criminal Code). The discharge also benefits the free-of-charge guarantors of the bankrupt trader, as well as the bankrupt trader's spouse.

V. INTERNATIONAL ASPECTS

3635. Despite the globalisation of trade, international harmonisation of judicial composition and bankruptcy law has remained minimal, probably owing to a tendency to protect the hierarchy of creditors from any foreign interference. This can result in major practical difficulties as recent prominent bankruptcies, such as that involving Lernout & Hauspie, have shown. At the international level, Belgium has concluded bilateral agreements with France, the Netherlands and Austria. Furthermore, Belgium has signed (but did not ratify yet) the Uncitral Model Legal Provisions on Cross-Border Insolvency.

3636. This section will only focus on EU Council Regulation No. 1346/2000 of 29 May 2000 on Insolvency Proceedings ("Regulation No. 1346/2000") (*O.J.* [2000] L 160) that came into force on 31 May 2002. Regulation No. 1346/2000 provides a framework for handling cross-border insolvency proceedings. Regulation No. 1346/2000 envisages 2 different types of insolvency proceedings within the European Community. The jurisdiction of the "main proceedings" is the jurisdiction where the trader has the centre of its main interests. The centre of the main interests of a legal person is presumed to be the place of the registered office. This presumption is rebuttable. Once the jurisdiction is determined, the determination of the applicable law follows the law of the proceedings. This choice of law principle is subject to exceptions regarding securities (Art. 5 of Regulation No. 1346/2000), immovable property, employment contracts, *etc.* The legal effects of these "main proceedings" must be recognised in all other EC Member States, except for Denmark. The office-holder appointed in the main proceedings, *i.e.*, in Belgium the so-called "trustee", must also be recognised and will be able to exercise his powers in other EC Member States without the need for a further court order.

3637. However, the universality and unity principles central to Regulation No. 1346/2000 are undermined by other provisions. Indeed, the Regulation also lays down the possibility to open local proceedings, known as "secondary or ancillary proceedings", the effect of which are limited to the assets in the EC Member State where the secondary proceedings are opened. This is mainly because of the substantial differences in significant law between the various EC Member States.

3638. A detailed analysis exceeds the scope of this chapter. However, key provisions of the Regulation No. 1346/2000 include Article 32, according to which creditors can declare their debts at the main proceedings as well as at the secondary proceedings, and Article 39, pursuant to which all creditors, including national tax or social security authorities, must be treated equally.

21. LITIGATION AND ARBITRATION

I. INTRODUCTION

3639. Litigation and arbitration are covered by the Judicial Code which was adopted by the Law of 10 October 1967. Its entry into force took place gradually over a period of 3 years. By 1 November 1970, the whole of the Judicial Code had entered into force. At the time of its introduction, the Judicial Code represented an attempt to unify and modernise the rules governing civil procedure.

3640. In its current version, the Code is composed of more than 1700 articles which are grouped into 6 different parts: general principles (Part I), judicial organisation (Part II), jurisdiction (Part III), civil procedure (Part IV), attachment and execution (Part V) and arbitration (Part VI).

3641. The Law of 3 August 1992 reformed the Judicial Code and has fundamentally changed the existing rules of procedure. The principal aim of the reform was to remedy judicial backlog. As the provisions of the law entered into force on 1 January 1993, only the new procedural rules are discussed here.

3642. Litigation and arbitration are by their very nature technical subjects. It is not the purpose of this chapter to describe them in a detailed manner. Rather, an overview will be given of the main features of the Belgian court system and of arbitration proceedings governed by Belgian law.

II. LITIGATION

A. Introduction

3643. This section will discuss (i) the principles of jurisdiction, (ii) the various legal professions, (iii) the way in which civil proceedings are conducted and, finally, (iv) the means of attachment and execution.

B. Jurisdiction

§1. Basic principles

3644. Jurisdiction is the authority of a court to hear actions which are brought before it (Art. 8 of the Judicial Code). In principle, the ordinary courts mentioned in the Judicial Code have jurisdiction to hear all actions (Art. 556 of the Judicial Code). Any exception must be provided by law and may only concern actions involving political rights (Art. 93 of the Constitution). These actions may be attributed to administrative courts. Actions concerning civil rights, however, are part of the exclusive jurisdiction of the ordinary courts (Art. 92 of the Constitution).

§2. Subject-matter jurisdiction and territorial jurisdiction

3645. The Judicial Code distinguishes between subject-matter jurisdiction (*volstrekte bevoegdheid/compétence d'attribution*) and territorial jurisdiction (*territoriale bevoegdheid/compétence territoriale*). Subject-matter jurisdiction determines the type of court which has the authority to hear a given action. It is based on the object and the value of the claim and, as the case may be, the urgency of the claim or the nature of the parties (Art. 9 of the Judicial Code). Territorial jurisdiction determines the venue where a given lawsuit must be tried. It is also the authority of a court to hear actions within a certain geographical area (Art. 10 of the Judicial Code). Territorial jurisdiction is determined by the existence of a certain link between the action to be tried and the geographical area in which the court may exercise its authority. Unless provided otherwise by law, the claimant may, at his choice, institute proceedings before a court which has territorial jurisdiction over the area:

  (i) where the defendant, or one of the defendants, is domiciled;

 (ii) where one or more of the legal obligations which are in dispute, has arisen, has been performed or should have been performed;

(iii) where the defendant has elected domicile; or

(iv) in cases where the defendant has no domicile in Belgium or abroad, where the bailiff has served due process on the defendant in person (Art. 624 of the Judicial Code).

3646. The principles governing subject-matter jurisdiction are principles of public policy and may not be modified by agreement between the parties, unless the law specifically provides otherwise (Art. 9 of the Judicial Code). Arbitration is one obvious example where the law authorises the parties to derogate from the principles governing subject-matter jurisdiction. Another example is provided in Article 573 of the Judicial Code which, under certain conditions, allows parties who do not qualify as traders (*handelaars/commerçants*) to act as claimants before the Commercial Court.

3647. As a general rule, the parties may derogate from the principles governing territorial jurisdiction contained in the Judicial Code. However, the Judicial Code lists numerous exceptions to this principle. In certain cases, such derogations are valid only if they are agreed upon after the dispute has arisen (Arts. 627, 628 and 629 of the Judicial Code). In other cases, no derogation at all is possible even if agreed upon after the dispute has arisen. For example, all claims relating to a bankrupt estate must be heard by the court in whose jurisdiction the bankruptcy proceedings were opened (Art. 632 of the Judicial Code).

§3. Territorial subdivisions

3648. In view of the territorial organisation of its court system, Belgium is divided into more than 200 counties (*kantons/cantons*), 26 districts (*arrondissementen/ arrondissements*) and 5 judicial areas (*rechtsgebieden/ressorts*).

§4. Courts at county level

3649. At county level, which is the lowest level, a distinction must be made between the Police Court (*Politierechtbank/Tribunal de police*) and the Justice of the Peace (*Vredegerecht/Justice de paix*). There are over 200 Justices of the Peace in Belgium, one in every county (Art. 59 of the Judicial Code). In larger counties, different magistrates will be appointed to fulfil the function of Justice of the Police Court. In smaller counties, Justices of the Peace have a double function. They serve both as Justice of the Peace and as Justice of the Police Court. Either way, these courts are always presided over by a single magistrate.

1. Justice of the Peace

3650. A Justice of the Peace is, in general, empowered to hear all cases involving claims of up to € 1,860 (Art. 590 of the Judicial Code). Article 590 lists 2 exceptions to this general rule: when the law expressly provides otherwise (*i.e.*, mainly in cases specifically attributed to the Court of First instance, the Commercial Court and the Labour Court), and when parties have made an agreement to submit their dispute to arbitration and one of them relies in due time on the arbitration agreement to contest the jurisdiction of the Justice of the Peace.

3651. In addition to his general competence, a Justice of the Peace has exclusive jurisdiction over a variety of specific claims regardless of the amount involved in the claim. The most important specific powers of a Justice of the Peace relate to disputes over all matters concerning real property leases, joint ownership and alimony (with the exception of alimony matters raised in the course of divorce proceedings) (Art. 591 of the Judicial Code).

3652. Appeals against decisions of the Justice of the Peace are, depending on the subject matter, heard by the Court of First Instance or the Commercial Court of the district in which the Justice of the Peace is located. No appeal is possible for claims with a value of € 1,240 or less (Art. 617 of the Judicial Code).

2. Police Court

3653. The Police Courts are empowered to hear all cases involving civil consequences of road accidents and cases involving misdemeanours (*overtredingen/contraventions*) (mostly minor traffic offences), which generally carry a maximum penalty of 7 days' imprisonment or a fine not exceeding € 0.62. Under Belgian law, the amount of fines is subject to a multiplier, currently set at 200, which is periodically adjusted.

3654. Appeals against judgments by the Police Court are heard by the Criminal Court (*Correctionele Rechtbank/Tribunal correctionnel*) which is a division of the Court of First Instance.

§5. Courts at district level

1. The Court of First Instance (Rechtbank van Eerste Aanleg/Tribunal de première instance)

3655. There is a Court of First Instance in each of the 26 judicial districts of Belgium. These courts are composed of 3 divisions: one dealing with civil law, one dealing with criminal law, and one dealing with juvenile matters (Art. 76 of the Judicial Code). Each division is composed of one or more chambers which, in turn, are composed of one or 3 judges (Art. 78 of the Judicial Code).

i. Civil Court (Burgerlijke Rechtbank/Tribunal civil)

3656. All claims which exceed € 1,860 and which do not fall within the specifically attributed competences of the Justices of the Peace, the Commercial Court or the Labour Courts must be brougt before the Court of First Instance. In addition, cases which are covered by specifically attributed competences of other courts (with the exception of those which must be brought directly before a Court of Appeals or the Supreme Court – *See*, Article 568 of the Judicial Code) may also be brought before the Court of First Instance, which may not refuse to hear the case on its own initiative. This is, however, without prejudice to the right of the defendant to contest the jurisdiction of the Court of First Instance (Art. 568 of the Judicial Code).

3657. Apart from its general jurisdiction, the Court of First Instance has a specifically attributed jurisdiction in a wide variety of matters. These are listed in Articles 569, 570 and 571 of the Judicial Code. For example: copyright claims exceeding € 1,860, all matrimonial matters except those which are specifically attributed to the Justices of the Peace, claims for indemnification based on the Law of 29 March 1962 relating to Zoning and Planning as well as *Exequatur* Decisions of Foreign Judgments in Civil Matters (*Wet houdende organisatie van de ruimtelijke ordening van de stedebouw/Loi organique de l'aménagement du territoire et de l'urbanisme*.

3658. The Court of First Instance is also specifically empowered to hear all cases involving disputes over the execution of judgments (Art. 569(5) of the Judicial Code). Most of these cases will be heard by the attachment judge (*beslagrechter/juge des saisies*), who is a magistrate in the Court of First Instance (Art. 79 of the Judicial Code). The attachment judge has jurisdiction to hear all claims relating to attachment measures and all other measures of execution (Art. 1395 of the Judicial Code).

ii. Criminal Court (*Correctionele Rechtbank/Tribunal correctionnel*)

3659. The Criminal Court division of the Court of First Instance hears all cases involving offences (*wanbedrijven/délits*), which carry a sentence of more than 7 days of imprisonment or a fine of more than € 25 (to be multiplied by 5) (Art. 179 of the Code of Criminal Procedure). The Criminal Court also hears appeals against judgments of the Police Court (Art. 174 of the Code of Criminal Procedure).

iii. Juvenile Court (*Jeugdrechtbank/Tribunal de la jeunesse*)

3660. The Juvenile Court, which is a division of the Court of First Instance, has general competence in most juvenile matters. Detailed provisions are contained in the Law of 8 April 1965 on Youth Protection (*Wet betreffende de jeugdbescherming/Loi relative à la protection de la jeunesse*), as amended.

iv. President of the Court of First Instance

3661. One of the principal competences of the President of the Court of First Instance is to order interim measures in all matters which he deems to be urgent (Art. 584 of the Judicial Code). Urgency is usually defined as a situation where an immediate decision is desirable in order to avoid damage of some magnitude or serious inconvenience (Cass., 21 May 1987, *Pas.*, 1987, I, 1160). Recourse may be had to summary proceedings (*kortgeding/référé*) whenever the use of normal proceedings would not lead to a timely solution of the dispute. The President has substantial discretion when deciding whether a given matter is urgent.

3662. Summary proceedings are handled in an expedited way. Orders given by the President in such cases are subject to appeal before the Court of Appeal.

3663. There are very few limits to the sort of relief which the President may grant by way of interim measures. For example, he may appoint trustees and experts; he may suspend the execution of agreements or of administrative decisions; he may even order the provisional payment of damages. One important limit to the powers of the President in summary proceedings is that the relief ordered may not bind the Court which will hear the case on the merits.

3664. Apart from his role in summary proceedings, the President of the Court of First Instance has specific competences in a series of matters listed in Articles 585, 586 and 587 of the Judicial Code. The most important among these competences are the designation of arbitrators, experts, liquidators or trustees when the law or the parties' agreement so provides and the granting of *exequatur* decisions in respect of Belgian or foreign arbitral awards.

2. *The Commercial Court (Rechtbank Van Koophandel/Tribunal de commerce)*

3665. Each judicial district has its Commercial Court. The Commercial Court is a court of special jurisdiction and is empowered to hear:
  (i) claims between traders (*handelaars/commerçants*) relating to transactions which are deemed commercial by law (*See*, Articles 2 and 3 of the Commercial Code, *See*, paras. 3465-3467) and which do not fall within the general competence of the Justice of the Peace (Art. 573(1) of the Judicial Code);
  (ii) commercial claims between a claimant who is not a trader and a defendant who is a trader, if the amounts involved are higher than € 1,860 (Art. 573(3) of the Judicial Code);
  (iii) claims involving bills of exchange and promissory notes if the amounts involved are higher than € 1,860 (*See*, Article 573(2) of the Judicial Code);
  (iv) claims arising from the Company Code (Art. 574(1) of the Judicial Code);
  (v) claims involving bankruptcy proceedings (Art. 574(2) of the Judicial Code).

3666. Other specific competences of the Commercial Court are listed in Articles 574(3) to 574(8) and 576 of the Judicial Code.

3667. The Commercial Court is composed of one or more chambers. Each chamber consists of 3 judges of which only one is a professional judge. He is assisted by 2 lay judges (*rechters in handelszaken/juges consulaires*).

3668. The Commercial Court hears appeals against decisions of the Justice of the Peace dealing with issues which fall within the specific competence of the Commercial

Court (Art. 577 of the Judicial Code). When the Commercial Court acts as appellate court, its judgments are only subject to review by the Supreme Court (*Hof van Cassatie/Cour de cassation*). When it acts as a court of first instance, appeals against judgments rendered by the Commercial Court are brought before the Court of Appeal of the judicial area to which the Commercial Court belongs. Judgments governing claims having a value of € 1,860 or less are not open to appeal (Art. 617 of the Judicial Code).

3669. The President of the Commercial Court may hear all matters which he deems to be urgent, provided they relate to the specific competence of the Commercial Court (Art. 584(2) of the Judicial Code). The cases are handled in an expedited way and the decisions are not binding on the court which is to decide the merits of the case. For further details, reference is made to the discussion of the powers of the President of the Court of First Instance in summary proceedings (*See*, paras. 3661 *et seq.*).

3670. The President of the Commercial Court also renders judgments on the merits in proceedings instituted in accordance with the Law of 14 July 1991 dealing with commercial practices and the information and protection of consumers (*See*, paras. 2792 *et seq.*).

3. The Labour Court (Arbeidsrechtbank/Tribunal du travail)

3671. In each judicial district there is a Labour Court. The Labour Court is a court of special jurisdiction which is empowered to hear claims:
   (i) relating to workers and dealing with employment contracts, the constitution and operation of works councils and health and safety committees, the termination of employment contracts, labour accidents, occupational diseases and social security issues (Arts. 578, 579, 580 and 582 of the Judicial Code);
   (ii) relating to self-employed persons and dealing with social security issues (Art. 581 of the Judicial Code).

3672. The Labour Court is composed of at least 2 chambers. Each chamber consists of a panel of 3 judges of which one or 2 are professional judges, assisted by one or 2 lay judges who are representatives of the groups to which the litigants belong (employers, employees, self-employed workers).

3673. Appeals against judgments rendered by the Labour Court are brought before the Labour Court of Appeal (*Arbeidshof/Cour du travail*) of the judicial area in which the Labour Court is located. Appeals may be lodged regardless of the value of the claim (Art. 617 of the Judicial Code).

BUSINESS LAW GUIDE TO BELGIUM

3674. The President of the Labour Court may hear all matters which he deems to be urgent, provided they fall within the specific competence of the Labour Court (Art. 584(2) of the Judicial Code). For further details, reference is made to the discussion of the authority of the President of the Court of First Instance in summary proceedings (*See*, paras. 3661 *et seq.*).

4. *The District Court (Arrondissementsrechtbank/Tribunal d'arrondissement)*

3675. The District Court is composed of the Presidents of the Court of First Instance, of the Commercial Court and of the Labour Court.

3676. The District Court is specifically empowered to rule upon conflicts of competence between the various courts at county and at district level. The District Court does not intervene in conflicts of competence between the Courts of Appeal. The District Court may be seized of a conflict of competence in 2 ways. Article 639 of the Judicial Code provides that when the defendant disputes the competence of the court before which the claimant has introduced the case, the latter may, prior to the moment the case is taken into deliberation, request the court to refer the case to the District Court. If no such request is made, the court will itself rule upon its competence. The second way in which the District Court may be seized of a conflict of competence is when the court raises its own incompetence *ex officio* (Art. 640 of the Judicial Code).

3677. The judgments of the District Court are not open to appeal, except that the attorney-general attached to the Court of Appeal (*Procureur-Generaal bij het Hof van Beroep/Procureur général près la Cour d'appel*) may bring the matter before the Supreme Court (Art. 642 of the Judicial Code).

3678. The District Court only rules on conflicts of competence between Belgian courts of ordinary jurisdiction. Conflicts of competence between Belgian and foreign courts, between ordinary courts and administrative courts and between ordinary courts and arbitral tribunals are, therefore, excluded from its competence.

§6. *Courts at the level of the judicial areas (rechtsgebieden/ressorts)*

1. *The Courts of Appeal (Hoven van Beroep/Cours d'appel)*

3679. There are 5 Courts of Appeal in Belgium (Antwerp, Brussels, Ghent, Liège and Mons). Every Court of Appeal is composed of one or more civil chambers, criminal chambers and juvenile chambers. These chambers consist of one or 3 judges (Art. 101 of the Judicial Code).

864

i. Chambers dealing with civil law matters

3680. The main function of the Court of Appeal is to hear appeals lodged against:
(i) judgments of the Court of First Instance and of the Commercial Court;
(ii) interim orders issued by the President of the Court of First Instance or by the President of the Commercial Court (Art. 602 of the Judicial Code).

3681. Apart from its competence in appellate matters, the Court of Appeal has competence in certain matters which must he introduced directly before it. For example, the Court of Appeal has competence to hear actions regarding the loss of nationality rights (Art. 604 of the Judicial Code), rehabilitation in bankruptcy matters (Art. 605 of the Judicial Code) and the homologation of decisions of a general assembly of shareholders or bondholders in a public limited company (Art. 606(2) of the Judicial Code).

3682. Every 1st instance judgment may, in principle, be appealed against unless the law expressly provides otherwise (Art. 616 of the Judicial Code). No appeal is available before the Court of Appeal if the amount involved is € 1,860 or less (Art. 617 of the Judicial Code).

ii. Chambers dealing with criminal law matters

3683. Judgments rendered by the Criminal Court (*Correctionele Rechtbank/Tribunal correctionnel*) may be appealed against before the Court of Appeal (Art. 200 of the Code of Criminal Procedure). The matter will be heard by a chamber of the court specialising in criminal matters.

iii. Chambers dealing with juvenile matters

3684. Decisions taken by the section in the Court of First Instance dealing with juvenile matters are appealed before a similar section of the Court of Appeal. As mentioned before (see para. 3660), a separate set of procedural rules is applicable in these proceedings.

2. The Labour Courts of Appeal (*Arbeidshoven/Cours du travail*)

3685. There are 5 Labour Courts of Appeal in Belgium (Antwerp, Brussels, Ghent, Liège and Mons). These courts hear appeals lodged against judgments of the Labour Courts and against interim orders by the Presidents of the Labour Courts (Art. 607 of the Judicial Code). All judgments rendered by Labour Courts may be appealed against regardless of the value of the claim which is at stake (Art. 617 of the Judicial Code).

3686. The Court of Appeal for Labour Law is composed of chambers consisting of 3 judges, of whom at least one is a professional judge. He is assisted by 2 lay judges who are representatives of the groups to which the litigants belong (employers and employees). In cases involving the social security obligations of self-employed persons, the Court is composed of 2 professional judges and of one lay judge (representing the group of self-employed persons).

§7. The Supreme Court (Hof van Cassatie/Cour de cassation)

3687. There is one Supreme Court in Belgium. It is located in Brussels and consists of 3 chambers. The first chamber hears civil and commercial cases, the second chamber hears criminal cases, while the third chamber hears labour cases (Art. 133 of the Judicial Code).

3688. The principal task of the Supreme Court is to review judgments that can no longer be appealed on the merits. The review by the Supreme Court is limited to issues of law. The Supreme Court will only verify whether the judgment which is being reviewed has applied the law correctly and has respected mandatory procedural rules (Art. 608 of the Judicial Code). Factual issues are not reviewed by the Supreme Court.

3689. Review by the Supreme Court must, in principle, be requested within a period of 3 months following the date on which the judgment has been notified (Art. 1073 of the Judicial Code).

3690. When the Supreme Court reverses and remands, the case is sent back to a court sitting at the same level as the court which rendered the reversed decision (Art. 1110 of the Judicial Code). That court is not bound by the views expressed by the Supreme Court. It is only when the judgment is reversed a second time on the same grounds that the court to which the case is remanded must follow the ruling of the Supreme Court (Art. 1120 of the Judicial Code).

3691. Apart from its powers to review judgments against which no ordinary appeal rights are available, the Supreme Court has other specifically attributed competences which are listed in Articles 609 through 615 of the Judicial Code.

3692. The procedure before the Supreme Court is governed by specific rules which are set forth in Articles 1073 through 1121 of the Judicial Code. In civil matters, only attorneys admitted to the Supreme Court may appear and file briefs before the Supreme Court (Art. 478 of the Judicial Code). Their number is currently limited to 16.

§8. Other courts

3693. The description of the court system above is by no means complete. Other courts which deserve to be mentioned briefly are the Court of Arbitration (*Arbitragehof/ Cour d'arbitrage*) and the Council of State (*Raad van State/Conseil d'Etat*) (*See*, Chapter 1). Both courts have constitutional and administrative law competences. In the area of criminal law, the Assise Courts (*Hoven van Assisen/Cours d'assises*), and the military courts and tribunals have to be cited. Internationally, the Benelux Court of Justice, the European Court of Justice and the EC Commission and Court of Human Rights also deserve to be mentioned. The scope of this book does not, however, permit any detailed discussion of their organisation and powers.

C. The legal professions

§1. Introduction

3694. The following sections describe the various legal professions in Belgium. The main legal professions are the judges, members of the public prosecutor's office, attorneys and bailiffs.

§2. Judges

3695. Judges are appointed by Royal Decree (Art. 99 of the Constitution). The conditions for their appointment are set forth in the Constitution and in the Judicial Code as amended by the Law of 18 July 1991 on the Training and Recruitment of Magistrates (*Wet tot wijziging van de voorschriften van het Gerechtelijk Wetboek die betrekking hebben op de opleiding en de werving van magistraten/Loi modifiant les règles du Code judiciaire relatives à la formation et au recrutement des magistrats*) – the "Law of 18 July 1991"). The Judicial Code contains requirements relating to the holding of a law degree, the number of years of relevant professional experience and, sometimes, the age of the candidate. In addition, the Law of 18 July 1991 has introduced a system whereby judges must either have passed a professional exam or completed a 3-year judicial training.

3696. In order to safeguard their independence, judges are, in principle, appointed for life. They are subject to disciplinary action only by other members of the judiciary. Their dismissal for disciplinary reasons may only be decided by a judgment rendered by the Supreme Court (Art. 409 of the Judicial Code). Mandatory retirement ages range from 67 to 70 years depending on the level of the court in which the judge exercises his functions (Art. 383, para. 1 of the Judicial Code). Judges may be mandatorily retired for reasons of serious and permanent infirmity which prevent them from properly exercising their functions. Unless the judge involved agrees, retirement for infirmity will be ordered by judgment of the Supreme Court, the Court of Appeal or the Labour Court of Appeal (Art. 385 of the Judicial Code).

3697. The exercise of a judicial function is incompatible with any elected public function and with any remunerated political or administrative function. Judges may not exercise the profession of notary public, bailiff or attorney. Neither may they perform military or ecclesiastical functions (Art. 293 of the Judicial Code). Their function is incompatible with any functions exercised in a trade union or a social security organisation. Judges may not, directly or indirectly, be engaged in commercial activities, nor participate in the management or surveillance of commercial companies or of industrial or commercial establishments (Art. 299 of the Judicial Code). They may not act as remunerated arbitrators (Art. 298 of the Judicial Code) nor represent any parties in court or provide legal advice (Art. 247 of the Judicial Code).

§3. The Public Prosecutor's Office (Openbaar Ministerie/Ministère public)

3698. The Public Prosecutor's Office is a service, acting under the authority of the Minister of Justice, which is attached to the various courts and tribunals. Its functions are mainly to act as claimant in penal proceedings and, in civil matters, to intervene in the cases specified by law and whenever the respect of public policy principles is endangered (Art. 138 of the Judicial Code). The list of matters in which the Public Prosecutor's Office must intervene has been shortened recently as a result of the Law of 3 August 1992 reforming the Judicial Code. Other functions exercised by the Public Prosecutor's Office are the control over the orderly functioning of the courts and tribunals (Art. 140 of the Judicial Code) and the supervision of the members of the judiciary police and of all public officials (Art. 148 of the Judicial Code). A separate section of the Public Prosecutor's Office (*arbeidsauditoraat/auditorat du travail*) is involved in labour and social security cases and is attached to the Labour Courts.

3699. Members of the Public Prosecutor's Office are appointed by Royal Decree. The conditions for their appointment are set forth in the Law of 18 July 1991 and are substantially similar to those applying to judges (*See*, paras. 3695 through 3697). The rules governing the incompatibility of certain functions or offices and those governing retirement and destitution are also substantially the same as for judges (*See*, paras. 3695 through 3697).

§4. Attorneys (advocaten/avocats)

3700. The exercise of professional activities as an attorney (*advocaat/avocat*) and the use of that title is subject to the following requirements:
   (i) Belgian citizenship or citizenship of one of the EC Member States;
   (ii) the possession of a degree of doctor of laws or an equivalent law degree;
   (iii) the taking of an oath as required by law; and
   (iv) being enlisted in a bar association (Art. 428 of the Judicial Code).

3701. There are 28 bar associations in Belgium: one for each legal district (*gerechtelijk arrondissement/arrondissement judiciaire*), except Brussels where there are 2 bar associations (Dutch and French-speaking). The limited number of attorneys allowed to practice before the Supreme Court also constitutes a separate bar association. The 13 French-speaking and the one German-speaking bar associations together constitute the Council of French-speaking and German-speaking bar association (*Ordre des barreaux francophones et germanophone*). The 14 Dutch-speaking bar associations together constitue the Council of Flemish bar associations (*Orde van Vlaamse Balies*). The main mission of these 2 councils is to unify the rules governing the profession.

3702. An attorney who is a member of a Belgian bar, either as a full member or as a trainee, is allowed to practice before any Belgian court, with the exception of the Supreme Court and the Council of State, where different rules apply (Art. 439 of the Judicial Code). Residents of other EC Member States who are allowed to practice in their Member State may exercise the profession of attorney in Belgium. Only attorneys have the right to appear before the courts on behalf of their clients. In that respect, and subject to limited exceptions (*e.g.*, before labour courts) they enjoy a legal monopoly (Art. 440 of the Judicial Code). In their role as legal advisors, attorneys do not benefit from a monopoly.

3703. Attorneys are not allowed to exercise any of the following functions or activities:
   (i) magistrate (except as a replacement), clerck at a court or state official;
   (ii) notary public and bailiff;
   (iii) any industrial or commercial activity; and
   (iv) any remunerated function or activity, be it public or private, which is liable to endanger the independence of the attorney or the dignity of the profession (Art. 437 of the Judicial Code).

§5. Bailiffs (gerechtsdeurwaarders/huissiers de justice)

3704. Bailiffs are state officials appointed by Royal Decree (Art. 509 of the Judicial Code). They are appointed to operate in a particular legal district and have a monopoly for the following actions: (i) service of process in general, including service of writs of summons, (ii) notification of judgments, and (iii) notification of attachment documents (Art. 516 of the Judicial Code). They may also obtain copies of all legal documents from clercks at a court, file applications where allowed by law, and conduct public auctions of goods (*Ibid.*).

3705. Documents drawn up by bailiffs are authentic deeds (*authentieke akte/actes authentiques*) (Art. 1317 of the Civil Code) and constitute valid proof of agreements or the facts which they contain. The content of an authentic deed may only be challenged by instituting a special procedure called *inschrijving tot valsheid/demande en faux civil* which is described in Articles 895 and following of the Judicial Code.

3706. Bailiffs, being state officials, are under an obligation to exercise their functions whenever they are so requested (Art. 517 of the Judicial Code). Their remuneration is fixed by law (Art. 519 of the Judicial Code) and each document drawn up by a bailiff must mention the exact amount of the bailiff's fee (Art. 523 of the Judicial Code).

3707. Bailiffs are subject to ethical rules administered by the various chambers of bailiffs, which are organised at district level.

D. Basic elements of procedure

§1. Introducing a claim

3708. Unless a specific exception provides otherwise, all principal claims must be introduced by the service of a writ of summons (*dagvaarding/citation*) (Art. 700 of the Judicial Code). This can only be done by a bailiff (Art. 516 of the Judicial Code). Counterclaims between parties in a procedure which is pending may be introduced by a simple motion contained in a brief (Art. 809 of the Judicial Code).

3709. A writ of summons must contain the following elements:
(i) the full name and domicile of the claimant;
(ii) the full name and domicile or, in the absence of a domicile, the residence of the defendant;
(iii) the object of the claim and a brief summary of the facts;
(iv) the judge before whom the case is brought: and
(v) the place, day and hour of the hearing (Art. 702 of the Judicial Code).

3710. In addition, writs of summons must meet all other formalities applicable to writs issued by bailiffs. These formalities are set forth in Article 43 of the Judicial Code.

3711. Writs of summons may be served on the person of the defendant or, if that is not possible, at his domicile (or in the absence thereof his place of residence) (Art. 35 of the Judicial Code). For legal entities, process will be deemed served to the person if the writ is handed over to a body or agent who, according to the law, the company by-laws or a proxy, is entitled to represent that legal entity in court proceedings (Art. 34 of the Judicial Code). If this is not possible, the writ may be served at the registered office or the administrative office of the legal person (Art. 35 of the Judicial Code). For defendants who do not have a known domicile or residence in Belgium, process will be served by the bailiff sending the writ of summons by registered mail to their domicile or residence abroad. For defendants who do not have a known domicile or residence in Belgium or abroad, service of process may take place at the Public Prosecutor's Office of the legal district in which the court hearing the case is located (Art. 40 of the Judicial Code). The above rules on service of process to foreign defendants are without prejudice to any other rules contained in international treaties.

3712. Service of process in legal actions brought against the Belgian State must be made to the Minister who is competent in the matter to which the action relates (Art. 705 of the Judicial Code).

3713. The service of a writ of summons is followed by an introductory hearing. The internal rules of organisation of each court will establish on what days of the week introductory hearings may take place. In addition, the Judicial Code specifies a mandatory minimum period between the service of the writ and the introductory hearing. As a general rule, this minimum period amounts to 8 days (Art. 707 of the Judicial Code). The minimum period is extended on account of distance by 15 days for defendants residing in The Netherlands, Germany, Luxembourg, France and the United Kingdom, by 30 days for defendants residing in any other European country and by 80 days for defendants residing in another continent (Art. 55 of the Judicial Code).

3714. Apart from the service of a writ of summons, legal proceedings may be started by:
    (i) voluntary appearance of the parties (*vrijwillige verschijning/comparution volontaire*) (only available for proceedings before the Courts of First Instance, the Labour Courts, the Commercial Courts and the Justices of the Peace) (Art. 706 of the Judicial Code);
    (ii) *ex parte* petitions (*eenzijdig verzoekschrift/requête unilatérale*), which are governed by Articles 1025 through 1034 of the Judicial Code; and
    (iii) petitions (*verzoekschrift op tegenspraak/requête contradictoire*) which are subject to Articles 1034*bis* through 1034*sexies* of the Judicial Code.

3715. As indicated earlier, these alternative means of starting a legal action may only operate when their use is expressly authorised by a legal provision. There is a tendency nowadays in favour of increasing the use of these alternatives to the writ of summons because of their flexibility and absence of formality.

§2. *Court appearances*

3716. Parties may appear in court either in person or represented by their attorneys (Art. 728, para. 1 of the Judicial Code). In certain limited cases mentioned in paragraphs 2 and 3 of this Article, special proxy-holders other than attorneys may act on behalf of the parties. Attorneys who appear before the court on behalf of their clients do not have to justify their appearance by presenting a proxy or mandate (Art. 440 of the Judicial Code). Judges may refuse parties the right to appear personally before the court and present their arguments if the parties' inexperience or strong emotions would not allow them to do so with sufficient dignity and clarity (Art. 758 of the Judicial Code).

3717. The first appearance before the court is the introductory hearing, the date, place and hour of which is indicated in the writ of summons. The defendant's failure to appear at the introductory hearing allows the claimant to obtain a judgment by default (Art. 802 of the Judicial Code).

3718. In cases where only short pleadings are required, it is possible to argue the case at the introductory hearing or to have it referred to a hearing which will take place shortly thereafter (Art. 735, para. 1 of the Judicial Code). Parties who wish to make use of the accelerated procedure must indicate this in the writ of summons and provide reasons.

3719. In all other circumstances, the case will be referred to the general docket (*algemene rol/rôle général*) in order to allow the parties to exchange exhibits and briefs.

§3. *Exhibits and briefs*

3720. The process whereby exhibits and briefs are exchanged between the parties starts by the claimant communicating to the defendant the exhibits (*stukken/pièces*) which he intends to use to substantiate his case. This normally happens shortly after the writ of summons has been served upon the defendant. Upon receipt of the claimant's exhibits, the defendant has, in principle, one month to file his brief (*conclusie/ conclusions*). A brief is a written document in which a party sets forth factual and legal arguments and requests the court to rule in a given manner on the claim contained in the writ of summons or any other claims filed at a later stage. The claimant has one month to reply to the brief filed by the defendant and, finally, the defendant has 15 days to file a rejoinder (Art. 747, para.1 of the Judicial Code). The parties may. however, agree among themselves to other timeframes within which they will file their briefs. At this stage of the proceedings, the failure to respect these timeframes does not carry any sanction.

3721. Where the parties do not respect the normal calendar set forth in Article 747, para. 1 of the Judicial Code and fail to reach an agreement on an alternative calendar, either one of them may request the President of the Court to determine the dates at which the parties must file their respective briefs. At the same time, a date will already be set for the oral hearing (Art. 747, para. 2 of the Judicial Code). When this procedure is used, any failure to respect the dates set by the President will result in the briefs being excluded from the hearing, unless the other party agrees to them being filed (*Ibid.*).

3722. Alternatively, when a party has not filed its brief in accordance with the normal calendar set forth in Article 747, para. 1 of the Judicial Code, or with the calendar agreed between the parties, the other party may request the court to set a date on which it will be allowed to request a judgment (Art. 751 of the Judicial Code). The party which has failed to file its brief will be notified thereof by the clerk of the court or by a bailiff. As of that moment, it will have 2 months to file its brief. Any brief filed after this deadline has expired will be excluded from the debates. The date on which a judgment may be requested must be set within one and 2 months after the expiry of the 2-month period allowed for the filing of the brief.

3723. In principle, the parties may decide for themselves which exhibits they will present to the court in order to substantiate their case. There is no equivalent of discovery proceedings in Belgium. However, if there are serious indications that a party to the proceedings, or a third party, is in possession of a document, which contains proof of a relevant fact, the court may order that the document, or a certified copy thereof, be deposited at the registrar's office (Art. 877 of the Judicial Code).

§4. *Investigative measures*

3724. Parties must provide evidence of the facts which they allege (Art. 870 of the Judicial Code). In order to assist them in gathering this evidence, the Judicial Code provides an array of investigative measures which the courts may order. These measures are: mandatory disclosure of documents (*overlegging van stukken/production des documents*), identification of handwriting (*schriftsonderzoek/vérification d'écritures*), forgery investigations (*valsheidsprocedure/faux civil*), witness testimony (*getuigenverhoor/enquête*), enquiries by court-appointed experts (*deskundigenonderzoek/expertise*), hearing of the parties (*verhoor van partijen/*

interrogatoire des parties), oaths (*eedaflegging/serment*), inspections by magistrates (*plaatsopneming/descente sur les lieux*) and (limited to divorce proceedings) certain affidavits made by bailiffs (*vaststelling door gerechtsdeurwaarder/ constat par huissier de justice*). All of these procedures are described in considerable detail in the Judicial Code.

§5. Oral arguments

3725. If the parties respect the time periods allowed for the exchange of briefs and exhibits, or if they have agreed on a derogation to these time periods, they will jointly request the court to set a date for oral arguments (Art. 750 of the Judicial Code). If they use the alternative procedures set forth in Articles 747, paragraph 2, or 751 of the Judicial Code, the date for the oral hearing will be set pursuant to a request made by one of the parties (*See*, para. 3721).

3726. As of the moment the parties make a joint request to set a date for an oral hearing, they will no longer be entitled to file additional briefs. Such briefs must be excluded from the hearing, unless the other party agrees to them being filed (Art. 748, para. 1 of the Judicial Code). Nevertheless, a party which has discovered a new and relevant fact or document may, at least 30 days before the oral hearing, request the court to grant an additional period of time in which to file a brief. This may, or may not, lead the court to postpone the date set for oral arguments (Art. 747, para. 2 of the Judicial Code).

3727. The presentation of oral arguments to the court does not amount to the equivalent of a trial as that concept is used in Anglo-Saxon legal systems. Oral arguments simply mean that the parties, generally represented by their attorneys, present their views to the court in oral pleadings. In simple cases, oral arguments may take less than half an hour. In complex litigations, oral arguments may take several hours.

3728. The parties may waive the right to present oral arguments and agree to limit themselves to a purely written procedure (Art. 755 of the Judicial Code). Within a month of the parties depositing their file at the registrar's office, the judge handling the case may request the parties to provide oral explanations with respect to certain points. In most courts, the written procedure is used only on rare occasions.

§6. Judgments

3729. After the oral arguments, the court declares the proceedings closed and takes the case into deliberation (Arts. 769 and 770 of the Judicial Code). In principle, a judgment must be rendered within a period of one month of the case being taken into deliberation. There is, however, no specific sanction other than the fact that no judgment has been rendered within one month must be recorded in the court's minutes and that, after 3 months, if no judgment has been rendered, the President of the Court of Appeal (or, as the case may be, the President of the Labour Court of Appeal) must be informed.

3730. A judgment must be signed by all the judges who rendered it and by the registrar (Art. 782 of the Judicial Code). It is a public document, except in the cases specified by law (Art. 757 of the Judicial Code). All parties receive a non-official copy of the judgment by mail within 8 days of the date of the judgment (Art. 792 of the Judicial Code).

§7. *Appeal*

3731. Unless provided otherwise, appeals may be brought against all judgments (Arts. 616 and 1050 of the Judicial Code). However, judgments rendered by Justices of the Peace involving claims not exceeding € 1,240 or judgments by the Courts of First Instance or the Commercial Courts involving claims not exceeding € 1,860 are final (Art. 617, para. 1 of the Judicial Code).

3732. Appellate proceedings must be instituted within a period of one month as of the moment the judgment is notified by the bailiff at the initiative of one of the parties (Art. 1051 of the Judicial Code). This period is extended on account of distance when the party to which, or at whose request, the judgment has been notified has no known domicile or residence in Belgium. The length of the extension is governed by Article 55 of the Judicial Code (*See*, para. 3711).

§8. *Costs*

3733. Any final judgment must order the losing party to bear the legal costs (Art. 1017 of the Judicial Code). Costs may be compensated as the court sees fit when all the parties fail on certain of their claims (*Ibid.*). Interlocutory judgments or judgments in summary proceedings will reserve the costs. The costs of execution of a judgment must be borne by the party against whom execution is sought (Art. 1024 of the Judicial Code).

3734. Legal costs which may be recovered from the losing party are:
    (i) stamp duties, registration fees and registration rights;
    (ii) costs and fees related to legal documents (for example, bailiff's fee for the service of a writ of summons);
    (iii) cost of authenticated copies of the judgment;
    (iv) costs of investigative measures such as witness testimonies and court-appointed experts;

(v) travel costs of magistrates, registrars and parties if these journeys are ordered by the court; and

(vi) the procedural indemnity (*rechtsplegingsvergoeding/indemnité de procédure*) (*See*, para. 3737).

3735. Registration duties on judgments currently amount to 2.5 per cent of the sum of the principal amount, the interest calculated by the court and the legal costs which a party is ordered to pay (Arts. 142 and 302*quater* of the Registration and Mortgage Tax Code). No registration duties are due on:
  – interlocutory judgments;
  – judgments imposing criminal, civil or disciplinary penalties;
  – judgments ordering alimony payments; and
  – judgments where the total amount which one and the same party is ordered to pay does not exceed € 12,394.68 (Art. 143 of the Registration and Mortgage Tax Code).

3736. Registration duties are payable by the defendant and by the claimant, but by the latter only if he has received payment from the defendant pursuant to the judgment and only up to an amount equal to one half of the amount which he has received (Art. 35 of the Registration and Mortgage Tax Code).

3737. Attorneys' fees borne by the parties are not recoverable apart from a small amount which is called the procedural indemnity (*rechtsplegingsvergoeding/indemnité de procédure*). The amount of the procedural indemnity is set by law and depends on the type of court before which a case is brought and on the amount of the claim. Procedural indemnities currently range from approximately € 250 to € 400. They are periodically adjusted to reflect the cost of living.

E. Attachment and execution

§1. Basic principles

3738. Judgments may be executed only on the basis of an authenticated copy or, exceptionally, the original copy of the judgment to which the executory formula has been added (Art. 1386 of the Judicial Code). Authenticated copies are called *uitgiften/expéditions*. The original copy of the judgment is referred to as the *minuut/minute*. The content of the executory formula, by which the King orders all judicial officers to assist in the execution of the judgment, is determined by a Royal Decree of 27 May 1971.

3739. Any execution of a judgment requires its prior notification (*betekening/significa-tion*) to the party against whom enforcement is sought (Art. 1495 of the Judicial Code). Only bailiffs are entitled to notify judgments (Art. 516 of the Judicial Code).

3740. The filing of opposition or appellate proceedings normally suspends the enforce-ability of a judgment (Art. 1397 of the Judicial Code). The Judicial Code provides a number of exceptions to this principle. One important exception is the possibility for the judge who rendered the judgment to provide that it shall be enforceable notwithstanding the filing of an appeal. This procedure is known as provisional enforcement (*voorlopige tenuitvoerlegging/exécution provisoire*) (Art. 1398 of the Judicial Code). Provisional enforcement may not be granted *ex officio* by the court, but must be requested by the claimant. If granted, the court may require the party seeking enforcement to first provide security (Art. 1400, para. 1 of the Judicial Code). Any enforcement of a judgment pending opposition or appellate proceed-ings is done at the risk of the party seeking enforcement. In case of a reversal, that party will have to reimburse the money received and provide compensation for any damage which the enforcement may have caused. The provisional enforcement of a judgment against which opposition or appellate proceedings are pending may be avoided by the debtor paying the amount requested into the hands of a bailiff or to a special government-owned financial institution (*Deposito- en Consignatiekas/ Caisse des dépôts et consignations*). This right of the debtor, which is called *kan-tonnement/cantonnement*, may be excluded by the judgment if a delay in paying the claimant is liable to cause the latter serious hardship (Art. 1406 of the Judicial Code). *Kantonnement/cantonnement* may be likened to payment into an escrow account. The creditor will have the security that he will receive payment if the opposition or appeal is unsuccessful. The debtor, on the other hand, will be shielded from risks related to the financial situation of the creditor if as a result of the oppo-sition or the appeal the initial judgment is reversed.

§2. Periodic penalty payments (dwangsom/astreinte)

3741. The Benelux Convention of 26 November 1973, approved by the Law of 31 Janu-ary 1980, introduced Articles 1385*bis* through 1385*nonies* into the Judicial Code. These articles relate to periodic penalty payments (*dwangsommen/astreintes*). Periodic penalty payments are civil penalties which may be imposed when the debtor does not voluntarily execute the judgment. Periodic penalty payments may only be imposed at the request of one of the parties (Art. 1385*bis* of the Judicial Code). They may not be imposed for financial judgments or for claims relating to the execution of employment contracts. The judgment will determine the amount of the periodic penalty payment and whether it will be due as a single lump sum, per time unit (for example, a sum payable for every day of delay in executing a judgment) or per violation of the judgment. In the 2 latter cases, the judgment may fix a total maximum amount for the periodic penalty payments (Art. 1385*ter* of the Judicial Code). Periodic penalty payments are only due if the judgment is enforceable and if it has been served by a bailiff (Art. 1385*bis* of the Judicial Code). Periodic penalty payments are due to the creditor and are not in lieu of any damages. The recovery does not require the prior intervention of a judge. Any dispute relating to the recovery of periodic penalty payments must be brought before the attachment judge.

§3. Attachment for security purposes (bewarend beslag/saisie conservatoire)

3742. Under the following conditions, any creditor may request the attachment judge for permission to seize the property of his debtor as security for the payment of his debt:
  (i) the matter must be urgent, that is, there must be serious risks that the debtor will become insolvent;
  (ii) the debt must be certain, that is, the debt cannot be reasonably contested;
  (iii) the debt must be due; and
  (iv) the amount of the debt must be liquidated or at least capable of being estimated provisionally (Arts. 1413 and 1415 of the Judicial Code).

3743. The request for permission to attach the goods of a debtor is made by means of an *ex parte* petition which must be addressed to the attachment judge and filed with the registrar (Art. 1417 of the Judicial Code). The attachment judge must rule on the petition within a period of 8 days (Art. 1418 of the Judicial Code) and must indicate for what amount the permission is granted (*Ibid.*).

3744. The prior permission of the attachment judge is not required when the creditor can rely on a judgment (Art. 1414 of the Judicial Code). This judgment does not need to be provisionally enforceable, nor must it have been notified to the debtor prior to the attachment. Since the judgment constitutes sufficient proof that the debt is certain and due, and that its amount is determined, the only additional requirement which must be met is the requirement of urgency (*dringendheid/célérité*).

3745. Attachments may only be made by using the services of a bailiff (Art. 516 of the Judicial Code).

3746. The Judicial Code provides the possibility for the creditor and the debtor to appeal against the decision which authorises or refuses the attachment (Art. 1419 of the Judicial Code). Where no prior authorisation is required, the debtor may also institute proceedings against the creditor in order to obtain the release of the attached goods (*opheffing van het beslag/levée de la saisie*) (Art. 1420 of the Judicial Code).

3747. The attachment is valid for a period of 3 years (Art. 1425 of the Judicial Code). This period will be suspended if the creditor starts proceedings on the merits (Art. 1493 of the Judicial Code).

3748. The Judicial Code distinguishes between various types of attachment, each of which is subject to specific rules.

§4. *Attachment followed by a forced sale (uitvoerend beslag/saisie exécutoire)*

3749. Attachments with a view to the forced execution of a money judgment require the following conditions to be met:
  (i) the judgment must be enforceable;
  (ii) the judgment must be served by a bailiff to the party against whom enforcement is sought; and
  (iii) the attachment must be preceded by an official summons (*bevel/commandement*) to the debtor to pay. This must be done at least one day prior to the attachment (Arts. 1495 and 1499 of the Judicial Code).

3750. In the event that the goods have already provisionally been attached by the creditor for security purposes, the enforcement of the judgment does not require a new attachment (Art. 1497 of the Judicial Code). In that case, the existing attachment will be deemed converted by the serving of the judgment and the summons to pay (*Ibid.*).

3751. The requirement that the judgment must be enforceable implies that judgments against which it is still possible to file opposition or appellate proceedings may not be enforced during a period of one month after they have been officially notified to the debtor, unless they may be provisionally enforced (Art. 1495 of the Judicial Code).

3752. All enforcement proceedings require the intervention of a bailiff. Bailiffs have a monopoly over the notification of judgments, the notification of official summons to pay and seizures of goods with a view to their attachment (Art. 516 of the Judicial Code).

3753. The attachment procedures applicable to the forced sale of the goods which have been seized are described in considerable detail in Articles 1494 through 1675 of the Judicial Code. They culminate in the forced sale of the seized goods by public auction. The creditor is paid from the proceeds of the auction.

III. ARBITRATION

A. Introduction

3754. The Belgian law governing arbitration is contained in the sixth and final part of the Judicial Code, that is, Articles 1676 through 1723. These provisions were enacted by the Law of 4 July 1972 which generally follows the Uniform Law attached to the Strasbourg Convention of 20 January 1966. Belgium is also a signatory to several international conventions on arbitration, both multilateral and bilateral. When applicable, the rules contained in these international conventions take precedence over the common rules on arbitration contained in the Judicial Code.

B. Arbitrability of disputes under Belgian law

3755. Article 1676 of the Judicial Code provides that any disputes which arise out of a defined legal relationship and which are capable of settlement by compromise may be submitted to arbitration. This provision is to a large extent inspired by Article II, para. 1 of the New York Convention on the Recognition and Enforcement of Foreign Arbitral Awards of 10 June 1958 (the "New York Convention") to which Belgium is a party. However, Belgium has not made use of the 'commercial' reservation, which is allowed by the New York Convention and which confines arbitration to disputes arising out of legal relationships which are considered commercial under the laws of the country making the reservation. Under Belgian law, disputes arising out of any type of legal relationship, whether commercial or not, may be submitted to arbitration.

3756. Despite the generality of its scope, this principle is subject to exceptions. Disputes may not be submitted to arbitration:
    (i) when specific laws provide otherwise; and
    (ii) when they are not capable of settlement by compromise.

§1. Statutory exceptions

3757. The most commonly referred to statutory exceptions to the general principle that all disputes are arbitrable relate to labour and social security matters and to distribution agreements covered by the Law of 27 July 1961 on the Unilateral Termination of Certain Categories of Distribution Agreements (*Wet betreffende eenzijdige beëindiging van de voor onbepaalde tijd verleende concessies van alleenverkoop/Loi relative à la résiliation unilaterale des concessions de vente exclusives à durée indéterminée* – the "Law of 27 July 1961"). In matters over which the Labour Courts have jurisdiction pursuant to Articles 578 through 583 of the Judicial Code

(*See*, paras. 3671 *et seq.*), the parties may not agree to submit a dispute to arbitration prior to the moment the dispute arises, except when the law specifically provides otherwise. Similarly, prior to the moment of contract termination, it may not be agreed that disputes concerning the termination of a distribution agreement covered by the protective Law of 27 July 1961 will be submitted to arbitration (*See*, paras. 1837 *et seq.*). Arbitration agreements which violate these principles are null and void, and therefore unenforceable.

3758. Other areas where the arbitrability of disputes may be subject to doubt are intellectual property and competition law. As far as patents are concerned, the Law of 28 March 1984 on Patents (*Wet op de uitvindingsoctrooien/Loi sur les brevets d'invention*) (*See*, paras. 2243 *et seq.*) makes it clear in Article 73, para. 6, that several types of dispute relating to patents may be submitted to arbitration. For example, disputes relating to the ownership of patents or patent applications, to the validity of patents, to the infringement of patents and to patent licences may be settled by arbitration. However, disputes relating to mandatory licences are excluded from arbitration.

3759. As far as other intellectual property rights are concerned, such as trade marks, design rights and copyrights, there are no express legal provisions clarifying that recourse may be had to arbitration. Nonetheless, legal commentators generally appear to have accepted, with nuances, that most disputes relating to these rights may also be submitted to arbitration.

3760. The arbitrability of competition law disputes raises similar issues. Under the old Law of 27 May 1960 on the Protection against the Abuse of Dominant Positions (the "Law of 27 May 1960" – *Wet tot bescherming tegen het misbruik van economische machtspositie/Loi sure la protection contre l'abus de la puissance économique*) (*See*, Chapter 13) it was clear that arbitrators had no authority to establish the existence of an abuse within the meaning of the Law of 27 May 1960 because such a conclusion required a finding that the practice at issue was against the "public interest". Such a finding could only be made by the administrative bodies provided in the Law. Likewise, certain decisions under the Law of 5 August 1991 on the Protection of Economic Competition (*Wet tot bescherming van de economische Mededinging/Loi sur la protection de la concurrence économique –* the "Competition Law") such as exemption decisions pursuant to Article 29 of the Competition Law, can only be taken by the administrative bodies provided in the Competition Law and are for that reason excluded from arbitration. This does not, of course, prevent arbitrators from taking into account the impact which the Competition Law may have on the validity of the legal acts which are the subject of the dispute. Arbitrators, like any other jurisdictional body, may not enforce contractual provisions which would be in breach of public policy principles (Cass., 5 September 1980, *Pas.*, 1980, I, 15).

3761. The above rules describe whether a legal dispute is arbitrable under Belgian law. However, when a dispute involves international elements, the analysis may be different. Under Belgian conflicts of law principles, whether a dispute is arbitrable must be determined in accordance with the law applicable to the arbitration agreement. At least, this is the rule which must be applied when a Belgian court decides on the validity of the arbitration agreement. If the issue of arbitrability arises in the context of recognition and enforcement proceedings in Belgium, Belgian courts will apply Belgian law, *i.e.*, the *lex fori*, (Brussels Court of Appeal, 4 October 1985, *J.T.*, 1986, 93). It will be recalled that the latter principle, that is, the application of the *lex fori* in recognition and enforcement proceedings to determine whether a dispute was arbitrable, is in conformity with the New York Convention (Art. V,2,a).

§2. *Disputes which cannot be settled by compromise*

3762. Article 1676, para. 1 of the Judicial Code limits the category of arbitrable disputes to those disputes which can be settled by compromise (*dading/transaction*). The notion of compromise refers to an agreement in which the parties make mutual concessions and thereby put an end to an existing difference or prevent a future dispute from arising. Compromises are governed by Articles 2044 through 2058 of the Civil Code. Not all disputes may be settled by compromise. Disputes which cannot be validly settled by compromise may not be submitted to arbitration either. Examples of such disputes are: in principle all matters relating to personality rights (*staat van personen/état des personnes*), alimony rights, matrimonial rights and agreements. With respect to most of these matters, detailed exceptions apply.

3763. The common denominator of all disputes which cannot be settled by compromise is that they involve rights which may not be waived. If parties are not allowed to waive certain rights, they may not submit to arbitration disputes involving these rights.

C. The arbitration agreement

3764. This section will discuss the validity requirements, the content and the legal consequences of arbitration agreements.

§1. Validity requirements

1. Capacity

3765. Article 1676 para. 2, of the Judicial Code specifies that persons having the capacity to settle disputes by compromise also have the capacity to submit disputes to arbitration. As a consequence, essentially all persons have the capacity to submit disputes to arbitration, unless they are covered by a specific legal regime which limits their legal capacity. Examples of such legally incapacitated persons include minors and persons assimilated thereto, improvident persons who must be represented by a court-appointed trustee and traders who have been declared bankrupt.

3766. Another important exception applies to public institutions. Article 1676, para. 2 of the Judicial Code provides that public institutions may not enter into arbitration agreements. Thus, the Belgian State, the provinces, the municipalities and all other institutions entrusted with public missions may not enter into arbitration agreements unless the law specifically provides otherwise. For the Belgian State, the derogation must be contained in an international treaty.

3767. Whether foreigners have the legal capacity to submit to arbitration will, under Belgian conflicts principles, be determined in accordance with their own national laws. For example, under Belgian conflicts principles, a French citizen will be deemed to have the capacity to enter into an arbitration agreement if French law grants him such capacity.

2. Representation

3768. Arbitration agreements may be entered into by proxyholders or by other legal representatives acting on behalf of the parties. In the case of a proxyholder, since the decision to submit to arbitration is regarded as an act which goes beyond the normal administration of the principal's interests, a specific proxy is required. In other words, the proxy document must specifically empower the proxyholder to enter into a defined arbitration agreement on behalf of the principal. A proxy which empowers the proxyholder to reach a compromise agreement does not by itself give the proxyholder the authority to submit the legal difference to arbitration. Similarly, an attorney who is charged by his client to represent him in court proceedings (mandate *ad litem*), does not have the authority to submit to arbitration. A specific authorisation to that effect is required.

3769. Legal entities must be represented in accordance with their articles of incorporation and with the legal provisions governing their status. Thus, for example, a public limited liability company (*naamloze vennootschap/société anonyme*) will normally be represented by its board of directors when submitting to arbitration.

3. Written agreement

3770. Arbitration agreements must be in writing. Article 1677 of the Judicial Code provides that arbitration agreements must be contained in a written document signed by the parties, or in other documents binding upon the parties, in which they have indicated their willingness to submit the dispute to arbitration. It is almost unanimously accepted that the requirement that arbitration agreements be made in writing is a requirement "*ad probationem*". In other words, disrespect of the requirement does not affect the validity of the agreement, but will lead to problems of evidence.

§2. Content of arbitration agreements

3771. Belgian law does not contain mandatory requirements as to the contents of arbitration agreements. The only (implicit) requirement is that the arbitration agreement must indicate the willingness of the parties to submit their difference to arbitration (*See*, Article 1677 of the Judicial Code). If the arbitration agreement expresses no more than a willingness to submit a dispute to arbitration, the parties will have to rely on the provisions of the Judicial Code for the rules of procedure which will be applicable to the arbitration. Thus, it is usually advisable for the parties to provide details on the place of arbitration, the language of the proceedings, the duration of the proceedings, the number and the selection of the arbitrators and other important matters. Alternatively, it is possible for the parties to refer to the rules of procedure of various national or international arbitration bodies. Most arbitration bodies recommend the use of specific clauses in the arbitration agreement. For example, CEPINA – a well-known Belgian arbitration institution – recommends the use of the following clause:

> "*Any dispute concerning the validity, the interpretation or the performance of this agreement shall be finally settled under the rules of CEPINA, by one or more arbitrators appointed in accordance with the said rules.*"

§3. Consequences of the arbitration agreement

3772. The main consequence of any arbitration agreement is that ordinary courts and tribunals lose their jurisdiction to hear the dispute which the parties have agreed to submit to arbitration. In this respect, Article 1679, para. 1 of the Judicial Code provides that the court before which such a dispute is brought must, upon request of either party, rule that it lacks jurisdiction, unless the arbitration agreement is invalid or has been terminated. The court may not rule *ex officio* that it lacks jurisdiction to hear the case. One of the parties must expressly rely on the so-called "arbitration exception" before the court may dismiss the case on the ground that it lacks jurisdiction. It should be noted that the court may not dismiss the case on the grounds that the dispute covered by the arbitration agreement is related to another dispute in which a third party not bound by the arbitration agreement is involved. This may take place only in the highly exceptional circumstance where these disputes would have to be considered indivisible (Cass., 9 May 1963, *Pas.* 1963, I, 956), *i.e.*, when the simultaneous execution of the decisions resulting from those disputes, had they been treated by different jurisdictional bodies, would be materially impossible (*See*, Article 31 of the Judicial Code).

3773. The parties may waive the rights resulting from the arbitration agreement and decide to have recourse to the ordinary courts and tribunals. They will be deemed to have waived these rights unless their first defence before the court is to invoke the existence of the arbitration agreement (Art. 1679, para. 1, *in fine* of the Judicial Code). On the other hand, the parties to an arbitration agreement will not be deemed to have waived their rights when they apply to a court or tribunal in order to obtain conservatory measures or interim relief (Art. 1679, para. 2 of the Judicial Code).

3774. As is the case with any other agreements, arbitration agreements will only be binding upon the parties thereto (Art. 1165 of the Civil Code). This principle has various consequences. First, it is generally accepted that a third party that has not entered into the arbitration agreement may not be forced to intervene in arbitral proceedings. A voluntary intervention by a third party will be possible only if all the parties agree. Several arbitral proceedings which are pending at the same time between different parties may not be consolidated into one arbitral proceeding on the basis that these proceedings would be related. In the absence of any specific provision to that effect, Belgian courts have no powers to consolidate arbitral proceedings.

D. The arbitral tribunal

3775. The arbitral tribunal must be composed of an uneven number of arbitrators and may consist of only one member (Art. 1681, para. 1 of the Judicial Code). The parties may determine the number of arbitrators in the arbitration agreement or leave it to be decided afterwards. If they fail to reach an agreement on this point, the tribunal will be composed of 3 members (Art. 1681, para. 3 of the Judicial Code). Where the arbitration agreement provides for an even number of arbitrators, an additional arbitrator must be designated.

3776. The parties may designate the arbitrators themselves or entrust this task to a third party. The arbitrators may be designated in the arbitration agreement or pursuant to a subsequent agreement between the parties (Art. 1682 of the Judicial Code). In the absence of any agreement between the parties as to the identity of the arbitrators or the manner in which they will be designated, each of the parties may designate one arbitrator or, if necessary, an even number of arbitrators. In this case, the notice of initiation of arbitration will contain, among other things, the identity of the arbitrator(s) designated by the claimant, as well as an invitation for the defendant to designate one or more arbitrators (Art. 1683, para. 2 of the Judicial Code). If the defendant fails to designate the additional arbitrator(s) within a period of one month, the claimant may request the President of the Court of First Instance to designate the additional arbitrator(s) (Art. 1684, para. 1 of the Judicial Code). The same rule applies when a third party has been entrusted with the designation of the arbitrators, but has failed to designate them within a period of one month as of the receipt of the notice of initiation of the arbitration. In that case, either party may request the President of the Court of First Instance to designate the arbitrators. Finally, if the parties have agreed to appoint only one arbitrator but cannot reach an agreement within one month after the notice of initiation of arbitration, the arbitrator will be designated by the President of the Court of First Instance (Art. 1684, para. 2 of the Judicial Code).

3777. If, as a result of the above procedure, the number of designated arbitrators is even, the arbitrators themselves must designate an additional arbitrator who will act as president of the arbitral tribunal. If the arbitrators fail to agree on the additional arbitrator within a period of one month after the designation of the most recently designated arbitrator, or if it is clear before this period has lapsed that the arbitrators will not reach an agreement, either party may request the President of the Court of First Instance to designate the additional arbitrator (Art. 1685 of the Judicial Code). In all of the above instances, the decision of the President of the Court of First Instance is final and not open to appeal (Art. 1686, para. 1 of the Judicial Code).

3778. A fundamental principle underlying the designation of arbitrators is that the arbitration agreement may not confer a privileged position on one of the parties. If this principle is not observed, it will result in the invalidity of the arbitration agreement (Art. 1678, para. 1 of the Judicial Code). Courts have used this principle, for example, to annul arbitration agreements which provide for the mandatory designation of members of one party's profession as arbitrators where not all parties are members of that profession.

3779. In principle, in the absence of any specific agreement between the parties, anyone who has the legal capacity to enter into agreements may serve as an arbitrator. Minors, persons who must be represented by court-appointed trustees and persons who are temporarily or definitively banned from exercising political voting rights may not serve as arbitrators (Art. 1680 of the Judicial Code). The parties may agree to exclude certain categories of persons as arbitrators (Art. 1692, para. 1 of the Judicial Code).

3780. Arbitrators can be challenged on the same grounds as ordinary judges (Art. 1690, para. 1 of the Judicial Code). These grounds are listed in Article 828 and following of the Judicial Code. The arbitrator(s) designated by a party cannot be challenged by that party if it was aware of the grounds justifying the challenge prior to the designation (Art. 1690, para. 2 of the Judicial Code). As soon as a party becomes aware of grounds justifying a challenge, it must inform the arbitrators thereof, whereupon they must suspend the proceedings. If the arbitrator being challenged has not stood down within a period of 10 days, the arbitrators must inform the challenging party. That party must then, within a period of 10 days, bring the dispute before the Court of First Instance by serving a writ upon the arbitrators and the other parties to the arbitral proceedings (Art. 1691 of the Judicial Code). Expedited appellate proceedings are available regarding decisions of the Court of First Instance.

E. The arbitral procedure

3781. Within certain limits, the parties are at liberty to determine the procedural rules which will apply to the arbitration. Parties often determine those rules by means of a reference to existing arbitration rules (*e.g.*, ICC rules, UNCITRAL rules, CEPINA rules, *etc.*). If they have not agreed upon the procedural rules prior to the designation of the first arbitrator, the arbitrators will decide which procedural rules will be applicable (Art. 1693 of the Judicial Code). The limits which must be respected in determining the rules of procedure are set forth in Article 1694 of the Judicial Code which guarantees that due process principles are respected. For example, Article 1694 of the Judicial Code provides that each party must be given the opportunity to present its case, that the arbitrators must render their award after having heard the oral arguments put forward by the parties (the parties may, however, waive the right to present oral arguments), that the parties have the right to appear in person, or to be represented or assisted by an attorney. In addition to the rules contained in Article 1694 of the Judicial Code, it appears to be generally accepted that other fundamental principles of due process, which any judicial body must respect, must also be respected during arbitral proceedings. Thus, the parties must produce the documents or other evidence on which they rely and have the right to receive that evidence which is used against them. The arbitrators may not base their award on factors or arguments with respect to which the parties have not been given the opportunity to express their views. These rules, aimed at protecting the rights of defence, do not prevent the arbitrators from proceeding or entering an award when a party which has been duly summoned has not appeared or presented its arguments (Art. 1695 of the Judicial Code).

F. The powers of arbitrators and the role of ordinary courts

3782. Arbitrators have the power to order the following investigative measures: the hearing of witnesses, the appointment of experts, on-the-spot investigations and the personal appearance of the parties. Arbitrators can also administer oaths and may, under the conditions set forth in Article 877 of the Judicial Code, order the parties to disclose certain documents (Art. 1698, para. 1 of the Judicial Code). However, the arbitrators have no powers to order a verification of, or decide on, the genuineness of documents, nor are they allowed to take decisions regarding the disclosure of documents held by third parties (Art. 1698, para. 2 of the Judicial Code). When issues such as these arise, the arbitrators must grant leave to the moving party to refer the question to the Court of First Instance (Art. 1696, para. 3 of the Judicial Code). The same rule applies when witnesses refuse to appear, to take an oath or to make a declaration (Art. 1696, para. 2 of the Judicial Code).

G. The award

3783. The award must be set forth in a written document signed by a majority of the arbitrators. If some arbitrators are unwilling or unable to sign, this must also be recorded (Art. 1701, para. 4 of the Judicial Code). In addition to the decision itself, the award must contain the following information: the names and addresses of the arbitrators, the names and addresses of the parties, the subject of the dispute, the date on which the award was rendered, the place where the proceedings took place and where the award was rendered (Art. 1701, para. 5 of the Judicial Code). Unlike most Anglo-Saxon systems, Belgian law requires that awards state the reasons on which they are based (Art. 1701, para. 6 of the Judicial Code).

3784. The President of the arbitration tribunal notify the award to the parties by sending to each of them a signed copy thereof. The original must be deposited at the registry of the Court of First Instance (Art. 1702, paras. 1 and 2 of the Judicial Code). Upon fulfilment of these formalities, the arbitrators' mission comes to an end (Art. 1702, para. 3 of the Judicial Code).

H. Legal effect of the award and possibilities of recourse

3785. Unless agreed otherwise between the parties, arbitral awards are final. Proceedings before ordinary appellate courts are not available and may not be agreed upon by the parties. Awards are only subject to annulment proceedings which must be brought before the Court of First Instance (Art. 1704, para. 1 of the Judicial Code), in most cases within a period of 3 months after the day the award was notified to the parties (Art. 1707. para. 1 of the Judicial Code). The grounds for annulment are limited to the following:

   (i) violation of public policy;

  (ii) the dispute was not arbitrable;

 (iii) there was no valid arbitration agreement;

 (iv) the arbitral tribunal has exceeded its competence or powers;

  (v) the arbitrators have failed to decide on one or more issues which cannot be separated from those on which an award was rendered;

 (vi) the award was rendered by an irregularly constituted arbitral tribunal;

(vii) violation of due process;

(viii) violation of Article 1701, para. 4 of the Judicial Code which provides that arbitral awards must be in writing, and that certain formalities regarding the signature of the award by the arbitrators must be respected;

 (ix) the award contains contradictory provisions;

  (x) the award is obtained by fraud;

 (xi) the award is based on evidence which is recognised to be false by a final judgment; and

(xii) subsequent to the award, evidence has been discovered which would have been decisive for the arbitration, and which was withheld by the other party (Art. 1704, para. 2 of the Judicial Code).

3786. Belgian law contains specific provisions on the annulment of international awards rendered in Belgium. Article 1717, para. 4 of the Judicial Code provides that Belgian tribunals may only hear actions to obtain the annulment of an arbitral award if at least one of the parties to the dispute in which the award was rendered is either a physical person having Belgian nationality or residing in Belgium, or a legal person constituted in Belgium or having a branch office or any other seat of business in Belgium. In other words, no recourse is available against awards rendered in arbitral proceedings in which no party has any of the above links with Belgium. In such cases, the parties may only challenge the enforcement of the award.

I. Execution of arbitral awards

3787. The execution of arbitral awards requires an *exequatur* decision which is rendered, at the request of the interested party, by the President of the Court of First Instance. Exequatur proceedings are *ex parte* proceedings. The party against which the execution is sought does not have the right to be heard at that stage of the proceedings (Art. 1710, para. 1 of the Judicial Code). However, in *exequatur* proceedings relating to foreign arbitral awards, the President may hear the applicant and the party against which enforcement is sought in chambers (Art. 1719, para. 5 of the Judicial Code).

3788. *Exequatur* decisions can only be given with respect to final arbitral awards or, when the parties have exceptionally agreed upon appellate arbitral proceedings, when the arbitrators have declared their award enforceable notwithstanding the filing of an appeal (Art. 1710, para. 2 of the Judicial Code). The *exequatur* decision itself is also enforceable notwithstanding the filing of an appeal (*Ibid.*), but may be suspended by the court hearing the appeal against the *exequatur* decision (Art. 1714 of the Judicial Code).

3789. With respect to Belgian arbitral awards, the President of the Court of First Instance must refuse to grant the *exequatur* decision when the execution of the award would violate public policy principles or when the dispute was not arbitrable (Art. 1710, para. 3 of the Judicial Code). For foreign awards, the *exequatur* decision will be refused when:
    (i) the award is not final, nor enforceable irrespective of the filing of an appeal;
    (ii) the execution of the award would violate public policy;
    (iii) the dispute was not arbitrable;
    (iv) there is a ground for annulment as defined in Article 1704 of the Judicial Code (Art. 1723 of the Judicial Code).

3790. Where there is a treaty binding both Belgium and the country in which the award was rendered, the relevant treaty provisions on execution of arbitral awards will prevail over the rules on execution contained in Article 1723 of the Judicial Code.

3791. The applicant must be informed of the *exequatur* decision by letter sent by the registrar of the President of the Court of First Instance within 5 days after the decision is taken (Arts. 1710, para. 4 and 1720 of the Judicial Code). If the *exequatur* is refused, the applicant has one month as of the notification of the decision to file an appeal before the Court of Appeal. This must be done by serving a writ upon the party against which enforcement is sought (Arts. 1711, para. 1 and 1721 of the Judicial Code).

3792. The *exequatur* decision, if granted, must be served by writ upon the party against which enforcement is sought. The latter then has one month to file opposition proceedings before the Court of First Instance (Arts. 1712, para. 1 and Article 1722 of the Judicial Code).

INDEX

References are to paragraph numbers